Gone with the Ivy: A Biography of Vanderbilt University

Old Main

Gone with the Ivy

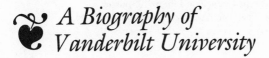 A Biography of
Vanderbilt University

by PAUL K. CONKIN

assisted by

HENRY LEE SWINT

and

PATRICIA S. MILETICH

THE UNIVERSITY OF TENNESSEE PRESS

Knoxville

The paper in this book meets the guidelines for permanence and durability
of the Committee on Production Guidelines for Book Longevity
of the Council on Library Resources.
Binding materials have been chosen for durability.

Library of Congress Cataloging in Publication Data

Conkin, Paul Keith.
  Gone with the ivy.

  Bibliogaphy: p.
  Includes index.
    1. Vanderbilt University—History. I. Swint, Henry Lee.
II. Miletich, Patricia S. III. Title.
LD5588.C66 1985   378.768'55   84-19714
ISBN 0-87049-452-X (alk. paper)

Credits

I n 1967 vague dreams began to mature into a project. Vanderbilt University, it seemed, needed a new history. Early discussions among administrators and members of the Board of Trust developed out of a reminder, by the Vanderbilt University Press, that Edwin Mims's 1946 *History of Vanderbilt University* was not only out of print but increasingly in demand in the used-book market. Why not update it? Could not someone supplement the Mims book by material taken from the collections so lovingly gathered by John T. McGill? Better still, could not aging Vice-Chancellor Emeritus Madison Sarratt write down his rich memories and thus build the needed historical bridge from World War II to the present? What project could better adorn the upcoming celebrations of Vanderbilt's centennial?

The book which I here preface grew out of Sarratt's wise response to flattering requests that he write down his memories. He counseled the university to sponsor something more thorough and balanced than anyone's memoirs. What it needed to do, he said, was to engage a trained historian who could commit the time and effort needed for a "full biography" of Vanderbilt, one that stretched "from its opening" to the time "the book is issued." Prophetically, he noted that 1967 was already too late for the university to enjoy such a full biography during its centennial celebrations from 1972 to 1975.

Through a series of improbable events, in 1982 I became the historian who agreed, perhaps unwisely, to complete such a full biography. I liked Sarratt's title. I have tried to live up to it. Although made up of many diverse individuals, Vanderbilt University is a type of living organism. It deserves a biography, beginning with its conception and birth and encompassing all the growth pains that accompanied its slow maturation. I have emphasized the problems and dilemmas it has faced, the hard choices that had to be made, the identity crises that were overcome. I have tried, above all else, to tell the full story suggested by a biography, to explore the rich texture of events, to probe the identity of critical individuals, to clarify some of the subtleties of campus intellectual life. I have tried to give equal attention to the major components of such a complex institution, to students, faculty, administrators, and trustees. Such a full biography cannot be brief. I have no apology for the length of what follows. I do feel apologetic about so much I had to leave out, so many

v

important events either skipped over lightly or ignored, so many loyal and giving individuals unreported, so many complexities ironed out by brief and simple descriptions.

I also accepted Sarratt's mandate that a new history go back to the beginnings, that it not merely update Mims's highly personal history. Insofar as possible, I have allocated equal attention to each decade of Vanderbilt's past. Admittedly, the sheer diversity and complexity of the post–World War II era has warred against this goal. As a historian, I found the first fifty years easier to chronicle than those that followed. This reflects not only the advantages of perspective and hindsight but also the greater unity and simplicity of the early, literate, classical, pious, securely southern Vanderbilt. The luxurious ivy that enveloped Old Main before the 1905 fire well symbolizes this early Vanderbilt and the ideals it exemplified. But that Vanderbilt has gone with the ivy. In a sense it had its final, belated apotheosis in the work of the Fugitives and Agrarians. The building that now houses the Medical School symbolizes the modern Vanderbilt, one in which strong professional schools and specialization in traditional disciplines have diluted the literary and humanistic ideals of the past. A little nostalgia for that past is in order.

Sarratt's recommendations bore early fruit. During 1968 Chancellor Alexander Heard consulted extensively with members of the Vanderbilt history department. He sought an appropriate author for what, by now, he referred to as the "Centennial History." Almost everyone agreed that the ideal peson was Henry Lee Swint, then McTyeire Professor of History. Swint received one of the earliest modern Vanderbilt Ph.D.s, had been a member of the Vanderbilt history department since the 1930s, was a pioneer in the field of social and intellectual history, and had taught and directed more graduate students than any other historian at Vanderbilt. By early 1969 he agreed to direct the centennial history project, and in April the Executive Committee of the Board of Trust approved the project and authorized the first funds to finance it. The committee noted that the expected publication date was 1975, the centennial of the first courses taught in the College of Arts and Science. Swint began research in the summer of 1969 and continued to work, on a half-time basis, until his retirement in the spring of 1977. Essie W. Samuels served as his associate director, and soon Swint and Samuels directed the work of up to four research assistants each semester. Most of these were graduate students in the history department. Altogether, over twenty-five people served, some briefly, as research assistants. Such a large research effort led to significant and enduring results. But with Swint's retirement in 1977, the Board of Trust, citing budget restrictions, suspended the project.

The products of this research effort are now on deposit in the Special Collections of the Heard Library. Even after working for over a year with these deposits, I have only begun to appreciate their scope. In effect, Swint created a university archives and for a period assumed the title of archivist. He and his crew located and gathered manuscript collections from all over the campus. They also created a greater historical consciousness on the part of faculty and administrators. The research assistants began compiling detailed research notes and writing preliminary briefs on almost every conceivable topic connected with Vanderbilt's history. A whole wall of file cabinets, which now contain the thousands of cards and dozens of briefs, form an enduring resource duplicated on few if any other campuses. Finally, working from these notes and briefs, Swint completed drafts of approximately half the topically organized chapters he planned in a projected two-volume history.

When I began work on this project in 1982, I inherited this gold mine of organized notes and completed briefs and chapters. Unfortunately, I could not use the notes as effectively as I had hoped, not because of any deficiency in them but because their sheer number overwhelmed me, and also because those who so conscientiously compiled them had often not probed the topics I thought most important or answered the questions that I, perhaps perversely, kept asking. But for focused questions, or specific topics, the notes almost always contained the answers, as I so often discovered after duplicating the earlier research in primary sources. Because possibly a fourth of the research for my history involved these notes, briefs, or chapters and almost all the other research involved the archival material that Swint and his staff had collected, I cannot began to express the debt I owe to Swint and to his team. Neither can I estimate how much longer it would have taken me to research and write this history had not so much preliminary work preceded my own effort. Unfortunately, I can think of no better way to acknowledge the work of Henry Lee Swint than to list him as an assisting author, although the title is inappropriate. It unfairly minimizes his contribution to my research and my understanding, even as it may suggest, quite incorrectly, that he is in any way responsible for my judgments or for the inevitable errors that remain in this biography.

My debt to those who preceded me is only slightly greater than to one who, in a sense, followed after. Patricia S. Miletich worked half time during 1982–83, even as I worked full time. She took over all my chapter drafts, carefully rechecked my sources, consulted new ones, and noted and corrected errors and misinterpretations. In this process she also compiled the notes. Since Patricia is the sole author of the notes as they now appear, her designation as assistant author is correct. But the title does not do full justice to her contribution, in part because it does not make clear how willing she was to work with almost no supervision, how many vital initiatives she took, or with what good will she lugged and then worked through the hundreds of newspapers, bulletins, minutes, and boxes of manuscripts. She seemed undaunted by the most boring of tasks.

Though no one was appointed for the task, Patricia and I nonetheless enjoyed the willing services of a research staff. All the people in Special Collections worked for us, in the sense that they advised us about, searched out, and carried to our desks all the archival materials that we requested. They did it gladly and never openly rebelled against my typical sense of urgency and my impatience over even ten minutes of wasted time. Most responsible for this help were Marice M. Wolfe, head of Special Collections, and her assistant, Sara J. Harwell.

For the photographic research, I turned always to Kay R. Beasley, Vanderbilt's photo archivist. I feel that she had a greater role in identifying, if not in selecting, the photographs than I did. Libby Byler had joined the Vanderbilt Photographic Archive by 1984, and generously contributed her artistic talent to the final selection and reproduction of photographs. Throughout the hot summer of 1983 Judy Williams typed into an unfamiliar computer console, which she soon mastered, over 1500 pages of messy manuscript. She not only worked rapidly and efficiently but with boundless good humor.

During the searching and writing of this history, I continually talked to Vanderbilt people—to professors, students, and former students. In fact, some of my colleagues in the history department became bored with the subject of Vanderbilt's past, but they kept talking. They shared more insights than they realized. I also arranged a few formal interviews. Since I took no detailed notes and compiled no transcripts for the archives, I have no reason to cite these interviews in my notes. They offer no resource for scholars. But I gladly acknowledge the information provided by Leonard Beach, Harvie Branscomb, Emmett B. Fields, Sam M. Fleming, Walter J. Harrelson, William C. Havard, Alexander Heard, Susan Ford Wiltshire, and David T. Wilson. Equally helpful were those who read all or part of the completed manuscript and who helped me avoid embarrassing errors or serious lapses in style: Harvie Branscomb, Jeff R. Carr, Emmett B. Fields, Alexander Heard, Robert A. McGaw, Rob Roy Purdy, V. Jacque Voegeli, and Henry Lee Swint.

More personal but not less important were those who gave support from within my families. I refer to colleagues, to the secretaries in the history department, and most of all to my wife, Dorothy. I was so absorbed in the project, so isolated from the normal tasks of home and shop, so neglectful of ordinary duties, as to require their constant indulgence.

Contents

Illustrations

EXECPT AS OTHERWISE NOTED, PHOTOGRAPHS COURTESY OF
THE VANDERBILT UNIVERSITY PHOTOGRAPHIC ARCHIVE.

Foundations

(1854–1874)

As UNIVERSITIES GO, *Vanderbilt is very young. It takes at least a century for a university to reach early adolescence, to gain a relatively stable identity. By then, some basic character traits are already established, but any rapidly growing university retains the impressionability of adolescents, their openness to new goals and new self-understanding. For a historian, writing a biography of an adolescent has its challenges and rewards. The early, rapidly changing years of a university are always exciting, full of soaring dreams and great hopes as well as stresses and strains, bright promises as well as great dangers and bitter disappointments. But the hazards are intimidating. Only in the light of a mature, if not a completed life, can one locate the more enduring and significant facets of childhood and youth.*

The Vanderbilt story has no clear beginning. Even the organic metaphor breaks down, for one can neither date its conception nor its birth. The legendary story of Bishop Holland N. McTyeire and Cornelius Vanderbilt marks as much a culmination as a beginning. The chronological ambiguities reflect the divergent histories of Vanderbilt's component colleges. Both the Medical School and George Peabody College for Teachers originated within the old University of Nashville and thus touch upon an institutional history that went back almost to Nashville's founding. The ambiguity also results from the several stages in the long effort of a few leaders of the Methodist Episcopal Church, South, to found a university. The first, abortive efforts came before the Civil War.

1

Birth Pains

THE METHODIST MOVEMENT split in 1844 over the issue of slaveowning. The southern branch eventually established both its publishing house and its missionary board in Nashville. Here annually met its bishops and here gathered its most able authors and editors, the nearest approach to intellectuals within the denomination. Thus Nashville, as the administrative and intellectual capital of southern Methodism, outranked other cities as a logical site of any denomination-wide university, one capable of providing advanced training for the graduates of the thirty or so struggling colleges supported by the annual conferences of the church.

The quadrennial General Conference of 1854 took the lead. This highest governing body within the southern church approved a resolution calling for a convention of leading Methodist educators, largely leaders from its colleges and academies. The Tennessee Conference subsequently endorsed this proposal. Thus, a convention met in Nashville in April, 1856, and formed itself into the Educational Institute of the Methodist Episcopal Church, South. This institute was to meet annually and work to improve southern Methodist education by raising larger college endowments, providing special training for teachers, and improving textbooks. The institute's membership consisted mainly of Methodist college teachers and, at least as honorary members, ministers concerned about education. Significantly for the later Vanderbilt University, a founding member of the institute was Holland N. McTyeire, then a minister in New Orleans but shortly to take over as editor of the Nashville *Christian Advocate,* the denomination's major periodical. The first head of the institute was Bishop Robert Paine.[1]

The first dream of a great Methodist university in Nashville matured among the members of the Educational Institute. Critical in the work of the institute was the special outlook, and the compelling interest, of those who represented denominational colleges. Important in comparison with later such efforts was the strength of the prewar southern economy and thus the realistic possibility of adequate funding from within the denomination. No records certify who, if it was one person, first conceived of a graduate-level university in Nashville. Possibly the thinking of several members of the institute converged on this quite logical next step in Methodist higher education. On April 16, 1857, the editor of the Nashville *Christian Advocate* reprinted a proposal from California (in the *Pacific Methodist*) that the forthcoming second meeting of the institute consider a central educational institution in Nashville.

The Educational Institute, meeting in Nashville in April, 1857, constituted a new committee on university education, made up of representatives from five Methodist colleges. One member, Professor W.J. Sasnett of Emory College in Georgia, presented the committee's major resolution—that the institute seek support for a central university in Nashville, consisting of the three departments of medicine, law, and literature. Notably lacking was any proposal for a theological school, an issue that had already stirred up a major controversy among Methodists. The resolution detailed the courses to be offered by the literary department and stressed their graduate level. Only graduates of regular colleges would qualify for admission to a two-year program leading to a Master of Arts degree. The university was to be controlled fully by the Methodist Episcopal Church, South, with its trustees appointed by the General Conference. Given the lack of competition with any existing colleges, it is no wonder that the institute delegates unanimously approved the resolution and set up a committee to procure a charter from the Tennessee legislature.[2]

With the adjournment of the institute, the fate of a central university passed largely into the hands of local, Tennessee boosters. Chief among these, and one of the heroes of Vanderbilt history, was Alexander Little Page Green. Born in 1806 in the mountains of East Tennessee, he gained the rudiments of an education in mountain schools, became a licensed Methodist exhorter at age eighteen, and later became a successful preacher and circuit rider, serving stations (congregations) throughout the Tennessee Conference. Settling in Nashville, he became a successful financier, a man of considerable wealth, but remained faithful to and active in the Methodist church. He used his credit to help establish the Methodist Publishing House in Nashville. Perhaps because of his own lack of education, his struggles as a young and handicapped preacher, he became a dedicated supporter of higher education and of the establishment of a central university. He also contributed later to Fisk University and to a small Methodist college at Florence, Alabama.[3]

Green and two other committee members, one the editor of the *Christian Advocate,* easily gained a charter from the Tennessee legislature in January, 1858, for a "Central University of the General Conference of the Methodist Episcopal Church, South." Unfortunately, they did not build wide support within the larger denomination. The charter, which closely followed the terms of the 1857 institute resolutions, had only one immediate effect—a group of leading physicians organized the Shelby Medical School of the Central University and began instruction in 1858. This fully proprietary school (fees paid all the cost) offered courses for three years, or until the war and the federal occupation of Nashville. Several graduates received Central University degrees. Two of the school's three organizers joined the Medical

Department of the University of Nashville after the war and thus were part of a medical school that subsequently affiliated with Vanderbilt University.[4]

Except for lending a prestigious name to a medical school, the first Central University never moved beyond dreams and a charter. The denomination betrayed the cause. Green brought his new charter to the combined meeting in May, 1858, of the institute and the General Conference. The Educational Institute welcomed the charter; not so, the General Conference. Acceptance by the conference seemed essential to any success. The educators in the institute now realized that they had failed in public relations. One of their own, McTyeire, faulted them for not publicizing the minutes of the 1857 meeting and thus circulating needed information about their proposed new university. The new charter contained the names of an original Board of Trust, yet the most eminent trustee listed, the beloved senior bishop Joshua Soule, insisted that he had not seen the charter and did not even know his name was on it.

The conference (then made up only of bishops and ministers) refused its endorsement after extended debate that revealed loyalties to other sites or to other aspiring universities, concerns about costs or sources of funds, and objections to the independence of the new medical school. The conference considered and rejected a motion to accept the charter but to defer any action on it until the next General Conference (1862). It even considered appointing a new committee to study sites, to consider methods of funding, and to form a new charter. In the winning resolution the General Conference refused to accept the charter allegedly because its quadrennial meetings made such inexpedient. It therefore referred the whole matter to the Tennessee Conference, which met annually.[5]

The lack of support by the General Conference probably doomed the Central University but did not end all efforts in its behalf. In October, 1858, Green and others persuaded the Tennessee Conference to accept the charter, with the understanding that they would secure needed changes in the name from the Tennessee legislature. Although the Tennessee Conference was willing to hold the charter, it could not fund such a denomination-wide effort, and so it appointed Green and James H. McFerrin, editor of the *Christian Advocate,* to seek general denominational support. The delegates to the 1859 Educational Institute continued their cheers for such a university, but it was clear that practical results would have to await a successful appeal at the 1862 General Conference.[6]

The war intervened. By May of 1862, federal troops occupied Nashville and the denominational buildings. But the story did not end. Attempts to establish this first Central University directly affected the founding of Vanderbilt by identifying Nashville as the most likely site of any major Methodist university and showing the organizers the need for wide support within the denomination. Further, it clarified the need for the advanced, possibly graduate, level of any such university. Above all, it created a loosely knit community

5

of the ablest Methodist bishops and ministers, all committed to a great university.

The war devastated the southern Methodist church. Disillusioned church leaders had fervently supported the Confederacy and the bid for southern independence. Somewhat defiantly, they resisted reconciliation or even missionary efforts by their northern brethren. In a critical General Conference at New Orleans in 1866, they reorganized the Methodist Episcopal Church, South. Among other changes, the church opened its General Conference to lay as well as ministerial delegates. This conference considered the problem of theological education but in the straitened economic situation recommended only biblical departments in the reopening southern Methodist colleges (only one had been open at war's end). Eventually, most of the older colleges did reopen, and Methodists throughout the South joined in a crusade for more if not better higher education. Within a decade the church had about forty colleges, although many were weak to the point of death and none was able to achieve the educational standards of better northern schools.[7]

In this postwar revival of the southern church, later Vanderbilt supporters or officials played a large role. McTyeire, for example, had fled to his Alabama farm in 1862, ministered to rural congregations for two years, then joined refugee Methodist intellectuals in Montgomery. From there he came as a delegate to the New Orleans conference. In Montgomery he joined an old friend, Thomas O. Summers (McTyeire had earlier succeeded him in the pulpit of the Mobile church) and A.L.P. Green, now a fellow refugee from Nashville. McTyeire, a key architect of the New Orleans reorganization, was therewith elected bishop and in 1867 left Montgomery to return to Nashville. His duties as bishop, presiding over and attending to the business of various annual conferences, left open his place of residence. The McKendree church in Nashville invited him to occupy their bishop's house, now vacant after the recent death of Soule. McTyeire was now located at the center of Methodism, and this, plus his outstanding administrative abilities, heightened his leadership among the other seven bishops. Summers also came to Nashville to work in the rebuilt publishing house (a project once again aided by Green) and to edit the revived *Christian Advocate*. Green came home with the old charter of Central University and took every occasion to press for its revival.[8]

The sequence of events leading to a second charter for a central university is not entirely clear. Later, several of those most involved disagreed on details or struggled to establish their own claims of priority. The first visible postwar support for a denomination-wide university appeared in four anonymous articles in the *Christian Advocate* in the spring of 1867. The writer proposed Bowling Green, Kentucky, as a site for a university sponsored by the Louisville, Tennessee, and Memphis conferences.[9]

Early postwar plans for a university soon became lost in a denominational debate over theological training, which had long preoccupied Methodists. A small cadre of Methodist intellectuals pushed for better ministerial training. McTyeire and Summers, speaking from the denominational center in Nashville, epitomized this "progressive" outlook. They deplored the deeply entrenched Methodist fear of elitism, formalism, and a ministry separated from the people. In 1868 or early 1869 they asked Landon C. Garland, then a professor of physics and astronomy at the University of Mississippi, to write a series for the *Advocate* in support of rigorous theological training. Garland, a devout churchman, was probably the best qualified educator among southern Methodists. He had taught McTyeire at the church's strongest prewar college, Randolph-Macon. His autumn, 1869, series of six thoughtful essays entitled "An Educated Ministry" preceded, by design, the General Conference of 1870. Garland proposed a central theological school to be located in Nashville. He did not tie such a school to any plan for a central university, and no evidence proves that at this time either McTyeire or Summers had such a linkage in mind. Coincidentally, another writer, using the pseudonym "Progress," contributed a three-part series in April, 1870, entitled "The Methodist University." A likely author was David C. Kelley, then minister of the local McKendree Church. These essays made a forceful appeal for a great university, comparable to Yale, Harvard, or Princeton, and thus one able to surmount the jealousy of the smaller colleges, to train professionals, and to attract to its faculty the most reputable scholars.[10]

The two schemes—for a theological seminary and a central university—did not merge at the critical General Conference of 1870, at least as revealed in the published record. The debate entirely concerned a theological school. Garland chaired the committee on education and persuaded the majority to report in favor of a theological institute. The arguments in its favor duplicated Garland's earlier article. A minority, although professedly just as interested in better-trained ministers, proposed a less expensive means—increased support for biblical departments in existing colleges. This minority report, which was less threatening to the boosters of local colleges and less alarming to opponents of formal theological training, won at the conference level after a long and bitter debate. Much later (in 1890), Garland recalled that McTyeire, Paine, himself, and others who supported the majority report had always viewed it in the context of plans for higher education as a whole. When the majority report failed, they placed all their hopes for quality theological training on a central university, one that could include an excellent theological school. A.L.P. Green, of course, eagerly endorsed this alternative. By Garland's account, bishops McTyeire and Paine joined Garland and Green in launching a campaign for such a university. They even planned to invite delegates from several annual conferences to consider it. But note that even Garland dated such planning after the vote in the conference. It seemed to be a fall-back position for all but Green. For the two bishops, at least, superior theological training remained a controlling motive.[11]

Whatever the plans they hatched at the 1870 General Conference, neither

McTyeire nor Garland rushed to implement them. McTyeire's letters to his wife reveal no compelling interest in a central university. Thus, these two greatest architects of Vanderbilt have to take second place to two other men in the next crucial move toward a university. In 1871 William C. Johnson, a Memphis minister and editor of the *Western Methodist,* began publicizing his own plans for a central university, possibly influenced by the informal discussions at the recent General Conference. He wrote McTyeire, who encouraged him, and met with Bishop Paine, who approved. In September, 1871, he wrote an editorial on the need for a great university to be supported by four annual conferences. He solicited endorsing letters from two friends. This, as he recalled it, was in preparation for the October meeting of the Tennessee Conference. He mailed copies of his editorial and one letter to the convening delegates. As Johnson later viewed it, his editorial triggered the appropriate resolution and was thus the critical necessary condition for Vanderbilt's later emergence.[12]

The scene shifts to the Tennessee Conference of 1871 at Lebanon. Here, recorded events again mix with the later memory of a key participant. Of all the founders of Vanderbilt University, David C. Kelley was the most colorful, the nearest approach to a maverick possible among the ministers of the southern Methodist Church. He later became a thorn in the sides of such addicts of orthodoxy, good order, and proper respect for constituted authority as McTyeire and Garland. Born in Wilson County, Tennessee, he had a varied career. A graduate of the local Cumberland University (a Cumberland Presbyterian college), he also took degrees in both medicine and law. He spent four broadening years as a missionary to China in the 1850s, commanded a cavalry unit in the Confederate Army, taught in a girls' school and helped found the Nashville College for Young Ladies (an early but short-lived complement to Vanderbilt University), ran unsuccessfully as prohibitionist candidate for governor in 1890, and was tried and suspended for six months by the Tennessee Conference for his campaign tactics. He pastored such leading Methodist congregations as McKendree in Nashville and was reputed to be a clever, powerful speaker. He seems, above all, to have had a lively, probing, open mind, receptive even to such new theories as Darwinism. He dreamed of a truly great university, one comparable to any others in America or in Europe. He backed his aspiration by a tolerance of faculty independence or ideological deviance that was practically beyond the comprehension of a McTyeire. Not particularly modest nor averse to controversy, and miffed by past run-ins with McTyeire, he used one of his own journals in 1890 to revise the by then orthodox version of Vanderbilt's origin. One feels he enjoyed iconoclasm. This time the dislodged idol was McTyeire.[13]

Kelley offered the successful resolution at the Tennessee Conference. It asked the bishop to appoint commissioners to visit surrounding conferences and get them to send delegates to a convention to plan a great university for the whole South, one that could command the respect of educated men everywhere. The resolution passed and Kelley became one of three commissioners. A second was the now venerable Green, the one link between all the groups working for a university. The old man made difficult trips to neighboring conferences out of his love for higher education. The third was Robert A. Young, who would long be associated with Vanderbilt as agent and secretary.[14]

More fascinating but less verifiable than this account of events is Kelley's later memory of what prompted his resolution. He had not attended the General Conference of 1870. He professed to have known nothing about any discussion of a great university, although he knew about the divinity school battle. By his account he had noted the decline or collapse of all the Methodist colleges in the upper South and had as early as 1870 conceived of a university supported by several contiguous conferences. He discussed these plans with the only nearby bishop, McTyeire. He did not note whether the visit preceded or followed the General Conference, but the story makes more sense if it preceded it. McTyeire was enthusiastic but only about a theological school. Kelley, as far back as 1867, had opposed separate theological seminaries because they did not provide a broad and liberal education. He wanted much better for ministers. As Kelley perceived his interview, McTyeire discouraged his whole scheme. Knowing the contrasting personalities of the two men, it is conceivable that McTyeire already wanted a Methodist university, one fully under the control of the bishops and one committed, above all else, to theological education. If so, his conception hardly matched Kelley's vision of a church-sponsored university but otherwise one without religious tests or even theological schools, one open to the latest science and scholarship. Kelley did concede the influence of Johnson's editorial in the *Western Methodist*. Reading it at the Tennessee Conference revived his enthusiasm for a university and helped prod him to introduce his last-moment resolution.[15]

The commission did its work well. Nine conferences appointed delegates to meet in Memphis in January, 1872. This convention created what subsequently became Vanderbilt University. The delegates included all the key figures—Green, Garland, Kelley, Johnson, and Young. Green brought along the old 1858 charter. Bishops McTyeire and Paine represented the larger church and shared the chair for several intense debates. The conferees slowly blended divergent conceptions into a resolution they could all support. Again, the theological school issue most divided the delegates. Two lay delegates, C. Jordan Stokes and Judge Edward H. East, both from the Nashville area, offered the original resolution—that a Methodist university be established, consisting of theological, normal, literary, law, and medical departments, as soon as $500,000 was invested for that purpose, except that the first department—theology—might open as soon as $100,000 was invested. A special committee worked out a broader, more general proposal, one congenial to Kelley and one that referred to a university of the highest order, built upon the broadest bases, in which the youth of the country might

9

pursue literary, scientific, and professional studies at a level comparable to any institution in America or Europe. It repeated the $500,000 requirement, made no exception for theology, but did provide for a theological school. Bishop McTyeire, a master of orderly thinking and clear exposition, fashioned the final, more detailed compromise resolution. Since it included the names of the original board of trust and would be incorporated into the subsequent charter, it remains Vanderbilt's most important founding document.[16]

The founding resolution called for the establishment, as speedily as practicable, of an institution of learning of the highest order, and upon the surest basis, in which the youth of the country and church could pursue theological, literary, scientific, and professional studies. At first, the Central University was to consist of five schools or departments (colleges, in today's language)—theological, literary and scientific, normal, law, and medicine. The provision for the theological school stipulated free tuition for "our young preachers," and opened admission to any recommended minister admitted on trial by any annual conference. The resolution emphasized that $1 million would be necessary to realize the desired objectives but provided for opening the university when $500,000 had been received (Garland fought for a full $1 million). Other resolutions involved governance. One left the site selection to the College of Bishops; another appointed the original Board of Trust (mostly made up of delegates to the Memphis Convention) and specifically empowered it to appoint agents and solicit funds. Another established a quorum rule of seven for board meetings. The charter opened membership on the board to other cooperating conferences. The final and somewhat ambiguous resolution stipulated that the bishops of the Methodist Episcopal Church, South, "be and are hereby requested to act as a Board of Supervisors of the University, or any of its departments, and jointly with the Board of Trust, to elect offices and professors, and prescribe the course of study, and the plan of government."[17]

On the day following the adoption of the Memphis resolution several of the delegates reconvened as the Board of Trust. They elected Judge Edward H. East of Nashville as their first president, with David Kelley secretary and A.L.P. Green as treasurer. These three, plus four others, constituted the first Executive Committee, charged by the board with three critical tasks—preparing a charter of incorporation, seeking approval from the bishops, and with the bishops' approval employing agents and launching the drive for funds. Incorporation proved the easiest task. Judge East, as president of the board, did the legal work and apparently even signed a fellow judge's name to the Chancery Court order of August 19, 1872, that legally established the Central University of the Methodist Episcopal Church, South. The new state constitution no longer required a special legislative act. Unfortunately, the charter did nothing to clarify the ambiguities of the Memphis resolutions. After a standard legal introduction, the court simply incorporated these resolutions into its action, making of them a university constitution. The final, standard judicial language gave to the petitioners (the first board) all the usual powers of an education corporation, such as suing and being sued, soliciting and receiving donations or legacies, buying, receiving, and holding real and personal property, appointing subordinate officers, awarding degrees, and making by-laws needed to carry out the objects of the resolutions. In light of the later controversies over the government of the university that led to separation from the Methodist Church, the key but standard phrase in the charter was the one providing for "perpetual succession," which meant that the board could determine its own new members.[18]

The board had more difficulty with the bishops. It met in Nashville concurrently with the annual meeting of the bishops in May, 1872, and instructed David Kelley, its secretary, to prepare an appeal for support. The bishops only briefly discussed the Central University before going off to dedicate the cornerstone of a new publishing house. The next day McTyeire pleaded with his colleagues but could gain only their limited support. The bishops agreed to the request of what they called the "board of curators"—that they choose the site of the university when $500,000 was in hand. But they carefully qualified even this cooperation; the new institution was not to be considered as "connectional to the damage of existing colleges and universities." They clearly did not want to adopt the university for the whole church, but only to approve the work of cooperating conferences, leaving it on par with other colleges sponsored by one or more annual conferences. In particular, they disavowed any active relationship to the proposed theological department and made as a condition of even their cooperation in choosing the site adherence by the Central University in its theological department to the minority report adopted at Memphis in 1870 (that biblical departments in existing colleges were the best available means of training young ministers). This was, at best, an unclear stipulation, at worst a mandate that the new university have only professors of Bible and no real seminary.[19]

The disappointed Board of Trust interpreted this begrudging action as sufficient for them to go on with their fund raising. Without the help of the bishops, the board faced an almost impossible task, given the poverty of the South and the other pressing appeals for Methodist contributions (for local colleges, for an old missionary debt, and to rebuild the publishing house, which burned in 1872). To make matters worse, an elderly and defiant bishop, George F. Pierce, wrote a series of four damning letters to the *Christian Advocate*, noting the lack of support for such a university, its forbidding cost, its potential monopoly of Methodist higher education, and, most important to him, its defiance of the denominational position against theological schools. Pierce, an old-fashioned Methodist orator, restated all the older Methodist objections to theological schools and praised the beloved circuit system. McTyeire wrote careful, moderate replies to the first three of the old man's emotional tirades, but the very fact of such a debate between

Part One: Foundations (1854–1874)

two bishops was bound to divide opinion and make fund raising for such a controversial university all that more difficult. Thus, as in 1857, the Methodist church as a whole subverted rather than supported plans for a major university.[20]

The next step for the board seemed most forbidding—raising $500,000. A.L.P. Green, as treasurer, headed the desperate effort, and soon he was almost the only board member who thought the task possible. The board, in frequent but increasingly ill-attended meetings, prepared a major address to Methodists, with a special appeal to the more affluent. It also appointed agents to roam the conferences and to solicit needed gifts or pledges. As then standard, the agents were to collect their salaries (a maximum of $1,000 a year) either directly from the gifts collected or from interest realized on such gifts. But returns invited despair. Four of the earlier conferences dropped out, and only one new one joined. In the first year most agents were unable to collect enough to pay their own salaries. But despite the early setbacks and the indefinite postponement of any university opening, the board enacted its first by-laws and prepared itself, administratively, to open a university. The by-laws provided for one annual board meeting each May and for the three officers to be elected annually. The by-laws formalized an Executive Committee made up of the three officers plus one board member from each cooperating conference. In a key bid for freedom from church control, the by-laws provided that the board fill all vacancies upon a "nomination" by the appropriate conference.[21]

In February, 1873, Bishop McTyeire went to New York. What happened there over the next month created the central legend of Vanderbilt history. Typical of legends, details and motives remain hidden, some controverted. McTyeire was the key figure. As a bishop he was not, and perhaps legally was not eligible to be, a member of the Central University board, since he was a member of the second governing body created by the charter, the Board of Supervisors. He had attended board meetings whenever possible, usually as the sole representative of the bishops. It is even difficult to measure the depth of his support for the early Central University, except for its theological component. But from this point on he played the key role. Besides soliciting the Vanderbilt gift, he would select the university's site, plan its grounds, direct the building of its physical plant, and have the final word in selecting its first faculty.[22]

McTyeire was born and spent his boyhood in a Methodist family in Barnwell County, South Carolina. As he began his ascent through Methodist schools, his family relocated in eastern Alabama. McTyeire did his college work at Randolph-Macon in Virginia. He began his first trial preaching just before the Methodist North-South split of 1844. President Landon Garland gave him his only earned degree, the B.A. from Randolph-Macon in 1844. Even with this he was better educated than nine out of ten of his ministerial colleagues. He served normally short ministerial terms in Williamsburg,

Virginia, in Mobile and at Demopolis, Alabama, and in Columbus, Mississippi. He preached often in rural pulpits but never really experienced the hardships of an itinerant. In 1849 he moved to a new mission station in New Orleans and there began his expanded service to his church. His brilliant ability in administration and organization came to the fore, as he unified struggling white churches, separately ministered to Negro congregations, and launched a successful religious periodical. To administrative skills McTyeire added those of a superb journalist. He had a gift for eloquent, often witty prose and obviously enjoyed composition above other arts, including oratory. His writing and editorial skills won him, in 1858, the editorship of the *Christian Advocate* and also began his association with Nashville.[23]

McTyeire was a bit out of place as a Methodist preacher. He won few plaudits from his first parishioners. He lacked the appropriate style and ultimately used other than preaching skills to win his ascendency in the church. Not that he preached poor sermons. Untypical of Methodist ministers, he wrote most of them, reused many of them, and preserved them for posterity. As literary exercises they exuded careful logic, modulated feeling, graceful literary allusions, compelling if sly wit, and withal a quite orthodox exposition of Methodist doctrines. His sermons, even the first ones, might have delighted an eighteenth-century Anglican audience. But this was not what his audiences wanted or expected, particularly those in rural churches or at outdoor campings. McTyeire knew this and tried to oblige his audiences. He dropped some of his early classical allusions and developed a pungent, even earthy style. He drew his images and illustrations directly from the life around him. Also, as he recorded in evaluations of his own preaching, he tried to extemporize, particularly in more evangelical contexts. On a few occasions, as he put it in typical Wesleyan language, he preached with "great liberty." A few sermons consist of little more than outlines, but McTyeire rarely depended upon the Spirit. By all reports his voice tended to be a bit loud and monotonous, his tempo slow and deliberate, the very characteristics that hurt him in a less formal context.[24]

McTyeire's sermons were literary, not theological. They abounded in practical and moralistic advice, but except for his earliest efforts rarely included much doctrinal analysis. In biblical analysis they revealed ingenuity but not daring scholarship or deep questions. Only rarely and with difficulty did McTyeire use personal experience even for illustrative purposes, another oddity for normally confessional Methodists. Thus, at least as written, his sermons seem detached and impersonal. They reflect a governmental, or juristic, approach to religion, not without genuine feeling but still strangely lacking in esthetic motifs or hints of intense, let alone ecstatic, religious experience. His was a dutiful, respectful piety, not a love affair with his deity.[25] As his role in the church shifted toward publication, his abilities began to better match his calling. He wrote an authoritative, lawyer-like manual on church discipline and much later, at Vanderbilt, wrote a scholarly but quite self-revealing and at times embarrassingly partisan southern *History of Methodism*.

McTyeire was tall, a bit stout with age, forceful and imposing. He looked like a bishop. As a bishop McTyeire was demanding, industrious, and very effective, setting high expectations for the ministers under his charge and demanding of them a meticulous accounting of their year's work. In leadership abilities, administrative talents, and literary skills he exceeded any of his fellow bishops; the other leaders of the church soon recognized this. His position began to dignify even his sermons. A final, rousing, inspiring sermon from the bishop was traditional at annual conferences, but McTyeire never adopted this style. Nevertheless, as he grew older people came to value, even love, his natural eloquence, his sincerity, even his deliberate style. The careful delivery, the logical arguments and wise instruction, seemed appropriate for a bishop, if not for a young minister taking his turn at a camp meeting.[26]

McTyeire kept his distance from most people. Almost all who knew him remarked his reticence; a detached or hidden person, he kept his own counsel. Enemies accused him of secretiveness. But his letters reveal a warm, even passionate husband, an intensely loving and concerned father, and by almost everyone's acknowledgment a person who loved children. Perhaps typical of very shy people, he dropped his normal defenses only when in the presence of children. He enjoyed the out-of-doors and particularly in his Vanderbilt days took special pride in the many trees and shrubs he had planted on the new campus. Barely concealed in his sermons, but clear in correspondence, was a man capable of intense partisan loyalties to his church, to the South, to friends. His mixture of loyalties, intense personal ambition, and rigid self-control made him an effective executive, or as those who admired him so often put it, a great and inspired leader. Had he not entered the ministry (and that without any explosive or instantaneous conversion), he might have excelled as a crusading newspaper editor or even as an innovative businessman. But he lacked a certain breadth of mind, just as he lacked the subtlety of an intellectual. He did not easily understand those outside the boundaries of his own loyalties, those who could not share his commitment to Methodism, the church as a whole, basic Christian doctrines, decent morality, or, later, his beloved Vanderbilt University.[27]

McTyeire was indispensable in the founding of Vanderbilt University. None of the other founders would have so skillfully dealt with Cornelius Vanderbilt; none would have moved so surely, so quickly, and so competently in making decisions about sites and buildings. McTyeire seemed immune to self-doubts, incapable of prolonged indecision. He took charge of tasks and completed them. But these same traits often made him a poor, at times almost disastrous, president of an ongoing university. But in 1873 he did not have to run a university; he only had to seduce a commodore.

On his extended trips as bishop, McTyeire frequently wrote back to his wife about a nagging medical problem. Apparently its private nature precluded open description, but it most likely involved the prostate. Thus, he came to New York in February, 1873, for some unnamed surgical procedure. The operation was serious enough to keep him flat on his back for four days. He reported to his wife that he had expected to stay in New York only ten days. Yet, despite the lack of conclusive evidence, one suspects a bit of a conspiracy—that McTyeire selected a New York surgeon in hopes of meeting Cornelius Vanderbilt and winning from him support for the Central University. It was now clear to McTyeire that only a wealthy benefactor could ever enable the board to meet the $500,000 condition. Other northern entrepreneurs had achieved favorable publicity, or possibly assuaged their guilt, by such gifts. Even Daniel Drew, the most corrupt and scandalous of speculators, had endowed a northern Methodist seminary. Unknown to anyone at the time, Vanderbilt had already contributed money to the bishop— $1,000 in 1872 to help rebuild the Methodist Publishing House. His willingness to do so had nothing to do with an ill-educated and anything but pious Vanderbilt's religious convictions (he never joined a church). Neither did he have any special sympathy for southern Methodism. Rather, it revealed the influence of his second wife, her mother, and possibly that of their minister. Perhaps his whole relationship to McTyeire proved the old adage: "Down South what counts is not who you know but who you are a kin to." To a few pious Methodists, it also reflected the contrivances of divine providence.[28]

While filling his second pastorate, in Mobile, McTyeire had met his future wife, Amelia Townsend. This marriage gave McTyeire entry into some of the most affluent families in Mobile. Here, unlike in most other cities save Nashville, the Methodist Church catered to the socially elite as well as to others. Among this elite was a half-sister to Mrs. Townsend, Martha (Mrs. Robert L.) Crawford. The Crawfords had a daughter over a decade younger than her cousin Amelia, but one destined to remain a close friend of her cousin throughout her life. This cousin, because of a foolish promise by the parents to name their first child, regardless of sex, after a close family friend, gained the unlikely and forbidding name of Frank Armstrong. Frank, seven when McTyeire served the Mobile church, later faced severe traumas—an unsuccessful marriage, the loss of a beloved father, and the hardships and impoverishment of war. She was inseparable from her mother, emotionally dependent upon her. Frank taught singing and music in a Mobile girls' school.[29]

At the end of the war the mother and daughter moved to New York, where Frank continued her teaching. Here the two Crawford ladies accepted (after indirectly soliciting) the hospitality of Cornelius Vanderbilt and his ailing first wife, since Vanderbilt's mother had been a distant relative of Mrs. Crawford's. The Crawfords became fixtures of the Vanderbilt household, comforting the aging Commodore during the death of his wife. Perhaps by intent they became almost indispensable to him. In 1869 the seventy-five year old Commodore married Frank, in a rushed wedding performed in Canada.

15

His marriage to a young lady forty-three years his junior occasioned endless gossip and numerous guesses about the motives of each party. From what is known, Frank was a dutiful, kind, helpful wife, a devoted companion during the Commodore's last six years. For this devotion she and her mother gained economic security plus a degree of unwanted notoriety. McTyeire now had direct access to perhaps the wealthiest man in America through his beloved cousin and loyal friend.[30]

Did Frank Vanderbilt and McTyeire plot their appeal to the Commodore? Probably. He had written Frank before his trip, suggesting that they try to get the Commodore "to do for us, what Daniel Drew did for the northern Methodists." Frank, according to letters she wrote later, used the occasion of a drive past the Astor Library to remind Cornelius of what needed to be done for the young men of the South, who had access only to debt-ridden colleges and inadequate libraries. In response to his query about what he could do, she suggested that he endow a southern university.[31]

The psychological preparation of the Commodore involved another figure in Vanderbilt history—Charles F. Deems. He was then Frank's minister at the nondenominational Church of the Strangers in New York City. A southern Methodist from North Carolina, Deems offered the Crawford ladies the type of warm and familiar religion they had known back in Mobile. Deems was a frequent guest at the Vanderbilt mansion and apparently without direct appeal received from the Commodore the funds to buy his church building. Deems never converted the suspicious old man, but he and Frank played upon his sentimentality, his greater openness to religion as he grew older. Vanderbilt revered his mother and her Moravian faith, had offered money for a Moravian women's college (apparently the church never met his terms), and loved the old Methodist hymns that Frank sang for him. Much later, with no supporting evidence, Deems made the doubtful claim that even before McTyeire's visit he had already persuaded the Commodore to endow a university rather than build a great Washington's monument for New York City, and that he, not Frank, subsequently persuaded a reluctant Vanderbilt to make added gifts to the university. The evidence suggests that Deems claimed far too much, but that he and his church may have helped to create enough sympathy for a warm, Methodist-style religion to help persuade Cornelius to endow what became Vanderbilt University.[32]

McTyeire received his expected invitation to visit, even convalesce, in the Vanderbilt home. Not only was he cousin to the Crawford ladies but a close friend and a revered bishop in their own preferred church. They were undoubtedly honored, as well as pleased, to have his company, quite apart from any university business. In letters to Amelia, McTyeire also recorded an increasingly friendly relationship to the Commodore. The two men, so alike in ambition and in powerful personalities, hit it off from the beginning. Respect and trust resulted. McTyeire could not help but like the old Commodore and admire his entrepreneurial achievements, in shipping and then in railroads. Wealth always impressed him. In a memorial sermon delivered after Vanderbilt's death, McTyeire, always the moralistic bishop, conceded world-ly facets of Vanderbilt's life (he did not condemn his business ethics) but he still struggled to find redeeming, if not redemptive, virtues. He made Van-derbilt something of a secular saint, establishing a pattern of praise that long punctuated the university's formal ceremonies. This retrospective whitewashing helped conceal the obvious—Vanderbilt University, like most other American private universities, was born of an unholy marriage of piety and plutocracy.[33]

McTyeire always boasted that he never asked Vanderbilt for any gifts. He was far too clever for such tactics. Frank had seen to it that Vanderbilt was already interested in plans for the Central University. He was seeking a suitable beneficiary for some of his money, a belated claim to a type of immortality. Sheer emulation of other wealthy men, if nothing else, led him in this direction. McTyeire needed only to air the plans and give vent to his own enthusiasm. Soon Vanderbilt was intrigued, even fascinated. By the final evening of McTyeire's visit, March 12, Vanderbilt had a proposition which he put in the form of a letter to the Central University's board. An exultant McTyeire wrote the news to Amelia, while an indiscreet Deems released it to New York newspapers. McTyeire rescheduled his trip home in order to visit the new universities at Syracuse and Cornell, plus older ones at Yale and Virginia.[34]

On March 26, McTyeire presented Vanderbilt's proposal to a specially called meeting of the Board of Trust at McKendree Church. The board enthusiastically accepted the Commodore's offer and set about modifying the charter to meet his terms, even as it also voted to change the name of the Central University to The Vanderbilt University. The charter change was entered on June 16, 1873. In almost all respects a simple change of name, the amendment included only one section that could be interpreted later as an increase in the status and power of the board. The court, without mentioning the Board of Supervisors (the Bishops), gave to the newly named university's Board of Trust the "power to pass by-laws, resolutions, etc., not inconsistent with the laws of the land, and to increase and diminish the number of its trustees and change the name of its schools, and do and perform any and all acts allowable by law to corporations of learning."[35]

Vanderbilt made his offer directly to McTyeire and only by way of him to the board of the Central University. He authorized McTyeire, not the board, to procure suitable grounds of "not less than from twenty to fifty acres," to submit to him plans and specifications for suitable buildings. Upon approval, Vanderbilt promised all needed funds and in addition to those expenses promised a total gift of "no less" than $500,000, with the excess over cost to go into endowment and library funds. Later letters made clear that Vander-bilt anticipated $300,000 for the endowment and $200,000 for land, build-ings, and library and scientific equipment, but that he was prepared to spend

*Bishop and Board President
Holland N. McTyeire*

*Chancellor
Landon C. Garland*

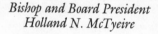

FOUNDING FATHERS

more if needed. Since he expanded his gifts to a total of almost $1 million (exactly $995,831) before his death in early 1877, it is possible he planned from the beginning to match the full charter commitment. He placed some ticklish conditions on his offer, conditions that either the Board of Trust or Supervisors had to swallow. McTyeire had to be elected president of the board and receive $3,000 in salary plus a free house on or near the campus. At his death the board was free to elect his successor. The board quickly obliged Vanderbilt on this point. But since McTyeire was already and automatically a member of the Board of Supervisors, his presidency raised a problem of propriety if not of legality. Vanderbilt also stipulated that McTyeire have veto powers over board action (only three-fourths could override his veto of motions approved by the board), that the university be in or near Nashville, and that all endowment funds remain inviolate. Vanderbilt offered only one motive for his munificent gift—sectional reconciliation. Later, he reportedly said he wanted to do something for the South because he had married one of its noblest daughters.[36]

Vanderbilt's offer brought speedy action at the expense of procedures

18

provided for in the original charter. One shudders to contemplate how long the bishops would have debated over sites. Vanderbilt, in effect, had turned a republican board into a monarchical one. McTyeire was not in a position to move quickly. Without checking with his board or even informing the treasurer, he committed the funds for land, buildings, and equipment, drawing directly on the Commodore for payment and rendering accounts only to him.

As soon as he returned to Nashville, McTyeire began scouting out possible sites. He insisted upon full control and thus refused any appropriated funds from the City of Nashville or any bargains with the now declining University of Nashville. He looked at proposed sites in many areas in and around the city, including one pushed by former neighbors of his across the Cumberland in Edgefield (he had lived there from 1854 to 1862). He settled on a small hill to the west of Nashville, off West End Avenue and Hillsboro Pike. In secret he first negotiated by May, 1873, the purchase of six parcels of mixed residential and farm land, all totaling about sixty-six acres and costing him just less than $75,000 (donations by owners cut the actual outlay by $15,000). By July he added a final lot, bringing the total for an amazingly symmetrical plot to approximately seventy five acres, at a cost of almost $90,000. After he had selected the site, he took his Board of Supervisors (the bishops) on tour and persuaded them to approve and thus legalize his fait accompli. The site, as purchased, had one residence (the present Old Central), a large boarding house near the present central library (renamed Wesley Hall and used as a residence for the first divinity students), and several smaller buildings.[37]

By July, McTyeire had engaged his architect, William C. Smith of Nashville, and sent him on a tour of other colleges. For both the physical and early academic plans he called upon his old teacher, Landon C. Garland of the University of Mississippi, and even took his architect to visit Garland while he was at one of his favorite trout streams in southwest Virginia. By the fall of 1873, McTyeire had planned campus walks and roads and the location of the first buildings. In April, 1874, he joined in laying the cornerstone of the first major building (now Kirkland Hall). This large building (to contain all classrooms, libraries, and laboratories) plus seven new faculty homes and a small observatory made up the original construction program. As the buildings went up, McTyeire and Garland recruited the original faculty, began buying books and scientific instruments, all in preparation for the opening of classes in 1875. McTyeire, aided by Garland, accomplished in just thirty months what might have taken five or six years. No deliberative body could have moved as rapidly.[38]

Cornelius Vanderbilt's original gift was open-ended. His purpose, as would become clear, was to provide McTyeire all he needed to build a great university that soon bore his name. He demanded only efficient, effective use of his money. In 1874 he increased his original commitment by $100,000. By the opening of the university in 1875, McTyeire's detailed accounts showed

Bishop McTyeire's campus home and later chancellor's residence

Chancellor Garland's residence

that the grounds, buildings, and equipment had cost almost double the expected $200,000 (actually $392,831). To bring the endowment back to the contemplated level of $300,000, the Commodore added another $92,831, for a then total committed gift of $692,831. Then, during his last illness, and during the final and third visit of McTyeire, he added another $300,000 in railroad bonds to the endowment, bringing it up to $600,000, where it remained for over a decade. The 7-percent bonds yielded $42,000 a year to Vanderbilt's operating budget. The Commodore also gave $3,000 to pay for medals, what became known as Founder's Medals.[39]

Even these gifts did not exhaust the Vanderbilt legacy. The original university buildings quickly proved insufficient, while the older Wesley Hall could not accommodate all the ministers who wanted training in the Biblical Department. Thus, in July, 1879, William H. Vanderbilt, the Commodore's son and also a friend of McTyeire, followed what he assumed would have been his father's wishes and offered $100,000 for three new buildings—a gymnasium, a hall of science and engineering (Old Science), and, by far the largest and most costly, a very large divinity building (the second of three Wesley Halls in Vanderbilt history). This building would have classrooms as well as rooms for students and single faculty. When the actual cost almost doubled the original $100,000, as McTyeire surely anticipated, W.H. Vanderbilt followed the example of his father and covered the whole amount. All in all, the two Vanderbilts gave almost $1.2 million to launch the new university. The amount is not nearly as significant as the fact that they were willing to give McTyeire a blank check for the capital expenditures that he believed necessary for a successful university. Had his vision entailed larger expenses, and had he been able to explain and justify them to the Vanderbilts, they might well have given even more. The Commodore, once committed to this venture, desired only the best. The seeming success of the new university was a great consolation to him in his last year; nothing more absorbed his interest than this, his last great enterprise. The $600,000 endowment, when supplemented by tuition and other fees and by smaller contributions, seemed sufficient for maintaining the facilities and paying the needed faculty.[40]

The magnitude of the original Vanderbilt gifts becomes clearer by comparison to present values. It is almost impossible to compare the value of a dollar in 1875 to one in 1984. In some areas of rapid technological advance, a dollar buys more today than then. Perhaps the most appropriate comparison for the beginning Vanderbilt are building costs and faculty salaries. The original professors (chairs) received $2,500 plus a free house, then calculated at a rent of $250 a year, or a total compensation of $2,750.[41] Comparable professors today receive from $60,000 to $75,000 in total compensation (stated salaries are lower), or a ratio of at least 20 to 1. This means that the $42,000 annually yielded by the endowment would today total at least $840,000, possibly even a million dollars. Building costs are now at least thirty times higher than in 1875 (Kirkland and Wesley Halls would cost, not

$100,000 each, but at least $3 to $5 million). Thus, the near $600,000 expended from 1874 to 1880 on buildings and equipment would today amount to $18 million. The $600,000 endowment, expanded even by a factor of twenty, would today total $12 million. This only proves that Vanderbilt University began as an exceptionally privileged institution, rich beyond any comparable university save the very oldest private colleges in the Northeast, a few new northern institutions such as Cornell, and only one southern university, The Johns Hopkins, which opened for students in 1876. No other southern Methodist institution had an endowment of even $100,000 or a physical plant worth over $125,000.[42]

2

Sect and Section

T HE SAME TESTIMONY came from all the founders—Vanderbilt was to be a great university, comparable to any in America. Green, Kelley, Garland all emphasized its university status, its uniqueness among southern Methodist institutions, its potential for leadership in southern higher education. Commodore Vanderbilt endowed it with these expectations. Such a conception of the university fit the times, although unfortunately it proved unrealistic for southern Methodism and for the South.

After the Civil War a university movement swept the United States. The word "university" was ambiguous, with structural, teleological, and qualitative meanings. Structurally, a university in contrast to a college encompassed and unified several diverse schools or colleges. The founders of Vanderbilt accordingly stressed its five contemplated departments. Teleologically, the various colleges within a university served not just the moral or cultural goals of a liberal arts college but also professional and career goals. That is, it trained people for various tasks. Traditional European universities contained colleges of theology, law, and medicine, but in the United States universities often included normal, agricultural, and mechanical schools. Through the Morrill Act, the federal government had provided land grants and continuing appropriations for agricultural and mechanical colleges in each state, most as a part of expanded state universities. This more practical or career-oriented movement influenced Vanderbilt; for years the Board of Trust talked vaguely about an agricultural college and quickly moved to create an engineering program that eventually matured into a college. Qualitatively, the word "university" stood for advanced levels of training and for original scholarship. Consistent with this meaning, the founders of Vanderbilt University at first anticipated only graduate work and even as late as 1875 hoped to limit beginning students in the Academic Department to those with at least two years of previous college work. At the same time they tried to hire professors who were at the frontiers of knowledge, those capable of making original and significant contributions to their own field of science or scholarship.

The University movement adopted two strategies—creating completely new institutions or expanding and upgrading older colleges. The new state universities all met the structural and teleological definitions, but only a few attained the qualitative standards in the three decades after the Civil War.

23

These were all in the Midwest, led by Michigan and then by Wisconsin and Minnesota. No public universities in the South so quickly met such qualitative standards, although Virginia and then North Carolina soon came closest. New, privately endowed universities provided the clearest models, and most influential of all was the one southern institution that quickly exceeded Vanderbilt in achievement and influence, the Johns Hopkins University in Baltimore. Close to it in influence was Cornell University and, later, the University of Chicago. Uniquely endowed by southern, not northern funds, Hopkins provided a convenient, although not exactly a fair, comparison to Vanderbilt. Johns Hopkins gave his Baltimore and Ohio stock to found a university that was incorporated in 1867, but because of delays in probating his will it did not open for classes until 1876. It attained all the early goals of Vanderbilt's founders, even as Vanderbilt had to give up or postpone one after the other. The reasons for the success of the Hopkins highlight all the constraints and special hazards that so early limited achievements in Nashville.[1]

Eventually most older, well-endowed colleges added new professional departments, introduced graduate work, and assumed the name of universities. Notable among these were the three universities almost always cited as role models for Vanderbilt—Harvard, Yale, and Princeton. Because of its intense religious and moral atmosphere, a Presbyterian Princeton provided a useful comparison to Vanderbilt. McTyeire was quite aware of Princeton's struggle toward university status, yet within a context of religious orthodoxy and a continued commitment to moral character as the highest end of a university education. In 1874 he visited Princeton, enjoyed the hospitality of its Scottish-born president, James McCosh, and, as he put it, found out how they did things in that great center of learning.[2]

One great irony attends Vanderbilt's early history. Its founders talked of a great university but, within a decade, ended up with little more than a struggling Methodist college. It took Vanderbilt a century to catch up with all the earlier expectations. In each of the three senses, the early institution failed to attain true university status. Structurally, it was a university only when one counted two appended proprietary, administratively autonomous professional schools—law and medicine. The board early postponed a normal school (until 1979, at it turned out), while the early Biblical Department in no wise qualified as a seminary. Its students helped depress the standards of the Academic Department. Teleologically, again except for the window-dressing provided by the two professional schools, Vanderbilt's guiding purposes remained those of a church-related liberal arts college—the forming of Christian character. Qualitatively, Vanderbilt struggled, with some success and many early compromises, to maintain the standards of a good four-year college. It would not soon have the libraries, the caliber of students, or even the breadth of faculty skills required for competent graduate training. To cite these depressing realities is not to brand the institution a failure. It failed only in the perspective of what turned out to be the unrealistic hopes of its founders. Given all the hazards, it may have achieved as much as possible. And, as Vanderbilt boosters so often insisted, it led all other southern Methodist and possibly all other southern universities. The realities that shaped the early Vanderbilt set limits to its achievement. Almost all of these involved not only the limitations of McTyeire's or Garland's leadership, but religion and geography. More specifically, they involved Methodism and the post–Civil War South.

Legally, Vanderbilt began as a Methodist-sponsored university, not as a denominational school. Neither the General Conference nor the six sponsoring annual conferences gave the institution any denominational funds or made any commitment to do so in the future. As the bishops insisted, it was not a "connectional" university. This would seem to give the denomination by far the best of the deal—all of the glory but none of the cost. Neither McTyeire nor the other founders so viewed it. Loyal, proud Methodists themselves, they always gloried in Vanderbilt's Methodist identity, or what turned out to be one of its most distinguishing characteristics in its earlier years.[3]

Southern Methodists, as intended all along, made up Vanderbilt's early constituency. From them came most of the original faculty, almost all the early students, the trickle of financial support, and most nonpecuniary support—the loyalty and pride and commitment among families and soon across generations that would sustain Vanderbilt well beyond severance of all its official ties to Methodism. It is good to remember—the founders too often forgot—that a university has to have students, and that parents are critically important in providing students. The early Vanderbilt was deliberately conventional, not at all daring in its curriculum. Unlike The Johns Hopkins, it offered nothing educationally that was not already available in stronger and more prestigious schools in the North. But unlike these universities, it was not only Methodist and thus morally and doctrinally safe, but also geographically convenient and culturally familiar. Without this combined confessional and regional appeal, the type of university conceived by McTyeire and Garland could not have gained enough students to survive. In time, this all changed. Strong academic programs at Vanderbilt eventually created a regional constituency, one tied to educational needs and to geographical convenience much more than to religious identity.

Its Methodist identity not only gave the early university its needed constituency but it also precluded any early attainment of the lofty goals of its founders. Kelley's vision of a great university simply was not consistent with the outlook, the attainments, the cultural resources of southern Methodists. To explain all this and thus to portray the early Vanderbilt requires a detour into American Methodism, its doctrines, polity, and religious behavior.

The Methodist movement emerged in England from approximately 1729 to 1745. It grew up within the Anglican church, a brilliant John Wesley its acknowledged founder. In polity, Wesley began and long remained high church—committed to the role of an ordained clergy as successors to the early apostles, to an ordered and liturgical type of worship, and to an hierarchical or episcopal form of church government. But Wesley, much influenced in his formative years by the Moravians, also emphasized a warm, experiential religion, the continuous consolation of the Holy Spirit, and the fruits of the Spirit in daily life, both in moral attainment and in a rich devotional life.[4]

Despite its innovations—open-field preaching, extemporaneous prayers, physical manifestations, and lay preachers—the Methodist movement remained within the English church. In the American colonies, Methodism spread after 1760 as informal societies within the loose Anglican establishment, usually without the blessings of ordained clergymen. Not a large movement before the Revolution (not over 4,000 members in 1776), Methodism grew rapidly during and after the Revolution. American independence dissolved the ties of Anglicans to their king and left the American church in disarray, with few remaining clergymen and even these with no clear legal status. Even more, the American Methodists were now orphaned, without a single ordained clergyman to administer the sacraments (a few Methodist lay preachers disobeyed Wesley and administered sacraments even before the Revolution). Meanwhile, the movement continued to expand, quadrupling its membership from 1776 to 1784, but all without any order or orders.

With no authority from his own bishops, but in response to fervent pleas from America, Wesley established an American episcopacy in 1784. He had concluded that, on scriptural grounds, elders or presbyters were the equals of bishops. Thus, as a presbyter (priest) in the English church, he had the authority to join other presbyters in ordaining the first superintendents of the American church. His reluctance to take such a step sprang from his support for the established church government as he knew it in Britain, but the lack of any legal American church after 1783 gave him the leeway he needed. Wesley selected Francis Asbury, a popular Methodist preacher who had remained in America during the war, and one of his able ministerial associates, Dr. Thomas Coke, to be joint superintendents of the American church. To conform to scriptural precedents, he ordained two other Methodist ministers as presbyters (or elders, the second level of ordination in an episcopal system), and they jointly ordained Coke as superintendent before the three all left for America. Wesley revised the Thirty-Nine Articles of the English Church into twenty-seven (leaving out the more Calvinist doctrines as well as irrelevant sections on church government), and also sent along a modified prayer book and a modified liturgy containing forms for ordination.

Gleeful American Methodists assembled in a general convention in Baltimore at Christmas time, 1784. Asbury awaited the unanimous vote of the assembled preachers before accepting Wesley's appointment. In succession, Coke and the two other ministers ordained Asbury as deacon, elder, and then superintendent (bishop). In turn, Asbury and Coke ordained all the qualified preachers as deacons, and then from those chose and ordained ten elders. Subsequently, and against Wesley's own advice, the Americans chose to refer to Asbury, Coke, and their elected successors as bishops. With a few exceptions they also dropped the liturgy and prayer book, as well as weekly communion and robes and other high-church practices.[5]

Early Methodists offered a clear doctrinal alternative to the Calvinist majority in America (Congregationalists, Presbyterians, most Baptists). In many respects Wesley was in the tradition of Luther and Calvin. He stressed justification, not by sacramental works but by faith (belief, trust, love). Critical to him, as to Calvinists, was the atonement, or the vicarious assumption by Jesus on the cross of all the penalties due man for his sinful pride or selfish works. This unmerited act of forgiveness reconciled all faithful mankind to the Christian God. Like Calvinists, Wesley emphasized that the initiative for salvation, the enabling grace or ability to love God, was itself from God, a gift. But at this point he broke with Luther and Calvin. He adopted the doctrine known technically as complete atonement. As he understood it, Jesus fully absolved human beings of any inherent or original sin, not that they were thereby any less inclined to disobey as soon as they become conscious of God's will. The Protestant reformers had affirmed conditional atonement; even infants and children gained reconciliation only conditionally, through an actual or imputed faith.

Wesley also rejected the doctrine of predestination, thus openly clashing with Calvinists, including many in the early Methodist movement. The subtleties are many; often the wide gulf seemingly separating avowedly Arminian Methodists from Calvinists reduced to verbal ambiguities. Wesley emphasized free grace, open to all. Calvinists shared this view, but they emphasized that the grace was open to all only in the sense that it was a human option, but not in the sense that everyone had the moral will to choose it. Without God's initiative, without the work of the Spirit, a person was unable to choose God or affirm God's glory above one's own selfish goals. It was God's grace that gave one the ability to love, and this grace came only to those whom God had selected for salvation. God's grace, once given, was irresistible and irrevocable. Calvinists did not properly mean by this that a person remained passive under the prompting of the Spirit. Far from it, for the resulting consent or love prompted by the Spirit dramatically transformed human affections and led inevitably to a fervent, even emotionally involving response. But at least in the American context, some Primitive Baptists (known as hardshells) did adopt the passive view and thus branded any human means used to win souls as blasphemous, since God had already chosen. Their rejection of revival techniques, of missions, and even of Sunday schools made them the prime antagonists, often a foil, for Southern Methodist preachers. McTyeire, for example, tangled with hardshells in his rural ministry.[6]

What in practice separated Methodists from mainline Calvinists? Both saw gospel preaching as one of God's chosen instruments of grace, both joined in fervent revivals, and both rejoiced in the rebirth experience. But in subtle ways they understood it all differently. In different beliefs lurked rather significant differences in styles of devotion and piety, and thus also in behavior. Whereas Calvinists emphasized God's initiative, or the irresistible role of grace, Methodists emphasized the human response, the active choice for or against God. As they expressed it, grace came as a free offer, which a person could accept or reject. Given their emphasis upon choice, or resistible grace, the Methodists easily, and by good logic, rejected a corollary of Calvinist irresistibility—the preserverence doctrine or, as usually expressed in the debates of the nineteenth century, "once in grace, always in grace." On this point Wesley and his friend, successful evangelist George Whitefield, parted company.

For the Methodist, one could reject grace, the work of the Holy Spirit, not only at the time of conversion but later. In fact, one rejected the Spirit whenever one willfully disobeyed God. Thus, by choice and action one could lose the promise of salvation, lose membership in the true or spiritual church. These doctrines led to a distinctive Methodist vocabulary, to their emphasis upon not only an original but a continuous response to the Spirit, to their fear of "backsliding," of losing their salvation ("lost my religion" became the vulgar but widespread reference). Methodists felt an obligation to turn continuously to God, to ask merciful forgiveness for their disobedience, else their salvation was at stake as it was not for Calvinists. Fervent revival preaching thus had two purposes—not only to redeem sinners but to reclaim or revive the laggard and the backslidden.

The doctrines of complete atonement, resistible grace, and the possible loss of one's salvation gave Methodism its distinctive flavor. They supported a distinctive Wesleyan tradition—a continuous and daily concern for spiritual attainment, for a close and loving, a warm and fulfilling, even an ecstatic relationship to Jesus or to God. They supported spiritual exercises and devotional practices, and led to the artful new methods of communal support behind such a warm, even happy religiosity, ranging from love feasts to watch nights to confessional services. In America, the Methodists perfected above all their annual outdoor religious retreats, or what soon became known as camp meetings.[7]

Spirituality is only one facet of nineteenth-century Methodism, comparable in some ways to an earlier Quaker tradition. The other tradition may seem contradictory; at its best it was only complementary. The first key to one's spiritual welfare, as much to Methodists as to Calvinists, was the proper fruits of the Spirit—preeminently moral attainment. But the belief that unforgiven sins, which had largely a moral meaning for Methodists, separated one from the church and the promise of salvation invited among less sensitive Methodists a moralistic or even legalistic as well as disciplined approach to religion.

Calvinists accused Methodists of reviving a religion of mere works. External observation sometimes reinforced their charge. Such legalism was nowhere more evident than in the early history of Vanderbilt. Insecure Methodists craved a clear, unambiguous test of their obedience and thus of their standing before God. It was simpler if one could list accepted or forbidden behavior. Thus, the standard Methodist prohibitions—against intoxicating drink, against the theater, against most games, frivolity, play, or any behavior deemed worldly. For nontheological Methodists, the Christian life could largely consist of adhering to the external rules, of not wearing rouge and thereby losing one's place in heaven. Such Methodists were often narrow and censorious, the most thorough going puritans, as most people now mistakenly use that label.

Properly understood, the quest for a pure and holy life was simply the external barometer of spirituality. If one could attain personal holiness and even spiritual intoxication, then worldly amusements had no place. Wesley even believed that a few people might attain complete sanctification, a type of holiness or perfection, in this life; they would grow in the Christian life to the point they continuously had a sense of complete love for God. Of course, such holiness was the attainment of all Christians in the afterlife. In America most early Methodists aspired to earthly sanctification, or what they called the second step, and in revivals they greeted this with all the emotional celebration and physical manifestations that accompanied earlier conversion. But the practice of the second-step experience began to lapse among a majority of Methodists by midcentury and was no longer preached by some of the founders of Vanderbilt. The minority of "holiness" Methodists eventually separated and founded the Church of the Nazarene in the early twentieth century.[8]

Methodist spirituality and moralism, when harmoniously blended, led not only to people of unusually strong character but to a type of prophetic religion. Methodists, like the Quakers, tried to be living witnesses as well as exhorters. At their best they denied any clear line separating a personal and a social morality. At Methodism's beginnings, Wesley led his followers into the prisons and ministered to the physical as well as the spiritual needs of poor people in slums. Always in early Methodism, a personal witness took precedence over intellectual attainments or theological disputation. Methodists not only eschewed alcoholic beverages but worked harder than any other denomination for temperance laws. Not only did early American Methodists give up the convenience of slave ownership but at their founding convention took the strongest possible stand in behalf of early emancipation (they made freeing of slaves a condition of church membership). Southern Methodists quickly forced compromises on the antislavery position, but as if in compensation undertook a very conscientious and effective ministry among slaves even as they tried to mitigate the worst cruelties of the institution. Yet, before 1875, northern and not southern Methodists led in the more daring or prophetic ministries. In the South, when the emotional tenor of revivals and camp meetings gave way to order and respectability, when all the fun and intoxication of having religion gave way to urbane propriety and increased intellectual sophistication, what often seemed left over was an unmoving orthodoxy and a reflexive legalism. To some extent, this was the Methodism that early and perhaps uncomprehending students often found, or thought they found, at Vanderbilt.[9]

Methodists were not only distinctive in doctrine and devotional styles but also in their institutions. The American church imported these institutions from England and then modified them to suit American conditions. The American church adhered to a tight, episcopal system, with the highest authority centralized in its bishops. It made the best possible use of its ordained ministers, few of whom had extensive theological training. The church won out in religious competition primarily because of its circuit or itineracy system and its use of lay preachers at the local level. As rapidly as itinerant ministers could win enough converts, they formed small societies or stations. In turn, these congregations organized themselves into classes (discussion groups or mutual support or encounter groups), each with a lay leader, who did most of the teaching or even preaching. Lay persons carried out most ministerial functions (visiting, praying, offering consolation, giving alms to the poor), freeing ordained clergy for circuit work, traveling week after week on a set schedule to their assigned stations, there to administer the sacraments and to preach. A single minister might serve six or eight stations in rural areas and travel a goodly distance each week. After a trial period, aspiring itinerants received ordination (first as deacons, later as elders). If they rose in the church hierarchy they might become district superintendents or presiding elders (supervising the smallest territorial grouping of Methodist congregations). If one achieved an outstanding reputation for piety, for oratorical skills, and for administrative ability, the General Conference might elect him a bishop. Bishops had almost dictatorial power over the assignment of ministers to circuits or, increasingly, to full-time pastorates in larger churches. Yet, even by Vanderbilt's founding the normal tenure in a circuit or a resident pastorate was still only one or two years.[10]

After the Civil War southern Methodism underwent significant changes. The lay representation backed by McTyeire was one symbol. Pressures for longer ministerial tenures grew. The class system gave way to Sunday schools. Annual in-church revivals remained the norm throughout the South, but the camp meeting had possibly passed its peak. In the more prosperous North the better developed camps, with ever more elaborate cabins built by the affluent, were on the way to becoming summer resorts or, as at Chautauqua, educational institutes rather than sites of fervent preaching. In the South the shabbier sheds and more spartan cabins fell into disrepair. Few Methodists any longer talked of stations and fewer in each generation aspired to full sanctification. The doctrinal differences with Calvinist churches became more blurred.

In this context of change, some said decline, the debates over theological education took place. The Methodists prided themselves upon a called ministry, one inspired if not informed by the Spirit. Willingness to utilize itinerant ministers had made possible Methodism's rapid growth. Now even this tradition seemed in jeopardy, with all the talk of theological education. As a whole Methodists had not been preeminent either in theology or in careful biblical scholarship. Experiential attainment took precedence over intellect, the commonsense understanding of a biblical text over scholarship. The experiential dimension of religion from the very beginning gave an ecumenical flavor to Methodism. From Asbury on, American Methodists cooperated with other denominations in what they saw as truly essential—spreading the gospel and saving souls. They argued theology, or more often points of doctrine, only during the coffee breaks of the religious vocation.[11]

This detour into Methodism now finally leads back to Vanderbilt University and the constraints it faced because of its Methodist identity. In 1875 Methodism was still young, not yet a hundred years old. Its first great period of growth came in the early nineteenth century. It was now finally making the transition from a fervent sect to an established, accepted church. Vanderbilt symbolized the transition but could not yet profit from it. Methodists won converts among all classes, but every ranking of local denominations in the mid-nineteenth century according to occupational status, and thus also by income and wealth, placed the Methodist toward the bottom. Even by 1875 Methodists did not have their share of professional people, of college graduates, of intellectuals and scholars. The older, more established churches—Espiscopal, Congregational, Presbyterian—far exceeded them, and so did Baptists in some sections of the country. So far, despite their energy in founding colleges, their desire to catch up economically with other groups, the Methodists did not have a single first-rate college, one comparable to Brown (Baptist), Yale (Congregational), or Princeton (Presbyterian).

Such facts frustrated McTyeire and Garland when they started looking for Methodist professors for a new Vanderbilt. Methodists lacked most Calvinist and Lutheran motives for high intellectual achievements—a tradition of theological disputation and inquiry, as much an intellectual as an experiential approach to religion, and the compelling necessity of a seminary-trained clergy. Methodists, unlike Presbyterians, simply did not have a bookish church that gave strong support to the life of the mind. Increasing numbers of Methodists like McTyeire recognized this as a handicap and set about trying to correct it. But cultural change is slow. The founders of Vanderbilt, if they had realistically surveyed their prospects, would have recognized that they had to cultivate the cultural context among Methodists required for support of a major university. McTyeire was too provincial, too loyal a Methodist, too reflective of its own intellectual deficiencies, to concede the problem. By recognizing it and struggling with it, Chancellor Kirkland later slowly converted a Methodist college into a regional university.

If anything, Vanderbilt's location better explained its early character and its lack of national distinction than did church affiliation. One meets the geographical refrain everywhere in the foundational records—Vanderbilt was to be not only the first high quality Methodist university but also the leading southern university. Geography always seemed as much a clue to its identity as religion. Cornelius Vanderbilt gave his money, not because Central University was Methodist but because it was in the South. Throughout its history, the "southernness" of Vanderbilt has played a multiple role. Often, it has excused mediocrity and encouraged smugness (Vanderbilt is, after all, the best in the South). At other times it has stimulated creative expression, fostered challenging goals, or stimulated rigorous self-analysis.

In 1875 the "South" meant the defeated Confederate states. No one thought of Johns Hopkins as a southern university; the Hopkins was indeed located in the Old South, but not in the South that lost the war. Its sectional identity was therefore incidental, an accident of its benefactor's residence. The architects of the Hopkins experiments, particularly in advanced graduate work and in medical education, never thought of their work in sectional terms. They recruited their faculty throughout the United States and even in Europe, and hoped to have a national and international impact on higher education.[12] Not so the founders of Vanderbilt. From the beginning they reflected parochial and provincial aims—to build a university for the church and for the South. In part, this narrowed focus reflected their sense of a compelling need, of the compelling educational deficiencies of sect and section. Given the magnitude of the need, there was little reason to search for any broader mission.

From the perspective of Cornelius Vanderbilt, or a succession of later Vanderbilt benefactors, Vanderbilt was always an educational mission station in a benighted land. It served an "impoverished, stricken, or defeated" South. McTyeire constantly played on the poverty of the South, on the lack of local support, on the need for northern benevolence. Given the images of sectional inferiority and backwardness, even small achievements at Vanderbilt easily gained the status of great victories, for they were exceptional, unanticipated, and thus all the more treasured, as if victories gained against impossible odds. This helped account for the self-congratulation that marked the official reports on Vanderbilt early in its history.

Southern poverty was a fact, not just a useful myth to woo northern philanthropists. The war marked a major transition in relative wealth and income among the sections. Until 1860, annual per capita incomes in the South, including slaves in the total, remained higher than those in the West (the present Midwest) and were not far behind those in the Northeast. A few southern counties had the highest income in the nation. But by 1870 the

South trailed all of the sections and by a wide margin (incomes in the Southeast remained below 50 percent of the national average until 1930). What is more difficult to explain is what happened to the South, why its economy collapsed and then stagnated.[13]

The South bore the brunt of war, in battles fought, in casualties, and, more generally, in the forced provisioning of the armies on both sides. Where battles or major troop movements had occurred, crops were disrupted and agricultural capital destroyed. The war also destroyed a good share of the ablest human capital in the South. But more has to be involved than the normally short-term impact of war. The economies of Japan and Germany, which suffered much greater wartime destruction than did the Civil War South, recovered in just over a decade, and in some areas even profited by the required new plant facilities. In part, their success depended upon outside aid (preeminently from the United States), but even more it reflected their own ingenuity and hard work, the exploitation of their own cultural resources in the form of skills, aspirations, work habits. But in the period after 1865, national policies toward the South were a drag on the economy, and in a changed political and social and perhaps even psychological context the people of the South simply did not have the cultural resources needed for sustained economic revival. The cumulative results of stagnation created a vicious cycle. Without the wealth or the will to foster the skills and the incentives, without the needed education, the impediments to recovery simply multiplied. Without the credit needed to create or convert capital, work became less efficient, not more. Thus, the South entered its long nadir, one that lasted until World War II and, despite all the present celebrations of a burgeoning sunbelt economy, one that still exacts its penalties.

What has all of this to do with Vanderbilt? McTyeire knew the answer. Impoverished southerners were unlikely to give money to found a university. But Cornelius Vanderbilt took care of that. In fact, his gift provided the perfect excuse for Methodists, southerners, or Nashvillians to give nothing at all to Vanderbilt, and in this sense the publicized gift retarded contributions and decreased local involvement. But the major constraints offered by the South involved other than gifts. The stagnant southern economy and the choices of local politicians practically precluded good public education in the South, and at all levels. Even before the war a cultural defensiveness had narrowed cultural opportunities. Now, with emancipation, a large pool of blacks lagged behind whites in almost every area except the immediate skills required in work. The South not only had the normal educational burden to face but a vast educational lag to correct. It could not, or did not, face the challenge, least of all for the blacks. The low support for public services tied either to a small tax base or to the lack of poilitical will joined the inevitable decline of private substitutes. Most of the earlier academies perished in the war or its aftermath. Northern efforts to educate blacks petered out just as the going got tough.

Throughout the postwar South, white literacy declined. Most blacks had, at best, only the merest rudiments of an education. At the same time, the better educated whites, in favored areas or from affluent families, faced almost irresistible temptations to move north, for higher education or for their careers. The vicious cycle plagued the South once again—with less training came less opportunity, and thus the fewer favored the fewer of those who remained. The effect was not just economic; standards in all areas of expression and appreciation declined. For Vanderbilt University, for any traditional college with high academic standards, this meant a very small pool of admissible students, even if they received subsidies or free instruction, but, on the other hand, a large pool of eager parents and students desperate to find educational opportunities and a way up. Unfortunately for the South, up too often meant out. The ablest graduates of Vanderbilt University would often use the university as a means of escaping the South. These hard facts also document the early irrelevance of Vanderbilt's contemplated graduate-level Academic Department. At best, it could have catered only to a small southern elite and could have had small impact upon the problems facing most southern Methodists. A great university neither fit the conditions of the South nor its most pressing needs. A struggling Fisk University, with standards scarcely up to those of a mediocre high school, made as much sense. In fact, as Vanderbilt faced the realities of the South it moved toward the Fisk example. Its growth toward university standing depended upon correlative changes in the South. It might lead in these changes but only if it was close enough to maintain contact.

Of course, Vanderbilt was not only in the South, but in the upper South, in middle Tennessee, in Nashville. These more local geographical environments never figured as large in the early conception of the university, perhaps because of its proposed denomination-wide constituency. But they probably did more to shape Vanderbilt than the South as a whole. The upper South shared all the economic problems of the section. But at least Nashville, with a population of about 35,000 in 1875, was one of the many scattered but favored spots in the South. Nashville is at the northern edge of the fertile central basin of Tennessee. Economically, it has always been a commercial hub for the surrounding, largely agricultural region. By good luck the city escaped most wartime destruction. Federal troops took the city in February, 1862, and without a siege; in December, 1864, they successfully defended the southern approaches of the city, preventing Confederate conquest and massive destruction. As a supply depot for federal armies, Nashville boomed during the war. It gained in population, and in particular became home to large numbers of newly freed blacks, among whom were many of the ablest black leaders that so distinguished Nashville in the postwar years. After the war, Nashville grew only slowly. Its banks, warehouses, religious publishers, wholesale and retail outlets, and small factories and shops enjoyed a growing transportation network tied to the crossroads of two large rail systems, the

Louisville and Nashville and the Nashville, Chattanooga, and St. Louis. At the same time, its citizens suffered from the grit and smoke that helped make Nashville one of the South's dirtiest and grimiest cities. In 1875 it had some claim to being a progressive city—an active fire department, a network of horse-drawn street railroads (one had its turn point at the edge of the new Vanderbilt campus), and a new water plant.[14]

For the Confederate South, Nashville was a large city in 1875, vastly outdistanced only by New Orleans. Soon both a younger Atlanta and Memphis would outgrow it, but not yet. Both McTyeire and Garland viewed it as a large city, with all the unwanted vices that came with such cities. In the early Vanderbilt University literature it always appeared as a modern Babylon, with its numerous saloons, its racetrack, its few amateurish theaters, and (unmentioned) its houses of prostitution. Given Methodist moral priorities, it seemed a terrible place for a university. Yet, when challenged, McTyeire thought up an imposing array of desirable features, ranging from its climate (neither too hot nor too cold), healthfulness (out of the malaria belt), centrality (for the church), and even the availability of boarding houses (Garland considered dormitories a moral curse).

Despite its later claim to be the Athens of the South (always a poor joke), Nashville had few cultural assets. Already it had the appearance and the structured class system of an older city, one that was sorely tempted to dwell on its past. Its golden age had been in the booming 1830s, when Nashville's Andrew Jackson was president, when the founding families still used their slaves to manage prosperous plantations around the city, and when the adjoining areas of Kentucky and Tennessee led the nation in grain and meat production. The war scattered or impoverished many of the older families, preparing the way for a largely new, outborn elite tied to commerce, transportation, or manufacturing. The more affluent families still affected the refinements of a provincial city and tried to give content to the leading shibboleths of their class system—"gracious living" and "southern hospitality." With over forty churches and two denominational headquarters, religion was already big business in Nashville. Educationally, the city had prominence on paper but its reputation was a facade, covering little of substance. The city developed a meager public school system before the war and at least kept it operating at a minimal cost in the difficult postwar decades. Of the several academies for both boys and girls, the graduates of only one consistently met Vanderbilt's early admission requirements. In higher education, Nashville's one traditional college (the University of Nashville) was now little more than a cluster of proprietary professional schools and a new normal school, which duplicated its surviving undergraduate college. Already, northern philanthropists and enterprising freedmen had launched Fisk and Roger Williams universities and Meharry Medical College, but each operated on a shoestring in 1875 and as yet neither had been able to attain college-level standards.[15]

Old Main, on completion in 1875, Chapel Wing

In such a Nashville the Commodore's gift had been big news indeed. The local population was enthusiastic about a new university, perhaps all the more so because they had no need to help pay for it. The local newspapers reported a sizable crowd at the ground-breaking ceremonies on April 28, 1874, a peculiarly cloudy and dreary spring day. Bishops and politicians joined in saluting the new venture and celebrating its assured future achievements. Already, the first chosen professors were making academic plans or off buying books and scientific apparatus. Into a special cornerstone the gathered dignitaries packed a revealing selection of symbolically significant documents: a Bible, a Methodist hymnal and Book of Discipline, church periodicals, a copy of Cornelius Vanderbilt's founding letter and the university charter, and portraits of the Commodore and of Methodist bishops. In a double sense, the foundations were all now in place, almost exactly twenty years after the 1854 General Conference first called a convention of Methodist educators.[16]

PART TWO

The First Vanderbilt

(1875–1887)

 VANDERBILT UNIVERSITY *had to suffer a frustrating,
often demoralized first decade. The early academic plans proved
unrealistic. The university had difficulty attracting students, even
greater difficulty coping with inadequately prepared students.
Enrollment goals conflicted with the desire for quality. The first
Academic and Biblical faculty soon engaged in a running cold war
with their assertive board president, Bishop Holland McTyeire.
Within a decade this first, increasingly disaffected full-time faculty,
save Chancellor Garland, all left Vanderbilt, some dismissed, some
pressured to move elsewhere. Early students chafed at the tight rules
and the lack of school spirit. They had to cope with the frustrations
of off-campus boarding houses. They had to fight, in the end
successfully, for the right to join fraternities, for cooperative messing
clubs, for a student newspaper, and for intercollegiate athletic
teams. Changes came, slowly at first and then rather dramatically
in a series of new policies adopted by a young and innovative faculty
in 1887. These changes created a second Vanderbilt, one closer to
the present university than to the blueprint of 1875.*

3

Academic Foundations

WㅎHILE McTyeire supervised the building of a Vanderbilt campus, Landon C. Garland planned its first academic program. He had no competitors. Alone among the founders of the university, he had extensive academic experience and a well-matured vision of a great university. In 1875 Garland was at normal retirement age, a small, erect, reserved, disciplined man of sixty-five, yet one frequently ill, hypochondriacal, and certain of his early death. During a lifetime in higher education, as teacher and administrator, he had conceived his own educational utopia. Now, through the generosity of the Vanderbilts, he had a rare chance to start over, to redesign a university so as to eliminate all the errors built into the ones he had served so conscientiously but with so much frustration. At first, Garland did not intend to join Vanderbilt himself but only help get it organized. Eventually, after entreaties and flattery, he reluctantly accepted an appointment as professor and then chancellor, a decision predicated in part on his loyalty to his church.[1]

Garland carried out all the expected educational inquiries. He traveled as far as Harvard to consult with President Charles Eliot, consulted frequently with an old colleague, Frederick A.P. Barnard, who then headed Columbia University, and wrote to university presidents as distant as Minnesota. But Garland sought advice not so much to learn of educational innovations as to confirm his own well-developed academic blueprint. From his earliest advice to McTyeire on through his years at Vanderbilt, nothing indicates that Garland ever altered any basic feature of his academic ideal. He had to compromise almost all of it in practice, but at every opportunity he proclaimed his dream anew and until his death seemed to nourish hopes that Vanderbilt might eventually fulfill it.[2]

Garland was born into a successful Virginia family and revered his home state. The University of Virginia provided the single most influential model for Garland's Vanderbilt; he long yearned for an appointment at that institution. He received his B.A. from Hampton-Sidney in 1829 and first taught at Washington College in Lexington, Virginia. There, revealingly, he praised a new organization of that college into distinct schools, away from a "ruinous" emphasis upon a four-year progression from class to class, from freshman to senior. In 1831, as a loyal Methodist, Garland moved to a lower paying job at a promising Methodist college, Randolph-Macon. Typical of mid-nineteenth-century professors, he taught courses in several disciplines, ranging from English to physics, but he most loved mathematics and the physical sciences. From 1838 to 1846 he served as president of the financially struggling Randolph-Macon and in this position awarded a degree to McTyeire in 1844.

After serious illness and a brief study of the law, Garland moved to the University of Alabama in 1847. By then, his letters revealed a man with heavy family responsibilities (six children with three to come later). In addition, he eventually owned up to sixty slaves, most of them dependent children. He had also moved to Alabama to find a more favorable climate for his wife. Here he taught mathematics, natural philosophy, and astronomy. He increased his appreciation of the various mechanical contrivances needed to teach advanced work in the physical sciences and became almost obsessed with plans for a new astronomical observatory. In Alabama a financially beleaguered Garland briefly yielded to entrepreneurial opportunities, also serving for two years as president of a new, speculative railroad venture. He reached a climax of his educational career in 1855 when he became president of the then thriving University of Alabama. He had become the most important educator in Alabama and, clearly, the most eminent educator affiliated with the southern Methodist church.[3]

As a university president Garland struggled with problems of student discipline. Few students at state universities shared his strict Methodist morality; many were wild, proud, and inclined to violence. Garland had difficulty understanding, or resisting, such youth and in the five years before the Civil War he developed what became a near paranoid fear of young men. He desperately craved order and deference but achieved this at Alabama only by converting the university to a military school in 1860, one under strict discipline. His experience at Alabama helped reinforce his aversion to residential colleges, to a system that required university officers to assume a parental role. He also came to believe that dormitories were, as he expressed it in the early *Announcements* of Vanderbilt, "injurious to both morals and manners." At Alabama his cadets made only a brief, futile effort to defend the university from federal troops in 1865. The invaders destroyed almost all the university buildings, including Garland's private library. The campus could not reopen even in 1866, although Garland remained for one year in a frustrating effort to rebuild. Desolate, threatened with financial ruin, desperate for a position, he finally found one at the University of Mississippi in 1866, at a university spared physical destruction in the war.

Garland was fortunate. Although broadly learned, and by most reports a very capable if old-fashioned teacher, he was never an outstanding scientist or scholar. He published only a small mathematics text and occasional articles, most of those on religion. By the end of the war he was not in the forefront of either mathematics or the sciences. As a respected academician he joined in the movement that led to the founding of the Central University in 1872. At the Memphis convention, he alone tried to postpone the opening of the university until $1 million was in hand. Even the original $500,000 gift by Vanderbilt in 1873 left Garland apprehensive. Ever cautious, he wanted to retain the full gift and slowly build a campus from its earnings.[4]

As soon as McTyeire received Vanderbilt's gift, he turned to Garland for help. McTyeire insisted that the board looked to him, "more than to any other man, for the shaping of our course." The venerable, dying A.L.P. Green wrote that the board felt it "must have you, and cannot do without you." For the next two years McTyeire carefully cultivated Garland's loyalty and slowly pulled him into a greater commitment to the university. McTyeire consulted with Garland about the campus, about the architectural plans, but even more on academic plans and the choice of the first faculty. Garland preferred a classical architecture, like that at Virginia, but was not greatly disappointed with the Victorian Gothic selected for the main building. He left such choices to others. But he was intensely concerned about the internal design of the scientific rooms. He also enthusiastically entered into the screening of early candidates for faculty positions. His broad contacts in the southern academic world, and in the church, lent authority to his preferences.[5]

By December, 1873, with the main building under construction, the final planning of a university program became imperative. Reasonably firm decisions had to be made at a January, 1874, meeting of the Board of Trust. McTyeire and the board were looking forward to the opening of classes in January, 1875, or only a too brief year ahead. In preparation for the board meeting (he could not attend), Garland wrote McTyeire detailed proposals for what he believed would be a great, new university. Without major changes, the board adopted his plan and made it the academic charter of the first Vanderbilt. Garland made clear that his was an ideal scheme, a goal for the future as much as for short-term realization. He wanted to show what a university "ought to be," impress educators elsewhere, and stimulate larger gifts from the Methodist church. Garland proposed only four departments (colleges), dropping the earlier board commitment to a normal school, perhaps in part because the Normal School of the University of Nashville also would open for classes in 1875. He proposed a Biblical Department made up of four schools or chairs—systematic theology, ecclesiastical history and church government, hermeneutics, and pastoral theology. The Department of Literature, Science, and Philosophy (soon referred to as the Academic Department) required eleven schools and chairs—Latin, Greek, modern languages, Oriental languages, English, mathematics, physics and astronomy, Chemistry, Natural history, applied mathematics and engineering, and mental and moral philosophy. By contemporary standards, Garland slighted the social sciences (all crammed into one school) to the benefit of classical and modern languages (five schools) and the sciences (five schools). By his perspective, he had properly married the classical emphasis of liberal arts colleges with the purely practical outlook of newer scientific schools.

41

Garland proposed a Law Department made up of a dean and six professors, and a Medical Department made up of a dean and ten professors. But by the time he wrote, it was already apparent that the university would of necessity affiliate with proprietary departments of law and medicine. Thus, Garland simply stipulated the conventional requirements here and never professed any competence to make detailed plans for such departments. Although his plan was in part a model for future realization, he recommended that the university not open until it had filled three of the four Biblical chairs and eight of the eleven Academic chairs (he was willing to postpone Oriental languages and to combine chemistry with geology, applied with pure mathematics). In effect, the board authorized McTyeire and Garland to begin the search for men to fill as many as possible of these chairs, even as it completed negotiations with affiliated law and medical departments and approved the first routine faculty appointments. The board appointed Garland as professor of physics and astronomy, but everyone assumed that he would also hold some, as yet undefined, administrative position. Shortly afterward board members followed Garland's advice and postponed the opening of classes until the fall of 1875.[6]

The reference to schools in Garland's letter had critical significance. From his days at Washington College, he had been committed to schools rather than to a conventional class system. He loved the scheme used at the University of Virginia and in many other southern colleges. According to this model, each school at Vanderbilt would be a minor college, headed by a chair professor and having its own prescribed courses and extensive exams. Upon completion of required courses and exams, a student graduated from each school, receiving a certificate to that effect and special recognition for high levels of proficiency. At the early Vanderbilt, various degree programs required different levels of achievement in certain schools. To receive a Master of Arts degree, Vanderbilt students had to complete all advanced courses offered in eight schools. This system meant that a beginning student at Vanderbilt could select work in any school (up to four a semester) and progress toward a degree at any chosen pace. The student who could not complete a degree still took from Vanderbilt certificates for completed work in each school. Although the early Vanderbilt degree requirements allowed no electives, one had a choice of three and soon even more bachelor's degrees, while the school system provided the greatest possible flexibility in arranging a college career. One could devise a schedule of college work that suited individual ability and interest.

Garland assumed that Vanderbilt students would be mature, self-directed young men, not the immature, wild, undisciplined undergraduates he had tried so desperately to control at Alabama. If academically ill prepared, students could pursue work, not in a maximum of four schools but in only two or three. Prior preparation and extensive entrance exams determined what level of courses one entered in a school, and thus how quickly one completed the degree requirements in that discipline. In a given school, well-prepared first-year students often mixed with third- or fourth-year students; bachelor's and master's candidates were indistinguishable within a school. Despite the flexibility, most Vanderbilt students never liked the school system. It prevented them from forming class organizations, from developing a peer group, and thus seemed to them to war against class competition and loyalty and a healthy school spirit.[7]

From the earliest prewar plans for the Central University the focus had remained on graduate-level work. This was also Garland's priority, essential to his definition of a true university. Ideally, the new Vanderbilt would have attracted the graduates of southern, and mostly Methodist, undergraduate colleges. Such an expectation was clearly unrealistic in 1875. McTyeire frequently warned Garland not to set his goals too high. Southern churches had few people who were prepared for university work, at least as Garland defined it. Besides, the seven supporting annual conferences did not operate a single, high quality college and clearly expected the new Vanderbilt to fill this need. Thus, almost apologetically in the first *Announcement,* Garland and McTyeire defined university courses as those at a level of junior and senior work in better northern colleges, plus master's-level graduate work. Students who came to Vanderbilt already prepared to enter the university could complete requirements for the bachelor's degree in two years, for the master's in three. This lowered definition of university work proved only the first necessary compromise, the only one easily accepted by Garland.[8] To meet the needs of students and to insure it had a student body at the time of its opening, Vanderbilt had to open with a Collegiate Department, a two-year course of study that prepared one for the "University." Thus, each of the schools broke their courses down into college- and university-level work. Since most schools set up two years of work in each, the course offerings ended up matching the progression found in most four-year colleges. The likely result—an influx of younger, less motivated, and less easily managed students—worried Garland.

Until it opened for classes, the university planned to build its own grammar school. Even Garland knew that some applicants would not have the background in math or in the classical languages needed for beginning college work. He clearly preferred to segregate such students in their own school. But in the absence of such an attached secondary school, Vanderbilt's first professors had to offer subcollegiate or high-school level courses. Otherwise, not more than a third of the inadequately prepared students could have gained entry into Vanderbilt. Without much public acknowledgment, and with a great sense of unwanted compromise, the Vanderbilt faculty quickly began hiring fellows to help teach the subcollegiate courses and continued to offer these in five subjects (Greek, Latin, English, modern languages, and math) until after 1887. Thus, in these early years the preponderance of teaching at Vanderbilt was much closer to that of a high school or junior college than to that of a great university. But note that the adopted strategies, which allowed young and ill-prepared students to find a place at Vanderbilt, helped preserve the high standards appropriate for university work. At first, few attained them, even as very few early matriculates ever earned Vanderbilt degrees, but such standards remained as testimony to Garland's utopian goals and to the university's long-range commitments. Rather than lower his standards, Garland was willing to wait until students rose high enough to meet them. As he put it in his first Founder's Day address, he hoped the time was not too distant when young men from the South and West would have no need to seek a superior education at Yale or Harvard, in England or Germany.[9]

For Garland two attributes were needed to establish Vanderbilt's advanced university status—its scientific equipment and the caliber of its faculty. From our perspective, Garland's obsession with laboratory equipment seems eccentric or perverse. One can only marvel at all the surviving machines and instruments, some probably never even used by students, now displayed in the Stevenson Center. But for the first two decades these machines constituted Vanderbilt's best claim to university status and a degree of even national distinction. The quality of its scientific apparatus was matched nowhere in America. Garland proudly showed all visitors his carefully designed and superbly equipped laboratories; no wonder that mere students must have hesitated even to touch some of the shining instruments. Scientific visitors could scarcely believe the quality of the instruments and expressed their wonder that a new institution, in the South of all places, had such distinction. Whenever anyone belittled Vanderbilt or criticized its achievements, not only Garland but almost everyone pointed to its great scientific resources. The machines had immense symbolic value. Although Vanderbilt compromised on almost every other front to survive, here remained a tangible pledge of its aspirations, of what it might some day become.

From the time he received his appointment as professor of physics and astronomy in January, 1874, Garland used every spare moment to acquire the needed scientific equipment. He wrote several university scientists in this country, scanned European scientific catalogs, wrote letters to French and German suppliers, finagled the lowest possible bids, incessantly besieged McTyeire and through him Vanderbilt for approval of more funds, and finally traveled to Europe in the summer of 1875 to complete his orders. In the plans for the university he had persuaded McTyeire to set aside $50,000 for scientific equipment and for the university library. He urged the geology and chemistry professors to compile lists of all the equipment they needed. The chemistry professor, Nathaniel Lupton, also traveled to Europe, both to upgrade his professional competence and to buy his own laboratory equipment. The two geologists placed their orders for samples and displays, or what they needed to stock the region's first geological museum. Eventually, Garland obtained almost $70,000 and spent the largest share himself, or over $30,000, for physics and astronomy, including a small telescope that re-

The Chapel in Old Main. Note the painting of the Founder, Cornelius Vanderbilt.

quired a new, separate observatory building completed during the first year of classes. Garland tried to keep aside at least $10,000 for the library for, as he said, "we must have books," but he seemed to regret that their cost cut down on his priority purchases. After all, any college had books, and Garland, mistakenly as it turned out, expected a continuous flow of gifts for the library. The six thousand original volumes, ordered through book jobbers in America and in Britain, often must have seemed almost a bothersome diversion from the critical job of equipping laboratories. But once his apparatus was in hand, Garland had his favorite plea—no southern college could afford, or should invest, in such superior equipment. Thus, Vanderbilt would become the one indispensable university for the whole region, playing in the South the same role in advanced training as did the great European universities. Given such an awesome capability in the physical side of advanced scientific teaching, all that Vanderbilt required was an illustrious faculty in the three central areas of its commitment—to biblical studies and the development of Christian character, to classical and modern languages, and to math and the physical sciences.[10]

For Garland, the development of character remained the central purpose of a true university. As he emphasized in a chapel address in 1876, and as all the early university *Announcement*s stressed, neither classical knowledge nor professional competence had any significance, was in fact only a sham, if separated from the development of Christian character in young men. Garland, steeped in Scottish moral philosophy, was fearful that moral training had been divorced from intellectual culture, that new universities had cast out the Bible and neglected "religious instincts," or that they had all succumbed to a transcendentalist appeal to conscience alone, neglecting the Bible, law, obligations, and contracts. Garland thus viewed Vanderbilt's mission, even in the sciences, as quite distinct from that of new scientific colleges or technically oriented academies. He so emphasized moral development, filled so many of his Wednesday chapel homilies with moral reproach or advice, that students quickly tired of it all. But in time they came to realize that Garland lived what he preached, that behind the rather stiff, always censorious demeanor of their chancellor lurked a kind and generous man, one of unimpeachable integrity, the finest expression of character produced by nineteenth-century Methodism. The students might be awed by a powerful Bishop McTyeire, but in time they came to love and revere only the slight, patient, quaintly old-fashioned Garland. Much less commanding than McTyeire, at times indecisive, never a great leader, Garland was yet the more devout of the two men, more "spiritually minded" as Wesley would have put it. As he and McTyeire began the selection of faculty, religiosity and moral character remained first in order of qualification, followed by professional attainments.[11]

Selection of a faculty proved very difficult. The choices were all-important to the beginning university. McTyeire and Garland, in their unguarded, confidential letters, documented all the hazards. They had to move cautiously, appease different constituencies, salve hurt feelings, make difficult political concessions. McTyeire, one feels, controlled the game and ended up with a faculty close to his own preferences, given the various constraints imposed upon him by his church. He soon regretted many of his choices. As usual, he played a crafty game, using logic or flattery to get others to do as he wanted. He also had to work very carefully with his board. For most of the early history of Vanderbilt, the majority on the board simply followed McTyeire's lead. As representatives of the seven supporting Methodist conferences, they were rarely in a position to challenge McTyeire or Garland on academic plans. On most issues McTyeire and the small Executive Committee could depend upon board endorsement of all their decisions. The board served as a ratifying body, and even had it asserted leadership, it then would have faced the veto power mandated for McTyeire by Cornelius Vanderbilt. But in the hiring of faculty the board briefly functioned as a political body that represented various geographical and church factions. Candidates for positions at Van-

The Observatory planned by Garland. Later renamed Barnard Observatory

derbilt often applied directly to board members or enlisted friendly members of the board to support their candidacies.[12]

On some appointments McTyeire had no real option. One of these, of course, was that of Garland, or the only member of the Board of Trust to take a faculty position. He also could manuever very little in choosing the staff of his beloved Biblical Department. The very name "Biblical," rather than "Theological Department" or "Seminary," was a concession to those Methodists still opposed to theological education, a capitulation to the conditions laid down by the Board of Bishops at the time of the original charter. The consensual choice for dean of the Biblical department (and, as a mere courtesy, also vice-chancellor of the university) was Thomas O. Summers, then editor of the prestigious *Christian Advocate* and by reputation the leading intellectual in the southern church. He would come to Vanderbilt only as a part-time professor, teaching one course in systematic theology. Ticklish negotiations preceded his nomination, for Summers always felt slighted and unappreciated by McTyeire. He felt, perhaps correctly, that McTyeire would have preferred another dean. The English-born Summers was self-educated, the guardian of both Methodist orthodoxy and good grammar, rather detached and impractical, not a philosophical theologian but a dogmatist with some logical skill, and by all accounts a tedious, uninspiring preacher. His quite formal lectures on theology, required of all Biblical students, flowed sonorously over the heads of all but a few, but Summers kept giving them, unaware of student ability or need. He lacked tact, rather bluntly condemned even colleagues for any deviance from Methodist doctrine, and was too busy, and too detached, to administer his department. His relationship with McTyeire remained tense until Summer's

47

death, and at times involved Summer's fiery and controversial son and namesake, who wanted an academic position at Vanderbilt and who gained, and then because of objectionable behavior lost, a position in the Medical Department. Later the youthful Summers, after a nasty fight with McTyeire over his mother's burial spot, disinterred the body of his late father from its original and honored resting place on campus.[13]

The two other Biblical chairs went to the best the church had to offer. Yet, neither appointee ever achieved national status in his field. Alfred M. Shipp moved from the presidency of Wofford College to become professor of exegetical theology. He also had the honorary title of assistant dean and later briefly served as dean after the death of Summers. Unfortunately, his voice had nearly failed; he taught only with difficulty and preached hardly at all. He was, next to Garland, perhaps the best known southern Methodist educator, with degrees and experience at the University of North Carolina and at Greensboro Female College before he came to Wofford. Later, he became a bitter enemy of McTyeire. The other chair—practical theology, or teaching young ministers how to preach—went to John C. Granbery. A minister of a prestigious Richmond, Virginia, church, he was accounted one of the ablest preachers in the denomination. An early, almost obvious choice of both McTyeire and Garland, he came only reluctantly and after much persuasion from Garland. He would leave Vanderbilt when elected bishop.

In the first year the Biblical Department also worked out a program in church music but did little more for the original instructor than provide facilities; he had to earn his way by instructional fees. The arrangement ended in a year, with some bitterness on the part of the young instructor, or what became the first hint of faculty disaffection over treatment at Vanderbilt. Throughout the next decade the Biblical Department frequently hired temporary instructors in music and in elocution but never raised such appointees to a professorial rank.

Lacking in the first Biblical faculty was anyone to fill the fourth chair deemed necessary in Garland's plan of organization—that of Hebrew and church history. In 1876 Thomas J. Dodd, president of Kentucky Wesleyan College, filled a chair in the Academic Department and also began offering Hebrew in the Biblical. Eventually, McTyeire unilaterally moved him completely within the Biblical. He was not a great scholar, although a gifted author of popular religious literature and very well known and respected in his church. He and Shipp both moved from a college presidency into a better paying but more dependent faculty position under the almost dictatorial authority of McTyeire, who especially wanted to control policies within the Biblical Department. They never easily fit such a role. Dodd, a very proud man, often alone among the early faculty opposed McTyeire's policies, all of which led to a bitter confrontation in 1885.[14]

McTyeire had fewer constraints in his choice of chairs for the Academic Department. He had much to offer able applicants. The board established a salary of $2,500 for all chair professors and in the early years provided all married appointees with a free house on campus. McTyeire supervised the building of the original crescent of seven houses, which he expanded to eight by the third year. These, added to the residence already on campus (Old Central), made up nine commodious and attractive houses, each backed by servants' quarters, privies, chicken coops, garden plots, and, for McTyeire and Garland, barns and carriage houses. McTyeire occupied the largest and most expensive house (one later displaced by the Medical School). Garland, because of his early choice and his later appointment as chancellor (he had a salary of $3,000), was able to supervise the plans for his home, a large two-story residence close to the present Rand Hall. The value of salary and residence (chair professors without access to a home received a compensatory $500, a sum soon reduced to $250) exceeded the compensation offered by any other southern university (save Hopkins), and in most cases faculty salaries at Vanderbilt exceeded administrative salaries in small colleges.Only prestigious northeastern universities paid more. The temptation to come to Vanderbilt was great. Yet, a few turned down the opportunity, most notably two professors who eventually joined the Vanderbilt faculty—William J. Vaughn and Charles Forster Smith. Garland badly wanted Vaughn, who had been on his prewar faculty at Alabama and who helped rebuild that university after Garland left in 1866. He had Garland's breadth of interest, was an avid book collector, and specialized in two of Garland's beloved subjects, math and astronomy. Smith was a favorite of McTyeire's, a classicist educated at Wofford and Leipzig. Both Smith and Vaughn joined the Vanderbilt faculty in 1882, after McTyeire displaced their predecessors.[15]

The board, with McTyeire's blessing, went after two prestigious but almost honorific appointments, needed to add luster to the new university. One of these was A.T. Bledsoe, a much published but bitterly partisan historian of the South, but also an academic mathematician and a leading publisher who gained some fame as editor of the *Southern Review*. The board wanted him to teach math only half-time and otherwise edit the *Methodist Quarterly*. Bledsoe was a nominee of southern Methodism's best-known politician, L.Q.C. Lamar of Mississippi, someone who was frequently in a position to aid Vanderbilt and who was then a member of its board. The board elected Bledsoe, with McTyeire concurring. McTyeire had second thoughts. He learned that Bledsoe was partisan, controversial, and uncooperative. McTyeire must have anticipated a man more strong-willed than himself, and thus a dangerous competitor on campus. He correctly sensed that Bledsoe would bring notoriety and controversy to the fledgling Vanderbilt, and McTyeire was almost as horrified of bad publicity or public controversy as he was of anything daringly innovative. For his only time as president he exercised his veto and persuaded the board to comply. The veto helped alienate Lamar, who subsequently declined to speak on campus and dropped his active participation on the board.

The other courtesy appointment worked out reasonably well. Andrew A. Lipscomb, then an increasingly frail man at the age of fifty-nine, had gained fame as an inspiring Methodist preacher, a popular religious writer with books on several New Testament topics, and a college administrator. He was, until 1874, chancellor of the struggling University of Georgia. Vanderbilt appointed him to a special part-time chair in philosophy and criticism, but his role was more that of a distinguished lecturer. He would come to Vanderbilt for one semester each year to lecture on the laws of thought and on art, with Shakespeare his specialty. The university so arranged the eloquent, poetic lectures, and so publicized them, that not only most students but townspeople could attend. Although his field was listed as a school, it never functioned as such, for Lipscomb did not require recitations or administer exams. Students were awed by his eloquence and learning, and after the board "elevated" him to an emeritus status in 1878 (McTyeire seemingly sought an end to his lectures, perhaps for financial reasons), the students began petitioning for a series of guest lecturers each year to fill his place.[16]

For Garland, the critical appointments were in the three fields most closely related to his own—geology, chemistry, and math. Each proved troublesome but for very different reasons. James M. Safford, state geologist of Tennessee and already a chemistry lecturer in the Medical Department, agreed to teach half-time in his field and received both an appointment and, for a time, even a campus residence. A Presbyterian, and thus a bit alien among Vanderbilt Arminians, he brought sturdy competence to his teaching and to his work with the new geological museum. Of all the faculty he seemed to remain most aloof from the gossip and intrigues on campus. He had scholarly credentials, based on his well-received *Geology of Tennessee,* could teach chemistry when needed, and seemed content simply to do his work without fanfare.[17]

To assist Safford and to complete a full-time staff in geology, the university appointed its one northerner and the one faculty member who already had a national reputation in 1875, Alexander Winchell. As it turned out, McTyeire must have regretted the choice, which remains the hardest to explain. Winchell was born in New York and attended Wesleyan University. In the 1850s he taught briefly in several Alabama academies. He then moved to the University of Michigan, where he taught geology until an all too typical 1873 controversy over supporting equipment led him to resign, although the family retained its home in Ann Arbor. In that year he became chancellor of the new Methodist-supported Syracuse University but soon relinquished this unwanted task for a part-time professorship, which allowed him to take the Vanderbilt position. Actually, Winchell was on the Vanderbilt campus for only about two months each spring (from April on), during which time he gave his lectures on historical geology to complement those of Safford. His selection made sense perhaps in part because of earlier southern connections. During the Civil War he had helped organize a land company in Ann Arbor to invest in cotton land in Union-controlled areas of Mississippi. He came south to help direct the company's plantations and, as did so many northern entrepreneurs who hoped to make a killing on high postwar cotton prices, watched his project plunge into bankruptcy. By 1875 he had published two widely circulated books about evolution but had approached his subject as a devout Methodist. No one made Darwin more tolerable to conventional Christians. Some of his developing theories about man's origins, original but speculative, constituted an ideological time bomb within the university faculty. It exploded in 1878, to the acute and lasting embarrassment of Vanderbilt. In Winchell, alone among early faculty appointments, Vanderbilt dared a bit and thus came close to hiring a person who flirted with originality. After leaving Vanderbilt, Winchell returned to a distinguished career in geology back at Michigan, where he is now known as one of the most eminent and published nineteenth-century scientists.[18]

Garland had a favorite candidate for chemistry but had to let others plead his case. This was his son-in-law, Eugene A. Smith, of the University of Alabama. In retrospect Garland was fully justified in his preference. Smith had a near-perfect academic record, a distinguished doctorate from his years in Germany, and would go on to an outstanding career. McTyeire seemed fully persuaded, or at least expressed such to Garland. But in the critical board meeting McTyeire lost. Smith had not, because of his family connection, applied for the position, so McTyeire presented his name and his credentials without mentioning Garland. But the board was not blind. Besides, it had a compelling applicant in Nathaniel T. Lupton, then president of the University of Alabama and a former faculty member under Garland. The intrigue was thick. Lupton, an active Methodist layman, marshalled support within the church, with Bishop Paine his advocate. Lupton did not play fair. In a letter to McTyeire he warned against Smith on religious grounds; Smith was not a Methodist and not particularly religious, and thus not fit to set the tone of scientific instruction in the chief institution of the church. Lupton had at least comparable credentials—European training, long experience in teaching, administrative experience, and broad contacts in the scientific professions. He lacked Smith's brilliance or his specialized, technical expertise. Smith indirectly pushed his own candidacy. He wrote a long letter to McTyeire, explaining his reasons for supporting a form of biological evolution, which did not appear to him inconsistent with Christian doctrine. He admitted his failures as a Christian in an unusually careful but yet honest letter. The board elected Lupton, to the despair and anger of Garland, who felt him to be a better politician than chemist. Lupton, incidentally, later became Garland's friend but McTyeire's enemy.

One suspects duplicity in McTyeire's handling of the Smith case. The later board, when under criticism for always bowing to McTyeire's will, would cite this as the one case in which it effectively opposed him. Maybe so. McTyeire's apologetic letter to Garland did not quite match the record of the board meeting. McTyeire never offered Smith as his candidate. He never spoke against Lupton. He simply did not want to take a stand on this issue against prominent board members. Given Smith's religious laxity and his views on evolution, McTyeire was undoubtedly quite happy to keep him down in Alabama. But he had to keep Garland on board; he desperately needed him. Thus McTyeire joined crass flattery with abject apologies in his letter to Garland. "I congratulate myself," he said, "in the prospect of being near you and your family, for the rest of our lives I hope. . . ." McTyeire tried to direct all Garland's disappointment at an overly "democratic" board, one that jeopardized the university by making faculty appointments a political issue. Garland feared for the future. Actually, at no other time did the board take such an initiative. One feels that, even in this case, it carried the ball for McTyeire.[19]

Mathematics presented a different sort of problem. Bledsoe lost out. Vaughn would not come at that time. And neither McTyeire nor Garland could settle on any acceptable alternative. They postponed the appointment until the last possible moment. The simple fact was that the church had no outstanding mathematicians. So, with some reluctance, they finally offered the position to William LeRoy Broun, president of Georgia Agricultural and Mechanical College. A graduate of the University of Virginia, an Episcopalian, a former Confederate official, he accepted the Vanderbilt position only reluctantly and in place of other tempting professional opportunities. He asked for and received assurances from McTyeire about the permanence of his salary and benefits and the early completion of his faculty house. When McTyeire later reneged on some of these promises, Broun correctly indicted him for a breach of contract and then, in effect, had his position stolen from him.[20]

For the other chair positions, McTyeire and Garland turned to younger men. They were free to look for promising talents within the constraints of religious orthodoxy and a southern orientation. They never found a fully qualified candidate for the Latin chair and thus appointed B.W. Arnold to an adjunct professorship. Garland had doubts of his linguistic ability, based in part on reports of his fumbling efforts to get an education in Germany. But he had some support in the church and McTyeire took the risk. He gained the respect of colleagues but had his position vacated after three years, leaving some of the usual hard feelings.

Two very able young men completed the original faculty. Edward S. Joynes, another Episcopalian, accepted the chair of modern languages. A graduate of Virginia and the University of Berlin, he was already a rising leader in his field, author of several language textbooks. He proved the most popular professor at the early Vanderbilt but lost his position in 1878 because of allegations that he had consumed alcoholic beverages. He went on, by way of the University of Tennessee, to a brilliant career at the University of South Carolina. An unusually happy choice for the chair of Greek was Milton W. Humphreys, a young man of only thirty but alone among early Vanderbilt professors, save Winchell, destined to become nationally preeminent in his field. He had moved from Washington College to Leipzig for his Ph.D., and then to the University of Virginia. More than any other early professor he was dedicated to serious scholarship and to the advancement of his profession. While at Vanderbilt he was president of the American Philological Association and published several significant editions of classical texts. A Presbyterian, he married one of Garland's daughters and became very much a part of the small, intense, clannish faculty circle. He too was a casualty of McTyeire's vendetta against all the original faculty and thus left Vanderbilt for the new University of Texas in 1883. He eventually moved on to the University of Virginia for an outstanding career. His was the greatest loss suffered by the early Vanderbilt, for he and Winchell were the only early professors to give Vanderbilt more than a regional standing.[21]

With Broun carrying up the rear, all the faculty were in place for the first classes in early October, 1875. Some had been on campus for months. Garland and Lupton had drawn salaries for the previous year. Most had used the time to work out a course of study for their schools, and the *Announcement* sent out in the summer of 1875 was amazingly complete for a new enterprise. The school system simplified academic preparations, for it minimized the need for coordination. In most respects Garland and McTyeire had reason for self-congratulation. They had the best equipped facilities and the most eminent faculty south of the Johns Hopkins. What more could one ask? No wonder the old Commodore seemed so pleased.

But yet, the historian has to hesitate before joining in all the cheers. At times, even above their desire for quality, caution and fears had guided the work of Garland and McTyeire. They feared controversy, feared scandal, feared to be different, to be anything but utterly conventional, respectable, and orthodox. They were intellectually old men. They never charted, never even thought about, new departures in higher education. In the context of a backward South, all they could think about was raising standards, catching up with the North, not setting a new course, not even a distinctively southern course, whatever that might have entailed. Their faculty was indeed impressive and distinguished, sure to awe both students and their parents. But, overall, the faculty reflected either slightly archaic (Lipscomb, Garland, Dodd, Granbery) or utterly conventional (Lupton, Safford, Summers, Shipp, Arnold) values and achievements. Only Joynes, Humphreys, and Winchell looked toward the future or approached the vital frontiers of science and scholarship. The majority were, at best, masters of past achievements, not architects of future ones. The university's opening profile, ironically, was not one of youthful enthusiasm but of age, order, stability, and propriety.[22]

The Law and Medical departments most reflected this lack of educational vision. Money was the limiting factor. McTyeire apparently never considered expending much of the Vanderbilt gift on any professional education save theological. The extended communications between Garland and McTyeire reveal almost no concern about, and no planning for, Medicine and Law, although a decade later Garland expressed keen regrets over the original arrangements. In 1874, Vanderbilt would open with a loosely affiliated and a proprietary medical school and an unsuccessful law school. The contrast with the new Johns Hopkins is most revealing, for Hopkins launched the first true university medical school and led in the battle for higher standards in medical education. But it had the needed funds; Vanderbilt did not.[23]

In April, 1774, the Board of Trust of Vanderbilt entered into a legally binding contract with the Nashville Medical College, a branch of the University of Nashville. This agreement consummated a marriage of convenience. From this time on the same school served as the medical branch of both universities and awarded both Vanderbilt and University of Nashville degrees. At first, almost all graduates opted for both, and from 1874 on apparently all chose Vanderbilt degrees. This medical college, a well-established and financially successful proprietary school founded in 1850, needed the prestige of Vanderbilt University to attract students. The Vanderbilt connection also provided a protection against the likely demise of the University of Nashville. As for Vanderbilt, this adopted school fulfilled, at no cost, its well-publicized commitment to medical education as a necessary component of any major university. The Medical Department pledged to employ men of the highest scientific attainments and to maintain up-to-date faculties and instruction. Vanderbilt accepted no pecuniary liability and, except for a courtesy approval of the dean, had absolutely no control over Medical Department policies, faculty, or standards. Since it gave nothing, it received nothing.

Fortunately, Vanderbilt adopted a financially sound, better than average proprietary medical school. It had a competent faculty and through the years had acquired the minimally necessary apparatus and laboratories. Consistently, spokesmen claimed it was the best in the South (Johns Hopkins excluded), and the evidence supports that claim, though it meant little. Medical education in the United States, generally, was a scandal in 1874, and the South lagged behind the rest of the country. The Vanderbilt Medical Department, with its limited clinical opportunities, was not comparable to the larger New York and Philadelphia schools, let alone to the new Hopkins experiment. Also, it was in no position to keep up with the few more daring innovations in medical education, and thus, in a relative sense, declined after 1874. It never enforced any admission requirements (not even the requirement of a high school diploma) and, as did most proprietary schools, practically assured anyone a M.D. if he completed the brief (October to February), redundant, two-year sequence of lectures and labs. Vanderbilt, so committed to standards in academic areas, was not in a position to demand any at all in medicine.[24]

McTyeire and Garland asserted themselves a bit more in developing a closely related Law Department. By giving more it gained more control than in medicine, although at first not much more quality. In what turned out to be a false start, the Vanderbilt board in early 1874 appointed a part-time law faculty, headed by Judge William F. Cooper and including some of the ablest jurists in the Middle Tennessee area, among them two of the founders of the Central University (Jordan Stokes and Edward East). In anticipation of access to two rooms in the new Methodist Publishing House, Vanderbilt advertised for students in the fall of 1874. Since the rooms were not complete, only four students actually enrolled, all receiving instructions from a younger faculty member, William B. Reese. One advanced student completed the requirements and received a law degree in May, 1875. Once this effort failed, most of the original professors resigned, allowing the university to start over.

This time it did not try to build its own law department. Instead, it entered a twenty-five-year lease with only three prospective faculty members—Reese, Edward Baxter, and Dean Thomas H. Malone. The university committed some resources to the effort—two rooms in Main, a guarantee of $1,000 salary for each of the three part-time faculty members, and free publication of an annual catalog. Although the faculty had the right to elect successors or additions, the university could remove a professor for cause. The three faculty members, all full-time lawyers, came to the campus to give lectures in the then standard requirements of law schools, but at first without any supporting legal library. In 1875 the fledgling Law Department enrolled twenty-five and awarded degrees to ten in the spring of 1876, to seven more in 1877. It grew to an enrollment of fifty-three in 1880–81, only to fall back to a level of about thirty each year in the late 1880s. Competing schools made it almost impossible to demand very much in the way of requirements. Almost anyone could enter the Law Department upon payment of fees ($120 a year until 1878, thereafter only $100), although entrance into the second-year courses required an exam. But, unlike in the Medical Department, the Law term soon matched that of the Academic Department, and Law students took a very active part in campus activities. Their moot court, at the time of commencement, became a well-attended Vanderbilt tradition. But to McTyeire and Garland, the Law students were a thorn in the flesh, since they did not clearly come under the rules that applied to Academic and Biblical students. The Law students early gained an enviable reputation among students as free and daring, the nearest approximation to radicals on the early and very staid campus.[25]

With a mixture of hope and apprehension, students began to stream into Nashville in late September, 1875. They came to enroll in the Academic and Biblical departments of the barely completed Vanderbilt University. The elaborate two-day opening ceremonies began on Sunday, October 3. Pushed by aspiring parents, or personally lured by the lofty academic promises contained in the university's 1875 *Announcement,* 115 students enrolled in the Academic Department, 52 young ministers (51 Methodists, 1 Cumberland Presbyterian) in the Biblical Department. These young men represented at least fourteen states, while one divinity student was a native of China, another of Mexico. Half did not travel very far, either by horse or by train. Over half hailed from Tennessee, and a majority of those (61 out of 96) came either from Davidson (41) or nearby counties (20). Most of the other Tennessee delegation came from Middle Tennessee or the Memphis area, joining nearby students from southern Kentucky. Most non-Tennesseans came from the adjoining states of Alabama, Kentucky, and Mississippi; smaller numbers from Arkansas, Georgia, and Louisiana. The early Vanderbilt drew very few students from east of the Appalachians. Except for the border state of Missouri, almost none came from the North. In this first year only a few came from Texas, but in subsequent years Texas often came in second only to Tennessee. The few records on early matriculates suggest an overwhelming Methodist student body, with most of these from the six supporting annual conferences. Non-Methodists were most likely to come from the immediate Nashville area, attracted more by the closeness of the university than by its religious identity.[26]

Very few of these first Vanderbilt Academic Department matriculates were the desired graduates of small colleges. Few even had the needed background for college work and had to enter hastily improvised subcollegiate courses. But at least eleven of these first students did eventually graduate, from 1877 through 1880. Those who eventually received bachelor's or master's degrees included one faculty child, two Nashvillians, three other Tennessee students, plus one each from Kentucky, Georgia, Mississippi, Texas, and Arkansas. Uncounted in the list was Vanderbilt's first woman graduate, Kate Lupton, who began courses in 1875 and eventually received an M.A. degree without matriculating. To the extent that these first graduates reflected the background of early students as a whole, Vanderbilt drew most of its students from the Midsouth's affluent classes—businessmen, physicians, lawyers, or large planters—and not from its small yeoman farmers. The first graduates ended up in law, medicine, teaching, banking, or merchandising, often joined with the management of family estates. The first matriculates in the Biblical Department were all licensed ministers, who did not enter a professional degree program but one leading only to a certificate at graduation. Presumably, many of these came from humble origins. These early ministers, as a whole, came woefully unprepared for advanced work in theology and thus most never even finished the two-year curriculum. The few graduates from the entering Biblical class all continued in either the ministry or teaching.[27]

One can only sympathize with the first, undoubtedly awed and frightened Vanderbilt students. On their arrival they met Chancellor Garland, signed their names in a matriculation book and thereby pledged to observe university regulations, paid their tuition of $35 plus $5 in fees, and if they had not already made housing arrangements, received from Garland a list of approved boarding houses in the area near campus. They had to negotiate their own living arrangements, although the university refused to certify houses that charged exorbitant rates. All out-of-town ministerial students roomed and boarded on campus, in the converted boarding house now renamed Wesley Hall. Since several Biblical students were from the Nashville area and presumably lived at home, Wesley apparently came close to providing accommodations for all the early ministerial candidates. Not only did these ministers have free tuition but if they could establish the need (almost all did), they received interest-free loans or outright grants to cover room and board, or Vanderbilt's first major program of student aid. This aid came from a special sustentiation fund for ministers, the largest result (eventually over $30,000) of the early fund raising in behalf of a Central University, and the only significant source of nonendowment income enjoyed by the early Vanderbilt. The Academic students often resented the free ride enjoyed by ministers, even as they scrounged to find suitable, or suitably cheap, board.

Academic students had to walk to campus each day from their scattered houses. Very few were close enough to return to their rooms when not attending classes. Since they were not allowed to study in the cramped library, most wandered the halls of Main or tried to study wherever they could find an area to sit. The hallway commotion bothered classes. The students, according to rules, all had to attend a brief chapel or prayer service that began each day. On the special, more extended chapel service each Wednesday morning Garland usually gave a long sermon on the moral dangers that faced students, or on observed deficiencies in their deportment. The image one gains is that of young, undertrained, but devout Methodist students, awed by their professors but rarely in a position to understand them, often homesick and lonely, endlessly thinking about parents or girlfriends back home and lamenting the lack of any active social life on campus. Their one sanctioned extracurricular outlet was the two literary societies (the Philosophic and the Dialectic), which met after classes ended at eleven o'clock on Saturday morning. Here, by the imprimatur of Garland and McTyeire, the boys were to debate weighty issues, learn how to run a meeting, develop speaking ability, and bend their hopes and energies toward the one authorized competitive challenge at the early Vanderbilt—winning the right to give an oration at commencement.[28]

From the faculty perspective, the first three years were more harmonious than any that followed. In the first year the Academic and Biblical faculties met jointly and frequently but rarely struggled over very weighty issues. They adopted rules, certified boarding houses, received student petitions, established degree requirements, set up examinations and grading requirements, made the rules for the literary societies, heard appeals on the discipline administered by Garland, approved scholarships and graduate fellowships, and on occasion heard eulogies for students who died in the midst of a term. Of enduring significance, on December 21, 1875, they established an honor system, requiring on all exams the following pledge: "I hereby pledge my honor that I have not given or received assistance during this examination." The faculty early sought graduate fellows to take over the laborious and demeaning work of subcollegiate classes and as early as the second year recommended the early termination of such high school work. In 1876 they approved courses of study for three Ph.D. programs, in chemistry, physics, and geology.

Pushed by Garland, and beyond him by McTyeire and the board, the faculty with some reluctance kept expanding the prohibitions placed on students. They were allowed no membership in secret societies and no attendance at horse races, at the theater, at billiard parlors, at saloons, or at any other place of "dissipation" (meaning brothels). Notably, the faculty was more cooperative in enacting such rules than in enforcing them. From the beginning students were on their own when off campus, and in the absence of any diversions on campus had little better recreation than wandering around in downtown Nashville. In October, 1877, the faculty learned that Vanderbilt students had announced a scheduled baseball game against the University of the South. Since they believed it had been arranged because of a misunderstanding, they allowed it to take place but strictly forbade any subsequent foolishness of this sort. Also in 1877, the faculty first responded, very slowly and then negatively, to student requests for a newspaper. But, more than on any other issue, the professors struggled over the details of campus ceremonies, which climaxed each year at Founder's Day and then with a rather elaborate commencement.[29]

4

The Reign of King McTyeire

In THE FIRST YEAR the administrative structure of Vanderbilt slowly became clear. Garland, nominally chancellor, really carried out the combined functions of a dean of faculty and dean of students. He had limited policy-making power. So did the faculty. By his own choice, McTyeire served as the chief academic officer of the university. His intense concern for its success, his intimidating presence on campus, and his penchant for leadership insured his involvement in every important policy decision. He did not easily delegate duties. And, very quickly, he seemed frustrated by the university's slow growth. Possibly, as his enemies later charged, the very prestige of the original faculty, of men with higher degrees, broader intellectual interests, and greater brilliance than himself, rankled, creating jealousy and insecurity. His status in the church created strains—he had to cater to too many demanding constituencies. In short, Vanderbilt created unending frustrations for the aging bishop, and this may have reinforced his tendency toward a secretive and imperious role. His power, his aloof manner, his special privileges, as reflected in his large salary ($6,000 combined from church and university), and his superior house created jealous responses on the part of faculty members, particularly those who left college presidencies to come to Vanderbilt.[1]

The first university crisis came in 1878. Under McTyeire's guidance the board fired three professors. Because one casualty, Edward Joynes, was a student favorite, his departure joined with other frustrations to provoke escalating student complaints and demands. In 1877 the board had considered a motion to dismiss Joynes for drinking but postponed action. Joynes was duly repentant, promised no further offense, and even under severe pressures in 1878 refused to resign his position. In a letter to a colleague he complained of an exaggerated report of one drinking incident only, and that back in 1875. Then, at the end of the 1877–78 academic year, the board vacated his chair. What is not clear is exactly when Joynes imbibed or if he was ever actually drunk. Perhaps not. He suspected pressures from within the church, was bitter because he was never allowed to speak up against any of the charges or appeal the decision, and suspected the true cause as something hidden, possibly his non-Methodist church affiliation. Not only was Joynes popular with students, but his daughter had provided a bit of feminine charm on an all-male campus. As a backhanded slap at McTyeire and the board, the unhappy students ostentatiously invited Joynes back in 1879 to address their literary societies and received from him a framed photograph. Also, it is clear that several faculty resented and regretted his dismissal.[2]

The second dismissal was far less controversial. B.W. Arnold was not reappointed to his adjunct professorship in Latin. In this decision Garland may well have played a key role, since he had early doubts about Arnold's credentials. The faculty, by a special commendation, expressed their distress, if not at his dismissal at least at the abrupt methods used by McTyeire. Arnold first learned of his dismissal from a Nashville newspaper. The departure of both Joynes and Arnold required early replacements. Neither replacement worked out. John Lee Buchanan, from an affluent Virginia family, remained only a year in the Latin chair before accepting the presidency of Emory and Henry College in Virginia. He had a distinguished later career at several other colleges and as superintendent of public instruction in Virginia. To replace Joynes the university hired John M. Doggett as adjunct professor of both English and modern languages. A son of a bishop, he gained his post in part through his church and family connections. Doggett became a burden for McTyeire and apparently lacked the academic skills needed for his complex task.

Buchanan was succeeded in 1879 by James William Dodd of Kentucky, a brother to Thomas J. Dodd, who had now moved from the Academic faculty into the Biblical Department. "Uncle Billy" Dodd, who stayed at Vanderbilt for the rest of his foreshortened career, was a widely renowned orator and became the most beloved faculty member on campus, although the evidence does not establish him as an outstanding scholar. In 1885 he helped establish an enduring Vanderbilt tradition—the Bachelor of Ugliness. At the whimsical conferral of the first such degree on Polly Branch, Dodd gave him a Barlow knife. After Dodd's early death in 1887, the awarding of the degree became a "sacrament" in honor of Uncle Billy, or what quickly became the most sought-after honor for Vanderbilt men, an honor bestowed after a hotly contested annual election.[3]

The third dismissal had limited academic implications but deeply tarnished the reputation of Vanderbilt. In May, 1878, the Board of Trust abolished the chair held on a part-time basis by Vanderbilt's most prominent professor, Alexander Winchell. As always, it acted in accord with the wishes of McTyeire. Winchell was only marginally a part of Vanderbilt. His brief spring lecture series took him away from wife and family but apparently provided a much-needed supplement to his income even as he pursued other possible academic openings. He was always the opportunistic entrepreneur, but he was also a man of commanding pride and enviable eloquence. The background to his dismissal is complex and, as with all such events at Vanderbilt, clouded by conflicting memories. Given the rigid Methodist orientation of Vanderbilt, one can only wonder why McTyeire ever invited

Winchell to the campus, particularly since his lectures on historical geology (evolution) and zoology made up only a small supplement to the teachings of Safford. At Vanderbilt, Winchell seemed quite popular and, a sensitive man, he was pleased by his warm personal reception. The Vanderbilt community both valued him and flattered him. McTyeire apparently respected him and seemed more gracious to him than to most of his faculty. But Winchell remained on thin ice. Dean Summers, a determined opponent of almost all evolutionary theories (they all conflicted with special creation), balanced his personal regard for Winchell with frequent expressions of dissent from his "heretical biology." Summers seemed to connect all of Winchell's theories with the omnipresent controversies over Darwin's *Origin of Species*. But, ironically, it was not Darwinist theory but a related and very speculative belief that triggered the showdown at Vanderbilt.[4]

Winchell spent years developing and defending a theory of polygenesis. He wrote about the numerous humans who occupied the earth before the Christian deity created a biblical Adam. Winchell had all but conclusive archaeological and even historical evidence of people on earth long before any realistic dating of the Adam described in the Jewish scriptures. And, in incidental ways, even the Book of Genesis seemed to entail pre-Adamites (whom did Cain marry after he slew Abel?). From today's perspective, Winchell's elaborate arguments seem largely an adjunct of nineteenth-century racial theories, for his pre-Adamites included all the "inferior" races, such as African Negroes. Incidentally, such a theory of multiple human origins placed him in opposition to Darwin as well as to most Christians. For Summers, these views meant quite simply a dangerous heresy at the heart of the church. Early in 1878 Winchell published back in Syracuse an abstract, or what he called a pamphlet, about his pre-Adamite theory, apparently under the auspices of the northern Methodist church. His major book on the subject did not appear in print until 1880. It was his early published argument that first raised the hackles of southern Methodists and, horror of horrors, first threatened embarrassment to Vanderbilt. Both the St. Louis *Christian Advocate* and Summers's own *Advocate* in Nashville cited the unacceptability of Winchell's novel theory, and by this gave the type of warning to Methodist laymen that was almost certain to bring criticism on the new university. Had the disagreement between Winchell and Summers remained a campus dialogue, McTyeire would have had no reason to fire Winchell. On all the evidence, he had much greater personal affection for Winchell than for Summers. But the church took precedence.[5]

Whatever his intent, McTyeire certainly mishandled Winchell's dismissal. Formally, the board did no more than eliminate Winchell's limited lectureship. None of the records even refer to any unacceptable beliefs, but it is inconceivable that any board member remained unaware of the real issue, for the 1878 board adjourned its annual meeting, as usual, to hear a special Founder's Day lecture on May 27, a lecture by Winchell in which he defended his pre-Adamite theory. The unanswerable question is whether McTyeire set Winchell up for the kill. Thomas Dodd, in later recollections colored by his hatred of McTyeire, believed it was all a trap; he even remembered McTyeire's earlier quizzing him privately about Winchell as he gathered information to justify termination. But McTyeire hardly had any need to trap Winchell or to set up a lecture to display his heresy before the board. Winchell's views were now in print, already a source of controversy in the church. Winchell had planned to air his pre-Adamite theory in a lecture series at David Kelley's McKendree Church but backed down because of Summer's protest. He now had his chance, not only to clarify his views but to disarm a growing number of critics. By inviting him to give the Founder's Day speech McTyeire bestowed on Winchell a signal honor, one not heretofore accorded any faculty member. He had also proposed the lecture as if on his side, as a vehicle for Winchell to defend himself. Thus, the fact that Winchell chose, as expected, to speak on the sensitive issue could not have had any influence on McTyeire's choice to drop him. If one wants to see a devious goal behind the invitation, it makes more sense to argue that McTyeire planned the speech only as a way of vindicating a much earlier decision to dismiss Winchell.

McTyeire approached Winchell about forty-five minutes before the speech. He requested his resignation, possibly a request triggered by pressure from some of the board members just now in from the Methodist provinces. McTyeire noted the criticism in the church and the need to avoid embarrassment for the university. According to Winchell, he was completely surprised by the request, argued briefly with the bishop over the content of his pre-Adamite views, and refused to resign "with indignation," calling the request "unjust and offensive." As Winchell remembered the exchange, he had acted out the role of a deeply wounded scientific martyr, the victim of a new inquisition reminiscent of the one that had silenced Galileo.[6]

Winchell gave his speech. Even Summers, who still stressed its heretical import, called it one "of the most beautiful lectures we ever heard." Winchell received a magnificent bouquet and much applause. That was the last kindness he received from Vanderbilt. The board reassembled the next day to abolish his position. Meanwhile, Winchell had left Nashville to return to his family in Ann Arbor. He received formal notification of his discharge by mail, along with warm expressions of continued friendship from McTyeire. Possibly a naive McTyeire expected it to end there. By his standards, in light of what he expected in the way of loyalty to church and university, Winchell should have remained silent, playing along with the face-saving charade. McTyeire always insisted that Winchell's views did not influence the decision to terminate his position. Even a suspicious David Kelley, who missed the critical board meeting, seemed persuaded by all the protestations that it was a limited, purely financial decision. It made sense to combine the loosely unified work of two professors into one chair under Safford.

Winchell was not one to avoid a fight. He sent a detailed narrative of events to the Nashville *American,* a newspaper that loved nothing better than to embarrass straitlaced Methodists. This letter made Winchell's dismissal a cause célèbre, a prominent example of the suppression of academic freedom in the name of orthodoxy. Several newspapers picked up on the *American* account and embellished it with editorial judgments. Only Methodist newspapers, and some of the annual conferences, praised Vanderbilt for its action; Summers's Nashville *Christian Advocate* could now proclaim that "Vanderbilt is safe." In far-off Paris, Andrew White of Cornell University heard of the case, praised Winchell for his courageous stand, and asked for all the documents relating to the case for inclusion in his projected book on the *Warfare of Science and Theology.* In his belated 1896 book, White of course featured this as a prime exhibit of the suppression of free inquiry. However understandable McTyeire's caution and despite all the ambiguities in the case, it did reflect quite clearly the narrow bounds of free expression at the early Vanderbilt. The disclaimers and public denials by McTyeire only added an element of hypocrisy to the repression. This is true even if one grants that Winchell rather enjoyed playing the role of an injured academic martyr.[7]

The board's summary and underhanded dismissal of two of Vanderbilt's ablest professors—Joynes and Winchell—posed a direct threat to all the Vanderbilt faculty. Only by indirect hints can one pick up the extent of their concern, even anger. Lupton, as the faculty spokesman for the sciences at Vanderbilt, wrote several supportive letters to Winchell and conveyed the sadness of his colleagues (some "very, very sad"). The lack of any hearing or appeal, of even the semblence of due process, made all their positions seem insecure. Faculty resentment of the board really meant resentment of McTyeire; all knew that he guided the board in all such critical decisions.

On his part, McTyeire seems to have survived the purge with increasing bitterness and resentment. The widespread approval of Methodists could not compensate for the unfavorable national publicity. A young professor from Michigan, already lined up at Winchell's suggestion to launch a new and important engineering program, refused to come to Vanderbilt in protest. Neither Winchell nor the faculty seemed to display the dutiful and unquestioning loyalty that McTyeire demanded from his Methodist ministers. To cap all this, in the fall of 1878 Vanderbilt's enrollment fell rather sharply, to the lowest number (156) in the history of the combined Academic and Biblical departments. On campus, the students seemed to be developing an identity of their own. Led by more daring law students, a few of them joined to publish a nonauthorized but a very high quality journal, *The Austral.* In it they offered their courteous, moderate, but well-taken criticism of the university, to the horror of both Garland and McTyeire. An angry Garland joined with his faculty quickly to suppress such an unsupervised and such a "gossipping and scandalous" newspaper. But the students would no longer submit in silence and fought for the next two years to get approval for their own publications.[8]

A few expansive notes relieved the gloom of 1878–79. One was the construction of three new, badly needed buildings. The new gymnasium would meet a student demand for physical training. The large new Wesley Hall provided more than enough space for divinity students. And Science Hall, by accommodating geology labs, helped end the crowding in Main. In 1879 Olin Landreth, formerly an assistant astronomer at the Dudley Observatory in New York, joined the faculty in order to launch a separate school of civil engineering. Recommended by the Reverent Charles Deems, he would guide engineering into the status of a full department (college) in 1886 and remain dean of Engineering until he left Vanderbilt in 1894. In the fall of 1879 a new, fully proprietary, downtown Dental Department also opened for students. Closely related, a nonproprietary Pharmacy Department opened on campus. The Dental School, at first very small, was conducted for five months each year by Nashville dentists. Pharmacy grew up as a "soft" adjunct to chemistry. Regular courses offered by Lupton and Safford were supplemented by two lectures a week, on materia medica and on the theory and practice of pharmacy, by two Nashville pharmacists. Students repeated the five-month course in their second year.

In 1877 Vanderbilt awarded its first two bachelor's degrees, while seven students graduated from the two-year nondegree Biblical program. By 1878 the number of bachelors rose to five; the Biblical graduates dropped to six. In 1879 Vanderbilt had twenty-three graduate students in residence, all with B.A.s or M.A.s from Vanderbilt or other colleges. In that year it would award twelve bachelor's degrees, three M.A.s, and its first two Ph.D.s. It now had an indispensable requirement for a university—a coterie of mature, able, advanced, but not always docile students. Slowly, it was also gaining a junior faculty, made up of fellows or instructors, some eventually referred to as assistants to professors or, in today's language, as assistant professors.[9]

In 1879 the uneasy harmony between McTyeire and "his" faculty gave way to bitter controversy. McTyeire persuaded the board at its 1879 meeting to reduce faculty salaries, a move that caught the faculty by surprise. McTyeire not only wanted more faculty loyalty but he wanted his "officers" to attract more students, and thus to work harder. The Academic and Biblical departments had seemed to flounder even as the proprietary Medical Department enjoyed increasing enrollments. McTyeire tried to adopt a modified proprietary incentive for his campus. The board reduced the contractual salary (paid quarterly) of all professors by approximately 20 percent; thus, full professors dropped from $2,500 to $2,000. Notably, this did not affect McTyeire's university salary of $3000. In partial compensation for these cuts the faculty now had a claim to one-half of all tuition income. The other half was to go into new student scholarships, calculated to increase enrollment. Given the existing enrollment patterns at Vanderbilt, the faculty share of tuition made up slightly less than one-half of their lost salary (full professors received a total of $2,213 in 1879–80), leaving them with an effective cut of just over 10 percent, a percentage that remained rather constant over the next decade. No financial squeeze justified the cut, for Vanderbilt operated in the black each year. It seemed to the faculty clearly a disciplinary measure. It was not as economically disastrous for teachers as it would be today, for this was a time of rapid productivity increases and generally falling prices. This deflation helps account for the lack of concerted faculty demands for regular salary increases. But whatever its economic impact, such an arbitrary change in salaries was a direct assault on faculty pride and self-respect. It also violated implied, if not written, contracts.[10]

The faculty fought back. In a meeting in late May of 1879, professors engaged in a full and acrimonious debate with McTyeire and then appointed a special committee to write a memorial to the board. They cited their "just and equitable rights" as established by their original terms of appointment. Garland chaired the committee, which included most of the full professors (Broun, T.J. Dodd, Granbery, Humphreys, Lupton, and Shipp). In its long, detailed 1880 memorial the committee credited the board members with no intentional damage; they surely expected tuition to make up the full difference in contractual wages. Thus, in light of the actual impact of the change, they asked for a reversal. To justify this petition they cited the original offers that enticed them to leave other jobs and come to Vanderbilt. They had assumed a contractual obligation on the part of the board, short of grave financial exigencies. For most professors, this was a matter of simple trust or an implied contract. Not so for Broun. He still had his telegram, which made acceptance of his position conditional on his position's being permanent and with a salary of $2,500 and a house. Some faculty came with hopes of future salary increases; others rejected outside offers because they considered their salary secure, a firm commitment from Vanderbilt. The memorialists carefully, and easily, demolished any financial justification for cuts, proving Vanderbilt's enviable economic situation as compared with other southern universities. The professors stressed their training, their family needs, as justification of a salary of at least $2,500. The memorialists also cited higher salaries in several New England schools and at the University of Virginia. They implored the board to reverse its action, to avoid injury to the university, to right a painful injustice, to uphold contracts, to prevent unrest and insecurity in the future, to restore mutual confidence between board and faculty, to keep faculty loyalty in a great university, and to prevent plunging the faculty into the position of mere hirelings.[11]

McTyeire was not about to back down. The faculty memorial incensed him. He now seemed determined to be rid of all such malcontents. The new Latin professor, Buchanan, left for Emory and Henry, at least in part because of the salary controversy. Before the board in May, 1880, McTyeire reported that the new salary system had worked well, that it had commended itself to "the judgment of our patrons" and that it was recognized as based on a sound principle of general economy. Notably, he identified none of the happy patrons. A special board committee of five considered the faculty memorial and denied any implied contract to continue the original salaries. Salaries were subject to annual determination by the board, and thus the board had no reason to grant the faculty claims. Judge Milton Brown, of the Memphis Conference, moved, in a substitute motion, to grant the petition, perhaps in recognition of its legal merit, but only one board member supported him (David Kelley abstained). The motion affirming the salary cut passed by fifteen to three, but with two powerful board members—Brown and Kelley—undoubtedly opposing. How many other board members reluctantly supported McTyeire one has no way of knowing. Unfortunately, the board minutes do not contain a detailed record of the extended and often heated discussions. Thomas J. Dodd later remembered that McTyeire stormed and raged before the board, and that Professor Doggett, although not one of the memorialists, spoke out very bluntly in its behalf and against McTyeire.[12]

In 1880 McTyeire began building his new Vanderbilt faculty. He did it in a tense atmosphere: both students and professors were disgruntled, campus morale was terrible, enrollments were moribund, and Vanderbilt's external academic reputation was all but destroyed by the Winchell affair and now by the salary cuts. This time, McTyeire tried to choose his faculty in behalf of institutional loyalty, even as he used every possible tactic to speed the departure of the current faculty. He began lining up replacements well before he gained the needed vacancies. In 1881 he hired the core of his new staff. He replaced Doggett with Charles Forster Smith of the University of Virginia, whom he had wooed unsuccessfully in 1875. Smith, although a classicist, briefly took over modern languages, as if in wait for the departure of a much more eminent Humphreys. McTyeire also hired a friend of Smith's, William M. Baskervill, to head a new and separate school of English. These two younger men were the beginning of a much heralded Wofford-Leipzig connection at Vanderbilt, a subject of many student jokes. Smith had taught at Wofford before completing his Ph.D. in classics at Leipzig. Baskervill, a Randolph-Macon graduate who had earlier completed his Ph.D. at Leipzig, filled in for Smith at Wofford and then remained on the faculty. The two became close allies at Vanderbilt, part of a clearly identified and much-favored McTyeire faction. They were much resented by some of the original faculty. Baskervill moved from adjunct to full professor at the end of the first year and further cemented his position by marrying McTyeire's daughter, Jane. He then by-passed older, waiting professors in order to move into one of the best-cared-for campus houses, displacing the ever obliging Safford.[13]

Smith and Baskervill were Methodists, as their Wofford connection suggested. They also came from a South Carolina institution, or from the state of McTyeire's birth. It seems that the bishop felt more at ease, more secure with these young men, who were dutifully grateful for his patronage. Later critics charged McTyeire with Methodist chauvinism, for at least three of his enemies on campus were non-Methodist. But the record scarcely bears out this charge. McTyeire wanted familiar, sympathetic, loyal officers in his tight command, people acceptable to his board. At least a nominal Methodist connection abetted this goal. Smith and Baskervill were not all that religious. They were broadly informed, cosmopolitan, and a bit contemptuous of older, more provincial Methodists such as the Dodd brothers, Summers, or Shipp. Also, unlike the old faculty, they did not have as intense sectional loyalties, the same bitter memories of the Civil War, or as deep racial or sexual biases. They horrified old-timers by reckless hints at black equality or by their support of coeducation. In scholarly attainments and professional specialization, they soon would rival Humphreys and were a world removed from the gentlemanly versatility of a Garland or a Lipscomb. Both became significant, honored national scholars (Baskervill published a pioneering book on southern writers), and both exerted critical educational leadership, within Vanderbilt and by their efforts to raise the standards of southern education generally, even at the high school level. In short, they represented a new South and a new professionalism.[14]

It is critical to note that the Wofford-Leipzig connection remained incomplete at Vanderbilt in 1881. The third member, a student and protégé of Baskervill and Smith—James H. Kirkland—was only then a student at Wofford. He would later complete his graduate study at Leipzig. Through correspondence with his two friends, he kept up his hopes of an eventual appointment at Vanderbilt, if only a popular "Uncle Billy" Dodd would retire or die at the right time. Dodd eventually obliged. Young Kirkland's letters from Smith and Baskervill reveal a final McTyeire goal—to bring Wofford's president, James Carlisle, to Vanderbilt as Garland's replacement. McTyeire apparently expected the elderly Garland's early death, or hoped that he would be decent enough to retire. Garland never obliged.[15]

Baskervill gained his Vanderbilt position, if not his house, before marrying into the McTyeire family. Not so a controversial John Tigert. Tigert first came to Vanderbilt from Louisville as an older divinity student in 1875, after a career as a public-school teacher. After completing the required two-year course and winning the first Biblical Founder's Medal, he became a Methodist minister back home in Kentucky. Crucial to his later career, in 1878 he married his Vanderbilt love, Amelia McTyeire. Perhaps as early as 1879 Bishop McTyeire began planning to get his son-in-law back on the Vanderbilt campus. In the spring of 1881 he met with the Biblical faculty to urge a new degree, a Bachelor in Sacred Theology. The faculty obliged, setting the course work requirements and the required thesis on the atonement. Only John Tigert, who had completed additional theological work at Southern Baptist Seminary, ever took advantage of this new program. In 1883 Tigert won his S.T.B., although some of the Biblical faculty felt he took shortcuts and never met all the tasks they had set for him. Meanwhile, upon his arrival at the campus McTyeire gained for him an original appointment as assistant instructor in the Biblical Department, although he never taught courses in that department.

In his first year, 1881–82, Tigert taught only an English course. By McTyeire's edict, this became a requirement for all Biblical students, even including those few with bachelor's degrees. Adding substance to the charges of nepotism, Tigert soon moved into one of the now scarce faculty houses, by-passing waiting full professors. The tactless Tigert was an able man, by both faculty and student testimony, and in some ways almost another McTyeire—large, strong-willed, with a powerful personality. He had gifts as both writer and teacher. But he soon faced a wall of faculty resentment, beginning with Chancellor Garland, who opposed any regular faculty appointment for the bishop's protégé even after he won his "advanced" degree in 1883. In 1883 Tigert in effect took over the vacant courses in both history and moral philosophy and by 1884 was so listed in the *Register* of the university. But he remained at the anomalous rank of assistant instructor, although well paid at $1,500. By 1885 McTyeire desperately wanted to elevate him to the chair of moral philosophy, but for this once he failed. McTyeire could not, for reasons of propriety, make the nomination. Garland absolutely refused to do so and when pushed even submitted his own resignation, which he subsequently withdrew when McTyeire humbly begged him to stay. Garland had immense prestige and ample board support on the Tigert case. Thus, in 1885 no one nominated Tigert for a professorship, but the next year a board committee nominated him for the chair of history and moral philosophy. The board elevated him unanimously, with what behind-the-scenes maneuvers no one knows.[16]

Like a row of dominoes, the rest of the old faculty, save a secure Garland and a detached Safford, began to fall. In 1882 Granbery left the Biblical Department to become a bishop, an elevation that suspicious faculty members believed had been arranged by McTyeire. Then, at about the same time, Dean Summers suddenly died, removing another thorn from McTyeire's side. This left the struggling Biblical Department in the hands of a crippled Shipp and a drastically overworked and vulnerable Thomas J. Dodd. But even then one could see the beginnings of a new era, as McTyeire brought youthful Wilbur F. Tillett to campus to serve as chaplain in 1881 and, the next year, to take over Summers's course in sacred theology. In the Academic Department the mathematician William L. Broun received an appealing offer from a new University of Texas in the spring of 1882. Even as he considered it, and before his acceptance, McTyeire jumped the gun and hired William Vaughn as his long-desired replacement. Thus Broun had to take the Texas job, leaving Vanderbilt with the now usual fund of bitterness. In the next year Broun helped inspire his new, well-funded university to offer a position to Milton Humphreys, now easily Vanderbilt's most distinguished professor. Humphreys faced an agonizing decision. Thomas Dodd recalled the concern among the faculty over his prospective loss. Faculty members urged McTyeire to appeal to Humphreys to stay; McTyeire refused to say one word, to do anything to sway him toward Vanderbilt. As a memorialist during

The first dean, Thomas O. Summers   *Dean Wilbur F. Tillett*

THE BIBLICAL DEPARTMENT

Wesley Hall, from Old Main with Science Hall in foreground

the salary controversy, he also remained an enemy. Under these conditions Humphreys moved to Texas in 1883. This enabled Charles F. Smith to move into the Greek chair, the one that best fit his training. The sorrowful Vanderbilt faculty voted to award Humphreys the first of two Vanderbilt honorary degrees, the LL.D. By 1883, of the original faculty only Garland, Shipp, Lupton, and Safford remained; the two Dodds also identified with this old faculty. Gone were Arnold, Joynes, Winchell, Broun, Summers, Granbery, Lipscomb (now listed as emeritus), and Humphreys, or two-thirds of the faculty assembled only eight years earlier. That McTyeire contrived the departure of most of this older faculty, as so often charged at the time, is borne out by his own advice to the university, given in an 1884 version of his last will and testament: "Keep no professor who is discontented with his salary or his situation—or whose family is so pronounced. For such, withdraw chairs, if they will not leave them of their own accord. This infection spreads; it makes disorders; it disaffects students. *Be rid of them*.."[17]

Vanderbilt possibly reached its lowest ebb in 1884–85. Combined enrollments in the Academic and Biblical departments shrank to 176, the second-lowest ever. Most disappointing, this included only 50 Biblical students, or only a third of the number needed to fill up the new, half-empty Wesley Hall. A frustrated McTyeire reported to the board that Vanderbilt's enrollment should have doubled by this time. When arsonists set fires in 1884 that came close to destroying Main and did burn a hay barn and McTyeire's stables and carriage house, morale sank very low and soon would get worse.[18]

In December, 1884, McTyeire began a complete reorganization of the Biblical Department. It was by now clearly the weakest link in the university and yet the one department closest to McTyeire's heart. In part, he was at fault for its weaknesses. He had insisted upon an open admissions policy against the advice of his faculty. Thus, near-illiterate young ministers kept coming to Vanderbilt, lowering standards even in the Academic Department and driving away the few able college-trained men who had mistakenly assumed that Vanderbilt had a seminary. The old faculty had proven ineffective. Summers had little administrative skill. The almost voiceless Shipp, Summers's successor as dean, had been unable to attend conferences or effectively publicize his department. Dodd, disaffected and with a very ill wife by 1884, had too many teaching obligations to keep his head above water. In the leadership vacuum McTyeire had intruded himself into the day-by-day operations of the department. Because his highest obligation was to the church and to the now eight supporting conferences, he was afraid to raise standards, to turn away pious applicants, or to risk lower enrollments. Rigid rules, poor food, and arbitrary or confused requirements all helped dampen morale among the ministers in Wesley Hall. The worst-prepared students left with Vanderbilt certificates, only to embarrass the department by their incompetence. The ablest students left Vanderbilt for better training in other seminaries. Such was the situation when a small study committee, composed of Chancellor Garland and Executive Committee members David Kelley and Robert Young, made a detailed analysis of the Biblical Department before submitting their reorganization scheme.

For once McTyeire did not dictate policy. Both Garland and Kelley had independent views and both had bruises from earlier fights with McTyeire. They reaffirmed the previous demands of Shipp and Dodd for higher admission standards. In the reorganized department, entrants would have to demonstrate the equivalent of two years of college work or, short of this, enroll in the Academic Department until they gained such competence. To facilitate the new policy, ministers or aspiring ministers could still live in Wesley Hall and receive support from the sustentation fund. In a concession to McTyeire, and perhaps to reality, the committee recommended the vacating of all Biblical chairs. The justification made clear its intent—the department needed four professors who could approach the church as ministers of great power (that is, do a better job at public relations). This would mean the forced retirement of an elderly Shipp, the departure of a quarrelsome T.J. Dodd, and a dismissal for the able Tillett, who would be quickly reinstated. Forewarned, Dodd submitted his resignation in March of 1885, but somehow McTyeire never presented it to the Executive Committee, making him look all the worse in the showdown.

Both Shipp and Dodd, incensed, wrote indignant attacks on McTyeire and cited all the failures of the early Vanderbilt. Shipp's attack found outlet in the Nashville *American,* apprising local citizens and, as the stories about Vanderbilt circulated in newspapers and church periodicals, Methodists everywhere of the bitter controversy. Both Dodd and Shipp had constituencies in the church, and both added ammunition to the older enemies of both Vanderbilt and of divinity schools. They aired again the salary dispute, lamented the forced departure of earlier faculty members, and charged McTyeire with the use of unchecked, arbitrary power. The new controversy posed the greatest threat yet to parent loyalty and church support, and thus to badly needed enrollment increases. Members of the board tried to refute charges that it had rubber-stamped all of McTyeire's decisions. In the next two years the university also launched its first concerted public relations effort. The new Biblical professors attended all the annual conferences, loyal professors spoke and wrote on Vanderbilt's strengths, and, perhaps most important, in 1887 the faculty completed a well-publicized, major reorganization of Vanderbilt's whole academic program.[19]

Within two years the new Biblical Department was at least a moderate success. An older man who first came to the campus to serve as chaplain, Gross Alexander, took the chair of Greek and exegesis and served as secretary of the Biblical faculty during its first year, carrying out the duties of a dean, but only until the appointment of McTyeire's favorite, Tillett, as dean in 1886. He would lead the department for the next thirty-three years as well as teach courses in theology. Tillett, from a southern Methodist family, had taken his seminary work at Princeton, which allowed Dodd and Shipp to charge him with clandestine Calvinism. He brought to Vanderbilt the respect for rigorous intellectuality so lacking in the early department, and to specula- tive theology a philosophical breadth so lacking in Dean Summers. In 1886 the Reverend W.W. Martin, from DePauw University, took over the Hebrew and Old Testament chair. Elijah Embree Hoss moved from the vice-presidency of Emory and Henry College in 1885 to take over church history and pastoral training. Because of new admission requirements, enrollment in the fall of 1885 dropped to only thirty-four, but increased numbers of aspirants each year entered the Academic Department in what became a distinct preministerial program at Vanderbilt. McTyeire never gained the 150 students he wanted to fill up Wesley Hall, but the morale of the Biblical Department zoomed. Now, finally, completion of the two-year Biblical course came close to meeting normal Bachelor of Divinity requirements, and those students who entered with a B.A. now received a B.D. on graduation.[20]

In 1885 and 1886 McTyeire completed the rebuiling of his Academic faculty. Of the full-time older faculty, only Garland, Lupton and "Billy" Dodd remained. Lupton had strong board support, particularly from David Kelley, and Dodd was by far the most popular professor on campus. McTyeire needed luck. He got it. Lupton, as a lonely survivor from the original full-time faculty, must have felt pressured. In a much publicized gesture the board approved a year of paid, postdoctoral work in Germany for John T. McGill, who earlier had received his chemistry Ph.D. at Vanderbilt and had remained on as one of a growing number of Vanderbilt instructors. Lupton incorrectly read into this another McTyeire plot, an opening move to replace him with the younger, more submissive McGill. Then, perhaps as a departing shot at Shipp and T.J. Dodd, perhaps as a warning to recalcitrant faculty or students, the board, in its May, 1885, meeting, issued an edict on university government. The extended statement referred to fundamental principles that had to be recognized by all officers—that the charter gave highest authority to the board, that it extended special powers to the president, and that the chancellor, deans, and faculty had only delegated duties and rights. They were under obligation to those in charge of the government of the university. The board acknowledged the likelihood of differences of opinion about policies, invited appeals to the board on such divisive issues, but nonetheless made clear that the faculty had to accept, sustain, and observe all rules in form and in fact, in behalf of harmony and unity of action. Finally, the board warned anyone who could not faithfully comply with these views to vacate his position, but stipulated that it had not directed this statement at any particular individual. Lupton felt it was directed at him.[21]

On September 2, 1885, just as the fall term was to open, Lupton submitted his resignation in an angry letter to McTyeire. He resigned to accept a position at Alabama A&M (Auburn), where he would also serve as state chemist of Alabama. He justified his abrupt departure by alluding to

McTyeire's recent course toward him and to the board pronouncement on government. Lupton violated the required six-months' notice before leaving, and, to make matters worse, he released his letter to the Nashville newspapers. In the worst of times, with the Biblical controversy still brewing, he struck back at Vanderbilt and at McTyeire with bitterness and, one suspects, a bit of glee. The Executive Committee had no alternative but to accept his resignation. McTyeire lamely tried to vindicate his behavior toward Lupton. Because McGill was already in Europe, Safford had to take over the scheduled chemistry instruction. McGill returned next year as adjunct professor of chemistry but did not replace Lupton. Instead, the university appointed William L. Dudley to the chemistry chair. Dudley was destined to make a great impact upon Vanderbilt, not so much as a pioneer scientist but as an able teacher, as a leader in intercollegiate athletics, and as a later dean of the Medical Department. To add to the woes of September, 1885, Professor James H. Worman did not show up for his modern language classes and then shortly thereafter submitted his resignation. He had come to Vanderbilt only in 1883; a native of Berlin, Worman had engrossed his students in the German language. He cited poor health and the agitated condition of the campus as reasons for his leaving but made clear his support for McTyeire. Replacing him in foreign languages was another foreign-born professor, Casimir Zdanowicz. Even Garland professed an inability to pronounce his name, but he turned out to be an immensely popular teacher, remaining at Vanderbilt until his premature death in 1889.[22]

Poor Uncle Billy Dodd. He fell ill in the spring and summer of 1886, necessitating a brief absence from his Latin courses. Then, in the early summer he asked for a leave of absence for the following year, to rest and recuperate. He trusted he would thereby recover his health and return to Vanderbilt duties. In a strange, seemingly heartless action, the board elected him emeritus professor as a reflection of "our high esteem for him as a man and officer" and out of the necessity of filling the chair of Latin. This only confirmed the earlier suspicions of his bitter brother that Baskervill and Smith were plotting to remove Billy. As Dodd died within a year, the action may have reflected only a realistic appraisal of his health. But, whatever the motives, Baskervill and Smith were overjoyed. Smith immediately wrote the good news to their protégé, James Kirkland, who at the age of twenty-seven became a chair professor with a salary of $2,000 and lodgings in Wesley Hall. The new, dominant faculty triumvirate was now in place, ready to undo much of Garland's original design and create a new Vanderbilt almost as modern and progressive as northern schools.[23]

The years of strife and stagnation from 1879–1886 were not unrelievably gloomy. While administrators and faculty fought, the campus blossomed. Main and Wesley were indeed imposing buildings, adequate homes for the Academic and Biblical departments. Main contained chemistry and the new Pharmacy Department in a segregated basement or first floor, business offices and physics labs on the second floor, and a library, lecture rooms, and the literary society meeting rooms on the third and fourth floors. Stretching to the west was the chapel wing. Wesley had rooms for up to a 160 students, a small divinity library, lecture rooms, and basement kitchens and dining facilities. Science Hall provided needed space for the geologists and the first home of a developing engineering program. The gym and the small observatory provided almost luxurious frills, the tokens of financial health. Most needed were separate buildings for a library and for the new, still ill-equipped engineering program. William H. Vanderbilt, who continued his patronage until his death, added $100,000 to the endowment in 1884, with the interest dedicated to civil engineering, and then on his death the next year left $200,000 more, bringing the endowment up to $900,000, for an annual return of $63,000.[24]

But the glory of the campus was the grounds, intersected by several driveways and numerous walks. Within a decade the raw campus of 1875 was already graced by adolescent trees, some fifteen to twenty feet tall, most, except for a few older oaks, dating back to a beginning 1,500 trees planted by McTyeire. In large part these came through a gift of 450 plants by Thomas Meehan of New York, drawn from his great nurseries at Germantown, Pennsylvania. The 1878 university *Register* could list 306 varieties of trees and shrubs on campus, or what it called the Vanderbilt Arboretum. McTyeire lovingly supervised the planting of every new variety he could identify and procure. Some exotics did not survive the Nashville climate. The close spacing often required later thinning, as did new construction. Few of the original plantings remain on the present campus, with a handful of venerable magnolias most distinctive. But in an age before most private families indulged in landscape planning, or even bothered with shrubs or trees, the campus was a haven of loveliness. In their publications, students frequently remarked the beauty of the campus, particularly in the spring and fall, and noted that it became a favorite destination for Nashvillians out, in carriage or buggy, for a Sunday afternoon drive.[25]

The faculty members suffered from the constant turnover and their cold war with McTyeire. But they tried to maintain academic standards, despite the need for additional enrollment, and fought continually to end the hated subcollegiate courses. From the students' point of view, standards of admission and grading went up each year (in 1881 only five students earned bachelor's degrees). The faculty was not as sanguine. In 1881 Garland admitted that Vanderbilt had opened with standards equal to the best in the land but had quickly backed away from such a demanding commitment. Entry remained too easy, and only after a year's work would Vanderbilt students gain entry to such excellent schools as Harvard or Michigan. The most glaring deficiency remained the high-school caliber library, still with no more than 10,000 volumes; students thought too many of these related to Methodism. In some years the university did not spend even $100 on book acquisitions, and the annual circulation of books remained under 1,000. Garland now emphasized this need at every opportunity. In 1884 a faculty committee addressed an urgent petition to the board, pleading for new library funds, but at first to no avail.[26]

Students perceived the instruction at Vanderbilt as very demanding. But it was so only in one sense—students had to attend recitations without fail, take notes on the text and lecture material, and render frequent reports as well as to take numerous exams. This old-fashioned approach placed a premium on constancy, endurance, and memory, not necessarily on creativity. In a modern sense, grades scarcely existed. Students with number grades over 80 received a certificate of high proficiency; those between 60 and 80 received credit. Lower grades meant failure. Failures on the long, five-hour final exams were frequent. The faculty achieved a few victories—increases in the number of graduate courses, the approval of several Ph.D. programs, an active poetry circle, and a bit of national fame from the astronomical discoveries (seven new comets, several stars or satellites) of Edward E. Barnard. McTyeire brought an impoverished Barnard from a nearby home to Vanderbilt in 1882 to use its telescope and to live in a small frame house behind the Observatory. He became a fellow in 1883 and an assistant instructor in practical astronomy in 1885, although he had no academic credentials. A very young man, he soon had all but a proprietary claim on the Observatory, which became his primary responsibility until he left Vanderbilt for a position at the Lick Observatory in 1887.[27]

Fortunately, the Vanderbilt students were in part insulated from the faculty bickering. They had their own problems and priorities. Despite Garland's continuing laments about their deplorable deportment and about all the temptations of a large city, the students remained deferential and obedient. They pleaded for their major goals, and in the long run they won everything they desired. They quickly gained a right to live in boarding houses east of the railroads, for otherwise they faced monopoly prices. Upon the completion of Wesley Hall a few Academic students briefly occupied some of the vacant rooms. Not for long. The Biblical faculty seemed afraid that lay students would somehow corrupt the morals of young ministers. Their exclusion from Wesley angered such students, who came to resent the segregated "theologs." But by 1883 the Academic students had much the better of living arrangements, or so they believed. A group of non-Nashville students rented a large, two-story, frame boarding house on West End, just across from the campus, and renamed it Liberty Hall. They formed a club, made their own rules, and established a cooperative, student-managed mess at a bare-bones cost of under ten dollars a month for each student. They even installed a telephone in 1885. Liberty Hall, in a sense, gave from fifty to sixty students the best of two worlds—the comradeship and proximity to the campus of dorm life joined with complete self-government. The "theologs," now more than ever resentful of their rigid rules and poor food, practically rebelled. In 1884 they won the right to establish their own mess and soon ignored most of the petty rules.

Once the students had de facto dorms (the university paid summer rents in order to keep Liberty open), even Garland relaxed his earlier opposition to on-campus housing. In 1885 William H. Vanderbilt gave $10,000 for four small dorms (two-story, eight rooms) known as Westside Row when completed by the fall of 1886. These rooms were designed to be as undormlike as possible, having only outside entrances. By selling a house given by another donor, the university was able to add two more such dorms in 1887. Then it began building a nearby dining hall (now West Side Hall), with eight more upstairs rooms, giving the university a total dorm capacity of 112. This almost met the need in the mid-1880s, as forty to fifty preministerial students lived in Wesley and several Nashville students lived at home. Although West Side was ostensibly built to supplement Liberty Hall, all references to Liberty disappear after 1888. Ironically, students, who had so often complained of separation and loneliness, now resented Westside Row. They hated to give up Old Liberty and lamented their relegation to the "hinterend" of the campus, behind the privies and stables of faculty row or, as they put it, just beneath the status of the campus's one ass (a mule used for several campus tasks).[28]

Four concerns dominated student agitation from 1879 to 1886—a desire for legal fraternities, for student publications, for intercollegiate athletics, and for a richer social life. On the issue of secret societies, Garland, his faculty, and the board suffered a galling defeat. Garland thought fraternities worse than every other youthful indulgence or vice, and he early gained a rigid faculty prohibition of all such at Vanderbilt. But even in the first year the effort proved futile. Sewanee and University of Nashville students recruited Vanderbilt students for Phi Delta Theta and procured a charter for a Vanderbilt chapter in 1876. Yet, for a couple of years, this chapter remained underground. In 1877 the students organized a chapter of Kappa Sigma, which seemed to expire about 1880. By 1879–80 Vanderbilt students were ready, quite openly, to defy the faculty rules. In 1883 students received their diplomas with fraternity badges in full view. Nothing so troubled Garland as open defiance of rules, particularly since each new Vanderbilt matriculate signed a solemn pledge to abide by all rules. He vainly preached in chapel about the evils of fraternities or lamented the declining popularity of the two literary societies. In 1882 the faculty recognized the now flagrant violations and voted to deny any graduation honors to those who joined secret organizations. At first, though, they left enforcement of the rule to the two literary societies, which nominated and chose the honored speakers at commencement. In the same year (1882), Phi Delta Theta asked the Board of Trust to allow it to form an open and legal chapter at Vanderbilt. The board, of course, refused the petition. But the faculty was about ready to give up. Even Garland disliked the hypocrisy, or the unwanted alternative of rigid enforcement,

The men of Liberty Hall, about 1884

which meant forcing young men to commit perjury or otherwise incriminate themselves.[29]

To the complete surprise of happy students, the faculty took a face-saving formula to the Executive Committee in October of 1883. They would suspend all unenforceable rules against fraternities, evil that they admittedly were, but from this point on the faculty, not student societies, would make the final choice of commencement speakers and thus those receiving honors. This turned out to be an unwanted, boring chore for professors, who had to sit numbly through endless orations, and a continuing point of resentment for students. But the dam was down and fraternities flooded Vanderbilt, five by December of 1883, another in January, 1884, eight by 1886. After recognition, fraternity men tended to dominate campus life, winning every Founder's Medal awarded from 1879 to 1887, gaining from 70 to 80 percent of all scholarships, controlling publications, and dominating social activities. Fraternity men captured the literary societies and for a time transformed their rather vicious fraternity rivalries to the Saturday morning debates. By 1886 Garland could say "I told you so" for, in his view, the campus was close to open violence because of fraternity conflict. He wanted, temporarily, to dissolve the now fractious literary societies. Even the fraternity leaders ac-

The stile on West End

knowledged the competitive extremes and after 1887 tried to moderate inter-fraternity bickering.[30]

Garland feared student publications almost as much as fraternities. The plight of the ill-fated *Austral* demonstrated what opposition the students faced. But the students, as always, persisted. In September of 1879 they requested faculty approval for a new paper, this one under literary society sponsorship. The faculty dillied and dallied but eventually set up such a stringent set of rules that one of the literary societies refused to go along. The issue festered for two years, or until December, 1881, when the two societies launched the most sophisticated student publication in the history of Vanderbilt—the *Observer*. A reluctant faculty had approved, and the board even at one time gave the societies $100 to pay costs. But all was under tight restrictions—the students were to indulge no personal attacks, say nothing harsh or unkind about Vanderbilt, do nothing to denigrate the character of Vanderbilt or to impair its interests. The publication was subject to the chancellor or a committee appointed by him, and the editors had to submit for review all doubtful material (the faculty promised kindly aid on all questions of propriety). Beyond this, the students were responsible for all content. In fact, the faculty scrutiny proved amazingly lax, and in a guarded way the editors of the *Observer* became powerful molders of campus opinion. The rules never prevented them from airing, indirectly if not directly, all controverted policies or from mobilizing student opinion on any issue that concerned them. The monthly *Observer* was not a newspaper, although it included campus notes invaluable to a historian. In part it was a literary journal, bound in the form of a quarterly and soon featuring the best essays from Baskervill's English courses. It was also a journal of opinion, containing editorials, borrowed materials from other campus publications, and even a few faculty essays. The editors, in almost every case, were the ablest and most literate students on campus.[31]

The professed religiosity of Vanderbilt, necessary to appease the supporting annual conferences, did not mean that the Academic Department was a typical denominational college. Except for the fifteen-minute morning chapel, religion remained extracurricular. The Academic Department offered no courses in religion or on the Bible and its faculty consistently voted down proposed requirements in this area. The faculty disingenuously justified this opposition by referring to the school of history and moral philosophy. That, they argued, was quite enough. The concentration of Methodist students gave way rather quickly to some degree of heterogeneity, possibly another reason for faculty restraint in the religious area. In 1885 students organized the first campus YMCA, which in the next few years became quite active, with its own meeting room in Wesley. At least from student publications, one gathers that Vanderbilt students were conventional, even lax in their own religious beliefs and behavior. But, on rare occasions, faculty members did refer to religious revivals on campus; notably, in February, 1886, Moody and Sankey held a well-attended revival.[34]

What students meant by an active social life was not more religious services but parties, particularly those including girls. At the almost all-male university, the absence of young women was constantly a topic of conversation and banter. The *Observer* carried an essay on the "art of embracing" and made frequent sexual references, from "lovely snowy bosoms" to whimsical references to topless and bottomless women at Nashville theaters. The students valued the few women on campus, including the daughters of faculty members. The broader Vanderbilt social circle included some neighboring families, who often boarded boys, and also many families associated with the central agencies of the southern Methodist church. From these circles came perhaps twenty or thirty young women, dependably present at most campus events—to observe gym demonstrations, to attend Christmas parties, and to attend Founder's Day and commencement exercises. At scheduled, official, well-chaperoned events, young men always had the opportunity to join in a promenade (the origin of the later "prom"), walking and talking with young ladies and, in theory, thereby learning needed social graces. The *Observer* complained of many shy, socially inept young men who only stood and gawked at young ladies without joining the promenade. By the early 1880s, some fraternities began sponsoring dances and in 1884 students organized a dancing club. By then, fraternity boys had gained the reputation of indulging in alcoholic drinks, a horrible affront to Methodist mores.[35]

Eligible young ladies were always tantalizingly out of reach—at Dr. Ward's Seminary (predecessor of the later Ward-Belmont College) and, after 1880, at the new Methodist-sponsored Nashville College for Young Ladies, usually referred to as Dr. (W.F.) Price's School. From the beginning Price tried to build a special relationship to Vanderbilt and in advertisements referred to his as a correlated school. He hired several Vanderbilt professors for lectures (which earned them extra income) and won the privilege of sending his girls to Vanderbilt for English and science lectures and to use lab equipment. But both girls' schools kept tight, almost perfect security around their charges, permitting Vanderbilt men little more than distant looks or furtive and brief conversations, although on rare occasions Price brought his carefully supervised girls to Vanderbilt promenades. Dr. Ward's school appeared to Vanderbilt men as something close to an impregnable fortress. For one young man to gain entrance through its gates deserved extended coverage by the *Austral;* one enterprising Vanderbilt student bluffed his way in by professing to Dr. Ward to be a concerned scout for his sister, a potential applicant. Beyond such insulated contact, Vanderbilt students were left on their own resources, to meet Nashville girls at downtown churches, in homes of friends or relatives, or in more unsavory settings, such as the forbidden but well-frequented theaters.[36]

By introducing a section called "Alumni Notes," the *Observer* soon qualified as Vanderbilt's first alumni journal. Vanderbilt alumni had been active almost from the beginning. They tried to form an alumni association almost before Vanderbilt had awarded any bachelor's degrees. An alumni group first met formally at the 1879 commencement and at that time set about drafting by-laws. From then on the association met for a luncheon or dinner during each commencement week. John T. McGill assumed greatest responsibility for the alumni group and began collecting information on all Vanderbilt graduates in 1883. In 1884 the association first asked for two alumni members on the Board of Trust; in 1887 McGill began regular "Alumni Notes" in the *Observer.* But in June, 1886, in a hint of cultural conflict, the alumni bowed to church pressures and gave up wine at their annual dinners.[32]

From the beginning Vanderbilt students complained about a lack of physical training or athletic competition. In their second year they played an unauthorized baseball game with Sewanee but thenceforth faced strong faculty rules against any but intramural or strictly informal competition. It is clear that students played at least semiorganized baseball games all along, and as early as 1883 they had regular football scrimmages on Tuesday and Thursday. By then a Vanderbilt baseball team had uniforms and played other Nashville teams or even more distant preparatory schools, and by all accounts it usually won. The students had access to a well-equipped gym from 1881 on. Garland and the faculty urged, even implored, students to make use of the weights and gymnastic equipment, all in behalf of enlarged musculature and added body weight. But since the gym exercises were individual and voluntary, student interest tended to wane, especially when the low-paid gym instructors seemed to change every year. By 1886 the allure of a new and winning baseball team seemed to subvert gym use, to the despair of Garland. He was horrified to find no effective rules to stop the shift toward team competition; the baseball team traveled that year as far as Sewanee.

One senses that Garland was increasingly alone in his opposition to sports. The new faculty preferred to join the students, not fight them. In 1886 Baskervill helped form the Vanderbilt athletic association; within a year Dudley assumed a key role in its evolution. From the beginning the association emphasized field sports and held a well-attended day-long competition each spring. Its field day, the first such in the South, was soon attended by all neighboring colleges. In combination with field events, the baseball team usually played one of the rival colleges. Just ahead lay two new developments—required attendance at gym classes and scheduled intercollegiate competition in track, baseball, and football.[33]

From the student perspective, the early Vanderbilt lacked school spirit and a fulfilling social life. Legalized dorms and fraternities helped allay the loneliness of young men, but the gripes about lack of holidays, festivals, and fun continued. Social opportunities were optimal only in the area of religion. In addition to the morning chapel, the rules required students to attend a Sunday afternoon service, featuring a sermon by local ministers or clerical professors. They were also urged to attend nearby churches on Sunday morning. As in so many other areas, the faculty never really enforced attendance at the Sunday chapel, and soon Garland took frequent occasion to berate student apathy. In this case nonenforcement involved matters of conscience; even Garland was reluctant to enforce rules pertaining to matters of private conscience. In 1882 the faculty gave up on the Sunday afternoon chapel and moved the university service to regular church hours on Sunday morning. The university chaplain (Tillett in 1882) preached at this service, which soon encompassed not only the university community but nearby Nashvillians. Some faculty members chafed at the almost obligatory financial support for one of McTyeire's pet projects. In time, this new university church merged with West End Methodist.

What about Vanderbilt coeds? That is a complicated story. Technically, Vanderbilt had no women students. In fact, it always had a few, even though none matriculated until 1895. In the planning of Vanderbilt everyone seemed to assume that it would be an all-male institution. Yet, the board never so defined it or enacted rules prohibiting women. Garland was so fearful of women students that he probably thought nothing needed to be said; why take the time to proscribe educational insanity? Yet, at least one woman attended Vanderbilt classes every year from 1875 on. Kate Lupton was first and by now is a legend in Vanderbilt history. The daughter of chemistry professor Nathaniel Lupton, she took advantage of her campus connection. Her father wanted her to get a university education, one a notch above that offered by female colleges. In 1875 an enterprising Kate asked permission from Professor Lipscomb to attend his lectures, a courtesy he gladly granted since townspeople also attended. In 1876 Humphreys not only admitted her but allowed her to do the assigned work and receive grades. The other professors quickly followed these precedents. In four years she completed the courses of study in eight schools and with high distinction in every one. This meant that she more than met all the requirements for an M.A. By special vote, the faculty and the board awarded her the degree in 1879. Her supportive fellow students elected her to class honors (valedictorian), but she refused that honor. At commencement Garland duly recognized her degree but chose to give it to her in private. Her name did not appear in the *Register*. Perhaps Garland feared the reaction of Vanderbilt supporters. In the late 1880s, when coeducation was the most debated topic on campus, Kate wrote a restrained letter from her new home in Alabama, citing her own experiences and trying to alleviate the apprehension of Vanderbilt men. Kate remained a vital, contributing part of the Vanderbilt social scene until her father's controversial departure in 1885.[37]

During the next decade no women rivaled Lupton's achievement. But for various reasons, several young women attended courses. Dr. Price's girls made up a special case. In 1882 the *Observer* mentioned three women students. Most prominent among these was Mary Conwell, who along with Kate Lupton was a vital part of campus society, one of two daughters of the matron of Wesley Hall (Mrs. M.S. Conwell) and a granddaughter of the late Bishop Soule. After taking courses and receiving certificates in German, French, and English, she became a governess for the Harding family at Belle Meade. Lizzie Kelley, undoubtedly the daughter of board member David Kelley, took Vanderbilt courses to support her teaching at Dr. Price's school. The *Observer* also identified a Miss Purnell in 1882 and a Miss F.C. Herrick in 1886. Often without giving names, it referred to perhaps a dozen female students or auditors during the 1880s. In 1882, in a bid for needed students, the Pharmacy Department opened its program for young women and even set aside a special room for them. But the graduation lists suggest that few women took advantage of this opening. In the next few years only such sexually ambiguous names as Dedie, Jo, and Isadore appear on Pharmacy graduate lists. By the mid-1880s, the issue of coeducation began to emerge as a highly controversial issue on campus, with a clear majority of students opposed. Then in 1887 a faculty committee began exploring the possibilities of coeducation at Vanderbilt, just one of the several winds of change that made 1887 such a watershed year.[38]

The early records of Vanderbilt make only oblique references to a final, essential part of the community—the staff. With the exception of a supervisor of grounds and a single campus policeman, all the workers at Vanderbilt seem to have been black. They cared for the grounds, cleaned and maintained buildings, cooked food in the student messes, and worked as porters or servants in professors' homes. They remained hidden, even resented components of the campus. One of the longest descriptions of Vanderbilt Negroes came from an editor of the *Observer*. He described the blacks on campus, and by implication all blacks, as "ignorant, superstitious, immoral, and with but small capacity for radical improvement. They are improvident, lazy, and easily imposed upon by designing men. They have a low order of intellect, learn with difficulty, and apparently make small use of what attainments they have acquired." Amazingly, this was in a preface to an article advocating more black education as the only hope for them to rise from degradation. They deserved a chance, although this editor feared that blacks might be worse off for their education, less inclined to accept a subordinate role. He assumed, as did all student writers on the Negro problem, that social equality for blacks was entirely out of the question. Beyond this certainty, students took varied positions on racial issues. A few sensed the unfairness of a caste system, tried to view it from the black perspective, and agonizingly sought answers. But even the generous analyses ended up where all the student editorials ended up—in a quandary. No one had an answer to the black problem. Equality was impossible, unwanted. Blacks, condemned to a perpetual subordinate, laboring role, could rise only through education, but this could only create impossible aspirations and new levels of frustration and bitterness. Thus, even the most generous student had no better answer than "to conciliate, to educate, to wait, to watch, and to hope."[39]

Vanderbilt students, as a whole, remained securely provincial or quite conventional on most political issues. Despite the campus emphasis upon Christian character, few students seem to have reflected much tolerance or any generosity of spirit. The early student publications reveal almost no concern for, or involvement in, the acute social problems of Nashville. The few hints of compassion toward blacks joined with harsh, self-serving criticism and a steady stream of nasty, even if unintentionally cruel, "nigger" jokes. Students probably shared their social beliefs with the first Vanderbilt faculty, largely made up of die-hard defenders of the Old South and the Confederate cause. The first significant break in official silence on racial issues came only at the 1887 commencement, when George Washington Cable spoke by invitation of the students. To the intense consternation of his audience, he chose to bring racial issues into this address. As he had before, he here advocated perfect personal freedom for blacks and in such a sincere, earnest way as to win applause from part of his audience, although his stand won him only abuse in most of the South. The *Observer* noted his deep love for his fellow men and criticized those, presumably in the majority, who condemned his topic as inappropriate for a Vanderbilt commencement.[40]

Not only on racial, but on other issues, the students seemed to take a conventional or fearful stand. They resisted coeducation long after the younger faculty embraced it and seemed hostile toward most forms of political radicalism. They were most open and daring on issues closer to students. An editor defended agnostic Robert Ingersoll's right to speak at the University of Kansas, and for years students fought against the censorship implied in the rules against theater attendance. In an essay printed in the *Observer*, a student even had a kind word for Christian forms of socialism before attempting his refutation of all the heresies of Henry George. But more characteristic was an 1887 debate on the Haymarket anarchists by the two literary societies. The issue was not whether the Chicago anarchists deserved hanging. All affirmed this. Not even about any of the troubling issues of fair procedures that haunted their trial; the students seemed oblivious to these. But only whether the convicted men should be allowed to make statements before their hanging. On this terribly important moral issue, the Vanderbilt students dutifully divided.[41]

In the history of universities, continuities always outweigh innovations. Change comes slowly. But in the history of Vanderbilt, 1887 was a major, transitional year. Academic reorganization opened a distinctive era, dominated by the new, younger faculty brought in by Bishop McTyeire. His boys were not content with the university created by Garland. By 1887 Vanderbilt seemed, belatedly, ready to recapture a lost youth. Even students noted the transition. In June of 1886 a student editor noted that the old faculty, the venerable gray beards, were now all but gone. Only Garland and Safford remained. Young men, representing a new South, were now in control. They had less reputation but more vigor. The editor predicted that the new faculty would bring higher standards. They had a reputation to make. They would be judged by the performance of their students. No doubt they would make a name for themselves and for Vanderbilt. He followed those wistful remarks, perhaps even more prophetically, by a brief profile of the newly hired professor of Latin, a young prodigy named Kirkland.[42]

PART THREE

The Almost Gay Nineties
(1887–1901)

 AFTER ITS TROUBLED FIRST DECADE, *Vanderbilt begn anew in 1887. For over a decade the university enjoyed peace and steady growth. Its Academic Department enjoyed a national influence and respect never regained until the mid-twentieth century. In competence and achievement its Academic faculty briefly rivaled that of major northern universities. The professional departments lagged far behind the Academic, but by the new century the chancellor had at last gained more control over the three semiproprietary departments (Medical, Dental, Law), had fostered the slow maturation of the Biblical Department, and had continued, as a virtual adjunct of the Academic Department, Pharmacy and an often lagging new Engineering Department. But in none of these did the university achieve more than regional leadership.*

All was not well. The golden age of the Academic Department proved ephemeral, a flowering of talent and energy based on able young faculty members, not on the sustaining resources of the university. The ticking time bombs were an inadequate and almost stagnant endowment and nearly frozen levels of income. The consequence was a steady, relative decline of Vanderbilt's resources when compared with better funded and growing state universities or better endowed private ones. By wisdom or luck, Vanderbilt recruited some outstanding young scholars; because of frozen salaries it could not keep them. With a great burst of enthusiasm its young faculty launched an ambitious graduate program, but it was unable to develop the libraries or the laboratories needed to sustain such work. Finally, by 1901 Vanderbilt had already begun to suffer from its ambiguous ties to the Methodist Episcopal Church, South. The church, despite some hopeful gestures, never provided needed financial support. As Vanderbilt's chancellors had to cultivate

other, secular sources of funds, the church ties often proved more an embarrassment than an asset. The boom in the Academic Department rested upon a more diverse, cosmopolitan, and less sectarian faculty, an increasingly pluralistic student body, and a slow but sure shift of Vanderbilt away from its Methodist allegiances. Even before the new century, these shifts produced tensions among traditional church leaders that presaged a growing controversy. That controversy would erupt in the open after 1904 and lead, in 1914, to a nasty separation of church and university.

5

A Bid for Greatness

By 1887 the faculty of the nonproprietary departments had gained full control over academic policies. The authoritarian rule of McTyeire was almost over. The old bishop was increasingly ill, unable or now unwilling to intrude into the detailed operations of "his campus." Besides, he had a justified pride in his young faculty, in their enthusiasm and loyalty. He tended to applaud, not resent, their innovations. Chancellor Garland had never tried to dictate to the faculty; he was one of them. Yet, he played an indispensable role in the university after 1887 and particularly after the death of McTyeire in 1889. Despite his reservations over some changes, particularly those contrary to his earlier educational ideals, he accepted the decisions of his faculty and ably advocated them before the board. Briefly, he became in effect the executive officer of the university, responsible and tactful if not always vigorous. But his role, indispensable as it was, still allowed power to shift to a coterie of young faculty members. Chief among these was the Wofford-Leipzig junta of William M. Baskervill, Charles F. Smith, and James H. Kirkland, ably supported by William J. Vaughn and by the smooth and diplomatic William L. Dudley. James M. Safford, as always, went along, while the controversial John J. Tigert seemed to remain an outsider. Of these new leaders, Smith was most capable and most prominent from 1887 to 1893; his contribution in these years easily rivaled that of a dean or a vice-chancellor.

Led by Smith, a committee of the faculty spent much of 1886–87 reorganizing the curriculum. As a prelude to this revision, and in a sense an indispensable part of it, the faculty successfully petitioned the board to abolish all preparatory work (subclasses) by the fall of 1887. In fact, the faculty had to continue a few of these courses for two more years. But Vanderbilt now took a courageous and unprecedented step in the South— admitting only those students prepared for authentic college-level work. This meant carefully specified levels of achievement in Greek and Latin, history and geography, English, and mathematics. All along, Vanderbilt had admitted students into its college courses only on the basis of extended entrance exams in these subjects but had shuffled the unprepared (a majority in the early years) into the subclasses. Now, for the first time, a passing grade on at least two of the four exams was a prerequisite for matriculation, and the students who failed on one or two were admitted only conditionally. They had to pass their failed exams by the end of their first year and on the basis of their own preparation.[1]

These tough new standards, long desired by both faculty and students, posed a grave danger—dramatically decreased enrollments. Smith and Baskervill, in particular, tried to meet this threat with new recruitment strategies. The new admission standards amounted to a gesture of support to preparatory schools and to the better public high schools. Vanderbilt would no longer duplicate their work or lure away their students before graduation. Smith and Baskervill began regular visits to such academies, to explain the new Vanderbilt exams and to help set up the needed curricula. They also began a program of dispersed exams in 1889. Both at the leading academies, and soon in most larger cities of the Southeast, Vanderbilt offered carefully monitored entrance exams each June to prospective Vanderbilt students. They even offered two prizes for the highest exam scores in two of the fields. These exams served as an early version of standardized scholastic aptitude tests, for many students took them even if they did not plan to come to Vanderbilt. Soon over half of the entering Vanderbilt students qualified through these local exams. Finally, returning to a policy tried briefly in the first two years, Vanderbilt in 1889 began certifying academies and public high schools that demonstrated very high academic standards. It accepted their graduates without entrance exams save in modern languages. This created a special partnership relationship with a few exceptional schools (only four in 1889; twelve in 1898), helped assure that a disproportionate number of their graduates would choose Vanderbilt, and initiated the first formal efforts in the Southeast to establish standards for secondary education.[2]

In their new course of study, the Academic faculty dropped the school system and the certificates granted by each school. In this they repudiated Garland's ideal and the model of the University of Virginia. Smith, once again, led in the assault on the separate, almost autonomous schools, and on the lowered standards invited by an elective system and the intermingling of beginning and advanced students. In its new plan, Vanderbilt adopted the standard class system, with courses fitted to the freshman, sophomore, junior, and senior levels. The faculty established two undergraduate curricula, one the then standard classical program leading to a Bachelor of Arts, the other a Bachelor of Science program with heavy science requirements and an emphasis upon modern, not classical, languages. Briefly, for a few years, the faculty also awarded a few Bachelor of Letters as a hybrid of the other two (a degree based on either Latin or Greek and on modern languages). All courses were mandatory for freshmen and sophomores in each degree program, but in the junior and senior years most became elective. For a B.A., freshmen and sophomores had to take two years of Latin and Greek, plus courses in English, history, and math; in their junior and senior years they had to add courses in physics, chemistry, and moral philosophy. B.S. candidates had to have four years of work in either German or French, and they began their science requirements in their first two years. In their junior and senior years they had to take logic and political economy but did not have to take any Latin or Greek, which for several years so stigmatized the degree that few students chose it.

The change in 1887 was not as abrupt as it seemed. The schools had already worked out what amounted to a progression of courses, and despite the school system the students had already begun to identify themselves by class. The new system retained much of the older nomenclature (departments in place of colleges; schools in place of departments), the old four-step numerical grading system with two levels of passing and two of failing, and the older emphasis upon entrance and final exams. Subsequently, the faculty did reduce the five-hour final course exam to only three for freshmen and sophomores, to four for juniors and seniors.[3]

For the first time the faculty now established a true graduate program, or what they called the "University Course." Heretofore Vanderbilt had simply awarded an M.A. for the completion of two more schools than required for a B.A., with no requirement of separate or qualitatively distinct courses. It had awarded a few Ph.D.s, based on superior work in the most advanced but essentially undergraduate courses and on completion of a dissertation. In theory, earlier Ph.D. candidates had pursued advanced work on an independent or apprenticeship basis. Now the university curriculum included a new series of separate graduate lecture courses or seminaries (modern seminars) offered only to graduate students, and normally offered only by chair professors or by adjunct professors with a Ph.D. The chancellor and four other professors served as a committee on university instruction, or what amounted to the first graduate committee. Graduate work could lead either to classical degrees (M.A. and Ph.D.) or scientific ones (M.S. and D.S.). Master's work required a year's residence and at least six hours of advanced course work, plus a five-hour exam and a thesis. The doctoral degrees required three years of work in a principal field and two subsidiary ones, up to fifteen hours of exams on these fields, a typed or published dissertation involving original investigations, and a final exam. To fulfill the added instructional burden, the faculty asked the board for more junior faculty and for a separate chair of history and political economy (granted in each case). To procure needed graduate students, it asked for ten graduate fellowships, which offered $100 in free tuition (granted in 1889). With these changes, the teaching responsibility of chair professors shifted decisively toward graduate seminars and advanced undergraduate courses. Soon, instructors or teaching fellows did almost all the freshmen and sophomore teaching, with a decided and noted drop in the quality of all too many junior courses. Falling math grades caused particular concern.[4]

Seventy-seven-year-old Chancellor Garland applauded all the new academic policies except the shift away from his near-autonomous schools. In a confidential, revealing letter to McTyeire in July, 1887, he lamented Vanderbilt's failure, thus far, to meet the standards of a great university. He used the phrase "start anew" to characterize the ambitious new program, talked of "a higher tone in character" and of a "higher stage of operation," and hoped, finally, that Vanderbilt would soon become "first on the continent" except in age. But he knew upon how thin a base his young "officers" had launched their new program. He doubted that McTyeire and the board realized it and so set about educating them for this one last time. Vanderbilt started strong in 1875; it had an adequate endowment for its early program. But since then, despite its head start, Vanderbilt had lost its momentum and its preeminence even in the South. He noted the $3.5 million endowment of Hopkins, the $5 million of Texas, and the larger annual income of Virginia, whereas Vanderbilt had only a pitiful and stagnant $900,000. He most emphasized the deficient library, which simply was not of university caliber. Already, true universities had a separate library building, a library endowment, and a professor of bibliography in charge. If Vanderbilt were to move, successfully, from the recitation of textbooks to original research and the use of primary sources, it needed to spend $100,000 for new books and at least $10,000 a year for new acquisitions. It needed a gift of $250,000 for the library, or about all it could judiciously expend over the short run. The Academic Department also needed a new chemistry building and some new laboratory equipment. Engineering desperately needed its own building.

Garland believed Vanderbilt had also failed to keep up academically. It needed new schools in sociology and political science, in psychology and hygiene, and in biology. Faculty salaries had lagged, until the contract salary of $2,000 trailed that of every major southern university and was insufficient to support a professor at his accustomed social position. The salary of chairs needed to go up to at least $3,000. All in all, Garland believed that the new adventure into the ranks of major universities required capital expenditures of about $300,000 and the additional annual income produced by $600,000 of new endowment. He also envisioned a completely new, endowed Medical Department much like the one at the Johns Hopkins. In his prophetic analysis, Garland probed the high costs of sustaining what his "boys" had launched in a burst of youthful but, he suspected, rather reckless idealism. It was characteristic of Garland, in this the last stage of his career, to look at Vanderbilt with amazing clarity and even detachment. Yet, he did so only to turn over all the financial problems to McTyeire and the board. Garland was ill prepared, not only by age but by temperament, to take a very active role in soliciting the needed funds. The old gentleman was too proud to beg, too honest to flatter any benefactor.[5]

On only one issue did the faculty fail in its proposed 1887 reorganization. It unanimously asked the board to approve the admission of young women "on exactly the same terms as young men, and that none but those who have thus been matriculated be admitted to our classes." This action led to a prolonged, intense student debate over coeducation, probably the most debated issue at Vanderbilt in the 1880s. The students interpreted the faculty action as an endorsement of unwanted coeducation. To some extent it was. The new admission standards, the ending of subclasses, created the need for qualified students, the more the better. The proprietary claim of faculty members to one-half of the realized tuition even added a small, pecuniary motive to their decision. Notably, in a subsequent action, the faculty asked to withdraw this proposal if the board refused to abolish subclasses, for they would not have the time to teach unqualified women. Actually, the intent of the proposal was ambiguous; it did not reflect all the varied faculty attitudes toward coeducation. Its implementation would not only have required the admission of women on equal terms but would have excluded a large number of women already attending courses. In this way it paralleled the abolition of subclasses.

Of seventeen young women taking French and German in 1888, only two stood for final exams. So far, women came to classes by courtesy of professors and most as special or irregular (nondegree) students. Few of those would be able to meet Vanderbilt's new entrance requirements. Thus, one can see in the petition not a plan to increase the number of women but rather an effort to regulate their admission to Vanderbilt. But the equality principle did open up the prospect of increased numbers of women in the future, and the board received the petition as if it were a license for coeducation. To them it seemed a political hot potato. During the first year a board committee tried to weigh opinions on campus, within the church, and within the South but still remained indecisive, requesting an additional year for study. Only in 1889 did it advise against equal status or even open admission, which it deemed "not advisable at this time." On the other hand, it did not terminate the existing, loose, irregular arrangement, leaving to faculty determination all rules controlling "courtesy" women. Thus, nonmatriculating women kept coming to Vanderbilt, and in 1888 a woman—Ella Freeman—gained their first faculty award; her essay was best in Baskervill's English course and merited publication in the *Observer*.[6]

The new academic program, fully implemented only by 1889, coincided with the death of McTyeire on February 15, 1889. McTyeire died with a sense of growing pride in "his" university, a belief that his policies had been vindicated. But his life on campus had not been a happy one. Governing the university had been the greatest trial of his life. In one version of his will he reflected his pent-up and unacknowledged frustrations. In his final advice for Vanderbilt, he recommended that future presidents of the board not live on campus, for such residence had been "my necessity and my misfortune." He had had to become intimately involved, receive all manner of requests, and then suffer the resentment of those rebuffed. He lamented his trials with incompetent, recalcitrant, or even immoral faculty members. In advice written in 1881, and which later proved embarrassing to the university during the protracted lawsuit with the Methodist Church, McTyeire asked the bishops, as "by Charter they have a right, to lay their hands on this University for guidance and governance." He wanted them to keep in constant connection with the university, and his will urged them to make and keep it a religious institution. On campus the eulogies were appropriately respectful and detailed. Students served as pallbearers for McTyeire's campus burial in the hallowed company of Soule and McKendree. The greatest single architect of Vanderbilt was dead, a momentous and mournful event. Yet, one senses in all the praise and all the regret more awe and respect than affection.[7]

A student editor of the *Observer*, with unprecedented frankness, gave an appropriate retrospective on McTyeire. He had been ubiquitous on the campus, knew it all down to individual trees, and loved it so much that he took too much unshared responsibility for it. He had been a friend to students, to his boys, perhaps more so than to his faculty. He always excelled in executive ability, in getting things done. He relied on his own judgments, too much said critics, but in rare confessional moments, in a few watch night services in Wesley Hall, he had acknowledged all his faults. He created many enemies, as powerful men always do. His caution, secretiveness, rigid self-control, and stubbornness all made him seem hard, unapproachable, and dictatorial, yet in private he was emotional and sentimental. Everyone at Vanderbilt was in debt to him. He had been a faithful servant. Yet, no one really wanted another McTyeire on campus, and in subtle ways his passing brought with it as much relief as sadness. Of course, the ghost of the old bishop continued to haunt his campus, was still tangible in Old Main, or flitted noiselessly through the magnolias that he planted. Perhaps fortunately, ghosts do not make policies.[8]

McTyeire's death required major changes in the government of the university. Could anyone, should anyone, try to take his place? Garland had always dutifully taken second place to McTyeire. He had often seemed unnecessarily deferential, fearful of making decisions. No more. The old man (he was seventy-nine years old) seemed to gain a new burst of energy, to thrive on his new responsibilities. He never served Vanderbilt better than in the next four years. By the time the board met in May, 1889, he had carefully prepared a special report to guide them into a new era. And "guide" is the right word, for behind his very careful phrasing one can see his own preferences. Garland had suffered in silence under the quite "anomalous" powers assumed by the "late president," powers not delegated by the board but acceptable to it as a condition of Vanderbilt's gift. Were these powers limited to the person of McTyeire or did Vanderbilt intend them as perpetual powers of the president? Garland left these questions for the board to decide. Clearly, he believed that they should terminate with McTyeire's death, but he asked the Executive Committee to consult about these issues with the Vanderbilt family (as he suspected, Cornelius Vanderbilt, the grandson of the founder, was not at all concerned about the details of university government, happy to leave such matters up to the board). The board then had two options. On its own initiative it could continue the existing scheme, which required it to appoint a bishop to succeed to all the powers and privileges of McTyeire. Or it could do what Garland clearly wanted—carefully redefine the nature, the powers, and the duties of the president of the board. Entailed in such a definition would be a needed clarification of Garland's own responsibilities as chancellor.

The board compromised in 1889. After extended discussions, and several votes on various details, it decided to elect a new president for life but without salary. It considered a motion to eliminate the veto held by McTyeire but defeated it, perhaps out of deference to the new president. But never again in the history of Vanderbilt did any president claim such power; the veto died with McTyeire. One other bothersome issue remained—McTyeire's campus residence. As early as 1881, in last words left for the board, he had requested that his wife be allowed to spend the rest of her life in the campus house and that she receive $1,000 annually. After Baskervill became his son-in-law, he updated his request to allow this family to move in with Mrs. McTyeire. The board did not have to honor these requests but gladly did so. The Baskervills soon moved into the president's home and lived with Mrs. McTyeire until her death, just two years after her husband's. This left no residence open for the new president; moreover, McTyeire had strongly urged him to stay off the campus. Thus, the board granted $1,000 commutation in lieu of a house, or the only compensation now attached to the presidency. During the financial stringency of the 1890s it eliminated even this. In these ways the board considerably diminished the prerogative of the president and by implication intended a diminished role for him. But in no formal way did it diminish any of his powers. He would remain executive officer of the university. In the subsequent election, four of the bishops received votes on the first ballot. The leader among these, Bishop Robert K. Hargrove, won the required two-thirds on the second ballot. Only a brash and daring editor of the new *Hustler* openly protested the choice; he said no bishop had the intelligence to head the university.[9]

Bishop Hargrove proved a very different sort of president than had McTyeire. Conscientious, restrained, he never took any responsibility for academic policies or the day-by-day operations of the campus. An Alabama native, a bishop since 1882, he had already served as the president of two small Methodist colleges and had brief earlier experiences as a math teacher at the University of Alabama. As board president he was legally responsible for almost every decision. Officially, he hired every professor and every teaching fellow, approved every expenditure of funds, and even endorsed rules pertaining to student conduct. Yet, so far as the record indicates, Hargrove trusted all these matters to Garland and to the faculty. In fact, he seemed to want to relinquish more of these responsibilities than at first he could. Garland, ever mindful of chains of command, took every decision to Hargrove or the Executive Committee, even those he knew would be routinely approved. At the annual meetings of the board, Hargrove's shrinking presidential reports proved only brief summaries of the more detailed ones rendered by Garland and by his successor. In his last years, as he grew increasingly deaf, Hargrove played an even less important role in university government. He was usually a loyal advocate of the more consensual policies developed on campus, not a source of new ideas, although he brought tact and wisdom to those few controverted policies that had to be fought out in the Executive Committee. His one area of responsibility, and one that constantly frustrated him, was financial. Here he played a major, constructive role.[10]

In 1892, as Chancellor Garland neared retirement (he first submitted his resignation in 1891), the board certified what had become, in fact, a new mode of university government. It made the chancellor executive officer of the university, with original responsibility for almost all academic issues, including the assignment of all personnel and the care of buildings and grounds. The board retained original responsibility only over financial issues. These changes finally eliminated even in form the special presidency created for McTyeire and brought Vanderbilt's government in line with most other universities. But, unlike most universities, the chief executive officer at Vanderbilt has always since held the title of chancellor, not president.[11]

Even as the board upgraded the office of chancellor, it searched for a successor to Garland, who kept his resignation before the board from 1891 on. Unfortunately, no detailed records of these board deliberations, official or private, have survived. The Board of Trust minutes simply report that on June 20, 1893, the board elected James Hampton Kirkland as its new chancellor. Later, Bishop Eugene R. Hendrix took credit for nominating Kirkland. After a few hours to consider and to consult colleagues, Kirkland accepted. And as if by prearrangement, Judge East then announced his retirement from the board. The board then elected Kirkland as his replacement from the Tennessee Conference, giving him the board position he needed. Edwin Mims, in 1893 a student at Vanderbilt, later the author of an eulogistic biography of Kirkland, remains the one source in the best position to infer what happened. He was also, as a student editor, an intensely involved supporter of Kirkland. From the campus perspective, the key concern was to protect the university from the one fatal propensity of boards—to elect one of their own kind. The board members might have been tempted to elevate religious over scholarly qualifications. Or they might have turned to an heir apparent, to one of McTyeire's sons-in-law, either Baskervill or Tigert, the latter now an increasingly respected minister in Kansas City. Tigert, insensitive and often brash, was still anathema to many at Vanderbilt, and some believed Baskervill did not have the required temperament to be chancellor. Mims believed the faculty had the key role, that the board wanted their guidance or advice and all along probably intended to elevate one of them to the post. Garland provided the only precedent, and in 1893 the key concern of a chancellor still seemed to be academic matters. No one in 1893 could foresee Kirkland's broader role in guiding the board, in fund raising, or in regional educational leadership. By Mims's account, based on hearsay and not records, the faculty could never agree on any one candidate, perhaps because so many secretly saw themselves as best qualified. Garland finally acted on his own, nominating Kirkland. The board then confirmed his recommendation.[12]

Kirkland became the most influential person in Vanderbilt's history. His subsequent forty-four-year career as chancellor so shapes one's images of him that it is almost impossible to characterize a thirty-three-year-old Latin professor in 1893. Very little in his background explains his sudden, and radical, promotion. Kirkland was the son of an upcountry South Carolina Methodist itinerant. He grew up in genteel poverty in Spartanburg. His father had died in 1864, when James, the youngest of five sons, was only five. His mother, well educated and refined, took responsibility for her seven children, often boarding students from their own, local Wofford College. Four of the five Kirkland brothers attended Wofford; one became a Methodist minister and editor. The two daughters both married Methodist preachers. It is no wonder that James took advantage of this local, family college. He had no other realistic options. But few entered it so young—fourteen. Here he followed the typical classical curriculum, graduating four years later at the ripe age of eighteen. At Wofford he came under the influence of the college's later president, James H. Carlisle, then a math professor, and Charles Forster Smith, the new, Leipzig-trained professor of Latin and Greek. Later, Smith would call Kirkland my "best and favorite pupil."

Upon graduation, Kirkland taught in a local preparatory school and took work for his M.A. In 1878, while still only nineteen, he became an instructor in Latin and Greek, surely one of the youngest faculty members in any respectable American college. As a faculty member he first met a new colleague, William M. Baskervill, and soon absorbed from him, and from conversations with the director of a summer institute at Wofford, Edward S. Joynes (formerly at Vanderbilt and then at the University of South Carolina), a new enthusiasm for the study of English. By English, he meant a thorough grounding in comparative philology and in the varying ancient roots of the English language. Encouraged by his mentors—Smith, Baskervill, and Joynes—he taught the classical languages at Wofford for five years and saved every penny he could. In the summer of 1883 he made the long trip to Leipzig, there to seek his Ph.D. in what, from a perspective shared by both Smith and Baskervill, was clearly the mecca of serious scholarship.[13]

No student ever went to Germany better prepared for, or more appreciative of, the opportunity. Guided by Smith, Kirkland had elaborately prepared himself. Gifted in languages, he quickly so learned German as to pass as a native. Serious, frugal, disciplined, he made every moment count. Even his trips, his recreation, fit his tight schedule, contributed to his goals. Already he had that remarkable ability to concentrate entirely on a task at hand, to ignore diversions, and to turn out an unbelievable amount of work in a short time. This work discipline joined a precocious, even brilliant mind. He was curious about everything, intellectually fascinated with a dozen disciplines, and quickly master of any of them. Of course, he paid a price for such an intense intellectual effort. Nourishing his inadequate savings, he lived as simply as a monk. He pushed his eyes to the limit, his health to the breaking point. He took out little time for friendship, for frivolity or fun, save for a few trips and a few fabulous days hiking in the beloved Swiss Alps. His educational goal became clear in his first term—to perfect his classical training and to master the roots of the English language. Thus, he not only took Latin and Greek but courses or independent study in all the older Germanic languages, including Anglo-Saxon, and in Sanskrit. Within a year he completed his dissertation—an intensely specialized study of an Anglo-Saxon poem—and in just over eighteen months stood, and passed, his final exams. He had his Ph.D. sooner than anyone, himself included, expected. This was only the first step in Kirkland's plans. Now he wanted to take postdoctoral work in Berlin and to study English linguistic roots in Paris and London, with a probable detour into Spain in order to learn that language. His hope was to return to the United States to fill a college position, teaching the new, scientific approach to English.[14]

Alas, Kirkland's plans ran aground on severe illness during the late summer and fall of 1885. For about the only time in his life he came close to despair, to acute depression. A fever and several severe complications—perhaps a physical collapse that followed naturally upon all the concentrated energy expended for his degree—left him weak, with his hair falling out. He feared he would be an invalid for the rest of his life. From then on, he attended carefully to his health, worked carefully at weights and at various exercises. After abbreviated trips to Italy and short stops in France and Britain, he returned to South Carolina in the spring of 1886, only two and one-half years after leaving home. By then his dreams all seemed dashed. He no longer had a position at an improverished Wofford, and in the mid-1880s academic positions were few and far between. As a matter of pride, or of an acquired arrogance, he told Smith and Baskervill that he would not teach modern languages even at Vanderbilt, where he and his friends, abetted by McTyeire, had long plotted to get him a job. He told his mother the modern languages were "too superficial and unscientific." He preferred English but would deign to teach either Latin or Greek. To a brother he bitterly asked if anyone knew of a good position as a "dray driver, streetlamp lighter or such like." He confessed he was about "to the end of my rope." He exaggerated. His friends pushed him for an appointment at North Carolina and, given his credentials, he would sooner or later have found a good academic position. But even as he searched he received the happy letter from Smith. Professor Dodd was ill and Kirkland now had the Latin chair at Vanderbilt. He and his aging mother made the joyous trip to Nashville in the fall of 1886.[15]

Kirkland came to Vanderbilt a loyal Methodist. He joined actively in West End Church and for many years taught a Sunday school class, mostly to his own Vanderbilt boys. His opening lectures to students each fall were as much lay sermons as those of Garland and not a whit less moralistic. Yet, his allegiance to Methodism never seemed so much doctrinal as a matter of family tradition and soothing familiarity. From his inauguration as chancellor on he always talked of Vanderbilt's "broad" or "liberal" religious identity. In effect, Kirkland reinterpreted Vanderbilt's church ties as a loose commitment to Protestant Christianity, and not at all to the distinguishing doctrines of the Methodist Episcopal Church, South. He defended only a loose Christian test in the recruitment of faculty. Obviously, Kirkland had no reason to speak out on doctrinal controversies in the church, but his Sunday school classes and his private correspondence indicate his rather loose, conventional Protestant orthodoxy, and his openness to higher criticism and to Christianized versions of Darwinian evolution. Kirkland reflected the most tolerant and accommodating wing of southern Methodism without ever moving to an avowed "modernist" position.

Kirkland never seemed deeply involved in serious theological issues. Here, more than in any other area, one might indict him as intellectually shallow. He seemed, without any deep anxieties or an acute awareness of intellectual flabbiness, neatly to harmonize his Methodist allegiances with all the eroding implications of modern scholarship, science, and philosophy. Such a broad but tolerant religious stance would shape all his work as chancellor. He always tended to translate "Methodist" into "Christian," and thus so broaden the religious ties of Vanderbilt as to include almost anyone in the South. He would not be sectarian or dogmatic, which is to say he would not be rigorous and thus exclusive on matters of religious belief. These religious views contrasted sharply with the sectarian loyalties of McTyeire and Garland, but the religious shift embodied in Kirkland seemed to parallel a similar shift from the old to the new Vanderbilt faculty.[16]

Little in Kirkland's early Vanderbilt career hinted at a future administrative role. He taught his undergraduate Latin courses, enjoyed the seminars made possible by the new graduate program, in part because they allowed him to move beyond the narrow boundaries of Latin. He gave most of his time to his teaching and to university committees, not to scholarship. The later, glowing tributes to his teaching are suspect. But no doubt he expected high levels of achievement, eschewed shortcuts to learning, was serious rather than folksy, witty but not humorous, and as always reflected a virtue of old McTyeire— the ability to get right to the heart of issues, to be clear and succinct. He related well to students, served for years as vice-president of the athletic association, tolerated some youthful pranks, but characteristically met even students at a more cerebral level, as when the young chancellor simultaneously took on every willing chess player at Vanderbilt (nine of them). In most ways he was the very opposite of his predecessor in Latin, the genial, relaxed "Uncle Billy" Dodd. Because of his assets he made the greatest impact upon the abler undergraduates and upon a young group of graduate students. His enthusiasm for the new, specialized Germanic scholarship rubbed off on several of them. As a scholar, he published a few technical articles and an edition of Horace's satires and epistles. The introduction to this edition, plus the articles, was a respectable showing for one so young, but to that point one could only demonstrate promise, not achievement, as a scholar. Already he devoted a share of his writing time to reviews, to popular articles in Methodist journals, and to articles dealing with teaching or education. These, alone, demonstrated his early involvement with not just the rigors of scholarship but with the supportive institutions that make it possible. That is, they show the budding interest of an educational politician. In scholarship Kirkland was too versatile, too curious, ever to restrict himself to any one subject or field. As a person and a professor he was too involved with Vanderbilt, too committed to the improvement of higher education, to the advancement of the South, and perhaps too ambitious, to be only a closeted scholar.[17]

Kirkland came to Vanderbilt at the end of the old battles with McTyeire. Although part of the new crowd, a protégé of Smith and Baskervill, he was not as tainted as they by past controversies. His intellectual and personal maturity, his intellectual quickness, his lifelong ability to maintain detachment from whatever he did, made him anything but a partisan. Garland undoubtedly appreciated these qualities. His colleagues all recognized Kirkland's skill on committees, his fluency, and his evenhanded approach to people and issues. He was not a politician in the ordinary sense. He did not flatter others or even develop the pleasantries of easy intercourse. From Germany he wrote his mother that he had no talent as an organizer, if that meant stomping the country for big money.[18] He never suffered fools gladly and as chancellor hated the fact that he had to smile at every inanity pushed on him by prospective benefactors, whether zealous Methodists or boring businessmen. He learned the skills of fund raising but always worked best with foundations or intellectually self-conscious philanthropists. His asset was his own ambition, his willingness to work and to endure unending frustrations. As a poor boy who had worked so hard, he loved fame and position. He also enjoyed power and loved to gain influence and use it for what he believed were righteous goals. He valued both intellectuality and action. The two compromised each other to some extent. He gave up on a scholarly career, and because of his work he remained a bit more conventional in beliefs, a bit more inflexible in his imagination, than his early brilliance would have suggested. That is, he absorbed some of the trademarks of an executive, the myopic perspectives of a manager. But at the same time he was for the first two decades of his chancellorship an unusually cerebral adminis-

Professor James H. Kirkland   *Mary Henderson before marriage to Kirkland*

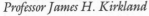

trator, and he kept alive earlier scholarly interests even after years of administrative labors.

The board had long since decided that McTyeire's large residence would
become the home of the new chancellor. Garland remained professor of
physics but chose to stay in his older house. After the death of Mrs. McTyeire,
Baskervill had moved into another faculty home. Thus Kirkland inherited the
now empty home. After his mother's early death, he had heretofore lived with
other bachelors in Wesley Hall, and with three close friends had been part of a
dining club (Club IV, pronounced Club Ivy) with its Negro cook. As
everyone now emphasized, Kirkland needed a wife and Vanderbilt needed a
first lady. In his busy life Kirkland had seemingly almost ignored the social,
and sexual, side of life. Now, with the deliberation that characterized so much
of his work, he began looking. He met Mary Henderson at a dinner party in
Nashville. She impressed him at once, although at first he seems to have
approached her in a quite reasoned manner. She was a quite eligible mate,
with talents befitting a chancellor's wife. The daughter of a prominent
Knoxville lawyer and historian, she had grown up in an atmosphere of wealth
and in an active, even frivolous social circle. But she had enough of an
education (in Boston and in Europe), enough literary and artistic interests,
and enough sensitivity to appreciate Kirkland. She also frightened him. Her

world of wealth, luxury, finery, and beaus was alien to his experience. Apprehensively, he wrote her of his serious intentions and later admitted that it was her initiative alone, her revealing signals of mutual respect and affection, that kept the tentative relationship going. Shy, socially inexperienced, and proud, he was ready to run at the first hint of failure.

Once the courtship began it blossomed in the glorious spring and summer of 1895. It culminated in a huge, well-publicized, fatiguing, and expensive wedding in Knoxville that November. Joyful Vanderbilt students tried, in vain, to get a free holiday to celebrate the marriage. The early affection quickly blossomed into an affair of intense passion, reflected in poetic and sentimental letters. Kirkland took every opportunity to visit Knoxville and then rejoiced in the opportunity for an almost idyllic summer tryst in the North Carolina mountains. Mary was soon quite clearly the most detached and rational of the two. She had lingering doubts about the prospective marriage; Kirkland none at all. She clearly feared her future role and had a rather dreary view of all those repressive Methodists. What would they think of her parties, her card games, her diverse and not always pious friends? How would they take to her upper-class habits—her annual shopping excusions to Atlanta and New York, her lavish dinners, her love of the theater? Kirkland minimized the problems and in a particularly revealing letter noted how much he loved beer and how much he would like to have it on his table each day. But he could not. A little enjoyment would hamper his work and cripple his influence. He favored moderate indulgence in these areas, and indeed indulged himself in social contexts far removed from student scrutiny. He promised to relax a bit more under her influence, risk a bit more, and perhaps her love of him would cause her to find less enjoyment in those pleasures he could not share.[19]

With marriage, the young chancellor settled into a domestic pattern that continued until his death. The marriage worked well, despite Mary's early fears. The couple remained very close, as affectionate years after as adolescent sweethearts. There were strains, particularly for Mary. She was often ill the first few years. Their one child, Elizabeth, was born in 1897, to the joy of students and the continuing delight of an adoring father. Serious surgery for Mary followed shortly thereafter. Mrs. Kirkland did not easily break from her family in Knoxville; she returned there frequently, perhaps as an escape from her duties as a chancellor's wife (she spoke to literary societies, helped form a Vanderbilt Woman's Club, and entertained an unending flow of important campus visitors). In some ways Mary had been pampered and must have suffered from Kirkland's seriousness. She also had expensive tastes, in clothes, in servants, in furnishings. Indirectly, in ways not to offend his pride, her family aided the couple in various ways (as a wedding gift the couple received a horse and a fine carriage). Their life on campus was comfortable, even luxurious. They had a cook, a gardener, and other servants. They managed long summer vacations and even one extended trip abroad. In other words,

Mary Henderson Kirkland and mother

they lived close to the level of the wealthy, not the normal penury of professors. But Kirkland, at least, did not move too far from his childhood experiences. An avid gardener, he shared vegetables with faculty colleagues and eventually made the hybridizing of iris first among a dozen hobbies. For many years he kept a cow in his back yard and even sold milk to his close friend Dudley. He loved the mountains, hiking, and most forms of hunting and fishing; dove or quail hunting often offered a brief respite from campus problems. As a token of their affluence and their interest, the Kirklands eventually purchased a summer home on a lake north of Toronto, Ontario, and there spent at least a part of each summer. Thus, in all private and personal areas Kirkland's life seemed fulfilling. He could therefore give full attention to his university; here, so much was frustrating.[20]

Kirkland became chancellor in a dark and gloomy depression year for the country but a good year for Vanderbilt. The end of subcollegiate work had triggered a momentary, severe drop of enrollment. In the fall of 1886 the Academic Department had enrolled 188 students, the most in its history.

Four years later this number had dropped to a frightening 112, the lowest in Vanderbilt's history. But in 1890 the new ties with preparatory schools plus the early and localized entrance exams began to pay off—slowly. Over the next decade, Academic enrollment rose by an average of 10 percent a year; in 1898 the undergraduate enrollment passed 200. And this steady growth came in spite of the highest entrance requirements in the South. Much more than before 1887, Vanderbilt was now an elite institution, accessible only to able students who enjoyed an exceptional secondary education. Also, the undergraduate growth reflected a steady reduction in the number of irregular or special students, and a stable graduate program averaged over thirty students each year.[21]

In 1893 the Academic Department had what is arguably the strongest faculty in its history. Able young men had helped expand the number of schools. When Casimir Zdanowicz died in 1889, Vanderbilt reorganized its always unstable foreign language program, setting up schools in both Teutonic and Romance languages. To teach in the Teutonic field it hired as instructor one of its former undergraduates, Walter Deering, just back with his Ph.D. from Vanderbilt's parent club—Leipzig. It appointed a young German Ph.D., a Leipzig friend of Kirkland's—Alexander R. Hohlfeld—to teach Romance languages. Unfortunately, in a beginning pattern, Deering moved to a chair position at Western Reserve in 1892. This allowed a very able Hohlfeld to take over his preferred Teutonic program, and in it he slowly rose to become chair professor and then the first dean of the Academic Department in 1900. Several junior faculty served the less stable Romance field.[22]

A comparable expansion occurred in philosophy and the social sciences. At the 1887 reorganization, John Tigert taught moral philosophy, history, and political economy. In that year the faculty brought to campus Edward W. Bemis, a new Ph.D. from the Johns Hopkins, to lecture on history and political economy. He repeated the lectures the next year, and then as adjunct professor he took over a new school in history and political economy in 1889. Bemis came directly from the famous Hopkins seminar chaired by Herbert Baxter Adams. He was the first Vanderbilt professor with a new style, German-influenced American Ph.D., and in his training compared very well with his five colleagues with Leipzig doctorates. He reflected the beginning of a new trend in both American higher education and in Vanderbilt recruitment—the slow turn away from German universities to major, new American graduate programs.

Bemis brought completely new perspectives to the campus and daring ones for any southern institution. His historical, institutional approach to economics successfully blurred the distinctions between his history courses (all institutional in approach) and his courses in political economy, which broke almost completely free from the English, Ricardian approach still dominant in most American colleges. Bemis wanted an expanded economic role for

The IV (Ivy) Club (front row: *James H. Kirkland, William Dudley, and John T. McGill;* standing: *William T. Macgruder and Austin H. Merrill*)

government, applauded labor organizations, and was sympathetic to limited government ownership or to milder forms of socialism. He tried to take his instruction beyond the walls of the university, supported and helped launch a branch of a new university extension movement at Vanderbilt, and with Smith and Baskervill gave adult lecture series in downtown Nashville. The extension effort never caught on, but the Round Table, a town-and-gown discussion group founded in part by Smith, did survive. Bemis pushed his students into detailed, local research. He had a group of abler students complete essays on state governments in the South, and with the help of Herbert Baxter Adams arranged their publication by the Hopkins Press. This was the only book published by Vanderbilt students until the Fugitive volumes came out in the 1920s.[23]

Bemis was lured in 1892 to the new University of Chicago by its aggressive head, William Harper. He left despite intense, organized efforts by his students to keep him at Vanderbilt. The South, they argued, badly needed someone with his perspectives and talents. At Chicago, Bemis received a salary of $2,500, above that of any chair professor at Vanderbilt. He probably regretted his move. During the railroad strike of 1894 he expressed sympathy with workers and indicted law breaking by monopolistic owners. In effect, Harper fired him in a celebrated academic-freedom case that tarnished Chicago much as the Winchell case had tarnished Vanderbilt. Harper frankly admitted that he had to get his financial support from large corporate interests and that he could not dare offend them. At Vanderbilt, Bemis would in all likelihood have survived such an honest but politically charged role. In 1894 churchmen, not corporate executives, still dominated the Vanderbilt board. Vanderbilt replaced Bemis with another young American Ph.D., Frederick W. Moore, just out of Yale. He was not as outspoken, or nearly as exciting, as Bemis, but a solid scholar who would make a continuing contribution to Vanderbilt, both as professor and as dean. By the end of the 1890s his own field had become too sprawling and unwieldy. Because he taught mostly in the field of history, one young instructor briefly took over economics. A subsequent young Vanderbilt M.A., Gustavus W. Dyer, introduced the first Vanderbilt course in sociology.[24]

Tigert retained the philosophy field until his departure in September, 1891. Already, people were beginning to refer to his field as both moral and mental philosophy. Emergent in it was the discipline of psychology. But the separation did not come until the middle of the next century. Tigert's replacement was Collins Denny, a former nominee for the preaching job in the Biblical Department. Denny was a well-known, gifted Methodist preacher. A Princeton undergraduate, he participated in what he considered the first American intercollegiate football game (Yale vs. Princeton, 1873), and captained the Princeton team in both 1874 and 1875. At Vanderbilt, Denny took an active role in shaping policies about football. After Princeton he took a law degree at Virginia and practiced law before converting to Methodism and entering its ministry. He remained at Vanderbilt until elected bishop in 1910. In Nashville he reared his family, among whom was his daughter, Elizabeth C. Denny Vann, whose Vanderbilt reminiscences have so enriched knowledge of campus life.

Denny was never a scholar in the sense of Smith, Hohlfeld, or Bemis. He did not transform either philosophy or psychology at Vanderbilt into highly specialized disciplines. He was also one of the last Academic chairs to gain his position, at least in part, because of church connections and active board initiative. Not that the teaching of this vigorous man necessarily suffered (reports on this varied), but only that, in training and academic outlook, he was a throwback to the first Vanderbilt. His qualifications perhaps still fit his unique academic slot. As professor of moral philosophy he remained uniquely responsible for cultivating a Christian character in Vanderbilt students. His teaching, almost alone among the courses offered in the Academic Department, continued to attest to Vanderbilt's Methodist allegiance. Notably, after the academic reforms of 1887 and the death of McTyeire in 1889, the Vanderbilt Academic faculty had seemed to forget all earlier sectarian and sectional criteria in its recruiting. Hohlfeld, Bemis, and Moore set the new Vanderbilt pattern—hire the ablest, best-trained scholars available. After about 1895, almost every new instructor had a Ph.D. from a major northern university.[25]

In 1892, before the departure of Bemis and Deering, the Academic Department at Vanderbilt, in faculty strength, had to rank just below that of Hopkins, Harvard, or Michigan. Scholars of ability or promise headed all the key schools save physics. Even there, young John Daniel ably backed up the venerable Garland. All chair professors except Garland, Denny, and Dudley had terminal degrees in their fields. Such was the tight academic market of the 1890s that Vanderbilt was able to hire new Ph.D.s even as instructors, some at less than $1,000 in salary. This meant a junior staff that, as a whole, matched the training of the chair professors. This superb staff gave some legitimacy to the new and very competitive graduate program. In the early 1890s, Vanderbilt's ten graduate scholarships attracted students from several elite northern colleges. To the delight of Garland, in 1890 the commissioner of education listed Vanderbilt as among the six leading universities in the country in graduate work. This was as much a quantitative as a qualitative achievement, but for a few brief years Vanderbilt was in the forefront of graduate instruction, for it had fully separate graduate courses, demanding degree requirements, and faculty members well qualified to train apprentices. But it could not maintain such a head start and because of a deficient library could never justify its limited Ph.D. program. It was clear by the time that Kirkland took over as chancellor that Vanderbilt's graduate program would serve a unique and important regional, not a national, role—to train young men, and increasingly also young women, for teaching in the better southern academies and liberal arts colleges. Those with a Vanderbilt M.A., or an M.A. plus some additional graduate work, were in great demand. Soon Vanderbilt almost controlled the market for such teachers through large sections of the Southeast. Because of its graduate students it had a larger role than any other institution in upgrading southern academy and college standards.[26]

The death of Garland in February, 1895, marked both an actual and a symbolic turning point. His death, much more than that of McTyeire's, produced a flood of heartfelt eulogies. He outlived all the earlier controversies. His age, his greatness, had long since disarmed student resentment of his moralisms. At his death, saddened alumni began a successful campaign to commission a bust of their old chancellor. A *Comet* writer (undoubtedly a professor and probably Vaughn) could easily proclaim Garland the "most striking and interesting figure in the Vanderbilt community." He symbolized older approaches to scholarship. In truth, said this writer, he had not read widely outside the Bible, and his knowledge of math and science extended little beyond an ordinary college curriculum. He was fascinated with telepathy but did not really keep up with astronomy. He was never a money raiser and, proud and austere, never a genial or affable man. But all this counted for little. He was a good, kind, generous man, devout and honest. He epitomized the old school, the earlier emphasis above all else upon character, a conception of education that he had gained from his beloved Scottish philosophers. In an intellectual sense, Vanderbilt had now moved from its Scottish origins to its Germanic and specialized present. Perhaps no one wanted to go back, to change direction. But in Garland one glimpsed the best of what was irretrievably lost. Only the most insensitive failed to shed a tear at his passing.[27]

Garland, who always celebrated its great possibilities, did not have to suffer through the gradual stagnation and even the relative decline of Vanderbilt. This decline, at least symbolically, began in 1894, a year into Kirkland's chancellorship. In that year Charles F. Smith reluctantly left Vanderbilt to head a classics program at the booming University of Wisconsin (his beloved wife had died only a year earlier). In the same year that Smith resigned, Dean Landreth left Engineering for a position at Union College. The faculty flight was on. In one sense, the loss of faculty was a healthy sign. Vanderbilt had recruited able men and profited immensely from their years of service. A university always suffers most, not from those successfully wooed and then lost, but from those who never leave, who attract no outside suitors. But a massive flight of talent is also a disaster, and this Kirkland feared by 1894. He was almost helpless. His leading chair professors received less pay ($2,000 plus about $300 in tuition fees) than the ones hired originally in 1875. Even worse, brilliant young men, such as Bemis, languished for years in assistant or adjunct positions at insulting salaries of under $1,500. Some left Vanderbilt for almost doubled salaries elsewhere. But by 1894 the university was in debt, needs mounted in every direction, and everyone seemed helpless. Even then, the university suffered less than it would have in ordinary times. A surplus of young scholars desperately sought work. A young Latin instructor, with a Ph.D., took over most of Kirkland's classes for only $700 a year, not much above factory wages. In 1898 a young Columbia Ph.D. in history accepted an assistantship (normally filled by graduate students) at only $500. He could do no better. But such exploitative opportunism did not serve Vanderbilt in the long run.

Kirkland most mourned the loss of his good friend and former mentor, Smith. He was irreplaceable, clearly the most valuable member of the Vanderbilt faculty. He left among frenzied student efforts to keep him at Vanderbilt and then after leaving came to regret his choice, maintaining until his death an emotional attachment to Vanderbilt, which tried to find a suitable replacement. In Herbert C. Tolman, a Greek and Sanskrit specialist then at North Carolina, it came close. A graduate of Yale and of the University of Berlin, Tolman became one of the most respected and most published scholars in Vanderbilt's history, and also a later dean of the College of Arts and Science. A non-Methodist, one mark of his competence and independence may have been the vocal protest of his appointment in conservative Methodist circles.[28]

After 1895 the quality of the Vanderbilt faculty noticeably declined. For years Vanderbilt was able to offer excellent instruction in both physical education and elocution without ever elevating either field to the level of a school, and without making such instructors fully a part of the faculty. This remained so even after Vanderbilt started giving credit (one hour for three hours of instruction) for mandatory physical education in 1893. But the Vanderbilt instructor, who unsuccessfully begged for years for at least $1,000 in salary, left for better opportunities, and the elocution instructor, beloved Austin H. Merrill, famous all over the South, accidentally died in 1900. The blows continued at century's end. In 1899, in a loss almost as severe as that of Smith, the great and respected Baskervill died, to be replaced by a less eminent Richard Jones. Baskervill had built his English program into one of the most respected in the whole country. In June of 1899 a former Vanderbilt Doctor of Science, youthful Paul M. Jones, drowned in Massachusetts. Almost alone, as a nominal subordinate of Safford, he had built what amounted to a new school of biology. The final blow came in 1901. Dean Hohlfeld, Kirkland's old Leipzig chum, moved to Wisconsin to take over a much larger program in German. He had served just a year as Vanderbilt's first dean of the Academic Department, appointed by Kirkland to help lighten his intolerable work load. By then the job market had tightened. Kirkland, who took the primary role in finding and hiring new faculty members, often had difficulty locating well-qualified candidates. In the loose and informal job market, he often detoured extensively from his travels to inquire after, or to interview, or even listen to lectures by likely prospects.[29]

In 1900, perhaps fittingly in the last year of the century, the aging Safford suffered a stroke and chose to resign his position. He set a needed precedent. Heretofore, Vanderbilt professors never retired; they died in office or had to be forced out (a lack of retirement benefits was one cause). Since Garland's death, Safford had been the sole survivor from the original faculty. He had served Vanderbilt well in his fourth of a century, as head of geology, as a chemistry instructor in the Medical Department, and for over a decade as dean of the small Pharmacy Department. In his letter of resignation he looked back twenty-five years to the original faculty: "A band of noble brothers was that faculty. I look back upon them with much affection. One by one they have dropped out of the life of the university, and now, with my withdrawal, no one of the band is left." He received the emeritus honor and, so typically, was replaced by a new Ph.D. from the Johns Hopkins.[30]

During the last decade of the century the Academic faculty made a few changes in their program. Beginning in 1894 in chemistry, a number of largely junior staff offered a proprietary summer school (they received the

*Academic guests for the 25th Anniversary Celebration.
Note the new academic gowns.*

fees as extra income), which grew slowly to about seventy students in 1900, almost half women and most of those school teachers. In 1898–99, in part as a result of student demand, possibly in part as a gesture to the church during a new canvass that promised to aid Vanderbilt, Kirkland asked for an undergraduate course on the Bible. Concerned students had already organized informal courses. The first year a temporary instructor taught fifteen students. None of the Academic staff would touch the course. Denny seemed an obvious choice, particularly since almost no one signed up for his history of philosophy. But he resisted strenuously; only Kirkland's authority forced him to teach it in 1899. In 1901, as Kirkland had long desired, the barriers between the Academic and Biblical Departments broke just a little; from then on undergraduates could take three credit courses in the Biblical, with the history of religion one of these. This, in effect, marked the beginnings of a religious studies curriculum.[31]

As the faculty approached the elaborate celebration of Vanderbilt's first twenty-five years, the only deeply embittered fight of the decade involved the Academic, Engineering, and Biblical faculties on the weighty issue of whether Vanderbilt should adopt mandatory caps and gowns for commencement. By a narrow vote the formalists won, but a cautious board made the new uniform optional for faculty. By 1901 the faculty had to feel a bit more somber than in the heady years of the early 1890s. The losses had hurt. In 1900 the number of chair professors—seven—remained identical to 1875. And, perhaps most ominous of all, the caliber of graduate students was falling. Fewer and fewer came from northern schools. More Vanderbilt undergraduates lingered on for their M.A. The brief, illusory flirtation with greatness was about over.[32]

6

Kirkland's Apprenticeship

As KIRKLAND CLARIFIED his early goals as chancellor, three had to take precedence. For Vanderbilt to grow, for it to attract more students, it had to raise educational standards in the South, at both the secondary and the collegiate level. Kirkland assumed a leading role in that effort. Second, for Vanderbilt to maintain its comparative eminence as other universities expanded, it had to gain a much larger endowment, increase its income, and expand and upgrade its plant. Kirkland largely failed in this financial effort, at least during his first decade in office. He gained only relatively small gifts from either church or private benefactors. But in these years he made essential contacts and learned needed lessons for his future success as a fund raiser. Last, he had to upgrade all of Vanderbilt's six professional schools and to gain more direct control over the appended departments of Medicine, Dentistry, and Law.

Smith and Baskervill, in their careful cultivation of select academies and the best public high schools, began in 1889 a type of de facto certification. The better secondary schools tried hard to make Vanderbilt's select list. Such certification aided them in recruiting students, even as the imprimatur of certification made it more likely their best students would choose Vanderbilt. But Vanderbilt still had recruitment problems. Without much additional cost, it could have taught double the number of students in its Academic Department in the 1890s. And, although student fees still paid less than 15 percent of Vanderbilt's operating budget, the additional tuition was badly needed. The laxity of secondary education meant that only a small proportion of southern students came close to Vanderbilt's admission requirements (these included fourteen units of carefully allocated and rigorously classical high school work). No clear standards governed high schools; in much of the South students attended only three years, whereas it was all but impossible to meet Vanderbilt's requirements in fewer than four. To make matters worse, the South had more purported colleges than any other section. Small, ill-financed colleges with minimal facilities and two or three unqualified instructors competed desperately for students. Some admitted any applicants, regardless of high school credits, and thus helped lure students out of high schools in their junior or even sophomore years. In other words, most higher education in the South was a scandal and a fraud, as Smith had pointed out in an article he published in the *Atlantic Monthly* in 1885. Vanderbilt had a difficult time bucking such a lax system alone. Partly as a commitment to the South, partly as a defensive effort, it sought cooperation with other like-minded institutions.[1]

As early as 1887, Smith met with other Tennessee colleges to seek uniform admission standards. He gained little cooperation. Then, in 1895 Baskervill presented a detailed paper to the Vanderbilt faculty, one in which he proposed that Vanderbilt invite colleges and academies to form a southern association of schools and colleges. Kirkland asked to be a delegate to the first meeting at Atlanta; Baskervill and Tolman accompanied him. Not only did Vanderbilt take the lead, but its delegates alone came to this organizational meeting with a specific agenda. Later, Kirkland gained almost all the credit for the new Southern Association of Colleges and Secondary Schools. In a sense he deserved it, but he gained his authority at Atlanta because he was chancellor at Vanderbilt. It is not at all clear that he contributed more to the original design than Baskervill. What Vanderbilt wanted and needed was a cooperative agreement among colleges to abolish all subcollegiate classes and establish uniformly high admission standards. The better colleges could then compete as near equals. The academies had to commit themselves to make such admission standards a condition of graduation. Only twelve institutions came to Atlanta, there to evaluate all aspects of southern education. These schools united in behalf of higher standards, a clear separation of secondary and college work, and mutual support and assistance. The first admission standards were far short of Vanderbilt's, save in English, yet only six represented colleges could meet them. Kirkland accepted the position of secretary and treasurer and for years was the key figure in the association. He coordinated its work and planned most of its meetings. At first the association linked only a few prestigious colleges. Later, when it evolved into a regional accrediting agency, colleges vied for membership.[2]

When Hargrove became president of the board, he quickly grasped the serious financial problems facing Vanderbilt. The recent building program—Westside Row and the Mechanical Engineering building (begun in the spring of 1888)—had cost much more than anticipated (the gifts had been for set sums). In order to provide a downtown home for the Law Department and new space for the Dental Department, the Vanderbilt board had sold railroad bonds from its endowment and constructed a new building on Cherry Street (presently Fourth Avenue) as an investment venture. It not only charged rent to the proprietary schools but hoped for well-paying outside leases, mainly to lawyers. But during the construction of a $93,000 building it lost interest on this amount of endowment and in the depression 1890s never gained close to 7 percent returns from rents.

Hargrove instituted tough accounting procedures. In an original audit he discovered a university debt of about $90,000 (some owed to banks, most borrowed from various university funds). Although the debt was small in ratio to assets, Hargrove and then Chancellor Kirkland wanted to save enough each year in operating cost to reduce it. This proved almost impossible. Annually the university had realized $63,000 from its $900,000 in 7 percent bonds, plus about $10,000 in tuition, fees, and such small items as sales of campus hay and timber. In the early 1890s the operating budget remained almost frozen at just over $70,000. This left little income for debt retirement or for unanticipated capital needs. The skimpy maintenance budget barely prevented a serious decay of campus buildings. By 1890 the budgetary squeeze was on.[3]

The financial crisis proved intractable. Tuition increases offered little relief. In 1893 the operating budget received only $5,700 from student fees and tuition, or only 8 percent of the total. That year the board raised tuition from $50 to $85 (fees made it $100 for each student), but that provided only an additional $3,000. In the depression decade any higher tuition threatened enrollment. Also, almost half of the students in the nonproprietary departments came tuition free—all Biblical students, all preministerial candidates, the sons of ministers, most scholarship students, all professors' children, and even public school teachers. In 1893, apart from the Biblical, ninety-four students in the Academic and Engineering Departments paid no tuition. Kirkland worked to reduce what he called Vanderbilt charity but removed only teachers and certain other scholarships from the long list. Financial salvation lay only in an increased endowment.[4]

Even the endowment threatened disastrously lower yields in the future. All the $900,000 endowment, by choice of the Vanderbilt family, was originally in 7 percent Lakeshore and Southern Michigan bonds, all maturing in 1901. Vanderbilt first sold some of these bonds to build its Law and Dental building and lost income as a consequence. After that experience the board, and an investment committee chosen from it, proved very reluctant to sell more. In the depression 1890s, high-grade investments yielded only about 5 percent, some even less. Hargrove saw the terrible prospect ahead; in 1901 Vanderbilt faced a loss of nearly 30 percent of its endowment income. Thus he prodded the board to sell the bonds, at up to 20 percent premium in the early 1890s, and to reinvest in diversified assets. In 1890, when he first proposed such sales, the amount received from the bonds could be invested at close to 6 percent, or in ways to produce an income equal to that of the bonds. But with each year of delay the premium dropped, and soon Vanderbilt could preserve its endowment income only through much more risky investments. It substantially completed its sale or conversion of bonds in 1897, but only after a fumbling, often ill-informed process. By then its endowment income had dropped from $63,000 to just over $59,000. In the process the premium on sales had raised the face value of the endowment to just over $1 million. Had the board waited to the maturation of the bonds, its income would have dropped to about $45,000, a disaster. But had it converted earlier, it could have increased the value of the endowment to over $1 million and maintained

111

an income close to $63,000. As Hargrove and Kirkland recognized, their board was simply not competent in areas of business management. Thus, in the midst of all the complicated selling and buying, they struggled to reconstitute the Board of Trust.[5]

In 1892 Hargrove and his Executive Committee first explored a major restructuring of the board. Advised by Judge East, Hargrove supported a charter amendment to reduce the number of board members from each of the eight conferences from two to one (they only dropped from four to two in 1888) and to make the bishops ex officio members of the board. The last change reflected a need to clarify their role. The original Memphis resolutions, as incorporated into the charter, made the bishops a Board of Supervisors and seemed to give them almost coordinate power with the Board of Trust. They never met as a separate body and, although no one was then aware of this, had they claimed the power of such a board they would have violated the general incorporation statute under which Vanderbilt received its charter (this statute required the governing power to be in one board). Thus, the bishops had simply attended regular board meetings but with no clear right to do so and no clear role at such meetings. Hargrove and Kirkland still hoped to get the needed new endowment from the church and so in the mid-1890s wanted to pull the bishops into a more active involvement (subsequently, Kirkland regretted this). Although a board committee signed a petition for a charter amendment in 1892, it never pursued it. Judge East, instead, helped secure a new Tennessee law that would have allowed Vanderbilt to so amend its charter as to come under an 1875 corporation act, but no one subsequently initiated this action. Instead, Hargrove and Kirkland, supported by attorneys, decided they could accomplish their goal through a simple by-law change, one allowing them to appoint needed businessmen. In 1894 they successfully proposed new by-laws that permitted four at-large appointees (those not confirmed by, or representative of, supporting annual conferences), and which made the bishops and the chancellor ex officio members. The board promptly nominated Cornelius Vanderbilt as one of the new business trustees (both he and his brother refused the honor) and in the next year added three new businessmen trustees to its investment committee.[6]

A second change in the board involved the church. In 1894, for the first time, the Methodist Episcopal Church, South, agreed to give major financial support to Vanderbilt. It launched a major new canvass, called the Twentieth Century Fund, and hoped to allocate up to $300,000 as an endowment for the Biblical Department. This dream, if realized, promised to resolve many of Vanderbilt's financial problems. For the next four or five years Hargrove and Kirkland did all they could to insure the success of the canvass. As it turned out, almost all that Vanderbilt ever received was what its own administration and faculty raised, or not enough fully to endow even a new chair in the Biblical Department. But in the heady opening phases of the canvass Kirkland moved Vanderbilt closer to the church, its only clear hope of financial salvation. Even as he did this, the university faced the first opening barrage of criticism from Methodists, criticism that it badly needed to smother. One largely friendly editorial in the Nashville *Christian Advocate,* undoubtedly written by former Biblical professor E.E. Hoss, subtly suggested that Vanderbilt was no longer in harmony with the church. Young Methodist scholars were refused appointments, and Vanderbilt professors derided or belittled Methodist beliefs and practices. The board denied the charges (they were partly true) and noted the lack of any proof. Meanwhile, Kirkland wanted to end the special Vanderbilt tie to conferences and make the university an adornment of the whole denomination. He played his political cards very well and won a victory at the General Conference of 1898 in Baltimore. Subject to the approval of the cooperating annual conferences, the church as a whole would now sponsor Vanderbilt and its Education Board confirm trustees. A new by-law eventually clarified the relationship and provided for staggered twelve-year terms for all trustees.[7]

None of the structural changes solved the financial problem, which only grew worse each year. Kirkland could not prevent a steady, slow increase in operating costs after 1895, as the budget grew to just over $80,000 by the new century. To have frozen expenditures would have imperiled the already straitened academic program and risked the loss of the ablest faculty. Kirkland turned in desperation to the Vanderbilts and began a long-term courtship of them and other new York financiers. The grandsons of the Commodore had only a peripheral interest in Vanderbilt, and that tied largely to its name. Their gifts had increasingly flowed into prestigious eastern schools, the ones they or their children attended. But in 1896 Kirkland was able to keep a balanced budget because of an anonymous gift of $5,000, a gift promised for only two years. He later revealed that the gift came from William K. Vanderbilt. The next year, Cornelius Vanderbilt added another annual $5,000 and promised it for up to three years. The university began a new policy—the use of gifts for operating purposes, not to increase endowment. The strategy kept the budget balanced and even helped retire a bit of the debt, but it offered no security for the future. Since 1884 the endowment had remained stagnant. It needed another large infusion. None came, although in 1900 Vanderbilt received $50,000 from the estate of Cornelius Vanderbilt (not enough to compensate for the loss of his $5,000 annual contribution).[8]

William K. Vanderbilt proved more munificent. He offered Vanderbilt an open-ended gift of a new dorm in honor of his mother. This dorm (Kissam), the last men's dorm completed at Vanderbilt until 1947, amounted to an addition of approximately $180,000 to the endowment, since Vanderbilt so assessed rents as to make it an income property. Kissam was to be the most distinguished building on campus. It had all modern conveniences (baths and toilets in the basement), a large basement dining hall, and suites for up to 200 students. Richard Hunt, whose father was architect for the Metropolitan Museum of Art and the Biltmore mansion, designed the new dorm, incorporating fire barriers and a room design copied from new dorms at Columbia University (two small bedrooms off a common study or sitting room). The Vanderbilt students were ecstatic; finally they would have a real dorm, with internal hallways and meeting spaces.[9]

Counting Kissam as an investment, Vanderbilt entered the new century with an endowment of just $1.2 million. Kirkland had no early prospects for significantly increasing it. The campus did receive the happy but soon ambiguous news of a new bequest from the estate of Mary Furman, whose will was soon contested. By its terms the university was committed to the construction of a Furman Hall at a cost of up to $100,000. When subsequently completed, it added needed facilities for chemistry; it did not add at all to the university income but, like all new classroom buildings, simply added new costs to the operating budget.[10]

To complicate Kirkland's financial problems, in 1899 he had to find means to rebuild both the campus heating and sewage systems. He had to borrow most of the $23,000. The original steam boiler was in Science Hall. As a gravity system, it connected by pipes to Main, to the public rooms in Wesley, and to at least some campus residences. Increasingly it failed in the coldest weather, even forcing several class cancellations after 1897. By 1899 it was virtually beyond repair. The university then installed an expensive new boiler in the Engineering Building and by a pump system forced steam through new pipes into radiators throughout the campus. Since this installation coincided with the construction of Kissam Hall, the new dorm opened with steam radiators (the fireplaces in each room were only supplements, rarely used by students). Now, for the first time, students in Westside Row and Wesley were able to give up their dangerous open grates. Also, for the first time in years students attended early classes without disrupting squeaks and bangs from radiators.[11]

In 1891 a young Vanderbilt engineer—William T. Macgruder—designed a new dynamo and what he hoped to be a more efficient source of electrical lights. He used a battery-storage, direct-current system reminiscent of later, rural systems. By it he provided electric lights for the chapel and the observatory. But gas continued to light public facilities and kerosene lamps the student rooms, with all the attendant fire hazards. As part of the 1899 physical revamping, the engineers procured a large gasoline engine for the Engineering Building and used it to power a large alternating current generator, which connected to a campuswide system of lights, including walk and street lights. As the system had a capacity of 900 bulbs, it furnished lights to each dorm room. Joined with several telephones that dated back to as early as 1885, and a typewriter on campus as early as 1888, Vanderbilt slowly joined the modern age. Bicycles abounded in the 1890s; in 1901 Kirkland took an automobile trip fifty miles outside Nashville. The streetcars had long since been electrified. But older technologies remained. The faculty had to pass rules to get certain colleagues to give up their chickens and chicken coops. It also tried to keep chickens and dogs out of campus buildings, improved the impressive West End stile, and built gates to keep wandering cows off campus. In 1899 it began looking for a replacement for the old, worn-out campus mule.[12]

Until 1899 the campus floated on its own sewage. In 1875 Nashville had not extended its new water and sewage system so far west as the new campus. A large cistern at the southwest corner of Old Main provided the first water supply. The students pumped their own water, often drank from a common dipper, and held luckless freshmen under the pump as a favorite hazing device. Toilet needs were served by privies near Old Main. Soon thereafter, these were supplemented by water closets within Main, including an extra one for women installed under the chapel stairway in 1893. These drained, by a short sewer line, into a so-called cave, shrouded in trees and located toward Science Hall. The "cave" apparently was a limestone sink or sinkhole; if so, Vanderbilt's raw sewage fed into, and undoubtedly polluted, the underground water supply. With the construction of Wesley Hall, the architect, at the request of William H. Vanderbilt, included modern conveniences, meaning bathtubs, urinals, and water closets. The water for flushing was held in holding tanks, periodically filled by pumps connected to another cistern. The water closets incessantly created problems (inevitably the subject of low jokes), either because of student abuse or deficient flushing mechanisms. With the construction of the new Mechanical Engineering building, Vanderbilt installed a large pool or holding tank connected to the untrustworthy Nashville water system. It used the pool as a pumping reservoir, both to provide regular water throughout the campus and as a resource for fire fighting. Because of dirty pipes and fears of epidemics, campus authorities urged students to drink only the cistern water. Even the Wesley Hall bathtubs caused leaks to lower floors; some had to be removed. The original baths in the gym basement rarely worked, and Westside Row dorms had no baths at all. Only in 1888 did the athletic association install halfway dependable showers in the gym. For the price of an annual bathing sticker ($2), Westside Row students were able to take advantage of these, although the water was rarely warm and never so when the steam heat was not on. Before this, one can only speculate about students' bathing habits, either in Liberty Hall or in the scattered boarding houses. Most students seemed to have reserved Saturday afternoon for this important but at times logistically difficult task.[13]

The sewage problem constantly worried Vanderbilt officials. They feared their cave would fill up. It never did, but the university at one point considered buying another sink off Church Street as an alternative. In 1891 the county health officer first condemned Vanderbilt's sewage system. Because Vanderbilt did nothing until 1892, it by then faced a stiff fine and had suffered damaging publicity. The complaint referred to a stinking privy and cesspool (possibly the cave) near Main. Garland authorized a complete clean-up—newly wrapped sewer pipes, the complete disinfection of all facilities, including the basements of buildings, and a thorough laundering of filthy bed linens (probably those used by Negro servants), all at an unbudgeted cost of $459. Better remedies became possible in 1899, when Nashville expanded its sewers to the Broad Street gate of the campus. The campus then built its own sewer lines from the cave to the city lines, now happily joining the city in the pollution of the Cumberland River. The elevations were such as to take care of Main and Wesley but not Westside Row, the anticipated new dorm, and most faculty residences. But within a year another line, close to the present Church Street, provided an outlet for the west slope of the campus. By purchasing a private easement the university was able to build its connecting line. Only two residences, those of Kirkland and Dean Tillett, had to await the later extension of lines up Hillsboro.[14]

Kirkland's struggles with budgets interacted with his efforts to improve the professional schools, particularly the three off-campus departments. As yet, the Engineering Department still functioned very much as another school within the Academic, although in 1886 Olin Landreth moved up from chair to dean. He remained the only full professor but gathered an instructional staff of four or five. With the completion of the new building in 1889, the new department had the facilities for a very ambitious program and offered a general four-year degree of Bachelor of Engineering and three five-year professional degrees in civil, mechanical, and mining engineering. In addition, the department added a special two-year course in manual technology, or what amounted to a high-school-level program in industrial arts. For the first two years city students attended these courses free but after 1888–89 had to pay tuition, although several scholarships kept the program open to poor boys. Despite facilities and staff, and an encouraging start, the Engineering program floundered throughout the 1890s. With free tuition, manual technology still attracted only twenty-five students; with tuition, their number fell to eight by 1893. The university dropped the program in 1895. The regular Engineering program could never attract more than thirty-five students, and by the mid-1890s they numbered as few as twenty-two. In prosperous times students took jobs before graduating. In the depression of the mid-1890s they did not come to Vanderbilt.[15]

After graduating as many as five Bachelor of Engineers in 1894, the department had only one B.E. in both 1897 and 1898. It never awarded more than two professional degrees in any year, and in some years none at all. With only a few exceptions, these were all Bachelors of Civil Engineering. Dissension among the junior faculty, and their desperate and futile efforts to get salary increases, depressed morale. Landreth left in 1894, to be replaced, first as professor and then as dean, by William H. Schuerman, who came to Vanderbilt from the University of Cincinnati. Then, in the next two years, the backbone of the program, two long-suffering and ill-paid adjunct professors,

William T. Macgruder, also the frustrated but very capable manager of campus buildings, and C.L. Thornburg, who also offered instruction in astronomy, left for better paying positions. Their replacements were low-paid instructors. At the turn of the century a recovering economy and slight increases in enrollment gave some promise of better days ahead in what so far had been a very disappointing department. As a symbol of that early failure, throughout the 1890s the Engineering Department was never able to use all the rooms in its new building, leaving space for a small elementary school for campus children.[16]

The small Department of Pharmacy remained a virtual adjunct to chemistry and the only income-producing department on the main campus. Since professors Safford, McGill, and Dudley did not charge extra to direct the department, from its founding in 1879 until 1888 the only cost to Vanderbilt was the part-time salaries of two local pharmacists. The students completed the two five-month duplicate sessions in order to graduate, but many found one year enough to gain desired jobs. In 1888, led by Dean Safford and by McGill, the department attempted some courageous reforms—entrance exams (at less than a high school level), a nine-month graded course of study, more academic requirements, including both Latin and modern languages, and an optional third-year course of study leading to a master's degree (only two were ever awarded). The result was disastrous; enrollments plummeted from forty-four to twenty-eight in one year and in 1889–90 fell to an unprofitable fifteen. Thus, a majority of the divided departmental faculty voted for a return to the original five-month course; the language requirements had already been dropped. The Board of Trust upheld the minority or more rigorous position (McGill's), which led the two part-time pharmacists to resign. At more cost, the university then hired its own full-time instructor in pharmacy, E.A. Ruddiman, who became the core of the program and who advanced to adjunct and then to full professor by 1900. As Paul Jones developed his biological program, several of his courses were added to the Pharmacy requirements. Enrollments remained low (only fourteen in 1896–97) until the economic recovery at the end of the decade. Then enrollment jumped to forty-two in 1899–1900 and to sixty-one in 1900–1901. At the retirement of Safford, McGill finally gained the title of dean. He had done most of the work for years and would now direct what was without question the strongest pharmacy program in the Midsouth.[17]

The Biblical Department, with its control over Wesley Hall, remained a first cousin to the Academic over in Main. But in the last decade of the century it remained a poor cousin. It never gained a comparable strength in its faculty or its leadership role in southern education. As a result of the 1885 reorganization, it did become a legitimate theological school and the only such in the Methodist Episcopal Church, South. Even as the university as a whole moved away from its sectarian origins, the Biblical strengthened its ties to the church. In most years every ministerial candidate was a Methodist. Its faculty remained securely Methodist, subject to constant and detailed scrutiny from the Board of Trust. For such key positions as practical theology (teaching ministers how to preach), it could only turn to prominent, politically well-placed southern Methodist ministers. Its faculty did not compare, on scholarly grounds, with those in leading northern seminaries. And despite all its solicitude, the church never translated its concern into significant financial support. Since all ministers received free tuition, the Biblical Department produced no income. Of all the departments of the university, it alone lived entirely from the general university endowment, a fact that produced resentment in other departments and made all the more galling the eventual failure of the Methodist Twentieth Century Fund.

Dean Tillett remained the key figure in the Biblical Department. Not always tactfully, he schemed and fought to expand and improve his department. In most respects he began the 1890s with a lackluster faculty. Gross Alexander continued in Greek and New Testament. Elijah Embree (E.E.) Hoss left the preaching chair in 1890 to edit the *Christian Advocate*, from which post he became a nagging critic of the department and of Kirkland's university. A. Coke Smith, not the board's first choice, briefly replaced him. Smith was a Wofford graduate, a gifted preacher, but not in any sense a scholar; he returned in 1892 to the ministry, leaving his chair vacant for several years. Like so many of the Biblical faculty, he later became a bishop in his church. Only in 1899 did a minister long sought for a position at Vanderbilt, J.A. Kern, then president of Randolph-Macon, take over practical theology. Gifts from benefactors helped pay his salary, making his the first endowed professorship at Vanderbilt. Also, for the first time since 1879, his salary of $2,500 broke the old barrier of $2,000. His post remained a uniquely political one, a means for the board to recognize and reward outstanding ministers in the fellowship.[18]

By 1892 a frustrated Tillett offered his resignation in a desperate ploy to gain more support from the board. In that year the board allowed him to make a long deferred appointment, Oswald E. Brown, to church history. A former Founder's Medalist in the department and subsequently a missionary to China, Brown would become second only to Tillett in length and depth of contribution to the department, remaining for forty-five years and later replacing Tillett as dean. But his strengths were in preaching, teaching, and administration, not in rigorous biblical scholarship. He later helped moderate, and reconcile, the split between so-called modernists and fundamentalists and helped make his department the recruiting and training center for the southern Methodist missionary effort in China and in Africa. The third member of the core triumvirate was James H. Stevenson, who came to Vanderbilt in 1893 as the first scholar in the department. A Canadian, he had a Ph.D. from the University of Chicago. He taught Hebrew and Old Testament, emphasizing biblical archaeology. He wrote several important articles and books on the ancient Near East. His scholarship joined that of the classicists in the Academic Department. His openness to the higher criticism and to evolutionary theories made him seem heretical to many Methodists, and his beliefs seemed daring and shocking to some of his fledgling ministerial students. In 1892 E.W. Cole of Nashville endowed Vanderbilt's first sustained lectureship. Periodically, the Biblical faculty and the Board of Bishops worked to select Cole lecturers "to defend and advocate" the Christian religion. The endowment also paid for the subsequent publication of such lectures. At first, the department used the fund primarily to bring outstanding bishops or Methodist ministers to the university, but after 1901 it would frequently move outside the church to attract outstanding theologians and scholars.[19]

The Biblical staff, although too small to meet Tillett's demands, was sufficient for the relatively small program. Enrollment stayed close to fifty in the department during the 1890s, with about half as many preministerial candidates in the Academic Department (they lived in Wesley and were part of the theological environment). By the end of the decade about three-fourths of the Biblical students were B.D. candidates (those who came with a B.A.), making it a true professional program. The department awarded from five to ten B.D.s each year. The young ministers came from all the annual conferences and upon graduation constituted an elite in the church. Soon, Vanderbilt graduates moved to the top of the church hierarchy—in publications, in missionary work, and in church offices. From the very beginning the department emphasized missions. The Wesley students had their own missionary society and briefly published a Wesley Hall *Missionary* in 1891. Walter R. Lambuth, perhaps southern Methodism's most honored missionary leader, had been one of the Biblical Department's first students. A Chinese graduate of the department, Charles Jones Soong, would head a powerful family back in China; his daughters married Sun Yat-sen and Chiang Kai-shek. At the turn of the century the Biblical had twenty-nine alumni in far-flung mission fields. In most years, the Biblical enrolled five or six foreign students, directed there by distant missionaries, the only reliable source of foreign students for the Vanderbilt campus.[20]

Before the century ended, Tillett had to fight to preserve Wesley Hall as a Biblical enclave. So many faculty lived in its apartments that they took almost half the rooms. Under Kirkland, Academic students also moved into any unused rooms. But Tillett received from the board the right to reclaim any of Wesley needed for the Biblical Department; he would never allow his ministers to live on Westside Row. He even tried to block their involvement in such frivolous activities as the glee club. In effect, almost all of them continued to live free in Wesley. The old sustentation fund, supplemented by some new private gifts, gave Tillett money and property worth over $70,000. He insisted upon using all the income for the support of young ministers. From the beginning the fund paid the room and board of Wesley "theologs," but they all had to sign a note committing themselves to later repayment of what

119

amounted to an interest-free loan. Many ministers never repaid, and except for sending solicitation letters the university never tried to collect. But many did pay, and thus the fund had a bit more than interest income. In 1889 Tillett began using sustentation funds for $100 scholarships (really, a concealed gift of free room and board). From ten, he slowly raised the number of fellows to twenty-six in 1894. These scholarships, alone, enabled him to maintain a stable or even growing enrollment. Such were the opportunities elsewhere in the church, or the low premium placed on a B.D. by the conferences, that a majority of young ministers had to have a free ride to come to Vanderbilt.[21]

The Law Department left the campus in the fall of 1889 and stayed downtown for a quarter of a century. The move from campus made easier the work of the law professors, who had their own private practices. Students were closer to the courts. But the key to the move was financial—Vanderbilt's desire to rent out prime legal offices in its new Law-Dentistry building. The lure was a new law library. Largely by fortuitous gifts, the Law Department collected over $10,000 worth of law books, a collection made up of the private library of Francis B. Fogg, of a library accumulated by the Nashville Bar Association, and of smaller gifts from several private donors or former faculty members. In 1891 it added the library of the late Judge William F. Cooper, a Tennessee Supreme Court judge and dean of the first, short-lived Law Department of 1874. His 1,700-volume library was reputedly the best in the state. To help flesh out the collection the Vanderbilt board appropriated $2,000, which was in theory but never in fact to be repaid by the Law professors. The result, out of almost nothing, was an instantaneous law library of 6,000 volumes, second to none in the Midsouth and a valuable resource for the Nashville legal profession. Tenants in the building had free access; other lawyers paid a fee. Since the Law Department gained an income from the library, it hired a full-time librarian to attend it, paid her a pittance, but equipped her with a new-fangled typewriter and expected her to supplement her income by stenographic work.[22]

The Law Department remained proprietary. The original proprietors had a twenty-five-year contract, which both parties fulfilled. In 1892 W.B. Reese died, and his wife joined the other two faculty in nominating as his successor Robert McPhail Smith, a widely acknowledged expert in constitutional law. This led to a troubling action by the board. Smith was no pious Methodist but in fact was a bit of a rationalist. Board members challenged, and held up, his appointment on the grounds that he had denied the "Divine origin of the Christian religion," or a charge so vague as to defy a clear response. But Smith was not about to defend himself on theological grounds. He noted that he had made no statement on this issue and promised, in his role as professor, to say nothing to offend anyone in the Biblical Department. He conceded nothing further and could not see how these issues related at all to his competence as a law professor. The board approved him. The next year, under pressure from Kirkland, the department raised its standards. Hereto-

Engineering Building (1889) with view of Nashville

PROFESSIONAL SCHOOLS

The Elm Street
Medical Department
Building (built in 1895)

Law and Dentistry
departments (1889)

121

fore it had offered only a single series of lectures, which most students took for two years but some for only one before standing their bar exams. Now the department adopted a graded, two-year required curriculum, a strategy facilitated by its multiple classrooms and use of simultaneous lectures. This system remained in effect until the contract expired in 1900–1901, although with several changes in faculty (both Dean Malone and Edward Baxter, still proprietors, often hired substitute lecturers, and Smith died in 1897).[23]

In 1900 Kirkland guided the reorganization of the Law Department but could not fund a conversion to a fully endowed school. Instead, he accepted a semiproprietary arrangement. The reorganized department had five part-time faculty, each with a guaranteed income. The university now took care of all accounts. The aged Malone remained as dean, but largely in an honorary capacity. Day-by-day direction went to a new secretary of the Law Department, Vanderbilt's own John Bell Keeble, who later would serve as dean. Among the three other faculty members was another Vanderbilt alumnus, James C. McReynolds, later a U.S. Supreme Court Justice. The proprietary element involved salaries. If, after paying all operating costs including building rental and contractual salaries, the department had any tuition money left, it paid half to the professors and half to the university. By this reorganization Kirkland gained several goals—effective governing and accounting control over the department, new intellectual standards (at least six hours of lectures during each of the four semesters, and with the lectures offered at convenient hours), and closer ties to the main campus. The faculty agreed to cluster their lectures so students could live on campus and come downtown only once each day. The new Kissam dorm made possible room and board on campus (Westside Row had been reserved for west campus students), and thus a more active participation by law students in the intellectual and social life of the campus. Finally, the move of the Dental Department into new quarters allowed Law to relocate its library and to develop two excellent lecture halls.[24]

In 1889 the Vanderbilt Dental Department moved from its first home, at Broad and Sixth, to the new Law-Dental building on Cherry (Fourth). It had all or part of four of the building's five stories, and by all accounts had the best facilities and equipment of any school in the South (that old litany again). The founder and dean, William H. Morgan, had received his M.D. from Vanderbilt's first medical class and maintained a close tie to the Medical Department, requiring the same standards for admission and graduation. In effect, almost anyone could enter and most found it relatively easy to graduate. But in relationship to the scope of training required in the two fields of medicine and dentistry, the Dental Department provided the more thorough training. Yet, in 1889 its students had to sit through the same five-month series of lectures for two years while they developed proficiency through guided clinical work. In other words, they filled and extracted teeth in the thirty chairs in the department's own infirmary. Financially, the department was quite successful, with rising enrollments throughout most of the 1890s. The department undoubtedly returned sizable profits to its proprietors, who were also part-time teachers. From around 100 students in 1890, it grew to 180 in 1898, then fell off a bit after a reorganization.

Like the early Medical Department, the Dental Department had only a tangential relationship to Vanderbilt. Kirkland, and Garland before him, waited for the opportunity to gain greater control. Pushed by Kirkland and by a national accrediting agency, the department expanded to a three-year course, of six months each, in 1895, and in 1896 advanced to a graded curriculum and required laboratory work. This seemed to keep it up to minimal national standards and as much ahead of nearby competitors as the tough competition for students allowed. Kirkland's chance for greater control came in 1899. The Dental Department faculty fought over policies. Several professors resigned. As some faculty asked for a complete reorganization, Kirkland and the board exercised their right to terminate the old contract. The new contract, signed in 1900, closely resembled that for the Law Department. By it, the Vanderbilt board acquired full control over budgets and approved all staff appointments. It guaranteed fixed salaries but allowed the five proprietary professors to collect one-half of all surplus income. The other half went into a sinking fund for future capital expenses.[25]

With reorganization it was apparent that the new department had to have larger quarters, which would require the use of endowment funds to build, or lease, new space. Vanderbilt refurbished a part of the now bankrupt Nashville College for Young Ladies (Dr. Price's School), located on Ninth Avenue just south of Broad. This move climaxed a complex series of maneuvers by Kirkland over the preceding three years. The Dental move testified to the frustrations of Kirkland's fervent efforts to develop a Vanderbilt women's annex.

In 1898, David Kelley, as president of the board of Dr. Price's School, had to watch the collapse of this Methodist college. He desperately wanted Vanderbilt to come to his rescue and begged its board to assume the debts and use some of its rooms as a required residence for Vanderbilt women. Kirkland wanted to keep Vanderbilt free of all the complicated entanglements of the bankrupt institution, but as soon as the property sold to creditors he then very much wanted it. Kelley had offered it at about $42,000. The new owners would sell for $48,000. Kirkland took a purchase option and then tried to raise the funds. He perceived the effort, not as a warranted investment for the endowment, but a means for adding a women's annex to Vanderbilt, perhaps on the order of Barnard or Radcliff. His motives probably varied. He was never happy with the irregular status of women on campus and always believed that coeducation was undesirable at the freshman and sophomore level. The annex could solve that problem. As he contemplated the prospects, he grew more and more enthusiastic and soon gained several allies in the effort to raise the needed money. The one coeducational option uniformly acceptable among all Vanderbilt's constituencies was a separate annex, with women taking basic courses separately, advanced work on the Vanderbilt campus. Kirkland also wanted to thwart other possibilities open to the Tennessee Annual Conference. As Dr. Price's School failed, Tennessee Methodists fell into quite a wrangle over women's education, a quarrel that eventually aligned Vanderbilt's board secretary, Robert Young, against David Kelley. Young helped get the board to reinvest some of its bond money in a new girls' college, Belmont. Kelley wanted it for his school.

In 1900 Kirkland and his later enemy, E.E. Hoss, joined a former Price teacher, Josephine Pearson, in maturing a formal proposal to present to the Tennessee Annual Conference. They won a partial victory. The conference voted to use 80 percent of its Twentieth Century Fund for either a dorm or an annex at Vanderbilt. The problem, again, was the lack of contributions. The pitifully small sums collected eventually went to several Methodist schools. Kirkland did all he could for the annex. He gave $1,000 of his own money to help purchase the Price properties. Some Vanderbilt professors gave as much as $500. But the purchase option expired before they could get half of the $48,000. The empty buildings remained a temptation. They seemed a possible answer for the Dental Department, as well as a promising investment for the endowment fund. Kirkland secured board approval and bought the three buildings. When repaired, they cost the university over $70,000. The Dental Department leased two, one as a dorm, one for classrooms and laboratories. Vanderbilt rented out rooms in the third. By the time it equipped its new quarters, the department had to pay interest and principal on $60,000.[26]

The final proprietary department—Medical—presented the greatest problems and challenges. In his inaugural report to the board in 1894, Kirkland aired all the problems of the department. Progress in medical education had passed it by. Needed was a three- or four-year graded curriculum and an endowment to pay costs. Of all Vanderbilt departments, the Medical alone scarcely advanced beyond its 1875 status. Each time a Vanderbilt University M.D. failed his state board, the reputation of the university suffered. Once again, the department gave Kirkland a needed opportunity. The old University of Nashville facilities were obsolete by 1894. The Medical faculty decided to erect new buildings and thus asked its two parent universities to accept a new, twenty-five-year lease. Vanderbilt refused the terms and countered with a twelve-year lease proposal, which included full Vanderbilt control over faculty appointments and an option to buy the facilities at the end of the lease period. This offer also required the department to sever all relationships to the University of Nashville and to offer an advanced, graded three-year course of study with each session not less than eight months. At first the Medical faculty accepted these terms but then backed off because of lures held out by the University of Nashville. In 1895 Kirkland decided to give the required notice and terminate the old contract in order to be free to build his own medical school. Many of the old faculty continued in what now

124

became the Medical School of the University of Nashville. It soon erected its own new building. A competing University of Tennessee school and Meharry for blacks gave Nashville more medical schools than the whole state needed.[27]

Kirkland had to move quickly in 1895. What he achieved was, at best, only an interim solution, although at the time he never admitted this. He selected a lot on Fifth and Elm, only two blocks from the department's earlier home near Franklin and Second. A special board meeting approved the use of endowment funds for a new building and accepted terms for a new contract. The building was completed in the summer of 1895 and drew raves from all sides (the "best in the South," of course). The new contract brought the department largely under university control. The new proprietors were mostly young professors, firmly committed to higher standards in medical education. Undoubtedly they also hoped for income, but as events proved they were willing to teach in some years for no salary at all, receiving their only compensation in the prestige gained or in the effect of their professorship on the recruitment of private patients. Vanderbilt built and owned the building, collected all fees, had a final vote on all appointments (two-thirds of the proprietors could nominate), and reserved the right to fire professors for cause. Complicated rules for evaluating and compensating proprietors of lost chairs were soon dropped. The eight new proprietors agreed to pay interest and principal on their building, to give up any tie with any other medical school, and to meet educational standards set by the chancellor. In 1895 this meant three, six-month graded sessions [extended to four years because of American Medical Association (AMA) requirements in 1899].

Most important to Kirkland, he now made his close friend, William Dudley, dean of the new department. This alone assured direct control from the chancellor's office. In 1896 Dudley claimed his to be the best three-year medical course in the United States. Perhaps. But by then all high quality medical schools required four years. More critical to the department's future, it had very low admission requirements and enjoyed no attached hospital. Its students suffered from the lack of clinical experience, which was calamitous in such fields as surgery. The department set up its own free dispensary (outpatient department) and gave students some experience at Nashville's General Hospital. In 1901 a new St. Thomas (near the west campus) offered a second alternative, but at such a distance as to be impractical. By then Kirkland saw the handwriting on the wall—either build a university hospital or eventually give up on medical education. But at the turn of the century such forebodings seemed misplaced. The Vanderbilt Medical Department maintained much higher standards for graduation than any of its nearby competitors and used its standards and its facilities to recruit a select group of students (it enrolled over 200 most years) from all over the country. In the perhaps myopic perspective of students, they received a superior medical training. By 1900 the Vanderbilt Medical Department already had 2,253 alumni, more than all the rest of the university combined.[28]

In 1901 Kirkland had begun a process that might lead to a real university. That is, he had begun to pull all the professional schools under his and the board's effective management, and to create the possibility of unified educational goals. By then it was clear that he had almost given up on his church as an agency that could or would support such a university. He had traveled frequently to New York, had cultivated the Vanderbilt family and other possible benefactors, and, except for the church connection, was in a position to claim any support available from new philanthropic foundations.

As early as 1898 Kirkland began exploring another possible avenue of progress. He wanted somehow to affiliate the George Peabody Normal School to Vanderbilt, with the Teacher's College at Columbia as his model. Already, the Peabody administration expected shortly to receive large new gifts at the final liquidation of the Peabody Fund. The school had a complex status—as part of the University of Nashville, as a special client of the Peabody Fund, and as a normal school in part supported by the state of Tennessee. Kirkland wanted to dissolve the now anachronistic tie to the University of Nashville but to keep Peabody as a quite separate college with its own board and with continued state support. This meant some ingenious, perhaps innovative mode of affiliation with Vanderbilt, and the move of Peabody near the Vanderbilt campus. If these plans worked, he envisioned a Peabody with much higher academic standards, a complementary sharing of courses between Peabody and his Academic Department, and improved levels of public education in the South.[29]

Daniel Coit Gilman, president of the Johns Hopkins, figured large in Kirkland's early plotting. Gilman first visited Chancellor Kirkland at Vanderbilt in 1894. They became friends and allies. Kirkland undoubtedly visited with Gilman in 1898 when he attended the General Conference at Baltimore. Sometime in 1899 he worked out a grand scheme for Peabody and shared it with Gilman. In it, he suggested that Gilman, on retirement from Hopkins, accept an appointment as president of Peabody, possibly through arrangements with the other trustees of the Peabody Fund (Gilman was a trustee). He appealed to him in a letter in January, 1900, to do this in order to uplift the South and intimated that some form of affiliation with Vanderbilt was at the core of his proposal. He wanted the Peabody trustees to suggest new members for a new Board of Trust for a new Peabody College, these to join local carry-overs from the old University of Nashville. He emphasized that a high-grade teachers' college was his first goal; proximity to, and affiliation with, Vanderbilt, a secondary goal, and one that he would sacrifice if necessary.[30]

Kirkland's efforts gained new momentum later in 1900. He invited Gilman to Vanderbilt's twenty-fifth anniversary and asked him to give the principal speech on the need for university development in the South. He wanted everyone to carry away enlarged ideas as to the needs of university work and the opportunities for progress. Gilman could not accept. In January, 1901, Kirkland wrote Gilman in strictest confidence, trying to engage him just as he resigned from his Hopkins presidency. His plan involved "an affiliation between the Peabody Normal and Vanderbilt University," modeled on Columbia. He wanted a distinct corporation entitled "Peabody Teachers College," to which the University of Nashville would convey all its real property. The state and the Peabody Fund could then agree on a permanent plan of support or endowment. And Gilman, the most venerated educational leader of the South, would head it and make it all work, yet without overtaxing his strength. As a department of Vanderbilt, Peabody would have much greater influence and power than heretofore. It could become less a high school and more a technical school for teachers, and could advance the profession of teaching in the whole South. With Vanderbilt's help, it could turn out educated, as well as technically equipped, teachers. He believed that, if Gilman accepted, they could consider further means of promoting it. If he disapproved he asked him to destroy the letter. Gilman approved the idea, foresaw difficulties with the University of Nashville trustees, promised to confer with others on the Peabody Fund, but discounted the one "unimportant" part of the proposal—that Gilman head the new Peabody. This exchange climaxed Kirkland's first merger effort. But the letters did plant the seeds for germination within the Peabody Fund. The first sprout reached the surface only in 1904. From it grew a new Peabody, much as Kirkland envisioned it and on Vanderbilt's very doorstep, but a Peabody not firmly affiliated with Vanderbilt until three-quarters of a century later.[31]

7

The Student Perspective

T HE STUDENTS on the main campus were not unaware of Kirkland's many problems. They lamented the financial crisis; several joined in noble even if disappointing fund-raising efforts. Much more than any other constituency, they often expressed openly their disillusionment with the role of the Methodist church. Their experience sensitized them to university needs and perhaps made them more generous alumni in the new century. The students also badly wanted a library building and vainly hoped that Science Hall would become such upon the completion of Furman.[1]

The library had only about $1,200 of fees to spend each year. Most of this had to go for periodicals. The library did expand into a second room, and then up its own walls, creating a type of balcony. Still, in 1900, many books remained on the floor. By 1899 librarian Vaughn was increasingly ill; he left all care of the library to three students. The library was not only insufficient, with its 20,000 volumes, but in a confused mess. In that year Kirkland hired Vanderbilt's first professional librarian, Edwin Wiley; although technically an assistant to Vaughn, he took over the library and in addition taught English courses. In 1900 he and student assistants began cataloging all the holdings, using the Dewey decimal system for an author-subject catalogue. But by 1901 the catalogers had progressed through only a few letters of the alphabet.[2]

In surveying student life at Vanderbilt, it is too easy to turn to the surface glitter, to what was always only a diversion from the serious goals of students. And late-nineteenth-century Vanderbilt students remained very serious indeed, although not quite as well behaved as those in the 1880s. They were generally studious and career-oriented. The high admission and grading standards insured, not brilliant students, but ones with developed study skills and self-discipline. Even then, student writers frequently complained of grade competition; student appeals to the faculty document some of the strain, the omnipresence of physical and mental stress, the immense pressures placed on students by parents and faculty, the almost desperate desire of many students to do well. The lighter side of student life—the pranks, the almost frenzied support of athletic teams, the first evidences of alcoholic abuse on campus—all testified to a need for relief or escape from the pressures.

Students were proud of Vanderbilt's eminence and of the notable achievements of its faculty. They saw themselves as an elite, as the ablest young men of the South, even as Vanderbilt was, to them, clearly the best university in the South. They had little reason to be anxious about later income or status or fearful about their vocational future. They were clearly the future leaders and shapers of a new South. They knew this. Such self-conscious elitism could lead to smugness, condescension, and arrogance, or to a sense of great responsibility and high moral commitment. What was increasingly absent at Vanderbilt were young men of lowly background, desperate to gain status and respectability, to move up into the ruling ranks. Because Vanderbilt catered to the socially and economically self-assured (at least such types dominated the fraternities and other student organizations), the basis of student anxiety shifted toward academic success and to problems of personal relationships. As Vanderbilt's standards made it accessible only to the more affluent families of the upper South, the percentage of Methodists on campus steadily declined to less than 50 percent by 1900. The non-Methodists tended more often to be Episcopalians and Presbyterians than Baptists or Disciples of Christ, further suggesting an upward shift of status on campus.[3]

From a student perspective, the last decade of the century was a golden era for the main campus. The mood was usually confident and upbeat. Unlike their predecessors in the dismal 1880s, students now had few major complaints and did not suffer under tight or repressive rules. They freely joined their fraternities; slowly the larger of these began acquiring homes near the campus (two owned and two rented by 1900). The core of students lived in Wesley and Westside Row and carried on a usually friendly competition, expressed even in arduous snowball fights. In 1890 the faculty repealed the last of the odious rules—those governing off-campus recreation and particularly attendance at theaters.

The ban on theaters had long since become a joke. In 1888 one student reported better attendance at the Vendome than at chapel. Another noted, quite seriously, that the only reliable place to meet faculty members was at the theater. But repeal of the unenforced rule, which invited disrespect for rules and enticed students to violate their pledge at matriculation, proved difficult because of the church. In 1887 a hilarious controversy erupted at McKendree Church. The minister, and later bishop, Warren Candler preached a tough sermon on the sinfulness of theater attendance. A young actress in the audience, part of a traveling company, stood up in church and defended her honor and her piety and Christian character, and argued the consistency of these with her chosen and honorable profession. The newspapers loved it and reported, perhaps in an exaggeration, that the congregation cheered at the end of her fervent statement. Although Methodists loved confessions, such an uninvited intrusion into a worship service offended people like Bishop McTyeire, who defended Candler's position as doctrinally sound. But other ministers, such as David Kelley, argued that Candler had taken an impossibly

129

narrow and extreme view. Vanderbilt students loved the fight, making it the subject of many jokes or lampoons. But the faculty waited until McTyeire's death before it replaced the rule, along with others governing private off-campus conduct. On campus, neither Garland nor Kirkland wanted to impose strict rules on students. Infrequent but well-verified reports of card playing and gambling in Westside Row led only to appeals to students, and to their own organized efforts either to stop the gambling or, one suspects, better conceal it. Ironically, within three years of the repeal of the theater rule, Vanderbilt rented the Vendome for the homecoming of E.E. Barnard, who came back to receive an honorary Doctor of Science (the last honorary degree ever awarded by the Academic Department at Vanderbilt). In 1899 Vanderbilt seniors even held a theater party at the Vendome.[4]

Somewhat incongruously, the uproarious 1890s coexisted with more overt public religiosity on campus. The YMCA played a key role. It helped initiate weekly prayer meetings in Westside Row (these, of course, had been routine all along in Wesley), and in the revival atmosphere of 1893 increased these to one each night. Students organized Bible courses during most years and demanded a credit course on the Bible. In 1895 David Kelley conducted a three-week revival. Students seemed more involved than ever before, and not just because they gained excuses from required recitations the next morning. They never showed the same enthusiasm for the required chapel services. Some students saw compulsory chapel as a coercion of conscience and noted the absence of most faculty members. The faculty tried numerous strategies to force attendance, including paid monitors to take the roll and examinations on what took place. In 1898 new rules were as much a confession of failure as a new enforcement strategy. In the first month, only 20 percent of unexcused absences in chapel merited a warning from the chancellor. If such a percentage of absences persisted, the chancellor could notify parents, assign extra work and exams, and in extreme cases (no attendance at all) suspend students. Behind the rules was an unnoted exemption—students could miss one day a week and everyone seemed to take advantage of this. Soon students protested the closing of the library during chapel; it was unfair to all the truants.[5]

In the 1890s young women struggled toward a position of equality except in numbers. Their saga remains one of the strangest in Vanderbilt's history. The 1889 refusal of the board to accept their admission as equals did not slow their increase. Already, three or four young women were enrolled in degree programs and up to twenty or so attended on an irregular basis. In 1891 Dora Johnson, the daughter of a trustee, received her B.A. along with the men and with no special notice. Hers was the first degree awarded a woman since Kate Lupton had received hers in 1879. In 1891 the faculty awarded an entering scholarship, based on local Nashville contributions, to Annie Paschall, a talented graduate of Webb School. A beautiful, serious young lady, she was class poet and, in the words of her friend, an ideal student exceptionally gifted

130

The Women in 1892 (all of them)

in languages. After receiving her 1894 B.A. she received fellowship offers from both Bryn Mawr and Vassar. She attended Bryn Mawr for a year, but then died back home in Atlanta in 1895 during a typhoid epidemic.[6]

In 1892–93, for the first time, the *Register* announced that young women would be "admitted by courtesy" to any of the courses of the Academic Department. They were subject to the same exams and rules as men and, although not formally matriculated, could complete and receive any of the degrees. In that year the *Register* also listed female students, most under the category of "irregulars." In 1893 the *Comet* noted twenty-nine women, fewer than half in degree programs. In a pattern repeated throughout the decade, women almost always served as class poets or historians. In 1892 a talented young woman, another trustee's daughter, Lilian Fitzgerald, received one of the two prestigious B.Litt.s awarded that year. As early as 1890 the *Observer*, the literary publication of students, welcomed women to its pages. Fitzgerald embraced the opportunity and under the pseudonym of Victor Shanet wrote several brilliant articles over a three-year period, becoming the publication's leading literary critic and the first Vanderbilt woman to take a strong role in shaping student opinion. She married in her senior year and then as a

Vanderbilt's first sorority, Phi Kappa Upsilon

graduate student continued to write for the *Observer* through 1893. Her degree led to a later, completely distorted legend about Vanderbilt. She worked hard for her B.Litt., which involved one classical language plus modern languages. For reasons unclear, the faculty voted to award no B.Litt.s in 1892 (they were phasing out the degree) but to give a less prestigious Bachelor of Science instead. Fitzgerald and one male student were affected. In a subsequent meeting the faculty reversed itself, as if under intense pressure. Undoubtedly, the forceful Fitzgerald demanded the prestige degree she had earned. Somehow, later student editors turned this into a very different story—that Fitzgerald received a B.Litt., not even a legal degree at Vanderbilt, and in anger tried to burn a worthless piece of paper pushed on her simply because she was a woman.[7]

From 1892 to 1901 women at Vanderbilt gained full legal equality except in one respect—access to dorms. Kirkland's effort to gain Dr. Price's School as a women's annex addressed even that need. In 1894 a divided faculty (7 to 6), and then the board, voted to allow women to compete for prizes. The Owens Medal in chemistry went to Gertrude Jones. In 1897 the faculty voted to charge women the $10 matriculation fee, or the last token of their equality in the Academic Department (only Pharmacy of the professional schools admitted women). By then, four or five entered with each freshman class. In 1894 women students joined faculty wives in a ladies' tennis association. A prominent Nashville singer even qualified, in a backhanded sense, as Vanderbilt's first female instructor; she taught voice to the glee club. In 1895 three women graduated in one year, a record. In the same year one of these, plus two junior women, gained associated membership "by courtesy" in Alpha Theta Phi, a student honorary fraternity formed by Professor Tolman and which in 1901 became a chapter of Phi Beta Kappa (another mark of Vanderbilt's growing status). In 1896 a woman was listed as member-elect. In 1897 the women even formed their own basketball team, and of five entering freshmen, three would hold class offices. Familiar names began to appear among the women—in 1898 Mary Amelia Tigert, granddaughter of Bishop McTyeire, and Marion Kirkland, a niece of the chancellor. Such family standing could not hurt. Kirkland became associate editor of the *Commencement Courier* (a daily news-sheet published during commencement week), a founding member of the first campus sorority, Phi Kappa Upsilon (organized in 1900 and followed a year later by Theta Delta Theta), and a full member of Alpha Theta Phi. In 1900 four women graduated; in that year twelve of forty-one sophomores were women. By then, women held more powerful class offices (secretary and vice-president), and a woman in Pharmacy, Martha E. Hunnicutt, won the 1900 Founder's Medal. Perhaps as a joke, a woman even briefly entered the Bachelor of Ugliness contest of 1897.[8]

Student activities burgeoned in the happy 1890s. Students met together in dozens of clubs, including some tied to states of origin or to the academies from which they graduated (such as Webb or Wall and Mooney). Their most ambitious effort, aided by the faculty, was a glee club accompanied by a small band, called the banjo and mandolin club. The glee club began tentatively in 1886–87 but gave its first Nashville concert in 1891. Dudley lent his organizing talents in 1892 and in another year it began extended tours throughout the South, a wonderful advertisement for Vanderbilt. For several years a few dedicated students, backed by Baskervill and other professors, tried to develop a dramatic club but never had the strength to stage a single play, to the continued embarrassment of student editors. Special interest clubs—camera, bicycle, chess, engineering—ebbed and flowed. A southern historical club survived but never lived up to its earlier hopes of great archival collections on the history of the South. A graduate club kept ties to such on other major campuses. The old literary societies largely ebbed. Briefly, to the delight of Garland, a third society, the Lyceum, struggled to survive as an alternate to the other two, both dominated by fraternities. It admitted no fraternity men but failed within a year. The literary societies now had only one clear role—to hold oratorical contests and thus help screen student speakers for commencement week.[9]

Even if they did not go in for drama, students loved journalism. The *Observer* continued as a polished literary journal, but one that gave up almost all campus news after 1890. Each year the fraternities, often in a desperate last-minute effort, published a yearbook, the *Comet,* which contained the pictures of each class, humorous skits and poems, and a review of the year's major events. But in its impact on campus nothing rivaled the new weekly newspaper, the *Hustler.* It began gloriously in 1888–89. Within a few years this first *Hustler* became famous, a campus legend. Unfortunately, no copies survived. Published without faculty approval or review, this newspaper was sharp, critical, deliberately controversial. It aired issues on all sides, freely criticized faculty and board, entered enthusiastically the debate over McTyeire's successor, and was a sounding board for student complaints. The faculty did not share student enthusiasm. It had Garland consult with McTyeire just before the bishop died, and in the spring resolved that students be forbidden to continue such a publication unless under terms and conditions set by the faculty and subscribed to in writing by all editors. The *Hustler* did not publish in 1889–90, but in the fall of 1890 seven students (Edwin

The men of Westside Row

Glee Club with Banjo-Mandolin Club, 1895

Mims included) petitioned the faculty for new rules governing a revived *Hustler*. The faculty complied but with rules tougher than those enacted for the *Observer* a decade earlier. The editor-in-chief had responsibility for all content, was deposable by faculty vote, and then if a newly elected editor failed to follow faculty guidelines for acceptable content the faculty could suspend the newspaper. Every student connected with the newspaper had to sign his name to show acceptance of the new rules. The students accepted and resumed publication for one year. In the spring of 1891 the athletic association, under the safe guidance of Dudley, took over responsibility for the *Hustler*. In the next decade it continued as a sprightly newspaper, full of campus news, editorially independent, even though up to one-half its space went to sports. Once again the faculty had imposed tough rules but then proved lenient in enforcing them. Notably, a 1901 Vanderbilt graduate, one H. Grantland Rice, never edited its sports page but did contribute articles.[10]

Intercollegiate athletics, and especially football, became the focus of student involvement in the 1890s. At the center of sports activity was the athletic association, founded in 1886 primarily to hold the annual field days but increasingly involved in team sports. In 1889 the student members first elected Professor William Dudley as president, a position he held throughout the 1890s. Perhaps as a political move, after 1893 they usually elected

The baseball team in 1888

Kirkland as vice-president. The officers, plus the student managers and captains of teams, made up an executive committee of the association. The popular Dudley smoothed the way for intercollegiate competition; at several critical junctures the tough rules enforced by the athletic association helped prevent the Board of Trust from eliminating all intercollegiate competition. The athletic association built the first almost successful showers in the gym, added a running track in the gym in 1895, managed the *Hustler,* collected dues and bathing fees, charged admission for all athletic contests, worked out all schedules and contracts with other colleges, hired and paid all coaches, and, subject to faculty review, made all rules governing intercollegiate sports. The association also made Vanderbilt a leader in southern collegiate sports. Its annual field days, attended by neighboring colleges, inaugurated intercollegiate track meets in the South in 1886.

In 1891 the boys of the athletic association graded a running course at the site of the present Curry field. Much more important, the association spent $2,500 of its own funds in 1892 to grade and lay out its own athletic field. As completed, it had a new and improved track, plus a level playing area for both football and baseball, with terraced slopes at the west for spectators and, eventually, for portable stands. In early 1893 a group of southern colleges (Vanderbilt not included) met in Richmond to found a Southern Intercollegiate Association; it tried to organize scheduled football and baseball games between two leagues of its far-flung institutions and offered trophies for winners. This association soon failed; its plans were too ambitious and perhaps too professional. In 1894 Dudley and Vanderbilt took the lead in forming a new Southern Intercollegiate Athletic Association among twenty institutions that met in Atlanta. This was not a league or conference but a rule-making and monitoring association. Dudley became its first president and, in an era of intense attack on college football, committed the association to the purification of rules. For years, he had the same dominating role in the association that Kirkland had in its academic counterpart.[11]

In 1891 football replaced baseball as Vanderbilt's favorite sport. By 1893 a football frenzy began to sweep the campus. Throughout the 1880s Vanderbilt boys played football and at times organized teams. In 1886 they even identified a single Vanderbilt varsity and apparently looked about for outside competitors. But the first enduring varsity team came together in 1890, practiced informally, and on Thanksgiving soundly thrashed an outmanned University of Nashville team, for Vanderbilt's first intercollegiate football victory. Then the new *Hustler* helped fan enthusiasm for 1891. An experienced student served as captain and coach. This team played home and away

PHOTO BY SANDERS

The football team of 1890

games with both Sewanee and Washington University of St. Louis, winning three of four. The team had to play at the Nashville Athletic Club downtown (later Sulphur Dell), which helped attract paying fans but not the most respectable audience. Women students were reluctant to attend, what with the boisterous yells, the all-too-obvious curses, and the very violence of the game itself. In 1892 this all changed with the new athletic field. But Vanderbilt lost its first two games, leading to student grumblings and the first effort to hire a coach. By then the freshmen had a football team and intense competition had begun among classes.[12]

In 1893 the team expanded its horizons, playing seven teams, one as far away as Auburn, and winning six in a glorious year. It had by then perfected its feeder system, arranging a play-off among academies at the Vanderbilt field. By 1893 the game had become a public spectacle, with up to 2,000 in attendance. Before the decade ended, 5,000 attended key games. By then Vanderbilt had a whole spectrum of cheers and yells and rallies, some before, some after the games. In 1894 Vanderbilt students adopted a button and flag, wrangled for years over the university colors (they eventually replaced the original "old gold," so hard to find and hard to reproduce, with simple gold and black), and began to use megaphones to stimulate and coordinate the cheers. The games, despite the sums paid to visiting teams, were profitable, helping pay the debts of the athletic association. Thus, in 1894, the association hired its first coach, a practice continued in subsequent years. The first "great" coach was Robert Acton, an M.D. from Harvard and an English physical fitness expert, who came to the campus only for his coaching and who combined the role of coach and trainer. His glory was the 1897 team, the greatest of the 1890s. It was not scored upon all season, although its record included a 0–0 tie with a national powerhouse, the University of Virginia.[13]

The football enthusiasm camouflaged a strong undertow of alarm and opposition. The game not only had its violent, gladiatorial aspects, but in its early college phase was as close to a professional as to an amateur sport. Few colleges were scrupulous in limiting players to bona fide students, let alone students taking and passing full course loads. The standards of officiating remained low; some teams routinely abused the rules; and fan behavior remained rowdy and at times came close to violence. Losing Vanderbilt teams always felt cheated on one or more counts, or felt they had to play huge local bullies. Some unfair teams had giants that averaged over 170 pounds, whereas early Vanderbilt players averaged under 160 (the average Vanderbilt male in 1890 was 5 feet 8½ inches tall and weighed 131.7 pounds). Vanderbilt always insisted that it would never tolerate any of the abuses so long condemned in the North. But even the *Hustler* admitted that one early Vanderbilt player was not a student, and early eligibility rules were, to say the least, loose. Any student in any Vanderbilt department, and at any level, could play. Thus older Dental and Medical students, who faced no admission requirements at all, often dominated early Vanderbilt teams. And a player

138

could stay on a team for five or six years (four in the Academic, then two more while in the Medical Department).[14]

The abuses, plus a national campaign either to abolish or clean up football, threatened the survival of the game at Vanderbilt. From the perspective of the board, of fervent Methodists and sincere Christians, the game detracted from the purposes of a true university. Students noted a falling-off in class work during the fall season. In 1894 a board resolution gave warning—it noted that intercollegiate sports were not beneficial to the interest of students, asked for no further promotion of such and, if continued at Vanderbilt, mandated that the faculty enforce proper precautions and restrain all excesses. The faculty resisted extreme board action. In 1893 it set up the first tough rules on eligiblity. Only matriculated students could play, and no one was eligible who matriculated just to get on a team. A new committee had to approve all dates and hours of games, none of which could interfere with the regular work of the university. Student athletes could be away for no more than four class days in each term. The faculty clearly wanted to preserve football by these tighter rules. They realized the depth of student involvement. Even old Chancellor Garland, in 1892, admitted the benefits of athletic competition. The athletic association was "a club of gentlemen," and the competition had heightened student loyalty to the university and had attracted the first broad and sustained interest on the part of Nashvillians. New financial support might lurk behind the football boom. Football seemed a safe path of discharge for youthful energy. A few even talked of some intrinsic benefits from football, such as physical development or training in cooperation.[15]

In 1897 the board came very close to abolishing all intercollegiate athletics. It had compelling reasons to do so. Just as the faculty gained some control and cleaned up the rules, the worst eventuality occurred—a near riot. In 1896 the rivalry between Vanderbilt and the University of Nashville reached a fever pitch, not only because of past incidents and a desire for revenge on the part of several players, but also because Vanderbilt had launched its own separate and now rival Medical Department. Medical students participated on both teams and dominated the one from the University of Nashville. The game, after several incidents, ended when the contending fans rushed on the field and joined in pitched battle. The newspapers, and then national news services, exaggerated the event. Vanderbilt students tried to minimize it, as if only a minor disturbance.

Kirkland was infuriated. The episode undermined the whole student cause. He had to play it tough. A joint Vanderbilt–University of Nashville faculty committee, aided by students and spectators, investigated. The excessive, unsportsmanlike partisanship on the part of the jeering crowd set the stage. A Vanderbilt player, in a grudge match, wanted revenge on a Nashville player and openly slugged him. The officials never seemed able to control the game (a frequent problem). Even before the melee the game had degenerated into very rough play, with several kneeings of downed players. This led to a

Prize racquet contest in 1889, when tennis was very popular at Vanderbilt

general fight among several players and a temporary suspension of the game. Then, when it resumed, a Nashville player struck the Vanderbilt star behind the ear. When a scuffle began among players, the partisans rushed the field (the two faculty committees disagreed on which student body came first). The few policeman were helpless. Some fans even seemed to enjoy the brawl. But only luck kept anyone from being killed. Several combatants drew knives or canes, and a few took out pistols but fortunately did not fire them. The Vanderbilt faculty at first suspended football for the year, but later relented. It canceled the eligibility of two players most clearly at fault; one of these was Vanderbilt's star. The students and alumni, incensed at this treatment of their heroes, countered with their own investigations, mass meetings, and petitions in behalf of a "blameless" team. A majority of the faculty bent a bit, reinstating one player with only a reprimand, all to the disgust of a minority of the faculty led by that old football legend, Denny. But the affair tarnished the reputation of Vanderbilt and gave the board the ammunition it needed. The question was whether quick, and tough, faculty action had been enough to preserve the game. The student behavior had not helped.[16]

At the 1897 Board of Trust meeting, Kirkland barely turned away a motion to abolish intercollegiate competition. The board substituted a five-member committee to explore the issue. The committee, in its report to the board in a calmer 1898, recommended only stiff enforcement of new faculty rules, which required for eligibility full-time status (fourteen hours); good standing, meaning no more than two third-level grades (50 to 60) or one fourth grade (under 50); and, as a sop to the pious, no Sunday travel. The political skills of Dudley and board respect for his ability both on and off campus probably made the difference. For good or ill, Vanderbilt would continue intercollegiate competition. By the end of the decade it even tentatively began basketball competition with neighboring colleges. From 1893 on, basketball had been a popular intramural sport, even for women. But the new sports—football and then basketball—tended to diminish student support of tennis, baseball, and track, although Vanderbilt consistently came in first or second in Southern Association track meets.[17]

Sports did not provide the only stimulus to student competition. The fraternities continued the competition of the 1880s, but in a much more friendly fashion (football absorbed much of their energies). The one big but unresolved policy issue, repeatedly debated in the late 1890s, was whether to delay "spiking" (membership recruitment) from the first two weeks of the freshman year to the second semester or even to the sophomore year, as Kirkland very much wanted. After 1887 the classes also organized each year, elected officers, and tried to engender a sense of competition. But one senses a lack of involvement and rather desperate efforts to give life to class cheers and

Undefeated women's basketball team, 1896–97

slogans. In 1887, in imitation of other colleges, Vanderbilt students staged their first, mournful funeral for a textbook, in this case Old Cal (Calculus). A long funeral cortege with a coffin led to an elaborate cremation ceremony. The novelty soon wore off such carefully planned rituals, but students revived the funeral march in 1901.[18]

College pranks now abounded. Vanderbilt students frequently serenaded downtown Nashville. Before a key game, after a crucial victory at home or away, or even when a Vanderbilt student won a national oratorical contest, large numbers of students loved to gather around huge, potentially dangerous bonfires, and then loudly and boisterously march through Nashville streets, invade hotel lobbies, or assault the locked gates of one of the female colleges. They rarely did serious property damage but sometimes captured streetcars or printed football scores on billboards. Such midnight marches kept Nashvillians awake and led to city council rules against such parades. A few campus incidents approached violence—one student, accidentally or not, set fire to a small shed on campus, and in 1901 a boisterous mob threw a rock through the Wesley Hall window of Professor Tolman.[19]

The climactic prank of the decade came in March, 1900. Six or more Engineering students painted circles of gold and black around a much-venerated downtown cannon, captured by Admiral Dewey at the recent battle of Manila, a gift to the state, and to Nashville's many chauvinists a great symbol of patriotism. The incident did not seem funny at all to many Nashvillians. Kirkland, at least in light of the hostile publicity, was incensed, more determined than ever before to set an example before increasingly reckless students. He was in the very midst of a campaign to attract new local support

Desecrated Dewey cannon

for Vanderbilt. The incident, he declared, was a cowardly act of desecration, not a joke. He was almost equally angry at Vanderbilt students who seemed to think it a quite normal prank, or at most a matter of poor taste, not at all an affront to citizens of Nashville, to Dewey, or to the goddess of liberty. To the extent that the faculty identified those at fault, either it or the board dismissed three and suspended for a year the three freshmen. The students easily cleansed the cannon, and Admiral George Dewey briefly visited the campus in May, 1900, ostentatiously to receive appointment as an honorary professor.[20]

Other student efforts could be more positive. Students joined in 1897 with the Vanderbilt faculty in helping celebrate a slightly delayed Tennessee Centennial (statehood came in 1796). The summer-long Exposition was practically across the street from the campus, at the old race track. By request of the Nashville planners, William Dudley took a leave from the faculty to help organize the affair. During the summer a group of faculty and students converted their dorms into Vanderbilt Hotel, accepting paying guests (the cost of preparation almost eliminated the profits). The Vanderbilt Engineering faculty prepared a rather elaborate Vanderbilt exhibit, and the campus received numerous prominent visitors. Professor Tolman dedicated his 1896–97 art and criticism class to the Parthenon, even as students observed the nearby building of its plaster replica. But the greatest effort went into the unveiling of the statue of Cornelius Vanderbilt, one based on private subscriptions and planned for over four years. Unhappy faculty members had to contribute; the bursar took the $10 or $15 from their salary. Monday, October 11, was official Vanderbilt day. Students gathered all morning at the Exposition and then united in a long procession before the afternoon ceremony in the auditorium. Later, they solemnly circled the bronze Commodore and unsuccessfully beseeched him to speak. Chauncey DePew, for the third Nashville occasion, gave a eulogy for the old Commodore. Later, with the closing of the exposition, the Commodore moved to his present perch in front of Main (Kirkland), although he then appropriately faced east toward the campus entrance and the city.[21]

The Tennessee Centennial preceded by only three years the twenty-fifth anniversary of Vanderbilt's 1875 opening. Kirkland decided to turn this into Vanderbilt's first major celebration. He had covert as well as obvious reasons. He hoped to present the new Kissam Hall in the presence of its donor. He also tried, without success, to lure Daniel Coit Gilman as featured speaker, a means of promoting his plans for Peabody. But the most obvious goal involved public relations—the free publicity and the prospect of increased loyalty and support. The planning was meticulous and justified by the result. The celebration was at first planned as a part of the 1900 commencement, but the committees of faculty and faculty wives eventually rejected this in behalf of October, 1900, for two major reasons—they did not want to compete with commencement ceremonies and they wanted a time more congenial to

Old Main with a new Commodore, about 1900

William K. Vanderbilt (despite the plans, he was unable to attend). Also, the October weather normally excelled that of June, and the delays in Kissam's construction recommended as late a date as possible. The celebration, as staged, covered three days, Sunday through Tuesday, October 21–23. Students enjoyed a holiday and, with one exception, the weather was cool and clear. Afterward, the historian of the event deemed it (what else?) the most notable educational celebration ever held in the South.[22]

The festivities began on Sunday. Bishop Eugene R. Hendrix gave an opening sermon in the crowded university chapel. He preached on the "mission of a Christian university," notably not on that of a Methodist university, an ecumenical emphasis that pervaded all the speeches. On that afternoon an aging Hargrove talked on the university's founders, with long quotations from McTyeire and a moving eulogy to Garland. On Monday morning the campus received the delegates from other universities and heard an address by Senator W.V. Sullivan of Mississippi, the first Law graduate of

Vanderbilt. This ceremonial occasion featured Vanderbilt's first use of caps and gowns and, given the number of represented universities, the colorful academic procession must have made a deep impression upon the Nashville audience. In the afternoon, on a muddy field, a lackluster football team played the University of Tennessee to a 0–0 tie. In the evening the ceremonies moved downtown to the huge Gospel Tabernacle (the present Ryman Auditorium), for another formal academic procession and an address by Edward E. Barnard on the recent history of astronomy. Students from all the area colleges and academies insured an enthusiastic crowd. The formal ceremonies climaxed on Tuesday morning. The Vanderbilt students gathered on the three campuses and then marched to the Tabernacle, with banners waving (the women from the main campus joined the marchers downtown). The hundred or so professors and visiting delegates (from twenty-four colleges and universities), in full regalia, boarded streetcars for the trip, for what must have been an amazing sight as the trolleys rolled along West End and Broadway. President Arthur T. Hadley of Yale gave the main address, an eloquent but rather general plea for more public-spirited leaders in business and government and on the vital role of universities in creating such leaders. The festivities ended with an elaborately planned reception in a lavishly decorated Vanderbilt chapel (Turkish rugs to replace the chairs, plants, and flowers, gold shades) and a late evening dinner in the just completed basement of Kissam.[23]

Kirkland not only introduced the various speakers but gave a brief retrospective on Vanderbilt at the main, Tuesday morning session. In it he asked the most encompassing of historical questions: What identity, what distinctive character, what worthy role had Vanderbilt achieved in its first quarter of a century? He gave a somewhat elusive answer. He was most proud of its role after the changes of 1887. By risking so much in the way of diminished enrollment, Vanderbilt had become an educational missionary to the whole South. The delegates from other southern colleges heartily endorsed this judgment. Involved in such a role had been a great deal of faith or hope, a willingness to dare more than the resources justified. And Vanderbilt's growth had been impressive. The Academic Department, Kirkland's principal point of reference, had expanded from ten instructors to thirty-three, from twenty-eight courses to seventy-three. Yet, its operating budget had increased by only 50 percent, a commentary not only on efficient management but on a dangerous lag in financial support. Of course, Kirkland put in his normal plug for new gifts, with a new emphasis upon alumni giving. But in a moment of celebration he dwelt not so much on problems as on possibilities, on the new glimmer of hope present in recent gifts. He ended with a brief review of the larger, moral purposes that had all along underlain Vanderbilt's mission—not to make specialists but to educate and thus shape young men, to contribute to the maturation of their Christian character. We propose, he said, "to be forever true to our position as a Christian institution." But what did that mean? How did "Christian" relate to "Methodist?" Was "Christian" consistent with either the worldly involvements, or the very specialized scholarly standards, that now characterized Vanderbilt? These unanswered and almost unanswerable questions would not go away. They struck at the heart of the identity issue and thus haunted the next era of Vanderbilt's history—its stormy divorce from the Methodist Episcopal Church, South.[24]

PART FOUR

Divorce Proceedings
(1901–1914)

 THE NEW CENTURY *marked a reversal in Vanderbilt's fortunes. It entered a troubled era. The 1890s had turned out to be a brief, almost golden age, but one haunted by intimations of future decline and impending conflict. After 1901 the conflict actually erupted and soon more than matched all the earlier portents. But, in the midst of this crisis, the university was blessed by clear intimations of future growth and prosperity. So much seemed at stake in the new century. Identity issues never were so omnipresent, as Vanderbilt struggled to define its relationship to the Methodist church and to a new George Peabody College for Teachers. The wrenching divorce from the church left a residue of bitterness, but by the final legal separation both sides experienced a sense of relief. Vanderbilt students rejoiced. Regrets on campus were few. Not so for the long and unsuccessful courtship of Peabody. Vanderbilt, as a rejected suitor, could only nourish its hurt pride by 1914.*

Fortunately, complex institutional relationships rarely impinged directly on academic affairs. In the midst of his legal battle, Kirkland slowly pulled the professional schools into the university, fought to preserve at least a strong Academic Department, and began his successful cultivation of new, northern foundations. Vanderbilt's students, now more numerous and more diverse, enjoyed a golden age of football but struggled, with insecurity and guilt, to assimilate cultural change. Significantly, at the end of this innocent era just before the Great War, Vanderbilt students joined in a series of emotional religious revivals.

8

The Bishops' War

Iɴ 1901 it seemed like a small, harmless cloud on the western horizon. Few noted it. But for Vanderbilt it turned out to be the harbinger of a massive storm. At the June board meeting Bishop Warren Candler, of Atlanta, introduced an innocuous motion—that all else being equal, the university give preference to Methodists in the hiring of professors. No one could really oppose such a motion, which passed without dissent. Literally interpreted, it was almost meaningless; rarely are any two candidates equal. And even under Chancellor Kirkland the university had always sought qualified Methodists when such were available. Kirkland kept quiet but recognized in this motion a concealed attack on himself and his policies and upon the type of university he was trying to build.

Candler's motion crystalized, before the board, the views of a growing minority of southern Methodists who were unhappy with policies or conditions at Vanderbilt. Elijah E. Hoss, as editor of the *Christian Advocate*, had since 1895 used this central organ of the church to make frequent even if indirect digs at the Vanderbilt faculty and students. He deplored a purported decline of real Methodists on the faculty, a growing contempt even among Methodist intellectuals for the old-time beliefs and practices of his church. He condemned the frivolous worldliness of students, as reflected in intercollegiate athletics, fraternities, and officially sanctioned dances.[1] Led by Candler, a minority of board members had already cast dissenting votes on some of Kirkland's most critical appointments or promotions. In 1901 the developing dissent remained unfocused and ineffective. For the next three years the board wholeheartedly supported Kirkland, while the campus experienced an interlude of unusual peace and harmony. Kirkland even took a type of sabbatical for the latter half of 1903, he and his wife touring Europe and the Near East. Intense controversy first erupted in 1904 and then recurred in frequent squalls, each with increasing fury, until 1914, or until the complete and bitter divorce of Vanderbilt from the Methodist Episcopal Church, South.

The complexity of the church-university struggle almost defies clarification. Half the critical issues never surfaced in the overt political and legal struggle. Also, the relationship of Vanderbilt to the new George Peabody College joined, and complicated, the battle with, and within, the church. The Peabody matter pulled into the fight various competing groups within the

Nashville community and assured for a time a rather incongruous coalition united only by opposition to the policies and the purported tricks of Chancellor Kirkland. To some extent the Vanderbilt controversy provided an outlet for increased but rarely identified tensions within the southern Methodist church.

The Vanderbilt struggle always involved Methodists against Methodists, even when the role of others was the occasion for conflict. A minority of broadly tolerant, ecumenical, socially concerned, or theologically liberal Methodists, often without clear intent, were subtly altering the very identity of their church. These groups sought an early unification with northern Methodists and almost captured Vanderbilt. Their more orthodox or traditional brethren sensed the changes even when they were unable to identify them. They fought back in behalf of the older Methodism they venerated, in behalf of the itinerant system, affectional revivals, spiritual and unworldly conduct, and literal, unqualified acceptance of biblical authority. They sensed, quite correctly, that Vanderbilt did not reflect these values, that its professors and students had negotiated an unholy alliance with the world, whether this was reflected in the frivolity of fraternities or football or in the shameful acceptance of grants from such northern robber barons and agnostics as Andrew Carnegie. Perhaps Vanderbilt had never reflected their Methodism or all their values, but it had come closer during the era of McTyeire and Garland.

Kirkland—his policies and asserted motives—remained at the center of the storm. Rarely in Vanderbilt's history has a chancellor played such a critical role; for over a decade he was much more at the center of events than faculty or students. As Kirkland's ego became involved, pride, or self-protection, conditioned many of his strategies. As he conceived it, he fought for the survival of Vanderbilt as a university and not just a sectarian college. He persuaded the overwhelming majority of faculty, students, alumni, northern benefactors, leading American educators, and Nashvillians that he was right. Eventually, a majority of southern Methodists saw it differently. These Methodists came to believe that Kirkland wanted to move the university away from the church, that he pursued this goal by clever calculation and devious strategies, and that he finally secured it through tricky maneuvers. The truth lies somewhere between the conflicting perspectives. The church never really threatened to turn Vanderbilt into a narrow denominational school. Kirkland never wanted a complete break from the church. But he did try to work out a new, very subtle relationship between church and university and then somehow persuaded himself that this relationship had prevailed all along.

Kirkland was often secretive. He tried to bring various Vanderbilt groups slowly around to his conception of a great university. This took time and diplomacy. Financial imperatives controlled most of his policies from the beginning. He had to find new endowments. His earliest efforts were all frustrating; only small annual gifts from the Vanderbilt family averted disastrous cuts in programs. But for a time—from 1894 to about 1900—the church seemed anxious to do more. The ill-fated Twentieth Century Fund proved disillusioning to everyone connected with Vanderbilt. Kirkland did not give up on the church, but by 1900 he expected from it only limited support for the Biblical Department. By then, new possibilities began to open up for the other departments. He first explored closer ties to a new George Peabody College, which brought him into contact with officials of the new Rockefeller-funded General Education Board (GEB) and, very shortly, also with representatives of the new Carnegie Foundation or, in short, with a growing community of northern philanthropists and prominent southerners or ex-southerners, all committed to the improvement of southern higher education. Now, Vanderbilt's ties to Methodism were an embarrassment, impeding successful fund raising.

Kirkland began asking hard questions about church-university ties. It was in his interest, the university's interest, to clarify these issues. By 1901 or soon thereafter he adopted the following strategy: To emphasize a special church tie only to the Biblical Department. The only possible support for this department was the Methodist church, and Kirkland wanted to force responsibility for it upon the church. The Bibilical Department was, in the fullest sense of the term, a denominational seminary. The church therefore properly controlled its policies, at least so long as it was willing to provide even partial financial support. But Kirkland wanted to deemphasize church ties to the other departments, ties that were more sentimental than legal or financial. No courts had pronounced upon the legal issues, and Kirkland was not yet willing to risk a court test. Until 1910 he tried to avoid controversy. Rather, he hoped to educate his own Board of Trust and lead it, as fast as it would be led, to a more independent stance, and at the same time to persuade officials in the church to go along with such a strategy. So long as the church appreciated the worth of a strong Vanderbilt, which it was unable to fund, why would it stand in the way of outside support? He hoped churchmen would be proud to remain "sponsors" of a largely independent, nondenominational Vanderbilt. Arguably, save for the Biblical, this was the only relationship the church ever really had to Vanderbilt. What Kirkland did not foresee was the intensity of the opposition within the church, or the degree to which certain bishops would now push their denominational claims. Much more than he expected, they resisted efforts to lead it in the well-trodden paths of Yale or Princeton.

Of course Kirkland could not announce these goals. But he could use them in bargaining for outside support. In a 1904 letter, apparently prepared for the Peabody Fund trustees, he offered his private interpretation of the ties between Vanderbilt and the church. Churchmen had conceived Vanderbilt but the Vanderbilt family had provided all the means. The church had contributed no funds except for limited donations to the "theological" department. The government of the university was "vested exclusively in its

Trustees. No conference or other ecclesiastical body elects them, nor can any such body give them orders or directions. They elect their own successors and no law exists requiring that they be Methodists." The board made the bishops ex officio members of the board "in order to secure the support and patronage" of the church, and for the same reason submitted the names of other board members *after election* to the General Education Board of the church for confirmation." In all likelihood, he said, the Vanderbilt board would soon change the role of bishops; some bishops desired a change. He insisted that Vanderbilt used no denominational test in appointing professors, save in the Biblical. His purpose, he said, was to make Vanderbilt a "genuine university, broad and liberal and free. Outside its Theological Department we do not wish it to be the exponent of any sect or any creed, save such as belongs to our common Christianity. This is the end to which I am working, and I work with faith and confidence that my policy is right and commands the support of my own Board and the thoughtful public." The validity of this characterization of Vanderbilt, he pointed out, was now a matter of board record, for earlier in 1904 he had forced the very issue upon his board and won a resounding victory. Unknown to him when he wrote this letter, he had only won a battle, not a war.[2]

From 1901 until 1904 Kirkland in effect served as dean of the Academic Department, for he did not immediately replace Dean Hohlfeld. Thus, at the June board meeting in 1904 he recommended the appointment of the dutiful, hard-working historian, Frederick W. Moore, as new dean. Moore had become chair professor only in 1901 but had taken over most of the work involving outside exams and entrance requirements. Moore was not Methodist but a devout Baptist and perhaps the most committed churchman on the faculty. Not until 1910 would Kirkland be able to recommend another comparable promotion or appointment. Thus, he took very seriously his recommendation and saw it and others as vital to the health of the Academic Department, a department always starved for funds and one increasingly staffed by a low-paid, junior staff. The promotion, plus the reappointment of Herbert Z. Kip as adjunct professor of German (he was Presbyterian), met resistance from the board, although the ensuing controversy involved Moore. At board meetings a committee always received, reviewed, and reported upon the chancellor's numerous recommendations. In this case Bishop Candler chaired the board committee. It asked Kirkland to confer, informed him of its reluctance to approve any further such appointments to non-Methodists, but then approved both Kip and Moore. No one questioned the ability of either man. But committee members knew that Kirkland could have chosen others for the deanship, including Collins Denny, professor of moral philosophy, a very close friend of Bishop Hoss, and a favorite of several bishops. Denny and Kirkland had been frequently at odds, and thus Kirkland was not about to nominate him. Covert support for Denny probably influenced Candler's protest.[3]

Before the whole board Candler aired his personal concerns and moved to postpone the Moore appointment. The motion seemed to pass on voice vote but on a call for division lost by one vote. Candler noted a developing problem at Vanderbilt—so many non-Methodists in key positions. They could not wholeheartedly serve the interest the university "was founded to serve." He claimed that eleven of nineteen professors in the Academic Department were non-Methodists (Kirkland disagreed; he included assistants and fellows and thus claimed seventeen Methodists and only eight others). Only the dean of one department (Biblical) was Methodist. This seemed all out of proportion and likely to estrange the university from the church. Candler's airing of this issue, and his implied censure of Kirkland, made this the most unpleasant, tense session of the board since the old salary controversy of 1879. But Kirkland chose not to defend himself; he later professed shock and surprise. Another committee of three effusively praised Kirkland and recommended a $1,000 addition to his salary, a motion that passed unanimously.

The politics within the board was significant. Although the bishops were all ex officio members, only five of thirteen attended this critical meeting. Of the five present, none was as concerned over this issue as Candler. His two most likely allies—elderly A.W. Wilson—and the newest bishop (as of 1902)—E.E. Hoss—were both absent. Hargrove, now almost deaf and near retirement, was in the chair. Present and most involved were the two bishops most knowledgeable about, and most committed to, the university, and both subsequently to serve as board president—Charles B. Galloway and Eugene R. Hendrix. Thus the narrow vote on Candler's resolution to postpone did not reflect deep resentment of Kirkland or his policies. Most of the lay trustees seemed surprised by the later repercussions of the vote and had simply wanted to think more about the issues. Some later profusely protested their innocence. Even Candler, although firm on the principle involved, probably did not anticipate, or desire, confrontation with an able and still valued Kirkland.[4]

After the boad adjourned, Kirkland fumed. But, typically, he found in the situation an opportunity. He knew he could win a crucial victory, one he needed in his overtures to northern foundations. He thus tried his first power play with a board that had always been loyal and supportive. Kirkland told President Hargrove he could not serve any longer as chancellor if he had to follow the sectarian principles pushed by Candler and almost endorsed by the board. He asked Hargrove to launch a search for a new chancellor and promptly left town. Within days rumors flooded the campus and cries of alarm rose from every quarter. Kirkland had traveled to Knoxville, there to explore the possibility of becoming president of the University of Tennessee. The discussions never advanced to a formal offer but, given his wife's attachment to Knoxville, the prospect had to be attractive. Students felt sure they were losing their still youthful (forty-five) chancellor.

In the midst of the apprehension, Hargrove called a special board meeting on June 23. Candler did not attend. Hoss was still absent. Thus, only friendly bishops and apprehensive laymen came to make amends to their chancellor. Both bishops Galloway and Hendrix played a critical role. The board had become dependent on Kirkland and faced with dismay the prospect of his resignation. The context was perfect. In a long, carefully written position paper, Kirkland clarified the action he required from the board. The Candler motion showed a lack of faith in his policies and presaged a completely new direction for Vanderbilt. Vanderbilt was Methodist in many ways, including the faith of board members. He even used the term "ownership" to express the church's claim. But Vanderbilt was a great trust, held for the good of society and the "upbuilding of Christ's kingdom." This could not mean that only Methodists had rights in the university. What about the Vanderbilt family? He had appointed suitable Methodists, which accounted for the higher percentage of Methodists than those of other denominations on the faculty. But to serve the trust given to Vanderbilt he sought those most suited to the task. Who, when ill, would choose a physician because he was a Methodist? Why was the teaching of young men different? Kirkland could not fill the Engineering or Medical faculties with Methodists. No one seemed to mind this. Why did they pick on the Academic? If Kirkland followed the policy suggested by Candler he would soon sabotage the university. Sectarian requirements would drive away all non-Methodists on the faculty and, even more critical, alienate major benefactors, for they endorsed only a "liberal Christian policy." He said he had no alternative but to resign, to give up the work he had barely started, a work that he wanted to complete. One can almost see the tears of his hushed audience.[5]

His friendly bishops further softened the board. Hendrix, from Kansas City and with the most friendly contacts with northern Methodists, stressed the difficulty of southerners in conceiving a real university. They only knew church colleges and thus tended to approach Vanderbilt not as a great university but as a denominational college. Since southern Methodists had not had such universities they had trained very few people to teach in them. Only now was the academic harvest ripening. In the meantime the university should enforce only a Christian test, by which he meant only the exclusion of profane men or libertines. No great university could tie itself to one denomination; to do so would discredit it in the eyes of scholars. In a nasty dig at fellow bishops, he suggested that young bishops, or those who did not consistently attend board meetings, were the ones raising the problems (he was right, or course, for constant attendance on board affairs clearly had a co-optive effect). The venerable Bishop Fitzgerald moved a vote of confidence in Kirkland. The board nominated a three-member committee of two bishops and a layman to draft the formal resolutions. It framed two, each quite to the point. In the first, the committee noted that the chief concern of the board, in "administering the great trust of a Christian university," was "to

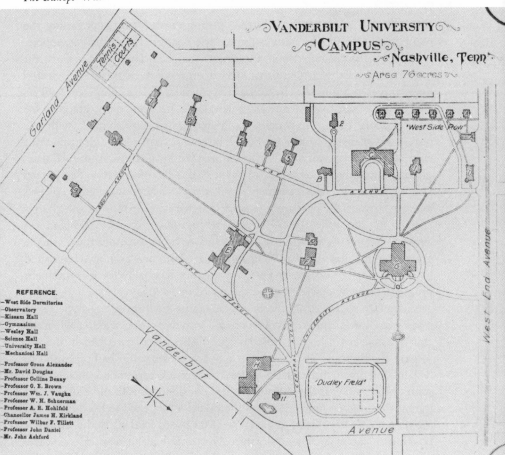

Map of Vanderbilt at turn of century

promote the highest type of Christian scholarship and Christian character."
In the future, as in the past, it would seek "for its Chairs the most competent
scholars, of unquestioned loyalty to Christ and of the highest attainments in
their several departments." Such a criterion might be of little consolation to
Jews or nonbelievers but it reflected well Kirkland's position. The second
resolution gave to a heretofore unwritten policy of the university the force of
a statute—that the chancellor be responsible for nominating to the board all
candidates for faculty appointments. Both resolutions passed unanimously.[6]

This first storm blew up rapidly, seemed very threatening, but was quickly
over with no danger, and it provided Kirkland with a needed clarification of
policy. Kirkland chose to press his advantage in 1905. As he intimated in his
confidential 1904 letter, he now wanted to alter the role of the bishops. The
Candler affair may have reinforced his commitment to this goal but it does
not explain it. Neither did Kirkland ever make public all his reasons. An
element of deviousness becomes part of his story. The overt reasons were

155

compelling. The church had thirteen bishops already and kept raising the number. The Tennessee statutes limited the board to thirty-three members, meaning that the bishops might soon gain a majority. This posed some threat to the other classes of board members, to the desire of alumni for elected board representation, and to the board's growing need for competent lawyers and businessmen. More critical to Kirkland, he needed to establish the independence of the university from denominational control; with the bishops soon able to control the board, he could not in good faith sustain this claim. One other possibility has to be noted. In April, 1905, Andrew Carnegie announced the establishment of a new $10 million foundation that offered very tempting retirement payments to professors from nonsectarian colleges and universities. Critics later charged that Kirkland instituted the charter changes in order to establish Vanderbilt's eligibility. Actually, Kirkland had already planned the proposed changes before he knew about the Carnegie grant, and in behalf of other compelling goals. But he was indeed fascinated by the Carnegie fund and at first very anxious to qualify for its retirement program, as he made clear before the board in 1906.[7]

Kirkland had supported the ex officio status for bishops in 1895, in the midst of a church canvass calculated to aid Vanderbilt and at a time when the church had fewer bishops. Until that time the board had tried, usually in vain, to woo the bishops. Then, automatic board membership had promised to help in fund drives and to clarify all the ambiguities surrounding their charter status. Now, ten years later, none of these considerations fit the realities, and the bishops, increasingly active on the board, threatened to become all too active. Note that Kirkland came to the 1905 board meeting in the strongest position so far in his chancellorship. Not only had he won his complete victory in 1904, but in the wake of a tragic fire that destroyed Old Main he had already headed a very successful campaign for needed gifts. Sure, able, competent, with increased national prominence, he never seemed more indispensable or more popular.

The 1905 board meeting was a Methodist love feast. Significantly, Bishop Hoss was in Brazil. Candler was present but in a conciliatory mood, since he found the board duties rather onerous and preferred to stay out of university politics. When Hargrove, increasingly ill, resigned as president, the board elected a pro-Kirkland Galloway on first ballot. Kirkland used his opening report to analyze problems with the university charter and suggested that the board petition the secretary of state for a new one. The background for this extended back to the era of McTyeire when the board voted for amendments to the charter in 1888 but never pressed their petition. Instead, Judge East secured a special legislative act in 1892 that allowed Vanderbilt, by a simple petition, to receive a new charter under the terms of the Incorporation Act of 1875. Kirkland now recommended such a petition. His analysis of the 1872 charter, and the 1873 amendment to it, revealed extensive consultation with lawyers. His was no casual proposal.

At the heart of the charter problem were the Memphis resolutions so awkwardly incorporated into the charter decree of 1872. Some of the resolutions had no place in a charter; others seemed to commit the university to policies never followed (that it have a normal school). Kirkland now questioned whether the resolutions, with their minute details, could be part of a charter granted under the State's general incorporation act. But Kirkland's concerns were not all matters of legality or clarity, but also of policy. The Memphis resolutions, if legally binding, might entail qualifications on the established practice of the board in controlling the election of new trustees. Beyond this, the ninth and final resolution made the bishops a Board of Supervisors, confusing their exact relationship to the Board of Trust. Kirkland wanted a new charter, not to deny the ties to the church but to establish the complete autonomy of the board and to divest the bishops of any possible claims to charter rights in university government. Under a new, standard charter the board would be free to pass by-laws to arrange "the status of the Bishops in accord with what may be deemed a wise and permanent policy." A five-member committee on the charter, including Kirkland, Galloway, Hendrix, later Board President W.C. Ratcliffe, and Bishop Duncan, endorsed Kirkland's proposal. The board unanimously adopted it and all present members of the board signed the required petition. The only reservation came from a few trustees who wished to add to the petition a statement about the friendly ties of the university to the church. The board did not await a new charter to deal with the bishops. The same committee proposed an immediate by-law change. As passed, it rescinded the ex officio category and thus automatic membership for the chancellor and all the bishops. In their place, the board elected the chancellor and the five senior, active bishops as regular board members. These changes passed unanimously. If any board members then harbored any doubts about Kirkland's motives they did not reveal them.[8]

In September, Bishop E.E. Hoss returned from Brazil. When he learned of the action of the board he interpreted the by-law change as an effort to remove him from the board. In an angry letter to Kirkland he demanded a full explanation and alleged that he "was thrust out of that body without having received the slightest hint or intimation that such a thing was intended. . . ." In a subsequent letter he referred to the bishops who, "without accusations of any sort, had been so unceremoniously stripped of their chartered rights and functions." Kirkland tried to conciliate, but to no effect. Hoss sent angry letters to Hendrix and Galloway, to their surprise and acute distress. To the mild, almost saintly Galloway he wrote, "I simply could not believe that my presence on the Board was so undesirable that you were willing to go the length of amending the Charter to get rid of me. Surely I might have been allowed the humiliation of being kicked out." He pointed out, quite correctly, that even Galloway now remained on the board, not by "charter right" but by sufferance of a board majority. Hoss also asked several, if not all, the bishops to withdraw their names from the charter petition. At least two did, which blocked any petition and new charter, since all board members had to sign. In all of this Hoss acted like a bull in a china shop. He arrogantly interpreted the changes as a direct attack on himself, assuming that he was the last stalwart defender of a thoroughly Methodist university. Now pushed, he was ready to fight. Almost singlehandedly he initiated the events that led to a protracted legal struggle and finally the separation of church and university.[9]

In the Vanderbilt epic Hoss is the one most easily identified antihero. He managed to antagonize everyone identified with Vanderbilt. Some students actually loathed him. Yet, Hoss was a colorful, brilliant, enduringly fascinating man. He loved the old Vanderbilt, the one he knew when he first joined the Biblical faculty in 1885, and loved it enough to fight to preserve its now threatened identity. "Love" is the key word for Hoss. He was a sentimental, visceral, passionate man, given to intense love as well as overwhelming hate. He loved his home country, the mountains of his birthplace in upper east Tennessee or those in the nearby Virginia that surrounded his beloved Emory and Henry College. He loved wife and children so deeply it hurt, and suffered through all their pains and trials. He was a loving, compassionate friend, generous in giving of himself, yet often ill during the struggle with the university and possibly more short-tempered as a result. His loyalties were all deep. His Methodism was passionate and personal, not nearly as doctrinal as such allies as Candler. He always had a sense of his own sinfulness, of undeserved mercy, and thus preached always the twin themes of atonement and redemption. Above all, Hoss was articulate, as preacher and editor. He had a direct, pungent, earthy style, leavened with keen wit. His eloquence helped insure his rise in the church from itinerant to college official to Vanderbilt professor to editor of the *Christian Advocate* and, later than he thought he deserved it, to bishop. He read avidly, was widely informed, but was never a scholar. Ever the protagonist, he could not distance himself from issues. He preferred to do battle for justice and right. He was not political. In fact, no one was more inept than Hoss in building bridges, effecting compromises, or winning a consensus. A proud, prickly, blunt, dramatic man, he was given to hyperbole and exaggeration. In these ways he was the very opposite of a careful, self-disciplined, reserved, conciliatory politician like Kirkland.[10]

From 1895 on, Hoss had fought what he referred to as new trends at Vanderbilt. He envisioned an ideal Vanderbilt as a thoroughly Wesleyan institution, one suffused with a warm spirituality, standing well apart from the secular world, from the temptations of both private sins and of dollars and cents. He minded not that it remained poor if it remained holy. He rejected Kirkland's vision of a liberal university that joined the world in order to get worldly support, that enlisted in behalf of all types of progress. He was not as narrow as he often sounded. He wanted to keep the university close to the church, but this did not mean he wanted every professor to be a Methodist or that he advocated piety as the key qualification for a teacher. His real quarrel was with fellow Methodists who compromised the older beliefs and practices or, worse, expressed contempt for them. It is possible that he had some traumatic experiences as professor in the Biblical Department. He may have felt a bit inferior in his contact with the new Leipzig Ph.D.s in the Academic Department or, as an old-fashioned Methodist preacher, have felt beleaguered or defensive in such a cosmopolitan setting. In his perspective Vanderbilt had become, by 1905, a campus of football frenzy and moral debauchery, of childish pranks and sinful indulgence. He fastened upon, and publicized, every actual or rumored scandal involving students. In a revealing letter to Bishop Galloway, early in 1905 but after it was clear Galloway would be new board president, Hoss warned him about local Nashville conditions, as if he were moving into a modern Sodom. In a key phrase, one often repeated in the court fight, he argued that the "whole inner drift and spirit of the University has been away from Methodism, and nothing short of a revolution can restore the original and true status."[11] Of course, as so often, he was correct. But how many people wanted to go back to the older Methodism? Not very many at Vanderbilt. But Hoss knew his real constituency, rank-and-file Methodists throughout the South. He took his appeal, his vision of Vanderbilt, to this audience. And in that context—no other—he fought Kirkland as an equal.

Hoss launched his fight against Kirkland's Vanderbilt without very clear goals. He claimed undefined charter rights as a bishop. He wanted to pressure the board to reverse its June by-law concerning ex officio membership, but at this point he did not challenge the right of the board to enact such by-laws. His opening barrage triggered conciliatory gestures from all quarters. In the *Vanderbilt Quarterly* Kirkland not only stressed that the proposed new charter would not change Vanderbilt's relationship to the church but even referred to the Board of Trust as, in a sense, a committee of the General Conference. Galloway noted his sadness at Hoss's interpretation of events and begged him to take up his complaints with the Executive Committee before airing them in the press or taking them to the 1906 General Conference. All to no avail, for Hoss had committed himself to a fight and stressed that he was not on the board by the grace of other board members but, in an analogy to Jeremiah, to discharge an obligation placed upon him by no choice of his own but by God's providence. He was, he said, in no way an agitator. But a prophet in a sinful Babylon cannot be bribed by flattery or conciliatory gestures. As bishop, Hoss was no longer an editor. The new editor of the *Christian Advocate*—George B. Winton—generally backed the university position and because of this later lost his job. But Hoss found friendly editors in other Methodist papers and carried his prophetic denunciations to several annual conferences, all in preparation for a showdown at the 1906 General Conference in Birmingham. Initially, his goals seemed to have been largely a vindication of his charges that Kirkland was deliberately moving the university away from the church.[12]

Hoss came to Birmingham to persuade delegates and to spread several charges about scandalous events on campus. He knew that the Education Board, in its report, or the conference as a whole could condemn the 1905 by-law changes, seek a clear statement of the exact legal relationship of the church to the university, or possibly even publicize some of the sinful influences at work on the campus. Any, or all, such actions would embarrass Kirkland and possibly wring concessions from the board. The generality of his goals is reflected by the Tennessee Conference, which was under his direct influence. It, as "one of the original owners and controllers of the University," asked the General Conference "to consider and act upon all matters involving the question of ownership and control of Vanderbilt University," and in general do what was necessary "more perfectly [to] conserve the university to our church and rally our church more fully and heartily to the support of the university." It is only fair to note that Hoss usually joined his criticism with appeals for greater financial support for Vanderbilt.[13]

The developing struggle, its exact issues still very fuzzy, reached its first climax at the May, 1906, General Conference. Kirkland came to defend Vanderbilt, to counter Hoss's extreme charges, and to win a positive report from the Education Board. He won. He hated church politics, the most petty he ever had encountered, but he was a calm and persuasive advocate and a superb tactician. Hoss, by his typical resort to extravagant charges, to verbal overkill, lost credibility at least among the bureaucrats of the church. He was in his element in the pulpit, or on an editorial page, not in hallways and lobbies. Kirkland managed to get the Vanderbilt issue to a small committee of five where bombast had no effect. The Methodist officials were not stampeded by Hoss's charges of heretical teaching in the Biblical Department (probably by J.H. Stevenson) or agitated up by lurid accounts of fraternity dances and drinking.

After hearing both sides, including the usual calm and logical brief from Kirkland, the committee recommended a commission of five prominent Methodist lawyers to inquire into all the legal ambiguities. Kirkland felt vindicted by this strategy and he approved the members subsequently appointed to what became known as the Vanderbilt Commission. He felt he had "wiped Hoss up" along with all his allies, including Hoss's friend Edward B. Stahlman, who kept writing nasty reports about Vanderbilt in the *Banner*. Kirkland also rejoiced in the widespread support for him and for Vanderbilt within the church, and particularly from Vanderbilt's friends and alumni everywhere. A supportive note from Edwin Mims, then at Trinity College, was virtually a love letter. In its key appointments, the conference generally elected moderate Vanderbilt supporters and repudiated the Hoss extremists. Hoss won only a few verbal concessions in the final report that established the

Vanderbilt Commission. It began with a loaded statement: "There can be no question as to the ownership of the university by the church, or as to the charter rights of all the bishops." None of the slanderous charges made it to the conference floor. Kirkland returned to Nashville full of confidence and even enthusiasm. He sensed that he had a growing, winning Vanderbilt faction within the church. His victory proved all too ephemeral.[14]

The high-powered Vanderbilt Commission completely changed the basis of conflict and betrayed all of Kirkland's hopes. The five-judge panel, headed by Kentucky Supreme Court Judge Edward O'Rear, had three assignments: (1) to inquire into and to determine the present relation of the Vanderbilt University to the Methodist Episcopal Church, South; (2) to take legal steps, if necessary, to perfect the transfer of the university from the patronizing conferences to the General Conference of the Methodist Episcopal Church, South; and (3) to define the charter rights of the bishops of the Methodist Episcopal Church, South. The second issue was not critical to the ensuing controversy. The commission held hearings in Nashville in August and again in October, 1906. Kirkland and Hoss made extended presentations; both sides engaged counsel, turning the hearings into quasijudicial contests.

In its response to the first critical issue—the relationship of the church to the university—the commission strayed onto completely new legal grounds. As against the brief presented by Kirkland, in which he defined Cornelius Vanderbilt as the real founder of the university, the commission decided that the church founded the university, that the original incorporators, although individuals acting in their natural capacity as only the state statutes allowed, were representatives of the annual conferences, and thus that the members of the corporation were the conferences, not the incorporators or subsequent trustees. This was a plausible historical argument, one defensible in law by a clever merging of common law precedents with the terms of the 1871 Tennessee incorporation statute. But what, if any, legal rights in the management of a corporation did such an interpretation give to the annual conferences or, after the transfer, to the General Conference of the church, since the charter quite clearly placed the right of electing trustees in the board? The commission found answers in an 1895 act of the Tennessee General Assembly, an act set up to clarify the rights of denominations in their own universities, colleges, and academies. If a religious society or denomination established and was maintaining and patronizing such an educational institution, then the governing body of such a society or denomination had the power, at its option, of electing the board of directors or trustees and filling vacancies among them. The key terms were "maintaining" and "patronizing." The commission concluded, or in fact never seemed to question, that the church maintained and patronized Vanderbilt University and that, by virtue of the 1895 law, it had the authority to elect its trustees despite the wording of the original charter. Not even Hoss had dreamed that the church had such awesome power, such ultimate and complete control over Vanderbilt. Until it was searched out by the commissioners, no one connected with Vanderbilt had even noted the 1895 law or thought it concerned Vanderbilt. The commission, by this clever but legally vulnerable ruling, created a new understanding within the church and set off maneuvers that climaxed at the General Conference of 1910. One can even argue that this opinion, alone, was a necessary condition for the eventual separation of Vanderbilt and the church. Without it, and the total control it assigned to the church, the issue could never have been drawn in such a way as to make compromise impossible.[15]

The commission offered an equally ingenious, and unexpected, solution to the "charter rights of the bishops." To a large extent it accepted the contention of Kirkland and his legal advisors. Resolution nine at Memphis made the bishops a Board of Supervisors, with coordinate powers with the Board of Trust in choosing a faculty and in determining educational policies. Kirkland doubted that the Memphis resolutions were properly a part of the original charter, except possibly in defining the objectives of the new university. But the commission decided otherwise on this issue and so incidentally would the two subsequent courts. Historically, Kirkland had a weak case here and legally he faced difficulties. But even conceding that issue, resolution nine still faced overwhelming problems. Nothing in the 1871 incorporation statute permitted a coordinate body to the board, or allowed control by nonelected trustees of any sort. Nothing in the charter made the bishops ex officio trustees. This seemed to strip resolution nine of any meaning, the bishops of any charter powers whatsoever.

The commission granted these arguments, as subsequently did the courts. But it found another role for the bishops. Even common sense suggested that the patron of a charitable or educational trust has some supervisory powers over the fulfillment of its purposes. The commission, therefore, interpreted resolution nine as a verbally inept effort to assign such supervisory powers to the bishops. The intent was lawful. What it really established was a board of visitors, an institution deeply rooted in English eleemosynary institutions and recognized in common law. The bishops were an overseeing body with essentially judicial powers—to insure that the board, the only governing body of the university, lived up to the trust given it by the founding church. As visitors, bishops could not participate in the board or intrude at all into the selection of faculty or the making of policy, so long as the board adhered to the charter and to the purposes of the trust. But on issues touching the meaning of the laws of a corporation, such visitors had the final say, much like a Supreme Court. Since the resolution establishing the commission mandated that the bishops immediately assume whatever role assigned them, Hoss from this point on asserted his charter rights as a visitor.[16]

Naturally, Kirkland and most board members were dismayed by the commission findings. The decision seemed to them partisan and, on legal grounds, tortured and contrived. The commission seemed to ignore most of the factual and legal points stressed by university witnesses. Hoss loved the report. It offered several new dimensions to his struggle and he soon made a proprietary claim to all the commission's arguments. Already the near-judicial context had begun to work its way. An adversary relationship was developing. Under legal tutelage, both sides were beginning to build briefs, very one-sided arguments. From now on neither side would ever again present anything close to a balanced position, attentive to all facets of past history or open to all the legal possibilities. In its 1907 meeting the Vanderbilt board adopted a carefully worded, cautious response to the commission report. It cordially received and filed it, expressed faith in the ability and fidelity of the commissioners, and recognized and rejoiced in the ownership of the university by the church, neatly avoiding any definition of the word "own." It welcomed any supervision by the College of Bishops "that may aid us in executing the great trust committed to our hands, so as to insure the observance of the charter, the conditions of specific gifts, and the statutes of the state." This final phrase came from the report, but its purpose was to make clear that the board would adhere to its understanding of the charter, to the conditions set by donors, and to state law, not necessarily to the findings of the commission. But the deliberate ambiguity of the language, the hint of cautious acceptance, led many in the church to believe that Vanderbilt University had conceded all the contested issues and that the controversy was now over.[17]

The legal issues remained in abeyance for four years, or until the next General Conference of the church. How it would interpret its "new powers" over Vanderbilt would determine whether the controversy was in fact over. Meanwhile, Hoss and his allies prepared for the clash and for their final victory. In 1908 the College of Bishops set out their first bait. Acting as visitors, with Candler as secretary, they ruled that a paragraph in the *Church Discipline* concerning church boards applied to Vanderbilt and that it required all board members to be Methodists. They therefore forbade the board to appoint any non-Methodists so long as "proper persons" could be found within the fellowship. The university board finessed the order and averted an open confrontation. It received the resolution, entered it in the minutes, and stressed that the board had acted with due regard for the *Discipline* but that it had understood that the *Discipline* justified the election of distinguished alumni or special benefactors, such as a Vanderbilt, and hoped that the bishops would concur with this understanding. That ended the matter but put the board on record as to what it faced if it dared enact any controversial new policies, particularly any touching upon the rights of the church.[18]

The commission report decisively altered the odds in the Kirkland-Hoss duel. Kirkland had supported the commission at first; Hoss had been reluctant. Kirkland had won his victory at Birmingham. But now he was in a most awkward position—either reject the commission report or concede the issues he had defended and turn Vanderbilt over to church control. He was trapped. Gestures of acceptance set him up for later charges of betrayal. Defiance seemed an ungraceful response by one who gambled freely and then lost. More critical, the report gave Methodists a proprietary claim to Vanderbilt. The well-publicized controversy created a new awareness of the university. Hoss had been right all along; the church did, by legal right, own the university. Now when Hoss talked of Kirkland's trying to steal their university, he made good sense. Methodists had scarecely recognized it before, but the university had been theirs all along. If the Vanderbilt authorities, by an act of bad faith, refused to accept the commission's report, then all the odium would lie on their side. Hoss, who appeared as the early aggressor, could now bask in the glory of defending the church against an aggressive Vanderbilt board. Before the commission had issued its report, he had persuaded and activated a small minority. Now, he easily rallied an overwhelming majority. In 1910 he could win; he delighted in the prospect.

But for a while the legal conflict abated. Instead, a seemingly unrelated one broke out on a quite different issue—the relation of Vanderbilt to a new Peabody College. Eventually the two issues joined, with Kirkland at the storm center. In 1867 George Peabody gave an original $1 million, and then another $1 million in 1889, to aid the cause of education in the defeated and

The Class of 1901, Academic Department

The Class of 1903 (note increase in women)

impoverished South. A group of prominent politicians, businessmen, and educators, from both North and South, became the trustees of the Peabody Fund and decided how to spend its earnings. By terms of the bequest, at the end of thirty years the trustees had the option of spending the capital and thus terminating the trust. One of the largest recipients of annual Peabody grants was the Normal School, soon named Peabody Normal, affiliated with the University of Nashville. As early as 1895 officials at this school anticipated a large grant at the expected termination of the fund. Many in Nashville talked of the possibility, even the likelihood, that the trustees would fund a large teachers' college in the South, one modeled after the one affiliated with Columbia University. The local goal, of course, was to gain the college for Nashville, to transform Peabody Normal into such a new teachers' college for the whole region. The change contemplated was a major one. Peabody Normal, which secured state as well as Peabody Fund support, provided the needed, certifying training for elementary and high school teachers in Tennessee, but at an academic level scarcely above that of a good high school. A teachers' college, as then defined, meant a degree-granting institution with graduate work, serving primarily educational leaders, those who served as county superintendents, as principals, or as model teachers.

As expected, after 1897 the Peabody trustees began the prolonged debates over the disposition of their trust, and at the outset talked of a single large gift to a new teachers' college. Chancellor Kirkland naturally wanted the teachers' college for Nashville and to strengthen Vanderbilt. He began his campaign in 1898 and, working behind the scenes, did more than anyone else to get the new college for Nashville. From his first secret plotting in 1898, he worked to duplicate the experiment at Columbia University. This meant, to him, a separation of Peabody from the old University of Nashville, the transfer of the college from south Nashville to an area on, or adjacent to, Vanderbilt, and some mode of affiliation with Vanderbilt that would allow a sharing of teachers and courses but permit a nonsectarian Peabody to accept both state and Peabody funds. In brief, he wanted to add a Peabody College to the educational resources of Vanderbilt without assuming any responsibility for its funding. This was not to be a one-sided arrangement, but a venture in educational cooperation, for Peabody students would gain needed access to Vanderbilt's Academic Department. Without such access, a new Peabody would have to provide its own very costly liberal arts college.[19]

Kirkland's first and friendliest contact among the Peabody trustees was Daniel Coit Gilman, president of the Johns Hopkins. As earlier recounted, Kirkland tried from 1897 to 1901 to gain Gilman's support for a Vanderbilt-Peabody affiliation, with partial success. Even as he wooed Gilman, the Peabody trustees moved slowly ahead with their plans. In 1901 the secretary of the fund first suggested a $1 million grant to Peabody Normal in Nashville. A fund committee came to Nashville to get the facts about Peabody Normal and to scout other sites. In 1902 Dean James E. Russell of the Teachers College, Columbia University, and Wallace Buttrick, secretary of the new General Education Board (GEB), met with the Peabody faculty. By then, the GEB was ready to cooperate in the creation of a new teachers' college, and Buttrick would from this point on play a key role.

Such opening gestures from the Peabody trustees triggered a needed, political response in Nashville. At Peabody Normal the two leading actors were former governor James D. Porter, an aged man who had accepted the interim presidency of Peabody in 1900, and Dean Wickliffe Rose. Porter also served as a trustee of the Peabody Fund, and Rose later would serve briefly as its general agent before moving on to the Rockefeller hookworm campaign. Thus, Porter and Rose provided the needed liaison between northern benefactors and local boosters. Porter's political skills were indispensable. The trustees made clear that, in locating the prospective new college, they would require strong local support, or something close to a matching of Peabody funds. Porter put together an $800,000 package. The University of Nashville would transfer all its property (optimistically estimated at $250,000), the State agreed to appropriate $250,000, Nashville committed $200,000, and Davidson County $100,000. As early as 1903 Porter secured legislation permitting the transfer of University of Nashville assets and in the next two years gained firm commitments from the three jurisdictions. In all of his efforts he apparently assumed that the new college would be at the old south Nashville site on Second Avenue and Lindner. But already the trustees of the fund had considered other sites closer to Vanderbilt, while the Tennessee Transfer Act permitted sale of the old campus if "necessary and expedient," so long as the funds were direted to a college for teachers within the Nashville vicinity.[20]

Gilman played a key role with the Peabody trustees. In 1903 he urged the trustees to establish a college for teachers and then chaired a special committee of five (subsequently six) to recommend a site. This committee worked for two years, rendering its final report in a crucial meeting in January, 1905. The meeting included President Theodore Roosevelt, the chief justice of the United States, and such prominent men as Richard Olney and J.P. Morgan. The political successes of Porter and Rose much influenced its final recommendation. In a close vote, the trustees voted to liquidate the fund and in a less divided vote decided to locate a new teachers' college at Nashville. This report mentioned cooperation with Vanderbilt but still seemed to assume the upgrading of Peabody Normal and the use of the existing campus. But behind the public announcement the political wheels were turning. Kirkland was at work. He continued his correspondence with Gilman. In 1903, as the committee of six began its work, he stressed his desire to cooperate through some type of affiliation. He made the same proposal to Wallace Buttrick at the GEB. During 1904, the crucial decision year for the committee, he practically became a member. In October he met in New York City for a long visit with Buttrick, clarifying the victory for nonsectarianism that he had just won over Bishop Candler. He talked of the need for a great university in the South and about whether Vanderbilt could be so liberalized as to be the foundation for such. He wrote home to his wife that Vanderbilt could win this goal—if it could get its affairs in shape, by which he referred to the problems of the church, and if it could get Peabody College. Then, there was "no telling whereunto we may yet grow." In these plans Kirkland had the support of Wickliffe Rose but did not negotiate at all with Porter, who was clearly committed to the south campus.[21]

Since the committee of six did not recommend the Vanderbilt site, Kirkland kept up the fight in 1905. He went a second time to Baltimore for a long visit with Gilman and then met with Andrew Carnegie, first approaching him to try to get funds for a new university library. In September, 1905, he asked for a conference with Buttrick and Gilman. By then he was afraid the trustees were going to turn all the money over to Porter at the old site and thus dash "our plans." Then, in a whirlwind of lobbying, he met with one of the more reluctant trustees, the elderly but powerful Robert C. Odgen, and considered but then decided against a meeting with J.P. Morgan. He was in an October meeting with Buttrick when Porter arrived. Kirkland slipped out the back door so as not to be recognized.[22]

Kirkland's efforts paid off on October 3, 1906. In 1905, upon approving the Nashville site, the trustees appointed yet another committee to explore how the new teachers' college could fit into the larger needs of southern education and to explore other ways of using parts of the Peabody Fund. Gilman and Buttrick wanted such a larger study, perhaps as a means of advancing a closer tie to Vanderbilt. The delays in local funding gave the committee plenty of time. Gilman was a member of the committee of three, which included Morris K. Jessup and Charles E. Fenner. The committee hired Buttrick to make the needed investigations of southern education, but the whole committee, plus Buttrick and Dean Russell of Teachers College, visited Nashville. In his trips to Nashville, Buttrick seemed to spend most of his time with Kirkland, who was an informed and persuasive host. In their conversations Kirkland also, for the first time, offered to sell, subject to board approval, a section of the Vanderbilt campus to the new Peabody College. Such an offer seemed essential to his goal, since it was not then clear that other land adjacent to Vanderbilt would be on the market. After all this work Kirkland gained everything he ever dreamed of in the final committee report, but he also gained a second, nasty controversy, one almost as prolonged and as productive of ill will as his developing struggle with the church.[23]

The committee, in a confidential report written by Buttrick, enthusiastically supported a new teachers' college in Nashville. This was the single most important need of southern education. Such a college could train teachers for the new secondary schools and serve as a graduate college for state normal schools. A self-sufficient teachers' college would require $5 million. Even at the best the fund had only $3 million. But cooperation with Vanderbilt could save $2 million. Thus, the committee called for "the most intimate and helpful cooperation with Vanderbilt University in so far as this can be done without interfering with the autonomy of either of the two institutions." In fact, thoughtful men no longer thought of creating teachers' colleges in isolation. The key recommendation followed—that the college "be located in immediate proximity to the campus of Vanderbilt University." The downtown campus was in an undesirable area and three miles from Vanderbilt. More important, Chancellor Kirkland had agreed to sell the highest and most desirable portion of his campus. The committee recommended immediate steps toward the creation of a $3 million college, so as to plant "in the South" a combined institution of learning to rank "with our very noblest in the North, Yale, Columbia, Hopkins, or Chicago, indeed a veritable Harvard for the South, the apex and crown of its whole educational system, a far-shining beacon light, raying forth true ideals and high inspirations. . . ." The committee also recommended the broader distribution of remaining Peabody funds—to state normal schools, to public school systems, and to Negro schools. The racial issue frequently complicated the plans for Peabody. Northern trustees forced Tennessee to remove a 1907 reference to "white teachers" in a bonding act, while local advocates of the Vanderbilt site frequently stressed the black bottom (Negro slums) adjacent to the old University of Nashville.[24]

The confidential committee report left Nashville in the dark about any contemplated move of the campus. But Porter saw the new scheme as a betrayal of past commitments. The local publicity began in 1907 after he resigned as a trustee of the Peabody Fund to fight for his south campus site. He still believed he would win and assured Nashvillians that no affiliation could develop between Peabody and Vanderbilt. By "affiliation" he meant something close to merger. He acknowledged that Rose, Kirkland, and others were "moving heaven and earth" to get the money and the college, and that he had been tricked into transferring the deeds to the University of Nashville campus before learning of the new location scheme. Thus began the charge that Kirkland was not only trying to steal the university from the Methodist church but that, as part of the same plot, he was also trying to steal the Peabody Fund. Porter was not opposed to some new university center. In 1906 he had joined another Peabody trustee, Episcopal Bishop William Lawrence of Massachusetts, in speculations about an expanded University of Nashville, with all the Nashville colleges, including those owned by Vanderbilt, as a part of it. In 1905 Kirkland had proposed to Buttrick a great, new George Peabody University, to which Vanderbilt could shift some of its professional schools (not, presumably, the Biblical Department). But for Porter all such schemes would have left the normal school at its downtown site. This became his pet theme and one abetted by the now anxious landowners of that area. His most telling argument was that this location was an implied commitment when he gained the local funding support. Porter had powerful political allies; he also gained the support of Bishop Hoss and for a time the backing of the Nashville *Banner*. In a December, 1909, letter to the Peabody trustees he stressed that Vanderbilt was a sectarian institution, despite Kirkland's claims, and that the Methodist church would soon assert its control over its policies. The one great hope of Porter was that the denominational status of Vanderbilt would block affiliation and that the Methodist church would suppress all of Kirkland's schemes. Thus, Hoss's successful fight for church control promised also to win Porter's battle in behalf of the south campus.[25]

The controversy raged throughout 1908 and 1909, particularly in Nashville newspapers. But the Peabody trustees had the trump card—the option of withdrawing their funds and locating their college elsewhere. This meant that, except for Porter and Hoss and the immediate southside residents, most of the leaders of the Nashville community, even Stahlman and the *Banner,* slowly swung behind the Vanderbilt site if it were a condition of having the college. In 1909 the Nashville city council at first blocked the issuance of bonds but, fearful of sabotaging the whole project, reconsidered and voted the funding, meeting all the local conditions in early 1910. Already the required deeds had passed hands, and on October 5, 1909, the new George

Peabody College for Teachers received its charter. At the first meeting of its board, Porter's supporters resigned to be replaced in part by Vanderbilt alumni and by two members of the Vanderbilt board. The fight had pushed octogenarian Porter into a corner. One can only feel sad for his plight, for he actually did more than anyone else to win Peabody for Nashville. In 1909, before the incorporation of the new George Peabody College, he resigned as president of the now doomed Peabody Normal, grandiosely suggesting Woodrow Wilson or possibly John Dewey as his worthy successors to head the new college. Through the intervention of several of Porter's opponents, and to induce the old man's retirement, Henry Pritchett, secretary of the Carnegie pension fund, voted Porter a new Carnegie pension.[26]

The Peabody Fund trustees tried their best to allay local suspicions. They formed yet another committee, the committee of five, headed by Bishop Lawrence. He traveled frequently to Nashville, consulted often with Kirkland but not with Porter, and tried to use his committee's November, 1909, report to end the controversy. In it he stressed the advantages of cooperation with Vanderbilt and noted how early such cooperation had become an essential aspect in the decision to locate the college in Nashville. He noted, ominously, that the trustees were not irrevocably committed to Nashville and that without the Vanderbilt connection they might well move the college elsewhere. But the committee emphasized that, by cooperation with Vanderbilt, they never meant any merger or even any affiliation (Kirkland's favorite term). They had only contemplated arrangements to avoid a duplication of plant, instructors, and courses, or a money-saving, complementary relationship. Such cooperation required a site either on the Vanderbilt campus or, if possible, in the immediate vicinity. Throughout, Kirkland had defined "immediate vicinity" as no more than a five-minute walk between classroom buildings. The Peabody College trustees reinforced this disclaimer and alleged that fears of a merger, or Vanderbilt control over Peabody, was a "bogey or phantom." Unfortunately, the committee used Kirkland's language in defining Vanderbilt's relationship to the church. It characterized Vanderbilt, not as controlled by the church but as under its "general auspices," and noted that its board was a self-perpetuating body, a statement contrary to the report of the Vanderbilt commission. In a last, failing effort to block the transfer of Nashville bonds, Bishop Hoss accordingly lambasted the committee and the Peabody Fund. The proposed "merger" was a menace to the Methodist church and he promised that the church would uphold its rights.[27]

Before the final site selection, a newspaper controversy further linked the Peabody and church issues and drew Kirkland into his first public statements about Peabody College. The background involves the Biblical Department. For several years Kirkland had tried to get a separate endowment and more church support for this department, and to draw more sharply the distinction between it and the rest of the university. No doubt, his hopes of gaining an affiliation with Peabody and of securing funds from GEB and the Carnegie

Foundation influenced this effort. Such a scheme pleased Dean Tillett. Thus, a special committee of the Biblical Department met in St. Louis in January, 1909, to perfect a proposal for the board. A detailed study of other seminaries informed the discussion. From this came a resolution to take steps to create a separate board for "the Theological Department of Vanderbilt University," a resolution that incidentally involved a new name. Kirkland susbsequently wrote William K. Vanderbilt of the plan, stressing the needs for the theological department to turn to church sources and of the rest of the university to seek a wider array of benefactors. Kirkland planned to turn over to the new corporation a share of the university endowment sufficient to meet its present level of funding. Vanderbilt heartily endorsed the plan and Kirkland had lawyers draw a special enabling bill for the 1909 Tennessee Assembly.[28]

Just as this innocuous bill was about to sail through, virtually unopposed, Horace M. DuBose, the editor of the *Epworth Era* (a publication for Methodist youth) and a close friend of Hoss, found out about it. Kirkland's bill would allow an educational corporation to donate a part of its endowment to a subsidiary corporation. DuBose frequently confused this with another bill, necessary for the completion of the University of Nashville transfer to the new Peabody, which would allow an educational institution to give away its land, a bill that subsequently passed. DuBose first rallied support in the Assembly to defeat the Kirkland bill, thus preventing a separate endowment for the Biblical Department. Then, in an editorial he rapped the committee of four, charged Kirkland with offering to sell part of his campus to effect a merger with Peabody, and in general indicted his defiance of the church. Kirkland replied not only with a stinging refutation of specific charges (he had no power to offer to sell a part of the campus; only the board could do that) but with a brief survey of his role in facilitating the establishment of Peabody College. But he underplayed his behind-the-scenes maneuvers, leaving the reader with the impression that he had merely offered whatever help he could to such a great educational undertaking.[29]

The now intertwined Peabody and church struggles came to a climax in 1910. By February, 1910, the new Peabody College board was on its own so far as site selection was concerned, but the deed of transfer of the University of Nashville property required them to locate close to Vanderbilt. The board decided to try to buy the fourteen Vanderbilt acres already offered by Kirkland (the strip from Garland north to South Drive, which was near the present northern edge of the old hospital). It pursued this option even as it sought additional land across Hillsboro. In all these negotiations Kirkland assumed that the main classroom buildings of Peabody would be on the Vanderbilt strip. In 1909 the Vanderbilt board had first approved cooperation with Peabody, a cooperation that had also included Vanderbilt's arrangement of purchase options on land south of Garland. Then in 1909 Kirkland first suggested an exchange of the Vanderbilt campus plot for the old south campus, which could serve as a new home for the Medical and

Dental departments. This helped him more easily win board approval and to some extent appeased the residents of south Nashville. By February, 1910, the negotiators agreed upon terms of exchange, with an equal valuation per acre. Since the downtown site of sixteen acres exceeded the fourteen acres on campus and had many more improvements, Vanderbilt eventually paid just over $33,000 additionally. Before the final details were complete, the Peabody Board, on October 22, 1910, bought the burned-out Roger Williams University campus, a defunct Negro university owned by the American Baptist Board of Missions. This land makes up the southern two-thirds of the present main Peabody quadrangle, stretching from Blakemore Avenue to just over the crest of the hill. Early in 1911 Peabody would also buy twelve acres from the Thompson estate, that part of the family estate just to the south of Edgehill and adjacent to the Roger Williams site. This plot makes up the present north side of the quadrangle. The other, unpurchased Thompson acreage, north of Edgehill, includes the present site of University School. Before the Thompson purchase, Kirkland assembled his board in a special session on October 25, 1910, in order to approve the Peabody exchange. But just before the board convened, the College of Bishops secured a court injunction preventing the board from alienating any of its present campus. At least briefly the fight with the church seemed sure to block Kirkland's dream of an affiliation with Peabody.[30]

The bishops acted as a board of visitors, consistent with their church's legal position as to the status of Vanderbilt. Then, at the May General Conference held in Asheville, North Carolina, the church finally asserted its full control over Vanderbilt, consistent with the legal arguments made by the 1906 Vanderbilt Commission. This General Conference was a complete disaster for Kirkland. Hoss, DuBose, and others had lobbied effectively in behalf of the commission's findings, and the overwhelming majority of delegates came to Asheville to support the report and ultimate control by the church. Most annual conferences had passed resolutions, some virtually drafted by Hoss, asking the conference to secure the church's ownership of the university. Yet, Kirkland came to Asheville with some hope of a last-minute miracle. He had always been effective before church committees and hoped once again that his careful logic might prevail. These hopes rested also upon the overwhelming support he received from the Vanderbilt community, including a mild but very effective resolution by the Alumni Association. All that Kirkland won at Asheville was a right to make a presentation before the Board of Education. Perhaps revealingly, Professor J.H. Stevenson was Kirkland's main ally, but Hoss and his friends viewed Stevenson as a heretical radical, one who had frequently been the occasion for their attacks on Vanderbilt. Since 1906 and the commission's findings, Kirkland had lost the support of the moderate center of the church. The majority of Methodists did not want repression at Vanderbilt and might have prevented basic changes had the church won in its ultimate court battle. But they would not give up on the ultimate authority of the church or concede to Kirkland's board its claim of autonomy.[31]

The issues were so polarized by 1910 that victory by either side had to be something of a rout. Until 1906 the church and the Vanderbilt board had shared power, had participated in an alliance based on mutual good faith. Whether or not the board had ultimate authority over board elections and by-law procedures was an ambiguous legal issue; in fact, the board had always deferred to the annual conferences or, after 1898, to the General Board of Education in the confirmation of trustees and whenever it used by-laws to change its governmental structure. Abetted by the commission, the General Conference now claimed final authority over the university, as expressed in the power to elect trustees, while the bishops claimed the judicial supremacy of visitors. In order to deny these aggressive claims, Kirkland and his board had to appeal to their charter as they undestood it and to assert just the opposite—that the board had ultimate power over the corporation and that the board had granted to conferences or to the Board of Education whatever role they had played in the government of Vanderbilt. The church thus had no legal rights at all. Not that Kirkland threatened to end the cooperation with the church; he insisted on just the opposite. But the church did not want a relationship based on the mere sufferance of the Vanderbilt board. The Vanderbilt board, which had gladly shared power with the church, believed it could not legally surrender its final responsibility for the university, a view backed by faculty, most students, and most alumni. By 1910 it was difficult to identify any possible basis of compromise, although some citizens of Nashville tried to facilitate face-saving concessions as late as 1912. Kirkland was more willing than the bishops to bargain; they confidently expected to win all.[32]

The maneuvering at Asheville was complex; the results, clear and simple. The only possibilities of compromise involved concessions by Kirkland and his board. He refused all such. Judge O'Rear, chairman of the Vanderbilt Commission, asked Kirkland to convene his board at Asheville and have it elect three new trustees (the number of vacancies then existing) acceptable to Hoss and the anti-Vanderbilt faction. Then the Board of Education could confirm them, thus averting any direct legal confrontation. After much hesitation and legal consultation, Kirkland pointed out that the board, by law, probably had to meet in Tennessee. By then O'Rear had become a leading partisan, determined to make the board accept his commission report, even demanding a signed concession on some of the legal issues. O'Rear, incorrectly but with some justification, believed that Kirkland was moving toward a complete separation of university and church, even toward a secular institution. After his, and other tactical maneuvers, and presentations by Hoss and Kirkland, the Board of Education almost unanimously recommended tough measures to the larger conference, which then overwhelmingly approved them. In brief, the conference voted to endorse the Vanderbilt Commission report, asserted its power to elect trustees, and voted to establish this power by electing three men to fill the existing vacancies. This was a pure power play, a way to establish a principle, not an acceptable way to run a university. The conference voted that, from this point on, the Vanderbilt board would again nominate all candidates for Board of Education confirmation. Beyond this all-important action, the conference approved the role of bishops in exercising the rights of visitors and voted them and the Board of Education the needed authority to sustain or defend in the courts the commission report. As partial compensation, it also took greater responsibility for the university, voting the first annual appropriations for the Biblical Department. By now it was clear—either the Vanderbilt board would concede all the disputed issues or face a lawsuit.

In retrospect it became clear that the church made a disastrous decision at Asheville. By pressing the most extreme claim—the right ultimately to elect board members and force them upon an unwilling board—the church risked a legal confrontation on its weakest claim. It had to stand on the 1895 Tennessee statute which, despite the commission's findings, probably did not apply to Vanderbilt. Had the church pressed a more moderate claim—that the nature of the trust reflected in the charter was such that the Vanderbilt board could not unilaterally elect board members, or unilaterally enact such by-laws as would threaten the role of the church—it could have won. That is, the church could have preserved the earlier, cooperative relationship, but it could not win a new, almost dictatorial one. It could have prevented Kirkland's subtle, but clear, efforts to alter the earlier partnership, to move all but the Biblical Department to the very brink of independence, leaving only a sentimental tie to Methodism.

The Vanderbilt board met for its annual session in June. In the month since the General Conference, Kirkland and the Executive Committee had consulted extensively with their attorneys. On the basis of this, and support by William K. Vanderbilt, who hired one of the lawyers, Kirkland decided to recommend against seating of the three "purported trustees" elected by the General Conference. By then, the leading university benefactors within the church, as well as those without, had expressed support for Kirkland. The General Conference action seemed, on the surface, a clear move toward a narrow, sectarian university. Two of the three contested trustees attended the board meeting. They were courteously received but their names not called in the role of delegates. Later, after a committee report, the board voted 19 to 8 against seating them, alleging that the General Conference did not have the required authority to elect them. Not all the eight dissenters meant to concede the legal issue but they wanted to maintain the ties to their church. Some preferred to legalize the Asheville action by reelecting the three. Only elderly Bishop A.W. Wilson fought back on principle; he resigned from the board and gave a moving, impassioned speech. In a legally more questionable action, the board then elected its own trustees in place of the three and in addition filled five other vacancies but submitted none of the names to the Education Board for confirmation. Instead, it repealed the by-law requiring such submission. Thus the board not only repudiated the unilateral action by the General Conference but for the first time in its history acted without consulting any agency of the church. In fact, if not in claim, the board declared its autonomy. As Thomas Jefferson in his 1776 Declaration, it of course placed all the odium of illegal aggression on the other side. But, consistent with its now infamous 1905 decision, the board elected two bishops to replace vacancies among the authorized five. Such was the developing controversy that neither of the two ever agreed to serve.[34]

The action of the 1910 board made it almost impossible for bishops to remain on the board. The College of Bishops would very shortly be a party in a suit against the university. Only Bishop Hendrix continued for another few months or until the legal action began. After the death of Bishop Galloway in 1909, the board had elected Hendrix president, the last bishop to hold the position. He remained loyal to Kirkland and to the board's legal claims to the end, and of all the bishop presidents he was the most talented. He had struggled against hopeless odds to unify the northern and southern churches, was a founder and first president of the Federal Council of Churches, and was at opposite poles from Hoss and Candler on most doctrinal and social issues.[35]

As of June, 1910, the gauntlet was down. Such defiance of the General Conference by the Vanderbilt board astounded Methodists. Most Methodist publications now joined in the condemnation of Vanderbilt, some in increasingly sharp language. Some predicted that a panel of elders would soon place Bishop Hendrix on trial and that the bishops planned to dismiss Kirkland and the majority of the board. They did not have the legal means to effect this goal, but on August 13, 1910, the bishops, acting as a board of visitors, declared null and void the action of the board in its unilateral election of new trustees. The board, it declared, was no longer a legally constituted body. In its response to the bishops, the Executive Committee only noted that it believed its action legal and in the best interests of Vanderbilt.

The bishops then hired attorneys and began developing their suit. On October 25, in a preliminary move, they secured temporary injunctions against the seating of the three replacement trustees, among whom was Judge Claude Waller, an early Vanderbilt graduate and a representative of the one family best represented in the early history of the university. The next day the bishops presented a seventy-four-page bill to the Davidson County Chancery Court. The complainants included all but three bishops (Hendrix and retired bishops Fitzgerald and Key) and the three unseated trustees. The defendants were the members of Vanderbilt's Board of Trust. In their complaint the bishops asked the court to affirm the right of the General Conference to elect trustees, to rule that the Methodist Episcopal Church, South, established

175

Vanderbilt, and to rule that it was then being maintained and patronized by the church. It further asked the court to confirm the rightful election of three trustees by the conference, to void the subsequent elections by the Vanderbilt board in June, to vacate any title to their office by Waller and the other two, to enjoin them from meeting with the board, to declare illegal the attempt to elect additional board members without the confirmation of the General Board of Education, to strip the five so elected of any powers, to install the three Asheville trustees as legal board members, and to enjoin any board meetings convened without their having an opportunity to participate, and to enjoin the Board of Trust from selling or exchanging any real property with Peabody. Note that nothing in this bill related to the visitorial rights of the bishops, but since they sought standing before the court as visitors to the university, the issue of their role in university government became involved in the arguments on both side. Over the next eight months university attorneys drafted their legal answer. But it was soon clear that this would be only a preliminary ruling, since each side planned an appeal to the state Supreme Court if it lost.[36]

The lawsuit had been expected. Not so the injunction against the sale or exchange of land with Peabody. The board approved the agreed-upon exchange but could do nothing to expedite it. At the same October meeting Hendrix resigned from the board to relieve himself from the terrible personal bind of being sued by his fellow bishops. The board elected Judge W.C. Ratcliffe of Little Rock as president for a four-year term. But the big news came in Kirkland's detailed defense of the Peabody exchange. He gave his usual idealistic justification of a close academic tie with Peabody and, in good faith, noted that, despite purchases and options across Hillsboro, Peabody would like to place its main buildings on the former Vanderbilt land. He also stressed the wondrous facilities now available on the south campus for the Medical and Dental departments. The very survival of these departments required university support, at least to the extent of providing them free use of buildings and laboratories. But of greatest concern to the board was the funding of the exchange, plus all the cost of relocating the two departments. Kirkland almost joyously announced that he had taken care of that up to fifteen months earlier. Buttrick, who had been godfather to the relocation of Peabody, committed $250,000 from the GEB if Kirkland could match this from other sources. William K. Vanderbilt promised a like amount. Kirkland allotted over $200,000 of this to the endowment. The earnings from up to $100,000 of this would be necessary to replace losses of income from rent on the Medical and Dental buildings and from four surrendered campus residences. These publicized gifts put the bishops in a squeeze. Kirkland emphasized that the university, whoever won the pending case, would gain immensely from the exchange and the subsequent gifts. The bishops did not want to be responsible for sabotaging such large plans and so in December asked the Chancery Court to withdraw the complaint, and the injunction, relating to Peabody. The bishops complained that Peabody got the better bargain. It did.[37]

Kirkland had not been so helpful in the complex Peabody negotiations for nothing. He soon gave up on any legal merger with Peabody. He never really expected to "steal" any of the funds. But he knew that proximity to Vanderbilt would create a great new university center and propel Vanderbilt to the very center of leadership in southern higher education. Such prospects could only open up new funding opportunities for Vanderbilt, but only if the Vanderbilt board retained the degree of autonomy from the church needed for such cooperation. His extensive discussions, even his virtual alliance, with Buttrick of the GEB, his early association with Henry S. Pritchett of the Carnegie Fund, his one personal meeting with Carnegie, all were preliminary moves in his plan to transform Vanderbilt into a major private university. By 1910 he had the needed contacts—with the Vanderbilt family, with the GEB, and with the Rockefeller and Carnegie people. He also had the needed southern contacts; in 1911 he was unanimously elected president of his Southern Association. Also in 1911 he became president of the Religious Education Association, a nice tool in his church struggle, and he was already a member of the prestigious Conference of Education in the South, an offshoot of the GEB. It included not only the Rockefeller people (Buttrick, Rose), but key southern or ex-southern advocates of education and economic progress, including Walter Hines Page, Edgar Garner Murphy, and Edwin A. Alderman. In 1912 Kirkland hosted one of its southern educational congresses at the Ryman Auditorium. Incidentally, Kirkland's heroes included both Page and Woodrow Wilson, who in 1912 won election to a new and important presidency of his own. Thus, after 1910 Kirkland was playing for big stakes indeed. It is likely he already had reasonably firm commitments from Carnegie for additional support for the Medical Department. He had not bargained for any final split from Methodism and did not want such. But if the church insisted upon complete control or nothing at all, Kirkland increasingly preferred a complete break. His educational dreams could not fit into a sectarian mold.[38]

The bishops' suit lingered in Chancery Court for two years, in part delayed by the time it took university lawyers to respond to all the charges made by the bishops. Meanwhile, the Peabody exchange took place, but with some ironic and even embittering consequences. In 1911 the new board of the George Peabody College for Teachers decided to locate their first public buildings on the Roger Williams and Thompson sites, the beginnings of what became its classic quadrangle. By then, Peabody very much needed to distinguish itself from Vanderbilt, to refute its bitter critics in Nashville, to end once and for all the allegations that Kirkland had captured it. The new president of Peabody played a key role in all of this. After Wickliffe Rose turned down the offer, the board turned, not to Woodrow Wilson or John Dewey, but to Bruce R. Payne of the University of Virginia. He seemed an excellent choice. A former student of Dewey's at Columbia, he was a recognized expert in educational philosophy. In 1910 Kirkland had tried to hire Payne to replace Collins Denny, who was elevated to bishop, after consulting very carefully with a special board committee (this was the most sensitive position he had to fill in the Academic Department). Payne had been an undergraduate at Trinity and a close friend of Vanderbilt alumnus Edwin Mims, with whom he had coedited a text. Kirkland visited Payne at Virginia in 1911 and enlisted his help in securing Mims for Vanderbilt. But soon he and Payne had, at best, only a very formal and polite relationship. Payne's educational philosophy, his concern for mass education and new teaching techniques, placed him at an opposite pole from the classical educational elitism of Kirkland. Payne's more equalitarian social outlook also contrasted with Kirkland's staunch advocacy of law and order and of highly nuanced southern racial and class relationships. Payne proved as much an educational entrepreneur as Kirkland, and for a time he seemed even more successful. He eventually raised $1.5 million to match an equal amount eventually awarded by the Peabody trustees, temporarily making Peabody a richer institution than Vanderbilt. Payne very much wanted to be his own man and Peabody to be a distinct and separate institution. He simply did not want Peabody's classrooms in Vanderbilt's backyard. He helped influence the architects in their original and grandiose plans, which copied the classical architecture of Payne's University of Virginia, and which placed almost all classroom buildings on the quadrangle to the east of Hillsboro, relegating the Vanderbilt strip mostly to dorms and residences. Payne's dreams were much too ambitious to fit the small tract along Garland.[39]

As the Peabody plans matured, Kirkland felt more and more betrayed. He had done so much to help Peabody, risked so much with his board and the church, and now only this as thanks. Kirkland had assumed, all along, that the area east of Hillsboro was too far away for effective cooperation. It was more than the mythical five-minute walk from Main. This five-minute rule had a long life and soon invited jokes. Various visitors and committees involved in the site selection so frequently walked the area with a watch in hand as to create permanent paths. By December, 1911, after disappointing talks with Payne, Kirkland tried to apply pressure. He stressed the understanding that led to the property exchange, the implied commitments made by Buttrick and Rose, the assumptions of his own board—that the Vanderbilt land was necessary for the realization of the whole cooperative scheme. In a sense, Vanderbilt had sacrificed the most valuable part of its campus to insure the success of Peabody College. Therefore, if the land was no longer essential for Peabody's main buildings, then he asked the Peabody board to return the land to Vanderbilt. Vanderbilt would buy from Peabody the south campus at a fair market price fairly determined by a committee from both institutions.[40]

In March, 1912, the Peabody board refused. It insisted it still needed the land and still promised all the cooperation Kirkland had dreamed of. Kirkland

would not give up. Residences and dorms did not fulfill the terms of cooperation that caused Vanderbilt to give up a part of its campus, or land it would
need in the future for classroom buildings. In particular, if cooperation did
develop with Peabody, Vanderbilt would need to grow in that direction. His
efforts were to no avail. By October, 1912, Kirkland turned to Dean Tillett,
who seemed to get along better with Payne. Later he also used Mims as an
intermediary. Tillett made some progress. He gained purchase options on
several lots to the east of Peabody (on present 18th Avenue), hoping to use
them to replace the acres lost on what Peabody now called its west campus (its
temporary library was already ensconced in Tillett's former residence, and
Payne prepared to move into the former chancellor's house). These first
negotiations floundered when the Peabody trustees asked for more than the
$125,000 paid, and when Vanderbilt had to ask for up to three years to
accumulate the needed money.[41]

By 1914 Peabody was more amenable. It needed the money and by then
had no early prospects for more than one classroom building on the site. As
part of very complicated negotiations, Tillett secured options on the north
section of the Thompson property (across from the present Vanderbilt
library). This valuable acreage seemed a likely basis of exchange, as did the
options Tillett kept alive to the east. Finally, in 1914 Payne even talked
directly to Kirkland and the two went to New York City to consult Rose and
Buttrick. The GEB no longer objected to the alienation of a part of the
Peabody campus. Peabody pressed the issue by threatening to begin a
psychology building on the site. By now, its tough board firmly rejected
$125,000 as being well below the market value of the land, and offered only
to exchange it for an equivalent fourteen acres to the north and east. Tillett
exercised his option on seven acres of the Thompson tract (the later site of the
Peabody Demonstration School) and about six and a half acres near present
18th Avenue. Vanderbilt paid over $162,000 for these tracts and then very
reluctantly used them to buy back its own former land. It also, as an investment, bought for itself the rest of the Thompson tract, a part of which it
would later sell for the YMCA College (the present Wesley Hall). Kirkland
accused the Peabody board of bad faith (true), but because of the long-term
needs of Vanderbilt swallowed his pride and, against some justified reluctance, pressured his board to go along. In effect, by its losses in the land deals,
Vanderbilt contributed about $37,000 of its endowment to the new Pea-
body. Only the prospective sale of the former law building, a poor yielding
investment, made the cost bearable. To add insult to injury, Peabody then
refused to pay over $4,000 of street assessments incurred while it owned the
property. Before this acrimonious suit came to trial, the two rival institutions
agreed to share the payments. In the same year (1915), the faculties of the two
institutions began a plan for shared courses, but the long-awaited and
tenuous marriage of Peabody and Vanderbilt had fallen prey to a stormy
honeymoon.[42]

The recapture of its lost campus followed the final decision in Vanderbilt's lawsuit. On February 21, 1913, Chancellor John Allison ruled completely in favor of the bishops. He accepted the intimidating arguments of the five-member commission—that the church founded Vanderbilt, that it maintained and patronized it, that the Memphis resolutions remained the "very essence" of the charter, that the annual conferences were the original members of the corporation, that the 1895 statute applied to Vanderbilt, that the General Conference had the authority to elect trustees in 1910, and that the subsequent elections by the board were invalid, as was the repeal of the by-law stipulating confirmation by the Board of Education. He even, somewhat gratuitously, ruled that the bishops validly exercised visitorial power over the corporation and that they had rightfully annulled the board action of 1910. Vanderbilt appealed, with guarded hopes of winning. Its seven attorneys believed the board had the strongest case; they tended to discount Judge Allison's ruling. They believed he had catered to a political constituency, that he had been intimidated by the prestigious judges on the commission, and that he had failed to address the most critical legal issues. He also had a very poor record on appeals.[43]

By the time the case was heard by the Tennessee Supreme Court in March, 1914, it had become one of the best publicized in the history of the state. Among southern Methodists everywhere the Vanderbilt issue had turned out to be the most divisive controversy since the southern church broke from the northern. The briefs in the case, all told, numbered over 8,000 pages, and each side minutely covered every aspect of university history. Because he was a Vanderbilt graduate and earlier involved on one side of the issue, Judge Samuel C. Williams recused himself. A Knoxville judge, William R. Turner, replaced him and as a presumably disinterested outsider wrote the unanimous decision of the court. His decision was not brilliant, not always well written, but he did a very fair job of dissecting the complicated issues. Contrary to the effect of this ruling—it denied the General Conference a right to elect trustees and thus fully reversed the lower court—it did not support all the contentions of the university.[44]

Of the briefs presented, the one by the church was more accurate in its historical interpretation, more vulnerable on legal issues. The university brief was so contrived and one-sided as to be historically useless for anyone who wanted to understand the beliefs and values of the founders of the university. But it devastated the case for the unilateral election of trustees by the General Conference, or the central issue in the case. By selective use of historical evidence, the university lawyers tried to discount the role of the church in the university from 1872 on, as well as to prove that the board had been self-perpetuating from the beginning. The counsel for the university minimized the church role, even imputing beliefs and motives to McTyeire and Garland that would have caused them to turn over in their graves. But on one crucial issue the brief was correct—the minimal financial support provided by the church. The university denied that the Memphis resolutions could be a legal part of the charter or that they survived the 1873 amendment, but even if they were part of the charter they did not give to the church any right to elect trustees. Thus the only shadow of support for the General Conference intervention was the 1895 statute. The university challenged even the constitutionality of that statute but hardly needed such arguments. If the 1895 act related to the Vanderbilt case, it still could not hold without amounting to an ex post facto deprivation of rights long vested in, and exercised by, the board. More important, it could not apply to Vanderbilt at all unless the church not only established Vanderbilt (a disputed point) but "maintained and patronized" it. Here the church's past penury did it in. There was no way it could claim much more than a spiritual or moral patronage; ironically, as university attorneys pointed out, the $25,000 cost of the court case against Vanderbilt exceeded the total of all its gifts to the institution until well after 1900.[45]

Turner, in his decision, vainly tried to reestablish the relationship between church and university that prevailed before 1905. He interpreted the relationship as one of trust, with obligations on both sides. He defined as "members of the corporation" the actual persons who met at Memphis, and not the annual conferences that sent them. The self-perpetuating rights of a corporation therefore accrued to them and to their successors on the board. In this sense the Vanderbilt board did choose its own successors. On the rather silly issue of who founded Vanderbilt (according to varying definitions, any one of several people or groups founded it), Judge Turner decreed that, at least in terms of money, Cornelius Vanderbilt was the principal founder and thus due the honor subsequently bestowed upon him by the university. In any strict legal sense the church did not own the corporation, although again by taking advantage of the ambiguities in the word "own" even Kirkland had in times assigned ownership to the church. Most devastating for the church, Turner ruled that in none of the concrete ways intended by the 1895 statute had the church maintained and patronized the university, and that by no valid argument could Vanderbilt's gifts be credited to the church. This ruling, alone, denied the claims of the bishops. His other technical arguments on the inapplicability of the 1895 statute amounted only to a devastation of this critical point, a further rebuke to O'Rear and the Vanderbilt Commission.

Since Turner accepted the charter status of the Memphis resolutions, he also tried to clarify the issue of visitorial rights for the bishops. But here his earlier findings of fact, about the lack of patronage from the church, indicated the answer he had to give to this issue. Of course, resolution nine did not even mention visitation rights. By analysis of its language Turner concluded that the Memphis convention had not intended to give such power. The commission had assigned this power only by some contrived implications. But even if the resolution had intended it, common law visitors represent the right of a patron or founder of a charitable trust. Since the bishops did not accumulate the funds for Vanderbilt, they were not its founders in that sense. And certainly the bishops did not represent the interest of Cornelius Vanderbilt, who did put up the money. Nor, for thirty years, had the bishops claimed this right of visitation. The early bishops even rejected any close tie to the university at all. Thus, Turner contended that the ninth resolution in no way supported the bishops' claim to visitorial supervision. He doubted that it gave any charter rights at all to the bishops, but that was not at issue in the case.[46]

All these judgments suggested an overwhelming victory for Vanderbilt, a complete defeat for Hoss and the church. On the technical complaints the church decisively lost and had to pay all court costs. Wild jubilation on campus contrasted with a Methodist gloom that still brings bitter memories to a few elderly Methodists who can remember the sweeping and shocking decision of 1914. But Turner balanced his denial of the key claim of the bishops with some rather clear rebukes to the Vanderbilt board. It had not lived up to the demands of a cooperative relationship. The Vanderbilt trustees had to serve the stated purposes of the university and to live up to the trust given to it by the church. The critical eighth resolution, which promised fair representation in the management of the university to any cooperating conferences, placed a clear responsibility upon the board and set limits to what it could effect by its by-laws. In recognition of this, the early board submitted important changes in procedure to the conferences as well as submitting to them for confirmation all elected trustees. The board and church then accepted the duty of helpful cooperation. Short of renunciation by the church, neither party could ignore these duties nor could the board unilaterally change the terms of cooperation. The board simply could not, on its own, change by-laws affecting the cooperative relationship, for such constituted a contract as much as if a literal part of the charter itself. Thus, its 1910 repeal of the by-law requiring Board of Education confirmation of new trustees was invalid, for the church had not renounced "its relationship of cooperation." The trustees elected in 1910 by the board, and all subsequent ones, served only in an interim capacity until the Board of Education either confirmed or rejected them. But in an ambiguous warning, the court noted that the General Conference could lose its role in the university by voluntarily surrendering or renouncing its trust relationship to the board, or if it should "contumaciously refuse to confirm members elected, and cease to cooperate with the university. . . ." Then the board would be autonomous as to by-law changes or trustee elections. This proved a very intimidating statement and much influenced the subsequent choices open to the church. Turner did not mean to foreclose Board of Education vetoes over trustees; confirmation would be a mockery unless the church had the option of rejection. But it seemed likely that the courts would define as contumacious wholesale vetoes over all or most nominees, or any pattern of retaliatory vetoes against the reappointment of board members party to the suit.[47]

The details of the decision were unimportant in 1914. The contestants had so defined the issues that there was no basis of continuing cooperation. Most Methodists were bitter at the decision. Church newspapers lamented a total defeat, the survival of only sentimental ties to the university. But the campus was delirious. Kirkland led a march of a reported 1,000 students in downtown Nashville. The celebration reportedly outclassed that following any great football victory. And in educational circles the decision was generally hailed as a victory for higher education or even for academic freedom. Leading journals of opinion, including *Nation* and the *Independent*, celebrated Kirkland's great victory. Most saw in the decision a bright new future for Vanderbilt. Few paid much heed to the losers. Hoss was devastated, but most people believed he got only what he deserved. Before the decision he wrote Denny that he had bought a new suit. A generous man, he rarely so indulged himself. He planned to buy a top hat if he lost his case, for he did not want his enemies to know how depressed he really was. Vanderbilt students were now unmercifully cruel. No longer afraid of a bishop, or of the harmful effects of their editorials, the *Hustler* took vituperation so far as to cause Kirkland to apologize. It lambasted Hoss for his opposition to their athletic teams and asked that he be thrown into a Davidson County jail for contempt of the court's decision. Every Vanderbilt student, it said, would like to see the Pope of Methodism in jail, so they could march by and stick out their tongues at him. The *Hustler* referred to him also as a czar, condemned his references to Carnegie, a new benefactor of Vanderbilt, as an impudent iron monger, asked the church to expel him, but promised that if he went to jail Vanderbilt students would bring him bread and water. It climaxed with an appeal: "cleanse the augean stables, the HOSS has been there." Hoss excused such extremes by innocent students and placed the full blame upon Vanderbilt officials.[48]

The rejoicing at Vanderbilt was premature and misplaced. Kirkland knew this. The prolonged struggle had placed the university in a no-win situation. The decision had been only the best of several possible undesirable outcomes. The task now was to repair the remaining ties to the church (it still confirmed trustees). In particular, the very survival of the Biblical Department seemed at stake, for it depended on the Methodist church for all its students and, increasingly, for much of its support. Tillett and the Biblical faculty had been walking a tightrope for ten years. They now made futile appeals for continuing denominational ties.

Conciliatory gestures were much too late. The reaction in the church was bitter and despairing. All was lost, Hoss acknowledged. Kirkland had stolen Vanderbilt. The issue could be quickly resolved; the General Conference, the last to be concerned with Vanderbilt, met in Oklahoma City in May. Very few except Vanderbilt alumni came to seek new patterns of cooperation. The only unifying issue was the perfidy of the Vanderbilt board. Even those most sympathetic to Vanderbilt or to the board admitted the now well-publicized "depravity" of its students. A majority report in behalf of complete severance won 154–131. Even the dissenting votes included not so much those who looked in favor upon Vanderbilt as those who wanted to use the surviving power of confirmation to get revenge upon the Vanderbilt board. The conference finally voted to reconsider the severance motion and ended up by approving a commission to consider the transfer of the church's rights in Vanderbilt back to the original supporting conferences. The conference debate was such as could only blacken the reputation of Vanderbilt. The church quickly cut off all funds to Vanderbilt, including all support for the Biblical Department. It authorized the same commission to consider church support of other universities and began efforts to construct two new theological schools: in Atlanta at a new Emory University (funded by Asa Candler, the bishop's brother and Coca-Cola king) and in Dallas at Southern Methodist University.[49]

In light of this conference action, the Vanderbilt board, at its June meeting, concluded the game. It decided on the basis of legal advice that the General Conference had, in effect, refused to accept the decision of the court and had rejected the type of cooperation mandated by that decision. Since Vanderbilt's board did accept the decision, it had no option but to take full responsibility for the university. This legally marked the completion of the divorce action. But the board postponed for a year any final, difficult decision about the Biblical Department. Subsequently, the commission established by the 1914 General Conference decided that the church had no legal rights to transfer to the annual conferences and, rather than arouse illusioned expectations, it dropped the issue in order to devote its efforts to its two new universities and seminaries. The divorce was now complete and final, but the aftertaste remained bitter.[50]

9

The Home Front

THE LEGAL BATTLE intruded upon campus life only at a few climactic points, as in 1906, 1910, and 1914. From 1906 on, the faculty knew how critical were the issues at stake, but the minutes of faculty meetings contain no references to the legal proceedings. The faculty took up most of their time and energy attending to the details of getting students through each semester. As long as the legal issues were pending, they were unable to make long-term plans. Students were insulated from problems of university government. They were pulled directly into the conflict only at critical junctures, and then, an overwhelming majority backed Kirkland. But in subtle ways the students were continually affected by the controversies in the church. Their conduct was always in the spotlight, the occasion of vicious attacks on Vanderbilt.

Both the church conflict and the Peabody courtship elevated Kirkland's role and power. He was the key figure on campus, the defender of faculty and student interest against all outside enemies. The siege mentality lessened internal resentment of authority and helped Kirkland gain an authoritarian role in campus government, both over faculty and students. He seemed almost indispensable and, at critical junctures, capitalized on outside threats or his own threats to resign to maintain a working consensus. Several times besides 1905 Kirkland came close to leaving Vanderbilt. Twice, in 1911 and again in 1913, as he seemed to be losing in the courts, he wrestled with beguiling offers. In 1911 he considered the presidency of the University of Alabama. Faculty, students, trustees, and even the Nashville Board of Trade begged him to keep up the fight. Even the Nashville *Banner,* often hostile to Kirkland, now applauded his administrative and business skills, his fund-raising successes. Then in 1913, when he was doubly frustrated—at the loss of his case before Chancery Court and at the developing cold war with Peabody—he nearly took the presidency of the University of Arkansas. The Arkansas trustees actually announced his appointment, and for a few weeks he gave them reason to believe that he would soon move. On the Vanderbilt campus the gloom deepened daily. *Hustler* editors speculated on his successor. But at the last moment, heartened by a new grant from Andrew Carnegie, he decided to stay on. By then Kirkland had the strongest student allegiance yet accorded any chancellor. The love affair continued through the victorious court decision of 1914 and then, predictably, slowly dissipated. Internal

185

conflict and difficult decisions led once again to a normal, and perhaps healthy, tension.[1]

As if to certify his value, the trustees steadily increased Kirkland's salary and prerogatives. By 1914 he had a salary of $6,000, double that of any chair professor.[2] Such salary discrepancies normally are evidence of inferiority in a university; strong universities are always able to attract scholars or scientists who can command salaries equal to or above that of any administrative officer. As a depressing matter of fact, Vanderbilt had few such distinguished professors in the period after 1901. Most deserved lesser salaries than Kirkland; they worked less and contributed less to the university, having neither his skill nor his national reputation.

In the Academic Department, still the standard for the university as a whole, stability also meant stagnation. Tight budgets precluded aggressive recruiting, particularly at the chair level. Vanderbilt did not suffer so many losses as in the 1890s, but this was largely because it had so few scholars in great demand. As of 1901 the department had only eight chair professors, and of those only Tolman in Greek had or deserved a national reputation. Moore, in history, was active professionally but, bogged down in teaching and by his duties as dean, he published only occasional articles. Dudley now excelled in administration, not as a research chemist, although he gained national recognition in certain applied fields and in the industrial applications of chemistry. The other chairs were occupied either by ill oldtimers (Vaughn in Math), by those not qualified in their field (Denny in philosophy), or by undistinguished or dated scholars (McGill in chemistry and pharmacy, Daniel in physics). In a 1913 editorial the *Hustler* decried the stagnation, the failure of the faculty to keep up with the times. It noted that the older faculty were content to rest on their laurels, ignore the latest scholarship, and boringly tell the same stories year after year. At the adjunct level, the two ablest men were L.C. Glenn in geology and Bert Young in Romance languages, but neither became outstanding in his field.[3] Such a description does not discount the enormous contributions made by Vaughn, who died in 1912, and Dudley, who died in 1914. Vaughn left a superb book collection to "his" library. Dudley, a man of charm, grace, and political skill, was irreplaceable. His contributions to the Medical School, to athletics in the South, and to various student organizations made him perhaps the most valuable member of Vanderbilt's faculty in its first forty years. He also left a valuable chemistry library to the university and bequeathed a final $5,000 to his beloved athletic association.[4]

New appointments could not improve faculty quality because Vanderbilt salaries were increasingly noncompetitive with those of major northern universities. In 1905 Kirkland asked the board to approve a new and by now conventional rank system, and with it a new salary schedule. In place of adjunct professors, he substituted both assistant and associate professors, keeping the rank of instructor for beginning or temporary appointees. The new, established compensation for a full or chair professor was $3,000, but this did not mean an increase over the previous, contractual salary of $2,000. A chair appointee still received $2,000 on contract, plus housing, which now had an established value of $600 for a two-story house down to $350 for a large apartment, and, if the university income allowed, enough of a share in the collected fees to complete the total $3,000. At times new appointees had to wait a few years to reach even this level. The established total compensation due associates was $2,000, for assistants only $1,500, and in many years their share of the fees did not quite fulfill this goal. But the new salary scale marked the first tentative shift from a pattern set in 1879. By placing a value on university houses, the university was finally moving toward fixed salaries and the straightforward renting of its houses and apartments. Yet, even as late as 1915 the faculty still fought over access to the better campus homes, suggesting that the university undervalued them in its rents. In two aspects the new scheme remained unchanged—Vanderbilt did not appoint more than one professor to any one school, and it did not yet recognize merit as a basis for unequal salaries. But by 1915 Kirkland already faced requests for extra professors in key departments, and in subtle ways he was already juggling compensation rates as a means of rewarding or retaining valued professors.[5]

New, senior faculty members were now few and far between. In 1901 Herbert Z. Kip came as adjunct professor of German, the last of a series of Leipzig Ph.D.s. In 1902 the Biblical Department made two important appointments—Thomas Carter from Tulane University to replace Gross Alexander in Greek and New Testament, and Henry B. Carré, president of Centenary College, as adjunct professor of biblical theology, a new chair funded in part by gifts solicited by Biblical students. For the next eight years all appointees were young men or, in one borderline case, a young woman (Stella Vaughn received first a $100 salary, and then after 1913 a munificent $200 for teaching physical education to young women and doing much of the work of a dean of women). Of the young men, a new instructor in 1908, a former Vanderbilt Ph.D., began a long Vanderbilt career—George R. Mayfield, in the field of German but later best known as an ornithologist. In 1910, when Denny became bishop and vacated philosophy and Dean Moore became ill with tuberculosis (he died in 1911), Kirkland had two critical appointments to make and worked hard at filling them within his salary constraints. Working closely with the board and endeavoring not to offend key Methodists, he resorted to an interim professor of philosophy—John P. Turner of the City College of New York. After a year Turner rejected a permanent appointment. Kirkland then hired Herbert Sanborn, from small Washington College in Maryland but before that a graduate student in about half the German universities. His degree was from Munich; his publications, highly technical articles mostly in German. A former student of American

Methodism's greatest philosopher—Borden Parker Bowne—Sanborn remained at Vanderbilt forever, coaching fencing long after his retirement, into the 1950s.[6]

As a temporary replacement for Moore, Vanderbilt first hired St. George Sioussat of Sewanee part time, and then offered him the chair of history the next year. He was more able than Moore, active in the American Historical Association, and a successful author; unfortunately, Vanderbilt kept him only six years. In 1915, and after a very careful search, Vanderbilt turned to James F. Norris from Simmons College in Boston as a replacement for Dudley. But Kirkland was unable to hire a professor of biology (no money) and did not replace Vaughn with a senior mathematician. He eventually appointed Tolman to replace Moore as dean of the Academic Department, thereby diverting his ablest scholar into supervisory and administrative details. In 1913 the Department of Engineering hired a second professor, Charles S. Brown, who had his professional degree from Yale. By then Dean Schuerman had become an almost indispensable professor, directing several building programs and teaching higher mathematics as well as supervising engineering. One irregular appointment deserves mention: in 1915 Will W. Alexander, an alumnus and a major figure in later southern reform efforts,

The great new dorm—Kissam

The bright new professor—Edwin Mims

began teaching part time in the Biblical Department to supplement local work with the YMCA.[7]

None of the appointments rivaled in significance that of Edwin Mims. He came to Vanderbilt in 1912 from the University of North Carolina and, two years before that, from Trinity College. Of the early Vanderbilt professors, only three—Smith, Baskervill, and Dudley—had as great an impact on Vanderbilt as would Mims. In sentiment Mims had never really left his alma mater. He had remained a very active and enthusiastic alumnus, a fervent supporter of all Kirkland's policies, and had meantime become a productive scholar. He had already published a well-received book on Sidney Lanier (echoes of Baskervill and his southern writers project), and had edited or contributed to several other volumes. Mims was somewhat pushy, always full of enthusiasm, a born booster. Characteristically, on the day of the Supreme Court verdict in the Vanderbilt case, Mims was first in line to get into the court building. He had Kirkland's love for, and commitment to, a new and more progressive South. Yet, his personal beliefs were utterly conventional, in no wise prophetic, innovative, or profound. A Methodist, enthusiastically religious, he began his career at Vanderbilt by abetting a moral and religious revival that swept the campus.[8]

Kirkland took great pride in Mims's achievements and for years sought the means to bring him to Vanderbilt. He never used McTyeire's tactics to force out professors but probably welcomed the departure of Richard Jones in 1910. Unfortunately, by then Mims had just taken his position at North Carolina and, short of a $1,000 repayment, was morally obligated to serve for two years. In the interlude Vanderbilt hired Carl Holliday from Southwestern Presbyterian College on a temporary basis. He proved extremely popular with students, who then resented his departure in 1912. Mims came to Vanderbilt in a typical whirlwind of activity—speeches, a new literary club, several outside lectureships, and absorption in campus politics. He moved into the very heart of the campus, to what is now called Old Central, and began teaching his students next door in Old Science. He promptly engaged in some nasty spats with students over grading and attendance standards, found his junior staff incompetent, and pressured Kirkland for a second professorship in English. Although as yet without the title, he was Vanderbilt's first department head. Pushed by Mims, Kirkland took an unprecedented step—he fired a junior English professor but then extended his appointment for a year so that he could find a new position. (Before the year was out the displaced English professor was able to take over some vacated German courses, thus remaining at Vanderbilt.) In short, Mims came to Vanderbilt with a high sense of his own ability, with great ambitions for his school, and thus demanded the support needed to build an empire. Given his friendship with Kirkland and the range of his contributions to Vanderbilt, he very often got what he wanted. Soon the school of English would be the strongest at Vanderbilt, the one school that would soon establish a modest claim to a national reputation. Vanderbilt needed many more such ambitious professors in 1912.[9]

During the court fight the west campus departments made no daring innovations in academic programs or policies. A gradual but steady increase of students in the Academic Department (from 220 in 1901 to 361 in 1914) required new courses and programs. At the turn of the century Vanderbilt added courses in Italian and in sociology. In 1908 a school of economics, including instruction in sociology, separated from history, all under the direction of a volatile Gus Dyer. Then, in 1913 sociology became a separate school, but neither of these social sciences yet rated a full professor. Slowly, Kirkland terminated the use of graduate fellows for teaching freshmen courses, substituting a slightly more costly corps of instructors. The resulting small sections improved academic performance in such difficult courses as beginning math. This change paralleled the gradual suspension of Ph.D. work and the continuance only of a small M.A. program, which strengthened undergraduate courses. The change amounted to a confession of failure. In 1912, as a money-saving gesture, Kirkland asked the board to withdraw the ten graduate scholarships, leaving all graduate students to pay their own way. He recommended, as he had privately since 1900, that graduate students go elsewhere, to northern universities with programs "beyond our reach." Unstated was his awareness that not only did Vanderbilt lack needed libraries and labs but that too few of its professors were on the frontiers of knowledge.[10]

The prestigious Vanderbilt B.A. program remained one of the most demanding in the United States. Until 1915 it required at least two years in both Latin and Greek. Vanderbilt continued to demand a classical preparation for its matriculates, with seven units required in Latin and Greek, and it continued to certify approved academies and high schools. It shifted its entrance exam to conform with one approved by the Southern Association, but Vanderbilt professors continued to grade the exams. This proved an arduous chore, as more and more high school students took the exam with no intention of enrolling in Vanderbilt. By 1910 Vanderbilt professors were reading up to 583 exams each spring, an educational contribution to the whole South. But in small ways the rigor began to relax. After 1906 Vanderbilt allowed its seniors to enroll in medical schools and to count the first year of medical courses toward their B.A. or B.S. The faculty refused continued student demands to make the final exams optional for those with high class averages, but they slowly reduced the length and the significance of the finals. In 1912 the faculty eliminated a second year of math for the B.S. program and began discussing a shift to more electives and fewer classical languages for the B.A. Seniors gained exemption from second-semester physical education and students gained a much desired spring semester holiday. After 1905 the faculty so relaxed the compulsory chapel law as to make it a joke; only those with eleven-to-twelve o'clock classes had to attend the twelve to twelve-thirty chapel, and those with five such courses each week could skip Monday, Wednesday, and Friday. Theological students were excused because they had their own chapel; women did not have to attend, no reason given.[11]

This relaxation of standards accompanied a decided growth in rules and bureaucratic procedures mandated by deans. In 1906–1907 professors first had to render formal attendance reports; these revealed an unbelievable laxity of record keeping among professors and a scandalous "cut" rate for students. From then on, three deans (Academic, Engineering, Pharmacy) and one faculty member made up a supervising committee to hear all student requests and to make delinquency reports. Dean Moore fought for years to lower absenteeism but found that students took advantage of all rules (if the university permitted three absences, most students cut three times). In 1907 a new committee of seven began acting as an elected student jury to enforce the traditional honor system. Although officially demanding, the course of study must have been more routine than the professors realized. In 1908 one of six Vanderbilt students graduated in only three years; the failure rate in courses was then under 10 percent. About one-fourth of the graduates qualified for Phi Beta Kappa. But by 1910 the problem of declining academic averages, particularly among fraternity men, joined a campuswide, even churchwide, crusade to clean up student morals.[12]

The only major physical changes on the main campus took place just after the great fire of 1905. Although at the time everyone talked about the disastrous loss, the fire probably proved a blessing to Vanderbilt. It broke out in the garret of Old Main at about 11:00 A.M. on Thursday, April 20. It had

The ruins of Old Main, 1905

considerable headway and had already engulfed part of the roof before students in the eleven o'clock classes smelled the smoke. When the blaze was discovered, the garret area that contained the now-useless water tanks plus a collection of books was already inaccessible. No one was able to find the cause; suspect were the electrical wiring or a faulty flue. The building burned for two hours, from the top downward, as frantic students carried or tossed out books and lab equipment from the lower floors. The Nashville fire department proved inept. It took over thirty minutes to hook up to any water at all, and by then the pressure was too low for effective fighting. When the fire was finally controlled, only the outer shell of the building remained. The beloved clock in the south tower was engulfed in flames but survived just to the noon hour, struck a desperate thirty times, and then fell into the rubble. The students threw over 4,000 books out the library windows; waiting

192

students caught them and carried them to safety. But the main library was next to the top floor; time proved so short that about 18,000 books burned. The basement labs went last of all. Students were able to save most of Garland's precious machines, although not without minor damage. Lost were most photographs and a new art collection situated in the library in 1902. Saved was the huge chapel painting of Cornelius Vanderbilt; lost, the one of Bishop McTyeire.[13]

The fire disrupted only the last classes of the day and the chapel service. Kirkland, in what became a legendary gesture, posted a letter to the anxious, begrimed, even crying students before the day was out. He thanked them, appealed to their loyalty to Vanderbilt, and asked that they not brood over the past but bravely face the future. He announced no interruption of the academic program. This became a matter of great pride—not one class was cancelled. At eight o'clock on the next (Friday) morning, students assembled in substitute classrooms, in the Observatory, in Kissam's and Wesley's parlors, in unoccupied Westside Row dorms, and in the YMCA building; chemistry and pharmacy students took essential lab work downtown in the Medical and Dental departments. For several years physics students had to give up much of their needed lab work. With such makeshift arrangements, Vanderbilt completed its spring semester. Campus morale was never higher than when it ended. At a mass meeting in the Kissam dining room on the Saturday after the fire, students began their own canvass to collect money for the rebuilding.[14]

The financial loss from the fire only slowly became clear. It was in Vanderbilt's interest to assess it as high as honesty allowed, for the impact of a great loss is the greatest single boost to fund raising. Thus, the optimum final estimate was $227,000, of which only $96,000 was assessed to the building, the rest to library, furnishing, apparatus, supplies, and art work. Insurance covered $115,000, leaving a net loss of $112,000. Kirkland saw in the disaster a chance to boost Vanderbilt's always critical financial situation. So far his fund-raising efforts had floundered. The board and the church had just failed to raise $100,000 to realize a $50,000 matching grant. The endowment seemed frozen at about $1.3 million. The debt was over $60,000, and operating expenses, by 1902 approaching $100,000, were creeping above annual income. The professional schools operated at an official loss each year, which translated into reduced rent payments on their buildings or little or no salaries for their proprietary professors. In 1903 Kirkland had asked the board for $5,000 to fund the expenses of a new university agent, or full-time fund raiser, but the church-oriented board then restricted his solicitations to the Biblical Department. And so Kirkland tried to exploit the fire for all it was worth. It was worth a great deal. William K. Vanderbilt contributed $150,000; the citizens of Nashville pledged over $50,000 and paid in over $40,000 by 1907; alumni outside Nashville promised more than they gave but eventually contributed about $10,000. After years of litigation, Vanderbilt finally negotiated an out-of-court settlement with the Furman heirs and gained downtown properties and almost $80,000 in cash. Later returns of near $60,000 on the sale of the Furman property downtown, plus the $80,000, almost exactly paid for Furman Hall. All in all, counting insurance, Kirkland accumulated a building fund of approximately $400,000. As a symbolically significant contribution to all this, the children of the campus collected $553 for a new clock and bell.[15]

Given such a financial boost, Kirkland planned a major building program in 1905. In 1902 the university had paid Hunt and Hunt, the architects of Kissam, to work out a landscape plan for the campus. In 1905 it paid George Kessler, who planned the grounds for the 1903 St. Louis Exposition, to refine and make more practical this original design (see map). Unlike the Hunts, Kessler actually visited the campus and took terrain features into account. Kirkland began immediate implementation of the Kessler plan. He paid for harmonized architectural plans for three buildings—the restored Main, a new library building at the apex of a new quadrangle that was to displace Science Hall and reach from near present Rand Hall all the way to the Broad Street entrance, and for Furman, which was to be the center of three planned buildings on the north side of this quadrangle. The engineering building already made up the easternmost of three buildings planned for the south side. Each of the three architectural plans featured the then popular college gothic, although the remnants of Main did not allow the fullest gothic effect.

Kirkland, as always cautious, tried to save money on the rebuilding of Main; he and his own engineers directed the work. They either hired their own laborers or subcontracted the tasks. Still, the costs mounted and by 1907 Kirkland gave up on an early construction of the beautiful new library, since he failed to get an expected grant from Andrew Carnegie. Desperate for increased operating income, he used the funds tentatively slotted for the library to increase the endowment. As a result of this decision only Furman ever contributed to the Kessler quadrangle; Science Hall had its first of several reprieves. But the Kessler scheme did, unintentionally, help locate future athletic fields. Furman Hall intruded into the edge of Dudley Field (present Curry Field), and the other buildings in the plan would have eliminated it. Thus, Dudley and the aggressive athletic association took an option on the Sperry track, an open field two blocks west of the campus, and borrowed from the university the $22,000 needed to buy it. During the next few, glorious football seasons the athletic association slowly paid this money back to the endowment and also developed practice fields on its new property, or what later provided the site for a new Dudley Field.[16]

In some ways Vanderbilt skimped on the rebuilding of Main. Yet, despite the awkward absence of one of the earlier two towers, everyone seemed to rejoice in the new product. Immunity to fire was now the controlling concern. Except for a few wooden floors, the interior and even the roof was of

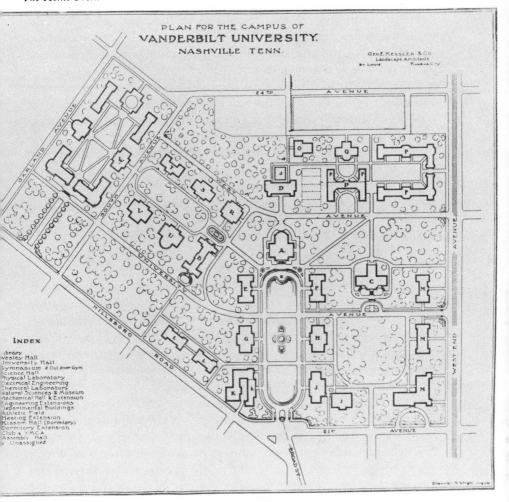

The Kessler plan for a new Vanderbilt, 1905

reinforced concrete. The flat roof was an esthetic comedown from the beautiful old gabled roof, but the considerably lower building now climaxed in a castle-like, terra cotta parapet, giving it a gothic twist to match the turrets of the new Furman. The resulting building was not nearly as impressive as the old, although the single clock tower was slightly higher and rather elaborately crowned by its own parapet, balconies, and gargoyle figures. The Seth Thomas Company built the four-fronted clock and the children's fund purchased a 2,000-pound bell, the largest of several planned for the tower. The tower turned out to be the most costly single part of the building, since the workers had to construct its foundation from the ground up. Otherwise, the old walls remained except for parts of the top floor. Dudley worked out a new composite, called lignolith, for several of the floors; it was soft to the walk.

Inside, the design changed only in minor ways. The basement included

195

lockers for men; the first floor had two rooms for young ladies. Both the restored chapel and the library to the east of it occupied both the second and third stories, but the chapel was a bit larger, now seating 750. It encompassed the earlier hallway, meaning that one had to go through the chapel, or its balconies, to move from the north to the south wings of floors two and three. The chancellor's office was on the first floor (above the basement). Since the building was fireproof, the Geology Department soon moved its museum to the basement and out of a now recognized fire trap, Science Hall. It was now the one building on campus that almost everyone believed would burn sooner or later. Only the less elaborately equipped biology labs remained in its basement, while the top floors now served as classrooms. By desperate efforts the work crews were able to have the basement of Main ready for temporary laboratory use in the fall of 1905, and to complete the whole building by the fall of 1906, all at a total cost of about $102,000.[17]

As so often before, the library ended up the loser. The librarians had gathered the remaining books into three rooms in a Westside Row dorm. Fortunately, some scattered and specialized libraries, such as those for chemistry and geology, survived the fire. During 1906 the library moved to its new quarters in Main. But these were only marginally larger than before, although the two stack floors could hold about 20,000 books. Wiley, the able director of the library (a crippled Vaughn only had the title), proved a wizard at rebuilding the collection. Everyone helped—private collectors, publishers, the Smithsonian Institution, the Library of Congress, the Bureau of Education, West Point, Yale, and several faculty members. Many libraries donated duplicate copies. Thus, within a year, and with an expenditure of only about $9,000, Wiley had the number of books back to 15,000, or well over half as large as before the fire and in most cases with more up-to-date books. Within two more years he had filled almost all the shelf space, proving how disastrous had been the decision to postpone building a new library. From 1910 on, the librarians scrounged for space. As a policy, they distributed needed books and periodicals to graduate seminar rooms around the campus, creating a series of small graduate libraries. A few of those, particularly the one in chemistry, became valuable assets. Of course, the Law and Biblical libraries remained fully separate entities, with the Biblical library moving into new quarters in Wesley in order to absorb over 5,000 volumes from the estate of John Tigert, who died unexpectedly soon after his elevation to bishop and after some very active years on the Vanderbilt board. By 1912 the main library was overrun with about 24,000 volumes, a still inadequate collection for a university. In 1913 the librarians had to find space for the magnificent 6,000 volumes bequeathed by Vaughn. By then the library featured a new interlibrary loan program and boasted that it was able to borrow any book it desired from the Library of Congress.[18]

While the library floundered, Vanderbilt ended up with an almost luxurious Furman Hall. As in 1875, the scientists got what they wanted. An

Glorious Furman Hall (1907)

enterprising Dudley did as well as an earlier Garland. Before all was complete, Furman and its furnishings cost over $144,000, or more than any previous building. It became the new campus showplace, the most modern chemistry-pharmacy building in the United States. It had everything, including pink marble in the grand entry hallway, pull-down screens for steroscopic slides, and special shields to cover the skylights in the large lecture theater. Professors Dudley and McGill had large office suites and private labs. The special subbasement included an ingenious system of pipes and ducts. Fans forced air through the building and to the outside, quickly eliminating odors. Special thermostats governed the mixing of hot and cold air to regulate temperatures. Compressed air and distilled water were piped to every lab. In the first such controversy on campus, students protested the cutting of large trees near Furman, purportedly to allow motorists on West End to view the new masterpiece. But the grounds crews quickly replanted sycamores, dogwood, and redbud trees in the barren space.[19]

197

Professor Dudley in new Furman office and laboratory

Furman ended construction on the main campus until the 1920s. But the exchange with Peabody forced the board to search for a new home for the chancellor. For several years, beginning in 1911, the university had bought up lots and houses along 24th Avenue, either for future expansion or for additional faculty residences. Meanwhile, Peabody took over four of the original campus residences, plus the old stables, forcing the university to build new ones near Westside Row. The board contemplated a new chancellor's residence, perhaps on 24th, but as the Kirklands fled the mad rush of Peabody people, they temporarily moved into the former home of Bishop Hargrove on West End. The university paid over $14,000 to buy and repair this house but considered it a good long-term investment. Before anyone could even plan the new chancellor's residence, Vanderbilt regained its lost campus and with it the old chancellor's home. The board decided to restore it. Because of decaying foundations, it ended up with a practically new building in 1915, and at the mansion-like cost of over $19,000, which a generous William K. Vanderbilt contributed.[20]

Although Kirkland never used all his potential building fund, the completion of Furman in 1907 left university finances in their normal, critical condition. The additions to endowment barely increased the annual income enough to meet steadily increased costs of instruction and the considerable new expenses occasioned by Furman. The university had to have more instructors just to keep up with enrollment increases in the Academic and

Engineering departments. The operating budget for the nonproprietary departments moved up from roughly $100,000 in 1905–1906 to about $120,000 by 1910. An endowment increase of $300,000 (to over $1.6 million) could not quite fund the increase. But gradually, through enrollment increases and the diminution of charity students, the tuition income took up the slack. In 1907, for the first time, students paid almost one-third of costs, or nearly $35,000; by 1909 they paid about $42,000, or more than a third. By then, in most years, Kissam and Westside Row were both full, adding to the endowment income invested in the dorms. But new salaries required $4,000 to $5,000 extra each year and suggested that the campus was still on the road to financial disaster. Someone always came to the rescue at the last moment. In 1911 the $300,000 from the GEB and William K. Vanderbilt, to assist in the exchange with Peabody and the conversion of the new south campus, added almost $200,000 to the endowment (now at $1,761,000), or about $10,000 a year to the operating budget. New Carnegie funds soon took care of the immediate needs of the Medical Department, but all this effort still left the west campus in a precarious situation as late as 1915. In a realistic analysis before the board in 1915, on the eve of dramatic new gifts that marked the next era of Vanderbilt's history, Kirkland stressed the needs of the former Academic Department, now renamed the College of Arts and Science. It alone required $1 million in new endowment. Williams and Amherst colleges each had double the income of the College at Vanderbilt; major departments in such colleges had double the faculty of those at Vanderbilt. Virginia spent 60 percent more for its college courses. By 1915 Vanderbilt still had only ten full professors, some of those still under the normal salary of $3,000. This was only two more than it began with in 1875, and these received slightly lower levels of total compensation than Vanderbilt's first professors. Eleven disciplines had not a single full professor. For this reason Kirkland was ready, by 1915, to launch a new drive in behalf of the College. By then the key professional schools, except for the Biblical, were comparatively better off than the College.[21]

The alumni offered one faint ray of financial hope. In 1908 a more active Alumni Association began a $250,000 campaign, to last over the next ten years. It was not up to such effort, but it expanded its campus presence and in 1912 began a subscription campaign for a full-time office. In 1914 it hired its first, and the South's first, full-time secretary for public relations, fund raising, and the recruitment of students. The university supplemented this with a new publicity bureau, which worked primarily with preparatory schools. Especially promising was a new, closer tie to the Nashville community, a tie cemented by the growing number of local alumni, by the gradually increasing economic role of the university, by an intense involvement created by the church and Peabody struggles, and by the growing success of the Vanderbilt football team. In 1915 the university decided upon more frequent contact with its alumni. It phased out the *Vanderbilt University Quarterly*, which began publication in 1901. The *Quarterly,* a subscription journal sponsored by both the faculty and the graduate club, never quite made it as a scholarly publication. In part, it failed because too few faculty made important contributions. It featured speeches delivered on campus, occasional articles on almost any subject, but devoted almost all of its space to university news. As a public relations effort the university bound the four annual news sections as additional *Bulletins* (a postage-saving device) and sent them, free, to alumni. In 1915 it replaced the *Quarterly* by the new *Vanderbilt Alumnus,* which it published monthly during the academic year.[22]

Both Engineering and Pharmacy continued as virtual affiliates of the Academic Department. After the decline of the 1890s, Engineering enjoyed a relatively stable period, with enrollment fluctuating from about sixty to ninety. With increasingly antiquated equipment and a minimal faculty, the department practically ended its small graduate or professional degree program, primarily awarding a four-year Bachelor of Engineering, which amounted to another degree option for Academic students. In 1907–1908 the two departments jointly announced a new course in agricultural engineering, but the program never fit Vanderbilt's resources. It reflected a continuing interest in the education of farmers and a recognition that many Vanderbilt graduates ended up managing inherited farms or plantations. But the contrived and short-lived program attracted almost no students. Then, after 1914, agriculturally inclined Vanderbilt students could enroll in Peabody's School of Country Life, which at least had specially trained professors. The enthusiasm for agriculture drew some inspiration from Bradford Knapp, a 1892 Vanderbilt graduate, son of Seaman Knapp, and successor to his famous father as head of the new cooperative extension program of the U.S. Department of Agriculture. The young Knapp was a featured alumni speaker on campus in 1912 and then served as alumni representative on the Board of Trust.[23]

The small Pharmacy Department limped along, despite the continued enthusiasm of Dean McGill. By 1915 it was the only subcollegiate program left at Vanderbilt (applicants did not have to have a high school diploma). Efforts to raise standards threatened the department's enrollment. In 1910 it even offered a Doctor of Pharmacy for those who came with a diploma, but it never had more than nine such graduates in any year. In 1914 it began requiring three years of high school (ten units) for entrance and in 1915 capped its collegiate offering (three years of course work) with a pharmaceutical chemistry degree. Even such moderate standards caused a drop from an earlier high of fifty students to only thirty-three in 1914–15. By then Kirkland had serious doubts about whether Vanderbilt should continue such a program.[24]

The Biblical Department enjoyed an ephemeral period of rapid growth, only to have it all turn to ashes with the court decision of 1914. All other departments won; it lost, for increasingly it had depended upon the church for everything—faculty, students, even its operating income. It had finally become what the church refused it in its first quarter-century—the seminary of southern Methodism. It began the new century at a low ebb. Enrollments had dropped to only 39 in 1901–1902. But then the church gave a hand. It paid the cost of a new correspondence course for itinerants, paid the salary of its director, Jesse L. Cuninggim, and, as it grew, for other graders or assistants. Through the generosity of Samuel Cupples of St. Louis, the Biblical slowly gained its own endowment, or over $60,000 by 1903, and much more in sustentation or scholarship funds. To help young ministers who filled Sunday pulpits and to align course work with the new correspondence courses, the Biblical Department shifted to a quarter system in 1904, or three sessions of twelve weeks each, with only four days of class work each week. It required only eight quarters of work for a B.D., one less than the former three-year program. In 1905, in a move designed to attract more students but justified as a greater service to the church, it deliberately lowered its admission standards (a rare tactic at Vanderbilt). It now allowed those without a B.A. to make up deficiencies and still receive a B.D., and it began admitting ministerial candidates over twenty-one who did not even have two years of college. Enrollment soared to 80 in 1903, 90 in 1906, and to peaks of 126 in 1909 and 134 in 1911. In some years almost 2,000 enrolled in correspondence courses prescribed by bishops. Such students read assigned books and then took exams offered by the appropriate professors in the department. Counting Gus Dyer, who taught a sociology course in the Biblical, a part-time elocution instructor, and the correspondence instructor, the faculty now numbered an impressive nine, making it comparable in staff to major northern seminaries. By this time the department was able to offer up to seventy scholarships each year.[25]

After 1900 Kirkland had one central goal for the Biblical Department—to make it self-supporting and stop its drain on the regular endowment. If it were self-supporting, and fully endowed, it could maintain its close ties to the church without implicating the other departments. Short of this, outside benefactors of the university knew that they supported a church-dominated seminary, one that did not even seek non-Methodist students. These concerns lay behind the aborted attempt, in 1908, to form a subsidiary corporation for the Biblical Department. Ironically, the same 1910 General Conference that tried to take over government of the university voted an annual assessment of $20,000 to aid the Biblical and also promised to endow a chair of religious education and Sunday school instruction. This tied in with the burgeoning correspondence work. In the enthusiasm of expansion, Tillett began planning for a new administration building so that he could use Wesley entirely as a dorm. But all the dreams lay shattered after the 1914 Supreme Court decision. Then, in effect, the General Conference disowned the Biblical and immediately moved the correspondence school. In the fall of 1914 only fifty candidates enrolled in the orphaned department, and many of these returned only to complete their last year's work for a degree. Even they risked censure from their bishops. By 1915 the number fell to thirty-three and even that involved some loose counting. By then, Kirkland was ready to give up. An independent seminary needed $1 million in endowment and not even a tenth of this was in the offing. But Tillett and most of his faculty decided to reorganize as a nondenominational seminary. Their new program, ready by 1915, helped launch a new era in Vanderbilt history. The details fit within that story.[26]

The Law Department rather quietly spent its last fifteen years downtown. After 1901 and the move of the Dental Department, it had quarters all to itself in what was now called the Law Building, a building largely leased out to city lawyers and a building that never yielded very high returns. The Law enrollment remained low until 1906 (then about fifty per year), when it moved up to around seventy. For the first time since its 1900 reorganization it enjoyed a balanced budget in 1907. In 1903 its most famous professor, James C. McReynolds, resigned. In the same year, Allen G. Hall, an active temperance advocate, a Presbyterian layman, but frequently bothered by ill health, took over as the department's first full-time instructor and secretary, moving to the deanship after the retirement of the venerable Malone in 1904. The law students now frequently lived on the main campus, formed their own literary society (the John Marshall), and soon after 1910 began lobbying in behalf of moving the department back to campus. The department could not raise its standards as high as it wanted; competition was too intense. It also had difficulty retaining students for even two years because of lax state bar exams. But in 1909–10 it moved to a three-year course and by 1914 came close to joining the Medical School in requiring a year of college work for admission. It was afraid to take such a daring step. In 1914 it hired a second full-time instructor, Charles H. Wilber from the University of Chicago. In the next few years it hoped to move to a full-time teaching staff. Dean Hall died in November, 1915. By then the university had already leased, and would soon sell, the Law Building to the Commercial Club (later the Chamber of Commerce). On January 1, 1916, the department moved back to the third floor of Main, with its law library housed in two large rooms.[27]

From 1901 to 1911, and its move to the south campus, the Dental Department floundered along in its new home at Vauxhall (9th) and Broad. Low enrollments at first forced it to operate at a loss, unable to pay its agreed-upon building rents. Then, in 1905–1906, it merged with another proprietary school, this one affiliated with the University of Tennessee. The merger boosted enrollments from 95 in 1904 to 157 two years later, but absorption of some of the merged property cost $6,000, salaries for merged faculty further added to costs, while the formerly separate faculties fought each other for years. By 1906 Kirkland found the Dental Department more a source of worry than an asset. After the merger, enrollment remained stable, averaging about 135 to 140 each year. This almost met expenses, since the fees in both the Medical and Dental schools went up from $100 to $150 in 1907. The problem was the required rents. When the Dental Department could not pay them, the operating budget of the west campus suffered. Thus, beginning in 1904–1905, William K. Vanderbilt made up the loss on Dental rentals, with his payments varying from the whole $5,000 in 1905 to under $1,000 in 1911, the last year in the old facilities and the last time Vanderbilt assessed rents against the department. The Dental Department took over one of the refurbished south campus buildings in 1912 but faced declining enrollments (109 in 1914–15), in part because it had to meet a new requirement of the American Dental Association—high school graduation as a condition of admission. In 1915 it had an increasingly tenuous status as it followed the Medical Department into a four-year program. Unlike the Medical School, it had no endowments of its own and even with free facilities barely met costs. By then, Kirkland was close to recommending its termination.[28]

The Medical Department survived, overcame almost fatal obstacles, and by 1915 seemed likely to become a first-rank institution. The department, as reorganized in 1895, successfully upgraded academic requirements but suffered from the lack of clinical facilities. By 1904 its graduates competed intellectually with those of better northern schools; none failed board exams in that year, an achievement equaled by only three other schools. Its staff included the ablest Nashville physicians and two or three men of national reputation, particularly John A. Witherspoon, a distinguished clinician and in 1912 president of the American Medical Association (AMA), and a brilliant researcher, William Litterer, Jr., a pathologist and bacteriologist who in 1905 discovered a new bacillus (comparable in importance to Barnard's earlier discovery of new comets). In 1905, for the first time, the Medical Department attained a collegiate status, for then it began requiring high school diplomas, a requirement met in most cases in the immediately preceding years. It also expanded its four yearly terms from six to seven months. In 1907 it became a first-class school by AMA classification standards, or next to the top rank. Enrollment increases led those of any other Vanderbilt department, moving up from 160 in 1901 to 215 in 1906 and to 278 in 1910. In 1909 its two competitors—the University of Tennessee and the University of Nashville—consolidated, driving several angry University of Nashville professors to Vanderbilt. Then, by 1911, as the University of Nashville went out of existence, Vanderbilt absorbed its last competitor and became the only white medical school in the city, with thirty-three instructors and an enrollment that leaped to an overwhelming 396. For the first time in Vanderbilt's history, a department tried to discourage enrollment because of crowding. In most years the proprietors were able to collect normal, part-time salaries of $500. But, increasingly, the key instructors were salaried nonproprietors, and in the key scientific fields such as anatomy, bacteriology, and pathology the department almost had to move to full-time teachers.[29]

Such impressive achievements masked problems. The Vanderbilt's M.D. was in reality only barely a bachelor's degree, not comparable in requirements to a B.A. on the main campus. The high school entrance requirements, unlike the ones in the Academic Department, did not involve certified schools or rigorous unit requirements. Given the quality of public high schools in the South, admission was still porously open. Other problems were more grave. The department lived on student fees, in itself a motive for low standards and few failures. The small Medical Building no longer provided adequate space for laboratories. Without an attached hospital, Vanderbilt graduates were ill prepared to enter their profession, although better prepared than most of those who practiced medicine in the South. In an almost pathetic gesture, the faculty added beds to the basement of their building in 1909 and called it a hospital. Most clinical experience still depended upon the charity outpatient service and work in the city's General Hospital, while some students had to travel to St. Thomas Hospital, near the main campus, in order to observe types of surgery.

Swift changes in medical education, nationally, forced Vanderbilt to choose between giving up on its Medical Department or spending large sums to improve it. In 1909 Abraham Flexner of the Carnegie Foundation visited Nashville and Vanderbilt. He toured the country in order to evaluate all medical institutions. His 1910 report, *Medical Education in the United States and Canada,* became a landmark in American medical education. Except at the Johns Hopkins Medical School, which served as a model for Flexner, the medical education he described was frightening, and most so south of Balti-

The University of Nashville, about 1900

more. Flexner met with Kirkland and began an enduring friendship. The two men soon had neighboring summer cabins in Ontario, Canada, and spent many a day fishing together on their lake. Flexner found no quality medical schools in Tennessee, but the best of a sorry lot, and the only one with real promise, was Vanderbilt's. But in his book, and in even more detailed discussions with Kirkland, he pointed out all its deficiencies. In the wake of this evaluation Kirkland decided not to sell land to Peabody but to swap it for the downtown campus. The downtown facilities offered new possibilities in medical education, but without a hospital the arrangement fell short of what Flexner recommended or of the reforms so quickly adopted by larger northern schools. Kirkland also turned to the GEB and to William K. Vanderbilt for the needed funds for moving and expanding, at the same time that he began early negotiations with the Carnegie people in behalf of a needed endowment.[30]

The new South Campus was plenty large enough for both the Dental and Medical departments. The old University of Nashville campus had six buildings, four quite spacious. Vanderbilt took the old demonstration school building, at the northwest corner of the campus, and enlarged and rebuilt it for use by the Dental Department. A dormitory, Lindsley Hall—at first considered for a hospital—proved too flimsy for repair and was soon salvaged. The main campus building, of sturdy stone construction, became the classroom building for the Medical School but not until after $22,000 in repairs. A smaller administration building, with minor changes, continued in that use. The old president's home became the home for nurses. They now

205

South Campus, Vanderbilt
(from top, clockwise: *Dental School, Administration, Gymnasium, Medical School, Nurses' Home*)

worked in the old Medical Department building, just two blocks away and now fully converted into a small clinic or hospital with sixty beds and fourteen nurses and even a small nursing training program. Finally, the YMCA took over the small, somewhat dilapidated gym and through it provided recreational programs for students.

What was conspicuously lacking in all this was an adequate hospital. The Methodists of Nashville proposed to meet this need. They launched a subscription drive for a new Galloway Memorial Hospital. After two years of difficult negotiation, Kirkland finally deeded it three acres of the south campus in exchange for clinical facilities for his students. Aided by loans from Vanderbilt, the trustees of this enterprise were able to get the shell of their hospital fully enclosed by 1915 but then ran out of funds to complete it. It was soon clear that it would not soon, if ever, be finished. The only final physical requirement for a quality medical school, at least in the post-Flexner era, was adequate laboratory facilities. The old stone building was not spacious enough for such labs. Thus, on May 1, 1913, after several earlier contacts, Kirkland set out the needs of the Medical Department in a long letter to Andrew Carnegie. He asked for $1 million, planning to use $800,000 for endowment, $200,000 to construct a new laboratory building. Carnegie was reluctant in light of his objection to the denominational status of Vanderbilt. But he gave the $200,000 outright and held the $800,000, promising the 4 percent annual interest to the Medical Department. This became a vital part of its operating budget from 1914 on. The Carnegie grant is a story in itself, for it interacted with the church controversy. After extensive planning, including even architectural drawings, in 1915 Kirkland gave up on the new lab building that was to rise behind the old stone building. He noted higher than expected costs as inflated prices spun off from the European war. The excuse for delay was a munificent gift by the senior William Litterer, a Nashville businessman, of the building that had housed the University of Nashville Medical School, and just across 2nd Avenue from the south campus. He gave it for laboratory use, and in honor of his son, the physician and researcher. This reduced the immediate pressure for lab space. Litterer's bequest, incidentally, allowed Vanderbilt to sell the building if it built duplicate facilities elsewhere.[31]

The Carnegie grant was big news, the largest single gift ever received by Vanderbilt. For a time students elevated Carnegie to a position close to Cornelius Vanderbilt. But, in a sense, Carnegie intruded himself into an ongoing court battle. By withholding the $800,000 he seemed enormously to increase the stakes at issue. Even more critical, he made his gift conditional on the formation of a separate, seven-member governing board for the Medical Department, a board that had to include Kirkland and three people experienced in the field of medicine, or a majority chosen by criteria in no wise tied to religion. Should the General Conference have won the right to appoint trustees, no one doubted but that Carnegie would have continued to withhold the $800,000. In fact, when the university won in 1914 he immediately turned the funds over to Kirkland. Thus, one could understand the anger of Hoss and his allies and their vehement attacks upon Carnegie. They saw the tentative grant, and the separate board, as a final trick by Kirkland, a way of making the Medical Department independent and a clever means of winning public support to his side.

Carnegie's money did have that effect. The gift added one more reason for many people to pray for a Kirkland victory, at least people in the Nashville area or those concerned about medical education in the South. Fear of losing the gift pulled the Medical faculty and students fully into the controversy, and for the first time in the university's history the whole student body was unified. Actually, Kirkland tried to keep confidential the terms of the grant until the court rendered a verdict. The publicity made him look devious. Kirkland had not bargained for a split gift or for the implied conditions. But he had supported the idea of a separate board and believed it would aid in the development of the Medical Department. It only paralleled the degree of separation he had tried for years to gain for the Biblical Department. Kirkland actually deplored Carnegie's extreme sensitivity to denominationalism and had earlier criticized the rigidity of rules enforced by the Carnegie Fund. But, in another perspective, Carnegie's qualms vindicated Kirkland's warnings that Vanderbilt would surely decline, by slow attrition and financial starvation, unless it retained an independent and self-perpetuating board.[32]

By 1914 the Medical Department seemed worlds ahead of where it had been only three years earlier. It had a campus, the necessary classrooms, and, for the short term, all the lab space it could use. It also had an endowment providing $32,000 a year and could expect up to $30,000 or $40,000 in income each year from student fees. Suddenly, financially, it was by far the most secure department of Vanderbilt. How did it use its new wealth? It tried to move up to the big time. In 1913 it decided to meet the AMA requirements for the highest grade school, a class A+. By then, it had six full-time professors and was seeking others. Entering students now had to have fourteen high school units plus a year of college credit in chemistry, physics, biology, and modern languages. This was far below the best schools (the Johns Hopkins required a college degree) but practically wiped out the entering class in 1914, when only twenty-one qualified. At the same time, the Academic Department instituted a one-year premed course; fifteen students entered it the first year. The Medical School (so renamed in 1915) now planned for a smaller but more able student body, with not much over 100 in regular attendance. The new buildings allowed the Medical Department to pull together scattered books, add to these a large donation by the Nashville Academy of Medicine, and initiate a new, staffed medical library with over 4,000 volumes. The new governing board first met in November, 1914, and took up again the aborted plans for a laboratory building. In all these ways the outlook was bright. As Flexner had urged, Vanderbilt had already taken the lead in improving medical education not only in the state but in the South. The one large, increasingly intractable hurdle remained a suitable hospital.[33]

In the memory of the alumni, the years immediately before 1914 later seemed innocent, golden years on the Vanderbilt campus. The alumni remembered, above all else, the glorious football team under Dan McGugin, the eloquent and poetic tributes of Grantland Rice, the last great era of hazing and popular pranks, the first dramatic club presentations, the grandeur of senior proms or "Germans," and the growing role of women. They too easily forgot the insecurities of the legal battle, the accumulating problems that plagued fraternities, the shift away from student self-government and toward *in loco parentis,* or the terrible sense of moral decay that engulfed the campus by 1912.

Vanderbilt gradually became larger, more diverse. In 1913 the west campus enrolled approximately 600 students; the south campus over 500. The comfortable little community of 1875 was no more. The growing number of junior staff, most forced to live off campus, helped create a more impersonal student-faculty relationship. But faculty wives still gave teas for freshmen and sponsored the senior prom. And the chair professors were all still in campus houses, still helping merge aspects of domesticity with college life. That is, students had daily contact with such domestic chores as laundering or gardening and knew the ever-present campus children. That is a story in itself, the unique experience of two generations of "faculty brats." The domestic and the academic occasionally clashed. In 1905 the Board of Trust formally banned all dogs on campus; they attended some classes in larger numbers than students. But the campus children, who had just raised their money for

Glee Club in 1906

the new clock, addressed a petition to the board, one of the most irresistible it ever received: "We the children of Vanderbilt campus beg that we may be allowed to have one little dog apiece. We will not let him bite." The board referred this petition to the Executive Committee, which granted it. But within two years the board was again passing rules to prohibit dogs and other animals on campus. No such rules ever had much effect.[34]

Students seemed ever more involved in activities. The outer boundaries of their social life involved fraternities and sororities on one hand, the YMCA on the other, with a certain tension between the two extremes. In addition to all the earlier clubs—the literary societies, the glee club, the history club, special interest groups—new ones abounded. In 1901 Gus Dyer formed a social science club to balance the existing history club. In 1903 or 1904 young men founded a commodore club to be made up of the leading seniors on campus. It was a cross between a snobbish fraternity, a male honor society, and a social club, since it soon sponsored annual dances. In 1910 it led in the formation of a floundering student association, an informal effort to introduce an all-student activities fee. Loyal students were urged to pay $10 a year, which gave them free tickets to all sports events and free subscriptions to the *Hustler, Observer,* and *Commodore* (the new name, after 1909, of the earlier *Comet*). These flourishing publications involved increasing numbers of students; such students formed a spectator club in 1912, open to all apprentice journalists. When Edwin Mims got to Vanderbilt he formed his students into a new

209

Marching Band, 1908

literary club (these rose and fell periodically). The glee club still dominated in music and took extensive tours each year, but by 1905 a pep band came to all football games and soon matured into something close to a regular marching band. Finally, after years of futile effort, Vanderbilt students put on a play. The women led the way with informal performances in 1909, giving the jealous young men the incentive they needed. They joined the women in 1910 in a first, and very impressive, performance of "The College Widow" at the Vendome. Their director and instructor was Pauline Townsend of Belmont College; she also played the lead role. A second performance in the spring of 1911, and still another the next year, kept the effort going, but interest declined after 1912, when religious revivals and moral reform took center stage at Vanderbilt.[35]

The student body still came, usually, from affluent or middle-class families, mostly southern and with increasing percentages from the immediate Nashville area. The Biblical students remained the poorest and the least involved in campus social life. Almost all of them had scholarships. A small percentage of Academic and Engineering students tried to earn all, or part, of their costs, and for years the YMCA maintained a local placement office. In 1907, for example, thirty-one Academic and Engineering students reported earnings from $25 to over $2,000 during the year. They worked either for local firms, as salesmen, as tutors, or in university cleaning and catering jobs. A rather inexact study indicated that they suffered a bit in their grades. As yet Vanderbilt offered no formal assistance in job seeking by graduates, but Kirkland served as virtually a one-man placement office, receiving job notices and directing students to employers. Vanderbilt students, when they graduated, flocked into the professions. Of all Academic graduates up to 1906 (565), 190 were teachers and 108 lawyers, with only 43 as ministers, but note that the survey excluded the Biblical graduates, almost all of whom remained in the ministry. Only business came close to the professions, with 79. Medicine had 29, but again note that college work was not yet needed for medical admission and that most of Vanderbilt's physicians had not graduated from the Academic Department. Except for farming, with 12, no other occupations counted more than ten, except that 14 of 49 women graduates simply classified themselves as wives. By then, 29 graduates had died.[36]

Campus life now had its annual rhythms. In the fall new students first gathered at a college night sponsored by the YMCA and then heard an opening address by Chancellor Kirkland. Immediately, those so inclined were swept up in what was then called "spiking" (rushing). They also quickly began attending football games and then in lesser numbers other sports. During the year each fraternity had at least one dance, often two, and several campuswide social events clustered around Christmas. The YMCA had ongoing activities— Bible classes, charitable efforts, and various social gatherings. West End Methodist had a large Bible class for young men, one earlier taught by Kirkland, and Stella Vaughn taught a small class largely for Vanderbilt women. The pace of events increased as commencement neared. The literary societies still vied for speaking honors. Factions formed around the highly contested election of a Bachelor of Ugliness, which occurred in a convention-like meeting in the chapel. Only once, in 1909, did the process become so corrupt, with so many ballots stuffed, that the innocent electee resigned and Kirkland did not make the award of this, the most prized degree of all, at the commencement. In 1908, and quite seriously, the *Hustler* first proposed a comparable award for women; it gagged on "old maid of ugliness" and opted instead for "maid of beauty," which sounded fine but was not a "degree." Commencement week was full of events—speeches, sermons, moot courts, and from 1902 on a senior prom, a senior banquet at the Maxwell House, a large gathering of alumni for their dinner (seniors attended), and the awarding of degrees, usually in the chapel but in 1905, the year of the fire, on the lawn in front of the chancellor's house.[37]

After 1900 diversity makes it difficult to characterize students' beliefs or values. The amount of internal conflict documents the broad continuum. Yet, in certain respects the students remained amazingly homogeneous. The campus simply had no rebels, no students who defied conventional political or social beliefs or who launched any visible campaign in behalf of radical change. A student poll at the election of 1908 showed 125 students for a Democratic Bryan, only eight for a Republican Taft, and a miniscule two for a Socialist Debs, who attracted a considerable student following on most northern campuses. Nothing in the student publications suggest that the strong Bryan support reflected incipient populism on campus. Kirkland led the students in condemning the violence of night-riders in west Tennessee and in decrying the ignorance of small farmers and other protesters. Race remained a compelling issue. Few students spoke up for Negro rights, not even for legal equality. But in addition to Bryan, the students did invite Booker T. Washington to address them in chapel, the first Negro to come on campus in a nonservile role. He used a well-rehearsed speech, close to the one he first gave at Atlanta. Perhaps more revealing of majority attitudes was the 1914 *Hustler* editor who asked that the "bunch of niggers" loafing around the gym be swept off campus, a campus that should not be "infected" by "niggers." One surprising speaker was the Socialist editor of *Class Struggle*, invited to campus by Gus Dyer, whose concern for urban reforms made him the nearest but very mild approximation of a radical on the faculty. Later, he seemed completely to switch his political allegiances.[38]

Each year a few exceptionally bright or popular students stood out from the mass. In 1904 John Tigert, Jr., the son of Bishop Tigert and the grandson of McTyeire, combined football stardom with academic excellence, winning an early Rhodes scholarship. In 1908 a brilliant brother and sister—Mary Florence Teague and Willard Conwell Teague—won the two prizes for the best entrance exams. Descendants of Bishop Soule, they went on to win membership in Phi Beta Kappa, to amass academic averages around 95, while Mary Florence took the Founder's medal. In 1909 Noel T. Dowling gained an enormous popular following, was editor of the *Commodore*, and was elected Bachelor of Ugliness. He excelled as much as any student of his generation in leadership skills. In 1911 a woman, Eleanor Richardson, was Founder's medalist and a Phi Beta Kappa. Finally, a son of a Tennessee Methodist minister won the most honors. John Crowe Ransom was Founder's medalist in 1909, editor of the *Observer*, an editor on the *Hustler*, Phi Beta Kappa, and finally a Rhodes scholar.[39]

As those achievements indicate, women were not only increasing at Vanderbilt but threatening to win all honors. Evidence of male resentment mounted with their every success. In the spring of 1915 the women published a special edition of the *Observer*, locally referred to as the *Observe-her*, the first such honor for them. They tried the most difficult genre—humor and satire—and of course could not sustain this for a whole edition, but they came closer than anyone before to publishing a humor magazine. Within two years envious male students would launch their own humor magazine. A junior editor of the *Hustler*, James G. Stahlman, became downright nasty in his cruel put-down of the women's effort. More threatening to the men, perhaps, was women's academic leadership. In 1914 their academic average was 81.72, that of men 71.47, and their lead had been even greater in earlier years, when the women had averaged as high as 87. From 1908 through 1912 Academic women were Founder's medalists each year, and in 1913 a brilliant male barely beat out a female in the Academic competition. By then, the student body contained 78 women, or just over 20 percent of the Academic enrollment. Their achievement, undoubtedly, reflected the self-selection involved in their applying to Vanderbilt, their lesser involvement in sports and other diversions, and possibly the absence of dorms. At the time all but twenty-two women were from Nashville and lived at home.[40]

Except for the lack of dorms, women faced no major legal impediments. They seemed exceptionally active, involved, and happy. They made it into every area of campus life, from a woman editor on the *Observer* to a reporter on the *Hustler,* from a basketball team that never lost a game for several years to a girls' club, which they formed in 1909. In 1915 they formed a YWCA, with a room reserved for them on Westside Row. They shamed the men by the calm, successful conduct of their two sororities. They fashioned rules for rushing in 1907 and for years apparently never turned anyone away who sought membership. For unclear reasons, the two independent local sororities chose to affiliate with two national groups and eventually became the two most exclusive on campus. Phi Kappa Upsilon became a branch of Kappa Alpha Theta in 1904, the first such in the South, and in 1909 Theta Delta Theta became a branch of Delta Delta Delta. Both sororities eventually bought their own houses. These coeds could also rejoice at the larger role of women on campus, from minor instructional roles in physical education, speech, and dramatics to prominent speakers, such as Jane Addams, to the 1913 recognition of a woman as librarian (Doris Sanders) and as the first university registrar (Mary W. Haggard).[41]

Women pushed their way forward. None of the men eased their way or even invited them. At the highest level of university government they were not yet fully accepted. Kirkland vacillated. He wanted to do justice to their aspirations. He and his wife entertained the women students in their home. Mary Kirkland was particularly helpful to them. But her husband somehow felt they violated the proper order. As late as 1915 he argued that it was not yet clear that coeducation was beneficial either to men or women. He wanted the board to consider whether the women should remain, or whether Vanderbilt should limit them by a quota. He was sure a continued increase would make Vanderbilt less desirable for men but never clarified exactly why he thought that was so. His goal, long deferred, was to get them off into a women's annex, decently segregated for at least the freshmen and sophomore years. The issue came to a head in a backhanded sort of way in 1914–15. The faculty, in the midst of formulating rules for practically everything, had to enact those governing women's teams that now proposed to play games at distant colleges. The faculty at first voted simply to apply the same rules of academic eligibility that applied to men's teams, but Mims objected and asked for a committee investigation.

This committee, in May of 1915, surveyed the whole range of issues affecting women. The survey was positive and favorable to women's role. Mims wanted an advisor for women, equal recognition for them in the

Bulletin, a dean of women as soon as possible, and their own social center or house. But the committee recommended the abolition of all women's inter-collegiate athletics. The women might continue physical education or in-tramural sports, perhaps at the new Peabody gym. But competitive contests were not allowed at other major universities (correct) and were not in accordance with the "best tradition and practice of the entire country." The faculty was not nearly as involved in the issue as Mims and tabled his recommendations. For years thereafter, Stella Vaughn continued to coach her girl's basketball team in games with neighboring colleges.[42]

The men did well in sports. Football remained dominant, although Van-derbilt fielded teams in baseball, basketball, and track, with the baseball team the southern champion in 1912 (15 wins and 3 losses) and with Vanderbilt consistently first or second in the annual Southern Intercollegiate Athletic Association track meet. Yet, the *Hustler* struggled in vain to maintain interest, or many paying customers, for these other sports, such was the appeal of football. The glory years actually dated back into the mid-1890s, when Vanderbilt first became the southern powerhouse in football. But for over a decade, from about 1895 through 1905, the game faced intense criticism nationally and repeated threats from the Vanderbilt Board of Trust. As late as 1904 a board committee condemned all off-campus games and recom-mended that the chancellor and faculty permit only intramural competition. From then on, Bishop Hoss led a group of churchmen who denounced football; they brought even athletics into the church-university struggle. But the students were not about to concede this issue to the bishops. By 1901 Vanderbilt football was an established tradition. The athletic association ran the best program in the South, save possibly at Sewanee. But the one-sided record (Vanderbilt lost only once in 1901, 1902, and 1903) largely reflected the lack of able opponents. In a pattern that lasted until about 1914, Vander-bilt played one season of five or six games with completely outclassed opponents, and a competitive schedule of from one to three games. This was not entirely Vanderbilt's choice; it was necessary to go outside the Southeast to find teams of Vanderbilt's caliber, which meant either high costs to lure such teams to Nashville or long trips to play them away.[43]

By a well-established myth, a new football era began in 1904. At the time nothing suggested a major transition. In the established pattern, the athletic association hired a coach for the fall season, paying him for his two or three months of part-time work. In 1904 the association lured Daniel McGugin down from Ann Arbor. A lawyer, McGugin had played on a very successful Michigan team and then had assisted the increasingly famous Michigan coach, Fielding H. Yost, which was why he was invited. He both inspired and perfected the team, by more discipline, more rigorous training, closer coop-eration, emphasis upon speed, and a few new strategies or plays. Against weak competition Vanderbilt won all nine games in 1904 and was scored on only once in a fluke play. It handily defeated its only worthy opponent

Sewanee game, Thanksgiving, 1902

(Vanderbilt 27 to Sewanee 0). It outclassed its opponents by a horrendous 452 to 4, coasting to such victories as 97 to 0 over Central of Kentucky. The problem, for the athletic association, was attracting fans to such one-sided contests. In 1905 McGugin returned and soon became the most popular person on campus. He eventually moved to Nashville, gained a part-time teaching post in the Academic and Engineering departments, and developed his own law practice. Yost visited Nashville frequently, joined in the preparation for some key games, and married a Nashville woman. This established a tie between Vanderbilt and the University of Michigan and led to the first big game of 1905—Vanderbilt at Michigan. Vanderbilt lost 18 to 0, but even that seemed a moral victory, the first southern team to play on a near equal basis one of the northern giants. In 1906 Vanderbilt came within an inch of beating Michigan (10 to 4) and in neither 1905 or 1906 came even close to losing another game. In addition, it played a special contest with the touring, and probably tired, Carlisle Indians, winning its first glorious victory by 4 to 0 in what local newspapers called the greatest game ever played in the South. Other representative scores in 1906 included Vanderbilt 78 to Alabama 0, 45 to Texas 0, and 20 to Sewanee 0. So dominant was Vanderbilt in the South that other struggling teams, such as those at Georgia, Alabama, and Tennessee, hesitated to play the Commodores or sour-graped their one-sided losses by charges of Vanderbilt professionalism.[44]

The greatest McGugin era lasted only a decade, until other southern

215

The football heroes of 1905
(young coach Daniel McGugin is second from left, front row)

universities adopted programs comparable to that at Vanderbilt. In 1907 Vanderbilt tied Navy and lost at home to Michigan (8–0) before a record crowd that included the governor of Tennessee. By 1908 the big games attracted much local publicity and earned sizable profits for the athletic association. The association updated the old Dudley field stands, made room for automobiles on both ends, elected the first of a series of "men of the cheer" in 1908, and even installed practice lights (strips of bulbs). But, as a type of warning, Vanderbilt lost two games in 1908 (to Michigan and Ohio State) and only tied Sewanee. Maybe McGugin had lost his touch. At the football banquet that ended the season Grantland Rice, who had written frequent, eloquent paeans to McGugin, ended a poem on "Alumni Football" with the famous lines: "For when the one great scorer comes to write against your name, he marks—not that you won or lost—but how you played the game."[45]

In 1909 Vanderbilt dropped Michigan from its schedule but lost to both Ohio State and, more embarrassing, to Sewanee. For the first time in years it

216

could not claim to be southern champion. But the circus atmosphere grew, with huge bonfires and rallies and after major victories a nightshirt parade by boys through downtown Nashville. Then came 1910, the greatest year of them all. Vanderbilt played neither Ohio State nor Michigan but instead traveled to Yale, one of the four or five greatest teams in the nation. It used its speed to "win" a 0–0 tie, and as the telegraph news reached Nashville the students set off the wildest demonstration yet; 500 students joined in the nightshirt parade in what they acclaimed once again as the greatest "victory" in history. When the students demanded a holiday, a clever Kirkland promised them one if President Hadley gave one to the Yale students, for they had as much right to be proud as did Vanderbilt students. A tie was a tie. That Thanksgiving almost 10,000 gathered to see Vanderbilt defeat a great Sewanee team by 23 to 6. The athletic association made this the first alumni homecoming game, a tradition in subsequent years. Vanderbilt had lost out that spring in its fight with the church but it made up for all that with its glorious undefeated season, the first since 1904.

In many ways Vanderbilt had an even stronger team in 1911, but lost 9 to 8 to Michigan, the only team to score on Vanderbilt. But an ominous note began to sound in 1912. Vanderbilt had another great team; it beat Virginia on homecoming and lost only 9 to 3 to a great Harvard team, yet it only tied Auburn 7–7. Other southern teams were improving; Vanderbilt dominance was about over. In 1913 a McGugin team lost, and decisively, to both Virginia and Michigan. Then 1914 was a disaster, incomprehensible to Vanderbilt and Nashville fans. Vanderbilt lost to Michigan, North Carolina, Virginia, Tennessee, Auburn, and Sewanee, winning only against smaller, warm-up teams. Vanderbilt would soon surge back and still lead all other southern teams throughout the 1920s, but it would never again so dominate southern football. And, in retrospect, it is noteworthy that, except for the Carlisle Indians, Vanderbilt gained its first national reputation in football, not by wins but by a series of ties or narrow losses. In the whole golden decade from 1904 to 1913 Vanderbilt never beat Michigan, Ohio State, Navy, Harvard, or Yale.[46]

As the church fight developed, student conduct at Vanderbilt became a subject of denomination-wide debate. On campus the earlier tradition of student self-government began to break down. After 1905 the chancellor and faculty felt they had to impose more rules. Then, after 1910, students became deeply involved in the issue of alleged decadence, an issue that eventually divided student against student and led to almost vigilante control. This joined with an emotional religious revival, and to the greatest, possibly the most repressive moral crusade in Vanderbilt's history.

The opening of Kissam Hall in 1901 launched dorm life at Vanderbilt. For the first time masses of students lived in proximity to each other and along hallways. By 1905 the dorm was full, although a growing number of fraternity houses drew increasing numbers off campus. With dorm life came an increase in the hazing of freshmen, particularly by sophomores. Also, some fraternities hazed their initiates. Hazing could take a humorous turn, as when freshmen in one fraternity had to carry roosters concealed in their trousers. Their crowing interrupted classes and, in one memorable case, even the chancellor's remarks in chapel. He laughed at the first crowing, not the second and third. The fraternity suffered probation. Another innocuous requirement, adopted in 1906–1907, was a required green cap (beany) for all freshmen. But the problem was enforcement of such childish rules. Sophomores frequently resorted to the paddle, to scalping (cutting off all hair), to tying freshmen to trees, or losing and stranding them at night out in the country. By 1905 freshmen and sophomores fought each other in the halls of Kissam, and Kirkland first used a chapel talk to condemn hazing and demand its termination. The faculty agreed. Hazing slowed a bit but did not stop, and it reached a violent climax in 1907. After only mild insults to the incoming freshmen, the sophomores interrupted a freshman dance. The freshmen retaliated, overwhelming and completely disrupting the sophomore dance. Two days of raiding by each group, with frequent scalpings, followed, ending in a midnight siege of about twenty-five freshmen clustered in a Kissam suite. After battering down two doors and some hand-to-hand combat, the now frightened boys called a truce, with six freshmen as sacrificial victims. Shorn and left stranded in the country, they hired a dairyman to bring them back to campus. Kirkland, then away from campus, rushed back at the frightened call of Dean Tillett. He spoke, separately, to both classes, disbanded the freshman club, and exacted a signed pledge from each boy to end all hazing. Officially it ended in 1907 but in ever new guises kept reappearing in subsequent years.[47]

Fraternities became the next problem, an insoluble one. Slowly their role had changed. In the early years they provided the needed social contacts for the scattered young men. At first the fraternities had been more open than exclusive and had competed with each other for the ablest men. The medal winners, the highest academic achievers, had almost all been fraternity men. This changed after 1900. One after another the fraternities bought or leased off-campus houses, establishing small, exclusive, often self-indulgent little communities. They retreated from active involvement in the campus. At the beginning of each fall semester they disrupted academic life by a highly competitive spiking season, an ongoing annoyance to the faculty. The fraternities united in 1902 in a council and in 1905 experimented with a delayed rush, initiating freshmen only in the second semester. They returned to the old system in 1906 and despite intense faculty pressure would not change in subsequent years. In 1908 Kirkland devoted a whole address on the fraternity problem, noting that the houses served a purely social role, that fraternities now impeded academic achievement, and that too many houses served as a cover for "dissipation." In 1910 he explained that fraternities simply had to lower costs to students, adopt a new rushing system, and give more emphasis to scholarship. He ominously predicted an end to fraternities at Vanderbilt if existing conditions continued.[48]

In 1908 a faculty committee, joined by representatives of fraternities, began a long inquiry. In 1910 the committee promulgated a set of stringent rules governing fraternities, rules that incensed the fraternity men on campus, who claimed they were being treated like children. The faculty felt they had been acting like children. The rules limited each house to two dances a year, set up strict chaperone requirements, mandated a midnight curfew on all dances or parties, denied students with grade deficiencies the right to attend parties in other than their own house, and reiterated strong rules against gambling, alcoholic drinks, or lewdness. To enforce these rules it required each chapter to appoint a supervising committee that had to render monthly reports to a faculty supervising committee. Violations led to penalties, from an end to rushing privileges up to and including suspension. By then, the fraternities were also under considerable student attack from the theological students in Wesley and from the roughly 50 percent of students not in fraternities. Campus leadership had gradually shifted toward non-Greeks. By 1915 nonfraternity students began a fight to wrest control of the *Commodore* from the fraternities; in 1914 a Vanderbilt club or student union was formed, with a new, specially furnished club room in the basement of Kissam.

Fraternity men were usually from affluent families and could be snobbish and clannish. They were also increasingly ill educated. A 1914 analysis of average grades revealed a deficiency rate in fraternities of over 50 percent to less than 40 percent for non-Greeks. The academic average of fraternity men was almost two points behind, and a few fraternities had terrible records—those in Kappa Phi averaged only a deplorable 63.94, the equivalent of a D – average. The fraternities would not act, so finally in 1915 the faculty mandated a delayed rush (until after November grade reports), restricted membership to regular students with good academic standing, and required all freshmen to live in Kissam. Some of the problems were alleviated by the new rules.[49]

The widespread concern about fraternities revealed a developing cultural clash at Vanderbilt. Counting divinity students, over half the students on the west campus remained Methodist, many quite faithful to the church and its traditions. For the most devout, any dancing or imbibing offended. Such students not only deplored the new vices but a frivolous, carefree approach to college so prevalent among fraternity men. Such serious students supported the organization that now symbolized the opposite values from those of the more socially oriented Greeks, the YMCA. With the completion of Kissam, this interdenominational Protestant organization moved into the old Westside dining hall and for years assumed the role of a campus ministry. In 1902 the "Y" employed its first part-time student secretary. Slowly the "Y" grew until, by 1913, it employed two full-time trained secretaries, one on each campus. It now offered over twenty noncredit courses on the Bible and other religious subjects, made the first efforts on campus openly to discuss the problem of race, and enlisted students in local service causes, such as boys' clubs, a prison ministry, and settlement work. It brought frequent speakers or evangelists to campus and in 1910 staged the first of a series of annual revival meetings. The YMCA engaged experienced and eloquent ministers to travel to campuses for a series of lectures; some were very effective speakers who knew their college audiences. Several of the ablest had trained in the Vanderbilt Biblical Department, which sent an increasing number of its ministers into YMCA work. The new revival approach was not heavily emotional or doctrinal but one that emphasized moral regeneration. A typical 1910 lecture was on "sex impurity," a talk that included warnings against all forms of social dancing. Out of this revival came plans for student rescue work in the downtown.[50]

The burgeoning YMCA role paralleled the 1910 condemnation of Vanderbilt at the Asheville General Conference. For the first time Methodists were publicly condemning student dissipation. The charges and rumors of immorality grew apace within church circles. Of course, any such charges are bound to contain a grain of truth. By 1911 Kirkland and the faculty at last conceded a serious problem and then began their crackdown on fraternities. The editorials by Hoss and others spread to the preparatory schools and led to some damaging warnings to prospective Vanderbilt students. Parents became apprehensive. The issue of moral decay became a central, widely debated issue on campus in 1911. The students met, argued, and finally came up with new, self-policing techniques. Tentatively, the students proposed an elaborate student council, made up of ten men empowered to investigate and try students charged with "poor conduct," those bringing discredit upon Vanderbilt; at the conclusion of a trial, the council would recommend penalties to the chancellor. Perhaps fortunately, the students eventually voted down such a powerful council, substituting instead supervising committees in the dorms to duplicate those already mandated for fraternities. These were to "revolutionize" student conduct and were to report all offenses to the faculty. As organized, the committees in Kissam seemed close to repressing all dissent. One proposed not only the goal of preventing students from wandering from paths of morality but promised to get them to lead a "Christian life." Campus revivals seemed to increase the zeal of such committees and made more perilous the life of the worldly or, possibly, even nonconforming rebels, if such existed at Vanderbilt.[51]

In 1912 a deeply divided faculty (the vote was 8 to 7) granted to upper classmen a supervising role over freshmen, one of the original demands of the supervising committees. The issue had many moral ambiguities and seemed to some a back-door reintroduction of hazing. Even before reporting to the faculty, the supervising upperclassmen could use "corporal" punishment "within reasonable limits." "Reasonable" meant that they could paddle all freshmen who disobeyed the requirement of green caps (upperclassmen confiscated all other headgear). The avowed purpose of the caps was to enable upperclassmen to identify all freshmen who entered a saloon, gambling house, or bawdy house, or who imbibed at any place. The paddlings had to stop short of "permanent injury," and upperclassmen had to report repeated offenses to the faculty. The faculty reluctantly granted such new hazing rights in their effort to retain student cooperation in the supervisory committees and in the enforcement of all the new rules. The strategy seemed to work for only a year or two.[52]

The moral crusade continued through 1915. In 1912 the issue came to a head at commencement. All the talk of dissipation came to rest on charges in three areas—gambling, drinking, and illicit sex. Even the glee club faced charges of gambling and apparently the illicit entertaining of women on one of its tours; Kirkland added new pledges concerning conduct and suspended one tour. Churchmen seemed to view social dancing and illicit sex either as identical or as intimately linked. In a reaction to church criticism, the faculty in 1912 voted to delete any reference in the official commencement program to a senior dance. A preacher had protested and some alumni were upset. This was all a bit hypocritical, since the faculty did not cancel any dances or impose any controls over student-planned activities. The theological students backed a student effort to follow the faculty precedent—to eliminate all references to dances from their own commencement programs. The students finally voted to have two unannounced dances, one for the juniors and one for the seniors. The dances had been part of strategies to get nonseniors to stay around for commencement. This issue caused no end of student wrangling, with the student "libertarians," or "libertines," denouncing the hypocrisy and snidely suggesting a new commencement made up entirely of prayers and sermons, climaxed by the awarding of certificates for "righteousness."[53]

By 1913 the crusades spread beyond the campus. Professor Carré enlisted his students to help clean up downtown Nashville. They investigated gambling dens and the "tenderloin district," and publicly described the local evils in what must have turned out to be a much sought-after guidebook. Dyer enlisted his sociology students in prison reform, all as part of a larger effort to take the gospel into the streets. Finally, to refute earlier charges from the proprietary schools, in 1913 Vanderbilt students first organized gospel teams to carry their own revival to the academies. For at least two years they visited and reported a very successful response. Presumably, reformed students would now enroll in Vanderbilt, causing fewer problems in the future. On campus the students gathered in a now frequent mass assembly to discuss persistent misbehavior in chapel. For the only time in the whole crusade, women were implicated. They promised reform but pointed out that they had to sit so far back in the balcony they had difficulty hearing speakers anyway.[54]

The climax of campus moral regeneration paralleled the winning Supreme Court opinion. In February, 1915, in the aftermath of the Supreme Court verdict, the YMCA sponsored a "campaign for Christian living," the largest campus revival effort in Vanderbilt's history. It was to be a revival of religion without any "crude emotionalism." Three evangelists, one just back from mission work in the Far East, gave the special chapel and evening sermons. Preparatory meetings even took place in fraternity houses. Kirkland opened the first session on a Sunday. The sermons followed. A former football hero came back to "take a stand for Christian living." The missionary proved a powerful speaker, winning over his audience. He preached largely on sin and the need for moral reform, joining an emphasis on personal piety with a social gospel emphasis on Christian service. The speakers also went to the south campus to preach to dentists and physicians. Beginning on the third day, the speakers began asking for "decisions for Christ" and by the final session on Wednesday had 200 signed cards of commitment. These pledged the student to lead a Christian life and to take part in one or more Christian activities on campus, such as the gospel teams, YMCA work, or social service in town. Leaders not only followed up on these cards but met with students to discuss personal problems. In so many ways this crusade parodied the modern, "up-to-date" revivalism that flowered later through the mass media. But the new techniques joined with more traditional values and methods. The faculty did not stand aloof; many joined right in. According to the *Hustler,* several virtually preached sermons in their classes and returned to "old time revival" doctrines. Edwin Mims, for example, enthusiastically involved himself as always, wanted even more "decisions," and gladly agreed to do follow-up work among those who signed cards.[55]

The great revival brought to a close the first phase of Vanderbilt's history. Even as the university won its emancipation from ecclesiastical control and entered a new and independent era, both students and faculty clung all the more to older values. One simply cannot imagine such a campus revival in 1875 or even 1895. Vanderbilt students participated in the gradual shift in basic beliefs and operative values that wracked the church with internal conflict. But they were far from rebellious in 1915. In spite of all the accusations, most remained almost frighteningly conventional in their be-havior, although they tried to imitate what students did elsewhere, to assume an appropriate student identity. But the worldly pose either did not work or led to deep feelings of guilt. From 1911 to 1914 faculty and students had endured, or possibly enjoyed, an orgy of self-analysis and moral flagellation. As they broke loose from their Methodist past, they also clung more zealously to it. The ill-defined tensions between orthodox Methodist beliefs and mod-ern revisions, between an older Methodist spirituality or moral asceticism and a new exploration of sensual indulgence, were not an issue just within the church. They challenged and confused Vanderbilt students, who did not march confidently into the new era. Rather, with much shame and guilt, they backed into it.

PART FIVE

Rockebilt University
(1915–1930)

 IN *1915 Vanderbilt entered a new and generally prosperous era.
As an independent private university it now qualified for major
gifts from northern philanthropists. Being southern, it did not need
to demonstrate its needs. Chancellor Kirkland, now at the peak of
his career, symbolized its integrity and trustworthiness. From 1915
to 1930 Vanderbilt received over $20 million from the Vanderbilt
family, from the Carnegie Corporation, and above all from various
Rockefeller charities. The Rockefeller-funded General Education
Board (*GEB*) gave over $14 million to the Vanderbilt Medical
School alone, and over $1.9 million to the rest of the university,
thus making Vanderbilt, by far, its largest single beneficiary.
Because of this aid, Vanderbilt was able to move beyond its stormy
childhood by 1930. The frequent moves and reorganizations were
over. The university was now settled on one campus, had all its
enduring schools, and enjoyed a stable academic identity.*

*After 1925 the new, almost luxurious Medical School almost
overwhelmed the university. It dwarfed the other professional schools
and far exceeded the College of Arts and Science in endowment,
faculty salaries, quality of staff, and national reputation and
influence. But the College grew rapidly and attracted a few very
bright young professors. By the late 1920s they had nourished a bit
of an intellectual renaissance, albeit one unappreciated and at
times almost unnoticed by students or by the older faculty. In the
long run, the influence of a few young poets, who called themselves
Fugitives, and a few social critics, who celebrated Agrarianism,
exceeded even that of the ablest scientists attracted to the new
Medical School. Ironically, neither the Medical School nor the work
of the young intellectual rebels sprang from older Vanderbilt
traditions or always reflected the goals of Vanderbilt's
administrators. Northern philanthropists planted the Medical*

223

School, shaped its early policies, and made Vanderbilt only the site of its flowering. It became an alien but very vigorous graft upon an old and undernourished tree. And the most vital intellectual ferment in the College came from young rebels, often frustrated and unhappy, who reacted against the small, utterly conventional oligarchy that controlled their College.

10

Nuts and Bolts

THE BREAK from the Methodist church changed little on campus outside the now threatened Biblical Department. But it symbolized a new beginning. The faculty in 1915 adopted new policies. First, it finally abolished the old, now quaint nomenclature it had kept as a legacy from Garland. It renamed the departments. The Academic became the College of Arts and Science. The professional departments became schools, while the old schools (i.e., English, chemistry, history) became departments.

To go along with these label changes, changes only gradually assimilated in campus use, the faculty of the newly named College inaugurated a new course of study, the first of such magnitude since 1887. The faculty came close to abolishing a Greek requirement for the B.A. and did reduce the requirements in both Latin and Greek to only one year, although a student might well choose more in order to fulfill rather complex language requirements. It slightly reduced the number of required courses; established requirements for a major (three courses of a year's length) and a minor (two such courses); changed the grading system from a numerical one, with two categories of passing, to the ABCDF system; and made class standing and graduation depend upon earned quality points in a 3.00 point system, a system changed only in 1982. Some changes were necessary to accommodate the new Peabody. The College allowed its students to take up to four year-long courses at Peabody, in certain approved academic areas, or in its own professional schools, such as Law or the reorganized School of Religion. The faculty somewhat reluctantly cut two weeks from the school year and moved from a semester to three twelve-week quarters. Students now faced three final exams in each year but of only two hours each. The College also gave up all efforts at a summer school, since Peabody offered a large program in its summer quarter, housed its students on the Vanderbilt campus, and hired Vanderbilt faculty for several key courses. Finally, as an aid to incoming freshmen, the College began a system of freshmen advisors, appointing and training a group of faculty to work directly with students in their first year, the beginning of an enduring tradition.[1]

The break from the church ended the earlier tensions within the Board of Trust. The bishops were all gone, along with the laymen who fought for a continued church tie. Kirkland in effect now chose his own board and chose largely in behalf of prospective gifts. Two recruitment trends now climaxed—toward businessmen and toward Vanderbilt alumni. From World War I on, corporate executives, bankers, and corporate lawyers made up at least three-fourths of the board. A sprinkling of physicians, planters, judges, and church officials made up the remainder. Even before the war, twenty-one of twenty-nine trustees were alumni; by the late 1920s Kirkland had to take special precautions to preserve even four or five nonalumni slots for outside benefactors or special friends. The Alumni Association continued to nominate two alumni members every other year and in the late 1920s formalized the process by mail ballot. The board always confirmed these special alumni trustees, who were distinct, if at all, only by their occasional youthfulness. The long-term board president, after 1915, was Whitefoord R. Cole, who loyally supported the university and became a valued friend of Kirkland's. He rose to the presidency of the huge, locally dominant Louisville and Nashville Railroad. Cole eventually had to move from Nashville to Louisville, but until that move he also played a key role in the Executive Committee of the board, largely made up of trustees who lived in the Nashville area. It increasingly had the major responsibility for governance. It met up to a dozen times during the year, made most important decisions even when these had to be legalized by the whole board, and spent an inordinate amount of time managing the university's investments.

Next to Cole, the most active and influencial board member in the 1920s was Frank Rand, the head of a large St. Louis shoe company. Rand, also an alumnus, headed the most critical canvass in Vanderbilt's history and would later serve as board president. An equally valuable but more distant trustee, at times a vital link to the Vanderbilt family, was Norman Davis, the financier and diplomat who held various government posts, including assistant secretary of state, throughout the 1920s. Of the few holdovers from the Methodist past, the most respected was George Winton, who had earlier supported the Vanderbilt position until fired as editor of the *Christian Advocate* and who eventually became a professor at Vanderbilt and even acting dean of the School of Religion.[2]

In subtle ways, the role of the board also changed after 1914. The break with the church left the board without a clear constituency. It no longer served as a trustee for the church. Unlike in a business corporation, it represented the interests of no stockholders. Legally, the board now owned the university. In fact, alumni and major donors now made up the de facto stockholders. From these two overlapping groups came almost all trustees, and on most issues the board members reflected the dominant opinion of such an informal constituency. Much more than before the divorce from the church, Kirkland could now manage the board by carefully preparing items for submission to it, by carefully cultivating and guiding the board's understanding of issues. If Kirkland had basic disagreements with his faculty, he could usually enlist the authority of a much more easily guided board to support his position. The board soon became an elite, exclusive men's club, one that bestowed considerable prestige and social status on members. A few trustees would gain membership because of some unique prominence or needed talent; most, because of their prospective financial patronage. Board membership qualified as the highest honor bestowed by the university, an honor that almost always elicited an intense loyalty to the university and, with this, new levels of generosity.

The most inaccessible aspect of university government is the subtle relationship of a chancellor to a board. The minutes of the Vanderbilt board are almost useless for gauging the nuances of such a relationship. But judging from all extant records, Kirkland by 1915 had become an expert at dealing with the critical half-dozen key board members. Normally, chancellors or presidents of private universities such as Vanderbilt have a very ticklish job of interpretation or translation. They have to interpret the unique perspectives, the professional biases, and the avant-garde or often unpopular political and social beliefs of academics to the more conventional businessmen who dominate such boards. A chancellor must also interpret to faculty members the special concerns of a board, particularly its solicitude for the external reputation of a university, for financial solvency, and for clearly identifiable or even measurable outputs.

In the 1920s Kirkland seemed to navigate well between these two competing outlooks. Few tensions surfaced. On only three occasions did faculty views directly clash with that of board members, each time over the outer boundaries of academic freedom. The reasons for such harmony lay not so much in the intellectual sophistication of the board as in the political and social orthodoxy of the Vanderbilt faculty. More often than not, the best-placed professors in the College worshipped the same icons as did board members. That is, the dominating faculty members were as conventional in religious beliefs, as enthusiastic in their support of prosperity and progress, as moderate and reasonable in upholding existing economic relationships, as unwilling to condemn racial or sexual inequities, as were a majority on the board. Thus, the range of opinion on the board, and in the faculty, encompassed a rather narrow spectrum somewhat to the right of center but never so far as to be radical or perverse. Extremists in either direction were distinctly unwelcome and unhappy at Vanderbilt. In fact, in the 1920s the board seemed very solicitous of faculty interests, often more so than Kirkland or the deans, who had a firsthand knowledge of the weakness, self-centeredness, laziness, or mediocrity of all too many professors. It was the Board of Trust that pushed most often for faculty salary increases; Kirkland and the deans of Arts and Science who most often demurred or even blocked such raises. Only the dean of the new Medical School fought consistently, and successfully, for his faculty, in part because he had by far the ablest and most productive faculty at Vanderbilt.

Kirkland's role on campus considerably changed by the 1920s. He had finally gained almost full control over his university and was one of the most respected university administrators in the United States. His well-publicized campaign for higher standards in southern higher education, his successful fight with the church, his intimate friendship with the heads of the leading foundations, and his long tenure all added to his prestige and accounted for his growing success as a fund raiser. For him, the years from 1916 to 1929 were years of solid achievement, ever greater eminence, and of praise and adulation from all sides. But the early years of struggle and financial insecurity left their marks. Kirkland, during the church struggle, had fought against a narrow orthodoxy and in behalf of a more pluralistic university. But by the war his role seemed to shift; not that Kirkland changed so much. But now the faculty and students no longer needed him as a champion of their interests. No outside enemies threatened. Suddenly Kirkland was the center of authority, the source of official policies. He never became a McTyeire. He never imposed his will in a dictatorial way. This was not his style. But in indirect and often clever ways, he molded a university more and more to his own taste. Perhaps more accurately, he molded the College and the School of Engineering to his own taste. These remained his part of the university, the areas of his

The Board of Trust, 1928

Chancellor and Mrs. Kirkland
with Dean of Men Sarratt and Dean of Women Stapleton

most direct involvement. In the changed perspective of the 1920s, an aging Kirkland seemed more and more old-fashioned and cautious, at least to his junior staff and to many students. He could not understand, let alone applaud, the various iconoclastic or radical intellectual innovations of the 1920s. His fiscal caution never fit the economic expansiveness of the decade, although as it turned out he well prepared Vanderbilt for the coming depression. His paternal but yet condescending treatment of blacks and women, what had earlier seemed enlightened for the South, now struck a few reformers as insensitive or even unethical.

Most important for the university, Kirkland slowly surrounded himself with a coterie of like-minded professors and deans. His alter ego, Edwin Mims, best represented this group. Kirkland craved peace and harmony. He had had enough of fighting. He also wanted to appeal to outside benefactors, to protect the reputation of Vanderbilt. Thus, in his recruitment of faculty one notes an increasing use of words such as "personable" and "safe." He sought professors who would "fit" at Vanderbilt, who would be cooperative and not rock the boat. To fit meant that one had to accept southern racial norms, although one might join Kirkland and Mims in their campaign against lynching. It meant that one either fit somewhere within the Christian spectrum or kept quiet on religious issues. Avowed atheists did not fit within

229

the narrow, repressive world of Nashville or the South. It meant that one could not openly espouse political or economic views outside the mainstream, not even to the extent of advocating milder forms of socialism. It meant that Vanderbilt professors should not openly attack their prime benefactors, the large corporate managers, those who had led in collectivizing production, in subverting an older proprietary society. They fit best of all if they joined Mims in celebrating a new South. The Vanderbilt Agrarians, most notably, violated this implied rule. These constraints, added to Kirkland's fiscal caution, meant that Vanderbilt cut itself off from many of the nation's ablest scholars. Kirkland would not pay enough to hire them in any case. In the changed perspective of the 1920s Vanderbilt was not nearly as much a part of, or as open to, the national community of intellectuals as it had been in the 1890s. But this very context helped stimulate youthful rebellion and may have better nourished the Fugitives and Agrarians than a more open or cosmopolitan university. One can also wonder whether such a cosmopolitan university was even possible in the South in the 1920s.

The divorce with Methodism left the university in an almost desperate financial plight, not from any lack of former church support, but because the struggle had so diverted energies, or so intimidated possible benefactors, that all the departments save the Medical had stagnated. By 1915 Kirkland decided to consolidate and strengthen at the same time. By his conception, the original Vanderbilt endowments had funded only the academic programs of the university, or in 1915 the College and its daughter School of Engineering. The appended professional schools originally paid their own way, although Vanderbilt had slowly absorbed them and took responsibility for them. But not too much responsibility. Kirkland was not irrevocably committed to the indefinite continuation of any one of them, although the Law School probably was his favorite. If necessary, Kirkland seemed willing to cut the university back practically to Arts and Science and to Engineering. He thus began a Vanderbilt tradition, a tradition reminiscent of many European universities—a clear financial separation among the several schools and colleges. By making clear the terms of survival for each of the professional schools, Kirkland was able to turn most of his energies to the College and the still appended School of Engineering, or to what he considered the heart of any university.[3]

The College desperately needed new support. It was about to fall behind four or five other southern institutions in both income and caliber of faculty. The quality of its faculty had declined for over a decade. Salaries remained lower than in 1875 or, as Kirkland put it, less than that received by a good bricklayer. Small gifts from William K. Vanderbilt made up operating deficits; funds he gave for the chancellor's residence had to be directed to operating costs. At Kirkland's request, his friends on the GEB had studied the needs of the College in 1914. Both Wallace Buttrick and Abraham Flexner agreed on its urgent need for another $1 million in endowment. Because the School of Religion took the earnings of $240,000 of the existing endowment, such an increase would mean a near doubling of the effetive College endowment. In 1914 the endowment yielded only slightly more for the College than its $900,000 had back in 1880. The GEB gave $300,000 on a matching basis to launch a new $1 million fund drive in 1915. Kirkland, at first unsuccessfully, turned again to the Vanderbilt family and eventually received a commitment of $300,000 from William K. and $100,000 from Frederick W. Vanderbilt. With this outside support, the board in February of 1916 approved a special campaign to raise the other $300,000. The new alumni secretary, Charles Cason, and the students helped organize the first public financial canvass in Vanderbilt history.[4]

The campaign of 1916 became almost legendary. The enthusiasm during the summer and fall of 1916, the last-minute successes in October, the appropriate thanks from Kirkland all disguised some of the hard realities. Actually, the main body of alumni pledged very little and paid in even less. The canvassing techniques were new and inventive—Founder's Day dinners for alumni in various cities, campaign chairmen with weekly meetings in Nashville, speeches and tours by Mims and Coach McGugin, and an incessant barrage of campaign literature. Though it would do so in later campaigns, Vanderbilt did not now engage professional fund raisers, although its students employed an attorney to help in the final Nashville effort. The pledges came quickly, at least at first. The board pledged over $60,000, the faculty over $15,000, students over $4,000, and Kirkland himself $4,000. In four days Nashville's alumni and other friends pledged $103,000; Kirkland had stressed the role of the university in Nashville's economy and capitalized on his personal friendship with affluent businessmen. But by September the drive had netted only about $175,000 in pledges, and some people who pledged would never make payments. Then, in October, the students launched a final, almost desperate drive for an additional $150,000, all to beat the announced end of the campaign on December 31. Students held downtown nightshirt parades, suspended classes, and painted the city with red paint. The efforts succeeded to the extent that pledges finally reached the $300,000 goal. Everyone celebrated at a great victory dinner. But Kirkland knew the problems ahead. The campaign cost $16,000, or more than the university ever collected from small alumni gifts or from students. The collections came in slowly. William K. Vanderbilt had to give an additional $25,000, and despite this the collections were still $10,000 short as late as 1918. The athletic association had to furnish the final $8,000 as a loan against future collections in order to meet the deadline for the last GEB matching grant. So, despite the fanfare, the great drive fizzled to a rather embarrassing finale. But by then no one knew it. The war occupied all attention. Soon after the war ended, the cumulative inflation almost exactly canceled the value of the added endowment. The university did not suffer the full effect of inflation only because it could pass most of the burden on to its professors, in the form of drastically reduced real incomes.[5]

The European war had small impact on the campus until February of 1917, when American entry seemed a near certainty. Until then, students or faculty had on occasion debated the issues raised by the contending sides, but few at Vanderbilt defended the Central Powers. Kirkland and Mims established the dominant view—enthusiastic support for Woodrow Wilson. Mims, as one would have expected, turned out to be the greatest cheerleader for the Allies and was always the 100-percent patriot. As early as 1916 he campaigned for compulsory military training. Philosopher Herbert Sanborn, more a German than most Germans, publicly and enthusiastically defended the Central Powers. When the United States entered the war, he had to remain mute. Kirkland made it clear that Vanderbilt would retain only silent dissenters from the great crusade. He declared in the fall of 1917 that individual "rights stop when they run counter to the whole current of national purpose." German sympathizers, he said, had had three years to get out and now had no option but to keep quiet and submit to the will of the majority. He backed the expulsion of Senator Robert La Follette from the U.S. Senate and stressed that "we cannot give enemies of America" positions of authority in private life. Sanborn—eccentric, often petty, hypercritical—long remained a thorn in Kirkland's side. Perhaps significantly, from early 1917 until 1923 his name never appeared in any university publication except the *Bulletin*.

Kirkland, usually balanced and restrained, gave himself completely to the war effort and could not comprehend those who would not do their part. He helped bring the prevalent war psychology to Vanderbilt. Yet, in contrast to many midwestern universities, Vanderbilt did not suffer deep divisions or lasting enmities or flagrant examples of repression. The consensus was too great. Sanborn seemed all alone; Vanderbilt had almost no students or faculty of German descent. Moreover, it had no contingent of socialists or representatives of the labor movement to condemn both sides in the war as imperialistic expansionists, equally opposed to the interest of the working classes. In the absence of vocal opposition on campus, Vanderbilt did not have even the occasion to deny anyone's civil or academic freedom, although the mood of enthusiasm and irrational patriotism was sufficient to silence potential dissenters. In retrospect, events on campus often seemed as comical as ominous.[6]

It soon became a point of local pride: Vanderbilt made a commitment to the war even before it began. In February, 1917, students held a mass meeting, agreed to cooperate with other universities, and began to organize a military company. Kirkland pushed such preparedness, proposed courses in military science, and promised that drill could substitute for gym. Quickly, ninety-nine students signed up for drill, possibly as a way of avoiding hated gym classes. By March almost every man voted to enter training companies, and apparently some Vanderbilt students, without uniforms or rifles, actually began parading around campus before the declaration of war. On March 28, as Wilson prepared his war speech, Kirkland preached a strong anti-German sermon to his students. He referred to 1776 and called German abuses a subversion of American rights. But in this and later anti-German propaganda, Kirkland seemed ambivalent. At the time he earned his Ph.D., he had been an enthusiastic supporter of German culture. He never condoned any suppression of German classes at Vanderbilt or denied the contributions of Germans to western civilization. He always distinguished between German art and scholarship and its militarism, and he liked to place the blame for German aggression either on the emperor or on the Prussians. In his first war speech, and later, Kirkland talked of his hopes for a new, peaceful Germany, often echoing the very words of Woodrow Wilson.[7]

Even though Kirkland jumped the gun in committing Vanderbilt to "the cause of righteousness," the campus felt almost helpless when the war began. The students canceled all spring athletic competition, but what else could they do except give speeches? On the day of Wilson's message the male students gathered for drilling sessions on Dudley Field, but for weeks they had to drill in civilian clothes and without weapons. It all seemed surreal. Eventually the Tennessee National Guard furnished some uniforms and antique rifles. And, just before graduation, the first contingent of Vanderbilt seniors moved to Fort Oglethorpe to begin officer training. Typically, the *Hustler* lambasted the small number of Vanderbilt applicants selected while the faculty voted to give such early volunteers full academic credit if they remained in classes until actually called to camp. The *Hustler* complained that this gave them no time to visit their homes. The first contingent returned to campus, in cadet uniforms, to receive their degrees. It was the closest anyone at Vanderbilt had yet come to anything military.[8]

A sense of reality returned by the summer of 1917. A prolonged war gravely threatened any predominately male university. During the summer, as mobilization for war continued at what seemed a snail's pace, Vanderbilt officials decided to go on as normal in the fall. In a bid for enrollment they converted year-long courses to quarter-length ones in order to make suspended work more easy, and also as a way of recruiting farm boys who needed to return home during the spring quarter for the planting of crops. By then, the official rationale was that educating young men also contributed to the war. Vanderbilt even fielded a football team in the fall of 1917. Enrollment dropped only about 20 percent (from approximately 455 to 388 in Arts and Science and in Engineering), and none at all in the freshman class. The majority of Medical School seniors enlisted but the entering class increased. The war, of course, was omnipresent. All the young men now drilled in uniform. Their former classmates wrote letters from training camps or, later, from France. Vanderbilt medical students organized a special hospital unit, which left for camps in November. The Medical School went to a year-long schedule to speed up the training of physicians. Women joined Red Cross units, enrolled in a home nursing course, and took up knitting. Only slowly did the cost, and the cruelty, break through all the sophomoric celebrations. James G. Stahlman of the *Banner* even wrote a sentimental celebration of patriotism in Vanderbilt football, turning football defeats into glorious events if they came because of wartime sacrifices. University costs soared. These, along with decreased fees, threatened major deficits. Key faculty members resigned or took leaves to enter war work; George Mayfield spent most of the war in France working for the YMCA. Such absences saved money on salaries. A campus speaker's bureau featured faculty willing to lecture in support of the war, while Kirkland asked Vanderbilt University students, as educated men, to go home and help inform the people on the evils of German policies and on American war aims. Finally, coal became so scarce in the winter of 1918 that the university suspended all chapel services and also turned off radiators in unused classrooms.[9]

Vanderbilt men distinguished themselves in various roles. Norman Davis, of the class of 1901, by then an affluent New York banker, gave his services free to the secretary of the treasury, helping to negotiate war loans. William Litterer of the Medical School helped develop a new, deadly gas that promised to penetrate any German mask and thus kill "thousands of Huns." Everyone read a letter written from a flying school in France by Irby "Rabbit" Curry, a 1916 graduate of the Dental School who had captained the 1916 football team and been elected Bachelor of Ugliness, the only Dental student ever to win that honor. At first the mood was upbeat, full of patriotic fervor and illusioned expectations. Not a single former Vanderbilt student died in the war until April 2, 1918, although on March 10 Nashville held its first memorial service at the Ryman; 6,000 gathered to hear Edwin Mims. On April 7, 1918, Vanderbilt students gathered in chapel, with poems and eloquent speeches, to dedicate their service flag, which already had 1,125 stars for alumni in the armed forces.[10]

By the fall of 1918 America had mobilized. Slowly the military equipped and trained all volunteers. It then turned to conscription. Normal college life was now impossible. And all the glory eroded with the mounting casualties of the summer of 1918. In this somber context, the War Department decided to form Student Army Training Corps (SATC) on major campuses, in effect converting universities into military posts. Vanderbilt signed all the contracts for such a unit; it seemed a way to insure a healthy enrollment, while the War Department committed funds for the needed changes on campus. Vanderbilt controlled the admission of the new student soldiers, relaxing a bit Vanderbilt's stringent admission requirements. The men gathered in October, or only a month before the Armistice. For young men this was not only a path to glory but a way to postpone the draft and to get a free college education. Vanderbilt agreed to enroll up to 500 cadets and eventually had about 315 on the west campus. They quickly crowded facilities because they joined with the

Students drilling without uniforms, 1917

Students drilling with uniforms, 1918

nonmilitary students—a record number of women along with men too young or too unhealthy for the training. The regular senior class had only one male. A ragtag football team managed to play an attenuated schedule. Except among the freshmen, the women were now in a majority among the regular students, taking over most elected offices on campus, including president of the senior class.

Vanderbilt Medical Unit at Fort McPherson, Georgia

The cadets followed a full military regimen. The three dorms (Westside, Kissam, and Wesley) became companies, and the Kissam dining room became an Army mess. Another company took over the south campus and housed troops in the old Montgomery Bell Academy, a prestigious private secondary school. The university opened new classrooms in the former YMCA building, reorganized courses to fit military needs, enlarged its labs, improved campus roads, all at an expenditure of about $13,000. It all happened so quickly that it led to utter confusion. Both the SATC cadets and the 250 regular students remembered the brief experience as a nightmare. After the Armistice, cadet morale plummeted as most awaited their discharge; some came close to rebellion on the south campus. Then, on top of all this, the influenza epidemic spread through the campus, leaving up to one hundred ill at a time. Several died. No wonder that the academic work suffered and that professors had mostly bitter memories of the SATC. But the university probably benefited financially—it gained the physical improvements, including furniture for dorm rooms. Even though most SATC cadets left at demobilization following the end of the first quarter, some enrolled as regular students. Without the SATC Vanderbilt would have had trouble opening in the fall of 1918.[11]

In January, 1919, Vanderbilt returned to civilian control. The men came back to campus in droves, quickly dispossessing the women of most of their elected offices. The *Hustler* led a crusade in behalf of reorganized classes, against any demeaning continuation of petticoat rule. But the women kept at least partial control over the *Commodore,* making the 1919 version exceptionally feminine in orientation, and the senior class retained its female president, Ednelia Wade, who tragically died of tuberculosis just before the commencement. Superficially, the campus seemed normal by the spring quarter. The fraternities reorganized and in most cases reclaimed their houses. The dramatic club produced a new play. The YMCA resumed its placement office, helping poor students find part-time work. Even the freshmen ordered green caps and tried to restore older traditions. But nothing seemed to work. Everyone decried the lack of the old school spirit. Returning soldiers did not easily return to sophomoric rites. The continuing SATC students often represented a different social background. Soon, demoralized students tended to blame all their problems on the SATC. Kirkland found the returning students unusually restless and excitable, the most unmanageable yet encountered at Vanderbilt. Besides some drinking and a few expulsions, it is hard to document such charges, except for a student rebellion against the new Reserve Officers Training Corps (ROTC). This, more than anything else, shaped Kirkland's perspective on the students. Never before had they so openly defied him or his faculty.[12]

After the Armistice, and during the demobilization of the SATC, the Vanderbilt faculty voted to establish an ROTC unit at Vanderbilt. In December,

Relief collections at football game

237

1918, they voted to make such training mandatory for College and Engineering men, except for seniors, thus doing away with compulsory gym classes. ROTC seemed an ideal, and cheap, substitute for the new gym facilities required for continued physical education. Also, the War Department would pay the drill instructors. Thus male students returned to campus in January, 1919, to discover that they had to sign up for ROTC. To some this was a surprise, since the *Bulletin* had not announced compulsory ROTC. The SATC remnants, or returning veterans, seemed particularly resentful. Even the *Hustler* took up the cause, and soon a campus that in 1917 had gone all out for drill now echoed with charges of coercion and militarism. The student mood was changing, reflecting disillusionment with the war and a more healthy cynicism toward the military. Only a minority felt the issues deeply; a majority became convinced that the faculty had unilaterally imposed rules on the students. The students held a mass meeting; several subsequently boycotted the drill. Kirkland refused to discuss the issue with students until they stopped the boycott. When they did, he appointed a faculty committee to hear the student complaints. The faculty voted to make drill optional for the rest of 1918–19, on the basis that students had not been forewarned. It made drill compulsory in 1919–20 for freshmen and sophomores. Given the option of drill or gym, about 85 percent of the students continued in ROTC in the spring.[13]

Student resentment continued the next year. The compulsory aspect grated most. The 1920 *Commodore* featured a doctored picture of Commodore Vanderbilt, facing west toward Old Main rather than as normal toward the east. He now looked away from assembled ROTC companies. He would not look "upon that horrible instrument of militarism," and thus "executed a snappy about face," so the world could see how much he disliked "the darn thing." If ROTC had this much effect on a statue, the *Commodore* asked readers to imagine its effect "upon real human beings." By then, even Kirkland and the faculty had become disillusioned with ROTC. It threatened new costs for storage warehouses, for needed new classroom space (instruction had been in the Wesley Hall dining room, now about to reopen as a cafeteria), and for extra drill officers. At the end of 1919–20 the university canceled its contract with the War Department, abolishing campus ROTC until World War II. It is impossible to gauge how much the student protest motivated the decision.[14]

By 1919 the hatred of so-called Huns gave way in America to wild fantasies about, and irrational fears of, the terrible Bolsheviks, a new, strange, grotesque subhuman species that had recently staged a successful revolution over in Russia. A frenzied assault on the civil liberties of certain aliens and socialists now rivaled that against German sympathizers during the war. The Red Scare peaked in 1919 and 1920, and fed on a few quite real bombings and scattered examples of violence by small leftist groups, most encouraged and inspired by the success of the Soviet revolution. But none of this violence came close to Nashville. Yet, almost desperate to join the politically popular crusade, some officials in Nashville found a victim in a confused, inarticulate, and idealistic young instructor of French at Vanderbilt, one Russell Scott. Before the affair ended, Vanderbilt officials became accomplices in an exceedingly cruel series of unjust and probably illegal abuses of this young man. No incident in Vanderbilt history, not even the earlier Winchell case, had exhibited so much insensitivity or so callous a disregard for individual rights.

Through it all, Scott remained a rather puzzling character. A British citizen, and thus an alien, he had first come to Nashville as a wartime YMCA secretary. Then the Romance language department had hired him as an assistant professor of French for 1918–19, although he seemed to have few scholarly qualifications. Apparently he was unhappy in his post, for in the spring quarter he asked to quit at the end of the term to return to England. He did not, perhaps because of the urging of his department. He was badly needed to teach a swelling number of students. Undoubtedly he planned to leave in June of 1919, as he was on only a one-year appointment. Scott's various statements, and his testimony before the Executive Committee of the Board of Trust, reveals more ideological confusion than a mature political position. As a young, would-be intellectual in England he had joined the famous Fabian movement and professed personal acquaintance with some of the key names in that movement, the embryo of what later became the successful Labour Party. He had always considered himself a socialist but he certainly was not a very militant or precise one, judging by his rambling efforts to give some content to the ambiguous label.[15]

Scott was probably a troubled and lonely young man alienated by what he viewed as the stifling political and social climate of Nashville and Vanderbilt. He looked for a cause, a way of affirming and reinforcing his own vulnerable identity. He seemed to find it among Nashville's small labor and socialist minority. On May 1, 1919, socialists throughout America planned rallies and public meetings. On this, the greatest holiday of international socialism, they particularly crusaded for the release from prison of their leader and hero, Eugene Debs. Because of his opposition to American involvement in the war, and on the grounds of antiwar and antiadministration statements he had made in a public speech, Debs was convicted and imprisoned under the notorious Espionage Act of 1918. Later, President Warren G. Harding would pardon him. But from his jail cell he gained over 1 million votes in the presidential election of 1920. At that time the American Socialist Party was the major third party in America, with widespread support among American intellectuals. That Scott was apparently the only avowed supporter of Debs among faculty or students at Vanderbilt must have made him feel even more alien in the strange political climate of the South. As one of his purportedly "dangerous" acts, he had posted a notice asking faculty and student support for those, such as Debs, who had been denied their American rights. No one responded.

Scott had a taste for the avant-garde, and thus for leftist literature, now

239

entering its golden age in America. He especially enjoyed an article in the February, 1919, *Liberator* (a successor to the banned *Masses*), and sought a copy to send his brother. As he correctly noted, any good library would have had a copy. But he could not find a copy anywhere in Nashville, which he correctly interpreted as evidence of cultural backwardness. Finally he heard of a shoe repairman downtown who sold the *Liberator*. This artisan, one Harry Goldfarb, introduced Scott to a small Nashville subculture—that of the labor movement and the supporters of Debs. Scott liked Goldfarb, found him intelligent and interesting. Goldfarb, as a Jewish immigrant, was from Russia, a distinct mark against him in 1919. From this contact came an invitation for Scott to address the May 1, 1919, labor rally, a rally advertised as one to urge the release of all "political, industrial, and religious prisoners." Debs was preeminent among those. Scott, who had noted the English precedent of an early release of all political prisoners soon after the Armistice, duly prepared his speech and came to the scheduled meeting. In doing this he was doing what Edwin Mims did all the time—speaking out on important public issues. Just as he arrived, a local federal district attorney, Lee Douglas, announced the meeting suspended. He did this because he found "seditious publications" on display—a copy of the new Soviet constitution and the speech for which Debs had been sentenced. Backing up Douglas was Mayor William Gupton of Nashville, desperately anxious to gain political capital from this one unanticipated chance to put down reds.[16]

What happened next was almost inevitable, given Scott's behavior. He did not know, or choose to play, by the local rules. As a result he, like most nonconforming outsiders, finally learned the hard truth about southern hospitality. He could have returned to Vanderbilt. Instead, he demanded to know the reasons for such an authoritarian denial of the right of assembly. He became an agitator; he challenged the local authorities. Instead of providing him an answer, the officials verbally abused him, thinking him one of what they called the "riffraff," a new term to Scott. When asked to identify himself, he at first concealed his Vanderbilt connection, avowedly to protect the university. He only identified himself as a citizen of England and was verbally abused as an impertinent foreigner. When he did reveal his Vanderbilt affiliation, Scott either ignored, or deliberately refused, a second chance to avoid a political incident. His Vanderbilt identity created a new basis of rapport with the district attorney, a Vanderbilt alumnus, and with the mayor. Scott, after all, was respectable, not a socialist or a labor agitator. His position elevated him to their social level and it is clear they sought extenuating circumstances to excuse Scott from any responsibility for the meeting. He was too honest to play the status game, too loyal to desert his labor allies. So he continued his demand for an explanation, slowly bared his socialist convictions, defended his wartime activities, and then finally returned to Vanderbilt, unsure of what would follow. He was not arrested; he had done nothing illegal.[17]

The district attorney was incensed at a defiant Scott. He came the same night to Vanderbilt to demand termination of his position, apparently on the grounds that he had attended the downtown meeting and was a dangerous radical. Kirkland was away. Dean Tolman listened, agreed with Douglas that Scott deserved dismissal but noted his lack of authority. Douglas next contacted Board president Whitefoord Cole, who immediately announced Scott's suspension. The two local newspapers vied with each other in airing the story, but both tried to absolve Vanderbilt of any responsibility for Scott's action. Scott, as always, fought back. He denounced his suspension without any justifying cause and asked for a hearing and a presentation of charges.[18]

The hearing took place. A stenographic record has survived. On the evening of May 4 Cole gathered his Executive Committee to examine Scott. By then, Cole defined the hearing as one to determine whether the suspension order should go into effect. This meant, technically, that Scott had not yet been suspended. Scott proved a trying witness, so rambling and incoherent as to confuse the ideologically naive trustees. Cole could have taught a lesson to a later Joseph McCarthy. He cleverly put words in Scott's mouth, showed his own ignorance of socialist thought, paraded some of the most fantastic legends about the new Soviet Union, and led the hearing to its foreordained and calculated conclusion—the Executive Committee voted suspension. In all of this no one ever precisely formulated charges. All that Tolman could later suggest was Scott's willingness to speak at the projected meeting and his caustic comments about his rights. Scott still did not know a sufficient reason for suspension. Was it because of his intent to speak in behalf of the release of political prisoners? Was it because of politically sensitive statements he had made before students? Was it because of several open-minded statements he had made about the Soviet Union during the hearing? Or was it because of several extraneous charges board members dug up from interviews with students, including even his advocacy of free love (he was married and a loyal family head)? No one ever said. Scott, despite his ideological vagueness, did try to raise the discussion to an intellectual level, to get people to define loaded words such as "Bolshevik," and to probe the largely unknown realities of recent Soviet history, all to no avail.[19]

Kirkland returned with all this a fait accompli. He would have handled it differently. Since Scott had less than a month of teaching left, Kirkland would probably have bottled the issue up in committee investigations until it became moot. As it was, he noted that Scott's conduct was reprehensible without clarifying what conduct he had in mind. No one ever did and, by any later standards, nothing at all in the evidence suggests any conduct at all unbecoming a professor. Kirkland refused to dismiss Scott, noting that his suspension had been sufficient punishment. He asked a faculty committee to investigate the case. Kirkland was in a bind, of course. He could not repudiate Cole, even though it is clear he felt Cole had acted too hastily and arbitrarily. Two members of the Arts and Science faculty, Walter L. Fleming and L.C.

Glenn, carried out the faculty inquiry. In the mildest language possible they rebuked Cole and the Executive Committee. The district attorney had the right to press whatever charges he wanted against Vanderbilt professors, but no right at all to intervene in university affairs or demand anyone's dismissal. Cole erred in suspending Scott without a hearing. The two faculty members also noted the absence of established procedures in such cases and begged the board at its next meeting to establish such. But even they referred to Scott's behavior as reprehensible, thereby joining the popular denunciation of him on no other stated grounds than unpopular political beliefs.

Before the committee even reported, Douglas had arrested Scott as an alien and set him up for forcible deportation. He had, purportedly, advocated the destruction of property and did not believe in the government of the United States, charges too vague to sustain criminal conviction but all too typical of noncriminal immigration hearings. Two Vanderbilt professors, Fleming and George P. Jackson, helped arrange his bail. Because of Scott's arrest and pending hearing, the faculty committee, rather than recommending reinstatement, accepted suspension until the legal proceedings concluded. Since they took their action in late May, Scott had no chance at all of returning to the classroom. No records survive of an eventual hearing for Scott; in all probability he voluntarily returned home to a familiar and much more tolerant England.[20]

Kirkland and his faculty were glad to survive the spring of 1919. But friction and repression did not monopolize the postwar era. Nor did a growing student disillusionment immediately snuff out the fervor of the war. On March 1, 1919, after intensive discussions in February, the Alumni Association board launched a campaign for a new building to memoralize the Vanderbilt men who fought and died in the war. At that point the alumni office had a record of thirty-five deaths, although this included some who died of the influenza or in other nonbelligerent accidents. Eventually, as the office updated its records, this list grew to forty-four. The contemplated building was to serve as an alumni office and a social center, was to provide such student services as a bookstore and post office, and was to contain an appended gymnasium and pool. Frank Rand of St. Louis headed the fundraising effort. The crusade began at a propitious time, as a response to the widespread feelings of guilt over wartime casualities and in an economic boom. Vanderbilt students enthusiastically joined in the drive. The students made the campaign their own. They pledged $30,000; Nashville alumni pledged $116,000; other Nashvillians added $30,000. Briefly, the giving seemed a test of patriotism. Within a short time the Alumni Association had pledges of over $256,000 toward an expanded goal of $346,000. But pledges are not gifts in hand. As the patriotic fervor subsided and as boom gave way to a recession in 1920, a large percentage of the pledges proved uncollectable. The alumni building became a new hurdle, haunting Kirkland for the next five years. The continuing collections made it impossible to launch needed new drives for other funds (Kirkland had pledged this to the alumni), and inadequate gifts in hand forced several postponements of construction. Eventually the Alumni Association collected about $240,000, or enough to build the modest, much reduced Alumni Memorial Hall finally completed in 1925 and still one of the small adornments of the campus.[21]

Even as the alumni solicited pledges, Kirkland matured some grandiose plans with Buttrick and Flexner. By September, 1919, he had an original commitment of $4 million from the GEB to build a new, regional Medical Center. This makes up part of a very complex story (see Chapter 11), but at the time it pointed up the severe problems facing the College. Thus, Kirkland entered the 1920s with two major but parallel goals—to help secure a prestigious Medical School and at the same time try, almost desperately, to revitalize the College, to keep it from being dwarfed or overwhelmed. In the two tasks he played a much more direct role in the College. The Medical School was in capable, largely outside hands. The College required constant attention. The other professional schools were much more peripheral to his conception of Vanderbilt's role in the South, so he left them to sink or swim on their own initiative.

The College faced three related inadequacies by World War I—in plant, in faculty, and in endowment. Its plant was barely adequate before the war, completely antiquated and much too small after the war. To the surprise of everyone, undergraduate enrollment soared after 1919. The combined College-Engineering enrollment barely reached 500 before 1917; it climbed to 600 in the fall of 1919, to 760 in 1921, to over 800 by 1923, and to over 900 in 1925. By then 162 law students also occupied the top floor of Old Main (now called College Hall), meaning over 1,000 students crammed into the four classroom buildings (Main, Furman, Science, and Engineering). Even more spectacular was the soaring number of degrees awarded, from only 40 B.A.s and B.S.s in 1916 to 91 in 1923 and 134 in 1928. Kissam was adequate only for male freshmen; upperclassmen rarely lived or boarded on campus, but in fraternities or boarding houses. Vanderbilt still had no dorms for over 200 women. It had only two rooms in Main for its library and adequate scientific labs only for chemistry. Classrooms, even counting those in converted Westside Row buildings, overflowed. The gym proved so inadequate that the board authorized funds for a temporary annex, which served various purposes until 1964. Physics and geology were both crowded in the basement of Main, with many facilities less adequate than those of 1875. Biology labs soon overflowed the ground floor of Science. Most apparatus for both physics and an increasingly dispersed Engineering School dated from the nineteenth century, much from the time of Chancellor Garland. The strengthening of the undergraduate program required, at the minimum, two or three new and costly classroom buildings, a library, a new gym, a large auditorium, and dorms for women.[22]

By World War I the brilliant senior faculty of the College of the 1890s had given way to stale, aged, and largely mediocre successors. The exceptions only proved the rule. Tolman remained the most eminent scholar, but he was now mired in the administrative details of the dean's office and would unexpectedly die in 1923. Only Tolman, assisted by a brilliant J.H. Stevenson from the School of Religion until his death in 1919, had continued to offer legitimate Ph.D. work. The only other departments that even flirted with excellence were English and history. Mims still dominated English, or as his junior faculty perceived it, almost tyranically controlled it. It is hard to offer an even-handed portrait of Mims, for faculty and student characterizations of him ranged the whole gamut from effusive praise to near hatred, of intellectual respect to complete contempt. But he had stature and recruited able young men, most notably John Crowe Ransom, Walter C. Curry, and finally John Donald Wade, all of whom deservedly gained national eminence. In short, Mims selected those more able than himself, whether by accident or design. As for himself, Mims came to Vanderbilt as a scholar and critic, with a reputation based on his biography of Lanier, but once at Vanderbilt he gave up serious literary scholarship. He taught what became famous and eloquent courses in literary criticism, began effective programs in creative writing, and became a sharp, pungent essayist, largely writing on the problems of the South. In a backhanded way he provoked a group of young poets; they had to succeed in order to torment old Mims. His work did not wear well because it was topical and conventional, at times even glib and superficial. But he had a gift for inspiring an audience and for meeting it on its own terms. Thus, Mims became Vanderbilt's most successful advocate to alumni and to the larger community.[23]

In history, St. George Sioussat excelled Mims as a scholar and in his reputation within a national profession. But Sioussat accepted an inviting chair appointment at Brown University in 1916. He was next to the last of a series of senior professors at Vanderbilt to move to prestigious northern jobs. The last was Bert Young, who left Romance languages for a position at Indiana in 1922. Few who were left deserved such recognition. That was not true of Sioussat's successor, Walter L. Fleming. He was the ablest possible candidate for what Kirkland desired—a prominent historian who fit the special Vanderbilt and southern context. Fleming's reputation has suffered in recent years, largely because of shifts in racial perspectives, but in 1917 he was in the recognized forefront of scholarship on southern history, the author of two important books, a professor at Louisiana State University, and one of the ablest students of William A. Dunning at Columbia, and thus a member of what later would be known as the Dunning School of reconstruction historians. Fleming published his third major book just after coming to Vanderbilt and then followed Tolman into the deanship, sacrificing scholarship and soon even his health to heavy teaching and administrative chores. Fleming, like Mims, hired a few able young men, beginning with Frank Owsley in 1920.[24]

The strength of other departments ranged from passable to pitiful. Most did not lack able teachers or even well-trained scholars. Rather, their key professors were not very active in research or scholarship and did not achieve, or maintain, a national reputation. After Bert Young moved to Indiana in 1922, Romance languages floundered because of a repeated turnover of staff. In German the two senior professors gained greater reputation for work outside their field than within—George Pullen Jackson in music and as founder of the Nashville symphony, George Mayfield as an ornithologist. After Tolman's death the classical languages never regained their earlier stature.[25]

The social sciences all lagged behind history. Political science remained part of history throughout the 1920s; its most promising scholar was Denna F. Fleming, who came to Vanderbilt in 1928 largely through the urging of Norman Davis, who loved his early work on the League of Nations. Herman C. Nixon, later distinguished for his work in southern reform, particularly relating to blacks, and for his association with the Agrarians, came to Vanderbilt in 1925 as an assistant professor. In the early 1920s a volatile Gus Dyer still headed a combined sociology and economics department. But, as a scholar, Dyer was something of a joke. He played a major role at Vanderbilt, as a gadfly and immensely popular outside lecturer. He forced students to confront new social issues, particularly the problem of blacks, and had involved himself extensively with local politics. He was Vanderbilt's only extension agent, but in the 1920s an increasingly embarrassing one. He seemed to reverse himself on social issues and became a paid publicist of the National Association of Manufacturers. By the 1930s his right-wing pronouncements proved almost as embarrassing as Scott's activism on the other side. Thus, Dyer eventually probed the limits of academic freedom at Vanderbilt and found them a bit broader than they had been in 1919. But by the mid-1920s Kirkland had eased him out of any directing role in what became two separate departments. By then, younger men began building a staff in sociology and economics, but not one as yet of national stature, although economist Roy Garis published extensively in behalf of immigration restriction and claimed the dubious honor of first advocating the racially and culturally biased national origins system, or what he called the "true American policy."[26]

Psychology emerged slowly and belatedly at Vanderbilt. Herbert Sanborn not only did all the course work in philosophy, with his older, idealistic approach, but also became enamored with animal behavior. He was thus reluctant to give up his one course in psychology or to welcome any younger faculty. An undistinguished Franklin Paschal, who came to Vanderbilt in 1927 as dean, helped develop a new program in psychology, but one that did not separate from philosophy. In 1929 a very able Lyle Lanier came to Vanderbilt as assistant professor of psychology and soon gained a bit of fame for his contribution to *I'll Take My Stand*.[27]

245

The natural sciences made up a new disaster area. The only glimmer of excellence came from geology and biology. Leonidas C. Glenn was the sole professor in geology from 1899 to the mid-1920s. He was unusually active in professional organizations, helped expand the geological museum, wrote a few articles, and rather extensively consulted for government agencies and oil companies. Thus, he made a name for himself and was a loyal and willing committeeman on campus. Kirkland trusted and admired him. In 1915 a youthful Edwin E. Reinke took over a small program in biology. He aggressively expanded the laboratory work and, in connection with the Medical School, struggled to build an excellent program despite pitiful facilities. In 1929, with the completion of Buttrick Hall, he finally inherited his kingdom. Reinke excelled as a teacher, not as a researcher. His local contributions made up for a lack of national eminence.[28]

Chemistry had the only adequate scientific facilities, but Vanderbilt had a hard time finding a deserving replacement for Dudley. In 1919 it hired a Ph.D. from Wisconsin, a Canadian by birth, J.M. Breckenridge, who headed a rather undistinguished department of four or five throughout the 1920s. Physics suffered most. An elderly John Daniel, who began as an able assistant to Garland, continued to give boring lectures. Students complained. Eventually Kirkland removed him from all lab instruction. By the mid-1920s the Vanderbilt physics program was scarcely of college caliber. Mathematics remained largely a teaching department with few creative or original faculty members. In 1916 a young and charming Charles Madison Sarratt came to Vanderbilt to teach math, but without his Ph.D. His students loved him. In 1922 he became dean of students, henceforth teaching only part time but gaining a full professorship on the basis of his administrative role (such inflated promotions were all too common under Kirkland). His success in teaching and in student affairs more than made up for his mathematical deficiencies. In 1925 Wilson Lee Miser, an Arkansas native who took his Ph.D. at Chicago, became the new professor of mathematics, remaining until retirement in 1951. He enjoyed teaching and published one textbook. Perhaps he reflected a Vanderbilt syndrome—loving devotion to students but too little engagement in scholarship or in professional activities. The College nourished all too many Mr. Chipses, thereby denying its students the latest understanding or the contagious enthusiasm that comes from contact with original investigations.[29]

Except for a few oldtimers such as Daniel, or exceptionally gifted people like John Crowe Ransom or the young poet Donald Davidson, all the senior College staff members had or soon acquired their Ph.D. Also, after the war, Kirkland finally began appointing more than one full professor in each department; the old title of chair now gave way to department chairman or head. The enrollment boom after 1920 forced Vanderbilt to hire an increasing number of junior staff members, most without a Ph.D. The surge in college attendance created a tight academic market; Vanderbilt often had to hire young men (and one woman; Kate Tillett became an instructor of history in 1918) with marginal qualifications or ability. For the first time, departments routinely dismissed instructors after a disappointing trial year. But they made appointments to assistant professor with more care; most such appointees stayed on at Vanderbilt if they chose. Most chose. The problem, in the perspective of a tough-minded Dean Tolman or an even tougher Fleming, was that too few chose to leave or had the credentials to rise rapidly in the academic marketplace. Thus, by the mid-1920s Vanderbilt had all too many loyal and faithful assistant and associate professors of middling ability and limited scholarly output, many of whom would eventually and very slowly rise to the later clogged rank of full professor (the College and Engineering had thirty-three full professors by 1930, or slightly more full professors than associates and assistants combined). As yet, no one had legal tenure at Vanderbilt. The word "tenure" was not even in vogue. But its absence did not so much mean harsh and arbitrary demands as the lack of any rigorous probationary period at all. No one had the heart to terminate loyal professors, particularly after several years of service. Thus, in a sense, a professorship at Vanderbilt, at any of the three ranks, meant complete job security. If insecurity existed, it never involved excessive professional demands but only the relatively small margin of ideological deviance possible within the South or within Kirkland's university.[30]

Until 1918 Vanderbilt had never officially used salaries to distinguish among professors at the same rank. The fiction of equal ability and equal merit died hard. This system gave few strong incentives for faculty development. Slowly this changed throughout the 1920s, particularly because of Dean Fleming. He constantly stressed the importance of good teaching and serious scholarship and helped establish a competitive atmosphere in the lower ranks. The need for teachers allowed departments to fire all too few mediocrities, but both Fleming and Kirkland made clear that promotion, salary increases, and several small prerogatives, such as clerical help or lower teaching loads or transportation to a professional convention, depended upon performance. In 1927 Fleming first requested, and received, $500 to pay travel expenses for professors delivering papers at conventions; the faculty eagerly used up all the money and the board soon raised the sum to $750. The first hint of national recognition came to the College faculty, most notably when Frank Owsley won Vanderbilt's first Guggenheim Fellowship in 1925 (John Donald Wade had a Guggenheim the same year but only came to Vanderbilt later). Thus, the College in the 1920s first moved slowly toward a highly competitive, even publish-or-perish environment, but not very far or very fast. Even by 1930 it had only a handful of professors who could have competed for positions, let alone chair professorships, in the best northern universities.[31]

Faculty salaries may help explain the lack of distinction in the senior ranks. Salary issues relate to the overall financial problems of the College. But the relationship was never one-to-one. Even when the College budget permitted, neither Kirkland nor his deans pushed salaries as high as they might have. Fiscal caution inhibited Kirkland. Dean Fleming, in particular, thought most of his faculty did not deserve more than they received, and at times he actively opposed across-the-board raises. An additional restraint was the national academic job market. To a large extent, Vanderbilt paid what it had to to get the new staff it wanted. When recruiting salaries went up, older salaries tended to follow. By the 1920s average salaries at Vanderbilt were just below those of the four or five other comparable southern universities, such as Virginia, North Carolina, and Texas. Kirkland, assisted by department chairmen or senior professors, tried his best to recruit the ablest possible appointees at any professorial level, but implicit in such a search were several constraints. The existing pattern of Vanderbilt salaries, or what Kirkland dared offer, was not as important as sectional constraints and the academic reputation of Vanderbilt. Only large salary increments could have lured a Yale or Harvard or Michigan professor to Vanderbilt. No one recruited such people. Kirkland was not daring or adventuresome in his searching. He got the faculty he deserved, in a sense the faculty he wanted, or possibly a faculty appropriate to Vanderbilt at that stage of its development. Perhaps without even articulating his criteria, he wanted people like Glenn and Mims, those happy in the South, those who were cooperative and supportive, those who fit in the unique Vanderbilt atmosphere. As an aging chancellor he did not want a staff full of egotists or prima donnas, more devoted to professional reputation than to the improvement of Vanderbilt or the South, or a staff dominated by a few eminent scholars with national or international reputations. When he received, almost as a gift, such an able and aggressive staff in the new Medical School he hardly knew how to cope with it. Likewise, a competent but not distinguished faculty will usually perpetuate itself. Only an infusion of outside leadership, or money, can quickly change the profile of a faculty, and this requires a cruel weeding out of loyal and faithful servants. A slow movement toward higher competitive standards was the only realistic choice for the College.[32]

Salary details reinforce such a general analysis. Until World War I, College salaries remained in the old ruts that went back to 1875 and 1879. Full professors in the College, and in Bible, Engineering, and Pharmacy, still received a maximum of $3,000, associates $2,000. Such stability was not as stifling as it would seem, since steady price decreases had increased the real income of faculty until after 1900. This changed with the European war and even more with the inflation of 1919. At the end of the war Vanderbilt professors suffered the lowest real wages in the university's history. Their plight led many to seek part-time teaching at Peabody or even at Ward-Belmont, a dissipation of their time and talent that detracted from their scholarship and from their duties at Vanderbilt.

Kirkland and the board recognized the financial plight of the faculty. Their first response to it involved retirement benefits. Before 1914, because of its church connection, Vanderbilt's professors had not qualified for the annuities provided by the Carnegie Foundation. Unfortunately, just as Vanderbilt became eligible the foundation had to curtail its grants for retirement or else deplete all its funds. Kirkland, who was elected to the board of this prestigious foundation in 1917, insured that Vanderbilt qualified for the new retirement scheme it established in 1919—the subsidized Teacher's Insurance and Annuity Association (TIAA). In 1919 Vanderbilt began contributing 5 percent of salaries to this fund; eligible professors contributed an additional 5 percent. The plan became obligatory for all new professors in the College and in Engineering after 1919; existing professors under forty entered on the same terms as new staff. Unfortunately, no one enforced the requirement, and many professors never joined TIAA to buttress the retirement benefits of older professors, the Carnegie Fund contributed $30,000 and Vanderbilt added $70,000, in what amounted to an invested fund used to purchase annuities for professors at retirement age. Poor old John T. McGill, now too deaf to teach, received the first annuity almost as a bribe to get him to retire in 1919. Late in the decade Kirkland opposed plans for group life insurance, but the faculty gained even this minor fringe benefit in the early 1930s.[33]

In 1918 Kirkland announced imminent salary increases as soon as funds permitted. For the first time he proposed to exceed the $3,000 maximum for full professors in the College and in Engineering. In 1919 he raised three key professors (Mims, Tolman, and Glenn) from $3,000 to $3,500, and Fleming to $3,300. An outside offer led to a quick raise of Fleming to $3,500 and began a matching of outside offers that continued throughout the 1920s. Despite the new merit system, the board in 1920 approved a new salary scale and thus gave raises to almost everyone in what amounted to a $20,000 boost in salary costs. Professors now received $3,000 and up, associates $2,500 to $3,000; assistants $2,000 to $2,500; and instructors $1,200 to $1,500. The open-ended scale for professors promised more than the university ever gave. The board approved $4,000 for some key professors, but this salary then stuck for most of the decade. The effect of the new scale was to narrow considerably the difference between junior and senior staff, which simply reflected the necessity of paying more to hire young men at the bottom. It also made it almost impossible to recruit outstanding men at the senior level. As a contrast to this maximum, in 1923 the athletic association paid Dan McGugin $4,500 for his part-time coaching duties, a discrepancy that worried board members more than it seemed to concern Kirkland, who then had a salary of $10,000, which rose to $12,000 in 1926, or by then three times that of Dean Fleming, who almost killed himself in working for the College and who never gained the salary he could have commanded elsewhere. After 1925, Medical School salaries almost doubled those in the College. The premium on beginning salaries in the College helped divert funds from key professors whose loyalty or age insured their retention. In 1924 Kirkland raised the scale once again but now set limits to full professors at $4,500. As assistants had a scale of $2,500 to $3,000, this further narrowed the range. Several assistant professors then earned $3,000, even as most full professors earned no more than $4,000. As a junior professor looked ahead in his career, he could anticipate salary increases of only about $1,000, unless he changed professions, universities, or detoured from serious scholarship into administration.

Kirkland held to these College and Engineering maximums until the depression, with only two exceptions. In 1925 he raised private funds to increase Edwin Mims's salary from $4,200 to $5,000; Duke had offered him $6,000. In 1927, after an expensive search for someone to replace Fleming as dean, Kirkland gave up on any scholar and hired Franklin Paschall from an administrative post at the University of Arizona. He had to pay him $5,000, although this was for eleven months rather than nine, but again for someone without Fleming's eminence. After 1925 faculty scales did not change, although competitive individuals gained significant raises. In 1926, when Kirkland repelled board efforts to raise salaries, he asked for a unique raise— to repay faculty pledges made in the recent canvass. This raise benefited only those who were loyal or able enough to have given. In 1927 the board almost rebelled against an unwilling administration and pushed through a series of individual raises. These raises elevated some assistant professors to over $3,000 and some associates to over $4,000. Finally, in 1930, just before the depression deepened, the university hired a new professor of education for $5,000, making him and Mims the only ones to reach such an elevated standard. William C. Binkley, the 1930 successor to Fleming in history, came with a salary commitment of $5,000 for his third year. By so narrowing the gap between beginning and senior professors, and by opening such a tremendous gap between senior professors and the chancellor, Vanderbilt financially discouraged outstanding achievement in scholarship, scientific research, or even innovative teaching. It seemed to value these much less than coaching; even the assistant football coach moved up to $6,500 in 1931 and several junior football coaches received $4,000, or the same salary enjoyed by Dean Fleming when health forced him to retire from all administrative duties.[34]

The history of the College of Arts and Science and School of Engineering in the 1920s was one of unending efforts to gain new endowments to keep the operating budget growing as fast as enrollments and costs. Kirkland was a dominating figure both in fund raising and in determining budgetary and even investment policies. He always ran scared. He feared debts like the plague. He would take no risks. He expected the worst of the future and would not build new facilities in expectation of increased enrollment or income. He never felt secure until budgets all balanced and until he had surplus funds to meet any emergency. His extreme fiscal conservatism carried over to investment policy; Kirkland worked closely with an investment committee of the board and largely determined its overall policies. Only in the 1920s did the complexities of the university portfolio force him to give up his detailed supervision of every investment. Kirkland had earlier supported investments in rental property, but in the 1920s the board sold almost all of this. Over 90 percent of the endowment remained in highly rated corporate bonds. In the mid-1920s the university received as a gift, and then retained, a limited amount of common stock, but only at the end of the decade did it divert even a small share of its investments into the stock market, and this as an avowed experiment. This strategy meant very secure investments but ones that yielded almost no capital gains and only about 5 percent interest during the decade. In fact, for all budgetary purposes, the university assumed a 5 percent yield and placed any surplus earnings into reserve funds.[35]

At the end of the war, as a result of the 1916 fund drive, the consolidated schools (Arts and Science, Engineering, and Pharmacy) had an endowment of just over $2 million. In 1919 this yielded $108,000, compared with $58,000 in student fees, which continued to grow as a percentage of the budget. The new income from the campaign funded the salary increases of 1919, retired some old debts, and helped cover the inflated costs for fuel and for common labor. Because the endowment was in bonds, the university had no effective hedge against inflation. In 1920 the board approved the first of a series of tuition increases, from $100 to $150, also ostensibly to cover faculty salaries. By 1920 the budget of these schools reached $176,000 and continued to rise rapidly with enrollment increases. In 1920 the GEB added $15,000 to the operating budget and $12,500 in 1921, to cover sharp increases in instructional costs. Early in 1920 William K. Vanderbilt gave the university $400,000. Kirkland did not immediately add this to the endowment because of efforts to get matching funds from the GEB. The interest earned from this noncommitted fund paid for the gym annex, at a cost of only $23,922. Then, at Vanderbilt's death in July, 1920, he left another $250,000 to the university, which the GEB matched. This raised the consolidated endowment to over $3 million but left it still far behind that of the Medical School. Kirkland might have used the Vanderbilt money for new buildings, such as a desperately needed library, but his caution led him to place it all in the endowment. In 1921 annual expenses moved to $238,000, but larger student fees and new endowment income provided over $240,000, a healthy situation but one too close to the balancing point to lessen Kirkland's anxiety.[36]

Two special gifts promised physical improvements in the very near future. Back in 1918, Mary Ella Calhoun Foote left her estate to Vanderbilt, to provide a classroom building in memory of her father, William H. Calhoun, a prominent Nashville artisan and merchant. But as with the earlier Furman estate, university lawyers had to fight off a challenge to the will. The university did not agree to a settlement until 1923. Meanwhile, the wife of a former board member and treasurer of the university, Mrs. George M. Neely, offered

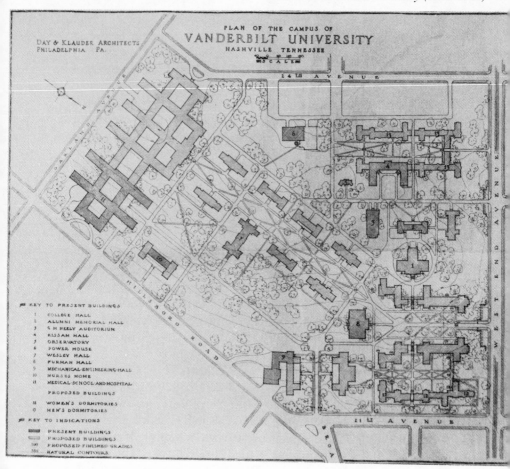

The Klauder plan for Vanderbilt

$100,000 for an auditorium. For two years the university planned to add this auditorium as part of the Alumni Building, but all the parties concerned fell into a protracted wrangle over an appropriate site. The Alumni Association wanted their memorial across from Furman, as part of the old Kessler map, but Neely held out for a building at the apex of the quadrangle, or not very far from the present site of Neely. Finally, Kirkland broke the impasse by paying $1,000 to Charles S. Klauder of Philadelphia to prepare a new campus plan, one that reoriented the campus toward West End and away from Broadway. Guided by it, the Alumni Association let contracts for a separate Alumni Hall while Neely upped her gift to $125,000 for a separate auditorium. The two buildings seemed to be rather expensive luxuries, given the cramped class-rooms, the inadequate labs, and the high-school sized library, but the auditorium actually served library purposes. It made redundant the old chapel, which now became the reading room of the main library. The stacks

Alumni Memorial Hall

Neely Auditorium interior at dedication of new organ

occupied one end, while the original library rooms now housed library services. It was a second-best answer to the library problem, one that would answer only for a few years. Both the new buildings were complete in time for the Vanderbilt semicentennial of October, 1925, or what became a milestone in the history of Vanderbilt, since it also marked the dedication of the new Medical School and Hospital.[37]

The faculty planned the semicentennial program for over three years. It turned out to be the largest celebration in Vanderbilt's history. Because of his prestige and his numerous friends in higher education, Kirkland was able to attract a glittering array of guests. Inevitably, the event turned out to be a long series of tributes to the chancellor, who was now at a normal retirement age of sixty-six. Many guests apparently thought of this as a farewell for Kirkland and came for that reason. Undoubtedly October 15–18, 1925, were the most important and rewarding days of his life. By the time the celebrations were over, everyone in Nashville was sure that Kirkland was correct, that this had been the "greatest educational meeting ever held in the South," and one of the most significant ever held in the United States. Over 300 delegates came from American and even several European universities. John Crowe Ransom headed a committee on local arrangements that went overboard in providing hospitality. Cole, as a railroad man, helped secure railroad passes or reduced fares, plus special Pullman cars, for all visitors. Students, happy to have their classes suspended, manned booths at the railroad stations and escorted guests to the campus, several of whom stayed in vacated dorm rooms.

The celebration had a serious purpose. It amounted to a survey of American higher education, with seminars on several key topics, with papers by college presidents or representatives of the major foundation and by leading journal or newspaper editors. Because the editor of the New York *Times* was one of the panelists, the festivities gained detailed coverage in the *Times* and thus in several other major newspapers. The seminars, in the new Neely auditorium and in the Peabody demonstration school, began on Thursday and climaxed on Friday afternoon. More ceremonial were an elaborate, quite formal presentation of honored guests at the downtown War Memorial Building on Friday morning; several luncheons and dinners, one in a part of the new Medical School; a visit to the Hermitage; an elaborate pageant on the history of universities presented by the Alumnae Council at a rain-drenched Dudley field on Friday evening; a memorial service as part of the dedication of the new Alumni Hall on Saturday morning, with Justice McReynolds, Norman Davis, and the French ambassador all participating; a football game with Tennessee on Saturday afternoon; and a concluding worship service as part of the formal dedication of Neely on Sunday morning.[38]

As Kirkland planned, his opening speech, "Vanderbilt University in Retrospect and Prospect," gained wide and favorable press coverage. He gave an eloquent but rather stereotypical history of Vanderbilt, in a speech so long that it surely tired guests. Almost incidental closing remarks caught the ears of dozing reporters and made newspapers across the country. Kirkland highlighted Vanderbilt's contribution to a growing South, not only to its purported prosperity but to its "spiritual and intellectual" life. Vanderbilt had stimulated a broad culture, scientific habits of thought, and scholarly attainments. Then, in a pointed reference to the just completed Scopes trial, he said "The answer to the episode at Dayton is the building of new laboratories on the Vanderbilt campus for the teaching of science. The remedy for a narrow sectarianism and a belligerent fundamentalism is the establishment on this campus of a School of Religion, illustrating in its methods and its organization the strength of a common faith and the glory of a universal worship."[39]

That sounded good. The reporters, keen to any reference to evolution, loved it. But it was misleading in almost every respect. No one at Vanderbilt in the 1920s honestly faced up to the issues raised by the theory of natural selection. Kirkland and his scientists insisted that organic evolution posed no threat to "religion," whatever they meant by that loaded word. In fact, Darwin's explanation raised crucial questions about the foundations of belief in most traditional versions of a Jewish or Christian deity. Fundamentalists were more honest than Vanderbilt professors in pointing out several areas of conflict between Darwinian evolution and the biblical tradition. And, despite Kirkland's latitudinarian sentiments, any honest survey proved that, even in the homogeneous South, no larger or common faith provided a basis for any universal worship. Only intellectual flabbiness or an irenic innocence allowed such confident assertions. But public relations, not the honest analysis of deeply rooted cultural conflict, best suited Kirkland's purpose. He spoke in order to flatter Vanderbilt's role and to identify its needs, to prepare the Vanderbilt community for a great new canvass. His litany of needs included not only increased endowments but two or three new laboratory buildings, a social science building, a new graduate program, and a dormitory annex for women. All in all, he itemized needs for the future that promised to cost several million dollars.[40]

In June, 1925, the board had already approved a new endowment campaign for the nonmedical parts of the campus. Such seemed a necessity if the College were not to become a minor appendage of the new Medical School, or what almost happened to the Johns Hopkins. Cole, Kirkland, and Norman Davis did the early planning. The board met again at the semicentennial to approve final plans and to announce and to launch the new effort. At first they had planned a goal of $3 million, but some large foundation commitments allowed them to raise the final goal to $4 million, or four times what the university had been able to raise, with great difficulty, in 1916. Of this, $3 million was to double the existing endowment, $1 million was to fund three new buildings. Frank Rand once again chaired the drive and soon had an elaborate organization, including an executive committee of trustees, alumni, and friends. The university also contracted with a New York fund-raising firm and depended upon it for guidance throughout an extended effort, which eventually cost the university just over $100,000. As part of the publicity effort, Kirkland called a conference of southern editors and publishers at Vanderbilt in February of 1926. The purpose was to explore the role of newspapers in the advancement of higher education, but he frankly admitted the relationship to his campaign. The flattered editors were enthusiastic and went home to write articles for almost every major southern newspaper.[41]

In some respects the campaign ended up as a great disappointment. The alumni did not contribute nearly as much as Kirkland had hoped. It is clear that the cost of contacting, pursuing, and finally trying to collect from the ordinary alumni (20 percent gave) cost more than Vanderbilt ever received. That is, the alumni effort, except for a few targeted and wealthy givers, yielded nothing. But garnering dollars was not its primary purpose. Kirkland had to get broad participation to prove good faith to the foundations. Even on that he almost failed. Once again, the early returns seemed very promising; altogether, students, faculty, alumni, and friends in Nashville pledged over $500,000; the board, another $217,000. Ultimately, these general pledges amounted to about $830,000, most from a few individuals, including $100,000 from Frank Rand. Unfortunately, the later collections fell well short of these sums. The big money came from elsewhere. The GEB eventually pledged a matching $300,000 for a new science building plus $350,000 for the endowment. Largely through the work of Norman Davis, members of the Vanderbilt family gave $650,000. This meant pledges of over $2 million by 1926. Then the GEB added another $650,000 as a match for the Vanderbilt funds, bringing the total up to about $2.7 million in mid-1926. The Laura Spelman Rockefeller Memorial eventually gave $750,000 for development of the social sciences, leaving a shortfall of only about $300,000 by early 1927. By counting the $140,000 gift for Calhoun Hall, Kirkland raised the official goal to $4.1 million. In 1927 the pledges came slowly, with at least $150,000 still to go in the fall. Then, in the summer of 1928 Kirkland received $200,000 from the Carnegie Foundation to advance graduate work, which allowed him to announce the successful completion of the campaign. In fact, pledges by then amounted to over $4.1 million, leaving a small surplus as a hedge against collection losses.[42]

As always in such drives, all the publicity attended the pledging. Few paid much attention to the collection effort. This turned out to be an agonizing process for Kirkland and for the professional fund raisers, who sent uncounted letters to get people to honor their nonbinding commitments. The process dragged on and on, even though Kirkland counted any small gift he could find during six years of effort. The collection effort was crucial, for a tightly audited GEB released matching funds only when the university presented evidence of matching pledge money in hand. In February, 1931, over $100,000 still remained uncollected, and by then the cost of collection had reached 50 percent of receipts. But even if it cost 100 percent, the GEB match would make the effort worthwhile in the midst of a deepening depression. The $800,000 of general pledges had now shrunk to about $675,000 collected, and a despairing Kirkland lamented the bad faith, the terrible message sent to the foundations. In June the collections came to within $10,000 and an audit of earlier accounts miraculously revealed an error of that amount. By late 1931 Kirkland could declare the drive over, but not with a feeling of jubilation. Despite all the campaign hyperbole, he now admitted the bitter truth—Vanderbilt remained a Yankee mission to an impoverished and ungenerous South. It still lived almost entirely on northern philanthropy, not on the generosity of its alumni.[43]

The new $3 million for endowment trickled in only slowly from 1927 to 1931. But the firm pledges of $900,000 for new buildings allowed construction to begin in 1927 on what became Buttrick, Garland, and Calhoun halls, all sited according to the new Klauder plan as part of a new, north-south quadrangle. The architectural style remained college gothic, but the more restricted gothic details, and the red brick, created a sharp contrast to the castlelike Furman. Old Science, now completely out of place on the Klauder map, was once again slotted for razing, along with Westside Row, the Old Gym, and the original faculty residences. In the fall of 1928 faculty and students exulted in the more than doubled new space; professors even had offices and could hold conferences with their students, which allowed them to offer a series of new independent study courses. In the final accounting the three buildings cost just over the allocated $900,000. For a time Kirkland feared two of them would come in under $300,000, forcing him to return funds to the GEB. To prevent this, and to buy books desperately needed for a revived graduate program, he persuaded the GEB to count books purchased for new seminar rooms, particularly in the social sciences, as part of building and equipment costs. In this way the departments that moved into Calhoun were able to spend over $10,000 for books. The three buildings came close to fulfilling all of Kirkland's dreams for a completed campus. Lacking was only a library, a women's dorm, a Law School building, and additional space for Engineering. By 1930 he began pushing plans for the library, but the depression helped insure that this would be a difficult, decade-long effort, as would also be his goal of more adequate housing for women. Law and Engineering had to wait until after World War II.[44]

The new collections from the fund drive slowly raised the College and Engineering endowment to over $5 million in 1929, or close to the $6.7 million of the Medical School (its endowment quickly rose by $5 million, once again more than doubling that of the College). Somehow, costs always rose as fast as income. Students continued to pay an ever larger share of their instructional costs. In 1923 the College had shifted from $150 tuition a year to $3 per quarter hour, which came out about the same for a student with a normal load (the change was in part intended to stop students from taking excess work). In 1924 the board raised the fee to $4 a quarter hour, or roughly $200 a year, making Vanderbilt the most expensive College in the South and leading to special efforts to find local employment or scholarships for needy applicants. In spite of costs, students continued to come to Vander-

257

bilt. But as enrollments finally stabilized after 1927, Vanderbilt stopped raising its fees. Ironically, by the time the new buildings had made it possible for Vanderbilt to absorb new students, they no longer wanted to come. A pattern of stable or falling enrollments lasted until the mid-1930s. The added tuition, plus new endowment income, raised the College budget to heights undreamed of in the past. In 1928 the College and Engineering budget climbed to $375,000 and then to $409,000 in 1928–29. In 1926–27 the total university budget first exceeded $1 million and rose to $1.3 million by 1929. By 1931 the university's total assets exceeded $25 million. Excluding the hospital, the two largest budget items—the College and the Medical School—each moved slowly toward $500,000 by 1930. Such spending never meant luxuries, but it did allow some indulgences. For example, Vanderbilt was able to hire a botanist, attend more carefully to its neglected campus trees, rebuild walks and runways, and even begin a periodic cutting of the grass, a luxury it could not afford in the early 1920s.[45]

11

Schools Large and Small

FROM 1915 TO 1930 Vanderbilt revamped its professional schools. This meant consolidation as well as growth. The university suspended the schools of Pharmacy and Dentistry. Religion and Law barely survived. But the revolutionary changes in the Medical School and the launching of a collegiate School of Nursing more than balanced the other disappointments. Here was the big story at Vanderbilt in the 1920s.

Technically, Engineering remained a separate school, to almost everyone's regret. For almost all purposes it functioned as a part of the College, and a quite inferior part. Despite verbal gestures toward the understaffed and ill-equipped school, which still claimed only antiquated facilities in the Engineering Building, Kirkland never allotted any of his new endowment funds to Engineering, except in the sense that faculty members gained from the new salary scales. The fund drives all related to the College, leaving Engineering as a bit of an unwanted orphan. Here, as for the more autonomous professional schools, Kirkland kept hoping for restricted gifts. In the mid-1920s he tried briefly, but unsuccessfully, to attract money for an aeronautical school at Vanderbilt. He frequently stressed Nashville's prime location for engineering and hoped that area businessmen would come forward to endow the school and add to its equipment. In 1916 he considered discontinuing the school and mandated that it restrict its offering to what its facilities justified—a single degree in civil engineering. As a limited response to his pleas, in 1920 the Nashville Engineering Association launched a fund drive for an engineering endowment but raised only $7,000 for the purchase of surplus War Department machine tools.[1]

In 1928, in a rare exhibition of poor judgment, a first faint sign that age might be catching up with him, Kirkland entered into a fantastic contract with an eager fund raiser. An entrepreneurial Willis Waldo maneuvered Kirkland into a self-serving agreement: He would raise $2.7 million for Engineering if Vanderbilt would pay him $5,000 a year for half-time work, pay all his expenses, and guarantee him a professorship in the school if he succeeded (in effect, a purchased chair). If not proffered a professorship, he was to receive double pay for all his work. Waldo wrote a beautiful and costly pamphlet about the school but did not raise a single penny for its endowment. After he eventually stopped his effort, and in the midst of a worsening

259

depression, Kirkland canceled his contract. Despite a lack of any new support, Engineering profited from the rising enrollments of the 1920s, reaching a high of 169 students in 1929–30. But only a disappointing small percentage of its students ever graduated: twelve in 1927, nine in 1928.[2]

Pharmacy simply petered out after World War I. In 1915 the school finally demanded a high school diploma for admission. Enrollment promptly dropped to twenty-five in 1916–17 and to only twenty-three in 1919–20. In 1919 Dean McGill, one of the few campus personalities who had been around almost from the university's founding, retired. The only pharmacist, E.A. Ruddiman, became dean for one final year. The board decided to suspend the school, as a contemplated four-year program would not yet attract any enrollment, given lax state licensing requirements. The implied commitment to a later resumption, given such standards, was mostly a gesture to a distraught McGill and Ruddiman. Ruddiman took a year's leave and then turned down a humane offer of a continued professorship (all along he had a joint appointment in the Medical School), while the chemistry department absorbed the needed offices and labs in Furman.[3]

The fate of the Dental School was tied to the Medical School. Briefly, in its new quarters on the south campus the Dental School thrived. Just before World War I its enrollment rose to 136, and student fees paid operating expenses and yielded small salaries for the proprietors. But it still barely kept up with national accreditation requirements. The National Association of Dental Faculties required a four-year program as of 1917. This, and the war, depressed enrollments to less than the 100 that Kirkland believed essential for survival. In 1918 the faculty asked the university to assume responsibility for salaries. Instructors wanted to follow the lead of the Medical School and give up the last proprietary arrangements in the university. The board finally accepted a new contract and guaranteed one-half of the stated salaries of professors, leaving them only a residual share in surplus funds. By then the Dental School was on notice—raise an endowment or die. This proved an impossible challenge. Nationally, dental schools gained almost no foundation support; most surviving schools would be within state universities. In 1919, with only fifteen freshmen in its new four-year program and a new, one-year college admission standard in the offing, the board dared the difficult decision—it voted to suspend all dental work at the end of 1918–19. But two faculty members would not give up; anxious alumni raised a supporting fund of over $3,500 per year for each of four years, and a reluctant Kirkland and the Executive Committee finally relented.

The school reopened in 1920 for its last short surge of renewal. Enrollment went back up to a booming 214 in 1922–23. By then, the Medical School was scheduled to move to the west campus in 1925, which doomed the Dental School. As of 1923 a one-year college requirement sharply cut its enrollment. No one offered any money to finance new facilities on the west campus, and in none of the planning for the new medical complex had anyone included dentistry. By 1924–25 enrollment was down to 141, with almost all of that in the junior and senior classes. Yet, the school still had a small surplus in its operating budget and thus Kirkland spared the ax for a final year. In 1925–26 the Dental School, now all alone on the south campus, struggled to survive. In that year it graduated its last class but had to bus its students to the west campus for part of their lab work. As long contemplated, the board suspended the still barely solvent school at the end of the year, leaving open the remote possibility that some future benefactor might endow a new school and provide it a building near the new hospital.[4]

The Law School floundered but survived. Kirkland loved it. It required no laboratories or costly facilities, although it gradually took over the third floor of Main in the period of greatest classroom scarcity. Before the war the school required only $10,000 a year to operate. With tuition at $100 a student, it needed only 100 to break even. It consistently failed to achieve that goal until after the war. After the death of Dean Hall in 1915, a part-time dean, John Bell Keeble, took over for the next fourteen years, or until his death in 1929. Keeble was a busy, successful railroad lawyer and thus was unable to provide the supervision needed by the school. Yet he was an eminent, proud, long-term friend of the university; no one dared supplant him. The school practically ceased operation in the war but, for no clear or expected reasons, enjoyed an enrollment boom in its wake. From a surprising 137 in 1919–20 the enrollment peaked at an astounding 230 in 1922–23 and then held firm for two more years. The tuition income paid off the earlier debts and funded two full-time professors—Holden B. Schermerhorn and Charles J. Turck—both of whom served a period as secretary, assuming many duties normally assigned a dean. Unfortunately, in 1925 Turck left for the deanship of the University of Kentucky Law School. By 1922 the Law School set a Vanderbilt precedent—it earned large annual profits, or as much as a $14,000 surplus in 1923. Its students, with fees up to $175 in 1920, were paying up to double their instructional cost. By 1925 it enjoyed an accumulative surplus of nearly $40,000 and invested $30,000 of this to create its first endowment. The school was able to replace Turck, to add a third full-time professor, and to assign over one-half of its courses to the on-campus staff.[5]

The prosperity of the Law School only masked deep problems. Too many proprietary patterns continued; to accommodate the Nashville attorneys who taught part-time, Law School courses remained in the afternoon, giving the school a part-time image. More critical, the school was not strict in enforcing admission requirements. In the boom year of 1922 it first required a year of college for admission but with little effect on the number of applicants. Then, in 1925 all schools that belonged to the American Association of Law Schools had to require two years of college for admission. The new rules threatened Vanderbilt's enrollment, since nonmember law schools never tried to meet such standards; consequently, in the fall of 1925 the Law School only laxly enforced them, even in effect nullified them by admitting many students conditionally. Keeble seemed out of sympathy with the ever-growing requirements, even using the school's location in the South as an excuse for lower standards. A tough examiner from the University of Iowa visited the Law School, developed a degree of contempt for Keeble and his nonprofessional school, and successfully recommended its loss of accreditation by the association in late 1926. Such well-publicized charges of lax standards stunned Kirkland, the long-term advocate of tough accreditation rules, and embarrassed the university as had few events in its history. In part, the problems involved misunderstanding about the number of conditional admissions allowed, but other charges—afternoon courses, part-time instructors, too great a dependence on College courses, poor facilities—all struck home. The loss of accreditation also had a devastating effect on the school, despite almost shrill protestations in the *Alumnus* that the charges were technical and that the school remained one of the most prestigious in the South. Students were afraid to enroll. Current students were afraid their school was disintegrating under them, and enrollments began a precipitous decline, falling from 212 in 1924–25 to a disastrous 83 in 1928–29. Now, like the Dental School four years earlier, the school was close to extinction.[6]

The loss of accreditation had the effect intended by the association. Vanderbilt immediately firmed up its admission standards and began offering morning courses. By 1929 the association ended its three-year suspension. But in every other respect things went from bad to worse. Kirkland almost desperately sought an assistant dean to be de facto dean, only nominally under Keeble. He failed. Schermerhorn, the secretary, became too ill to do much work; consequently, two women—the law librarian and a secretary—practically ran the department in the mid-1920s until even they resigned during the crisis. Kirkland futilely appealed to the prestigious alumni of the school for the $500,000 needed to save it and to provide it a new but small building. To complicate all the problems, the declining enrollment began to use up the accumulated surplus. By 1929 the financial future seemed bleak indeed. No wonder that Kirkland and members of the board openly debated its closure. Even a small summer school, which had yielded a reliable income, suffered a deficit by 1928. In 1929 higher tuition ($200) helped only slightly, for the school was in the red by over $15,000. By 1930 it promised to exhaust all its surplus and soon use up all its $30,000 endowment.

As the board agonized over future options, Dean Keeble died. This was a blessing for the school, for it opened up the possibilities of a full-time dean. In February, 1930, the board reached a rather daring decision—to try to build a prestige school. It agreed to loan the school needed operating funds for up to five years, drawing the money not from the endowment but from the earnings of $265,000 of profits gained on the recent sale of securities. In effect, the board allocated this much to the Law School as a temporary endowment. It approved the appointment, on a five-year contract, of Earl C. Arnold as a full-time dean, at a competitive salary of $7,000, much above any professor in Law or in the College. Vanderbilt lured Arnold from George Washington University and placed on him the burden of reviving the school in the midst of a developing depression.[7]

The School of Religion came even closer to extinction than did Law. After 1914 the Methodist church not only withdrew all financial support but used economic pressure to get its young ministers out of Vanderbilt. It also refused to grant conference standing to those clergymen who chose to continue teaching in the school, forcing them to give up their fellowship in the Methodist ministry. By 1916, after he failed to find any formula for continued church support, Kirkland was ready to discontinue the school. Dean Tillett and his faculty fought to save it and for the next fifteen years effectively argued their case before the Board of Trust. The school entered the new era with minimal funds and embarrassingly few students. It had less than $100,000 in endowment, but, by an agreed-upon formula, continued to receive $12,000 a year from the general endowment of the university. By a somewhat arbitrary decision, based primarily on an earlier division of costs, Kirkland attributed $240,000 of the original Vanderbilt endowments to the School of Religion. He believed donors, including the Vanderbilts, had given their funds primarily for the College of Arts and Science, and so he adamantly refused to transfer any more general funds to the school, leaving it on its own resources to sink or swim. It almost sank. The school had a secure income of roughly $15,000, plus a temporary surplus of $9,000 still uncollected from the Methodist church but committed before 1914. It also enjoyed a small rental income from Wesley, since its few students occupied only a minority of the rooms. It received almost nothing in tuition income, for ministers continued to come tuition free while the old sustentation fund easily paid all their room and board. Even with all these inducements, only forty enrolled for the regular term of 1915–16.[8]

Tillett and his faculty worked out a new scheme for a nondenominational seminary. They planned to educate not only ministers but YMCA secretaries and social service workers. In their terms, they would now emphasize ethics over theology and reflect a "reverent scientific spirit." They would emphasize convergent paths to religious truth and grant equality to students from all denominations. Although its new name—School of Religion—suggested a broad comparative approach and did mark a gradual increase of interest in non-Western religions, the school remained heavily Christian and Protestant, with the Christian Bible as the core of its curriculum and Christian ethics its central emphasis. It tried to model itself after Yale and Union and tried to engender enthusiasm for such a daring innovation in the South. To broaden its appeal, the school listed professors, and related courses, in the College (in English, philosophy, and history), established ties with the School of Country Life at Peabody, soon worked out new agreements with the YMCA, and enlisted several Nashville ministers, from six denominations, to offer what amounted to practicums for ministerial students. Desperate for more students, its faculty now offered two summer terms, all without extra salaries. It also welcomed its first women students, or what Kirkland called a "less meritorious clientele."

Kirkland was apprehensive. He feared a relaxing of standards, a school deliberately shaped to appeal to several ephemeral but nonscholarly and nonprofessional constituencies. Short summer terms, workshops, and institutes might appeal only to those who sought entertainment, momentary diversion, or a small taste of university culture, all provided at no expense by an overly solicitous school. He had wanted a strong, nondenominational seminary, or what he all too accurately described as a school for the "Kingdom of God rather than for any denomination, that emphasizes religion rather than theology, service rather than creeds." Such a vague goal characterized most so-called liberal seminaries in the 1920s. Such appeals to religion in general, or to nonspecific forms of Christianity, well expressed Kirkland's own religious taste. But in 1916, and for the next five years, such a seminary had little appeal. The School of Religion limped through the war and immediate postwar years with an average enrollment of only about thirty full-time students. But the school was able to survive on its meager income, and its faculty kept persuading Kirkland and the board to extend its lease on life, often on a year-to-year basis.[9]

In the first of a series of moves toward termination, the Executive Committee began a year-long evaluation of the School of Religion in 1918. In retrospect, the members believed they would have voted to close if it had not been for the unexpected request from the YMCA. It began a new Training College (see chapter 12), with up to fifty students enrolling in courses in the School of Religion. The program often enabled the school to meet its budget in the early 1920s. By 1921 the school had a slight surplus. Ironically, since its students came free, low enrollments helped the school financially by lowering instructional cost and freeing more of Wesley Hall for rentals. The death of Stevenson in 1919 took the school's ablest scholar but also cut its salary budget. In 1920 Tillett retired as dean but continued to teach theology; Oswald E. Brown took over as dean. To the joy of everyone, in 1921–22 the new Wesley Hall cafeteria opened with great success, soon earning $3,000 to $4,000 a year for the school. In 1922 the Methodist College of Bishops offered to absorb the school if Vanderbilt would surrender Wesley Hall and turn over $240,000 of its general endowment. The Vanderbilt board refused to give so much but asked for further negotiations. At that point the enrollment seemed hardly enough to justify the staff. In 1923 the school granted only four B.D.s; of its twenty-three students, ten were M.A. candidates, some clearly using the school as an easy back door into the graduate program of the College. In spite of its nonprofessional emphasis, a majority of its students remained Methodist, while only the Disciples of Christ welcomed and supported an independent seminary. By 1925 the enrollment slowly climbed back to 60 and soared to 103 by 1929–30. But even this modest success required extensive new strategies and a lowering of academic standards.[10]

In 1925 Professor Henry B. Carré launched a new effort to save the School of Religion. In a sense he gave his life to that effort. He traveled to New York and spent a year of paid leave trying to find benefactors for his school. He wrote a wonderful brochure but met repeated frustrations in his fund raising. Finally he persuaded John D. Rockefeller, Jr., to offer a matching gift of $25,000 a year for five years, not for endowment but to expand the program of the school. Rockefeller, so involved with several medical efforts in the South, saw the five years of his patronage as an experimental period, a testing of whether there was a need and a role for an independent seminary in the South. The matching feature was frightening in 1925 for a school that had been able to raise almost no funds. But, going on faith, the school planned a large campaign, began expanding its offerings, and hoped to be able to match the Rockefeller gift and in addition raise $300,000 in the next five years.[11]

The expansion decided upon, and of greatest interest to Rockefeller, involved new programs for small-town and rural ministers. All along, the school had offered short courses or institutes for ministers, most at no cost to the university. In April of 1927, consistent with its new goals, the school announced a two-week Rural Church School, planned in part by Carré. Already the school had offered a few courses on the country church, in one of several experiments in ethics or applied Christianity. The Rural Church School was a huge success and won Vanderbilt publicity and praise throughout the South. In the first year 168 rural ministers attended, hearing lectures from faculty members and almost sixty invited lecturers. The second effort, in 1928, so boomed as to force subsequent quotas on those admitted. For two weeks the university hosted 377 minister-students from twenty denominations, although over half were southern Methodists. By 1929 the school had to turn away hundreds of applicants. This pioneer effort, which so caught the imagination of the whole region, became the crux of the new, ongoing campaign. Spurred on by small-town newspapers, ordinary people throughout the South pledged money for the School of Religion. The new pledges, by 1928, amounted to $168,000 and thus more than matched Rockefeller's annual gifts. The success of its rural program and its nondenominational or social service emphasis helped persuade a tiny Congregational school—the Atlanta Seminary—to merge with Vanderbilt, bringing with it one paid professor.

In the enthusiasm of the fund drive and in the midst of soaring hopes for the future, the school increased its staff to the largest in its history. In 1928, alone, three new professors joined the faculty—Robert M. Hawkins to take Carré's place in Old Testament, Mims T. Workman in religious education, and Alva W. Taylor in social ethics. Taylor, who came from the Board of Social Welfare of the Disciples of Christ, cemented a close relationship with that movement, and by his social activism added a strong, prophetic emphasis to the school. The Disciples also funded a new chair of theology, filled by George N. Mayhew. Two or three other junior staff members came largely to work with the Rural Church School.[12]

The successes of the school concealed continuing problems. The Rural Church School helped secure funds for regular terms but in itself was hardly an academic undertaking. Kirkland acknowledged its public relations value but deplored its rising cost and its lack of solid academic content. He feared the School of Religion was off on a binge of service-related work, to the neglect of scholarly attainments. He also seemed to fear its prophetic role, its increased involvement with pressing social problems and its increased willingness to address the problem of southern blacks. More critical, the fund drive soon floundered. Once again pledges did not bring gifts. The growing expenses of the campaign, and particularly of collection by professional fund raisers, joined the soaring cost of the Rural Church School, absorbing all the new funds and leaving the school in a more precarious position in 1929 than it had been in 1925. By then, it had a growing debt to the university, a debt loosely secured by unpaid pledges. Then, in 1928, the architect of the canvass, Carré, unexpectedly died. By 1930–31 the depression made it increasingly difficult to collect pledges, and by then the school was in debt by $38,000. Its basic faculty already included seven full professors, and its annual budget had soared to as high as $70,000, including the funds earmarked for the Rural Church School. Campaign costs often exceeded collections, and in the final go-around the whole fund drive had realized, for the benefit of the regular program, little more than Rockefeller's gift.

Kirkland was increasingly at odds with the direction of the school and distressed at its financial mismanagement. He closed down the floundering campaign and suggested the development of a "respectable" winter term for ministers as a substitute for the Rural Church School. But Kirkland was happy with the new, acting dean, George B. Winton, his old Methodist friend and former board member. Brown had retired because of illness and Tillett, back in the deanship, had finally succumbed to age and illness. The only hopeful note, by 1931, was Rockefeller's renewal of his $25,000 annual but matching gift. The problem in 1931 was how to raise the other $25,000. Rockefeller also promised to match gifts of up to $500,000 for an endowment, but only a miracle in 1931 would have enabled the school to raise $500,000.[13]

The success of the Medical School made up for all the problems of the other professional schools. The complexity of this story defies brief explication. Slowly, scattered people matured a conception of a new Vanderbilt Medical School. The pieces all came together by 1921; the new school opened in 1925. The changes wrought in less than a decade were revolutionary. In no other Vanderbilt school, in no other period, did change come so rapidly. Very few people on the campus, in any of the older schools, quite comprehended what was going on, at times least of all the professors in the old Medical School. Even Kirkland, at times, was less a guiding architect than an astonished observer.

Only in a very limited way did the old Medical School grow into a new one. The continuities were few. After the old school moved to the south campus in 1912 and received its $1 million gift from the Carnegie Corporation, it entered a short period of prosperity. The $800,000 placed in endowment, plus student fees, allowed the school to hire three full-time professors in the scientific fields and to operate its small clinic and hospital. In effect, it ran a small charity hospital, with patients paying little or nothing. By choice, the school moved down to an enrollment of about 170 by the war, further reducing tuition income. In 1916–17 it ran an operating deficit of $10,000, which it drew from the $200,000 given by Carnegie for laboratories. Its annual budget now rose to over $100,000.

The school had other problems. By 1918 it had to require two years of college work for admission, which was sure further to depress enrollments, Kirkland addressed an appeal to the Carnegie Corporation in 1917 for additional endowment funds in order to meet minimal requirements for an A-class school. The war intervened, leaving near chaos in the Medical School as it speeded up its training and donated a large share of its faculty and senior students to a special Vanderbilt medical unit. At war's end the school had used up all the lab monies and faced an imminent deficit. More critical, all wartime schemes to complete the Galloway Hospital had fizzled. Given the new standards in medical education, Vanderbilt had to have a hospital or, quite soon, give up on its Medical School. Everyone now recognized this. Simultaneously, Kirkland worked at both sides of the problem—to complete a hospital and to get new endowments. In 1919 he was able to negotiate a settlement with the trustees of a bankrupt Galloway Memorial Fund. They owed Vanderbilt almost $100,000 and other creditors about $30,000. Vanderbilt agreed to assume these debts and to take over all the assets of the trust in exchange for a full title to the uncompleted hospital building. It committed itself to preserve the name, to complete the hospital, and to use it for its intended purpose. Kirkland quickly contracted a firm to plan its completion. For the needed endowment he turned to his old friends, Wallace Buttrick and Abraham Flexner, both with the Rockefeller-funded GEB. In 1919 they committed $4 million to the building of a new Medical School, the largest gift they had ever made to any university. Therein lies a complex story.[14]

John D. Rockefeller, Sr., has been Vanderbilt's most generous benefactor. Such a statement needs a few qualifications. Rockefeller gave Vanderbilt several times over what Cornelius Vanderbilt gave, but this does not diminish the importance of the founding donation. No later gifts could be as critical. Also, in the inflationary period after World War II, Harold S. Vanderbilt contributed much larger sums of money than ever provided by the GEB, but in constant dollars these later gifts did not quite match those of Rockefeller. Yet, surprisingly, Rockefeller has received little recognition at Vanderbilt. No building is named after him, no statues or portraits of him adorn the campus. Few people even associate him with the university. Why this is so involves a man, the times, and a new style of philanthropy.

John D. Rockefeller became the richest man in America by the turn of the century, a billionaire by 1913. He also became one of the most unpopular men in America, the symbol of unfair business practices, the architect of new market-controlling techniques, usually collectively referred to as "trusts." He was the hated oil baron. Personally, Rockefeller hardly deserved the hate. Much more conventional in personal behavior than Vanderbilt, much more conventional in philosophical and religious beliefs than Carnegie, he remained a rather simple, devout Baptist layman. He loved the game that soon brought him so much money he could hardly comprehend its magnitude, but he was neither extravagant nor miserly. From the time of his earliest success he gave away bits and pieces of his income, but at first in an unorganized way. Most early gifts went to Baptist organizations. But as early as 1890, plagued by solicitations and influenced by Carnegie's attempt to launch a new, carefully organized and administered philanthropy (a "gospel of wealth"), Rockefeller began to organize his own charities, which grew in the new century into the largest such in the world. After 1891 he probably gave more attention to these charities than he did to Standard Oil, and with complete sincerity placed all his giving in the context of Christian service, a profession of piety that only persuaded many of his critics that he was a hypocrite trying to camouflage his rapacity. By organizing his charities, by setting up several chartered institutes or foundations, Rockefeller was also able to insulate them from his own reputation. Often, recipients of gifts from a Rockefeller-funded board or institute scarcely associated the gift with the old man.[15]

In March, 1891, Rockefeller selected Frederick T. Gates to organize and manage all his philanthropies, and as it turned out also brilliantly manage his personal investments in behalf of higher yields. Indirectly Gates was responsible for the new Medical School at Vanderbilt. As an educational official in the American Baptist Church, he had already wooed Rockefeller successfully in behalf of the new University of Chicago, although it is worth noting that Rockefeller's original gift of $10 million to Chicago would soon be outdistanced by his grants to Vanderbilt. Gates, a graduate of the University of Rochester and of the Rochester Theological School, was an ordained Baptist minister. He well reflected a growing emphasis at Rochester Theological, one symbolized by its most famous professor, Walter Rauschenbusch, an emphasis upon Christian ethics or a social gospel rather than on the doctrinal controversies that followed in the wake of Darwin. Such a deliberate social strategy considerably outran the intellectual sophistication of an orthodox John D. Rockefeller, Sr., but captured the imagination of John D., Jr., who also played both a direct and an indirect role in Vanderbilt history. It also matched the outlook of another Rochester Theological graduate and ordained Baptist minister, Wallace Buttrick, whom Gates selected to head a new General Education Board.

In the late 1890s Gates began guiding the Rockefeller charities toward science, medicine, and education. Inspired by the new work at the Johns Hopkins Medical School, incensed by the incompetence of so many American physicians, Gates helped set up the Rockefeller Institute for Medical Research in 1901. Significantly for Vanderbilt, he hired as its first director Simon Flexner, a pathologist, a brother of Kirkland's later close friend, Abraham, and a University of Louisville M.D. who had taken postdoctoral work at the Hopkins. In 1903 Gates formed the GEB, with Buttrick as its secretary. Although the title did not suggest it, this board placed almost all of its early emphasis upon the South. In many ways it was a better-funded successor of the Peabody Fund and, as the earlier Peabody story has demonstrated, Buttrick and the GEB closely cooperated with the Peabody trustees in arranging for George Peabody College's move adjacent to the Vanderbilt campus. At its origin, and because of the intense moral concerns of John D., Jr., the directors of the fund planned to emphasize black education and saw their work as a complement to the older Slater fund, a fund dedicated to improved black colleges in the South. Buttrick had served for a time as its general agent, and Kirkland eventually became a member of its board. Slowly, a coalescing body of southern educational reformers, with Kirkland at its periphery and Walter Hines Page at its core, persuaded Buttrick and his board to embrace the full range of southern educational needs. In its early work, when it had very limited funds, the GEB involved itself with agricultural extension and backed the work of Seaman Knapp, whose son and successor in the developing Extension Service was a Vanderbilt alumnus and member of its board.[16]

Eventually medical education attained a special status in the GEB, accounting for about $94 million in disbursements. This concern sprang in part from yet another of Gates's new agencies—the Sanitary Commission, or what is often called the Hookworm Commission. Largely through the advocacy of a persuasive physician, Charles W. Stiles, Gates and Simon Flexner persuaded Rockefeller in 1909 to fund a regional effort to eradicate hookworm disease in the South. Although Stiles probably exaggerated the medical hazards of this parasite, the drive highlighted terrible sanitary conditions throughout the South, conditions tied to poverty, illiteracy, and a nearly total lack of public health services. To head the hookworm effort, Gates turned to Peabody's Wickliffe Rose, Kirkland's loyal ally in the then current Peabody negotiations. To further illustrate all the numerous networks, Rose had been general agent of the Peabody Fund, executive secretary of the ill-funded Southern Education Board (a board committed to the reform of public education), and a member of the Slater fund. He later served as president of the GEB. Until 1915 the Hookworm Commission carried out a complex program of surveys, examinations, treatments, and various hygienic and public health efforts in conjunction with state and local governments. The program at least reduced the incidence of hookworm disease but floundered all too often in broader southern problems—racial separation, poor education, and inept local governments. In particular, the hookworm staff soon realized that their effort interacted with all other social problems and could not be solved in isolation. One problem was the lack of physicians in the South, the incompetence of most, or even the unwillingness of a few able physicians to take any responsibility for broader public health issues. Thus, in 1915 Gates and Rockefeller decided to disband the Sanitary Commission. Under the auspices of a new, blanket agency—the Rockefeller Foundation— they turned to an international hookworm program but left the medical problems of the South primarily to the rapidly expanding GEB.[17]

One more interrelationship is needed to set the stage for the Vanderbilt Medical School. In 1910 Abraham Flexner completed his famous survey of medical education for the Carnegie Foundation. In its aftermath, Carnegie gave his $1 million to Vanderbilt, but the corporation was unwilling to provide funds for a new school. Fortunately, Abraham Flexner had moved on to the GEB in 1912, as secretary under president Buttrick, but kept close ties to the Carnegie charities. By 1917 Kirkland had an ideal opportunity. By then, the GEB had committed up to $50 million for improved medical education nationally, but with the South still a favored region. The Hookworm Commission had not only demonstrated the need for better medical training but for a different sort of medical school, one committed to research on the special diseases of the South, to broad public health efforts, and to an emphasis on disease prevention. These needs—for specialized scientific research and public health outreach—meant completely new or reorganized medical schools and hospitals. This in turn meant large sums of money, money not at all available in the South.[18]

As soon as the war ended Kirkland resumed his correspondence and his personal discussions with Buttrick and Flexner. Letters document only the surface of the story. By February, 1919, the members of the GEB gave a blank check to Buttrick and Flexner, and indirectly to Kirkland; they were to prepare a detailed proposal for a reorganized Vanderbilt Medical School. Buttrick and Flexner also visited Kirkland in Nashville. From this point on, the relationship was not one of a petitioner to benefactors. Flexner and Buttrick took a personal responsibility for the new school, and Flexner was as much or more involved in its planning than Kirkland. A dedication to Christian service guided all three men. At critical junctures Kirkland seemed more cautious, less willing to think in terms of huge sums of money, than his two friends. From these discussions came plans for a reorganization that promised to cost at least $4 million. This the GEB granted in July, 1919, but Kirkland postponed any announcement until November. The new plan was quite ambitious and entailed a new, full-time, research-oriented faculty, or a faculty modeled as closely as possible on the one at the Johns Hopkins and on

Flexner's standards for a modern medical school. In its original grant the GEB emphasized medical training, research, and organized hygiene, particularly relating to venereal diseases, typhoid, malaria, pellegra, and hookworm disease. No medical school in the South (Hopkins they did not count as southern) had the personnel or faculty to train physicians for these tasks or to carry out the needed research. The GEB selected Nashville as a strategic location, noted Vanderbilt's reputation for scholarly standards, and complimented the vision, energy, and leadership of Kirkland.[19]

Significantly, the GEB did not mention the existing Medical School. Few, if any, of the existing faculty fit the new plan. Thus, Kirkland had to confront his faculty with schemes so grand as to eliminate or drastically diminish their future role. Kirkland presented the developing scheme to the medical faculty in September, 1919. He faced bitterness and resentment. But, with varying degrees of reluctance and with no good alternative available, they all tendered their resignations, to be accepted at the pleasure of the board (when it appointed a new faculty), and joined in a statement justifying a new hospital, increased endowments, and a reorganized staff. Kirkland, throughout the transition, did all he could to appease the old faculty. He made a humane but a costly decision—to continue the existing school through the new building program and the reorganization process. Two factors probably influenced this decision—he still contemplated only a series of new buildings on the south campus and he did not yet realize the magnitude of the changes that would occur.[20]

Since the work on the south campus could begin as early as 1920, the GEB encouraged Kirkland to make an early appointment of a dean for the new school. The dean needed to help plan the new buildings and to begin recruiting a new faculty. In a sense, Flexner picked the dean. He asked Kirkland to go to the Medical School of Washington University in St. Louis to interview Dean G. Canby Robinson. This was a fateful trip, one that opened up problems and opportunities undreamed of by Kirkland. The early visit went well. Robinson visited the Vanderbilt campus and seemed enthusiastic about the new opportunity. Kirkland offered him the deanship, but Robinson demurred on the salary offer of $7,500. This began three-way negotiations, with both Kirkland and Robinson turning frequently to GEB officials as arbiters. Robinson tried one ploy vetoed on principle by Flexner— the privilege of a small private practice to raise his income. He finally accepted the $7,500 on January 26, 1920, but with special provisions—$6,500 salary as professor of medicine, $1,000 extra as dean, but with a guarantee that his professorial salary be as large as that of any subsequent professor.[21]

Unknown to Kirkland one dark omen lurked—the depressing realities of the south campus. On his visit Robinson had privately bemoaned the existing facilities. So had the superintendent of the Johns Hopkins Hospital, who investigated in behalf of the GEB in November, 1919. But despite such doubts, the New York architectural firm of Coolidge and Shattuct had completed preliminary plans by May of 1920 for several new buildings on the south campus; to please Robinson, all buildings were to be tied together by tunnels or corridors. The result clearly involved the many compromises required by limited funds, the inadequacy of existing buildings, and the costly legal requirement that the new hospital have separate black and white wards. In the summer of 1920 Robinson gave up on such a makeshift compromise. He decided to push with all his might for a new, ideal, even utopian medical center, whatever it cost.[22]

Robinson joined idealism and aggressiveness. Without these traits Vanderbilt would never have had a prestigious Medical School. In 1920 Robinson was a portly, balding, forty-two-year-old physician. He was, as a Johns Hopkins M.D., a student of the great William Osler, an accomplished teacher, and committed to medical research. He had not been a brilliant student and in some ways remained a quite conventional person, but he had already proved himself an able administrator. Perhaps most important, he became a favorite of the Rockefeller people, serving from 1910 to 1913 as the first resident physician in Simon Flexner's Rockefeller Institute Hospital. He absorbed the idealistic, altruistic outlook of the GEB staff and he had worked effectively to improve the school at Washington University. He had also developed a clear image of an ideal medical school. On a summer vacation in 1920 he wrote these dreams down in an extended memo, which he sent both to Kirkland and the GEB.

Robinson did not write a utopian dream just to stimulate discussion. Instead, he all but demanded a new Vanderbilt School and Hospital on or near the main campus. His plan needs little explication, for the new School and Hospital completed in 1925 followed his suggestions in almost every detail, except for some cuts in scale and cost. His plan presented several main points. The first was that the GEB should spend its funds only for a model medical center, not a patched-up compromise. What did a model center require? A large, unified building to bring classrooms, laboratories, and hospital wards into a harmonious interaction; a location close enough to the College of Arts and Science to enable coordinated research and teaching in the related sciences; a school dedicated as much to research into diseases and their cure as to teaching; and a school staffed, at least at the top, by well-paid, full-time scientist-teachers.[23]

Robinson's memo hit Kirkland like a bombshell. Even the minimal cost of a completely new school stretched beyond $5 million. Of course, Kirkland could not help responding to Robinson's idealism. He, too, had dreamed of a medical school on the main campus. His old friend Dudley had wanted such. But the high cost had deterred any planning for such a school. Kirkland, above all, felt embarrassed. He had worked so hard from 1917 to 1919 to get the $4 million. He could not go to the GEB and ask for that much again; it would seem ungrateful. Besides, he had other commitments—to complete Galloway Memorial and to keep an educational institution on the south campus. Thus, Kirkland's immediate response was one of avowed disappointment and chagrin, even a bit of anger at Robinson's impetuosity in submitting his plan to the GEB without Kirkland's approval.

Robinson would not back down. He eventually put his deanship on the line, forcing the GEB to respond to his plans. In December, 1920, the GEB appropriated $10,000 for a study of alternatives. Buttrick and Flexner asked Kirkland for a detailed analysis of the two alternatives. All planning for the south campus ceased, to the puzzlement of Nashvillians. For a time Flexner and Buttrick did not know Kirkland's real views, but his report, although ostensibly a detached analysis of alternatives, clearly favored the west campus except for the problem of cost. Charles Cason, the old alumni secretary and now a Rockefeller employee, helped sway the GEB toward the new scheme and apparently also communicated Kirkland's increasing enthusiasm for it. Flexner, as much a utopian as Robinson, was soon persuaded, but the GEB was unwilling to pay all the costs. Kirkland came to New York in April, 1921, to make a formal application both to the GEB and the Carnegie Corporation for an additional $4 million. The two foundations gave $1.5 million each, or $1 million short of the minimum that seemed necessary. But Kirkland had the funds necessary for a new building, enough to get the enterprise under way. He remained anxious about the future. Not so Robinson. He knew the early commitment was all-important, that once the GEB had invested so much money, and Flexner so many hopes, it would never let the finished school flounder for lack of funds. He was right.[24]

Kirkland never revealed the true story of the move to the west campus. Apparently he feared the condemnation of his older medical faculty, who had deep loyalties to the south campus. Thus, in rare but deliberate circumlocution, he always talked of "someone" who raised questions about the old site. In his history of Vanderbilt a loyal Mims attributed the original initiative to Cason. Both Kirkland and Mims thus concealed Robinson's true role. Kirkland had two reasons. Since Robinson acted as a dean under Kirkland, Robinson's initiative was in a legal sense also Kirkland's. Also, to have revealed the true story even to the board would have aired a lack of a harmonious chancellor-dean relationship, damaging Robinson's authority in his subsequent planning of the school. Mims probably had a different reason for concealing the true course of events—he did not want to concede to Robinson the credit he deserved for the move. To Mims, Kirkland had to be the chief architect of all Vanderbilt's achievements.[25]

Robinson proved an ideal person for the detailed planning. He sought the best available professors, unstintingly supported them in their early work, and kept aiming for ever higher goals. He proved enthusiastic, expansive, even pushy, and as a result was not always circumspect in his spending. He fought for the highest possible beginning salaries for himself and his faculty. At times he seemed to take university budgets as a type of floor on his spending, a point of reference or departure but not at all as a ceiling. His

273

independence, his free-wheeling style, his strong emphasis upon research as against teaching, and his budgetary overruns would constantly astound or even infuriate a cautious and disciplined Kirkland. But this developing tension at least awaited the opening of the new school in the fall of 1925. Until then, Robinson was a dean largely in absentia, one who made the decisions about staff and buildings that were beyond the competence of Kirkland. With an occasional sense of surprise at the pace of events, Kirkland and the board simply approved Robinson's various suggestions.

The old school functioned under its death notice until the very end. It even continued to appoint new faculty, yet with little hope that any of them would carry over to the new school. The school tried to hold its entering classes to fifty, or all that it could possibly train given the limited clinical facilities. In 1921 it moved its last labs out of the old Elm Street building, thus converting all of it to a crowded hospital of 100 beds. Doing this and rebuilding the nurses' home to absorb increases cost over $100,000, or as much as the building had cost when new. Since student fees yielded only $23,000 of a $144,000 budget, the old school ate up most of the interest yielded by the new endowment, whereas Kirkland had hoped to gain from the delay a surplus fund of up to $300,000. He begged the strictest economy at the old site, but new and unexpected expenses came up each year. The empty shell of Galloway stood as a symbol of past dreams and revoked commitments. Kirkland and his lawyers had to struggle for years to find the old Galloway trustees and to get a signed release from their contract, all eventually gained by a promise to name a wing of the new hospital for Galloway. Then in 1923 Nashville General Hospital suspended the clinical privileges of Vanderbilt students, a move justified by charges that Vanderbilt students were inconsiderate of patients but more likely a reflection of area bitterness against the move. Vanderbilt patched up the dispute and saved its accreditation.

In the last year morale at the old school plummeted, leading in the spring of 1925 to some final concessions by Kirkland. The resulting face-saving announcement was that all the part-time faculty would become clinical professors, at existing rank, in the new school. They would make up only a part of over 75 such clinical professors during the first year, a number that soon soared to over 100. They did not receive a great honor, since almost any well-trained Nashville physician could secure this position, either with token salaries or no pay at all. Only former Dean Lucius E. Burch gained a regular professorship, and this on a part-time basis. The three full-time faculty members in the old school lost their jobs and their income but received one extra year's appointment. The underclass students at the old school did move to the new, with no impediments and a distinct gain in the value of their eventual degree. Only the freshman class of 1925 had to meet the stiff new entrance requirements—a B.A. or three years in Vanderbilt's special premed program.[26]

The planning of the new hospital and medical school took two years.

The never-to-be-completed Galloway Memorial Hospital

Robinson surveyed facilities all over the country and worked closely with the chief architect, Charles A. Coolidge of New York. In a chapel speech at Vanderbilt in 1923 Robinson predicted a medical complex as efficient as any in the country, as perfect as possible. During the long wait he served for a year as head of the Department of Medicine at the Hopkins and also toured European medical centers as a part of his preparation. At least six other waiting professors also spent up to a year in Europe, at Vanderbilt's expense. In September, 1923, the university finally approved contracts for the one large building and for a new power plant and a dorm for nurses. At least in its window details, the final plan reflected the now traditional collegiate gothic. The contract to a New York firm for the 4 million cubic feet of buildings was for almost $2 million, one of the largest ever signed in the Nashville area. Separate contracts for heating, plumbing, and electrical work pushed the total original contract to just over $2.9 million; some inevitable later additions raised this to about $3 million, a tremendous sum in 1925. The completed hospital included Galloway and Carnegie wings but not a Rockefeller wing.

Since little of the old equipment was worth moving, the equipped hospital cost approximately $3.5 million. But the result was universally admired, the first unified school and hospital in the country, a showplace to visitors from all parts of the country and even from foreign countries, and a widely copied model for other new medical schools. It had every known convenience to greet the few patients who moved in November, 1925, from the old Elm Street building. Of course, the hospital quickly proved too small. The architects had anticipated this and had planned for future extensions. Only one sour note accompanied the chaos of construction. One of the loveliest groves of trees on campus had to be sacrificed, along with one of the original and now historic faculty houses. The new hospital stretched along Garland to the very edge of the chancellor's garden; patients looked down upon his iris. His lovely home and grounds had only a temporary reprieve.[27]

By its opening for students in the fall of 1925 the new Medical School had already been in existence for five years. Some faculty members practically deserved tenure before they taught their first course. The careful preparations paid off. Within a few months Robinson could write exultant letters back to friends at Johns Hopkins. It all worked. The government of the Medical School came under the nonclinical professors, the senior and junior men and women handpicked by Robinson, often at the suggestion of the GEB staff. This faculty, like the one in the College, made the original decisions about academic policies. A small body—the executive faculty—included key staff members and all department heads. It had supervisory control over the hospital and immediate responsibility for the administration of the school. Two other committees—one made up of key members of the hospital staff, the other composed of lay visitors from the outside—supervised the hospital. The new hospital superintendent received a salary of only $4,000, lower than most assistant professors in the Medical School. This indicated very well Robinson's priorities. He also appointed an assistant superintendent to take charge of the outpatient department and also paid her $4,000. To the surprise, even the shock, of Kirkland, Robinson treated women equally and

The great new Medical Center under construction, 1925

276

Medical Dean G. Canby Robinson

welcomed them into his faculty. In 1926 he appointed Katherine Dodd as instructor in Pediatrics (she quickly rose to higher ranks) and at $2,500, the same as male instructors. Robinson also insisted upon admitting women to the school, as did all "prestige" schools in the north (two women entered with the class of 1926). The old Medical School had boasted of its all-male student body.[28]

The faculty most distinguished the new school. Comparative judgments are almost impossible in matters of faculty strength. How does one compare age and achieved prominence with youthful brilliance and innovation? But across the board Robinson recruited a faculty that was better than any ever before convened at Vanderbilt. Of course, he could not pluck off the big stars from Columbia or Hopkins, but he did choose some young men who became key stars in those institutions, perhaps most notably young Alfred Blalock in surgery. What he hired were the best professors available in each field, from institutions all over the country. He paid what he needed to get them. The result was a faculty that ranked among that of the four or five best schools in the country. Above all, he selected men and women with proven research skills or achievements. Almost all had additional training beyond the M.D., then still only a bachelor's level degree. Some had both Ph.D.s and M.D.s. In the academic specialities he hired not physicians but distinguished scientists, most with a true doctorate. These included Glenn E. Cullen, a Columbia Ph.D. who came from the University of Pennsylvania as professor of biochemistry; Walter E. Garrey, with a Ph.D. from Chicago, as professor of

277

Vanderbilt's first great scientist,
Ernest A. Goodpasture

physiology; James M. Neill, a Ph.D. from Massachusetts, as associate professor of bacteriology; and Frances H. Swett, Ph.D. Yale, as associate professor of anatomy. The full professors came at salaries of from $7,000 to $8,000, or almost double those in the College. By 1925 Dean Robinson's salary was up to $9,000. In one year the Medical School gathered a group of eminent scientists that put to shame the professors in related fields in the College. They began offering the Ph.D. work that would normally have been part of an arts and science program. The center of scientific strength at Vanderbilt thus shifted in 1925 to the Medical School.

The faculty in the more specialized medical fields was equally distinguished. Consistent with its concerns, the GEB appropriated $10,000 a year for five years to fund a department of preventive medicine and public health. Waller S. Leathers, a graduate of the University of Virginia, a former dean of the University of Mississippi Medical School, and state director of the Mississippi hookworm program, came to Vanderbilt to head this special department, again clearly by contrivance of the GEB. He was also one of a minority of southerners to assume key positions in the school. He later replaced Robinson as dean, to the delight of Kirkland. An equally important appointment, by a later perspective, was the one new full professor who came from the Nashville area, a brilliant pathologist and a Vanderbilt alumnus, Ernest W. Goodpasture. A medical graduate of the Johns Hopkins, he came from the Singer Memorial Research Laboratory in Pittsburgh and had earlier experience at both Hopkins and at Harvard. He would become one of

278

Vanderbilt's most accomplished and most honored scientists. Barney Brooks, professor of surgery and a former colleague of Robinson's at Washington University, was a disciple of the great William S. Halsted. As a special favor, Brooks was allowed to collect limited fees from private patients, an early compromise of Flexner's full-time prescription. Robert S. Cunningham, professor of anatomy, also was a Hopkins man. Paul D. Lamson, professor of pharmacology, came directly from the Hopkins faculty, even though his Ph.D. was from Harvard. Associate Professor Horton Casparis, in pediatrics, took his M.D. at Hopkins; Associate Professor C. Sidney Burwell in medicine had taught there before moving to Vanderbilt. Hugh J. Morgan, an associate professor of clinical medicine (a part-time post), a pioneer in syphilis research and a second Vanderbilt alumnus, had taken an M.D. at Hopkins before joining Flexner's institute. The appointments reveal a few clear patterns. Several appointees had ties to Rockefeller charities or an association with Robinson. Even more had ties to the Johns Hopkins. In a sense, Vanderbilt was a copy of the Hopkins Medical School and Hospital, perhaps even a type of farm club. Unfortunately for Vanderbilt, the movement of staff went in both directions; often its ablest stars ended up at the Hopkins.[29]

When he had completed his scientific and clinical staff, Robinson had approximately as many professors as he had students (182 professors of all types by 1929–30). The new school set tough admission standards, tried to limit enrollment to 50 in each class, and soon had about 400 applicants to choose from, and these from all over the country. It quickly raised tuition from an opening $250 to $300 in 1928 and then added a $25 application fee to cut down the number of applicants. In addition to regular students, who usually numbered from 185 to 195, the school soon had a growing number of graduate or postdoctoral students, some back for special courses, others for a year of advanced training. In 1929 the school began a program in postgraduate studies, with 52 students the first year.

Despite the apparent success of the teaching, medical students still seemed almost lost in all the activity. The full-time professors spent as much time as possible in their own research, to the astonishment of Kirkland. All they seemed to want, year after year, was more apparatus, more assistants, and more salary. They published more research reports than anyone could count, traveled frequently, and held leading positions on specialized medical boards or in professional organizations. Most disturbing, almost no department ever seemed to live within its budget. As new staff came aboard and costs soared, the school seemed headed straight for bankruptcy. And Robinson did nothing about it; he even seemed to rejoice in new expansions or new achievements, whatever they cost. Thus, within a year of the school's opening he and Kirkland began to struggle over priorities. Soon, the contrast of style and personality was so acute that one or the other had to yield, or perhaps leave. By 1927 the best answer probably would have been the retirement of

Kirkland. The university might have gained from a younger chancellor. But it was Robinson who gave up on his golden dream at Vanderbilt; in the spring of 1927 he accepted a similar position at the new and much larger Cornell Medical Center then abuilding in New York. He gave part of his time to Vanderbilt in 1927–28, but increasingly Associate Dean and then Dean Leathers took over leadership of the school. In most respects his leadership was more lackluster.[30]

Robinson's deficits may have reflected not only his idealism and his enthusiasm but a temperamental inability to accept budgetary discipline. He later lost his position at Cornell, in the depression 1930s, in part because of disagreements over finances. But at Vanderbilt, Robinson's policies had a certain logic to them. The GEB wanted a model school, and Robinson tried to achieve this, whatever the cost. He expected the GEB to pick up the tab, and in fact it did just that. Robinson's exuberant optimism raised Vanderbilt to a much higher level of quality and eminence than it would have achieved under Kirkland's always prudent management. One has to pity Kirkland as all this happened, his sleepless nights worrying about the future, his constant anxiety about what Robinson would do next. Perhaps this was the normal tension that develops between an able, aggressive, self-confident dean and faculty and a prudent administrator. In part, it reflected the divided authority in the early school—the GEB on one side, Kirkland and his board on the other. Also, Robinson never fit in a proper chain of command. His faculty loved him, largely because he was their advocate. But he did not consult often with Kirkland, took major decisions on his own, and was not a dutiful, cooperative subordinate. Given the problem, Kirkland played a critical role even if he did not enjoy it. Reluctantly, he tried to interpret what was going on in the Medical School to an uncomprehending board, even as he did all he could to rescue Robinson's booming utopia from financial disaster. He turned again and again, until embarrassed, to the GEB. It kept rescuing him. After 1928, with a dutiful and cooperative Leathers, he finally brought the budget under control. Robinson's talents helped build a great school; Kirkland's caution helped consolidate and preserve it.[31]

The new Medical School revolutionized university budgets. Kirkland was able to retain about $5 million of Medical School endowment after completing the new buildings. This, with student fees and patient fees in the hospital, provided a total income of only $400,000. It was never enough. In the first year, 1925–26, the Medical School spent its income of about $240,000 but increased its budget to $284,000 for 1926–27. In that one year it came through with a small surplus, but already up to $90,000 of its budget represented special three-to-five-year foundation appropriations. These grew to $116,000 by 1928. For example, the GEB not only gave $50,000 over five years for public health, but $50,000 over four years for bacteriology and pediatrics, and other gifts for a revitalized Medical School library. By 1930, professors received over $30,000 a year in research grants. Kirkland never felt at ease with such soft money. He wanted an endowment that guaranteed needed income, and so he worried about the Medical School's future.[32]

From Kirkland's standpoint the early hospital was a disaster. In the first year it ran an $80,000 deficit. Accrued interest, accumulated during the long building period, easily covered the deficit and even left $120,000 for the future, but Kirkland was afraid one more extravagant year would absorb all of it. The hospital staff seemed unable to control costs or unwilling even to try. The director of the outpatient department, Augusta Mathieu, seemed to take every charity case in the city. Kirkland resented her salary, as high as that of men, and the fact that Robinson hired a woman from Ward-Belmont to head the housekeeping department. Mathieu accepted Negro patients, few of whom could pay. Kirkland had joined Robinson in excluding plans for black wards, and apparently had intended to exclude blacks from the clinics. He had wanted an excuse to appeal for donations for a special Negro ward. He also believed that the city of Nashville, not just the GEB, should subsidize charity work. But Robinson backed up Mathieu and emphasized the need, for teaching purposes, of all the patients the hospital could handle. Foreseeing a financial crisis by another year, Kirkland appealed to Flexner and the GEB, in what became a tug-of-war between Robinson and Kirkland. Kirkland insisted on a deficit of no more than $100,000 for the hospital in 1926–27 and stressed that the university would fund only half of this. The GEB would have to cover the other $50,000. Actually, the GEB decided to repay Vanderbilt for about $144,000 in equipment, freeing that much as a surplus to meet hospital deficits for two or three years. Although Buttrick and Flexner deplored waste, they did not want to circumscribe the work of the new hospital.[33]

The hospital situation slowly improved, although Kirkland fretted that budgets seemed meaningless in hospital operations. No one seemed able to control costs; Kirkland compared the hospital to a great machine with its own laws. The deficit in 1926–27 was just over $100,000, but rising patient income gave hope for the future. At this point Robinson left, and Leathers began to ride herd on costs. He also talked to Kirkland, reflecting more caution and discipline than had Robinson. But before Leathers clamped down, 1927–28 Medical School costs soared above the budget by almost $25,000. Kirkland called this reprehensible for the school was unlike the hospital, where costs were unpredictable; the faculty had no excuse at all. Even a departing Robinson was chagrined. This deficit, plus $29,000 beyond the last of the surplus funds in the hospital, left the school and hospital in debt for $53,000. Besides, the two faced a $75,000 drop in income in 1928–29 because of terminating grants. Consequently, Kirkland had to petition the GEB for another large grant. With the prospective annual deficit in the hospital up to $200,000 by 1928–29, he believed it would take $7 million more endowment to secure the school and hospital at its present level. The GEB immediately added $2 million to the endowment but asked Vanderbilt to

281

raise $250,000 locally (it expected help from Nashville, which enjoyed all the benefits plus extensive public health surveys carried out by Leathers and his staff). Since this was far from enough to cover deficits, the GEB continued library funding for three more years and agreed to contribute $625,000 to the operating budget over the next three years. Kirkland still ran scared. He was unable to raise even $25,000 locally. He feared he would still be $25,000 short each year, and what would happen after three years? He thus asked Leathers to cut charitable work by $25,000.[34]

The fears turned out to be unjustified. The hospital was by now saturated with patients and patient income continued to climb. The Medical School, by exercising economies, realized a healthy surplus of over $20,000 for 1928–29. And, glory of glories, the hospital spent $3.94 less than budgeted. The only problem—how to survive after 1930–31. The GEB responded in 1929 by adding $5 million to the endowment (this replaced the annual payments promised in 1929–30 and 1930–31). The Medical School endowment now totaled $12,405,000. The GEB had contributed just over $14 million to the Vanderbilt Medical School and Hospital, the Carnegie Corporation a bit over $1.5 million, or almost exactly what Kirkland, back in 1920, had guessed would be necessary fully to realize Robinson's impossible dream. Kirkland finally had his fiscal security. Typically, he cast about for savings to retire a small debt and to accumulate a reserve of $50,000 to meet any emergencies. Also, by then the Medical School faculty was already desperately short on space and demanding new additions to the hospital.[35]

By a back door route, the new Medical School and Hospital secured a new college for Vanderbilt—the School of Nursing. It moved toward true college status in 1925–26 but attained it only in 1930. When the Medical School, in 1909, first placed some beds in its Elm Street building and pathetically called it a hospital, it had had to establish a small nursing service. In the same year it also had announced a training school for nurses, but no details survive from this early date. In any case, such a school was in no sense a collegiate program or part of the educational mission of Vanderbilt. In the South, in 1909, almost any hospital large enough and sophisticated enough to have a nursing staff also established a so-called training school. Such schools provided cheap labor, labor often devoted not only to the care of patients but to housekeeping tasks. In the worst cases, such "training" represented a form of peonage. Presumably, the Vanderbilt "school" never stooped this low, but at best its early training program was a typical apprenticeship system, involving largely long hours of "student" work in the hospital under the supervision of the regular nursing staff. But by then such a program was respectable enough to attract country girls or girls from low-income families into a closely supervised, almost military form of service. At least in the South, nursing was not yet a preferred vocation for socially prominent young women.

Even the respectability of small training programs, which had existed even earlier at other Nashville hospitals, reflected the trickle-down effects of

The Nursing Class of 1917

Florence Nightingale's famous nursing reforms in mid-nineteenth-century England. She established new schools that had a double emphasis—upon rigorous training that justified a professional status, and upon the almost monastic dedication, the military supervision and discipline in hospitals and nurses' homes that for the first time made it respectable, open to women of breeding and high moral and religious character. After 1873, when Bellevue Hospital in New York formed the first American Nightingale school, aspects of the new reform spread throughout the country, but only a few large hospitals committed the resources necessary for a truly professional training course. The new Johns Hopkins soon took the lead here, as in medicine. These early pioneers in nursing education paralleled, in organization, the better medical schools. They separated their schools and teaching staff from the hospital and the regular nursing service. They included a rigorous preclinical or academic course, taught in part by medical school professors, and followed this by carefully supervised clinical training in various specialities. After three years, such disciplined training led to a prestigious certificate of graduation, and such graduates easily gained registration through state exams. They either went into private practice (the choice of the majority in the nineteenth century), into hospital wards, or, in the new century, increasingly into public health nursing. The new model for nursing education was well established by 1909 and promoted after 1893 by the National League for Nursing Education.

Nursing graduates of 1924

It is doubtful that, apart from Baltimore, the South had a single high-caliber hospital school before World War I. In the absence of state controls, hundreds of hospitals established their own schools. Most were very small. Few had a staff separate from the nursing service; few required any high school work for admission. Most were not even attached to a medical school and had to employ local physicians for a few lectures, if they offered any preclinical academic work at all. Clinical training was strictly on the job. In the hierarchy of such schools, Vanderbilt probably began in 1909 near the middle. At least shortly after its founding, records attest, it offered preclinical training; it at least enjoyed the resources of a medical school. But the clinical facilities were as inadequate for nursing as they were for the physicians.

The move to the south campus in 1912 considerably boosted nursing education. The nurses acquired their own home, and soon the Elm Street building became something close to a true hospital. In these crowded quarters the Medical School tried to bring patients of all types in order to develop physicians' skills. After 1912 the Nursing School set up a standard three-year course of study, admitted students only at designated times, and used the Medical School staff for preclinical lectures. After the new George Peabody College established a program in public health nursing, the Vanderbilt school, along with others in Nashville, could send interested students there for courses. In 1923, just before the move to the west campus, Peabody granted Vanderbilt's graduate nurses ten credit hours toward a degree. In 1918, for the first time, the *Commodore* included photographs of eighteen beautifully uniformed Vanderbilt nurses (only some of these were students), a token of their enhanced reputation during the war and the first hint that

284

they might become recognized as part of the Vanderbilt community. Only in 1924 did the *Commodore* begin including the four or five annual graduates of the Nursing School, listing them incorrectly in 1925 as registered nurses. But before 1925 the school was merely a property of the Medical School. It never gained entry into the Vanderbilt *Bulletin* and its graduates never participated in commencement exercises.[36]

The School of Nursing enjoyed few immediate changes when it moved west in 1925. The patients did not move from Elm Street until November, and at that point the nurses and nursing students also moved. Only during that academic year did Dean Robinson formally appoint a new director of nursing, who was also superintendent of nurses in the hospital. Thus, the new era, such as it was, began only in 1926. The impetus for change once again came from Robinson. Since 1920 he had assumed that a new and stronger Nursing School would parallel the new Medical School. Kirkland, on the other hand, seemed to be unaware of the magnitude of the new departures planned in nursing education and by 1925 was peeved when he realized that potentially expensive plans were abuilding. In 1924 Robinson petitioned the Rockefeller Foundation for funds to sustain a stronger Nursing School, for what he estimated as a $25,000 cost added to an already underfunded hospital budget. One complication was the existing public health nursing program at Peabody, a program tied into existing courses in nursing education. In its own specialized sphere, this program was one of the few academically respectable nursing efforts in the South, but it was seriously handicapped by the lack of a nearby hospital or rigorous training in the medical sciences. Nationally, public health nursing had developed almost as a separate profession and, unlike hospital and private duty nursing, more often had developed in conjunction with colleges than with hospitals.[37]

Robinson, optimistic and expansive as always, proposed a happy marriage of the Peabody program and a new Vanderbilt program in public health nursing. The people at the Rockefeller Foundation were hesitant at first. Concerned about Kirkland's reported antipathy to female education, they were nonetheless attracted to the concept of a model nursing program as a demonstration to the South. They had already provided small endowments to Yale and to a nursing school at Western Reserve. The South clearly needed nursing schools almost as much as it needed medical schools. The people at the foundation particularly relished an emphasis upon public health and, like most funding agencies, wanted to further closer cooperation between Peabody and Vanderbilt. The upshot was two grants—one of $20,000 for each of the next five years to upgrade the existing hospital school; another of $15,000 for five years to both Peabody and Vanderbilt for the joint public health nursing program. For the latter program, the candidates continued to enroll in Peabody but took work both at Peabody and at the Vanderbilt hospital, all under the supervision of a joint committee. Leathers, the physician most involved in this program, never gladly accepted the Peabody

285

Nursing Class of 1926 with instructors

involvement. Also, by 1926, the two institutions began to wrangle over what Vanderbilt saw as a misstatement in the Peabody *Bulletin.* By 1930, in the reorganization of Vanderbilt Nursing School, the cooperation ended and Vanderbilt established its own public health nursing specialty.[38]

In 1926 the Nursing School moved slightly closer to independence. In December, 1925, Robinson selected Edith P. Brodie to be director of the school as well as nursing superintendent. Heretofore, the school had been quite literally a part of the hospital staff. Brodie was an educator and came with the hope of raising the school, as soon as possible, to a true university school with a faculty all its own. She was a Smith College graduate, a registered nurse, and a candidate for an M.A. degree from Washington University, where she had practically assumed the role of a dean. She was also coauthor of a textbook on nursing. But in 1926, except for Brodie, the School of Nursing had no separate faculty. It continued the old pattern of four months of preclinical instruction, after which the nurses went into the wards. The teachers there were the supervising nurses on the floor. Admission into the new program (seventeen entered the first class in 1926) required a high school diploma. The *Bulletin* also announced a degree program, but very few took advantage of it. The College faculty agreed to award one and one-half years of B.S. credit for the 28-month nursing program, thus allowing a student to complete a degree in about five years. Alternatively, a College student could, after three years, enter the nursing program and receive her B.S. upon completing it (no men entered the early program). Such a combined degree program was still rare in 1926, even held in contempt by a few of the great hospital schools. Also note that this amounted not to an integrated program but to an awkward gluing together of two separate educational efforts.[39]

The Nursing School could never gain the status of a true college while under hospital control. By 1928 Dean Fleming of the College, as a member of a university committee on the Nursing School, offered his perceptive critique of its status. It was not at all what the Rockefeller Foundation wanted. Dean Leathers and the other physicians showed little interest in the school as an educational endeavor and treated Brodie much as a clerical subordinate, not at all as an equal. The young women did not receive the status of other university students. The school, like most hospital schools, was mainly a convenience to the hospital, a source of labor. Fleming wanted to confer privately with the Rockefeller people; perhaps he did. Kirkland was not very sympathetic to the school. The Rockefeller grant paid all of its expenses, but soon the forty to fifty nursing students threatened to take up over half the space in the new nursing building. This meant that nurses at the hospital might have to live off campus, require higher salaries, and thus add to the strained hospital budget. Kirkland apparently never conceived of the nursing dorm as a home for students.[40]

In February, 1930, the Rockefeller Foundation raised its annual support for the School of Nursing from $20,000 to $35,000, and this for the next three years. Although Vanderbilt did not hold and invest the principle, the Nursing School now received what amounted to the earnings of a $700,000 endowment, or more than the whole university opened with in 1875. But the new funding was contingent upon a reorganized and independent school, which would require a dean and an instructional staff separate from the hospital and the regular nursing staff. For dean, the Committee on Nursing appointed Shirley C. Titus at $4,000 plus room and board, or a salary comparable to senior professors in the College. Titus, a native Californian, a true pioneer in nursing education, completed her nursing training in San Francisco, took her B.S. from Columbia and her M.A. from Michigan; she had most recently been director of the School of Nursing at the University of Michigan Hospital. Titus began hiring a teaching staff of approximately eleven; an associate professor of public health even received a very competitive salary of $4,000, without board.[41]

The reorganization placed the Vanderbilt school at the forefront of nursing education. It raised it almost to the position in nursing education that the Medical School had attained in the field of medicine. But the new funds did not yet give it the strength, either in its academic or clinical staff, of a few of the most prestigious hospital schools. And, in spite of the reorganization, the

287

school did not fully break with the hospital and would still have to be classified as a modified hospital school. Since the Bachelor of Science program still required a separate sequence in the College, the degree course was not truly an integrated university program. Titus had only a coordinate position with the Superintendent of Nursing, and until 1935 the budget of the school and the hospital remained linked. Both remained under the overall control of the Medical School. The Rockefeller support paid for the new staff; it did not pay the hospital for extra nurses. Thus, to the despair of Titus, the nursing students still served as cheap labor in the wards, often working night shifts. Titus fought to free her students from such an apprenticeship role. But short of financial inducements, the university was unwilling to give up the student labor. Despite such continuing ties to the hospital, the nursing students, unlike 99 percent of those in nursing schools in the South, took even their clinical instruction not under floor nurses but under professors or instructors from the school. At least in this sense the School of Nursing became one of the leading hospital schools in the country by 1930, and one well on its way to complete autonomy within the university. This achievement in nursing completed the building of the modern Vanderbilt University.

12

College Life in the 1920s

AMIDST all the fund drives and the constant building, undergraduate academic and extracurricular life changed only slowly. The College gradually backed away from its earlier classical emphasis. At the end of the war the faculty finally removed Greek and Latin requirements for the B.A. degree. Vanderbilt could not get enough students with high school preparation in both these languages. Thus ended the longtime distinction between the B.A. and B.S. degrees. Only a few students who preferred a B.S. continued to receive it.[1]

The College faculty made other concessions to modernity. It lessened the number of required courses—to one each in English, math, and chemistry, plus a complex range of options in languages. The distribution requirements were lower in the 1920s than in subsequent years. Apparently lowering its standards, the College gave a more vocational slant to its chemistry offering, tied the department more closely to Engineering, and established a new department of commercial science or, as it was soon called, business administration, though it emphasized that this was no vocational program, no typing or shorthand route to college credit. Most of the required courses for a special Bachelor of Science in Commercial Science were in economics and other social sciences. The new staff set up a downtown extension, offering nondegree evening courses taught in part by Nashville businessmen. In 1921 the faculty also converted earlier gym instruction into a department of hygiene and physical education, thereby giving faculty rank to some coaches.

Such compromises only brought Vanderbilt more in line with other American universities. They did not sully its reputation for maintaining high admission requirements and high grading standards. Only Chicago among major universities still had a Greek requirement. Vanderbilt continued to require fifteen carefully selected high school units, and in 1921 it stopped accepting conditional admissions. These fifteen units had to include four units in foreign languages and, in the absence of four units in Latin, an applicant had to have completed solid geometry. The faculty flunked out twenty-two students in 1919–20; Dean Tolman became concerned that too many professors gauged their own performance by a high failure rate. Still, inevitably, he found all too many other professors who casually taught their courses and only loosely graded student papers.[2]

289

By 1921 the College faced a new problem—too many students. This happy situation allowed sharp fee increases and a continuation of tough high school requirements. No one at Vanderbilt had ever before had to compete for admission. Anyone who met the stiff requirements had been automatically welcomed. The women, of course, suffered first. In 1921 the faculty voted a limit of 50 on entering women, since it had no dorms for them. Then, in 1924, it set a limit of 250 on freshmen. This admission goal was intended to produce 50 women, 50 engineers, 50 premeds, and 100 men taking the general B.A. course. But the registrar could not calculate enrollments so exactly and new fees seemed to restrict the flood almost as soon as the quotas went into effect. Even women applicants fell below the allowed 50. By 1928 the registrar had no waiting list at all. The enrollment continued to rise modestly after 1925, but by then transfers accounted for almost all of the increase. More than half the students now came from Tennessee, most from the Nashville area, making Vanderbilt a more regional university than it had been in the late nineteenth century. Its admission criteria also kept it an elitest institution, since it favored the graduates of academies or exceptional urban high schools. In 1928 it changed policy slightly, largely as a bid for more students to fill its new classrooms. It began the selective admission of "unusual" students who had only two of the four language units or only one-half of the math requirement. Too many brilliant students from rural high schools had been excluded by the earlier rules. Also, several high schools had dropped most languages from their curriculum. In this case, accommodation with reality may also have served the cause of greater equity. But given the high tuition, the change did not mean a flood of students from poor rural families.[3]

The most important academic innovation of the 1920s involved graduate instruction. In 1920 Vanderbilt awarded its last Ph.D. under the old graduate program developed in the 1890s. For several years before that, it had accepted no Ph.D. candidates except in Dean Tolman's specialized field. It had also suspended all graduate scholarships. This left only an orphaned M.A. program, without financial support and, increasingly, with few separate graduate seminars. It was a vicious cycle: The evident decline in the quality of the faculty required the curtailing of graduate work; a lack of a vigorous graduate program made it increasingly difficult to recruit able faculty. Laboratory and library deficiencies were equally discouraging. Nonetheless, the College slowly turned back to graduate work in the mid-1920s. The faculty wanted it. The burgeoning enrollment in all southern colleges created a demand for more Vanderbilt M.A.s. Kirkland believed that several young men who could not or would not attend major northern universities might profit from a Ph.D. program at Vanderbilt. The new Medical School added the needed staff and labs for Ph.D. programs in medically related sciences. Perhaps most compelling, Kirkland found by 1925 strong foundation support for improved graduate work, particularly in the lagging South, a propitious opportunity that almost matched what existed in medical education.

Thus, in the campaign of 1925 Kirkland stressed graduate work, particularly in the social sciences. In the campaign, the $750,000 Laura Spelman Rockefeller Memorial gift for improvements in the social sciences, particularly in graduate and advanced areas, and the $200,000 Carnegie gift both specifically supported a new graduate program. Given the funds, Vanderbilt had to produce.[4]

The effort proceeded slowly. In 1920 Vanderbilt revived its older graduate scholarships (ten of $100 each), but then only for M.A. work. In 1923 Kirkland still discouraged professors who asked to enroll Ph.D. candidates. In 1925 he noted that Vanderbilt would offer Ph.D.s in the near future but only in a few fields. In his faculty recruitment after 1925 he tried to get people able to direct graduate work, and he undoubtedly used such prospects as a recruiting tool. In 1926 the university established a new department of graduate instruction, made up of the chancellor, the several deans, and a few senior professors from the College and the Medical School. The department was necessary to provide the needed rules and procedures for a few Ph.D. aspirants already enrolling in the Medical School. In 1927 the College formally announced Ph.D. work and also divided itself into three divisions—physical sciences; social sciences; and humanities, languages, and literature—each with a head. In 1928 Vanderbilt awarded its first two Ph.D.s since 1920, both to students who did their work in anatomy and bacteriology in the Medical School. In 1929 the College presented its first candidate for a new Ph.D., in history, and of the other two Ph.D.s—both in biochemistry—one went to a woman, the first such in Vanderbilt history. In 1931 Vanderbilt awarded five Ph.D.s, with English and history now providing one or two candidates almost every year. From 83 in 1927, the total number of graduate students swelled to 113 in 1929. By then most of the social sciences and English had reinstituted separate graduate seminars. The physical sciences only slowly began advanced work and, except for English, the humanities lagged even farther behind.

In 1927, with the new Laura Spelman Rockefeller funds, the university began expanding in the social sciences. It brought mature scholars to Vanderbilt for one year as research professors and added ten new scholarships. The library was the serious problem. The 50,000 volumes in Main were inadequate even for undergraduates, although interlibrary loans helped. The social science faculties selected 20,000 volumes for the new seminar rooms in Calhoun specifically to meet graduate needs. These proved adequate only for selected fields. For example, the history department at first never attempted Ph.D. work except in American, primarily southern, history. By 1929 Kirkland proposed to move, within a few years, to a separate graduate school with its own dean. Had he found a suitable dean in the existing faculty (Fleming was now ill), he might have taken such a course in the early 1930s. Thus, in the 1920s Vanderbilt finally began cautiously to develop its modern graduate program.[5]

One troubling omission marked all the planning for graduate work. Almost no one ever mentioned George Peabody College. What had happened to the dreams of 1914 of a great integrated University Center? The dream had little substance by 1920, almost none by 1929. Part of the problem remained the stubbornness of both President Payne and Kirkland. Both acted like spoiled children throughout the 1920s. Payne believed, correctly, that Kirkland had always wanted a close affiliation with Peabody, one in which Vanderbilt could determine overall educational policies. He argued that Kirkland wanted a dependent college of education in his backyard. Kirkland could not accept the fully independent and even brash new Peabody. He kept bemoaning the failure of his earlier courtship, what he once described as "the real disappointment of my life." The two men, and thus the two institutions, remained intensely jealous and suspicious all during the decade. Nevertheless, a type of cooperation ran rather smoothly from 1914 until the early 1920s. The exchange of students increased very slowly, with over 100 Peabody students enrolled each year at Vanderbilt (121 in 1927) but only a fourth that many Vanderbilt students reciprocating (32 in 1927). Almost no Vanderbilt students took the allowed twelve hours at Peabody. But Peabody paid for the difference and also worked out amiable arrangements on the use of Vanderbilt dorms and facilities in the summer. Yet, the ties began to loosen early in the 1920s and almost broke under Dean Fleming. He had less respect for Peabody professors, course standards, and educational philosophy than did Kirkland.[6]

Many of the irritants seemed trivial. These included special fees and other restrictions that Peabody used to limit Vanderbilt student use of its swimming pool; the belated threat of Peabody to hold its own semicentennial in May of 1925, thus upstaging Vanderbilt; a series of undocumented charges by Vanderbilt that Peabody instructors discriminated against their students in grading; charges by Peabody students, particularly women, that they faced ridicule and unfair grades from Vanderbilt professors; a series of imperialistic statements by Payne that belittled traditional liberal arts programs; Vanderbilt faculty resentment over lower teaching loads and purportedly higher salaries at Peabody; purported misrepresentations in Peabody catalogs of the cooperation in graduate work or in the new public health nursing program; frequent, undocumented statements by Vanderbilt professors about the frivolous courses offered at Peabody; and frequent charges by Peabody professors and students that Vanderbilt graduates knew almost nothing at all about teaching. But the friction also developed around some important issues, issues that had to be resolved before effective educational cooperation would be possible.[7]

During the 1920s Peabody developed a huge graduate program in education. Over 40 percent of its students sought graduate degrees; in the summer the proportion rose to over 50 percent. Teachers flocked to the huge summer quarter, even as Vanderbilt professors flooded Peabody to earn extra money, there teaching the same advanced courses that they taught during the regular session at Vanderbilt. But Peabody graduate students who wanted to continue advanced work during the regular academic year had to take these same courses at Vanderbilt. From Payne's perspective, the availability of graduate work at Vanderbilt was the primary reason for Peabody's cooperation with Vanderbilt. Thus, Peabody early negotiated an agreement with Vanderbilt and advertised it in its catalog. It referred, quite properly, to a joint graduate program and listed all the available courses in both institutions. Its graduate students could take half their work at Vanderbilt but had to complete their thesis at Peabody. The agreement was reciprocal, but few Vanderbilt students took advantage of it; Vanderbilt M.A. candidates rarely chose work in education. As early as 1923 the Vanderbilt faculty clearly wanted out of such a one-way arrangement, because Peabody students might flood their seminars, because many judged Peabody students inferior, and because in a few cases graduate students who could not meet Vanderbilt language requirements used Peabody as a back door to the same courses.

The issue came to a head in 1927 when Vanderbilt announced its new Ph.D. program. During the year a joint Peabody-Vanderbilt committee worked out a new, essentially unchanged plan of cooperation for undergraduates. But Vanderbilt asked Peabody to deny its students admission to Ph.D. work at Vanderbilt. The request struck a sensitive nerve, for what it communicated to Peabody was a Vanderbilt effort to segregate its graduate program. Such an interpretation accurately reflected the feeling of at least Dean Fleming and some of his faculty. In addition, Vanderbilt soon refused to open its library for Peabody summer students, the first of many irritations that impeded the construction of a joint library. Payne was angry, along with many of his faculty, and so took his complaints to the GEB. In fact, both Vanderbilt and Peabody kept trying to make their case before the GEB, which still urged more institutional cooperation. The GEB eventually persuaded Vanderbilt to relent—to allow Ph.D. candidates in education to take Ph.D.-level work at Vanderbilt—and then turned down petitions from Peabody for funds to inaugurate Ph.D. programs in the arts and sciences.[8]

The quarrel deepened in the next three years. As early as 1926 Dean Fleming had proposed to Kirkland that Vanderbilt give up on Peabody and establish its own education department. Kirkland had to demur, because such a move openly and flagrantly would violate the cooperative agreement. He asked Fleming to move cautiously and to consult with Peabody and the GEB. The excuse was scheduling difficulties for Vanderbilt students. By 1929 Kirkland used this as a basis for a justifying letter to the GEB; Vanderbilt students often could not schedule the courses they needed for state certification. The GEB accepted the logic, and so Vanderbilt established its own department in 1930, with Joseph K. Hart as its head. At the same time Fleming, who recognized the need of summer work for graduate students, began formulating plans for a new summer quarter at Vanderbilt, another

293

direct slap at Peabody and possibly a ploy to woo Vanderbilt professors away from their summer teaching at Peabody. By then, the estrangement was almost complete. The long road back to more effective cooperation began in the 1930s and blossomed only after the retirement of Kirkland and the death of Payne.[9]

Meanwhile, two other colleges moved into Vanderbilt's neighborhood—the YMCA Training College and Scarritt College. Willis D. Weatherford, a Vanderbilt alumnus and former YMCA secretary, first proposed in 1919 a southern college for YMCA secretaries to complement two such in the North. His proposal to Vanderbilt largely concerned the struggling School of Religion and its half-empty Wesley Hall. He wanted to set up a four-quarter program of training, with the summer quarter at the YMCA's Blue Ridge assembly grounds and the three regular quarters at Wesley. The aspiring YMCA secretaries would be able to take, and to pay tuition for, courses in the School of Religion, plus others at Peabody and in the Medical School. Weatherford sought a $500,000 endowment and hoped to erect his own building in the future. Since his plan offered hope for the School of Religion, Kirkland welcomed the venture, which amounted to a two-year, upper-level professional course for applicants with at least two years of college. The YMCA College opened in 1920 with its own staff of three, and with plans for up to 100 students each year. In 1925 the new college purchased from Vanderbilt a site just north of the Peabody Demonstration School and with a loan from Vanderbilt completed its wondrous new gym and classroom building in 1927. Broader cooperation soon evolved, for Vanderbilt now used the YMCA gyms for physical education instruction and helped pay the salary of YMCA gym instructors. Vanderbilt students, for the first time, had ready access to a swimming pool and women students enjoyed their first facilities for physical education. Later, when the YMCA venture failed and after old Wesley burned, Vanderbilt acquired the building and renamed it Wesley Hall, the new home of the School of Religion.[10]

The Scarritt story is a briefer one. In 1923 Jesse L. Cuninggim, of the old Biblical correspondence school and then president of the Scarritt Bible and Training School of Kansas City, persuaded his board to move the college to Nashville, after extensive conferences with Kirkland, Payne, and several Methodist officials. Scarritt was a small Methodist missionary training college with advanced and graduate-level instruction. It would now, for the first time, admit men as well as women. Cuninggim wanted partial affiliation with Peabody, for in a sense Scarritt was another, specialized education college. As a southern Methodist institution it could not yet even hint at affiliation with Vanderbilt. The bishops were even concerned that it was too close to the Vanderbilt campus. Yet Cuninggim consulted with Kirkland and relied upon the School of Religion for some of the courses needed by his students. The college opened in Nashville in 1924, in Peabody facilities and with 125 students. In 1926 it began construction of its first complex of gothic stone buildings (the core of its present campus). Apparently from the very beginning, Vanderbilt granted library privileges to Scarritt faculty and students and welcomed its students into courses.[11]

In popular mythology, the decade from 1919 to 1929 marked a period of cynicism and rebellion on campuses. Little at Vanderbilt supported such images. Sharp breaks in student morale, beliefs, or behavior are not visible in the surviving records. Of course, change was continuous but often noticeable only when it had accumulated for years. A few changes did support the popular myth. In the 1920s Vanderbilt students clearly moved away, in greater numbers, from the evangelical religion that had so agitated the campus back in 1914. The role of the YMCA declined and revivals all but ceased. More students seemed wary of conventional religion, suspicious of churches, or reluctant to be preached at by professors or anyone else. But at Vanderbilt one finds no moral revolution and no evidence of repudiation of conventional sex roles, family pieties, or traditional political allegiances. Students did talk more openly, and with greater anxiety, about sex, did condemn prohibition and more openly sanctioned alcoholic drinks, and did, for the first time, begin open and serious discussions of southern racial policies. To some extent Vanderbilt students picked up all the fads and fashions of the decade, just as they had in earlier decades. They had always resented tight rules and regulations and still did. But in the 1920s they faced more of those than ever before at Vanderbilt. *In loco parentis* arrived, which may, more than anything else, account for mild protest, beginning with the anti-ROTC crusade. But most Vanderbilt students still loved football and parties, and a higher percentage than ever before joined fraternities. In fact, a survey of student concerns in the 1920s would include little else but football and fraternity dances. In their publications, students probed the limits of propriety; male students commented endlessly on the "new woman," although she was barely visible on campus. That is, few Vanderbilt women smoked, drank gin, or drove sports cars.

The war helped change student life. To meet SATC requirements the university had to furnish the rooms in Kissam and to hire a caterer to operate the dining hall. When the war ended, a $10 increase in room rents covered the cost of furniture, but this "progress" ended earlier, innovative student efforts to furnish their own rooms. Also lost was the old, student-run boarding system. The university tried to furnish board at fixed rates after the war but faced incessant student complaints and a flight of students from the Kissam dining hall to fraternity eating clubs. The Wesley mess did not open immediately after the war. To preserve the dining hall, the faculty in 1919 required freshmen not only to live in Kissam but also to take their meals there, a very unpopular rule. As an experiment, in 1921 the School of Religion decided to reopen the dining room in Wesley as a cash-only cafeteria. This proved immensely popular, for soon Peabody students and townspeople joined Vanderbilt students to enjoy the purportedly "home cooked" meals.

Up to 358 came each meal, and soon up to fourteen students had jobs. Thus, in 1923 Kissam, which had already featured a small cafeteria as an adjunct to the dining room, converted its large dining room into a student cafeteria. The voluntary features seemed to please students, and the complaints about food fell to their normal level. Here, also, students, including the women, received needed employment. But, to the despair of Kirkland and the faculty, Kissam was no longer the center of campus life. In the 1920s almost no students except for a few poor boys chose to live in the inadequate rooms of Westside Row, and very few upperclassmen chose rooms in Kissam. Since the resident male freshmen had to room there, their dominance probably stigmatized it for older men. Also, with the passage of time the glorious Kissam of 1902 now seemed antiquated, even foreboding to students. Improvements did little to enhance it. Just before the war the building crews had broken doors through the fire walls, so that north wing students could have indoor access to baths and toilets in the basement, ending their famous, partly undressed parade across the courtyard. In 1919 the administration added new baths and began converting some rooms into toilets on each floor.[12]

The unpopularity of the dorm only meant an ever greater role for fraternities. Their problems plagued the faculty throughout the 1920s, but no one could find a solution. By the mid-1920s over 70 percent of the College and Engineering men belonged to fraternities, up from 50 percent at the turn of the century. With few exceptions, all upperclassmen roomed in boarding houses or in their own fraternity houses. The degree of dispersion rivaled that of 1875; at times only the on-campus freshmen seemed to have any loyalty to the university as a whole. In the 1920s Vanderbilt became the fraternity school of the South, famous for the strength of its major houses and for the fanatical loyalty of members. Except in scholarship, fraternity men dominated every activity on campus. The dispersion into autonomous little communities created problems of centralized control and discipline and added to student costs. Kirkland often lamented the evils of the fraternity system. On two or three occasions faculty committees investigated, but little changed. Despite over thirty years of faculty pressure, the fraternities would not give up their fall rush, which meant anarchy for freshmen as soon as they arrived on campus. When, in 1929, Dean Sarratt first tried to develop a special freshman orientation, he feared it could not work if he did not find some way to keep eager fraternity men from molesting the freshmen, all in an effort to get ahead start in recruiting the ablest. In 1919 the faculty tried a lure, an offer to lease lots on campus and to advance loans for new, clustered fraternity houses along 24th Avenue. Elaborate rules insured the rough equality of the houses. None of the established fraternities, with increasing revenues from new members in the early 1920s, was interested in moving. As enrollment increased the old chapters simply expanded and new ones moved to the campus area, including the first Jewish fraternity in 1928 (in 1915 Jewish students had established a Menorah Society).[13]

Moves to create a counterweight to the fraternities never worked for long. The latest of such efforts was a commons club, formed in 1921 for non-fraternity men. It had strong faculty support, stressed cooperation with fraternities rather than criticism, and emphasized unity and university spirit, but it faded from the scene in a year or two. In 1925 the students all joined in a student union as part of the new Alumni Hall program. The union was not much more than a cover for a new $5 activity fee, which funded a director and student activities in the new building. It never replaced, or even competed with, fraternities.[14]

In an attempt to exercise stronger control over increasingly dispersed students, Vanderbilt began in the 1920s to build an elaborate system of student supervision. New forms of student government emerged. As a new generation of students gathered in 1920, Kirkland became a bit frightened. They seemed so bent on parties and fun, so casual about academic work, and in too many cases downright immoral. In 1919–20 he dismissed increasing numbers of students for cheating and a few others for gambling. The honor system seemed in jeopardy. As a partial answer, and to take from his busy schedule the increasing disciplinary burden, he recommended a new officer, called either a secretary of the faculty or a dean of students. He persuaded Mims to accept this position for one year, in 1921–22. Then, in a move he never regretted, he transferred the young Charles Sarratt to the job in 1922. Kirkland soon had complete confidence in Sarratt and for the first time in Vanderbilt history moved almost all student issues outside the chancellor's office. Sarratt had lived in Kissam before his marriage and had become an artist in managing his boys. He talked their language, used indirect means of gentle persuasion, and always gave them a feeling that he was supportive. He made rules flexible, and in students' numerous off-campus scrapes he always served as a solicitous advocate. He served on all faculty or joint faculty-student committees dealing with student life. In 1925, with the appointment of a dean of women, his title became dean of men and eventually his authority extended beyond the College to the whole campus. Sarratt had the backing of a new university committee. Its origins went back to a special 1919 committee on university relations, made up of faculty, students, and alumni, and which tried to find solutions to dorm and fraternity problems. Then in 1922 the university formed a new committee on student life and interests, with Sarratt as its coordinator. It did its work through several specialized subcommittees, such as one that regulated all student publications.[15]

The publication committee had a difficult task, both in stimulating student journalism and arbitrating the outer limits of student freedom. Unlike their counterparts on many campuses, the *Hustler, Commodore,* and different literary or humor magazines had to pay their own way through advertisements and subscriptions. They barely survived year after year. A publication board was born in 1916, along with the beginnings of an elected student council. The board included faculty, alumni, and student members but did not really begin to function until after the war. In part, it grew out of a famous controversy that erupted in May, 1916. A small group of anonymous students launched a new, clandestine humor sheet, *The Vampire*, published by the "Circle of Five" to "knock" certain conditions at Vanderbilt. Its first number proved its last. It defied all the conventions and was as irreverent as any campus publication until the 1960s. The writers referred to Kirkland as "Jimmy Chance" or as "His Baldness," made several vicious attacks on student council president and later board member Robert Garner, referred to a prim and pious student council as the committee on public safety, accused Garner's girlfriend of enjoying a dirty joke, and, most scandalous of all, referred to a popular sorority as a "cess pool of iniquity." Administrators and faculty found the edition anything but funny, as did most students. A special investigating committee of students eventually identified one of the three "publishers" and by faculty approval tried him and voted his expulsion. He refused to identify his cohorts.[16]

The new publication board tried to avoid another *Vampire*. It began by altering the ownership of authorized publications, taking the *Hustler* from the athletic association and the *Commodore* from the fraternities. Both continued into the 1920s without major problems but with fluctuating quality. The old literary journal, the *Observer*, died with the war, and by then with few regrets. Fewer and fewer people wanted to read student term papers or the speeches delivered in chapel. What Vanderbilt students seemed to want was a humor magazine, which they launched in 1919 as the *Jade*. Modeled after the Harvard *Lampoon*, it proved a difficult chore for various editors. It remained a thin but sparkling little journal, with some excellent poetry to balance its jokes, short stories, and often heavy satire. Then, in 1923, it exceeded the limits of propriety permitted by the publicity committee, leading to the first suppression since 1878 of an ongoing student publication. The last *Jade* of 1922–23, as was by then traditional, was a women's issue, not only written largely by women but oriented to women's issues. The editors, though, all were male. This famous final number, often referred to on campus as the Lady Godiva issue, unfortunately has not survived. After the women submitted copy, the editors doctored a drawing of a "perfect 36" bathing girl; the male editors so contrived a broken shoulder strap as to bare too much breast, at least by contemporary standards and to the considerable embarrassment of the women and the horror of faculty members. After about twenty-five of the offensive issues had been distributed at an evening party, the faculty impounded the rest and destroyed them. It then closed the *Jade* forever and two of its editors were denied their degrees. In the fall of 1923 new editors launched its successor, the *Carpet Bagger*, but the title offended southern chauvinists. Finally, in the winter of 1924 students successfully launched the *Masquerader*, which continued throughout the decade and, except for the absence of any further indiscretions, was a virtual twin to the earlier *Jade*. It probed the limits of frankness about sex, not by nudity but by innuendo. It is

298

also worth noting that Vanderbilt students considered *The Fugitive* another, and soon very famous, student publication.[17]

Formal student government began in 1916. As early as 1914, students had bid for some power in the university, some check upon the unlimited authority of the faculty. By 1916 two committees—one made up of faculty, a broader one appointed by the chancellor—worked out a plan for a student council, one that won student approval. The members of the all-male council were elected by the four classes. Its first goal was to own and supervise publications; it made a name for itself by its enthusiastic leadership in the new endowment campaign, particularly in the final city campaign of October, 1916. Its first political success came over the issue of compulsory chapel. The students resented the compulsion and won a faculty ally in 1917 when George Mayfield described such chapel as a medieval carryover. Kirkland, as always, defended it for its moral and religious role. But drawing from the various proposals, the faculty reduced compulsory chapel to a special Wednesday convocation, at noon, which faculty had to attend. Students also had to attend one other less significant chapel each week, on Monday or Tuesday. Thursday was reserved for voluntary religious services, usually led by the YMCA, and Friday for student assemblies, completely under their own control. The new plan eliminated most student complaints. During the war the student council seemed to lose any clear role, but it at least continued to function throughout the 1920s. Its work joined that of a new honor council, completely in student hands after 1920–21. The women, excluded from both the councils (how could a male student ever press charges against a female?), had to form their own duplicate councils, or what became, in the 1920s, a policy of separate but not equal for everything touching upon women.[18]

The story of women at Vanderbilt grew more complex in the 1920s. They made impressive gains, but their status on campus became more insecure than a decade earlier. Victories won seemed to have to be won over and over again, in what became by the 1920s an open battle by women for elementary equity. The two exceptions involved the new School of Medicine and the developing School of Nursing. Here, women were accepted as equals, but these schools were quite distinct from the traditional parts of the campus. Two changes seemed to underlie a revived challenge to women—their increasing numbers and influence on campus and the enrollment boom of the early 1920s. During the fall of 1918 women briefly took over the campus. They had already come close to monopolizing academic honors. After the war they were numerous enough, and self-conscious enough, to organize and to battle for their rights. To all, from Kirkland on down, the development seemed threatening. Before the war women helped build needed enrollment. By 1923 they seemed to be taking slots that young men craved and were more resented as a consequence. In the 1920s women broke all earlier enrollment barriers; they first entered the School of Religion, the Dental School, and the Law School in 1916, the Medical School in 1926, and Engineering in 1929.

Alumnae historical pageant, 1923

The firsts multiplied: first class presidency in 1918; first representative on *Commodore* staff, 1918; first loss of a women's basketball game, 1918; first alumna to address an alumni dinner, 1921; first female athletic association, 1929; first Ph.D., 1929; first girls' premed club, 1929; and first Lady of the Bracelet, 1929 (after this, the men threatened to disallow female voting for the Bachelor of Ugliness).[19]

From 1920 on, the women staged an annual stunt night, often before standing-room-only audiences. In 1923 a new Alumnae Council staged Vanderbilt's first historical pageant (men and children took part) in the new and darkened Dudley Field, by far the most elaborate staged event heretofore in Vanderbilt's history. It included four historical scenes on Nashville history, featured over 100 actors, had large sets and even horses on the field, used several dances and pantomimes, and tried out new spotlights. The event was only a prelude to the pageant the women staged for the semincentennial. During the decade they formed four new sororities, organized their own panhellenic council, and founded several literary societies or honor clubs. By 1929, 348 women students were on campus, scattered in all the schools and constituting about 25 percent of the total. Throughout the 1920s they won more than their share of M.A.s, served as teaching fellows, and rejoiced at five or six women instructors in the College. The new Student Health Service, begun in 1927 in a Westside Row house and directed by physicians Thomas B. and Kate Zerfoss, was particularly accommodating to women, since Kate Zerfoss devoted a great deal of attention to their health needs, a type of care enjoyed by women at few other campuses. The women still enjoyed the highest academic average of any classifiable group on campus (1.808 on a

Alumni reunion in Gym Annex, 1925

The old grads at Semi-Centennial Celebration of 1925

3.00 system, or close to a B average). In comparison, the highest academic average for the most brainy fraternity was 1.742. Of the women, 177 lived at home in Nashville, 50 in boarding houses, 19 in sororities, 65 in the nursing dorm, 34 in three small dorms, and 3 at Ward-Belmont. Perhaps less complimentary, beginning in 1923 the football team elected two women as sponsors and displayed them on the team bench at each game. Women could not yet play in the marching band or lead cheers.[20]

These achievements did not come easily. The *Hustler* was frequently hostile and used women only as lowly reporters. As late as 1929 almost all *Hustler* references to students were to "men." In 1929 the all but defunct literary societies, in a desperate bid for attention, held a debate on whether women should be allowed at Vanderbilt, a throwback to the debates of the 1880s. Almost no one ever mentioned them or included them. Until the new Neely forced their integration, they sat in the chapel balcony to hear speeches directed at "Vanderbilt men." Kirkland, in his references to students, almost never mentioned women. An alumna in 1923 struck back, and with some effect. The Alumni Association worked for years to compile and publish an *Alumni Directory,* an effort that eventually almost bankrupted the association. For months the *Alumnus* contained appeals for information, all to go into what the association referred to as a *Directory of Vanderbilt Men.* A former student wrote a bitter letter; she was tired of being ignored by everyone. The *Bulletin* contained only masculine pronouns. The honor system pledged one's honor "as a gentleman." Her degree had been conferred upon a "him." Speakers always directed their addresses to the "young gentlemen." Even most of her letters from the Alumni Association were addressed to a "Mr." She did not like to be invisible. This protest worked. From then on alumni references were to both men and women, the book became the *Alumni Directory,* and so far as possible letters went out addressed to Mr. or Miss or Mrs. But the minor victory did not symbolize any genuine acceptance of women. Perhaps Kirkland put it best, and officially, at his speech at the semicentennial. He noted that Vanderbilt was founded as a university for men. He alleged that its general tone would so remain. He acknowledged women's unsatisfactory position at Vanderbilt. He suggested that Vanderbilt should do more for women or refuse to admit them. But refusal was now impossible. The cooperative agreement with Peabody brought women on the campus all the time (Kirkland often seemed to resent Peabody's feminine atmosphere). Thus, the only good answer was the old one—a separate women's college with separate courses at the elementary level, innovations that could require at least $1 million.[21]

Kirkland hit at the nub of women's status. He followed a consistent path. After the divorce with the church, he decided, without any evidence, that all past donors had given money for the College and for men's education. This meant that neither the professional schools nor women had any claim to endowment income. They came to Vanderbilt, at best, as guests. He had tried, with great enthusiasm, to raise money for a women's annex in 1900. This became his fixation. Consistent with those views, he would gladly use endowment income to hire Dean Sarratt but never considered using such funds to hire a dean of women. Thus, beginning in 1921, with the quota of fifty women, he kept insisting that the women would have to solve their own problems, get their own money, attract donors. He even solicited a women's dorm from Vanderbilt descendants. With the quota he made a promise—if women raised $1 million for an annex, then Vanderbilt would admit 200 women from outside Nashville, another 100 from Nashville. From that endowment they could also have a dean of women plus women teachers for their segregated courses.[22]

In a very limited way the women tried to follow his advice. In 1923 they formed their Alumnae Council in order to raise money at least for a dorm, a dean, and physical education facilities. In what Kirkland referred to as women's "agitation," they set out to win certification by the American Association of University Women (AAUW), which required these three marks of women's acceptance to accredit Vanderbilt. Kirkland gave them a rather backhanded blessing—the effort was a brave one and the women could do no harm by it. The effort, even if unsuccessful, might end all the absurd criticism of Vanderbilt for purported unfairness to women.[23]

The women moved rapidly. Their project income joined with pledges from the University Woman's Club and with other small gifts. By 1925 they offered to pay $3,000 a year for their own dean; Kirkland accepted their offer and hired Ada Bell Stapleton as the first dean of women and also professor of English. Stapleton had just won her Ph.D. from the University of London and had credentials equal to any of the younger male faculty. Her salary rivaled that of associate professors, and Kirkland followed the precedent set by Sarratt's case in giving her an undeserved professorial rank. She was no feminist and believed in a strict double standard. She soon placed the women under tougher rules than ever before. They could not afford a real dorm, but the university provided them two houses, the former Harry Vaughn house on 24th Avenue and the old Plummer house on Garland; one of these became the freshman dorm. In addition, the women who boarded with Stella Vaughn accepted the new dorm rules, making this a third approved residence. The new YMCA gym, beginning in 1927, finally provided the needed physical education instruction, and thus Vanderbilt women finally became eligible for AAUW approval in that year, but one wonders if the university attitudes justified it.[24]

Blacks, of course, hardly made up a minority at Vanderbilt. They still held only servile jobs. But among faculty and students, one can find hints of coming changes in racial beliefs. The YMCA offered courses on race relations, both before and after the war. Gus Dyer also organized discussion groups to help improve interracial understanding. The new School of Religion, with its increased emphasis upon "applied ethics," tried to lessen racial tensions and, by the end of the 1920s, had a nucleus of faculty members committed to equal rights for blacks, still a very radical position in the South. Mims and Kirkland took the lead at the end of the war in a law-and-order movement against lynching. These were straws in the wind, but they documented an increased sensitivity to racial issues. "Nigger" jokes continued, but they mixed with student concerns over racial policy and with some willingness to consider alternatives. Often the basis of the new concern was a developing commitment to "separate but really equal," a position much more radical in its implications for the South than most people realized. Of course, in most cases the concern was still paternalistic, but paternal concern may be an improvement over hostility or unjustified fears.[25]

A few interracial meetings at Vanderbilt hinted at future change even as they illustrated the intensity of southern resistance to racial progress. Notably, the impetus toward racial reform at Vanderbilt came from the School of Religion or from YMCA secretaries, not from either the faculty or students of the College. After 1925 one can identify a small group of daring or even radical students in the University Center. Those who took the lead on racial change came from Scarritt, the YMCA College, and Vanderbilt's School of Religion. In 1926 a socially active and widely resented YMCA secretary, William B. Jones, held an interracial forum in Alumni Hall, attended by blacks as well as whites. Vanderbilt students protested such racial mixing; Dean Sarratt urged Jones to avoid such incidents in the future. He did not. In January, 1927, Jones arranged a conference of Tennessee Student Volunteers, from both black and white colleges, at Alumni. Blacks and whites, men and women ate and talked together. An enraged Sarratt now ordered Jones to end all such daring experiments.

The climax came in March, 1927. Socially involved representatives of all Nashville colleges held a mass meeting in Wesley Hall to mature protests against avowedly imperialistic American policies in China. This meeting was arranged, not by the YMCA, but by concerned students and professors, particularly in the Vanderbilt School of Religion. John L. Kesler, professor of religious education, and several divinity students spoke to the mixed audience. The meeting gained coverage in both Nashville newspapers, led to much outside and inside criticism of Vanderbilt, and embarrassed Kirkland and other administrators. The concerns all involved the racial mixing at the meeting, not the content of the resolutions. Dean Fleming investigated the meeting, rejoiced that only one College student had attended, and recommended stricter university controls over biracial gatherings on campus. Notably, such did not soon resume, and at the end of the year a resented Jones was replaced as YMCA secretary by Henry Hart, whom Fleming enthusiastically supported for the position. Ironically, in 1943 Hart would lose the same job because of a later controversy involving race.[26]

Such new departures in race relations joined with an increased recognition

Bowling Fitzgerald,
Kissam porter and football trainer

of the role of blacks on campus. Particularly in the memory of alumni, three or four blacks became beloved campus characters, comparable even to the one policeman, James H. "Cap" Alley, who finally had to retire in the 1920s. One venerated black was Bowling Fitzgerald, a porter at Kissam and the de facto trainer for the football team for three decades. Fitzgerald accumulated extensive property, drove late-model cars, and late in his life took courses in chiropractic to improve his training skills. Equally respected was Robert Wingfield, for years the chef of the dining hall, first at Westside and then in Kissam. He died in 1921, but before this he served a special banquet each year for a restricted, and honored, group of students. He was also comparatively well off. At his death a faculty member, with no intended condescension, called him "the best negro I have ever known." But most loved, and belatedly a campus institution, was John E. Fulton, or "Uncle Remus." He began his service in old Wesley in 1885 and became a servant to the famous Club IV of bachelor professors. As this petered out to only Dudley, Fulton became his valet and thus suffered a grievous loss in 1914 with Dudley's death. By then he had packed his basement room in Wesley with photographs of practically every past Vanderbilt student. By the 1920s students flocked to his room as a sort of required pilgrimage, to hear him reminisce about the past, to hear him play his guitar or recite the now famous "Uncle Remus" stories of Joel Chandler Harris. When feebleness forced him to give up all janitorial duties in Wesley, he moved for a year to California and there, as a famous campus

305

John Fulton (Uncle Remus) with his collection of student photographs

character, met with alumni groups, competing for attention with Coach McGugin. He came back to Nashville in the late 1920s, and in 1929 was voted a $5 a week pension by a grateful Vanderbilt.[27]

In the 1920s a considerable shift occurred in student organizations. The YMCA remained the largest and only subsidized student group. The university contributed up to $4,000 annually to its support, but somehow the association was not able to adjust to new student interests. A series of unsuccessful secretaries tried to build effective programs but with such a poor response that Kirkland almost cut off the subsidy. The annual religious campaigns were only shadows of the enthusiastic prewar revivals, and Bible courses attracted little student attention. But the YMCA still kept up its placement effort, tried to focus student social concerns, and brought able speakers to campus, including a youthful Reinhold Niebuhr. The other sources of able speakers was the Cole lecture fund, which brought a very popular Harry E.

Fosdick, and a very prestigious science lectureship in the Medical School, funded by Bernard Flexner in honor of his brother Abraham.[28]

The old glee club remained popular through the war but then declined in the 1920s, even as it added more serious music to its repertoire. In the summer of 1920 a small portion of the glee club faced serious charges after a performance at Bald Knob, Arkansas. As an encore, the small group of eight staged their version of a Negro revival, which a sensitive local lady saw as sacrilege. She published her charges in a Little Rock Baptist journal, to the acute embarrassment of Kirkland. He canceled all such summer tours that used the Vanderbilt name but decided the only offense had been poor taste. In 1926–27 professors George P. Jackson and Mims helped organize a chapel choir, with Arthur Wright of the Medical School as the director. This coeducational musical effort was the first officially sponsored by Vanderbilt. The Dramatic Club fluctuated like alternating current. The students could sustain only a series of three or four plays, and then the club would peter out. Thus, dramatics kept reviving about every two years throughout the 1920s. Saddest of all were the old, prestigious literary societies. They struggled on throughout the 1920s, but with no more than six or eight members in some years. In 1929 the two societies combined in a futile effort to survive. They failed to generate any enthusiasm and quietly died in the next few years. In part, the competitive debate teams stole their thunder, and genuine coeducational literary societies and publications absorbed Vanderbilt's greatest talent, with the *Fugitive* only the best-known.[29]

By the 1920s student social life revolved around fraternities, football games, and dances in the gym. In football these were still glory years, even though the won-and-lost records were not quite as impressive as during the McGugin decade of 1904–14. But from a spectator standpoint, football improved with stronger southern competitors and more close races for the mythical southern championship. In the wake of McGugin's disastrous 1914 team, Vanderbilt came back in the two prewar years of 1915 and 1916. It also produced its most famous hero—Irby "Rabbit" Curry, who led the 1915 team as quarterback and then captained the 1916 team. In 1915 Vanderbilt lost only to Virginia, and the 138-pound Curry (he was the only player in history who never gained any weight, for in all legends he always weighed 138) led the way. In 1916 the team won easily a glorious victory over Virginia but floundered at the end of the season when Curry hurt his ankle. Tennessee beat Vanderbilt 10 to 6, one of the first losses ever to the Vols, and then Sewanee fought them to a 0–0 tie, one of the last moral victories ever won in football by the University of the South. Curry had powered his team to a fourth-quarter rout of Sewanee in 1915; he was unable to stimulate any offense in 1916, but somehow the two games became confused in athletic legends. Even Mims, in his history of Vanderbilt, had a crippled Curry leading Vanderbilt to four touchdowns in the final quarter of the 1916 game.

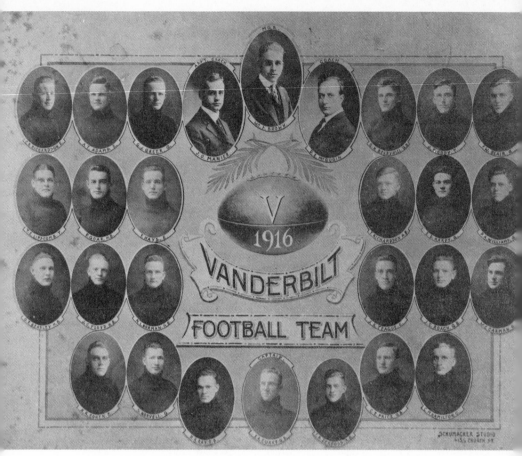

The team of 1916

In the war, Curry served with a flying squadron in France and subsequently died as a result of enemy fire and a subsequent plane crash, adding a patriotic aura to his athletic heroism. McGugin had much admired him and so joined Nashville newspapers in elevating him into an inspiration for all subsequent Vanderbilt teams.[30]

After makeshift teams for the two war years, Vanderbilt began another decade of football preeminence in 1919. It lost only to Georgia Tech in 1919 and tied Tennessee and Kentucky. In 1920 it suffered a poor year, losing to Georgia Tech by a record score of 44 to 0 at home, and to Auburn 56 to 6, before scrambling back to beat Kentucky and Sewanee. In 1921 Vanderbilt beat Kentucky, Texas (a glorious victory), Tennessee, and Alabama, but tied Georgia to lose its claim as the unchallengeable best in the South. In that year the athletic association hired a second full-time coach, Wallace Wade, and gained faculty status for McGugin. The sports program now came under a new faculty committee on athletics, which had ultimate control over the hiring of coaches. The athletic association nominated and continued to pay all the coaches for other than their instructional duties on campus. By 1921 Vanderbilt was also involved in a rather nasty battle with other southern teams. After the war Vanderbilt had resisted a majority of fellow Southern Intercollegiate Athletic Association (SIAA) schools in their effort to enforce a one-year rule, a rule that prohibited freshmen or transfers from playing football during their first year. Without such a rule, universities with lax admission standards could bring almost anyone onto their teams, and all could lose their best players to opposing teams. Because of Vanderbilt's admission standards, this was never a local problem and, as a small team, Vanderbilt very much wanted to play its freshmen. Because it blocked the rule in the SIAA, several of its strongest competitors formed a new league, the Southern Intercollegiate Association (SIA), and from the beginning it accepted the one-year rule. In its 1921 organizational changes the Vanderbilt faculty also mandated the one-year rule. By then, the SIAA was an empty shell, and so in 1922 Vanderbilt joined the new association.[31]

Even more important, the athletic association began construction of its new stadium. In November, 1921, the association completed a preliminary fund drive in order to build a stadium on the site formerly acquired to the west of the campus. It planned a stadium that would eventually seat 40,000 but proposed to complete stands for only 20,000, in a horseshoe stadium modeled, in part, on the famous Yale Bowl. It asked the Vanderbilt University board for a loan of $75,000 against future gate receipts and hoped to raise another $75,000. Board chairman Whitefoord Cole headed a downtown fund drive, and both the Chamber of Commerce and civic clubs joined in the effort. Typically, the early enthusiasm peaked all too soon, but the athletic association still gained pledges of over $80,000 and contracted the building of the stadium for the fall, 1922, season. It was barely ready by the Michigan game in October and opened with a great flourish. Cornelius Vanderbilt, great-great-grandson of the founder, attended. Somewhat disappointing, slightly less than a capacity crowd came. A parade from downtown, bands, the first Vanderbilt float by the Engineering students, numerous flags, a handkerchief display by student fans (a prelude to cards), and even the game ball dropped from an airplane all marked the celebration. For the first time, Vanderbilt tied a Michigan team, another moral victory. Grantland Rice composed a new song to honor the occasion: "Come On, You Commodores." The team then went on to an undefeated season and an unchallenged southern championship. In 1923 it lost only to Michigan and Texas, but except for one tie won all its conference games. Sports writers voted it the best in the South, for which it received a new cup. Even in 1924, when the team lost to Tulane, Georgia, and Sewanee, it won over the new southern powerhouse, Georgia Tech, and, in a pleasant surprise, over Minnesota. None of these glories drew a full 20,000 to the new stadium. Despite the fervor of some local fans, Nashville simply never gave overwhelming crowd support to the team. It always played to its largest crowds when away from Nashville.

The new stadium under construction, 1922

The athletic association suffered. The stadium cost much more than antic-ipated; on a cost-plus basis, the final sum soared to $232,000, an overrun of $82,000. The association borrowed $75,000 from the university, eventually collected about $82,000 in pledges, and took a bank loan for over $75,000. As late as 1929 the athletic association still owed $70,000 to banks and over $80,000 to the university. Nonetheless, it again borrowed $152,000 from the university to buy vacant lots to the east of the stadium as a site for a fieldhouse.[32]

McGugin remained the symbol of football preeminence. Almost everyone attributed Vanderbilt's success to him. As of 1928 he had won 163 games and lost only 42 in twenty-four years at Vanderbilt. But coaching had become a team affair, and from the early 1920s on, McGugin had increasingly received assistance from one full-time coach and from up to four part-time assistants. The scope of ticket sales also necessitated a full-time business manager. Thus, the athletic association could never retire all its debts, even though its football income soared to almost $150,000 in 1927–28.

All in all, Vanderbilt remained the strongest team in the South for the whole decade. After three losses in 1925, it lost only to a Rose Bowl–bound

310

Alabama in 1926. In 1927 it lost only to Texas, but tied both Tennessee and Georgia Tech, thereby losing a chance to win the southern championship. In 1928 it again lost to Georgia Tech, the conference champion, but in an otherwise victorious year directed its efforts at the much-heralded game with a strong Tennessee team. Finally, six years after its construction, fans jammed the new Dudley field to overflowing, but all to no avail. Vanderbilt lost. It no longer faced easy games within the conference, and Tennessee had finally surpassed Vanderbilt. Yet, the glory was not all over. In 1929 Vanderbilt won all games except Tennessee and Minnesota, and in the decade as a whole came in first or second in the conference in all but two years. No other single team did as well. But the great era was finally at an end. In the next decade Vanderbilt declined to somewhere in the middle of the conference; rarely would the fans fill even half of the seats in the new stadium.[33]

The very success of football concerned Kirkland and the board. The budget of the athletic association was often over half that of the College; coaches earned much more than professors, and McGugin received lavish gifts (silver service, an automobile) from Nashville supporters. The larger share of time required of players hurt their academic work. Kirkland sought much tougher eligibility rules in the SIA, but to no avail. He also actively opposed players' joining in postseason bowl games. In the South only Vanderbilt enforced a rigid two-sports rule—no student with under a B average could play more than two sports. Thus, the football team faced increasing difficulties.

The pressure for victory mounted, with Nashville newspapers much more concerned about football prospects than academic achievement. Informal gambling marked each game, and the crowds, the bands, the fanfare all denoted a developing professionalism. Vanderbilt could not keep up. McGugin was already full of complaints or apologies—lower coaching salaries at Vanderbilt, higher academic standards, no scholarships, high tuition, tough faculty controls, and his own reluctance actively to recruit players. Fortunately, these problems did not haunt other sports, but neither did any of these gain any great loyalty from fans or contribute money to the athletic association. The basketball team, now playing either in the Annex or the nearby Hippodrome skating rink, had moments of excitement, as when it won the SIAA championship in 1920 and the SIA tournament in 1927. But often the basketball team suffered from academic disabilities, or from such faculty limitations on classroom cuts as to preclude participation in distant tournaments. Basketball never paid its way in the 1920s but lived on football receipts. In 1925 Vanderbilt began interscholastic competition in golf; in 1926, in tennis and swimming. Even before that a Vanderbilt student, Frank Godchaux, Jr., became a local golfing hero, winner of several tournaments.[34]

The football fervor also warped campus values. Football heroes such as Jess Neely or Lynn Bomar not only won all-American notices but became big men on campus. Only rarely did anyone but an athletic hero now win the Bachelor of Ugliness. The athletes easily gained needed jobs in town (McGugin required them actually to work for any pay) and entry into Nashville society. Such preferences distracted local attention from the academically or artistically gifted students on campus, such as all the young poets. In 1923 Lynn Bomar's football heroics outshone William Scott Vaughn's first all-A record; Vaughn also won membership in Phi Beta Kappa, the Founder's Medal, and a graduate fellowship to Rice. He maintained a family tradition, as did several members of the Waller family, the largest of the early family dynasties at Vanderbilt. By 1923, twenty-one members of that former Kentucky family had attended Vanderbilt. Football success also overshadowed a considerable achievement in 1928, when two Vanderbilt graduates won Rhodes scholarships; Robert Penn Warren, B.A. 1925, Founder's Medalist, and then a graduate student at Yale; and Cleanth Brooks, Jr., a 1928 graduate and class poet. These names are only tokens of an outpouring of student talent in the 1920s, or what arguably was the most stimulating decade ever at Vanderbilt. The Fugitives and Agrarians proved that.[35]

13

Fugitives and Agrarians

Ⅰɴ 1915 a half-dozen Vanderbilt men began gathering periodically for some heavy if sophomoric philosophical discussions. After the war these few, joined by an equal number of younger men, switched their concern to poetry and for three years published a small poetry journal, the *Fugitive*. After 1925 four of these Fugitives, joined by other Vanderbilt intellectuals, turned their attention to political and economic issues, to the problems of the South. These discussions found outlet in a famous book, *I'll Take My Stand*, and in an intellectual stance called Southern Agrarianism. This fifteen years of intense intellectual dialogue directly involved no more than twenty people. Only two remained in all the groupings from 1915 to 1930. But, for complicated reasons, these discussions eventually made up the most important single chapter in a now widely recognized renaissance of literature in the South and stimulated the most extended twentieth-century debate about the cultural identity of the South and about the economic and social institutions appropriate for such a South.

The young intellectuals who argued in Vanderbilt hallways or in Nashville homes never agreed on all issues. They did share a common geographical origin, educational experience, and religious heritage. Brilliant, creative, eloquent, they managed only ephemeral alliances at the level of broad, general, but inherently ambiguous platforms. Neither Fugitives nor Agrarians shared enough common goals to make up a movement. Just as it is more accurate to refer to a remarkably similar group of young men a century earlier in New England as a Transcendentalist circle, so these Nashville intellectuals made up a loose circle, with vague outer boundaries and frequent shifts in membership.

Equally ambiguous is the connection between these intellectuals, their beliefs and productions, and Vanderbilt University. Three of the fifteen officially recognized Fugitives, and two of twelve contributors to *I'll Take My Stand*, had no formal connection to Vanderbilt. In no official sense did the university recognize or support either the work or the publications of Fugitives or Agrarians. The bulk of the university community, students and faculty, never read or understood the Fugitive poems, read or sympathized with Agrarian arguments. The Agrarians brought as much unwanted notoriety as prestige to the university. Old Chancellor Kirkland was mystified by most of the poems, embarrassed by the political and economic controversies, and therefore not supportive of either group. But this is not surprising and not important. The chancellor's role was not that of an intellectual or esthetic arbiter. Little in Kirkland's responsibility prepared him for such a role. His uninformed opinion about poems deserved no particular respect, just as one would have no reason to respect a young poet's judgments about university investments. Local indifference, or hostility, in no way impeded the work of the two groups, who spoke for the university as much as any other constituency. Such opposition even allowed young men to enjoy the role of rebels.

Thus, Vanderbilt was the site, the occasion, for an unexpected and still unexplainable surge of intellectual ferment. Such fruitful ferment has been rare in American universities. When it has erupted, an almost accidental coming together of a group of people and their catalytic effect upon each other has been all-important. The intellectual resources of a university—courses, professors, libraries—have always played a secondary role. But even this is a necessary role. Without Vanderbilt the groups would never have gathered; without some supportive university assets the intellectual renaissance could not have occurred. Intellectually, most original or influential products of a university are spontaneous, uncontrived. One can locate necessary but never sufficient conditions. The rich harvest, always unexpected, is an academic form of unmerited grace. The Fugitive and Agrarian phenomenon became the one unexpected flower whose blooming gave Vanderbilt a truly distinctive position among American universities.

It is appropriate that Vanderbilt had its most enduring impact on American intellectual life in literature and criticism. Its achievement matched its academic strength and thus reflected its major academic commitments. Until 1925 and the new Medical School, Vanderbilt had compiled an undistinguished record in the physical sciences, as all too well reflected in its faculty. It began strong programs in the social sciences only in the 1920s. But from its beginnings it had at least flirted with preeminence in English and in classical languages and literature. Here clustered all its ablest professors—Humphreys, Smith, Baskervill, Tolman, Stevenson, and Mims. Such faculty strength joined with the classical degree requirements to give a literary emphasis to Vanderbilt's curriculum, which rubbed off on students. They had to spend over half of their high school years in Latin and Greek, and then completed over half of their required courses at Vanderbilt in these two subjects plus English.

The atmosphere at Vanderbilt, even before the turn of the century, was literate, not scientific or philosophical. Students revealed this bent in the high quality of their publications, in their various literary societies and clubs, and in their choice of major subjects and fields of subsequent study. For the more able students at Vanderbilt, vigorous scholars usually exerted the most decisive influence, although at times they were not always the most popular teachers. The seedbed of the Fugitive circle reached back toward the turn of the century, to the time John Ransom matriculated in 1903. Consistently, the more able of his generation of Vanderbilt students had the highest regard for Professor Tolman, and thus their estimate confirms later scholarly judgments. Perhaps more surprisingly, the Fugitives who attended Vanderbilt before the war all listed Herbert C. Sanborn, the somewhat eccentric, dogmatic, but impressively scholarly philosopher, next to Tolman. Edwin Mims came to Vanderbilt in 1912, and in quite complex ways he also had a tremendous impact on Vanderbilt students and on young Vanderbilt poets. He did not share the taste of the Fugitives, but he helped establish a community of appreciation for poetry, rather daringly counted creative expression the equal of scholarship for academic promotion, and provided a foil for the more rebellious young men. Finally, a critical part of the seedbed was the Calumet Club, an honorary society of Vanderbilt journalists or would-be writers. In its meetings the student intellectuals of Vanderbilt gathered to debate literary trends and to criticize their own largely journalistic productions. The tradition of literary talk early spread from here to just beyond the campus, where it eventually spawned the *Fugitive*.

In 1914 or 1915 the literary discussions in the Calumet Club took on a new dimension. The catalyst for change was an unusual, thirty-year-old Nashville man—Sidney Mttron Hirsch. Eccentric, independent-minded, Hirsch had not attended Vanderbilt or completed degree work at any university. But a half-brother, Nathaniel Hirsch, took his degree at Vanderbilt and first brought able classmates to his home, to the delight of Sidney, who loved nothing more than presiding over brilliant conversation. The awed students included several future Fugitives: William Yandell Elliott, who later became an eminent political scientist; Alec Stevenson, son of Professor J.H. Stevenson of the School of Religion, editor of the *Observer*, and a later Nashville businessman; Stanley Johnson, later a disaffected instructor in the Vanderbilt English department and a novelist and free-lance writer; and Donald Davidson, who had begun a B.A. program at Vanderbilt in 1909, dropped out for financial reasons, and returned only in 1914. In 1914 John Crowe Ransom, the brilliant graduate of 1909, rejoined the Vanderbilt English department as an instructor after three years as a Rhodes scholar at Oxford and a year as a preparatory school teacher in New England. Davidson, almost as old as Ransom, enrolled in his Shakespeare class and then invited Ransom to join in the discussions and good hospitality at the Hirsch home on nearby 20th Avenue. In the fall of 1915 a new Vanderbilt assistant professor, Walter Clyde Curry, began joining some of the sessions. Curry, who was to become a great Chaucer and Shakespeare scholar, enjoyed philosophical and esthetic discussions. He completed a circle of seven young, unmarried intellectuals who continued to meet together until the disruptions of war in 1917. By their later memories, the discussions ranged far and wide but usually came to rest on deep philosophical or metaphysical issues. They did not yet involve, at least in any sustained sense, a discussion of poetry. The two dominant figures remained Sidney Hirsch and Ransom.[1]

Hirsch played an essential role in the flowering of the Fugitive group, and not just as a host. He was the cultural outsider. The young Vanderbilt men, except for Curry, were all from Nashville or the surrounding countryside, and all were native stock, evangelical Protestants. Hirsch was Jewish, from a prominent mercantile family in Nashville. But his Jewishness scarcely accounts for his special identity. Vanderbilt already had a sizable Jewish contingent, gained support from the Nashville Jewish community, and had one Jew on its Board of Trust. Jewish-Gentile interaction was a normal aspect of campus life. Hirsch fit no labels. He was a bit of an intellectual dilettante, with special enthusiasms. He had had a rather strange career, one undoubtedly embellished with each fascinating recounting. A large, handsome man, he had served in the peacetime Navy, traveled in the Orient, served as an artist's model in Paris, and purportedly knew many famous people around the world. He successfully projected a worldly, cosmopolitan, sophisticated outlook to his awed guests. More important, he professed familiarity with much ancient and hidden wisdom, Occidental and Oriental, much present in the occult meanings hidden in ordinary words. His position drew upon Cabbalist or Rosicrucian traditions and properly mystified his young guests. More recently, Hirsch had dabbled in drama and the theater and in 1913 had directed a spectacular Greek pageant in front of Nashville's replica of the Parthenon.

None of the young men fully understood Hirsch. His mind seemed undisciplined by logic, as he leaped from one topic to another or professed to derive half the secrets of the universe from a detailed etymological investigation of a single word. For Hirsch, ordinary surface appearances always masked deeper truths, truths that often emerged, unrecognized, in poetry. Hirsch loved people, loved to talk, and thus flattered his guests by his attention and often by his uncritical praise. They flattered him by taking him seriously. For unsure youth just venturing into creative endeavors, Hirsch's praise provided a needed self-confidence. In some ways Hirsch was already a pathetic man, with evidence of major psychological problems. He had no real career, no direction in life, no chance of major achievements. He lacked the needed discipline. His only glorious achievements, in part mythical, were now all in the past. Thus he gained much from the Fugitives and took an almost parental pride in all their achievements. But, in time, the young men all outgrew Hirsch. They continued to respect him, to love him for his generosity of spirit, but they eventually came to recognize that his beguiling obscurities concealed not some deep truth but only his own confusions. Out of pesonal respect they never let on that they knew.[2]

Ransom was the perfect counterweight to Hirsch. When he joined the emerging discussion group he tried to discipline Hirsch's scattergun insights. No one ever succeeded in that. But the two stimulated the best in each other, even as their soaring interchanges often left the undergraduates completely mystified. Ransom had a native brilliance, as reflected in his academic successes. He also had extensive philosophical training at Oxford. Despite all the claims about him, he did not have the temperament, or the skills, of a professional philosopher. He never easily traveled back and forth between basic assumptions and working theories, but rather worked out, often with an exacting logic, the implications of his unrecognized assumptions. This would lead him, over the next twenty years, into a series of often conflicting intellectual crusades. But Ransom, in discussion, seemed unusually detached and logical, always on guard against verbal obscurities or needless flights of fancy. For the young men he was mentor and critic. Yet they did not approach him in fear and trembling. Ransom seemed so detached from the critical game, so far removed from any intellectual insecurity, any ego vulnerability, that no one saw any personal animus in his most devastating remarks. He was able, therefore, to remove from what soon became an ongoing seminar any deadly ideological explosives. Not only did he raise his comments to a seemingly impersonal and therefore nonthreatening level, but he kept pulling those of others back to the pure intellectual game. Not that Ransom was as detached as he seemed; he later suffered some bruises to his own ego. But he was able to establish game rules that allowed a dialogue to continue for years, a dialogue that placed ever heavier demands on participants, yet in an atmosphere that reinforced a growing sense of self-mastery. Discussion groups rarely achieve this for very long. They either break up or settle into a comfortable rut. Hirsch, half guru and half clown, always ready to find great truths in any sophomoric comment, provided the needed stimulus toward originality; Ransom, with his dry detachment, set the standard for rigor and for intellectual self-discipline.[3]

The prewar seminar remained, at best, a preparation for poetic creativity. The members did not meet to criticize poems, although they talked a great deal about art and esthetics. But back on campus the participants read and discussed poetry in the Calumet Club, in Mims's famous course in English literature (he required his students to memorize long sections from Browning and Tennyson), and in Ransom's course on Shakespeare. And, largely in private, they did what many college students do—they wrote verse. In about 1916, according to the later memories of Donald Davidson, Ransom sheepishly approached him with a poem, inviting comments. This, surprisingly, was Ransom's first effort, at least as he understood the demands for a poem as contrasted with mere verse. Perhaps characteristically, Ransom made the intellectual decision to write a poem and then carefully crafted it. He was never a natural poet; composition for him involved choice and deliberation as well as the assumption of certain formal constraints. Davidson applauded the poem, and Ransom soon successfully submitted several poems for publication. Just before the war he submitted a bundle of them to a press and through the critical support of Christopher Morley and Robert Frost was

317

able to publish the small volume in 1919 under the title *Poems About God*. Ransom later felt apologetic about this early effort; the poems received little critical acclaim, at least in America. Conventional in form, they were nontraditional in subject matter. In the poems Ransom aired some of the metaphysical concerns explored, and not resolved, in his discussions with Hirsch. Even this early he flirted with an unresolved dualism, between head and heart, between abstract reason and the qualities of immediate experience, that would shape his later critical theory. This early volume incited Ransom's interest in poetic theory and the writing of better poetry. It also gave him a professional reputation, a degree of eminence not enjoyed by his students or young colleagues. Had the war not intervened, the discussions at Hirsch's apartment would have turned to poetry at least by 1918.[4]

The war only postponed the next, poetic stage of the discussions. The emerging Fugitive circle led charmed lives. None died or were even wounded in the war. Ransom and Davidson both joined the first officer candidates who left Vanderbilt for Fort Oglethorpe in May of 1917. Here they met from time to time and even read each other's poems. Elliott, Stevenson, and Johnson all volunteered or were drafted. Of the group, only Hirsch and Curry remained in Nashville. Lieutenant Ransom went early to France but instead of front-line duty served in an officer training program at Saumur. Davidson moved into combat only a few days before the Armistice, taking with him a manuscript of *Poems About God*. Vanderbilt graduates, by their education eligible for officer training, flocked to Saumur, creating there an alumni group that revolved around Ransom. Stevenson trained there, as did another Vanderbilt student—William Frierson—who would briefly join the Fugitive circle after the war. At war's end, Ransom, Elliott, Stevenson, and Frierson were able to enroll in French or Swiss universities at army expense and in this interlude gained a direct acquaintanceship with the new schools of French poetry. In 1919 these future Fugitives slowly returned home, presumably much wiser for all their adventures. Not surprisingly, they sought out Hirsch and resumed their prewar seminar. Sidney Hirsch had meantime moved to the home of his sister and brother-in-law Rose and James Frank, who lived two miles west of the campus. The Franks became generous hosts to the group, and in a supportive sense James Frank, a businessman and not a poet, became a member of the Fugitive circle and so gained a listing on the editorial page of the magazine.[5]

Very soon poetry dominated the discussions. Ransom's absorption in the problems of poetics insured this. Hirsch welcomed the subject, one always related to the universal wisdom he espoused. The two men once again worked their magic with the growing number of newcomers. Curry, who occasionally wrote sonnets, rejoined the group but soon would be too involved in scholarship to attend all the sessions, which soon fell into a biweekly, Saturday evening pattern. Elliott was back in graduate school; Frierson completed his senior year. In 1920 both had to leave the magical group as

318

they moved to Oxford on Rhodes scholarships. Stevenson soon returned to Nashville because of the death of his father (he had worked for Philadelphia newspapers), and after brief assignments with the *Tennessean* and the *Banner* went into banking and securities. Davidson, now married and in desperate financial straits, taught briefly in Kentucky and then, in the fall of 1919, began M.A. work at Vanderbilt while teaching freshman English. Stanley Johnson did not return until 1921 to enroll in the English department and to complete his Ph.D. Before that, he had taught two years in the Philippines and written his first novel. A later 1925 novel, *the Professor,* satirized the Vanderbilt English department. A few other students came occasionally, including Alfred Starr, subsequently a local moving-picture entrepreneur and an infrequent contributor to the *Fugitive*. Of this younger group, Davidson was most committed to a career in literature and to poetry as a profession. But the others all dabbled in poetry, even though they would never become as engaged in critical theory as Ransom and Davidson.[6]

This was not true of a new member of the group. As of about 1921, Davidson invited John Orley Allen Tate, then a junior at Vanderbilt, to attend the seminar. Tate was an *enfant terrible,* a slim, wiry, intense, large-headed prodigy out of Kentucky. To Hirsch the mystic and Ransom the disciplined professor, Tate added an entirely new intellectual ingredient—youthful rebellion joined with a sympathy for poetic experimentation. As yet he was a rebel without a clear cause, a somewhat obscure high priest of poetry as contrasted to Ransom's lucid philosophizing. Unlike the other young men, Tate had no secure background or identity. A ne'er-do-well father, a near psychotic mother, and frequent moves had left him insecure, at times bitter, and in rebellion against most forms of authority. He barely managed the discipline to remain in college, enjoyed challenging old Mims, became a lifelong burr under Mims's usually comfortable saddle, and shocked more conventional students by his avowed atheism and radicalism. Tate joined the Fugitive group not as a deferential undergraduate but as a cocky, even arrogant, protagonist. He also contributed a vital ingredient—a familiarity with all the new, often ephemeral schools of poetry, including the most avant-garde. Tate soon made T.S. Eliot his hero and celebrated formal experimentation and free verse. Tate, as much an irritant as a companion, strained the tolerance of the group. But his radical proclivities alone made possible a wide-ranging discussion of modern poetry. The magical ingredients—the mix of brilliant personalities, even an element of intellectual tension—were now all in place.[7]

Early in 1922 Hirsch urged the young men to publish some of their emerging poems. Throughout the country, small poetry magazines seemed to sprout almost monthly, so why not one in Nashville? According to later memories, Stevenson suggested the title of *Fugitive* but drew the title from one of Hirsch's poems. It is not clear what, if any, meaning the group intended by it. A fugitive is a wanderer, perhaps an outcast. Some assumed a connection to Hirsch, to the diaspora of Jews. The more likely meaning was their intended escape from an older sentimentality. In the preface to the first *Fugitive* number, in April, 1922, Ransom said the Fugitive "flees from nothing faster than from the high-caste Brahmins of the Old South," but he gave no clues as to exactly what he had in mind. The group hired a Negro, in a small shop, to print the first edition and then set about trying to gain subscribers. Despite optimistic claims made in the magazine, it never sold well and was always on the brink of financial disaster. In the first two numbers the poets assumed humorous and revealing pseudonyms—Ransom was "Roger Prim"; Davidson, "Robin Gallivant"; Tate, "Henry Feathertop"; Hirsch, for his one contribution to each issue, "L. Oafer." By issue three, in the fall of 1922, the authors now proudly came forward and identified themselves. By then, critical praise insured the continuation of their venture; the December issue contained an explanation of how the magazine began and how it functioned, plus an editorial by Tate.[8]

By December, 1922, the *Fugitive* gained three new contributor-editors. After the first number, Merrill Moore, an undergraduate poet and, along with Tate, an editor of the *Jade,* submitted a poem for the second number and very quickly joined in the discussions. Moore was the son of John Trotwood Moore, a much venerated Middle Tennessee poet, and the young Moore quickly became the most prolific member of the group. He was a natural poet, later writing up to 100,000 sonnets while he pursued a very busy career as a Boston psychiatrist. Moore never became deeply involved in subsequent critical arguments. He strove for a pure poetry, one tied to no theory. He turned poems out at a phenomenal speed, writing several sonnets in a single setting. The other poets had small success in disciplining his verse; he usually responded to criticism of one poem by writing and submitting ten more. The other additions were cousins—Ridley and Jesse Wills. Ridley, a popular but controversial and irrepressible *Hustler* editor at Vanderbilt before the war, came back in 1922 to complete his degree. Jesse had come to Vanderbilt with the SATC unit in 1918, stayed on to earn his degree, and then joined his businessman father as a rising young executive in the National Life and Accident Insurance Company. The two Wills helped very much in the early promotion of the *Fugitive.*[9]

The Fugitives never tried to form a new poetic school. Their views varied too much, but the editorial process helped camouflage their differences, leading some to the false conclusion that Ransom wrote all the poems. Each contributor brought poems to their Saturday evening discussions and the whole seminar acted as an editorial board. The group interaction was vital. The seminar provided a critical but appreciative audience, forced the effort needed to write so many poems, and gave crucial support for all the work involved in preparing them for publication. By force of personality, and by their more self-conscious even though still developing theories about poetry, Ransom and Tate had the largest critical impact. The *Fugitive* thus exemplified careful craftsmanship and struck many readers as much too intricate or too cerebral. Most poems remained conventional in meter and rhyme, even when they involved a somber or cynical content. For one versed in romantic poetry, the *Fugitive* poems seemed difficult to read, uninspired and uninspiring in content. Thus, to the larger public, at Vanderbilt or in Nashville, the poems often seemed puzzling, dense, even a deliberate affront to intelligibility. Actually, they were quite intelligible but often required care and work on the part of readers. The sympathetic editors of the *Jade* raved at the success of the first volume; a puzzled reviewer in the *Hustler* noted that the poems were "beyond the grasp of the average Philistine of the campus." Nashville newspaper reviewers never developed much understanding of or appreciation for the poems, but Nashvillians soon rejoiced in the critical success of the little journal. Thus, in a proprietary sense, they were proud of the Fugitives and gave honor and respect to them. So did Edwin Mims, who never liked the poetry but rejoiced in the prestige that soon accrued to his department from the magazine and then from the spinoff volumes of poetry published by his two colleagues, Ransom and Davidson.[10]

The *Fugitive* continued through 1925, or for four volumes. Its peak years were 1923 and 1924. Because of numerous European admirers or contacts (Robert Graves and two ex patriates, the Arkansas imagist John Gould Fletcher and T.S. Eliot), the *Fugitive* gained an early and appreciative foreign audience. Tate also developed several New York City contacts. With increased tensions, the joint editorial process continued through 1924, although a faithful Davidson often assumed too much of the hard work. In the second volume the editors were able to announce a $100 prize, donated by Nashville businessmen, and a $50 Ward-Belmont prize for the best poem by any female college student. Despite the number of poetry magazines, hundreds of frustrated poets submitted entries. The outside judges had a hard time agreeing on winners, but the contest further established the reputation of the *Fugitive*. By the second volume it always contained a few poems by outside contributors. Because of its high standards of craftsmanship, its aversion to ideology, the sheer talent of its poets, and the high quality of a majority of its poems, the *Fugitive* soon gained a uniquely lofty status among small poetry journals, a status reinforced later by the careers of Ransom, Tate, Davidson, and Moore. It reflected a gentle form of revolt and suffered none of the ephemeral qualities of more extreme literary experiments, from imagism to Dada.[11]

In 1923 a young, red-haired undergraduate from the nearby Kentucky border town of Guthrie, Robert Penn Warren, first submitted a poem to the demanding seminar. He joined the editorial board for the final two volumes. Warren roomed with Tate when Tate came back in 1923, after a bout with tuberculosis, to complete his delayed degree, and used his two years with the *Fugitive* as an unexcelled apprenticeship in literature. But Warren remained an apprentice; his poems revealed only a hint of his later success as both poet and novelist. Even for Tate the Fugitive years were apprenticeship years—only a few of his more mature poems appeared in the *Fugitive,* and at its termination in 1925 he was still almost as confused about his identity, as tentative and obscure in his critical stance, as he had been when he came to Vanderbilt. Davidson, the lyrical balladeer of the group, was much swayed by Ransom and by his closest lifelong friend, Tate. Always a bit awed by the intellectuality of the group, so happy to be part of it (this was his taste of utopia), Davidson experimented with more complex forms and subjects, and in retrospect he has received more critical acclaim for his early *Fugitive* poems than for most later ones, which were simpler, more lyrical, and soon also more didactic. For Ransom, the Fugitive years were critical for his poetry and at least helped lay the basis of his later critical theory. Tate pushed him as no one else ever did, forcing constant reevaluation and new refinements in his poetry. Ransom completed many of his greatest poems in the Fugitive years, which is not surprising—he was reaching full maturity and his years of poetic composition were about over. In summary, the Fugitive enterprise guided the maturation of Ransom as a poet, forced Tate to the brink of his final poetic style, offered a rich apprenticeship to Warren, and pulled a somewhat more reluctant Davidson into critically acclaimed experimentation. Given the significance of Ransom, Tate, and Warren in American literary history, these modest claims take on their full significance. The *Fugitive* was by far the most influential publication ever tied in any sense to Vanderbilt University.[12]

By 1923 the Fugitive group had begun to break up. The early volumes included Elliott and Frierson only as editors in absentia. Jesse Wills and Alec Stevenson were increasingly absorbed in business. Curry, by 1923, took a leave to complete his book on Chaucer and ceased to have any role in the discussions. Moore entered the demanding Medical School. Tate, away in the North Carolina mountains for much of 1922, left Nashville for good in the spring of 1924, to teach briefly in West Virginia and then to launch a difficult career as a free-lance writer in New York City. He practically withdrew from the *Fugitive.* By then the problem of editorship caused new strains within the group. Ransom, because of his seniority and national reputation, gained the most professionally from the *Fugitive.* Critics saw him as a mentor to the group, the real editor, and often offended the other authors by so characterizing the journal. Ransom was not unaware or unconcerned about the professional side of the enterprise, and never quite went far enough in setting the record straight. Yet by 1924 Davidson did more of the actual work than Ransom. Neither young professor had a Ph.D., and with poetry as their only publications were struggling up the academic ladder. To his credit, Mims helped win Ransom his full professorship, but Ransom, never a workaholic, had to give most of his time to campus duties, including such tasks as planning for the semicentennial of 1925. Further threatening the earlier harmony was Ransom's fight with Tate over critical standards. Tate took offense at a Ransom attack on Eliot's "Wasteland," and in an outside journal, and then in the pages of the *Fugitive*, the two developed their debates about free verse and formal experimentation, with Ransom the advocate of more traditional forms, Tate the advocate of modernity.[13]

Beyond such manageable tensions, the *Fugitive* faced grave financial problems by the end of 1924. A gullible business agent who financed volume three almost lost his shirt. The *Fugitive* clearly had to have a managing editor to go on. Ransom strenuously objected to an elected editor. But he relented in 1925, since he joined Warren on the masthead as "Editors serving for 1925." Warren did most of the work for the final volume, now published only quarterly. The final numbers listed one additional editor-contributor—Laura Riding Gottschalk—but one who never functioned as part of the seminar, itself now almost defunct. Riding (her professional name) had entered the first poetry contest, winning a rave review from one judge and effusive praise from several of the Fugitives. She rejoiced in the honor and the recognition, worked hard but unsuccessfully to sell subscriptions, and contributed several poems to the final two volumes. But by the end of 1925 it was clear that the earlier group had so dispersed, or shifted their interests, that the *Fugitive* had to die. The December number announced the suspension, not because of any financial need (not entirely accurate, despite a group of patrons who subsidized the final year's effort), but for lack of a sacrificial editor.[14]

Almost nothing in the *Fugitive* suggested what later became Southern Agrarianism, even granting all the ambiguities in the label. Neither the poems, the few critical essays by Tate, Ransom, Davidson, nor the reviews introduced into volume four hinted at any special identification with the South or commitment to any specific social order. The poems were remarkably abstract or universal, not contextual or provincial. The poets had rejected local color and clearly did not want to be tarred with any southern image. Such symbolized the sentimentalism, the sweetness and light, the romantic lost cause that they had repudiated. Not only for a rebellious Tate, but also for Ransom, Davidson, and Warren this was a time for breaking away from home ties, from parental and provincial values, from the verities of childhood Methodism. Home loyalties remained most beguiling for Davidson, and local, even pastoral themes kept breaking into his poetry, but all his confessions showed him vainly trying to break free of village attachments. The group was simply not very political, not clearly committed on broad social issues. Whatever their private opinions, few of these entered into their lofty philosophical dialogues or into their poetry. Yet, within two years of the demise of the *Fugitive*, its ablest, most professional architects were already planning a symposium in defense of the South and in defense of a social order they increasingly called "Agrarian." The chief architects of this venture were Tate, Ransom, and Davidson; Warren was a willing but less involved accomplice. But behind the label lurked very different conceptions of the South and quite ambiguous references for the word "agrarian." Yet, these chief architects still had more in common with each other than with some of the other contributors to *I'll Take My Stand.*

At Vanderbilt in the 1920s no one could escape some involvement with the South. Debates over southern problems were incessant. Even less could young intellectuals ignore the southern component of their identity. But for Tate, Ransom, and Davidson an absorbing concern with southern problems seemed to await the Butler Act (anti-evolution) and the famous Scopes trial of 1925. The publicity, the sharp barbs of H.L. Mencken (an earlier hero of Tate and one who had complimented the Fugitives), the superficial press treatment of the issues involved at the trial, the widespread airing of purported southern backwardness, all created a defensive stance among southerners. But, in the eyes of the three Fugitives, almost all the defenders of the South accepted the uncriticized and sinister assumptions of the detractors. This was true of Chancellor Kirkland, who used his semicentennial address to defend education—more laboratories and ecumenical divinity schools—as a solution for the problems of southern ignorance and bigotry.[15]

In 1926 Edwin Mims published his upbeat response to Dayton, *The Advancing South,* a tremendously popular book both North and South. Even Davidson was impressed with many of its arguments, but Tate and Ransom found it fatally flawed. For underlying its optimism was Mims's contention that the South, despite such setbacks as lynchings or the embarrassing display of the fundamentalists, had already made tremendous strides, and that progress, not reaction, had best characterized its recent past. Implicit in this was a claim that the South was slowly catching up with the North in industrial growth, in educational facilities, even in artistic achievement. Thus Mims accepted the values of the critics, whereas Tate and Ransom wanted to challenge just these assumptions. Actually, Mims's analysis was more subtle than a resentful Tate could ever concede. Typical of other New South cheerleaders, he noted distinctive and desirable cultural traits in the South, not the least being a pervasive religiosity that of course appealed to the evangelical Mims. But he believed southerners had to face up to deep social and economic problems, get rid of blind optimism, eschew escape into the mystique of a lost cause, and then, by a very selective and intelligent borrowing of northern and English techniques, set about the laborious task of reform. Mims advocated black progress along with white, fought against lynching or overt repression, but even he could not accept social equality for blacks and in North Carolina had supported so-called progressives who had worked to disfranchise blacks. Ironically, his approach to racial issues very closely paralleled that taken by Robert Penn Warren in *I'll Take My Stand.*[16]

Each of the three key Fugitives moved to their Agrarianism for different reasons and ended up with very different perspectives. Ransom came closest to being the philosopher of the group, and he wrote both the opening manifesto and the opening and theme essay for *I'll Take My Stand.* The

Fugitives' reunion, 1956 (from left: *Tate, Moore, Warren, Ransom, Davidson*)

FUGITIVES AND AGRARIANS

Agrarians' reunion, 1980 (from left: *Warren, Lytle, Lanier, and Brooks*)

complexity of his views do not yield to brief treatment. To some extent he clarified after 1925 certain preferences tied to heritage and temperament. His father and a grandfather were Methodist ministers. His father was a college graduate, a former missionary to Brazil, a bit of a linguist, and a very able, literate, cultured man. Ransom's academic and literary successes grew naturally out of his family environment, an environment that was culturally refined, even aristocratic, and far removed from the competitive pressures, the pecuniary values, of the much-venerated business civilization of the 1920s, or what Ransom came to hate. Of course, Ransom was ambitious, academically and professionally competitive, but he never celebrated competitive values. He always espoused the virtues of a country gentleman. While a Rhodes scholar he found as much to criticize as to praise in Britain. But the manners and mores of Oxford, of the British upper class, rubbed off on him. One key word in his vocabulary became "leisure." In Britain, and then back at Vanderbilt, he loved good conversation, his tennis and golf, card games. He reacted to the tension, the endless committee assignments, that plagued his career at Vanderbilt. He thus yearned for a peaceful retreat, plenty of time to write poetry, or a life less frantic, hurried, and abrasive.[17]

From his Fugitive experience, Ransom was led to consider the social and cultural conditions most conducive to artistic creativity and, in particular, to the writing and reading of poetry. This too suggested a society that allowed leisure, at least to a talented few. Thus, even esthetic imperatives led to what he made his new credo—a society aristocratic in social relations and in political leadership, traditional in its culture, and orthodox in its religion. Such a society, which seemed almost feudal in some of his celebrations, fit his developing critique of modern, Western intellectual life and its economic offshoot. Of course, he indulged stereotypes and caricatures. But he picked up, from sources rarely acknowledged, a widely shared perspective on scientific thought and on the dangers of applied science and technology. In brief, he saw abstract reasoning and a scientific ordering of our experience as inherently dangerous, the serpent in the garden of experiential fullness and innocence. As William James put it earlier, the abstract classifications, the general or even universal relationships sought by scientists, do not bring us closer to reality but in a sense insulate us from it. These conceptual nets, justified only when recognized as narrowing abstracts and when put to humane uses, can beguile us, lead us away from the wholeness, richness, and conceptually irreducible nuances of experience. They can dwarf us, lead to abstract or imperial relationships and foster a purely practical scale of values. In brief, such an outlook can dehumanize. Like Emerson a hundred years earlier, Ransom saw any capitulation to the abstractions of the physics workshop, any temptation to dwarf reality to fit such abstractions, as well as efforts to order economic relationships around such a partial and impious world view, or what he often called materialism, as the great enemy of modern humanity. Ransom never unraveled these issues with the rigor of a philosopher; his insights remained loose and imprecise. But such an analysis clarified, for him, the terrible cultural heresy advocated by Clarence Darrow and the other defenders of Scopes at Dayton. Their scientism, with all that it denied, was a much greater threat than the mere stupidity of a William J. Bryan. The fundamentalists, with their inadequate tools, were really on the right side. Thus, Ransom sprang to their defense.[18]

Even as Ransom helped collect the essays for *I'll Take My Stand*, he also published a very self-revealing book—*God Without Thunder: An Unorthodox Defense of Orthodoxy*. He dedicated the book to his father. In a sense he remained, or wanted to remain, a good Methodist. But that was impossible. The book is a strange one, but it contains the same attack on "industrialism" that he presented in *I'll Take My Stand*. It is a book on gods, one in which Ransom bared his taste in gods. He liked the old style, or a god of thunder, a god that invites fear and trembling, that created both good and evil. He went back to the Old Testament, and in arguments very close to those of modern neo-orthodox theologians, from Kierkegaard to Barth, castigated those soft, sentimental, indulgent gods of modernity, those without thunder. He placed himself squarely on the side of anthropomorphic and supernatural gods, those rooted in natural wonder and manifested in compelling stories or myths. Such gods do not mesh with scientific intelligence, even stand as an affront to it. In a rather eccentric analysis, he identified such a god with the ancient Orient and traced the Western or Greek perversions of such a god. Even the Christ, the Logos concept of Western theology, was a perversion, and in the abstractions of early Greek theology he found, quite suggestively, the origins of the later scientific, materialistic outlook that produced a modern industrial society. But the flavor of the old god lingered in the superstitions and myths of the middle ages, and just a bit lingered still in southern fundamentalism. His demotion of Jesus made him, technically, a unitarian, even as he made modern American Unitarianism the symbol of all the compromises he despised in religion. The new gods, and the modern liberal religion of a Kirkland or a Mims, were products of essentially impious men, of men who denied evil, defied fate, and foolishly claimed human omnipotence. An industrial, artificial, consumer culture was only one result.

Despite Ransom's cleverness, *God Without Thunder* leaves a reader more perplexed than persuaded. One of similar taste may well applaud Ransom's god. His choice might even be most consistent with an openness to poetry or even to a stable and humane social order. On this one can argue. But one has no sense that Ransom, personally, stood in fear and trembling before any god. The book is artful social criticism, not confession. If, perchance, such a god was beyond his own vital belief, then Ransom could not in good faith recommend such a god to the peasants.[19]

From these intellectual strands, Ransom constructed his image of an idealized South. The South became the "concrete universal" of his ideology, and industrialism came to symbolize all the evils of modernity. Agrarianism stood for an ordered, stable, orthodox alternative. But his South had the same cerebral character of his god. To confound his own analysis, it came through as an overly abstract product of a philosopher's workshop, not as a living reality.

Allen Tate followed a different path back to the South, but at several points a path that converged toward Ransom's. Religion united the two. But Tate was not given to professorial games or cerebral abstractions. He would, like Jeremiah, argue with his god or else have no god. In 1924 he moved to New York and there struggled to make a living from his writing. He suffered from a stormy marriage and from deep financial insecurities. Largely to make a living, he wrote biographies of Stonewall Jackson and then Jefferson Davis, and as these progressed toward publication he wrote his most famous poem in 1927, "Ode to the Confederate Dead." These efforts, on the heels of the Scopes trial, not only forced his attention on the South but raised deep and troubling problems about his own identity. Tate still struggled to find a cause and to find himself. The "Ode," for example, was not really about Confederates, as Davidson protested, but about modern man's estrangement from the past. Tate's mother, fallen on hard times and married to a man her social inferior, nourished fantasies of her Virginia childhood, of an aristocratic and romantic past. Tate grew up on these and on summer visits to Virginia. For years he thought he had been born in a genteel Virginia, not a plebeian Kentucky. Thus, to turn to southern history was to open up heretofore unchallenged anxieties about class and status, anxieties that Tate could not resolve.

In 1928 Tate used a Guggenheim fellowship to live in England and France. Here, so far away from home, he struggled toward a personal resolution; he almost joined the Roman Catholic church. Davidson tried to dissuade him. But by then Tate desperately craved some deep and energizing loyalty, some humane ideal that he could believe in and fight for. The consequence of this was a heightened distaste for the more imperial, dehumanizing features of cities and of factory employment. To some extent he absorbed the critique of Marxist friends, but he sought a quite different resolution of all the problems. It was in Paris that he wrote his friends at Vanderbilt, first suggesting a symposium on the South, and beyond that an ongoing academy or institute with continuing projects and publications. This new enthusiasm postponed his affair with Rome (he converted in 1952) and constituted a major commitment for Tate, almost a conversion. In his developing views of the South he found the order, stability, and authority he sought. Typically, he invested much more emotionally and financially in the emerging cause than anyone else, more even than Davidson. The others had academic jobs. To some extent they dabbled in Agrarianism, never risking their careers. Not so Tate. In 1930 he plunged completely into the cause, moving to a farm near Clarksville, still dreaming of a great crusade. He had found his church.[20]

Donald Davidson was never caught up in all these philosophical and religious abstractions. He never navigated well in ideological waters. And, despite his later fervor, he moved to his version of Agrarianism much more slowly than Tate and Ransom. But, as with the *Fugitive*, he ended up doing most of the actual work of compiling *I'll Take My Stand* in 1930. Tate was not in Nashville. As usual, Ransom, the senior colleague, was too busy to take charge of the practical details.

Davidson came from the same Methodist, small-town, Middle Tennessee background as Ransom. They were practically relatives. But Davidson's father, a school teacher, had to struggle to educate his children. Davidson, as had Ransom, attended an excellent academy and then secured a small loan to finance his first year (1909–1910) at Vanderbilt. But four years of school teaching delayed his graduation until 1917. He loved Vanderbilt and, reflecting a lifelong sense of inferiority, rejoiced that he was able to share the intellectual feast. Warm, responsive, loyal, he formed close friendships, admired both Mims and Ransom, and eagerly entered the Fugitive group. The discussions, the friendship, marked the high point of his life. He never quite got over the breakup of the club. Simple, responsive, touchingly vulnerable, he needed the support of others and tended to flounder—in melancholy, self-pity, bitterness—when intellectually and emotionally alone. Then he could become cranky and defensive. He became particularly close to, and dependent on, his friend Tate.[21]

It is almost impossible to characterize Davidson ideologically in the late 1920s. He seemed tentative, open. He absorbed and reflected many of the themes pushed on him by Tate and Ransom. But at times he also shared the point of view of Mims or Kirkland. His views on the South, even after 1925, remained ambivalent or confused, as he tried to do justice to different points of view. Meantime, life was a struggle for him. With no Ph.D. and only a Vanderbilt M.A., he remained a somewhat stigmatized work horse in the English department, struggling to gain favor and promotion and a living wage. From 1924 to 1930 he devoted enormous time and energy to his task as editor of the book page of the *Tennessean*. Tate could never understand the professional demands that haunted Davidson. Life for Davidson was a grind; he always seemed to have some new problem or complaint. Privately he was much more conventional than Tate or even Ransom—straitlaced, old-fashioned, a near teetotaler, as much or more a moralist than Kirkland. Although gifted in music, a charming companion, he rarely entertained and held back from social involvement, again as if unsure of himself.[22]

The Scopes trial touched Davidson personally. He felt the barbs of Mencken. He had none of Ransom's detachment. For the next three years he struggled to find an appropriate response. These were very difficult years, now that the old support group had dissolved. He seemed in a trap in the English department, going nowhere. At Tate's urging he considered a possible position at Columbia University but did not finally want to leave Vanderbilt. Home loyalties were deep. He needed a cause, a program, to justify his

329

staying at Vanderbilt. He also wanted to form another magic circle of friends, working together on some unifying project. Thus, he avidly greeted Tate's suggestion for a symposium on the South. He early capitulated to much in Ransom's and Tate's newly honed defense of a "South," although it is clear that his response was more personal than ideological. In various guises their theories began to appear in his developing critique of modernity. But, at the same time, he began to assert his own identity as a poet, breaking loose from Tate's earlier critical constraints. In his first published book, *The Tall Men* (1927), he returned to his instinctive bent—lyrical poems with simple, even pastoral content, those that revealed a growing fund of sentiment. Davidson embraced a type of provincialism and began to write almost epic poems about heroic Tennessee pioneers, his home folk, and against the impersonal aspects of urban life. He had a message and began preaching it in verse. He committed an unpardonable sin by the critical standards of Tate and Ransom—he began to mix ideology and esthetics.

What is not clear in all this is what Davidson committed himself *to* in 1927 or 1928. To the South, surely. To the land, to a simpler life, also, but not clearly to the refined image of a good society as envisioned by Ransom and clearly not to the comforting church sought by Tate. Later, at least, he placed more emphasis upon "southern" than on "agrarian" and identified the evils of industrialism more with an imperial central state—the Leviathan—than with private corporatism. Thus, much more than his two friends, he defined not an ideal South, not a contrived intellectual model, but the actual South, at least the South he knew best. His defense of it soon evoked no qualifications, no exceptions. His loyalty was complete, and for the rest of his life the South was his only real cause.[23]

Out of such complex motives came *I'll Take My Stand*. Ransom, Tate, and Davidson were its authentic parents, pushing it through publication in late 1930. They knew not what they wrought. The book was a uniquely successful disaster, stimulating extensive debate upon publication and attracting new audiences even today. Typical of gathered essays, it had no unity. It still defies full understanding unless one is willing to probe deeply into the background of each essay. Few people ever read all the book, and well-insulated from its diverse and elusive content almost everyone has some oversimplified view of what it was about. The trouble is that, in some place or another, it was about almost everything. Much of the language is loose, ambiguous, suggestive, as language always is when valuative issues are at stake. These problems have allowed sympathetic readers to find what they want in it and critics to erect damning stereotypes or caricatures. The only pretense of a unifying statement is in Ransom's introduction, a set of principles or, better, a manifesto. To this the various contributors, with varying levels of critical attention, eventually subscribed. It at least permits a bit of content analysis.

The opening manifesto is both truistic and involves a vacuous comparison. That is, few people could possibly reject the values portrayed in it, and the implied comparisons are vacuous because no other side really exists. What Ransom did here, as in *God Without Thunder,* was to pile on a series of damning descriptions of what he called industrialism or the modern American system. The South had until recently struggled to resist the dangerous virus of industrialism, but lately seemed to be increasingly infected by it, with the infection often spread by the advocates of a new South. The contributors to *I'll Take My Stand* wrote in order to help southerners, or other regional minorities in America, resist industrialism. What is "industrialism?" Ransom's answer was, at best complex, at worst unclear. First of all, it is a mode of economic organization, involving large collections of capital, of plants and tools, centralized management, and dependent wage employees. Ransom emphasized that such collectivized production amounts to a "capitalization" of science. The cruel effects of such collectivism afflict those who work; their "hard, fierce, insecure," brutalizing, servile labors alienate them from the ends and purposes of work and deny them any leisurely or joyful involvement. Workers also face the threat of redundancy, as machines take over more and more work. In other words, in an industrial society work ceases to be an art, for it is dedicated not to any intrinsic rewards but only to extrinsic products. It contributes only to a deceptive goal—more and more mindless consumption. Ransom, in one of his few original arguments, noted that the logical end of such industrialism is communism. In fact, as he used the terms, "industrialism" and "communism" are all but synonymous, for people, in their desperate response to the evils of industrialism, turn to socialism or communism, to a more complete form of collectivism than that already prefigured in large corporate enterprise.[24]

Ransom wanted much more than a purely economic definition. But, notably, he began with economic realities and saw these as determinate of all else in a society. The only effective check to industrialism would be direct changes in the mode of organizing capital and mobilizing workers. Welfare tinkering, or sentimental religious or esthetic reproaches, would only play at the surface. Given an industrialized economy, then, all areas of life are affected by it. Authentic religion, which entails a submission to an inscrutable nature, can not survive in an industrial society, one in which people process nature, convert it into cities, manufacture it into artificial commodities. Such a transformed or corrupted nature invites the illusion of power, a loss of any sense of mystery and contingency, and turns the gods of yore into amiable and superfluous entities. Likewise, the arts can not cohere with industrialism, for they depend on a right (mythic, religious) attitude toward nature and require leisure. The arts of living—manners, hospitality, sympathy, romantic love—also yield before an industrial order, since they are complementary to religion and art. The ravages of industrialism, immune to meliorative reforms, increase through time because the system has an internal dynamic, a constant need for more production and more consumption. The modern stimulants for this are advertising and salesmanship, means of persuading innocent people to want all the new goods made possible by applied science.[25]

The opposite of industrialism is "agrarianism," a word Ransom said did not "stand in particular need of definition." But Ransom tied it down a bit—to a belief that agriculture, pursued with intelligence and leisure, is the model vocation, approached by other necessary tasks as much as possible. An agrarian society makes the culture of the soil the preeminent vocation, one that has preference in public policy and one that attracts the most people. Beyond indicting industrialism and elliptically celebrating agrarianism, Ransom eschewed specific policies or programs, although he did list some possibilities. He ended his manifesto on a note of hope. If a section, or race, or age is "groaning under industrialism" and is aware that it is an evil dispensation, it must find a way to throw it off. Unfortunately, he did not pen the appropriate ending: "Farmers and poets of the world unite."[26]

What is wrong with this manifesto? Nothing at all. It is very persuasive. It is also commonplace. The very same sentiments reverberated through almost all the social criticism of the prior one hundred years, and most forcefully in that of Karl Marx. When, subsequently, both Tate and Ransom occasionally substituted capitalism for industrialism one sensed the unintended verbal similarities with the "Communist Manifesto." But some such critique of an overly commercialized, overly centralized, dependency-creating economic order were present in Emerson and in American Transcendentalism, in John Ruskin and other English rustic socialists, in several strains of Roman Catholic criticism, in extreme antimodernist or neofeudal advocates, in some forms of European corporatism or fascism, even in the social criticism of such a nemesis as John Dewey. Such a generalized critique touches on almost every profound concern of the twentieth century, from the problems of alienated workers to the hazards of unchecked economic growth to a lost respect for nature and the environment to laments over religious or artistic decline. This is not to say that *I'll Take My Stand* touched upon every social problem. Given the southern context, its omission of racial justice was the most obvious. But the scope was so encompassing that the manifesto still defies any conventional classification, whether right or left, radical or reactionary. All categories fit.

By refusing to advocate specific programs, Ransom left a set of glittering principles that are almost as obvious as respect for motherhood. Of course, all the key words are loaded with private meanings. One does not have to attach Ransom's ugly images to science or machines or his pleasant ones to nature or to art. But granting his definitions, it is hard to imagine anyone who would dissent from his principles. Their very generality and universality seem to strip away any very specific content for the word "southern." The lack of specific economic programs make "agrarian" practically a synonym of everything good.

The twelve essays in *I'll Take My Stand* did not build consistently upon the opening manifesto. This is not hard to explain. The editors rather hastily recruited contributors and gathered together the final essays. The group was unable to gather and hone contributions through debate as they had in Fugitive days. Two authors—Frank Owsley and John Donald Wade—simply submitted essays largely, or wholly, composed for other purposes. One contributor, a former Vanderbilt student and young journalist, Henry B. Kline, submitted a rambling monologue not worthy of a B in a freshman English class but, lacking an alternative, the editors still included it. The summary essay by Stark Young is disjointed, largely a series of rambling sermons on the foibles or achievements of southerners and not always consistent with the earlier essays. But Young, a Mississippian who succeeded in the North as novelist, dramatist, and editor, lent prestige to the volume. Only three essays consistently developed the themes of Ransom's manifesto—his own, Davidson's, and John Gould Fletcher's. Even Davidson never fully accepted the hierarchical or feudal social order embraced by Ransom and Fletcher. Thus, attempts to group even three essays soon fail, and sweeping statements about what all the southern Agrarians proposed or wanted are simply not worth the paper they are written on. A brief excursion into the essays illustrates this point.[27]

Ransom used his opening essay to plug the South into the theoretical framework of his manifesto. Here he used what Michael O'Brien has correctly described as his "Idea of the South," one only tangentially related to the history of that section and one that Ransom himself referred to as a "southern idea," in contrast to an "American idea." Too briefly stated, he pictured the South as an established, ordered, conservative society, one after the European or English model, and one committed to leisure as against profits. This society contrasted with the pioneering, and thus dynamic, mobile, nonestablished, ever-changing, materialistic society of the North, a society given over to economic progress. Ambitious Yankees remained at war with nature, nourished commercial ambitions, and then reaped all the evils of Ransom's industrialism. Now, long after military defeat in the war, the South trembled under a cultural invasion by an alien industrialism. It was at the point of crisis and of choice. Ransom wrote to persuade southerners to fight back, not blindly and beligerently as in the war, but by forming alliances with like-minded people all over the country and then working within the existing political system.[28]

In "Education, Past and Present," the erratic, mentally beset Arkansas poet John Gould Fletcher seemed to share Ransom's vision of an aristocratic and hierarchical society. But in Fletcher the elitism became more belligerent, the tone more reactionary. Fletcher hated representative democracy and the leveling downward that was, he perceived, an inevitable product of mass public education. He yearned for the old academies that educated the rich or the few exceptional and qualified students. He scored some hits, as any sophomore can, in his identification of the inanities present in any existing school system, but all in all he wanted to return to pauper schools for the masses, those who in a properly ordered society exist only for the sake of their superiors. His bent was to destroy the public schools, but since that was impossible he proposed a second-best answer—the creation of truly elite secondary schools for the few, and the routing of Negroes and less intelligent white children into manual training schools.[29]

Davidson's "A Mirror for Artists" closely paralleled one of his earlier publications, but it well fit *I'll Take My Stand*. In some ways, his was the most persuasive essay in the book. He followed up Ransom's argument that industrialism is hostile to the arts, which flourish only in stable, religious, and leisurely societies. In an industrial society the arts may indeed have value—they sell well. But art as a commodity soon ceases to be art as an object of appreciation. In an effective ploy, he joined John Dewey in castigating museums and libraries, those patronized by the wealthy, those which collect and disseminate art and literature as decorative objects to a noncomprehending public. His plea was to make the arts an integral part of life, an adornment of both work and leisure. Mass consumption has severed art from the objects of daily life; specialized factory labor, under the command of bosses, had severed art from work. He believed over the long term that the conditions of modern urban life could not nourish creativity, or when it did survive it would necessarily take a false detour into a type of sick romanticism.

By this approach Davidson was able to say something refreshing about the South, even while admitting its meager past contributions to the more fashionable fine arts. Instead, he suggested, with what degree of truth one is hard put to judge, that the old South, a harmonious agrarian society, and in his view as much or more a democratic than an aristocratic or feudal society (his images came from Middle Tennessee, not from an English gentry), did produce the integrated arts of good living. He stressed folk arts, home crafts, oratory, and rustic humor, not "great art," although this might have come later had the war not intervened. Already Davidson rejoiced in the revival of southern literature and in subsequent years celebrated this as if it were a key strategic victory in the ongoing battle of the sections. Self-revealingly, he ended his essay with a note that would have gladdened a Marxist—that the artist, in critical times, cannot separate his art from his larger role as person and citizen. An artist has to fight against the evils that threaten art. He has to join crusades. By implication, even his art is a tool in that larger game, in creating the highest form of beauty, the greatest work of art—a harmonious and fulfilling society. Never again would Davidson separate his politics from his poetry.[30]

An important essay—Robert Penn Warren's "The Briar Patch"—was rather out of place in the volume. Warren was not vitally involved in the Agrarian enterprise. Now away at Oxford, he wrote his assigned essay on the Negro with small understanding of the goals of the group back in Nashville, and one feels without a deep personal commitment to these goals. After the early Fugitive days at Vanderbilt, he had passed through some stormy years, despite outward academic success at an uninspiring California and then at Yale. Just as he left Vanderbilt an earlier eye injury worsened, leaving him almost blind in one eye and severely depressed, even to the point of attempting suicide. From the suffering, and from his earlier career in literature, he slowly matured his own philosophy and one very different from that of Tate and Ransom. He turned loose of older certainties, dared live in a universe without ultimate meaning, and in such a universe probed the meanings various people create for themselves. He was not given to great crusades and yearned for no church. But at Oxford the world of little Guthrie, Kentucky, and of Nashville seemed more appealing than ever before. Thus, a bit homesick, he welcomed the volume on the South and of course easily concurred in the opening statement of principles. He seemed to invest little in his somewhat strained essay, and later seemed to remember it, quite mistakenly, as a defense of segregation. Actually, in the context of 1930, and with the editors he had to face back in Nashville, he took as daring a stand as he could. Simply put, he argued that the southern Negro would gain more from a continued agricultural economy than from new manufacturing, but only with a major qualification that Warren wanted to emphasize to his white audience. In all areas except social mingling, the Negro had to receive completely equal justice. In effect, Warren threw out the enormous demands implicit in "separate but equal" and, in terms reminiscent of Booker T. Washington, demanded for blacks the same economic rights, including land ownership, already enjoyed by whites. Even such a moderate attempt at fairness offended Davidson and led to some minor editorial changes as a condition of publication. Very clear in this essay was an outlook, and a growing sense of guilt, that would soon lead Warren to embrace full racial integration.[31]

Warren's essay, alone, tangled directly with the problem of race. Ransom evaded the issue, but his hierarchical society clearly suggested Negro subordination. In part, his evasion reflected the dominating concerns of time and place. Public awareness of black suppression, at least among whites, reached a record low in the early 1930s, as broader economic issues dominated public concern. But in several essays the issue lay just beneath the surface, quite deliberately suppressed or evaded. This most compromised the beguiling moral preferences aired in the book and at least made problematical the various pictures of a South, old or new. From other sources it is clear that, in 1930, Owsley, Lytle, and Davidson took an inflexible stand on segregation and supported this by a belief in some degree of Negro inferiority.[32]

Owsley, the historian of the group, was intimately invoved in the planning of *I'll Take My Stand,* as he was on the scene and a friend of Ransom's. His essay developed themes he had explored before Tennessee historians, themes intimately involved in his own scholarship. Owsley was a rising star in the history department. His book on state rights in the Confederacy had been

335

well received, and he used his 1928 Guggenheim to pursue European research for his first major book—*King Cotton Diplomacy*. But 1930 was not a
great year for the Alabama native. He was passed over as department chairman to replace the ailing W.L. Fleming, to whom *I'll Take My Stand* was
dedicated, and had engaged in a vicious fight against Kirkland, Mims, and
L.C. Glenn (the oligarchy) to prevent the appointment of a mediocrity from
the outside to head the department. He professed respect for the ultimate
choice—William C. Binkley—but in all the struggles he had come close to a
nervous breakdown and would be ill during the next year. He seemed to
welcome the new Agrarian effort as an outlet, a needed crusade.

What came through in Owsley's essay was, on one level, a then conventional historical thesis. He argued that the Civil War largely reflected an irrepressible conflict between an industrial North and an agrarian South, or the
very theme of much of the symposium. But some of his words were bathed in
vitriol, revealing a frustrated, bitterly defensive southerner, an old-fashioned
populist who carried a huge personal grudge against the North. The North,
in his terms, stood as the perennial imperial aggressor, now bent on the
spiritual conquest of the South as well as its continued economic exploitation.
He minimized the role of slavery in the road to war, denied it any essential
relationship to the southern economy, and referred to "half savage blacks"
hardly three generations removed from cannibalism, statements that were not
as intentionally mean-spirited as they seemed. Owsley had not yet explored
the topic, but he would soon develop his thesis that the backbone of the
South was the small yeoman farmers, those with few or no slaves, and not the
few large plantation owners. But in 1930 Owlsey was angry and he showed it.
Free from the constraints of scholarship, he bared his animus in a forceful,
pungent prose. As he noted at the Fugitive reunion in 1956, he suffered
plenty of scholarly scorn for such bluntness and such honesty.[33]

Poor Allen Tate. He invested so much in the cause. He saw the effort as a
defense of religious humanism and chose for himself the critical essay entitled
"Remarks on the Southern Religion." But he flubbed the opportunity,
ending up with a dense, obscure, often unfocused argument, written in a
clever but rather sophomoric style. His first goal was to give a definition of
religion or, more accurately, to clarify why a verbal definition is always
inadequate. Drawing on themes from Ransom, he insisted that true religion,
not the attenuated forms that flourished in America, is always holistic,
encompassing both the intellectual and experiential aspects of life, the objec-
tified but always inadequate reports about experience and the actual, vital
qualities that are experience. He used the awkward image of a horse to make
his point—words, abstractions, the sciences deal only with half a horse, with
the dynamic and manageable half. A half-horsed religion is one that deals only
with how things work. This led him into his understanding of the modern,
false religions of production, consumption, and progress.

Next, Tate expanded this whole-part analysis to views of history. The highly abstract long view of the past, which drops out most particularities, is another half horse, as compared to the vital, concrete personalities and events present in a short view. The short view alone accommodates the details of religious myth and allows a wholehearted commitment to specific gods or, in brief, to provincial or parochial verities, all of which dissolve in the long view. In all of this Tate revealed his own dilemma, that of one whose intellect led toward the long view, which dissolved traditional loyalties into skepticism or agnosticism, but whose personal needs, and search for identity, pushed him toward the Roman church. But he wanted to become part of the church in a natural, simple, mythical, wholehearted way, not in the typical Western, defensive way, which leads to elaborate and, to Tate, irrelevant and diverting rationalizations or dogmas. He wanted to be part of a tradition, not argue it or defend it. This put him at cross-purposes with *I'll Take My Stand,*, for most of the essays defended both tradition and a particular southern tradition. Painted into a corner, Tate finally, and one feels with some reluctance, turned to southern religion.[34]

In Tate's view as necessarily oversimplified, the South developed a feudal economy, one tied to soil and climate, but was never so spiritually isolated as to be able to develop the religion that best fit its social order. In religion it remained part of Protestantism, of a nonagrarian or trading religion, a half-horse religion that served as a mask for secular ambition. The South tried, in vain, to use the catchwords of this essentially alien religion to defend its society, but caught up in contradictions, the South was doomed to defeat. The aggressive North, meantime, developed its own parasitic and imperial society, living economically on such colonies as the south, culturally on England. As Tate put it, New England became a European museum. The South did not borrow from Europe in this way, for in a sense it was Europe, a traditional society rooted in its own native soil. But thus the tragedy—a false religious life, a false mythology, false gods. For rationalization, southerners turned to an artificial Jeffersonian rationalism, a rationalism that did not fit their social order any more than the dogmas of fundamentalists provided a fitting religious rationalization. Now in the crisis of a South under economic and spiritual siege, the section was all but helpless. It had no short view, no mythic resources, no appropriate religion to turn to as a defense. How could the southerner defend himself? Only, said Tate, by violence, by a radical or revolutionary use of political tools to get back to the roots of his heritage. But Tate saw the paradox, if not the helpless obscurity, of this elusive prescription, and ended his essay with the question: could southerners use an alien instrument—politics—to recover a "private, self-contained, and essentially spiritual life?" Clearly Tate doubted it.[35]

The other essays revealed the various linkages and divisions among contributors. Lyle H. Lanier, an able young psychologist at Vanderbilt, linked to Ransom in university politics, wrote a very balanced, almost scholarly analysis of "The Philosophy of Progress." It included a long, informed critique of

John Dewey's views and ended with an analysis of the excesses of the new industrial order that would have fit very well into the discussions at a social science convention. Its clarity and balance made it the best essay in the volume, but it did not very clearly advance the philosophical purposes of Ransom. One feels that Lanier, although a native Tennessean and quite loyal to the South, was not as committed to the South as a cause as he was to a more humane economy.[36] Andrew N. Lytle, a former English major at Vanderbilt, later a playwright and novelist, coined the most memorable title, "The Hind Tit." He used the second half of his long essay to paint a highly idealized verbal portrait of an actual farm in the upper South. In the early, more analytical section he used more pungent language than either Lanier or Ransom to indict the gospel of progress. Like Owsley and Davidson, he pointedly emphasized the yeoman farmer and denied any class rivalry between such farmers and the small number of planters. Like Owsley, he also reflected a bit of countrified anger at northerners. His essay had one unfortunate effect—it helped people identify the book primarily with subsistence agriculture and thus helped conceal the more subtle philosophical issues that most concerned Ransom and Tate.[37]

Since John Donald Wade was, briefly as it turned out, in the Vanderbilt English department, he submitted an already completed biographical sketch of "Cousin Lucius." He did not write it to further Agrarianism and apparently was not yet strongly committed to the joint effort. The essay adds nothing to the whole, although one can find in it a living example of at least some of the ideals included in the opening manifesto.[38]

Herman C. Nixon, a member of the Vanderbilt history department until 1928, shared a strong attachment to the South and was particularly interested in its now suffering small farmers. His bias was strongly populist, but he shared none of the racial animus of Davidson or Owsley. Even more than Warren, he would soon join the fight for racial justice. In "Whither Southern Economy?" he resorted to an almost offensive display of economic statistics, stuck largely to historical description, and presented a series of arguments justifying southern agricultural reform, including the usual plea for greater diversification. He did not oppose manufacturing but only its rapid and unregulated growth, with all the new economic vulnerabilities this entailed. His ideal was a balanced economy, certainly not a fully agricultural one. Little in his essay related him to Ransom, Tate, or Davidson.[39]

Ironically, just after publishing *I'll Take My Stand,* several of the contributors moved on to a true agrarian position. They developed an economic program, joined in larger political efforts, and had at least a limited impact on national policy. The controversies that ensued upon publication of the book, and major debates about it (Ransom debated Stringfellow Barr at Richmond before a standing-room-only audience and with extensive national coverage), might alone have pushed them in this direction. But the developing depression was crucial. *I'll Take My Stand* came out of the 1920s; it was in fact a stinging rebuke of the popularized values associated with prosperity and corporate expansion. Even as late as its publication in November, 1930, the economic recession had not yet developed into a deep depression. No one could yet foresee the depth, or the duration, of the great depression. Thus, the self-called Agrarians had attacked an ascendant industrialism, but within a year or two the context changed dramatically. As unemployment soared to near 25 percent in 1932, as the great industrial and financial machine floundered, as consumer values paled, the Agrarians seemed more and more like prophets. Agrarianism ceased to be just an intellectual foil for profound philosophical and religious criticism; it now appealed to many as a practical strategy for a shrinking economy, an economy that had perhaps already probed the upper limits of economic growth. Ransom had deferred any commitment to specific principles. But Davidson and Owsley saw the high-falutin' discussions of general principles only as a prelude to action. Now, when people demanded programs, not just principles, these three plus Tate, joined at times by Lanier, Lytle, Warren, and Wade, eagerly tried to fill in the programmatic implications of *I'll Take My Stand*. As they did so, they returned to an etymologically correct and economically radical meaning of the word "agrarian."

In 1930 Ransom refused to define "agrarian" but identified it with agriculture. He certainly wanted it to carry a great deal of cultural content, to suggest an ordered, stable, traditional, nonacquisitive, leisurely, and religious society, whatever the exact ordering of occupations or the details of economic policy. All the essayists gave lip service to the often vaguely identified virtues of farm life, although at the time this was not very important to Tate or even to Ransom. The word "agrarian," by its Latin roots, relates to the soil and to problems of tenure and ownership. It is an inept synonym for agriculture, either as an occupation or an economic sector. But in twentieth-century America the word came to connote the virtues of farm life, or not at all what it meant in the nineteenth century—an often radical effort to provide everyone access to land, to one's natural birthright. Organized agrarians, since their Anglo-American origins with one Thomas Spence in late eighteenth-century England, had fought against land monopoly, against large landowners, and against tenancy. So did the "dangerous" agrarians of the 1830s in America, men such as Thomas Skidmore. Echoes of this meaning lingered on in Henry George, in some of the Populists, and in certain native, midwestern socialist movements. But in the early twentieth century such an agrarianism had a more vital constituency in England than in America. The Vanderbilt Agrarians were not unaware of this English tradition. Tate, Ransom, and Fletcher knew of the political activity of two English literary figures, Hillaire Belloc (*The Servile State*) and G.K. Chesterton and of a movement they helped launch, one now generally called "distributism." Belloc, an antimodernist Catholic, wanted to return to a propertied society, which would entail the radical redistribution of real property, particularly land. But in *I'll Take My*

Stand the key organizers of the volume chose not to engage those issues. Had they done so, they would have altered the cultural focus of the essays toward more narrow economic problems and would also have risked the loss of some contributors. But in 1931–32 they could no longer evade such economic issues. They slowly became economic as well as cultural agrarians or, if already persuaded in this direction, at least came out of the closet.

I'll Take My Stand remained deliberately ambiguous on problems of ownership, not only of capital goods but even of land. Behind the vague language one critical issue divided the contributors. They had sharply contrasting images of the good life. On one side, Tate, Ransom, and Fletcher seemed to prefer a class-based, hierarchical, organic society, although this commitment by both Tate and Ransom remained a bit halfhearted and tentative. Owsley, Lytle, and Nixon were more equalitarian; they wanted no aristocratic elite, no feudalism, no English gentry. They minimized the role of an older planter class even in the South. They venerated the small proprietor and with some very limited justification made Jefferson their hero. Davidson, somewhat ambivalently, generally sided with the proprietary or yeoman cause. The other contributors did not engage these issues directly, but none of them seemed at all attracted to, or even familiar with, the elitest, premodern perspective. This basic division complicated issues concerning agriculture and very much involved the problem of race. The hierarchical model suggested ownership by a few, perhaps in large plantations or in other forms of extended household production, and a large peasant class, either made up of tenants or of those who owned plots but under the regulations of a nobility. Obviously, in this scheme, the blacks would fit in a subordinated but, by the theory, not necessarily servile peasant class. Even Owsley accepted some aspects of the feudal model for most blacks and for less talented whites.

These tensions, which so blurred the focus of the book, did not prove a major hurdle to an agrarian program. Fletcher was rarely a part of the political effort. The aristocratic bent of Tate and Ransom related primarily to cultural and literary issues, not directly to the southern economy. Soon both of them emphasized the small, landowning producer. This meant that the agrarian activists could join, at least for four or five years, in a rather coherent crusade for a broader distribution of productive property, for a return of as many people as possible to the land, and for an increase in subsistence as opposed to commercial agriculture. Such a program, radical in implications just because so atavistic, seemed persuasive only during the worst years of the depression, and thus had a built-in time bomb—the eventual return of prosperity and economic growth. But for a brief and strange interlude the Southern Agrarians were able to link up with several like-minded groups and to lead a crusade for a decentralized economy, for property and free enterprise when almost no one enjoyed either. All recent economic trends had favored more centralized ownership and control and a work force largely excluded from the ownership or management of property. In a sense, by 1933 no policy, not even communist proposals for complete collectivism under state auspices, was so radical in implication, in challenges to the existing order, as the one preached by the Agrarians. For cautious administrators such as Kirkland, the Vanderbilt professors now had a double mark against them—they were at one and the same time cultural reactionaries and dangerous economic radicals.[40]

Ransom, Tate, Owsley, and Davidson became most involved in political advocacy. Tate, free of professional obligations out on his farm, had always wanted an agrarian party and gladly sought political allies outside the South. In fact, his agrarianism had, all along, much less of a southern content than anyone else's. Ransom, always the master of logic and consistency, was now driven to a detailed investigation of the concrete historical and economic issues implicated by his earlier, more cerebral critique. He became, for a few years, a student of economics, a political partisan, and all but suspended his scholarly work in literature to write a continuing series of agrarian articles and reviews. Owsley, a bit of a rural-minded populist all along, proved most adept at communicating agrarian views to southern politicians. Davidson joined the effort but was most leery of outside allegiances and most skeptical of any success in Washington. Of the other four activists, Lanier was perhaps more deeply involved than Wade, Lytle, or even Warren, who again made important contributions but with a degree of detachment or diffidence.[41]

In the years after 1930 this group first planned for some follow-up volume, one much more practical and programmatic than *I'll Take My Stand*. Davidson very much desired this; he also craved the support of a close and familiar circle, something like the old Fugitives. But the group was never able to complete a second symposium or to arrange any suitable format for collecting and publishing such a book. Several publishers turned down specific proposals. Meantime, the group found a sympathetic outlet for a series of articles and reviews in Seward Collins's new (1933) *American Review*, which featured articles by representatives of all the major traditional or antimodern movements, including New Humanists, neo-Thomists, and distributists. Here, in over sixty articles in the next few years, the Agrarians publicized their developing program. But in the ideological confusions of the mid-1930s the ties with Collins later proved embarrassing. To the chagrin of the Agrarians and other contributors, he openly gave his support to a type of fascism.[42]

Tate, who arranged for the publication of *I'll Take My Stand*, eventually gave up on any very practical program by his colleagues or even on any subsequent book. He believed, perhaps unfairly, that only he had fully sacrificed his career in behalf of the cause and seemed disappointed that it never developed into something close to a political party. After coming to admire the historical writings of a Louisville journalist, Herbert Agar, he joined with Agar to plan a broader symposium and book. Their plan involved all the groups that supported a redistribution of property and even those who joined in sentimental back-to-the-land efforts, or specifically the English distributists, a Catholic Rural Life Movement, Ralph Borsodi and his rather

341

eccentric back-to-the-land followers, and some nonattached intellectuals such as Agar. The group met in Nashville in 1936 to celebrate the publication of their new book, *Who Owns America?* Eight of the original Agrarians contributed, and by this time Ransom and Tate were key members of an enlarged but exceedingly loose coalition. The book attracted little attention, an omen of the precipitous decline of agrarian sentiments. The same group, with Agar's leadership, had already launched a weekly magazine from New York, *Free America*. Tate backed the effort; Ransom served briefly as its book-review editor. But it soon became largely a guide for modern home-steaders, an early version of *Organic Gardening*.[43]

Given all this organized activity, what was the Agrarian program? The nuances varied from group to group, but all joined in advocating a society based on property. The distributist position was rather simple—fulfillment depends upon freedom, and this in turn requires personal ownership of, and control over, the means of production. The theme does relate very much to Jefferson, and to the eighteenth-century belief that property is the basis of independence and thus of liberty. But in the context of the depression 1930s, the position represented a deliberate inversion of the Marxist program, but one that shared a large part of the Marxist critique of something called capitalism. Tate, in his condemnation of the existing society, often sounded very much like radical Marxists; his hatred of corporate capitalism was intense. Marxists proposed to solve the problem of alienated workers, and an increasingly inequitable distribution of wealth, through cooperative worker ownership, by a more complete collectivism. Distributists believed that this would only lead to a slightly different form of servility under a powerful state. Thus, they proposed a redistribution of property. Unfortunately, as Tate so eloquently argued in *Who Owns America?*, few people seemed to understand what property meant. They confused it with legal claims to corporate profits, or with other paper wealth totally bereft of direct managerial rights. What one does not control is not property, at least in the moral sense. Thus, the only primary property is land, and next to it other productive tools (capital). Such elementary definitions clearly revealed a very distressing fact—property had all but disappeared in America and the few remaining property owners were under attack. Given this perspective, the Vanderbilt Agrarians worked to reduce the size and power of corporations, to decentralize economic decision making, to aid existing farmers to stay on the land, to end tenancy and sharecropping through land-purchase programs, and to encourage more subsistence agriculture. Given market gluts, the only way that larger numbers of Americans could farm was to increase home consumption. Given massive unemployment, such subsistence strategies made sense, for even nonfarmers might survive on part-time wages if they could utilize a small homestead. The enemy of such a program was large corporate enterprise, not small shops or stores. In a sense, the Agrarians fought for a return toward (they knew the change could not go very far) an earlier, proprietary, household-based economy, and of course they easily linked their esthetic and religious and moral goals to such an economic program.[44]

For a very brief time the Agrarian program received favorable attention in the press and even in Washington. In 1933 the new Roosevelt administration established a small Subsistence Homesteads Division and soon resettled some unemployed workers in several small, planned communities. With the exception of Davidson, who very soon developed an intense fear of New Deal initiatives in the South, the Vanderbilt Agrarians gave enthusiastic support to this small program and also to other New Deal agricultural efforts. Herbert Agar was a strong Roosevelt supporter; so was Owsley. Growing out of the Subsistence Homestead effort and subsequent community programs developed by a new Resettlement Administration came a major effort in 1936 to pass a new tenant-purchase bill, or the subsequent Bankhead-Jones Farm Tenancy Act. Owsley and Nixon were heavily involved in the lobbying effort behind this bill. In 1935 Owsley drew up his own agrarian platform, which he published as "The Pillars of Agrarianism." He sent copies to Bankhead and other congressmen. Bankhead acknowledged its influence on his thinking, although it had limited impact on the final legislation.[45]

Owsley's "Pillars" came closer than any other statement to being the manifesto of economic Agrarianism. He submitted it to his comrades and they all endorsed it, although one senses unvoiced reservations or qualifications on some of the points. Owsley referred to the existing Scandinavian countries, not the historical old South, as the best model for an agrarian society. The central problem of modern America, he said, was concentrated ownership. Agrarians wanted to get rid of the twentieth-century robber barons and to break up their large property into small units controlled by real people. As his first and most complex pillar, he advocated a complete rehabilitation of southern agriculture. For existing farms he applauded easier credit and several other New Deal programs. He supported special credit to help the better class of white tenants and even a few Negroes purchase their existing land. To get land for the landless he asked the federal government or state governments to buy up all land owned by insurance companies and absentee owners, and excessive land owned by large planters, and use it for a new homestead program (eighty acres, a rough home, two mules and two cows, and living expenses for a year). The homesteads were to be nonalienable, subject neither to sale nor mortgaging, or a traditional agrarian position. As an answer for an even larger number of the urban unemployed, he proposed their gradual reintroduction to farming, including an apprenticeship as tenants on plantations before they moved on to their homesteads. This, he hoped, could lead to a better balance between farms and cities.[46]

As a second pillar of agrarianism, Owsley advocated a major effort in behalf of soil rehabilitation and conservation. For homesteaders, a failure to follow approved methods would cost them their land. He even condoned laws to prevent the mortgaging of land or the speculative sale of land. In his third pillar he urged a new balance between subsistence and money crops, with greater priority to subsistence. As a fourth pillar, he argued that, if manufacturers benefited from tariffs or monopolies, then compensatory subsidies should go to southern farmers, or a program that went back to old Alliance and Populist platforms of the late nineteenth century. Finally, and fifth, he wanted to anchor such economic changes through major constitutional changes, reminiscent of those proposed by John C. Calhoun. He proposed to divide the country up into regions, each with a regional government, and thus to decentralize economic decision making, the one plank that was probably most congenial to Donald Davidson.[47]

As a quite subversive political and economic program, Agrarianism floundered after 1937 and quietly died in World War II. Events all moved in the opposite direction from what the Agrarians had predicted and preferred. Not only did a new and more equal balance between farming and other occupations fail to appear, the 20 percent of farmers shrank to less than 3 percent in the next half century. Instead of greater decentralization of ownership or political power, the concentration in larger and larger firms, balanced by a larger and larger government, increased with each decade, until the degree of collectivism in America rivaled that of communist countries. By the 1980s fewer than 10 percent of workers owned productive land or tools or were self-employed. Private property, in the Agrarian sense, had all but disappeared and free enterprise, as they understood it, was now only a nostalgic slogan.

Success need not determine preferences. Most of the aging Vanderbilt Agrarians kept the faith, as revealed in their response to a 1952 questionnaire or by a few nostalgic memories they shared at a reunion of the old Fugitives at Vanderbilt in 1956. This reunion, organized by English professor Randall Stewart, marked the first, much-appreciated official recognition of the Fugitives by Vanderbilt University. But even as early as 1952 the surviving Agrarians had amazingly diverse views of what Agrarianism had earlier meant. Ransom came closest to outright defection, for by the end of World War II he openly accepted the new economy, acknowledged Agrarianism as a lost cause, and rejoiced that blacks were sharing more equally in the benefits of an industrialized order. By 1952 Tate minimized the political side of Agrarianism and insisted, as a brand-new Catholic, that it primarily meant a unification of Christianity. Wade also emphasized religion, as did even Davidson and Owsley, or themes that they had hardly hinted at in the early 1930s. Both Lytle and Davidson reflected an almost apocalyptic gloom at all the recent developments and now saw the federal government as the great tyrant and civil rights as the Trojan horse. In Davidson's terms, the subversion of constitutional rights now joined wasted resources, corruption, and treason. In that year of rampant McCarthyism, of a second Red Scare, both Davidson and Owsley emphasized the anticommunist side of Agrarianism. Thus, time, changed circumstances, and a variant understanding of Agrarianism had produced an amazing diversity of beliefs and programs. For example, H.C. Nixon, during World War II and at the time he returned to the Vanderbilt faculty, placed his career in jeopardy by a courageous defense of Negro rights and by enlisting in politically radical reform organizations. During the postwar years Donald Davidson jeopardized his academic reputation, and eventually embarrassed Vanderbilt, by a courageous if cantankerous and increasingly desperate defense of segregation; he enlisted in some far-out organizations that stopped barely short of the KKK. Each fought his battle in behalf of a beloved South and in furtherance of what he saw as the noble ideals of Agrarianism.[48]

Even as political and economic Agrarianism expired, the broader principles of *I'll Take My Stand* kept taking on new meaning and appealing to new audiences. Like a well-cut diamond, the various facets of philosophical agrarianism alternatively flashed with every shift in the position of the cultural sun. In the 1950s, intellectuals lamented the advent of a mass society, of plastic other-directed people, of conformity and mediocrity, of lagging educational standards, of a society given over to quantity at the expense of quality. Just what the Agrarians had prophesied. In the 1960s both rural and urban poverty became a national embarrassment. Political rebels now charted the evils of monopoly capitalism, consoled alienated workers or students who had to cope with large, impersonal managers, and tried to escape from false, consumer values. *I'll Take My Stand* became a campus bestseller, appealing both to campus radicals and to advocates of a counterculture. In the early 1970s concern shifted to humanity's alienation from nature, to its distorting role in the environment, and to the need for ecological balance and a regained respect for the earth. And no one had expressed these sentiments more eloquently than the Vanderbilt Agrarians. Finally, by the late 1970s and early 1980s, Americans tried to adjust to energy shortages, to the prospect of depleted resources, and suddenly realized the waste involved in large cities, in a mad rush to ever higher levels of consumption. Conservation became a watchword. A new generation at least yearned for a return to the land; homesteading once again became fashionable. Folk arts revived, and sheepish suburbanites began growing gardens and burning wood. Small is beautiful! And all right out of *I'll Take My Stand*, by now clearly the most influential document of cultural dissent in American history.[49]

Ironies marked the relationship of the Fugitives and Agrarians to Vanderbilt University. In a national perspective, Vanderbilt long enjoyed, or suffered, an identity tied closely, if not exclusively, to the products of these intellectuals. To an extent rare in American higher education, Vanderbilt gained a philosophical identity. It stood for a point of view, even though one, on close examination, that always tended to vary slightly from one observer to another. The one constant was that Vanderbilt had a closer identification with the South than ever before. Such an ascribed identity brought some benefits, particularly in the recruitment of able graduate students, not only in the English department but for the social sciences. Vanderbilt's poets and critics also exerted an influence upon American literary culture rare for those identified with any university, let alone a small and underfunded southern university. For example, one necessarily arbitrary list of the most eminent American writers reveals that more had ties to Vanderbilt than to any other university save Harvard.

But the fame of the Fugitives and Agrarians posed risks, at least from the perspective of Vanderbilt administrators. A private university needs to be many things to many people, else it risks a loss of financial support. The Agrarians launched a massive attack upon corporate America, the very source of most of Vanderbilt's gifts and most of its board members. Agrarian antimodern beliefs challenged, at times scandalized, advocates of a new or progressive South. Any defense of purportedly southern values also worked against what soon became an announced goal for Vanderbilt—to break out of its provincial mold and become a truly national university. No wonder that Chancellor Kirkland tried to distance himself from the advocacy of Agrarians. No wonder that these prophets, as others, gained least honor in their own back yard. Finally, the beliefs and preferences of both Fugitives and Agrarians ran counter to the views of a vast majority of Vanderbilt's faculty, a fact vouched for by frustrated students who enrolled at Vanderbilt in order to drink in the agrarian gospel. Thus, instead of reflecting the real identity of Vanderbilt, as so often believed by those far away from Vanderbilt, the Fugitives and Agrarians simply added another, uniquely self-conscious ingredient to the developing pluralism of a university that, each year, moved closer to national patterns.

PART SIX

In the Worst of Times
(1931–1946)

❧ THE RECESSION OF *1930 gave way to a deepening
international depression by 1931 that lasted in the United States
until 1941. The worst collapse came early in 1933; a second low
point came in late 1937 and early 1938, or after a period of
moderate recovery from 1934 until 1937. The decade of depression
meant problems for all colleges and universities. Some did not
survive. Generally, enrollments declined, faculty members lost jobs
or faced sharply reduced salaries, endowments declined in value and
in returns, and sources of private benevolence dried up. Vanderbilt
fared better than most. Yet, for five years its enrollment lagged as
its income declined. But by 1936 the worst seemed over. From then
until Pearl Harbor, Vanderbilt resumed a pattern of slow growth.
But overall, it remained in a holding pattern in the 1930s, a
period of arrested development. It awaited full economic recovery.
War brought recovery, but under exceptional circumstances that
posed new and greater problems for universities. The earlier pattern
of expansion resumed only in 1946.*

*At the end of fifteen years of depression and war, Vanderbilt remained
an institution remarkably similar to the one of 1930. Except for a
new library building and a few hospital additions, it had the same
campus. The number of students and professors remained
remarkably similar; the College of Arts and Science had 799
students in 1929–30, 728 in the spring of 1945. The quality of
faculty, the caliber of education, changed in no significant way.
From a national perspective, Vanderbilt still had only two
distinguished schools—Medicine and Nursing. The College had
only regional prominence in 1930 or in 1945. In quality of staff
and in academic standards, it remained the leader only of the
upper Midsouth, the one institution between Duke or the University
of North Carolina and the University of Texas qualified to offer*

347

graduate work in selected fields. It remained second-rate in comparison with leading northern universities, public or private. Lamentably, even this status eluded the schools of Law, Religion, and Engineering. The declining Law School had to suspend classes in 1944, Religion still struggled to find a role and a constituency, and although in World War II Engineering enjoyed an enrollment boom it still lacked adequate facilities or a distinguished faculty.

Depression and war held immense significance for the South and in the long run for Vanderbilt. Of course, contemporaries could not grasp the magnitude of impending changes. The depression simply further impoverished an already poor South. Falling agricultural prices led the way into depression in 1930, with greatest impact on such export crops as cotton and tobacco. But the depression helped realign party allegiances. The Democratic Party, under Franklin Roosevelt, became the majority party. The South regained some of the leverage in Washington it had enjoyed before 1860 and briefly in the Wilson administration. In response to the hard times, the Roosevelt administration increased federal expenditures, particularly for relief. It also began several small social welfare programs. The South increasingly became an object of national concern. It not only received a disporportionate share of relief funds because of greater need, but also such special public works programs as the Tennessee Valley Authority. New Deal agricultural programs, which subsidized commercially successful farmers, abetted new efficiencies and, particularly in the South, pushed millions out of agricultural employment. The painful consequences included major migrations from the rural South to either southern or northern cities. During World War II, which accelerated all the trends of the 1930s, a new South finally began to emerge, but a South increasingly like the North. From 1870 to 1930 incomes in the South had remained at approximately one-half the national average. During World War II the gap slowly began to narrow and continued to narrow into the 1980s. In most areas of the South, outside the Piedmont, agriculture had remained the primary industry. In World War II the South began a momentous shift toward manufacturing. Climate and political clout lured a disproportionate number of military bases and new defense industries to the South. Even racial mixtures began to change, with larger migrations of blacks to northern cities.

Depression and war helped make the South a special client of the federal government. A section that had long chafed under discriminatory federal policies now luxuriated in special programs and in special solicitude. But federal solicitude brought with it inevitable demands for greater conformity. Southern states had to revamp their institutions, bring them closer to national patterns. They also had to follow federal standards or guidelines in the administration of subsidized programs, from welfare payments to aid to public education. Local differences eroded. Congruent economic and social patterns meant that the South could no longer rest at ease with older racial codes. Blacks not only became more self-conscious, more demanding, but they could appeal more effectively to national norms and to federal power. The Democratic Party, the fount of so many material blessings for the South, became also the preferred party of self-conscious blacks. Northern solicitude soon embraced blacks as well as whites. Finally, the federal courts eventually embraced the full logic of the Fourteenth Amendment—national citizenship and equal rights. Thus, one implication of southern economic progress was a major assault on legalized segregation. Changes in racial relations became both an effect and then a cause of a new South, one molded more in the image of the North both in achievements and in problems. Vanderbilt University not only enjoyed, or suffered, from changes in the region, but eventually lost an early facet of its identity, its special mission to a backward South. As the South became less distinct, and less a problem, Vanderbilt had to give up old sectional apologies for its weaknesses. Increasingly, it would have to stand comparison on a national level. But these shifts only began in the 1930s and 1940s; their implications lay well hidden in all the new policies.

14

Hard Times

THE DEPRESSION threatened Vanderbilt. On the positive side, falling prices and lower wages cut costs. But impoverished parents could not send their children to Vanderbilt. Beleaguered alumni would not make generous contributions. The major foundations suffered serious losses in earnings and, out of caution, temporarily curtailed gifts. Most critical, Vanderbilt depended on endowments and these were now threatened, but not in the sense one would anticipate. By 1932 the Vanderbilt endowment had declined, in estimated market value, by about 13 percent, largely because of falling bond prices. Beginning in 1931 a few companies began defaulting on interest payments. A few declared bankruptcy. These defaults grew exponentially in 1932 and 1933. By the end of 1932 Vanderbilt had failed to collect about $40,000 of interest due on bonds; by 1935 the accumulated loss rose to $228,000, a sum that grew only slowly for the next few years. Yet, in comparison with most universities, Vanderbilt defaults were very low. It suffered an annual loss to its operating budget of about $50,000 a year, or approximately 5 percent of its predepression level of funding. Lowered costs more than made up for this, seemingly meaning an improved endowment situation for Vanderbilt. In fact, most defaulting companies eventually resumed interest payments; Vanderbilt lost very little of its capital during the depression.[1]

The real threat to Vanderbilt's future came, not from bankruptcies and defaults, but from the long-term effects of falling interest rates. Given lower rates (down from 5½ percent in the late 1920s to about 3 percent by 1939), Vanderbilt's portfolio actually gained market value after 1934 or 1935, since its older 5 or 5½ percent bonds now sold at a considerable premium. But companies recalled bonds as soon as legally possible, forcing Vanderbilt to seek new but ever lower yields. The trend threatened a one-third reduction in Vanderbilt's endowment income, since Vanderbilt could not attract many additions to its endowment during the worst years of the depression.[2]

Earlier fiscal caution saved Vanderbilt in the early 1930s. Until 1933 Kirkland had served as de facto treasurer. He joined with other trustees on a special investment committee but tried to guide investment policies himself. The task took an increasing amount of his time and attention, but it remained manageable, largely because the university continued to invest largely in highly rated corporate bonds, a tradition that stretched back to Cornelius Vanderbilt's original gift of railroad bonds. Such fiscal conservatism suited Kirkland's style and removed the need for constant attention to a portfolio made up of common stock. In 1933, roughly 90 percent of the portfolio of about $20 million (face value) remained in corporate bonds, with the largest shares in utilities and a considerable number still in railroads. Largely because of gifts, or a few experimental purchases, a small 6 percent remained in common stock, 4 percent in real estate. The ratings of Vanderbilt's bonds protected the university from the worst ravages of the stock market crash, or from the numerous bankruptcies of 1932 and 1933. The long-term bonds also provided a hedge against short-term falls in interest rates, for the value of existing, high-interest bonds eventually rose. But the portfolio turned out to be vulnerable in unexpected ways. Over half of Vanderbilt's utility bonds were invested in large regional holding companies. These suffered from intense public scrutiny in the late 1920s, from a few highly publicized scandals in the early depression, all leading to demands for strict regulation. This culminated in the Public Utilities Holding Company Act of 1935, which forced such companies to accept detailed regulation and threatened a few with dissolution. Vanderbilt had its most extensive holdings (one-tenth of its endowment) in Commonwealth and Southern (a generally honest utility in the Southeast, headed for many years by Wendell Willkie) or in its production companies, or the very companies which seemed threatened by Tennessee Valley Authority (TVA) competition. Few of the feared catastrophes ever materialized, but Vanderbilt's trustees ran scared for several years. Most were intense opponents of Roosevelt. They hated him for what they considered his frequent "encroachments on private business." Annual financial reports to the board contained frequent references to the "TVA menace" until 1939, when the TVA, instead of duplicating facilities, bought out desired Commonwealth and Southern affiliates at a fair price.[3]

In 1932 Kirkland sought investment help. He asked the board to appoint a salaried treasurer. For $4,000, it hired Andrew B. Benedict, who took over direction of all university investments. For the first time the Vanderbilt endowment enjoyed day-by-day management and frequent changes in the portfolio. Benedict gradually shifted about one-third of the total from corporate bonds to common stock. In a sense, he took advantage of artificially low prices but with no immediate vindication (stock prices remained low through World War II). But by the late 1930s stock dividends consistently outyielded bonds. By the war this shift spared Vanderbilt acute financial embarrassment, for Benedict kept overall university returns at about 4 percent even when prime interest rates sank as low as 2½ percent. This was still a serious drop from the 5 percent rate of the 1920s, but by then higher tuitions and increased enrollments made up the difference. Although the worst never happened, Vanderbilt officials remained apprehensive from 1931 until 1936.[4]

The shrinkage in endowment earnings joined declining enrollments in all the schools except Medicine and Nursing. The College fell from 799 in 1929–30 to a depression low of 665 in 1933–34; Engineering, from 169 to 128. Overall, enrollments fell by only about 10 percent, but even this threatened budgets. With a few exceptions the university could not cut its faculty to match the decline. It could not raise tuition, outside Medicine, since already many of its students could hardly afford to attend Vanderbilt. By 1932 the university struggled unsuccessfully to meet a ballooning demand for scholarships, loans, or part-time work. The hard times precluded any new fund drives. Then, in the midst of all the financial problems, Wesley Hall burned in 1932. Only after a long struggle with the insurance company was Vanderbilt able to collect close to the face value of its insurance policy— $158,000 for building and contents. After attorneys' fees and protective work on the remaining outer shell, it had only about $135,000 to pay for a new building; in the depression it had to use the income from this to keep the School of Religion operating. For years the fenced-off skeleton of old Wesley remained as a symbol of depression hardship.[5]

As early as 1931 Kirkland contemplated salary cuts at Vanderbilt. Other universities had to resort to such cuts. But Vanderbilt ran no deficits and the board kept delaying any action. In effect, the Vanderbilt faculty enjoyed major increases in real wages (up to 20 percent) because of sharply falling prices. Finally, in February, 1933, Kirkland asked the board temporarily to cut total salaries by approximately $20,000 for 1933–34, even as the schools, particularly Medicine, dropped staff employees in order to lower costs. The salary reductions were emergency measures; faculty and administrative salaries were still listed at their earlier level. The cuts amounted to approximately 8 percent. Salaries for coaches dropped by about 12 ½ percent; for administrators and faculty members earning over $4,500, by 10 percent, graduating down to only 4 percent for those earning under $2,000. Kirkland shared in the cuts. He had never accepted more than $13,400 of his $18,000 listed salary, and he reduced this to $12,000 in 1933–34. The board eventually created a trust fund from his uncollected salary, later using this to pay annuities to his wife. At her death, the fund reverted to the university and was always listed as a gift from Kirkland. The faculty accepted cuts, not happily but gracefully. Professors knew that they fared better than faculty at most institutions. Those with higher salaries never lived quite as well as during the depression. In fact, the cuts proved unnecessary. They relieved Kirkland and the board of anxieties, but the university, by a few additional economies, could have met its payroll each year. Even in the years of the cut the College budget began a pattern of consistent annual surpluses. Because of these surpluses, in 1936 Kirkland asked the board to distribute to the faculty 50 percent of their loss in 1933–34, and then in 1937 the board finally canceled the cuts, reinstating the salaries of 1932–33. During these years only a select few professors received promotions or raises. Outside the Medical and Nursing schools, almost all appointments reflected necessary replacements of departing instructors or temporary appointments for faculty on leave.[6]

Almost as soon as the salary cuts went into effect, enrollments began to climb once again. No one at Vanderbilt expected the dramatic turnaround in 1935, when the College gained over 100 additional students. It maintained the growth for the next three years. College enrollment climbed from 665 in 1933–34 to 1,046 in 1938–39. One can only guess at the causes. In a period of massive unemployment, college was an inviting alternative for those who could afford the tuition. A degree of recovery began in 1934, particularly in agriculture. New Deal subsidies and controls raised farm income dramatically, boosting the economy of commercial centers such as Nashville that largely served rural areas. Perhaps more critical, the Federal Emergency Relief Administration (FERA) began a campus work program in the spring of 1934. Government agencies eventually employed up to 215 students at Vanderbilt. These students worked, at $15 a month, in the library, on the grounds, as aids or research assistants to professors, and in legal aid or office work. Henry Hart, the YMCA secretary, directed federal employment programs on campus. The most needy students were now able to pay their way through Vanderbilt, and the work program freed other scholarship funds for those who could not qualify for federal assistance. The aid continued throughout the decade, although as part of a new Works Progress Administration—National Youth Administration after 1935. Finally, the faculty of the College lowered admission requirements and began actively recruiting in local high schools. In early 1933 the College faculty voted to allow special admission for all those in the top one-half of high school classes, in effect waiving stringent language and math requirements. Later in the year it lowered the language requirement from four units to two, the math requirement from three to two and one-half, purportedly to bring Vanderbilt in line with the work offered in local high schools. In 1934 it accepted high Scholastic Aptitude Test (SAT) scores as a substitute for deficient requirements, and began offering special qualifying exams for exceptional applicants. Almost any bright student could now come to Vanderbilt; with the government assistance almost any poor student could pay his or her own way.[7]

Vanderbilt entered the depression with an elderly leadership. Kirkland was seventy-one in 1930 and in the following years revealed the effects of age. Growing old with him was a younger but more frail board president, Whitefoord Cole. The board, of approximately thirty members, retained its business-banking-legal profile and remained securely under the management of Kirkland. Much more than ever before, the outlook of the board diverged from that of students and faculty. With a few exceptions, board members looked with increasing fear and loathing upon Franklin D. Roosevelt's New Deal; an overwhelming majority of students and faculty applauded Roosevelt. The board, and even Kirkland, symbolized an old order and were often perplexed and even scandalized by student beliefs and values.[8]

As everyone now realized, a change of leadership had to come very soon. The omens were everywhere. John H. Dye died in 1930; he was a former board member from Arkansas and the last surviving member of the Memphis Convention of 1872. On campus, only the career of retired John T. McGill stretched back to within a year of campus beginnings. Now the great second generation at Vanderbilt, the ones who came to replace the original faculty, had all reached a normal retirement age, and in the next fifteen years all of this generation would die. In August, 1931, Kirkland received the sad news from Wisconsin: Charles Forster Smith was dead. Few on campus even remembered him. A year later, Dean Schuerman of Engineering died. When Kirkland opened classes for 1932, his fortieth year as chancellor, only four people in the audience had been on campus at his inaugural—John McGill, John Daniel, Dean Tillett, and Edwin Mims.[9]

A worse blow came to Kirkland in 1934. Whitefoord Cole died at a relatively young sixty. As anticipated, Frank Rand replaced him as board president, but this did not assuage Kirkland's sense of loss. Since before World War I he had worked closely with Cole, who had come to symbolize what Vanderbilt sought in its trustees and in its board president—corporate leadership, wealth, and social prominence. Cole had all the credentials— Louisville and Nashville presidency, when in Nashville a member of the prestigious Belle Meade Country Club, a member of Christ Episcopal Church. Rand, as a St. Louis shoe executive, was an equally loyal Vanderbilt alumnus but not part of the Nashville elite. He would not be able to play as effective a role in the Executive Committee and never became as involved as Cole in the actual day-by-day operations of the campus. With Cole's death, Kirkland felt his age, his mortality, more than even before. By then he kept before the board his resignation as chancellor. The board continued to reject it and seemed reluctant to face up to the impending necessity of governing Vanderbilt without Kirkland. Although many young faculty members eagerly awaited his retirement, it was difficult for students or most faculty to imagine Vanderbilt without Kirkland or to face such a future without a degree of fear and apprehension.[10]

The board, under Kirkland's guidance, acknowledged the problem of transition as early as 1929. It began the process of selecting a new chancellor in 1932, appointing a new committee on administrative appointments to study the needs of the university. Kirkland joined his friends Cole, Norman Davis, and Frank Rand on the original committee (subsequently, the board added a fifth member). This arrangement, in effect, gave Kirkland leeway to select his own successor. The board stipulated that its primary goal was to keep Kirkland as long as possible, but to find ways of helping him do his work. The new treasurer made up half of the needed relief. The other half, as it turned out, involved a new dean of the Graduate School and an heir apparent, but not until 1935, after three years of study and searching.[11]

The change in university leaders was closely tied to gradual changes in the

College. These changes began with the revived graduate program of the late 1920s and with Kirkland's expressed intent to appoint a dean of a new graduate school. In 1930 the College faculty first opened up the always controversial issue of curriculum requirements. The existing committee on schedule and course of study began an extended review of required courses, or what would later become known as the distribution requirement. The committee surveyed requirements at other universities; Kirkland provided needed information. Out of the study came a 1931 reorganization, the division of the College into a lower and upper level, with separate admission requirements for each. In connection with this change, the special faculty-advising program was extended to sophomores as well as freshmen. Left in abeyance were several faculty schemes for a new set of course requirements for the two levels, an issue not fully settled until 1937–38.

The first step toward these changes involved adminsitrative organization. In 1933 Kirkland asked the College-Engineering faculty to approve a new committee on educational policies, constituted by the two academic deans (in the College and in Engineering), by Dean Sarratt, and by the three divisional heads (natural sciences, social sciences, humanities). Kirkland soon referred to this as his cabinet. Its makeup symbolized the chancellor's special relationship to the College. He still presided at its faculty meetings and tried to direct its policies. His new committee, made up only of his friends and appointees, promised to increase his leverage. The first assignment for the new committee proved its significance—to help find a dean of a new graduate school and, in all likelihood, also the next chancellor.[12]

Legally, the Board of Trust elects chancellors and all administrative officers. But the board had earlier surrendered effective control over all lower appointments to the chancellor. Thus, its elective role had shrunk to the choice of a new chancellor, or an infrequent role that rivaled in importance its overall management of university finances. So far, the board had never really elected a chief executive officer. When it appointed Kirkland back in 1893, no one could foresee the future and dominant role of the chancellor in university government. Kirkland, by ability and force of personality, created a strong executive; he led and eventually totally dominated his board, with their willing acquiescence and deference. Everyone realized how critically important was the election of Kirkland's successor and how difficult it would be for anyone to fill his shoes. For this reason the board joined Kirkland in an unofficial strategy of selecting a likely successor, of giving him an administrative role, and allowing him time to prove himself and time to learn how to do his job. Kirkland had valuable contacts in the foundations, among other university officials, and with several wealthy patrons of the university. A transitional period would allow a new man time to gain the needed contacts, to build a working relationship with the board, and to develop a needed reputation among the faculty. This strategy allowed the board to delegate the selection of a graduate dean to Kirkland and to his close board associates, since a trial period removed most of the risk of a disastrous choice. Given the realities of such a search, the strategy also assured that the original screening would take place in Kirkland's new committee on educational policies, another committee completely loyal to him but one obviously in the best position to evaluate the qualifications of a dean.

The active search took place in 1934 and early 1935. As Frank Rand remembered it, the board committee eventually evaluated about fifteen people. The committee on educational policies eventually focused on two candidates, W.K. Greene of Duke University and Oliver C. Carmichael, president of Alabama College, a small, state-financed women's college in Montevallo, near Birmingham. They settled on Carmichael. Rand believed they thus avoided a nearly disastrous choice but gave no grounds for such a judgment. Edwin Mims and one other faculty member first interviewed Carmichael in Alabama, and then Kirkland met with him in Atlanta. They openly emphasized his likely succession to the chancellorship, a determining factor in his acceptance.[13]

On paper the selection seemed to make little sense. Carmichael was president of a small liberal arts college. Little in his career suggested any qualification as a graduate dean, let alone the status required for an effective chancellor. Carmichael grew up on an Alabama farm, one of ten very talented children, several of whom had distinguished careers. From small rural schools he matriculated in a small Alabama Presbyterian college and then transferred for his final two years to the University of Alabama, graduating in 1911. He took work both in the social sciences and modern languages. After graduation he taught German and French as a lowly instructor at the university, but then moved to Florence Normal School as an acting professor of languages the next year, meanwhile completing his work for an M.A. at Alabama. In 1912 he won a Rhodes Scholarship from Alabama, much to his own surprise. He went to Oxford in 1913, taking work in psychology and philosophy and, later, in anthropology. The war offered new opportunities. He served on Herbert Hoover's Belgian Relief Commission and had a key role in smuggling back to England a famous, inspirational letter written by a Belgian church official. Later, he served for a year in India and in East Africa as an employee of the YMCA, adding further adventures to his youthful career. Only in 1917 did he complete an Oxford research Bachelor of Science and earn a diploma in anthropology. Back in the United States he finally enlisted in the army, using his language skills in intelligence work. He survived the war with a wealth of exciting experiences but with no advanced degree and without notable scholarly achievements. Thus, he could find a teaching job only as a high school principal until 1922, when he gained a position as dean at small Alabama College. He helped revamp the curriculum, moved up to the presidency in 1926, and proved adept at gaining increased state appropriations. But he was, by then, a big duck in a very small pond, head of an undistinguished college.[14]

Carmichael won his appointment because of perceived personal qualities and because of his reputation among Alabama and southern educators. He was personable, engaging, knowledgeable on issues affecting higher education, and an able public speaker. Not a scholarly specialist, he had become a bit of an expert in educational philosophy, or on issues directly relating to such matters as curriculum reform. In short, he had the political and administrative skills Vanderbilt needed. Eventually, each member of the committee on educational policy voted for him. Mims, an early advocate of Greene, decided Carmichael was the ablest educator in Alabama, and with his brilliance and charm an ideal candidate for chancellor. Carmichael realized the hazards of being heir-apparent to Kirkland. Kirkland stressed to the board that "no agreements and no intimations have been made as to any promotion or advancement that might come to him in future years." But even the *Hustler* identified him as the next chancellor. If he did well as dean, he knew he had the job and a very significant advance for his own career. He later noted that he took a cut in salary and lost a degree of independence as part of this gamble. He came to Vanderbilt at a listed salary of $7,500, but an actual salary of $6,750 because of the temporary cuts. Carmichael came as dean not only of a new graduate school but of the Senior College, a new name adopted for the upper two years of the College. Paschal remained as dean of the newly named Junior College. In 1936, after Carmichael received an offer of the presidency of the University of Alabama, the board changed his title to vice-chancellor and all but guaranteed his subsequent election as chancellor.[15]

The depression had varying effects upon each college or school. For most purposes, College and Engineering remained one unit, and both suffered the same drop in enrollment during the early 1930s, the same growth after 1935. Fred J. Lewis became dean of Engineering in 1933, following the death of Schuerman in 1932. Lewis had just organized a summer school for surveying at Bon Air, the new Cumberland Mountain branch of the campus. He had no national reputation as an engineer, but in Kirkland's terms he could "conserve what we have, prudently and faithfully." What Vanderbilt had in the early 1930s was a mediocre Engineering School. Despite several additions, the now aging Engineering building was completely inadequate, and engineering paraphernalia spread all over the campus—in Old Science, in Main, and even in Furman. Until the late 1930s Engineering did not attract many able students, probably because of the lack of jobs. The only innovation in the depths of the depression was a new, special course for sanitation officers, a course of study paid for by the U.S. Department of Public Health. It continued into the war years.[16]

The College suffered about five years of decline or arrested growth. The faculty was the most stable in Vanderbilt history, a blessing in some cases, a curse in others. The strongest department—English—proved least stable, or a predictable effect of excellence. In 1931–32, while John Crowe Ransom was on leave, the department hired Robert Penn Warren as his temporary replacement. Warren remained on in the fall of 1932 as a replacement during Davidson's sabbatical. Despite all the later regrets over Vanderbilt's losing Warren, he never had a regular appointment. In the fall of 1933 he had no work, and so Mims hired him to teach part time during the fall quarter. John Donald Wade, never happy away from his Georgia plantation, asked for a leave in January and then resigned in March to take a part-time position at the University of Georgia, a serious loss to the department but not one that anyone could prevent. Warren then took over Wade's upper-level courses and completed his final three years at Vanderbilt. At the time he did not have the scholarly credentials, or even the fame as a novelist or poet, that suggested him as a likely replacement for Wade. Ironically, the department let him go in order to maintain its scholarly standing. Thus, Warren moved on to a low-level position at Louisiana State University and to a brilliant career, not only as a writer but, with Cleanth Brooks, as editor of the new *Southern Review*. The department, in a rare depression appointment, lured Randall Stewart, an alumnus, from Yale. With Curry, Mims, Ransom, and Davidson, he completed an imposing array of talent, or arguably one of the two or three strongest senior English faculties in the United States. It attracted by far the ablest graduate students at Vanderbilt.[17]

No other appointment for 1936 rivaled that of Stewart; no other loss duplicated that of Wade. The College did hire some able instructors and assistant professors, but they gained distinction only much later. A few younger professors began to establish names for themselves, most notably D.F. Fleming through his book on the United States and the League (1932). George Pullen Jackson finally gained fame for his pioneer work on white spirituals (1933), and Walter C. Reckless, already an acknowledged expert on race because of his detailed investigations of black religion, published extensively on juvenile delinquency. Young men also began very slowly to upgrade the sciences at Vanderbilt. The longtime problem in physics finally came to a head. An increasing flood of student complaints forced Kirkland to subordinate the work of aging John Daniel. Daniel would not quit and like so many before him probably could not afford to retire. Kirkland urged Daniel's retirement and gave Francis Slack, the rising star of the department and already its lab instructor, a leave to prepare himself for the major lecture courses. Young men of ability now backed up Glenn in geology, Reinke in biology, Breckenridge in chemistry, and Garis and Eberling in economics, Sanborn and Lanier remained an odd couple in philosophy and psychology.[18]

In the most overt way since the Russell Scott case of 1919, issues of academic freedom and secure tenure agitated the faculty in the mid-1930s. Minor incidents had arisen in the 1920s. A few parents complained about the biases of professors or textbooks, only to receive mollifying letters from deans or from Kirkland. More serious were charges by the one Jewish trustee, Lee Loventhal, that Frank Owsley had mishandled his treatment of Jews in

American and European history courses. He suggested Owsley leave out all references to Jews rather than distort the truth. The dean believed Loventhal overly sensitive and that no intentional distortions had occurred. In 1921 the ablest law professor, Charles Turck, published in a union newspaper his belief that Nashville employers, in the midst of a printer's strike, had been guilty of "a spirit of brazen indifference." Whitefoord Cole was incensed that any professor would involve himself, not in general principles but a specific labor dispute. Kirkland refused to intervene and tried unsuccessfully to convince Cole of the futility of trying to control public utterances of professors. He noted the rightful complaint of union leaders against Gus Dyer's crusade for the open shop. Indeed, Dyer eventually provoked more letters of protest than anyone else, particularly by his virulent attack on New Deal programs in the 1930s. Even congressmen, who resented his unfair attack on their voting record, complained to Kirkland. After Dyer debated economist Eberling on the merits of the New Deal in a well-publicized campus stand-off, Kirkland received irate letters from those who considered any defense of the New Deal as evidence of communist loyalties. But all such outside pressures amounted to little more than a problem of public relations, or in the case of Loventhal and Cole, of the needed education of a board by a chancellor. The case of education professor Joseph K. Hart raised but left unsettled much more serious issues.[19]

The decision to hire Hart, and to launch a department of education in the College, was risky from the start. The decision further fanned resentments at Peabody, for it undermined the one serious contribution Peabody could make to Vanderbilt students' educations. Kirkland tried to minimize the damage. He emphasized that Vanderbilt would never duplicate any professional courses at Peabody. Instead, it would only introduce courses that were an integral part of a liberal arts curriculum, which seemed to mean courses only in the history and philosophy of education. By all objective criteria, Kirkland employed a man superbly qualified in these two fields. Joseph Kinmont Hart, fifty-four years old in 1930, was one of the two or three best-placed educators in America, with over ten significant books to his credit. A farm boy from Indiana, he had moved from a small sectarian college to a heady graduate program at the University of Chicago. Here he worked with George Herbert Mead and in the shadow of the recently departed god of American educational theory—John Dewey. He was also much influenced by Thorstein Veblen. He had intermittently taught for twenty years in the College of Education at the University of Wisconsin, taking off several years for editing and publishing work in New York. His educational philosophy closely followed Dewey's, and his books on educational history and theory had a broad market. It was his recognized eminence that led Kirkland to write him for suggested candidates for Vanderbilt's new position. To Kirkland's surprise, Hart intimated his willingness to move from Wisconsin, and from this ensued a long correspondence about Vanderbilt's needs and Hart's impressive plan for such a department. The two seemed in perfect accord as they worked out a curriculum, which included undergraduate courses on the history and philosophy of education and on the principles of education, plus a graduate course on the problems of teaching in colleges. To get Hart, Kirkland had to offer him $5,000, a lofty salary then enjoyed within the College only by Mims. But, again, this seemed a bit low for someone of Hart's prominence. In fact, his move seemed a bit suspicious. Hart joined a faculty much less distinguished, and less published, than himself, to set up a new program in an alien environment and with a suspicious Peabody next door. There was, in fact, much more to the move than Kirkland realized.[20]

In all likelihood, Kirkland never read any of Hart's books. They ranged widely, including several related to adult education or education within a community, including one book on Danish folk schools. But Hart published his broadest theoretical book in 1929 as *A Social Interpretation of Education*. In it he followed a consistent instrumentalist or Deweyian approach, one in some ways more sharply radical than Dewey's own. He attacked traditional schools, with their emphasis on dead cultures, on the disciplining of unruly behavior, and their authoritarian imposition of irrelevant subjects and old values. He deplored the institutional tyrannies that marked the public schools. With echoes from as far back as Rousseau, he begged for new schools, committed to the unique needs of each child, to the natural flowering of native abilities, to self-development in a context of freedom or cooperative mutuality. Hart filled in these rather standard progressive motifs with some concrete detail and thus moved a good way beyond abstract generalities.

Hart paralleled his vision of new schools with a vision of a new society. Much more even than Dewey, and in images surprisingly similar to some of those of Donald Davidson, he lamented what modern man had lost when he moved from earlier, simpler, more primitive but more holistic communities. A new industrial order had destroyed the integrity of such communities, leading to a disoriented, competitive, alienating modern world. Science and technology made possible the new order, but Hart, unlike his new Agrarian colleagues, saw the problem not as applied science or collectivized production, but as distorted social institutions, primarily acquisitive capitalism, dogmatic religion, and authoritarian and antiquated schools. A fulfilling education was all but impossible in such a disordered context. The restoration of cooperative communal life was the first requirement, and this meant educational reforms that began with adults. In all his theory Hart stressed the larger educational role of all institutions and minimized the educational role of schools, particularly those that were separate from the concerns of daily life and work, those that tried to pass on an antique culture. He was not as precise in identifying the solution to such deeply entrenched social ills. He vacillated between a return to local, decentralized communities, but ones blessed by modern technology, and the achievement of a truly national community or

361

cooperative commonwealth. In either case, he believed corporate capitalism was inimical to true community, its modification or displacement a prerequisite of a new economic and educational order. His key terms came from Dewey—cooperation, evolution, democracy, intelligence, science. But he never quite raised his discussions to the level of academic philosophy or overcame a tendency to oversimplify. His books functioned at a more practical level, or at exactly the same level as the books of Edwin Mims.[21]

In educational outlook Hart had already repudiated everything that Vanderbilt stood for. His attacks upon a separate academic culture, upon elite educational standards, upon dead languages such as Latin or useless tools such as algebra, joined with his insistent efforts to reform American society. This alone prepared him for a degree of resentment within the traditional Vanderbilt faculty. But he had other problems. As it turned out, he was widely hated at Wisconsin, even close to losing his position there. He had been a carping critic of colleagues, a disaffected and contentious teacher—in short, an unhappy misfit. At Vanderbilt he almost immediately ran into problems. He won a following among students but he created among them a contempt for other professors and other courses. Perhaps without naming names, he nonetheless communicated his own critical rejection of what most colleagues taught or of how they taught it and made clear how irrelevant it was to all the immense social problems of the decade. He accepted none of the conventional rules in grading or in exams. Early on, he criticized the ancient but beleaguered honor system; one of his students led a campus crusade against it. This was a prelude to a cyclical wave of concern over the system, to student mass meetings in 1933, and to the usual series of inquiries and then to a new honor code and a fervent rededication to its ideals.[22]

Hart had other difficulties. One student followed him to Vanderbilt and, without Hart's knowledge or approval, cohabited with an unmarried girl and created a minor scandal by advocating free love. Hart attracted, and inspired, a small nucleus of campus radicals, those most likely to criticize the small faculty oligarchy led and controlled by Kirkland. Hart never related well to most of his colleagues and was, in his own words, thoroughly ostracized by a resentful Peabody faculty. He frequently faced charges about his exams and grades. He easily countered charges of lax standards. But the registrar's office reveals a much more serious problem of capricious grades. In his defense, Hart stressed creativity and originality above all else; he rewarded the critical students, those who rejected the system. He penalized the conventional, hard-working, dutiful Vanderbilt students, those who were career oriented and who made As in all their other subjects. A large number of otherwise A students made Cs or Ds in Hart's courses, and they went complaining to their major professors, probably for very good reason. But Hart might have remained at Vanderbilt for a while longer if it had not been for a famous *Hustler* editorial of March 30, 1934. It cost Hart his job.[23]

The unique editorial was, in part, a cooperative effort by the *Hustler* staff, headed by Ben West, later a mayor of Nashville. Entitled "Sign the Pledge on This Quiz, Faculty!," it vaguely mocked the honor system and then laid down an unclear challenge to the faculty. Some of the phrasing came directly from Hart's books and lectures; West was taking his course. But the inspiration for the editorial, and a close model for it, appeared in the *Saturday Evening Post* and in several college newspapers. The editorial attacked a majority of "administrative officers and faculty members" who, it said, had failed "to foster an eagerness for understanding" in an era of change. The Vanderbilt faculty did not realize that once highly respected traditions of culture and living were about as alive as the Commodore statue. Faculty members did not help the Vanderbilt student understand the new order, and few were helping create the new order, presumably a reference to the New Deal. Thus, it was not strange that the Vanderbilt student seldom concerned "himself with the ideas of liberal leaders of social and economic thought, when hypocritical 'dispensers of truth,' pretending to be interpreters of the concepts of the ages, shove at him a dead, outlived dogma which must be recopied and spouted back in total to receive approbation." Students were young, they wanted to live actively and dangerously, and had the same burning love for understanding that inspired Charles Darwin (one of Hart's great heroes). Professors at Vanderbilt were, in effect, "throwing up handfuls of sand into the new national atmosphere, with charges of Communism and radicalism," or they went about making speeches crying out for the old order (here the clear target was Gus Dyer). The faculty had fed thirsty students only biased disillusion, only petty, childish outlooks "which the day-laborer at which you sneer would be ashamed to assume." They had wanted the "advanced ideas of civilization," a "cultivation of living," but had to endure a dried-up thought, a "four year quibble over grades," a "pseudo-intellectual passivity."

The editorial ended with a five-question quiz for faculty members. Did they seek to enlighten students or force them to repeat fundamentals? Did they appear as guides to truth or as ingratiating actors? Did they give the students all they could of scholarship, wisdom, and understanding even when students appeared immune to learning? Were they enthusiastic about their subject, free from pedantry and dogma? Were they personal friends of students, their guides and exemplars? Faculty members were not to answer "yes" unless they were ready to sign the honor pledge. If any was unable to answer all five questions in the affirmative, then, the agitators maintained, "the Chancellor went once too often to the bargaining counter when he brought you to Panderbilt!"[24]

The front-page editorial hit the campus like a bombshell. For anyone who lived through the student protests of the 1960s, this is hard to understand. The editorial was relatively mild and in any case so oblique as to miss any specific targets except, possibly, Gus Dyer. But never before had students at Vanderbilt so openly impeached the integrity of faculty and administrators, or so mercilessly held them to a high standard both in teaching and in community involvement. A week later the *Hustler* staff acknowledged the poor taste of the editorial, excused "Panderbilt" as a typo, and denied any effort to pillory all the professors. They had the good of the university at heart and only wanted to improve the quality of courses and teaching. One tangible consequence of the editorial was a well-publicized debate on the New Deal by bitter opponent Gus Dyer and glib apologist Ernest J. Eberling, a debate that drew a large audience for rather stereotyped arguments. The various programs of the Roosevelt administration were too varied and too confused for any clear ideological verdict. The College faculty met, at first moved to request Kirkland to reply to the students, and then it decided to leave him free to do as he wished.[25]

Kirkland was incensed at the editorial, which was widely quoted in newspapers, "to the joy of our enemies and the mortification of our friends." He blamed Hart for influencing if not directly instigating it, and wrote a long and bitter letter to the *Hustler*. He read the editorial as a blanket condemnation of the whole faculty, denied that any editor had the range of experience needed to evaluate 80 professors and 226 courses, and made the telling point that all education is self-education, that students could join various organizations, and could read and study all they wanted, and that the faculty could only help them in this process. He asked the editor to come forward and identify, for possible discipline, all "hypocritical instructors and pretenders." He noted the traps involved in the five questions. He was most snide about the alleged political passivity and the suggestion that the age of Tolman and Barnard was gone. He gave the students a lesson in historical continuity, on the "relevance" of ancient wisdom, and identified the heralded "new order" with Hitler's Germany. He invited students who loved communism to get a passport and go to Russia. He admitted problems, faults, but affirmed an "honesty of purpose and a degree of faithfulness in execution." Drawing on the famous words of Daniel Webster, he said, "Vanderbilt has many faults, but there are those who love it." He ended: "Before I lift my hands to tear down the work others have tried to do, may my arm be palsied and sink helpless at my side. Before I use my pen or my voice to bear false witness against the Vanderbilt faculty or student body, may my tongue cleave to the roof of my mouth and remain silent forevermore."[26]

The punishment of Hart was swift and sure. Even before Kirkland published his reply, his new committee on educational policies met on April 5, 1934, and recommended discontinuance of the department of education (and thus of Hart) at the end of the "present session." They cited two reasons—the need for economy and the failure of the department to meet expectations. It had not stimulated a desire among students to enter the teaching profession and had not brought Vanderbilt into more friendly contact with high schools; the courses offered did not meet state certification requirements and, if expanded, new courses would mean more duplication with Peabody. This amounted to hypocrisy of the highest order. The College budget balanced in 1934, and what college would choose to fire its most eminent professor to meet a budget problem? Hart had taught the exact courses proposed to him by Kirkland, and no one ever expected these, alone, to meet certification requirements. Kirkland was conveniently absent at this meeting but had already shared his feeling with some or all its members. He presented the committee's recommendations to the Executive Committee and eventually to the board in its June meeting. He did give Hart the opportunity to respond to the committee's recommendation. In a moving ten-page document, Hart tore its logic to shreds and correctly identified the action as an underhanded means of terminating his job. He noted the past bitterness of faculty toward him, the malicious rumors circulated by some of his enemies. He cited a series of rather silly charges made against him and refuted all of them.[27]

Hart's letter availed nothing. The board abolished his position but, without acknowledging any legal requirement to do so, gave to the Executive Committee (that is, to Kirkland) the authority to arrange "equitable" payments during the coming year. Between the decision of the committee on educational policies and the June 11 board meeting, Kirkland received comments and letters from several professors. The most moving letter came from Hart's closest friend, historian Curtis Walker, who first mentioned Hart's name to Kirkland in 1930 and who lamented all the slander against him, particularly that relating to his tenure at Wisconsin. Walker felt that Hart had started a work of profound educational benefit and significance. Dozens of Hart's students, past and present, signed petitions in his behalf. The most damning letter against him came from his principal enemy all along—David C. Cabeen of Romance languages. Cabeen differed profoundly from Hart on educational philosophy, denounced his arbitrary grading, and cited some carefully solicited gossip, only in part correct, about Hart's career at Wisconsin.[28]

Hart fought back, but helplessly. He had no contract with the university, no tenure. He first asked, and failed to receive, a hearing before the College faculty. After the final board action, he noted several examples of duplicity on the part of Kirkland and threatened to make all the documents public, to appeal to the American Association of University Professors (AAUP), and to carry the matter into the civil courts. Given such threats, Kirkland refused to negotiate any "equitable" payment. Hart then appealed to the AAUP, ending the increasingly bitter exchange between him and Kirkland. W.W. Cook, general secretary of the AAUP, asked Kirkland for full details on the university action. From Hart's letters, he believed Vanderbilt had violated tenure standards adopted by the AAUP and subsequently endorsed in the same year by the American Association of Colleges (ironically in 1925, the very year that Kirkland served as its president). Cook noted that Hart had received an appointment no less permanent than that of any of his colleagues. He had been dismissed, apparently with no charges of misconduct or incompetence, and thus with no hearing on any charges, and also without any prior notice. The AAUP could accept the termination as justified if it rested entirely on financial constraints, but even then a professor had the right to a full year's prior notice. This meant that Vanderbilt, at the very least, owed Hart an additional year's salary.[29]

The correspondence became a bit strained. Kirkland did not want to make the termination only a financial matter but yet was unwilling to specify any charges warranting termination. Finally, in October, 1934, Kirkland relaxed his guard enough to share some of the hidden facts. He admitted both financial and educational reasons for termination. He most emphasized the judgment of faculty leaders about the disappointments of the department and emphasized their decision to rely henceforth on Peabody for all educational work, or a very good rationalization for the decision but one not heretofore introduced into any of the letters. Kirkland emphasized that the substantive issues were matters of practical failure, not of academic incompetence. Cook, seeking a satisfactory financial settlement, chose to interpret this as a justifying reason, one not requiring charges or a hearing. When he assured Kirkland that Hart contemplated no legal effort, the Executive Committee approved a lump payment of $2,500 just before Cook suggested the same figure. It would have been more had Hart not found a part-time job in New York State. There he continued as a prolific writer and sometime teacher at Columbia Teachers' College, but with only bitter memories of Vanderbilt and some continued threats to sue Cabeen for libel. Ironically, the book that he and his graduate students wrote while he was at Vanderbilt—on the technological and educational challenges offered by the TVA—came out just after he had left Vanderbilt and Tennessee.[30]

Present-day professors can only shudder at Hart's fate. The most prestigious professor in the College (comparable to a distinguished professor today) received a termination notice only a month before his last paycheck, a termination that resulted, at least in part, because one of his students wrote a critical editorial. Hart, with believable emphasis, made clear that he did not write, or encourage, or even know beforehand about the editorial. All he did was establish a critical perspective on the part of students. The real reason for Hart's dismissal was never concealed at Vanderbilt. For years, Dean Sarratt rejoiced over how student agitation diminished as soon as the university dismissed troublemaker Hart. But the dismissal itself further divided a College faculty that seemed to be gravitating toward internal conflict. It also raised crucial questions about faculty rights, particularly among the minority who defended Hart.

As usual, Herbert Sanborn spoke out for the faculty and against Kirkland. He still loved to torment the aging chancellor and jealously insisted upon the rights of the faculty. In December, 1934, he introduced a seemingly innocuous motion to create a faculty committee to study the tenure issue. Sarratt seconded it. But in January, Sarratt withdrew his second (illegal from a parlimentary standpoint) because of antiadministration criticism circulated to the faculty by Sanborn. In it, Sanborn pointed out the implications of the Hart case for all faculty members. No one had any protection against such a dismissal, despite the American Association of Colleges' endorsement of the 1925 AAUP position. In effect, Sanborn indicted Kirkland for inconsistency, for not living up locally to what he had supported in the association. When Sarratt withdrew his second, Owsley took his place. Then Sanborn unilaterally withdrew his motion (also technically illegal under parliamentary rules) until such time as it could be considered objectively and more favorably by the administration. Despite the confused parliamentary situation, a discussion of tenure followed. Some faculty reflected fears over a lack of tenure. Kirkland, sensitive as ever to faculty criticism, denied several implications in Sanborn's contentions and particularly denied that member colleges had any legal or moral obligation to adopt the 1925 statement. But, he said, the faculty could have contracts if they wanted them. He felt they were undesirable, not in harmony with the cooperative spirit of Vanderbilt. This ended the matter in 1935. George Mayfield, chairman of the local AAUP chapter (it soon died only to revive after World War II), noted that the national officers of the AAUP had congratulated him on how well Vanderbilt had responded to their initiative in reaching a settlement with Hart.[31]

The next controversial dismissal of a professor involved not the College but the School of Religion. This school barely survived in the depression, but it had flirted with suspension from 1915. Hard times were normal. By 1932 it was barely able to raise $25,000 a year to match the gifts from John D. Rockefeller, Jr., and thus keep going the rather ambitious program of outreach it developed in the mid-1920s. Because of Rockefeller's concern, it had to keep alive its Rural Church School, which absorbed many of the gifts. The annual Rockefeller gift expired in 1936 and by then the university had to match his $500,000 commitment to the endowment. Kirkland clearly anticipated an end to the school at that time and thus did not go outside to get a permanent and well-qualified dean.[32]

In the midst of all this, on February 19, 1932, Wesley Hall burned. The fire destroyed much of the school's library, all its offices and classrooms, and even the books, manuscripts, theses, furniture, and clothing of the seventy-five students and ten faculty who lived in the building. The human cost was much greater than the 1905 fire at Old Main. A few graduate students lost all notes and chapters for dissertations; Jesse Stuart, the poet who came to Vanderbilt for M.A. study, even lost forty-five of his sonnets.

Local charity provided some students with enough clothes to keep them coming to class. The fire also destroyed one reliable source of income—the popular cafeteria. The school's faculty moved to offices in the front of Neely; most students moved, free of charge, into vacant rooms in Kissam. Classes continued and the Rural Church School met at West End Church. Instead of breaking the will to survive, the fire even seemed to inspire the faculty to make greater efforts to raise funds, in this the very worst of times. As an ironic footnote to the fire, old John "Uncle Remus" Fulton, now ninety-five years old, the long-term resident of old Wesley, died only two months later. A former slave, purportedly born at the Hermitage, he more than anyone else had symbolized the old Wesley in its glory years. Kirkland and several faculty joined a Negro clergyman for his funeral at a Nashville home.[33]

In the fall of 1932 the School of Religion staff began its drive for survival. Following the early example of Carré, Professor William A. Harper devoted full time to fund raising, with almost no early results. Aging Dean Tillett came before the board in February, 1933, to plead for the continuation of the school despite the gloomy prospects. By 1934 the board was ready to give up. Approaches to the Vanderbilt family had failed. The board approved, as a temporary alternative, a request to Rockefeller that he spread out his remaining $65,000 commitment over six and a half years, at $10,000 a year, and that he extend the time needed to meet his $500,000 endowment offer. If he would do that, the school could cut staff and programs enough to go on at a $30,000 reduction in budget. Rockefeller refused. The faculty then received notice of a possible termination of their jobs as of June, 1934, although in that case a favored two or three would have received appointments to a new religious studies department in the College. Instead, the faculty and Kirkland worked out a reorganization for 1934–35. George B. Winton remained as part-time dean, the major members of the faculty remained at reduced salaries, and three were allowed to remain only if they raised half their own salary, since the Rockefeller fund would match such gifts. This reduced the school's budget from $78,000 to $40,000, or a sum that required only $10,000 of Rockefeller gifts. Tillett then successfully appealed to Frederick W. Vanderbilt for $150,000 to rebuild Wesley. Since this gift met the matching conditions of Rockefeller, the school eventually gained $300,000 for its endowment, but at the reduced interest rate of 4 percent. The fund yielded only $12,000 of annual income and involved a commitment to rebuild Wesley. A board member, E.J. Buffington, then gave an additional $50,000 ($100,000 when matched), and the future looked more promising for the beleaguered school. The problem remained the 1936 death warrant— when Rockefeller's commitments of up to $25,000 a year ended.[34]

The reduced program even yielded a small budget surplus in 1934–35. Harper continued to win a trickle of gifts as the economy improved. Then in 1935 the faculty began plans for the reorganization of 1936, for surviving in the post-Rockefeller era. The school would have an endowed income of roughly $21,000, plus the traditional $12,000 from the general endowment, plus fees and annual gifts, or enough for a minimal program. It had just over $100,000 in a scholarship fund, or enough to recruit twenty or so able students. The new goal was a drastically reduced school but one of higher quality. The enrollment had steadily fallen from 103 in 1929–30 to only 42 in 1935–36. The new plan meant that it would become a more academically

Chancellor Kirkland at age 77

Edwin Mims after retirement

OLD TIMERS

Retired Dean Wilbur Tillett

oriented school and one much less committed to public service. The faculty divided sharply in an effort to recruit a new dean. No one on the faculty enjoyed general support. After one or two false starts, the school agreed on Umphrey Lee of Southern Methodist University, a Vanderbilt alumnus and an able scholar and administrator. He assumed Tillett's old chair in Christian doctrine and philosophy of religion, at a salary of $5,000. Kirkland, advised by Tillett and Winton and others, then made the hard decision about which of the existing faculty to retain. The net effect—all nine remained, at least on a part-time appointment, except for Professor Alva Taylor. His department of social ethics was eliminated. For two years he had raised half his own salary. Now, as of 1936, he was out of a job, even though in recent years he had taught the largest number of students and directed the largest numbers of theses. Herein lies another complicated story.[35]

In no sense did Taylor have Hart's personality problems. The two men shared only certain political or social beliefs. Taylor was a mild-mannered, generous man with few enemies, at least among people who came to know him. He grew up in Iowa, where he absorbed the religious ideals of the Disciples of Christ and the populist politics of William Jennings Bryan and of fellow Iowa farmers. His youthful hero was the Iowa social gospel leader George Herron. From Grinnell College he went to the University of Chicago Divinity School, where he became primarily involved in the social issues that confronted his church early in the twentieth century. He did not then graduate but went into the Disciples ministry, with uncommon success. He soon published a small book on missions, wrote articles for the *Christian Century,* and became immensely involved in the social action work of his church and of the Federal Council of Churches of Christ (FCCC). He supported, and helped write a report on, the steelworkers' strike of 1919 and shared with John D. Rockefeller, Jr., a pro-union stance in labor-management problems. After 1921 he worked as a full-time director of the Board of Temperance and Social Welfare of the Disciples, an agency headquartered in Indianapolis. He remained a lifelong temperance advocate but decisively shifted the concerns of his agency toward three issues—equal rights for blacks, more democracy in industrial relations, and peace among nations, all popular causes among the leaders of a continued Protestant social gospel movement in the 1920s. He joined ecumenical social action groups, such as Reinhold Niebuhr's Fellowship for a Christian Social Order, or what became in 1928 the pacifist Fellowship of Reconciliation. He also associated with a southerner and a Vanderbilt alumnus, Will W. Alexander, in a Committee on Inter-racial Cooperation. He became deeply involved with the Mexican Revolution from 1926–29 and tried to create a favorable image toward it among American churchmen. His family suffered from his activities, from his incessant lecture trips and long absences. His first wife committed suicide in 1924. He later married a sympathetic YMCA worker he met in Mexico, a woman sixteen years his junior. By the time the Taylors moved to Vanderbilt, he was in the unusual position for a man nearing sixty of heading a house full of children.[36]

Taylor first visited Nashville in 1927 to lecture at Fisk and Vanderbilt. George Mayhew, a friend and fellow Disciples minister, had helped establish the Disciples Foundation at Vanderbilt and taught part-time in the School of Religion. After teaching in the Rural Church School in 1928, Taylor was offered a position at Vanderbilt, to establish a program in social ethics and to work each year with the Rural Church School. He moved to Nashville in the fall of 1928, but for the next four years continued to give one-third of his time to his board back in Indianapolis. He lost that position and its salary in 1933, or just as the School of Religion had to curtail its program. For two years Taylor rather easily raised one-half of his salary (Rockefeller matched this) and by 1934 he was the most successful fund raiser in the school.[37]

At Vanderbilt, Taylor had enormous influence, both directly and through his students. He was never a scholar, but a Christian activist. Although he eventually completed his Bachelor of Divinity, he never had a doctorate. He wrote not books but an unending stream of articles and reports. In every spare moment he left the campus for lectures or investigations. When the numbers were so few, the work so dangerous, he became the key FCCC representative in behalf of southern workers. He lobbied for labor legislation, boosted union organizing efforts, and raised relief funds for strikers. He also spoke out loudly and clearly for Negro equality. All of this should not suggest that he was a flaming radical. Rather, he was an aging Christian minister, a mediator, a man of goodwill, as much at home in a rural pulpit as a picket line.

Very soon after coming to Vanderbilt, Taylor became the hub of a growing network of courageous southern reformers, half of them his own students. Out of either Christian or Marxist loyalties, or fascinating combinations of the two, they battled against overwhelming odds in behalf of those they believed the South exploited. A Taylor student, Donald West, was cofounder of the Highlander Folk School, and both Taylor and Mayhew served on its board. West gained much of his enthusiasm for a type of adult education from courses he took with Joseph K. Hart, and from Hart's studies of Danish folk schools. Another student, Howard Kester, served as the southern representative of the Fellowship of Reconciliation and later as a leader in the Southern Tenant Farmers Union. Claude Williams, perhaps the most radical of all Taylor's students, came to Vanderbilt University from the socialist Commonwealth College in Arkansas, took only Taylor's courses, and then became perhaps the ablest representative of the American Communist Party in the South, working effectively for labor and racial progress. In Nashville, Taylor tried to be a living witness to a new social order; he lectured at Fisk, arranged early interracial meetings between Vanderbilt and Fisk students, entertained blacks and whites at his house, and frequently provided room and board for Negro students. Long after his retirement he stopped attending a segregated Christian church and moved to an integrated Congregational chapel at Fisk. Needless to say, he was not the most popular person in Nashville. But, and

371

this is testimony to his personality, he did not seek confrontation and usually cultivated friends from all points on the political spectrum.[38]

Even before 1934 Taylor realized that Chancellor Kirkland wanted to abolish his chair. Kirkland had no special animus against Taylor, but all the way back to the 1920s he had looked askance at the Rural Church School and at the involvement of the School of Religion in so many service or reform activities. Old Dean Tillett apparently shared some of his reservations. Kirkland knew the risk of such involvement, particularly among Vanderbilt supporters, although Taylor believed Kirkland to be more frightened of racial than of labor reform. By 1935 Taylor had some hopes of keeping his position, since he had raised funds so successfully and since he expected Kirkland's early retirement. Thus, he turned down an inviting pastorate in 1935. For a time he also withdrew his name from more radical or controversial petitions or platforms, a clear example of how tenure vulnerability can intimidate a professor. He learned in May, 1936, of the suspension of his chair. But he kept hoping he could get it back, since the only official reason for its suspension was necessary budget cuts. Taylor was nothing if not a politician. He pleaded his cause with Kirkland and with a majority of the board; he knew many board members. He had a large personal constituency, not only in the FCCC and among the action agencies of major denominations, but among politicians, within New Deal agencies, and, as he liked to note, also among blacks, Jews, union leaders, and even progressive businessmen. Even without his complicity, his large circle of admirers launched a concerted drive in his behalf. His appreciative former students mailed in identical, mimeographed petitions. Most of his colleagues in the Divinity School were supportive. Some well-placed Methodist officials pleaded his case, either to Kirkland or to Frank Rand. An official of the FCCC asked information and expressed concern. Many if not most of his supporters assumed, correctly, that not only money but his reform role in the university and in the South lay behind the loss of his chair.

Several of Taylor's advocates pledged money to continue his salary. In effect, they proposed that he keep his chair but at no expense to Vanderbilt. Since Taylor was sixty-five years old, this arrangement promised to be a short-term one and promised a facesaving solution for all parties. In a careful letter Kirkland rejected it. He welcomed funds for a new chair in the school but would not commit the university to any one candidate for it. The university could not, honorably, appoint a professor with no salary, even if outside funds maintained his support. To rely on outside benefactors for one person would endanger other fund-raising efforts and would leave the university under obligation should the private collections fall short. In brief, Kirkland did not want Taylor on his faculty and had very good reasons for dismissing outside offers. Taylor described Kirkland as a "hard boiled old Czar" and soon gave up all hopes of reinstatement. When he gained a one-fourth time lectureship at Fisk for 1936–37, Kirkland publicized this fact in the *Banner* to make clear that he was no longer eligible for reappointment, both because he had a part-time position and even more because of the peculiar nature of Fisk.[39]

Taylor lectured for only one year at Fisk. Because he had joined the Vanderbilt annuity system, he technically retired with a small stipend. But he had to support a family. Now, a gentle martyr to a cause, he basked in the support of friends all over the country and, if anything, increased the pace of his reform efforts. Largely because of him, Nashville became the capital of daring liberal or radical causes in the South. Several agencies made his home their headquarters. Until the war he headed a small organization supporting the League of Nations and led a Save the Children Fund, with most of his work in the southern Appalachians. In 1939 he became, for a year, the manager of Cumberland Homesteads near Crossville, a New Deal community for stranded miners. His brother, Carl Taylor, by training a rural sociologist, served as a high-level official in the Farm Security Administration, the agency then in charge of the homesteads. Taylor proved a very successful labor mediator during World War II and gave much of his effort to the new Southern Conference on Human Welfare, which had its headquarters in Nashville and which he served as secretary-treasurer. Howard Lee, a former student, was very active in the conference and was another Taylor student to move far to the left politically. After the war, now aged and crippled by arthritis, Taylor enlisted in the idealistic political campaign of a fellow Iowan whom he had always admired, Henry A. Wallace. Before Taylor died, he even received the high honor of being cited by the House Committee on Un-American Activities.

Taylor, in his political ideology, was ecumenical and rather loose, not doctrinaire. He joined most liberal Protestants of his generation in supporting some form of socialism, but Taylor was never very insistent upon any one economic program. He supported the work of students who varied in their political allegiances from support of a mild New Deal to membership in the American Socialist Party, or even those who joined the American Communist Party. Taylor honored all such choices by his students, so long as they battled for what they saw as social justice. As he knew, anyone in the South who stood for full racial equality, or even those who joined cio unions, would soon be radicalized by the scope and the repressive violence of local opposition. In the 1930s only a few people, most with a radical Christian vision or an intense Marxist commitment, could long stand the strain. On the battle lines they fought side by side.[40]

Taylor's fate did not raise any legal issues concerning academic freedom. But his treatment did continue a sporatic pattern at Vanderbilt, one stretching back to the Winchell case in 1878. Once again, in both the Hart and Taylor cases, a Vanderbilt chancellor abolished positions and dropped professors for reasons never made public or defended. Hypocrisy became the one constant. In Taylor's case, no tenure issue was involved. By 1935 all the professors in the School of Religion had temporary appointments. All had received notices of possible termination. Kirkland simply used a good opportunity to be rid of Taylor. The decision seemed largely his, although supported by Tillett and probably by Winton. In fact, it was a decision about the future direction of the school, not just about Taylor, but again Kirkland did not use this to justify the termination. Undoubtedly, Kirkland had faced criticism because of Taylor's political advocacy. But no evidence suggests that it had been strong enough to force his hand; it never came to a head over any particular incident. Taylor, in his contacts with board members, found only three bitterly opposed to his continuation. Two of these he identified: John Edgerton, a former head of the American Association of Manufacturers and one who resented Taylor's labor activities, and of course James G. Stahlman of the *Banner*. Taylor had directly involved himself in a labor dispute at the *Banner* and stood for everything that Stahlman bitterly opposed. Taylor cultivated two or three active supporters on the board. But most, as usual, took their lead from Kirkland. Unfortunately, both the Hart and Taylor cases came in the waning years of Kirkland's administration, when the old man was increasingly authoritarian. By 1937, in his reaction to opposition, he could become almost paranoid and, in many ways, often seemed almost pathetic. The board deserved all the censure—for keeping Kirkland on much too long.[41]

Fortunately, in the early depression the other professional schools did not suffer as many problems as the School of Religion. That would have been difficult. But the Law School, in a more quiet and peaceful way, moved gradually toward bankruptcy and suspension. It needed over 100 students to meet minimal costs. Its enrollment slowly dropped from 84 in 1930–31 to only 63 in 1934–35. With six full-time and four part-time professors, this was an invitation for disaster. Dean Arnold, brought in to rebuild the school, was able only to reestablish its academic credentials. The long-anticipated fund drive simply was out of the question in the early depression. The board, which all along had been generous toward Law, had to pay almost one-half the operating cost of the school, or exactly what it would not do for the School of Religion. With this level of support the school was able to maintain its staff, even replacing Holden B. Schermerhorn, who died unexpectedly in 1935 after sixteen years with the school. In 1934–35 the Law students shifted away from class organizations and formed their own Bar Association. The Law School had an enviable reputation in the South but did not come close to the admission requirements, or the caliber of course work, that was already standard in the prestigious schools of the Northeast. For example, the best schools already required three or four years of college; Vanderbilt required only the minimal two, and even this made it difficult for it to recruit students. Easy Tennessee bar exams and a lack of state requirements for legal education continued to undercut efforts to establish a strong school in Nashville.[42]

The Medical School, after the dramatic achievements of the 1920s, drifted along in the 1930s. It remained a model school in the South, equal except in size to the best in the North. Under Dean Leathers it did not generate the excitement that came under G. Canby Robinson, did not undertake any dramatic innovations. It simply held its own in difficult times. Slowly, but surely, the brilliant staff recruited by Robinson began to disperse. In 1932 the school lost James M. Neill, its professor of bacteriology. In 1935 C.S. Burwell, chair of the critical department of medicine, left to become dean of the Harvard Medical School, his alma mater. Such losses only documented the quality of the school, and to a large extent Vanderbilt would keep nourishing young professors of equal caliber. But Burwell's departure forced a careful search for his successor. In the past, personnel searches at Vanderbilt had been all too informal, based on personal networks or the inclinations of the chancellor. This was changing by the 1930s, and the Medical School led the way. A search committee wrote to all the major schools, screened fifty-six serious candidates, evaluated each on the basis of six carefully stipulated qualifications, and ended up with a final list of ten, three of whom were at Vanderbilt. After all this, the school ended up appointing Hugh Morgan to the post. Since he was a very close, even intimate friend of Kirkland, one could suspect the search of having a foregone conclusion, but that would be unfair. Morgan was eminently qualified and moved from a part-time professorship to what, increasingly, the Medical School defined as full time. Morgan received $9,200 in salary but was allowed enough limited consultation or private practice to bring his total income to $12,000. Such arrangements meant a new source of income for the school and hospital—the earnings of professors that went beyond the allowed salary accrued to the school.[43]

In the depths of the depression only the Medical School dared expand. The hospital was inadequate from the beginning. Robinson had planned an early addition, particularly one to care for the diseases of women and children. The depression only temporarily blocked these plans. Kirkland tried, unsuccessfully, to qualify for Public Works Administration funds. When this failed, he and Leathers had to turn once again to the GEB. By 1935, with its investments secured, it awarded Vanderbilt $2.5 million, with just over a third for hospital construction, the rest for endowment to operate the expanded facilities. This was its first large gift in six years, proving once again the esteem it had for Vanderbilt, although the gift came after a tough fight in the board. The days of GEB funding were about over. When completed, the large eight-story addition almost overshadowed the original building in front of it. The new wing, completed in 1937, added 155 beds, or 1.5 million cubic feet. It pushed the hospital to the very edge of the chancellor's residence, forcing Kirkland to move to a private residence in Belle Meade (he received a housing payment in compensation). The new addition also provided space for psychiatry and for a program on infectious diseases. But it was not entirely a godsend. The added endowment of $1.5 million did not yield nearly enough to cover the new costs. The hospital even delayed the opening of some of the completed wards. Fortunately, during the two years of construction Vanderbilt already had the new endowment and used its income as a reserve fund against future deficits. The related financial problems of the hospital and school worried Kirkland until his death in 1939. By heroic economies, Leathers had kept budgets balanced up until 1935. A key to this had been the continued, but never fully reliable, inflow of soft money, amounting to about $135,000 a year in the mid-1930s. The tuition, up to $300 a year by 1935, was also a vital part of the total income for the school.[44]

The Nursing School presented a mixed picture in the early 1930s. The newly independent school had an enviable position in nursing education and soon served as a model for visitors from around the world. With only two other Rockefeller-supported schools, it had its own outside financial support, in this case $35,000 a year from the foundation. This severed the normal dependence of a nursing school upon hospital or medical school funding. It was this independence that lured Shirley Titus as its first dean and allowed her to recruit an able staff, many with major publications. But, to some extent, the new school struggled from the very beginning against cross-currents generated by the Medical School and hospital. Titus was another G. Canby Robinson, almost unlimited in her aspirations for the school. She wanted a school completely independent of the hospital, which she achieved to a large extent in 1933 when the school stopped paying part of the salaries of supervising or head nurses in the hospital. She wanted one with a fully integrated Bachelor of Science program. In a sense she achieved this in 1936, when all entering nursing students at Vanderbilt had to enter a Bachelor of Science program, but she achieved this goal only by requiring two years of college for admission. Finally, she wanted a program oriented more heavily toward public health nursing, health specialties, nursing administration, or nursing education than to bedside nursing in hospitals. This emphasis also reflected the sentiments of the supporting Rockefeller Foundation. But it ran against the chronic budget problems in the hospital and the use of student nurses to lower costs. In a sense, the contradictory goals aligned resentful men against suspicious women, Kirkland and Leathers against Titus and her staff.[45]

In a critical meeting with representatives of the Rockefeller Foundation in 1933, Titus complained of exploitation of her students and came close to resigning. But this would have meant, almost certainly, an end of Rockefeller funding. After all, the university did not contribute any money directly to the school. Titus had to live on fees and on the Rockefeller grant. But even by the mid-1930s Dean Leathers wondered if the work performed by student nurses adequately compensated the hospital for the services provided students—room and board and laundry. After 1933 the school paid hourly fees for physicians who gave lectures to nurses and also contributed a small sum for support provided for its freshmen students, who did not perform any nursing duties. Privately, Kirkland and Leathers continuously bemoaned, or ridiculed, the grandiose schemes of Titus, and clearly would have preferred a less prestigious school, one that directly served the needs of the hospital in the sense of furnishing it with cheap, apprentice labor. In 1935 an increasingly wary Rockefeller Foundation capitalized $25,000 of its annual gift but continued $10,000 in annual support. But the $500,000 it gave as an endowment, at depression rates, promised less than a $25,000 yield, suggesting coming deficits. In fact, increased enrollments and soft money prevented this, but in 1935 the Nursing School was both a great success and a major headache for Kirkland. The showdown with Titus would come three years later.[46]

The depression had less impact on student life than one might have expected. Hard times curtailed the spending pattern of some students, forced more than ever before to seek work. By the mid-1930s about 12 percent of Vanderbilt students were relief clients of the government; 25 percent received some type of aid. Faculty concern over educational costs never led to tuition cuts, but for a few years the fraternities agreed to curtail formal dances and other expensive frills. In 1933 the students gave up their junior prom. But the most threatening effect of the depression seemed to be an ever greater provincialism. Vanderbilt had practically ceased to be a southern university, becoming in effect a local college. Only a sprinkling of College undergraduates now came from distant parts of the South, let alone from the North. Over three-fourths came from the Middle Tennessee–southern Kentucky region; in 1933 exactly two-thirds came from the Nashville area. The Graduate School and School of Religion drew from a larger area, but only the Medical School had anything close to a national constituency. Such a narrowed background meant greater homogeneity, again most evident in the College. The middle- to upper-income profile of most students added to the sameness of appearance and outlook noted by visitors and deplored by some professors.[47]

Even if diverse students came to Vanderbilt, they had little opportunity to meet and to mingle. Vanderbilt was now largely a federation of scattered fraternities and sororities. It had become, essentially, a campus without dorms. Old Kissam, ever more forbidding to students, was rarely full even after the burning of Wesley. Twice in the 1930s demoralized students in the half-empty building seemed bent on destroying it; in 1932 they hurled furniture from the fourth floor to the basement and came close to a riot. Later, they used candles to set off a new sprinkler system, flooding rooms and ruining ceilings beneath. For freshmen, Kissam was at best a temporary way station as they moved as soon as possible to a fraternity house. Only a few misfits, nonconformists, or extremely serious day students remained outside the Greek system. In the fall of 1933 only twenty-five young men failed to pledge a fraternity. Almost the only unifying or rallying focus was football, dancing, and possibly student publications. After 1933–34, the *Hustler* received support from student activity fees; students received it free and for most it was the sole source of news about overall campus events or problems. In many respects, student life at Vanderbilt had degenerated into a nearly pathological state. But no one knew what to do about it. The university had no money to build dorms, no way to bring a majority of students onto, and into, the campus. Students did not even have to attend chapel but twice a month.[48]

Another looming problem was intercollegiate athletics. From 1930 to 1934 Dan McGugin completed his successful reign at Vanderbilt. The football team remained competitive, winning a majority of games each year but always missing a championship or bowl bid. In 1932 the team tied Tennessee (McGugin never beat Tennessee after 1926) but probably lost a bowl bid because of its loss to Alabama. In that same year, one of the last glory years, McGugin served as president of the American Football Coaches Association, and Vanderbilt helped form a new Southeastern Conference (SEC) made up of thirteen colleges, thereby splitting up the old, sprawling, and unwieldy SIC. But even spectacular wins in 1932 rarely filled the 20,000 seats in the stadium, and the beleaguered athletic association barely met expenses and paid interest on its $180,000 debt. In 1930 the Nashville Optimist Club had sent out questionnaires to probe sentiments toward the team, to find out why so few attended games. Most people wanted better schedules, which seemed to translate into five games each year with the University of Tennessee. Finally, even McGugin's conservative brand of football came in for criticism; some people craved a more exciting offense. In 1932 only Georgia Tech and Tennessee drew a full crowd, in this the tenth anniversary of the stadium. In 1933, without a home game with Tennessee, the total annual attendance slipped to a paltry 43,000; Alabama drew the most, or just over 13,000. To the despair of many alumni, the athletic association for years refused to allow WSM to broadcast Vanderbilt games that were not sold out, which meant almost no broadcasts at all. Attendance did not improve in 1935 and only slightly in 1936 and 1937. But poor attendance only symbolized deeper problems with football, which became the basis of an extended policy debate that began in 1936 and extended to 1946 (see chapters 15 and 16). Vanderbilt moved uneasily, and unequally, into the era of paid football players. By 1935 it already offered "scholarships" to players; alumni gifts already funded some of these.[49]

McGugin retired at the end of the 1934 season. He would die a year later, at the young age of fifty-six. By then he was a living legend, still the senior and most honored coach in the South. His overall won-and-lost record, although dimmed a bit in the last years, was still unmatched. But, as much as Chancellor Kirkland he now stood for older values and an older style. The eulogies for him came from far and near. Among alumni, two people had come to symbolize Vanderbilt—Coach and Chance. Coach was dead and Kirkland could not last much longer. Clearly an era was ending. Characteristically, the Vanderbilt faculty did not dismiss a single class to honor McGugin. Football was extraneous to the purpose of the university. But, as Kirkland found out, it was central to alumni interest. At times it seemed that the real arbiters of Vanderbilt athletic policy were local or national sports writers and the faithful alumni who echoed all of their demands. While McGugin lived, the pressures built in behalf of Ray Morrison as his successor. Morrison had been a football hero at Vanderbilt, was then a very successful coach at Southern Methodist University. He commanded a considerable salary. Kirkland, against his better judgment, finally gave in to alumni and appointed him head coach for 1935–36 at a salary of $10,000, exactly double that of any professor in the College and above any but Goodpasture in the Medical School. Kirkland deplored such an imbalance, and out of this experience launched a long and complicated debate over athletics. In the long run, after he died, he decisively lost the debate. So did the Vanderbilt faculty.[50]

Politically, Vanderbilt students responded to national student trends. But, except for a handful of Hart and Taylor disciples, they did not move as far to the left as did northern students. Most supported a mild, if somewhat puzzling, New Deal. Roosevelt became their hero. Fewer than in northern schools supported socialist alternatives or even temporarily flirted with Marxist movements. In a 1932 straw vote, Roosevelt won 186 undergraduate votes to 45 for Republican Hoover and only 29 for Socialist Norman Thomas. Graduate students voted 63 for Roosevelt to 21 each for Hoover and Thomas. Among the 33 faculty who joined the poll, 16 were for Roosevelt, 8 for Hoover, and 9 for Thomas. As the varied, often contradictory New Deal programs developed, student support remained firm, or a "perversity" of outlook that Kirkland and his board attributed to student immaturity. In 1934 a *Hustler* poll revealed three-fourths of the students still backing Roosevelt. In 1935 another poll raised the approval rating to about 80 percent and even recorded 2 percent of the possibly unrepresentative students supporting the Communist Party, but as the *Hustler* noted this was much lower than on eastern campuses. In November of 1934, FDR visited Nashville, merely driving through the campus. Students treated him like a visiting god. Classes let out at ten o'clock and students waited over two hours to receive no more than a smile and a wave from a speeding automobile (Roosevelt was off schedule). In 1936 a poll of students and faculty in history and political science showed that eight out of nine were gleeful over a recent Supreme Court decision favoring the TVA, despite the feared effect upon Vanderbilt's endowment.[51]

By the mid-1930s a peace movement spread to all American campuses. Once again, Vanderbilt students followed behind the eastern schools. At Vanderbilt, the work of D.F. Fleming on the United States and the League, and his certainty that Americans had betrayed the League and the Wilsonian dream, had some impact on student opinion. Vanderbilt students wholeheartedly approved collective security as a way of avoiding future wars. In 1935 Fleming helped organize a week-long series of lectures under the rubric of an Institute of Public Affairs, an early precedent for later Impact programs. In this one, students heard lectures by eminent visitors on the European situation and on Latin America, already a much emphasized interest at Vanderbilt. In 1935 Vanderbilt students joined in the famous, but in-herently ambiguous, *Literary Digest* poll on student attitudes toward war. At Vanderbilt, 227 students said yes, to only 99 no, on a statement that the United States could stay out of a future war; 332 to 41 said they would fight if the nation were invaded (only one-eighth of Vanderbilt students said they would not fight to one-sixteenth nationally); only 62, compared with 303, said they would fight if the United States were the aggressor (even this yes vote was above the national average); while 202 as against 265 still favored entry into the League (above the national sample). In 1935–36 the Student Strike for Peace became big news on campus. In March of 1936 students also organized a chapter of the half-whimsical, half-serious Future War Vets and thereby tried to "laugh war to death." On April 22 it joined in a national antiwar demonstration but without any of the huge parades, rallies, and even near riots that erupted in New York City and on a few large campuses.[52]

In April of 1936, following the great success of a humorous edition of the *Hustler* (called the *Rustler*), a group of antiwar students published a broadside called the *Vanderbilt Patriot,* a "Hurst" paper. It was a clever take-off on the popular hysteria of World War I on the Vanderbilt campus. The headline announced "War is Declared." Arkansas had invaded Tennessee and thus Vanderbilt. Memphis was under siege, with razorback atrocities already resembling earlier ones in Belgium. An economics professor declared the war a god-ordained solution to unemployment. The first great martyr and hero was a former Vanderbilt student, Holtus Poltus. Bishop Hypocritic, of the Do Punk Foundation, came to preach a sermon to the chosen of God as they marched off to slay the heathen of Arkansas, and by this somehow "make them children of Jehovah. . . ." The battle hymn began: "Commodores lift your voices,/Pray and Roar and Grunt/That Our Men May Conquer/on the Beale Street Front!" The satire was heavy, an ironic commentary on what would happen only five years later. The key editorial was addressed to women:

> Of late women have become brittle, artificial, useless toys under the despoil-ing effects of peace and other evils of modern civilization. We must go back to the fundamental principles of the universe as laid down by the All-Wise. Tear away the life sucking parasite, Peace, and give to our abnormally anemic people—*War!* Clean and brave and glorious! Women, demand your chance to fulfill yourselves! As student after student rushes eagerly to the battle-field, to receive there a glorious death or magnificent mangling as God in his mercy decrees, let each woman's heart swell joyfully within her. For it is *her* brother, *her* sweetheart, *her* father, out there 'mid muck and mire and murder—and as their glory accumulates, so does hers. Ye women of Vanderbilt—kneel and pray for *War!* And looking ahead, marry now and produce multitudes of fresh, strong sons, that in the future still another War may be possible, and ye may gain more and more glory, —even unto the end of life, to which we all strive.[53]

So much sooner than students ever dreamed, an unprayed-for war did come. Fortunately, not before Vanderbilt enjoyed a brief interlude of near prosperity, in at least better times.

15

Better Times

For Vanderbilt, the depression ended by 1935 or 1936. The American economy had not recovered, but a lower level of production had become the norm and Vanderbilt had made its adjustments to a slow economy. The years of fear were over. Soaring enrollments boosted confidence. Administrators and faculty dared to start new programs, to plan again for modest growth. The brief interlude before World War II saw a minor boom on campus. Not that problems had disappeared; they are endemic to universities. But most were now internal, home grown, the kind that stimulated further growth and development. Three major issues marked these immediate prewar years—controversial curriculum changes in the College, the transition of leadership in the chancellor's office, and a new cooperation with Peabody and Scarritt reflected in the new Joint University Libraries (JUL).

The curriculum fight overshadowed new developments in the College. These included the institution of a fine arts program, starting with an appropriation for a band and choral director in 1934–35. In 1935 the College faculty approved a course, by Professor William P. Jackson, in choral music. A College faculty proposal for a fine arts department in 1935 listed courses on music, the theater, and the plastic arts. The effort climaxed in 1941 when the Carnegie Corporation gave $15,000 for fine arts. Marion M. Junkin, a painter from the Richmond Professional Institute, became associate professor and head of the new program in 1943, with work offered in art history and studio skills. Work in drama began in 1942 when Jonathan Curvin came to Vanderbilt as assistant professor of public speaking and drama and began the professional direction of a university theater. The only other new department was political science, which finally separated from history in 1940, with D.F. Fleming as its head.[1]

After Carmichael took over direction of the new Graduate School, he planned a new emphasis upon faculty research. As early as 1933, William C. Binkley, head of the social sciences division, had proposed special research in the social sciences, particularly on the problems of the South. He hoped to find funds for a research council, comparable to a GEB-funded fluid research fund ($50,000 a year) in the Medical School. Carmichael strongly backed such an effort, as part of his goal of quality Ph.D. programs in ten departments. His greatest love was public and business administration, or skills he felt essential for southern progress. In the fall of 1935, soon after coming to Vanderbilt, Carmichael first met with the GEB in Washington to solicit such a research grant. However, at this time, the library needs were most basic, and this was what the GEB was most willing to support.[2]

In 1939 Chancellor Carmichael added $1,500 to the College budget to fund the first competitive Graduate School research grants. Faculty members quickly submitted proposals to use this amount and much more. Carmichael could boast, by 1940, that half the College faculty was engaged in some type of research. In 1940, with a $30,000 commitment from the GEB and a $40,000 commitment from Vanderbilt's own budget, Carmichael estab-lished a new Institute of Research and Training in the Social Sciences, with special funding in public and business administration. The institute funded special internships for students, either in local businesses or in government offices, and provided released time for faculty members. Five professors became the first recipients of institute grants in 1940–41. Closely joined to this was the creation in 1940 of a Vanderbilt University Press, in part to publish the results of all the new research. The press began on a shoestring, without a director or any but temporary revolving funds. It first funded the publication of Edwin Mims's eulogistic biography of the late Chancellor Kirkland, and then a revised dissertation by a young assistant professor of history and recent Ph.D., Henry Lee Swint. The press hoped, in each case, to recover costs. A press committee, headed by the dean of the Graduate School and aided by a student assistant, selected manuscripts but provided limited editorial help. In effect, Vanderbilt established its imprint and contracted for the various publishing and printing services. But, to Carmichael, the press, the fifth such in the Southeast, further emphasized a new and very serious Vanderbilt commitment to scholarly research and publication. He always claimed the press as one of his greatest achievements at Vanderbilt.[3]

The almost frozen College faculty of the early 1930s thawed quickly after 1936, in a series of losses, retirements, appointments, and promotions. The academic marketplace began to work once again. Rising enrollments forced some expansion of staff by 1937, an expansion largely reflected in junior appointments in such understaffed departments as math, English, history, and chemistry. The resignation of D.C. Cabeen because of ill health (he thus left closely behind his old enemy, Hart) led to Charles Zeek's appointment as professor and head of Romance languages. Zeek was a Southern Methodist University professor and a Grenoble graduate. When Carmichael moved up to chancellor in 1937, he and a committee on educational policy launched a major search for a dean of the Graduate School and Senior College and, also, someone to guide the new efforts in social science research. From eighteen names seriously considered, they ended up with two prominent professors, one each at Harvard and Princeton. Carmichael interviewed both in New York and settled on John Pomfret, a historian and associate dean at Prince-ton. A Pennsylvania Ph.D., he had two significant books to his credit and, more important, was secretary of the Social Science Research Council, a position he continued part time during his first year at Vanderbilt. Unfortunately, after five years he moved on to the presidency of William and Mary. In 1938 the university lured John Van Sickle as professor and soon head of economics. A Harvard Ph.D., a longtime employee of the Rockefeller Foundation, he came to Vanderbilt as a prospective director of the planned institute. Except in English, a story in itself, the only other notable appointments of this period included in 1938 Normal L. Munn in experimental psychology, immediately from Peabody but before that from the University of Pittsburgh and the author of important books and articles; and in 1940 Herman C. Nixon, back as a special lecturer in political science, supported in part by the Rosenwald Fund.[4]

The economic distresses of the early 1930s had created a backlog of delayed promotions. With greater prosperity the dam broke, at least for some. In 1938, alone, E.J. Eberling in economics, Arthur W. Ingersoll in chemistry, D.F. Fleming in political science, and Edwin L. Johnson in classical languages all became full professors, followed in 1939 by Francis Slack in physics, Walter Reckless in sociology, and Richmond Beatty in English, and in 1941 by Willard B. Jewell in geology. The long delays in promotion contributed to the loss of Lyle Lanier in 1938 and Reckless in 1940; ironically, both directed inquiries involving race. Almost as significant as these highest promotions were the advances of the young men who just now gained associate rank. In 1940 these included Charles S. Shoup in biology, Waite P. Fishel in chemistry, and Daniel Robison in history, joined in 1941 by Paul Manchester and Juan Castellano in Romance languages and Philip Rudnick in physics. By now, the new emphasis upon graduate work and upon research meant that all these promotions reflected scholarly attainment and in most cases an active involvement in professional organizations. The rising generation of College professors were more narrowly specialized, more attuned to their profession on the national level, than the older generation they replaced.[5]

The older generation seemed to fade away quickly. Kirkland's retirement in 1937 began the exodus, in many cases a painful one. Many of the oldtimers had not joined the TIAA and so kept on teaching out of economic need. In 1939 Carmichael dared do what an aging Kirkland never had the heart to do—move out those at or past normal retirement age. In effect, he forced John Daniel in physics and R.B. Steele in Latin to retire. He gave them emeritus status, and, after some haggling, awarded them one-half salary as the substitute for a retirement annuity. Daniel's retirement allowed Slack to become head of physics; he had been doing much of the work for several years. In 1940 Ada Bell Stapleton resigned as dean of women to give full time to her teaching; she was succeeded by Blanche Henry Clark, who moved over from Ward-Belmont College.[6]

The long, drawn-out negotiations with Daniel seemed to make imperative a compulsory retirement system. No one dared say it, but so did the abnormally prolonged reign of Kirkland. The sensitivities were high and the fears palpable, but Carmichael pushed ahead with such a scheme in 1940 and secured board approval for it in February, 1941. The new plan encompassed all parts of the university. Now, professors and all administrative officers had to retire during the year of their sixty-eighth birthday. They could retire, voluntarily, at sixty-five. By recommendation of the chancellor and special action by the board, one might extend this for up to two years, or until age seventy. All existing professors under forty had to join the TIAA (still at a 5 percent university, 5 percent personal rate); those over forty were urged to join, and if they did not, they had to take responsibility for their own retirement. All new faculty employees after July 1, 1941, became TIAA participants after five years and could join by their third year if the board approved. If they came from a TIAA college, they could enter as soon as they moved to Vanderbilt.

When the new plan went into effect in 1941 it forced the immediate retirement of all professors over age seventy. Two in the College were affected—Gus Dyer, the controversial sociologist, and Albert Harris, the old elocution teacher back at the turn of the century who had lived on to head what amounted to a developing speech department. Mary Haggard, the longtime and much beloved registrar, also chose to retire that year. Three key professors—Glenn, Mims, and Sanborn—were sixty-seven or older. Glenn, Vanderbilt's preeminent geologist since 1900, was granted one extra year but gave up his administrative duties. Jewell was his department replacement and Reinke became the new head of the physical sciences division. Mims followed this pattern, with Curry taking over both as English department chairman and as divisional head while Mims worked at his planned history of Vanderbilt. Sanborn also continued for one additional year.[7] For him, retirement came too soon, just after he finally got rid of his old enemy, Kirkland, and also at a time when he was still vigorous. He continued to coach his fencing team for over a decade. These important retirements ended the Kirkland era in the College; Mims and Glenn had been his closest allies, Sanborn his only constant critic. He needed both. They had served him well.

When Carmichael came to Vanderbilt in the fall of 1935 he began organizing the new Graduate School. It never became a school in the sense of Medicine or Law, but rather coordinated graduate work for the whole university. At first, though, its scope extended primarily to the College and Medical School. As first organized, the graduate faculty included most full professors in the College (not the few, such as Dyer, who offered no graduate-level work) and six key professors in the Medical School, including the preeminent research scientist then at Vanderbilt, Goodpasture. This arrangement seemed a bit unfair to the younger staff. It led to such an anomaly as Daniel's being on the faculty and Slack's not; Dean Sarratt was on it and D.F. Fleming was off. Accordingly, in 1936 Carmichael added the names of all

Chancellor Oliver C. Carmichael
and Dean of Women Blanche Clark greet students

YOUNG LEADERS

Provost Philip Davidson

Dean of Nursing Shirley Titus

associate professors who taught graduate seminars or directed theses. Finally, in 1943, the dean listed all full and associate professors in the College as members of the graduate faculty, a policy as unrealistic in its sweeping inclusiveness as the earlier one had been in its narrowness. By then, the assumption seemed to be that Vanderbilt would not promote anyone to associate professor who was not eminent enough, or skilled enough, to offer graduate work.[8]

Growth in Engineering paralleled that in the College. Enrollment grew from 163 in 1935–36 to 236 in 1940–41. The school was not yet independent, but expansion pulled it slowly away from its College allegiance. Before the war, in addition to several instructors, the school appointed two new junior professors—in 1939 Roy S. Hanslick, of Yale, and in 1941 E.E. Litkenhaus (Ph.D., Minnesota)—both in a developing department of chemical engineering, a fourth degree program in the school (joining civil, mechanical, and electrical). In 1939 Samuel Schealer replaced Wesley Brown as professor of electrical engineering. By 1939, for the first time ever, the school had to limit incoming freshmen because of a lack of facilities and equipment. In addition to its ongoing program for sanitation officers, in 1940 it began a preflight training program for the Civil Aeronautics Administration.[9]

After 1935 enrollment climbed in all schools except Law. In 1941 its enrollment was down to 55 and falling each year. By 1936 the board had already spent $125,000 to keep the school going (in effect, by normal university accounting, the school had a deficit of this amount). In 1936 a board committee studied the problem; Kirkland seriously considered suspending Law. Since the School of Religion kept a fund drive going, it seemed pointless to try to raise any funds for Law in the Nashville area. Then, in 1937, it again faced accreditation problems. A visitor for the Association of American Law Schools cited two grave concerns—a lack of space and too few full-time professors (it needed seven instead of six). Given a new building and a slightly larger staff, it could be one of the two or three best in the South, for it had an able faculty. But the warning was clear—the Law School could not retain its accreditation in its existing quarters in what would soon be officially named Kirkland Hall. The library was impossibly crowded and students had no lounge and toilet facilities except those in the basement. The school tried to keep up with minimal requirements. It moved to a semester system in 1939–40, to match that of other schools; inaugurated new courses in labor law; sought a now required full-time librarian in 1940; and looked ahead to its planned expansion into the old chapel upon completion of the JUL in late 1941. By then, student discontent was widespread. Students believed Dean Arnold to be arbitrary in many of his decisions. Perhaps mercifully, the war practically eliminated its enrollment and by 1943 left only Dean Arnold of its former full-time staff, and by then a complete new beginning after the war seemed the best hope of eventual survival. But the school only suspended classes in 1944, when the Association of American Law Schools finally approved rules for temporary suspension without any loss of accreditation.[10]

After 1936 the School of Religion gained an identity, a reasonably clear mission, and a new home. Under Dean Umphrey Lee it had to move ahead on a financial shoestring. The reorganization that eliminated Alva Taylor placed heavy burdens on all professors; full professors taught four courses each quarter for an annual salary of only $3,300, by far the lowest in the university. Four professors could get only one-half time appointments. A new assistant professor of practical theology had to work part time for the library to get even a meager salary. Here, as in the College, the oldtimers departed. On June 4, 1936, just four days before his official retirement was to begin, Tillett died, fifty-four years after the young chaplain had come to an almost new Vanderbilt in 1882. Then in February, 1937, the other emeritus dean, O.E. Brown, resigned his teaching position and then died in October, 1939, just after a campus memorial service for Kirkland. George Winton, the former acting dean, died in 1938. In 1937, Dean Lee further reduced his staff and began relying on Scarritt College for courses in music and soon in other practical or applied fields. At the same time he moved to raise admission requirements. He wanted a more restricted school, one strong in history and theology, not in vocational areas. He believed that four or five distinguished scholars could make his school an academic leader in the South, a school for scholars or the ablest of ministers. In 1938 the school established a Tillett chair but awaited an endowment to fill it. Just as the new program got under way, Lee resigned to become president of Southern Methodist University.[11]

The new plans made sense in part because the school now had its new home, the old YMCA College. By 1935 this college was unable to pay interest on its debt to Vanderbilt. President Willis D. Weatherford struggled to find some way of salvaging his small training school but could not raise money in the depression. Its impending demise created great problems for Vanderbilt students who used its gyms and swimming pool and received instruction, for a fee of $20 per student, from three of its faculty. Vanderbilt faced horrendous costs if it lost access to these services; without the Vanderbilt student fees the YMCA College would have already folded. For almost a year Weatherford and Kirkland exchanged proposals for some type of merger that would save the identity of the college. Weatherford, in particular, wanted to surrender the building to Vanderbilt to cover its $166,000 debt, but to retain a right of later repurchase. Vanderbilt might have accepted this except that a second mortgage precluded clear title. Eventually, in 1936, Weatherford gave up on any continuation and actively sought foreclosure on the mortgages. He was able to retire a second mortgage and turn the property over to Vanderbilt for about $176,000 of canceled debt. The building and land were easily worth double this. The insurance from old Wesley more than covered the cost of the part of the building that went to the School of Religion. Vanderbilt would continue to use the gyms and swimming pool, and it even hired the existing instructors to teach physical education courses. In fact, Religion lost a bit on the exchange of insurance funds for its part of a building, but the board had provided it free facilities during the interim. Rooms for seventy students on the fourth floor promised enough rental income to maintain the building. Totally apart from the gyms and the swimming pool, the long building contained space for a rebuilding religions library (out of the debris of old Wesley, Tillett and students had slowly salvaged a surprising number of the old books), a small auditorium, dining facilities, and many offices and class-rooms. It was not a perfect home, but it was a cheap one, for it left the school all of its existing endowment for operating expenses. Appropriately, in 1937, the school voted to rename the building Wesley Hall and gained from Frederick W. Vanderbilt his approval for this alternative to a new building, for which he had donated $150,000.[12]

The challenge in 1938–39 was finding a new dean to replace Lee. After a thorough search by the faculty and university administrators, Carmichael appointed John Keith Benton from Drew University, significantly, a north-ern Methodist school. Benton, a professor in the key fields of religious philosophy and psychology, had his B.D. from Yale, his Ph.D. from Edin-burgh, yet came to Vanderbilt for a salary of only $5,000. In the year before his move he had served as visiting professor at Duke and had been closely related to the work of the National Council of Churches of Christ (the former Federal Council). In most respects Benton shared Lee's commitment to academic excellence, but he shifted the school a bit more toward ministerial training. In 1940 the school moved back once again to a four-day week to accommodate active ministers, and replaced the old thesis requirement with independent study. Since 1938 the school had required a B.A. for entrance and would soon emphasize graduate work. Benton brought in new profes-sors, most notably Roy Wesley Battenhouse (Ph.D., Yale) as professor of church history in 1940, and J. Phillip Hyatt (a Brown B.D., a Yale Ph.D.) as associate professor of Old Testament. By 1941 the school met all accredita-tion standards and the requirements of most denominations; the southern Methodist church finally approved it for its ministers, on the same level as their own seminaries. Under Benton the school offered work in five broad fields: the religions of mankind; the Bible and its interpretation; Christianity and its historical development; the religious interpretation of the world and of man; and the work of the church at home and abroad. Instead of limiting enrollment, the new focus and direction proved appealing; enrollment grew from a low of twenty-five in 1937–38 to fifty-two in 1940–41 and kept rising in the early years of the war. The school also lived on its own income. Thus, for the first time since 1914 the school seemed secure. Talk of suspension finally ended.[13]

The Medical School moved toward war without major changes. The most serious faculty loss was R.S. Cunningham, head of anatomy (replaced by Sam Clark). The most significant research, among the dozens of grants and projects, was the viral investigations by Goodpasture, inquiries that yielded enormous returns in immunization during World War II. His use of eggs as a culture for virus caught the public fancy and led to considerable national publicity for his work. From 1937 to 1943 Vanderbilt offered a special postgraduate training program for Tennessee physicians, under grants from the State Medical Association and the State Department of Public Health. In a sense, the bulk of its educational work involved, not its 200 regular students, but dozens of postgraduate courses or institutes, plus its work with its own interns and residents. As expected with the completion of the new wing, the hospital soon suffered annual deficits, met for a time from built-up reserves. The school raised its tuition to $400, and then in 1940–41 to $450. Increasingly, even chair professors enjoyed limited private fees, from consulting or from private patients, and these extra fees earned small additional income for the school. But by 1940 a major budget crisis forced reluctant administrators to decide to charge all patients in the wards and even in the outpatient clinics. The university hoped to collect fees from the city for indigent patients, but added $1,000 annually to the hospital budget to pay for special charity cases. The hospital staff feared the fees would sharply curtail patients, undermining its teaching role. So far, the hospital had functioned as a huge laboratory for the school, one that was expected to live largely off its endowment and only marginally off fees from a few affluent private patients. It seems unbelievable today, but the new fee schedule was $2 a day for ward patients, fifty cents for the first visit to a clinic, or about 40 percent of the actual cost of the services rendered. No one even thought of charging patients full cost. The new policy regarding charges coincided with rises in new defense spending and rather rapid economic recovery, and so they did not lead to a significant drop in the number of patients and rather quickly solved most of the deficit problems in the hospital. For the first time, university administrators began to perceive the hospital in a new light—as a potential source of income.[14]

The impending crisis in Nursing came in 1938. A frustrated Dean Titus, unable to realize her dreams, disappointed in the support she received in behalf of them, resigned. Ultimately, nine of her faculty also left, leading to a nearly complete turnover in two years. Just as she left, she gained one final goal—the board approved the awarding of a Founder's Medal in Nursing. In the same year the school stopped admitting anyone without two years of college, and thus anyone not able to earn a Bachelor of Science after the three-year program. The school turned to a nursing educator from the University of Virginia, Frances Helen Zeigler, as its new dean, at a modest salary of $4,200. Among the new faculty, Lulu K. Wolf, who followed Zeigler from Virginia in nursing education, and a new instructor, Julia Hereford, would play major roles in the subsequent history of nursing education. A later, key appointment, Helen M. Howell, came in 1941; Howell, with an M.A. from Columbia, worked in the important field of public health nursing. In 1937 the Rockefeller Foundation added $200,000 to the nursing school endowment (making $700,000 in all), completing its capitalization of annual gifts. But because of lowered earnings and threatened deficits, the foundation also contributed small operating sums for the next few years, but on no guaranteed basis. Despite some reservations about how the hospital continued to use student nurses, the foundation seemed proud of this, its only gift, so far, to Vanderbilt. It sent even its international visitors to Nashville. Along with the nursing education department of Peabody, the school hosted the Association of Collegiate Schools of Nursing in 1939.[15]

One should not forget the suspended schools. Echoes from the past kept appearing, particularly among alumni. Several Vanderbilt alumni gathered at a reunion of the Tennessee Dental Association in 1939 and talked about raising funds for a building and a new dental school. Pharmacy graduates also met in Nashville to honor E.A. Ruddiman, with John T. McGill, aged eighty-nine, also present. They actually organized an association to work toward a new school of pharmacy. The war soon intervened, and the echoes of these schools slowly died away. Suspension became extinction.[16]

No changes in the schools rivaled in significance, or created as intense conflict, as a new curriculum in the College. The 1937 curriculum fight in the College also became entangled with university government. The story is complex. When Carmichael arrived on campus in the fall of 1935, he took over as dean of the new Senior College prepared for him. Dean Paschal, already the frequent object of student complaints and criticism, in effect accepted a demotion to dean of the Junior College. He would be eased out in the war years. For several years the College faculty had made tentative moves toward major curriculum reforms. The earlier division into lower and upper levels had begged a differentiated curriculum for the two levels, a move now made imperative by the creation of junior and senior colleges. Carmichael seemed the perfect person to lead this reform. He had helped devise the new curriculum at Alabama College and frequently wrote and spoke on the purposes of a liberal arts college. In other words, he had some rather clear beliefs about a proper mix of required courses in a college.

Scarcely had Carmichael arrived than he asked the faculty to appoint a committee to study other institutions with junior and senior colleges. Sanborn, eager for a new regime, seconded such a motion. Carmichael chaired the all-important committee, made up of Ransom (English), Eberling (economics), Lanier (psychology), and Jewell (geology). His choices were unusual, exactly the opposite of what one would have expected from Kirkland. Unlike senior professors, reliable and loyal veterans, these four men reflected the ablest talent among the younger, ambitious, middle-level, and to some extent frustrated faculty. Lanier, in fact, was still an assistant professor after almost a decade of very able service; he was an experimentalist of promise, a member of a new Association of Experimental Psychologists. Eberling was a long-term associate professor, awaiting what he believed was a deserved promotion. Jewell was also an associate, still in the shadow of L.C. Glenn.

Ransom alone was a full professor, but he remained under the tight rule of aging Edwin Mims and had the outlook of many younger faculty. At the same time, Ransom was arguably the most brilliant, and on the way to being the most prominent, professor in the College, in fact the only College faculty member who rivaled in achievement and promise the abler chairs in the Medical School. In short, Carmichael picked a superbly qualified committee but one clearly with a bent toward independent judgment. They would not play political games or submit to the guidance of their "superiors."[17]

By December, Carmichael had decided on two committees. He converted his original committee into one on the Senior College. He had Paschal chair a new committee on the Junior College, made up of Curtis Walker (history), J.M. Breckenridge (chemistry), Randall Stewart (English), and George R. Gage (biology), all full professors. But Walker, at least, was an independent man and after the Hart affair clearly outside the circle of loyal Kirkland admirers. The two committees worked for the next year, at times separately, at times jointly. By his position, Carmichael had to assume responsibility for what they achieved and clearly made major contributions to the final reports, rendered in December, 1936. In the reports the two committees recommended a truly sweeping reorganization of the College and its work. In addition, the joint committee proposed even more basic changes encompassing the whole approach to liberal education. In brief, the committees jointly proposed that credits be assigned by quarter hours, not yearly hours, and that as many courses as possible be one-term, five-hour courses. Such a change would give students opportunities to take a much broader range of subjects. In addition, it recommended that Junior College students take a minimum of twenty-five hours in each of the three divisions (or seventy-five out of the ninety required quarter hours), leaving the ticklish problem of internal distribution to each division. Finally, the two committees proposed optional final divisional examinations at the end of the two Junior College years, to enable students to make up deficiencies in grades or to improve their grade-point averages. The Junior College committee elaborately defended the new five-hour, one-term approach. In addition, it recommended that there be a wider use of achievement tests for credit, that each department offer an introductory one-term, five-hour course, and that the existing political science course in problems of citizenship be converted into a one-term survey of the social sciences. The survey would serve as a required introductory course for the social science division.[18]

The Senior College committee, under Carmichael, did an enormous amount of work. It surveyed colleges all over the country and read much literature. It also met with all department heads at Vanderbilt. One feels that Carmichael used this committee as a way of demonstrating his qualifications as next chancellor, and he obviously invested his educational idealism in the effort. The committee report included a broad, philosophical vindication of its work, with special emphasis on intellectual initiative and independent thinking, on greater student freedom, and challenging individual goals instead of the mere accumulation of credits. Ironically, some of the idealistic language seemed remarkably familiar—as if Joseph Hart had written it, although the committee emphasized how conservative and practical its new program would be, how little change it would require. For the Senior College, the new focus was upon a major and a minor. To graduate, a student would have to have a minimum of sixty quarter hours in a field of concentration, with forty in his major department, twenty in a related field. To enable students to profit from such a concentration, the committee recommended two levels of courses in the Senior College. Junior level courses would be open to nonmajors, but majors would do extra assignments. Each student also would have to complete a senior-level, integrative course in his major. For the humanities and social science departments, the committee mandated a new course (Number 20), a five-hour, quarter-length seminar for no more than ten students. It stipulated a nonlecture format, with assigned papers, tutorial conferences, and a final comprehensive exam covering the major subject. In effect, this turned a part of the senior year into an early experience of graduate work. Instead of such seminars, it asked the science departments to incorporate historical and comparative content into a special senior lecture course, culminating with a comprehensive exam. When necessary, preprofessional students could by-pass the new requirements.[19]

At the December faculty meeting Lanier moved acceptance of the reports as read. But the faculty was not about to accept such sweeping changes without major debate. On motion, the professors voted to postpone consideration until December 15. During the week the inevitable political juggling began. The committee received four written communiques, and faculty members met frequently and long to discuss it—all a normal response to any proposals touching so directly upon faculty educational beliefs and preferences. When the faculty reconvened, Paschal moved acceptance of the proposal in principle but with the faculty to use a later meeting to modify the details of a final draft. Also, each department was to prepare an outline of its likely new program under the new rules. Curry read a paper explaining his reservations, but even this was referred to the committee for the final draft. The rather innocuous motion then passed, with all the policy issues unresolved. Dean Carmichael moved that the administrative committee (deans and divisional heads) plus one member from each of the two committees comprise a new committee of direction to assist in implementing the new program.[20]

Everything seemed to be proceeding smoothly. Not so. Kirkland was already involved. Several faculty members, particularly in the sciences, had come to him full of complaints. He knew a fight loomed, possibly a very divisive one. Kirkland had always, as chancellor, tried to run a tight ship, working hard to maneuver and persuade in order to avoid open controversy. He knew that a good manager never allows issues to come to a sharp confrontation, and Kirkland had been very successful in this game, in part because he devoted enormous energy to preparation before finally bringing anything to a vote, and because he so shaped the distribution of effective power as to leave opponents without any leverage. Now, he believed Carmichael had bungled the whole affair. What was at stake was a smooth transition to a new chancellor. If the faculty sharply divided, many would inevitably be angry at Carmichael. In fact, Kirkland had already received just such intimations from many of his older and most loyal faculty. The new reforms were clearly most popular among the more disaffected faculty, the younger and more independent-minded individuals that Kirkland most resented. He began to take over the direction of the faculty and to guide Carmichael out of dangerous waters.[21]

Why did these issues raise so many perils? They need not have. But any major change in curriculum, such as in distribution requirements, is certain to involve a faculty in extended debate and political conflict. Given certain habits, or certain institutional forms, such conflict can serve constructive purposes, as can any dialogue over fundamental principles. Such does not necessarily lead to disruptive, enduring factions or intensely personal conflict. But the College had neither the habits nor institutions needed for such a debate. The chancellor had, heretofore, chaired the monthly faculty meetings, carefully guided the issues that came before the faculty, and had allowed the departments much autonomy in all academic matters. The heads of key departments, along with deans and divisional heads, constituted a friendly little oligarchy that gave the required general policy direction to the College. An army of committees did the required work, even up to the critical approval of new courses. But not since 1887 had the faculty ever come close to an intensive analysis of aims and objectives, of courses and requirements. These issues struck at the heart of faculty interest, both at the level of educational philosophy and at the very concrete level of the work that one had to do. The curriculum proposals were full of red flags—for older professors who now faced the task of completely changing courses they had long taught, for departments that enjoyed larger enrollments because of existing requirements or well-developed student habits, for professors who sensed that the senior seminars would increase their teaching loads or force them to tear up well-worn lecture notes, for traditionalists who saw some faddish or fashionable new but foolish educational theories behind the new plan. In the minds of some, the university had just as well kept Hart around if Carmichael was going off on a binge about intellectual challenge or independent work or self-mastery. Several professors in the sciences and the humanities saw the plan as a power grab by the social sciences, the alleged pets of Carmichael. Heretofore, the College had had no course requirement in any social science departments. Even Kirkland, as informed by his old cronies, suspected this was one ulterior motive, since social scientists Eberling, Lanier, and Carmichael could control the five-member senior committee.[22]

394

The reaction to the proposed changes revealed the inertia, the resistance to structural change, that lurks in all faculties. In a modern university the reformers, the idealists, even the would-be utopians, are most often administrators. Either they move into administration as a way of effecting their educational ideals, or the holistic perspectives of administrative work propel them in this direction. Great new, fascinating schemes for curriculum reform almost always originate at the center, as with Carmichael. These often dominate the serious deliberations at meetings of deans or vice-chancellors for academic affairs, but rarely conventions of specialized scholars. The resistance to change comes from the academic provinces, from the tough oligarchs that run departments, those who often are brilliant and innovative in their own scholarship, possibly leftist in their political leanings. They tend to defend their property and thus the status quo. Or they have learned how to bargain with other oligarchs and in the process have become somewhat cynical realists. The Carmichael committee also illustrates another common phenomenon: he was able to pull younger, less entrenched, inherently idealistic professors into a committee that tried to deal with College-wide issues. They flirted briefly with academic utopia and became deeply, personally, philosophically committed to their new blueprint. As lambs they threw it out to the wolves, totally unprepared emotionally or intellectually for how quickly the wolves would ravage it. And they were too committed to drive a bargain. The brewing controversy began to erupt in February, 1937, but in a minor way. The faculty easily approved a new proposal from the junior committee, one that clarified the degree of separation between the two colleges. A second motion, from Carmichael, had a more ominous twist to it. The two committees were not to resubmit their finished drafts to the faculty after all, but to a committee of review made up of the chancellor and the two committee chairmen, both deans. Only what the three officers agreed upon would then come to the faculty. It seems strange that a self-confident faculty could approve such a resolution, but this one did, 46–9. By that vote the faculty gave up almost all control over the new reforms.[23]

On April 6, Kirkland presented the results of his review committee in the form of a considerably revised and watered-down proposal. He began with a lecture on university government, with a rather odd twist. Heretofore the faculty had determined all academic policies, subject to board review. Now, a committee had proposed to set requirements and the faculty had approved a committee of directors representing the three divisions to make subsequent decisions about courses and admission requirements. That, said Kirkland, was very unwise and gave unintended legislative power to the three divisions. Thus, he and the two deans proposed a new college committee on the curriculum, appropriately made up only of the administrative offices of the faculty, those charged with general responsibility and those wholly independent of any one discipline. His recommended committee was to be made up of the chancellor, the two College deans, the dean of Engineering, and the three divisional heads. This committee was to recommend all future implementing actions in behalf of the new curriculum. But the faculty was to retain the right of final approval, a nice way of expressing Kirkland's firm belief in responsibly guided democracy. The new committee was also to study all existing courses and try to prepare a rational schedule of courses.

The review committee also considerably weakened the original report. It now made the five-hour, term-length course only one option among many. It stressed the advantage, in some departments, of traditional two- and three-term courses, or those that carried only three hours. Likewise, the committee members gave in to department pressure and suggested voluntary introductory courses, not mandated ones. They retained the provision for term credits, kept an eighteen- instead of a twenty-five-hour requirement in the social sciences, and otherwise retained existing requirements in languages, English, math, and for a laboratory science. The committee kept the requirement for a major (with a minimum of thirty-nine and a maximum of fifty-one hours), and kept the required course for seniors but changed it from a seminar to a lecture format. In effect, the committee moved the College back perilously close to where it had been all along. It took the sting out of the surviving reforms; the most basic changes were now optional.

Kirkland faced a more independent faculty than he had anticipated. The frustrated, out-maneuvered reformers fought back. Dean Sarratt, as always, supported Kirkland and moved acceptance of the report of the board of review. Ransom offered an amended or substitute wording that would, in effect, have sent the report back for further study to an enlarged committee containing six elected faculty members, two from each division. This lost by only one vote, 26–27. D.F. Fleming, in a gesture of reconciliation, then moved a small amendment—to add one member from each division to the proposed committee on the curriculum, these three to be appointed by the chancellor. Sanborn moved to amend the amendment to make these three elective. Lanier seconded this, and it passed by an impressive 37–16 vote. With this concessionary amendment as a gesture to the reformers, the whole report passed unanimously.[24]

Kirkland almost blew his top. He was now seventy-eight years old, in failing health, and trying to survive to his retirement in July, which perhaps explains what followed. So far, in long and rather conspiratorial letters to president of the board Frank Rand, he had justified his intervention, his ploys to keep the faculty from ever discussing any details of the reports, as a way to protect Carmichael. To some extent this made sense. The informal meetings about campus, the new suspicions and accusations among the factions, frightened him. He also saw in the divisions a widespread hostility to the administration, in some cases directed at Carmichael, at times against himself. He even professed a martyr's role—"let them hate me for I am leaving." He correctly sensed a beginning demand for more faculty self-government and knew from other sources that a number of junior faculty had already tried to rush his retirement. Two even contacted a trustee, apparently in a mistaken assumption that the GEB was awaiting a change in the administration in order to make large grants for the University Center and a joint library. Owsley, in complete honesty, circulated such rumors as he had picked them up in Alabama. So, even before the climactic meeting, Kirkland believed that a growing body of agitators were at work.

The votes at the April 6 meeting confirmed his deepest suspicions. He wrote an angry letter to Rand about "a large group of anti-administration agitators," led by a dangerous John Ransom. He applauded Sarratt's loyal support but described Ransom's remarks as "ridiculous," for his plan would have imposed six antiadministration members on the new committee. If Kirkland meant this, then the antiadministration forces made up an overwhelming majority of the faculty, enough to control an election in each of three divisions. The close vote of 26–27 distressed him, for it showed "a burning desire on the part of a well organized group to control the faculty in opposition to all the administrative machinery. . . ." In effect, he argued that in a guided democracy it is treason to vote against the already ordained outcome. The right to vote does not mean a right to support an independent, antiadministrative position. Then the rebels, headed by Sanborn, won on the final vote, and with that victory the "rebellious crowd" seemed satisfied. Again, Kirkland believed the effect was to push on the committee three hostile members, as if his point of view would not prevail in a forthcoming election.[25]

If Kirkland had expressed these strange sentiments only to Rand, then no harm. But even before the faculty adjourned, he preached to them. He argued, with no basis whatsoever, that their "antagonism" extended not only to himself but was "an offensive gesture against the Board of Trust." One can only wonder—why have a vote at all if a negative vote is an insult to the board? Kirkland's logic was that the board appointed administrative officers (it also appointed every faculty member present). To Rand, he argued that the only hope of successful administration was the cooperation of faculty members with the appointed officers. The trustees were not going to relinquish control to "any insurgent group." He even listed the men the insurgents planned to place on the committee—Ransom, Lanier, and Slack, all completely unacceptable to him. Again, how these three could control the election is unclear. Thus, Kirkland took the matter to the Executive Committee of the board and had its astonished and somewhat confused members dutifully veto the faculty action, because the added members would cut down on the efficiency of the committee, because the faculty revealed an obstructive purpose, and because the action gave an illegal legislative power to the three divisions. No trustees wanted to oppose the retiring chancellor. Rand was concerned about a developing rift within the faculty, as anyone should be, particularly since Kirkland believed the two factions to be about equal in size.[26]

On May 4 Kirkland communicated the Executive Committee's decision to his faculty. They could do nothing. The committee of the board, unprecedented as was its action, simply exercised its ultimate power to override any vote by the faculty even on purely academic matters. Finally, in the most pathetic aspect of the whole affair, Kirkland dragged Frank Rand to the faculty meeting and had him address the faculty on peace and harmony. To its credit, the faculty members repressed any overwhelming urge to laughter, showed compassion for poor Rand and the awkward situation he was in, and perhaps generously responded to his goodwill and even the unusual courage that brought him before them. They applauded his speech. This ended the great curriculum fight. By the next year, the catalog began to reflect the few changes, along with a new 100-200-300-400-500 numbering system for all courses. Number 450 was assigned to all special senior courses in the major.

The effects of the curriculum fight lingered on. Sanborn kept agitating the issues among the faculty. Carmichael had lost some faculty support by leading his committee into the storm and then deserting it in the middle of the fight. With a few exceptions, the "insurgents" were the ablest faculty members. The fight left a bitter taste in their mouths, and most of all for Lanier and Ransom. In 1938 Lanier left Vanderbilt, moving from a lowly assistant professorship to become professor and head of psychology at Vassar. He later had a successful career in university administration and possibly gained some understanding of the strange behavior of Kirkland. Notably, in the curriculum fight the surviving Agrarians at Vanderbilt were all among the so-called insurgents.[27]

Even as the curriculum fight came to a climax, Ransom was agonizing over a compelling offer from Kenyon College. Gordon K. Chalmers, the new president of Kenyon, asked Ransom to come to Kenyon to write poetry and teach philosophy. The offer included a free home and a somewhat higher salary (possibly an additional $1,000, but probably only about $500). Chalmers made his case personally and approached Ransom with the profound respect that Ransom had never received from Kirkland. Mims, in his way, tried to keep Ransom, but his way was not always very helpful. Mims considered trying to raise some additional salary locally (he once received such a supplement) to help Ransom pay off family debts, an approach that seemed patronizing. As it turned out, Ransom this time was not able to wrestle the problem out in private, as he had for earlier offers. His move became, quite literally, a national issue, publicized in every literary journal. Allen Tate, by then one of America's most respected poets and, unlike a more retiring Ransom, a close friend of almost every writer and critic of note, wrote an open letter to the *Tennessean*. In it he quite correctly stressed Ransom's international reputation as one of the most distinguished men of letters in the world. He noted the caliber of students Ransom attracted and emphasized that young Robert Lowell had left New England to enroll at Vanderbilt just to study with Ransom (Lowell, of course, moved with Ransom to Kenyon, as did other able students). Tate stressed the dimensions of the loss, the need for every possible effort to retain Ransom for Vanderbilt and for the South. He ended with some caustic cracks about the inability of chancellors and trustees, men of "organization and finance," to evaluate the work of professors. If Kirkland knew of Ransom's eminence and still remained indifferent, Tate said he could "only pity you, and meditate upon emotions that I shall not easily get my consent to express."

Tate was correct in his harsh judgments. Kirkland had never been quite so irresponsible, so narrowly personal and small-minded, in his whole career. He did not like Ransom and clearly wanted him to leave. As far as the record indicates, Kirkland never once expressed to Ransom any confidence in his ability or even asked him to remain at Vanderbilt. He also refused to make major counteroffers in salary or lowered teaching loads. In fact, his cold but logical response to Tate's letter amounted almost to a recommendation that Ransom go on to Kenyon. Kirkland noted that the "financial conditions" of the offer were so favorable that Ransom "cannot afford to decline the invitation."[28]

The reasons Ransom decided to go to Kenyon are not clear. They seldom are in such cases, not even to the one who moves. Financial considerations were probably not critical, although Ransom did have pressing needs. He never revealed the exact terms of the Kenyon offer. Mims recommended against any matching offer; Kirkland adhered to an old policy of balanced salaries. Since the cuts were still in effect in 1936–37, Ransom's salary for 1937–38 was first set at $3,822, or comparable to his colleague Curry but well behind that of Mims, who was both departmental and divisional head. Kirkland eventually promised $4,200 for the next year, a sum close to the average for full professors in the College. But, as Ransom's friends bitterly pointed out, the football coach received $10,000 and several Medical School professors close to that. Kirkland did not balance salaries on a university level. To critics, this seemed to tell the world how little Vanderbilt valued a distinguished poet and critic. Kirkland did agree, with some reluctance, to add an additional $500 offered by an anonymous donor, but Mims eventually vetoed even this. Kirkland did not even bring up this matter in June, his last board meeting as chancellor. Meanwhile, the university was besieged with letters, telegrams, and petitions. In a few weeks the autograph value of the chancellor's files doubled. Most noted critics and poets enlisted in the cause. *Time* and other national magazines sent reporters and aired all the facts and many of the rumors. Students, led by Randall Jarrell, personally petitioned Kirkland; many graduate students noted that they had come to Vanderbilt to study with Ransom. Newspapers throughout the South felt Vanderbilt's honor at stake if it allowed a small, weakly endowed northern college to steal away its most famous professor.[29]

On June 10 Ransom announced his expected decision to leave. It is possible he would have accepted the offer even if there had been no curriculum fight, even if Mims and Kirkland had begged him to stay, even if Kirkland had gone to the board with an attractive counteroffer. Ransom craved peace and quiet, more time to devote to his criticism. He had tired of the Agrarian effort, felt pressured by so much teaching and committee work, and saw an almost idyllic opportunity at Kenyon, one that allowed him, shortly, to launch the prestigious *Kenyon Review*. These enticements warred against his loyalty to Vanderbilt and to the South. From the perspective of American letters, he made the right choice, for the Kenyon environment was much more conducive to the full flowering of his critical skills. He announced his departure at a special honorary dinner arranged by Tate and Lytle. This dinner, informal, with open invitations and at a local dinner club, was a perfect counterculture affair, a standing rebuke to the formal ceremonies marking the meetings of the Board of Trust and Kirkland's retirement. To one hundred guests, Ford Madox Ford, who presided in white duck trousers, read telegrams from T.S. Eliot, Edmund Wilson, Mark and Carl Van Doren, Henry Canby, Carl Sandburg, Louis Untermeyer, Archibald MacLeish, Katherine Anne Porter, and many others. Students and colleagues testified. In editorials lamenting his decision, some newspapers at least extended the hope that it would be possible to lure him back to the South in the future. In a much more bitter comment, rendered in 1947, a former student of Ransom's, Cleanth Brooks, tried to explain why so many Agrarians moved north, and in part tried to explain his own departure from Louisiana State University. He noted the indifference or hostility of southern universities, particularly toward professors who challenged administrators. Southern universities sought a public reputation, tried to keep up with the times, and thus preferred bowl games to poets, technocrats to humanists. The comment was unfair.[30]

Ransom left Vanderbilt just before he made his greatest impact as a literary critic. He had burned himself out in Agrarian advocacy from 1931 to 1936. He floundered in the complexity and ambiguity of economic policy, and as the depression lessened he realized that he had backed another lost cause. Even the South, so neat and appealing in his earlier, more cerebral descriptions, turned out to be impossibly diverse. With his move to Kenyon, Ransom shifted his interests almost completely to literary matters. Even his philosophical loyalties began to shift. Industrialism in America, now hedged in by humanitarian rules, seemed to allow room for the life of the mind and the flowering of the spirit. Leisure is still a condition of poetry. But the world of the arts is always in some sense an elitist world. He believed students of the arts had always made up a minority culture, in some sense even a subversive one. So long as an industrial society allowed such a minority culture to exist, or provided the material foundations for its flowering, then Ransom could be content in his academic retreat, as he embraced a less catholic and more sectarian view of literary culture.

Ransom kept his increasingly commonplace view of the sciences as sets of mental abstractions, justified if at all only by their humane use. But he no longer defended a thundering god, one he never really encountered or believed in. He once acknowledged that a pious naturalism could meet the ends he earlier tried to fulfill through religious myth. In the later thought of John Dewey, with Dewey's profound respect for the arts, Ransom found a persuasive philosophy. Nature, when given the fullest meaning the word deserves, is much more than the material ball of the physicist. It is the fount of all multifaceted experience, the rightful object of awe and wonder, the content for all our creative efforts. It inspires piety; it sustains art.[31]

At Kenyon, Ransom became best known as one of the founders of a "New Criticism." The label obscures his contribution. He simply recognized, as anyone should, that a critical understanding of any human contrivance—a philosophical argument, a scientific theory, a history, a poem—requires an understanding of the problems faced, of the disciplines or tools used, and of the degree of successful resolution achieved. Literary criticism is, by definition, directed at literary objects, poems in the case of Ransom. Related and peripheral studies—of the poet, of the cultural context—constitute forms of knowledge. They answer questions, but they do not constitute literary criticism. Given this perspective, Ransom tried to hone the tools needed for a critical understanding of poetry. His achievements all relate to very technical problems about the structure and texture of poems, about the involvement of poetry in both cognitive and qualitative experience, and about his complex efforts to develop objective and nondidactic standards of criticism. The subtleties of his views defy any brief explication.[32]

Ransom's former Vanderbilt students, Robert Penn Warren and Cleanth Brooks, did more than Ransom to introduce such a critical perspective into English courses. They published a series of textbooks, beginning with *Understanding Poetry* in 1938, that revolutionized English instruction. Or, perhaps more correctly, they helped turn English courses away from cultural history and toward technical criticism. Whether this shift was desirable or not is a problem for curriculum planners. In any case, a coterie of former Vanderbilt people led this crusade and, this time, they won at least a temporary victory.[33]

Ransom's move broke the back of Vanderbilt's great English department, which for a few years had been the strongest College department ever assembled at Vanderbilt. Even before Ransom made his decision, Randall Stewart chose a better position at Brown University. Mims had to put together a somewhat differently oriented staff. He hired Claude Finney of the University of Illinois, a Harvard Ph.D. and an able Keats scholar, comparable in some ways to Curry. Richmond Beatty, a prolific author and an alumnus, came as an assistant professor but because he published a new biography almost every year would soon rise to full professor. For any other department at Vanderbilt, these two would have been distinguished additions. But neither was a Ransom. The department remained strong, still without an equal in the College, but it lost its preeminence, not so much in scholarship as in poetry, criticism, and creative writing, with only Davidson, now finally a full professor, to maintain that tradition. Until Nixon came back later, he and Owsley were also the only two Agrarians still on campus.[34]

Kirkland must have retired with a great sense of relief. His last few months in office were full of storm and strife. In June, 1936, Kirkland had tried his best to effect an immediate transition to Carmichael. In retrospect, it seems that the university might have gained from this and Kirkland would have retired with more honor. Carmichael, in his later autobiography, took exception to Kirkland's high-handed role in the curriculum fight; he undoubtedly would have let the political process proceed even if it had ended in a few internal fights. And if the Senior College committee had been honored by an open debate and not effectively silenced by administrative fiat, Ransom and Lanier might well have remained on the faculty. Of course, one cannot be sure about such might-have-beens. From Carmichael's standpoint, the year's delay helped. It cleared the decks of controversy and tarnished just a bit the image of Kirkland. He succeeded a fallible mortal, not a god.

Kirkland submitted his formal letter of resignation on January 2, 1937, to be effective not later than July 1. He meant it this time. The board finally saw that the change was in the interest of the university. His forty-four years had now set a record for the head of any major university. In accepting his resignation, the board insisted upon retaining his services as a continuing member of its finance committee and as vice-chairman of the Executive Committee. Kirkland wanted time to write a history of the university and indeed during the next two years wrote several rather thin chapters in pursuit of this goal, chapters that Edwin Mims used, or at times even incorporated, into his history of Vanderbilt. At the February board meeting, next to his last, Kirkland made a strange confession—that the board had left him too much alone, that he had "been permitted to map out the course of the University and its destiny too arbitrarily." The board, he said, had in effect been "me," with major policies conceived and executed by Kirkland. As a strange gift to Carmichael, he now urged the board members to discontinue such deference, to become more involved, to give the new chancellor the benefit of their judgment. At the June board meeting Kirkland offered a graceful little speech, with a brief summary of the achievements of over fifty years, and lamented the new era of necessary retrenchment. His retirement was news, warranting a widely copied and appreciative editorial in the New York *Times*. The praise came from all sides. Kirkland gave an eloquent, moving farewell address at the commencement, blaming the board for keeping him around too long. He left with a final wish list, with goals not yet achieved—primarily more endowments all around and a new Law School building. But implicit in this wish list was a great sense of pride, a sense that the university that Kirkland conceived, and fought for, was now all but complete.[35]

As planned, the board unanimously elected Carmichael as third chancellor, at a salary of $10,000, which they soon raised to $12,000. Carmichael had already attended board meetings as vice-chancellor and had rendered several reports to the board. His formal inaugural came in February, 1938. It led to a published symposium on higher education in the South, and by Carmichael's wishes was more of a scholarly gathering than a ceremonial occasion. The symposiums ranged over arts colleges, law, medicine, engineering, theology, and graduate work. In his inaugural address, Carmichael gave effusive praise to the achievements of the past but yet tried to suggest new directions, to give clues to his goals as chancellor. But not very clear clues. He lacked Kirkland's penchant for terse, direct expression. Carmichael usually floundered in abstractions and generalities, talked fluently and at length without ever taking a firm stand on issues. Loosely, he suggested more flexible admission standards at Vanderbilt. As for college work, he emphasized the most elusive and unchallengeable goals—teaching students how to think, how to be creative or original, how to synthesize facts. He defended the Vanderbilt shift to an intensive major, not just to improve skills but to support a "spirit of learning." He defended both the traditional humanities and the new emphasis upon the social sciences, and hoped that somehow Vanderbilt could enjoy the best of both worlds. Characteristic of so many speeches in the 1930s, he talked of a spirit of unselfishness, of cultivation of the "social interest." Even in plugging a stronger graduate program, he stressed the need for "coordination" and "cooperation," other catchwords of the decade.

Unfortunately, such loose appeals to every conceivable goal or strategy marked most of Carmichael's speeches on higher education. The speeches apparently sounded good; audiences responded well to him, but his mind seemed untidy, so unlike Kirkland's. But, by his very lack of precision, Carmichael became the better politician, the mediator, reconciler, trimmer. He always left himself maneuvering room and somehow managed to be on the winning side. He never confronted anyone; his was always a moving target. He never wielded power in a dictatorial way, but no one ever quite knew where he stood, personally, on controverted issues. The politician swallowed up the person. But, typical of a good politician, he was warm, responsive, much more of a flatterer or charmer than Kirkland, and in these traits most comparable to Dean Sarratt.[36]

Carmichael contributed to some significant changes at Vanderbilt. He did work for a new balance between courses directed primarily at intellectual discipline or self-understanding (English, history, philosophy, math, fine arts, and languages) and those directed at practical mastery (the social and physical sciences). His bias was toward the developing social sciences, not basic research in the physical sciences, and thus toward improved economic and political institutions. He was, as much as Kirkland, an advocate of a new South, but one that Carmichael defined in terms of new administrative and executive skills, new industries, more efficient and effective governments, and a spirit of cooperation and service—once again, goals that easily degenerated into platitudes. He wanted to turn out industrial and political leaders, to offer thoroughly humanized but yet practical courses. He wanted a College better

403

McTyeire Hall, the first real women's dorm

attuned to contemporary southern problems than in the older, more elitist Vanderbilt. These goals did not translate into any major changes at Vanderbilt, beyond those he had already guided—a more flexible curriculum, more specialized training, more emphasis on graduate work, a new emphasis on faculty research, or, in total, what he believed conducive to a "philosophy of social progress." He seemed to blend the new and the old, to wrap modern trends in traditional icons, to have his cake and eat it too. But in one critical area—coeducation—Carmichael was much more sympathetic than Kirkland. Thus, in 1940, the university completed its first real women's dorm, a beautiful McTyeire Hall.

Carmichael's political skills and his emphasis on cooperation had one immediate benefit for Vanderbilt. Even before he became chancellor he began repairing the old rift between Vanderbilt and Peabody. The eventual retirement of Kirkland and the death of President Payne, both in 1937, made this task even easier, but it was the very challenge that best suited Carmichael's diplomatic skills. Thus the creation of a workable University Center and the completion of JUL remained the most tangible achievement of his decade as dean and chancellor.

Kirkland's advice proved prophetic. The board did become more involved in university affairs under Carmichael. Whether this benefited the university or not, such was almost inevitable. After all, Kirkland never achieved his complete dominance of the board until after the church battle of 1914, or halfway through his chancellorship. Carmichael never had so much time. He maintained a very harmonious relationship with the board, although he never gained from it the respect, even the devotion, granted to Kirkland. Board members sensed that they worked with a clever politician. Individual board members seemed a bit wary or suspicious of Carmichael. Kirkland guided the

404

board, at times educated it; Carmichael consulted it, even negotiated with it. When necessary he altered his policies or his language to keep harmony. The results did not seem so different, but in subtle ways the policy-making process was very different—less predictable, more open, tentative, and precarious. This new form of leadership became evident even in the financial management of the university.[37]

When Carmichael became chancellor, Vanderbilt had a total listed endowment of roughly $23 million, but with more reliance on common stock the face value was becoming rather meaningless. In 1937 the treasurer estimated the market value at about $19 million, or an endowment not much larger than in 1930. Negotiations were then well advanced for a GEB grant for a joint library, but the university by then had almost exhausted all foundation support until after World War II. Carmichael was not necessarily a worse fund raiser than Kirkland. In fact, he probably negotiated more successfully with the new generation of foundation directors, and he spent much of his chancellorship on trips to New York and Washington, in traveling the foundation circuit and in all types of consultative work for foundations and government agencies. He soon had more contacts with politicians and government agencies than Kirkland had had, and he moved easily in such circles. This was probably his greatest asset had he remained chancellor in the two decades after World War II. But he took over at a time of dismal prospects.

He soon drew an ace, without which his chancellorship would have floundered in either economic stagnation or red ink. In June, 1938, Frederick W. Vanderbilt died, leaving Vanderbilt a 15 percent share in his total estate and a contingent half-share in another 47 percent, little of which could be realized. The value of the estate was not immediately clear, but before Carmichael resigned in 1945 Vanderbilt had realized over $5 million (again, the securities had fluctuating market values). Before the will was probated, Carmichael had an idea. Why not draft an ambitious plan of development, a wish list, before the Vanderbilt money began to trickle in? If he had such plans, then the Vanderbilt money might qualify as a matching fund for foundation or private gifts. A 1938 board committee worked out a $9 million want list, and in June, 1939, the board approved a new program of expansion in what seemed to be a great new fund drive. Yet, in the publicity the board noted that it did not plan any public canvass, only the quiet solicitation of major givers. More truthfully, the fund drive was a paper scheme artfully contrived to get added mileage out of Vanderbilt's gift. One senses that Kirkland would have vetoed such a scheme, although in his last speech before the board he gave a moving statement in behalf of it.[38]

The development scheme was heady enough to excite everyone. It was Carmichael's blueprint for a great, dominating university in what he often called the south central United States. At the time it was hard to think of anything not included. The Law School was to get $1.25 million ($250,000 for a building); Religion $750,000, most for endowment; Medicine a needed $2 million in additional endowment; Nursing a needed $300,000 in endowment plus $40,000 for small building changes; Engineering an open-ended amount sufficient to provide it a new building and equipment (it still took its operating funds from the general endowment); the College about $3.5 million for educational programs, plus a social science building, a gym, and the new women's dorm; the Graduate School $1 million for research funds, fellowships, film, library materials, higher salaries, and special research professorships, or enough to enable new Ph.D. programs in political science, mathematics, physics, Romance languages, and philosophy and psychology. The key emphasis was on the College, on Carmichael's goal of raising it to the level of the Medical School and of major northern universities.

Nothing much ever happened to fulfill this new scheme. Everyone seemed to forget it during the war. Yet, Carmichael felt bound to prove it a success or his whole administration would have seemed a failure. By some bizarre logic, he declared the goal met by 1945. First of all, he had the $5.25 million Vanderbilt gift as a good starting point. Then Mrs. Neely died and left $250,000, the only significant new gift. The new fee system in the Hospital realized the equivalent of an added $2 million in endowment, so Carmichael counted it. Finally, he decided the new joint library building yielded benefits to Vanderbilt that matched an endowment of $1.6 million. Added together, this made over $9 million. As for specific new needs, the university simply used the Vanderbilt gift. The so-called fund drive yielded nothing. Now, of course, alumni gifts came in each year, at about the rate of $23,000 a year by 1944 (with a 20 percent participation rate). But when alumni wrote embarrassing letters about their contribution to the Living Endowment, about what buildings or programs their gifts helped fund, the university had to admit that, so far, educational programs had never gained a dime from such gifts. All of them, and even additional appropriations, went into the cost of the alumni office. To avoid further such embarrassments, in 1944 the university started budgeting the whole cost of the alumni office, and thus its public relations and development effort, so that it could assign gifts to specific, identifiable projects.[39]

Under Carmichael the university did continue to improve its techniques of financial management. It was now a tremendously large enterprise, with an annual budget of $1,831,000 for 1941–42. The College and the Medical School each had budgets approaching $400,000. After the war the annual budget would quickly rise to over $3 million, while the endowment grew to over $30 million. In 1939, in behalf of fairness and to maximize investment leverage, the treasurer pooled the four endowment funds (Medicine, Nursing, Arts and Science, Religion), and from then on distributed income by a common formula. Each of the four schools simply had a proportionate claim on the whole. In 1941 the university began its first studies on central purchasing. It never implemented such a plan until after the war, but this again indicated the new concern for managerial efficiency.[40]

Prefab barracks, 1946

Library needs proved a magical wand. They brought Vanderbilt, Peabody, and Scarritt together, something all the foundations had failed to achieve for over forty years. As the preceding chapters reveal, Vanderbilt kept talking about a new library just as frequently as it found reasons to postpone building one. In the crunch, the library always had the lowest priority, below observatories, four major classroom buildings, the gym, dorms, the stadium, an auditorium, and a student union. The final and successful effort to build a library went back to 1929. Kirkland finally accepted this as the last major goal of his administration. The need was imperative. In 1930 the main library, located in the old chapel, seated only 120 in its main reading room and operated on an annual budget of $25,000, most contributed by student fees and bookstore income, but with a few periodic grants from the board for special improvements or purchases. In 1930 the university libraries subscribed to about 800 serials, but almost half of these were in medicine, the most favored of the specialized libraries (medicine, religion, law, and several departmental collections, with geology the largest). Altogether, these libraries contained approximately 130,000 volumes, but a large share of these were not available to most students.[41]

In 1929 Kirkland wrote his first formal petition to the GEB for $500,000 to endow a new central library at Vanderbilt. He hoped to raise elsewhere the $500,000 needed to construct a new building. Fortunately, or unfortunately, Peabody submitted its own library request to the GEB at almost the same time. The GEB, as always, jumped at the opportunity for institutional cooperation and expressed its sympathetic interest in a plan for a joint library. The GEB also launched its own study of the library needs of all institutions in Nashville. Two librarians visited Nashville in September, 1931, and reported to the GEB, recommending a library building on the Vanderbilt campus to serve four institutions, not only Peabody but Scarritt and the YMCA College. Peabody was not happy with this original proposal. The GEB made clear that the cooperating universities would have to develop and approve a plan of joint ownership and also raise part of the required funds. After several complex, often tense negotiating sessions, Kirkland and Payne eventually worked out plans for an independent corporation to own a joint building. But any GEB plan required that the two institutions raise matching funds, a near impossibility in 1933. In November, 1934, GEB officials came once again to Nashville to meet with Kirkland and Payne. They gave the two only one more year to complete plans for cooperative ownership and a local fund drive. When the deadline arrived in December, 1935, the GEB noted enough preliminary progress to extend its deadline indefinitely. By then, several things had happened. Carmichael was on campus and would take a larger role in the negotiations. In 1934 the American Council on Education, in its survey of graduate work in the United States, found no adequate facilities in the South. Only twenty-five academic departments were deemed adequate to Ph.D. work; only one was distinguished out of 233 in the United States. No southern university really qualified for a major graduate program. One limitation for almost all southern universities was inadequate libraries. At the very least, this publicized need helped keep the GEB involved.[42]

The institutional logjam yielded only to an initiative from librarians. In March, 1934, Edwin Mims communicated to the GEB a suggestion from Dean Louis R. Wilson of the Graduate Library School at the University of Chicago, one of the two visitors in 1931. Wilson suggested that Vanderbilt procure the services of a competent librarian and let him coordinate plans for the joint effort. A month later Kirkland applied for a $15,000 annual grant, over five years, for some outside person to help solve "the difficult library situation in this locality." GEB officials read Wilson's letter and discussed the plan at Vanderbilt in May. The board granted $15,000 for two years, in part to upgrade the Vanderbilt library, particularly in bibliographical tools. But Kirkland could not find the professional he wanted, and in a less-than-ideal arrangement hired Rudolph H. Gjilaness from the University of Arizona, at an inflated salary of $5,000 for only part-time work. While Gjilaness tried to upgrade the library, A. Frederick Kuhlman came to Nashville in November, 1935, as a representative of the American Library Association to study the libraries of all four adjoining colleges. He became the key to a successful effort

408

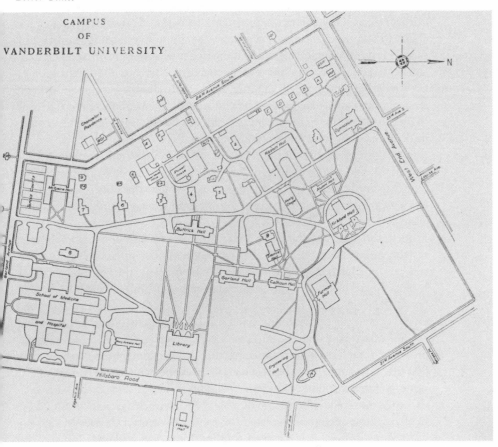

CAMPUS
OF
VANDERBILT UNIVERSITY

The campus as of about 1942

and rightly deserves the title of "Father of JUL." Kuhlman noted not only library needs but a foolish duplication of courses among the four institutions. He quickly grasped the hard message in all this—the foundations would, and should, insist upon a broader cooperation in academic work before they funded any joint library. In a meeting with representatives of all four institutions, in the neutral YMCA College, he impressed everyone with his dazzling vision of a great experiment in regional cooperation, or what everyone now referred to as a developing University Center. Equally important, Kuhlman turned out to be another G. Canby Robinson—the more he explored the possibilities the more enthusiastic and involved he became. He developed a prospectus, as required by his survey, and in it talked of joint libraries as the most challenging and interesting development in modern library work. Such joint efforts could mark a turning point in the development of American university libraries.[43]

Kuhlman set the wheels in motion. A new, joint Vanderbilt-Peabody faculty committee began work on new plans of academic cooperation. Carmichael chaired this joint committee and took the effort as a key test of his ability to become chancellor. Eventually, the committee helped eliminate 280 quarter hours of duplicating work at the two institutions; restricted Peabody courses to education, fine arts, and practical arts; assigned all content courses to Vanderbilt; and left all summer work to Peabody. For junior college students, course exchanges were now fully open, subject only to the approval of the home dean. Senior college students had to major in their home institution but beyond this faced no limits on the amount of work they could take across 21st Avenue if their major professor approved. The same rules applied to graduate work, except here the thesis had to be completed in the home institution. If a graduate student took more than one-fourth of his work away, then he had to accept a joint graduate committee for his final exams.

Such academic cooperation cleared the way for final plans for a joint library system, one including Scarritt and the YMCA, a plan agreed to by the four colleges on March 25, 1936. Vanderbilt University and Peabody set up a Library Board made up of three faculty members from each institution; this board then appointed Kuhlman as the new director of libraries. He very much wanted the position but made some logical demands: that he receive $6,000 salary and that the director's office receive $8,000, that he have professorial rank in both institutions, that he have indefinite tenure (he was first offered a three-year contract), and that he be general director of all the scattered libraries on the two campuses. This evidence of progress was sweet music for the GEB, a culmination of what it had struggled to achieve for years. In effect, these agreements created the Joint University Libraries (JUL) even had the institutions never gained funding for a new building. But only in 1938 did the three institutions (the YMCA College had folded) work out a legal trust agreement on ownership of JUL. By the inauguration of Carmichael in 1938, he could announce a new GEB grant of $1 million (approved in December, 1937), a grant contingent upon the three institutions' raising an equal amount by December 31, 1938. This was Carmichael's first and greatest coup as chancellor, but it faced one enormous peril—the problem of raising great sums in 1938, when a brief but brutal new panic pushed the economy back toward 1933 levels.[44]

Even as the institutions perfected the legal documents, the GEB gave $15,000 a year to pay the director and for the gathering of bibliographical aids. The JUL staff began assembling a joint catalog of all Nashville libraries. The Library of Congress contributed copies of its card catalog. Legally, the new JUL would be owned by a Vanderbilt-Peabody library trust. Faculty members from each served on the Board of Libraries. Each of the three institutions was to assess $25 library fees for all students and in this way share the cost. According to the trust agreement, Peabody and Vanderbilt could amend, modify, or abolish the trust at any time, provided they respect the rights and obligations of Scarritt, which meant Scarritt would receive back all funds it contributed in case of abolition. If either Peabody or Vanderbilt ceased to function, or moved from Nashville, all its rights, duties, and obligations ended, and the rights accrued to the remaining trustee. This meant, in 1979, with Peabody's merger with Vanderbilt, that all rights resorted to Vanderbilt, which continued to protect the interest of Scarritt. It also nullified the familiar old title of JUL.

Despite all the hazards, the fund drive largely succeeded. The Carnegie Corporation contributed $250,000, and the three colleges tried to raise the remaining $750,000, with a major share sought in the Nashville area. The largest gifts often came from business firms. James G. Stahlman chaired an imaginative local drive and deserved credit for its success. For once, the three colleges were in a position of cooperation rather than competition for gifts, and the new library, more than most buildings, represented a major asset for townspeople and won gifts from outlying parts of the South. But the drive never quite reached its goal. Vanderbilt eventually turned over $150,000 of its own funds to the new trust in order to meet the December, 1938, deadline.[45]

Kirkland took an active role in the fund drive. But, increasingly, he showed the frailties of age. He kept on at his history, came to his office almost every day, continued an active role in Medical School financing, and even attended the Board of Trust meeting in June, 1939. In July he moved to his lakeside cabin in Ontario and upon arriving took ill. His close friend and personal physician, Hugh Morgan, attended him during the final weeks; his wife and daughter were at his side. The letters back to Nashville were not very hopeful. He died on August 5, 1939. The eulogies came from all over. The body came back to Nashville for burial at Mt. Olivet. The campus was not in session. But with the fall opening, students and faculty joined for a moving memorial in the auditorium. They sang "O Vanderbilt, Dear Vanderbilt" and the "Iris Song." None of the students present, few of the faculty, could grasp the extent of Kirkland's contribution to Vanderbilt. Not even a present historian can do justice to it. Often mistaken on small issues, less successful in his last years, he proved right on all the major issues. In a fitting gesture the board renamed Old Main (called College Hall in recent years) for Kirkland. It remains the center and core of the campus. Kirkland remains the central figure in Vanderbilt history.[46]

During 1939 Kuhlman and his architect, Henry Hibbs, planned the new JUL building. Vanderbilt donated the site, the one closest to the convergent points of the three campuses. Kuhlman visited twenty libraries to seek out new ideas. He based the final plan on enrollment projections for the three institutions, projections that proved much too modest after the war. The architect chose the collegiate gothic of the Vanderbilt campus, not the more authentic Crab Orchard gothic of Scarritt or the classic revival style of

The new building for the Joint University Libraries, 1941

A reading room in the JUL

JUL *Director A.F. Kuhlman*

PHOTO BY CHARLES WARTERFIELD

Peabody. The style well fit the completed, four-story building, in many ways the most pleasing on the Vanderbilt campus until later architecturally sabotaged by an ill-grafted graduate wing at its front. The seating capacities of the large reading rooms, in the end wings, seemed more than adequate (undergraduate reading room, 160; reference, 135; graduate reading, 150). The School of Religion library moved into the south basement; the other professional libraries, including Peabody's education collection, remained separate. The eight stack floors provided room for about 500,000 volumes; the faculty enjoyed 44 studies; graduate students, 83 carrels. Compared with the old Vanderbilt library, this was the next thing to heaven, particularly in the summer. It was the first centrally air conditioned building on campus, a costly and even somewhat experimental effort predicated not so much upon human comfort as the endurance of books. On opening (a gradual process which began in September, 1941), the library contained fewer than 250,000 books, or not quite half its capacity. The total system contained just over 400,000 volumes; not until 1966 would the JUL collection contain 1 million volumes. But in the South below the Potomac, only Duke, North Carolina, Virginia, and Texas had larger libraries.

The dedication of the glamorous new building took place on December 5 and 6, 1941. Carmichael and Presidents S.C. Garrison of Peabody and J.L. Cuninggim of Scarritt joined in the ceremonies. W.W. Bishop, one of the godfathers, came from Michigan to give a key speech. On Saturday morning speakers from Duke, Emory, and Tulane joined Carmichael in a symposium on university centers. In the afternoon Kuhlman joined two other librarians

413

in a panel on the role of libraries; significantly, one of the two panelists was Harvie Branscomb from Duke. In the evening representatives of the GEB and the Carnegie Corporation spoke at the dedication. The tired guests left the long evening program with no intimations of what lay immediately ahead, but before some tired participants awakened the next morning, Japanese planes were on their way toward Pearl Harbor.[47]

16

War Times

W<small>AR</small>. It came so soon again, as if an inevitable affliction of each generation. But this time the issues seemed very different than in 1917. Competing ideologies confused earlier and simpler forms of imperial conflict. More was now at stake. In a larger perspective, the two world wars were part of a single complex era of change and struggle, or what future historians may characterize as the Thirty Years' War of the twentieth century, a war broken by a long but uneasy truce. The destructions of the first phase, dynastic and traditional as it seemed, created deep class and ideological tensions, as well as national frustrations and jealousies, that insured that the next open conflict would have the intensity of past religious wars. This time, war would be total, with civilian populations as major targets.

The United States gradually increased its involvement in the world struggle after 1938, but not without deep internal policy conflicts. Pearl Harbor clarified the issues, all but ended the disagreements over policy. Consensus prevailed as in no earlier war. Without the anxieties, the secret or open doubts, of World War I, Americans went to war with greater maturity— without the fantastic execesses, the romantic expectations, the hysterical patriotism, the ugly repression of 1917–18. For Vanderbilt, World War II threatened much greater disasters than in fact occurred. Problems, and thus deep insecurities, were inescapable. But the threatened collapse of enrollment, the expected budgetary deficits, always lurked just ahead, for next year. Next year never came.

In their foreign-policy outlooks the majority of Vanderbilt students and faculty seemed to follow closely the gradually increased commitments to the Allies that characterized the Roosevelt administration. In the mid-1930s a majority of Vanderbilt students had joined in the student peace movement, but not in as large numbers, and not as intensively, as students on northern campuses. In the Student Strike for Peace in 1935 and 1936, Vanderbilt students marched in Nashville with other area college students, but the strongest leadership came from Scarritt. Neither pacifist nor fervent noninterventionist sentiment ever prevailed at Vanderbilt.

The peace movement drew much of its strength from political radicals, from socialists and communists on northern campuses. Vanderbilt had no more than a dozen such radicals. In the Midwest, traditional Anglophobia, or pro-German sentiment, added a special flavor to revisionist attacks on World War I involvement, another perspective all but absent at Vanderbilt. What one senses, from the new *Hustler* polls, was a Vanderbilt student body strongly inclined to support national policy, to go along with the president. On campus, the pervasive advocacy of D.F. Fleming in behalf of collective security and an early support of the Allied cause undoubtedly influenced some of the Arts and Science students. So, perhaps, did the strong internationalist position taken by Chancellor Carmichael. But such commitments should not suggest a campus up in arms against fascism. For the most part, Vanderbilt students remained fully absorbed in local or campus concerns.[1]

Unlike Americans at the beginning of World War I, most Americans by 1939 considered the merits of the Allied cause to be obvious, a viewpoint shared by most of the Vanderbilt community. The one exception, as elsewhere, was within the German department. In 1933 John Frank, a German professor who had been born in Germany, defended Hitler's new order and emphasized that nothing was further from his mind than to wage war. Frank took twenty students on a summer tour of Germany in 1936. For a time, Sanborn was a near ally, for he still nourished bitter memories of World War I and still believed the League of Nations reflected the "sinister purposes" of international bankers. Soon the only acknowledged pro-German sentiment was in the German department, but even this was enough to support a wild campus rumor in 1940 that the FBI had Vanderbilt faculty members under investigation. To squelch the rumors, Carmichael had to solicit a denial from J. Edgar Hoover. Polls of the faculty in 1940 showed overwhelming support for the Allies. But a few, such as Sanborn and Owsley, still wanted complete neutrality. D.F. Fleming took the strongest interventionist stand and helped organize a new international relations club. Of course, draft-age students were ambivalent. They hoped somehow that American aid could help the Allies win short of actually going to war. In contrast to student fervor in 1917, few students now yearned for the glory of combat. *Hustler* editorials consistently stressed the horrors of war, one lingering echo of the earlier peace crusade. In 1941 Vanderbilt students voted four to one in favor of Roosevelt's decision to convoy American ships all the way to England. By May, 1941, half the Vanderbilt students believed the United States would be at war with Germany by October. In the same month, students joined in a strongly interventionist Student Defenders of Democracy, and 224 faculty and staff members wired Roosevelt urging immediate entry into the war. But despite such a growing belief in the inevitability of war, or open support for immediate intervention, the Pearl Harbor attack still came as a shock. Students gathered in silence and occasional tears to hear Roosevelt's war message on December 8.[2]

Vanderbilt was ill situated for war. Not only in 1920, but again in 1935, the faculty had vetoed an ROTC unit on campus. In 1937 the army approved an ROTC unit for the Medical School, the only military organization on campus at the time of Pearl Harbor. By 1940, and the first military draft, the university had realized its vulnerability—male students began to choose competing universities with ROTC units. The university suffered a frightening enrollment drop in the fall of 1941. By then, Vanderbilt officials were trying their best to get an ROTC unit, either army or navy. Army investigators came, inspected, and approved Vanderbilt's facilities, but in 1941 the army did not have the officers for additional units. A spring 1941 application to the navy came closer to success. The faculty voted for such a unit, Carmichael enlisted the support of Tennessee congressmen, but Vanderbilt ended up ninth in a competition among twenty-eight colleges. The navy established only eight new units, and not until the last year of the war did it approve such a unit for Vanderbilt.[3]

The declaration of war had little immediate effect on Vanderbilt. The draft was already in place and the military could not immediately call up all eligible men. It had too few training facilities. Already, in the fall of 1941, students had organized a home guard unit, and volunteer officers had begun drill for about sixty students. Throughout the war this remained the only military organization open to regular students. Because of military preparedness efforts, the College had already added defense-related courses and advisors helped young men select majors that might win them exemption from draft boards. After Pearl Harbor the faculty tried almost desperately to find ways of retaining students. It so revised admission requirements in the College as effectively to eliminate the foreign-language requirement. It established a summer school to allow a three-year degree program, and soon both admitted and graduated students each quarter. Later in the war it added evening courses. The Medical School began an intense, twelve-month training program, even as many of its professors entered the military. Then, in July, 1942, an all-Vanderbilt medical and nursing unit (the 300th General Hospital) went on active duty, further reducing the hospital staff. Early in 1942 the College first required two hours of military drill for freshman and sophomore students, and then extended this to reluctant juniors and seniors before the year ended. To save gasoline, college students agreed to schedule meetings and even social events in the afternoon; in the fall of 1942 the opening classes moved from 8:00 to 8:30 to help relieve congestion on Nashville busses.

Such modifications and adjustments still left the campus vulnerable as mobilization progressed. The fullest mobilization came only in 1943. To the surprise of everyone, Vanderbilt's enrollment climbed slightly in the fall of 1942; only the Law School and the Graduate School suffered severe losses. Since fifteen professors were already on leave, many classes were crowded. But the erosion really began during the year, as 659 dropped out, shrinking the total university civilian enrollment from 1,835 in the fall to about 1,100 by the next June. By the fall of 1943 the College and Engineering school had only 600 civilian undergraduates, a number that dropped even more in 1944. Special military units on campus more than made up for the civilian losses, but only in a most chaotic sense. Units came and left during quarters, creating endless confusion. Yet, the various military contracts saved Vanderbilt from major deficits.[4]

Military contracts most benefited Nursing and Engineering. The Nursing School moved to an accelerated schedule and soon worked closely with the military. In 1943 all its graduates volunteered for the armed forces, for all became part of a Cadet Nurse Corps. The government paid all expenses and a small stipend; the candidates agreed to serve in the military after graduation. This program ended all financial problems in the school and boosted enroll-ment after 1943 (to 200 by war's end). By 1943, almost all medical students were also involved in one or another military units.[5]

The Engineering School boomed as never before. Civilian students flocked to its militarily approved programs up through 1942, and then several military contracts took up the slack. Already, the school had the preflight training program, which now began to give early training to military pilots. In 1940 the Tennessee Department of Education used Engineering facilities to train WPA workers for special defense jobs. Such contractural arrangements brought money to the school; the trainees did not earn regular college credits. Engineering also most benefited from other training programs. Vanderbilt, along with most universities, accepted Navy Reserve V-7 trainees, a program that allowed juniors and seniors to remain in college until graduation. Eventually, Vanderbilt also recruited a few freshmen and sophomores for a Navy Reserve V-1 program. In April, 1942, Vanderbilt gained permission to recruit students into the Army Air Force Reserve Corps, or a type of preflight preparation well suited for seventeen- and eighteen-year-olds. Most who entered as freshmen had to go into active duty long before gaining a degree, but such an arrangement attracted beginning students, most of whom chose work in Engineering. In November, 1942, Vanderbilt contracted with the Army Air Force to offer a one-year, premeteorology training program for up to 200 men. This, the first active duty unit at Vanderbilt, was in residence from February, 1943, to February, 1944. The overworked trainees attended specified courses mainly in math, physics, and engineering, but with limited time for lectures in history and English. They took over Kissam Hall.

The largest active duty program involved an Army Specialized Training Division (ASTD), which began at Vanderbilt in April, 1943. This large training program involved about 700 men, who so dominated the campus as to provoke almost as much resentment from civilian students as did the SATC during World War I. The women were most inconvenienced, for they had to surrender McTyeire Hall to the troops, moving into nearby homes. Over half the ASTD boys enrolled in basic engineering courses; other groups took medical courses or foreign area studies. Again, Vanderbilt trained only one group in this rigorous, one-year program, which began and ended in the middle of normal quarters.[6]

The men of the 300th Hospital Unit in Italy, 1943

The women of the 300th Hospital Unit in Italy, 1943

The military programs never displaced regular, civilian students. Only in 1943–44 did active duty, full-time military students come close to equaling the regular students, many of whom were in various reserve units. This time, unlike 1918, women only briefly outnumbered regular men students. Vanderbilt refused to raise the quota of fifty for entering freshman women in the College. Chancellor Carmichael explained that the policy was intended to insure that Vanderbilt would continue, primarily, "to serve the needs of men students." A higher percentage of women "might have in time a definite effect on the outlook and program" of Vanderbilt. Inevitably, tensions developed between soldiers and civilians. One Army Air Force commander practically threatened vigilante action when regular students refused to stand or salute the lowering of the flag. Professors in the humanities and social sciences bemoaned the military requirements, which almost by-passed or made cursory their courses. Even the Board of Trust had to reiterate its support for a broad liberal education. The cadets, under speeded-up programs, had little time for extracurricular activities; they joined no fraternities or clubs and rarely even had time to attend dances. But at odd moments they ogled the women.[7]

The Vanderbilt faculty suffered in the war. Younger men faced the draft; older ones often left for special war work. Francis Slack, and eventually several graduate students in physics, worked on the atomic bomb project. The remaining faculty faced chaotic schedules, extra teaching loads, and a twelve-month schedule. Worst of all were the hot summer months, before air conditioning came to classrooms. In the humanities, courses often enrolled only women and a few physically unfit (4-F) men. Because only a few teaching fellows or female instructors remained on campus, senior professors had to teach beginning work and grade enormous stacks of exams and papers. Up until 1942 professors gained salary increases to compensate for higher wartime prices, but after that a wage freeze stopped most raises except at times of promotion. Of all the faculty, those in the Medical School suffered the most from a lack of adequate staff and from the speeded-up program. The Engineering faculty suffered the most from inadequate facilities and during the war began planning a new building. The School of Religion remained the most normal. The faculty in the College and in Engineering had extra committee duties and had to go through all the motions of patriotic commitment, including leadership in war bond and community chest drives. Carmichael formed a faculty war council to develop special war-related programs.[8]

Even in the midst of war Vanderbilt had to recruit new faculty members as existing ones took leaves, resigned, or retired. The retirement of Sanborn in 1942 led to the appointment of Robert Calhoun Provine as professor of philosophy and psychology; he had his Ph.D. degree from Brown but was a Vanderbilt alumnus. The departure of Dean Pomfret in 1942 created a critical vacancy. Carmichael had a major role in choosing his successor. He picked a friend, Philip G. Davidson, Jr., from Agnes Scott College. Davidson was a forty-year-old historian (colonial United States), a Mississippian, with graduate degrees from Chicago and one important book to his credit. Later, Davidson came within an inch of being chancellor and served for years as dean. Departures included Dean Paschal, who resigned in 1944; Dean Clark, who married historian Herbert Weaver and left to join her husband in the military (another historian, Nora Chaffin, came from Duke as the new dean of women); and, quite unexpectedly, division head Edwin Reinke, who died in January, 1945.

Several junior men gained promotions or received them upon their return from military services. Meredith Crawford, who moved as assistant professor from Barnard to Vanderbilt in 1940 in psychology, returned from a brilliant military career to become new dean of the Junior College and a full professor. In 1944, after a long search, Vanderbilt appointed William Stead as head of business administration and director of the Institute for Research and Training in the Social Sciences and Business Administration. (By 1945, the institute had an annual budget of $20,000, and after a wartime suspension once again revived an internship program for students and awarded up to $6,000 annually for faculty research.) Stead came from the deanship of the school of Business Administration at Washington University, at what many colleagues believed an inflated salary of $8,000, only to leave less than two years later. Even during the war the College faculty increased its involvement in scholarship. In 1941, the GEB granted $25,000, on a matching basis, for research in the natural sciences. During the war the university funded up to $10,000 of such research each year. This left only the humanities without a research fund. The Vanderbilt University Press continued to turn out monographs, some written by Vanderbilt professors. As of 1942, William C. Binkley assumed the editorship of the *Journal of Southern History,* moving its offices to the Vanderbilt campus. Dan Robison also edited the *Tennessee Historical Quarterly* at Vanderbilt.[9]

In the Medical School fully half of the senior staff left for military duties, with Hugh Morgan rising to the rank of brigadier general. In order to insure his return, the university supplemented his military salary. Sadly, the great staff assembled in 1925 slowly faded away. Horton R. Casparis, in pediatrics, died in 1942, to be succeeded briefly by Vanderbilt's first female acting head outside Nursing—Katherine Dodd. The next year Amos Christie came from California to head the department; Dodd resigned in 1945. In 1945 both Walter Garrey, physiology, and Dean Leathers retired. Leaders gained widespread recognition during his last years, serving as president of the American Public Health Association in 1940 and as president of the Association of American Medical Schools in 1942. Early in 1946 he died. William W. Frye took his place as head of the department of public health and preventive medicine. Goodpasture took the deanship. Why is hard to explain. He had rejected a deanship at the Johns Hopkins in 1942 and already had the highest professorial salary at Vanderbilt ($11,000). He was, by the war, the most honored scientist in the South and a member of the National Academy of Sciences (an honor not yet achieved by anyone in the College). Administrative duties now diverted him from his research and proved personally unrewarding. His talents clearly lay elsewhere. Once again, in an old pattern, Vanderbilt asked its ablest scholars and scientists to take on administrative duties.[10]

Wartime needs helped account for a major new effort in university cooperation—the Nashville School of Social Work. The need for such a school had seemed obvious for years. In 1934 the Federal Emergency Relief Administration first contracted with Vanderbilt for the training of social workers, a limited contractual arrangement that continued for two years and largely involved the sociology department. The Medical School also had offered several special courses for social workers. But the founding of a separate school awaited the completion of JUL and closer cooperation among Vanderbilt, Peabody, and Scarritt. In 1942 the GEB offered $40,000 to support a new school in Nashville during its fledgling first three years. Lora Lee Pederson of Scarritt took the lead in seeking such a grant and became director of the school, which opened in the fall of 1942. It used a Scarritt-owned house just to the north of Wesley Hall. The school offered a two-year master's degree, with a combination of courses and field work. In 1942 forty-three students enrolled, and the number grew slowly each year. Its board consisted of the administrative officers and two trustees from each of the three cooperating institutions. Vanderbilt acted as fiscal agent and awarded degrees. Scarritt furnished the quarters. Peabody provided dorms for its largely women students. By 1945 it had gained full accreditation. Social service agencies in the area provided the opportunity for field work and funded several scholarships. The school had one major problem—insecure funding. The GEB extended its support for a second three years in 1945, but by 1948 the school had to gain its own endowment.[11]

Vanderbilt was somewhat less involved in another University Center venture—the Southern Rural Life Council. Planned in 1942 and 1943, this council brought together community leaders in such fields as education, agriculture, health, religion, and industrial development. Peabody took the lead in its creation and early direction of the council, including its conferences and a series of publications directed at rural problems.

War meant a serious time for civilian students. They joined in bond drives, gave blood, gathered old magazines for servicemen, collected scrap metal, and joined in a dozen other morale-boosting causes. Women students attended obligatory dances for area servicemen. By edict of the faculty, the fraternities had to give up all remnants of hazing and cancel hell week. Disobedience meant suspension. With so many students tied to the military, the women gained an enlarged role in extracurricular activities. In 1942–43 a woman became editor of the *Hustler,* the first in its history. The honor system, now perennially in crisis, once again floundered in wartime chaos. Another committee, at least the tenth in the history of the College, investigated, found cheating most prevalent among freshmen and football players, and urged tough new enforcement measures.[12]

The major wartime controversy on campus involved, of all things, a new institution—Religious Emphasis Week (REW). During the 1930s the old YMCA and YWCA joined in a more inclusive Student Christian Association (SCA). Henry Hart, the former YMCA secretary, continued as director of this campuswide religious organization. Because he received his salary and budget from the university, he was in reality the campus chaplain. As part of his duties he had coordinated all the federal work programs for students, even as the old YMCA had operated a campus placement office. Hart typified YMCA leaders in his tolerance, his liberal theological stance, and his concern with social issues. Even though nominally Christian, the SCA activities often included Jewish students in the 1930s (one of these was Fannye Rose "Dinah" Shore). During the 1930s the SCA brought to campus several eminent speakers each year but discontinued the old YMCA revivals. These did not fit the age or the campus. In 1942 Hart, assisted by a student and faculty committee, inaugurated a new, concentrated series of lectures and discussions and, following the lead of many other campuses, called this REW. With one keynote speaker and up to a dozen other lecturers or discussion leaders, the 1942 experiment was deemed a great success by everyone. Local churches cooperated, as did a Jewish rabbi.

Hart joined student and faculty leaders in planning an even more elaborate REW for January, 1943. Significantly, Herman C. Nixon was the faculty sponsor. He and Hart shared advanced views on such controversial issues as Negro equality and the role and place of labor unions. They decided to adopt as a theme "The Campus and the Changing World." They invited E. McNeil Poteat, a Baptist minister from Cleveland, as the principal speaker. Of the thirteen other invited speakers, four or five represented the socially radical side of Christianity. Hart and Nixon chose them, quite deliberately, to inform and challenge Vanderbilt students on the two issues of Negro rights and labor management relations.[13]

The events of REW brought to a head brewing ideological conflict at Vanderbilt, conflict that always involved race. From the heyday of Alva Taylor in the 1930s, a small, loose group of radical students, some in Religion and some in the College, had continued to speak out on controversial issues at Vanderbilt. They had allies at Scarritt and at Peabody. On the faculty, H.C. Nixon in the College and George Mayhew in Divinity were most sympathetic. In April, 1942, the Southern Conference for Human Welfare met in Nashville. Nixon was very active in the organization. A friend of Alva Taylor and of Mayhew, James Dombrowski of the Highlander Folk School, helped plan this conference. The first such conference had met in Birmingham in 1938. It developed out of an ugly kidnapping and beating of a liberal-left

Jewish prolabor reformer in Alabama, and his early plans for a conference on civil liberties in the South. The victim of the kidnapping, Joseph Gelders, joined with Lucy Randolph Mason, a descendent of founding father George Mason and a deeply involved racial activist and later CIO representative in the South, to plan the 1938 conference. Mason conferred with her friend, Eleanor Roosevelt; Gelders sought out H.C. Nixon and other southerners. As a result of such contacts, the planned conference grew into a major event, a rallying of a vast array of southerners from the center to the left of the political spectrum. The conference had the official blessings of Franklin D. Roosevelt and became entangled with his efforts to purge his party of "conservatives" such as Georgia's Senator Walter George. Thus, loyal New Dealers, including governors and congressmen, several editors, CIO union organizers, a few Catholic workers, several representatives of the American Socialist Party, six communist Party members, representatives of native American radical causes such as Highlander Folk School and the Southern Tenant Farmers Union, and a group of social gospel ministers all united at the first conference. One of Alva Taylor's more radical ministerial students, Howard Lee, became a leader in the continuing organization and helped establish its offices in Nashville. What turned out to be most newsworthy about the first conference was the equal participation of blacks and, until the Birmingham police intervened, integrated seating in all the meetings. From 1938 to 1942 and the Nashville Conference, the organization floundered and lost some of its more moderate membership. But it continued to support civil liberties and civil rights, and from the beginning it had led campaigns against lynching and the poll tax.[14]

The Nashville Conference of 1942 attracted national news coverage. The 500 delegates included Eleanor Roosevelt (a *Hustler* reporter even interviewed her) and as guest singer the great Negro baritone, Paul Robeson. H.C. Nixon headed a panel on agriculture. A *Tennessean* editor chaired a panel on citizenship and civil liberties, a panel that advocated poll-tax repeal and the right of laborers to organize and bargain. Clark Foreman, a close friend of Will W. Alexander, a leading advocate of Negro rights in the New Deal, chaired the conference. About one-third of the delegates were blacks, a good share from the Nashville area. The Vanderbilt student delegation was led by Howard Katz, a brilliant Vanderbilt student, a championship debater, a *Hustler* editor, and the ablest chess player on campus. For many in Nashville, the integrated meetings at the War Memorial Building, and the appearance of Robeson, were close to scandalous. Eleanor Roosevelt presented one of two Thomas Jefferson awards for distinguished contributions to the South to Mary McLeod Bethune, a Negro educator; the other went to Frank Graham, then president of the University of North Carolina. Robeson, in comments before his singing, urged the release from prison of former Communist Party leader Earl Browder and identified Browder as the first American to warn against fascism.

All of this was too much for most people at Vanderbilt. Hill Turner, the cranky editor of the *Alumnus,* could not restrain his distaste for Eleanor Roosevelt, even as he presented two contrasting student views. In fact, the conference did not take as radical a stand as the critics suggested. Even Eleanor Roosevelt, although firm on the need to end all racial barriers of a legal sort, did not advocate social equality. A panel that condemned racial and religious bigotry still defended segregated facilities. But a Vanderbilt student—Jack Paul Jones—published a warning about the Southern Conference in the *Hustler.* He acknowledged the need for better race relations but wanted all steps to achieve this goal to be taken by "democratic, conservative" groups, those of a balanced mind. The goal, he said, was ill served by integrated meetings, by an award by the First Lady to a Negro. Such radical "off-beam people" only angered the majority of whites in the South. He used Robeson's remarks, not to characterize the view of most delegates, but as evidence that the leaders of the Southern Conference used racial issues as a front for Communist loyalties. He also, quite correctly, pointed to a small Communist element in the Southern Conference. Katz, who also debated with Jones over this issue on campus, wrote a stinging letter in reply. He said charges of communism diverted attention from the fundamental issues, noted that the conservative solution to the race issue was to do nothing at all, and defended the Southern Conference as the one organization that tried to "extend democracy to all groups" and "to combat bigotry and prejudice and fascism . . . ."[15]

The controversy over the Southern Conference for Human Welfare set the stage for the REW controversy. Three of the same personalities would be involved—Nixon, Katz, and Lucy Mason. As a lead-in to the religious activity, one of the most radical social activists within American Protestantism came to Nashville in November, 1942. Harry F. Ward, then in the Department of Social Ethics at Union Theological School, came to Nashville on a speaking tour sponsored by the American Committee on Soviet Relations. He visited D.F. Fleming's course and used the occasion to argue that the Soviet Union enjoyed democracy and religious freedom. His speech was so flagrantly pro-Soviet, so much a one-sided apology, that students perceived in his mission the illegitimate use of religion as a cover for political propaganda.[16]

The REW lasted from January 18 through January 22, 1943, and received a small financial contribution from the Board of Trust. Poteat led the noncontroversial morning meetings in the auditorium. The other invited speakers held over 100 meetings, some in fraternity houses. Some visited classes at professors' invitation. Some joined in six forums or debates. One each of the special forums dealt with race and with labor relations, the only issues that became sources of controversy. Lucy Mason, now public relations officer of the CIO, led the discussions on labor, and both in a forum and in classrooms took such a prounion stand as to shock many Vanderbilt students. Joseph Fletcher, dean of the Graduate School of Applied Religion in Cincinnati, a deeply committed young Episcopal clergyman, later famous as an advocate of "situational ethics," took the strongest stand against what he called "capitalism." Howard McClain, a theological student and former undergraduate, a minister committed to the welfare of blacks, personally defended black equality. Dean W.J. Faulkner of Fisk University, a black educator, came by invitation to the forum on race and in his remarks celebrated the Negro struggles in behalf of equality, noted in a rather conciliatory way the obstructions used by whites, and during a heated discussion, and in response to badgering questions from some disruptive medical students, seemed to endorse black-white intermarriage. In fact, he only noted the 8 million people of mixed blood already in the country. He did support complete social equality.

The discussions fulfilled one purpose of the organizers. They stimulated intense student reactions. From the perspective of Hart and Nixon, the controversial issues were all essentially related to religious faith, even at the heart of religious commitment. The more shocking statements came from clergymen or from Lucy Mason, who placed her work for unions in the context of Christian obligation. Of course, definitions of religion are a dime a dozen and, as many students defined the word, some sessions were not about religion at all. Students believed protagonists used a religious excuse to push private racial or economic views. Notably, these charges never arose except in the context of what students perceived as radical opinion. Poteat and other ministers addressed social issues in general terms, or talked about the war and postwar issues from a religious perspective, all to no protest.[17]

In the immediate aftermath of REW, a group of campus leaders drafted a petition and gained for it over 300 signatures. According to one participant, the instigators were members of the leading honorary leadership society, ODK, represented the fraternities on campus, and had as one goal the removal of Henry Hart from the campus. George Ed Wilson, president of the student council; William Freeland, president of the honor council; and Ann Stahlman, the daughter of Board of Trust member James Stahlman, headed the petition drive and also protested directly to Chancellor Carmichael. The petition, drafted with the assistance of Donald Davidson, was more restrained in wording than in its total effect and did not reveal the underlying antipathy toward Hart or toward such student activists as Harold Katz. The 320 students protested certain regrettable features of the week, namely, a failure to consult a representative student group in selecting speakers; the questionable philosophical views of certain speakers who confused students, a confusion harmful to students and damaging to the nation and to the national welfare; an inadequate representation "of the conservative viewpoint held by the great majority of Vanderbilt students"; the promotion of "disturbing social and economic questions" of an inflammatory nature in the name of religion, and particularly racial and capital-labor issues; and the use of an ostensibly religious awakening to propagandize the views of "a radical minority" on campus and to suggest to outsiders that such views represented the opinions of Vanderbilt students and faculty.

The petitioners requested an end to the circumstances that allowed such "embarrassing conditions to arise." An "observer" contributed an editorial to the *Hustler* that reflected the same views. The Nashville *Banner* carried a story about the student petition and in an editorial defended it. The *Tennessean* gave a more detailed account of events on campus and justified the discussion of controversial issues. The wire services picked up on the local accounts and aired the campus controversy to the country as a whole, to the embarrassment of Vanderbilt administrators and the Board of Trust. On campus, a few students defended the most radical speakers, while the *Hustler* deplored the outside agitation. Harold Katz took advantage of the controversy to rally students from the three campuses into a new interuniversity forum, both to discuss and act on social problems. For its first biweekly meeting it invited Joseph Fletcher, for the second Kenneth Boulding of Fisk, and before the year ended began abortive plans for a cooperative, student-owned dormitory.[18]

Given all the publicity, Carmichael quickly lost control over events. The board took over, the first time it had ever so directly involved itself with internal campus issues. James Stahlman, although on military duty in New Orleans, was soon at the center of the controversy. Both his daughters, students at Vanderbilt, gave him detailed accounts of REW and of the petition effort. His managing editor, Charles Moss, also wrote, blaming the whole incident on Henry Hart and Harold Katz, who had "a field day for racial equality and Communistic ideas. . . ." Moss lambasted Fletcher for urging workers to vote for the CIO, for bringing "liberal" speakers to his Cincinnati campus, and for backing the Spanish loyalists. Stahlman wrote Frank Rand, president of the board, expressing his bitter resentment of the whole proceedings and indicting Henry Hart as an improper minister for Vanderbilt students, suggesting that it "would do well to rid itself of such unwholesome influences." Stahlman protested even more vigorously to Carmichael, stressing that this was no time for Vanderbilt students "to be subjected to more confusion . . . over such highly controversial matters as the race issue and the doctrines of labor organizations tainted with Communism." He stressed the harm of having a Fisk professor on campus and suggested the race issue was coming to a showdown soon enough. That these issues were discussed under the cover of religion amounted to a fraud on Vanderbilt students.

Stahlman asked Carmichael to launch a full investigation and to supervise campus programs in the future so as to prevent Vanderbilt from becoming a sounding board for radicalism. Fitzgerald Hall, Stahlman's fellow board member and the one who most clearly shared his political outlook, was, if anything, even more incensed by the affair after Stahlman wrote him about it. Hall did not believe it was "within the realm of 'academic freedom' to advocate doctrines inimical to the American system of government. . . ." He asked for a thorough investigation by the board and raised the possibility of firing Hart from his position. Given such pressures, Carmichael as always bent with the wind. He offered a brief report on REW at the February 10 board meeting, praised Poteat's lectures, but called the program "not as well balanced" and student reaction "not as favorable" as he would have wished. He cited the controversial issues as inappropriate for REW and promised that such programs would not continue in the future. An extensive but unrecorded board discussion followed; Stahlman later described it as heated and noted that the board insisted on the removal of Hart from the campus. Carmichael held out for, and won, a one-year extension so that Hart would be eligible for retirement. The board, in its final action, mandated that Carmichael carry out a full investigation "and handle the matter at his discretion." The last phrase reflected a board effort to downplay any internal division or any hint of any lack of confidence in Carmichael. In fact, Carmichael's discretion was very limited. On February 5, both in response to students and his board, he asked the committee on student life and interest to investigate the REW program, with Dean Sarratt as chair.[19]

Sarratt's committee rendered its report on March 17 to the Executive Committee of the Board of Trust. The committee included an assistant dean, the dean of women, and the deans of the Junior College, of Law, and of Engineering. It gave a detailed report on the various programs of the week, extensively investigated the sessions conducted by the four most controversial speakers, and in general placed the events in a clear perspective. As the *Hustler* had pointed out, as astonished speakers testified, student reactions had not been all that negative. Possibly as many students approved the more controversial programs as those who signed the petition. In a modern perspective, the report leaves one wondering what all the excitement was about. The committee nonetheless rendered an adverse report and thus confirmed the intentions of the board. It stressed that any program protested by 320 students had to involve serious failures. Its members argued that the planners placed too much emphasis on "racial, social, and economic issues," especially deplored the airing of racial problems in a "time of great racial tension," argued that the program was too ambitious in topics covered, and stressed the unfortunate choice of certain speakers (presumably the four radicals). They recommended that such large-scale programs in the future be cleared by the faculty. They denied that either the students, or the committee, saw these precautions as any threat to freedom of speech or discussion, which were Vanderbilt traditions. They only protested the airing of controversial issues under the auspices of religion. The committee said the university, in presenting controversial issues, "should undertake to see that they are handled by those equipped to handle them wisely." It should not "provide a forum for crackpots or extremists." The committee never defined "crackpots" or suggested who had the authority to exclude them. Its report was as weak a defense of free discussion as one could imagine. It also amounted to a vote of no confidence in Hart and in such faculty members as Nixon and Mayhew.[20]

The climax came at the June, 1943, board meeting. In the most polite way possible, Carmichael not only announced the intended termination of Hart but the elimination of his office. After a full review of the religious program, he and Dean Benton had decided to shift away from the existing SCA pattern. The faculty and students of the School of Religion were to take over the chaplaincy role performed by Hart; Benton was also to be dean of the chapel. For 1943–44, Benton and his crew would limit themselves to the military units, leaving the SCA to function for one more year. In other words, Hart would be out as of July 1, 1944. As it turned out, this proved too soon for his retirement, and Carmichael, by subsequent board permission, continued him in his position until March, 1945, and paid his salary during a leave that lasted until September 1, 1945, the earliest the YMCA would grant him an annuity. This was, at least, a series of humane gestures to a man who had served for seventeen years, and who now had to leave under board attack. Hart's wife, Helene, continued to teach speech courses for another decade in the College, and Hart gained some additional YMCA assignments. Carmichael also recommended in 1943 that the formerly independent SCA now come under the supervision of the committee on student life and interest. This meant, in effect, that a dutiful Sarratt would replace a controversial Hart as arbiter of religious programming, or what in fact meant the end of an independent religious voice on campus. The SCA student advisory committee became just that—merely advisory.[21]

Even as the REW issues boiled, another troubling policy issue surfaced, the status of intercollegiate athletics at Vanderbilt, an issue that eventually aligned the faculty against the board. The story began in the mid-1930s, possibly at the death of Dan McGugin. A reluctance to hire Ray Morrison, at $10,000, for the first time brought the Vanderbilt administration into conflict with alumni groups and, beyond them, a rather substantial local constituency for a stronger football program. Kirkland hated what was happening and with his usual bluntness made his views known before the board in 1936. Football, he argued, had ceased to be a campus activity; it was a "public spectacle." Alumni had helped make it so, with all the pressures for victory. Now, coaches were higher paid than anyone except chancellors. Winning was necessary. Colleges competed for players. Football had ceased to be an amateur sport, as colleges bought or hired players under the euphemism of "scholarships." The new Southeastern Conference had abetted, not prevented, such trends. In 1936 it openly approved pay for players, if not in grants at least in loans for made work. Vanderbilt players earned $600 a year by Kirkland's calculations. The Vanderbilt faculty was helpless, the athletic association increasingly in debt as it struggled to make it in a professional league. Kirkland received no answer and addressed a board already quite sympathetic to winning football. Kirkland thus began a debate but for a time no one took up his challenge. Only Dean Sarratt published a defense of athletic scholarships, a position that endeared him both to alumni and to board members.

But the football problems only worsened. Not that Vanderbilt fell immediately to the conference cellar, but notably it would never win a conference championship in football. In 1936 Coach Morrison, in his second year, suffered a near disaster; even Southwestern of Memphis defeated the Commodores. But Morrison earned his pay in 1937; the team beat Tennessee and might have gone to the Rose Bowl had it not lost to Alabama by a score of 6–7. Next year it lost to its three strongest SEC opponents. By 1939 it won only one major victory, after which Ray Morrison "escaped" to Temple. Vanderbilt hired Henry R. "Red" Sanders as new head coach, at a much lower salary. In 1941 Sanders was SEC coach of the year; his team lost only to Tennessee and Tulane. Paul "Bear" Bryant was one of his assistants. After a so-so season in 1942, Sanders left for war duties, the eligible civilian players shrank toward zero, and the board suspended SEC competition for the duration.[22]

During these years of competitive football, attendance remained low. The old athletic association, deeply in debt, was unable to continue its nominal funding of all athletic contests. In 1940 the Board of Trust appointed a committee to explore the athletic program. Already, at the time Vanderbilt absorbed the YMCA building in 1936, the College had established a department of physical education, in part as a means to hire former YMCA instructors. It then brought the athletic staff under this department, but the athletic association continued to pay coaches' salaries. By 1940 the athletic association could not meet interest payments on a $180,000 debt, even though it did not pay the support for players. In 1936 the Board of Trust began funding ten so-called scholarships for freshmen, but these really amounted to grants-in-aid for football players. Certain alumni contributed funds for ten more "scholarships" but reserved the right to nominate the holders to the faculty scholarship committee; they always nominated outstanding football prospects, with no apparent concern for academic promise or financial need. The alumni soon increased these scholarships to twenty, awarding ten to upperclassmen. In effect, this began a full maintenance scheme for players under the guise of "scholarships." In 1940 the Board of Trust did away with the hypocrisy. The University assumed the valuable property (stadium, land) owned by the athletic association, canceled its debts, and assumed financial responsibility for the whole athletic program. The Board placed responsibility for athletics in a new seven-member committee on athletics (called an athletic board in most institutions), made up of faculty and alumni. Dean Sarratt became its first chairman. The committee agreed to offer twenty football grants each year, the SEC maximum, but restricted the amount to two-thirds of tuition and rent. It discontinued the alumni scholarships. In

430

1941 it followed this by approving postseason bowl games, a policy Kirkland had fought to his death.[23]

Suspension of SEC competition in 1943 reflected hard necessities, not any policy decision to demote athletics, although suspicious sports writers read such an intention into the decision. But the suspension did make possible an open discussion of the proper role of athletics, and particularly football, at Vanderbilt. In any case, resumption required a decision by the board to reappoint needed coaches and to appropriate funds for grants-in-aid. During suspension Vanderbilt played both football and basketball on a nonsubsidized basis and with physical education instructors as coaches. Its strictly amateur football team had great fun and won all games in 1943. Some students joined faculty members in demanding a continuation of such amateur sports. On January 11, 1944, after the first nonseason, Donald Davidson moved, in the College faculty meeting, that the faculty go on record in favor of a full intramural program to benefit all men and women, and that it support the continuation of intercollegiate athletics only "on a strictly amateur basis, in the best spirit of college traditions, without undue emphasis on any one branch of sports or commercialization of any one branch." The faculty did not favor a return to the "large-scale, subsidized, and semi-professional athletics" that had characterized prewar football. It specifically deplored any return to athletic grants, which injured scholarship, hurt academic standards, and lowered the dignity of the university. Davidson asked that Carmichael communicate this resolution to the board, after the faculty passed it at the end of an extended discussion.[24]

Carmichael did report the action to the board, and the board took it very seriously. The board as a whole postponed for a year action on the motion of its athletic committee to resume SEC competition in 1944. A board committee wanted to meet with faculty members to exchange views. University attorney and board member Cecil Sims did address the Arts and Science faculty. The board committee accepted many of the criticisms of the faculty but wanted to stress the positive benefits of football, and not only in developing leadership abilities and good sportsmanship among players. It believed that sports upheld a great Vanderbilt tradition, cemented alumni loyalties to the university, and thus helped procure more gifts. It acknowledged the high cost ($33,000 paid in scholarships from 1938–43) but believed football could yield profits if Vanderbilt remained in a reformed SEC. In any case, Vanderbilt already had the fixed cost of its stadium and other facilities. In response to the board suggestions, the Arts and Science faculty appointed a committee to meet with other SEC colleges to try and achieve Davidson's goals at that level. As far as the records show, the majority of board members loved football. Most were alumni, several had played football, and their memories all went back to the golden era, and to the amateur tradition, of Dan McGugin.[25]

The Vanderbilt faculty committee spent six meetings in preparing its proposed reforms for the SEC. It took them to a meeting at Birmingham in October, 1944. The committee took not a blueprint, but varied proposals based on various eventualities. For example, it recommended an end to all athletic scholarships, but if the SEC retained such awards, it suggested that faculty committees select students on the basis of academic ability and qualifying exams. If the SEC supported aid based on football ability, then the conference should refer to these as grants, not scholarships. The faculty wanted to prohibit all recruiting, but failing that to prohibit contacts before high school graduation, limit the number of visits to campus to one per candidate, and allow no more than 10 percent of grants to students from outside the SEC area. The committee wanted to limit to twenty-five the players eligible for any game, to limit football to September, October, and November, with no bowl games; to require a C average for eligibility; to release athletes from no more than one course and that by a dean's permission; and to allow no coaches' salaries above that of full professors, but to give tenure rights to coaches (note that faculty members at Vanderbilt had only de facto tenure rights). Several of these recommendations reflected faculty concern over the academic progress of Vanderbilt football players. In the last normal prewar season (1941), the thirty-six football players had compiled a very poor academic record (fifteen had at least C average, four were just below a C, and seventeen were deficient).

As the more realistic expected, the Vanderbilt delegation to the August meeting of athletic boards at Birmingham failed almost completely. On October 16, 1944, it reported its failure back to the Arts and Science faculty. On motion to reaffirm Davidson's prior resolution, the faculty amended it to affirm the reforms proposed at Birmingham and voted to instruct Carmichael to fight for them at the upcoming meeting of SEC presidents. The vote was unanimous. Before Carmichael went to Birmingham for this December meeting, he led a long discussion of the issues in a November faculty meeting. But instead of assuming a neutral role, he ended up defending football. Very much aware of board sentiment, he begged the faculty to look at the broader issues—to football's appeal to Anglo-Saxon youth, to the image of Vanderbilt if it gave up its fight within the SEC, to the hallowed memory of Dudley. Sarratt moved that the faculty leave the final decision up to the chancellor and board but withdrew his motion because of strong opposition. Carmichael went to Birmingham, presided at the president's meeting, and won only a minor concession that limited the total number of grants to seventy-five. The presidents rejected new limits on recruiting, refused to eliminate freshman competition, and even defeated, by seven to five, a motion to require athletes to make normal progress toward a degree. This meant the faculty had failed in their reform efforts; it also left them on record in opposition to a resumption of SEC participation.[26]

The athletic issue had to be settled quickly. If Vanderbilt were to reenter

Cheers at a 1945 football game

the SEC in the fall of 1945, then it had to engage coaches, recruit players, and fund the needed grants. Thus, in December, 1944, the Executive Committee began the process. The decision to resume was all but inevitable, given strong board sentiment. President Frank Rand very much favored resumption. But the board feared an open clash with faculty. It was also under intense alumni pressures, fanned by continuing rumors spread by sports writers. Technically, the board faced only one decision—when to resume competition—since all it ever had done was suspend games because of the war emergency. In December, 1944, the Executive Committee voted unanimously to resume competition in the fall of 1945. At the February board meeting Carmichael summarized his statements before the faculty and thus placed himself firmly behind the resumption. He stressed the value of athletics to an undergraduate college and the few minor reforms accepted by the SEC. The path of courage, he said, was to stay the fight, to try to gain the new reforms sooner or later. The full board simply endorsed his report without further discussion. In December, 1944, Carmichael had rather apprehensively presented the Executive Committee's decision to the Arts and Science faculty. He sweetened the report by noting that the board would continue fifty Founder's scholarships, competitive scholarships that began during the war as a means of attracting outstanding students to the campus, and the first major scholarships for the College in the history of Vanderbilt. The faculty took their defeat without protest. Some recommended that Vanderbilt follow the Birmingham resolutions (impossible) and that it use more care in selecting players for its grants. Later, Carmichael expressed surprise and joy at how well the faculty had accepted the board decision. Meanwhile, the new or returning coaches prepared for the fall 1945 season. Sanders was unable to return until 1946; McNeil "Doby" Bartling led a team through a disastrous season, in part because he had to play teams that had not suspended football during the war.[27]

The controversy over athletics had some enduring significance. It brought to the fore an issue that has continued, periodically, to incite debate and controversy on campus. It represented the first open challenge by the faculty to board policies and left a residue of mutual distrust. Big-time sports became a major issue in the subsequent selection of a new chancellor; the board made support of competitive football a condition of candidacy. But football was only one divisive issue as Vanderbilt moved toward a new era of peace and growth. The REW episode only brought to the surface some explosive ideological issues that had to be confronted sooner or later. Race and economic policies remained at the center of these issues. On the board, James Stahlman and Fitzgerald Hall reflected the most extreme positions on social and economic issues, positions not fully characterized by such labels as "far right" or "reactionary." They kept a lookout for any form of liberal or radical heresy on campus, whether that be advocacy of greater Negro rights, a challenge to the prerogatives of business firms large or small, or support of New Deal regulatory or welfare policies. Fortunately for Vanderbilt, other more moderate board members, or the chancellor, usually diverted or modified their frequent efforts to clean up the campus, efforts predicated upon their sincere love, and loyalty to, a Vanderbilt they never quite understood. Their enthusiasm usually challenged academic freedom. One example of this occurred in early 1945.

Fitzgerald Hall had an idea. An alumnus, the son of the former dean of the Law School, himself a past instructor in that school, for a time president of the Nashville, St. Louis and Chattanooga railroad, he became a very active member of the board. In February, 1945, as an ailing and perhaps increasingly senile old man, he wrote Carmichael from a sickbed in Sarasota, Florida, asking him to introduce a motion in the upcoming board meeting, one requiring every candidate for any degree at Vanderbilt (even in the Medical School) to take and pass three courses—one each in American history, American government, and constitutional law. This effort soon became a crusade for Hall. He corresponded with a friend who was vice-chancellor of the University of the South, and with other board members. Out of kindness everyone expressed sympathy, but each had reservations. His efforts raised several issues. Had the board acquiesced, it would, for the first time, have dictated academic policies to the faculty. In the post–World War II period not only university boards but some state legislatures did mandate college courses in American history or American government, but none involved three courses or required them in all colleges and schools. More sinister was Hall's understanding of what he was about. He wanted to instruct students in "true Americanism," to inspire students to love the constitution, not as recently interpreted, but as it was in its pre–New Deal purity. He thus admitted that a study of American government under someone like Justice James G. McReynolds was what he wanted, not study under a Hugo Black or a Felix Frankfurter. In other words, Hall not only wanted particular courses but wanted to control how they were taught in order to thwart rising "subversive tendencies" in America.[28]

Hall did not want to run roughshod over the faculty. He acknowledged that they normally could decide what to teach and how. But he stressed strict limits to their freedom, arguing that the board should fire anyone for advocating communism (Hall defined this ambiguous word very broadly) or the abrogation of segregation laws. In the same sense, and on the positive side, the board could rightly stipulate a few key courses. He lamented the lack of such courses and incorrectly believed that the Vanderbilt history department primarily emphasized European history.

Eventually, under pressure from other board members, Hall changed his motion to a more innocuous one–that the chancellor and administrative officers study the issues and find out the best way to teach students "to revere more the American system of government." Even the watered-down version bothered some board members, particularly those with more experience with or a clearer understanding of university government, because it still involved the board directly in controversial curriculum issues. Significantly, a much more sophisticated Frank Rand believed the motion "exceedingly unwise." Hall would not concede and argued that "we have carried this question of 'academic freedom' and 'administrative prerogative' to absurd limits. . . ," so far, in fact, that "Harvard College has become the greatest menace to good Government in America." At Harvard, any foreign crackpot could teach "false foreignisms" and he used the "foreign born Jew," Frankfurter, to illustrate the point. The board at Harvard should long ago have fired him, without consulting president or faculty. He also argued that the board should have similarly fired Henry Hart, not just eased him out. Under intense pressure, Hall eventually decided not to offer his motion at the June, 1945 meeting. His failure to gain support reveals the increasing moderation and sophistication of the Board of Trust.[29]

Hall's aborted motion coincided with the winding down of World War II. By the spring of 1945, Vanderbilt was already in transition. Victory was assured and the major military units had all left campus. Finally, in 1944–45, Vanderbilt was able to gain its navy ROTC unit; through 1945–46 the 200 members of this unit remained on active duty status, thus making up the only uniformed students on campus. The spring and summer proved a lull before a storm. In the fall semester of 1945 only seventy-five veterans were back, and the enrollment began at a lower level than during the war. But the less than 1,500 students rose to over 1,800 in the winter quarter, to almost 2,000 by spring. By then, over 450 veterans were enrolled, with the major surge, under the new GI bill, still to come. Fortunately, many faculty members also returned, but not enough to teach the flood in freshman English (751 students) and chemistry (540). Vanderbilt thus entered a brief, eventually self-correcting reconversion boom, a period as chaotic as during the war but one full of promise and hope.[30]

The boom created no end of problems and challenges. Vanderbilt hired a full-time counselor, a psychologist, to direct veterans' education. Prices rose, creating a need for salary increases. In a tight market the departments had to search for additional faculty members. Classroom space became a premium. A textbook shortage plagued the bookstore. But the one great problem was housing. The naval ROTC unit took over most of Kissam. Fraternities and boarding houses were crowded and inadequate, and these did not appeal to most veterans, many of whom were married and with families. Even new faculty members could not find apartments anywhere close to the campus. As temporary, emergency measures, Vanderbilt constructed twelve faculty houses near the stadium, built a fourteen-unit apartment complex for young faculty, and moved eight navy prefab barracks to the north of Kirkland to hold 240 students. In addition, it began constructing twenty-eight semi-permanent concrete-block apartment units for married veterans just south of Garland ("the Settlement"). It used another temporary barracks as a dining hall, which it soon converted to a bookstore (near present-day Rand).

These temporary expedients were far from adequate. Thus, in 1945 Chancellor Carmichael persuaded the board to approve a huge new complex of seven men's dorms (750 rooms in all) in a quadrangle off West End. These, when completed, were to supplant both Kissam and the old gym. Work on the first two of these began in 1945 (McGill and Tolman), but delays and shortages prevented completion as planned in the fall of 1946; the first students occupied Tolman in March, 1947. Even as the dorms went up, new fund drives looked to the early construction of two major buildings—a new gym to honor Vanderbilt's World War II veterans and a desperately needed Engineering building. Half of the veterans seemed to choose courses in Engineering, a school now engorged with students and desperately hiring junior staff as rapidly as possible. The Engineering faculty finally requested separation from Arts and Science in 1945, and henceforth met separately. The school launched an ambitious fund drive, raising only $165,000, but the board added $85,000 to help it plan a new building after 1947.[31]

The heady years of reconversion invited new plans and a few dreams. The departments of economics and business administration merged. The board first discussed a graduate school of business and public administration. Several people tried to reorganize a school of dentistry. In the College, three or four additional departments began to offer Ph.D. work, including those in the physical sciences. Physics, a two-person department before the war, expanded to eight people; in 1946 Carl K. Seyfort came to Vanderbilt from Case University to begin a new program in astronomy. Biology, with largely a premedical program before the war, now expanded into a large academic department, with courses listed in botany, zoology, and bacteriology. To consolidate an expanding number of research funds, the board approved a Research Council in 1944, made up of representatives from each of the schools. It began seeking new funds from foundations and government and established research policies. The School of Religion added a new Ph.D. program. The old Rural Church School gave way to an endowed circulating library for rural ministers named after J.L. Kesler. An influx of new faculty members, most at the junior level, allowed an expanded and more specialized program in most departments. The pace of faculty publications increased, with both Donald Davidson and H.C. Nixon publishing important books in 1946. Vanderbilt University also published, and effectively promoted, Edwin Mims's *History of Vanderbilt University.* One sad note: John McGill, the one surviving link to Vanderbilt's origins, died at age ninety-five on April 11, 1946. He had retired in 1919 but had continued to live in a faculty house between Kissam and the gym, a house doomed by the new dorms.[32]

Peace brought relief to the Nursing School. The frenetic activities of war and the depletion of staff had strained resources and nerves to the breaking point. Fortunately for its finances, the Nursing School was able to extend the cadet program through 1945-46. By then, it had developed a major program in psychiatric nursing, through an agreement with a Veterans Administration hospital in Murfreesboro. At the end of the war it accelerated its public health program and began plans for an M.A. degree in that field. Tensions over the nursing duties of students remained. By 1946 Dean Goodpasture of the Medical School gave up counting on very much work by Vanderbilt students and began plans for a licensed practical nursing program in the hospital. The Nursing faculty, instead of going on with its M.A. program, soon made early plans for an integrated four-year Bachelor of Science program. It still enrolled students only after two years of college.[33]

The Medical School gladly returned to a nine-month schedule in 1946. It established a new department of anesthesiology in 1946 and in 1946–47 signed a contract to provide professional services to the local Veterans Administration Hospital. The VA connection was a godsend to the school, providing desperately needed clinical facilities for students. The VA connection took the place of a long-promised state tuberculosis hospital, which the state never built but which it had planned for land adjacent to the campus. The school continued to lose and gain eminent staff members. John Youmans moved in 1946 to the deanship at Illinois; Glenn Millikan, son of the famous

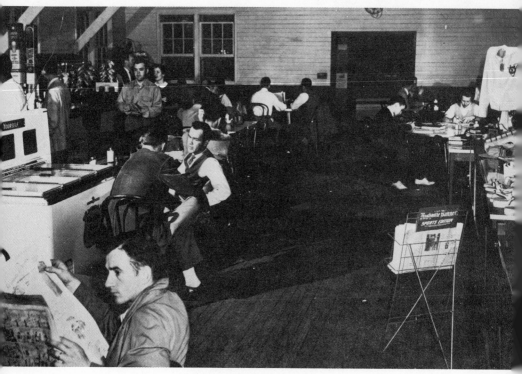

The new, prefab bookstore (replaced later by Rand)

physicist, with his Ph.D. from Cambridge, took over as head of physiology. But the postwar inflation played havoc with hospital costs. By 1946–47 the school and hospital ran a deficit of over $300,000, or a 33-percent overrun on the budget, leaving grave problems for the future. Basil C. MacLean came from the University of Rochester to make a detailed study of hospital operations and cost. He left over fifty recommendations, some of which helped guide changes enacted in the next era of the school's history.[34]

The Law School started over, and with more optimism than at any time since the 1920s. During the two years of suspension (1944–46), part-time instructors had offered courses to five or six seniors in order to enable them to get their degree. The librarian kept the collections up to date. The suspension allowed the board to concentrate on a fund drive, which began in 1944. The board committed $500,000 from the Frederick Vanderbilt estate and hoped that Law School alumni could raise $500,000, enough for a building and a beginning endowment. Dean Arnold, while on leave, decided not to return, a decision welcomed by the board, which wanted a completely new start. The search for a dean began in 1945, with no early success. From a list of seven names, including some of the most prominent legal scholars in the country, the search committee picked two. When one of these withdrew, it hired L. Dale Coffman, a rather surprising choice, for he was not a legal scholar. A

Harvard S.J.D., he had only a brief stint as a teacher at the University of Nebraska and then had pursued his career on the legal staff of General Electric. He started at a salary of $10,000, or much more than several eminent scholars on campus. Because of a large gift from Frank Rand, the school also hired another Harvard S.J.D., Rollin M. Perkins, for $8,000 to fill the Rand Chair, the first such outside the School of Religion. Older, with numerous publications, he gave distinction to a staff of nine people, four of whom taught part time. The two most eminent were Jefferson B. Fordham, a public law scholar from Louisiana State University who, unfortunately, remained only a year at Vanderbilt, and a brilliant young man, Hugh Lawrence Sowards, Jr., just out of Yale. Most encouraging of all, an astonishing 153 students enrolled in the fall of 1946. Within a year the students and staff began a prestigious, ably edited *Vanderbilt Law Review*. The fund drive fizzled, yielding only $375,000, but the university contributed enough funds to balance the school's budget.[35]

Financially, the university survived the war in excellent shape. To withstand postwar inflation, the university raised tuitions in most schools (in Arts and Science, up from $285 to $315 in 1945; in Law, to $350; Engineering, to $330; and Medicine, to $500). Because of successful investments and rises in interest rates the endowment yield also rose after 1945. By then, the university listed the value of its total endowment at $30 million, but its market value approached $36 million. Until 1946 the university held the over $5 million of Frederick Vanderbilt bequests in escrow. In that year it assigned over $3.3 million to various purposes—$2 million for College endowment, $200,000 to Nursing, $185,000 to Engineering, $353,000 to Law, and $600,000 to Religion. The College was to use the income from the $2 million to upgrade its faculty and to expand research. As a beginning effort to reduce hospital deficits, the board in 1946 raised the fees of private rooms from $8 to $10 a day and semiprivate rooms to $5, and increased most laboratory fees. By 1946–47 the soaring annual university budget approached $3 million, but almost half of this was for the hospital. Among hopeful signs, alumni giving began to increase after the war; in the immediate postwar years the Living Endowment yielded a net surplus for the first time. Except for the hospital, the university continued its hallowed tradition of balanced budgets.

The new income allowed the first of a series of faculty raises. By war's end, Carmichael was embarrassed over salaries, particularly in the College and the School of Religion. Living costs had effectively reduced professors' incomes by 30 percent since 1941. In 1946 the board approved raises of at least 10 percent for those with salaries over $2,400, 15 percent for those under that figure. This brought the average professor's salary up to about $4,500, about one-half that at Harvard but just below the median for eighty-eight graduate-level universities. In the area of fringe benefits, the university now added faculty members to the TIAA after one year of employment and in 1947 began

439

a group health (Blue Cross) plan, paying the full premium for each faculty member but still requiring private payments for other family members.[36]

In the midst of all the boom and bustle, Carmichael announced his impending resignation. In July, 1945, he visited with Frank Rand in Michigan to discuss an offer for him to head the Carnegie Foundation for the Advancement of Teaching. He subsequently met twice with board members in the Nashville area and in August made his final decision to leave. The public announcement came in September. He hoped to leave Vanderbilt by early 1946. For the board, this was a surprising and disturbing resignation. It had seemed to warm to Carmichael during the war years and had praised him unstintingly at its end. Continuing small tensions and distrust by board members perhaps explained the overt compliments, but certainly nothing suggested that Carmichael was unhappy at Vanderbilt. And, in fact, he left with kind feelings toward the university and as a foundation president remained a friend and valuable counselor. The search for his successor was assigned to a newly appointed board committee on administrative appointments. The five members of the committee included Carmichael; Frank Rand of St. Louis, president of the board; W.L. Hemingway, vice-president of the board; George Sloan, a New York City banker and chairman of the committee; and P.D. Houston, another prominent banker. This committee trusted Carmichael and was very much influenced by him in their selection of candidates. Carmichael met at Vanderbilt with all the major officers of the university to seek their advice. From these meetings, and from other sources, came an avalanche of suggested names. When the board committee met at Rand's St. Louis home in early October, 1945, it had to evaluate twenty-five candidates. It selected four names for final review. Carmichael brought the four to a faculty committee, composed mainly of the various deans. After two meetings, the faculty committee agreed to recommend to the board their own dean of graduate work, Philip Davidson. Carmichael, in several meetings with Vanderbilt area trustees, mistakenly believed they also favored Davidson. The committee rejected, at least temporarily, the other three prime candidates: Rufus Harris, president of Tulane, a lawyer, politically astute, personable, dynamic, but not a scholar; Francis P. Gaines, president of Washington and Lee, a skilled orator and a favorite of Frank Rand; and John E. Pomfret, president of William and Mary and Davidson's predecessor at Vanderbilt.[37]

The board committee on administrative appointments accepted the faculty recommendations and formally made its nomination to a special meeting of the board on October 19. The full board freely discussed Davidson's credentials (no stenographic record was taken), aired many doubts, and voted to continue the search. One can only speculate about their reluctance to go with Davidson. He was a Carmichael friend and appointee, and Carmichael had carefully engineered his nomination. The board refused to concede to Carmichael, who resigned rather than retire, what they gave to Kirkland—the right of choosing his successor. Some board members (Stahlman said a majority) resented Carmichael's effort to "cram Davidson down our throats." Besides, Carmichael and the faculty had chosen Davidson for his job as graduate dean, not at all as an apprentice chancellor. The analogy to 1935 did not fit. The stated objections of the board members was that Davidson lacked the ability, or the eminence, for the job. A secondary consideration may have involved his faculty loyalties, or a quite understandable fear that he was too much a part of the College faculty, too likely to shape his policies according to the wishes of former colleagues. He would not be sufficiently independent, not able to transfer his primary allegiance to the board. Tied to this was athletic policy. Davidson might be soft on football, a concern that remained behind all the board deliberations. Finally, according to Stahlman and others, Davidson was not popular among alumni, particularly in the Nashville area. Stahlman opposed Davidson from the beginning and believed that most board members from the Nashville area joined in that opposition. What is clear is that Davidson remained a bit suspect among the more right-wing board members.[38]

The rejection of Davidson created a new problem for Vanderbilt—an extended and eventually divisive search for a new chancellor. By December, 1945, it was clear that the task would be difficult and time-consuming. Thus, the Executive Committee decided to poll board members about a new position of vice-chancellor. All but one member approved the position and the only candidate for it—Dean Sarratt. He took over as acting chancellor in February, 1946, when Carmichael left. Sarratt did not want to be chancellor and knew he lacked the scholarly credentials for the post. This made him more effective during the holding period. His election allayed the fears of the alumni. Sarratt had built up a tremendous following during his years as dean of students and he was safe on all issues, from racial policy to athletics. For Sarratt, the promotion meant a near doubled salary ($10,000). More important, his vice-chancellorship was permanent, assuring him an important role in any new administration and the board an element of continuity which it craved.[39]

By the fall of 1945 the university community reflected the uncertainty and anxiety posed by the vacancy. The future of Vanderbilt seemed at stake. The board, without a clear line of succession to follow, now faced its most critical task, but also the one for which it had almost no qualifications. The board was a club of old men, all alumni, whose images of Vanderbilt were fixed by their own student experiences back at the turn of the century. The faculty gathered in discussion groups, generated possible names, and passed these on to the board, but never agreed on any one preferred candidate. The faculty did not have the power, or the objectivity, to choose a chancellor. It was also too self-interested. Students had little basis for judgment. Alumni were too far removed from the existing Vanderbilt, too scattered and too diverse to make any decisions. Somehow, all the university constituencies needed to come together in the search, but that was almost impossible. Hill Turner, secretary of the Alumni Association, set down what he saw as the qualifications required by any new chancellor. Hill's first requirement was that he be an alumnus, or at least intimately acquainted with Vanderbilt; he also preferred that he be a professional administrator, that he have the scholarly eminence needed to win the trust of faculty, that he be a southerner who knew and respected the special qualities of the section and who would not leave for a northern job, and that he not try to change the character of the existing Vanderbilt in any fundamental way. (Turner mentioned as dangerous innovations the dropping of football, the formation of a School of Education, a commitment to a huge university of 3,000 to 4,000 students, a desire for a heterogeneous student body, or a diminution of academic standards). The board agreed with most of these criteria, except possibly Turner's fear of size and heterogeneity.[40]

The search began in earnest after the October, 1945, rejection of Davidson. None of the four finalists was out of the running, although Davidson was now the least likely choice and Pomfret next to the bottom, for he was considered soft on football. Rand preferred Gaines, although Carmichael had downplayed his scholarly credentials as part of his advocacy of Davidson. Perhaps fortunately, Gaines took himself out of contention. That left only Harris, a candidate strongly pushed by board member Frank Godchaux, head of a rice company in Abbyville, Louisiana. Then in November or December the board committee identified a new candidate, William DeVane, an English professor, dean of the College at Yale, and a tremendously popular administrator. DeVane hailed from South Carolina and had the appealing assets of a southerner who had made good in an elite institution of the North. He also had symbolic assets—he was from the state of Kirkland and also of Sarratt. The New York alumni, particularly Sloan, nominated him and compiled what must have been an overwhelming vita. Unless he flunked the football test, DeVane could have received the offer. He disappointed everyone by removing his name and nominating instead Dean Harvie Branscomb of the Divinity School at Duke. Branscomb had to have been on earlier lists, but somehow he had not made the prime list. He had lectured at Vanderbilt, had advised on JUL, and had briefly considered the post of dean of the School of Religion. He was already the scheduled Cole lecturer in the school for 1947. Carmichael knew this fellow Alabamian well and undoubtedly ranked him just below Davidson. As the author of two scholarly books, he had the credentials sure to please the Vanderbilt faculty. But the road to his nomination proved rocky. He was now in contention with Rufus Harris.[41]

By early April the board had settled on Branscomb. They had interviewed him in St. Louis. In a genial meeting, Branscomb remembered only two pointed tests—an offer of an old-fashioned before dinner, which he accepted, and a very pointed question about intercollegiate athletics. His remembered answer on this one was "it is like sin. We all have it, and we have to make the

442

best of it." George Sloan consulted, in New York, with the members of the GEB and the Carnegie Corporation, another important Vanderbilt constituency. These foundations, which had practically built the university, were enthusiastic about Branscomb, leery about Harris. Sloan's committee planned to present Branscomb at a special April 19 board meeting, a meeting somewhat delayed because of scheduled interviews with Harris. On April 12, Branscomb, in the dark about the board plans and under pressure to remain at Duke, wired his withdrawal from candidacy, leaving the distraught committee with no reason for a meeting. By then, tensions were building in the board. Rand was desperately anxious to fill the position. By May the members of the committee had decided to recommend Harris, which they did with some reluctance. Although Carmichael praised Harris, it was soon clear that he seemed to lack the scholarly credentials prized by the foundations. He had no Ph.D. Thus, Rand and Sloan cooked up a compromise proposal—elect Harris and elevate Davidson to a second vice-chancellorship, one keyed to higher educational work at Vanderbilt. Davidson also made the trek to St. Louis and agreed on this arrangement, which was also a bit of a concession to the Vanderbilt faculty. The proposal was soon in trouble. James Stahlman, who all along viewed Harris as too much a politician, too little an intellectual, began rallying votes against the Davidson scheme. The Davidson promotion also raised fears among Sarratt's supporters, those who wanted him as the only second man. Fortunately for the board, Harris declined any further considerations, rescuing it from what could have developed into a very divisive fight. By then, local board members, or those from the deep South, were increasingly suspicious of Rand, Houston, and Sloan, or the banker-northern members, those closest to the foundations and still most influenced by Carmichael. A national outlook clashed with a more provincial one. Stahlman and Sloan exchanged angry letters.[42]

After Harris declined, Sloan again contacted Branscomb. He found him still interested. Branscomb was also in an enviable position—the only serious candidate for an almost desperate board. He could bargain freely. Branscomb met in New York City with Sloan and Carmichael on July 22. From the discussions came the offer, which the whole board approved in a special meeting on August 2, 1946, setting his beginning salary at $15,000. Branscomb had asked for a prompt decision by the board and also asked that his appointment be approved by Sarratt. He had one small embarrassment—he had moved toward ordination as a Methodist clergyman to better complement his deanship of a Methodist divinity school. The board asked him to drop such plans, for ordination would have raised again the old Methodist issue and possibly blocked his selection. Branscomb refused any direction from the committee (he did not want it publicized that the board stipulated these terms) but simply on his own dropped the plans. He took up his new duties at Vanderbilt on October 1, 1946. Except for alumni status, he seemed to meet every criteria cooked up during the long search—a brilliant southerner with scholarly eminence, proven administrative skills, beloved by the foundations, and willing to keep football.[43]

On the prior February 4, Carmichael had rendered his last report to the board. Typically, it amounted to an extended apology for his chancellorship. He took responsibility for lowering tensions on campus, for the new curriculum reforms, for the growth in graduate education, for the research institute, for a beginning program in fine arts, for an expanded University Center and the completion of JUL, for the Nashville School of Social Work, for the University Press, for a new retirement system, for early efforts to develop Latin American programs, and even for the almost $9 million gained in endowment. In addition, he took credit for the new building program already under way—the men's dorms, a new bookstore, the proposed memorial gym. In his address at a special convocation to honor him, one would have concluded that Vanderbilt was never as prosperous, its prospects never as bright. Such are the perspectives of departing chancellors.[44]

New chancellors see things from a different perspective. Branscomb, in his later memoirs, offered a most depressing evaluation of Vanderbilt in the fall of 1946. It was surrounded by privately owned, deteriorating property and thus was increasingly isolated on its own meager acreage. It was virtually a campus without permanent dorms—only old Kissam for men and an inadequate McTyeire for women. The only dining hall was in Kissam, with aluminum trays and poor service. He found an impossibly provincial campus, with half the students from Nashville, two-thirds from Tennessee. Vanderbilt was no longer a pacesetter for the South, for it had almost no impact on the South. Three of its professional schools—Law, Religion, Engineering—had woefully inadequate facilities. The School of Social Work, an illegitimate child, had no permanent facilities at all. Faculty salaries were low, fringe benefits few, and in spite of the rules too many faculty members were not yet members of the retirement system.

The university had one dubious financial asset—no major debts. But one-half of the $30 million endowment belonged to the Medical School. Income remained low; unrestricted gifts for 1946–47 totaled only about $8,000. Four campaigns in eight years had yielded diminishing returns. The bright side included some high academic standards, an able faculty in Medicine, and a handful of distinguished faculty in the College (in retrospect, he could name only three professors in the College with national prominence). The university did have a favorable location, with no nearby competitors. But these few bright spots hardly relieved the somber ones. On the day following his election, Branscomb wrote a friend that Vanderbilt had "almost all the problems." But, as he admitted, these were problems endemic to southern universities. Like each of his predecessors before him, he wanted to establish a great university in that part of the South. He spent the next sixteen years in that effort, and came closer than any predecessor to achieving the goal.[45]

PART SEVEN

The Great Leap Forward
(1947–1963)

 IN THE *1950s Vanderbilt slowly but painfully began to outgrow its provincial roots. It began to measure its achievements by national standards, to recruit more of its students from a national pool, to break from the barriers of region and race and traditional ideologies. The changes came quickly; the growth was phenomenal. By its ninetieth anniversary, in 1963, Vanderbilt for the first time ranked in the top twenty private universities in the United States. It remained behind any likely list of the top ten (Brown, Chicago, Columbia, Cornell, Harvard, the Johns Hopkins, Pennsylvania, Princeton, Stanford, and Yale) but now competed for first rank among the second ten, along with such universities as Duke, Northwestern, Pittsburgh, and Rochester. Such rapid change meant severe growth pains. Sharp conflicts of belief and value accompanied traumatic changes. Doubts, regrets, angry confrontations haunted the maturation of Vanderbilt, its rapid transition into a modern, complex, pluralistic university.*

External factors supported Vanderbilt's change and rapid growth. Higher education enjoyed unprecedented prestige and support after World War II. New federal programs helped even private universities. Despite periodic recessions in the 1950s, most Americans enjoyed sustained economic growth. In particular, the South benefited from both the growth and new federal policies. By the late 1950s demographic trends insured a boom in college-age youngsters, even as the proportion of young people going to college increased each year, ushering in a time of great expansion on most campuses.

To take advantage of such favorable conditions, Vanderbilt needed the kind of effective, imaginative leadership that Chancellor Harvie Branscomb provided. He navigated carefully, but not always

445

smoothly, among intense competing pressures. He had to educate, to lead with infinite patience an elderly, old-fashioned, ideologically naive Board of Trust. Constant alumni pressures were often atavistic. Aging alumni rallied in behalf of their remembered Vanderbilt, not the one abuilding after the war. On the other side, the ablest and most sensitive professors and students chafed at moral compromises, the painful slowness of change, the dictatorial power of administrators. Sectional differences continued to plague the university, which had to chart a course between the national perspectives of northern benefactors and of many faculty and the narrowly provincial beliefs of southern alumni, parents, and students. In addition to coping with the strains of Cold War and demands for loyalty and political orthodoxy, Vanderbilt and other southern institutions had to navigate through the treacherous problems of racial integration. No chancellor could please all constituencies. Thus, the story of Vanderbilt at the level of the Board of Trust and the chancellor, at the very top, was not only a story of great achievement but of tension and ever lurking controversy.

Success at the top meant new strengths at the middle. The quality of a university rests upon the quality of faculty instruction and research, upon the dedication and ability of scholar-teachers, upon the academic programs they develop and implement. The postwar expansion of Vanderbilt offered opportunities for improved academic quality as well as new programs, but the hazards were many. The results seemed uneven, as ever, with some schools at the pinnacle of success, others threatened by decline. The 1950s turned out to be the golden age for Religion, a prosperous and growing period for a newly organized Law School, of growth but less than great distinction for the College and for Engineering, a period of crisis and relative decline for Medicine, and an era of absolute decline for an ill-supported Nursing School. Under Branscomb, the university remained exceptionally centralized. Yet professors gained a greater role in university government and finally attained security of tenure. In an increasingly favorable market for their skills, the Vanderbilt faculty also gained salary increases that outdistanced the cost of living. They bettered their economic conditions by the early 1960s, at least in comparison with the period just after the

*war, not necessarily in comparison with their status and income
back at the turn of the century or even in the 1930s. But all was
not well at the middle. Despite guarantees of academic freedom, the
Vanderbilt faculty still faced intimidating pressures for conformity.*

*Students make up the bottom tier of a university. They constitute an
ever-changing community and have limited impact on a
university's policies, though they remain the focus of its central
purpose. Postwar growth at Vanderbilt helped add new strains to
student life. In just over a decade students had to accommodate a
shift toward much higher and more competitive admission
standards, higher academic demands, a more pluralistic student
body, an enlarged body of graduate students, and the shift from
decentralized fraternities to a true residential campus. To the
traditional but intensified issues of fraternities, the role of athletics,
the vitality of student government, and the survival of the honor
system, Vanderbilt students added new concerns over national and
international problems (nuclear energy, the Korean war, the
peacetime draft, loyalty and subversion, racial integration). They
faced ever-increasing tuition charges, accepted and then struggled
to escape charges of conformity and passivity, and for over a decade
lamented a purported lack of intellectuality on the campus. Strains
and tensions surfaced repeatedly in panty raids, in a few near riots,
in all manner of fraternity foolishness and excessive drinking, and
in a decade-long cold war between students and the Nashville
police.*

*Race was one issue that engaged all elements of the university
community. From 1952 to 1962 Vanderbilt gradually, reluctantly
removed all racial restrictions from its admission requirements. In
no meaningful sense did it integrate either its faculty or student
body, and it would not do so until the mid-1960s. But even
minimal concessions to national opinion, to foundations, and to
Negro pressures raised a storm of controversy at Vanderbilt and in
its southern constituency. The depth and breadth of resistance to
integration will seem unbelievable to later generations. Until 1960
Chancellor Branscomb successfully, but not without difficulty,
walked a tightrope over the volatile passions of a racial revolution in
the making. But all political maneuvering ran aground in 1960 in*

447

the complicated case of one James Lawson, the most divisive episode in all of Vanderbilt's history. Such are the surviving memories, the still smarting hurts of this episode, that a historian can only try to unearth the record with trepidation.

17

At the Top

HARVIE BRANSCOMB took over as chancellor in October, 1946. In the next two years he clarified his own goals for Vanderbilt. They reflected his personality and educational philosophy, the lessons learned from his years of academic work, and his early efforts to understand the history and traditions of Vanderbilt.

Branscomb's background was surprisingly similar to his predecessor's, but his personality was almost the opposite of Carmichael's. Carmichael was a bit heavy, genial, warm, eloquent, and often vague; Branscomb was lean, intense, reserved, direct, and precise. Branscomb was born in Huntsville, Alabama, the son of a Methodist minister. He took his B.A. at Birmingham-Southern, a quality Methodist college, and then won a Rhodes scholarship, joining Carmichael at Oxford. He also joined Carmichael in the Hoover relief effort in Belgium and in escaping with the famous letter from the Belgian church official. At Oxford, Branscomb was a brilliant student and an able athlete (crew, tennis). He became fascinated with biblical studies and earned a distinguished M.A. in that field. After serving briefly in the army, he planned his career in high school teaching, taking summer courses at Teacher's College, Columbia University. In 1919 he reluctantly took a position in the philosophy department of the young, struggling Southern Methodist University. After a year he moved up to an associate professorship in the School of Theology. In Dallas he also met and married Margaret Vaughan.

In 1923 Branscomb took a year's leave to complete course work for a Ph.D. at Union Theological Seminary and Columbia University. Back at SMU he soon became embroiled in a crisis involving academic freedom. Branscomb wrote a letter to a Dallas newspaper in support of a younger colleague and former student who was dismissed for his liberal theological teachings. Summarily fired for his impertinence, Branscomb was hardly in a desperate situation, since he already had a job offer from Duke University. Rather than pursue an appeal to the SMU Board of Trust, he accepted the Duke position and moved to Durham in the fall of 1925 to be a professor in the Divinity School (much later, SMU would award him an honorary degree). He remained at Duke from age thirty to fifty-one, or until he moved to Vanderbilt. He took a summer's leave in 1927 to complete his dissertation back at

Columbia and enjoyed a Guggenheim year in Europe in 1931–32. In the depression he used part of his time at Duke to serve as director of libraries, and out of the library experience and a related book came his advisory role in the founding of JUL in Nashville. Library duties also led him to a study of college libraries for the Association of American Colleges, and to a brief advisory role in Brazil at the end of World War II, cementing his lifelong interest in that country. In 1944, after several job offers from other prestigious seminaries and two important lectureships, he rose to dean of the Duke Divinity School, the springboard for his appointment as chancellor at Vanderbilt.[1]

Despite his heavy teaching and administrative commitments, Branscomb gave time and attention to scholarship. While at SMU he wrote a popular, straightforward book on the teachings of Jesus, one much informed by his Oxford studies. Of two scholarly books, the first was his Union-Columbia dissertation, *Jesus and the Law of Moses*, which he published at his own expense. In it he carefully analyzed Jesus' views of the Mosaic law as revealed in the synoptic gospels. His conclusion, out of the often conflicting statements attributed to Jesus, was that Jesus, despite his firm rooting in the Jewish tradition, broke with the Pharisaic scholars in his willingness to follow general ethical principles even when those conflicted with the ritualistic or ceremonial demands of the law. This conclusion supported a thesis of Branscomb's that he argued in other contexts—that Jesus anticipated Paul's more self-conscious, coherent treatment of the Mosaic law and thus is correctly viewed as the founder of Christianity.

More important for Vanderbilt, Branscomb revealed in this scholarly monograph certain characteristics that lived on in his work as chancellor: a fully detached, nonconfessional approach to his subject. The scholarly restraint had a purpose—to by-pass all the sensitive doctrinal issues so much in conflict within Protestantism. Except for those fundamentalists who feared any scholarly approach at all to the Bible, Branscomb's books proved acceptable and useful across the liberal-conservative spectrum. This same quality marked his next book, his last scholarly effort—a commentary, in the respected Moffatt series, on *The Gospel of Mark*. He successfully reduced problems of New Testament interpretation to factual ones. This very factuality had one effect—it separated Branscomb clearly from the more extreme liberal and iconoclastic biblical scholars of that generation. His work had a reconciling, not a divisive, impact.

From reading Branscomb's two scholarly books one gains no insight at all into his own religious beliefs. He was never confessional. His treatment of biblical topics was always that of the fascinated scholar. He was in temperament never a clergyman. As a divinity professor at Duke he had to preach sermons, which he did with success. As chancellor he kept his own views so hidden that he easily negotiated with people in all theological camps, and by his detached understanding of arguments on all sides left various protagonists with the mistaken impression that Branscomb fully agreed with them.[2]

When Branscomb came to Vanderbilt he seemed much younger than fifty-one. Not handsome, a bit reticent and retiring, he could not win his way by personal magnetism. Branscomb relied on substance, not form, and at times suffered from a lack of tact or polish, although not from any lack of a ready and subtle wit. He did not woo people so much as awe them, even intimidating the unprepared or incapable, and this by his very tough-minded intellectuality. He never suffered fools gladly. He quickly understood complex issues, grasped the magnitude of a problem, and moved on to a solution while most ordinary people were still trying to get their bearings. He became a respected chancellor, not a beloved one. Few students, few professors, ever felt they really knew him. He could be imperious, impatient with the slow processes of discussion. He preferred direct statements, and as an administrator increasingly appreciated direct, effective action, preferences that endeared him more to trustees than to faculty members. All of this is not to suggest any ultimate detachment. Branscomb held deep commitments and loyalties, and in ways he rarely revealed in public he suffered intensely from such controversies as the Lawson affair. He had an intellectual's love of consistency, of principled conduct, and when beleaguered could become defensive and inflexible. Some found him downright stubborn; others, a bit arrogant and insensitive. Branscomb incessantly had to make decisions that deeply offended someone. He was constantly under attack from some side or another, although he usually managed to outmaneuver critics or to keep most of the power on his side.

Branscomb at times almost delighted in his unpopularity, in his willingness to risk criticism in order to build a new Vanderbilt. But behind the scenes the criticism of people he respected hurt him deeply, and in the last three years of his chancellorship such criticism even began to affect his decisions. He felt besieged and personalized his administrative style. By then, he was much less a reformer than when he first came to Vanderbilt. The rapid changes in society, particularly in race relations and economic policy, had passed him by; he had been out front in the South, a progressive, in 1945, but his desire for gradual and reasonable change, guided by an able elite, seemed ever less in fashion. By 1963 he seemed to campus critics to be old-fashioned, an opponent of change, a defender of the past, and thus ever more closely attuned to the outlook of his own Board of Trust.

The Branscomb family moved into the modest chancellor's residence on 24th Avenue. Just before World War II the university had purchased and repaired this house in order to bring Carmichael on to the campus, at his own request. This, the former Kirk Rankin home, included two acres of land and, with its Spanish stucco style, became an attractive addition to the campus, serving later as a sorority house, the first University Club, and finally as the admissions office. In 1952 board member Brownlee Currey left $200,000 in his will for a new chancellor's home. Subject to the consent of his wife (given), his own house was to go to the university for this purpose; his wife received $125,000 back again out of his gift. The details were complete by 1953, and Branscomb moved into a large, historic mansion at the intersection of Lynwood Boulevard and Harding Road, far to the west of the campus in the wealthy town of Belle Meade. This gift had its cost—the university had to maintain and staff an older house. Its use considerably altered the lifestyle and the real income of the chancellor. Branscomb had a salary of $15,000 in 1952, and because of the ever tight financial situation, he refused a raise to $25,000. But as part of his move he now received $200 a month as an expense and entertainment bonus, plus free use of a very large and stately house. From this point on, one cannot estimate the total compensation of Vanderbilt chancellors. They gained many of the prerogatives of the wealthy. The move to Belle Meade also had symbolic significance. Branscomb was now in a better position to host wealthy benefactors, such as the Harold S. Vanderbilts. He moved more easily in the Nashville social circles from which came both board members and financial support. But his large house and its servants widened the social distance between the chancellor and Vanderbilt professors, who struggled to make payments on modest houses in the campus area. More critical, the chancellor's residence, and its Belle Meade location, helped reinforce the class resentments of many Nashvillians toward a purportedly elite Vanderbilt, resentments that reached a peak in the 1950s. In short, Vanderbilt seemed to them a wealthy school patronized by the upper classes and attended by snobbish rich kids.[3]

Branscomb came to Vanderbilt with a reasonably clear understanding of what the university needed to compete with the best universities of the North. His work with Duke administrators, his intense involvement with the building of the Duke Divinity School, his national work with the Association of American Colleges, all provided him the needed perspectives and examples. He quickly established contacts with several other university presidents, moved onto the boards of national foundations, and accepted numerous consulting assignments with the federal government. But he had to match his vision of a great university with Vanderbilt traditions. His first attempt was his inaugural address on February 4, 1947. After carefully reading Mims's *History of Vanderbilt University,* he identified the heart of the school's tradition as a type of integrity. He honored the usual qualities celebrated at Vanderbilt festivities—high standards, tough degree requirements, the rejection of merely practical or vocational courses, and the traditional liberal arts emphasis upon individual character. He thus correctly identified Vanderbilt's best claim to a distinctive tradition in higher education. The evidence of such integrity were all around—the honor system, the rejection of honorary degrees or any other pandering to benefactors, the refusal to establish degree programs in physical education, industrial arts, or in business, unceasing efforts to screen out "crip" courses, and the reluctant abandonment of classical language requirements. Even Vanderbilt's frustrating effort to clean up big-time athletics reflected its basic integrity; the guilt that accompanied continued Southeastern Conference participation reflected this sense of integrity violated.

Upon this tradition Branscomb wanted to draft the other, missing requirements of academic leadership. In his inaugural address he sketched in his more general goals—to serve the development needs of a resurgent South, particularly in manufacturing and government services, which meant improved facilities and research programs in the natural and social sciences; to escape not only sectional but national provincialism; to build new programs in international relations, which would entail stronger departments in languages, area studies, and the social sciences; to transmit and enhance the broad values of a Western, or Christian, civilization; to add to the pursuit of truth a concern for preferences and taste, for moral engagement and a sustaining faith, a faith that Branscomb characteristically expressed in the broadest possible language (in man, in nature, or in God).

From such broad goals Branscomb soon clarified several specific needs: To buy land and break the stranglehold that private property owners placed on a too small campus; to build new dorms to entice more distant students and thus enable Vanderbilt to break from its provincial shell; to expand classrooms and, even more, research facilities, so that Vanderbilt could contribute to the basic knowledge needed in a growing South; to develop a pilot international studies program (it would, of course, involve Brazil); to gain higher faculty salaries and thus be able to recruit outstanding scholars and scientists in several key departments; to develop stronger Law and Religion schools, with special concern for Religion; to begin a more rigorous screening in faculty appointments and promotions; and, finally, somehow to find a way to deemphasize intercollegiate athletics and to bring social fraternities under the control of Vanderbilt administrators. These were goals aplenty, few completely original to Branscomb. But as a newcomer he was in an excellent position to identify Vanderbilt's problems and to develop new strategies to solve them. Unfortunately, all the needed reforms required the cooperation of the Board of Trust, plus incalculable increases in Vanderbilt's endowment and operating budgets.[4]

The board remained as it had been since 1914—a club of old alumni, mostly businessmen, all deeply committed to Vanderbilt but usually suspicious of innovations. As Branscomb remembered the board that appointed him, it was made up of good friends, almost all well over sixty-five, who enjoyed their twice-a-year reunion on campus. Frank Rand, the now aging board president, died on December 2, 1949, to be succeeded by W.L. Hemingway, another old man with fewer than five years to live. Branscomb believed the board needed more youth, more diversity, and, if possible, greater wealth. To gain this he had to take time and proceed cautiously. In

1948, on request of the Alumni Association, the board approved a special new committee on membership. The Alumni Association wanted restricted terms for their specially nominated candidates, since by a hallowed tradition the board always reelected trustees at the end of their eight-year terms. In effect, a position on the board brought life tenure, even for the elected president. Carefully guided by Branscomb, the new committee proposed a limit of thirty-three on the active members of the board but proposed honorary, nonvoting membership for all those over either seventy-two or seventy-five. Even this touched sensitive nerves on the board, but in June, 1950, it approved a mild reform. At seventy-two, board members had to retire from active duty but could be elected as life trustees with full voting rights. Such life trustees would be in addition to the thirty-three active members, a change that soon increased the board to over forty members and increased the effective power of the chancellor.[5]

From 1950 on, the board in effect did much of its work through two standing committees, the Executive Committee, made up largely of trustees from or near Nashville, and the Finance Committee, made up of most of the other very active board members. In 1952, as the work of the board increased, it asked for longer meetings (two days instead of one day of business). In 1956, in a mild revolt against the powers of the Nashville trustees, who made up a small, socially prominent, and very exclusive club of their own, the board took from the Executive Committee the power of nominating new board members and placed this crucial responsibility in a nominating committee of five, no more than two of whom could be also on the Executive Committee, and thus in all likelihood from Nashville. These changes led to a slow shift to a somewhat younger and more dynamic board, including a shift toward non-southern trustees, to a few crucial nonalumni trustees, and to two ex-faculty appointees. This was as far as the board would go in "modernizing" its structure. These shifts changed only slightly the board's homogeneity and conventional outlook. But they helped the board recruit new talent and insured that it would continue to follow the chancellor's leadership. Except on the divisive issue of integration, it remained a consensual, harmonious club.[6]

The critical nonalumni appointee was Harold S. Vanderbilt. He first agreed to board membership in 1950, at age sixty-six. Branscomb rightly considered the successful wooing of this modern Commodore as the greatest coup of his chancellorship. In importance for Vanderbilt it easily compared to McTyeire's courtship of the old Commodore. Harold Vanderbilt was, by 1950, the best-known descendant of Cornelius Vanderbilt. He kept up the family business enterprises and had chaired the board of the New York Central. He served in the navy during World War I and then became internationally known for his success in racing yachts (he was a three-time winner of the America's Cup) and for compiling rules for yacht racing. He was also the inventor of contract bridge. Branscomb began writing Vanderbilt soon after he took office as chancellor and eventually persuaded him and his young wife to make a one-day visit to Vanderbilt in November, 1949. They walked into a carefully prepared process of courtship. Branscomb showed the couple the campus, pointed out the portraits of progenitors, and carefully avoided any request for money. He flattered Vanderbilt by a request for a portrait of the late Frederick W. Vanderbilt and asked his help in soliciting a contribution from his aunt. The chancellor and a board member poured on the southern hospitality. Trustee Frank Houston further deepened the relationship on a world cruise. In May, 1950, Vanderbilt accepted a two-year term on the board and thus became slowly more involved with the university. Branscomb carefully cultivated his growing interest, which culminated in his acceptance of the board presidency in 1955. His financial contributions eventually made him Vanderbilt's greatest personal benefactor. But it is unfair to emphasize only one side of Harold S. Vanderbilt's role. He gained even as he gave. His earlier fame rested on corporate management, on investment success, and on his achievements as a sportsman. The university pulled him into a socially important, personally rewarding enterprise, into what became his most compelling vocation in the last years of his life. For him, this educational role was both an opportunity and a privilege.[7]

Even as Branscomb did as much as possible to shape a board as open as possible to his reforms at Vanderbilt, he slowly began to assemble an administrative staff. When he took over in 1946 he inherited Madison Sarratt as vice-chancellor, Andrew B. Benedict as university treasurer, and the various deans, with Philip Davidson of the Graduate School and Senior College in the most critical position. In 1948 Branscomb changed Davidson's title to that of provost of all the undergraduate colleges as well as dean of the Graduate School. Branscomb had some disagreements with Benedict but kept him on until his death in 1953. Benedict's task then went to two capable men—Edwin S. Gardner, treasurer, and Overton Williams, comptroller and bursar. Sarratt worked most effectively with alumni relations and on athletic problems but had a limited policy role. In 1958 he reached mandatory retirement age (seventy) but remained on the payroll as a special consultant or an honorary "Dean of Alumni." As he lived on and on, he became a beloved living symbol of Vanderbilt traditions, a perennially displayed centerpiece for every fund-raising effort.[8]

Slowly, Branscomb was able to form his own administrative team. In 1948 he appointed Robert McGaw, an alumnus with journalistic and publishing experience, as a special assistant in charge of public relations. McGaw would also serve for a time as alumni secretary and as editor of the *Alumnus*. In 1956, after he had decided to resign as alumni secretary, he moved up to direct a reorganized Office of Information and Publication. He became Branscomb's chief campus spokesman, the one who tried carefully to encourage more and better news about Vanderbilt. In 1951, after Philip Davidson moved to the

Chancellor Harvie Branscomb, 1949

Vice-Chancellor Rob Roy Purdy

Robert McGaw

456

presidency of the University of Louisville, Branscomb eliminated the office of provost. Already the College had eliminated the administrative distinction between junior and senior colleges and was now headed by one dean. In 1951 Leonard Beach moved from chairman of the English department at the University of Oklahoma to become dean of an expanding graduate program at Vanderbilt. He worked closely with Branscomb and did more than anyone else to develop creditable Ph.D. programs. In 1956 Branscomb appointed a former Eisenhower administration official, John H. Stambaugh, as vice-chancellor for business affairs. Stambaugh was an able, cautious business manager, sharply divergent from most faculty members in beliefs. But he served Branscomb well in budgetary and investment policies and in a sustained program of campus expansion. He also worked with all the details of faculty fringe benefits.

Because of the increasing demands of fund raising, the board established a new office of development in 1955, one briefly headed by Oliver C. Carmichael, Jr., and then later by Don R. Elliott, who became a vital member of Branscomb's emerging management team. Finally, in 1959 Branscomb asked the board for a new executive officer, a vice-chancellor for academic affairs. For this he turned to Rob Roy Purdy of the English department, an able teacher, a conscientious committeeman, and an eloquent speaker. Purdy completed a small cabinet that supported Branscomb during the Lawson controversy of 1960. In this crisis period it included McGaw and Purdy in the inner circle, with Stambaugh and Beach in the outer circle, critical in their more restricted areas of responsibility. At the top it now took six men to do what Kirkland had done by himself in the 1930s, and just beneath the cabinet was a growing administrative staff—deans of men and women, a growing alumni and development staff, housing and food service directors, an admissions director and a registrar, associate or assistant academic deans in Arts and Science and in Medicine, and so on and on, with one addition almost every year.[9]

The one increasing task of the board and central administration was finding the new income needed to support Vanderbilt's rapid growth. In a fifteen-year period the university budget exploded, from $2.7 million in 1946–47 to $12 million in 1961–62, and that exclusive of over $4 million of grants. By 1963 total university expenditures reached $22 million, and more than that if one included student payments to the university for books, room, board, and other services. This sevenfold increase in cost accompanied a much more modest increase in the endowment—from approximately $38 million in 1946 to $88 million in 1963 (market value). The endowment, the largest source of income during the first seventy-five years of the university, slowly shrank from approximately 50 percent of income in 1947 to only 17 percent in 1963. Despite a steady increase in tuition fees, the percentage of income gained from students stopped growing just after the war and then declined steadily, from over 50 percent in 1950 to only 25 percent in 1963.

By then, annual gifts, grants, hospital fees, and a few rentals accounted for 57 percent of income, and these were growing in importance each year. In addition to finding ways to meet such increased costs, the board also raised or borrowed money for an unprecedented increase in capital expenditures, including over thirty new buildings or major additions to buildings. Of course, inflation accounted for almost half these increases and also helps explain the decreasing role of an endowment. But even calculated in constant dollars, the rate of expansion was unprecedented in Vanderbilt's history. How did the administration and board get all the money? Since almost half of the budget went to the hospital, the single most important source of new income was increased patient fees. This complex story will be told later. For all other budget accounts, and for capital expenditures, the increased income came from foundations, from individuals, from government or corporate grants and loans, and from higher tuition.[10]

Before World War II almost all gifts had gone to Vanderbilt's endowment. Then, almost all universities lived on tuition payments and endowment income, with only a small trickle of operating grants or gifts. Such a strategy fit a period without inflation, with almost no direct corporate or governmental support for private higher education, and with no public funding of medical care. After World War II universities concentrated more of their income in their operating budgets. In effect, they also began to sell more of their services. In theory, such a sale of services earned no profits, which was certainly true for Vanderbilt's deficit-plagued hospital. But a largely self-sustaining hospital is, from another perspective, a huge, indispensable laboratory. For federal and corporate grantors, universities also provided a full measure of research services. Such research brought more, and abler, professors to the campuses and helped procure needed facilities and equipment for students. In this sense Vanderbilt followed the pattern of all large universities and, in fact, lagged well behind most in the proportion of its budget funded by research grants.

Parallel to the increased role of services was a gradual change in foundation policies. Before World War II, Vanderbilt's chief patrons, the GEB and the Carnegie Corporation, gave almost all their gifts to Vanderbilt's endowment or, as they put it, they "capitalized" a reasonably secure level of annual income. For brief periods, usually to inaugurate new programs, they made limited-term grants to the operating budget but either withdrew these at the end of the stipulated term or capitalized them. But after the war the foundations made as many gifts for capital expenditures, or for the improvement of specific academic programs, as to endowments. Along with this, alumni organizations placed their greatest emphasis on annual unrestricted giving, or what Vanderbilt and a few other universities call a Living Endowment. The postwar pattern of financing was highly fluid, complex, and insecure; Kirkland would never have borne up under the strain. Each year a university had to rely upon inputs from thousands of sources. Some of this income came from generous individuals, but the gifts ranged all the way down to alumni donations of $10, which probably did not cover the cost of solicitation. Each year grants of all kinds expired and had to be replaced by new ones. Income that came from consumer services (medical care) was always vulnerable, not only to recession or depression but to market competition or abrupt changes in government welfare policies. In the case of the hospital, Vanderbilt had to sell a product in a very competitive market. The reason Vanderbilt administrators did not succumb to ulcers was the very diversity of income sources, the symbiotic ties of university services to government and business, and the predictability of the work carried out by key university faculty and bureaucrats, including those in public relations, development, alumni support, and sponsored research.

When Branscomb first came to Vanderbilt, he emphasized three areas of expansion—new dorms, expanded graduate programs, and higher faculty salaries. Before he came, funds and plans for a new gym and a new Engineering building were all but complete. Two new dorms (McGill and Tolman) were almost completed, but if Vanderbilt was to break out of its insularity it needed many more. Budgets were tight, despite the great postwar bulge in enrollment. Tuition in the College was only $315 in 1946–47 and still only $500 in Medicine. The rapid inflation of 1947 quickly undermined the value of the endowment and shrank the real wages of faculty members, although rising interest rates and an increased investment in common stock helped raise the endowment's annual yield. Alumni gifts barely covered the cost of alumni services. Eventually, the gifts collected for the gym were insufficient to complete the building as planned. Only F.W. Vanderbilt's undistributed estate enabled Vanderbilt to expand during the reconversion period. Yet, new possibilities began to open up. Not only were dorms self-liquidating, but soon the U.S. Housing and Home Finance Agency advanced very low-interest loans for such projects. Foundation support soon reached an all-time high, largely because of the new Ford Foundation. In one case the sheer entrepreneurial ability of a professor took over. Carl Seyfert, the popular university astronomer and television weatherman, began in 1951 the almost single-handed development of a new observatory for a hill site far to the south of the campus. He received $25,000 from Arthur Dyer, plus construction work from his Nashville Bridge Company, and solicited most of the other needed materials and work from Nashville businesses.[11]

In 1947 Branscomb was elected to the GEB. He served during the final liquidation of that Rockefeller charity and secured more than a fair share for Vanderbilt. This distribution began in 1948, with a gift of $130,000 for three years to fund research in the social sciences and to help develop new Ph.D. programs. In December, 1949, the GEB granted $1.2 million, on a matching basis, for improved graduate education and another $1 million to begin a separate Graduate School endowment. The university raised the matching funds with great difficulty. In late 1951, as part of one of its last major grants, the GEB offered an additional $1.5 million as a matching grant for faculty development in the College and Graduate School ($500,000 for operations, $1 million for endowment, to be matched over ten years by $2 million of additional gifts). To back up this support, the Carnegie Foundation gave $30,000 for graduate education in 1951 (spread over five years), and in 1952 the Rockefeller Foundation gave $112,000 for social science research and training. When fully matched, all these gifts meant a Graduate School endowment of $5 million. These funds provided the basis of new faculty recruitment and improved faculty salaries, plus research support for most graduate fields. Note that support for the Graduate School, although some funds went to both Religion and Medicine, largely aided the College. But the era of GEB support was now almost over. In its final liquidation, it gave $1 million in 1959 ($250,000 for research labs, $750,000 for the Graduate School), to make a final total of over $23 million given to Vanderbilt. As the GEB faded out, the Ford Foundation took over. It, and then the enormous private gifts of Harold S. Vanderbilt, became the primary source of outside income for Vanderbilt after 1955.[12]

In 1955 the Ford Foundation committed $500 million to private universities and hospitals. In its first major distribution, Vanderbilt received $1,249,000 for the College and $186,000 for the hospital, or the twenty-fifth largest gift and third largest in the South (behind Hopkins and Duke). Vanderbilt added two-thirds of the College gift to endowment and used one-third to fund increasingly higher faculty salaries. In 1957 the Ford Foundation granted $2.3 million for the almost desperate Medical School. In 1960 the Foundation selected Vanderbilt as one of five favored sectional universities and offered it an original $4 million, nonrestricted gift on a two-to-one matching basis to be paid out over three years. This proved the seed money for a great $30 million campaign launched in 1960. Such a sum seemed preposterous even to some board members, but the university achieved it in two years, clearing the way for additional foundation gifts in the 1960s.[13]

This successful campaign, the last triumph of Branscomb, in a sense his departing gift to the university, also revealed fundamental shifts in the nature of fund drives. Even before the public campaign opened, board members had pledged over $11 million, or more than enough to balance the Ford grant. This meant that the remaining fund drive was for only $15 million, not really $30 million. Most of the additional $15 million came from a few large donors. In addition to a large trust that accounted for much of the $11 million, Harold Vanderbilt gave a challenge grant of $2 million in 1962 in order to complete the drive. But success did not mean an early receipt of $30 million. In fact, the immediate return was largely the Ford grant, not only because of continuing pledges (many scheduled their gifts over several years), but because the whole focus of alumni giving had shifted toward bequests or trusts, each unrealized until the death of a donor. Such gifts, led by those of

460

Harold S. Vanderbilt, accounted for the speed, and success, of the fund drive.[14]

Huge foundation and private gifts should not obscure the importance of tuition. It has a special status among sources of income. In a financial crunch, tuition increases often enable universities to balance their budgets. But at some peril. In periods of slack enrollment, tuition increases can cut off a flow of needed students. Even when applicants are plentiful, tuition increases, short of plentiful scholarships, cut off students from lower- or even middle-income families, which means the exclusion of some of the most talented students and an unwanted homogeneity. During the years from 1946 to 1963 tuition grew much more rapidly than living costs, but probably at about the same rate as family income among those parents most likely to send children to Vanderbilt. The 1950s brought bountiful gifts to the business and professional classes of the Midsouth.

As one would expect, tuition increases at Vanderbilt correlated with enrollment and application patterns. After the GI boom, enrollments fell rapidly in the early 1950s, an effect of the low birth rates in the depression. Small colleges struggled to survive. Even Vanderbilt wanted more students than it attracted in several of its schools. Thus, tuition increases through the mid-1950s roughly matched inflation; in the College these rose from $405 in the fall of 1947 to $525 in 1955. Medicine and Law were higher, Engineering comparable, the Graduate School and Nursing somewhat lower. But by 1955 enrollments began to climb. For a decade everyone had been anticipating the great enrollment boom that would begin about 1959, a boom that reflected increased birth rates from the beginning of World War II all the way through the 1950s. And, indeed, by 1959–60 the applications soared, admission standards rose sharply, and so did tuition. The total enrollment reached an early peak of about 3,700 students in the fall semester of 1948–49, and then steadily declined to a low of approximately 2,900 students from 1951 through 1954, and from then rose continuously to an enrollment of almost 4,000 in 1962–63. By then, only carefully maintained quotas kept the enrollment so low. Throughout this growth period the university justified a series of tuition increases by the need to raise faculty salaries (in fact, what income goes to what purpose is largely a matter of budget juggling). In the fall of 1958–59 the College tuition rose to $750, to $900 in 1960–61, and to $1,000 in 1962–63, plus a new $10 application fee. Yet with each year the rising tuition paid a smaller and smaller percentage of university costs.[15]

Annual alumni gifts, unrestricted or not tied to pledges made in fund drives, had always constituted a tiny part of Vanderbilt's income. Until after the war, small alumni gifts at Vanderbilt had never really paid the cost of collecting them, if one attributes to them the cost of alumni personnel and publications. At the end of World War II annual unrestricted contributions to the Living Endowment finally rose to about $10,000, or a total of $93,000 for all gifts. About 20 percent of all alumni contributed. In 1948 unrestricted

461

gifts dropped to a postwar low of $17,000, largely because alumni shifted their pledges to the gym or to other restricted purposes. After that, expert efforts by the alumni office gradually increased alumni giving. By 1951–52 the total received reached over $300,000, but unrestricted gifts made up only $32,000. Only in 1956–57 did unrestricted gifts reach even $100,000. In 1960–61, during the great campaign, these climbed to $250,000, with one of the highest participation rates in the country (by comparison, the Living Endowment reached over $8 million in the 1980s). Such small alumni gifts were only a pittance, but the purpose of alumni solicitation was not so much to bring in money as to sustain the interest and involvement of alumni. From some of these alumni would come the large gifts and the great bequests.[16]

As alumni gifts slowly increased, one result of postwar economic changes became apparent. The South moved toward parity with the North; the sunbelt phenomenon first became visible. With each passing year Vanderbilt was able to turn more often to southern benefactors. In the South, and in Nashville, several alumni were becoming wealthy, not in the sense of the Vanderbilts and Rockefellers, but millionaires nonetheless. For example, in the $30 million campaign, Eldon Stevenson, from the local National Life and Accident Insurance Company, not only gave large trust funds but added a final $250,000 to help the drive achieve success. One other notable gift of $1 million, the largest yet from any individual outside the Vanderbilt family, came in 1958 from W. Alton Jones. A native of Missouri, a Vanderbilt alumnus, Jones had moved up in the oil business to head the Cities Service Company in New York City. As Branscomb remembered it, Jones gave this munificent gift when he felt burdened to turn down a flattering offer from Harold S. Vanderbilt to become a Vanderbilt trustee. He received the offer at the Kentucky Derby during an outing by the whole board (the boys of the club enjoyed such special treats but never used university funds to pay for them).[17]

The university had two large capital costs in the postwar period—new buildings and the purchase of extra land for eventual campus expansion. Except in one case—the new Divinity School building—the board never dipped into the endowment, or its earnings, for these costs, and it did so in this one case in order to qualify for a huge gift from John D. Rockefeller, Jr. The rebuilding of the campus began, in a sense, in 1947. The university then retained Edward Durell Stone Associates as supervising architects. Stone, then a young and far from famous architect, completed another plan or map for the campus, one that guided the placement of most subsequent buildings. He recommended that the main campus retain malls and open areas, that internal roadways be closed to automobiles, and that new buildings make a wall around the campus at its outer edges. This plan has created the present campus profile with its seemingly impenetrable exterior. Many Nashville visitors never really see the campus; those who walk into the campus are often entranced by the internal vistas. Stone's plan had some hidden snares. It, as

Air view of campus, looking south

many previous ones, assumed the razing of Kissam and Old Science. Painfully, with nostalgic resistance even from board members, the university finally demolished Kissam early in 1958, six years after it first voted its demise. The demolition helped create one of the internal malls. But Old Science survived all the plans and still basks in its refurbished glory, defiant in its unique and absurdly illogical orientation.[18]

New buildings soon began filling in Stone's plan. Cole Hall added another dorm to the contemplated quadrangle. In 1951, with federal loans, the university began what became Vanderbilt and Barnard Halls, the first wall along West End. In 1951 it also began the Rand dining complex, one of the planned interior buildings to serve students. In 1956 the wall expanded to the northeastern part of the campus, to the six-dorm Kissam complex (designed by Stone, but of flimsy construction and shabby design). In 1961 construction began on the Law School, or part of the wall to the east, a wall only

463

completed in 1981 with the new Owen Graduate School of Management. A huge federal loan ($3 million, later increased) funded most of the cost of the Branscomb quadrangle, a huge complex for women planned as early as 1951 but completed only in 1962. The government also funded two apartment complexes for married students (Lewis and Morgan houses), also completed in 1962. These became imperative in 1958, when the new Veteran's Administration Hospital displaced most of the settlement, the old temporary postwar apartments to the south of Garland. Athletic funds paid for two small additions to the football stadium, which increased its seating to 34,000, and for additions of small gyms and extra seats in Memorial Gym. In 1954, as part of its payment for use of the stadium, the Billy Graham Crusade contributed almost half the cost of new stadium lights. Several income-producing expansions of the hospital, including the large west wing with its circular wards (1962), depended upon government grants or loans, some under the Hill-Burton Act.[19]

Income-producing buildings were the easy ones to finance. In fact, one of the mysteries of Vanderbilt history is why the university lagged so long in the development of self-liquidating dorms. But classrooms and laboratories not only yield no direct income but increase operating costs. Here, a major construction program began only late in the Branscomb period and was not completed until the mid-1960s. The belated completion of Divinity and Law buildings make up part of the story of those two schools (see chapter 18). The Engineering Building (1950) utilized funds solicited at the end of the war plus a share of the old Frederick Vanderbilt estate. During the 1950s private, largely local gifts helped fund additions to the building, including a much needed mechanical engineering lab. The greatest needs in the College involved the natural sciences. The labs in Buttrick, Garland, and Furman were now antiquated. Because of the enrollment sag in the early 1950s and a scheduling of classes over most of the day, classrooms remained adequate. Minor new projects helped. In 1948 the Federal Works Agency gave Vanderbilt a temporary frame theater, located on the south side of Garland Avenue. Its huge stage became the site of the greatest flowering of theater in Vanderbilt's history, and for years it housed a well-attended series of foreign films. The move of the Divinity School into its new home in 1960 cleared space in Wesley for the philosophy and psychology departments, after the Vanderbilt board had refused to sell the building to the University of Tennessee as a home for the School of Social Work. It took only $150,000, in 1961, to convert the old gym into a small museum and a lovely home for the fine arts department. Otherwise, the College departments all remained in facilities dating at least as far back as the 1920s.[20]

The first effort to solve the problems of the natural sciences involved more cooperation with the Medical School. In the early 1950s the Medical School used grants and gifts to begin two new laboratories, both attached to the hospital. It completed, and named after the prime benefactor, a smaller Light

Air view of library addition and Medical Center

Laboratory for surgical research. It was able, at first, to complete only a three-story shell of a graduate research building, at the north end of the original Medical School building. The location, toward the main campus, was carefully planned, because the laboratories were to be used by both College and Medical School scientists. But a lack of money meant that, for over two years, only a few of the medically oriented labs had any equipment. In 1953 A.B. Learned gave $75,000 to complete the three bottom floors of what was to be a nine-story building. Only in 1958 did the Surgeon General's Office give $700,000, on a matching basis, to complete the upper stories of the Learned Laboratories. The completed building enormously increased the resources for basic research at Vanderbilt, but it did not provide the scientific laboratories needed for teaching students or nearly enough space to accommodate growing faculties in physics, chemistry, and mathematics.[21]

As part of the $30 million campaign, or what the board considered a great

465

Air view of the Old Gym and nearby campus

"modernization effort," Vanderbilt began planning for a huge science center, later named after the fund chairman, Eldon Stevenson, Jr. This was by far the most elaborate classroom facility ever completed at Vanderbilt, and even early, modest projections set its cost at over $4 million. By 1963 only one part of the new center was complete—a circular computer center, rushed to completion to accommodate a new IBM 7072, the first transistorized computer at Vanderbilt. The system cost approximately $460,000, the building to house it only $325,000. The early funding of the center represented a new financial tactic for Vanderbilt, which borrowed the money using as collateral trust funds given during the campaign. To make this financing even more painless, Harold S. Vanderbilt gave $500,000 to pay the interest. By Branscomb's retirement the only future buildings envisioned, except for self-liquidating dorms and a new student center, were several additions to the Medical School, including already planned expansions to the front and new x-ray facilities in the center; a major addition to JUL (then contemplated as

466

additional floors added to the old building), and rather vague plans for a new graduate school of business, or plans that the board first discussed just after the war. Despite all the frustrations over the now aging hospital, and many dreams about a beautiful new one, the straitened financial situation of the early 1960s allowed no plans for such in the foreseeable future.[22]

Branscomb, when he first visited Vanderbilt, professed his dismay at the small, hemmed-in campus. Plans for expansion seemed thwarted by a lack of space. Scarritt and Peabody cut off any expansion to the east. Despite futile Vanderbilt protest, the city of Nashville slowly zoned the north side of West End for commercial development; it became an ugly business strip marked off by one gaudy sign after another. Older residential blocks filled the areas to the south and west. As far back as the Kirkland era, the board had approved various administrative requests to purchase homes between 24th Avenue and the stadium when houses came on the market and Vanderbilt could drive a good bargain. The siting of the new gym required a more expansive policy. Vanderbilt purchased the playing fields of the old Duncan School and later the school itself, thereby gaining parking space adjacent to the gym and stadium. The university delayed the Branscomb quadrangle for years in

Branscomb Quadrangle

Kissam Quadrangle

order, slowly and with reasonable prices, to buy up several houses not already owned by the university. These purchases joined the two parts of the campus, although several private plots remained to the north of Vanderbilt Place, mixed in with fraternities and sororities. Meanwhile, Branscomb secured permission from the board to purchase, without prior board approval, other property to the south whenever it came on the market. By 1957 the university owned several scattered properties as far west as Natchez Trace, and along 24th and 25th avenues as far south as Blakemore. Its immediate needs included more playing fields south of the stadium and land south of Garland for new apartment buildings for married students.[23]

Campus expansion took off in 1956, after the appointment of Stambaugh as vice-chancellor. One of his tasks was land acquisition. In 1957, fully familiar with the possibilities because of his work within the Eisenhower administration, he first suggested that Vanderbilt join Scarritt and Peabody to have a large area around the campuses designated as an essential urban development area. If so designated, then any approved developer, including Vanderbilt, could use the right of eminent domain to acquire needed property at fair market value. This strategy, alone, promised to hold down real estate prices in the area. Stambaugh drew up a map of likely Vanderbilt expansion and marked off the whole area to Blakemore and Natchez Trace. He believed all the unpurchased plots, many with decaying houses, was then worth only about $1.25 million, or a relatively small cost as compared with the estimated $4 million for a science center. The board rejected such grandiose plans, opposed any scheme for the use of eminent domain, but began appropriating for, or retroactively approving, an expanded annual purchase effort. Stambaugh often spent more than his targeted budget. While he aggressively purchased, the private colleges of the state succeeded in having the Tennessee legislature pass a bill granting them the right of eminent domain, justified by the constitutionally dubious argument that these colleges served a public interest. Branscomb and other administrative officials participated in the legislative effort, but Cecil Sims, board member and long-time university attorney, believed the bill unconstitutional. In fact, no private colleges used it and the bill has remained unused and untested.[24]

In 1961 Vanderbilt joined Peabody and Scarritt in an application to the Nashville Planning Commission for a large urban renewal project. The designated area stretched from 18th Avenue to Natchez Trace, and from West End to Blakemore. Vanderbilt had by far the largest stake in this effort. Scarritt and Peabody sought access only to land along 18th Avenue and immediately south of the Peabody campus. The Nashville Planning Commission made the needed federal application. It gained preliminary approval in 1962, a year in which urban renewal was strongly supported by a Kennedy administration committed to economic recovery after the recession of 1961. The U.S. Housing and Home Finance Agency also granted $7,907,000 to Nashville to support the renewal effort. But several snags plagued the project, postponing final approval until the mid-1960s. By then, resentful private owners, now legally forced to sell to Vanderbilt at market prices, charged that Vanderbilt had tricked or defrauded them. But Branscomb left office with a great sense of achievement—Vanderbilt had finally broken out of its earlier shell.[25]

How much Vanderbilt should grow had become a critical issue by 1960. For the first time in its history it had to turn away highly qualified young men from most of its schools. Because of its continued quota system, it had had to turn away highly qualified women as far back as the 1920s. One welcome result of enrollment pressures was an intensely competitive admission process and steadily better qualified students, particularly in the College and in Engineering. In 1957 the College made the Scholastic Aptitude Test (SAT) scores mandatory for women and a year later applied this rule to men, excepting good football players. The early scores helped shatter a consoling myth at Vanderbilt—that its male students made up an elite comparable to the students in better Ivy League schools. Not so. Vanderbilt's male freshmen in 1959–60 scored just 496 on the verbal, 553 on the math, for a combined score of 1049 (in Ivy League schools the mean combined score was above 1200). Vanderbilt women, as always, did better, with a combined score of 1077. These test scores subtly began to alter admission policies. The other bases of selection, the high school record or letters of recommendation, declined a bit, particularly the more informal and personal criteria. Another subtle, often unintended effect was a favoritism for nonsouthern applicants, since SAT scores were higher outside the South. The proportion of Nashville students in the College declined to a low of 16.6 percent in 1960–61. Another result was steadily improved SAT scores; by 1962–63, both male and female scores rose above 1200. Such changes created intense pressures from alumni parents, including those who loyally supported Vanderbilt fund drives. Their children often could not get admitted to the College.

The problem was most acute for young women. By 1960 only one out of four women applicants gained admission. The College, which tried to hold maximum enrollment to 1,800, had long maintained a quota of one-third women. Since Engineering was almost all male and about four times as large as Nursing, women made up only a bit more than one-fourth of undergraduates at Vanderbilt. In the College, of the 125 women admitted each year, only about 25 were accepted from Nashville, creating enormous pressures among Nashville alumni. In 1961 Vanderbilt had to reject thirty-two daughters of alumni, accepting only thirty-one, while it admitted ninety-seven sons to twenty rejected. The admissions office read alumni applications first and accepted all clearly qualified alumni children before moving on to other applications. Given the pressures, and increasing administrative support for expansion, the board in 1962 reluctantly raised the target enrollment in the College from 1,800 to 2,000, the first of a series of increases in the next two decades. These came in spite of wailing and gnashing of teeth over the loss of the small, intimate Vanderbilt so beloved by board members and older alumni.[26]

Vanderbilt cooperated with Peabody and Scarritt on urban renewal but on little else. The dream of a great University Center, so important to Carmichael, faded during the Branscomb years. It is difficult to assign responsibility for the failure. Jealousies abounded on both sides. And, as Vanderbilt outgrew Peabody, both in size and in prestige, the old Peabody fear of Vanderbilt imperialism again made negotiations very difficult. During Branscomb's early years cooperation seemed easier. By 1949 both institutions again had overlapping requests for GEB funds. Branscomb asked for some negotiated cooperation and pledged not to duplicate education courses at Vanderbilt. In 1952 Vanderbilt and Peabody representatives worked out the details of a joint graduate scheme in teaching for submission to the Ford Foundation. Even these negotiations at times proved difficult, but President Henry Hill of Peabody and Branscomb met in New York to work out the final details for a grant that led to a popular two-year Master of Arts in Teaching program, with substantive courses at Vanderbilt and education courses at Peabody. At the end of the three-year grant period, in 1955, Peabody refused to continue the cooperation; Vanderbilt decided to continue the M.A.T. program on its own. By then, the Vanderbilt faculty was pushing hard for a return to the semester system (achieved in 1957) and for an education department at Vanderbilt. Branscomb had concluded that lasting cooperation with Peabody was impossible without some organic unity, although one that preserved separate boards and endowments. Branscomb consistently held to such a view, which aroused all the old fears of imperialism on the Peabody campus. Any such relationship, he conceded, would require an initiative from the two boards and a genuine desire for such unity by both boards. But in the next few years the ties gradually loosened, with even the exchange of students dropping after 1957. In contrast to the 1930s, more Vanderbilt students now took courses at Peabody than the other way around, for Peabody had developed duplicate courses in most content disciplines. Its students were dependent on Vanderbilt instruction only in the more advanced or graduate areas.[27]

Abetted, as always, by the foundations, in 1961 Peabody and Vanderbilt opened new negotiations. Within a few months of each other the two universities also began a search for new heads, continuing the old pattern of tandem terms for their chancellors and presidents. The Peabody board desired closer relations with Vanderbilt and initiated the process. Dean Rusk, of the Rockefeller Foundation and a close friend of Branscomb, boosted the early effort. The Executive Committee of the Peabody board drafted a "Statement of Position," which became the basis of a large, outside study. In it, Peabody committed itself to a coordinated educational effort that would better serve the cause of higher education without subsuming the traditional identity or purpose of either institution. In May, 1961, the Vanderbilt board appointed trustees to a joint committee of trustees and approved a joint study by a prestigious outside educator, advised by a study committee composed of the chancellor of Rice, a high official in the Methodist Board of Education, and the dean of the School of Education at the University of Wisconsin. The paid director was John Dale Russell, a former commissioner of education, who established his study office in JUL. Both the GEB·and the Ford Foundation joined in offering $40,000 to fund this elaborate study, which eventuated in a ninety-six-page report and several longer staff studies.[28]

Russell, in his report, developed a very ambitious plan, but one that stopped short of the merger anticipated by Branscomb and his trustees. Russell wanted to bring all areas of academic cooperation under one administrative agency, called the Nashville University Center, with a board of trustees all its own (comparable to the board that governed JUL), and either a president or chancellor to head it (the executive officers of Vanderbilt and Peabody would take the alternative title). This board would establish a common calendar, review the budgets of each institution in order to determine where it needed to add supplemental funds, and approve all new programs of instruction and research. Other possible functions for it included supervision of a foreign language center, area study programs, a center for the performing arts, research contracts, a faculty club, a university press, intramural and intercollegiate sports, musical and dramatic clubs and presentations, and the urban renewal project. It might appoint distinguished professors, carry out common testing and counseling and placement efforts, administer financial aid, and possibly even take over a joint maintenance and purchasing program. To monitor these coordinated functions, the overarching board would appoint officers, or what might have become Center deans. The plan was to be open to participation by other Nashville institutions, not only Scarritt but possibly even Fisk. Basic to the plan was major foundation support to finance student interchange, to raise Peabody faculty salaries to the Vanderbilt level, to enable Peabody to reduce teaching loads to the level at Vanderbilt, and to establish the joint faculty club. In light of later developments and the expectations of the Vanderbilt board, it is significant that Russell considered and rejected, largely because of opposition at Peabody, a full merger, with Peabody becoming a College of Education within Vanderbilt University, but with a high degree of retained autonomy and with representatives of the Peabody board joining the Vanderbilt Board of Trust.[29]

The Russell report included a detailed and almost utopian dream for a great University Center. But the administrative structure—the super board and super chancellor—had no chance for acceptance by either institution. The Vanderbilt board, which had anticipated imminent merger, was bitterly disappointed. It considered the report on June 9, 1962, and simply concluded, after an extended discussion, that the larger, structural proposals were not "feasible and workable." It asked for joint institutional efforts to develop a more workable basis of cooperation. Indeed, the Vanderbilt board appointed members for a joint trustee committee to develop such plans. Peabody did not reciprocate, although at an informal level members of the two boards continued discussions. From these came a formal proposal, endorsed by the Vanderbilt board, for a joint study committee composed of three board members from each institution, chaired by the Vanderbilt chancellor. This was shot down by Peabody because it seemed stacked in Vanderbilt's favor. Unfortunate newspaper publicity, late in December, 1962, gave the erroneous impression that Peabody had thus rejected an imminent merger. Chancellor Branscomb, nearing the end of his administration, supported but minimized the importance or the durability of voluntary forms of cooperation and still sought some organic relationship. By then, all the study and effort and cost had led to no major new cooperation. The only immediate changes involved minor programs, including a university club for faculty, a combined Vanderbilt-Peabody band, and the continued sharing of coursework.[30]

Unknown at the time, this was also a last opportunity for Peabody. In the 1960s Vanderbilt enrollments and finances continued to grow while Peabody went into a slow decline. By the late 1960s it could no longer bargain

472

The Peabody campus at the time of merger talks after World War II

with Vanderbilt as an equal, but could only accept, or defiantly resist, merger with or absorption by Vanderbilt.

By choice, Vanderbilt gave up on one of the prime exhibits of institutional cooperation, the School of Social Work. In 1948 the final GEB grant expired. In 1947–48 Vanderbilt had to contribute nearly $9,000 to balance the school's budget and in 1948–49 budgeted an additional $10,000. By the original agreement Vanderbilt was alone responsible for such deficits. The school had done an outstanding job, was well regarded throughout the South, but had failed to gain a sustaining endowment, in spite of the fact that it rendered vital services to many public agencies. Branscomb recommended to the board that Vanderbilt not take further responsibility for the school at a time when he was struggling with horrendous deficits for the Medical School and Hospital. Although a joint effort, the Scarritt and Peabody contributions had become minimal. Branscomb invited the University of Tennessee to absorb the school, beginning such negotiations in 1948, at first with no success. In 1949–50 Vanderbilt had to cover a $28,000 deficit but limited what it would pay to $12,500 for one final year, 1950–51. With all Vander-bilt's support to end by June, 1951, the school seemed doomed. Its able director, Lora Lee Pederson, resigned in March, 1950, to move to the University of Texas. The GEB accepted Branscomb's explanations and agreed to the termination of Vanderbilt's financial support. Although the University of Tennessee was originally uninterested, Governor Gordon Browning wanted the school to continue. The state contributed a needed $15,000 in 1950–51 to a still growing school and, as part of a decision to begin a limited University of Tennessee program in Nashville, persuaded the University of Tennessee to take over the school for 1951–52. It remained for a time at its old but inadequate site, and it continued to enjoy JUL privileges and other types of cooperation from its institutional parents.[31]

The challenges, and frustrations, at the level of board policies are all clearly part of the story of any university. In the case of Branscomb, one other story best fits here—faculty development. In a still tightly centralized university, one without any hint of faculty government, it was largely up to Branscomb to take the initiative in revitalizing the faculty. In his judgment, Vanderbilt in 1946 had able teachers but precious few outstanding scholars and scientists except in medicine. And no wonder, given the lagging salaries, the almost nonexistent fringe benefits, the heavy teaching loads, and the scarcity of those few academic stars who set standards of performance for younger professors.

Branscomb found a lack of understanding on the part of the board and alumni of what a university had to commit, and sacrifice, in behalf of an outstanding faculty. It was quite clear that the most innovative, and often most cantankerous and unmanageable, intellectuals had not been attracted to Vanderbilt, at least since the demise or departure of most of the Agrarians. Even they had not fared well at Kirkland's Vanderbilt, or in the repressive intellectual environment of Vanderbilt, Nashville, and the South. One can only imagine how a John Dewey, or a preeminent Marxist scholar, or a persuaded and outspoken socialist, or even an avowed atheist, would have fit in at Vanderbilt. Such views, although commonplace among leading intellec-tuals in both America and Europe, were still a form of heresy in most of the South. A greater openness to a wide variety of beliefs, to daring and innova-tive research or teaching, including that with radical implications for prevail-ing beliefs and values, was a prerequisite for any great university.

Branscomb realized this. Carefully, he tried at first to educate his board on what recruitment of a high quality faculty really involved, but in the later stresses and strains of his administration either forgot, or beat a strategic retreat, from the degree of freedom by then considered normal at a Harvard or a Michigan or in English universities. In three areas—purported deviation from Christian orthodoxy, rejection of "fundamentally American political beliefs," and advocacy of equal rights for blacks—Branscomb faced enormous pressures in behalf of the status quo, and either as a matter of conviction or as a defensive ploy to preserve as much freedom as possible at Vanderbilt, he considerably qualified his commitment to an open, pluralistic university. These compromises are part of some complex and fascinating stories concerning the various schools, and as such become a part of the next chapter.

One clear mark of Vanderbilt's lagging status was its lack of a tenure system. From 1925 on, the American Association of University Professors (AAUP) had struggled to gain tenure for faculty members. In 1940 it published a famous statement on tenure that became a guide for most new tenure systems. Branscomb wanted such a policy at Vanderbilt and secured both faculty and board support for it in 1948. The new rules provided for the standard six years of trial for junior staff members. If an assistant professor survived the trial period (two three-year appointments), the university either had to grant him or her tenure or, after an additional year for job seeking, terminate his or her employment. The university could, of course, grant tenure before six years or terminate at the end of the first three-year appointment. Those faculty members who received tenure had a permanent position, contingent on satisfactory "service and character." This meant they could be removed only for cause and after an adequate hearing. Such rules had a double purpose. They gave assurance and security to able professors and thus reinforced their desire to remain at Vanderbilt. To a limited extent, such security also protected academic freedom, making it more difficult to remove a professor because of his or her beliefs or because of controversial teaching. But most people overestimate the role of tenure in this area. For universities such as Vanderbilt, numerous constraints against arbitrary dismissal already existed—adverse publicity, damaged recruitment, and lagging faculty morale. Tenure does not, in itself, protect an unpopular or trouble-making professor against all manner of penalties short of dismissal—no raises, no committee assignments or honors, and subtle administrative pressures to seek jobs elsewhere.

The second purpose of tenure was more important to the goal of upgrading the faculty. This was the careful screening of junior faculty to eliminate all but the most promising. Heretofore, the retention or dismissal of instructors and assistant professors had been on an informal basis, with varying rules from department to department. The result had been, more often than not, lazy retention. After two or three years of faithful service, competent but average professors simply never left Vanderbilt. Only the brilliant left; they attracted plenty of offers. After 1948 this pattern began to change. Not dramatically. The demand for professors was too intense in 1948 for Vanderbilt to exercise tough tenure judgments. Then, after a stable and more rigorous screening process in the early 1950s, the market began to toughen once again. By the early 1960s few junior professors failed to get tenure at Vanderbilt or almost anywhere else.[32]

Branscomb and his board literally bent over backward to fund increases in salaries and benefits. Consistently, throughout Vanderbilt's history, the Board of Trust had worked zealously to raise faculty salaries. The opposition to salary increases had almost always come from administrators. As postwar inflation joined with severe budget crises at Vanderbilt, the university could not begin to match salaries to increased living costs. Few universities did, as real salaries of professors plummeted all over the country. From 1939 to 1948 living costs increased by 60 percent, Vanderbilt salaries by only 25 percent. In 1948 the average professor at Vanderbilt (outside Medicine) received only $4,800, or just $1,200 over the $3,600 required to lure assistant professors and to give them a living wage. To add insult to injury, football coach "Red" Sanders moved up, in 1948, from $8,500 to $10,000.

As a gesture, the board in 1948 voted bonuses, or supplemental grants, to all faculty members earning less than $6,000 (that meant all but three or four in the College). In 1949 some key faculty members resigned to take better paid positions elsewhere, including Frank Owsley, one of the last three Agrarians. The board voted a needed $75,000 in 1949 to bring the College scale up to $6,000 for full professors, $5,000 for associates, and $4,000 for assistants. This was the target goal, but one met in individual cases only after a few years and one already exceeded for a few abler professors. In 1951 the board raised this goal to $6,500 for full professors, and by then one professor in the College had a salary of $10,000; two had salaries over $8,000. But as late as 1952 the average for full professors was only $6,440 (slightly less in Engineering and Divinity, a great deal less in Nursing, in a year in which six professors from the College left for better jobs and a dozen others had good offers). The raises only kept professors at the real income levels of 1946 and left them well below those of 1939. Coincidentally, a new coach moved to Vanderbilt for $12,000 in 1953. In 1954 the median salary climbed to $6,115 compared with $7,887 for North Carolina, $7,700 for Duke. By then, the highest paid professors in the Medical School earned $25,000.[33]

After 1955 Vanderbilt finally made substantial progress on faculty salaries. For the next eight years gains outpaced living costs while Vanderbilt gained ground on most of its southern competitors. It was Branscomb's goal to bring Vanderbilt salaries close to those in the largest and most prestigious universities of the North, both in order to retain able staff and effectively to recruit the best, including a few key professors at the highest rank. Increasingly, the university used merit raises to achieve those goals, leaving a few underpaid, often older professors to depress the averages. In 1955 Harold S. Vanderbilt added $75,000 to the $75,000 voted by the board for merit increases, and in subsequent years he, more than anyone else on the board, fought the battle for higher salaries. Income from tuition increases all went to salary budgets. In 1956 professors in the College received from $6,000 to $12,000, with an average of about $8,000. The ablest chair professors or those with outstanding scholarly records all were above $9,000. These climbed every year, and gradually the highest salaries in the College closed in on that of the football coach. The average full professor earned about $9,300 in 1958–59; $10,785 in 1961; and $12,000 in 1962. The gap between top and bottom widened; instructors and assistant professors now averaged only one-half as much as full professors. In 1962 one new professor, who also served as a chair and dean of graduate studies in the sciences, came at $18,000, a record for the College and comparable to most salaries in the scientific fields of the Medical School. At least two professors in clinical departments in the Medical School now earned as much as $30,000. By the comparative figures compiled by Committee A of the AAUP, Vanderbilt had moved its salary up from a D rating in the mid-1950s to a strong C in 1962–63 and very close to a B in most ranks for 1963. By then, its professors earned only about $2,000 less than those in the rare and enviable A institutions. Vanderbilt salaries, given regional differences in living costs, finally matched its academic standing. No longer did Branscomb compare Vanderbilt salaries with southern schools; the goal and standard were now national.[34]

The stated salaries joined with increased fringe benefits. Vanderbilt contributed an added 5 percent to the TIAA, sponsored a group insurance plan, paid the cost of Blue Cross coverage for individuals, and granted approximately one-half tuition discounts to faculty children. In 1951, as part of a decision to qualify Vanderbilt faculty for the Social Security system, the board changed the now fully mandatory retirement system in a way designed to allow part-time work, or a gradual evolution to full retirement. It made the retirement age sixty-five but granted a three-year extension when such was justified. In extraordinary cases it could also grant two one-year extensions to age seventy, or allow part-time employment in the years after sixty-five. Already, in 1948, and at Branscomb's suggestion, it had set a retirement age of sixty-five for all administrative offices, but with additional one-year appointments permissible up to age seventy. In 1960 the university increased its contribution to TIAA from a straight 5 percent to 5 percent up to the maximum Social Security base and 10 percent beyond that. Counting all benefits, the total compensation of professors was roughly 12 percent above their stated salaries, and more for those few who enjoyed the tuition benefit. And the gains had only begun—both the $30 million campaign and future Ford grants would sustain the pattern of rapid increases for the next several years.[35]

As Branscomb went through the formalities of retirement in early 1963 he had reason to be proud of his achievements as chancellor. He left in the wake of three years of crisis, with all manner of hurts and resentments, but these now seemed behind him and behind the university. The campus had never enjoyed such a boom, higher education such fervent support, as in this post-Sputnik, New Frontier era. Since his coming to Vanderbilt, the full-time faculty had doubled to over 450, faculty salaries had almost tripled (in current dollars), the endowment had more than doubled, the number of buildings on campus more than doubled, and the full-time enrollment in 1962–63 had reached an all-time high even as SAT scores continued to rise.

Branscomb had failed to deemphasize football, to gain an organic tie with Peabody, and to solve all the problems connected with fraternities. He was still dissatisfied with faculty salaries and was increasingly concerned that highly specialized scholars had transferred too much loyalty from the local campus to their professional organizations; he feared the loss of independence and integrity that might follow from increased federal aid and lamented a lack of scholarship funds to balance ever higher tuitions. But such concerns never overbalanced his pride in great achievements. Reinforcing cheers came from all sides. Even faculty members and students who had fought bitter battles against Branscomb now acknowledged his role in Vanderbilt's great leap forward.

18

In the Middle

E XPANSION, new buildings, and increased endowments are justified only if they produce an abler faculty, more inspired teaching, a wider array of courses and programs, and more and better scholarship. It is almost impossible to evaluate such returns for the university as a whole. The schools became, if anything, even more autonomous in the postwar years, and their problems and achievements varied widely. Throughout Vanderbilt's history, a law of compensation has seemed to apply. Any time a school has reached greatness, another one has fallen into decline. No board and no chancellor has been able to keep them all strong or to foster growth in tandem. Each school has had its day of glory, usually followed by new problems and relative decline.

The College remained the core of the campus. If anything, it gained status during the Branscomb years. It had by far the largest enrollment, provided indispensable courses for Engineering and for Nursing, and employed the most full-time faculty. Qualitatively, it came closer to parity with the Medical School than at any time since 1925 but not, unfortunately, entirely because of its own achievements but also because of the Medical School's relative decline. Although the Graduate School had a separate administrative status and encompassed work in four schools by 1963, the bulk of its faculty and courses remained in College departments. Most of the growth in the College reflected new grants to the Graduate School.[1]

The College faculty slowly altered the controversial but watered-down structural and curricular reforms of 1937. In 1950 it did away with the confusion of two deans, when Meredith Crawford became dean of the whole College and Philip Davidson provost for all undergraduate instruction. In 1951 Crawford resigned for a job in army research. Branscomb then made Ewing Shahan, an economist with extensive philosophical training, the acting dean and then, a year later, dean. Shahan, although at first only an assistant professor, fully justified the confidence placed in him. Unfortunately, the hard work did not help his often fragile health or leave him time for the scholarly research needed to advance in his own field. Because of Shahan's illness, chemist George M. Smith briefly took over as dean in 1954, only to leave Vanderbilt the next year. Shahan then resumed his duties and remained until 1960 when, at his request, he returned to full-time teaching. He was replaced by Emmett Fields, a former Vanderbilt Ph.D. in history who had returned to Vanderbilt in 1957 as associate dean of the College. The increased work in the College had also justified the appointment of an assistant dean, a position held for several years by John L. Bingham of Romance languages.[2]

Because of its expanding faculty, the College moved to a more efficient form of government in 1955. Very carefully guided by Branscomb, who still chaired faculty meetings and despaired of the endless debates, the faculty voted to delegate original policy-making authority to a council, made up of four administrative officers (chancellor, dean of the Graduate School, dean of the College, and director of admissions), nine elected members (three from each of the academic divisions, with no two from any one department), and six members appointed by the chancellor. This design weighted the council heavily toward administrative guidance, but Branscomb had asked for more elected members than at first proposed by the faculty committee. The inclusion of the director of admissions reflected a faculty desire to retain control over admission standards. In 1952 the faculty had very reluctantly approved, as an exception for brilliant students, admission without any high school language training, and remained very leery of any further relaxations of standards. The faculty as a whole retained the right to approve or reject all council actions and continued to exercise this power in less frequent meetings.[3]

Curricular changes came slowly and without the divisive conflict of 1937. In 1947 a newly appointed chancellor's committee considered distribution requirements in the College, an issue before the faculty almost continuously from then until 1955. In 1947 the faculty agreed in principle on the prerequisites of a liberal education—at least a year's work each in English composition, mathematics, philosophy, the history of Western civilization, American history, and the natural sciences, plus a selected course from economics, psychology, and sociology. A student also needed competence in one foreign language. The first implementation of this scheme came in 1952, when all College students first had to take a one-year, lecture-discussion course in Western civilization to replace an earlier introduction to the social sciences. In 1952 Dean Shahan used a grant to visit other colleges and came back enthusiastic about curriculum reform. Extended discussion and committee efforts culminated in 1956 in a new distribution plan that replaced the simpler 1937 requirement of eighteen quarter hours in each of the three divisions and thus eliminated the last administrative role for such divisions. The new requirements included a year in English (select students took a special honors-level course, while students who were inarticulate had to take a special speech course in addition to English), a year of Western civilization, a year of math (with four options set up to accommodate different levels of achievement and ability), as many courses in a language as required to attain the intermediate level, a year of a natural science with a required lab, nine quarter hours of humanities in addition to the English and language require-

ments, and ten hours in the social sciences in addition to the history requirement. For some students this distribution requirement could take up to
eighty quarter hours. It promised great breadth. Continued requirements for
a major, and more restricted requirements for a minor or related work, could
absorb another seventy hours, leaving only thirty-nine hours as assured
electives. But very few students had to take all eighty hours, since few had to
begin a language or take the required speech course.

Such detailed requirements joined with some concessions to students.
They gained a new advisory system that encompassed all students, could
count up to twelve hours in studio arts for College credit, and could take
independent or honors work in selected departments (a formalized, Ford-
funded honors program began in 1961). The faculty also spent an inordinate
amount of time in the 1950s on the issue of excused absences from classes. No
proposal seemed to please the majority. But after 1959 juniors and seniors
had only to meet the attendance rules of professors (an unlimited cut rule if
professors so desired), and professors no longer had to file absence reports on
sophomores who had achieved a B average as freshmen.[4]

Shahan sought some even more idealistic reforms. The faculty had
approved one interdisciplinary major, with courses taken in three fields and
without a minor. Shahan wanted to expand this approach into a major
program in coordinated liberal studies. Such programs flourished on several
campuses that he visited. A committee appointed by Shahan, and in part
guided by him, spent months in preparing a detailed blueprint, or a plan fully
as innovative and utopian as the one originated by Carmichael's committee
back in 1937. The program would have included a coordinated four-year
curriculum. The core was to have been nine new seminar-type courses, all
developed to provide a needed integration or synthesis of studies in addition
to the specialized major. Four of these new courses were to encompass the
broad culture of the West, or something close to a great books series. Up to
fifty students each year were to enter this integrative honors program. But the
plan ran directly against departmental interests, for it was predicated upon a
partial breakdown of departmental or disciplinary boundaries. After almost a
semester of debating, the faculty finally tabled the program by a vote of
thirty-two to thirty-one. A despairing Shahan noted the lack of clear reasons
behind the rejection and lamented the two years of hard work that had gone
into the proposal. This episode, like the one in 1937, proved the difficulty of
winning any major curriculum changes or educational innovations in the face
of entrenched departmental interests. Shahan could rejoice in only one
vindication of his dream. A new interdepartmental course, Humanities 250,
quickly gained one of the most enthusiastic student responses of any course in
the College. Taught by nine professors from four or five departments, it
integrated Western literature, fine arts, and philosophy.[5]

The College faculty approved a new curriculum even as it kept urging the
board, year after year, to allow it to return to the semester system. The new

distribution requirements were so designed as to fit a conversion to semester hours. In 1957 the board finally approved, and the shift occurred with few problems in the fall of 1957. The change promised many tangible benefits for the faculty: less time for registration, less disrupted work, fewer exams, and several savings in time and administrative costs. Students vehemently opposed the change, for reasons not always very clear. They welcomed the larger diversity of courses allowed, at least in theory, by quarter terms, and saw greater hazards to grades in less frequent exams. For those undergraduates seeking certification in education, or graduate students under the Master of Arts in Teaching (M.A.T.) program, the shift created problems in taking courses at Peabody, which retained the quarter system. To appease these students, Vanderbilt continued to offer a few education courses on a quarter basis.

For the first time since the 1930s Vanderbilt added courses in education. These began in 1953 with a Ford-funded, special Ph.D. for teachers, which paralleled the joint Vanderbilt-Peabody M.A.T. program. Ford fellows now worked toward a special Ph.D., which included courses to improve college teaching. Roger P. McCutcheon, former dean of the Graduate School at Tulane, came to Vanderbilt as director. He set up special seminars on teaching attended by all the fellows and supervised their teaching internships, mostly as teaching assistants in departments. The special Ford program did not achieve its intended goals—the teaching seminars became a joke to too many of the fellows, while most regular Ph.D. candidates gained just as much teaching experience. More threatening to Peabody, which refused further cooperation on the M.A.T. program in 1956, Vanderbilt added a small program in education in 1956. Under the guidance of a full-time director of teacher education, it gained the right to certify teachers and approved several courses that counted for certification, courses offered in history, philosophy, sociology, and psychology. For secondary school certificates, Vanderbilt students had only to take their practice teaching and a single methods course at Peabody. Elementary school candidates had to take several technical courses at Peabody but could take all their core or substantive work at Vanderbilt.[6]

With growth came an expanding curriculum and new programs. Between 1950 and 1963 Vanderbilt added a fine arts department and a Latin American studies program, instituted new courses in the Russian and Chinese languages, and in many departments more than doubled the upper level courses. But of all the special programs, the new Institute for Brazilian Studies (1947) attracted the most publicity and added most to Vanderbilt's prestige. A special interest in Brazil at Vanderbilt stretched back into the Carmichael era, but Branscomb did the most to launch the institute, which easily gained foundation support. It involved four new professors and new courses in Romance languages, history, economics, and anthropology. Vanderbilt's offerings in Portuguese and in the culture of Brazil soon exceeded that of any other American university. Vanderbilt also became the best-known American university in Brazil, a country that was immensely flattered by all the attention up in Nashville. The president of Brazil visited the campus in May, 1949, when the institute faculty elected him its honorary director. The faculty interchange, and visits by the Brazilian ambassador, maintained these close ties. The State Department never loved the university more. Unfortunately, the early enthusiasm slowly waned in the 1970s.[7]

The great new emphasis in the College was on graduate work. The effect of this trickled down to undergraduates, most of all in the form of better qualified professors and more specialized work available in major subjects. Undergraduates were more dubious of one effect—a greater use of teaching assistants in most freshman courses. Almost all the major grants from foundations targeted graduate instruction, beginning with a Carnegie Foundation program in 1947 that provided research grants for faculty members in four university centers throughout the South (Nashville was at the center of one of these). Within the decade, grants provided $5 million of endowment for the Graduate School, and almost as much in various grants directed at faculty improvement and research support. The rate of expansion was unparalleled. At war's end, Ph.D. work at Vanderbilt, with a few rare exceptions, had been restricted to only six departments, and only three of these—history, English, and chemistry—had had a substantial track record in advanced work.

Branscomb saw graduate work, and advanced research, as Vanderbilt's major contribution to the South, and he exploited this theme very effectively with the foundations. The needs were overwhelming—for library expansion, for new laboratories, and above all for more eminent professors. Weakest of all were the most costly programs—in the natural sciences. Branscomb considered eliminating all graduate work in the sciences, to concentrate on Vanderbilt's greater strengths in English and the social sciences. But scientific knowledge related most closely to southern economic needs and to the funding priorities of foundations and the federal government. So, by 1950, Branscomb decided to attempt the almost impossible—quickly to build quality graduate programs in a minimum of ten College departments. He hoped to attract at least one nationally recognized scholar or scientist to each and began by appointing Dean Leonard Beach, the architect of Vanderbilt's modern graduate program. With the help of the GEB and the Ford Foundation, Branscomb and Beach reduced the teaching loads of graduate faculty (to an average of less than eight hours a week by 1960) and supported the ablest faculty with research grants, research assistants, and extra library or laboratory facilities. By the late 1950s able faculty members in the College were usually able to win periodic research leaves funded by the university.

In 1949, long before these efforts bore fruit, Vanderbilt was accepted for membership in the American Association of Universities (AAU), an association of the best graduate institutions in the country. The prestige of the Medical School largely accounted for Vanderbilt's membership. Vanderbilt followed Virginia, North Carolina, Texas, and Duke into this select company, and had the smallest enrollment of any member. In 1954 Vanderbilt took the lead in the formation of a new Council of Southern Universities, made up of the leading graduate institutions in the South (Duke, Emory, Tulane, Rice, Virginia, North Carolina, and Texas), a council that won and distributed a $2.5 million GEB grant for graduate fellowships in the liberal arts.[8]

Just as the new fellowships and expanded faculty came together in the early 1950s, graduate enrollment began to sag nationally. In the boom period just after the war, graduate enrollment at Vanderbilt had climbed from about 200 to over 300 in 1950–51, but with the Korean War then declined for the next two years. The quality of students, by most accounts, also eroded. Growth began again in 1954, with graduate enrollment climbing to approximately 600 by the fall semester of 1962–63 (or over 700 for the year). Even this was a minimal enrollment. Without at least twenty graduate students in a department, it proved difficult to offer a needed diversity of seminars or to create an intellectually stimulating community of scholars. Enrollment patterns shifted slowly, both as a reflection of student interest and the changing strength of departments. In the early 1950s a vastly improved physics department joined English as the top choice of graduate students; each had over sixty students. Chemistry and a growing new psychology department (it separated from philosophy in 1950) attracted about forty students. Biology was close behind. Only two other College departments—history and economics—had the critical mass of twenty. In 1960 the Graduate School enrolled 611. By then, ten departments had the critical mass or very close to it. English and physics remained in the lead, with history and psychology close behind. The strongest program was then in economics, divided between regular Ph.D.s and largely foreign students in a special economic development program. Two weaker departments—biology and math—also had a critical mass, but not so such other departments as sociology and political science or new Ph.D. programs in German, Spanish, French, philosophy, and Latin American studies. From 1946 to 1962 Vanderbilt awarded 421 Ph.D.s, 1,285 M.A.s or M.A.T.s. It had the twenty-sixth highest number of Woodrow Wilson Fellows in the nation. It had the third highest number of new National Defense Education Act Fellows, largely because these funded new graduate programs, and Vanderbilt began five or six new Ph.D. programs in 1960–61. Dean Beach, in his role as advisor, had also helped shape the National Defense Education Act.[9]

One possible support for faculty research, the Vanderbilt University Press, never lived up to its possibilities. Until 1959 the press stumbled along without a full-time director or any focus or direction. It published five or six books a year but selected them on a hit-and-miss basis, provided almost no editorial assistance, did nothing to recruit manuscripts, and had no budget to advertise beyond the Vanderbilt bookstore or a few notes in the *Alumnus*.

484

For several years after the war, H.C. Nixon kept all the accounts and, for a small additional salary, gave limited direction to the press. Then, in 1956, the press became a part of the public relations operation of Robert McGaw. McGaw could not give much time to the press, but he did bring professional competence. The result was a few well-designed, well-edited books.

To continue at all, the press had to have a director. From 1957 to 1959 Rob Roy Purdy served as a part-time interim director. In 1959 he and McGaw won from the board $15,910 a year for the press (this was, of course, in addition to what it earned on book sales). They then hired David Howell Jones, an editor at the University of Texas Press, as director at a salary of $7,500. He used the rest of his budget to hire an assistant editor and designer, an account supervisor, and a secretary. On a commission basis, Jones also paid for the services of a sales representative and a publicity agent in New York City. A committee of eight faculty members served as an editorial board. But such a limited staff could not expand much beyond five or so books a year and could not even begin the development and editorial work necessary for a successful press. The subsidy from the board was a small Band-Aid to keep alive an imprint and little else. To add insult to injury, in 1959 the inventory had to be moved to the university storerooms, well away from the press offices in Kirkland Hall. Every time the press removed a book for sale, or even for its own use, it had to pay a twelve-cent storage fee.[10]

Usually one measures the strength of a graduate faculty not only by the degrees granted, but by the quality and quantity of research completed and published. By quantitative standards, the College faculty certainly became more productive after World War II. The university proudly gathered annual reports on research in progress and periodically advertised the number of books and articles emanating from the faculty. On the record, over 80 percent of the College faculty, by the late 1950s, was actually engaged in research. Such statistics mean very little, for many professors dabbled at projects for years and never completed them. Also, any list of books and articles always contained a great deal of fluff, of edited works, or noninnovative textbooks, or simply very dull and unexciting monographs.[11]

Judgments have to be impressionistic. The record of completed research suggests that the College faculty, as a whole, moved up rather dramatically at the bottom and middle but that it did not gain very much distinction at the top. That is, the higher salaries, lower teaching loads, research support, and tougher tenure requirements did insure a competent faculty, both in teaching and in research. To remain at Vanderbilt, or to join its tenured faculty, one now had to meet all the rules followed in graduate universities—proven teaching skills and early research achievement, meaning a varying number of refereed articles or books according to the standard of a given professional discipline. By 1960 only a few oldtimers flunked these tests. But the College could not hire, or keep, many individuals at the very frontiers of knowledge, those who were pacesetters in a discipline, those who gained the most prestigious awards and prizes, or those who attained the presidency of their national professional organizations. Too many Vanderbilt professors remained close to entering level qualifications—one important scholarly book or five or six important articles. As at all major universities, some Vanderbilt professors continued for years, or decades, without major new publications, let alone fresh excursions into new intellectual terrain. Students said it all the time, and perhaps they were partly correct—Vanderbilt was not an intellectually alive and stimulating campus. Its College faculty did not, as a whole, reflect a contagious enthusiasm based either on continuous, rigorous intellectual dialogue or on vital and important research. Vanderbilt also seemed either terribly unlucky in its appointments or failed to provide the needed stimulants for intensive scholarly engagement. Over and over again it hired very promising scholars, often to head departments, and then after they came their scholarly work seemed to slow down or completely stop. Such judgments, of course, beg an impossibly detailed survey and evaluation of individual departments.

In 1946 the strongest College departments at Vanderbilt were English and history, with chemistry close behind. Traditionally, classical language had been strongest, but enrollment shifts had transformed Greek and Latin into a small and undistinguished classics department. By divisions, in 1946 the social sciences remained strongest, the natural sciences undistinguished, and the humanities, with the sole exception of English, very weak. During the Branscomb years the natural sciences gained near equality with the social sciences, while, relatively, the humanities remained weakest, with even English no longer an exception to that rule. Within the social sciences, economics pulled away from the other departments (history, political science, sociology, and psychology). George Stocking came to Vanderbilt at the end of the war to head the Institute for Research in the Social Sciences and remained the College's most distinguished professor for over a decade. In national stature he rivaled the three or four most distinguished professors in the Medical School. His accomplishments—both his publications and his professional involvement—led to his election as president of the American Economics Association in 1958; he was the only College professor to attain so high an office during the Branscomb years. Stocking brought to Vanderbilt three other able, younger economists—William H. Nicholls, a Harvard Ph.D. and, of all things at Vanderbilt, an agricultural economist (he came to Vanderbilt in 1948 and eventually served as departmental chairman); Nicholas Georgescu-Roegen, a Romanian exile and able theorist who joined the department in 1949; and Rendigs Fels, who came as assistant professor in 1948 and later worked with the specially funded economic development program.[12]

The other social science departments lagged well behind economics. History lost its two most eminent scholars—Owsley in 1948 and Binkley in 1953—to competing southern universities. The department had some able younger scholars—Charles Delzell in Italian history, Dewey Grantham in American—but it took years for younger men to attain national eminence. Consistent with Branscomb's desire to appoint eminent outsiders in key departments, the College replaced Binkley with Harold Bradley, a Californian with a prize-winning book and great promise. He served Vanderbilt well as department chairman and in university government as well as in important service to the larger community, but as was the case with so many others he did not add much in the way of new scholarship. At war's end, political science had only one well-known scholar, D.F. Fleming. Fleming had a unique impact on scores of students, continued to write a stream of articles, and worked at a long book on the Cold War, but he was more an old-fashioned historian than a political scientist. Even his historical standards began to give way to subjective interpretations. Branscomb eased him up to a special research professorship in 1951. In 1952, in another and successful search for eminence and new beginnings, the department appointed Avery Leiserson of the University of Chicago to the chair. He reoriented the department toward analytical and behaviorial studies. Another able scholar and theorist, Robert Harris, came to Vanderbilt from Louisiana State University in 1953; the department later lost him to Virginia, the best possible evidence of successful recruitment. Even as Vanderbilt lured Leiserson from Chicago, it employed one of his colleagues, Albert J. Reiss, Jr., an expert on population mobility, to head sociology and anthropology. He remained only to 1958, followed in his chair by Wayland J. Hayes, who was an expert on small communities and who had been at Vanderbilt since the war. In 1963 Vanderbilt employed Ernest Q. Campbell as professor and chair of sociology, a young man who helped build a still undistinguished department into at least an average one. In the newly separated department of psychology, the longtime chair was Stanford C. Ericksen until he moved to Michigan in 1962. By then, the growing department had a number of able young men, most notably Jum C. Nunnally.[13]

The postwar years proved a golden age for physics. It built upon wartime connections to Oak Ridge and exploited a growing interest in nuclear physics. Its leader, and one of the most eminent professors in the college, was Robert T. Lagemann, who also held the Landon C. Garland professorship. Unfortunately, the university astronomer, Carl Seyfert, died in a tragic automobile accident in 1960. Able younger men in physics included Ingram Bloch and Wendell Holladay. Otto Bluh joined the department in 1961, with his salary completely covered by grant money, a new departure for the College. Physics had an able research faculty on almost all levels. Geology, long headed by Willard Jewell, remained a very small, nongraduate department with only three instructors. Biology remained a department without prominent or nationally recognized professors. By 1963 it did not have a single professor at the highest salary levels. As a promised cure, in 1962 Vanderbilt lured an eminent biologist and scientific journalist, Graham

DuShane, to head biology and serve as dean of graduate sciences. He came from the editorship of *Science* and at a princely salary of $18,000. Tragically, he died the next year. Chemistry, alas, declined somewhat from its earlier preeminence. As in biology, it had an able teaching staff, young men involved in important research, but few stars at the top.[14]

Vanderbilt graduate students in the sciences, and even some undergraduate majors, could take advanced work in the scientific departments of the Medical School. Here, they could study with some of the outstanding scientists in the country. For example, Oscar Touster, in biochemistry, won a major award in 1957 for enzyme research, and a young but nonteaching professor of physiology, Earl Sutherland, would later win a Nobel Prize. It was the presence of related professors in biochemistry, physiology, microbiology, and even anatomy that gave an extra edge of quality to the natural science program at Vanderbilt. Without this backup support, graduate programs in the natural sciences outside physics would have remained marginal at best.[15]

The humanities lagged far behind. The language departments expanded, developed new courses, but remained comparatively undistinguished. No language professors gained the highest salary levels in the 1950s. Only in 1960, or later, did the language departments begin Ph.D. work. The new fine arts department had no full professors and no graduate program. The newly separated philosophy department remained small, with three or four professors, but gained as chair an administratively talented Samuel E. Stumpf, who moved to the College from the Divinity School. The only well-developed graduate program in the humanities remained in English. Alas, that grand old department began to decline by the late 1950s. It survived the war with strength in people such as Claude Finney, Walter Clyde Curry, and Donald Davidson. But the beloved Curry retired in 1955, after a much revered and now famous final lecture. Davidson slowly became a fanatic in his opposition to integration, to the embarrassment of the university, but he remained a creative and highly original teacher until his retirement in 1964. Finney never lived up to his early promise; his scholarly production all but ended with his one great study of Keats. Richmond Beatty took ill in 1956 and had to retire. To ease the loss of Curry, Randall Stewart came home from Brown to spend his last years at Vanderbilt, heading the department until just short of retirement in 1962. But by then the formerly great department had all but dried up or blown away. Symbolically, even Edwin Mims died in 1959. The department attracted able younger men, but as of 1963 it did not have a single distinguished full professor, save for the elderly Davidson, and was critically in need of major new appointments.[16]

As in the case of the natural sciences, so the humanities derived some strength from a related school, Divinity. Already, the College had a small program in religious studies, headed by George Mayhew, and students in the College could choose several courses cross-listed with Divinity, including a few taught by some of the most distinguished scholars or theologians in the country, such as Nels Ferre. In addition, in 1949 the Carnegie Foundation provided funds, over three years, for a new associate professor of Jewish literature and thought, a joint appointment for the College and the Divinity School. B'nai B'rith Hillel Foundation subsidized the original salary and then took over the full cost for several years. For three years the post was filled by Samuel Sandmel, and then for two decades by Lou H. Silberman.[17]

The Engineering School seemed to drift throughout the 1950s. Even Branscomb confessed that it was a bit dull. Outwardly, it enjoyed one success after another. After all the fund drives, the loving plans, and a long delay, the school moved into its new building in 1950. It had been literally swamped by veterans before the move. Ironically, just as it moved, the enrollment pressures abated, with a drop from 746 in 1948–49 to only 418 in 1951–52. From that low, enrollment climbed gradually to 673 in 1958–59 and then, as a result of imposed quotas, leveled off at just over 600. At least in the 1950s, Engineering students were less well qualified than those in the College and a higher percentage commuted from the Nashville area. Until his death in 1959, Fred Lewis continued to head the school, for a total tenure of twenty-five years. A balanced, conscientious dean, he was also part of the problem. Never a distinguished engineer or scientist, he simply did not have the drive to raise Engineering above its status as a good training school for mid-level professionals, almost all of whom gained excellent jobs upon graduation. His engineering students took only one required course outside their technical training—English composition. The packed four-year curricula left only twelve or even fewer elective hours for students, and almost none took advantage of courses in the College. As a whole, Engineering students made a very limited contribution to the intellectual life of the campus.

Another problem involved faculty recruitment. Vanderbilt faculty salaries were insufficient to lure top-flight engineers away from corporate jobs, or to attract engineering scholars from prestigious engineering schools or universities. Yet, faculty salaries in Engineering lagged behind those in the College, not because of any discrimination by the central administration but because Lewis simply could not recruit, or retain, outstanding people. A cycle, if not of mediocrity at least of contented stagnation, took over. Small innovations never seemed to have much impact. In 1952 the school announced a division of engineering research and development, but this led only to a few small contracts each year and to almost no basic research. In 1958, just before Lewis died, the school began a new M.S. program in both nuclear science and nuclear engineering, a program tied closely to scholarships offered from Oak Ridge.[18]

For Engineering the revolution came in 1960. Dean Lewis's death paved the way. After an extensive search, Branscomb appointed Robert S. Rowe as the new dean, at a then astronomical salary of $20,000. He earned it. A civil engineer with a Yale Ph.D., he came to Vanderbilt from Duke in order to build a university-level engineering program. This meant a new emphasis on

Dean Robert Nelson, Divinity School

Nels Ferre, Divinity

DISTINGUISHED AND CONTROVERSIAL PROFESSORS

graduate work and advanced research. He could not fire unproductive professors, clear out all the dead wood, but he began pushing his staff and tried to recruit only professors who had a Ph.D. and research interests. By 1961 he had seven of his faculty on leave to get their Ph.D.s and used Ford funds to add seven new Ph.D.s to the school in 1961. By 1965 his faculty of fifty would contain thirty-eight with such advanced degrees. In no other school in Vanderbilt history did faculty development proceed so rapidly. To some extent, Rowe deemphasized technical or merely practical work. For example, he discontinued the pedestrian summer courses in surveying at the Bon Air camp and turned the land over to the university for sale. He also began building closer ties to the College. By 1962 Engineering students took up to thirty hours of required and elective work in the social sciences and the humanities, received credit only for advanced work in math, and had to take more rigorous courses in the basic sciences. Rowe's faculty now were expected to do research and to publish; a Ford grant of $250,000 in 1960–61 helped fund new faculty research projects. All of this allowed Engineering to become fully a part of the graduate program. By 1963, with the cooperation of the College and Medical School, it had M.S. and Ph.D. programs in electrical, civil, chemical, and mechanical engineering. Rowe's plans included a new chemical engineering wing, a new research building or wing, new space for the growing engineering library, and even an auditorium. In only five years

490

Economist George Stocking

Political scientist Denna F. Fleming

Engineering had moved from relative obscurity to one of the most lively and promising schools in the university.[19]

The great leap forward came a decade earlier in the Law School. The new start in 1946 had been a blessing. Dean Coffman was able to hire his own full-time staff and that staff designed its own curriculum. Unfortunately, the school suffered from an early exodus of its key professors that climaxed in 1949 when Coffman moved on to become dean at UCLA. Rollin Perkins, the Rand professor, served briefly as acting dean. Then, a young whiz kid from Tulane, William Ray Forrester, accepted the deanship, only to return to Tulane in 1952. Even before this, Perkins had moved elsewhere, as had another distinguished professor, Harold E. Verrall. The losses hurt, but they only proved how much the new Law School differed from the old one. Coffman had largely turned away from the local bar and recruited the ablest men he could find anywhere in the country. But the rapid postwar expansion in law schools made such a staff subject to repeated raids. Vanderbilt could not compete in salaries and above all in facilities with leading schools, but that it tried to do so was encouraging. In various ways it was able to recruit and then in the less competitive 1950s retain a staff almost as eminent as the one Coffman originally assembled. In 1950 the school brought Edmund Morgan from Harvard for a one-year lectureship, in order to expose Vanderbilt students to a world authority on procedure and evidence. Since Morgan had

491

just retired at Harvard, Vanderbilt was able to persuade him to continue on at Vanderbilt as Frank Rand professor, necessarily on a year-by-year basis. The new retirement rules allowed such temporary appointments of retired professors only from outside Vanderbilt. In 1947 a young John W. Wade, already a rising expert in the field of torts, joined the new school at Vanderbilt, not only to teach but to work with students on a planned *Vanderbilt Law Review.* In 1952 Branscomb appointed him dean, and with that the school finally gained the stable leadership it needed.

Just after the war the Law School began raising funds for a new building but had to postpone the actual construction for over a decade. It was to the special credit of Wade and his faculty that they built a quality Law School in spite of the inadequate facilities in Kirkland Hall. From 1950 to 1960 the school grew to a full-time faculty of twelve. The *Law Review* won high praise, and Vanderbilt students competed successfully in national moot court contests. In 1956 Robert Hutchinson's controversial Fund for the Republic (Ford money) selected the Vanderbilt Law School as publisher of a new *Race Relations Law Reporter;* this new, objectively edited, and widely circulated journal brought two new staff members into the school and in the controversial integration struggle helped gain Vanderbilt new friends outside the South.[20]

The Law School did have problems. The great enrollment boom after the war (an unprecedented 382 students in 1948–49) enabled the school to balance its budgets and accumulate reserve funds. But a decline in students (down to 131 in 1953–54) threatened disaster and even with new tuition increases led to annual deficits. For a few years the school seemed to be in the same bind as in the late 1930s. But enrollment growth resumed after 1955, much as in the College, and by 1959–60 the enrollment was up to 200, as large as facilities allowed. This enrollment growth paralleled that in other schools and, joined with the tempting salaries available in private practice, made it once again difficult to recruit eminent faculty. Dean Wade turned down a lucrative outside offer in 1957. To keep him, the board not only raised his salary to $15,000 but set up a board committee to work out funding for a new building; the board also increased funds for the library and approved more tuition scholarships. In 1958 a $350,000 Ford grant enabled the school to raise salaries generally and to meet most outside offers. But in spite of large merit raises, Vanderbilt lost F. Hodge O'Neal to Duke in 1960. In the same year the board approved a new building, not to exceed $1.25 million, a building completed and occupied in 1962. By then the Law School promised to become a prestige school for the South, with most of its students still from that section. It had high standards but did not yet compete with a Harvard or a Columbia. It continued to emphasize legal practice, not legal scholarship or legal philosophy.[21]

The Medical School entered its time of troubles after 1945. For fifteen years one crisis followed another. The crises should not conceal its stengths. It still competed in a national arena; its full-time faculty remained the most productive, the most eminent, of that of any school except possibly Divinity. It continued to lead the College in research and in winning national awards and honors. It had enormous resources: in endowment, laboratory equipment, and above all in an established national reputation. But the changes were all too painfully obvious. The school had been a pacesetter in the late 1920s and 1930s, with a staff fired with zeal and enthusiasm. In the postwar years all that great staff left or died. They proved very hard to replace. Now, the school entered a defensive period, one in which it desperately tried to remain solvent and to hold its position. It could not, for other schools moved far ahead of it. By the mid-1950s it was close to being the smallest medical school in the country (a point of pride) but only somewhere in the middle rank in quality and prestige. An almost unending financial crisis held down faculty salaries, until they fell toward the bottom of American medical schools by the late 1950s. Even the caliber of students dropped off by the mid-1950s. Fewer applied (a national pattern); more important, the ablest students now chose other fields. Medical Board scores revealed that Vanderbilt students were, at best, only in the middle third of applicants nationwide. Finally, because of the financial strains, the school and hospital moved back a way toward the earlier proprietary pattern. That is, increasing numbers of the Medical School staff had to earn their own salaries, even though these were laundered through the university budget. By 1960 the worst seemed over. Hopes grew afresh out of several large financial windfalls. But the road back proved treacherous, the gains slow.[22]

The first crisis began in the hospital even before the war ended. The hospital had to depend on a fixed income even as prices soared. By 1947 it suffered an annual deficit of over $200,000; by 1949 it had exhausted all the reserves built up early in the war. Temporary expedients helped balance the budget briefly by 1950, but by 1953 the heavy losses resumed, mounting to a cumulative postwar deficit of about $2 million by 1955. Because of interdependent budgets, the hospital drained income away from the Medical School, leaving it either with deficits or with such tight budgets that it could not raise salaries or even make needed appointments. By 1949 the Medical faculty debated, and quarreled, over what to do. Some wanted to save the school by returning to a more overt proprietary system—to a prestigious, profit-making clinic staffed, in part, by the faculty, one modeled after the famous Mayo Clinic. This would have required new hospital wings, but the fees from private patients might have covered the cost of staff patients in the wards.[23]

Ernest Goodpasture, the beleaguered dean, made the most daring proposal. He wanted the school to suspend its four-year teaching effort and to convert itself into a medical foundation for research and post-M.D. training. This had been the school's forte all along; government funds and endowment income were adequate to fund such a mission. As it was, the school faced a gradual erosion toward mediocrity. Goodpasture was sick at heart from the endless strain of seeking money, from skimping on budgets, and from watching his ablest faculty leave for better paying jobs. Freed of the teaching needs of a school and the unending effort to get the staff (i.e., the nonpaying or indigent) patients needed for each clinical specialty, the hospital would be able to survive with paying patients. The faculty, freed from teaching and problems of hospital management, could get along with their real work. Those faculty members in nonclinical or academic research could develop closer ties to the College. He did not say it but implied that those with an odd taste for teaching could always take over certain College courses. The board rejected this radical proposal; shortly thereafter Goodpasture resigned his deanship to return to his own research.[24]

The board and Branscomb chose a third option, but one that never worked very well in the 1950s. They believed the hospital simply had to pay its own way, without cost to the endowment or to the Medical School. They wanted to channel all endowment income to the school. But for the hospital to succeed, it first had to win more paying patients. The board contributed $250,000 to spruce up the wards and rooms in 1949. Its second requirement was public aid to compensate it for the care of indigents. The City of Nashville had to cooperate in funding the hospital or risk the loss of a great medical center. Branscomb believed Nashville did not deserve the school if it refused to help. As early as 1948 he made a formal offer to the city, one coordinated with a similar offer from Meharry. The two schools were to take over the care of Negro indigents, those presently cared for in a sagging and partially condemned General Hospital. The city could then save the cost of refurbishing General. Vanderbilt wanted the city to pay $8.60 for ward patients, $1.00 for outpatients during the first year, and actual costs thereafter, for up to 200 patients at Vanderbilt. If the city would so contract, Vanderbilt agreed to add 100 extra beds and to add outpatient facilities, both supported by Hill-Burton funds. Meharry and Vanderbilt agreed to operate General Hospital during the transition. Without such a contract, Vanderbilt would have to stop accepting indigents and this, in turn, threatened the school, for it had to have a continuous flow of staff patients for teaching purposes.

The situation at Vanderbilt highlights the role of indigents generally in American medical education—they were the willing, nondemanding guinea pigs required for students to learn their trade. Only patients under the care of the hospital staff would submit to the frequent and sometimes fumbling ministrations of students. The small hospital was already short on the needed patients, particularly for rare diseases. Thus, the school literally scrounged for additional patients of the type that would seem to flow from the proposed contract, or what seemed mutually advantageous to both sides. Of course, in a sense, Vanderbilt wanted to have its cake and eat it too—to have both amenable patients and fees. In another bid for patients, the school had already, in 1946, signed an agreement with the Thayer Veterans' Administration Hospital to provide needed services to white patients (in effect, this meant that Vanderbilt selected and supplied the house residents, who in turn allowed Vanderbilt students to observe or work with patients).[25]

Briefly, the new strategy seemed to work. In 1948 Nashville rejected any contract. True to Branscomb's threat, the hospital stopped all free services, except for emergency cases. Elaborate publicity before implementation of the new policy avoided most complaints, and the $8.50 per day fees began to eat away at the deficits. The only problem—staff patients dropped to such a level as to threaten the school. Then, in 1949, the city finally agreed to a contract with Meharry and Vanderbilt, with a majority of the ward patients cared for at Meharry but with Vanderbilt providing staff services at General. By 1950 the school and hospital achieved the first balanced budget since the war, but the crisis abated for only two years. In 1952 Vanderbilt took over complete operation of General Hospital for a contracted $750,000. This led to an unanticipated loss of over $10,000 a month, and once again new deficits to contend with. Difficult new negotiations in 1953 led to a new contract, one based on actual costs. By then, Vanderbilt faced increasing opposition from the City Council and from Nashvillians. To complicate matters, the patient census dropped at Vanderbilt Hospital; few Negroes came (General and Hubbard seemed to draw them away) and even the number of paying ward patients dropped. Low-paid nurses were now up in arms and secured a reduction in hours from forty-four to forty. Other costs also rose, and it was obvious that the hospital was ill suited for an increasingly competitive market. Its dull rooms joined the extra aggravations of the teaching effort to push patients elsewhere. Then, with the new crisis developing, the Nashville City Council canceled the contract for indigent care and for operation of General Hospital. The jealousies and resentments boiled over, with Vanderbilt taking a raking in the local press. The charges were old ones—that Vanderbilt was a rich man's university, aloof and basically uninterested in Nashville's problems unless it received full pay. The attack gained support from several resentful physicians who had not been able to gain the right to practice at Vanderbilt. It also came after three years of panty raids and student-police skirmishes, episodes that led to city charges of excessive drinking and rampant immorality on campus or in fraternity houses.[26]

Once again the Medical School seemed doomed. To protect the school, the university finally separated its budget from that of the hospital. A special board committee investigated the mess. It suggested the only available option—to try to make the hospital pay its way. To attain this goal, Vanderbilt hired a special consultant, spent a million dollars to improve the facilities (new elevators, new paint, air conditioners in private rooms), and began successfully to exploit new technology such as cobalt treatments not otherwise available in the area. Fortunately, the Ford Foundation gave $169,000 toward the repairs. By the fall of 1955 the patient load began to rise, particularly among the more profitable private patients. The hospital was simply more competitive, which meant first of all that it was a more attractive hotel. Then, in 1956–57, a Ford grant of $2.3 million allowed the hospital to begin plans for a new, modern west wing (the circular wards), with construction beginning in 1960. By 1957, miracle of miracles, the hospital budget finally balanced, in large part because of the effect of prepaid (Blue Cross) medical plans and the ability of the hospital to raise rates to cover costs.

The only problem that remained was supplying enough staff patients for training purposes, but even this changed for the better. In 1958, after some complex and perilous negotiations, and even some political lobbying, Vanderbilt successfully wooed the new VA hospital to an area adjacent to its campus. The VA began planning its hospital for just south of Garland and, despite protests from Meharry, signed an exclusive staffing contract with Vanderbilt. Finally, in 1959, the Medical School received a new, and what turned out to be a profitable, contract to provide staff services at General Hospital. From 1960 on, three hospitals directly catered to Vanderbilt medical students, together barely meeting its teaching needs. Unfortunately, hospital problems had allowed the Medical School to decline to a low ebb by 1957. Only then could the chancellor and dean try to rebuild it.[27]

In 1949, when Goodpasture resigned as dean, John B. Youmans returned to Vanderbilt to take the difficult position. He had been dean at Illinois for three years. The financial crisis had taken its toll, in declining graduate work, less research, several critical staff vacancies, and a lack of clear rules and procedures. Clinical physicians had no nearby office space, and the small hospital pharmacy was not as profitable as it should have been. Youmans asked for funds to build an office building, a self-financing if not a profitable investment, which by completion in 1955 was named the Medical Arts Building. By asking the board to raise tuition to $800, Youmans tried to raise key salaries, which had virtually stagnated since the war. But the one overwhelming problem was staff. Four critical departments were without heads, and in the Medical School, much more than elsewhere on campus, the department heads were little gods, presiding over kingdoms often consisting of forty or fifty instructors. In key departments, heads had much of the power and the prerogatives of a dean in the College. The most critical loss had been William W. Frye, head of preventive medicine and public health, who moved to Tulane in 1948. By 1950 the old curmudgeon Barney Brooks faced imminent retirement in the key department of surgery, and Ernest Goodpasture would shortly retire in pathology. The giants of old were falling. Youmans appointed Robert Quinn, from Wisconsin, as chair in preventive medicine and, after the most critical search of all, Henry William Scott to surgery. Scott came from Hopkins, a disciple of former Vanderbilt surgeon Alfred Blalock. To get him, Youmans had to probe new limits on salary— $15,000 plus up to $5,000 in retained fees. In addition to key appointments, Youmans slightly expanded the program. Bacteriology (microbiology as of

1955) became a separate department in 1952, moving out of pathology. The curriculum, a rigid schedule of required courses over four years, had heretofore involved a year and a half of preclinical scientific work before the students moved into hospital wards. Youmans and his faculty now tried to get beginning students more involved in patient care; entering students each took an assigned patient family, which they observed or worked with for a year. And, in the fourth year, rather than make a routine shift from one service to another, students now adopted patients from each service. In 1951 the school also made one other affiliation; it began a Master of Science in Audiology in cooperation with what later became the Bill Wilkerson Speech and Hearing Center. Vanderbilt students, mainly out of the College, took their work at the center but received a Vanderbilt degree, while professors in the center gained nonsalaried professorial status in the Medical School.[28]

Youmans suffered through the second budget crisis of the mid-1950s and then, like Goodpasture, gave up the struggle. In 1958 he resigned for more peaceful work in army research. By then the future of the school looked brighter, largely because of the new Ford grants and the promise of a nearby VA hospital. Youman's replacement was John W. Patterson, formerly a dean at the University of British Columbia. He had gained a Ph.D. in organic chemistry before completing his M.D. at Western Reserve. He launched a major self-evaluation study in the school, talked about the need for a new hospital, and seemed to have more administrative skills than his predecessors. He succeeded in the fiscal side of administration, relieving some of Branscomb's burdens. In 1959 he even gained a new title—vice-chancellor for medical affairs. His immediate problems involved personnel, staff morale, and the low quality of medical applicants. Symbolically significant, in 1960 both G. Canby Robinson and Ernest Goodpasture died (Goodpasture had received the honor of election to the Vanderbilt Board of Trust after his retirement). By 1958 the financial crisis seemed to be over. Grant income climbed to over $1 million a year, and then to over $2 million by 1963. New formulas for the recovery of indirect costs also made such grants more profitable for the school.[29]

Except for a few recent appointees, Medical School salaries had fallen to the lowest level of any major school in the country. Patterson successfully attended to this problem. In 1959 he worked out a new salary scale with Branscomb. As soon as possible, he wanted to raise salaries for nonclinical or scientific heads of departments to $18,000, for the heads of clinical departments to $25,000. Thus, when another of the giants, Hugh Morgan of the department of medicine, retired in 1959, Patterson paid his replacement, David E. Rogers, a salary of $25,000, with all his fees to go to the school. In 1961 Robert W. Noyes, new head of OB-GYN, also received $25,000 without fees. But in 1962, to the consternation of Branscomb, Patterson twice broke his own rule; he appointed heads of both anesthesiology and radiology at a total compensation of $30,000. The justification was not only that competition required such salaries, but that both men would earn the school much more in fees than their salaries would cost it. In other words, these were profitable appointments. Perhaps high demand would have necessitated such salaries in any case; in 1962 Patterson had to break the other, nonclinical barrier and pay $22,500 to get an eminent anatomist. Though such scientists brought no patient fees to the school, they did bring large research grants. As early as 1957 biochemist Oscar Touster earned all his salary for three years under a research contract with the Howard Hughes Foundation, which has maintained a continuing research program at Vanderbilt. In such cases, higher salaries cost the university nothing and even added to its income. Thus, in a pattern soon repeated again and again, faculty salaries in the Medical School increasingly reflected one's potential for attracting patient fees or sustaining research grants, the modern version of the old proprietary system.[30]

Patterson administered efficiently. He ruled arbitrarily. Or so charged his staff. By 1961 the school was in turmoil. Patterson had a few loyal supporters, some of whom he had appointed. But most of the older, eminent staff, including several key department heads, led an organized opposition movement. The charges against him, as communicated to Branscomb, all involved arbitrary or high-handed decisions, made without consultation with his faculty. Patterson chose his own committees, changed rules without notice, and was insensitive in personal relationships. In part, the resentments involved the opposition of an old guard to a new dean. Possibly, political and ideological issues were in the background, for Patterson had tried to make changes in many areas and was not a part of the older Vanderbilt tradition.

One product of dissension was more faculty self-government. Following the lead of the College, the medical faculty formed its own council and worked out what amounted to a constitution for the school. Its 1962 bylaws specified the duties of the dean and the executive faculty, and in ways that severely limited the dean's authority. Patterson most resented a requirement that a new faculty committee on tenure promotions and appointments would have a dual role in setting up all search committees. Patterson engaged in a running fight with Robert Noyes, his own appointee to OB-GYN, a man who tried to run his own empire. In another critical clash, pediatrician Amos Christie openly defied what he saw as irresponsible orders from Patterson. Both sides pleaded their case with the central administration, but Branscomb felt he had to go with the major department heads. He fired Patterson as vice-chancellor and dean but offered him an appointment in physiology or a year's paid leave. To replace him, Branscomb followed the older pattern of Leathers, Goodpasture, and Youmans—he elevated a professor, Randolph Batson, a relatively young pediatrician, to the acting deanship. The change at last brought harmony to a troubled staff. Patterson, in his perhaps dictatorial way, had already expanded the staff, brought salaries up once again to the upper third among medical schools, and had balanced all budgets. What seemed lacking was a new vision, plans for innovations that might give the school a distinctive role once again.[31]

In the end, the Nursing School suffered most from the financial crisis in the hospital. Vanderbilt had a great Nursing School at the end of the war, but few loved it or even took it very seriously. As Nursing enrollment sharply declined after the war, from 224 in 1946–47 to only 80 in 1949–50, the school seemed headed toward extinction. The faculty made needed adjustments. Dean Frances Helen Zeigler resigned in 1949 to marry a New York banker. Julia Hereford, a longtime professor in the school, moved up to dean and helped work out a complete new program. Until 1949 the school had offered a rigorous three-year professional course leading to a prestigious Bachelor of Science in Nursing. But admission to the program required two prior years of college, meaning five years to earn a degree. Since only a handful of nursing schools required so much college preparation, Vanderbilt simply had to lower its sights or risk a loss of all students. Thus, in 1950 it moved to a four-year Bachelor of Science program for high school graduates. In four years, plus three summers, students now completed both their academic work in the College and their nursing courses. By 1954 the school eliminated almost all summer work. This program placed Vanderbilt in the vanguard of what soon became a standard for college schools, as distinct from three-year nondegree programs in hospital schools.

Strenuous recruitment made the new plan work. Enrollment gradually climbed back to 171 in 1954–55, but then backed off. By the early 1960s Nursing was the only school that faced enrollment declines, a reflection as much on the profession as on Vanderbilt's particular program. With the new curriculum came the full integration of nursing students into the undergraduate life of the campus. By 1963 they paid tuition comparable to other schools and took part in all extracurricular activities.[32]

Despite such achievements, the school slowly starved to death in the 1950s. Its salaries ranked far below those in any other school, in many cases not much above half of those in the College. Staff turnover became a near scandal, with few instructors remaining more than two or three years. The ablest professors, such as Lulu Wolf, moved to better positions elsewhere. The Nursing School seemed always to come in last—in chancellor's reports, in board concern or attention, and in status in the Medical Center. In part this reflected sexual bias. Being women, the nurses were simply not taken very seriously by male administrators. The university files abound with slighting remarks or resentful gossip whenever the dean of Nursing became too "pushy." Had the Hospital and Medical School been prosperous, the Nursing School might have gained from the trickle-down effect, but as it was, it faced constant hostility and, at least twice, a threat to its very survival.

The Nursing School had originated through the generosity of the Rockefeller Foundation and the vision of G. Canby Robinson. It was almost an unwanted graft from the outside. From the beginning, the school had seemed a burden to physicians and to the hospital. The hospital needed cheap nursing care, not an independent school; a dorm for staff nurses, not for Vanderbilt undergraduates. After 1950 the new curriculum fully solved the old problem of how much work the students would give the hospital in pay for room, board, and uniforms. The nurses now paid their own way, except for a limited amount of work in the junior year. But by the early 1950s the hospital was short on nurses, largely because of low pay tied to annual deficits. It already operated its own hospital school for licensed practical nurses, including a few nurses to work the black wards. By 1954, when the hospital was most desperate, a special Board of Trust committee that sought means of solving its problems looked almost angrily at the existing, nonhelpful Nursing School. The committee then issued a warning—if the existing school would not cooperate (give free nursing care), then the board should replace the college school with a good, old-fashioned hospital school, one with a three-year diploma course and free nursing care. The committee argued that it made only good sense to sacrifice the existing Nursing School in order to save the hospital. Fortunately, the larger board never pursued this option, since the crisis soon abated in the hospital. But this proposal, more than anything else, suggested the status of the Nursing School in the university.[33]

Even as hospital finances improved after 1955, the Nursing School continued to slide toward bankruptcy. Year after year Dean Hereford tried herculean means to balance, or almost balance, her budget. Impending deficits meant that she had to turn repeatedly to tuition increases, which threatened enrollment. Few southern girls, as she knew, were willing to pay $1,000 a year to become nurses, especially when so many other schools were tuition free. In 1960 the National League of Nursing evaluated the school and lamented its decline from one of the best in the nation. The League granted only two and a half years of conditional accreditation. It noted the low salaries, low faculty morale and instability, and the noneducational ward work still required of juniors. The school had used W.K. Kellogg Foundation funds, after 1954, for a limited Master of Science program, but it attracted few students and the grant ran out in 1959. The school then lost its accreditation for graduate work. In 1962 the hospital director demanded one floor of Mary Henderson Hall as a residence for his licensed practical trainees; without it, he said he could not staff the new west wing of the hospital. This was simply the last of a series of efforts by hospital administrators to use nursing facilities for their own purposes. Again, the school refused the request. But by 1962 the fate of Nursing was in doubt. As Branscomb retired, here was one dramatic failure of his administration. In his final report to the board he asked for some "angel" to rescue the school. He sounded like Kirkland on coeducation back in the 1920s—the women could enter the kingdom if only they would raise their own money.[34]

As Nursing declined, the School of Religion briefly entered into its kingdom. Branscomb, of course, was a great ally. He believed the school, or its graduates, had done more than anyone else to keep his own southern Methodist church from surrendering to the "fundamentalists." Thus, he and Dean Benton took extraordinary measures to expand its program and to recruit distinguished professors. To such able professors as J. Philip Hyatt, they added William Kendrick Grobel in New Testament (1947) and two outstanding theologians, Nels Ferre and Langdon B. Gilkey, a distinguished Baptist scholar with degrees from Harvard and Union. Gilkey gave the school national visibility and helped attract able students to the expanding graduate program, a graduate effort that threatened for a time to eclipse the more pedestrian B.D. curriculum. Briefly, the scholarly output of the faculty exceeded that of the College and rivaled that of the Medical School (Ferre published two books in one year). The signs of progress were everywhere—enrollment soared to 150 in 1951–52, more and better students came from all parts of the country, and by 1957 the school began screening applicants and rejecting those with poor college records, an innovation never before possible. The Cole lectures became the intellectual event of the year; lecturers included Paul Tillich, Pitirim A. Sorokin, and Rudolf Bultmann. Wesley Hall was not an ideal home, but somehow it also fostered a brief, fleeting moment of close fellowship. A benefactor helped create in it a small but beautiful chapel. One final symbol of success came in 1955—the Tennessee Conference of the Methodist church asked for a relationship of understanding and cooperation, and appointed an advisory committee to work with their ministers in the school. In 1956, to avoid misunderstanding and to follow the national pattern, the school changed its name to Divinity School, a name that pleased Branscomb.[35]

All the progress paid off financially. In 1955 John D. Rockefeller, Jr., through one of his charitable funds, awarded the Divinity School $2.9 million for endowment. In total, Rockefeller gave $20 million for theological education, much of it going to six private nondenominational seminaries. Unspoken, but undoubtedly a necessary condition of the gift, was Vanderbilt's 1953 decision to admit blacks to the school. The new riches were committed to an improved program—new courses and new faculty, library improvements, higher faculty salaries, and more service to the community, all key conditions of Rockefeller gifts. In 1956, alone, the school recruited three new professors. The gift had one qualification—Vanderbilt had to contribute at least $1 million for a new building. The board decided against a hasty fund drive and committed the needed funds from the earnings of the endowment, a rare strategy at Vanderbilt. The early plans involved four buildings, all just northwest of the JUL, but by 1958 the architects combined these into a chapel-classroom quadrangle, a beautiful complex completed early in 1960. It would have the most generous faculty and student facilities of any building on campus. Even as the planning began, Dean Benton died, at age sixty, in August, 1956, and Ferre announced his resignation in October. These blows considerably muted celebrations within the school.[36]

The search for a new dean ended in a surprise appointment—J. Robert Nelson. Like past deans, he was a Methodist, but otherwise he was outside the common mold. At a youthful thirty-six, he came to Vanderbilt from the staff of the World Council of Churches at Geneva, Switzerland. A Yale B.D., he took his Doctor of Theology at Zurich under the world-famous Emil Brunner. He had published one book on theology but seemed to have his brightest future in church administration and in ecumenical advocacy. Nelson came to Vanderbilt with youthful enthusiasm, grateful for such a prestigious appointment; he was originally paid $10,000, and promised $12,000 by 1959–60. He loved being dean. And, in many respects, he lived up to the high expectations. He became an eloquent spokesman for the Divinity School, deeply impressing the board in a speech before it. He worked closely, and deferentially, with Branscomb, who was so taken with him that he asked the board to grant him his $1,000 raise a year early, and in 1959 he raised that above the committed figure, to $12,500, very high by Divinity School standards. But Nelson was much more an effective spokesman than an effective administrator. He proved ineffectual in handling details. At times he did not consult effectively with senior colleagues and often seemed indecisive. Neither his age nor his personality prepared him for firm, consistent leadership.[37]

Under Nelson the growth of the school continued. Higher admission requirements slowed enrollment, but the caliber of students, and the number committed to Ph.D. work, grew each year. Rapid faculty turnover continued, another sure sign of academic strength. Nelson made several key appointments, climaxing in 1959 with the announcement that Walter Harrelson, of the Divinity School of the University of Chicago, would come to Vanderbilt in the fall of 1960 as professor of Old Testament. In 1960 the faculty approved a new advanced degree in the practical ministry, a Master of Sacred Theology. By then, the school threatened to become more a graduate institution than a training school for ministers. But just as the faculty began moving into its new building in early in 1960, the dismissal, by Branscomb, of one of its students, James Lawson, precipitated a devastating crisis in the Divinity School. For the next three years its tragic history became largely an aspect of the Lawson affair and of the troubled history of integration at Vanderbilt (see chapter 20).[38]

Even before the Lawson affair exploded on campus, the fascinating career of Nels Ferre at Vanderbilt had put to test the university's announced commitment to academic freedom. Ferre's is a complex story. The background begins with the appointment of Branscomb. He recognized one implication of Vanderbilt's effort to attain national stature: it would have to recruit a distinguished faculty. And, in the social sciences and humanities, distinguished scholars were likely to hold nonconventional beliefs, particularly those that would seem radical in the South. Branscomb tried to prepare his board for this possibility. In 1950, as security and loyalty became the national obsession, and as blacks began gaining admission to southern public universities, Branscomb urged the board to accept the need for complete freedom of thought and writing for Vanderbilt's faculty. Without this commitment it would be impossible to recruit the most distinguished scholars and scientists, for no self-respecting professor would accept any limits on his or her freedom. But even then Branscomb hedged. He promised to try to secure men of balanced personality and good sense, and to try to keep them that way, leaving open what he meant by "good sense." He also said that those who admitted to, or proved to be, members of the Communist Party should be dismissed, for they taught principles which would deny academic freedom to colleagues.[39]

In 1950–51 the postwar concern for loyalty reached an hysterical extreme. Americans suffered great anxieties in the developing Cold War and searched for explanations or scapegoats. The word "Communist" became the verbal symbol of disloyal, or possibly even subversive, activities. But the images that attached to the loaded word were so multiple, and so varied from one user to another, that it could not communicate any clear image at all. For some people, a Communist was simply a member of the Communist Party of the U.S.A., a party that, even though small, had exerted tremendous influence in the 1930s and even in the war years. The party had gone through several phases, shifted rather abruptly some of its policies, and, in spite of efforts to maintain tight discipline from the top, had recruited diverse people. Several brilliant academic intellectuals had joined the party, or cooperated with many of its fronts, in the 1930s. But party membership was far from being the primary definition of the word "Communist." For many people in the South, as the unending flow of letters to Branscomb indicate, the word encompassed all those who considered themselves Marxist in philosophy, all who wanted a state-owned or socialist economy, and even at times those who did not believe in any one of the various Judeo-Christian gods, those who espoused racial integration or racial equality, or those who wanted to maintain closer cooperation with the Soviet Union. Of course, according to how one played on definitions, the Soviet Union was or emphatically was not a Communist, Socialist, or Marxist country. Even this superficial semantic analysis suggests the complexity of issues wrapped up in the anti-Communist crusade. Equally crucial ambiguities lurked behind such words as "loyalty," "security," and "subversive."

In 1951, in the midst of the McCarthy era, Tennessee threatened to follow the lead of several other states and set up a state loyalty oath for all its public employees. Such state oaths supplemented the elaborate security screening system established by the federal government in 1948. Eventually, the Supreme Court would void all such state oaths, but while they prevailed the oaths created a crisis of conscience for thousands of professors, who felt morally compromised when they signed them and feared dismissal when they refused. Fortunately, professors in private colleges were exempt from taking such oaths, but not from the public mood that created them. In state after state, professors from private universities led the efforts to repeal, or to challenge, the constitutionality of state loyalty oaths.

Vanderbilt professors had their own limited skirmish. In 1951 three professors in the College (H.C. Nixon of political science, William H. Nicholls of economics, and David Hill of physics) submitted a strong motion to the College faculty. They wanted the faculty to go on record against the Taylor bill (named for Senator H. Frank Taylor), a pending subversive control bill before the Tennessee General Assembly. The heated debate revealed that roughly one-half of the faculty was against the motion, and in turn this group was divided between those who favored oaths and a larger group that believed the Vanderbilt faculty had no reason to involve itself since the oath did not apply to private colleges. On a point of order, Branscomb ruled the original motion out of order. But he did rule in order a revised statement that the faculty, rather than sending a memorial to the legislature, consider and approve a statement against any limits on freedom of thought. After protracted discussion, the faculty voted to adjourn for two days. Instead of seeking a formal vote, the concerned faculty circulated such a statement and gained for it 142 signatures. In response to the publicity it engendered, a few professors, led by Donald Davidson, publicly disassociated themselves from the petitioners. But the faculty action, as published, gave the impression that the overwhelming majority of the Vanderbilt faculty not only opposed such legislation but was willing to take a stand in state politics.[40]

Senator Frank Taylor quickly put his foot in his mouth and enabled Branscomb to turn the episode into a brilliant public relations victory. Taylor not only condemned the faculty petition but charged the Vanderbilt faculty with teaching communism on campus. Since Vanderbilt had no professors of even a mildly leftist persuasion, Branscomb saw a perfect way to respond. The only possible target of Taylor's attack was Alexander Dragnich's political science course on comparative governments, about a third of which he devoted to governments in the Soviet Union and Eastern Europe. Branscomb, in a statement soon repeated in journals and newspapers all over the country, pointed out that Vanderbilt University opposed communism (still undefined) not by silence, not by refusing to talk about it, but by exploring its "vicious doctrines or practices." Even the Nashville *Banner* joined the New York *Times* in endorsing his statement. The Taylor bill died in committee and Vanderbilt won wide respect for its tiny tangle with Communist witch hunters. But, as no one seemed to notice, this was a cheap and evasive victory. If Vanderbilt professors, in their courses, set about exposing the "vicious doctrines" of communism, then they seemed to be using their courses for a propagandistic purpose. Even if they offered balanced, descriptive lectures on the Soviet Union or on Marxist theory, as did Dragnich, a defense of such courses hardly touched on the issue of academic freedom at Vanderbilt.

Could a professor at Vanderbilt who honestly believed in Marxist theory, one who preferred a socialist economy, or one who belonged to or had formerly joined the American Communist Party, teach at Vanderbilt? By skirting this issue, by emphasizing the need for Americans better to understand their "enemy," Branscomb left in doubt the amount of leeway for unconventional or unpopular opinion in his faculty.[41]

Fortunately, at the height of the McCarthy era, no incident at Vanderbilt forced any testing of the university's commitment to free expression. But Branscomb continued to speak out on the issue, treading a very careful path among divergent constituencies. He was frightened by some of the congressional investigations, the pillorying of academicians elsewhere. To his board he balanced his emphasis on the need for academic freedom with concessions. In May, 1953, he stressed that universities should not become "temples of refuge for disloyal citizens," that universities "should not harbor Communists." He thought no such were at Vanderbilt and welcomed any "careful investigation," one that followed judicial safeguards and rules of evidence. He wanted no public charges, no hearsay evidence, no trial by television, and was very frightened of the tactics used in campus investigations by a Senate subcommittee headed by Edward Jenner of Indiana. He conceded that, in the past, the Communist Party had been a legal party and that "loose thinking individuals" had joined it, thereby hinting that Vanderbilt might employ past members of the party if they were now repentant. But, as always, he qualified. The right to freedom in research and teaching was no license "to be either a fool or a scoundrel." In England in the summer of 1953 Branscomb ran into criticism of his views, and those of other American university administrators. British professors believed the exclusion of Communists from access to the classroom compromised any belief in academic freedom. Branscomb concluded that the difference lay in the meaning that both sides gave to the word "Communist." His British friends welcomed committed Marxist theorists, not clandestine conspirators, which is what Branscomb meant by the word. In 1954 Branscomb denied that academic freedom gave any professor the right to refuse to answer questions about loyalty posed by proper authorities, but left open the exact prerequisites for such authority.[42]

Nels Ferre helped change the focus from abstract discussion to hard realities. In the spring of 1949 Ferre came from Andover-Newton to give the Cole lectures. Then a youthful-looking forty, he inspired his audience as had no former lecturer. A native of Sweden, his slight accent probably gave added appeal to his speeches. Although no one was aware of it at the time, Ferre had a restless, almost childlike trait—he developed easy enthusiasms, yielded completely to appreciation or approval from others, and could never say no to any request. He loved his reception at Vanderbilt and quickly identified with the building Divinity School. When asked, he indicated his openness to joining its faculty, given certain professional considerations. This seemed like a gift from the gods for the school, and in a sense it proved so. At the time,

Ferre was widely considered among the brightest theologians in the country. His most significant book—*A Christian Understanding of God*—won him worldwide acclaim. Ferre, as always, wanted extra time for his writing. Thus, he bargained with Branscomb and Dean Benton for a special professorship, one that involved a one-course teaching load and abundant research opportunities. This represented the first time Vanderbilt had ever offered such special privileges or committed itself to bringing in great "stars" to help boost a program. Ferre, who often reflected a childlike sweetness and generosity, could also be petulant and demanding. He frequently sparred with Dean Benton over the terms of his appointment and eventually pushed to the very limits his special privileges. After accepting an appointment, at a reasonably modest $6,500, he suddenly had doubts and wrote asking assurance about academic freedom. Someone had warned him he would not have it at Vanderbilt. Beyond a general impression about southern universities, the informant may well have known some of the widely circulated details about the Alva Taylor case of 1936. Both Benton and Branscomb assured him that he would have freedom at Vanderbilt. They did not know the trouble to which they committed themselves.[43]

Soon after coming to Vanderbilt, Ferre became the bête noire of evangelical and fundamentalist groups, now on the attack. They used carefully selected quotations from Ferre's books to damn the whole liberal or ecumenical sector of American Christianity. In many ways, Ferre was an unlikely target. In a larger perspective, he was part of the loose new "orthodoxy" that swept American Protestantism during and after World War II. That is, Ferre helped resurrect serious theology and doctrine in the churches, had a soaring, almost Platonic view of the incarnation, joined Reinhold Niebuhr and others in exploring the heart themes of sin, grace, and redemption, and personally reflected a deep and even mystical personal religiosity. But he was completely honest in writing about his beliefs. As anyone who took the Bible seriously, he had to understand it in the light of a century of critical scholarship, and in books even for popular audiences he aired the textual and historical problems, and the internal contradictions, that were part and parcel of his trade.

Such biblical sophistication was sadly lacking among most church people, perhaps most of all among those in the South. Thus, Ferre joined Paul Tillich in bemoaning the biblicalism so rampant among modern Protestants, an authority of the book that, as he put it, placed an effective, totemic umbrella between individuals and the Christian deity. As a way of subverting this totemic by-pass, he loved to toss out small barbs. His view of Jesus was broadly orthodox—Jesus was in all senses a person, but the incarnate Christ was in all ways God. Such a view led him to speculate widely about Jesus' human characteristics, even to the likelihood of his sinning. He discounted the importance of the virgin birth theory, not only because of weak biblical authority behind it but as a theological red herring, an issue that diverted attention from the reality of the incarnation. He did not believe a physical resurrection necessary for the spiritual truth and thus aired the grounds for rejecting such a literal doctrine. His cosmic version of God was such that, on purely technical grounds, Ferre was fully monotheistic or unitarian, and his irenic confidence in God's love made him a universalist (God will save all mankind). Finally, his political and social views matched his cosmopolitan background and his fervent belief in a coming kingdom. He was not as open to Marxist theory as Reinhold Niebuhr was but acknowledged its wide appeal, an appeal that at points overlapped traditional Christian themes. Typical of most eminent theologians, he found the values underlying modern corporate capitalism to be profoundly un-Christian and thus he supported a form of democratic socialism. Finally, as a Christian, he preferred as his ideal social order a type of Christian communism, a view widely shared by Christian intellectuals. Such a brief résumé does not do justice to Ferre's elusive theology, but it does suggest why he was so vulnerable a target of the religious right.[44]

In the early 1950s the indictments of Ferre gained momentum, culminating in a decision to cancel his scheduled lectures at the Methodist summer camp at Lake Junaluska, North Carolina, in 1955. The cancellation led to as many condemnations of the camp as attacks on Ferre. At times, he seemed to float above the battlefield, becoming only the occasion for deep cultural conflict that never personally engaged him at all. He lectured all the time, and with such sincerity and profound piety as to win over most critics. But among his critics were many Vanderbilt alumni, and soon they barraged Branscomb with hostile letters. By 1955, answering the repetitious charges took up half his time, for by then critics included wealthy alumni and three or four board members. The crusade against Ferre was led by evangelists Carl MacIntire and Billy James Hargis, by a southern Methodist group called the Circuit Riders, and by dozens of fundamentalist radio ministers. These critics of Ferre, whatever their motives, were dishonest. They deliberately quoted him out of context, misread his intentions, and refused to engage any of the textual or scholarly issues. They abundantly proved his point—an ignorant biblicalism had become the god of many purported Christians. Eventually all the critics emphasized one brief statement in Ferre's *The Christian Understanding of God*. He had noted the possible correctness of an old Nazi and racist claim—that Jesus was somehow Germanic and not fully Semitic. Mary, he said, could have been impregnated by German soldiers from a nearby Roman garrison. Ferre had no way to substantiate such a wild theory and did not take it very seriously. Whether this statement haunted Ferre or not, it certainly came to haunt Branscomb.[45]

To critics, Branscomb patiently tried to talk reason. He pointed out the unfairness of the quotations, noted Ferre's larger purposes, stressed his good standing in the Congregational church, and asked critics, if possible, to hear him lecture or at least read some of his books. Almost no critics had read his books; they gained all their information through right-wing religious tracts.

One most persistent critic—board member Vance Alexander—required much more careful handling. Alexander, an alumnus and a prominent banker in Memphis, was ill informed on religious and ideological issues. He kept receiving the ugly tracts, struggled through Ferre's books, and still found offensive passages. He circulated his concern among other board members and effectively rallied a number of Memphis alumni to his demand that Branscomb get rid of Ferre. Alexander believed Ferre was ruining the reputation of the university, even as his sources of information kept backing him up on this point.

Branscomb tried to appease Alexander as much as possible and in so doing very seriously narrowed the implied definition of academic freedom. As so often, he granted to critics the validity of their concern but then denied guilt. Ferre was a Christian in good standing in a major denomination. This was all the Divinity School required. But such a concession implied that Vanderbilt would not keep him if he were not in good standing. Branscomb went all the way to the FBI to get letters to clear Ferre of a charge that he had signed a petition on behalf of the Communist Party members convicted under the old Smith Act. His name did not turn up on any of the petitions, although the *Daily Worker* had listed him as a petitioner. Ferre could not remember whether he had signed or not, apparently felt that he should have signed it even if he did not, and could not see anything in the issue important enough to take seriously.[46]

The more ominous responses of Branscomb need to be taken in proper context—he was appeasing critics in the interest of public relations. In 1955, to an impatient critic, he acknowledged the tactless nature of Ferre's reference to Jesus' paternity, and then said: "If this had been repeated the University would have had a practical problem calling for action. The book I refer to was written before he came to Vanderbilt. Although he has written four or five books since he has been here, and many articles, all of which I have carefully watched, there has been no comparable slip." To Alexander he finally conceded: "writing to you as a trustee, I will say that if this kind of tactlessness were frequent, I would have a clear responsibility to do something about it." To a friend of Alexander he promised "to watch everything which Professor Ferre writes and says. . . . If there is anything wrong in this case, I assure you that we will not overlook it, and neither will we disregard it." Such assurances would not have reassured Ferre or his faculty colleagues. Such words seemed to document a very restrictive intellectual environment at Vanderbilt. But they helped keep the wolves at bay so that Ferre, oblivious to many of the agonies of chancellors, eventually left Vanderbilt with a grateful acknowledgment that Branscomb had lived up to his original promise. Despite all the attacks, Vanderbilt had never in any way restricted his freedom.[47]

Then why did Ferre leave? For complex reasons, some tied to personality problems, some to hard decisions made about him at Vanderbilt. Ferre, lovable and generous on most occasions, was a bit of a headache in his school.

508

Like a supernova, he exploded in all directions, burning out all too quickly. He was always away on a lecture tour or on leave. His teaching was minimal and he rejected most onerous committee work. Other professors resented his privileges; Dean Benton tried to harness him, to get some sustained departmental work from him. Ferre was always tempted to take off for elsewhere and enjoyed a rather constant flow of ego boosting. In 1956 he tried to get university permission, and some financial support, to spend up to three years in Japan. Vanderbilt was generous, but not generous enough for him to complete the arrangements. After some difficult negotiations, Ferre, in a typical gesture, pledged his full devotion to the school and his willingness to give more time to students and to his own writing.

Deeper personal problems loomed. Ferre was too distracted, too pulled in all directions, to maintain serious scholarship. His voluminous writings, often a fallout from lectures, continued, but the repetitions increased, the quality declined. Recognizing this, he floundered in trying to correct it. Branscomb saw in him a crisis of self-confidence. Although he gave up on his Japanese trip, Ferre was off to Oxford in the summer of 1956. In letters he helped join in the search for a new dean and welcomed the appointment of Nelson. But Branscomb knew he was restless. In one letter he talked wistfully about the chance he had of resuming his old chair at Andover-Newton. Branscomb expected him to leave soon and in almost fatherly letters came close to supporting his choice. He did nothing to persuade him to stay, offered no new salary or privileges. The separation was friendly, a bit of a relief to both sides. Ferre was never quite as well loved as when he left, and he retained warm feelings toward Vanderbilt. To Vance Alexander, Branscomb revealed his own personal feelings. Six days before Ferre's expected October 12, 1956, resignation, Branscomb conceded that, on entirely different grounds, he had come around to Alexander's position. "I have come to feel that there is in this instance a certain emotional instability, so that if this gentleman should get an offer from another institution, we are not going to do one thing to keep him, and, in fact, I would encourage him to take it."[48]

The only other tenured professor who probed the limits of academic freedom was D.F. Fleming. Fleming suffered through the early Cold War and through the labyrinth of government loyalty programs. An old Wilsonian who had dreamed of a new world order tied to collective security, he saw American foreign policies, from Truman on, as Russophobic and disastrous. In his very popular courses on campus, and in a series of articles, he became an outspoken critic of a new, self-centered American empire. He bent over backward to see world events from a Soviet perspective. His position bothered some students, most of whom chose other courses. His publications attracted some public attention, but in the early 1950s not enough to bother Vanderbilt's administrators. But after 1952, when Branscomb made Fleming the first research professor in the College, Fleming became a burr in the shoes of his successor—Avery Leiserson. Quite apart from whether he had any right on his side, he was a complaining obstructionist in the department. Fleming kept up a continuing, friendly, almost fawning relationship to Branscomb, sending him all his publications and begging for praise and professional rewards. They were both members of the off-campus Round Table discussion group.

Fleming would have been shocked to read a Branscomb letter to Vance Alexander in December, 1953, a letter largely related to Ferre. In it, Branscomb referred briefly to the communist issue on campus. He had found no party members in his faculty and rejoiced that no Vanderbilt faculty had yet taken the Fifth Amendment. But he did have ideological concerns about four or five cases, including two nontenured faculty who "were discouraged from continuing, and have gone elsewhere." A third junior professor (Norman Parks in political science) presented more problems. He declined to leave short of his contract period and tried to create an issue over it. In Branscomb's language, "we handled the case carefully in a way which, though it took a couple of years, resulted in his resignation last summer." The fourth case was that of a former departmental chair, obviously Fleming. "He is no longer the chairman and he no longer teaches freshmen and sophomores." If taken literally, Branscomb's letter suggests major penalties for politically sensitive professors. Perhaps they did suffer. But the context helps defuse its more sinister implications. In his desperate efforts to defend Ferre, Branscomb wanted to show active concern about the communist issue, to take credit for steps already taken. In the Parks case, Branscomb had indeed received some pressures from Nashvillians. Parks had moved to Vanderbilt from the *Tennessean*, was as outspoken an internationalist as Fleming, and had some bitter local enemies. But he did not have the scholarly credentials for tenure, and not only Branscomb but colleagues made him aware of this. Parks did insist upon fulfilling a three-year term appointment and then, as expected, moved elsewhere. Branscomb even wrote an enthusiastic letter in his behalf for a deanship at another college. In no sense did Parks's political views hasten his departure. The case with Fleming is a bit more complex. But the research professorship of 1952, which relieved him of the duty of teaching a lower level course, did not seem, at the time, at all related to any disturbing content in his courses. Possibly, if one takes Branscomb's letter literally, course content was a contributing issue. But, once again, Branscomb simply seemed to have been retroactively milking these two personnel decisions of all possible ideological content in order to get a board member off his back.[49]

The Fleming case had a sequel, one that did eventually involve serious issues of academic freedom. In 1955 the Post Office, in accordance with a new law, notified Branscomb that it held extensive communist propaganda addressed to a D.F. Fleming. Unless the university supplied justifying educational reasons for receiving such materials, the Post Office would not deliver it. Branscomb asked Fleming about it and received a rather nasty reply, one reflecting impatience with stupid bureaucrats. Fleming wanted the right to decide what was communist propaganda and did not recognize that right in the Post Office. He included a sharp sermon on growing American police state policies. Since he did not provide justifying educational reasons and perhaps could not have until he screened the material, Branscomb notified the Post Office that Vanderbilt did not want to receive any more of the mailings.[50]

In July, 1957, the university had to decide on whether to extend Fleming's appointment for an additional three years, or to age sixty-eight. For such a distinguished professor a refusal to extend would have been a serious vote of no confidence. Dean Beach recommended extension even though, at first, Fleming's departmental chair would not recommend or oppose. Branscomb concurred with Beach. Again, in this case, ideological issues remained peripheral. But shortly thereafter, Fleming came under national attack in a radio address by the far-right newscaster, Fulton Lewis, Jr. Of all things, he picked up on an internationalist article Fleming wrote for a Sunday school publication of the Board of Education of the Methodist Church. The Daughters of the American Revolution took up the issue, and Branscomb received angry letters of protest. In each case he defended Fleming's right to express his views but noted his personal disagreement with them. In 1960 Fleming received a small salary increase, but by then he had lagged behind most other professors of comparable age and stature, a subtle hint of administrative disfavor, but a disfavor that certainly concerned far more than his political views. From Europe in 1960–61 Fleming wrote long letters to Branscomb about his just completed two-volume book, *The Cold War And Its Origins,* noting the eminent publisher (Doubleday) and the enthusiastic British response. But from Fleming's recent articles, Branscomb believed the book one long apology for the Soviet position, a repetitious indictment of American policies. It is important to note that, even before final publication and before any reviews of the book could reach Vanderbilt (only leftist scholars approved its point of view and some of them noted serious problems in documentation or objectivity), the administration had already decided to deny Fleming any extension beyond age sixty-eight, although he pleaded for such. The consoling letter from Purdy came on January 6, 1961. Purdy noted no extraordinary or emergency reason for such an extension and expressed "our hope, and expectation, that you will be able to offer your distinguished services in scholarship and in teaching at other institutions of higher learning." Fleming accepted the decision as one based on continuing good faith.[51]

Unfortunately, the story did not end with Fleming's retirement or Purdy's note. As mounting criticisms of his book began to flood Vanderbilt, Branscomb happily noted his prior retirement and emphasized that Fleming spoke for his own point of view in the book, not that of Vanderbilt. Branscomb personally believed Fleming to be almost obsessed in his fault-finding with the United States and disassociated himself from his arguments. On June 11, 1962, Branscomb wrote such a response to a critical Mary Low Weaver of

Orlando, Florida. She had sent along a vicious attack on Fleming from the Fundamentalist Church League of America, headquartered at Wheaton, Illinois. It began with his allegedly pro-Soviet Sunday school article of 1957 and ended with a detailed denunciation of his book. Branscomb wrote a frank but impolitic letter. He said he did not think Fleming was a Communist, but rather "an individual who has gone sour over the years, and has lost his perspective and his balance of judgment." Many scholars would have agreed with this judgment, whether fair or unfair. It was, to say the least, ungracious, but not so much so as his follow-up: "Professor Fleming was retired a year ago in spite of his request for continuation," which seemed to make his retirement a form of punishment meted out by a concerned chancellor. Branscomb ended by noting that Fleming was now transferring to a college in Florida. Branscomb later regretted the letter, for it soon became public knowledge all over the country and part of a major academic freedom controversy at the University of South Florida.[52]

Consistent with Purdy's hearty recommendation, a healthy Fleming sought postretirement lectureships. In January, 1962, he received a seemingly firm offer to go to the University of South Florida for a year, on a half-time basis. Fleming accepted, visited the campus in March, and even bought a house. When President John S. Allen announced the appointment to newspapers in April, right-wing groups began to organize a protest. By July, Allen decided not to submit the appointment to the State Board of Control, the final appointing authority. As justification of his refusal to submit Fleming's name, Allen cited new and damaging information about Fleming received after July 26, 1962. This led to Fleming's appeal to the AAUP, a long investigation by that organization, and eventual censure of the University of South Florida for flagrantly violating academic freedom. The new information involved concerted attacks by right-wing political groups in Florida and, above all, Branscomb's letter to Mary Weaver. Because of the ambiguity of the loaded and often inaccurate public charges against Fleming, Allen had to rest his case on Branscomb's damning comments. It turned out, contrary to Branscomb's previous knowledge, that Weaver was affiliated with a Florida Coalition of Patriotic Societies, the source of the original protest against the appointment. He had provided it with needed ammunition. Allen subsequently telephoned Branscomb, who stood by the content of the unfortunate letter. The AAUP investigation led to solicited letters from almost all Fleming's Vanderbilt colleagues. All of them disagreed with Branscomb as to the implied reason for Fleming's retirement, and most disagreed with Branscomb's adverse judgment about his having gone sour. The national publicity for the case made Vanderbilt, because of that one letter, seem a party to the actions of the University of South Florida. The letter also helped abet right-wing groups in Florida and embarrassed those who had rallied to Fleming's defense.[53]

Branscomb's letter deeply wounded Fleming. The sequel came in December, 1963. Branscomb attended a Round Table meeting in Nashville at which Fleming read a paper entitled "The Turn Toward Peace." Branscomb complimented him privately on the paper and tried, in what had to be an embarrassing moment, to explain the Weaver letter. He even said that, had he heard the paper then delivered, he would not have written the letter, and that he regretted having done so. Such an apology could not have come easily for Branscomb. In a subsequent letter Fleming rejoiced in the apology but was still bitter. The apology left unexplained several disturbing facts—Branscomb had written the Weaver letter only four days after an earlier meeting of the Round Table at which Fleming had announced his South Florida appointment; in the Weaver letter Branscomb had expressed very strong interest in a right-wing diatribe written against Fleming; he had made clear his views that Fleming was unfit to teach; and he attached great opprobrium to Fleming's retirement at age sixty-eight, when this simply followed the rules of the university. As Fleming suggested, it took a lot of apologizing to erase all the damages to his reputation. He further accused Branscomb of adding even more damaging comments in his telephone call to Allen. Because of the letter, Fleming pointed out that he lost a year's employment, suffered acute embarrassment, and probably lost several opportunities to teach at other universities. Beyond his private losses, Fleming argued that the letter added a blow to higher education in Florida, armed special groups to do further battle with universities, and helped create the type of fear that worked to lessen freedom on campus. He asked Branscomb to back up his belated apology by expressing his regret to the AAUP for all the harm he had done.

Fleming outlived this episode. He went on to a well-received lectureship in Arizona, and with the rapid shift of ideological outlook became a darling of the new left by the middle and late 1960s. His work anticipated many revisionist arguments offered, often with more scholarly rigor, by subsequent diplomatic historians.[54]

Branscomb's involvement with the South Florida case came at the embattled end of his administration. The Lawson case, although not directly related to academic freedom, sharply divided the campus. It placed Branscomb on the defensive against many professors. In this context the leeway for faculty independence shrank. In an exchange of letters between Branscomb and Purdy in August, 1961, when Branscomb was in France, Purdy even talked, with some hyperbole, about a purge of malcontents, those who could not adjust to "our way of doing things. . . ." But, again, such loose talk exaggerated the pressures for conformity. Close investigation reveals that terminated professors always suffered from incompetence as well as from noncooperative behavior.[55]

The problem was that the Vanderbilt faculty had small protection against subtle pressures from the administration. The government of the university remained highly centralized, a situation that did not change significantly in 1959 when Branscomb authorized a new University Senate. He felt the need for an all-university "consultative, deliberative, and advisory" body, one that could serve both the chancellor and the board. This Senate, justified by an old by-law dating from the university's beginning, included as ex officio members all six academic deans and all vice-chancellors, or nine members; balancing these were ten elected faculty members (three from Arts and Science, two from the Medical School, and one each from the other five schools). The faculty in each school elected its members by ballot. The Senate was to meet at least twice a year. It would play its first constructive role during the Lawson affair, but it did not represent any major approach toward faculty government. The chancellor chaired it, its powers were limited, and appointed officers had a balancing power. But it was a beginning. Out of the integration conflict, and in the new Heard administration, the expanding and improving faculty would press for a more representative campus government and for firmer protections of academic freedom. It gained both.[56]

19

On the Bottom

As THE FLOOD OF VETERANS subsided after 1948, campus life returned to something close to the prewar norm. But not completely. The simple, small, homogeneous campus with only two dorms quickly expanded into a residential campus housing up to 4,000 students. The outer world remained tense and threatening but the campus was scarcely a refuge. The 1950s and early 1960s turned out to be the most troublesome in Vanderbilt's history. The perennial issues of athletics and fraternity policy heated to new intensity. Student disturbances or near riots reached their peak. Students rarely seemed happy or content, and by the early 1960s were increasingly restless and hypercritical.

In the years of rapid growth Vanderbilt continued to attract the same type of undergraduate students as before the war—affluent, Protestant, career-oriented, from the South, and politically either Republican or state-rights Democrats. In one sense, and as a policy, Vanderbilt did become less provincial. In 1946–47, 63.3 percent of its students came from Tennessee, 37.4 percent from Nashville; by 1960–61 only 44 percent in the College came from Tennessee, 16.6 percent from Nashville. But the more distant students came largely from the South, with a few from the Northeast and Midwest. Higher tuitions excluded most young men and women from small farms or from laboring class families. The typical Vanderbilt students had parents in business or the professions in southern small towns or cities. Limited scholarship funds brought in a few students from less affluent homes, but never enough to challenge the elite-wealthy image reflected by students. In 1955 both the College and Engineering were able to award only 221 scholarships. Only twenty-eight Founder's scholarships covered full tuition and attracted able and on occasion poor young men (not women). Other undergraduates worked for wages, gained tuition reductions as sons of teachers or of preachers, or qualified for a variety of special endowed scholarships. In addition to university aid, by 1955 approximately fifty-four graduate students enjoyed corporate or federal scholarships. Most other graduate students graded papers or worked as teaching assistants. Unlike the undergraduates, the typical graduate student came from a low- or middle-income family, often graduated from a small denominational college, had a strong

Miss Commodore contestants, 1957

service commitment, prepared for low-income but intellectually rewarding careers, and supported the national Democratic Party.[1]

Women students remained second-class citizens. In proportion to their numbers, they received fewer scholarships, were last to get new dorms, faced much tighter restrictions on their conduct, and were discouraged from entering many professions. The percentage of women enrolled in Law, Medicine, and Engineering actually declined after the war. But they still made the best grades and won a disproportionate share of medals and awards. They now had a role in all student activities and even gained a right to join the marching band in 1958 (the administration quickly vetoed a girl twirler after one controversial trial at a football game).[2]

The most obvious symbol of female inferiority remained the quota system. The board feared too many women on campus and thus allowed only one-third in the College, or roughly one-fourth of all undergraduates. Briefly, in the early 1950s, the university relaxed this a bit when faced with sharp enrollment declines. Branscomb asked the board to raise the quota from 33 percent of the College to 700 women in both the College and Engineering, or what amounted to 38 percent in the College. But he warned against further changes, since he wanted to preserve the "traditional character of the college." He believed that, once "the number of women rises too high, the men cease coming. Then the women cease coming." The logic of this explanation is not apparent. No one ever offered a persuasive explanation of why Vanderbilt men had to outnumber women by three to one in order not to feel threatened. But, after taking care of the men, Branscomb and the board eventually did build enough dorms to take care of the full female quota. Before beginning

516

the plans for what became Branscomb Quadrangle, Vanderbilt briefly considered, in 1951, buying bankrupt Ward-Belmont College in order to convert it into the women's annex so long dreamed of by Kirkland. The cost, and the considerable distance from the campus, discouraged such a plan. The Tennessee Baptist Convention then purchased the campus.[3]

By later standards, women students in the 1950s suffered sexist repression. They bore the brunt of most humor. A careful statistical analysis by a *Hustler* reporter revealed that two-thirds of the content of campus humor magazines involved sex, with most of the humor directed at the women students. From reading the *Hustler* one could conclude that Vanderbilt women were primarily sex objects, at the university to be the playthings of men. The women offered few published protests, and polls revealed how conventional their values were, how many made marriage and the raising of children a greater goal than a professional career. The *Hustler* carried a steady series of cheesecake or sweater-girl photographs, such as a "Coed of the Week" series. It was the decade when men turned attention away from their World War II fixation with shapely legs and fixed their attention instead on big breasts. Women made the news most often for their beauty, as a Miss Vanderbilt or homecoming queen, or for their charm, featured in an annual charm week.[4]

Women students became the subject of a serious debate in 1961. Tom Templin, editor of the *Hustler,* wrote what became a famous editorial, "The Vandy Coed." The "typical coed," he said, was cold, aloof, and snobbish, not because of any fault of her own but because of a false value system on campus. When innocent and warm and unaffected females arrived, they immediately confronted a vicious social game. Campus prestige depended on pledging the

Miss Charm contest, 1958

517

right sorority, dating the right man, and moving in the right social circles, circles that extended to alumni and into proper Nashville society. The snobbish city reinforced the same evil on campus. The men either supported the game by going along with it or else retreated from it. That is why so many could hardly wait for vacations, to get back to authentic hometown girls. Hope remained. After two years the most sensible, and most talented, coeds saw through the system, outgrew it, and repudiated all its false values. This took exceptional courage and sincerity because it was so difficult to break through "Vanderbilt's Great Social Barrier, paper thin but very high and absolutely opaque." Templin hoped the editorial would help, that the courageous and the sincere would vanquish the system and tell incoming freshmen the hard truth. The editorial elicited a huge response, with numerous denials from the women. It fed a near orgy of self-criticism then sweeping the campus. It also began an enduring debate over the characteristics, and foibles, of a typical Vanderbilt coed, a title soon shortened on campus to TVC.[5]

Women did gain a role in an integrated student senate. In 1951 a committee appointed by the chancellor matured a new system of student government. The students overwhelmingly approved a new constitution by a vote of 616 to 39. It replaced the old, all-male student council and did away with organized classes in the College. It replaced all this with a single representative elected senate that encompassed all undergraduates (the College, Engineering, and Nursing). The complex apportionment of twenty-seven senators included a man and woman from each Arts and Science class, a single representative from each Engineering class, and one representative for all the nurses, plus several other represented groups and one at-large member. Six standing committees of this senate governed all student activities, with the publication committee most often in the news in the next decade. The student senate, much more than the earlier council, assumed a vital role on campus. On most controverted issues it took a stand and usually conducted a student referendum. But it faced incessant criticism and ridicule from disaffected students, and in some years bogged down on routine issues, temporarily losing student support or interest.[6]

The one issue that engaged the senate the longest and divided it most consistently was Vanderbilt's membership in the National Student Association (NSA), a rather innocuous federation of students that offered certain services to colleges and tried to serve as a national spokesman on student issues. In 1958 the NSA, at its summer meeting, gave wholehearted support to equal opportunity and condemned all racial segregation. Since such a stand offended many Vanderbilt students, the senate voted not to withdraw from the NSA but to dissent from this one policy. In October, 1959, the senate held a heated debate on NSA membership but voted 16–6 to renew. By then, few southern universities remained in the NSA, although Fisk and Tennessee A&I were members. Lamar Alexander, a *Hustler* reporter, led the fight to remain in the NSA. After a heated students' forum in Furman Hall, the senate received a student petition with 537 names asking for a binding student referendum on membership. The constitution of the senate precluded any binding action, but the students voted 775 to 362 against membership. By then, support for integration was only one symbol of an NSA viewed as ideologically unacceptable to "southern and conservative" students at Vanderbilt. In the summer of 1960, Vanderbilt students attended the annual NSA meeting, tried to represent the views of southern white students, and at least found northern students willing to listen. Consistently, those Vanderbilt students who became most involved with the NSA were the ones who desired to retain membership and thus a voice in national student politics. In the fall of 1960 the senate ignored the referendum and voted 13–7 to keep membership; many students interpreted this as a tyrannical act.[7]

The NSA issue came to a climax in 1961, just prior to Vanderbilt's adoption of an open admissions policy. In 1961 the NSA had endorsed sit-ins at lunch counters, and a few northern students joined a special motorcade to Nashville to show their solidarity with local demonstrators just after the infamous Lawson case. The NSA, in a policy statement, endorsed civil disobedience in order to test the constitutionality of laws. In February, 1961, a sharp Vanderbilt debate on another motion to withdraw ended when the tired students tabled the motion. A week later Lamar Alexander, now president of the student senate, broke a tie vote to block a resolution condemning NSA's sit-in policies, though subsequently the senate voted its own opposition to sit-ins. Vanderbilt sent effective delegates to the 1961 NSA meeting, and this time they became part of a "conservative" group within the organization. This considerably shifted the basis of conflict on campus. Some politically able but socially conservative students now wanted to remain in and work to change the NSA. The senate, in the fall of 1961, voted 17 to 8 to remain in the NSA. But by the fall of 1962, a new senate voted withdrawal by 14 to 12, a motion subsequently vetoed by the chair as provided for in the constitution. History professor Alexander Marchant made a stirring appeal for the continued membership and for the national and international responsibility this symbolized. By 16 to 11, just short of the required two-thirds, the senate failed to overcome the veto and Vanderbilt remained in the NSA for one more year. By now the issues had begun to shift. Much of the debate centered on cost and practical benefits received, as well as on ideological differences.[8]

Student publications in the 1950s probed the limits of administrative toleration and of student rights. Humor magazines had a hard time on campus. The old *Jade* of World War I was eventually suspended because of the daring Lady Godiva issue. Its eventual successor, the *Masquerader,* revived after World War II but became more risque, more daring, than ever before. Increasingly a ribald, sex-obsessed humor sheet, it still had to use insinuation to make its points. In the fall of 1950 the *Masquerader* cover featured the back view of a nude woman, allegedly a Vanderbilt student. With

Cheesecake in the Commodore

PHOTO BY WALTER COURTENAY

this the publications board, then headed by Robert McGaw, suspended the magazine. The reasons offered involved the whole tenor and pattern of the publication, not just this one example of bad taste. The discipline proved mild indeed, for some of the same editors launched a new humor magazine, the *Chase,* which except in title seemed to be a continuation of the *Masquerader.* Then, in honor of Mothers Day in 1954, *Chase* published a mocking, somewhat salacious issue. One page included four illustrations. The top left one was simply dark, with the caption "Father loves mother." To the right appeared a snapshot of a beautiful, fully clothed young girl, about age two, the type sent in Christmas cards by adoring parents. The editors had found the photograph at a downtown print shop. The caption read: "Daughter loves mother (and wants to be one too)." On the left bottom appeared a picture of a sailor, who also purportedly loved mother. All in all, the page was a model of decorum for the *Chase.* But it had plenty of sexual nuances, even more, it turned out, than the editors ever imagined.[9]

It so happened that R.L. Langford, minister of the Dalewood Methodist Church in East Nashville, recognized the snapshot as an earlier one of his daughter, Pamela. He claimed great embarrassment and enduring harm. He was so chagrined that he doubted he could remain in Tennessee, and could not stand the thought of his daughter growing up and finding this "hideous thing." Langford targeted more than the offensive photographs; he inter-

520

preted these in light of the context, an obscene magazine from a morally corrupt campus. His reaction came in the midst of a nationwide religious revival and just before Billy Graham's great campaign in Vanderbilt's stadium. Despite sincere apologies from the editors, Langford sued the *Chase* and its publishers in January, 1955, for $180,000 in damages. As a reaction to the developing controversy, the publications board adopted a new standard of editorial decorum in December of 1954. The *Hustler* and other publications had to consider the effect of each article upon "the public relations of Vanderbilt" and could not deal with sex in an "obscene or vulgar manner."[10]

A defiant *Hustler* staff, on January 28, 1955, challenged the new rules. It published, on the front page, a picture of the offending *Chase* photographs and then in titillating detail quoted the more lurid charges filed by Langford. Langford believed the caption to his daughter's photograph suggested that she was "interested in and amenable to acts of illicit sexual intercourse or carnal knowledge . . ." and that the black frame suggested that Mrs. Langford was engaged in sexual intercourse in a dark room. Finally, the proximity to

More of the same

PHOTO BY WALTER COURTENAY

521

the picture of the sailor suggested that she was amenable to "acts of illicit sexual intercourse or carnal knowledge" with him, and thus that his wife was a common whore. He read such meaning into the cover because of the "lewd, bawd, vulgar, lascivious, suggestive and sex-laden stories" throughout the magazine. The *Hustler* article gave the original feature ten times its former circulation. Consequently, Langford filed a new damage suit for $440,000 against the two *Hustler* editors, against Vanderbilt University, and against *Hustler's* publisher. The publication board promptly suspended the two editors.[11]

The Langford case proved costly. The university attorneys had to defend the case all the way to the Tennessee Supreme Court, while Branscomb and other officials had to submit to extensive and hostile legal questioning. In 1956 the Supreme Court exonerated the *Hustler* editors from any violation of privacy. They had simply repeated certain details of a case already filed in the courts. It remanded the case back to the lower courts to determine if the editors had been accurate in what they reported. In July, 1956, the lower court judge directed the jury to render a verdict in favor of Vanderbilt. Subsequently, the Langfords also lost their original case against the *Chase*. In the fall of 1956, after the successful outcome, Branscomb reported to the alumni on why he had not followed numerous demands that he censor student publications. If the administration could control content, then students would lose interest in such official publications or resort to wild, outlawed newspapers. He noted that students were not children and that the university was not an army. The students deserved free speech. They should have their say about campus matters, including their opinion of how well "the Chancellor discharges his duties. . . ." After all, he said to his critics, "we are training them to be alumni." He described student journalism as a maturing process. Of course it was risky, for "it is risky to have young people about . . . , it is risky to be a young man or woman." But to let students manage their own affairs is "society's wisest and most rewarding investment."[12]

Other student activities expanded as rapidly as the enrollment. Dozens of special interest organizations catered to every need, but with shifting patterns of popularity. The 1950s, above all else, was the golden age of Vanderbilt's theater. Joseph E. Wright directed most of the plays. Stimulated by the new frame building on Garland, with its huge stage, the directors attempted the most difficult Shakespeare plays by the early 1950s. An outstanding student actor in many of the toughest roles was Cecil Jones, Jr., who would later return to Vanderbilt to teach and direct. In the spring of 1952 the students took on the challenge of original material and received national recognition for their effort. They first staged Brainard Cheney's "Strangers in This World," a haunting musical about a snake-handling sect. No one who saw the play could ever forget the choral music or the actual snakes on stage. Charles F. Bryan of Peabody composed the music, as he did for a follow-up opera, "Singin' Billy," based on a poem by Donald Davidson.[13]

The 1950s marked the apex of conventional religiosity among Americans. A higher percentage belonged to churches than ever before or since. Various forms of religion seemed to sweep the country, and belief in a god no one seemed to define very precisely was almost universal. Such a consensus affected even campuses, and particularly Vanderbilt. In fact, the celebration of religion seemed to grow in tandem with a greater frankness about sex, with more drinking and more alcoholism, with panty raids, and with a widespread sense of moral decay. In 1946 the Student Christian Association (SCA) reorganized at Vanderbilt. Sam C. West, the director, began with only 50 members and expanded this to over 1,600 in 1950. The SCA welcomed Jews and emphasized socially oriented programs. It skirted doctrinal differences. It served for many years as the only universal campus organization, the only one that brought independents and Greeks, Christians and Jews, together. It was not like the prewar SCA led by Henry Hart. Its leaders did not assume a reforming or prophetic role but did direct students into local charitable work.

In 1958 the SCA board decided to adhere to its title. It proposed to change its constitution by adding the phrase "A fellowship of Christians." The board (nine faculty, eight students, and the personnel deans) wanted to be honest, not exclusive. The worship services sponsored by the SCA had, all along, been not only entirely Christian but fully Protestant, a reflection of the YMCA background and Vanderbilt's heavily Protestant student body. In its social activities the SCA had been inclusive, truly an interfaith organization, and the board did not mean to change this role. But the constitutional change did reflect a new emphasis among American Protestants—back toward doctrinal and theological self-consciousness. The board wanted to give some specifically religious content to the SCA, and to shift away from merely social activities. Behind this was a desire to serve the religious needs of students, or at least of most of them.[14]

This change provoked another extended controversy on campus. A Jewish professor resigned from the SCA board. The *Tennessean* ran an editorial on the new exclusiveness, on a developing rift between Jews and Christians. The controversy followed the dynamiting of the Jewish Community Center in Nashville. Consequently, in May, 1958, the student senate, the governing body over the SCA board, vetoed the constitutional changes in order to keep the SCA inclusive, to thwart a purported "Protestant power drive." The chagrined SCA board so redefined its statement of purposes as to please everyone—"a fellowship of believers and doubters, of Protestants, Catholics, Jews, and others—who are endeavoring in our relationships with one another and with God to be a redeemed and redemptive community." One issue raised in the debate remained unsettled. Vanderbilt paid the SCA director and provided a house for the organization. Should an avowedly nonsectarian university fund a sectarian religious organization? The almost vaporous statement of purpose hardly seemed sectarian, but even it excluded a few Moslems already on campus and did not clearly encompass nontheists.[15]

Perhaps appropriately, a more prophetic form of religion flourished just off campus, out from under the controls that were implicit in university funding. After the war four student religious organizations ministered to all the adjoining campuses—the Wesley Foundation (Methodist), Canterbury House (Episcopal), Westminster House (Presbyterian), and a Baptist Student Union. A Newman Club (Roman Catholic) and a Jewish Student Organization also met on campus. The directors of the four houses joined in several cooperative activities, or the nucleus of what later became the Office of University Ministry. Of the houses, the Wesley Foundation, in a heavily Methodist context, exerted the greatest intellectual impact. Under the direction of Ruth and Joe Brown Love, it staged its own plays and for years sponsored a Sunday evening symposium that featured the most controversial and the most cerebral debates anywhere in Nashville. From courses in sex education to overt advocacy of integration, the foundation provided a refuge for the most daring or socially committed students.[16]

Not that social commitment bothered many Vanderbilt students. As a whole they were committed to the status quo and reflected the preferences of their parents. In 1948 Vanderbilt students organized a (Strom) Thurmond for President organization on campus, while the *Hustler* backed the East Tennessee Republican E. Carroll Reece for the senate against notorious "liberal" and "left of left" Estes Kefauver. But despite the majority view, Kefauver gained some fervent followers on campus, who lamented his failure to receive the Democratic nomination in 1952. Possibly that disillusionment helps explain the most one-sided national election poll ever taken at Vanderbilt—84 percent for Eisenhower to 16 percent for Stevenson. Eisenhower remained the student favorite throughout his eight years. In 1960, in a campus poll, Nixon led Kennedy by three to one, despite Kennedy's reputed appeal to youth. But among registered voters on campus (older students, including graduate students), Nixon barely led Kennedy, with only 56 percent of the total. For a Democrat to be so popular meant something close to an emerging political revolution at Vanderbilt. Incidentally, sixteen of twenty faculty members willing to express a favorite voted for Kennedy. After Kennedy's speech on campus early in 1963, and then his assassination early in the fall, he seemed to command the loyalty of a vast majority of Vanderbilt students.[17]

After World War II Vanderbilt students never recaught the football madness that had possessed them in the 1920s and 1930s. In fact, athletics dropped dramatically as a compelling student concern. Twenty years earlier the fate of the football team had been headline news in the *Hustler*. In part, the loss of interest simply reflected the effects of so many losing seasons. It would be too flattering to suggest that Vanderbilt students finally grew up and left behind all the childish antics of old, for too many other even more destructive forms of infantile mindlessness marked the 1950s.

The relative decline of football paralleled a new prosperity for basketball,

524

which, in an era before giants dominated the sport, was yet a game of artistry and finesse in contrast to the gladiatorial contests on the gridiron. Robert Polk took over as head basketball coach in 1947 and gradually built a winning team. Vanderbilt students, in increasing numbers, traveled to the David Lipscomb gym to see their new heroes, who won the SEC tournament in 1950. With the completion of Memorial Gym in 1952, students and towns-people began to pack it for every home game. The first great basketball hero, the first to match the football heroes of the past, was Billy Joe Adcock. Throughout the 1950s the basketball team flirted with greatness and, if it had not been for its one great nemesis, Kentucky, would have led the SEC over the decade. In 1956 the team ranked as high as tenth in the United Press poll and in 1957 rose as high as eighth in both polls, only to lose to Kentucky in the SEC tournament. Again, in 1961, Vanderbilt lost its chance to play in the NCAA tournament only because of a final loss to Kentucky. Polk, victim of an early heart attack, retired in 1961, to be followed by Roy Skinner. Basketball receipts by then joined those of football in paying the cost of the whole athletic program.[18]

Football remained the big money sport. It also caused the most headaches for the chancellor and board. "Red" Sanders returned to Vanderbilt for the 1947 season, which briefly hinted at a return to prewar glories. The 1947 team had notable victories, including a 14–7 win over an Alabama team that had whipped Vanderbilt 71–0 in 1946. This set the stage for 1948 and Vanderbilt's strongest post–World War II football team. After two opening losses and a tie with Alabama, this team won its last eight games, many by large margins. It beat Tennessee 28 to 6, the first such victory in eleven years and the widest margin since 1925. The stars were quarterback Jamie Wade (another Wade, Billy, was then a freshman) and kicker Zack Clinard. At the end of the year Vanderbilt ranked twelfth in the Associated Press poll, an end-of-the-year rating never matched by any subsequent Vanderbilt team. On the strength of this success, Sanders moved on to a more prestigious and lucrative job at UCLA.

In 1949, under new coach Bill Edwards, the team fell to a lackluster 5–5 record. Another poor season in 1950 prepared the way for what seemed sure to be a great team in 1951, a team led by a candidate All-American, Billy Wade. The team floundered, to the great disappointment of fans. Attendance fell to a disastrous total of 85,000, and everyone blamed Edwards. He resigned at the end of the 1952 season, when the stadium filled only once to see Vanderbilt lose to Tennessee 46–0. The new coach, Art Guepe, came from Virginia with a great reputation for building strong teams out of mediocre material. At first he justified all the hopes. In three years he built a winning team, which in 1955 won against Auburn in the Gator Bowl. Although not one of the top four bowls, in 1955 the Gator Bowl seemed like heaven for starving Vanderbilt fans. Briefly the old football fervor seemed on the way back. Guepe received a five-year contract. But subsequent Guepe teams fell back into the new Vanderbilt norm—one losing season after another and increasingly rare victories within the SEC. Guepe, with administrative support against increased criticism from alumni and even from students, who once hanged him in effigy, held on until 1962, when he resigned under pressure.[19]

Just like Kirkland and Carmichael before him, Branscomb had to seek solutions to the football problem. He found none, although his efforts were more imaginative. By now, football success depended upon the active recruitment of fully subsidized players. Briefly, just after the war, the NCAA made some effort to preserve fully amateur teams. In 1948 it limited grants-in-aid to tuition payments, leaving the student to pay room and board. A reluctant SEC had to go along, but by subterfuge the teams all subverted this limitation. So did Vanderbilt. It set up new scholarships for students of general excellence, awarded on the basis of scholastic record, promise of leadership, and participation in school sports. For some reason these scholarships all went to athletes, but still only to those in the upper third of their high school classes. The NCAA in 1950 accused Vanderbilt of violating its rules. The NCAA would accept such full scholarships only if they were limited to the top 20 percent of high school graduates and to students with 550 or better on SAT verbal and mathematical scores. The Vanderbilt Athletic Committee protested an intervention by the NCAA in purely academic policies and refused to change the basis of its selection. But at least the standards for scholarships helped Vanderbilt football players attain almost average grades. In 1951, under pressure from the SEC and other conferences, the NCAA relented and allowed full-ride athletic grants. These raised Vanderbilt's costs even as its gate receipts went down. In 1950 and 1951 the athletic program operated at a deficit, with the largest cost being the grants-in-aid. As Branscomb put it, Vanderbilt had to bet from $250,000 to $500,000 each year on having a winning team, and thus secure enough gate receipts to meet its expenses.[20]

In February, 1951, Branscomb first presented the developing dilemma to his board. With characteristic wit, he stressed Vanderbilt's need for an Ivy League of its own, but "we are located in a spot where ivy does not seem to flourish." Branscomb was by then irked with the SEC and remained a critic of its priorities over the next decade. Vanderbilt seemed cursed by its location, for it competed largely with land grant universities noted for weak academic programs and whose winning football teams were their claim to fame. The greatest offenders were such rivals as Alabama and Tennessee. Branscomb briefly pursued his vision of a new, less professional football league. He consulted with several likely universities but found only the University of Virginia and Washington University strongly interested. Duke, Tulane, and Rice—all likely members—were not interested for a variety of reasons.

This left Branscomb only one option—to battle once again for reforms within the SEC. He gained board approval for a new list of reforms, even as the board talked seriously of leaving an unreformed SEC. The board did not have the means to subsidize a losing athletic program year after year, and already Vanderbilt awarded fewer grants than any other conference school (106 in 1951). Branscomb asked the board to consider suspending big-time football, as had Washington University, Emory, and the University of the South. He noted that a winning team, and thus balanced budgets, seemed to require a physical education program, an active quarterback club, and frequent trips to bowl games.[21]

Branscomb began his reform effort in the SEC in the fall of 1951. He sent letters to Vanderbilt alumni, urging a deemphasis on football. He wrote other SEC conference presidents, asking support for reform. He applauded a suggestion from the president of Mississippi State that SEC presidents meet to consider reforms. Branscomb, in what he called a six-point deemphasis program, asked for an end to spring practice, agreements to reduce the numbers of scholarships as football income fell, a limit of 80 on all athletic grants in a given year (down from 140), a restriction to keep physical education majors from participating in athletic games, an end to unlimited substitutes or two-platoon football, and rules against all special clubs or funds to support athletic programs. The presidents met in Birmingham on November 18, 1951, in a unpublicized meeting. As so often before in similar meetings, the presidents achieved almost nothing. On most issues they talked but took no action or appointed committees to consider critical issues. Branscomb found that too many presidents came to protect their big teams, and on more extreme measures, such as abolishing bowl games, he faced solid opposition. But the presidents of winning teams did agree to share a portion of the profits from bowl games with the losers. In a follow-up meeting in December, the presidents voted a slight restriction on the number of freshmen and transfers allowed to play each year, reduced spring practice to twenty days, and recommended to the NCAA an end to the two-platoon system. An SEC committee to study a limitation on scholarships also met in December and, even though chaired by Sarratt, ended up with no firm proposals. Vanderbilt, as always, seemed helpless to do much more. Branscomb kept pushing his more radical reforms, preached them in an article prepared in 1952 for the Southern Association of Colleges and Secondary Schools, and at least gained favorable national attention for his idealism.[22]

In the wake of these failures a special board committee headed by Cecil Sims studied the athletic situation and reported to the board in 1952. It defended the value of football for increasing alumni support and raising student morale but argued that football now violated sound educational policies and even principles of moral conduct. The board voted unanimously to give the chancellor and the Executive Committee power to withdraw from the SEC and join a new conference. The board also followed the committee in endorsing new guidelines just voted by the American Council on Education. These guidelines, which followed closely the reforms sought by Branscomb in the SEC, included full faculty control over all athletic policy, coaches as tenured faculty members, no admission favoritism for athletes, normal prog- ress toward a degree in four years as a condition of eligibility, no freshman participation in varsity sports, no recruitment payments or paid visits to campus, grants-in-aid only to needy students and on the same competitive basis as those awarded nonathletes, a limit of aid to actual educational expenses, no termination of aid for discontinued participants, no special employment or any employment without honest work, clearly stated rules, and a full disclosure to competing schools of all athletic data (number of grants, aid given, grades earned). For football, the guidelines designated a season lasting from September 1 to December 1, which would allow no bowl games. In the SEC only Tulane joined the Vanderbilt board in endorsing all these guidelines. But Vanderbilt could not follow many of them and remain in the SEC. It did cut down on the number of its grants (to 75 or less), and in 1952 also cut the number of assistant coaches from six to four. Coach Art Guepe also served without any athletic director, eliminating another high salary. Such a shrinking budget, and program, contributed directly to Guepe's teams' losing record. By the mid-1950s Vanderbilt was in an im- possible bind. Low gate receipts curtailed expenditures, while losing teams contributed to the poor attendance. Even Guepe's early success, through 1955, in part rested on a temporary gift from the NCAA—a limited substitu- tion rule that favored small football programs as against larger ones.[23]

Through the late 1950s Vanderbilt remained in the SEC and tried to compete effectively. Its basketball program helped, as did such small sports as baseball and tennis. But even halfway competitive teams seemed to demand moral compromises. One had to join the big sports system or quit. For example, in 1957, when Vanderbilt moved to require SAT scores, it had to exempt football players. They were recruited before the exams were normally taken, and in many cases prospects scored so low as to have prejudiced their admission if they had been less brawny. When charged by professors with unequal admission standards, and thus of a violation of Vanderbilt's heralded academic integrity, Branscomb could only weakly protest that in the "realm of intercollegiate sports one does not live in the world of pure logic." Vanderbilt maintained a sense of slightly flawed righteousness because it had no physical education major and established no courses just for athletes.

Branscomb, just before retirement, tried one final time to form a new conference. He met in complete secrecy with the presidents of five other private universities. Southern Methodist University and Rice did not want to give up their share of Cotton Bowl receipts. Duke did not want to join a conference that did not include the University of North Carolina, while Georgia Tech did not want to lose the University of Georgia as a competitor. In May, 1962, Branscomb reported his failure to his board. In a parting sermon he sounded like the retiring Kirkland. The universities, he said sadly, had come to provide athletic entertainment for the whole country, even though this had nothing to do with the business of education. Vanderbilt

528

should either get out of the entertainment business, associate only with likeminded institutions, or try to be reasonably competitive in the SEC. The last seemed the only alternative by 1962. In this one area Branscomb left as great a problem for his successors as he had inherited in 1946.[24]

On another inherited problem—the multiple evils of uncontrolled fraternities—Branscomb won at least a partial victory. Despite intense friction, he considerably abridged the role and the power of fraternities and sororities. After the war, social fraternities regained almost as much prestige as they had enjoyed in the 1920s and 1930s. In several respects they seemed to Branscomb to be inimical to the academic goals of the university. Social life continued to center in the scattered, aging houses. As late as 1959, 76 percent of men, 79 percent of women belonged to social fraternities and sororities, one of the highest percentages in the country. A young man or woman who rushed but failed to gain the desired membership usually felt devastated. Independent students were virtually frozen out of campus politics and the largest share of social life. The most eccentric, unconventional, and original students, the glory of any campus, rarely fit within the Greek system. A few of the very ablest students often rebelled against it and ended up as part of a small, reversely snobbish intellectual elite. The highly decentralized houses practically precluded common campus activity. Some of the houses were extremely snobbish, choosing members because of parentage or prep school background. The social life of fraternities diverted freshmen from course work and, consistently, fraternity (not sorority) members had lower grades than independents. The fraternity houses rather flagrantly violated campus rules, particularly those that prohibited alcoholic drinks, and thus protected a de facto double standard of conduct. Despite constant effort by the faculty or deans, the fraternities and sororities had tenaciously held on to the earliest possible rush—as soon as freshmen arrived on campus each fall. Balanced against this was the role of houses as cheap substitutes for dorms and the sense of community they provided for immature young men and women.[25]

In 1951 Branscomb began the reform. He announced a plan for deferred rushing, possibly as late as the sophomore year, his preference. The proposal set off a minor explosion on campus; 635 students signed an interfraternity council petition containing nine reasons against any deferral. In December, 1951, a student-faculty committee began preparing a final proposal. The committee favored rushing at the beginning of the spring term but offered, as a more modest two-year experiment, a procedure for rushing in the middle of the fall quarter, just after mid-term grade reports. Those with deficiencies could not rush, or what turned out to be a very harsh rule. In the fall of 1952 over 40 percent of the men were deficient and the fraternities could not begin to fill their quotas. The faculty changed the rule to allow one deficiency. Still, the system was a disaster, for it meant continuous surreptitious rushes for half of a term. Instead of freeing freshmen for academic work, it constantly diverted them from it. The faculty soon hated the system as much as did the students. In 1954 a faculty poll revealed eleven for opening rush, thirty-one for the beginning of the second term, and twenty-five for a later date, usually meaning at the beginning of the sophomore year. What is significant in this limited poll is that not one faculty member voted for the existing plan.[26]

In 1954 Branscomb announced one more year of the hated system, while a new faculty committee carried out an enormous study of the whole fraternity problem. This committee, chaired by a psychologist, released its much awaited report in February, 1955. Unfortunately, it was so pompous and full of jargon that one needed an interpreter to read it. It was short on concrete proposals. The faculty, in good social science form, had submitted twenty-five questions to students. To no one's surprise, 92 percent of the students favored a return to September rushing. The committee noted the major problem areas—few explicit rules, a pattern of arbitrary blackballing (based on family income, religion, or lack of social graces), a lack of programs for independents, intense competition among fraternities, and too great interference by alumni in some houses. The committee recommended a faculty-student advisory council, nonrestrictive membership (fraternities and sororities had to take all who rushed), stronger efforts to control drinking, required records and reports from each house, and, as a goal if not an immediate policy, a deferral of rushing to the sophomore year. The two Greek councils rushed out a counterreport, written in plain English, which challenged each faculty finding and recommendation. An alumni group also wrote a critique. The College faculty endorsed a watered-down version of the somewhat befogged committee report. But, as enacted, it left the final decision about rushing up to the faculty-student advisory council. This council then voted for a January pledge, with a C average in the first quarter as a prerequisite. In a sense it did away with rush because it stipulated no rush week. The fraternities and sororities could rush freshmen at any time, which led to a continuous process of evaluation and recruitment each fall.[27]

The new plan went into effect in the fall of 1956 but did not settle the ongoing debate. Students circulated rumors that Branscomb planned to force all students into dorms, thus threatening the solvency of their houses. Branscomb assured them that he had no such plans. But the change to the semester system in 1957 forced a revision of the rules. Fears over their fraternities may have influenced students in their strong opposition to the new semester system. The advisory council had to fight through another tense battle before approving a pre-Christmas rush for 1957, and at the end of the first semester for all subsequent years. So long a delay horrified the fraternities. But the Board of Trust seemed to give a sop in compensation—it approved a special fraternity district to the west of the campus and worked out financial arrangements to assist those houses that wanted to move. Unfortunately, the offer remained an empty gesture. No fraternities or sororities could afford to move, since they required a small and expensive dorm to house and feed their members. They had acquired their large, often rambling boarding houses when prices were low, and even though some houses were in bad repair or were fire traps, they had no alternative but to hang on.[28]

In as complete secrecy as possible, a committee of deans began working on a final solution in 1958. It completed a plan early in 1959, one submitted to Branscomb and then discussed by the Executive Committee of the Board of Trust. The Executive Committee endorsed, in principle, a gradual three-year transition to a completely new fraternity system. The heart of the new plan was a conversion from residential houses to club or chapter houses, without sleeping quarters or kitchens. As dorm space became available, the residents of existing houses would have to move. Meanwhile, the university would lend money (up to two-thirds of the cost) at low interest to enable the majority of fraternities and sororities (those outside a slightly larger designated area) to sell their old houses and build a new club house, at a cost of no more than $100,000. As for rushing, the deans recommended the existing rule but asked for minimal grade averages before a fraternity or sorority could pledge new members. The board, aware of a near rebellion on campus, postponed a final vote until the fall of 1959, meanwhile inviting a response from students.[29]

The response came in many forms. Long before the board heard the new plans, rumors leaked to students. The fears grew apace. The students joined in mass meetings, signed petitions, formed a vigilante organization, and wrote thousands of letters to alumni. They saw the new plan as the death of the Greek system at Vanderbilt and could not contemplate any compelling fraternal life without live-in arrangements. Branscomb now became their devil. When the chancellor and his wife attended the final dance in Greek Week, they were shocked to confront placards ridiculing his plan. Hostile alumni letters swamped his office. The *Hustler* editorialized against the plan and even talked vaguely of possible violence to block it. To Branscomb, the wild student response seemed to certify the wisdom of the plan. Clearly, students gave more loyalty to their fraternities than they did to the university. Student protest had limited impact on the final board decision in October, 1959. In its final plan the board allowed up to four officers and two student workers to live in each club house. It set a final limit of $90,000 on construction costs and provided for Vanderbilt's architectural supervision of what soon became a cluster of attractive, architecturally varied houses. Perhaps most important, the university surrendered on the rush issue, leaving all rushing rules to the fraternities. They, of course, returned rush to the fall semester.[30]

At one point the fraternity issue did contribute directly to violence. This story began with the new carillon installed in Kirkland Tower in April and May of 1959, just as the fraternity debate heated up. In the midst of student protest meetings, all orchestrated by a clandestine united Greek organization, four young men hatched plans for an ingenious prank. The senior class voted, not without some vocal protest, to contribute to the carillon. Behind this was the desire of the Alumni Association to renew an old tradition of class gifts. As so often in campus fund drives, the pressure to cooperate and to pledge was well orchestrated and intense. Thus, some of the dissidents had a double grudge—almost forced payments for some silly bells and the impending death of their beloved fraternities. The young men ingratiated themselves with the engineer installing the carillon, helped do some of the work, and easily located the various cables that ran from the console in Neely to chimes and speakers in the tower. They spliced in a wire to the speaker cable and stretched it through the attic to the student-run radio station (wvu) in one of Neely's towers. There it remained, ready for use any time the students wanted to connect it to the radio record player and amplifier. On Sunday, May 17, at near midnight, they regaled the campus and much of west Nashville with a prerecorded program relayed through the wire to the powerful new speakers in the tower. This "broadcast" preceded the dedication, and the first playing, of the carillon. The broadcast began with voodoo drums and opened with a sonorous voice which declared itself to be either the "spirit" or "ghost" of Kirkland Tower. What followed was a ghostly indictment of the new fraternity scheme.

The joke had more than its intended effect. As so often before, the dorms opened and up to 500 boys gathered in front of the tower, many in pajamas. They shot off firecrackers, threw water-filled bags, and moved to a women's dorm shouting "panty raid." They did not enter or do damage that early Monday morning. On Monday evening they gathered again for what turned out to be only a harmless bonfire. But on Tuesday a more determined group of about 250 marched on two dorms and tried to gain entrance, even scaling walls. The dean and assistant dean of men, in what had become one of the occupational hazards of their office, came to campus to try to break it up. The assistant dean had his glasses knocked off. The two deans gathered as many names as possible before the boys returned to their dorms. Thus, the "ghost of Kirkland Hall" could be accused, in an indirect sort of way, of inciting three near riots among a volatile student body. The electronic geniuses suffered a suspension for the rest of the year but were allowed to make up exams the next fall, when they remained on probation.[31]

The carillon caper made up only one incident in a pattern of senseless, usually unfocused violence that stretched back as far as 1952. This violence made up a puzzling episode in Vanderbilt's history. On the surface, the various panty raids or snowball fights or aimless milling about the dorms seemed to be a continuation of earlier pranks, or evidence of high spirits or even school spirit, but the incidents sometimes had a darker side—fear, even sheer terror, considerable property destruction, and a high risk of serious injury or death. Only luck, it seemed at times, prevented fatalities. It is difficult to explain the disturbances. Different student generations were involved, and the inciting incidences varied through time. One could not explain any of this without noting imitative behavior and then what became a campus tradition. Freshmen learned about former skirmishes or battles and yearned for their own excitement or glory. The worst violence occurred during the years when the fraternity issue was unsettled. Panty raids began nationally, during the Korean war and amid new fears about the draft. In several cases the Nashville police unintentionally or even intentionally incited or helped worsen such behavior at Vanderbilt. The restriction of freshmen to dorm residence at least created the needed critical mass of immature young men. In a few cases the women helped invite raids by challenges and dares. Nashville newspapers dramatized and magnified each incident, while the *Hustler* downplayed them or deliberately ignored them. A few came just before football games. One could go on and on, to weather conditions (deans prayed that snowstorms would miss Nashville), to barometric pressure, to phases of the moon, and possibly even to sunspots.

The disturbances began as early as 1950. A fraternity serenade of a sorority led to boisterous songs and catcalls, neighborhood protest, and police intervention. By 1951–52 the boys felt that they were special objects of harassment by Nashville police. Twenty boys received traffic tickets during the year, often for very minor infractions. Near the end of the year, with warm weather and exams looming, the dorm boys staged their first panty raid on May 18, 1952. Approximately 250 boys from Kissam marched on McTyeire and then in larger numbers on Mary Henderson (the nursing dorm). Some also invaded sorority houses and even stole the clothing of a house mother, hurled stones and eggs, and in two cases slightly wounded the greatly overpowered Nashville police force, which came to the scene. Expensive women's clothing soon hung on trees, as the boys did at least $700 worth of damage to buildings. Newspaper stories referred to greetings from girls. Actually, the vast majority of women were frightened half to death. Three nursing students in a top floor room of Mary Henderson locked their door and then, fearful that the boys would scale the wall, tried to fasten a screen that accidentally fell, injuring one of ten policemen. Next morning the newspapers had a story of how women had thrown screens at the men. Eventually, the university suspended five men and placed twenty-five on probation. The students collected money to pay for damages.[32]

In one sense, this inaugural raid is easily explained. Well publicized panty raids had swept from campus to campus across the country. If, as suggested at the time, the search for women's intimate garments symbolized the various sexual frustrations of young men on campus, then Vanderbilt men were no different than those on other campuses. They outnumbered Vanderbilt women by four to one, and the women were notoriously cold and unresponsive. Students in the 1950s learned what was almost obvious—that campuses offered few opportunities for sexual intimacy. Studies showed that college males were less sexually active than any other class of young men, which in part helps explain all the titillating humor about sex. Back seats of cars make poor bedrooms, and Vanderbilt coeds—from proper families, and under very restrictive codes of conduct—rarely "went all the way." But all this had been true before the war and scarcely explains the raids.

Once the pattern of disturbances began, almost anything could trigger the formation of an uncontrollable mob. No major incidents occurred in 1953. But on January 8, 1954, an innocent student snowball fight ballooned into a near riot. When Nashville police arrived, the students rallied to bombard them with snowballs, some filled with stones. The battle became vicious, stopped traffic, and led to several minor wounds. Students, and the *Hustler,* insisted that the event was largely for fun and that reports in the Nashville newspapers exaggerated its seriousness. Several arrested students faced a tolerant judge, who made them write essays as their only punishment. The university expelled some ringleaders for the rest of the term. The snowball battle only intensified police-student hostility. Two weeks later the police arrested a Vanderbilt student for loitering and possession of a pocket knife (the judge quickly dismissed the absurd case). From now on, almost any snowfall on campus led to snowball battles and a high risk of a near riot. A year later, in January, 1955, a snowball fight among boys led to a panty raid on the women's dorm, to the breaking of windows, and the theft of some women's clothing at McTyeire, but to no arrests. In both 1955 and 1957 freshmen mounted small panty raids, breaking into hallways but doing little damage. Then the carillon raids came in May, 1959. Interspersed with these were several near riots—explosive gatherings of students outside their dorms. Deans became proficient at talking down the students, at cooling them off and getting them back into their rooms. The youngsters, perhaps out of boredom, seemed to rush out of their dorms at the slightest provocation. In one case the harried dean of men rushed to campus to deal with a mob in front of the West End dorms, with traffic already blocked. Critical to effective crowd control, he knew, was getting there before the Nashville police. In this case the dean could not find anyone who knew why they were out. Each one just followed others. It turned out that the triggering incident had been a police car stopping speeding vehicles on West End, to the accompaniment of whistles and jeers from Vanderbilt students.[33]

The climactic raid came on November 26–27, 1957. Vanderbilt students had petitioned for a Thanksgiving break but under the new semester system the faculty had voted it down. This was also the week before the football game with Tennessee, and in these lean years students had tried desperate measures to whip up school spirit. The evening of November 26 began with a freshman pep rally. The students moved from the rally to the clock tower but could not get into it. Almost all the freshmen were out of their dorms by 10:30, when the growing mob marched on McTyeire, breaking in and taking undergarments captive. They then besieged Cole but could not get in. They moved by the Kissam quad and picked up several upperclassmen. They came back to Tolman and broke several windows. By 11:15 over 500 boys came back again to McTyeire, invaded it in larger numbers, broke windows and screens, and stole some very valuable clothing. After visits to sororities and to Mary Henderson, they set fire to trash cans and then invaded Peabody shortly after midnight. The uncontrollable mob broke into Confederate Hall and then moved on to a graduate women's dorm, where they reportedly stole not only clothing but wallets and money. Unlike Vanderbilt women, now inured to raids and not very frightened by them, many Peabody girls were terribly frightened. Some foreign women feared for their lives, became hysterical, and at least one had to be hospitalized. For them, the incident remained in their memories a moment of terror. The Nashville police, by now more reluctant to intervene on campus, arrived only at 12:45 when students had blocked all traffic on Hillsboro. The mob was by then beyond control, as students slashed the tires on police cars. Slowly the mob broke up, and as the crowd dispersed the police arrested anyone they could catch, including several innocent bystanders. Thirty-seven students were booked by 2:00 A.M.

For once, students realized the seriousness of their actions. The *Hustler* no longer talked of fun or about school spirit. The student senate called a special convocation and confession became the order of the day. The senate also sent a letter of apology to Peabody. Judge Andrew Doyle arraigned the arrested students and assigned to them the responsibility of identifying all the guilty, those actually involved in break-ins. He challenged students to prove how much honor Vanderbilt students really had. Eventually, 265 boys came forward to confess, which in each case meant disciplinary probation by the university. The students also pledged to pay all damages, including a bill presented by Peabody College. Judge Doyle, impressed by the confessions, dropped all criminal charges against those arrested, and this just before Christmas. Briefly the town-gown conflict seemed to cool off. But students had a hard time raising the damage money. The student senate first assessed every student fifty cents, only to make this a voluntary payment after heavy protest by the innocent, including some female victims.[34]

The great panty raid of 1957 did not end the disturbances. But the worst was over. In November, 1959, when students burned Coach Guepe in effigy, policemen came and met a barrage of water balloons and firecrackers. Fearful of renewed police-student violence, the student personnel deans and safety director tried to win a truce. The student senate even debated a $25 gift to the policemen's benevolent association to buy peace. None ensued. But Vanderbilt officials were now dedicated to avoiding further confrontations. The policemen seemed to resent, almost hate, Vanderbilt students, and much more so than students on other Nashville campuses. The Nashville policemen were not college-educated and did not have the highest professional standards. They came from families that could not afford a Vanderbilt education. They saw Vanderbilt students as rich, frivolous, arrogant, contemptuous, and reflected the same hostilities felt in the 1960s by policemen who battled Vietnam protesters on northern campuses.

The police hostility fed on a series of incidents that involved Vanderbilt in conflicts with Nashvillians, most involving hospital policies. Vanderbilt, in a symbolic sense, was not really part of Nashville. Half of its strongest local supporters lived, with the chancellor, out in Belle Meade. When Vanderbilt faculty or student groups moved off campus for banquets, they were much more likely to go to the Belle Meade Country Club than to the downtown Labor Temple. The police seemed to feel, and internalize, these resentments and jealousies and to take them all out on students. They constantly over-reacted. The students returned the contempt, and so the battle raged. The last major skirmish with police came on March 1, 1963, when another snowball fight led to a melee on West End. The police arrested only four students, but students shot pellets at the policemen, broke car windows, and could easily have blinded someone. This angered Judge Doyle as no earlier episode had done. He made the students pay $215 in damages.[35]

After the fraternity controversy of 1959, student protest began a subtle change. In the fraternity battle it had a focus and a target—the arrogant chancellor and unsympathetic faculty. By then, the students, or at least those who joined in protest or wrote for student publications, seemed extremely unhappy with Vanderbilt. The students had picked up all the fashionable criticisms of American students in the 1950s—that they were other-directed, passive, plastic people, given to conformity and status seeking. The students worried that this was an all too accurate description. In addition to conformity based on peer pressures, Vanderbilt students faced some of the restrictive rules, and the impersonality, that had begun to agitate students at Berkeley even before the 1950s ended. Larger enrollments and dorm life meant new rules, such as required parking permits in 1950 and student ID cards in 1958. The administrative crackdown on fraternities, their last bastion of independence, reinforced their sense of a dependent relationship, of not being treated like adults.

Joined with all this was a developing sense of intellectual inferiority. The post-Sputnik emphasis upon educational failures and the new pressures for academic excellence gave outside support to the internal criticism. As students looked carefully, the campus seemed dull, classes unexciting, professors remote. *Life* magazine, in a 1960 issue, taunted Vanderbilt students for their low SAT scores (it used out-of-date figures). This sense of inferiority helped explain the enormous pride Vanderbilt students felt in a victorious College Bowl team in 1960, one that won four matches and appeared for the maximum fifth time in this quiz show for brainy college students.[36]

After about 1957, Vanderbilt students constantly expressed disillusionment with their faculty and with the quality of their education. They wanted more contact with professors, an old demand that usually concealed other concerns. In part, they got what they wanted. The 1955 curriculum reforms permitted independent work, and by 1961 the College had a full-fledged honors program. In 1957 willing but shy faculty members began meeting students in specially scheduled forums, although they found it hard to match the student vision of pipe-smoking professors sitting around a fire batting around great philosophical ideas. In 1961 Branscomb appointed a student committee to study undergraduate needs, an attempt to turn pervasive criticism into focused recommendations. The report must have surprised the faculty. The students bemoaned the lack of an academic atmosphere, which made Vanderbilt's claim to be the greatest in the South a sheer fraud. They found no stimulus to higher intellectual attainment, little encouragement of individual study and research. The committee proposed, and soon began, formal course evaluations, carried out with the voluntary assistance of faculty. They felt that most courses were not demanding enough, had too few exams, required too few papers, and lacked rigorous grading standards. The committee felt that the College curriculum was too provincial, containing no history courses on Africa or Asia, too few on Russia, no geography courses at all, and no non-Western philosophy. Too many freshman courses were led by teaching assistants, with Western civilization the most dull, boring, severely factual, and intellectually sterile course on campus. The dorms had too few study rooms. The library was open for too few hours. Engineering courses were too specialized. The alumni system stank and, of course, Vanderbilt provided for too little student-faculty interaction. Within a week of the report, eight departments within the College approved new honors programs.[37]

Such student criticisms have to be evaluated with care. Only more able and more demanding students gave their time and effort to such committee work. The purpose of criticism is reform; the focus precludes the celebration of assets. Implicit in the student complaints was an ambivalent goal—on one hand, all the special attention and faculty concern and warm communal support of a small liberal arts college, and on the other, the specialized competence, the intellectual confrontations, and the wide range of courses featured by large state universities. Vanderbilt could not have it both ways.

The students did raise serious questions about Vanderbilt's achievement in undergraduate education. Had it failed its students? One can doubt it. On a comparative basis, Vanderbilt offered more to its undergraduates in the College (not yet in Engineering) than it did in graduate work or in any professional area save possibly Medicine. The College had always emphasized teaching responsibilities, and the unending debate over curriculum and programs revealed a faculty thoroughly committed to the teaching role. The College retained several characteristics of a small liberal arts college—a high faculty-to-student ratio, numerous courses with small enrollments, and enough staff to allow independent work. It tried to avoid the inescapable evils of small colleges—an overworked faculty, specialized courses taught by nonexperts, and the inevitable erosion of course content by professors unchallenged either by graduate students or by engagement in scholarly or scientific inquiry. If Vanderbilt lacked in intellectual atmosphere, the fault had to lie in the personalities of professors and in the personality and intellectual mix of students. In a sense, all the complaints about a lack of intellectuality may have been the best possible evidence not only of concern but of a campus that did stimulate students.

20

The Unwanted

By 1945 black Americans slowly began mobilizing in behalf of equal rights. In the next twenty years they moved from moderate demands and crucial litigation to effective organization and massive protests. During one of the most dramatic epics in all of American history, they eventually won their legal demands and, at least in the South, precipitated a social revolution. Southern white resistance was intense, yet in retrospect what is surprising is how quicky it crumbled before the civil rights movement, in part because most defensive positions rested on morally decayed foundations. No representatives of southern institutions could for long stay above the battlefield. Vanderbilt administrators tried to do just this and thanks to political artistry and defensive policy changes came close to success. But the effort fell to pieces in the Lawson case of 1960. For a brief time Vanderbilt became, in the national press, one of the most widely reviled universities in the country.

For public universities the death knell of segregation came as early as the Gaines case of 1938. The U.S. Supreme Court ruled that southern states had to offer equal opportunities for blacks in all areas of higher education, including such professional fields as law and medicine. This proved impossible under the old rules, for the postwar courts would accept neither tuition payments to northern schools nor inferior black professional schools as viable alternatives. No new black professional schools came close to white counterparts in faculty, facilities, or academic prestige. In a series of cases between 1948 and 1950, the federal courts in effect denied the possibility of separate but equal higher education, and forced formerly all-white state colleges and universities to admit blacks. In most cases the first successful appeals involved professional or graduate education, but this proved only an interim defense against full integration. In the early 1950s Louisiana was the first deep South state to open its four-year colleges to blacks. None of these decisions directly affected private colleges and universities. But the decisions did, by implication, nullify state laws requiring segregation in higher education and made all but certain that private universities would face increased pressures to integrate. For a university such as Vanderbilt, with so many northern patrons, the handwriting was on the wall as early as 1950. In the next decade it finally had to face up to the race issue. What no one foresaw, including Chancellor

Branscomb, was how quickly the pressures would escalate, how rapidly Vanderbilt would have to make hard decisions about admission policies.[1]

When Branscomb came to Vanderbilt he considered himself progressive on racial issues, more willing than most white southerners to accept a gradual modification of discriminatory laws and customs. In a 1948 letter to Jonathan Daniels, the editor of the Raleigh *News and Observer,* he revealed his own thinking. He wanted slow progress, led by the moderate gradualists of each race. He favored greater equality only among the more gifted and educated classes of both races. Let only those blacks with superior ability enjoy progressively greater educational and economic opportunities. Of course, this would not entail social mixing. Southern whites would never accept this because of the bitter and still remembered experience of post–Civil War reconstruction. The impulse to change should properly come from white southerners, he thought, from those who were willing to assimilate those blacks who could make an important contribution to the South.[2]

By 1948 Branscomb could not avoid some consideration of racial issues. The organized civil rights movement still lay several years ahead, but early challenges to old policies already frightened southerners. When Vanderbilt played Yale in football in 1948, some alumni protested that southern white boys had to play against a Negro, one Levi Jackson. In a response to one such letter, Branscomb displayed a characteristic of his whole chancellorship—time-consuming efforts to appease critics, to meet them on their own terms, even when this meant a degree of misunderstanding. Branscomb often did this in order to educate his readers. Thus, he opened his letter with the concession: "I don't think any of us enjoyed the experience of playing against Levi Jackson." Branscomb even noted that the Yale dean had given him reason to believe Jackson would flunk out before the game. Then to the point: Vanderbilt had already played against a Negro at Northwestern and did not want to pull itself "into an increasingly limited area." His attempt to get his correspondent to take a broader view prompted Branscomb to ease the needle in so painlessly as to take away all its sting.[3]

Branscomb used the February, 1948, board meeting to send out an early warning signal. It was typical of the early Branscomb to educate the board, stimulate thought, long before he had to ask for a new policy. He began on what he assumed was common ground. President Truman's important Commission on Higher Education had just recommended an end to an expensive dual system of black and white colleges. When polled by the education editor of the New York *Times,* Branscomb made public his solidarity with four dissenting southerners on the commission. He also noted his apprehension over a bill before Congress to deny tax exemption to discriminatory private colleges and deplored the fact that the American Association of Colleges had almost passed a resolution against segregation. But he was not happy with such negative reactions by the university. Already on campus, opinion was sharply divided on racial issues, and Vanderbilt needed to clarify its relationship to Fisk and Tennessee A&I universities. In fact, librarians at these black colleges had already asked permission to use the JUL's Library of Congress catalog. Branscomb had recommended that they buy the printed catalog but conceded that their librarians could consult the records at JUL in special cases. Given the strong commitment of the JUL's prime patron, the GEB, to black education, Branscomb could hardly refuse such privileges. But he wanted no pattern of regular or routine use, no "recurring inter-racial patterns . . . ." As so often on racial issues he seemed to walk on eggs, to do all he could to mollify the fears of board members. He ended with an eulogy to Booker T. Washington, to his policy of encouraging those blacks who tried "to lead their race along the slow path of hard work, educational advancement, and moral improvement . . . ." He considered President Charles Johnson of Fisk such a leader, one who would support moderates and resist "radical and revolutionary" agitators. Later, in 1950, Branscomb noted the several southern states that, under court orders, had admitted blacks to public universities.[4]

By 1949 racially pregnant incidents began to multiply. A black veteran applied to the Law School. The university attorney advised that state laws precluded his acceptance. Branscomb did not want President Johnson of Fisk to appear on a platform at Vanderbilt, since this might have suggested that Fisk was a member of the University Center. When the Medical Society asked about inviting Meharry professors to scientific meetings, Branscomb discouraged but did not veto such a plan and asked the faculty if it did invite them to do so informally, without publicity. By 1951 several small or border area private colleges or universities in the South had admitted blacks (Berea, the Johns Hopkins, St. Johns, Loyola of New Orleans), and so had almost all denominational seminaries, including Southern Baptist at Louisville. The Vanderbilt Divinity School, in particular, stood little chance of foundation support if it continued to reject black applicants. As a type of precautionary warning, in the summer of 1952 eight faculty members resigned from the School of Theology at the University of the South when their board refused black admissions. Branscomb wanted to avoid such a damaging struggle at Vanderbilt.[5]

The occasion for a defensive change of policy came in the fall of 1952. Scarritt admitted two blacks. This meant that Vanderbilt, if it were to honor its commitment to the University Center, had to admit them to its courses if the students chose to take them. Blacks were also now eligible to use JUL. By the October, 1952, meeting Branscomb planned to present this issue to his board. He also had a letter from Rufus Harris of Tulane, asking if the two universities could join in announcing a common policy of admitting blacks. By the terms of its founding bequest, Tulane could not admit blacks short of a test case to break a will. It wanted to move in that direction and hoped that Vanderbilt could lend support. Finally, Branscomb had solicited a resolution from the School of Religion in behalf of open admission. The Religion

541

faculty very much supported such a policy on moral and religious grounds, as the only policy in "accord with the Christian gospel." It already had a request for Hebrew study from a black Nashville minister. The board postponed any vote on the petition of the School of Religion, completely rebuffed Tulane's request for cooperation, but voted to honor the Univesity Center agreement. James Stahlman, a board member not likely to endorse integration, offered the motion and the board approved it unanimously. To an extent they could not realize, this was the proverbial foot in the door. Branscomb pointed out in his remarks that the "honest and sincere" proponents of equal citizenship included the national philanthropic foundations, although so far only the Ford Foundation had made this policy an explicit condition for awarding its grants. Branscomb predicted that in five years all foundations would end grants to segregated institutions. Money thus proved a powerful persuader.[6]

By agreement, the chancellor did not publicize this 1952 policy. He did not want to offend southern benefactors. But he conveyed the news to the New York foundations, and particularly to John D. Rockefeller, Jr. Thus began a strategy of emphasizing racial progress to northerners, minimizing it to southerners. In New York City, James Pike, a later and famous bishop in the Episcopal church, heard about the board action, talked to a local trustee about it, and as part of his active involvement in the Sewanee controversy announced that Vanderbilt now admitted blacks to its Divinity School. His letter made the United Press wires and alerted Nashville newspapers to what seemed a local secret. The *Tennessean* referred to a cover-up. Its reports met with awkward local denials, which then led to terrible publicity. The denials embarrassed Vanderbilt with its national constituency even as the early reports worried southern alumni. Branscomb feared the publicity would throw Vanderbilt into the race controversy and damage it as much as Sewanee. He felt that these issues had to be settled privately, not in the public arena. In a statement released to the competing newspaper, the *Banner*, Branscomb clarified the earlier board action. To defend this small gesture of cooperation with Scarritt he appealed to the Christian gospel; Christianity, he said, was not the sole or private possession of any one race or nation. It was one of the last times Branscomb used a moral or religious arguement in public statements on the race issue. It seemed to work. Over half the incoming letters approved the policy. One of these, ironical in light of the later Lawson case, came from the local branch of the Fellowship of Reconciliation, a highly regarded, socially active, and strongly pacifist alliance of Protestant churchmen. Among a few letters of condemnation was one from Donald Davidson. He pointed to the conspicuous lack of any faculty involvement in such an important policy decision, one that might require him and other College professors to teach blacks.[7]

The next, and by now anticipated, step came at the May, 1953, board meeting. By then the School of Religion backed up its earlier petition with a strong black applicant, Joseph A. Johnson, Jr., a thirty-eight-year-old minis-

542

ter in the Colored Methodist Episcopal Church and president of its Theological School in Jackson, Tennessee. Johnson did not want to leave the region in order to complete his education. Much later he would serve as the second black member of the Vanderbilt Board of Trust and the first nominated by normal board procedures. The board voted, again unanimously, to admit local blacks into the school. It justified this by the lack of any comparable seminary in the area and made clear that it would not admit blacks that qualified for Fisk, A&I, or Meharry. By implication, it would not admit even seminarians from outside the Nashville region. This basis of selection left open the possibility of black admissions to the Law School and to Ph.D. programs in the Graduate School. Johnson went on to complete his B.D. in 1954, by which time several other blacks had enrolled in the School of Religion. The most reassuring aspect of this original integration was the lack of local controversy or coordinated alumni protest. In the years before the Brown decision of 1954, southerners seemed relatively unconcerned about such token integration, now that several state schools, including the University of Tennessee, had also broken the barrier. To James Pike, Branscomb explained Vanderbilt's willingness to defy an extant Tennessee law against integrated facilities. He noted that "in a conflict between the Supreme Court and the Tennessee law, I see no moral strength in the argument that we are bound to abide by the established local but probably invalid ruling." If challenged, he announced his willingness to appeal all the way to the Supreme Court.[8]

For two years Vanderbilt did nothing to extend this first small opening toward integration. But in these two years the racial issue came to a boiling point in the South. The *Brown* decision of 1954 portended a dramatic change in southern race relationships. Not that any school integration immediately followed except in border states. Within two years southern politicians had worked out evasive strategies, frightened whites had organized in White Citizens' Councils and other resistance organizations, and southern moderates began to form organizations to back at least token compliance. In the glare of national publicity no new policy at Vanderbilt could go unnoticed or unprotested. Never had an administration at Vanderbilt faced such a perilous problem in public relations.

The Supreme Court mandate for school integration encouraged blacks to bid for full rights in other areas, helped inspire the successful year-long Montgomery bus boycott of 1955–56, and boosted the membership and prestige of several growing civil rights organizations. In 1956 the first black gained admission to the University of Alabama, only subsequently to be expelled. In the same year Orval Faubus of Arkansas closed the schools of Little Rock to prevent integration, while Governor Frank Clement of Tennessee took strong steps to protect integrated students at Clinton, Tennessee. In January, 1956, Clement sent a telegram to several select individuals about his attempt to counter groups whose activities he considered "both legally

543

and morally wrong." In one of these telegrams to Branscomb he asked for prayer that he might have "the wisdom to know what is right and the courage to stand by his convictions." Branscomb responded warmly, applauded his courageous stand, and noted that actions against integration would never succeed in the long run. But, characteristically, he also praised action by southerners to solve their own problem and condemned intervention by northerners.[9]

As a whole, white resistance succeeded in the mid-1950s. In hundreds of separate incidents, southern officials or white citizens used threats or violence to suppress and, in a few cases, to kill black activists, and this in spite of the widely adopted policy of nonviolence clarified by Martin Luther King, Jr., the black minister who vaulted to national prominence as a result of the Montgomery bus boycotts. In this period of southern white reaction, Vanderbilt officials pulled back as much as events allowed from the developing conflict. Above all, Branscomb, who had taken a very cautious lead in behalf of civil rights, now withdrew behind a cloak of neutrality or even prosouthern defensiveness. To some extent his own heritage pushed him toward resistance. He resented pressures for hasty change and the attack upon his South by northerners. As most southerners of his generation, he also expressed some personal aversion to full racial mixing. In September, 1954, he recounted an experience at nearby Fort Campbell, an experience that "so amazed me that I have not yet recovered from my sense of surprise and almost shock." Some blacks from a college in Ohio were assigned common barracks with Vanderbilt ROTC cadets. Branscomb said he "was fighting mad," ready to protest. But the Vanderbilt boys assured him there was no problem, that it all worked very well, a fact which he used to soothe outside critics. Branscomb's most fervent hopes by 1956 was to keep the race issue away from the campus. When Martin Luther King, Jr., visited Nashville in 1956, in the midst of the Montgomery boycotts, he spoke at the Wesley Foundation, threatening unwanted publicity when he noted that "ninety percent" of Vanderbilt students "favored racial integration." From any but a southern perspective, this was great public relations for Vanderbilt but it seemed to trouble Branscomb. He correctly assured angry correspondents that King was completely wrong about student opinion, and through a series of such responses seemed almost to be on the side of segregationists.[10]

In 1955 the Law School asked the board for advice. In 1951 the American Association of Law Schools had endorsed integrated student bodies and finally in 1955 seemed ready to enforce such a policy. The Law School's accreditation might be at stake. What was the school to do about increasing numbers of black applicants? Branscomb submitted the petition, which led to a long board discussion. Eventually, a motion to admit carried without dissent, but several board members remained unhappy. Vanderbilt viewed this policy not as a new one but as a reaffirmation of the one adopted in 1953. By implication, blacks could now apply also for Ph.D. work and, shortly, a few did. Branscomb defended the policy as consistent with "the best southern viewpoint" and as fully consistent with state rights. The South had never wanted to deny opportunities for qualified blacks. Men of good will in the South had to solve such problems for themselves. In 1956–57 the Law School admitted its first two black students. In the changed atmosphere of 1955 the Law School policy elicited a barrage of protest, although the campus remained quiet. Branscomb received forty-one critical letters to only thirty letters of approval. He stressed to alumni how very limited the policy was.[11]

Disaffected alumni picked up on the Law School issue. Trustee Vance Alexander, who missed the board meeting, wrote in opposition from Memphis. A group of former Law School students formed an Independent Alumni Association to "preserve the traditions of Vanderbilt" and to protect it from the "interference" of the federal government or the foundations, and to resist "socialistic and communistic principles." The alumni rebellion centered in a few cities, particularly Memphis, and soon fizzled out. A few alumni threatened to stop all gifts, but even some of these subsequently relented during the Lawson episode. The local president of the Alumni Association, Vernon Sharp, wrote a rather hostile letter to the board asking clarification of the policy, since he received most of the flack from angry alumni. The climax came in the meeting of the Alumni Association in the fall. Branscomb and Harold Vanderbilt came, talked, and appealed. They denied any government or foundation pressures and noted board loyalty to all southern traditions. They presented such a minimalist program as more a way of resisting significant integration than of furthering it. No one seconded a motion of disapproval at a meeting of the Alumni Board, while a larger meeting of Law School alumni ended up tabling a hostile and passionately defended motion by a vote of fifty-six to twelve.[12]

As so often on racial issues, Branscomb ended up conceding too much to critics. To those who applauded, he presented the Law School policy as a courageous first step, although quite enough for a while. To critics and celebrants alike he defended it as a defense against more complete integration. In long personal letters to important critics, such as Vance Alexander, he expressed himself on a whole range of issues. He believed in a middle way, one that allowed only a small black elite to attend white schools. He deplored the 1954 decision, one that opened all-white public schools to any and all blacks, because "a large percentage of negroes have certain well-known deficiencies . . . ." In light of the use of "armed force" at Clinton, an unexpected development after the board decision, he even admitted that Vanderbilt probably should have reversed its decision in favor of the two law students. Above all, he said he wanted to maintain a strong state rights position.[13]

As the two law students matriculated, and then the first graduate students, Branscomb kept insisting on how minimal their campus role would be. The

545

two law students were aksed not to eat in campus dining halls, even though they had the right. They were not allowed to play against undergraduate intramural teams. They were advised not to buy the tickets that allowed graduate and professional men to use the gym, but were eventually allowed to sit in the student sections in athletic contests. Fortunately, none of the early black students asked to live in a dorm, a problem that sent shudders through the whole Vanderbilt administration. By 1961 the plan was to have any unwanted black dorm applicants reside with the socially liberal divinity students. To one critic, Branscomb rejoiced that the "two boys" (Sarratt, with no intended slight, consistently referred to them as "colored boys") had kept to themselves, that they were rarely seen outside the Law School. In 1959 William Nicholls tried to apprise a black applicant of the "annoying, embarrassing, or very distasteful" experiences he would face as a Ph.D. candidate in economics. Since he could not live on campus, he would have to find housing in distant black residential areas, be refused service in white restaurants and at all major motels, and face all manner of subtle disapproval from white Nashvillians. The Law School integration accompanied a moderate plan for the integration of Nashville schools, one grade at a time beginning with the first grade in 1957. A citizens' group to facilitate peaceful integration included several faculty members, most notably Hugh Morgan of the Medical School and Walter Sharp of the fine arts department. A beleaguered Branscomb refused to serve as a sponsor of the group.[14]

Why did so many alumni oppose blacks at Vanderbilt? The opposing letters reveal an amazingly consistent position. Almost no one broached widely accepted moral or religious issues or seemed willing to argue at that level. Few rested their case on racial arguments. Conceivably, many opponents believed in some undefined way in black inferiority. In measurable areas, such as educational attainment and economic status, southern blacks were in fact inferior, as any observer would quickly note. But even if one believed the basis of such inferiority was genetic, and not just a matter of cultural differences or denied opportunity, no such issues had any logical relationship to the problem of equal rights or to open admission at Vanderbilt. If anything, Vanderbilt officials were extra scrupulous in applying normal standards of admission to blacks; such standards obviated any problem of poorly qualified students and any lowering of standards.

The critics seemed to accept these facts. Thus, almost all the letter writers appealed, not to principles, not to universally applicable moral standards, not even to problems of academic standards, but over and over again to the violation of Vanderbilt or of southern traditions. They spoke of betrayal, of capitulation, of treason. Vanderbilt was disowning the fathers, the great ones who came before, snubbing historical traditions, disowning ancestral racial conventions. The university was now about to force white students to violate deep family, clan, or sectional loyalties. Those who so argued included many lawyers and physicians, even the recipients of past Founder's Medals. Implicit

546

in such arguments was intense wrath against northerners, against aliens or outsiders who would try to impose a new pattern on Vanderbilt or the South, no matter how well such a pattern met some abstract sense of justice. The motif throughout was one of our country or our university, love it and defend and, above all, do not change it. In all such letters one grasped how much such alumni retained traditional loyalties, how insensitive they were to universal moral principles. The only alumni group that consistently supported integration and did so by appeals to abstract principles, or to supportive biblical commands, came from the School of Religion.[15]

Racial conflict first erupted in Nashville in September, 1957, when the city schools integrated the first grade. John Kasper, a notorious agitator from New Jersey, came to Nashville and helped provoke a near riot. Kasper was arrested, and a majority even of whites condemned such violent efforts to impede the enforcement of law. Donald Davidson, as chairman of the Tennessee Federation for Constitutional Government, a diehard segregationist organization, was called as a witness in Kasper's defense, but even Davidson would not condone his behavior. Kasper would seem to have no direct relationship to Vanderbilt, but as an ironic twist the basis of opposition to Kasper, a strong affirmation of law and order, would become the justification offered for the expulsion of James M. Lawson, Jr., in 1960. Kasper kept returning to Nashville and even once came on campus to speak in a dorm before a largely hostile audience. By then, Vanderbilt administrators loved to point to such speakers as a vindication of freedom of speech on campus, but they were more fearful of and less generous toward civil rights leaders who came on or even near the campus. The strongest outside pressures now came from segregationists, not from civil rights activists. In this context the Lawson case exploded like a bomb.

James Lawson, a native of Ohio, an ordained Methodist minister, a graduate of Baldwin-Wallace College, a student at Oberlin School of Theology, first applied to the Vanderbilt Divinity School in May, 1958, for the 1958–59 term. Because he was a black from beyond the Nashville area, Dean Robert Nelson approved his admission. Lawson, then thirty-one, had a dual purpose in coming to Nashville—to complete his B.D. at Vanderbilt and to continue his ministry, not in a local pulpit but as a regional director of the Fellowship of Reconciliation (FOR). He had already planned some form of service in the South for the FOR and was deeply committed to the cause of civil rights. He believed in the nonviolent strategies of Martin Luther King, Jr. He considered Atlanta as a possible base but chose Nashville largely because of its excellent Divinity School.[16]

Lawson had already taken a very strong stand in behalf of Christian pacifism and believed strongly in the pacific and reconciling purposes of FOR, then headed by the famous Presbyterian minister, A.J. Muste. As a college student he had asked to have his draft registration canceled because he had become a conscientious objector. His draft board refused and Lawson de-

547

clined to do anything further to cooperate with the system. When he refused induction into the army in 1950, he was tried, convicted, and sentenced to a three-year term in a federal prison. He served only eleven months, was transferred from one prison to another because his interracial work created hostility among whites, but by the testimony of prison officials was a cooperative and constructive prisoner. This record justified his early parole to work with a Methodist mission in India. There the teachings of Gandhi helped reinforce his pacifism and provided new insights into the virtues of passive resistance.[17]

Lawson was a new type of black student at Vanderbilt. Age, broad experience, self-confidence, and northern racial patterns ill prepared him for any deferential role. He did not accept the second-class status of earlier black students, refused to be an invisible man on campus. He joined in intramural competition, took his meals in the dining hall, and took an active role in student activities in his school. His part-time ministry largely involved black students. He joined other black ministers in a Christian Leadership Council, an affiliate of King's Southern Christian Leadership Conference. By the fall of 1959 the Christian Leadership Council decided to press for the integration of lunch counters in Nashville department stores. As early as November, 1959, black college students sat-in briefly at Harvey's and subsequently at Cain-Sloan's department stores. Their purpose was to demonstrate an injustice and to force negotiations with owners. They were unable to achieve their goals. These unpublicized sit-ins preceded the famous ones in Greensboro, North Carolina, and placed Nashville in the forefront of what turned out to be a milestone in the civil rights struggle. But, clearly, the Greensboro sit-ins early in February, 1960, the attendant publicity, and direct communications from North Carolina, encouraged Nashville students from Fisk, A&I, and the American Baptist Theological Seminary to begin a much larger effort.[18]

James Lawson was no more the instigator of such sit-ins than any number of other ministers or the students themselves. But he applauded their efforts and tried to do all he could to insure their success. Rather than joining the students in the stores, he gave them careful instruction on nonviolent methods. He knew the immense self-discipline required to adhere to such a policy. By February 27, the fourth of a series of sit-ins included up to 300 students, with some from Vanderbilt. This time the students met active resistance, as they had in several other cities. A group of young whites gathered at the Woolworth store in downtown Nashville, hurled insults at the sitting students, spat on them, and even put out burning cigarettes on their backs. The police, so often in attendance, were strangely absent when the violence began. When they came the whites scattered, but on orders of a local judge the police subsequently arrested eighty-one nonviolent students, charging them with disorderly conduct.[19]

This confrontation became the first controverted factual issue in the Lawson case. Subsequently, Branscomb always described it as a near riot; the demonstrators saw it only as an example of unprovoked assault. More critical were subsequent judgments about what impended for Nashville. City officials, like Branscomb on campus, believed or came to believe that a very ugly confrontation was likely in the near future. Rumors of armed whites from the outside, and blacks ready to fight back, became rife. The Nashville *Banner*, in lurid language, denounced the nonviolent students, and even the *Tennessean*, more balanced in its reporting, begged a suspension of the sit-ins and the use of legal efforts to attain worthy goals. In the publicity the newspapers first identified Lawson as a leading organizer of the sit-ins, an at least half-true description. The potential for violence much concerned Mayor Ben West, the old Vanderbilt radical of the 1930s, who returned from a trip to meet with various civic groups in order to mediate some solution. On the evening of February 29 he appealed to about 200 black ministers at the First Baptist Church. West conceded the legal right of students to sit-in as long as lunch counters remained open. But he stressed that they violated a state law when they remained after owners announced the closing of the counters. He wanted assurances that the students would obey this law, allowing him time for negotiations even as he promised impartial enforcement by his police.[20]

Lawson clearly took a very active role in these discussions. He did not follow those of his colleagues who wanted to fall back into an old pattern of deference to authority, and ended with some much publicized statements. No one could ever agree on his exact words. But reporters from both newspapers made clear that following policy position, one that Lawson never denied— that, since the arbitrary closing of lunch counters at any time by owners was a deliberate effort to crush the student movement, the law referred to by West was a gimmick to deprive blacks of their rights. Thus, Lawson recommended that students continue their sit-ins. Apparently it was Mayor West, not Lawson, who interpreted this as a minister's advising young people to "violate the law." West referred to John Kasper's earlier flaunting of the law and suggested he would apply the same principles to this case. The *Banner* followed with a vitriolic attack on Lawson, one that again drew the parallel with Kasper. Publisher Stahlman concluded that there was "no place in Nashville for flannel-mouth agitators, white or colored—under whatever sponsorship, imported for preachments of mass disorder; self-supported, vagrants, or the paid agents of strife-breeding organizations."[21]

Because of Lawson's alleged statements before Mayor West, his unwillingness to retract them, and thus his unwillingness to abide by the existing laws in Nashville, Branscomb eventually expelled him from the university. Lawson, at first, could scarcely comprehend the reasons. He had done nothing wrong. His perception of events matched that of most Divinity School faculty members and students; the perception gained support from the dominant voices in the national press. The sit-ins, in the same sense as the Montgomery bus boycott, provided a perfect case for demonstrating injustice to blacks. Just as blacks paid equal fares on buses but then had to take stigmatized back seats or even yield seats to whites, so patrons of department or variety stores paid equal prices for goods, helped assure profits for owners, but could not sit down at a lunch counter to order refreshments. Such discriminatory treatment failed to meet conventional standards of justice and won sit-in demonstrators support among many southern whites. The sit-ins also helped demonstrate that blacks were victims. And, given recent Supreme Court interpretations of the equal protection clause of the Fourteenth Amendment, Lawson could argue that the store owners were, in all likelihood, in violation of the federal Constitution. The students thus had a constitutional right to service, whatever state laws said about the issue. Subsequent federal court decisions justified this interpretation of the law.

Given these perspectives, Lawson's position as against Mayor West made perfect sense. As he viewed it, those sitting in the stores were victims, the wronged party. The store owners were guilty of injustice and at least of bending the law to their purposes. Why should public authorities ask the victims to make further sacrifices? Why not make the store owners, the exploiters, change their policies? Short of this, Lawson advocated continued sit-ins. He made clear all along that his central goal was not simply gaining access to lunch counters, or even testing the constitutionality of local laws, but rather changing the self-image of blacks. They had to stand up for themselves, gain self-respect, demand equal treatment, or else flounder in a sense of helplessness, or what follows whenever victims apathetically submit to injustice. Since such a stand for justice, and a justice in all probability now supported by federal laws, seemed beyond reproach, then he wondered why Vanderbilt authorities treated him as guilty of a crime? They were capitulating to the old pattern, joining city authorities in placing blame on the victims of injustice. Lawson kept emphasizing that his main role had been to assure that the protest by the victims had been nonviolent.[22]

It is much more difficult to communicate the sharply different perspective of Branscomb. In the battle of rationalizations, he lost in almost all courts of opinion except most southern ones. He had difficulty articulating his position and almost always hurt it by loaded or oversimplified statements about events or ad hominem references to his opponents. Branscomb had an enormous commitment to an ordered community. It is not fair to say he valued order above justice, but rather that he saw order as the prerequisite of any secure justice. In a tense city Mayor West had taken on the difficult role of an executive—to seek compromises, to calm tempers, to minimize the damage to the larger community. Lawson had refused to lend his efforts to that cause and in effect even undermined it. In such a situation larger issues of abstract right, even of constitutional guarantees, may rightly condition long-term goals but must not dictate short-term strategies. As an executive, West worked out the terms for restored order. Maybe he should have asked more of the merchants, less of the demonstrators. But such debatable issues were beside the point. He chose policies and with good will sought the cooperation of different groups. Lawson thus risked peace in order to adhere to abstract principles. Given the traditional basis of social stability in Nashville, given the laws still on the books and not yet successfully challenged in the courts, given the traditional alignments of political power, then it was clearly the students who disrupted the existing order, not the merchants. Had the students acted only in order to initiate a legal test, Branscomb would have had no qualms about their tactics. He had earlier endorsed Vanderbilt's violation of Tennessee segregation laws in order to get a test case. And as his critics pointed out, in other contexts he had made the obvious point for any Christian—man has a higher obligation than that to any state and in certain situations must follow conscience or a higher law. He simply believed this was not such a situation, that legal processes already under way would correct much of the injustice. The system offered means of redress and thus did not require the extreme weapon of civil disobedience.[23]

In the whole Lawson affair, Branscomb unfailingly exemplified the perspective of a realistic executive officer. He calculated policies in behalf of institutional survival, not on the basis of personal preferences. He hoped, as do most administrators, that more often than not moral rectitude and institutional welfare would eventually converge. He knew the dilemmas and pressures that could confront decision makers and at times was impatient with students or faculty members who seemed incapable of appreciating the constraints that he faced. He valued those who tried to understand, who would cooperate, who were helpful in times of crisis. He became almost obsessively hostile toward those he called agitators or troublemakers, those who quibbled or blocked what he perceived as sensible, moderate policies. He easily translated loyalty to Vanderbilt into loyalty to its appointed officers and to the policies they adopted. This joined a sentiment reflected by most of his board—a bias in favor of the existing order, support only for gradual changes within it, and a deepening fear of outside agitators. Only those within a system, those who knew how it operated, and those who had gained a stake in it by years of loyal service had a right to criticize or to rule. Throughout the Lawson episode, Branscomb stressed what to his Divinity School professors could only seem a series of ad hominem arguments—that Lawson was from the North, that he was a paid reformer or agitator, that he never tried to understand the way the system worked in Nashville or the South. Later, Branscomb, the earlier advocate of a great national university, kept pointing out how many of the Divinity School faculty came from the North or how many had been at Vanderbilt for fewer than five years, as if such details not only explained but undermined their moral stand.[24]

In the aftermath of the controversy Branscomb felt betrayed. Events had overtaken his own careful timetable of racial change. His goal remained the gradual, peaceful, limited integration of Vanderbilt. By a very complex political strategy he wanted to move a reluctant board and the always suspicious alumni toward this goal. He feared above all else any incidents that might trigger concerted resistance. Once Lawson's activities were public knowledge, they posed a grave threat to that larger goal. From Branscomb's perspective, an unchallenged Lawson threatened to arm southern supporters of segregation, on the board and off, with needed ammunition, postpone more liberal admission policies, further damage Vanderbilt's relationship to foundations, and thus direly threaten its continued progress. Viewed politically, Lawson's campus defenders, by raising the episode to one of high principle, endangered not only Vanderbilt but moral goals much more critical than Lawson's personal fate, moral goals that remain empty abstractions or a private indulgence when they do not encompass political realities. Branscomb thus could argue that expelling Lawson was a rational, even necessary, tactic in his own effort to move the board toward a policy of open admissions. His enemies, if sincerely concerned about a more righteous society, should have understood these realities and thus have accepted, however reluctantly, Branscomb's tactical moves.

On March 1, with the newspaper publicity about Lawson's defiance of Mayor West, Branscomb decided he had to act. Yet, he was never able to explain why he needed to do anything at all, at least on his own initiative. Perhaps (as Stahlman's inflammatory editorials suggested) Branscomb knew he might not long have the option of inaction. The Executive Committee or the Board of Trust might well take the initiative. Branscomb's first step was to call in Dean Nelson of the Divinity School. During the whole episode Branscomb avoided direct contact with Lawson and offered a persuasive reason for this—he feared that Lawson might publicize and distort his personal comments, an ever-present problem for chancellors. He asked Nelson to talk with Lawson, to see if he had been misquoted or if he had misspoken in the tense atmosphere of the meeting. Robert McGaw accompanied Nelson to evauate Lawson's response. If Lawson had denied the position attributed to him, or if, on reflection, he had repudiated his stand and agreed to instruct students to stay within the law as Mayor West defined it, then there would have been no Lawson affair. Lawson, who professed shock at the request from the chancellor, could not give the reply Branscomb wanted. He did not accept the exact positions attributed to him by the newspapers, but it was clear that he would not ask his trained students to end a sit-in any time an owner announced the closing of a counter. To do so would have been to disown his own teachings and moral commitments. Nelson and McGaw reported his response back to Branscomb on Tuesday afternoon.[25]

Branscomb then tried a second strategy. He sent Nelson back in the evening to make Lawson aware of a new regulation in the student handbook that forbade students to participate in disorderly assemblies, or assemblies likely to lead to disorder, a regulation created as a tool to control panty raids. Since heretofore no one had applied this rule to other than undergraduates, neither Lawson nor any other professional or graduate student had read it or even had any reason to be aware of it. Whether it even applied to Lawson became a much-debated point on campus. Since no other professional students had to agree, beforehand, to abide by the rule, applying it to Lawson did constitute discriminatory treatment. Insofar as Branscomb's subsequent dismissal of Lawson related to Lawson's refusal, Lawson suffered not from overt violation of university regulations (he had never personally participated in sit-ins) but from refusing to pledge himself beforehand to obey them, or the first such disciplinary procedure used at Vanderbilt since the era of Garland. Yet, by this time, Branscomb had pushed too far to retreat, given his personality. He so far had not consulted with the faculty. He had initiated none of the procedures that would normally precede the suspension of a graduate student, such as consulting the relevant dean or faculty, and also none of the time-consuming maneuvers that might have delayed actual dismissal until the issue became moot with Lawson's contemplated graduation in May.[26]

Unfortunately, a regular meeting of the Executive Committee of the board occurred just over a day later, on March 3. Branscomb subsequently acknowledged that he made a mistake in deciding to bring the Lawson matter before the committee. But it is doubtful the committee would have passed it over in silence. Branscomb asked Dean Nelson to attend a part of this critical meeting, to make prepared statements, and to provide information. By this time Nelson had become the third key member of the cast in a developing drama. He proved very inept, although in the early negotiations he was also bothered by a cold and suffered from a lack of sleep. He began as a messenger boy for Branscomb. Nelson thought he could work out some agreement to keep Lawson as a student. He failed. More important, he proved to be weak and vacillating. He did not take a clear, consistent position at first, did not stand up to Branscomb, and did not turn to his faculty for advice. Nelson had an almost son-father relationship to Branscomb. He had deferred to Branscomb, constantly sought his approval, and now wanted to maintain a close personal relationship. He also very much wanted to remain dean. Briefly, as an innocent, he tried to play politics in the big leagues and perhaps rejoiced in his opportunity to influence events at the top.[27]

Nelson did not help Lawson by his performance before the Executive Committee. He began with a pre-Easter reference to his coming before Pilate's court, suggesting, quite plausibly but very undiplomatically, that neither he nor Lawson would get a fair hearing. Nelson asked for additional time to consider the case and to consult his faculty. But he lost credibility when he was not forthcoming about all the facts of Lawson's admission and left the board members with a mistaken understanding of Lawson's prison record (they assumed he had been a prisoner of war). Lawson, before the Executive Committee meeting, finally had time to write a statement to clarify his position, a statement that Nelson read to the committee. It was conciliatory, flattering to the university, and full of regret that such a confrontation

553

ever developed. Lawson denied claims that he was the key leader in the sit-ins, or that he condoned lawlessness in the sense that Kasper did. He said, "defiant violation of the law is a contradiction to my entire understanding of and loyalty to Christian non-violence." He condoned civil disobedience only when a law or law enforcement agency had, in reality, "ceased to be the law," and then he chose it only in "fear and trembling before God." He ended with a reiteration that he believed God had called him to his work. After these presentations, and discussion, the Executive Committee rendered its unanimous verdict. Note that in no sense was it an impartial jury, given Stahlman's earlier and intemperate attacks on Lawson and the fact that John Sloan, as owner of a department store, had been a resentful target of the sit-ins. The committee offered Lawson two choices—withdrawal by 9:00 A.M. the next day or expulsion. Lawson chose expulsion.[28]

The Vanderbilt faculty had to gain most early information about the Lawson matter from the newspapers. Nelson had given his Divinity School faculty only a five-minute briefing on Tuesday, or barely enough to prepare them for the unwanted expulsion. Just before he appeared before the Executive Committee, nine of his faculty handed him a note expressing support for him in his difficult position. Some already suggested that they might have to resign if Lawson was expelled. Then, just after the Executive Committee meeting, the chancellor met with the Divinity School faculty, gave his version of events, and announced the pending expulsion. This was the worst possible news for the Divinity faculty and began a four-month trial of conscience for each one of them. The faculty expressed sharp disagreement with Branscomb, noted the inevitable condemnation from the rest of the world, and again talked vaguely of resignations. Eleven faculty members released to the press a statement denying any adequate justification for the dismissal. They knew that Lawson had not been more involved in the sit-ins than any number of other Vanderbilt students. Branscomb seemed to single him out only because the newspapers chose to air his views and not the similar views of other demonstrators. For Branscomb, the publicity was the critical issue. In his press release he argued that Vanderbilt could not "be identified with a continuing campaign of mass disobedience of law as a means of protest" and noted the newspaper identification of Lawson as a Vanderbilt student. Thus, Branscomb wanted Lawson to withdraw from the university for as long as he worked with the sit-ins, and by doing this spare the university from public embarrassment. It is important to note that a compelling concern of Branscomb, Purdy, and McGaw all along was public relations. At times, this concern seemed to control policy.[29]

The sit-ins went on to a successful climax. On March 4 Lawson was arrested at the First Baptist Church, charged along with seventy-five students with violating the state trade and commerce law, the law that justified owners in closing their counters. A faculty committee from the Divinity School personally bailed him out of jail and soon launched a defense fund in his behalf. The mayor's biracial committee continued negotiations, several clergymen backed Lawson and the sit-ins, and the *Tennessean* aired a surprising number of letters supporting them. On March 17 black students gained service in the restaurant at the Greyhound bus terminal. But after only such token concessions the students resumed sit-ins in late March. Finally, on May 10, seven stores opened their counters to all races. The city then dropped all charges against Lawson and the students and, at the city level, the sit-in demonstrators seemed to have won their first major goal. Note that restaurants all remained segregated. The larger struggle had only begun.[30]

The war had also only begun at Vanderbilt. Although the student senate unanimously upheld Branscomb's action, many students protested Lawson's expulsion. Divinity School students briefly picketed Kirkland Hall. A clear majority of faculty members in both the Divinity School and the College believed the expulsion unjustified. On March 10, 111 faculty members published a statement condemning the injustices that provoked the sit-ins, or an oblique challenge to Branscomb. But by March 30 a counterpetition backing the chancellor gained 97 names, with majority support in the Medical School, in Engineering, and in the English department. John Aden, of English, published his personal dissent from the 111. In a March 8 statement to the Arts and Science faculty, Branscomb reiterated the reasons that he had earlier offered to the Divinity School faculty. Unfortunately, the context did not allow debate. To make matters worse, the Divinity School faculty began to fall apart under all the strain. Nelson's early role in the case had left his faculty ignorant and suspicious, and now many blamed Nelson for not taking an earlier and stronger stand. The Divinity faculty even used a special retreat to try to regain an earlier level of mutual respect.[31]

Because of the depth and breadth of faculty concern, Branscomb turned to the newly formed University Senate. He appointed an ad hoc Senate committee to recommend procedures for all future suspensions. Chaired by Dean Beach, the committee had a report ready for the Board of Trust on June 3. It proved a thoughtful, even an eloquent document. The committee affirmed freedom of thought without restriction, freedom of speech and action in behalf of what one believed true, freedom of peaceful assembly to redress grievances, and a right for a hearing to decide complaints against any member of the university community. Citizens of the university could exercise all the rights of citizens in the larger community but should also give "thoughtful consideration to the image of the University reflected in his position before the public." When members of the university community violated laws out of conscience or to test their validity, the university would not protect them from the processes of law. But, regardless of court decisions, the university remained free to determine a person's suitability for continued membership in the academic community. For disciplinary cases, such as Lawson's, involving matters of conscience or academic freedom, the dean of the college or school was to act with the advice of a new Senate committee. If accused of misconduct, one had the right of hearing before the committee. The dean and the committee were to recommend appropriate punishment to the chancellor. Anyone accused and convicted had a right to appeal that decision to a special new committee on appeals, appointed by the chancellor and representing the whole university. If this committee granted a second hearing, then both sides could make presentations. This appeals committee made the final recommendation to the chancellor. Had such a procedure been in effect for Lawson, he would likely have retained his student status and, in any case, the procedure might have prolonged the case until his graduation.[32]

The dedication ceremonies for the new Divinity School complex came in the midst of the Lawson controversy. The ceremonies proved embarrassing to Branscomb and to administrative officials. Instead of the normal Cole lecture, the school invited a series of able speakers in the spring of 1960, a series that climaxed with the actual dedication on March 21. Three visiting speakers commented on the Lawson case or criticized his expulsion; at least two talked with Lawson. In his dedicatory address, Liston Pope, dean of Yale Divinity, was most outspoken. He said: "I could not be faithful to my own views on the race question if I did not say that my presence here today is by no means to be construed as an endorsement of the recent action of the University." He believed the action of the students and faculty on behalf of Lawson had preserved the reputation of the school. After such a strong, and to many such an embarrassing platform statement, he praised Branscomb, a former teacher, for first opening the school to blacks. This episode created a lasting bitterness on the part of Purdy and Branscomb. At the same dedication, 150 Divinity School alumni urged the readmission of Lawson. More critical, by then the Sealantic Fund asked for assurances of continued open admissions in the school as a condition for releasing promised new endowments. Slowly, pressure built for some reconsideration of the dismissal. And, as events indicated, Branscomb was not entirely opposed to some compromise.[33]

For two months the Lawson issue preoccupied the Divinity School faculty. On March 4 it voted to make an appeal to the University Senate, an appeal that focused upon how Branscomb had by-passed the faculty in making a decision affecting one of their students, a procedural point that would soon worry the national AAUP. On March 8 the same faculty asked Branscomb and the board to reconsider the expulsion. On March 11 it issued a long statement justifying its petition for reconsideration, again with the emphasis upon a series of procedural lapses (no inquiry, no hearing, no witnesses, no right of appeal, a misapplication of a student rule, judgment on intent rather than actual behavior). In accordance with these petitions, Dean Nelson asked Harold Vanderbilt to allow him to speak before the upcoming board meeting in June. On March 17 the aging president of the board granted the request, but in a very discouraging letter, one in which he noted no board dissent at all from the Executive Committee action. His letter, in every sense, said "come on but expect nothing."

Benton Chapel

Meanwhile, a committee made up of James Sellers and Lou Silberman, and representing an informal junta within the Divinity School, carried out extended negotiations in late March with Purdy and, on one occasion, Branscomb. Purdy prepared, and in one session Branscomb seemed to approve, a plan to let Lawson finish his work in absentia (he eventually moved to Boston University, one of countless seminaries that welcomed him), or by transferred credit receive a B.D. from Vanderbilt. The various informal and often secret conferences climaxed on May 4 when Branscomb met with the whole Divinity School faculty. In these private conferences the faculty and Branscomb had often seemed close to some possible compromise.[34]

On May 4 at the meeting with Divinity faculty, Branscomb joined Harold Vanderbilt in pointing out the discouraging prospects before the Board of Trust. Only one trustee, Hugh Morgan, was likely to take the Divinity faculty side. In this last friendly meeting, Branscomb even talked of resigning, of making himself a scapegoat for the Divinity School. After all the discouraging reports about board opinion, the faculty came to see the board as the critical obstacle to any settlement and to believe that a more conciliatory Branscomb was under intense pressure from his trustees. In the complicated negotia-

The new Dyer Observatory

tions, the faculty tried to find, and drive deeper, a wedge between Branscomb and the board, while Branscomb and Purdy tried to find allies on the Divinity School faculty and exploit factional divisions within it. After several discussions on May 19, the faculty decided to withdraw their request for a hearing before the board. This proved a disastrous decision for the Divinity School. Branscomb, ever the astute politician, subsequently painted this as a refusal of the faculty to bargain in good faith and thus placed on them the odium for the failure of any compromise.[35]

The Divinity School had no effective head, which hurt. Nelson kept on trying to control, or at least influence, events. By May he seemed more pathetic than helpful. Branscomb had long since given up on Nelson and under no circumstances planned to keep him on as dean. Nelson could not accept this, continued to write conciliatory letters to Branscomb, and seemed to believe, somehow, that the Lawson episode was a temporary aberration, that men of good will could somehow find a solution and that he could retain his cherished position. His faculty increasingly told him otherwise, frequently caucused without him, and even formally decided to support him as a continuing colleague but not as dean.[36]

By May 18, when they withdrew their request for a hearing before the board, the Divinity professors had developed a new strategy. Lawson was on the verge of leaving Nashville to complete his degree at Boston University. Thus, they decided to ask for his readmission into the school for the summer so that he could then complete his degree. In a University Senate meeting in March, Branscomb had referred to the possibility of Lawson's readmission through normal channels by way of reaffirming his support for the new rules being worked out by the Beach committee. Thus, Nelson compiled a new dossier on Lawson, the school's admission committee voted to admit him for the summer term, and on May 26 Nelson submitted this to Branscomb as a formal request. But, because of Lawson's imminent need to respond to an offer from Boston University, Nelson asked Branscomb for an answer within two days, a request Branscomb interpreted angrily as an ultimatum coming in the midst of a busy commencement week. Once again the dean mishandled ticklish negotiations. The dossier contained a fourteen-page philosophical statement from Lawson on his views about nonviolence and civil disobedience. It also contained additional letters of recommendation and noted his recent resignation from FOR in behalf of pastoral work and writing. And, since the board had become intensely concerned about his prison record, Lawson included detailed notes from a prison diary (in letters to the Department of Justice, Branscomb had secured an official record of his imprisonment, a record that sustained Lawson's own statements). Since the admissions committee had followed correct procedures, Branscomb called its members to his office on May 30. He rehearsed his grievances over some of Nelson's actions, interpreted this new ploy as a publicity effort, and refused readmission.[37]

By this time several other professors from the College and the Medical School had joined with the Divinity School faculty. This meant a larger and more representative coalition of professors, all committed to some compromise plan that would allow Lawson to complete his B.D. and redeem Vanderbilt's national reputation. This informal coalition had placed great hope on the readmission effort. It seemed to them the last basis of a just settlement. Several faculty members had talked of resigning if it failed. Already, on May 30, Dean Nelson announced his resignation, effective as of August 31 of that year. This gained him added respect from his faculty. Then, on the fateful evening of May 30, nine assembled Divinity professors decided to submit their resignations, effective at the end of the next year (August, 1961) as required by AAUP procedures. The nine professors also stressed their commitment to next year's seniors, their solicitude for the continuation of the Divinity School, and their need for time to find new jobs. Their letter of resignation, as submitted to the chancellor, marked a new phase of the Lawson affair, one much more serious and tense and more threatening to the university than the one that began on February 27.[38]

The faculty resignations led to bitterness and confusion. Even the number of professors involved, as well as their motives, invited conflicting judgments. The original list included well over two-thirds of the staff. Notably, the nonresignations involved two oldtimers—George M. Mayhew, now close to retirement and not eligible for jobs elsewhere, and James Philip Hyatt, the very distinguished professor of Old Testament, quite eligible for jobs elsewhere but philosophically opposed to the gesture. Hyatt believed the welfare

559

of the school, its future role in the South, outweighed the injustice to Lawson, and thus he wanted to let the Lawson issue die so as to move on to a constructive rebuilding of the school. Hyatt was the only professor to argue this position, but one other full professor, William H. Kirkland, and one associate professor, Paul S. Sanders, refused to resign. Those who submitted resignations on May 30 included Langdon B. Gilkey, an eminent professor of theology and director of graduate studies; Lou Silberman, professor of Jewish studies in the College and a graduate teacher in Divinity; Ronald E. Sleeth, professor of preaching; James D. Glasse, associate professor of practical theology; Gordon D. Kaufman, associate professor of theology; Bard Thompson, associate professor of church history; Arthur Foster, assistant professor of pastoral theology; Leander E. Keck, assistant professor of New Testament; and James Sellers, assistant dean and assistant professor of theology. Bard Thompson already had another job offer and now chose to accept it. Thus his resignation had only symbolic significance. Everett Tilson, who was still on the staff in the spring of 1960, had already resigned for another position in the fall of 1960 and could not take even such a symbolic gesture. He wanted to. Of all the professors he most strongly supported Lawson and most sharply and brutally criticized Branscomb. He believed Branscomb to be a hypocrite and a segregationist, in part because Branscomb had allegedly penalized him for earlier social advocacy. In a series of published letters and articles he unmasked all the elements of hypocrisy in Vanderbilt's treatment of blacks and read the worst possible motives into all Branscomb's behavior.[39]

The appearance of only nine names considerably underplayed the seriousness of the situation in Divinity. William Kendrick Grobel, another of the giants in the school, was in Europe and as soon as possible wired his resignation. From the Chicago Theological Seminary, Walter Harrelson, who was to join the department in the fall, submitted his resignation. Finally, two staff members with joint appointments—Herman Norton, with the Disciples Foundation, and Frank Grisham, with the Divinity School Library in JUL, announced their solidarity and firm intentions to resign later if necessary. By counting Dean Nelson, twelve professors or prospective professors actually resigned, two more were ready to resign, and only four refused. Under these circumstances the Divinity School could not continue either as a quality or even an academically accredited school. The resignations made news all over the country, all the academically respectable seminaries voted some type of solidarity, and several promised to hire those without work. Under these circumstances no professors of national stature would have accepted employment at Vanderbilt and no foundation would have offered any support. Yet, one of the distressing sidelights to the controversy was the large number of opportunistic people who applied for the vacant positions in the school.[40]

Branscomb now faced very high stakes indeed. He either had to relent on the Lawson issue or give up on the Divinity School, now at the height of its strength and just moving into its great new quadrangle. Dean Nelson had believed at the time of the dedication, and with some justification, that his school now ranked in the top five nationally. It also had become the brightest southern bastion of liberal Christianity and in 1960 was comparatively the strongest school in the whole university. Branscomb knew all this and he loved the school. But a majority of the board wanted to accept the resignations. Stahlman thought it all good riddance and applauded the resignations in the pages of his *Banner*. He, and other Board members, had never liked the prophetic role of the Divinity School. Its professors were always raising bothersome moral issues or subverting the conventional beliefs and values of southern youth. And here is a huge irony. When Branscomb first came to Vanderbilt he warned the board of what a distinguished faculty meant in the way of independent judgment and advanced moral and social advocacy. Now he was the target of such professors, accused of capitulating to a narrow, immoral sectional outlook and thus of jeopardizing the school's national standing. The Divinity School faculty had long tried to serve as the conscience of the university, much more so than the cautious and more conventional professors in the College. And now look at what it all cost![41]

Branscomb was in a very difficult position. For the first time he had to contemplate the possibility, even the likelihood, of his own resignation. His pride was involved, not his ambition. He was close to retirement age and might have welcomed a way out of the impasse. But he had to consider the university. He could resign, responsibly, only if he used this extreme weapon in such a way as to extricate the university from its troubles. No such way seemed open. His immediate response to the resignations was not to act on them, to refer them to the board. The national wire services now almost daily covered the events at Vanderbilt, meaning an airing all over the country of each new development or rumor in newspapers. The publicity triggered a deluge of mail (eventually over five cubic feet of letters, over half opposing Lawson's dismissal), led to several reports in *Newsweek* and *Time* (in a June 20 article *Time* located Vanderbilt in Alabama), brought cries of alarm from liberal church groups even in the South, and added new installments to a continuing series of articles in the *Christian Century*. From this point on, reporters hovered around every meeting and somehow gained access to many confidential documents. Vanderbilt professors often learned about new initiatives from the *Tennessean* or even from the New York *Times*. The most biting editorial, in the Washington *Post*, noted that this was the inevitable outcome "of allowing Christian Doctrine to be taught in such places" as Vanderbilt or Nashville. It emphasized the lack of any guilt on the part of Lawson, the subsequent settlement of the lunch counter issue, and stressed that Lawson had followed the precepts taught by his own teachers. But, "if excuses like these were allowed to prevail, the whole country might be affected by ethics."[42]

In this tense atmosphere several groups tried to find a face-saving compromise. Branscomb seemed open to one. The first successful effort in that direction began on June 1. Harrelson, accompanied by the president of Chicago Theological Seminary, flew to Nashville, ostensibly to close the deal on a house he might now never live in. Branscomb met him at the airport. While Harrelson closeted himself with Branscomb, his president offered all the resigned faculty a position at his school. In their meeting Branscomb confirmed earlier talks and asked Harrelson, as an outsider, to take over either as acting or full dean. Harrelson, of course, was open to this only if Branscomb made concessions on the Lawson issue, and only after consulting Dean Nelson, as well as the Divinity School faculty. The faculty discussions with Harrelson went on way into the night of June 2. On June 3 the Executive Committee of the university met, accepted Nelson's resignation, and officially offered the position of either dean or acting dean to Harrelson, who still hoped for a compromise of some sort. From discussions with the faculty, Harrelson clarified two key demands—the readmission of Lawson and the retention of a professorship for Nelson. This became his bargaining position with Branscomb, who acceded to Nelson's professorship but not Lawson's readmission. But Branscomb did offer a compromise—he would grant Lawson a Vanderbilt B.D. in absentia on the basis of transferred credits from Boston University.

His terms unmet, Harrelson flew back to Chicago on June 4 and then on to the American Baptist Convention. He returned to Nashville on June 6. Branscomb, anxious to get a settlement, then requested a meeting with the Divinity School faculty and Harrelson in his office on June 7. In a politically inept move, the faculty declined on the basis that Branscomb had made no new offer. Thus Harrelson had to shuttle back and forth to keep any negotiations going, with the Divinity School faculty meeting in continuous session. A bit later the faculty also rejected an invitation for a conference with Harold Vanderbilt, who was on campus for the Executive Committee meeting. Since Harrelson could not get Branscomb to readmit Lawson, he finally gave up his arbitrating role on June 7, resubmitted his own resignation, and returned to Chicago. Branscomb then asked for a meeting of the whole, anxious university faculty, to announce the failure of the negotiations and to lambast the Divinity School faculty for its refusal to meet and to talk.[43]

The chancellor scored a political point but could take small consolation in such a small victory. As never before in its history the university was in peril. Without some settlement that would retain the Divinity School faculty, several professors in the College and in other schools were likely to resign. Four in the Medical School had already made firm commitments to do just this. But that would only be the surface of the danger. Distraught faculty members who did not resign would be filled with guilt and resentment; the most able might seek jobs elsewhere, beginning the erosion of quality that would quickly cancel all the gains achieved in the Branscomb years. The ones who remained would include the mediocre who could not move, and those professors (up to half, including some very distinguished men) who agreed with Branscomb's handling of the Lawson affair. The remaining and talented faculty would all be on the conservative side politically or share a distinctively prosouthern bias, constituting a narrowly sectional and provincial faculty. In order to remain nationally prominent, Vanderbilt simply had to find a compromise on the Lawson issue, not one that would please everyone but one that would allow most Divinity School professors to withdraw their resignations, one that would save face for Branscomb, and one that could gain at least begrudging acceptance by a board that was not about to acquiesce to what it saw as faculty blackmail. The achievement of such a compromise filled the most critical week in Vanderbilt's history.

The needed compromise emerged from two days of intense negotiations. Much more than ever before, faculty members from throughout the university became involved. On June 8 the local chapter of the AAUP met for a critical session, one open to all faculty members and ostensibly called to consider the new Beach committee report. By then, the national AAUP office had become intensely interested in the resignations and in the status of academic freedom at Vanderbilt. It had asked for continued reports on new developments. Inevitably, the AAUP meeting moved quickly to the Lawson impasse. Both Silberman and Gilkey, in the first faculty forum open for a full and free discussion of the Lawson case, clarified the views of the resigning faculty and noted their frequent efforts to find a solution. For many professors, this was their first opportunity to get behind the official actions and glimpse some of the dynamics of the conflict or even hear the Divinity School side of the controversy. What emerged from the meeting was an acute faculty awareness of its own impotence. A great, dramatic crisis developed and matured, with the faculty, outside Divinity, playing almost no role at all. So far, the chancellor had run the university, and the faculty, generally satisfied with his policies, had accepted a centralized system.

Avery Leiserson of political science pointed out that professors could now side with Branscomb or the Divinity School but had no other role. The chancellor had even so orchestrated their access to information that they heretofore had heard only one side. He urged the faculty not to resign but instead, perhaps through the AAUP, to press for a larger role in policy making. He offered a resolution, which passed 70 to 0, noting the failure of Branscomb to consult the faculty at any time from March 4 to June 7 and his refusal to negotiate the issue of Lawson's readmission until pressed to do so by the resignation of faculty members. Clearly, Vanderbilt lacked machinery for ascertaining the opinion of faculty leaders other than those the chancellor chose to consult. The assembled faculty voted that it was "our considered opinion" that the present tragic situation could have been avoided if a representative body, chosen solely by the faculty, had existed and consulted with the chancellor. This first expressed the faculty pressures that led, later, to a stronger Faculty Senate. The group debated, and then divided, over a proposal to send a letter to Harold Vanderbilt. The actual members of the AAUP, in a follow-up and closed business meeting, decided to explore within the next week a request that the national AAUP offer its help in resolving the controversy. Implicit in much of this discussion was a sense of gloom, a feeling expressed by physicist Ingram Bloch that the crisis had already all but destroyed Vanderbilt, that it could not be saved so long as the chancellor ran it the way he was now doing.[44]

Fortunately, even as the faculty debated, smaller groups moved toward the critical compromise. On June 7, just after Branscomb's second report to the university faculty, five Divinity School faculty met with four supportive Medical School professors—Victor A. Najjar, head of microbiology, two of his colleagues, and David E. Rogers, head of the largest department, medicine. The four had submitted their resignations to Dean Patterson, who held them awaiting developments and who frequently also joined in efforts to find a compromise solution. The four Medical School professors played both a crucial and a courageous role. Rogers and Najjar had the eminence needed to protect them against the hostility of colleagues. The majority of Medical School professors rallied behind Branscomb or even applauded his role in the Lawson case. On June 12, sixty Medical School professors telegraphed Harold Vanderbilt, deploring the threat of resignation on the part of their four colleagues and expressing their contrary view that "the Board of Trust has handled the Lawson case fairly and correctly." A nonsigner of this telegram, Amos Christie, assured the chancellor of his wholehearted support by telegram. This response isolated the four Medical School activists and to some extent lessened their influence. But even board members flinched from their publicized threats of resignation and at least glimpsed the type of internal conflict that could grow out of the bitter soil of the Lawson case. The four Medical professors, working through Dean Patterson, finally got the five Divinity professors together with Harold Vanderbilt, who left the Executive Committee meeting for this purpose. He gained his earliest, direct understanding of the Divinity School point of view and, even as he defended the chancellor's decision, seemed open to some compromise.[45]

Another helpful intermediary was Charles E. Roos, professor of physics. He met with the other Divinity School faculty on the same afternoon (June 8). He conveyed his impression that Branscomb wanted very much to seek a settlement. That evening all the Divinity School faculty still on campus met with Roos and finally began to hedge on their heretofore absolute stand in behalf of Lawson's full readmission. Exact wordings became all important. The faculty eventually decided that the former injustice might be rectified through some provision by which Lawson could complete his semester's work, either by oral conferences or by examinations. This meant, to them, that he in effect be reinstated and not readmitted. Yet, the terms could be such as not to require him to take courses on campus. For the first time the

Divinity School faculty moved toward the type of deliberate ambiguity that alone made possible the resolution of principled conflict. The faculty knew this and suffered the guilt normal to moralists who have to enter the political arena. Branscomb clearly preferred the transfer of credits. But before noon, on June 9, he conceded the point during talks with Silberman. The Divinity faculty gathered and agreed to the very wording they had worked out the night before. The final details all concerned Dean Nelson. Branscomb was, of course, unwilling to retain him as dean, and on this the faculty members concurred. But, now impressed by his moral integrity during the final weeks of conflict, they never loved him quite as much and still hoped that he could remain as a professor. Silberman worked out an informal agreement with Nelson and by telephone secured Branscomb's assent to it. It provided only for Nelson's return to his professorship until August, 1960. After Branscomb had convened the most critical Executive Committee meeting in university history, at 4:00 P.M. on June 9 in Rand Hall, Nelson codified the agreement concerning himself in a letter that Roos took to the Executive Committee and read before leaving.[46]

The Executive Committee rejected the agreed-upon compromise and thus sabotaged all hopes for a settlement. The Divinity School faculty had, all along, feared just this. They knew the position of Stahlman and always doubted that Branscomb could budge him from it. But the process that led to the compromise had allayed their doubts. In the university faculty meeting on June 7 Branscomb had stressed the good faith of the board in upholding hard-won agreements, and Harold Vanderbilt had noted that the board had never turned down a Branscomb recommendation. The critical Executive Committee meeting put a fateful decision in the hands of very few men—trustees Cecil Sims, Stahlman, Orrin H. Ingram, John Sloan, Eldon Stevenson, Jr., and William Waller, along with Branscomb and Harold Vanderbilt. The decision had to be made by a group of Nashville cronies, men who loved the university but who were already leery of Branscomb's softness in moving toward compromise with a rebellious faculty. They wanted to uphold not only the Lawson decision but, even more, the authority of the board, and to demonstrate that faculty rebellion or blackmail could not work. Without intending it, they risked the survival of Vanderbilt as a quality university.

The proposal, as agreed upon in the faculty negotiations and as submitted to the Executive Committee, contained only two provisions. When Lawson had fully met the requirements for the B.D. degree, the chancellor would recommend the granting of the degree to the board. He was to receive credit for his uncompleted spring 1960 courses by "passing written examinations." The second point stipulated the return of all resignations by the dean and faculty of the Divinity School, and reinstitution of their status to that which prevailed before May 30, 1960. It was Branscomb's intent, and his understanding of the compromise, that he would subsequently dismiss Dean

565

Nelson. On these crucial points, the substance of the compromise, the Executive Committee took no action, which was tantamount to rejection of the carefully negotiated agreement. They did vote to reject one procedural detail contained in Nelson's belated letter—that within twenty-four hours after the release of the compromise settlement to the press, and thus his interim reinstatement as dean, he would submit his resignation as dean, effective immediately, and as professor, effective August 31, 1960. This was consistent with the telephone agreement except for his early resignation. By gaining his moment of vindication and then turning immediately to the press with his announced resignation, and on his own terms, probably with an elaborate statement, Nelson made bid to have the last word and to go out as a glorious martyr. Neither the board nor Branscomb wanted to give him that privilege and thus rejected his formula. But the critical point is that these procedural details had not been part of the negotiated agreement but were conceived at the last moment by Nelson. The Divinity School faculty had not even been a party to such procedures, which were in no way integral to the crucial compromise or vitally involved with the fate of Vanderbilt.[47]

Branscomb was now trapped. His Executive Committee had reversed his recommendation and thus his good faith agreement with the faculty. In a later letter Stahlman tried to explain what had happened. The Executive Committee believed Branscomb had the case "licked to a frazzel" after his statement to the faculty on June 7, when he had lambasted the Divinity faculty's refusal to negotiate and had announced that he had no alternative but to accept their resignations. Stahlman and the Executive Committee believed that acceptance of the subsequent compromise "was inimical to the best interests of the university." Surprisingly, a majority were willing to award a degree to Lawson so long as it was in absentia but were not willing to reinstate the rebelling faculty. Such a move would reward the faculty for their power play and undermine university government as the Executive Committee understood it. Just after the disappointing meeting, Harold Vanderbilt returned to New York; Branscomb left for Williamsburg without announcing any results to the anxious faculty or public. In a sense, both men had lost, for Vanderbilt had twice assured the faculty that the Executive Committee would approve a settlement recommended by Branscomb. The whole episode caused him deep distress, and the now frail old man was soon in the hospital because of heart problems.[48]

On campus the faculty only learned of the fatal nonaction in the evening, and this from Purdy. Before leaving, Branscomb had told Purdy (Purdy was not present for the critical part of the meeting) that the procedural details in Nelson's letter had sabotaged the agreement, and this was what Branscomb always argued in the next few weeks or, for that matter, the next several years. This excuse served him well and perhaps served the university well. It allowed him to remain as chancellor when immediate resignation would only have had disastrous results. It unfairly placed the odium of a failed settlement

566

on Nelson, an injustice, but one almost justified by Nelson's fumbling effort. The evidence, though, is conclusive—the Executive Committee would have rejected the proposal even without Nelson's letter. After Branscomb publicly announced the Nelson "betrayal" as the reason for the Executive Committee action, Stahlman reminded him that the committee had acted "for more reasons than the one which you indicated in your statement . . . as having been the principal cause for the Executive Committee's unanimous rejection of these proposals . . . ." At another point he noted that both he and Ingram had called his attention to "the difference between your interpretation and ours of the reason given . . . for the Executive Committee's refusal of the Roos proposals. . . ." But the members of the Executive Committee believed it best to support Branscomb in his public statements, and thus to leave as part of the accepted record the Chancellor's explanation of what seemed by far the most crucial Executive Committee decision in Vanderbilt's history.[49]

For the next four days chaos reigned on campus. The Executive Committee action, the "great betrayal," was devastating news to the faculty. Reporters rushed to campus to get the details, and once again Vanderbilt made all big city newspapers. A group of Divinity, Medical, and College faculty, plus Purdy and McGaw, met late on the fateful evening. All seemed hopeless. They could only rehearse the events of the last three days, commiserate on how all had come to nought. Silberman lamented that he could not "go through another single day of negotiations. Today was the most humiliating day in my life. Today I became an old man." Nelson turned over to the press the letter he sent to the Executive Committee. The faculty also shared with the press some heretofore confidential details of the negotiating process, including a commitment by Branscomb that, if he could not get the board to award Lawson's degree after he had met the agreed-upon terms, that he would resign along with the faculty, a report that got garbled in the newspapers and even led to false rumors that Branscomb had resigned.[50]

The next day, a Friday, the faculty recovered enough to resume the struggle. By then several additional professors had threatened resignation. All the way from South America, William H. Nicholls wired his intent to resign and his expectation of an early demise of a distinguished economics department. Representatives from several departments met at the Divinity School to draft a rather clever, politically charged proposal, subsequently signed by 161 of 195 faculty members contacted (out of 428) in this interim period. In the statement the faculty commended the action of Harold Vanderbilt and Branscomb in negotiating an agreement, expressed shock at the failure of the Executive Committee to accede to it, and urged the "responsible officials of the Board of Trust" to resolve the crisis without delay and according to the terms worked out by the chancellor and the board president. They stressed that it was crucial to the future of Vanderbilt to resolve the crisis immediately. They gathered the names in time to make the Saturday, June 11, *Tennessean*, another mark of developing political savvy. As a follow-up, the

Divinity faculty sent a note of appreciation to a hospitalized Vanderbilt. Now, with skill, but little prospect of success and a reckless disregard for consequence that seemed justified by their sheer hopelessness, professors tried to drive a wedge between Vanderbilt and Branscomb and any far-flung board members inclined to support them, on the one hand, and the resented Nashville trustees on the other.[51]

Branscomb now faced dangerous pressures from two sides. For a time from Thursday until Sunday, while in Williamsburg, he was out of reach of any of the protagonists. Briefly, the Nashville trustees confronted the false rumors of his resignation. When they learned better, they were still disturbed at what Branscomb had said to the faculty about resigning. The Nashville trustees met, and consulted, throughout the weekend. On Saturday, June 11, Stahlman wrote a long letter to Harold Vanderbilt, after checking details with Purdy, Ingram, and even Fred Russell, president of the Alumni Association. Stahlman, like most trustees, did not know Harold Vanderbilt in the close, intimate sense that the local trustees knew one another. In his letter, which sounded amazingly like some of his editorials, he castigated all the protesting faculty on campus, those who were dedicated to the "venomous task of damaging and, if need be, destroying" the university. "They will stop at nothing." He deplored their recent statement, published in the *Tennessean,* a statement which threatened to separate Branscomb and Vanderbilt from the board and drive Branscomb from the chancellorship. He wanted to enlist the aging Vanderbilt in a great effort to rid the campus of all the disloyal and rebellious element. He rejoiced in the mounting support from the American Legion and from conservative church groups in the South, as well as from the "loyal" faculty in the Medical School. He welcomed the early departure of the few discontented Medical School professors. There was no way to reach agreement with such emotionally disturbed and fanatically driven "rebels." Without being specific as to the final tactics, he urged Vanderbilt to join in a final showdown, a type of shoot-out at high noon. In the early morning hours of June 13, Stahlman and Ingram put on paper their specific proposals for ridding the campus of trouble makers: to commend all involved in efforts to solve the problem; to announce the Lawson case closed; to authorize the chancellor to accept all the resignations from the Divinity School; to instruct him to take necessary steps to keep the Divinity School open, if possible, and to take such other steps necessary to restore order and tranquility; to authorize him to accept immediately all subsequent resignations that appeared in the best interest of the university; and, if the Executive Committee would not approve these measures, to call a board meeting to consider them.[52]

On the telephone Harold Vanderbilt listened politely to these proposals. He did not overtly reject them but instead read a statement he had prepared in his hospital room, one much milder than Stahlman's. Vanderbilt preferred to give Lawson his B.D., either for transferred credit or upon completing exams, and in this keep faith with the faculty. He wanted to deny Lawson any right of subsequent readmission to the Divinity School or to the Graduate School. This would be the final word on the Lawson case, but the resignation of faculty members would be handled individually, presumably by the chancellor. Ingram and Stahlman dropped their own harsher recommendations, helped shape and toughen the wording of Vanderbilt's, and sent it to Branscomb as partial preparation for an afternoon Executive Committee meeting on June 13.

Branscomb, for good reasons, feared such a meeting. He asked the Nashville board members to call it off and read them his own statement, which he planned to release later in the day. Ingram and Stahlman were not happy with Branscomb's statement, and on two counts. It again suggested that the Executive Committee rejected the earlier compromise largely, or even solely, because of Nelson's letter, and it allowed the Divinity School faculty to withdraw their resignations. They argued with Branscomb, pointed out the opposition of the alumni and the general public to such concessions, but could not dissuade him. As Branscomb remembered this critical phone call from the perspective of twenty years, he had asked Stahlman and the other local trustees to yield responsibility in settling the crisis to the chancellor. They had refused. Branscomb then remembered telling them he planned to proceed on his own responsibility, and that he thus in effect challenged them to fire him if they wanted. In this sense, a courageous Branscomb took more than the usual degree of responsibility for what followed.[53]

Branscomb prepared a rather terse statement, checked it with three members of the university Senate, and then issued it as a statement to the faculty. He stressed that the escalating controversy had to end. No one disagreed with this. Viewed from either side, the dangers grew each day. Up to half the faculty, despairing of any solution, were mobilizing for a direct confrontation with the board. The faculty at least planned to go down fighting. More frightening, the Executive Committee was becoming more militant each day, and if it met seemed likely to take actions that violated academic freedom. This which would ruin Vanderbilt's academic reputation and mobilize a vast majority of the faculty, including those heretofore supportive of the chancellor or not involved. Branscomb's statement was brilliantly ambiguous. In his prefatory comments he administered another sharp spanking to the Divinity School faculty, accusing it of bad faith for refusing to negotiate. He also again placed sole blame for the failure in the Executive Committee on Nelson's letter. But, except for wording and minor details, his solution combined the wording of the one the Executive Committee had unanimously rejected and of Harold Vanderbilt's newer version. In four brief parts he (1) accepted Nelson's resignation, immediately; (2) allowed Lawson to receive his B.D. either by transfer of credit or by written examinations but without readmission; (3) permitted the other members of the Divinity School faculty to withdraw their resignations within a period of ten days; and (4) announced that the matter was now closed.[54]

Of course, no statement could really close such a troubling controversy. But, legally, it was now over. As Branscomb anticipated, his board backed him in this unilateral action. Had it not done so he would have had to resign. Even Stahlman, keenly disappointed by the leniency of the statement, fearful that some of the Divinity School faculty might stay on to corrupt Vanderbilt students by their false values, still wrote an editorial commending Branscomb, although not without a few shots at his failure to act so decisively much earlier and some final cheers for the final elimination from Vanderbilt of both Lawson and Nelson. Unfortunately for the university, Branscomb's imposed solution did not end the continuing dialogue in religious journals. Nelson gave his version in the *Christian Century;* Branscomb wrote a reply. Not surprisingly, both were self-serving. Correspondence about the case continued for months. Branscomb's final statement, a carefully prepared white paper drafted in order to minimize the effects of bad publicity, appeared only in the fall. The one person least happy with the settlement—Everett Tilson—continued his verbal shots at Branscomb for years. But the statement did calm the campus. Newspaper reporters moved to other beats and Vanderbilt finally moved out of the national spotlight.[55]

It is impossible to gauge the long-term consequences of the Lawson affair. But some effects upon the various protagonists are clear. Lawson, the occasion for so much conflict, chose not to complete his B.D. at Vanderbilt but rather at Boston University. He refused the terms offered in deference to his friend Dean Nelson, who had sacrificed his position in Lawson's defense. Lawson, in all of this, never seemed bitter but rather generous. He deeply appreciated the support of students and faculty and in his reaction to Branscomb's statement noted that he bore no ill will to the Vanderbilt community. Strangely enough, he seemed to love Vanderbilt and returned to the campus for graduate work in 1970, in a very revealing and complex sequel to this story. Nelson gave up a position he deeply loved, had to take a temporary position at Princeton for the next year, but was gracious enough to say the words that allowed his colleagues to withdraw, in almost good conscience, their resignations. Branscomb suffered enormous mental duress during the affair. For a time the conflict drove him far toward the defensive, inflexible stance that his critics had accused him of all along. He was hurt by his critics, by the enormous flood of hostility from national journals, church leaders, and fellow biblical scholars. The support, the plaudits, came almost entirely from the South, and often from strict segregationists or from very conservative churchmen. Beleaguered, Branscomb had a hard time forgiving many of his outspoken critics on campus.[56]

To what extent the highly publicized Lawson affair, and its troubled aftermath, influenced the career choices of professors is impossible to evaluate. To what extent it scared eminent professors away from Vanderbilt positions is also incalculable. It seemed to have small effects outside the Divinity School, and for two reasons. In two years Branscomb retired, and

Vanderbilt continued to admit blacks to the Divinity and Law schools. Within two years it also moved, at least formally, to open admission in all schools.

The Lawson case devastated for a time a great Divinity School. Yet it survived, and in 1960 that seemed reason for rejoicing. The ambiguities in Branscomb's statement gave its professors a few face-saving possibilities. They could interpret it as a great victory for their cause, a concession by Branscomb. As far as Lawson was concerned, they gained their fall-back or compromise goal. As in negotiating the compromise, they chose to interpret the provision for his completion of his semester's work through examination as a type of reinstatement. It took away any penalty of expulsion and in that sense nullified the earlier injustice. They interpreted the right to take exams as a right to come back on campus and complete his work; the stipulation that he not be readmitted meant, not a penalty, but a concession. Of course, neither Branscomb nor the board read this into the words. The Divinity School faculty also faced intense pressures from their colleagues in the College and other schools. Practically everyone at Vanderbilt urged them to stay, for only their retention could restore harmony to the campus. Although not a reason they would cite in the context of agonizing self-justification, career concerns also had to play a major role. Few wanted to face disruptive moves, and now, with all the national publicity subsiding, the job offers declined. Once again the faculty members met and agonized and prayed. They resented Branscomb's attacks on them, nourished a deep sense of guilt over Dean Nelson's fate, but at the same time regained some hope in the possibilities of their school, of its potential role in a morally backward South.[57]

On June 15 all those who had resigned, except a departing Bard Thompson, prepared a statement withdrawing their resignations. Five of them carried it to Chancellor Branscomb late in the evening, even as another took a copy to the *Tennessean* in order to make the morning headlines. Branscomb expressed his deep sense of relief, in a moving if formal exchange. In their prepared statement the professors took exception to Branscomb's interpretation of the Lawson case and to his summary dismissal of Nelson, but they saw in the terms for Lawson an honorable resolution. They stressed the continued role of their school in solving the racial crisis. At they expected, their capitulation shocked many of their northern sympathizers and thus left a large residue of self-doubt and guilt. Maybe they had betrayed the cause of civil rights, compromised the prophetic role of their school. Had Lawson returned for his exams, and degree, they would have felt so much better.[58]

The immediate problem for the distraught Divinity faculty was to put their school together again. This proved a herculean task. Branscomb appointed a mild, conciliatory, respected Herman Norton as acting dean. His problems multiplied rapidly. In the midst of the controversy, Paul Sanders decided to take another job. Nelson was already gone. Thompson was leaving. Three vacancies had to be filled. This turned out to be only the beginning, for in the next two years Gilkey, now arguably the school's most distinguished professor, and Kaufman both resigned to take positions in prestigious northern seminaries. The school immediately began a process of self-analysis and launched a search for a dean. The faculty leaned toward Harrelson, who was now back on board for the fall of 1960. He had the national reputation and the administrative experience needed. But he was one of the "rebels" to board members, and thus Branscomb vetoed him. Purdy did urge Branscomb to keep his name in the running as long as possible, for he could help the school in its developing accreditation problems with a committee of the American Association of Theological Schools (AATS). Some people even suggested a temporary dean, perhaps a Methodist bishop, and Branscomb actually inquired about several bishops.[59]

Out of the self-study, and a position paper prepared by Sellers, the remaining faculty began to question the whole recent direction of their school— toward graduate work, ecumenical achievements, and scholarly eminence. The school had developed a national reputation, but in its lofty intellectuality and rigorous moral standards had failed to serve many churches in the South. Here, in local pulpits, where the battles for racial justice had to be fought among real, prejudiced, troubled people was a significant mission for the school. From this sense of a new direction, back toward sectional problems and a ministry to the church, the faculty worked out the desired qualifications of a new dean—that he have a primary interest in serving southern churches and that he be familiar with the attitudes and problems that faced southerners. Branscomb, in his stated qualifications for the new dean, stressed that he be a Methodist, a southerner, an ordained minister with a B.D. and a Ph.D., and someone with administrative experience. He wanted no second Nelson. In one sense, these qualifications seemed a perfect prescription for mediocrity and did reflect a planned retreat. The school temporarily gave up on being the Yale of the South. Consistent with these guidelines, Branscomb eventually appointed as dean William C. Finch, president of small Southwestern University in Georgetown, Texas. A charming man, an able administrator, he lacked scholarly credentials or national prominence but provided the administrative skills and tact needed to bring stability to the school. He left after four years to take over as president of Emory and Henry.[60]

In November, 1960, the AATS sent an investigating team to Vanderbilt. To the surprise of Branscomb and others, the AATS, in its December meeting, placed Vanderbilt Divinity School on probation for one year. Unless it corrected some critical problems, it risked a loss of accreditation. The investigations grew directly out of the Lawson case and the doubts and suspicions of member schools, largely northern. The AATS was most concerned about faculty morale and the relationship of the faculty to the central administration. The committee specifically cited the following concerns: that the interests of the school were not sufficiently represented on the board (an understatement); that rules for admitting students or recruiting faculty were not clearly defined in written statements (meaning, of course, that the chancellor played too large a role and the faculty too small); that clear lines of communication did not exist between the faculty, administration, and board; that the faculty might have too limited a role in the selection of a new dean; that the administration might retaliate against students and faculty; and that the board might even dissolve the school. The investigating committee found that the faculty did not exercise control over admission, curriculum, and other academic aspects of the school, another clear reference to the handling of the Lawson case. The committee worried over continued factions in the faculty and doubted that it yet had "all possible freedom to pursue its calling responsibly within the University, Church, and society." The report caused great concern and had much of its intended effect. Faculty members helped Branscomb select the new dean, the faculty gained formal rights to control admissions, and most procedures were now clarified by written rules. By May, 1961, the faculty was able to give careful, honest, and in most respects reassuring answers to each of the queries. The AATS removed probation at the end of the year, and a chastened school slowly regained the good graces of its peers. On a few points the faculty admitted continuing problems and tensions. Notably, among those concerns was a new university rule about the faculty role in admissions; it stipulated that the faculty act with "discretion with respect to the admission of qualified Negro students from outside the region."[61]

A final, and complex, issue was the relationship of the Lawson episode to racial integration at Vanderbilt. Note that race was not overtly an issue in the Lawson case. Branscomb did not single out Lawson because he was black but because of the role he played in the developing civil rights movement. He would have taken the same action against a white student in the same highly charged and well-publicized situation, as he always insisted. Only a few bitter faculty members ever accused Branscomb of allowing racial bias to influence his handling of the case. On the other hand, Lawson's race almost certainly affected the reactions of a few board members, although possibly no more so than the fact that he was a Yankee and a pacifist. Clearly, Lawson's race very much shaped the news coverage of the controversy and led interested people outside the South to view the dismissal of Lawson as both hostility toward the sit-ins and as an effort to keep blacks in their place. From a public relations perspective, the Lawson case began and ended as a test of the depth of Vanderbilt's commitment to racial equality. Not only did northern journalists so consider it, but so did those many southern newspapers that applauded Vanderbilt for the first time in its history. Segregationists wrote approving letters to Branscomb from all over the South.

The Lawson case did not impede a painfully slow process toward open admission. It complicated the process, for from now on Vanderbilt could do nothing outside the glare of publicity. In small ways the controversy may have speeded up new initiatives. Branscomb reassured the foundations that nothing had changed, that the professional schools remained integrated. During the Lawson case the first large Ford Foundation gift was pending, and in his correspondence with the foundation, Branscomb committed the university to full integration within the next few years, before he retired as chancellor. This was no small commitment in the wake of Lawson and given the strong feelings of so many members of the board. Thus, the story of the final, legal moves is a strange one. Quite literally, the Vanderbilt board and administration backed into a formalized open admissions policy.[62]

During the two years leading up to a decision on open admissions, and in the even more critical months just after it was announced, the central administration at Vanderbilt worked assiduously to avoid incidents, and publicity, involving any aspect of race. In 1961, when Branscomb was away, Vice-Chancellor Stambaugh joined Dean of Women Nora Chaffin and the Vanderbilt police in forcing a group of white and black students off campus. Students from six Mennonite colleges had met at Fisk for an international peace fellowship conference (attended by a few Vanderbilt students), and then spread out to local campuses to circulate notices of a planned workshop at the Highlander Folk School. A horrified Stambaugh talked of the "invasion" of a mere twelve students and used a purported nonsolicitation rule to get them out of the dorms, the same dorms that had invited John Kasper to speak.

Branscomb took every possible occasion in 1961 and 1962 to defuse the racial issue. As a gesture to segregationists, he praised Donald Davidson's new book, *The New South and the Conservative Tradition.* In 1961, when he received from a black educator a request to intervene with restaurants near campus that had refused service to blacks, Branscomb chose to work quietly, and by persuasion, and out of fear of a possible racial incident. Then, in December, 1962, after the board vote for open admissions, two uninvited incidents infuriated Branscomb.[63]

On December 8, 1962, a visiting assistant professor of physics, David Kotelchuck, joined black students picketing before downtown restaurants. He wanted to show his support for the students and apparently could not understand what was wrong with Vanderbilt professors. Not a one joined the effort, whereas on many northern campuses hundreds of faculty members had joined such demonstrations. Kotelchuck only walked on the sidewalk and never violated any law. But on this occasion, when the police were not present, white ruffians challenged the marchers while angry employees fought them. One black passerby, after being knocked to the ground, drew a knife but was persuaded to leave. In the midst of all this, when a restaurant employee slugged Kotelchuck on the face, a lucky newspaper photographer caught the blow just on impact. The picture made the AP wire services and appeared in newspapers all over the country. This one incident gave Vanderbilt the most favorable northern publicity it had received in years, made a

Vanderbilt professor a minor hero in the civil rights movement, and helped erase much of the damage from the Lawson affair. But the Vanderbilt administration did not so view it. At the time Purdy stressed that "a member of the Vanderbilt community should always give thoughtful consideration to the image of the University reflected by his posture before the public." In a form letter written to angry southerners, Branscomb noted Kotelchuck's temporary status, as a "quick" replacement, and noted that he conformed to the law but ended with a chilling rebuke: "What I might say with reference to his judgment, good taste, and sense of corporate responsibility is another matter." Implicit in this was a signal to faculty members—do not become actively involved in the civil rights movement. Do not take an active role in the most significant moral crusade of the century. Kotelchuck remained at Vanderbilt for six years and felt more at home in the new Heard era.[64]

The next incident came only three weeks later, just after Christmas, 1962. The Southern Regional Council and the Fellowship of Southern Churchmen organized a special conference, "The South: The Ethical Demands of Integration." The group contacted the Law School and rented the Underwood Auditorium at the new Law School building for the December 27–29 conference. Apparently no one in the central administration knew about the arrangement. The conference gained national attention and again very favorable national publicity for Vanderbilt, largely because Martin Luther King, Jr., spoke on December 28, for the first time on campus (he spoke earlier at the Wesley Foundation). The publicity frightened Branscomb. In a letter to critics he stressed that Vanderbilt did not sponsor the conference and that university administrators were not even aware of its scheduling by a minor official of the Law School. He concluded: "Needless to say, steps have been taken to prevent anyone's lending Vanderbilt facilities to outside organizations again except with central administrative approval." Robert McGaw tried to control press coverage, since the sponsoring organizations gave out a press release that announced the conference at Vanderbilt University. He deplored this and asked newspapers not to publicize Vanderbilt's relationship to the conference, pointing out that Vanderbilt had no more relationship to it than did a hotel that hosted a conference. If the newspapers had to mention Vanderbilt, then they should mention the sponsor first.

Embarrassed by King's appearance, Branscomb moved to the other extreme as compensation. A Nashville contractor sent him a copy of a notorious tract written by Wesley C. George for Governor George Wallace of Alabama and entitled *The Biology of the Race Problem*. The book contained every vicious racial stereotype then prevalent in the South, and backed up its arguments for black inferiority and the dangers of intermarriage by a distorted, intellectually dishonest use of scientific data. But Branscomb wrote back that he had glanced at the book and found it "a forthright and useful document" which "certainly deserves a place in all of the present discussions on race matters."

He said it would "certainly be proper to have this point of view expressed on the Vanderbilt campus," and if any group invited him, the "university would certainly approve the scheduling of the lecture."[65]

In 1961 Branscomb began preparing the board for a vote on open admissions. By then, almost everyone on campus realized that a decision was in the offing. The issue was constantly discussed. By now, not only the Tennessee public universities but Peabody, Scarritt, Maryville, Tusculum, Sewanee, and Madison colleges had all integrated. Even Tulane, a favorite comparison for Branscomb, encouraged a test case in the courts in early 1962, broke a benefactor's will, and admitted blacks. By then, Dean Wade of the Law School pointed out some implications of the Tulane decision by Judge Skelly Wright—that even the degree of public involvement of Vanderbilt (it operated under a state charter and was tax exempt) might bring it under the Fourteenth Amendment. On campus, the *Hustler* editor, Lamar Alexander, strongly supported open admission, and did so in part because of Branscomb's urging.

The student senate next tackled the issue. After a torrid three-hour debate, the senate defeated a resolution favoring integration of the undergraduate colleges by 14 to 13, and in a subsequent referendum, in February, 1962, students voted 862–661 against recommending such a policy to the board. But the senior class in the College and in Nursing approved; the strongest opposition in this record turnout came from Engineering. Also, some students said they voted "no" because students had no business advising the board. Branscomb could have better used a "yes" vote at this point. He soon gained the support he wanted from other constituencies, and with this the needed evidence for a board meeting. In March a new organization, the graduate student council, recommended open admission to all divisions of the Graduate School. It held that racial discrimination was "contrary to the spirit and aims of any university." On April 17, 1962, the College faculty, after a long and intense debate, recommended by 79 to 27 that all restrictions involving race be removed from College admission requirements. Finally on April 26, 1962, all members of the University Senate present and voting recommended open admission. Throughout April the *Hustler* kept pushing the open admission issue; both the editor and the assistant editor stressed that the board had to consider the policy in its May meeting, since the *Hustler* believed a large Ford Foundation grant was at stake. Without fuller integration, Vanderbilt would lose it.[66]

The University Senate's resolution summarized the reasons that the board could not any longer postpone open admissions. It also, as much as the *Hustler,* conveyed Branscomb's own position. The Senate noted the action of other southern universities, pointed out the possible loss of tax-exempt status, stressed the eventual loss of government grants and loans and foundation gifts, and noted the rapidly changing racial climate in the South. It tried to minimize the effect—few blacks were qualified; without recruitment few would come; the experience with twenty-seven students in the professional schools had been favorable; and all Vanderbilt constituencies except the lower level undergraduates now favored it. Only after a barrage of such realistic and factual arguments did the senators turn to moral and religious reasons, to the equality of blacks before God and under the Constitution.[67]

In the month before the critical May 6, 1962, board meeting, Branscomb worked carefully to mature a resolution that could win even a majority vote. For once, everyone realized the board would not approve a major new policy unanimously; without Branscomb's and Vanderbilt's careful spade work, it might even vote against open admissions. The Lawson affair had left bitter feelings. Yet, once again, so much was at stake. With the help of the Vanderbilt administration, Harold Vanderbilt prepared informational placards, with tables and supporting information, for each member of the board, all written in large capital letters so as to be readable by a group of old men. He also carefully arranged a series of speakers to help boost its passage. By prearrangement, Branscomb did not commit himself and came to the meeting as if he were neutral on the policy issue, although he was prepared to present factual data and clearly wanted the resolution to pass. At the critical session the careful planning paid off. The board first received the University Senate resolution. Vanderbilt read his prepared statement in support. Sarratt noted the likely opposition of some alumni groups. Finally, William S. Vaughn moved the open admission resolution and Cecil Sims seconded it. Heated and sharply divided discussions followed.[68]

The resolution provided for admission to all schools and colleges of the university, "without regard to race or creed," on the basis of "scholastic achievement, intellectual capacity, moral character, and promise of leadership." The qualification came in a second part of the motion, or what could be called the "all-deliberate-speed" clause. The chancellor, in consultation with the vice-chancellors and deans, was "to use administrative care and discretion in implementing this policy, with the view of insuring a continuous atmosphere conducive to learning, study, and good conduct compatible with the high traditions of Vanderbilt University." This motion passed. Out of thirty-four present, six asked to record votes in opposition and, out of courtesy, two other absent trustees recorded negative votes by proxy. Three of the eight were elderly men and thus life trustees. Stahlman reluctantly voted yes. But he did so only because he had assurances that a follow-up motion would also pass. He had first submitted, and then withdrawn it, in the form of an amendment. This might well be called the "Nelson-Lawson reservation." It specified that any admission coming under the administrative discretion phrase (blacks), or any other application considered questionable, could not be acted upon without the prior approval of the appropriate dean and vice-chancellor and finally of the chancellor himself. This resolution became a dead letter, for legal reasons as well as the disinclination of administrative officers to follow it.[69]

Board President Harold S. Vanderbilt at retirement of Chancellor Branscomb

The board vote in favor of open admission was in no sense a vote in favor of significant or full integration. A majority of the faculty probably supported real integration. That is, they now wanted and expected Vanderbilt to welcome black students as equals. The board intended no such result and the administration at least equivocated on the meaning of the new policy. In their response to southern critics, Branscomb and Purdy stressed the small number of blacks qualified for admission to Vanderbilt and predicted that few if any undergraduates would enroll any time soon. The board, in approving Stahlman's motion, tried to cut off what they now saw as the one possible source of qualified blacks—the North. By giving final administrative authority to the chancellor, they expected him to block what H.S. Vanderbilt referred to as those "bright colored boys from Chicago," or other potential trouble makers like Lawson. Their letters revealed a widespread assumption—that very few southern blacks could meet Vanderbilt undergraduate requirements, and of that few, almost none would be able to pay the high tuition. The repeated administrative assurances that blacks would receive no special favors became, by sheer reiteration, an implied promise to the board that Vanderbilt administrators would discourage black applications.

The early record seemed to confirm such an understanding. By the time of the board vote in the spring of 1962, the admissions office announced a full quota of undergraduates for the next fall. Blacks had no reason to apply. In the spring of 1963 the admissions office accepted applications from four black high school graduates, but in a scrupulously fair evaluation judged none of them qualified. Thus, the new policy produced not a single black undergraduate until 1964. The policy turned out to be a politically brilliant maneuver by the board; it disarmed the foundations but did not immediately change anything on campus. Since they were still unsought and not clearly wanted, it is not difficult to explain the pitifully few black applicants. Why should blacks want to come to a university without a single black instructor, and as late as 1964 without one black secretary? In 1964, as much as 1875, the only black employees at Vanderbilt performed menial tasks.[70]

Because no black undergraduate came to Vanderbilt in 1962 or 1963, the new board policy never triggered a major controversy. All the fears about integrated dorms, mixed physical education classes, dining room mingling, or, horror of horrors, interracial dating or pressures for integrated fraternities proved groundless, at least in the short term. Most alumni seemed to join most board members in accepting the new policy as inevitable, a necessary concession to the social and political changes taking place in the country and

Chancellor Branscomb's campus residence until 1953

in the South. But, now much more quickly than the board members could ever comprehend, the pace of racial change was about to quicken.

The interlude of effective southern resistance was almost over. The sit-ins had led to a new, largely student civil rights organization, the Student Nonviolent Coordinating Committee (SNCC), an organization founded, in part, through the active work of James Lawson, but one that eventually rejected his nonviolent strategy. By 1961 the focus of civil right activities shifted to segregated trains and buses, in the year of the famous freedom rides. The violence heaped on freedom riders invited the first, hesitant federal intervention in the South by the Justice Department and helped mobilize northern opinion as effectively as had the sit-ins. In 1962 the several civil rights organizations began active voting registration drives among southern blacks, with SNCC leading the way. In 1963 Martin Luther King, Jr., carried his movement to Birmingham, where nonviolent protest led to several violent confrontations, to King's incarceration, to his eloquent and philosophical "Letter From a Birmingham Jail," to marches by, and arrest of, black children, and out of it all a partial victory—integrated restaurants and other facilities, more jobs for blacks, and some biracial committees. In 1963, with a show of force, federal marshals forced the integration of the University of Alabama. In August, 1963, a quarter-million blacks and whites came for the march on Washington, to hear King deliver his most famous and dramatic speech. The mass rally had all but official federal support and symbolized the political success of the civil rights movement. In 1964, in the wake of Kennedy's assassination, the federal Congress enacted the first of three major civil rights acts, and in 1965, the year of the Selma marches, passed a major voting rights act. These legislative initiatives made illegal virtually any form of segregation and joined early federal efforts to insure equal employment opportunities. Thus, Vanderbilt "enjoyed" only a brief interlude of defensive or token integration. By 1965 Vanderbilt welcomed black students in all schools. In the next year it began actively recruiting them.[71]

PART EIGHT

Into the Second Century
(1963–1982)

❦ IN THE SPRING *of 1963 Vanderbilt's future never seemed
brighter. Higher education in America enjoyed boom times;
enrollments soared, an ever more generous federal government
steadily increased its support, and the prestige and income of faculty
members rose. The nation enjoyed an unprecedented decade of
prosperity and economic growth. President Kennedy spoke at
Vanderbilt and added his blessings on its ninetieth anniversary.
Nashville and Davidson County entered a golden age, one
symbolized by a new Metro Government, by steady population
growth (from 399,000 in 1960 to 456,000 in 1980), and by a
rapidly expanding economic base, with the new country music
industry supplementing commerce, government, banking,
insurance, religious publishing, higher education, and small
manufacturing. The upper South, soon to be blessed by the ending
of legal segregation and freed from the rigors of its climate by air
conditioning, began to enjoy the benefits of growth. As wealth and
income and population drifted toward the Southeast, the area from
which Vanderbilt drew most of its students moved toward equality
with the rest of the country. In 1980 per capita income in the
Southeast, when corrected to account for living costs, rose to
approximately 90 percent of national averages. Per capita white
income exceeded the national average. Finally, Vanderbilt had a
new chancellor, one committed to a more open and pluralistic
campus.*

*Vanderbilt took advantage of the new opportunities. In the next twenty
years it added three new schools, doubled its enrollment, and in
most schools recruited a more distinguished faculty and achieved
new levels of quality in both teaching and research. It at least
retained its relative position among graduate-level private
universities.*

*The achievements did not come easily. The golden promise of the summer
of 1963 faded all too quickly, as symbolized by Kennedy's
assassination in November, 1963. Controversy, strife, disorder
marked the next decade, particularly on campuses. The tension
repeatedly posed challenges for Vanderbilt's administrators and
faculty. But at Vanderbilt, as much as at any comparable
university, the tension usually led to constructive outlets. The
campus gained more than it lost in the turbulent late 1960s and
early 1970s. The more dire problems came after 1974, after the
abeyance of racial, urban, and antiwar strife, after students once
again settled down to dutiful study largely in behalf of career goals.
Then, in an era of energy shortages and runaway inflation, of
recurrent recessions, of diminished federal support for higher
education, of a declining college-age population, of a faculty
demoralized by declining demand for their services and continuing
erosion of their real income, Vanderbilt's leaders struggled to find
new sources of funds, to battle lagging faculty morale, to maintain
the quality of student applicants, particularly in the Graduate
School, and even to appease the escalating demands of women.*

21

Leadership and Stewardship

GEORGE ALEXANDER HEARD assumed the chancellorship during the brief, golden interlude that marked most of 1963. The peaceful civil rights movement had almost reached its climax. Having enjoyed several partial victories, it had not yet broken apart over the issue of black power. President Kennedy had already committed American advisors and support troops for what would become a major war in Vietnam. But in 1963 few Americans realized the magnitude of that commitment or sensed the controversies that lay ahead. After the embarrassment of the Bay of Pigs in 1961, the agonies of the Berlin crisis, the dangerous confrontation over defensive Soviet missiles in Cuba in 1962, the two superpowers seemed, in 1963, to move toward detente, a detente reflected in calmer words and in a ban on open nuclear tests. The mood nationally seemed unusually hopeful, even upbeat and idealistic, as economic growth easily paid for, and smothered political opposition to, increased social welfare and educational expenditures, or what seemed a major effort to alleviate inequalities of opportunity in America.

Heard came to Vanderbilt as a result of the most thorough search ever conducted by the Board of Trust. Given early warnings from Chancellor Branscomb about his planned retirement, the board began searching for his successor in 1961. It formed a five-member committee on the succession to the chancellorship, effectively chaired by Henry Alexander, then a New York City banker. The board also approved an advisory faculty committee, chaired by Willard B. Jewell of the geology department. It included some of the most eminent professors on campus—John W. Wade from the Law School, J. Philip Hyatt from Divinity, Amos Christie from the Medical School, and economist George Stocking from the College.[1]

The search was open. Unlike Kirkland and Carmichael, Branscomb did not push his own candidate or prime any successor. Vice-Chancellor Rob Roy Purdy had strong support among local alumni and from most local board members. Branscomb remained loyal to his good friend but never tried to push his candidacy upon the board. Purdy had critics on campus in the wake of the Lawson affair and lacked the scholarly eminence sought by key members of the search committee. The faculty committee played a critical role in the screening. The board committee received scores of suggested names and numerous self-serving applications, but it chose to work with a list of qual-

583

ified candidates referred to it by the faculty committee. This procedure gave the faculty a type of veto over the new chancellor but left the final decision fully up to the board.[2]

The faculty committee rendered its report in October, 1961. After screening about seventy people, it recommended ten, each of whom seemed qualified "to continue and expand the excellent leadership of Harvie Branscomb. . . ." The committee stressed "intellectual integrity, social tolerance, moral courage, and sound judgment. . . ," and particularly a commitment to academic freedom. They looked for a candidate between forty and fifty-five, with an earned advanced degree, with teaching experience on a college faculty, an understanding of scholarly research, and administrative experience as dean, provost, or college president. First on their list was Don K. Price, Jr., dean of the Harvard Graduate School of Public Administration, a Kentucky native, a Vanderbilt alumnus, a former Rhodes scholar, then fifty-one years of age, with extensive consulting or advisory experience with both the federal government and the Ford Foundation. He had written several books or articles in political science. The nine other candidates included four presidents of smaller colleges, a provost, two deans, and two directors of major university programs. The committee grouped the ten nominees in five ranks—Price alone made up the top rank, two names each made up groups two, three, and four, and three names made up the fifth rank. Among those three was Heard, then dean of the Graduate School of the University of North Carolina.

Every nominee had a distinguished academic career and notable publications. One was an outstanding scientist, another a brilliant lawyer and professor of law. Only Price was a Vanderbilt alumnus or had a prior connection to Vanderbilt. Five of the ten grew up in the South, five in the North. Given the eminence of the faculty list, it is hard to see how the board could have, in good conscience, gone beyond it. Above all, Don Price had the qualifications that had to appeal to the board. He was a southerner and a brilliant alumnus, he could best appease the Purdy supporters, and his field of public administration fit the interest of many board members. He was personable, made a good impression in a speech at Vanderbilt (not given as a candidate), and impressed the board committee in New York interviews. Thus, the board committee notified him of their intention to present his name to the board. His selection seemed assured.[3]

Price was tempted to return to his alma mater. He enjoyed the hospitality of the committee, which wooed him assiduously. But on February 4, 1962, he reluctantly rejected the impending offer. His role in the selection did not end there. On February 17 he wrote a telling letter to Henry Alexander in behalf of someone he knew only slightly, Alexander Heard. Price had surveyed the list of ten and found Heard the most interesting possibility. Price knew V.O. Key, Heard's mentor and then colleague on the President's Commission on Campaign Costs, and very much valued his enthusiastic support for Heard. Moreover, he believed Heard desired a career in university administration, that he was probably blocked from the presidency of North Carolina, and that he would welcome the Vanderbilt position.[4]

Price's letter raised Heard to the top of the board committee's list. Within a week or two Henry Alexander clearly favored him. Informal interviews reinforced his confidence. But Heard was not well known on campus. The failure of the Price courtship raised new hopes, locally, that Purdy could now win the position. From late February on, the search became more complex and more interesting. Although the faculty committee had been asked to evaluate only people off campus, Harold Vanderbilt had written Jewell personally asking for confidential evaluations of Purdy and a friend of his on campus, Samuel Stumpf. Jewell vetoed Stumpf in a January, 1962, letter and suggested that Purdy was not vigorous and dynamic enough to succeed Branscomb, although he would have more campus support than any other member of the faculty. Such reservations probably reinforced the board committee's determination to bring in an outsider. Yet, on campus and in Nashville it seemed by April of 1962 that the Purdy boom was almost unstoppable. He had fervent alumni support, including supportive letters from the officers of the Alumni Association. At this late date, on May 20, Jewell wrote a second letter, taking back his earlier reservations about Purdy. On close observations of Purdy's talents and administrative skills, Jewell now concluded that he was equal to the names on the original faculty list. Dean Beach, on the other hand, continued to support a strong outsider. Retired vice-chancellor Stambaugh strongly supported Purdy and insisted that only the extremely "liberal" faculty opposed him.[5]

As if largely unaware of the Purdy boom back in Nashville, the board committee began its courtship of Heard. On April 8–10, Harold Vanderbilt flew the Heards to his Florida estate in his own jet plane, there to meet with members of the committee. His plane then brought the whole party to Nashville. The Heards briefly toured the campus and then Vanderbilt's plane returned them to Chapel Hill, leaving the committee in Nashville. Heard was now almost certain to be nominated by the board. But the inquiry continued. The committee was much influenced by what it expected from a pending Vanderbilt-Peabody study—an expanded Nashville University Center headed by the new Vanderbilt chancellor. This, as much as any other factor, precluded Purdy or anyone closely tied to the existing institution. The committee had only minor doubts about Heard—could his wife entertain with four children to raise, and was Heard too "liberal" politically?

Harold S. Vanderbilt conducted his own personal inquiry. In each case he asked if Heard were a radical or leftist or if he would bring such people on campus. Each bemused respondent gave him the wanted assurance. Malcolm Moos, of the President's Commission, cleverly characterized Heard's views as radical in the mid-nineteenth century but conservative by contemporary standards. A pleased Vanderbilt concluded that Heard was perfect—"liberal"

George Alexander Heard with wife and children, 1962

enough to get along with the faculty, "conservative" enough to please the board. No one defined these ambiguous labels. By the annual board meeting on May 7, 1962, the committee was unanimous in support of Heard but decided to delay submission of his name. This meeting, as they anticipated it, faced two other critical decisions—on open admissions and a possible merger with Peabody. The latter issue fizzled, but the admissions issue led to a very tense and divisive meeting.[6]

The climax of the search came in a special board meeting of June 9. The committee did all it could to prepare for the meeting. O.H. Ingram and Eldon B. Stevenson, the two Nashville members, were crucial, for it seemed all other local board members supported Purdy. On May 16 Heard flew to New York to talk over the final details of the offer at Harold Vanderbilt's apartment. On June 2 Heard accepted an offer, subject to board approval. By then, he had settled several details, including salary terms and arrangement for expense accounts, a university car, and some minor repairs and changes at the house. Ingram and Stevenson worked hard to win over the remaining Purdy supporters. H.S. Vanderbilt compared this search to the one in 1946, when all the alumni and local Nashvillians had backed Sarratt (Look how well Branscomb turned out!).

Vanderbilt tried to involve Branscomb in the final persuasion. Branscomb's earliest reaction to Heard had been mildly negative—he feared he was too young. But after Beach attended a common conference and came home full of enthusiasm for Heard, Branscomb seemed fully persuaded. Just before the June 9 meeting, Vanderbilt grew fearful about the strength of the Purdy backers and telegraphed Branscomb, asking him to speak against Purdy. Such a speech proved unnecessary, but in any case Branscomb refused to say anything "against my loyal and devoted colleague" but promised to speak in support and praise of Heard. All the fears proved groundless. On the evening before the board meeting, Purdy informed relieved board members that he was not, and had never been, a candidate for the position. The committee answered some hard questions, most about Heard's qualifications, and then voted unanimously for his appointment.[7]

Alexander Heard had grown up in Savannah, Georgia, a son of able, college-educated parents. His father was an engineer, inventor, and businessman; his mother, a public school administrator. After high school he entered the University of North Carolina in 1934 to work on a degree in chemical engineering. After one year he transferred to political science, a discipline that reflected his own growing involvement in public policy issues during the depression and New Deal years. At North Carolina, significant for a later Vanderbilt, he chaired the Carolina Political Union, a student forum that featured diverse speakers, including political extremists. Of all southern universities North Carolina in the 1930s was the most open, pluralistic, and intellectually vibrant. In many ways the university reflected a southern version of the University of Wisconsin, both because of the involvement of its administrators and faculty in public affairs and, so rare in the South, because it also became a gathering place for political radicals. It was the only southern university that nourished small Marxist or Communist Party groups in the 1930s and just after World War II. When Heard moved to Vanderbilt in 1963, he carried with him an image of a great university molded by his North Carolina experience, as well as by his graduate work at another, even more pluralistic university—Columbia. He moved there in 1938 to begin graduate work but suspended this in 1939 for a six-year interlude of government service—in the departments of Interior and War, from 1941 to 1943 as vice-consul in Ecuador, and then from 1943 to 1946 in the Navy. Thus, very early, Heard mixed his intellectual interest in politics with firsthand observations. From then on he related easily to working bureaucrats and politicians, used interviews with politicians as a base for his scholarly inquiry, and continued to serve governments in a wide variety of advisory roles.[8]

At war's end Heard, after some indecision, finally settled for a career not in government but in scholarship. Before this he won a position as research associate in the Bureau of Public Administration at the University of Ala-

John F. Kennedy at Dudley Field, 1963

bama, assisting V.O. Key, Jr., in a monumental and now classic study of southern politics, a huge three-year project sponsored by the Rockefeller Foundation. Heard became Key's closest associate and, alone among all the researchers, gained recognition as assistant author of the resulting book, *Southern Politics in State and Nation* (1949). Heard's work on this study complemented his earlier graduate work at Columbia, which he decided to resume in 1949. He came to Columbia with his dissertation already written, as a spin-off of the Key project, and with a firm offer of a subsequent position at the University of North Carolina. He completed his Ph.D. course work and exams in one academic year, received his Ph.D. in 1951, but had moved to the University of North Carolina as associate professor of political science in the fall of 1950. His successful, much-acclaimed work with Key made Heard one of the identified bright young men in his chosen field. Aided by tempting job offers from several universities, including a proffered chairmanship at Vanderbilt, he moved up to full professor at North Carolina in January, 1952. From the Key project came not only a coauthored 1950 book, largely statistical, on southern primaries and elections, but in 1952 a revised version of his dissertation, *A Two Party South?* In it he carefully analyzed the continued role of the Republican Party in the South, evaluated a bit too sanguinely the emerging power of southern black voters, and predicted, correctly, the early emergence of a two-party system in the region.[9]

Even though these publications easily gave Heard national prominence, they still remained in the shadow of his friend and mentor, Key. Heard soon launched a major research project of his own. Largely with the help of his graduate students at North Carolina, he began the first extensive study of campaign financing, a project that moved him away from his earlier concentration on southern politics. Aided immensely by a research professorship at Harvard in 1957–58, Heard pulled the data together in a major publication, *The Costs of Democracy* (1960), a book published after he had become dean of the Graduate School at North Carolina in 1958. This pioneer book—careful, thorough, balanced, fact-filled, but eloquently written—established Heard as one of the three or four leading students of American government and helped secure his precocious election as president of the Southern Political Science Association in 1961–62 and his appointment by President Kennedy in 1961 as chairman of a special bipartisan Commission on Campaign Costs. Yet, even before the book appeared in print, Heard at least tentatively committed himself to a new career in university administration, a career that allowed precious little time for additional scholarship.[10]

His books revealed some of Heard's enduring personality traits. They did not reveal a troubled intellectual or a person given to much abstract philosophical discourse. Heard easily and smoothly blended empirical theory with data, asked searching questions about the actual rather than the apparent functioning of American institutions, but bared no deep doubts about the American political system or its underlying values. Typically, he wanted to understand it, repair its weaknesses, make it function more smoothly. His books illustrated traits noted by his colleagues at North Carolina—smoothness and polish, attentiveness to every detail, promptness, and scrupulous accuracy. Heard could also turn out an amazing amount of work. In other words, Heard exemplified in all areas an unusual degree of self-control, conscientious preparation, and almost formally eloquent expression. Even his appearance—neat, crisp, fashionable—and his manner—pleasant, gracious, warm, formally correct—exemplified these traits. Behind the urbanity and polish lay the private person, one not easy to glimpse or to know. One sensed a great deal of pride and a very strong ego. But, unlike Branscomb—sharp, pungent, overwhelmingly brilliant, and often quite self-revealing—Heard rarely if ever relaxed his public self-control. In his own disarming way he could be as tough as Branscomb and on critical issues maintained just as much control over policies. But, whenever possible, he preferred to orchestrate the contributions of others and, if possible, anticipate and by careful planning avert sharp conflict.

Heard believed in what he called a "democratic" process. He wanted an open society, one in which divergent views could find expression, one in which varied preferences or values competed for public acceptance. Despite all the friction he had to contend with, the occasions when he confronted what seemed to be bad faith or intractable ignorance or sheer prejudice, Heard usually kept faith—out of tangled competition or even open conflict truth would usually emerge. Thus, more than any previous chancellor he emphasized the process of decision making as much or more than precise or preset goals. The proper response to felt problems, present or anticipated, was always a new planning study or an ad hoc investigatory committee. His bent was toward conciliation, the harmonizing of what often seemed irreconcilable differences. This always meant compromises, even the acceptance of ambiguity, as Heard tried to appease contending factions.

From his inauguration on, Heard repeatedly spoke of a Vanderbilt community. He stressed common interests that properly united all constituencies in a context of open discussion and equal access to power. Given the characteristics of Vanderbilt students and faculty, and Heard's skills as a mediator, this strategy worked in one sense—it maintained order, alleviated open or violent conflict, and prevented extreme alienation on the part of any constituency. Such a political strategy may be the only principled way to proceed in a heterogeneous or pluralistic context. But it had its costs. Those with strongly held commitments often felt betrayed by what they saw as fluidity or ambiguity in Vanderbilt policies. Others felt coopted, bought off by all the reconciling concessions that came their way. Another effect of consensual politics is that those who are most aggrieved or who are better able to concentrate or focus their demands have inordinate power.

As does every new chancellor, Heard tried to assess the strengths and weaknesses of Vanderbilt. He was not nearly as pessimistic in his analysis as Branscomb had been in 1946. And for good reason. In most respects Vanderbilt reflected the prosperity common to higher education. Heard always acknowledged Branscomb's achievement in building the modern Vanderbilt, a university with some claim to a national constituency. But what most appalled him was the lack of what he found at North Carolina and Columbia—a lively intellectual dialogue, the airing of diverse points of view, and an ongoing contribution by faculty and students to university policy making. He agreed with *Hustler* editors—Vanderbilt was staid and dull and unexciting, heretofore governed dictatorially by an antique Board of Trust and strong-willed chancellors. Heard's first priority was to correct these problems, to open up the campus, to create an atmosphere of freedom and self-government.

He began with symbols. As chancellor he first met with student leaders. He gave his first major speech to the assembled faculty in February, 1963. Characteristically, he talked about Vanderbilt as a community, about common unifying concerns, about the need for goodwill, for an open interchange between faculty and administration. He stressed that great universities are "basically self-governed by their faculties," and that they depend upon the faculty feeling an identity with the institution. His professed goals all had a pluralistic flavor—the need for greater diversity among students, meaning those of diverse sections, classes, and races, and for a higher level of public service on the part of the faculty. At his inaugural on October 4, 1963, he placed greatest emphasis on freedom of inquiry and expression and noted the need to bridge the developing gap between the sciences and cultural studies. He celebrated the struggle of blacks for equality and applauded Vanderbilt's new policy of open admissions. He climaxed this speech with an appeal for a Vanderbilt as a place where pleas for fuller freedom could be calmly heard and clearly debated, and at which conclusions could be freely stated. Beyond this plea, his priorities tended to be a bit heuristic, even vague. He stressed national standards but service to the South. Of course he noted the need for stronger and better paid professors, for new courses and programs, for larger endowments. But, typically, he left all the details to a vast new planning study that he used to launch his administration.[11]

Heard inherited his Board of Trust. Like Branscomb before him, he wanted changes but had to move slowly. To the limits of his influence, he supported a gradual shift in the board toward diversity and youth. In 1964 the board, with some opposition, ended the power of entrenched Executive Committee members from the Nashville area; members now had to rotate on this most powerful committee. In 1969, as the board ballooned in size, it stripped all subsequent life trustees of any right to serve as chairmen of committees, thereby reducing the future influence of older men. In 1968, when Harold Vanderbilt's ill health forced his resignation as president, the board replaced him with a brilliant William S. Vaughn, from the old Vanderbilt family and then chief executive of Eastman Kodak in Rochester. Vaughn brought to the board an urbanity and sophistication lacking in many former trustees.

Much more significant, both symbolically and in fact, was the board's decision in 1964 to elect its first female trustee—Mary Jane Werthan. She proved an invaluable member of the board, possibly contributing more, except in money, to the life of the university than any other board member. She gently worked to advance the cause of women faculty and students, brought a new social sensibility to the board, particularly on issues affecting blacks, worked directly and effectively with students during a time of troubles, and in a series of interviews and articles offered amazingly perceptive comments on the board and on her own anxiety about her role among all the old men. As she later sheepishly confessed, she asked her husband if she could accept the offer and came fearfully to her first board meeting in hat and gloves. The men accepted her graciously and soon applauded her contribution.[12]

A final critical board change came in 1968, and in part as a deliberate effort to anticipate and disarm rebellious students. At the suggestion of Heard, the board enthusiastically approved a new class of trustees made up of four recent Vanderbilt graduates. Each year, the Alumni Association was to convene a committee of juniors and graduating seniors to recommend three candidates from among the graduating seniors of the undergraduate schools. From these three candidates, the members of the junior and just-graduated senior class were to choose their nominee for a four-year board term. To launch the new scheme, the Alumni Association used this procedure to nominate four youthful board members, with terms from one to four years. Three of the four were women; within two years the voting students also nominated Vanderbilt's first black trustee. These young men and women had limited influence (they rarely served on the major board committees) but freely entered into policy debates and on many issues tried to speak as representatives of student opinion on campus.[13]

The changes in the board made it more pluralistic, although dominant power remained in the hands of businessmen. Increasingly, the now inflated board had to become largely a ratifying body, with actual policy making centered even more than earlier in the Executive Committee. In 1968, not counting the four young alumni members, the board contained nineteen corporate executives, ten bankers or financiers, five lawyers, two governors or ex-governors, two physicians, one publisher, and one film director. On most issues the board reached a consensus and voted unanimously. For the young alumni members, the board proved a very different institution than they had expected. The students had expected long and divisive discussions of basic university policy. Such debates rarely occurred, at least not before the full board. The board members sought a consensus and almost always ratified the policies of a strong chancellor and their own Executive Committee. The board seemed, to the ex-students, a club of gentlemen, of old cronies unified by long association, a similar political outlook, and gracious manners. As one ex-student characterized the board, it wanted to provide Vanderbilt students with an experience that approximated a "country-club-in-training." It was not that dissidents never spoke up on issues or complicated the procedures, but that no real vote ever seemed to take place. The trustees were reluctant to vote until they reached a consensus; negative votes were a confession of failure. The young men and women gained a gracious hearing in the club, were sought out by older board members on social occasions, and slowly entered into the outer fringes of the network of private associations that lay behind matured policies. To an extent, women, blacks, and ex-radical students intimidated the older board members, who now modified their more expressive language and moved toward a somewhat broader view of issues. Young trustees came to appreciate the loyalty of board members to Vanderbilt, their dedication to their one major role of keeping it solvent.

To former student activists, the most disappointing aspect of board decision making was an absence of larger philosophic or moral issues. Unlike students on campus in the 1960s, board members never talked about building a better world or about how Vanderbilt could contribute to such. They worked at the intractable issues of balance sheets, rates of interest, and the means of attracting gifts and grants. In time the youthful members were able to raise some larger moral issues, particularly on investment policies and proxy votes and, once such subjects had been broached, they found board members more sensitive and more concerned than they had at first expected. All in all, the election of ex-students turned out to be a very successful pioneer effort, one which won praise from several other universities.[14]

Heard challenged his faculty to take a larger role in university government. An elaborate Planning Study in 1964 endorsed several new faculty initiatives, especially in establishing and enforcing rules for tenure and promotion. In 1964 a special faculty committee began work on a charter for an enlarged and more independent University Senate. After extensive suggestions from a member of the board, it submitted a new constitution to the board in November, 1966, or what amounted to a limited charter of faculty self-government, much like those in effect at most major universities. The faculty overwhelmingly (95 percent of those voting) endorsed the new scheme in April, 1967. It required at least one regular meeting of a Faculty Assembly each year, with the chancellor or his representative presiding. This turned out to be, except for amendments to the constitution, not a business but more nearly a ceremonial occasion, with the chancellor giving a required State of the University address. More critical, the constitution provided for a more independent University Senate, one chaired by an elected faculty member and not by the chancellor. This was to be a representative, deliberative, legislative body of the faculty, with an original thirty-eight elected members representing proportionately the schools and colleges and joined by the deans of each. Ex officio but nonvoting members included the chancellor, vice-chancellor, provost, the director of JUL, and any other administrators invited by the Senate. All full-time faculty, from assistant professor on up, were eligible for three-year, nonsuccessive terms and were elected by secret ballot by the professorial faculty in each school and college (soon amended to include as voters all full-time instructors). The University Senate, or Faculty Senate after a 1971 name change, worked out a pattern of monthly meetings and elected, a year before they were to occupy the positions, a chair and secretary from among those senators beginning their second year.[15]

The Senate has major responsibilities. It reviews and evaluates all educational policies and programs, advises and consults with administrative officers on all academic issues, consults on all new degree programs or on the establishment of new schools or colleges, and defines policies and procedures relating to matters of conscience or academic freedom. The chancellor retained the right to accept or reject actions recommended to him by the Senate but has to render at least an annual report on the status of pending Senate recommendations. In fact, the chancellor and other administrators have accepted the responsibility for detailed explanations of any vetoed Senate legislation. The two officers and two officers-elect make up an executive committee of the Senate, while third-year senators serve as a special consultative committee, advising the administration on a wide range of issues. The Senate also established several standing committees to carry out its assigned functions and to mature motions for the monthly meetings. A secretary, paid by the university, assists the chair and types and distributes all minutes and reports.[16]

Almost from its establishment in 1966–67, Vanderbilt professors have debated the new Senate's significance or bemoaned its weaknesses. At its beginnings a few professors lamented its lack of power, its largely advisory role, even as a few board members reluctantly approved such an immense delegation of power. Actually, the Senate constitution contained as broad a delegation of powers as those enjoyed by faculty assemblies or senates in universities with a long tradition of effective faculty self-government. The explanation of the Senate's role at Vanderbilt hardly relates to formal mandate, for in fact the Senate has never probed the extent of its constitutional powers. By general consent on campus, the Senate never became a vital institution during the Heard era. That is, faculty members rarely took it very seriously, few professors campaigned for election or even welcomed membership, and those faculty members who exercised greatest influence on campus policies did so through other channels.

At first the Senate had to work hard to establish its identity and role. It actually had to seek out issues to fill its monthly meetings. The Vanderbilt faculty, traditionally as passive as any in the country, had no experience with representative government and, short of a major crisis such as the Lawson case, proved very reluctant to give the time and attention needed for self-government. The near autonomy of the schools and colleges, and the diversity of concerns from one to the other, meant that on vital academic issues, on policies largely controlled by the faculty, the significant governing bodies remained either in the departments or within school and college assemblies and councils.

The only university-wide issues that have aroused any general faculty enthusiasm have largely been such ones as salary, benefits, academic freedom, and rules for appointment and promotion. These issues have dominated the work of the Senate, including its standing committees. The Senate has, at least, focused such faculty concerns and in a mild way served some of the roles of a faculty union or other bargaining agent. A tradition of gentility at Vanderbilt and its very informal and nonpolitical modes of decision making, combined with the elusive, conciliatory, and consensual style of the Heard administration, tended to alleviate tension or antagonism dividing the faculty from the administration, thereby removing the most powerful incentive for intense faculty involvement. Devils were hard to identify. By the late 1970s and early 1980s, with lowered faculty morale and some aggravating tensions, particularly concerning women, the Senate became slightly more active and vital, suggesting a stronger role in the future. Perhaps it takes two decades to establish mature habits of self-government. Only some major new crisis will reveal the real significance of the Faculty Senate.

No period of Vanderbilt history has opened with such a clear benchmark of progress as the most recent one. The huge Planning Study of 1963–64 provided a detailed analysis of every facet of Vanderbilt, plus hopes and dreams for its future up through 1975. Robert T. Lagemann of physics chaired the overall self-study effort; under him were twelve specialized committees of about fifteen members each, covering the scope of the university, its administrative organization, students, campus environment, graduate studies, interdisciplinary relationships, libraries, faculties, research, institutional relations, staff, and even public relations. In addition, planning committees evaluated each school and college and in a more informal way committees functioned in each academic department. The reports make up about two cubic feet of material; the study abstracts take up 263 pages. Overall, the study reflected a hopeful if not sanguine outlook. Most schools, with Nursing the dramatic exception, had experienced recent growth and expected more in the future. Thus, the overall judgment was—we have made progress, we are on the way, but we need this and that to fulfill the "passion for excellence" that inspired the study.[17]

The Planning Study chartered new needs in central administration. The committee recommended four immediate subordinates to the chancellor—a vice-chancellor to oversee alumni relations, development, and athletics; a provost to supervise all academic policies; a treasurer; and a director of medical affairs. To a large extent Heard followed this advice. Rob Roy Purdy continued as vice-chancellor, offered advice in all areas, but gave most attention to alumni, students, and athletic policy. After an extended search, Heard in 1966 appointed a provost, not a new title at Vanderbilt but a much more critical position than in the past. He turned to an energetic psychologist at Peabody, Nicholas Hobbs, the architect of the Kennedy Center for Human Development and then president of the American Psychological Association. As a gesture toward Peabody, Hobbs retained for two years a one-fifth time appointment as director of the center. Hobbs shared Heard's bent for consensual or nondirective management and tried to gain support at Vanderbilt for several educational innovations. In 1965, Don Elliott took the title of vice-chancellor for alumni and development, and in 1966 William W. Force became vice-chancellor for business affairs; these were vice-chancellorships not contemplated in the Planning Study. Robert McGaw surrendered some of his duties in public relations and publishing to become the new secretary of the university. These reassignments and appointments accompanied a more rapid growth in the central administration than envisioned even in 1963. A growing array of governmental regulations and pressures from within the university seemed to require increasing administrative effort. Faculty concern over administrative growth led, as always, to a committee investigation in 1969. By then, administrative growth entailed a growing number of assistant or associate vice-chancellors and deans.[18]

The Planning Study did not push Vanderbilt off into dramatic new directions. A committee on students considered several formulas for enrollment

595

growth but recommended gradual expansion from an undergraduate enrollment of 4,272 in 1963 to 6,960 in 1974. It recommended much higher
admission standards, since Vanderbilt undergraduates scored below those of
most rival schools on SAT scores (among comparable universities, only Tulane
and Southern Methodist University students scored lower). This was primarily a problem for Engineering and Nursing, neither of which rejected
many applicants. But it also reflected too many special admissions to the
College, preeminently athletes and alumni children. Consistently, those
admitted with lower than normal requirements usually either flunked out or
managed barely passing work. In 1963, for example, 42 percent of specially
admitted athletes were dismissed each year for academic failures, a horrible
attrition rate for Vanderbilt.[19]

The committee on the scope of the university did not contemplate early
expansion into new programs or new schools. It rejected as premature or
unneeded any restored school of dentistry (it did support a department of
dentistry in the Medical School), any school of architecture, and recommended cautious progress toward a graduate school of business, or an actual
launching only after $6 to $7 million were in hand. Other committees
pointed out urgent needs in the library (more than a doubling of space and
over $5 million of acquisitions over the next decade), the urgent need of
expanded offerings in music and the arts, and the need for a fine arts center
and new classrooms for several departments. A faculty survey revealed minor
problems of inbreeding (23 percent had their highest degree from Vanderbilt, the majority of those in Medicine) and of provincialism (46 percent had
their bachelor's degree from southern institutions), a high attrition rate in
recent years, and too high a percentage of faculty in the lower ranks, a
problem almost reversed in the next twenty years. The Planning Study helped
speed several changes affecting faculty—a *Faculty Manual,* a new codification
of rules relating to promotion and tenure, the more independent University
Senate, new efforts to improve salaries and fringe benefits, and the establishment of a new rank of distinguished professor. Although the Planning Study
committee endorsed a more diverse faculty, it did not mention any need to
recruit either more women or more blacks, concerns that would surface
within the next decade.[20]

It was not easy in 1964 to evaluate the caliber of graduate students. Until
1963 most departments did not require Graduate Record Examination (GRE)
scores for admission, and without this it was impossible to evaluate or
compare standards in graduate admission. Clearly, in many weak departments these were distressingly low, as suggested by the high percentage of
applicants accepted. The faculty profile also made clear that Vanderbilt had
its share of able, young, research-oriented assistant and associate professors
but that, outside the Medical School, its senior faculty did not yet compare
with those at major graduate centers. Vanderbilt had gained admission to the
American Association of Universities largely because of the distinction

596

gained by its medical scientists, and in 1963 by all rankings remained near the bottom of association institutions. Now, at a time of burgeoning graduate enrollments, Vanderbilt had a chance to move up in the quality as well as the quantity of its graduate programs. The Planning Study noted fifteen possibilities for new Ph.D. programs at Vanderbilt, projected a rapid growth from 585 graduate students in 1962–63 to 1,500 by 1975, and a tripling of Ph.D.s awarded (from 50 to 150). It stressed lower teaching loads for research-oriented faculty (to six hours), the need for twenty new, top-rated professors, for a program of visiting distinguishing professors, and for a stronger university press.[21]

One administrative suggestion may not have helped the Graduate School. From the time of the postwar Ford Foundation grants on, the Graduate School had retained its own endowment; the graduate dean contributed to the salaries of upper level staff and thus had a financial role in the recruitment of able graduate teachers. But these funds applied only to the College, not to graduate departments in Divinity, Engineering, and Medicine. Thus, the planning committee on administration recommended, and the board soon endorsed, a transfer of all Graduate School endowments to the College and the paying of all Arts and Science salaries from a single source. This simplified accounts but took power away from the graduate dean. Along with this shift, the committee recommended a new and prestigious dean of the Arts and Sciences faculties, a dean who could take over certain Graduate School functions, and along with this a new dean of graduate faculties to coordinate all graduate programs. The changes in titles were never implemented, but the roles changed as suggested. Dean Beach, in his final years before retirement, moved upstairs to dean of institutional relations, where he did invaluable work with black colleges and universities. A younger Robert Lagemann moved from the self-study to the graduate deanship in 1965. The committee did not intend that these administrative changes weaken the Graduate School. It stressed the need for a strong graduate council under the dean's direction, and the dean's continued participation in all decisions concerning the appointment of professors, the granting of tenure, allocation of research support, or decisions about increased salary. But, in fact, the effective power of the graduate dean declined sharply after 1965, perhaps in part because he lost control over his $5 million endowment.[22]

All the dreams of expansion in the Planning Study depended on money. Because of inflation, the costs soon soared beyond any envisioned by the committees. The increases in Vanderbilt annual income over the next twenty years seemed staggering—from a then mind-boggling sum of $25.6 million in 1963–64 to $269 million in 1982. But, in the meantime, the value of the dollar dipped to one-third of its 1963 value. Thus, in constant dollars, income grew by a still impressive 360 percent. Total university assets rose from $109 million to $730 million, or about 250 percent in constant dollars. One has to note that many of these new assets balanced large debt liabilities, as for new dorms and the new hospital. Nonetheless, the university raised enormous sums for capital improvements. In the same two decades the endowment grew from approximately $90 million (market value) in 1963 to $167 million in 1982, helping Vanderbilt rank approximately twentieth nationally in size of endowment. Corrected for inflation, this meant a near constant endowment over twenty years, although much higher stock prices rapidly raised its market value in 1983 (to $240,000,000 in mid-1983). Endowment income grew from $2.4 million to over $14 million in 1982 (at the then set rate of 5.5 percent payout; the actual return was higher), or almost a 50 percent increase in constant dollar terms.

These changes meant a continuing shift away from endowment and even tuition as a support for university budgets, a continued dependence on annual gifts and corporate grants, and a major shift toward higher returns from various university services. For example, in 1963 tuition contributed 25 percent of the operating budget, endowment 17 percent, and gift and grants 4 percent. In 1982, out of a total income of $255 million, tuition contributed approximately 17 percent, endowment only 8 percent, and gifts and grants 20 percent, leaving over 50 percent from the sale of services and from patient fees. But excluding $90 million of hospital income, tuition still contributed 26 percent (more than in 1963), endowment 12 percent, and gifts and grants 30 percent. This left about one-third of academic income to derive from nonhospital services, a large proportion of this being patient fees in the new professional practice program of the Medical School.[23]

How did Vanderbilt get all of this needed money? By a steady increase in tuition and student fees, by selling certain services in a competitive market, and by effective appeals for gifts and grants. For income-producing assets (dorms, the hospital), it was able to secure low-interest government loans or utilize tax-free bonds, and thus assess certain capital costs against future students and patients. The critical component of income has always been gifts and those grants which do not pay for services but for academic improvements. Tuition is self-limiting, else Vanderbilt cannot attract students. Self-financing services, whether dorm rents or professional fees, are all tied to the scope and quality of educational programs. Likewise, most research grants are self-generated by the faculty and, in a sense, pay for services rendered and are thus dependent on the academic quality of the faculty. All this means that the financial strength of a private university depends on gifts and grants, whether from individuals, foundations, or, in rare cases, from the federal government (such as a 1979 challenge grant to the College of Arts and Science from the National Endowment for the Humanities).

The Planning Study provided the data needed for a large grant proposal to the Ford Foundation. The board submitted a series of ten-year projections of university growth, updated from the Planning Study, and of needed increases in funding. On the basis of these 1965 projections and the past record of Vanderbilt, the Ford Foundation approved an unrestricted challenge grant of

$11 million in June, 1966, the largest it had ever given to a southern university. On its part, the Vanderbilt board committed itself to raise the $44 million required to match the conditions of the Ford grant, which was to help Vanderbilt attain parity with northern universities through capital improvements, new faculty appointments, and higher faculty salaries.

Trustee Sam F. Fleming headed the new $55-million fund drive. The Ford challenge, a matching $11 million from Harold S. Vanderbilt, $5.5 million from other board members, and early gifts opened the drive with half already achieved. Over the next four years (1966–70) Vanderbilt gained pledges for the other $27 million and, as the funds or irrevocable trusts came in, slowly collected all the matching Ford money. The campaign funds were tentatively committed as follows: $26 million for new buildings, $7 million for faculty recruitment, $3 million for student aid, $4 million for library improvements, $6 million for a new Graduate School of Business, $4 million for Law School endowment, plus other smaller payouts. As usual, it never worked out as planned. Too many of the projected allocations, such as to Law or to a Graduate School of Business, were predicated upon a successful appeal to special donors.

The $55-million campaign helped carry Vanderbilt through the era of greatest growth, the era of campus tensions, and the first tremors of a later runaway inflation. But—foreshadowing future problems—the drive might not have succeeded without the unprecedented generosity of Harold S. Vanderbilt. To add to the over $20 million he had already committed to the university, he now made Vanderbilt a primary beneficiary of his will. Because of age and poor health, Vanderbilt resigned the presidency of the board in 1968; on July 4, 1970, he died. At the time of his death the university expected to receive about $20 million from his estate, perhaps $15 million more at the death of his wife. It realized this and more as the value of securities rose. In its final calculation, the university recorded gifts and bequests of $56,915,448 from Harold S. Vanderbilt and another $6,419,417 from his wife, making him by far the largest individual benefactor of Vanderbilt. His death posed a new challenge. In 1970, for the first time in decades, Vanderbilt had no solicitous patrons and no ready foundations to come to its rescue.[25]

As its great fund drive came to a close, trustees, faculty, and students met in a special retreat in 1970 at Montgomery Bell State Park. They updated the earlier Ford profile and made plans for the next five years, which would mark Vanderbilt's centennial. During these five years the Vanderbilt development office worked hard to cultivate major benefactors and to sustain the recent surge in the annual Living Endowment (up to $2.6 million in 1969, with a national record of 52.7 percent participation). Thus, the board committed $10 million from the Harold S. Vanderbilt estate, on a one-to-one matching basis, to the Living Endowment, and used it all up in only four years. In 1970–71 the Living Endowment collected over $3 million, with a 59.1

percent participation. The Mellon Foundation gave $1 million to enhance intellectual life at Vanderbilt, even as federal grants stabilized or began to fall during the Nixon administration. But as the impetus of the fund drive ran out by the mid-1970s the university once again faced a perilous financial future. This led to early plans, in 1974, for a new centennial campaign and to a new administrative organization that would free Chancellor Heard largely for fund raising.

By 1974 the university faced almost certain deficits. Budget-cutting efforts were under way on campus, causing faculty anxiety. At this point the board met for a special planning session at the Cloisters in Sea Island, Georgia. Heard spent weeks of research and effort preparing a special position paper with a title drawn from the words of Chancellor Garland: "Fulfilling the Conception of a Grand University." At this meeting the board made several momentous decisions—to reorganize the executive administration at Vanderbilt, to free Heard for fund-raising efforts, to develop a new campaign to double the annual income of Vanderbilt over the next ten years, and to set goals for several areas of campus development. The actual planning and launching of a new centennial fund drive took almost two years, but the contributions of board members began at Sea Island. By 1976 the board decided on a five-year effort to raise a staggering $150 million. David K. (Pat) Wilson of Nashville headed the campaign. By the time of the public announcement, over $50 million was already in hand, the amount deemed necessary by the professional fund raisers who assisted in the campaign. As originally projected, the $150 million was to add $60 million for the endowment, $25 million for endowed chairs, $15 million for student aid, $10 million for the library, and $40 million for construction and renovation. Because of restrictions on gifts it never came out according to this formula, and in fact the university raised approximately $180 million by the deadline of June 30, 1981.[26]

This successful campaign scarcely allowed comparison to earlier ones. It involved no single major benefactor such as Harold S. Vanderbilt, few matching funds from foundations. It reached a much broader array of wealthy contributors, and now, more than ever before, much of this wealth was in the South. It is almost impossible to evaluate the success of the drive. Most of the $180 million pledged was not immediate income but took the form of long-term pledges, trust funds, or hard-to-value bequests (approximately $63 million). The board members pledged over $60 million during the years from 1974 to 1981. Conceivably, the university would have received all or most of this even without the campaign, but it better served fund-raising purposes to cluster as many such gifts as possible. Early commitments in the form of special gifts or bequests may have reduced the value of later gifts. Some losses were inevitable during the almost indefinitely extended collection period, but inflationary increases in the value of most property would more than balance the loss. The value of such a campaign lay not only in the commitments garnered between two dates, but in its effect upon habitual giving patterns. A campaign succeeds, gloriously, if it raises the consciousness of alumni and moves them to more generous habits. In any case, from 1977 to 1981 the Vanderbilt University family had never before been so assiduously wooed. During the drive Heard traveled 117,537 miles, or 2,100 each month, visiting sixty cities in twenty-five states. Most impressive of all, by 1981 the Living Endowment reached a formerly undreamed-of figure of $8.2 million, with a new emphasis upon unrestricted gifts. By the end of the drive the university had more than a balanced budget and, for a time, enjoyed the sheer luxury of several targeted efforts at university improvements, including a number of endowed and centennial professorships. In a period of retrenchment on most campuses Vanderbilt dared embrace further growth.[27]

A steady rise in tuition accompanied the various fund drives. In 1962–63 undergraduate tuition reached an even $1,000 ($1,200 in the Medical School). This rose rapidly to $1,460 in 1965–66, to $2,200 by 1971–72, to $3,650 in 1977–78, and then zoomed in each inflationary year, to $3,950 in 1978–79, $4,260 in 1979–80, $5,300 in 1980–81, $6,100 in 1982–83, and $6,800 by 1983–84. By then, the Medical School tuition reached $8,900. Thus, in a twenty-year period, during which the cost of living rose by three times, Vanderbilt undergraduate tuition went up just over six times, or double the rate of inflation. But this rate of tuition increase remained below that of costs and by careful calculation remained close to that of competing private universities. The increases also reflected what the market would bear. At least until 1982–83 the sharp increases did not curtail enrollment, although high tuition rates further lessened Vanderbilt's ability to attract a more socially or economically heterogeneous student body. The decline of attractive student loan opportunities meant that Vanderbilt students more and more came from very affluent households. Various estimates suggested that the income of families of Vanderbilt students were near the top for universities throughout the whole country. By 1983 the high tuition seemed increasingly to threaten either the desired level of enrollment (in Nursing and at Peabody) or to lower the average quality of enrolling students (in the College and Engineering). In 1982–83 even the College suffered a slight enrollment decrease, based on miscalculations of those who would come and not on any shortage of applicants. Threats of enrollment decreases lead either to more intensive and costly recruitment efforts, or to a modest lowering of admission standards. By 1984, with inflation slowing and the number of high school graduates declining each year, Vanderbilt faced a period when it either would have to stabilize its tuition charges or have recourse to very modest and less frequent increases.[28]

One frequent justification of tuition increases is higher instructional costs. Throughout Vanderbilt's history, administrators and the board have used faculty salaries to justify higher tuition. But from 1963 to 1983 faculty salaries rose at only slightly over half the rate of tuition increases. In 1962–63 the average Vanderbilt professor (outside the Medical School) received $10,084 in wages and fringe benefits. By 1981–82, this had increased to $33,200, or only a very slight increase in real wages over two decades. Comparably, Vanderbilt salaries reached their apex in the late 1960s, or before the ravages of inflation and very tight budgets in the mid-1970s. As a matter of great pride, in 1965–66 Vanderbilt was able to raise its faculty, in all but the full professor's rank, to the A level as set by the AAUP; it even came close to the $18,720 average required at the full professor's level.

Shortly thereafter, AAUP changed its rating system to one based, not on a set amount for each rank in all colleges and universities, but to percentile rankings within major categories of universities. Thus Vanderbilt in category I (major Ph.D.-granting universities) competed with the most prestigious universities in the country. It had to struggle to keep total compensation near the average or median of its category (40–60 percent), or a 3 ranking on a 1–5 scale. In 1972–73 it was able to gain a 2 ranking overall (professors at an average of $24,900 rated 2, as did assistant professors at $14,900; associates at $17,700 rated only a 3, but instructors at $12,600 rated 1). By 1977–78 Vanderbilt professors (at an average of $32,400) and associate professors ($23,700) remained in 2, but assistant professors ($17,900) and instructors ($14,800) fell to a 3. By 1979–80, Vanderbilt was able to maintain only an average 3 rating overall. Double-digit inflation ate away at professors' salaries nationwide, and Vanderbilt suffered a bit more than the average in its category. By 1980–81 it barely managed to remain at 40 percent of the average. In 1981–82 its full professors (average compensation at $43,400), barely gained the 60–80 percent bracket (2), while associate professors ($31,300) remained at 3 and assistant professors ($24,200) at an embarrassing 4. By then, Vanderbilt's compensation rates were below those at Texas, Rice, Duke, North Carolina, and Virginia; paralleled those at Emory; barely exceeded those at the University of Kentucky; but remained well above those at Tulane and the University of Tennessee. It still compared well with Ivy League schools in the lower ranks but was not close at the full professorial level (Harvard, Princeton, and Yale all paid full professors an average of over $50,000). Such comparisons can be misleading. Living costs are exceptionally low in Nashville. State taxes are as scandalously low as the level of state services. But, overall, faculty salaries at Vanderbilt lagged in the 1970s, leading to herculean efforts to raise them in 1980–81 and again in 1982–83. Such raises, averaging from 10 to 12 percent each year, in part explain the sharp tuition increases of these same years.[29]

What else did all the new income purchase? First of all, a continued expansion in the campus and in buildings. Since the 1950s, Vanderbilt had been buying up any land offered for sale to the south and west of the campus, as far as Blakemore and across Natchez Trace. Even before Heard took over as chancellor, Vanderbilt had committed itself, tentatively, to cooperate in developing an urban renewal district that included its expansion area and more land to the south and east of Peabody. Vanderbilt had proposals ready by 1963; detailed plans by 1965. By 1967 the early plans ran aground, in part because of smaller than expected federal funding. Thus, the Metro Council (the legislative body of the New Metropolitan Government of Nashville–Davidson County) gave up on immediate development in what has become the Music Row area and instead made application for only the first stage, which meant largely Vanderbilt's proposed expansion area. In 1967 Vanderbilt updated a campus map, first developed in 1965, which indicated its proposed uses of the area. In 1968 the federal government approved Phase I. According to federal regulations, all the money Vanderbilt expended in land purchases benefited Metro, for it received matching federal subsidies for public improvements. Vanderbilt's involvement was, in this sense, a boon to the metropolitan area, and through improved streets and sewer lines a boon to many businesses.

In 1968 Vanderbilt finally contracted with the Nashville Housing Authority to buy up all the renewal land it did not already own, or 41 percent of the land from Garland to Blakemore and west beyond Natchez Trace to 31st Avenue. By 1974 it had expended over $8 million in new purchases, plus the $6 million expended before 1968. By contracting with the Nashville Housing Authority, Vanderbilt could have let the authority do all the actual purchasing, since it had the power of eminent domain. The university, for public relations and humane reasons, chose to continue negotiating with private owners. But the residual power to condemn meant Vanderbilt could purchase at or near market values, a fact that infuriated some private owners. More critical, many older residents of the area did not want to move and had no place to go if they did sell their modest homes. Thus, urban renewal quickly exploded into another, uninvited controversy, one that soon interacted with student protests on campus.[30]

As soon as the Metro Council began hearings on the urban development plan, affected residents organized a United Neighbors Association. Those most incensed developed an array of charges against Vanderbilt involving at least several half-truths. One charge was never borne out by any facts—that Vanderbilt forced people to sell at below market prices. The university had no power to do this and could prove that it usually paid more than appraised values. It is true that, without the residual condemnation rights of the city, holdout property owners might have been able to drive prices for a few lots much above what owners ever received. The other charges, all aired nationally in a damaging and irresponsible October 11, 1971, article in *Newsweek*, proved embarrassing to Vanderbilt simply because they had an element of truth in them. When, in the mid-1950s, Vanderbilt began buying property as far south as Blakemore, and when it became generally known that it planned to extend its campus into these residential areas, then some degree of conflict was inevitable. Two factual issues dominated the controversy—the condition

603

of the neighborhood before Vanderbilt "invaded it," and the subsequent effect of Vanderbilt policies. The development area included too many blocks for any easy description, but by and large it contained small, densely packed homes built near the turn of the century. By 1955 almost everyone at Vanderbilt referred to the area as a whole as declining or decaying, although it was by no means a slum area. No doubt, as charged, Vanderbilt's purchases and its known intentions discouraged rehabilitation efforts by some owners. To that extent Vanderbilt did contribute to neighborhood decay, although it is difficult to see how it could pursue its expansion goals without having such an effect.

The more serious charge against Vanderbilt involved intent—that it bought up homes scattered throughout the area, waited too long to demolish the worst ones, stopped all repairs on better homes, and by thus allowing its properties to deteriorate drove property values lower and helped make the whole district eligible for renewal. This charge made Vanderbilt out as an insensitive slum lord, a wolf feasting on the poor and elderly lambs of the neighborhood, a charge that gained some credence among rebellious Vanderbilt students. The recalcitrant owners filed suits against the Nashville Housing Authority and thus Vanderbilt in 1970. In 1974 they lost before a federal district judge, and in 1975 the U.S. Supreme Court refused to hear their appeal. No one ever proved any conspiracy on Vanderbilt's part and the extant records do not suggest one. At first, Vanderbilt officials may have been insensitive, so committed to campus expansion that they failed to anticipate all the human costs. Also, totally without intent, Vanderbilt may have contributed to increasing decay. It bought up houses for eventual destruction, not for other than temporary residential use. It is hard to see any alternative open to Vanderbilt, given its need for a much larger campus. However Vanderbilt proceeded, it could not buy up, and demolish, all the houses in a twenty-block area without causing many people to suffer.[31]

Vanderbilt officials eventually became very sensitive to the plight of those displaced. It made several concessions to help aggrieved owners and to minimize devastating publicity. As the project began in 1968, Vanderbilt began a relocation program for displaced residents, helping them find alternative houses, or, in a few cases, offering modest rents in houses owned by Vanderbilt. Instead of asking the Nashville Housing Authority to use condemnation proceedings against recalcitrant owners, Vanderbilt kept negotiating in good faith up to and even beyond the 1975 purchase deadline for the project. By 1973, as purchases proceeded, Vanderbilt submitted revised and more modest plans for conversion of the area to its own purposes. This new map had to be approved by the Metro Council and so led to three public hearings in 1973. By now, only 78 of the 501 properties remained unpurchased, but the aggrieved had gained enormous public sympathy. Consequently, the council, in the first of three hearings in July, amended the "Vanderbilt plan" so as to exempt 68 properties from it. Vanderbilt quickly made concessions. It discovered some additional flexibility in the federal regulations and agreed to allow certain families to live, rent free, in their former homes until 1977. Such an amended plan passed in the second hearing in September. By the final hearing in November, Vanderbilt further conceded the right of such special tenants to live on until the actual redevelopment occurred. This amended contract passed. By the end of 1974, under these generous terms, Vanderbilt had purchased all but fifteen properties. But the problems were not over. In 1974, because of new federal laws, the aggrieved parties forced Vanderbilt to prepare an environmental impact statement, which it did, successfully, but not without delay. In 1975 Vanderbilt finally had to turn to the Nashville Housing Authority to secure its first forced purchase. The angry elderly woman who formerly owned the house simply moved away, leaving her household goods as a type of eloquent protest. Vanderbilt stored them. By early 1976 only eight owners still held out. This was down to four in 1977, with the university now offering 10 percent above appraisal. By 1980 only two holdouts remained, but they continued to fight in the courts to keep their property.[32]

Now that it had more than doubled the size of its campus (110 added acres), what would Vanderbilt do with the land? In the heavy growth years of the late 1960s this seemed to pose only one problem—how to plot out all the new buildings. In 1965, when Vanderbilt first submitted its urban development proposals, it contracted with Clarke and Rapuano, Inc., of New York, for yet another campus map, this one encompassing the urban development area. As revised in 1967 it marked the climax of visionary planning in the booming 1960s. The map showed an integrated campus stretching all the way to Blakemore and to 31st Avenue. Except for a narrow commercial strip along 21st, it envisioned Hospital and Medical School expansion all the way to Blakemore and behind the Veteran's Administration Hospital to 24th Avenue. A new Engineering quadrangle was to stretch along the west side of 24th, from Garland to Lewis and Morgan houses, which were to be supplemented by additional married student apartments. The area south of Dudley Field and along Natchez Trace was to become playing fields, the only part of the plan fully implemented. New dorms were to stretch along Blakemore from 24th to Natchez and along 31st to Vanderbilt Place. Nine parking garages dotted this expanded campus, ironically none planned for the site of the garage actually built at the future Medical Center.[33]

In 1970 Richard T. Dober of Cambridge, Massachusetts, made a six-month study of Vanderbilt. He issued a 280-page, almost utopian but largely unused planning study that modified details of the 1967 map and contained an array of planned modifications for the urban renewal district, most subsequently rejected by the university. Among other changes, Dober suggested that some high-rise apartments on Blakemore be opened to displaced families from the renewal areas, and that the university rehabilitate some existing houses in a few of the acquired blocks. Dober scaled down the dorm projections of 1967, even though he still planned for 11,000 students by 1985. He proposed no new dorms along distant 31st Avenue and pulled all proposed dorms back away from Blakemore. In the older campus he rejected earlier plans to demolish Old Science and Central and shifted plans for a planned social science center to the area of the existing Kissam Quadrangle, long a candidate for early demolition. By 1970, and even more clearly by 1975, it was clear that most of the acquired land would not be needed for building purposes in the near future. Yet Vanderbilt rejected Dober's more ambitious plans, repented paying him so much for the study, and went ahead with its planned demolition of all existing houses. Then, in what seemed a vindication of many charges by critics, Vanderbilt slowly moderated its planned dorm expansion and ended up with a large, virtually unused area to the west of Natchez Trace, and more open land or low-demand parking along Blakemore. It has not yet used a third of the contemplated space for its new Medical Center, has never expanded Engineering beyond Olin Hall, and except for two clusters of apartments around Lewis and Morgan, has never built any dorms on the new land. Except for a lease to the Blair School of Music, it never developed the community-use area along Blakemore. In part, this slowed expansion reflected a national pattern of a slower growth in higher education, in part the changes in campus planning occasioned by the unanticipated absorption of Peabody in 1979. Thus, the south part of the campus, in 1984, remained largely an empty campus.[34]

Despite scaled-down plans, Vanderbilt seemed always to be building in the late 1960s and early 1970s. Instead of building parking garages, it steadily

PHOTO BY J. CLARK THOMAS

Aged Dean Sarratt supervises groundbreaking for Sarratt Center

PHOTO BY RICHARD DEASON

Sarratt Center as completed

expanded its surface lots. Instead of building multiple dorms to the south, it opted for two high-rise, fourteen-story complexes (four towers at 24th and West End, or what would be named Carmichael Towers). Planning for the first two towers began in 1964; they opened in 1966. The second two opened in 1970. These towers cost over $8 million, housed 1,200 students, contained some apartment like, almost luxurious suites much valued by students, and were almost entirely funded by low-interest, federally guaranteed loans. These towers, plus a few apartments for married students around Lewis and Morgan, virtually completed dorm expansion at Vanderbilt (it had purchased Oxford House, a twelve-story apartment building on 21st, in 1967), although it had to begin leasing available space at Peabody even before the 1979 merger.

The other construction of most interest to students was what became the Sarratt Center. Heard first asked for a new student center in 1966, and in the subsequent 1967 plans it was located on Garland. By 1970 the university had raised $2.5 million for the center but still had trouble locating it. Construction began in 1973 after architects worked out an ingenious plan that merged it harmoniously with Rand Hall. Athletic expansion, largely funded by football and basketball receipts, included six balconies added to the gym, which expanded its capacity to over 15,000, the McGugin Athletic Center (1969), an indoor tennis facility (1977), playing fields along Natchez, and in

Carmichael Towers and enlarged Memorial Gym

1981 the renovation of Vanderbilt Stadium. One old landmark disappeared with the razing of the Old Gym Annex in 1964.

Administrators and faculty gained a few luxuries. In 1964 Harold S. Vanderbilt gave money to buy a new chancellor's home. The historic but aging Belle Meade mansion on Lynwood Boulevard needed extensive and costly repairs. The board decided to sell it and to buy another large, almost palatial, but aging estate at 211 Deer Park Drive. Since 1964 this large and elegant home, supplemented by a swimming pool and other minor luxuries, has served as the chancellor's residence and a site for frequent receptions for students and faculty. As of 1983, it underwent a $500,000 refurbishing. Back on campus the faculty received, mostly as a gift, a new and luxurious University Club. Former Vice-Chancellor John Stambaugh originally contributed $100,000 for the club and eventually expanded this to $234,000. The Board of Trust contributed $200,000 and then added $100,000 when ambitious plans pushed the cost close to $1 million by completion in 1969. Members are drawn from all Nashville area universities. The new club contained a beautiful dining hall, a bar, several small dining rooms, a well-appointed reception hall, and game and meeting rooms. It has appealed, largely, to university administrators and senior faculty, in part because most junior staff either cannot afford the lofty dues or do not feel comfortable in its country-club atmosphere.

The expansion of academic facilities slowed after 1963, despite ambitious expansion plans tentatively approved by the board. During the $55-million campaign the board contemplated new buildings for Nursing, for social science, for general biology, and for geology, none ever completed. Preliminary planning also began for a new Medical Center, completed only in the early 1980s. What the university achieved was completion of the second phase of Stevenson Center ($7.3 million for facilities for molecular biology, mathematics, and a science library); Olin Hall of Engineering (built with a $4 million gift from the Olin Foundation); and the expansion and renovation of Kirkland Hall (1966); of Furman (a 1967 conversion of the former science building into charming facilities for the humanities); and of the former Mary Henderson Hall (the home of the Nursing School and as of 1971 renamed Godchaux Hall). In 1970 the university added a new section at the front of the hospital, in part from a gift by Joe and Howard Werthan.[35]

The most controversial building—a new social science center to match Stevenson—never got beyond architectural drawings. In December, 1968, the Executive Committee approved the site for a social science complex—the space between Rand, Kirkland, and Calhoun, which meant the razing of Old Science and Old Central. The site caused concern among many, because building on it would not only destroy the open area in the center of the campus, contrary to Edward Stone's older plans, but also threaten the oldest and most majestic trees at Vanderbilt. A student group organized a committee to Save Open Space (SOS). By 1969, the architectural drawings included an eventual six buildings, with four connected towers, or a virtual twin to Stevenson. But it was not to be. The existence of SOS offered one excuse for postponement and restudy; a lack of funds, a much better one. Thus, in the Dober plan of 1970 the social science complex had shifted to near Kissam Quadrangle. By then, the plans were vague, with no architectural renditions. Board members protested the demolition of dorms as young as Kissam and slowly all plans for a social science building faded. The disappointed social scientists had to make do with a later renovation of Garland and Calhoun halls.[36]

The next wave of construction followed the special Sea Island board meeting of 1974 and became part of the justification for the huge centennial campaign. At Sea Island the trustees projected a fine arts building, a new College classroom building, an addition to the Law School and, most ambitious, a new medical education building, a health science laboratory building, and a new hospital. This was to parallel the renovation of Old Science, Mechanical Engineering, Kirkland, Neely, Alumni, Calhoun, Garland, the

609

Engineering lab, and the stadium. In fact, the university had to make several compromises. The fine arts building, a dream of years, never reached fruition before 1979 and then faded after the Peabody merger. But one intended section of such a building, a new theater, became embroiled in controversial plans for a medical education building, the first unit planned for the new Medical Center (along with a self-financing, largely underground parking ramp begun in 1976). Before 1974 all the campus plans had placed this medical building to the north of Garland, which would have required demolition of McTyeire Hall and residence number 7 (the home of the Center for Health Services). Both students and trustees resented the loss of the historic house, and women revered their first and still most distinctive dorm. Thus, in 1974 the board enthusiastically greeted a new plan—to move the medical building to the south of Garland, to demolish the prefab theater building, to spare McTyeire and number 7, and to convert Neely Auditorium into a new university theater.[37]

In 1976 the board first decided to add an auditorium to the medical classroom building, or what was by then Light Hall. Langford Auditorium (1978) did not give the university the needed facilities for major musical events, lectures, or convocations (the gym still had to serve), but a medium-sized facility of 1,200 for Medical School lectures and to replace many functions of the old theater. Neely, when totally converted, turned into an amazingly flexible and intimate theater. The shift of Light Hall across Garland still left room for the new hospital, the largest building project in university history. One effect of the tight clustering of the new Medical Center was to leave a large expansion area to the south of the Medical Center. The university had planned for a new hospital for at least two decades, had begun detailed plans in 1969, but waited until the existing hospital showed operating surpluses and its patient load seemed adequate to finance a new building. This opportune moment came in 1975. Plans were complete by 1977, when the university contracted with Nashville-Davidson County to sell $74,000,000 of tax-free health-educational facility bonds. Fortunately, this came just before interest rates soared; the bonds sold at just over 6 percent. Technically, Vanderbilt now leases the hospital from the city and uses its "rent" payments to retire the bonds. The huge, 514-bed hospital opened in September, 1980.[38]

A few other building projects completed the campus as of 1984. In 1977, as a second-best answer to longtime plans for a new Nursing building, Godchaux Hall went underground. A complex of classrooms connected it to Stevenson Center. In 1978 empty shell space in Stevenson was completed for the geology department. By 1978 the university was committed to an expansion of the Law School (largely for extra library space), to a new building for the Owen Graduate School of Management, and to a badly needed classroom building for the College. Contracts for Law and Owen were let in 1980, but no one could agree on plans for a College building. Rather than following through with a planned demolition, the university designed the new Owen School so that it would wrap around, and interrelate with, the main section of the original Mechanical Engineering Hall. By most opinions, the resulting stark red brick building was the ugliest on campus when viewed from the outside but had some of the loveliest internal vistas.

Until 1982 the board debated the fate of Old Science. Demolition seemed more economical, at least according to most engineering surveys. But students and faculty organized a Save Old Science Committee, held hearings on campus, and helped stir the nostalgic memories of older alumni. In the midst of a continuing debate over the fate of Old Science, Robert Green Benson gave $1 million to the university for the renovation of Old Science (renamed Benson Science Hall in 1983). In 1982 the firm of Street and Street began the renovation of both Old Science and Old Central and completed the work early in 1984. The two refurbished, largely new buildings now house the departments of English and history and have helped relieve some of the pressures in Calhoun on the economics and political science departments. Joined with the Peabody merger and the new hospital, these have all but solved classroom and office problems at Vanderbilt. Only the College still has space problems, most pressingly for psychology, which remains in a deteriorating Wesley Hall. It is hard to envision many major new capital expenditures over the next decade, except for continued renovation (as for Kirkland Hall in 1982–83) and repairs.

This too-brief survey of physical expansion has ignored smaller projects—the costly extensions of utilities, the purchase by Vanderbilt of a new, internal telephone system, several small apartments bought or built for married students, and even the agonizing decisions that lay behind the replacement of the aging Sigma 7 computer in 1976 by a new DEC-10. It also ignores efforts to maintain and improve the grounds, including the labeling of many campus trees, underwritten by donations from Mrs. James Mapheus (Willa) Smith, and in 1982 the employment of a landscaping architect, the development of a new beautification plan, the beginnings of an endowment for campus beautification, and the employment of a full-time horticulturist.

22

The Chancellor, the Kids, and Some Old Men

Soon after Alexander Heard assumed the chancellorship, national attention began to focus upon the new concerns and demands of college students. The free speech movement at Berkeley set off the first shock waves. In 1965 Heard and student deans began planning ways of averting such confrontations and violence at Vanderbilt. For the next five years Vanderbilt officials were able to pick up clues about impending student demands before imitative Vanderbilt students got into the act.

In a speech to the Alumni Board of Directors in June, 1965, and again before the Board of Trust, Heard analyzed the student situation at Vanderbilt. He noted the lack of a partisan political climate comparable to the one at Berkeley, the conservatism of Vanderbilt students, the lack of any tradition of faculty protest, and the nonprovocative environment of Nashville. He also listed, with some pride, the positive features of Vanderbilt—no restrictions on student freedom of expression, the attention devoted by administrators and faculty to undergraduates, the existence of active and meaningful student self-government and free student publications, and several new outlets for student energies, including a new orientation program for freshmen (VUCEPT), a new parents' weekend organized by students, and above all several new, student-administered programs to bring controversial speakers to campus.[1]

In part through Heard's insistence, students had already organized a continuing series of student forums involving outside speakers. More ambitious was a new Impact series that first opened in 1964, originally funded by outside gifts and soon self-supporting. For Impact, students each year chose a critical topic, sought out a wide array of highly visible or controversial speakers, and charged admission to a series of well-publicized speeches and seminars, all introduced by a slick annual publication with articles related to the subject and advertisements for the coming speakers. Heard always considered Impact, in particular, and his emphasis upon the campus as an open forum as major antidotes to student violence. But in 1965 he also pledged several other initiatives to prevent a Berkeley—to try to keep student leaders responsible, to keep close contact with student organizations, to understand and anticipate their demands, to establish and maintain clear procedures for chartering student organizations, and to keep alumni and friends informed of university policies in order to prevent inflammatory counterprotests from outside the campus. Already, on the basis of several vehement letters protesting early Impact speakers, Heard knew that he faced intense outside pressures, and so he spoke to try to gain the understanding of an older generation. In more informal ways he tried constantly to educate the Board of Trust on new campus realities and on the concessions necessary to avoid violent confrontations. In fact, as Vanderbilt entered the new student era, Heard was generally most successful in his dealings with students. He was better able to establish with them an atmosphere of goodwill and trust than he ever was with certain board members and alumni. From his perspective, the greatest threat to Vanderbilt often came not from protesting students but from extremist attacks by outside critics.[2]

Given the traditional political views of the great majority of Vanderbilt students and all the preventive strategies adopted by administrators, why all the fear of student protest? First, as proven on several campuses, a small minority of students could cause major disruptions, which could feed on the conflict of political factions within a campus. The political right as well as the left could become involved. Vanderbilt was a peculiarly vulnerable campus. It had a well-established tradition of student volatility and violence, as earlier revealed by panty raids and continuing skirmishes with Nashville police. Also, the Vanderbilt undergraduates, more so than any other in the South, fit the profile of protesting students in the North and West—almost all came from affluent families, a large proportion majored in the arts and sciences, and very few were status-anxious, lower-income students fighting for middle-class status (the students who proved most immune to protest or violence). One opposing factor, not then obvious, was the almost total lack of second-generation radicals at Vanderbilt—the sons and daughters of Marxists or socialists from the 1930s—a class of students that provided the early leadership for politically motivated protest at Berkeley, Wisconsin, and Columbia.

One final circumstance has to be stressed. To some extent the seriousness of student protest always lay in the eye of the beholder. Politically oriented protest at Vanderbilt, even defiant gestures toward established mores and values, seemed very mild in comparison with those at Berkeley or Wisconsin, perhaps not even worth administrative attention. But they did not seem so mild in an ideologically naive Nashville, in the South, or in the eyes of Vanderbilt's very conventional Board of Trust. Consequently, moderate protest at Vanderbilt triggered as shocked a reaction from outsiders as did the more radical activities of protesting students at other schools in the North. In some circles in Nashville even those students who accepted the ambiguous label "liberal," the very people who became the much hated targets of northern radicals, remained suspect. And anyone who accepted one of the more canonical versions of Marxism, or even desired some form of socialism, was beyond the pale, whereas in the national perspective such students were often only slightly to the left of center. Widely shared southern political perspectives help explain the strong reaction to the mild, almost always civil and nonviolent strategies adopted by Vanderbilt students.

When Heard came to Vanderbilt in 1963, little on campus suggested the ferment to come. Politically, the student body continued to reflect the views of affluent, Republican parents. In October, 1963, the Student Government Association (SGA) finally dropped its membership in a purportedly too "liberal" National Student Association, and by a unanimous vote. Dissenting students, outside the SGA, who saw the action as a symbol of racism and a blow to the new and open Heard regime, were shouted down by the campus majority. Russell Kirk, the advocate of a new conservatism, was the featured campus speaker. The student-faculty publications board reprimanded the *Hustler* for publishing an editorial condemning the *Banner*, which condoned on its front page a vicious anti-Kennedy book. The *Hustler* resorted to low language to make its point—a reference to "journalistic diarrhea" and a suggestion that Stahlman's newspaper would make "bad toilet paper." In the spring of 1964 Vanderbilt students hosted a mock Republican convention. In April they staged a large panty raid, inflicting $1,000 of damage at Peabody. And in an October, 1964, election poll, undergraduates favored Goldwater by 51 to 44 percent over Johnson, a preference fully reversed by both graduate students and faculty. In a follow-up mock election, undergraduates favored Goldwater by 1,349 votes to 1,099 for Johnson. During the year the new Vanderbilt Forum featured a member of the John Birch Society and Strom Thurmond. The well-publicized and well-attended Impact, on "The South in Transition," featured two able journalists—James Kilpatrick and Ralph McGill—who debated the merits of integration, a not very daring interchange to say the least, but even McGill's appearance provoked sharp protests. In 1963–64 a few other intimations of the future ruffled the calm of Vanderbilt. The *Hustler* began probing the limits of its freedom. Nora Chaffin, dean of women and an advocate of older values, noted the instability of "her girls"—more pranks, more sex, more drinking. It seemed to her they were willing to defy all standards and all Vanderbilt rules, to tolerate almost any obscenity in print, to slight all decorum and rules, and to resist established authority. Her lament seemed to be quaint, and even she, with perhaps unjustified optimism, noted some improvements in 1964–65.[3]

The stirring events of 1965 seemed to have more effect on busy Vanderbilt administrators than on students. Impact for 1965 did tentatively broach a bit more controversy. George Wallace, Roy Wilkins, and Robert Wagner all spoke, once again and typically reflecting a broad political spectrum. But Wallace's appearance led to hostile student demonstration that may have inspired the burning of two crosses on campus. The Vanderbilt Forum also dared controversy. It invited Norman Thomas and, much more controversial, Carl Braden, a leading victim and opponent of the House Committee on Un-American Activities. Because Braden had helped integrate a neighborhood in Louisville, had gone to jail on a state sedition charge, and later had returned to prison rather than answer questions from a congressional committee, he was considered quite a radical in much of the South, particularly because of charges that he had earlier belonged to the Communist Party. His appearance at Vanderbilt, although scarcely an issue on campus, led to intemperate newspaper editorials and the first flood of angry letters to Heard, almost all protesting his open-forum policy. Perhaps more threatening to the campus, deans reported a sharp increase in student depression and other mental problems.[4]

In the spring of 1965 the escalating Vietnam war finally became a campus concern, not only for young men who faced the draft but for a very small coterie of campus antiwar activists. A small Vanderbilt delegation attended the first national teach-in on the war at Washington, D.C., in May. There, former Vanderbilt professor D.F. Fleming gave one of the most moving and impassioned speeches against the war. Briefly, the first of two Students for a Democratic Society (SDS) chapters formed at Vanderbilt and helped secure a campus broadcast of the proceedings of the teach-in, all mild initiatives condemned by the Nashville *Banner*. The fledgling SDS did not survive the summer of 1965, but the same students re-formed in the fall as the Student Political Education and Action Committee (SPEAC), which in 1966 issued the first politically radical publication at Vanderbilt, a news sheet called *Prometheus*.

Such antiwar activities gained remarkably little support on campus and triggered a brief but intense reaction. A committee of campus leaders in December, 1965, formed a Students for the Support of the Soldiers in Vietnam and launched a blood donor's drive in their behalf. The football team lent its support, although it turned out that no one really needed the blood after the student association spent $400 collecting it. Over 2,000 students and faculty members signed a petition in support of the boys in Vietnam, not of the war itself, an ambiguity that led some to sign the petition even though they opposed the war. Nonetheless, a general came by helicopter from Fort Campbell to accept the petition in what turned out to be an obviously prowar rally. He assured his audience that the Vanderbilt gesture would help counteract demonstrations on other campuses. Then, in February, 1966, students gathered in Benton Chapel to honor William Settlemire, the first known Vietnam casualty from among former Vanderbilt students. Before his death Settlemire had written a moving letter to fraternity brothers at Vanderbilt. This marked the apex of prowar sentiment at Vanderbilt, but in early 1966 such demonstrations distinguished Vanderbilt students from those beginning to assemble on northern campuses.[5]

Continuing peace on campus in 1966–67 (no panty raids and no snowball fights) belied a major crisis in campus public relations and within the Board of Trust over the 1967 Impact. Finally tensions had increased on campus, but they still fell short of any action either illegal or violent. Students were already rebelling against in loco parentis and petitioning in behalf of women's visitation in men's dorms and a more liberal policy on alcoholic beverages. In a countercultural vein, a few students launched an underground newspaper in the spring of 1967, the *Dirty We'jun*. In February, 1967, a Marxist study group formed and gained recognition, supplementing SPEAC, but neither avowedly leftist organization enlisted more than a handful of students. Counter groups, including a conservative club, also attracted few active supporters. Continuing teach-ins against the war were ill-attended, and few professors seemed involved in active Vietnam protest. In spite of all the efforts by a concerned few, and by the now fashionably rebellious editors of the *Hustler*, the campus remained apolitical. The few rebels, much influenced by well-publicized events on other campuses, protested in vain Vanderbilt's continuing identity as a southern finishing school full of politically immature, career-oriented students, quick to ostracize anyone with long hair or even unfashionable clothes. From the outside, the increasingly alarmed *Banner* did all it could to rouse opposition to radicals on campus.

In such an inhospitable setting, the few politically involved or radically inclined students had only one effective outlet—to try to bring the larger world of political conflict to campus in the form of controversial speakers. As Heard had intended back in 1963, the Forum and Impact series ended up providing what he believed to be a constructive outlet for student frustrations as well as for their healthy, moral idealism. On campus this strategy worked as planned, particularly in 1967, when Impact planned the most absorbing and exciting interlude in recent Vanderbilt history. The students poured their energies into the now very successful Impact and thought they had found a perfect forum for voicing basic dissent—they welcomed notorious and effective speakers from both the right and left and then turned to leading academic speakers to moderate from the center. It is hard to fault their balancing. For example, in 1966 the Forum included not only Thomas Hayden, founder of SDS, but Richard Nixon. The 1966 Impact was unable to attract any famous antiwar activist and thus allowed right wing speakers—Goldwater and Alexander Kerensky—to gain the largest audiences and headlines. Impact by then had become rather famous, gaining national news coverage and imitations on other campuses. Even celebrities often found it a desirable platform.[6]

The 1967 Impact theme, "The Individual in American Society," was broad and elusive enough to allow the students a wide, and desired, leeway in inviting speakers. Impact was not only a forum but a self-sustaining student organization. It needed celebrities and controversy to draw a paying audience. This time, the radicals of the left seemed to overbalance the right, since only the old reliable, Strom Thurmond, really represented a rightist perspective. The most sought-after celebrity was Martin Luther King, Jr., who gave the keynote address. Ironically, unlike a few years earlier, almost no one opposed his appearance, although he seemed a bit tired and gave a lackluster speech. Allen Ginsberg, the old Beatnik and now countercultural guru, added color, stimulated some local opposition, but was not yet as notorious as he would soon become after voicing a series of shocking platform obscenities. Three middle-of-the-road speakers all added balance, but eventually all of the attention centered on Stokely Carmichael. By 1967 Carmichael had the needed notoriety. Chairman of a declining but increasingly violent Student Non-violent Coordinating Committee (SNCC), outspoken advocate of black power, he loved to give inflammatory speeches to blacks and deliberately shocking, even if carefully reasoned, speeches before white audiences. On campus his April 8 speech went smoothly. For a measly honorarium of $200 he drew a packed and profitable audience in the gym, while dire predictions of on-the-scene violence proved groundless. Carmichael's speech, by most accounts, was both literate and informative. Except for an opening series of sneers at the *Banner*, he simply read from an article, "Toward Black Liberation," which he had already published in the *Massachusetts Review*.[7] But because of repercussions in the city and in the Board of Trust, the Carmichael visit led to a Vanderbilt crisis second in gravity only to the Lawson case of 1960. Again, the behind-the-scene complexities defy brief narration.

Much of the deep and embittering controversy preceded Carmichael's speech. Although invited up to six months before the symposium, along with dozens of well-known people (Billy Graham declined an invitation, for example), Carmichael delayed his acceptance until March, 1967. On March 17, as student Impact leaders began publicizing the upcoming program, Heard routinely gave his blessings, complimenting the students for another successful effort in arranging an appealing forum. Only at that point did alumni, or even most Board of Trust members, become aware of the speakers and particularly of Carmichael's planned appearance. The first letters of opposition began to pour into the chancellor's office, and several key board members telephoned or wrote about their concerns. On March 23 Carmichael received national television coverage for incendiary speeches, including references to killing and burning which, out of context, seemed even more outrageous than they were in fact. On March 24 Carmichael came to Nashville for a SNCC meeting. At this time he was trying to build a new SNCC and hoped to find support in Nashville, particularly among its Negro college students.

James Stahlman was among those most horrified at Carmichael's tactics and most distressed at his invitation to appear at Vanderbilt. From the time he heard about it, he blamed Heard and other administrators for not blocking the invitation, for not setting stricter limits on student organizers. Thus, Stahlman reported on the SNCC meeting on March 24 and then on March 25 featured a story on Carmichael's devious plans for Nashville. Carmichael, after being denied formal permission, nonetheless addressed Tennessee A&I students and then spoke, again without an invitation, at Fisk. Stahlman responded to these speeches with a rare front-page editorial: "Hate-Spieling Carmichael Unwelcome In City." He indicted those campuses that invited him, stressed limits on freedom of speech, but did not refer directly to

Chancellor Heard with James G. Stahlman, 1972

Vanderbilt. These editorials helped arouse the concern of Vanderbilt alumni and possibly gave Carmichael the publicity he needed to get a larger audience in Nashville. In any case, Stahlman's obsessive crusade against Carmichael turned his April 8 speech at Vanderbilt into a highly publicized event and also added enormously to racial tensions in the city. It is worth noting that, by this time, Stahlman had enormous contempt for Heard, both for his political views and for his capitulation to "liberals" on campus. He relished any published embarrassments for Heard but balanced this with concern for the welfare of his beloved alma mater. Now an old man, increasingly bitter about the course of recent history, Stahlman entered enthusiastically into the developing controversy.[8]

As events in Nashville moved toward a climax, the Board of Trust became involved. A Nashville member of the board, Sam Fleming, then heading the major $55 million fund drive, for obvious reasons fearful of the impact of the Carmichael issue on gifts, not only expressed his concerns to Heard but to the now aged and infirm board president, Harold S. Vanderbilt. The success of the campaign depended upon H.S. Vanderbilt. Because his plan to leave a large bequest to the university was also still reversible, no one wanted to go against his wishes. Heard returned from a trip off campus to find what had to be a bombshell, a March 31 telegram from Vanderbilt. Contrary to views earlier expressed and after much reflection, Vanderbilt now believed it ill-advised for Carmichael to speak on campus. He suggested that Heard ask the

618

students in Impact to withdraw the invitation. If they refused, then he recommended that at its upcoming April 4 meeting the Executive Committee (he could not attend) take responsibility for withdrawing the invitation. H.S. Vanderbilt seemed unaware of the enormous consequences of this strategy— damaging nationwide publicity, the embarrassing repudiation of Heard's much publicized open-forum principle, and perfect justification for all manner of student and faculty protest on campus. An aged Vanderbilt may have been a bit senile and forgetful; he seemingly acted almost entirely because of Fleming's urging, perhaps even sending a telegram largely worded by Fleming. Heard traveled to Florida to consult with Vanderbilt as soon as possible and was soon able to report that Vanderbilt now believed it unwise to prevent Carmichael's speech. His wife had already helped change his mind. But his switches in position raised suspicions about the degree to which either Fleming or Heard influenced H.S. Vanderbilt's thinking.[9]

Ironically, Stahlman, as vice-chairman of the Executive Committee, had to chair the April 4 meeting. He joined all the other attending trustees, at Heard's urging, in supporting no action in respect to Impact. The terse minutes conceal the agonizing discussion that preceded this nonaction. Stahlman knew of Vanderbilt's telegram as of April 1 but still rejected any intervention by the Executive Committee. One could ascribe this to his wish to see Heard stew in a mess of his own creation, but at the next Board of Trust meeting he explained that he and other trustees felt that they could do nothing at so late a date. The chancellor had approved the invitation. To have rescinded it would have been tantamount to a request for his resignation. The issue was then an administrative matter, not one for the Executive Committee.[10]

Just before Carmichael's appearance, the pressures against the university mounted. Predictably, the local American Legion asked Heard to withdraw the invitation. More seriously, the Tennessee State Senate passed a resolution in which it denounced Carmichael's racist views and deplored his opposition to the Vietnam war; the "whereas" clauses referred to his invitation to speak at Vanderbilt and the Senate sent its resolution to Vanderbilt. Note that it did not include any specific demands on Vanderbilt, but in the context it seemed to place the state in opposition to the open-forum principle. The chairman of Impact argued directly with state senators. Several campus spokesmen, including the new university chaplain, made statements in defense of the open forum. Heard felt no need to issue any statements at all. In the largest volume since the Lawson case, letters flooded the campus, with the vast majority opposing Carmichael's appearance (the files contain over a cubic foot of letters from those opposed). Heard, unlike Branscomb, never argued the issues with critics but instead sent noncommittal cover letters thanking people for their interest and noting how people of goodwill could disagree on such controversies. He typically enclosed a former speech or policy statement, in this case a 1965 address on campus speakers delivered to the

619

Nashville Junior Chamber of Commerce. When he had no such speeches, he worked closely with his staff to develop an appropriate position paper.[11]

Carmichael's eloquent and moderate speech at Impact might have vindicated Heard's good judgment even in the eyes of his opponents, save for what followed. Carmichael left Vanderbilt, briefly visited Fisk, and then motored on to Knoxville for another speech. Some of his associates in SNCC remained in Nashville. The areas around Fisk and A&I were tense, in part because of inflammatory speeches and the organizing work by Carmichael and his colleagues. At about 8:00 P.M., on the same Saturday evening, a proprietor of the University Dinner Club, near Fisk, called the Nashville police to evict a rowdy student. The first police came and the student left voluntarily. But meantime black students began gathering and taunting the police, setting off a chain of events in a fearful city. For two days Nashville riot police had been waiting for an expected incident, one incited by Carmichael. Thus, when alerted of a developing problem, the police came to the Fisk area in large and intimidating numbers, a move that may either have prevented more violence or triggered it. No one could say for sure, and the conflicting arguments in Nashville went on for months. In any case, a dangerous confrontation ensued. Students rallied behind the stone wall of Fisk, threw bricks and stones, overturned automobiles, and set fires. Apparently some students also fired guns. The police, to their credit, fired guns only into the air but used tear gas directly against the students. The whole area became engulfed in sporadic outbursts of violence before most of the students returned to dorms.

The tensions continued on Sunday and broke out in new student-police confrontations at Tennessee A&I. Once again, massive police efforts restored order. These riots represented the first major social disorders in the nation in 1967 and the worst ever in Nashville. On the other hand, they did not compare to the urban violence that struck other cities by 1968. By good luck no one was killed, but out of approximately twenty wounded, three suffered severe wounds from apparently stray bullets. Several stores suffered from window breaking or lootings. The police never doubted that Carmichael planned the riots and that students set up the triggering incident. They arrested and charged Carmichael's associates even when they were not in the area of the violence. Whatever the several necessary conditions for what happened, the city had an easy answer—Stokely Carmichael. And as the *Banner* kept repeating this easy explanation, it seemed that Vanderbilt was equally guilty.[12]

It is impossible to relate Carmichael's Vanderbilt speech to the riots, except insofar as publicity about him increased racial tensions. To the extent that Carmichael instigated the riots, he did so by his inflammatory speeches at Fisk and A&I, not by his almost scholarly analysis at Vanderbilt before a largely white audience. For Carmichael, the Vanderbilt speech was an almost incidental aspect of his organizing work; he would have come to Nashville even without that engagement. But even to "blame" Carmichael for the violence was undoubtedly to oversimplify complex causes. Blacks in the campus areas worked out a very different analysis, one that placed greatest blame on the overreactions of Nashville police.

None of these complications concerned Stahlman. On Monday, April 10, he wrote a new editorial for the front page, right between stories of the riots. Stahlman condemned the university administrators for avoiding their duty to the campus and to the larger community. Their "colossal stupidity" made them a party to all that happened in the city. The Pandora's box of violence was opened by "academic hands and with high official consent." He concluded: "In the final analysis, the ultimate responsibility for what occurred lies at the door of the Chancellor . . .," since he approved the speakers in a public statement. Stahlman sent the editorial to board members. It, along with the riot, became part of the national publicity. Several state newspapers analyzed the possible damage to the campus and to Heard's chancellorship. The *Tennessean*, on April 11, called for reason, not hysteria, and labeled "absurd" charges that the speech at Vanderbilt provoked the violence. *Time* magazine reported that Heard had said he would resign if he did not get a substantial vote of confidence at the upcoming board meeting. Heard strongly denied the statement in the April 28 issue. Yet, the analysis rang true. Heard would have had to resign had the board repudiated his open-forum policy.[13]

The May 5–6 Board of Trust meeting was the most critical for Vanderbilt since 1960. Stahlman wanted a confrontation over the Impact invitation. He wanted Heard to eat crow, to acknowledge that he had erred in not preventing the students from inviting Carmichael and in giving his imprimatur to the final arrangements. Both before and after the board meeting he corresponded constantly with friends on and off the board, or with what amounted to the aging and dying remnant of an older Vanderbilt Board of Trust and now venerable Vanderbilt alumni, men who were by temperament and background unable to comprehend or accept the ferment of the 1960s or the type of open Vanderbilt valued by Heard. Stahlman lost his battle. Heard quickly boxed him into a corner, in part by cementing a tight alliance with Harold S. and William H. Vanderbilt as well as with almost all the newer trustees. Wealth, foundation support, and thus the future of Vanderbilt seemed clearly to require board endorsement of Heard's policies respecting Impact. Heard put it directly to the board—vote confidence in his policies, vote restrictive measures (and thus implicitly invite his resignation), or appoint a committee to investigate the issues. Except for two trustees—Robert Garner and Frank Houston—the whole board deserted Stahlman and gave Heard his desired vote of confidence. Many board members complimented Stahlman for his long, defensive, and passionate speech concerning his role in the whole Impact controversy. Yet, Stahlman emerged from the meeting bitter, unable to understand Heard's political style, certain that his friends on the board had been brainwashed and browbeaten, that they sold out principle on behalf of

Harold Vanderbilt's wealth. Thus, Stahlman was completely pessimistic about Vanderbilt's future but, as he put it, unwilling to gratify Heard by resigning from the board.[14]

The complex sequel to the Carmichael debacle concerned Nashville. It involved conflict among several members of the Nashville elite and among churches and ministers, all of which touched on conflicting racial attitudes. After his board defeat, Stahlman no longer tried to disguise his contempt for Heard—for "that bird," that "cocky liberal" and all his "jack assery." He decided that he would vote gladly for his dismissal, rejoiced in any discomforts that came his way, and exulted briefly in 1967 at word that Heard had an outside offer and might leave Vanderbilt. Actually, Heard entertained several outside offers in the next three years. But through it all Stahlman maintained a dogged independence and integrity. He loved Vanderbilt, although, as many on campus suggested, his was a Vanderbilt that no longer existed and perhaps never had existed. In a sharp letter to *Time* he made clear that he had never asked Heard to withdraw the invitation to Carmichael. He was incensed when a local businessman, Horton Early, joined by two other men with ties to the John Birch Society, formed a Committee for Vanderbilt and in an overtly racist letter asked alienated alumni to express their views to Stahlman, to help him clean house at Vanderbilt, beginning "with Chancellor Heard if necessary," all to prevent "communists, anarchists, one-worlders, and misguided do-gooders" from destroying "our school. . . ." In an editorial, Stahlman dissociated himself from any members of the John Birch Society and from any organized effort to harm Vanderbilt. He preferred to offer his own criticism, to maintain his own independent and incorruptible voice.[15]

The Impact controversy had diverse effects. It even had a mildly intimidating effect on freedom of speech at Vanderbilt. Without repudiating any policies, administrators now more closely monitored student invitations to outside speakers and in a few cases effectively used appeals to good judgment, or to the larger interests of the university, to prevent invitations, a policy followed unsuccessfully in the case of a return engagement by Allen Ginsberg. More critical, though, the publicized reports of Heard's problems with a few vocal members of the board, even his erroneously reported threats to resign, cemented a deeper alliance between students and their chancellor. Not only the few leftists but most students backed the principle of an open forum and with it the freedom of students to manage their own affairs. On campus, Stahlman became the greatest devil since old Bishop Hoss back in 1914. Heard, in seemingly placing his career on the line in support of student interests, became a hero. His enormous prestige among students endured until after 1970 and was a major factor in Vanderbilt's ability to avoid violent confrontations. Heard was also able to isolate Stahlman and his few cronies on the board and build further support for his policies among a clear majority. In 1969, when he received a much publicized offer to head a beleaguered

Martin Luther King, Jr.,
as Impact speaker, 1967

Columbia University, he gained strong endorsements and petitions from students of all political persuasions, from his faculty, and from his Board of Trust. This probably influenced his decision to "complete his assignment" at Vanderbilt. In any case, his growing national prestige, his receipt of a dozen or so offers or feelers from other universities (including the universities of Alabama, Georgia, Texas, and Johns Hopkins) gave him increased leverage with the board, although he still faced one final confrontation in 1969.[16]

The Carmichael affair had one almost comical sequel. The Marxist discussion group and other student organizations had already invited Mike Zagarell to speak on campus. Zagarell was youth director of a weak American Communist Party and purportedly an expert on something called communism. Stahlman rose to the bait and wrote yet more sharp articles. The publicity led to a near circus at Neely, as right and left, campus and town, gathered to uphold their causes. The townspeople brought American flags; the campus radicals, Marxist literature. For the first time, and the only time at Vanderbilt, a crowd effectively but only briefly prevented an audience from hearing a speaker, but in this case the hisses and catcalls came from the right. Fortunately, after Zagarell vainly tried to give what turned out to be a low-keyed and dull speech, the townspeople all marched out singing the "Star-Spangled Banner" even as "We Shall Overcome" rang out from those who remained. The remaining students, at least those in front rows, heard a cliché-ridden speech. Zagarell's incompetence and the overkill of the opponents worked in Heard's favor. He used Zagarell as an example of why it is desirable to let students confront unpopular ideologies directly.[17]

623

Zagarell's speech helped mute the most serious alumni challenge to the open forum. Meeting in June, the venerable class of 1917, the so-called Quinqs, drafted a resolution urging those in authority to follow the example of their beloved "great Chancellor Kirkland and our other following chancellors" and never allow "Communists and self-confessed enemies of our country to address students on the campus as invited guests of our beloved alma mater." Stahlman gladly published their resolution in the June 10 *Banner*. Heard had to take this resolution very seriously. After all, these were the alumni most able to aid Vanderbilt, whose past gifts or bequests, and their age itself, gave special poignancy to their petition. Heard wrote them a long, forty-page letter, a letter matured through an elaborate staff process and through several editions. As completed, it constituted an unusually eloquent and cogent position paper on the open-forum issue, a paper informed by the best libertarian thought from John Stuart Mill on. It began with a long prelude on the five functions of a university and continued with a dissertation on the means of developing independent thought among students. Heard stressed changes in American society since 1917 and carefully explained that the appearance of ideologically diverse speakers on campus no more suggested university approval than the existence of diverse books in the library. He supplemented his argument by examples such as Zagarell, cited similar policies at the greatest American universities, and only then gave a detailed justification for Carmichael's speaking on campus. After all, as at Tennessee A&I, he could speak at the edge of campus any time he wanted, and in any case the university had no way to insulate students from his widely aired views. Finally, should the university censor or restrict opinion on campus it by that policy capitulated to the very repression supported by certain varieties of communists.[18]

After 1967 Impact played less of a role on campus. Vanderbilt students became more directly involved in their own multiple causes. In the 1968 Impact, William Buckley debated Julian Bond, but they did not draw near the audience of Robert Kennedy, who spoke to 12,000 in March at a pre-Impact appearance. In 1969, in what proved a financially disastrous shift in emphasis, Impact began to feature primarily academics or prominent politicians, and with this attendance and revenues plummeted. By 1970, with the second appearance of James Kilpatrick, a sense of déjà vu set in, although William Kunstler and Roy Innis tried to spark some controversy. In 1971 Impact actually lost $8,000, or most of the surpluses accumulated in the glory years. Its stars—from a flamboyant Bella Abzug to a dull George McGovern—failed to excite anyone. Financial problems and less able student organizers led to Impact's temporary death after an even less successful 1972 effort, although students revived an attenuated version of it in 1977.

In the years that Impact flourished and then died, a complex student phenomenon, what came to be called "The Movement," flourished and then after 1970 withered on large university campuses. Vanderbilt students staged at least a pale imitation of "The Movement" in each of its four emphases—radical politics, an often shocking attack on established beliefs and values (a counterculture), strong assertions of student power, and support for the demands of black students.

In comparison with the more publicized campuses, radical politics at Vanderbilt seemed a tame show indeed. But in comparison with Vanderbilt's past, what happened from 1967 to 1970 seemed almost revolutionary. In 1966–67 campus demonstrations against the Vietnam war became violent throughout most of the North and West, with several confrontations between students and police, usually related to anti-ROTC demonstrations or student efforts to prevent campus recruitment by the military services or by Dow or other chemical companies. As always, alert to campus trends elsewhere, Vanderbilt students began their local versions of such protests a year later, in November, 1967. A relatively few protesters carried signs and a coffin across campus to protest Dow recruiters. Larger numbers of counter-demonstrators tore the signs and damaged the coffin but characteristically then offered to pay damages. Earlier, a well-publicized but satirical threat to burn a live dog on campus led to an extremely negative reaction on campus and in Nashville.

It should be noted that, at the time of these first demonstrations, a poll showed 77 percent of Vanderbilt students still favoring a victory in Vietnam (89 percent of fraternity members favored a victory). Two-thirds of the faculty favored some alternative to victory. Nonetheless, a growing body of activists staged a large teach-in on February 19–20, 1968, with William S. Coffin as the keynote speaker. As he had already been indicted for draft counseling, his visit aroused intense local criticism but, as always, Vanderbilt students tried to be fair and invited a well-known prowar priest, Father Daniel Lyons of New York City. To the embarrassment of organizers, some members of the audience heckled the speakers, although no Vanderbilt audience ever prevented anyone from speaking. After the teach-in Vanderbilt students formed a Vietnam action committee, which supported conscientious resistance to the draft while the board of presidents (the new student governing body) asked the administration to provide adequate draft counseling for students. The Vietnam action committee organized a February 23 protest of Dow recruiters in the Stevenson Center, where the campus police arrested two protesters for blocking a doorway. A minor melee occurred, much more of a tussle than a riot, but enough slightly to injure a policeman. This turned out to be the gravest personal injury suffered at Vanderbilt from any politically motivated demonstration (compared with dozens of injuries during panty raids). Even this small fracas seemed to rest upon a misunderstanding; the students had not planned to prevent access.[19]

In 1968 student political attitudes slowly but clearly shifted. For example, the board of presidents voted in February to rejoin the National Student Association, which no longer seemed a radical organization. In April, just as the campus mourned the assassination of Martin Luther King, Jr., students rallied in support of ex-football player Terry Thomas. He left the team because of pressures from the coaching staff. Thomas, a white boy, signed a campus petition in which he said he would not serve in Vietnam. The coaches believed this would reflect badly on the team, as stories in the *Banner* seemed to bear out. He was also pressured to get a haircut and then counseled by Coach Pace after he dated a Negro girl. The finale came when Pace either told him he could not bring his Negro date, or at least discouraged him from bringing her, to a football awards dinner at Hillwood country club. The episode gained national publicity, embarrassed Vanderbilt, and led to an athletic committee investigation.

Equally revealing of a changing student perspective was the response to an unusually representative mock ballot in April, 1968. The most popular candidate was antiwar candidate Eugene McCarthy (609). Joined with strong support for Robert Kennedy (447), the vote placed Vanderbilt students clearly against prowar candidates Nixon (560) and Johnson (52). As to alternatives in Vietnam, the students voted 1,118 for a phased withdrawal, 302 for an immediate withdrawal, and only 290 for an all-out military effort or 244 for an increased military effort. On the bombing of North Vietnam, 937 students favored a temporary suspension and 677 a permanent suspension, to only 492 in favor of intensified bombing and 58 who favored the use of nuclear weapons. Such votes were inconceivable even two years earlier. But that the votes largely reflected attitudes toward Vietnam, and not a major shift in overall political outlook, became clear in a preelection poll in the fall, when Vanderbilt students favored Nixon by 57.19 percent to 23.6 percent for Humphrey and 7.1 percent for Wallace. The 10 percent or so of persuaded radicals liked neither major party candidate and wrote in 41 votes for McCarthy and 38 for the one black candidate, Dick Gregory, the *Hustler's* choice.[20]

In 1968–69 student political action broadened a bit. Students supported the grape boycott in California, while a new but mild sds organized some community work in Nashville, preeminently in the nearby urban renewal district and among residents "mistreated" by Vanderbilt. In the spring, and in support of equalitarian goals, a student refused election to Phi Beta Kappa and denounced its overemphasis on grades, while the officers of odk, the senior honorary, voted to suspend that "elitist" organization (the charter remained and students later revived it). The board of presidents also opposed the Bachelor of Ugliness, Lady of the Bracelet, and Miss Commodore competitions, traditions all suspended in the early 1970s. But Vietnam remained the largest issue. Students around the country called for a Vietnam moratorium in October, 1969, one marked by demonstrations and the suspension of classes. At Vanderbilt the board of presidents, young Democrats, and a coalition of radical organizations backed the moratorium, while the young Republicans, a new young Americans for freedom, and the junior class cabinet officially opposed it. On October 15 about 700 students and faculty participated in various planned and orderly activities. The campus chaplain organized sermons in Benton Chapel. The speak-out on Rand terrace included twelve opponents of the war, two for it. Some students distributed antiwar literature downtown or heard students read out the names of war dead on the terrace (eighty alumni were now among the casualties). Others attended a citywide rally downtown. Some professors canceled classes, others did not. As a follow-up, a Vanderbilt contingent chartered a bus to take part in a larger November march in Washington, D.C. In all these rallies the administration was generally supportive but clearly did everything possible to moderate student demands and to avoid any direct confrontations. Typically, on such issues as class closing, the administration tried, if at all possible, to avoid any central policy at all, leaving the issue up to individual faculty members. Heard was amazingly successful in these nonpolicies, never giving students a clear target.[21]

Finally, in the spring of 1969, the new SDS launched its attack on naval ROTC. What followed seemed, in retrospect, almost comical or surreal, but at the same time it revealed some of the basic characteristics of Vanderbilt students. The SDS first challenged academic credits for ROTC courses and induced the university subsequently to appoint a committee to evaluate all such courses. By then almost any constructive student demand would have led, at the very least, to a new committee. On May 8, 1969, SDS planned a major demonstration at the annual ROTC review. It dutifully followed the rules and registered its plan with the administration, a pattern never violated at Vanderbilt. On the fateful day it managed to rally about thirty radicals and soon encountered a much larger body of opposing demonstrators. The radicals planted crosses and carried antiwar signs. During the parade, a disruptive "grim reaper" interrupted the marching cadets and was escorted from the field by police. This, alone, of the protest activities violated campus rules. But no one unmasked the "reaper." Soon the rumor circulated on campus that he was an alumnus, not a student. Heard, one feels, without any careful checking accepted the report and did nothing, a politically brilliant nonresponse. Meanwhile the SDS students moved on to their main act. They carried a tub of water onto the sidelines, poured detergent into it, and then made ready to wash the American flag of its Vietnam blood. The counter demonstrators surrounded the tub, chanting "Go to hell, SDS," and physically prevented the washing. A personnel dean intervened and converted a possible confrontation into an ongoing and intense argument. After an hour of discussion the two sides reached a compromise settlement. The SDS members were permitted to sprinkle drops of water on the flag, and everyone went back to the dorms at least half happy.[22]

The climax of Vietnam demonstrations came nationally with the American incursion into Cambodia in early May, 1970, which coincided with the shooting by national guardsmen of four students on the Kent State campus.

Cambodia-Vietnam protester, 1970

Massive student protests closed several campuses and led to canceled final exams at others. At Vanderbilt these disturbing events triggered the most politically intense week in Vanderbilt's history. The faculty and administration were more apprehensive than ever before, and seemed intent on keeping the students as busily involved as possible in a whole series of activities. Over 400 students attended a rally at the federal building, others sponsored a forum on campus, staged a memorial for the Kent State students on the Rand terrace before an overflow crowd, and took part in several classroom discussions organized by professors. Toward the end of a busy week, many distributed pamphlets or petitions in the city. A student rally led to a two-hour debate on whether the students should call a strike (really a boycott of classes) and ended up with another typical Vanderbilt compromise—to stage a "work for peace" day instead. Heard noted the intensity and the sincerity of student concerns, emphasized freedom of expression, complimented students on their "orderly events" and their "peaceful and lawful" techniques, or what came close to an endorsement of their opposition to President Nixon. The students maintained a telegraph table at Rand, staged three workshops, and carefully organized for community work. All did not join the protest, although, for the first time at Vanderbilt, a clear majority of the students united in some protest activities. But up to 400 students attended a pro-Nixon rally on campus to hear a pro-Nixon speech by Congressman William Brock. Thomas W. Mar-

628

tin, Jr., wounded in Vietnam and the son of a Vanderbilt chemistry professor, spoke from a wheelchair in support of the war. Civility reigned. All speakers had their say. No one was shouted down. At Vanderbilt, as elsewhere, many students petitioned for relief from final exams, given all the diverting events. The College faculty refused to change the exam schedule but some individual professors made concessions on requirements or in the assignment of final grades.[23]

In the midst of the campus protest Heard announced his acceptance of an invitation to serve as a special advisor to President Nixon. The Danforth Foundation paid his expenses. This occasioned criticism and mild protest by Vanderbilt students, including a nonblocking demonstration in Kirkland Hall. From May 8 to mid-July Heard was in Washington, preparing several reports and briefing papers, and offering advice on campus disturbances. He took with him, as an assistant, the most politically active student at Vanderbilt, student association president-elect John Gaventa, who had just joined

Protest at Kirkland Hall, 1970

other campus student leaders in calling for Nixon's impeachment. Already Nixon had met with university presidents, including Heard, and in part as a result of Heard's work would appoint what became known as the Scranton Commission. For a brief time in the spring of 1970 Americans listed campus unrest as the number one domestic problem. Heard was not coopted by the Nixon administration. His reports were often sharply critical, offending the conservative press and disappointing Nixon staffers. Heard did not help them solve their public relations problems. He tried, rather, to clarify the perspective of students, the concerns of college administrators, and thus placed much of the blame for the "gulf of understanding" on Nixon's policies and on the exaggerated rhetoric of his staff.[24]

In many ways all the concern soon seemed misplaced. By the fall of 1970 student political protests abated almost as suddenly as they began. At Vanderbilt, the *Hustler* lamented that the campus was virtually dead even as student government had become moribund. And, out of the political calm came a series of atavistic panty raids by now bored students. One, in December, 1970, involved water dropping, egg throwing, and breakage at Branscomb Quadrangle, or what the boys called "good, clean fun." One on a Sunday evening in October, 1971, led to a break-in at Cole Hall. But the amazed women not only welcomed the men but pointed out they were welcome to visit any time. In the new era of open dorms, of almost nothing foreclosed or forbidden, the raids turned into empty gestures, so that even sheepish freshmen soon discontinued such pointless efforts. In the new, more indulgent era, Vanderbilt student political attitudes soon returned to the old norms. Briefly, in 1969, a poll revealed more Vanderbilt students who considered themselves "liberal" than "conservative," but even then most chose the label "moderate." In 1973 a national poll revealed that entering Vanderbilt freshmen were unusually "conservative" except on the one issue of women's rights. By 1976 an intensive survey by psychologists Hans Strupp and Suzanne Hadley found Vanderbilt students conventional on most issues—they were career oriented, generally happy with their Vanderbilt education, and quite satisfied to receive expert knowledge from their professors.[25]

Lifestyle changes among Vanderbilt students did not lead to organized protest. But student defiance of parental mores caused more concern on the board and by parents than did campus political activity. Sloppy clothing, long hair, four-letter words, rock concerts, overt homosexual activity, and drug use became symbols of such protest. Student publications became the main exhibit of shocking new mores. Unlike political radicalism, these changes in mores did not end in 1970 or 1971 but in some ways continue to the present. Because of the lag effect at Vanderbilt, the most telling symbols of lifestyle changes peaked not in the late 1960s but in the early 1970s. Despite some overlap, the political radicals and the cultural rebels were quite distinct groups at Vanderbilt. Identifiable radicals remained relatively few, but the

630

Pro-war rally on Rand Terrace (the speaker is Thomas Martin, Jr.)

advocacy of libertarian cultural change, by a daring few, soon affected almost all students. They altered their dress or hair styles, became tolerant of obscenity or drug use, and changed their musical taste. Obviously such widespread, basic change is elusive and thus difficult to chronicle.

Cultural revolt often interacted with issues of student power. For example, some parents suffered agonies enough over new rules allowing alcohol on campus or in dorm rooms and then collapsed into sheer horror at the establishment of coeducational dorms. But neither the consumption of alcohol nor greater convenience in the mating game reflected any great cultural breakthrough. Parents had often indulged both alcohol and sex, and memories of their own campus escapades often lay behind their expressed concerns for sons or daughters. But toleration of psychedelic drugs or of homosexual activity was a quite different story.

The first publicly expressed concern over drug use at Vanderbilt dated back only to 1967 and accompanied new regulations placed in the *Student Hand-*

book. Disciplinary action, or dismissal, were the penalties for the use of narcotics or hallucinogenic agents or the misuse of prescription drugs. This harsh policy proved a losing strategy, almost by necessity arbitrary in effect. One marijuana bust led to four suspensions and to forty assessments of probation, a selective enforcement bitterly resented by students. By 1970 the administration's policy changed radically. It removed all prohibitions of drug use, kept rules against the sale or distribution of drugs, and began drug counseling programs. The extent of drug use, of course, cannot be measured. It seemed much less a problem at Vanderbilt than on most campuses, always clearly less a problem than the excessive use of alcohol. What is clear is the widespread tolerance of at least marijuana by Vanderbilt students. At times, marijuana use was public and open, as at the most ballyhooed rock concert in Vanderbilt's history—the glorious coming of the Grateful Dead on October 21, 1972. Student organizers planned for 15,000 fans, but only about 5,000 gathered on alumni lawn on a chilly day for the almost hypnotic music that continued well into the evening. Students did come from distant campuses, hippy dress was the rule, and the use of marijuana, if not LSD, was commonplace.[26]

Tolerance of homosexual activity, or recognition of organized gay liberation groups on campus, proved an explosive bombshell. In all the ferment of the 1950s and 1960s this was the one issue that seemed to catch Vanderbilt administrators most by surprise, without a developed policy and without ready answers. The issue also provoked intense antagonism on the part of many alumni. On December 9, 1972, the young socialist alliance, a newly chartered student organization, sponsored a campus dance widely advertised as for the benefit of homosexuals in the larger community. The *Banner* rather routinely carried news stories of the dance, publicizing it beyond the campus. In a sense the young socialist alliance carried the ball for an organized Nashville homosexual group, one interested in forming a gay rights organization at Vanderbilt. About 150 people attended the famous Alumni Hall dance, about two-thirds of whom were estimated to be homosexuals. But, as a gesture of respect, several heterosexual students and even faculty members also came, and only later in the evening did many couples of the same sex take to the dance floor. Cameras were forbidden.

The dance elicited a flood of mail, almost 100 percent in opposition to such a lenient policy. Several ministers from local Baptist churches or Churches of Christ protested, and the affair became notorious in Nashville. During the next few months Heard tried to respond to hostile letters, but with an untypical hesitancy and uncertainty. He then launched a staff study of the whole issue. On campus the issue was now in the open and occasioned rather frequent films and discussions, with one ill-attended forum sponsored by the Office of University Ministry. Homosexuals, in general, found a friendly outlet for their views in the *Hustler* and other student publications. In both 1973 and 1974 the *Hustler* featured long, informative series on homosexual-

Grateful Dead concert, 1972

ity. As early as 1974 a small group of Vanderbilt students first attempted to form a gay rights group; the twelve persons who attended the meeting may not have been all gays, for many supported the rights of homosexuals without necessarily being homosexuals. Only in March, 1977, was a small gay rights association able to hold together long enough to get a charter from the community affairs board. By then, several critical court decisions had severely curtailed the ability of Vanderbilt to exclude such organizations, and Heard made much of this in responding to critics. He also noted that the organization's program was educational—to create understanding and acceptance for homosexuals and not to facilitate homosexual activity. This tack seemed to work, although a few alumni continued to protest.[27]

The university never quite formalized a policy toward homosexuals. Unfortunately, Heard's original response to complaints about the dance gave a somewhat misleading history of past policies. The pressures were intense; feelings on this issue ran much deeper even than earlier ones on race. Several alumni actually canceled their pledges, creating concern in both the alumni and development offices. Heard, in an unusually defensive form letter, explained the origins of the dance in the plans of a recognized student organization, and pointed out legal constraints against prohibiting gay organizations on campus. He also noted the complex and controverted medical, ethical, and educational questions involved. But, in a strategy most reminiscent of Branscomb's responses to critics, he seemed to concede a validity to the complaints.

633

He reported on Vanderbilt's policy toward "homosexual practices" on campus, noting that Vanderbilt officials had taken action against any "offender" after someone had lodged a complaint or brought charges. He also noted that the university had "separated" practicing homosexuals. This imputation of guilt, and of uniformly harsh university action, not only got him into trouble with homosexuals but also with many students.[28]

In March, 1974, in conjunction with a *Hustler* series on the subject, Heard qualified his earlier position. He sent to board members an increasingly nuanced position paper. In it he referred, not to the former separation of homosexuals, but to their having "separated themselves" from the university. He also noted that, traditionally, the Vanderbilt response had involved counseling or medical attention, or a much more humane position than the earlier one noted, although one that still implied guilt or at least illness and thus did little to appease some homosexuals. Heard ended up endorsing no set policy but rather a constructive effort in each individual case. He noted ambiguities even in the label, the diversity of behaviors, and therefore the impossibility of any fair, uniform policy. One implication of Heard's statement was that the university would now deal with homosexual activity much as it did with heterosexual—when it involved coercion or was so conducted as to give offense to others, then it was a punishable offense. Since most Vanderbilt students were eighteen and legally adults, he implied but did not say that private consent for sexual behavior of all types was no longer subject to university surveillance or discipline, the policy actually followed by the university. What Heard wanted to avoid was any university policy at all touching upon this highly sensitive issue.[29]

Most continuing problems of "good taste" involved student publications. The Board of Trust preferred to let administrators handle such touchy issues as gay rights but could not at times restrain its distaste for the *Hustler*. Small indiscretions worried the board even before 1967. By then, the *Hustler* carried on a running battle of ridicule and political hyperbole with the *Banner*, and consequently Stahlman frequently led the board in its criticism. The problem came to a head in November, 1968, when the trustees came close to cutting off funds for the *Hustler* (collected as part of student activity fees); Stahlman and William Waller were the most vehement in their complaints. Heard persuaded them to let it be, pointing to an incorporated publications board that protected Vanderbilt from any libel action. Also, a new advisory board included professional journalists and an attorney. Equally important, in the same year *Versus*, at first a news sheet and then a full-fledged weekly newspaper, began as a "conservative" reply to a purportedly "radical" *Hustler*. *Versus* defended ROTC, called the Vietnam moratorium "goof-off-day," unmercifully caricatured the university chaplain, but gave as full attention to black students and black issues as did the *Hustler*. Its editors had short hair, but were, in contemporary terms, more "square" than "reactionary."[30]

In retrospect, the problems that people had with the *Hustler* are hard to identify. Its worst offense, at times, was sloppy reporting. Politically, it never moved far to the left and in the perspective of a Berkeley or a Columbia seemed a rather conservative student publication. It moved furthest politically in 1968–69, when it tried, unsuccessfully, to become a daily, and when the editors used sensationalism to capture student interest and support. One editor flunked his courses and thus lost his job but was succeeded by an equally aggressive and defiant editor who, ironically, had the name of Jeff Davis. The *Hustler* soon gave up on such sensationalism and steadily improved the quality of its reporting. After 1970, because of a series of in-depth features on a variety of issues, it won and deserved a series of awards in national competition. In the early 1970s it was, in many ways, one of the best nonprofessional campus newspapers in the country.

In one area the *Hustler* would never change—its use of four-letter words and its increased frankness in matters sexual. In 1972 it even emulated *Playboy*, featuring a fully nude photograph of Heaven Lee, a local stripper. But *Versus*, the avowedly conservative paper, gained the greatest notoriety and the strongest board reaction for a type of frankness. On September 17 and again on September 27, 1971, *Versus* published advertisements for mail-order condoms. The first began with the headline "Making love is great. Making her pregnant isn't." The company offered thirteen assorted types for $4.00 and for 25 cents extra threw in an illustrated brochure. When complaints poured in from board members, the *Hustler* captured some of the notoriety by a series of news articles about the developing controversy. The *Versus* editor refused to write a letter of explanation to the trustees but dropped the ads when he found out that they were illegal in Nashville. On its part, the *Hustler* carried ads for prewritten term papers and thus gained the righteous condemnation of the honor council.[31]

A concerned board, in its November, 1971, meeting, tried to solve the problem of campus publications. It passed a Stahlman resolution directing the administration to alter the publication board, to include on it outside professionals, and to "formulate guidelines which would permit freedom without license." The new board was not to censor publications but could penalize editors or business managers who violated its own policies. The new Vanderbilt Student Communication, Inc., did recruit an outside journalist. But by 1976 it suffered a long, complex struggle over the role of student editors on the governing committee. At one point the *Hustler* staff threatened to strike, and by now Heard was a designated enemy, since he vetoed a vote for editors on the committee.[32] By then, the most defiant and sophomoric shenanigans were all in the past. In most ways the competition of the two newspapers improved both—each had more zeal, better reporting—but it also invited sensationalism. In 1972–73 *Versus*, although still in newspaper format, turned to literature and the arts. In the fall of 1973 it became a literary magazine, one slanted toward countercultural issues. Much later, in 1979, under an able but rebellious editor, Alexander Heard (no relation to the chancellor), *Versus* pushed publication to its ultimate in a special satirical edition called *Versux*. It carried an explicit, purported poll on student-faculty sex, with very unfair digs at Nursing students (for example, 100 percent of Nursing students engaged in fornication compared to only 5.5 percent of engineers; 100 percent fornicated once a week to 11.2 percent for Arts and Science women; 100 percent knew what fornication meant to 1.2 percent in Engineering). A sign of the changed times was the fact that this edition received a concerted attack not from the administration or the Board of Trust but from campus feminists.[33]

Cultural changes on campus had major impact on fraternities and on student religious life. The role of fraternities declined to the lowest level since their recognition in 1883. By 1969 campus newspapers aired several discussions about their likely demise. The number of freshmen pledging fraternities, once as high as 80 percent, declined to about 50 percent in the early 1970s. A few fraternities could not meet payments on their houses. The more radical students considered fraternities reactionary and irrelevant. For the first time since 1882 independents now began to dominate campus life. In 1969 a joint faculty-student committee studied Vanderbilt fraternities and in its original report recommended an end to the blackball (an individual veto on new members), the delay of rushing until the sophomore year, and a five-week limit on the initiation or training period for new pledges. As always, such recommendations triggered strong responses from the fraternity councils and from alumni. The fraternities and sororities accepted the principle of nondiscriminatory membership by 1972 (meaning that they accepted the eligibility of blacks) but fought for continued control over their own membership. Here conflicted two impulses of the era—concern for blacks and for equalitarianism and the students' demands for autonomy in their private lives. After hearings and reports from concerned groups, the student activities committee recommended to Heard that the chapters be permitted autonomy in regard to membership and that rush be held in the second semester, or the policies that were actually implemented. In the early 1970s Greeks slowly regained much of their lost status, particularly in campus social life, but they were never again to so dominate the campus as they had in the 1950s.[34]

The officially recognized religious organizations at Vanderbilt generally abetted, rather than resisted, the changes wrought by student activists. By 1964 the old, university-supported Student Christian Association had become only a shadow of its former size and role, even as organized religion lost support among an increased number of students. At the beginning of the Heard administration, the board, following years of discussion and some abortive searches, again approved a search for a university chaplain, one who would work independently of the SCA and who would be able to coordinate the work of denominational representatives on campus. Chancellor Branscomb had conceived of the post and modeled it after the university minister at Duke. Before the new office was filled, the "liberal" campus denominations—Methodist, Presbyterian, Disciples, and United Church of Christ—combined in 1964 into a University Center cooperative ministry, with the Methodist and Presbyterian chaplains serving all four groups.

After a difficult search, a faculty committee finally recommended a candidate for chaplain in the fall of 1966, one Beverly A. Asbury, a Georgia native, a Yale Divinity graduate, and a Presbyterian minister who had pastored a church at Wooster College in Ohio. He began his work in January, 1967, with the assigned title of "preacher to the University," a title earlier recommended by Branscomb. By religious labels he was liberal and very ecumenical in outlook. He was skilled in working with students and in addressing their concerns in what became regular Sunday sermons in Benton Chapel (administration of the chapel was transferred from the Divinity School to the chaplain's office). In student language, Asbury was "with it," aware of avant-garde theological developments, often sympathetic to the most faddish student concerns, very deeply involved in large moral and ethical issues. He early came to oppose the war in Vietnam, committed himself to greater equality for blacks and the poor, rationalized most changes in lifestyle and, because of these very emphases, placed less importance upon traditional doctrines, upon confessional differences, and upon traditional and largely private moral standards. Both the political and religious right distrusted him. The early *Versus* almost declared war on Asbury and unmercifully ridiculed him as "an aging Holden Caufield," or as one out not "to convert the world to Christianity" but "Christianity to the world." It joked about his agonizing personal dilemmas, ridiculed his refusal to vote in the presidential election of 1968, and noted in his sermons a predominance of confessional self-references over references to a god. Yet even the *Versus* staff had a hard time hating Asbury and begrudgingly acknowledged his oratorical skills and his goodwill.[35]

To some extent the sca had served as an interfaith association, despite its confessional name. In the fall of 1967 Asbury supported a student decision to change the name of sca to the Vanderbilt Inter-Faith Association (vi-fa), embracing not only Christians but Jews, Moslems, or any other interested religious group on campus, and largely committed to voluntary service. It launched a University Center neighborhood project, helped white families in nearby renewal projects, and formed volunteers in service, an organization under whose auspices Vanderbilt students gave their time to a number of Nashville organizations. Out of this came a later, major prison project. On campus, Asbury helped organize boycotts and fasts, launched open-air speeches on the Rand terrace, and tried to get Vanderbilt students involved in social issues. In 1967 David Stroh became the first associate chaplain and worked most directly with vi-fa. He represented the United Church of Christ. His appointment facilitated what Asbury had planned from the beginning—a Joint Campus Ministry (1967), with all denominational clerics cooperating to serve all students except possibly in the area of worship.

In 1971, even as the university cut funds for the chaplain's office, Asbury became both chaplain and director of religious affairs. This reorganization reflected the elaborate work of a chaplain's advisory committee, chaired by philosopher John Compton. Asbury directed a newly named Office of University Ministry (OUM). At first this broadened office encompassed the work of four campus ministries (Episcopal, Presbyterian, Roman Catholic, and Jewish), but soon the Methodists also joined. The cooperating chaplains, although paid entirely by their own confessions, received office space, university certification, and certain campus privileges. A faculty-student committee on religious affairs supervised the work of OUM. In most respects OUM continued, until a redefinition of mission in 1983, to reflect the original concern of Asbury for a cooperative, even corporate ministry. But by the mid-1970s it represented only about one-half of campus religious life—that of the mainline churches and synagogues, or those with an ecumenical outlook and a primary concern for social action. Major confessions (the Churches of Christ, most Baptists, and smaller evangelical denominations) remained aloof from OUM. By the early 1970s students began encountering more evangelical, born-again Christians on campus, and even some Pentecostal proselytizers (unfairly labeled as "Jesus freaks"). Also quite separate from the OUM were interdenominational evangelical groups, such as the very active Campus Crusade for Christ and the Fellowship of Christian Athletes.[36]

Vanderbilt protesters were most effective in abolishing in loco parentis and in gaining access to campus decision making. In 1965, before the years of activism, the old student senate voted to abolish itself. A new constitution provided for a new board of presidents, not directly elected but made up of actual leaders on campus. For a few years it rallied student opinion on behalf of various versions of student power. It began, in 1967, with demands for a student center, for more courses on current affairs, for a broader leeway in course selection by students, and for more informal contact with professors. Already, students had begun course evaluations of their professors. Within two months the board of presidents first intervened in a tenure case; it asked the university administration to reconsider tenure for a popular German professor who had published nothing at all. This is the one issue on which students never won any concessions. For over a decade they campaigned for student representation on appointment and tenure committees in the College, but the faculty refused to yield any power in this area.

As an alternative to dull or "irrelevant" courses offered by the faculty, the students formed a Free University of Nashville (FUN) in 1969, the first such in the South. It grew out of a report on campus by a Stanford student and was to cover important subjects not taught at Vanderbilt. The courses were, for the most part, informal student-run seminars; the budget of $200 all came from the board of presidents. The provost applauded the effort and thus

638

stripped it of "illegal" connotations. In an early burst of enthusiasm 600 students signed up for 37 different courses, but the enrollment soon dropped off to about 150. Student concerns over academic matters also led to a special committee to study the freshman year, to successful protests against compulsory physical education, and even to a board committee to consider the size of the College (students resented any increase in enrollment). In a famous case in 1968, about fifty students walked out of a Western civilization course because of poor lectures and no allowed cuts.[37]

Out of the same student frustrations over normal academic processes came a special student-faculty inquiry, soon generally referred to as the "what the hell are we here for?" study. In December, 1969, the university devoted a "day of self-reflection" to Vanderbilt's programs, a clever and effective way of directing student criticism into constructive channels. Arts and Science Dean Wendell G. Holladay published a series of articles on the question, as did several faculty members. Out of the studies came influential reports on Vanderbilt and effective challenges to various constituencies. For the first time students raised questions about a conflict of interest on the board (the university owned stock in corporations owned by board members or gave its business to such firms, particularly to Nashville area banks). In October, 1970, a high-powered commission on university government tried to adjudicate the emerging student role. But neither the faculty nor student members could agree and grudgingly ended up with two conflicting reports. John Gaventa, the most involved student leader, fought hardest for major student representation in all areas. What the students gained was major representation on all university committees directly affecting student affairs, including those involved with curricular issues. But in the fall of 1970 the students had difficulty finding enough volunteers for the thirty-five slots now open to them. Just after these victories, John Gaventa helped mature plans for a new student government. In February, 1971, the board of presidents voted to abolish itself. A new constitution for student government transferred most of its powers to a new student affairs board. This joined a potentially powerful faculty and student community affairs board, a joint Greek council, and interhall (a new form of self-government for the dorms). Unfortunately for Gaventa and other dreamers, the more complicated governmental structures soon ran aground on massive student indifference.[38]

What the students won, clearly and decisively, was a right to run their own lives outside the classroom. In the past, the double standard had prevailed—dorm students had to follow stricter rules than ever observed in fraternities, while women came under much tighter rules than men. Access to alcoholic drinks came to symbolize all forms of the double standard. In 1966 both student and faculty groups asked to serve drinks on campus, a privilege heretofore limited to alumni reunions and to such ceremonial occasions as board meetings. By then the faculty had gained a bar in the University Club, and they voted to allow seniors to serve drinks at special functions. The board deferred any decision but in 1967 allowed alcohol in men's dorms. In 1970 the university adopted a new policy for men—almost full dormitory autonomy. Each dorm made its own rules, including those relating to alcohol, consistent with state laws. In effect, this ended university supervision of drinking and paralleled the end of university supervision of drug use.[39]

In 1967, even as the men first asked for alcohol at social events, they asked for extended visiting hours for women in their dorm lounges and for more social events at dorms. This began a series of escalating demands and concessions by the administration. In six years the concessions added up to a near capitulation. As early as 1967 the men won the right to entertain women in the dorm lounges during the weekend, and even in suite living rooms in Carmichael (doors open). After 1970 they practically made all their own rules regarding women visitors, and in the fall of 1970 the university began experiments with the first coeducational dorm (twelve men and twelve women on separated floors of small Landon Hall). In the next three years women moved into several formerly all-male dorms, but either on separate floors or wings or suites.

The liberation movement soon encompassed women. As late as 1965 women lived under tight check-in rules, with a curfew of 11:00 P.M. on weekday nights. But in that year Kensington House, a converted apartment building, became an honor dorm with no check-in requirements. In 1967 McTyeire became an honor dorm for seniors with no restrictions except that girls had to note expected time of return (up to 5:00 A.M.). In 1969 the university abolished all curfews for women over twenty-one and even for sophomores who had parental permission. This included the right to spend a night away from the dorm. The women saw this as the end of a double standard, even as the women in Cole demanded the right to have liquor in their rooms. Beginning in 1970 the shift to mixed dorms gave women the same privileges as men. In effect, Vanderbilt dorms became apartments, leaving to the tenants the same rights as adults in off-campus housing. The shift was widely but not universally acclaimed on campus. But the older generation fought back; for years the chancellor or able, long-suffering Dean of Student Affairs, Sidney Boutwell, received critical letters, but they were soon able to defend the policy on legal grounds. The courts narrowly circumscribed the parental role of universities and the lowering of legal maturity to eighteen made almost all students legally adults. Contrary to all the assumptions, the new dorm rules did not lead to an orgy of campus sex, although visitation rights certainly made sexual intimacy easier than ever before.

In 1979 the *Hustler* carried out a detailed survey of campus social life. Only about one-half of a sample of 550 responded. This survey suggested that women were happier than men, that fraternities contributed to fulfillment on campus, that students suffered a disturbingly high rate of alcoholic consumption (67 percent imbibed once a week or more), but a very low rate of drug use. The response on sexual behavior documented no revolution, although 59.3 percent of males admitted to having had sexual intercourse, three-fourths of these having begun sexual activity before entering Vanderbilt, where they presumably continued it. Those males who came as virgins usually remained so until their senior year. Only 41.1 percent of Vanderbilt coeds had had sexual intercourse, and again most of those either came with sexual experience or began it late in their college career. Given the existing pressures toward sexual achievement, it is hard to believe these respondents concealed sexual activity, and it is equally doubtful that those who were less sexually active responded in larger numbers to the poll.[40]

By the late 1960s escalating demands from black students led to major demonstrations on many campuses. No issue touched as deep a reservoir of guilt or mobilized as many white students. The story at Vanderbilt involved only a small echo of national explosions, and thus led to a very mild administrative and faculty response. It was hard for Vanderbilt students to find any chink in the moral armor of the administration. Heard clearly and even courageously committed Vanderbilt to equal opportunities for blacks and began by appointing an advisory committee on race relations. He early explored closer ties to Fisk and A&I and in 1968 welcomed Fisk and Meharry into an expanded University Center, which opened up new courses for Vanderbilt students, particularly at Fisk. He also worked to increase the number of black students, since only in 1964 did Vanderbilt admit its first eight black undergraduates. Two women moved into Branscomb without incident. Beginning that year Vanderbilt participated in a special scholarship program funded by the Rockefeller Foundation for four southern private universities. This provided $250,000 for up to ten scholarships, which the Vanderbilt board funded after 1970. The Vanderbilt board of presidents joined the administration in the active recruitment of disadvantaged students, who received special treatment in the admissions process. In 1966 a Danforth grant, gained in part through the efforts of Dean Leonard Beach, funded special scholarships for underprivileged graduate students. Heard met periodically with black students, out of which came a Human Relations Council. The council provided a vehicle for blacks to make their concerns known to top administrators.

By 1969–70 Vanderbilt had a miniscule 18 black undergraduates, most with some type of aid. This number increased rapidly to 35 in 1970–71 and to 104 in 1973–74. From 1968 to 1973, 21 of 35 entering blacks in the College remained to graduate, or a higher retention rate than in most universities. Vanderbilt also had the first black athlete in the Southeastern Conference—basketball player Perry Wallace. He was elected both sportsman of the year and Bachelor of Ugliness in 1970. In the same year a black graduate, Walter Murray, became the young alumni trustee, thus integrating the Board of Trust. Murray had helped found an increasingly militant Afro-American Association on campus in 1967 and later worked as the first black recruiter in the admissions office. But these marks of progress coexisted with some lingering problems.[41]

The black presence remained pitifully small. Blacks suffered from loneliness and often seemed angry or unhappy, although not more so than on many northern campuses. With Heard's chancellorship the university became officially pro–civil rights. Vanderbilt students and faculty now engaged freely in demonstrations. The numbers were never large, whether in the local battle to integrate the Campus Grill or in joining the famous march from Selma to Montgomery (eight Vanderbilt professors took part). Despite honest recruitment efforts, the number of black faculty remained miniscule, or only four by 1968, and one of these a nutritionist not actually on campus, another a joint appointee with Fisk. Few blacks were willing to pledge fraternities; few fraternities really wanted blacks. When, in 1968, a black rushed a fraternity, he gained membership and then, along with another, dropped out before graduation. The Inter-Fraternity Council (IFC), in its most responsive stance toward social issues, voted in 1968 to boycott a nearby recreational center that refused to host an integrated fraternity. By 1970, despairing of effective fraternity integration, the IFC began efforts to secure a black fraternity at Vanderbilt and soon succeeded. In some ways Vanderbilt students seemed to go overboard to welcome blacks, but the tensions remained. Perry Wallace, although overwhelmed at all his honors, never felt relaxed at Vanderbilt or felt that he knew many white students. He suffered from heckling at SEC gyms and was unsure of himself on campus.[42]

Blacks at Vanderbilt slowly organized and effectively worked for their own interests. In 1968 the Afro-American Association, which took over house number 5, gained IFC membership. It had thirty-six members. Black students in the Divinity School followed an example on other campuses and pushed a list of demands in November, 1968. They wanted more courses on the black experience, including black churches, and more courses taught by black instructors. Unlike blacks on northern campuses, their demands were reasonable and supported by arguments rather than force. But the pressure for a larger faculty response mounted. Black student protest mobilized thousands of students on some northern campuses and led to a massive destruction of property. Agents from Health, Education and Welfare (HEW) also investigated Vanderbilt along with other southern institutions to test its compliance with civil rights legislation. The HEW staff suggested special recruitment programs and more guidance and academic help for black students. It noted Vanderbilt's lack of compliance in several, essentially minor areas, mostly involving staff. The university filed an affirmative-action plan in April, 1969, but it most clearly failed to meet its announced goals for black faculty. By 1970 it still had only two full-time black professors and none at all in the College or in Engineering.[43]

It was in this embarrassing context that the board of presidents, led by John

Gaventa, passed two resolutions on institutional racism and demanded special recruitment of blacks. The pressures helped inspire the Arts and Science faculty to approve an Afro-American studies program for the fall of 1969–70, while a College committee began a frustrating search for a director. Even as it searched, black enrollment threatened to decline as applications dropped off in 1969. The new Afro-American studies program never amounted to much. Ill conceived, poorly planned, it finally all but expired in 1981. But briefly it led to a sprinkling of black related courses and facilitated the recruitment of the first black professors in the College. In 1971 the College appointed Akbar Muhammad, an Islamic historian and son of the head of the Black Muslims, as chairman of the Afro-American studies program. He became the first of three chairmen, or acting chairmen, as one black scholar after another left Vanderbilt for better paying or more congenial jobs elsewhere.[44]

Even as the university tried to respond to black demands, the Board of Trust almost ran the university aground because of one black student. James Lawson, Jr., reappeared like a frightening ghost out of the past. After his expulsion from Vanderbilt in 1960 he had helped found SNCC, taken part in the freedom rides of 1961, moved to Memphis as a minister, there led the sanitation workers' strike that provided the occasion for King's assassination, and through it all remained a firm advocate of nonviolence. In November, 1968, he asked the Divinity School faculty to nominate him for a new parish minister's fellowship in the school. He wanted to resume formal education. The faculty nominated him. The dean then informed Heard that, if he won the award, he would likely apply to the Divinity School for graduate work in 1969 (he actually did not begin studies until the fall of 1970). This sent shudders down Heard's spine.

The dean who talked with him was Walter Harrelson, elevated to his post by the board in 1967 in the very midst of the Impact controversy. Harrelson's role in the 1960 Lawson affair, plus his theologically liberal position, made him anathema to many old board members, most emphatically to James Stahlman. The nomination of Harrelson astounded an aging Stahlman, who began to lobby for enough board votes to block it. He failed. But the effort led to some careful plotting before the board meeting in May, 1967, and to elaborate efforts by Harold S. Vanderbilt to make sure that no one refought the Lawson case. The planning worked. The board approved Harrelson with only five recorded negative votes, although some of Stahlman's closest friends were unhappy. Branscomb abstained. Stahlman felt betrayed once again and condemned the board for abject cowardice.[45]

In the fall of 1969 Heard sensed that he faced a new fight on this most sensitive of issues, and one which involved former Chancellor Branscomb. He felt he had to take the issue to the Executive Committee for, on reading the record from 1960, he was not sure whether the earlier action allowed Lawson's admission. He believed it did and so informed the Executive

Committee on December 3, 1968. But because he had been unable to consult with Branscomb, he asked to postpone any discussion to the meeting of January 7, 1969.[46]

In preparation for the January meeting, Heard consulted extensively with Branscomb. The problem he faced was that of unraveling the ambiguities in the action of Branscomb in June, 1960. Were the provisions for Lawson to complete his degree without reenrolling a matter of convenience to Lawson (the interpretation of the Divinity School faculty) or an absolute prohibition against his reenrolling? Heard now, for obvious practical reasons, wanted to follow the Divinity School interpretation. Branscomb disagreed and by all odds chose the correct historical position. His statement had meant no reenrollment. He preferred that Lawson go elsewhere. But, as an unwanted alternative, he believed that if Lawson, in writing, now agreed to abide by the rules of the university he was technically admissible provided the Executive Committee approved. But Branscomb's concession posed problems because it entailed a special pledge or oath on the part of Lawson, one he was almost certain to reject. Heard then launched an inquiry into admission rules and on statements required by entering students. These varied from school to school. The administrative staff then worked out a statement that henceforth would require the signature of all new students: "in applying for admission or in accepting admission to Vanderbilt University, I agree to abide by the rules of the University."

Heard made this new rule the crux of an extended memo he prepared for the Executive Committee meeting. In the memo he recounted his meetings with Branscomb, the last of which occurred on the evening of January 6. He concluded the memo to the board with a politically effective statement: "I have shown a copy of this statement to Chancellor Emeritus Branscomb and he has said that it sets forth his own position in the matter." If the Executive Committee also accepted it, he considered Lawson admissible. This turned out to involve another ambiguity. Stahlman and John Sloan, in private talks with Branscomb, gained the clear impression that Branscomb did not endorse Lawson's admission on the basis of such an innocuous general statement, and said so at the January 7 meeting. After the meeting, Heard asked Branscomb to write Stahlman and Sloan to set them right. Branscomb demurred. He told Heard that his words "set forth my position in the matter" referred, not to the full strategy, not to the tenor of the memo as a whole, but only to Heard's several references to what Branscomb had actually said in their consultations. In other words, Heard had correctly quoted him but beyond that Branscomb was still opposed to any routine admission of Lawson.[47]

As far as the record indicates, the action of the January 7 Executive Committee did not turn upon any interpretation of Branscomb's position. Stahlman simply reflected the view of a majority of a committee already dead set against Lawson's return to Vanderbilt. Stahlman believed, correctly, that

Branscomb's reference to a statement meant a special agreement by Lawson "unequivocally" or "without reservation" to abide by the existing rules. Heard tried unsuccessfully to add the phrase "without reservation" to the statement in his memo. But such an addition was beside the point. The Executive Committee clearly wanted to single out Lawson, to force him to go through a special and humiliating ritual. This was, therefore, simply another way of forbidding his entry. Stahlman framed a motion that by-passed all the verbal confusions; he simply moved that the Executive Committee reaffirm the action of 1960 in regard to Lawson. This led to over an hour of intense discussions. The Executive Committee agreed that this motion prevented Lawson's admission and that the university faced unknown and potentially very dangerous repercussions if it refused admission. For Stahlman, these were less threatening than the results of admission, for "if he comes back here, the first Lawson episode will be a pink tea or a garden party. . . ." Heard anticipated disasters ahead—faculty resignations and student demonstrations. He also denied any personal responsibility for the Executive Committee action and said he could not be an agent of the Executive Committee in defending it on campus, a possible hint of his pending resignation. Vice-Chancellor Purdy and Provost Hobbs both attested to the disasters that lay ahead. In a final vote six trustees voted for the Stahlman motion. Dan May opposed it. President William Vaughn and Heard did not vote but both bitterly deplored the action.[48]

For a week it looked as if an unfortunate Vanderbilt was in for a repeat of 1960, perhaps worse. Heard was in a trap. Fortunately, the exact action of the Executive Committee remained confidential, known by only a few people on campus. Had it made the news all hell would have broken loose on campus. As it was, faculty and students only knew that tense negotiations were in process. Heard met with his deans, with the Senate consultative committee, and everyone saw only disaster ahead if the Executive Committee did not reverse its decision. Provost Hobbs submitted to Heard a handwritten letter of resignation as provost, effective at any time Heard was forced to resign.[49]

President Vaughn fully appreciated the enormous risk and called a special meeting of the Executive Committee for Sunday morning, January 12. Neither he nor Heard wanted to take the matter to the large, unwieldy board, where confidentiality could not be preserved and where deep and divisive conflict seemed likely. Heard prepared another memo for the meeting but deferred his presentation until Stahlman read his own careful remarks. For very different reasons the two men agreed on what the Executive Committee had to do. Stahlman stressed that as early as December he wanted to keep the Executive Committee out of any second Lawson case. But if reopened at all, he believed, it was a matter for the whole board. Heard had forced the issue in the Executive Committee and then lost in the showdown. The Executive Committee expressed its honest view in the vote and could not reverse that. But that vote did not mean a contest between the chancellor and the Executive Committee. The Lawson case, now as in 1960, was properly an administrative matter, one which the chancellor should have handled on his own responsibility. Earlier, Heard had disclaimed any responsibility for the Executive Committee action to block Lawson. Now let the Executive Committee disclaim any responsibility for his return. Thus, Stahlman moved that the whole matter be returned to the chancellor for his disposal.

Heard also reviewed the whole case. He noted his surprise at the January 7 action, stressed his campus consultations, and emphasized the deep and lasting damage that threatened the university if it rejected Lawson. Unstated in this were the events of the last seven years—the civil rights legislation, the militancy of black students, the agitated Vanderbilt student body still looking for a compelling moral cause, and a more independent Vanderbilt faculty. Thus, rather than trying to get a reversal of the January 7 vote, Heard also asked the committee to transfer full responsibility to the chancellor to handle the situation as he deemed best. The Stahlman motion passed, without dissent, although Dan May stressed that he did not agree with the rationale offered by Stahlman. In 1970 Lawson reentered the Divinity School, quietly worked on his doctor of ministry degree for most of a year, and even served as an advisor to a new course on the Theology of the Black Experience.[50]

The new Lawson controversy, with all its explosive potential, also symbolized the early end of tension and sharp disagreements on the board, or of tension between students and the board. As so often before, the campus atmosphere changed rapidly. The revived Lawson case marked the last stand of the older men, of Stahlman and his close friends, of all those who graduated from Vanderbilt back in the years before World War I. With their early silence, or death, the old order passed. Stahlman, ever loyal to his Vanderbilt, was stricken by a stroke in a Board of Trust meeting in 1976 and died before the Board ended its sessions. On campus the very student militancy that had so exacerbated generational conflict evaporated within two years. By 1975 the social and political outlook of a majority of the board closely matched that of a majority of Vanderbilt students.

23

Academic Update

Recent changes in academic programs at Vanderbilt are much harder to describe, let alone evaluate, than budgetary or physical growth. Such changes have taken place in each, relatively autonomous school and college. But the College and the Graduate School have to begin such an evaluation, not only because of their large enrollments but because the university's national reputation largely depends upon its strength in the traditional disciplines.

Both the College and the Graduate School enjoyed the enrollment boom of the 1960s. For the College, with its enrollment quotas, this meant a steady upgrading of student abilities, whatever the balancing diversions of campus protests. The Graduate School expanded from 650 students in 1963–64 to 1,171 in 1969–70. The College, with an enrollment of 2,101 in 1963–64, expanded only as the board set new limits. In 1964 it set the quota at 2,600, raised it to 3,100 in 1971, and finally to 3,280 in 1983. Enrollment pressures peaked in about 1966. Beginning in 1970, the SAT scores of entering freshmen, which had risen to a combined score of over 1200, leveled off and then, mirroring the national trend, began to decline (to 1160 in the College by 1975).

A gradual move to equal female admissions helped ease the problem of so many alumni children denied admission to Vanderbilt. All along, the admissions office had given some preference to alumni children as part of an overall admissions category called "other" (weighted at 20 percent), if they came very close to other applicants in their high school grades (50 percent) and SAT scores (30 percent). In 1977 the university compromised a bit more on equal requirements for admission (most compromises had involved athletes or disadvantaged students) by giving special consideration to sons and daughters of alumni with special developmental potential, all to the despair of the *Hustler*.[1]

Despite all the ferment on campus, the College of Arts and Science enjoyed relative stability in the 1960s and 1970s. In 1969, when Emmett B. Fields left to take a dean of faculties position at the University of Houston, physicist Wendell G. Holladay became dean and remained in that office until a major administrative reshuffling in 1976. A relatively young historian, Jacque Voegeli, then replaced him as dean. At the Graduate School, Dean Robert T.

647

Lagemann was followed in 1973 by a very articulate and able sociologist, Ernest Q. Campbell. He remained dean until 1982. In 1984, Russell G. Hamilton, from the University of Minnesota, accepted new, expanded responsibilities as Dean of Graduate Studies and Research.

College administration has remained closely tied to academic departments. Associate and assistant deans move from teaching and research for short-term appointments in the dean's office. The Arts and Science faculty, in regular meetings, and particularly through its elected council, determine academic policies. The most divisive issues in the College have remained those related to tenure or to curriculum requirements. Despite stability and relative harmony, professors in the College have also worried about its relative decline in the university as a whole. As they saw it, a new Graduate School of Management first threatened to divert funds and board attention away from the College. The later merger with Peabody and the Blair School of Music threatened an additional diversion of resources. National trends in higher education, by the end of the 1970s, favored professional training over liberal education. In most College departments, jobs became scarce and placement of even exceptional graduate students grew more difficult. Overall graduate enrollment in the humanities and social sciences declined. As urgent fund drives, or loans and grants by the board, increased the funding of other schools, the College depended more and more on tuition. Relative to Engineering and Law, its share of endowment income decreased by almost 23 percent between 1969–70 and 1976–77.[2]

In just over a decade the College faculty twice debated and approved new distribution requirements for undergraduates. The first reflected a response to intense student pressures for greater flexibility; the second, a reversion to detailed requirements and basic skills. The student power movement on campus led to several concessions, including the formation of two student faculty committees, one on the freshman year, a second on teaching and learning at Vanderbilt. Out of these committees came more honors work, more independent studies, better advising, and several strategies to increase student-faculty contact. One departmental faculty—philosophy—adopted McGill Dorm and conducted informal sessions with its students. The one area of agreement between protesting students and old-fashioned board members was a mutual distrust of too much research and publishing, and great enthusiasm for what they defined as superior teaching. Early in the Heard era, pressures from both groups led to the establishment of two faculty awards for excellence in teaching.

The most focused curriculum demands came from the committee on teaching and learning in 1969, but similar concerns were aired in special campus-wide seminars and even an auditorium session presided over by Heard. From this ferment came student demands for "relevance" in requirements. In March, 1970, the Arts and Science faculty approved new and more flexible requirements that remained in effect until 1981. Students had to take

648

work in English plus six of seven designated fields, meaning that an individual could escape one tough area, such as mathematics, the physical sciences, or languages. The requirement allowed optional courses in American or Far Eastern history as well as the traditional and often resented course in Western civilization. The concessions only whetted the appetites of students for more change and for a greater role in effecting such changes. They battled successfully for observers in Arts and Science faculty meetings and gained membership on student-related College committees.[3]

Along with flexible requirements came many new educational programs. In 1971, when Vanderbilt joined Peabody in a new calendar, with the first semester ending before Christmas, it tried without much success a 4-1-4 plan with an intersession in early January. In 1974, as a partial substitute, it introduced a three-week term in May, preceding the regular summer school. The earlier Vanderbilt in France program expanded to Spain (1965), to Germany (1970), and to England (1972). Nothing added so much to the intellectual life of the College as new Harold Sterling Vanderbilt honor scholarships, first approved by the board in 1970 and later expanded. This highly competitive scholarship covers most student expenses for four years. By 1983 the College awarded nine of these scholarships each year, attracting to the campus some of the brightest students in the country. Many able students who lost in the competition also ended up coming to Vanderbilt. To existing seminars for juniors and seniors, the College added some well-received freshman-level seminars in 1975, guaranteeing to every beginning student an opportunity to take one low-enrollment course. New interdisciplinary programs and offerings (East Asian, Afro-American, and women's studies) joined new or expanded departments (molecular biology, and religious studies), and the conversion of McTyeire Hall into a language house. In 1975 the College approved an artist-in-residence rank and used it to bring distinguished people to campus for one or two semesters. The related expansion of the fine arts department offered Vanderbilt students, by the late 1970s, studio work in several plastic arts, while cooperative arrangements with the Blair School allowed each College student up to six hours of credit for instruction on musical instruments. The merger with Peabody also strengthened Vanderbilt's resources in the arts (an excellent music library and an art museum).

In the completely changed atmosphere of 1980 the College faculty began debate on an imaginative but complex new distribution plan. In it, Vanderbilt joined a national trend away from an academic smorgasbord and toward tougher and more extensive course requirements. But, since the College had relaxed its requirements only slightly in the late 1960s, a faculty committee wanted to do much more than merely restrict student options. It tried to work out an idealistic, almost utopian new Program in Liberal Education. The original committee proposed basic skill requirements in foreign languages, mathematics, and writing; complex overlapping distribution requirements based on familiarity with a variety of disciplines and cultural traditions; and a final integrative seminar for all seniors. In a long and often bitterly contested debate, the College faculty eliminated the senior seminars as impractical and hard to staff and, out of the normal adjustments of often myopic self-interest in the various departments, compromised one committee intention—to keep the number of eligible courses small enough to insure a roughly common experience for all College undergraduates.

By the plan as finally approved, entering students had to demonstrate a defined level of skill through tests or, short of that, take specified courses in mathematics, writing, and foreign languages. The required scores meant that even though many Vanderbilt freshmen could opt out of freshman composition, only those who scored above 700 out of a possible 800 on a tough achievement test could by-pass six hours of required writing courses offered in various departments. The required competence in math meant that few students without strong high school mathematics preparation could avoid a year-long sequence at Vanderbilt. Qualifying scores in some of the languages were lower, meaning that students with two years of excellent high school language instruction could meet Vanderbilt requirements. Beyond these skills, students had to take nine hours from a limited list of courses in the humanities, eleven hours in the natural sciences, six hours in the social sciences, six hours in American studies, and from three to six hours from a complicated series of options, including advanced language work, in international studies, with a history requirement blended into the last two categories. The new plan, despite its complexity, seemed to work well despite sharp attacks from the *Hustler*. As campus wags suggested, any entering freshman who could decipher all the options, particularly in international studies, was almost sure to graduate four years later with honors.[4]

Most College departments offer graduate work. Graduate students serve as graders, as teaching assistants, or as research assistants. Most senior professors in the College teach both graduate and undergraduate courses. Thus, the national reputation of the College depends primarily on the strength of its graduate-level faculty and the quality of its M.A. and Ph.D. graduates, those who usually end up teaching at other colleges and universities. To a limited extent, the growth in graduate enrollment in the 1960s accompanied gradual improvements in the quality of academic departments. Yet, most rankings of graduate programs proved disappointing to Vanderbilt administrators.

Faculty development is a difficult and painfully slow process. Whether fairly or not, the prestige of departments depends largely upon senior staff, those with significant research and publications, those with an active involvement in national professional societies, and those who have trained a large number of graduate students. Since 1963 Vanderbilt has tried to upgrade its faculty, not only by making excellent beginning appointments and by making more rigorous the requirements of tenure, but by making a few costly appointments at the top. Out of the Planning Study of 1964 came the new rank of distinguished professor or, in a few cases when people have interests that cut across disciplines, university professor. Appointment to these ranks helped bolster a few departments in the College, although in no sense did Vanderbilt opt for a "star" system, for purchased and immediate prestige through a few highly paid celebrities.

One handicap continued—a lack of endowed chairs. This prompted the successful effort in the centennial campaign to secure eventual commitments, at the university level, for eighteen fully endowed chairs of $1 million each, and eleven centennial professorships at $250,000 each. Such key appointments and the retention and promotion of able young professors should enable a few College departments to attain or approach a critical mass of excellence. That is, in a few departments the expectation levels, the implicit demands upon junior staff, will become intensely professional and rigorous, both in research and in teaching (the two are complementary, at least as to the substance of what is taught, not necessarily for argumentation skills or even the time given over to students).

Since 1963 most strong departments at Vanderbilt have remained strong. A few weak departments have improved. To the embarrassment of the College, the strongest departments in the sciences have remained in the Medical School. Consistently, and in all national rankings, pharmacology has scored highest and has been the only Vanderbilt department to rank in the first ten nationally. The biological sciences in the Medical School (anatomy, physiology, biochemistry, and microbiology) have consistently outranked general biology in the College, and shared appointments with the Medical School have in part accounted for the strength of molecular biology in the College. Thus, the Vanderbilt Graduate School maintains some strong degree programs in the biological sciences, but in the College the biological sciences remain weakest among four conventional divisions (physical sciences, biological sciences, humanities, social sciences).

When Heard came to Vanderbilt, he fell heir to an intense struggle in the then single biology department. He solved the problem by splitting the department into general and molecular biology. Oscar Touster moved over part-time from the Medical School to head a tiny molecular biology department, but his eminence immediately established a qualitative advantage for this subcellular offspring. General biology, primarily botany and zoology, floundered for years and has never quite recovered. In the early 1970s the department spent four frustrating years looking for a new chairman, as older and younger staff battled for advantage. By then, graduate students complained of low academic standards. The department gave up on an extended outside search and promoted one of its own professors as chair (usually a confession of failure) and began a rebuilding effort. But as recently as 1983, in an evaluation of graduate programs published by National Academic Press, Vanderbilt faculty in both botany and zoology ranked at the very bottom of Ph.D.-granting institutions. On a scale that starts from 50 as the average rating, these programs scored a miserable 35 (botany) and 33 (zoology) on faculty quality, or very close to the lowest ratings in the whole poll. On the other hand, molecular biology, though small, scored a near-average 48 on faculty strength and an above-average 52 on prestige or familiarity.[5]

Since World War II the physical sciences and mathematics have challenged the social sciences for academic leadership at Vanderbilt. They have come close but never quite caught up. The two strong departments remain physics and chemistry, with mathematics weak but gaining in recent years, and geology very small and without a Ph.D. program. In a 1964 American Council on Education survey (the Cartter Report) of graduate schools, the chemistry faculty joined those in psychology, English, and history as "adequate plus," below "distinguished," "strong," and "good" (only the pharmacology faculty ranked as "strong," but that in economics, political science, physiology, and biochemistry ranked as "good"). In a 1969 follow-up, both physics and chemistry moved into the "good" category, along with five other departments. By 1982 the chemistry faculty ranked in the middle of departments nationally, with physics just a notch below average. The math faculty, by 1982, scored a fair 44, or not too far below the average of 596 doctoral programs. These results, for whatever they are worth, well reflected the prestige of the two relatively small, research-oriented departments of chemistry and physics, each with two or three very distinguished senior scientists, many able young researchers, but neither with the breadth of specialities nor the long tradition enjoyed by universities having much larger graduate programs.[6]

The social sciences and history have remained the strongest departments in the College, a position of strength gained in the World War II period. In the 1950s, economics briefly took the lead, in eminence of staff and diversity of programs. It has remained a strong department but has declined, relatively, and today ranks close to psychology, political science, history, and even a late-blooming department of sociology and anthropology. The social science departments are remarkable, not for national eminence, but in each case for three to six nationally prominent scholars and for solid strength in the middle ranks. It is notable that in the 1964 survey, the economics and political science faculty made the good category and that history, psychology, and sociology all joined them by 1969. The most recent data supports such modest compliments. In the 1982–83 scales the faculty in the social sciences at Vanderbilt consistently ranked just above the national average of 50—economics (51), history (55), political science (52), psychology (56), and sociology (53). Comparatively, Duke, North Carolina, and Virginia social science departments outranked those at Vanderbilt, but Vanderbilt's ranked above those at Emory and Tulane. Note that such ratings are not very reliable, for to a large extent they reflect the overall reputation of a university (Harvard faculties rarely score low), and often are out of date, reflecting few very recent changes. But such rankings do establish, with some accuracy, the perception

Provost Nicholas Hobbs

of Vanderbilt Ph.D. programs held throughout the country. Since, as a group, the social sciences outrank departments in the other divisions, the rankings show that Vanderbilt has not yet made good on its bid for national preeminence. Note that in each of the social science departments a few scholars have gained national recognition. In political science, Avery Leiserson has served as president of the American Political Science Association, an honor comparable to that of an earlier George Stocking in economics. Hans Strupp in psychology, Ernest Campbell in sociology, William C. Harvard in political science, Charles Delzell and Dewey Grantham in history, and several others have earned such honors at a regional or a specialty level.[7]

In the humanities Vanderbilt has made its most dramatic recent efforts at improvement, and with some noted successes. Two departments—fine arts and classics—have built from almost nothing in the 1950s into small but

*Dean Igor Ansoff of the
Graduate School of Management*

energetic programs, although not strong enough as yet for major graduate work. Vanderbilt has no Ph.D. program in linguistics. But its language departments are much stronger than two decades ago, with the one lamentable exception of Slavic languages. In 1964 and 1969 surveys of graduate programs, no Vanderbilt language department made the third or good category. By the 1982–83 survey, French and Spanish ranked near the national average. French has enjoyed one special distinction. In 1968 William T. Bandy moved at retirement age from the University of Wisconsin to Vanderbilt as distinguished professor of French. He brought along with him his unexcelled Baudelaire collection, the largest in the world. It is now housed in Special Collections at Vanderbilt University Library. Replacing Bandy, who is now emeritus, was Claude Pichois, a Distinguished Professor of French and one of the world's leading Baudelaire scholars.

Philosophy has become one of Vanderbilt's most dynamic departments. It has received numerous rewards for excellence in both graduate and undergraduate teaching. It has never ranked as well as it deserves on national surveys, in part because it has not had one or two "stars" and in part because it has not pursued the more fashionable specialities but has sought to maintain a diversity of viewpoints. In 1982 the department was able to fill a newly endowed chair by the appointment of Alasdair MacIntyre, an eminent and lively expert on moral and political philosophy.[9]

English has remained the largest humanities department, the one with the greatest history and tradition. But the department almost steadily declined from the 1930s to the early 1960s and has only recently built back to at least a shadow of its former glories. With the retirement of Donald Davidson in 1964 and the death of Randall Stewart in 1965, the last of the Fugitive generation was gone. In 1965 the department lured as chair a young associate professor from Princeton, Russell Fraser, who came to try to rebuild a lagging program and who, with more courage than tact, dared challenge what he viewed as a reactionary old guard. He left for the University of Michigan after two unhappy years of struggling against the grain in the department. Eventually, all his youthful appointees voluntarily left Vanderbilt or failed to get tenure. Thomas Daniel Young, in many respects a latter-day successor of the Fugitives and Agrarians, took over as chair and began a second rebuilding effort. The department gained two endowed chairs (for a time the only two in the College) and was able to make a few outstanding appointments by the end of the 1970s, the most eminent being that of Donald A. Davie, an English-born poet and critic who moved from Stanford to Vanderbilt as Mellon Professor. Thus, the English department ranked with the stronger social science departments by the 1982–83 surveys, or slightly above the perceived national average.[10]

National rankings of graduate departments often conceal as much as they reveal. The focus upon graduate programs tends to slight achievements in undergraduate teaching. In the College, for example, even the most eminent professors devote the largest share of their teaching to undergraduate courses. More critical, national surveys, tied by necessity to acquired reputations, never take full account of present realities. Beginning by 1979, when its annual budget deficits finally gave way to surpluses, the College was able to

Dean Howard Hartman of the Engineering School

Nobelist Earl Sutherland

embark on the largest faculty development effort in its history. Aided by the early returns from the centennial campaign, by 1985 it had recruited approximately twenty senior professors, about half of these as distinguished professors or occupants of endowed chairs. This does not include half again as many searches underway in 1985, or new positions already approved by the dean. Such key appointments joined with the attainment of distinction by several professors already at Vanderbilt, and with very tough standards in both the recruitment of junior staff and in the awarding of tenure.

The successful recruiting and retention of an able faculty depends upon research support, in the form of funds, released time, research-oriented institutes, library and computing resources, and publication outlets. Out of the Planning Study came an additional $100,000 a year for the Vanderbilt Research Council. Other gifts and grants steadily supplemented the council's work, enabling a majority of faculty applicants to win limited grants for special projects or for summer salaries. Vanderbilt has never adopted a formal sabbatical policy, but in some college departments, professors with a proven research record have gained an implicit right to a one-semester research leave every fourth year (or one-half of a year's salary plus all fringe benefits for a year), paid through adjustment of teaching assignments. The office of sponsored research keeps the faculty apprised of grant possibilities and helps process grant applications. Yet, outside the medical specialities, most studies suggest that the Vanderbilt faculty has not been as successful in capturing grants as those at major, northern graduate centers. To cope with the problems that arise when many professors remain for years without any direct cost to the university, often doing little or no teaching, a 1968 Committee on Faculty Responsibilities drafted strict rules governing outside consultations by faculty members, rules that clarified conflicts of interest and set up formulas for allocating outside income between the faculty and the university. These rules joined earlier tough rules relating to the patent rights of faculty members.

The library has been a perennial problem. Out of the $55 million campaign came major commitments to the library, including $1 million for back purchases, plus major additions to annual purchases. The Planning Study committee on the library set a goal of doubled book budgets by 1975 and stressed as an absolute imperative a near doubling of library space. By then, the JUL general library was almost filled to capacity. The study also led to changes in the Trust Indenture with Peabody, giving to Vanderbilt, in case of termination, a claim on all its subsequent disproportionate contributions to the joint collections. The first critical response to the study was a new, aesthetically disastrous addition to JUL, the $2.1 million H. Fort Flowers (he gave $250,000) graduate wing, which added shelf space for 350,000 volumes and furnished an area for special collections, library offices, and faculty studies. The largest contribution for the building came from the U.S. Office of Education ($700,000). In 1967 JUL was forty-first in holdings in the country but losing ground. In the same year JUL's second director, David Kaser, moved to Cornell, to be succeeded in 1969 by Frank Grisham, who moved up from the Divinity Library. In 1968 the library provided space for a new, externally funded project—a video archive of television news broadcasts. This archive provoked a much publicized but ultimately unsuccessful suit against Vanderbilt by Columbia Broadcasting System, led to abundant publicity for Vanderbilt, and now receives extensive requests by scholars for use of the tapes. In 1971 a Mellon Foundation grant of $1 million helped to fund a new library excellence program. To further strengthen its holdings, the board used money from the Harold S. Vanderbilt estate to match, on a one-to-one basis, all outside gifts to the library. Partly through the effort of Jean Keller Heard, a new organization, Friends of the Library, began raising money in 1973.[11]

Despite these efforts, by 1975, the target date of the Planning Study recommendations, the 1.3 million-volume JUL had fallen to sixty-fourth among university libraries in its rate of annual additions. Out of the centennial campaign came a tentative commitment of an additional $10 million to what, in 1979, became the Vanderbilt University Library, but only a disappointing $3.5 million was raised by 1981. Such heroic efforts still barely enabled Vanderbilt to hold its position relative to other universities, even those in the South. It suffered, as do all libraries, from the explosion of expensive scholarly periodicals and serials and from the higher cost of buying the ever-enlarging output of scholarly monographs. It also, unfortunately, remained heavily dependent on faculty book orders, not on specialized bibliographers. In 1982 Frank Grisham left, creating a new problem of leadership. In 1983 a committee began the crucial search for a successor, which led to the appointment of Malcolm Getz, a former associate professor of economics at Vanderbilt and an expert on library financing.

Traditionally, the College had supported only one specialized research institute, the old Institute for Research in The Social Sciences. This undertaking petered out in the late 1950s when George Stocking fought, unsuccessfully, for continued foundation and university funding. With it died also one of the few resources at Vanderbilt for research on local economic and social problems. Vanderbilt remained embarrassingly short on extension or service organizations. Yet, by the late 1960s Vanderbilt students were incessantly pressing the faculty to become involved in local problems, to move beyond abstract theory or classroom discussion, and to improve the lives of people outside the university. Vanderbilt faculty did become involved in the Urban Observatory (1969), a Model Cities project dedicated to research and action on major urban problems. Complementing this was a fledgling Urban and Regional Development Center (URDC), the brainchild of Daniel Grant of political science. In 1970 Gilbert Merritt of the Law School briefly headed it, only to turn it over to an assistant professor in sociology. With limited Ford Foundation support and a constantly shifting leadership, it was not able to complete much of its intended research on the problems of inner cities. Its grants ran out in 1973.[12]

At that point Heard successfully petitioned the Board of Trust for from $800,000 to $1 million to fund a new URDC over the next ten years. In 1973 James Blumstein, from the Yale University Law School, came to Vanderbilt in part to direct URDC, establishing its offices in the basement of the Law School. In 1974 an advisory committee on urban affairs and related studies worked out a charter for an expanded research institute, named the Vanderbilt Institute for Public Policy. Heard, in approving the report, changed this to Vanderbilt Institute for Public Policy Studies (VIPPS). Also in 1974, Provost Hobbs, as he planned his 1975 retirement from administration, became acting director of VIPPS and began planning his own research effort in the area of human resources, one of three recommended research priorities for VIPPS (along with urban and regional development and problems of the environment).[13]

The new VIPPS really began work in 1976. Erwin C. Hargrove, a political scientist at Brown University with extensive research and publications in the area of public policy, came to Vanderbilt to head an expanded program. VIPPS has remained the only major research institute tied closely to the College faculty, although it has a university-wide clientele (fifty-eight faculty research associates by 1982). As Hargrove developed the institute, it decentralized into four centers—for the study of families and children (Hobbs's show), executives and bureaucracies (Hargrove's major interest), health policy (which involved many ties with the Medical School), and educational policy (an early link to Peabody). Through 1982 VIPPS had expended only one-half of its committed $1 million, had solicited over $5 million in grants, and had gained a $500,000 endowment from the estate of Winthrop Rockefeller. In 1980, after suffering temporary rented quarters off campus, VIPPS moved into the former quarters of the Blair School of Music and into two additional buildings, all on 18th Avenue to the east of Peabody. It supports a wide array of research efforts, sponsors lectures and seminars on public policy issues, and offers seminars for graduate students. It has come closer than any other Vanderbilt organization, save possibly the Center for Health Services, to fulfilling a service goal.[14]

A final support for faculty research, particularly in the humanities and social sciences, is a strong university press. The one at Vanderbilt petered out after 1972. Out of the Planning Study and a board commitment of $60,000 a year, and later $80,000 a year, came the first true university press, one with up to six professional staff members under director David Howell Jones, and up to seventeen titles published each year. But the days of glory proved ever so brief, or less than a decade. In 1972 Provost Hobbs announced a slow strangulation process, after a faculty committee investigated the press's financial and personnel problems. The board slashed its annual subsidy from $80,000 to $50,000. By then it was clear that a successful press cost money, that no press could survive without considerable subsidies. Perhaps a new and less abrasive director might have saved the press, but Jones could not. Instead, under pressure, he resigned. In 1974 a committee took over supervision of the press and first considered a merger with another university press. Before any detailed negotiations took place, Hobbs resigned as provost, leaving the unsolved problem to Heard. By then, the remaining staff worked in a difficult holding pattern, accepting no titles except for committed series or special publications related to Vanderbilt, but maintaining the imprint and continuing to sell back copies. In 1976 the board ended all subsidies, leaving the press to live, in effect, from sales of its inventory. John Poindexter added the role of director to his other duties as alumni secretary. In 1979 the reassessment panel appointed by President Emmett Fields seemed to sign the press's death certificate; it argued that the cost of rebuilding a viable operation outweighed any possible benefits to the university. But, like the proverbial cat, the press had many lives and would not go away. It enjoyed a limited, restricted endowment, which Vanderbilt would lose if it stopped all publishing. This small financial incentive, by 1983, helped provoke new and successful efforts to work out a cooperative arrangement with the University of Illinois Press, one that preserved the imprint and the endowment and which made it possible for a small Vanderbilt University Press to publish up to five volumes a year.[15]

Each of the professional schools deserves at least a full chapter covering the critical years since 1963. The brief and elliptical sketches that follow do a disservice to complexity and subtlety and will at points astound, or offend,

659

the several actors. In general, the schools have fared well. Only Nursing has fallen below an earlier eminence. The Medical School has remained the strongest, closely followed by Law and Divinity. Engineering, after struggling with serious problems in the 1960s, roared back in the 1970s. Finally, a new Graduate School of Management, born prematurely, afflicted with numerous early maladies, long confused about its identity, finally began a normal maturation process in the mid-1970s. The two new grafts—Peabody and Blair—have full billing in the next chapter.

In 1963 the Divinity School still floundered in the ugly shadow of the Lawson case. Dean William Finch presided over a strategic retreat, back toward the South and even toward greater orthodoxy. Such an identity did not fit the school or match its traditional role. In 1965 Finch moved on to the presidency of Emory and Henry, and to a more congenial intellectual and theological environment. A rapid turnover of faculty created an almost new school after 1965. Three major professors had left in the aftermath of the Lawson affair. Then, in 1965, William Kendrick Grobel died of a heart attack, just after he had planned a move to Oberlin. Among the new faculty was an expert on Hinduism, Winston King from Grinnell College, and a future dean of the school, H. Jackson Forstman. With Finch's resignation, Assistant Dean James Sellers became acting dean and then dean. He helped move the school back toward its pre-Lawson priorities—ecumenical concern, an emphasis upon rigorous scholarship, and new outreach efforts for lay people. A new $25,000 addition to scholarship funds helped enlarge the number of Bachelor of Divinity applicants in 1966.

In the midst of this growth the school worked out a merger agreement with the Oberlin Graduate School of Theology in 1965. The arrangement brought Vanderbilt about $1.25 million in additional endowment, six Oberlin professors (one, Herbert G. May, was an internationally respected Old Testament scholar, although close to retirement age), fewer than expected library books, and a few transfer students. Vanderbilt tried to respect the Oberlin tradition through name professorships or the names it gave to parts of its quadrangle. Vanderbilt carefully evaluated each transferring professor, paid moving expenses, and assumed all scholarship commitments for transferring students. This merger helped reestablish the Divinity School's image as progressive or liberal and fully committed to social action.[16]

Such changes did not endear the Divinity School to some of the older trustees. The old tensions revived with Walter Harrelson's election as dean in 1967 and even more with the decision to readmit Lawson in 1969. But this time the chancellor successfully defended the Divinity faculty and spared them a sequel to 1960. The school's faculty continued to take progressive stands on social issues. In 1970 the school not only hired a local black minister, Kelly Miller Smith, but made him assistant dean, the first such appointment for a black at Vanderbilt. In 1975, when Dean Harrelson returned to teaching as a distinguished professor, the school elected Sallie

TeSelle, the first female dean outside Nursing and the first in a major theological school in the United States. In 1979 she gave way to H. Jackson Forstman. By most evaluations, the Divinity School remained one of the top nondenominational seminaries in the country. One survey ranked it among the top eight nationally. It continued to broaden its scope—more Roman Catholic involvement, more programs on Judaism, more exchanges with other schools—and, following national trends, converted its B.D. program into a Doctor of Ministry in 1971. The M.A. and Ph.D. remained scholarly degrees, while a new S.T.D. allowed advanced practical work for ministers.

Success, even a degree of eminence, paralleled some grave problems—in attracting able students, in keeping the enrollment up to capacity (it was down to 188 in the B.D. program by 1972), and in balancing budgets. By the late 1970s enrollment in divinity schools everywhere dropped, and so did the academic ability of too many ministerial candidates. Thus, the Divinity School had some of the most distinguished scholars at Vanderbilt, but they often taught some of the least gifted professional students. From 1970 on, the school also suffered annual deficits, deficits met from general university funds. In 1976 the board offered up to $2 million of Harold S. Vanderbilt estate funds to the school, as part of a matching grant (3 to 1) and by this strategy helped raise its endowment during the centennial drive. But as late as 1980–81 the school still suffered an annual deficit of $234,000, although only half that of just a year before.[17]

Since 1963 the Engineering School has taken a ride on a roller coaster. Problems have matched achievements. When Heard took over as chancellor, Engineering seemed to be thriving. Dean Robert S. Rowe had upgraded the faculty, initiated a new research emphasis, and created several new Ph.D. programs. The boom continued until at least 1967. By then, the faculty had increased from thirty-two in 1960 to fifty-seven, faculty Ph.D.s from six to thirty-eight. Bucking a national trend, enrollment grew from 658 to 810, graduate enrollment from 6 to 108. In addition to the traditional departments in civil, chemical, electrical, and mechanical engineering, Vanderbilt had an older department of water and sanitary resources engineering and, under a division of engineering sciences, offered curricula in biomedical engineering, engineering mathematics, engineering machines, and information engineering (the name for a new computer science program). In 1966 Merritt A. Williamson moved from a deanship at Pennsylvania State to become the school's first distinguished professor, offering master's degree work in the comparatively new field of engineering management.

Such a growth in both the quality and breadth of programs disguised some developing problems. The enrollment grew in part because of very low admission standards. Engineering students remained less sophisticated and more provincial than those in the College. And after 1967, with the student movement on major campuses, the image and prestige of engineers sank to an all-time low. Fewer able students chose the profession and even Vanderbilt suffered small enrollment declines by 1970. By then, the school ran annual deficits, or over $800,000 in 1970. The school used every strategy it could to attract students, including a jazzy course on "Man and His Environment," aimed primarily at College undergraduates. Because of the budget crunch, and the termination of its instruction in applied mathematics, the school gave notice, in December, 1970, to seven of its junior staff. Such an extreme action, so exceptional in Vanderbilt's history, led to an extensive airing of the problems in Engineering and to student sympathy for those "fired." In the end Vanderbilt rehired three of the seven. It did not renew two instructors and two assistant professors, all former Vanderbilt students. One had already planned to leave. But the school clearly needed a new boost.

The stimulus came in the form of a new dean after Rowe's resignation in 1970. After an extended search, the school made a rather daring choice— Howard Hartman, a mining engineer and dean at Sacramento State. He came to Vanderbilt singing the praises of "relevance" and the need to meet "people-oriented problems." He tried to reform and rejuvenate the school, leading to a five-year period of ferment that might best be dubbed "the greening of Engineering." Hartman began by abolishing departments and replacing them by a then fashionable grid system, one used at Peabody and favored by Provost Hobbs and other educators. In Hartman's grid plan, all the professors were grouped, for administrative purposes, in four divisions—chemical, fluid and thermal sciences; electrical and computing sciences; materials, machines, and structures; and sociotechnological systems. The faculty taught courses in eleven focused programs, some traditional, some as new as a much publicized, interdisciplinary program in socioengineering. The structural changes and the emphasis on social need dismayed many of the older faculty, who lamented change for change's sake or deplored the decline of rigor that they perceived in some of the new courses. The chair in environmental and water resources engineering resigned, in part out of personal bitterness against Hartman. He noted low morale and high-handed tactics on the part of the dean. Another chair professor resigned in 1977, before Hartman resigned his deanship in 1978.[18]

At whatever cost, Hartman created a very unusual Engineering School. He exuded a type of moral idealism, shared many educational goals with Dean Igor Ansoff of the stumbling new Graduate School of Management, but, like Ansoff and other educational reformers, expressed his ideals in vague or highly general terms, often in futuristic gobblydegook. Hartman shared, or absorbed, much of the ill-focused reform zeal of students. He loved to talk about a new, social direction in engineering, of a social orientation to technology, of a new era of socially as well as technically efficient and responsible engineers. This meant a concern for values, a consciousness of the social, environmental, economic, and political factors that impinged upon an engineer's work. His pride and joy was the new program in socioengineering, which involved a series of courses on technology and society, with a historical

662

and philosophical base and with several professors borrowed from the College. The series of courses culminated in one on "ecological systems." How could one be more fashionable? The motivation for such courses was not moral concern alone. Engineering desperately needed students and a larger endowment. The interdisciplinary courses pulled in an enrollment from the College. The school also gained approval in 1974 for a new Master of Engineering degree, a nonscholarly degree for practicing engineers. Even more suspect academically was a new Bachelor of Science degree, a degree without the specific and rigorous curriculum requirements of the conventional Bachelor of Engineering. It particularly fit loose degree programs in social, environmental, or computer areas, and often involved considerable coursework in the College. To tradionalists, it symbolized a further decline of standards. But it helped woo students, particularly athletes; to some extent the new degree was a response to entreaties from the athletic department.[19]

Under Hartman the Engineering School, along with the early Graduate School of Management, led the university in its opening for minorities. Already, in 1968, the school agreed to make two cooperative appointments with Meharry in biomedical engineering. In 1972, aided by a DuPont grant, it signed a cooperative agreement with Fisk, one that allowed Fisk undergraduates to move to Vanderbilt after their junior year, to get their Fisk degree a year later, and to complete a Bachelor of Engineering at the end of their fifth year, one of the few University Center programs that really worked. Just after Hartman resigned, the school's first black professor, William Mills, took charge of minority recruitment and with dramatic success. Within a year Engineering had a higher proportion of black students than the College. Women also flocked to the school. In 1980 the 30 percent women in its freshman class was the highest in the nation. One explanation was Hartman's innovations, his concerns for the larger society, his socially oriented outlook, and the new programs that overlapped with those in the College. By 1980 the largest overlap involved computer science (the replacement for informational engineering). When Dean Rowe resigned in 1970, the school reluctantly gave up its department of applied mathematics, transferring staff and courses to the mathematics department in the College, a move much resented by engineering students. In exchange, the Engineering School gained full responsibility for all courses related to computers, or what turned out to be a boost for its enrollment. Not only does Engineering now offer a degree in computer science but it attracts increasing numbers of College students into these courses. Unfortunately, for a time, the computer science department brought as many problems as benefits. By 1979 the understaffed department was without a chair and had only three continuing professors. It carried out four different searches in one year.[20]

Fortunately for Engineering, trends in employment and in student preferences favored the school by the mid-1970s. In 1975 beginning engineering students for the first time had SAT scores higher than those for students in the

College. By then, enrollment pressures had begun to build even as the new problem became one of faculty recruitment. But increased enrollment did not solve all the financial problems. In 1972 Dean Hartman joined with a committee of visitors (such committees, made up of eminent lay people, now existed in each of the schools, but not in the College) to launch a major fund drive. The school had only $2.5 million in endowment, and annual corporate and alumni gifts scarcely exceeded $50,000. As a special incentive, the board offered up to $4 million from the Harold S. Vanderbilt estate, on a generous two-to-one matching basis. This strategy worked, as Engineering gradually raised its endowment to a targeted $7 million and by 1981 to approximately $10 million. But success in fund raising accompanied a gradual retreat from Hartman's early reforms, even as the student activists of 1970 gave way to those with narrow career goals by the mid-1970s. In 1976, as a financial move, Hartman began to consolidate departments, allowed larger enroll-ments in courses, and tried to adjust to fewer professors. After he resigned, and under the new dean, Paul Harrawood, the school finally returned to its traditional roots. It merged water resources engineering into a department of chemical engineering, blended biomedical engineering with electrical, and merged material sciences with mechanical engineering. It had long since dropped socioengineering and now did away with program directors, the last echo of the grid system. Consolidation paralleled a clear return to basic courses and to a more narrowly professional focus. These shifts in Engineer-ing matched the new program in liberal education in the College. But, compared with the College, Engineering had wandered farther away from its traditional and conservative roots and thus had to move farther to get home again.[21]

The Law School suffered, or enjoyed, few of the ups and downs of Engineering. It began the recent era in a new building in 1962 and ended it with the completion of a major extension in 1982. Through the two decades it enjoyed a steady increase in the popularity of law as a profession, and in the last decade has been able to be highly selective in its admissions, unlike Divinity. It gradually raised its enrollment from about 300 in 1963 to 430 in 1970 to a quota of approximately 500 in 1983. It began and ended the two decades as one of the three or four most prestigious law schools in the South, below Virginia or Duke but above Tulane and most state schools. In the Planning Study its ambitious goal was to move from a very competent to a truly great school. Its students by 1979 ranked fourteenth nationally on LSAT scores, a rough index of the school's eminence. It has continued the conven-tional case method of instruction, but with greater opportunities for special-ized work in the second and third years. A majority of its graduates enter established law firms; a minority work for corporation and governments or enter into individual practice. The strengths of the school remain traditional ones, with a curriculum slanted toward commercial practice (tax, corporate, trial procedures, and international law), not such fields as labor, consumer, environmental, or public law. The emphasis remains upon training for legal practice, not so much on training in jurisprudence or in legal scholarship.[22]

As always, success in some areas has matched problems, particularly in finances and faculty recruitment. Given its small endowment of approximately $1 million in 1963, the Law School simply could not balance accounts by the early 1970s despite increased enrollment. Here, as in Divinity and Engineering, the Harold Vanderbilt estate came to the rescue. The board gave the Law School $2 million on a two-to-one matching basis, and with this aid the school increased its endowment to over $5 million by 1981. But by then, the largest share of its income came from sharply higher tuition, enough income to keep its budget more than balanced.

After World War II the modern Vanderbilt Law School built its national reputation by recruiting eminent jurists after their retirement from other institutions. Its most famous professor, Edmund M. Morgan, gave up teaching at Vanderbilt only in 1963 at the age of eighty-six. In the 1960s the school continued its program of recycling professors. Elliott E. Cheatham, another former president of the Association of American Law Schools and an international expert on conflict of laws, came from Columbia in 1960 at age seventy-two and remained on the Vanderbilt faculty until 1968. The last of the emeriti professors, E. Blythe Stason, former dean of the University of Michigan Law School, taught at Vanderbilt from 1964 to 1969 and briefly held the Rand Professorship.

By the 1970s the school once again had to rely on normal appointments, creating continuous recruitment difficulties. Law School salaries, in a period of deficits, lagged behind those in competing schools, although they still exceeded those in the College. The lure of outside opportunities made it difficult to recruit or retain gifted young professors. Competing universities also raided Vanderbilt, as in 1972 when Lyman Ray Patterson left for the deanship at Emory. The most deeply felt loss was the retirement of Dean John Wade, the most important architect of the modern school. He wanted out of the arduous deanship duties by 1970. In 1971 he retired as dean but continued as the school's only Distinguished Professor. His replacement as dean, Robert L. Knauss, an expert in regulatory law, came from a vice-presidency and professorship at the University of Michigan. He helped increase the faculty to approximately thirty full-time teachers plus a steadily enlarged affiliated or clinical staff, made up of lecturers or visiting professors. Several of the most popular or eminent post–World War II professors retired (Paul J. Hartman, Paul H. Sanders, and Theodore A. Smedley). Able new appointees helped fill gaps in the curriculum—James W. Ely, Jr., in legal history; L. Harold Levinson in criminal law; Jonathan I. Charney in international law; and a former Vanderbilt philosophy professor, Samuel E. Stumpf, in the heretofore neglected area of legal ethics. Despite such appointments, the school, except possibly for Wade, lacked stars, and in the early 1970s the quantity of faculty publications began to decline. Knauss constantly stressed

665

the need for more top-rank appointments. Yet when Knauss gave up his deanship in 1979, a search committee, after a frustrating two-year effort, failed to hire an outside replacement. Acting Dean C. Dent Bostick moved up to the position of dean.[23]

In many ways the Law School proved responsive to the demands of students during the late 1960s and to outside pressures for change. It continued to recruit black students, welcomed women, and in 1972 appointed its first part-time female lecturer. Others followed. Allaire Urban Karzon became the school's first regular female professor in 1977. Several student activists worked out of the Law School, and in two areas—environmental protection and women's rights—these students clearly led the campus. Student concerns in the late 1960s contributed to added clinical programs. By 1972 juniors and seniors ran a legislative reference bureau to help improve the quality of legislation in Tennessee, worked with Legal Services of Nashville, with the Public Defender's office, and with the Juvenile Court. Such clinical work, when tied to classroom lectures, counted for credit. Out of such programs came Vanderbilt's own Legal Clinic, a legal aid office staffed by students and supervised by professors. Student work, largely with indigent clients, made up one of Vanderbilt's most valuable services to the Nashville community.

In several ways the Law School remains the most isolated in the university. Unlike Nursing and Engineering, it teaches no undergraduates and thus does not rely on the College for instruction. Unlike Engineering, Divinity, Medicine, and the Owen Graduate School of Management (OGSM), it has no graduate degree program, although it does join Divinity and OGSM in some joint degrees and facilitates those among its students who want to take parallel Ph.D. work in the Graduate School. Its faculty has often lamented its relative isolation, although it has its representatives in the Faculty Senate and several of its professors still serve as research associates with VIPPS, which grew in large part out of Law School initiatives. For its external relations the school publishes two respected journals. In 1963 these included its own *Law Review* (published by able students under faculty supervision) and the *Race Relations Law Reporter*. Ford funds for this second journal expired in 1969, possibly after the need for it had peaked. But a year earlier the International Law Society sponsored at Vanderbilt a new journal eventually named the *Journal of Transnational Law,* with Vanderbilt students doing most of the work under the direction of Professor Harold G. Maier. The Law library, under the direction of Igor I. Kavass, the very blood supply of the school, has continued to grow, occupying as of 1982 its beautiful new quarters funded by a gift from the Jack C. Massie Foundation.

Nursing has enjoyed little of the success of the other schools. It has remained the problem child of the university. The roots of its problems lay in the past—in the lack of any strong university commitment to quality nursing training. Over and over again the Nursing School came out last in competition for university funds. In 1965 Dean Julia Hereford resigned after serving as dean since 1949. She had fought for years to survive inadequate budgets but saw her school steadily decline from one of the pioneer collegiate schools to one that barely met accreditation requirements. The Planning Study addressed the problems in 1964—an unstable faculty with exactly one-half employed during the last three years; an inbred faculty with 68 percent earning both their bachelor's and master's degrees at Vanderbilt. Since Vanderbilt's ill-funded and fledgling master's program lost its National League of Nursing accreditation in 1962, this was even more of an indictment than it seemed. Too often, the school had to turn to its own immediate graduates to meet its teaching responsibilities. The school had only one professor with a Ph.D. and almost no ongoing research. Its 200 students came almost entirely from Tennessee and the Southeast, and the average nursing student had an embarrassingly low combined GRE score of 962, compared with approximately 1200 in the College. The attrition rate for nursing students was the highest in the university. The school occupied severely limited facilities in Mary Henderson Hall and still had a rather tense relationship with the hospital, whose directors continued all the way into the 1980s to talk about adding their own training school for nurses.[24]

The new Heard administration proved sympathetic to the Nursing School. In an almost emergency situation, the board finally began allocating funds. When Harold S. Vanderbilt sold his private jet plane, he donated $500,000 to the school, or a fund from then on known as the Jet Star account. A special $100,000 foundation gift and $75,000 from the original Ford funds also helped boost morale. In 1965 Alma E. Gault left retirement to serve as interim dean while a committee launched a major search for the new dean needed to rebuild the school. This led, in 1967, to the installation of the first male dean, fifty-one-year-old Luther Christman, who moved from an associate professorship at the University of Michigan. He was a registered nurse, had a Ph.D., had published widely, and thus qualified as an expert on nursing education. For better or worse, and his staff quickly disagreed on this, he launched a series of rapid changes, some reminiscent of those made by Hartman in Engineering and including even the grid system. He began hiring outside professors with advanced degrees, presided over a three-day self-study by faculty and students, helped secure a $500,000 HEW grant (this was matched by the board), shifted the emphasis in the school toward primary care, began a new graduate program in family nursing, and boosted research by his faculty.

The changes over five years seemed dramatic. The faculty grew from 28 to 55, including a new clinical staff; enrollment rose from 165 to 455; the students shifted rather dramatically from an emphasis on hospital care to theory and to what Christman called "applied science"; and the school even began planning for its first Ph.D. program. The new grid system, with five divisions and several defined programs, broke down the older departmental oligarchies, allowed younger staff members a greater role in course planning, and abetted a new flexibility in student requirements. Although Christman claimed the support of 80 percent of his faculty, his reforms and his methods (he joined in firing an instructor in 1969 because she missed three lectures to attend a conference) created a deep enmity among senior professors. They found him insensitive and dictatorial. Six of them sent a bill of accusations to Heard and forced a confrontation that seemed to mean either his resignation or theirs. Because of this pressure and what he felt to be a lack of full administrative support, Christman resigned in 1972 to take on an even more prestigious deanship at Rush College of Nursing at the University of Chicago.[25]

The resignation of Christman did not mean a reversal of his reforms, but it did initiate a decade of troubles and a continuing identity crisis. Another Ph.D., Sara K. Archer, a nursing educator who joined the school in 1969, took over as dean in 1972. Then in 1976 a local benefactor endowed the Valere Potter Distinguished Professorship of Nursing, the first such position in the Nursing School. The new appointee, Ingeborg G. Mauksch, came from Chicago, emphasized nursing as a science, and devoted much of her time to her own research and to numerous professional contributions. In most respects Archer continued Christman's emphasis upon the scientific side of nursing, upon research, and upon a broader role for graduate nurses in health care. She continued the grid plan. She also took over at a happy time, for students flocked to nursing in the early 1970s and federal grants still came easily. Enrollment climbed to over 500 by 1978, the year the school moved into its new subterranean classrooms. A $728,000 HEW grant funded a new training program in primary health care for existing RNs, allowing many of them to assume a new job status as nurse practitioners.

Problems continued. In 1977 a student study was particularly critical of nursing, citing serious internal conflicts. In 1977 Archer solicited comments and criticism from her 102 professors (this included a growing clinical staff in the hospital), with mixed results. The rapid turnover of staff remained a problem. The school continued to face accreditation problems with the National League of Nursing. In 1973 league visitors had pointed to critical problems of staff turnover and to a need for improved programs in psychiatric and community nursing. It granted only temporary accreditation until the school responded to its warnings and, by implication, suggested a possible future loss of accreditation. In a 1977 accreditation study the school passed muster, gaining approval of its undergraduate program until 1983. But in 1979 the National League for Nursing found severe problems in the school's Master of Science program and threatened to cancel accreditation. The problems cited seemed all too familiar—one-third of the Vanderbilt faculty still had Vanderbilt degrees, eight of ten in one department had Vanderbilt degrees, only 20 percent of the faculty had doctorates, five professors in the graduate program did not have a master's or its equivalent, the Master of

Science and Bachelor of Science requirements were too similar, and theory and practice were not well integrated in the curriculum.[26]

The identity crisis involved the place of nursing in modern medical care. All the new specialities created a confusing jumble of career possibilities while the low pay and status of nurses, particularly in comparison with physicians, led by the early 1980s to a serious drop in nursing school applications. Able women chose other vocations. And even a favorable market—an acute shortage of nurses—began to ease by 1983, suggesting an end to market pressures for higher salaries. In this confused context the nursing professors had to grapple with their mission. The research orientation launched by Christman and the enforcement of more rigorous tenure standards by the university created great anxieties among many nursing professors. By sufferance, some professors had continued on the staff for years without any tenure decision and thus were technically subject to termination. The paucity of Ph.D. programs in nursing further increased the anxieties of those nurses without doctorates. And the clinically oriented staff had no opportunity to carry out research and thus could not meet some of the new standards for tenure.

In 1981 a major task force in the Nursing School tried to define the field and to chart Vanderbilt's future priorities. It emphasized nursing as a discipline, a label not easily clarified. In the sense of learned skills, nursing as much as medicine does constitute a very complex discipline, but if discipline refers to a reasonably coherent body of knowledge or to the research skills needed to expand such knowledge, then nursing, again like medicine, draws upon a number of disciplines in the physical, biological, and social sciences. But whatever the definitional problems, the task force emphasized nursing's autonomy as a discipline and even as a method and its place in the broader field of scientific research. It endorsed the Vanderbilt emphasis, in its undergraduate degree program, upon theory and scientific courses as a prelude to clinical experience. It anticipated an early shift from the Bachelor of Science in Nursing to a combined five-year Master of Science program and outlined as a next step a Ph.D. program at Vanderbilt, one tied to discipline, theory, and basic and applied research, not to practice.[27]

In 1980, after the resignation of Sara Archer, Helen Bigler took over as acting dean. This was a prelude to the appointment of a committee to pick a new dean, and this in conjunction with even more soul-searching in the school. By 1980 the school suffered acute embarrassment because so many of its graduates failed state board exams (16.8 percent in 1978; 15 percent in 1980), giving it the second worst record in the state. Students alleged poor preparation in certain courses, the failure of team-taught courses, and the lack of clinical experience in some fields. The faculty hoped the failures on objective exams largely reflected a lack of cramming for the tests or poor test-taking ability on the part of their graduates, who largely wrote essay exams on campus. The test results raised serious questions about Vanderbilt's curriculum, with approximately one-half of its courses in the College. Maybe students gained too much theory, even too much abstract science, and not enough rigorous training. But this was only one final blow, out of a series, that left the school in 1983–84 still desperately trying to define itself and still awaiting new leadership (in 1984, Colleen Conway, a nurse midwife from the University of Colorado, became the new dean). Hauntingly in the background of all this waiting and planning was the memory that, for a brief time in the 1930s, the school had led the nation into new paths of nursing education.[28]

The Medical Center—large, well-funded, prestigious—still threatens to become the tail that wags the Vanderbilt dog. The Medical School and Hospital account for over 70 percent of university income and expenses, employ 45 percent of the full-time faculty and almost 58 percent of part-time faculty, employ over half the Vanderbilt staff, and exercise the greatest impact on the larger community. Except possibly for athletic contests, a majority of lay people gain their direct impression of Vanderbilt from some aspect of its medical program, even if this be only a short visit to a patient in the hospital. The Medical Center has also become a very distinctive branch of Vanderbilt, in the sense that its educational role is a tiny tail that wags no dog at all. It is easy to lose sight of the medical students in the huge hospital, in the numerous outpatient clinics, or in the professional practice program operated by the Medical School faculty. It is impossible, in any fair way, to isolate the educational cost of the center from its numerous other costs. To a much larger extent than in any other branch of the university, the Medical Center is like a complex company largely selling its services to the public. Even the school draws a miniscule percentage of its income from student tuition (5 percent) and from endowment (just over 2 percent). For the most part, the salaries of faculty and the maintenance of buildings now depend on grants and patient fees. The typical Medical School professor, if in the nonclinical sciences, lives on "soft" money (mostly from the National Institutes of Health); if in the clinical specialities, on the fees of the Vanderbilt Professional Practice Program (VPPP). The hospital lives entirely on fees for services rendered. Thus, the Medical Center, like an engorged giant, goes its own way, so powerful as to intimidate anyone who would try to control it.[29]

The story of the Medical School is increasingly a separate story from that of the hospital. The two intersect at many points, both come under the vice-chancellor for medical affairs, but they face increasingly different problems. The Medical School has grown but it has not changed its basic character or purpose. One might chart a critical change of outlook in the 1960s but only with trepidation. A few older professors still hearkened back to the General Education Board origins of the modern school, to the early emphasis upon preventive over curative medicine, to a special concern for the health needs of the South, and to the early commitment to a full-time teaching staff. Such commitments became impossibly idealistic and expensive by the 1960s. Perhaps Hugh Morgan was the last of the older tradition as he served on the

Vanderbilt Board of Trust and struggled for the peaceful integration of schools in Nashville. Morgan, more than any successor, fought against the AMA emphasis upon the status quo and tried to get it to take the lead in opening medical care to all people. The other outstanding "progressive" in approach to medical politics—David E. Rogers—left the important department of medicine in 1967–68 to take over as dean at the Johns Hopkins, both an honor to Vanderbilt and a severe loss.

One other loss hurt even more, at least symbolically. In 1971 Earl Sutherland, already one of two Medical professors to win election to the prestigious National Academy of Science in the period after 1963, and already amply honored for his hormonal research, won the Nobel Prize, the first and so far only such award to go to a Vanderbilt professor. The university duly celebrated his fame; Chancellor Heard attended the award ceremonies in Stockholm. Yet in 1973, Sutherland moved to the University of Miami, only to die the next year. In 1975 Allan D. Bass, chair of pharmacology, the strongest department at Vanderbilt, retired with all due honor. Such giants were, quite literally, irreplaceable. The trend in medicine, as in other disciplines, was away from strong, dynamic leaders and toward cooperative research and a generally higher level of technical ability. But, by 1984, the school could boast another much celebrated research scholar and a possible candidate for a Nobel Prize, biochemist Stanley Cohen.

In the last twenty years the school has doubled in size from 200 to approximately 400 students. At one point it considered an even more grandiose plan. In a utopian twenty-year plan for the Medical School, drafted in 1967, the goal had been as many as 1,700 students, taught by 1,600 faculty in the South's largest school, joined to a new twenty-story Hospital. In 1970–71 a more modest five-year plan entailed only the doubling of enrollment, which actually occurred. A commitment to such an expansion was built into several federal grants, and for a time expansion warred with Vanderbilt's limited facilities. Such expansion also necessitated new classroom facilities and laboratories.

The status of physicians constantly rose after World War II. From salaries below lawyers and comparable to college professors in the 1930s, physicians' earnings soared to the highest of any profession and to more than double that of average professors. This helped insure a plethora of Medical School applicants with only a slight diminution of enthusiasm in the midst of the student activism of the late 1960s. In the 1970s Vanderbilt admitted only a minute proportion of applicants (83 entering students out of 5,400 applicants in 1974–75). Such carefully screened students, among the best according to their national board scores, usually did as well as they should. In 1969 Vanderbilt seniors ranked first nationally in surgery, second in medicine. Vanderbilt scored eighth out of sixty-nine schools in overall national board exams and easily placed its students in preferred internships or residencies. Vanderbilt's medical students enjoyed an enviable but rather typical student-

The old Medical Center

faculty ratio (about one student for every two faculty members). As late as 1981 the school accounted for over $18 million of sponsored research, compared with only $4.8 million for the College. Its faculty, by 1966, published over 300 articles a year, and the number has kept growing. These obvious strengths, joined with the new facilities of the late 1970s and early 1980s, at least maintained the school's rank as one of the best, albeit one of the smallest, medical schools in the country, a school only a step behind the four or five most prominent medical training centers.

The student movement of the late 1960s had one lasting impact on the Medical School. A few of its students caught just a tinge of radicalism, suffered some guilt over the grave medical problems of the area. In 1968 the Macy Foundation gave a small grant to Meharry and Vanderbilt to support student medical work in Nashville's slums. In the summer of 1969, advised by Professor Amos Christie, medical students joined Divinity and College students to work in community centers funded by the Office of Economic Opportunity (OEO) and located in a mountain valley in Campbell County, Tennessee. Medical students also aided a Head Start program in nearby

672

Williamson County. In 1970–71 such concerned students expanded their projects to five Appalachian counties, or what became known on campus as the Appalachian Project. In 1971 the Commonwealth Fund gave $300,000 to further this work, which was now guided by a new student health coalition. In 1972 fifty students from all divisions of the university helped direct health fairs in rural Appalachian counties under new grants from the Appalachian Regional Commission and the TVA. The program tended to radicalize students and to distinguish them from the majority of nonactivists on campus, making the program, in a sense, the only countercultural movement to affect the Medical School. This particular outlet engaged the moral idealism of Vanderbilt students and grew year by year. The health fairs involved massive examinations of people who normally had no access to physicians, and student groups often successfully organized local cooperatively owned clinics. The program, with its cooperative orientation, was immensely popular in local communities. To consolidate such outreach efforts, the Medical Center formed a new organization, the Center for Health Services, and in 1975 hired a young political scientist, Richard Couto, to head it. The range of voluntary work, funded by various grants, has grown each year. The program not only offers a continuing outlet to students but has created much goodwill for Vanderbilt and for the Medical School.

PHOTO BY LIBBY BYLER

The new Hospital and Medical Center

Each decade, it seems, the Medical School has suffered from serious internal friction. In 1962 a rebellious faculty had pushed out Dean John W. Patterson. His successor, Randolph Batson, director of medical affairs and dean, fell prey to problems of his own by the early 1970s. He was increasingly ineffective. The school drifted without forceful leadership while poor faculty morale threatened an early exodus of key staff. In 1973 Batson was eased out of his administrative position. In 1974 a national search led to the appointment of Vernon Wilson, a pharmacologist from the University of Michigan, as vice-chancellor for medical affairs. He was strongly committed to primary care and to community health. He came with commitments from the university to begin, within a year or two, the first stages of the long-contemplated construction program, including a new classroom building and a new hospital. The new administrative structure provided for a separate Medical School dean; in 1975 John Chapman, who had already served as associate dean for education, became dean of the school and by faculty demand assumed primary responsibility for academic policies. Under Wilson and Chapman the school not only expanded into its new quarters but continued to add new programs, with the most publicity going to a center for fertility and reproductive research, with its in vitro fertilization program (1980). By the early 1980s the most energetic department probably was radiology. It vied for national leadership in the area of imaging, not therapy, and in 1982 committed almost $2 million for a nuclear magnetic resonance (NMR) imaging system, a move that probably insured it national leadership in this newest of a series of new imaging techniques. A final, but smooth leadership change came in 1982 when Roscoe R. Robinson (shades of G. Canby) moved from Duke to become new vice-chancellor for medical affairs.[30]

Through all the expansion and the ballooning costs, the Medical School continued to balance its budget almost every year—a remarkable shift from the recent past. The secret to this financial success lay almost entirely in the new Vanderbilt Professional Practice Program (VPPP). Recommendations for faculty-operated clinics went back at least to the financial adversities that followed World War II. In the Planning Study of 1963–64 the Medical School committee recommended a new compensation scheme tied to faculty practice. Already in such departments as anesthesiology and radiology, faculty consulting fees often exceeded salaries, but when earned by full-time faculty these fees all went to the Medical School. Thus in 1964 Dean Batson formally recommended a professional plan to Heard, who recommended it to the board. The implementation took time. David Rogers, who would soon leave Vanderbilt, fought it on principle. The plan clearly violated the hallowed principles of Abraham Flexner or the ideals that had formed the new Medical School of 1925. Flexner had insisted upon full-time professors, those who gave all their time to the school and who received their salaries directly from the university. This did not mean that professors in clinical departments gave up on all medical practice. Competence as teachers required continuing work with patients. But in the 1925 scheme the assumption was that this clinical experience would relate directly to the teaching role and would be gained through work with staff (indigent) patients in the hospital, which served as their laboratory.

By the mid-1960s one of these working assumptions no longer applied— Vanderbilt had fewer and fewer indigent patients and now wanted as few as possible. With widespread medical insurance, with the new Medicaid and Medicare programs, most hospital patients became private or paying patients. If Medical School professors continued to practice at all, even in hospital wards, they were already involved in the fee system. More critical, most patients in the hospital now had their own private physicians, which made it difficult for professors to get needed clinical experience. The problem was how best to organize a program of clinical practice to gain the needed medical experience for professors and at the same time help the Medical School. Batson's original plan addressed these issues. He proposed to move back to a version of the old proprietary system but with few of its abuses. That is, he wanted to formalize mechanisms that allowed the clinical staff to earn their own salaries and that gave them incentives to recruit more private patients.

By the original 1964–65 plan, as worked out by Batson and a faculty committee, clinical professors at Vanderbilt now had a choice of participating in a new salary scheme. If they chose not to participate they continued to draw their full salary directly from the university. Their consulting fees, if any, continued to go to the Medical School development fund. But any faculty member willing to commit 15 percent of his efforts to a new VPPP could participate in a new dual salary plan. The professor now signed a contract specifying the percentage of time devoted to patients (up to a maximum of 50 percent) and reduced his or her contractual salary by such a percentage. The other or supplemental part of the salary came, as contracted, from fees earned from patients less 20 percent (adjusted as needed) for private practice rooms, secretarial services, and other costs. All surplus earnings beyond those needed to meet the supplemental salary went to the professor's department (75 percent) and to the Medical School development fund (25 percent). The extra departmental income was committed, first of all, to paying the salaries of any unlikely professor whose practice did not cover the supplement, and then to exceptional departmental expenses (those not in the annual budget) as determined by the chairman and the contributing physicians.[31]

The dangers in the plan were obvious to all—a diversion of faculty interest and time away from teaching, subtle pressures to participate and thus help the Medical School, and an early dependence upon this extra income by departments. The original plan had verbal assurances on each of those points. It emphasized that "private professional activities" should not "interfere with the proper performance of other academic duties," and that the plan was not

675

"a means of effecting a radical upward adjustment" in faculty salaries. The last point particularly concerned Heard, and in the negotiations at the beginning of the plan everyone agreed that participating professors would retain their existing salaries and enjoy only normal raises. But informally it was soon clear that faculty members had all manner of incentives for participation (they could count such professional expenses as trips to meetings against costs and not as part of their supplemental salary), and that the new plan justified a steady rise in faculty compensation, much in the same sense that salaries tended to go up faster for Medical School scientists paid entirely from "soft" money. These professors who had been earning large consulting fees already tended to have higher salaries. It is hard to turn down raises for professors who more than earn their own keep.[32]

This early plan, as implemented in 1965, was the acorn that grew into a large oak. The early participants saw patients in their regular offices or in special examining rooms provided by the hospital. By 1969 the annual fees collected rose to between $400,000 and $500,000, not close to what now seemed their potential. Thus a new Medical School study led to a much enlarged VPPP housed in new quarters prepared during renovation of the outpatient wing of the hospital. In effect professors now joined in a more structured group practice with an eventual potential of from 75 to 100 participants. The distribution of the earned income remained the same, but Batson now talked openly about some incentive formula for salaries, some way of rewarding those who brought in more patients and more income.

Such a formula came into use in 1972. By then, the clinic practice was booming, with fifty-two participating professors (including all thirteen in the department of anesthesiology) and an annual income of $1.4 million (equal to a $28 million endowment). The practice also became a major recruiting tool for the hospital; at one time over half of hospital inpatients had been referred by VPPP. Medical School administrators wanted to encourage VPPP as much as possible and thus opted for a variable salary system, one already tried at several medical schools (Abraham Flexner must have groaned in his grave). Clinical professors continued to get a contractural percentage of their salary from collected fees. But now one could increase the total salary. After payment for overhead and the stated supplemental salary, the professor had a claim of 60 percent of the first $10,000 of surplus, 50 percent of the second $10,000, and 30 percent of all the surplus over $20,000. The school and department shared the rest of the surplus as before. In 1975 this formula changed to a more variable one, with professors negotiating for from 30 to 50 percent of the total surplus income. Dean Batson called this the "best private practice system in the country," since physicians now taught medicine in the context of active practice. John Chapman, later dean of the school, said: "We must be able to attract the practitioners who can attract patients. We must have a system of compensation related to practice, and we must relate that practice to the educational program." We must also, he said, "be careful that the practitioners are also teachers of students." One can still wonder where the primary loyalties of professors lay. By 1981 VPPP grossed over $20 million each year, with six departments each collecting over $1 million and with surgery collecting over $3 million.[33]

With even the Medical School selling its services in a highly competitive market, the hospital was right at home. In the 1960s the same changes in health care that justified VPPP began to alter the role of the hospital. Soaring medical costs, based in part on higher salaries for physicians but much more on extensive new medical technology and almost luxurious care, forced the United States along with other advanced countries to socialize the widely unequal burden of medical care. Few families could afford medical care in extreme situations. Typically the United States resorted to a crazy patchwork of programs, but a patchwork that was comparable in results to more centralized and fully tax-supported schemes in Europe. In almost all families in which husbands or wives enjoy stable employment, health care risks are now shared through group insurance contracted with private or cooperative insurers. In effect, workers pay for such protection through a concealed employee tax, a deduction from their gross earnings. For people over sixty-five the Social Security system pays basic costs through Medicare. For most indigent or uninsured low-income people, the federal government pays most medical costs through Medicaid, a major income transfer system. A few people fall through the holes in these multiple programs. The system, by its variability and flexibility, has avoided many of the problems of centralized European health plans, most notably a paucity of health care personnel, less technologically sophisticated hospitals, and long waits for routine services. It has avoided these problems by retaining the fee system of payment for hospitals and physicians even in the case of governmentally funded care, and with the fee system come the many incentives to get people into medicine and to get physicians and hospitals steadily to upgrade their skills and machines. The system has its obvious costs or deficiencies—almost no patient and little public leverage over escalating costs, greater financial rewards for curative than for preventive medicine, and a developing hierarchy in health care. In effect, low-income and indigent patients go to crowded outpatient clinics, not to private physicians. Except for rare or complex illnesses, when they often inherit the best, they also go to ill-funded public or charity hospitals.

For Vanderbilt, the hospital now had to compete successfully in the complex medical marketplace in order to survive. It had to pay its own way. The university had long since given up on a subsidized laboratory; it even transferred former hospital endowments to the Medical School. Unfortunately, the hospital faced handicaps in the 1960s as Medicare and Medicaid came on board. Its aged facilities did not bear comparison with new hospitals such as St. Thomas or to profit-oriented corporate hospitals (those set up often near large medical centers largely to cater to the most affluent or best-insured private patients, usually without any commitment to a full range

677

of hospital services, to basic research, or even to the most expensive technologies). What Vanderbilt had competitively was the exceptional talent attracted to the Medical School and to a teaching hospital, in a few areas the most sophisticated and most expensive machines, and in other areas the benefits of very recent research. It also soon had VPPP and thus the direct patronage of the most specialized and talented group of physicians in the Nashville area, those able to compete very effectively for patients, most slotted to Vanderbilt Hospital when they needed such care. This two-pronged competitive advantage—technical sophistication and a successful recruiting device—kept the aged hospital going in the late 1960s and into the 1970s. A few smaller programs helped, such as the separately funded Nashville Children's Hospital, the best in the region, which moved to the Vanderbilt Hospital in 1970.

It was clear by 1969 that Vanderbilt could not remain competitive without a new hospital building. The old one, after all the additions, had become an impractical, ill-planned maze. All the planning focused on a new building, but this could not be funded until the existing hospital balanced its budgets and demonstrated a need and the funding capacity for a new building. Fortunately, the developing health care system allowed hospitals to pass along mounting costs to patients, or beyond them to those agencies that paid the bills. Vanderbilt raised its fees, often dramatically, but it still could not raise them much above its neighbors in Nashville. And so the hospital in the 1970s tried to maintain a precarious balance—to maintain a high patient census, to maximize fees as much as consistent with this goal, and still to offer some noncompensated services to the region, a commitment present from its origins in 1925 and required because of several federal subsidies. By 1977 it had so juggled these priorities as to justify the planning of its new building. In this sense it succeeded, but to do so it had to cut its service function to the bare minimum.

Throughout its history the hospital has had to minimize its indigent load, or what Chancellor Kirkland always referred to as its charity work. Long efforts to get the city to pay at least part of this cost largely failed, an effort that fed into the tortuous negotiations concerning General Hospital. But in the 1960s the federal government assumed much of the responsibility. Thus, the hospital worked to reduce the number of nonpaying patients even as it tried to collect unpaid bills. It could not reject emergency patients. And, consistent with earlier federal subsidies, it could not turn away some usually unclear percentage of charity cases. But it usually tried to divert indigents elsewhere. On several occasions its tough screening of patients to determine their ability to pay, and its rejection of prospective patients, led to hard feelings, to adverse publicity, and to one successful 1975 legal challenge based on its use of Hill-Burton funds. As late as 1983, in a national television program on exclusive private hospitals, NBC used Vanderbilt as a prime example of a cold-hearted and legally dubious screening policy and of course found individual cases to back up its very uncomplimentary portrait. The hospital increased its budget for public relations, made more clear to prospective patients its legal obligations for free care, negotiated formulas that would meet criteria of the courts, but never appeased all its critics, including some private physicians in Nashville. It raised the amount of acceptable charity care in 1981 to approximately $6 million, to approximately $10 million by 1983. In a consent agreement, which resulted from successful legal action in behalf of an indigent patient, in 1975 Vanderbilt accepted an obligation to provide uncompensated services to a percentage of its indigent patients. In 1983, in response to motions to hold Vanderbilt Hospital in contempt for violating this decree, a federal court ruled that, despite minor problems, Vanderbilt had substantially fulfilled the obligation incurred by acceptance of Hill-Burton funds.[34] But in December, 1984, in an admitted but a very embarrassing mistake, a new Vanderbilt burn center rejected a non-insured burn victim who then had to fly all the way to San Antonio to enjoy comparable facilities.

A second and related public relations problem involved both the Medical School and the hospital. Vanderbilt stood accused of monopolizing clinical facilities in Nashville at the expense of a financially beleaguered Meharry. When Meharry suffered an acute financial crisis in 1981, it demanded equal access for its physicians to the clinical facilities of both General Hospital and of the Veteran's Administration Hospital, both bound to Vanderbilt by long-term service contracts (Meharry students did have access to General). This led to a complex controversy, one aired even in the New York *Times,* and once again to a controversy that painted Vanderbilt as smug, insensitive, monopolistic, perhaps even racist. The controversy continues. New federal funds rescued Meharry by 1983, while Vanderbilt's help in securing it clinical privileges in the Veteran's Administration Hospital in Murfreesboro half appeased its local demands, but Meharry is likely to gain a cooperative role at General and is bound to continue its appeals for access to the Nashville VA Hospital. In this controversy Vanderbilt bent over backward to show concern, took part in several joint meetings, seemed always to be conciliatory, but never offered to give up its exclusive clinical rights at the VA Hospital.[35]

In 1967 a rare event occurred at Vanderbilt—a new school was born, the first since Nursing. This new Graduate School of Management (GSM) came into the world prematurely despite a long gestation, suffered from acute early malnourishment, and almost perished within its first seven years. The conception went back to the Branscomb administration. Guarded guidelines for its development appeared in the Planning Study of 1964 and in a detailed report by a 1965 faculty committee. Thus in July, 1965, at a special retreat of the Board of Trust in Hot Springs, Virginia, Heard raised the issue for an extended board discussion. Heard believed such an effort desirable, in part because it offered one avenue of community service. But he saw the prospect as a long-term one, a goal and not an early reality, since he wanted $5 million to $7 million in hand to assure its early success. The prospect tantalized a few board members, perhaps most of all Sam Fleming, who saw its possible value in the $55 million fund drive, which he subsequently chaired. The board thus authorized planning for such a school, one to be established as soon as funds were in hand. After this vote, a faculty committee began on-campus consultations and considered several specific models or plans all the way down to sample curricula.[36]

Fleming brought the issue to an early head at an Executive Committee meeting in April, 1967. He now believed that continued planning of such a school would not aid the existing fund drive, but that a school already in operation would stimulate giving. Several trustees still wanted to wait. Faculty resolutions favoring such a school all stipulated prior funding. Heard was already sensitive to faculty concerns, particularly in the College, and to realistic fears that a new school would divert gifts from existing programs. Thus, as throughout its development, Heard took the role of a critic, of one who asked hard questions and advocated delay. He made it clear that if the board chose to proceed, it would have to accept the burden of funding the school and only then through new sources, not already developed ones. In May the board, with some reluctance, and at least strong doubts on the part of a minority, voted to use reserve funds of up to $1.25 million as a 5-percent loan to launch the school and support it over its first five years. A fund drive would repay the loan. Heard reluctantly went along, accepted the risk as worth taking, but ended with a precautionary warning about the loss to the university five years later if the fund drive failed. Heard's tactics made sense, whatever his personal feelings about the new school. He did everything possible to place key board members on the spot, to insure that they would personally raise or contribute the needed $5 million or $6 million. Very shortly thereafter, Fleming and others worked out a plan by which those who gave $250,000 to the school earned the title of "Founder," with their portraits to hang in the new school. Lesser donors became "associates" and received special certificates.[37]

No one could fault the planning efforts that went into the new venture. Provost Nicholas Hobbs directed an extended study of existing schools. The new Holiday Inn–Vanderbilt hosted an unending stream of business school deans or other consultants. But the critical first decision involved the selection of a dean. The search involved dozens of names, but many prominent people were not interested. Of all the proposed names, one—Igor Ansoff, professor of industrial administration at Carnegie-Mellon—most appealed to Hobbs, who sensed in him kindred educational ideals. Ansoff was the first and only candidate invited for an interview, made a favorable impression on Heard and other administrators, and received generally enthusiastic letters from numerous outside referees. Ansoff also had credentials that pleased hard-headed board members. He had spent most of his career with Lockheed, working his way up to vice-president before moving in 1963 to Carnegie-Mellon. He had written one book and had tried to shift business

680

training away from the conventional casework approach (made famous at the Harvard Business School) to what he called an analytical approach.

Ansoff, trained in engineering, turned out to be an almost utopian visionary. He was devoted to anything new or innovative, was inspired by the magnitude of recent social and technological change, and was bursting with enthusiasm for all the immense possibilities opening in the near future. To him, a new school meant the opportunity to start over, to break from outdated methods, to make a great impact on management education in America. Whenever possible, he tried to distinguish Vanderbilt's new school from others, to make it open and experimental in approach, to broaden its constituency well beyond business, and to take the lead in recruiting blacks and women and other heretofore excluded groups from the area of management. An enthusiastic Ford Foundation executive predicted, under Ansoff, a new "spark in management education." Behind Ansoff's idealism lurked conceptual fuzziness and a proclivity for pretentious jargon and abstract generalities. The mystique of revolutionary change, the passionate visions of a wonderful if cloudy future, elicited a favorable response from most audiences, but more precise thinkers often went away confused and doubtful.[38]

Ansoff sent Hobbs his preliminary dreams for the school in May, 1968. By

PHOTO BY LIBBY BYLER

The Owen Graduate School of Management

September, 1969, he had drafted a thirty-five-page plan for a "Graduate School of Management." Even the title had significance. Ansoff did not want to use the word "business," as did most such schools, and finally chose "management" over "administration," a change approved by the board (it subsequently insisted upon an optional Master of Business Administration to complement Ansoff's planned Master of Management). Ansoff's goal was to achieve distinction instantly, largely through educational innovations. He foresaw a standard two-year master's program, an executive training program for existing managers, and a Ph.D. that would "focus on research in change processes." Although business would provide most students, he wanted to attract people from all "purposive" social institutions. Instead of narrow vocational training, or low-level skills, he wanted to emphasize theory or generalist skills, those appropriate for top-level managers, those who worked at the intersection of scientific and humanistic cultures. He particularly stressed new computer skills, behavioral theory, and problem solving, without very careful definitions in any case. The student somehow was to become a constructive agent of change, a favorite theme of Ansoff's. Beyond this he frequently lost himself in educational or corporate jargon.[39]

Certainly Ansoff's original plan exuded idealism. His emphases resembled Howard Hartman's in Engineering and echoed themes of the student movement. He always stressed opportunities for the underprivileged and from the beginning tried to open his school to a diverse student body, with special efforts to recruit blacks in what he called "project equalizer." He joined Hobbs in supporting a "trajectory concept," which apparently entailed a gradual move from theory and facts to actual clinical experience in a "real world." He talked enthusiastically about "modular courses," "total mastery learning," variable pacing, and the elimination of all student failures. On the nuts-and-bolts issues, which did not excite him, he projected a $6 million endowment for an originally small school with a faculty of only ten to twelve and from 100 to 120 students. Student concerns would determine the scope of the curriculum. The faculty was to include an expert on pedagogy. Other "problem-oriented" professors would enlist in five "knowledge areas"— behaviorial science, management science, information science, middle-management decision making, and general management decision making. In student recruitment he emphasized "life history information" over grades and test scores. Finally, he proposed to begin some instruction in 1969, with only six or eight students joining the new faculty in developing the final curriculum.[40]

The Ansoff dream proved unrealistic. It eventually failed. And so in many respects did the early school, despite all the promotional gimmicks. The original fund drive never garnered $6 million. The largest gifts involved slightly over $1 million from Valere Potter for a distinguished professor in American competitive business, an endowed chair in banking from Frank Houston, $500,000 from the Sloan Foundation, and from board member

PHOTO BY BILL LEFEVOR

The Blair School of Music

David K. Wilson and his wife a gift of the school's first home, a former funeral home on West End, subsequently refurbished and named Alexander Hall. By the end of the 1969–70 experimental year, Ansoff had assembled a fledgling staff but his two chairs remained open. He hired nine young assistant and associate professors; recruited two part-time professors from Engineering; fulfilled his commitment to blacks by the shared appointment (with Fisk) of Flournoy A. Coles, Jr., from the Wharton School in Pennsylvania; and appointed one new full professor, James R. Surface, who would soon move into the central administration.

So much went wrong. The school had difficulty attracting able students and as a result went ahead with marginal ones. Its pass-fail grading and too many easy courses scandalized professors on other parts of the campus. Students criticized the school or were unhappy with their education. The "core models" concealed serious deficiencies in such basic areas as economics. The school scarcely cooperated at all with the College department of economics and business administration. In 1972 it secured board approval for a completely premature Doctor of Management degree, one it would subsequently have to suspend. The early gifts and the early enthusiasm soon ran out, creating a deficit budget by 1972–73, a deficit overcome by a transfer of funds from an unused endowed chair, but a deficit that suggested the early need to transfer funds from other parts of the university, or exactly what

Heard had promised would never take place. In 1972 two black students sued the school for racial bias after they lost a case before the honor council. The students, backed by the NAACP, eventually lost their case, and it was ironic that they charged bias in the one school that most eagerly sought blacks.[41]

Such problems concealed limited progress. The school slowly did raise its standards, the entering board scores of its students moved up from pitiful to almost average, and able faculty members, some increasingly disillusioned with Ansoff, did their best to help improve the school. The school, from the beginning, turned out a few well-qualified and well-placed graduates. Ansoff, despite the problems, had fervent supporters, some among prominent businessmen. But he failed in several critical respects. He was an egotist, insecure and defensive, abrasive when challenged or criticized. He had no skills in fund raising, antagonized many would-be supporters in the Nashville area, and spent enormous amounts of time in petty fights with other schools or with administrators (Heard had to mediate a nasty quarrel over who controlled parking at GSM). By 1972 Ansoff had exhausted almost all of his early support, had finished out his original contract, and under pressures from all sides, including some board members, submitted his resignation as dean effective at the end of the 1972–73 academic year. He remained on for three years as the Potter Professor before moving to Belgium and to consulting work.[42]

Ansoff announced his resignation in September of 1972. Very quickly a committee began what turned out to be a frustrating search for a dean. By February, 1973, the committee had evaluated 146 possibilities. A flow of candidates came to the university. No one seemed very interested. In what turned out to be an extended interim, James V. Davis served as acting dean. In the first year he bettered the school's image locally. Whereas Ansoff had been prickly and quarrelsome, Davis was always obliging. He wanted to become the permanent dean and soon began enlisting local support. Davis established better relationships with local firms and reinvigorated the fund drive, which had languished for two years. Even without a new dean, the morale of the school temporarily improved. In 1974 J. Dewey Daane, a banking expert with experience on the Federal Reserve Board, came as the Houston Distinguished Professor of Banking, sharing his time with Commerce Union Bank. Other key appointments followed in the next two years. But the interval of renewed hopes could not last long, not without a new dean. The extended interim jeopardized student and faculty morale, as did increasing rumors that the school might have to close.

The rumors had all too much basis in fact. Continuing deficits, too few students, and the failure to find a new dean made 1974–75 a good time to call it quits. In January, 1975, board members debated two alternatives presented by Heard—close the school or risk the money needed to expand it from 100 students to 350, and from 11 to 30 faculty members over the next five years. It could not go on as at present. As normal in such cases, because of all the

684

embarrassment of closing, the Executive Committee finally voted for expansion. In February it allocated $1.25 million from the Harold S. Vanderbilt estate to meet expected operating deficits for six years and also promised to lend funds for a new building. This meant a possible deficit of $1.2 million plus interest plus building costs by 1981, or from $5 million to $13 million. Could the school ever repay so much? Heard had doubts and once again passed the burden of fund raising to the board. It had pledged that it would never draw funds from other schools; he already faced criticism from his faculty. In May, 1975, the full board spent over two hours discussing options for GSM; twenty-seven trustees spoke on the issue, a record number. Heard wistfully said that in a sense "I told you so back in 1967." After considering various options, the board voted to work toward a minimal expansion costing $7.5 million, rejecting other options that would have cost as much as $13 million. In a rare lack of consensus, eleven of thirty-four trustees abstained on the vote. Although the $7.5 million was to derive, eventually, from new fund-raising efforts, the board committed itself to the early loans needed for such expansion.[43]

With this crucial vote, Heard promptly appointed a task force, headed by James Surface, to plan the needed changes. Out of its work came the blueprint of what amounted, in many ways, to a new business school. The task force proposed that Vanderbilt move as quickly as possible to a middle-level business school, one with a faculty of twenty-one and approximately 250 students. Instead of a new building, it recommended additions to Alexander Hall, thus sparing as much as $4.7 million of the planned $7.5 million for an endowment. Effectively, the task force repudiated Ansoff's earlier model. He had tried too much too quickly and ended up with low standards. It recommended a more limited curriculum, more attention to the business sector, a faculty committed more to teaching than to research, or what it perceived as a school comparable to the one at Dartmouth, not one comparable to such great schools as those at Harvard and Stanford. In letter or telephone votes in July, 1975, the board approved the task force recommendations. The file of their votes contains a fascinating array of expressed opinion. The three "no" votes and two abstentions do not begin to reflect the depth of the expressed reservations, many from those who voted "yes."[44]

Board action in 1975 saved GSM, gave new hope to its faculty and students, and revived the search for a dean. In the school the faculty rather quickly conformed to the task force recommendations. In 1975 it ended all doctoral programs and moved to a single Master of Business Administration degree, eliminating even a Master of Management. By then, almost all its students planned careers in the corporate sector. As a follow-up, the school faced and escaped rather painlessly from a second embarrassing lawsuit. In 1976 seven students in the older Doctor of Management program charged a breach of contract. Stiffened degree requirements had prejudiced their chances of success. The court did not find any breach of contract in the new Ph.D.

requirements but nonetheless awarded the students a full refund of about $30,000 in tuition. The school had not provided a quality graduate program and thus had not lived up to its contractual obligation to graduate students.[45]

Most important of all, the new board commitment made the school attractive to prospective deans. A new eight-member search committee first recommended Harvey W. Wagner of Yale. He was interested, entering into long negotiations about the school. He wanted the board to commit Vanderbilt to a much larger and more expensive program. The negotiations with him ended in 1975, delaying an appointment for another frustrating year. The board finally elected Samuel B. Richmond, a statistician and transport specialist from Columbia University. This was perhaps the most eagerly awaited appointment of a dean in Vanderbilt's history. Richmond had served the Columbia Graduate School of Business both as associate dean and acting dean. Still in his fifties, quite vigorous, he brought to the school the leadership required for rapid growth. He also helped to complete the switch back toward rigor and conventional courses in what, in 1977, was renamed the Owen Graduate School of Management in honor of two local benefactors, Ralph and Lulu Owen. Richmond supported a shift in curriculum—mainly to requirements in such basic areas as math, statistics, economics, accounting, and finance. In 1976 tentative planning for a new building began, with the old Engineering Building then first identified as a possible base.

The school also applied for accreditation with the American Assembly of Collegiate Schools of Business. A favorable response required the College to drop its undergraduate major in business, a prospect that appalled many undergraduate students, led to an extended controversy in the *Hustler* in 1977, and to a debate in the Faculty Senate. Somewhat reluctantly, but soothed by much closer cooperation with OGSM, and by a new undergraduate minor in business administration, the department of economics and business administration, and then the College, capitulated, allowing OGSM to win its accreditation in 1977. Architects first began developing plans for a new $6.7 million building in 1978. In 1980 the school celebrated its first graduate in a new, widely publicized, largely weekend Master of Business Administration degree for executives. The school expanded by 1979 to a full-time equivalent of 20.5 faculty, with 280 students in its regular Master of Business Administration program and 70 in the program for executives, or close to the targets set by the task force in 1975. In 1982 the board approved an early Ph.D. program in finance and operations management. At least by estimates of its own faculty, the school had already attained the status contemplated by the task force—a very strong second-level school.[46]

The solid achievements spurred fund raising. After very successful appeals in the centennial campaign, the school seemed to have an assured financial future, although through 1982 it still had to depend upon loans from the university. It never, in the six years after 1975, used more than one-third of $1,386,000 in loans authorized by the board to cover deficits but had to ask for an extension of such loan privileges for 1981–82. By 1981 it had amassed an endowment of over $5 million and had raised $2 million for its new building and used bonded debt to pay the rest. From an annual budget of approximately $2 million in 1982, the school hoped to expand up to a $4 million budget in the next decade, to grow to a faculty of up to forty, and to enroll up to 400 students. Thus, after a sickly early childhood the school seemed to move toward a secure and reasonably healthy adolescence, although not necessarily a popular one. Resentments against it, jealousies over its recent progress, or continued doubts about the academic integrity of its courses still lived on in some of the College faculty.[47]

24

Presidential Politics

As EARLY AS 1973, at the end of his first ten years as chancellor, Alexander Heard began studying ways to reorganize Vanderbilt's central administration. In part, the motive had to be personal. The preceding decade had pushed him to the limits of patience and energy, had placed cruel burdens on his family, and the future seemed to require more of him than any one person could tolerate. He needed relief, more time for himself and his family, and some escape from the incessant pressure of campus constituencies. Heard, given his personality, could not ignore problems but rather tried to meet all of them, to bring everyone together, a task that was time-consuming and often nerve-wracking.

Heard's interest and capabilities increasingly were directed to the external relations of the university. He had to be away frequently, even to the extent that his former allies, the students, began complaining that they never saw their chancellor, although he maintained his open-door policy for students and still met with and entertained student groups. Heard believed consulting work, such as his advisory role in the Nixon administration, and his membership on the boards of Time, Inc. and the Ford Foundation was not a diversion of time but directly worked to the benefit of Vanderbilt. In 1972, with board permission, he became chairman of the board of the Ford Foundation, a demanding task. After 1973 he was also frequently involved in a series of university centennial celebrations, for he chose, in a break with tradition, not one large event or conference but a series of smaller events keyed to the different founding events of a century earlier. One very thoughtful, much-appreciated, and yet financially brilliant undertaking was a reunion on campus of the carefully identified descendants of Cornelius Vanderbilt, many of whom had never met one another. But most of all, Heard realized that he would have to give a much larger share of his time to fund raising. All of this lay behind the Sea Island conference of 1974, the opening plans for the centennial campaign, and early studies of various plans for executive reorganization. Out of this came a new office of president of the university and a fascinating, unprecedented, unrepeatable interlude when Vanderbilt had both a chancellor and a president.

After informal meetings with key board members—William S. Vaughn, Sam F. Fleming, David K. Wilson—Heard had a tentative reorganization plan ready for the Executive Committee meeting in April, 1976. At this point, and through much of the intense discussion on campus, Heard assumed that he would become president of the university and that a new chancellor would take over most of his campus responsibilities. He wanted to devote his time increasingly to institutional planning and financial development. So far, the provost had not relieved him of all academic responsibilities; his title still pulled him into critical issues on campus. He talked of making the board presidency an administrative post (echoes of Bishop McTyeire) and of asking the board to elect him to that post. As board president he could chair a new committee on planning and development, serve on all other committees, in a sense direct fund drives, handle governmental relations, and continue certain ceremonial functions, such as opening the commencement exercises (Heard always took these formalities very seriously). The new chancellor could serve as chief academic and administrative officer. The discussions, as ones that followed, revealed some ambivalence and a great deal of ambiguity. The new scheme both intrigued and concerned Heard. He wanted to move upstairs but not surrender his administrative authority. He wanted to be much more than a ceremonial head of state. As the discussions continued, his pride became involved, and more than ever before he revealed a personal sensitivity and at times an untypical impatience.[1]

The board, in 1976, delegated all the detailed arrangements to a new ad hoc board committee on executive organization, but in a sense Heard's views remained determinant. He served on the committee. On July 13, 1976, the committee made its preliminary report. It recommended that Heard become president of the university and that a screening committee, chaired by Heard but made up of trustees, faculty, administrators, and students, begin the search for a chancellor. The exact details posed several problems and invited various views on campus. The committee thus held a series of meetings from July until October, meetings that involved administrators, faculty, alumni, and even five students. Out of this came significant changes from the preliminary July report. One was semantic. Heard would retain the title of chancellor, avowedly to avoid confusing people off campus, but perhaps also as a way of affirming the continuity of his slightly more than coordinate authority. In subtle ways, this change of title downgraded the new office and also made more problematic the continuation of its occupant at the time of Heard's retirement. It also meant name changes everywhere. Since the new executive officer would be president of the university, this meant that the president of the board became chairman. All the vice-chancellors on campus became vice-presidents. Heard, as chancellor, now became vice-chairman of the board and of the Executive Committee and kept his ex officio position on the Faculty Senate. The new president would also be an ex officio member of the board and of the Faculty Senate. He or she was to report directly to the board, and all other lower offices would report to the president.

The sticky issue became that of the relationships among board, chancellor, and president. No listing of duties could quite clarify the subtleties here. As the Executive Committee conceived it, Heard would have responsibility for the "general welfare" of the university, would work directly with the board, have primary responsibility for fund raising, remain Vanderbilt's representative to the American Association of Universities, and continue to open and close commencement exercises. The president was to run the former chancellor's office in Kirkland, address the Faculty Assembly each year, award degrees, prepare the agenda for Heard and for board meetings, render reports to the board on the state of the university, draft annual budgets, and carry out most ceremonial roles on campus.[2]

The board, in its final deliberations over the new plan, came quickly to the crux of the issue—did the new president have a coordinate or subordinate position? Who outranked whom? Where did the buck stop? With the issues so drawn, the answer was clear—Heard would have authority over the president. Thus, to prevent future confusion and conflict, the board almost changed the crucial provision that the president report directly to the board, not to it through the chancellor. But such a move would have symbolically downgraded the president's position and jeopardized the search. Who wanted to take a thinly disguised provost position, even when dignified by a new title? The board decided to risk confusion and adopted the committee report (the new president would report directly to the board). But when the new screening committee, chaired by Heard, publicized the job description for the new president, it qualified the Board language on the critical issues of status and authority. It noted that the president, "pursuant to authority delegated by the Chancellor, act as the Chief academic and administrative officer of the University." The president was "along with the Chancellor," to "report to the Board of Trust. The Chancellor will be the President's point of communication with the Board. . . ." The new by-laws provided that the president, "in consultation with the Chancellor," was to "acquaint the Board of Trust with the state, interests, and needs of the University at every meeting of the Board."

These ambiguous statements caused considerable concern in the Faculty Senate. Generally, professors wanted their new president to have direct access to the board. The faculty also wanted the president to appoint all administrative officers and deans on his own authority. Thus the Faculty Senate petitioned the board to add by-laws clarifying specific areas in which the president would be able to exercise independent authority. The faculty action clearly disappointed Heard, who wondered how intelligent professors could be so suspicious. The board rejected the petition and let the job description stand. Significantly, Heard later referred to the plan as one "I proposed to the Board" and seemed anxious that people understand, correctly, that the powers of the president were ones that he "delegated" or gave up voluntarily.[3]

On paper the new scheme seemed awkward, an invitation to a confusion of

690

President Emmett Fields

authority or to frequent conflict. The board adopted it with the hope that Heard, whom they knew, and some future president would sort out the divergent responsibilities, would create a complementary working relationship. Whether it in fact worked out that way is still a debated point on campus. From the perspective of the university, it probably worked much better than one could have expected, even better than such an ambiguous scheme should have worked. Much of the early credit goes to Heard, much of the later credit to the new president, Emmett Fields.

The presidential screening committee, with all constituencies represented, worked very hard, but yet with the outcome already all but settled. Heard had first approached Emmett B. Fields about a new executive appointment as early as 1973. Board members Fleming and Wilson had wooed him for the presidency before the search officially opened. The position was created, and defined, with him in mind. In most high-level recruitment, success often depends upon adventitious factors—someone is at the right point in a career, has personal reasons for a move, needs to cater to health or to special family needs, or is strongly loyal to an institution. Fields, an Arkansas native, a Vanderbilt Ph.D. in history, a former dean of the College, had deep loyalties to Vanderbilt and lesser loyalties to the South. Without those incentives, it is unlikely that he would have considered the job, since in professional terms it was a risky move. He had left Vanderbilt for the University of Houston, had risen there to senior vice-chancellor, and from there in 1975 moved to a major executive position as president of the State University of New York–Albany, or close to the top in university administration. Although the whole New York system had a head, the president was the highest administrative officer at each of the campuses, and Albany was one of the two most prestigious campuses in the system. Ordinarily one in this position would not move to an ambiguous, second-level administrative position elsewhere. Fields did. One aspect of the gamble was the prospect of becoming chancellor when Heard retired. He came with this expectation, not because any board members ever promised it, and despite the necessary statements that no such was entailed, but because such a prospect seemed to him to be an unspoken assumption throughout the bargaining process. Another factor was the pressure he faced in his new job at Albany. He had served to some extent as a "hatchet" man, getting rid of dead wood, setting priorities, and trying to strengthen key departments. He had created enemies as well as friends and functioned in a system with severe financial problems. A final lure was the ample prerogatives given him at Vanderbilt, in salary, fringe benefits, and use of a luxurious Belle Meade home.

Fields had to make the presidency what it was. He came determined to be chief administrative and academic officer, and quickly asserted himself to establish the needed authority. He made critical decisions. Very early he made the board his source of authority and worked carefully to coordinate policies with it. He behaved just like a new chancellor. On campus he took charge in a much more direct way than had the early Heard, a matter of a very different personality and a different conception of administration. Heard was a politician; Fields, primarily a manager. What seemed to be ambiguous on campus was Heard's continuing role. Of course, everyone understood his work in fund raising and in the university's external relations, but many wondered about his authority in Kirkland. In the crunch did he still run things? Did the critical issues all move up from the large president's office on the second floor to Heard's more modest office on the third? Not normally. The records show a magnanimous, surely at times a frustrating early defer-ence on the part of Heard. He tried to keep in the background, to surrender real authority, not an easy task for anyone who had served so long as chancellor. Heard pushed Fields to the fore not just as a gesture, not to screen himself from tough decisions, but because he wanted the new system to work. In this case, history did not repeat itself a hundred years later; Fields was not a Garland, Heard not a McTyeire.

Yet, on several critical issues, Heard had to become directly involved. This was not because of his office as chancellor so much as the fact that Fields had hardly arrived at Vanderbilt before a series of crises erupted, one after the other. They were of such a magnitude that they related to the "general welfare" of the university. That is, they were so serious that they overlapped

Heard's designated areas of responsibility, even as they also necessarily involved the direct role of the Board of Trust. Thus, on such issues as athletic policy, affirmative action, and the merger with Peabody, Heard had to play a key role, not in such a way as to take all responsibility away from Fields but in ways that required both men, for the welfare of the university, to arrive at and defend a common policy.

In the midst of these crises the early harmony between Heard and Fields slowly degenerated into distrust and tension. Outwardly, except on two public occasions, their relationship remained correct and even cordial. Disagreements on major issues never escaped the confidentiality of staff or board meetings. The university did not suffer. But the personal costs were high on both sides, particularly for Fields, not only in the frustrations of his job but in his ultimate loss of the chancellorship. Perhaps a degree of distrust and suspicion, if not conflict, was built into the ambiguous new administrative plan. Personality differences added to structural pitfalls. Heard had trouble accepting Fields's administrative style and initiatives. Fields wanted to change basic policies, to occupy a truly coordinate leadership position. Whenever he tried to establish priorities of his own, to shape a distinctive administrative program, then he felt that Heard became uneasy and hypercritical. Heard often felt that Fields had by-passed him or had taken too much responsibility or credit for policies, that he had usurped the role of the chancellor. He also felt that Fields procrastinated on important policy decisions in areas not central to his own priorities.

Fields tried to honor Heard's position and in all formal ways did so. He consulted when appropriate and routed most decisions through Heard's office. But in the somewhat ambiguous situation, he felt that he had to take charge. From his perspective, Vanderbilt needed strong leadership, and if he were to gain the respect of the board and establish his credentials as a future chancellor, he had to do the hard work that justified his appointment. He saw his role as that of an able and tough manager, brought to Vanderbilt to arrest a trend toward drift and indecision. He believed that Heard lacked needed managerial skills and that several key members of the board agreed with this view. He acknowledged Heard's enormous strengths as a fund raiser, as an eloquent spokesman for the university, as a superb diplomat in handling the university's external relations. But in an era of limited resources, of hard decisions and needed retrenchment, he also felt that Heard's collegial and conciliatory style, which had served Vanderbilt so magnificently in the fractious 1960s, was now antiquated. Thus, Fields could not help but reveal his own sense that Vanderbilt was a slack ship in need of a strong commander. This helps explain what Fields soon viewed as obstructionist tactics by Heard and, in two cases, what Fields viewed as Heard's embarrassing assertions of authority before a university and then a board committee.

The differences in temperament and style made a warm, harmonious partnership almost impossible. Heard simply could not understand the

693

aggressive, at times almost confrontational style of Fields, a style much closer to that of an earlier Branscomb than to that of Heard. He distrusted Fields's managerial preoccupations, felt that at times Fields tried too hard to win favor from the board, and believed that he lacked the needed human sensitivity for an executive position. Heard, characteristically, worried about those whom Fields offended, about how various Vanderbilt constituencies might react to what Heard saw as an often abrasive manner, about the feelings of those who might lose out in a managerial approach that entailed losers as well as winners. Heard remained the conciliator, concerned as much with process as with results, with form and grace and style as much as with content. From his perspective, Fields turned out to be a very different administrator than he had expected or desired. Fields seemed to create, rather than alleviate, tensions. He put off or offended people rather than pulling them into the community. He was, in this view, inept or even cruel in dealing with subordinates, either vice-presidents or professors. Heard soon concluded that Fields was not qualified as his successor, and indeed Fields would have been a very different sort of chancellor. What Fields saw as obstructionism on Heard's part seemed from Heard's perspective only necessary intrusions to protect the university from divisive policies or tactics. Heard wanted to minimize the damages or to pacify this or that constituency.[4]

Fields came to Vanderbilt in August, 1977. His one conspicuous handicap in gaining the respect of his faculty came from his lack of scholarly attainments. In compensation he had long and varied administrative experience, was informed on issues affecting higher education, and was conversant with management theory. In working papers, in reports to the board, he occasionally sounded like a stereotyped educator or a corporate manager, with his convoluted, abstract, and jargonistic prose, with his models and his management teams, but in more self-revealing speeches to the public he could be effective, even moving. He reflected an intense, even sentimental affection for Vanderbilt. He was open, frank, and direct in working with committees. He was not given to pleasantries and to small talk. If anything, he most prided himself on making tough decisions, on choosing among options, on developing a few clearly focused goals and working toward them. He had developed this administrative style and some guiding convictions about higher education from his experience at Houston and Albany. These very much shaped his beginning administration at Vanderbilt.

Fields assumed the presidency at the beginning of the centennial campaign, at a time of looming deficits, lagging faculty salaries, and a cacophony of dire predictions about the future of higher education. Thus, in what amounted to his inaugural speech to the faculty in September, 1977, he set a theme for his early years at Vanderbilt—the need for a few carefully focused missions and the elimination of all peripheral or unsuccessful programs in a "steady state" era of limited resources. He stressed the problems in higher education, emphasized dramatic changes in the larger society, and then tried to assess Vanderbilt's strengths and weaknesses. In follow-up talks and papers, to the bemusement of some professors, he spoke often in the language of systems theory, with his models and flow charts and other mystifications. Fields noted a slowed pace and slipping energies at Vanderbilt as compared to the Vanderbilt he knew back in the 1960s. The core concerns were now less focal, the entrenched bureaucracy less sensitive, the relationships between administrators and faculty less harmonious, the campus less exciting, and the goals less clear. These somber themes were not new to him. He had been through all this before at a much more beleaguered Albany. His purpose then became clear—to launch a new self-study at Vanderbilt, the typical first step for a new manager. Vanderbilt had had many of these before. But Fields would give this one a personal stamp, beginning with his chosen label—reassessment. Reassessment suggested hard decisions, sacrifices as well as gains. It meant that every department or program had to justify its existence. It suggested not only overall university growth, but the suspension or curtailment of weak programs in order to focus energies on strong ones.[5]

Fields waited a year to launch his reassessment, or until the fall faculty meeting of 1978. He had little choice. A nasty controversy over the Davis Cup tennis matches in the spring of 1978 and a long brewing crisis surrounding the whole athletic program took up most of his time. These athletic issues placed his leadership skills on the line, tested in a way no one had planned the effectiveness of the new administrative scheme, and plunged Fields all too quickly into the one issue that, traditionally, had most separated faculty opinion from that of the board and thus had traditionally posed the greatest perils for chancellors.

It is not easy to describe the role of intercollegiate sports at Vanderbilt. The subject invites cant or hypocrisy, as much so on the side of those who want to abolish specially recruited and subsidized teams as those who want to do anything necessary to produce winning teams. The past, as always, sets the terms for later policy making. In the age of innocence, and of truly amateur competition, Vanderbilt made a wholehearted commitment to football and then to basketball. McGugin contributed almost as much to Vanderbilt's developing identity as did Chancellor Kirkland. By the end of that golden era, by the 1930s, when recruiting and grants-in-aid and special admission and special treatment slowly became essential for winning, Vanderbilt could not easily repudiate its past, give up its teams. The tradition was too fixed, the loyalties among alumni too deep and abiding. From the elderly Kirkland on, every chancellor had tried to find solutions to the problem, with nothing gained but futility and frustration. They tried to reform the sec but with little result. They contemplated new conferences but largely met indifference on the part of other universities. They made fewer moral and academic compromises than did other sec competitors, a source of pride that yet never quite compensated for athletic mediocrity. But all this seemed to lead, by the 1960s, to the worst of all possible worlds—most of the evils of the system and few of its glories.

The evils were inescapable, essential to sec competition. Pained innocence did not become Vanderbilt. Competitive athletics undermined the fairness of the admission process and slowly forced compromises in Vanderbilt's academic programs. For example, in 1967 Vanderbilt students on athletic grants scored 178 points lower than the average of College men on the sat. Only 40 percent graduated in the normal four years (lower than that for football players), and only 60 percent ever completed Vanderbilt degrees. Those who did graduate, on average, had grades near the minimum required, and athletes had double the average number of honor code violations. By 1973 a board survey showed limited improvements (65 percent had completed degrees). But athletes were three times as likely to have disciplinary problems. As 5 percent of the student body they caused one-fourth of the damage in student dorms. They also ate 50 percent more food, smoked less marijuana, and almost never sought psychological counseling.[6]

Those who fervently fought to abolish all big-time college sports often revealed an unflattering, or dishonest, naivete. Of course, football victories on Saturday do not directly further the educational goals of Vanderbilt. But victories on Saturday may sustain the level of support needed for educational goals. The issues here are not fully resolvable on any evidence. No one can say for sure how giving patterns would shift if Vanderbilt, in a moment of academic righteousness, repudiated its sec commitments and experimented once again with truly amateur sports (no grants, no preferential admission, and no high-powered coaches). A few people would rejoice and increase their gifts. For some, the shock might be shortlived. But there is always the possibility that the cost would be very high, so high that Vanderbilt would suffer deep and lasting damage. In any case, the risk has been too high for the gamble. Whether it should be so or not, Vanderbilt teams have remained the most visible link between Vanderbilt and aging alumni. Television has tremendously enhanced the continuing bond. Most alumni, however attentive they are to Vanderbilt academic programs, become more emotionally involved with its football or basketball teams. However much pride evoked by Earl Sutherland's Nobel Prize, alumni become more intensely concerned about the success or failure of the most recent football coach. This lesson, if not already obvious, had to be learned quickly by any new chancellor.

Heard did not have to learn this. The clues from the board at the time of his appointment were as clear as when Branscomb came. The one unalterable condition of his appointment was his willingness to continue big-time athletics. In an early address to the quarterback club, Heard tried to clarify his views on athletic policy. He emphasized the value of sports, stressed physical education, intramurals, and recreational sports over the "publicized" and "self-supporting" big two. He ended with all the pieties—about high

Dean John Wade, Law School

academic standards and the need for Vanderbilt to adhere to its primary educational mission. Disillusionment came early and intensified as one football coach after another failed to win in the SEC. In 1967 Heard somewhat ruefully informed the board that Vanderbilt, beyond teaching, research, and service, had a fourth mission—entertainment. He asked a frank acceptance of this mission and suggested the possibility of leaving the SEC and buying a professional team to entertain Vanderbilt fans.[7]

How poorly did Vanderbilt teams do in the SEC? In the 1960s they remained competitive in minor sports, competed for preeminence in basketball, but did miserably in football, the one sport with greatest earning potential. In 1963 Jack Green came from Florida as new football coach, or what turned out to be a disastrous decision for him. In 1963 his team beat only George Washington, losing even to Furman. His teams improved only marginally during the next three years, leading to his resignation at the end of the 1966 season. Fortunately, this debacle in football paralleled a glorious era in basketball. In 1963–64 Roy Skinner's team won nineteen, beat Kentucky, and remained in the top ten much of the season. A sophomore, Clyde Lee, made the all-SEC team, foreshadowing even greater success for the next two seasons. In 1964–65 Vanderbilt won the SEC title (its first), barely lost in the NCAA tournament to national champion Michigan, and Lee made all-American. Fans practically fought for tickets, a boom that led to all the new balconies in the gym. In 1965–66, Lee's senior year, the team started strong, rose to second place in the polls, but two crushing losses to Kentucky denied it the SEC crown and an NCAA bid. Skinner's magic continued even without Lee; in 1966–67 a less talented team again made national rankings, tied for second in the SEC, and Skinner won national coach-of-the-year honors. The next year he compiled a 20–8 season. By now, Vanderbilt basketball fans expected only winning teams.[8]

Basketball success helped deflect alumni attention away from the football program. After Green resigned, a new, special university committee began an extended study of the athletic program. One early, and quickly implemented, suggestion was that Vanderbilt join other conference teams by hiring an athletic director. In the fall of 1967 Vanderbilt brought a retirement-aged football hero, Jess C. Neely, back from Rice University, where he had coached since 1940. Neely appointed a younger man, Bill Pace, as football coach. But such shifts changed nothing at all on the field.[9]

From 1967–68 on, the board tried to find an answer for Vanderbilt football. In doing so, it allowed athletic priorities for the first time to affect basic academic policies. And already, even though on paper the athletic department was self-supporting, the university had accepted limited subsidies for the teams. The tuition paid the university by the athletic department as part of its grants-in-aid was now less than the rate for other students. After 1969 the university also paid subsidies for some nonincome sports. The great debate began with a report from a special committee chaired by former Dean Ewing Shahan. It recommended that Vanderbilt, at least temporarily, remain in the SEC. In addition to the new athletic director, the committee recommended and the university implemented several additional new privileges for athletes: special academic advising, the segregation of athletes in a section of Carmichael Towers (as a cheap substitute for a separate athletic dorm), a training table for athletes (special meals), and more carefully devised class schedules so as to accommodate players.

A final proposal provoked years of controversy—that the university expand its course offerings and degree programs. This was, in part at least, a euphemism for degrees in health and physical education and for other less demanding programs in education or in engineering. This suggestion led to a series of proposals during the next four years and influenced the decision of Engineering to add a less rigorous B.S. degree. By 1972 the dean of a new division of allied health professions in the Medical School proposed an almost academically respectable Bachelor of Science degree in health and physical education. Provost Hobbs submitted a proposal for a divison of teacher education. But a resistant College faculty had enough strength in the Faculty Senate to block or defer all such proposals.[10]

In 1969 the despairing board concluded that Vanderbilt could not compete in the SEC with its existing high academic standards. Success in recruiting required a physical education department and opportunities for athletes to get teaching degrees so as to become high school coaches. The Shahan committee had explored joint programs of this type with Peabody, a possibil-

Walter Murray, the first black trustee

ity now eagerly pursued by the board. The Peabody board welcomed such prospects of cooperation and, in November, 1969, proposed a whole series of joint degree programs as part of the University Center. But the Vanderbilt faculty retained the power to veto all such programs. In 1971 the Vanderbilt board appointed a trustee committee on athletics, which was to work with a comparable Peabody committee in developing a joint physical education program. But even this risked the hazards of a likely negative vote in the Vanderbilt Faculty Senate.

The trustee committee found an almost magical solution. In a wide-ranging report in 1972, it aired such options as becoming independent, joining the Atlantic Coast Conference, or returning to amateur status. But it preferred another option suddenly available to Vanderbilt—to use Peabody students on its athletic teams. After learning of NCAA approval for joint athletic teams at two small California colleges, Vice-Chancellor Purdy successfully petitioned the NCAA for permission, over the next two years, to use Peabody students at Vanderbilt. The NCAA renewed this permission at the end of 1976. This option tremendously improved recruiting possibilities, since prospects now had the option of enrolling in a less rigorous Peabody and of majoring in physical education. Within a few years up to half of the football team came from Peabody, and Peabody students rightly argued the team should also carry the Peabody name, else Peabody would become an athletic colony of Vanderbilt. For example, in 1976 six basketball players were from Peabody and forty-one football players, or roughly two-thirds of all freshmen players. The most valuable defensive player in the 1975 Peach

Bowl was from Peabody, although none of the media accounts ever mentioned Peabody.[11]

During the four years of debate over athletic policy, the basketball team remained strong while even the football team began winning a few games. Bill Pace got off to a bad start in the fall of 1967. For two years, his 2–7 teams did not win an SEC contest. Then in 1969 Vanderbilt upset Alabama and beat Kentucky at homecoming, for a 4–6 year, a great season for Vanderbilt (Watson Brown was the great hero). In 1970 Vanderbilt won 4 and lost 7, still a comparatively good year. But in 1972 hopes of improvement gave way to near despair. The team lost eight games, students lost interest, and attendance, up to an average of 25,000 in 1969, dropped to a pitiful 17,600 average in 1972, or not more than half of other SEC schools. Even the basketball team had a losing year in 1969–70, but led by Jan van Breda Kolff it bounced back to another SEC championship by 1974 and a second but unsuccessful trip to the NCAA tournament. In 1973, with Neely at retirement age and Pace on the ropes, the Athletic Committee appointed a new coaching team, Clay Stapleton as athletic director and Steve Sloan as football coach.

Sloan seemed to perform miracles. In an expected weak first year, his team at least beat Kentucky at homecoming and came close to beating Tennessee. After impressive improvements in 1974, his 1975 team set a post-1948 Vanderbilt record (7–3–1). After tying Tennessee, it accepted an invitation to the Peach Bowl and tied Texas Tech, which turned around and hired Sloan. Just a year later Skinner retired as basketball coach. Gloom pervaded Vanderbilt. Its new football coach from Memphis State, Fred Pancoast, suffered two 2–9 seasons and could not win in the SEC. Thus, despite all the efforts, and despite the 1972 Peabody agreement, Vanderbilt remained a loser. Immense pressures mounted to get rid of Stapleton and Pancoast. Students, who had downgraded athletics in the early 1970s, were once again football fans and signed petitions for a coaching change. To add to the pressures, a small stadium and small attendance jeopardized continued SEC participation. Finally, even basketball did not provide much relief; under a new coach, Wayne Dobbs, the team had losing seasons in 1976–77 and 1977–78. It was this gloomy situation that greeted President Fields in his first year and which led to the one most agonizing reassessment of his brief five years as president of Vanderbilt.

One aspect of the developing athletic crisis was financial. By 1973 the athletic department carried a debt of $3.5 million, most related to new construction. The debt would have to be retired by 1981. Gifts and ticket sales barely paid its annual budget, which rose to $2.6 million by 1978. By then, the very survival of football seemed to require a new stadium. Most agreements with SEC teams expired by 1979 and few of these teams were willing to continue 50–50 gate splitting on both home and away games. Vanderbilt, to its own embarrassment, earned much more from its games away from Nashville than from those at home. To remain in the SEC, and to earn needed income, it seemed that Vanderbilt would have to have a stadium seating close to 50,000. Already, when Fields came to Vanderbilt, a board committee was at work exploring various stadium options. The least expensive option seemed to be a Vanderbilt contribution to a new Metro stadium, but since this threatened to remove football from the campus, students vociferously opposed the plan. But for over three years Vanderbilt officials carried on negotiations with the Metro Council. In November, 1977, just as Fields settled in, a committee to study the long-range future of the athletic program stressed the unrealistic prospects downtown and recommended that Vanderbilt move ahead on at least a renovation of Vanderbilt Stadium to add 10,000 to 15,000 seats. This recommendation led the Executive Committee to explore all other options, and the issue quickly became very sensitive on campus. In January, 1978, Fields personally took responsibility for a new "management level" task force study of the stadium issue. But even as it started work, the campus exploded in controversy over an event planned by the lowly tennis team.[12]

The plans began in late 1977. Vanderbilt bid for and then contracted to host the North American zone finals of Davis Cup competition on March 17–19, 1978. At the time the contest was contracted in December, the almost certain contestants were the United States and South Africa (the South Africa team needed only one victory over a weak team to qualify). That a South African team would provoke criticism, if not large demonstrations, should have been clear, but apparently no one at Vanderbilt foresaw the magnitude of opposition. Recent South African repressions of blacks and of demonstrating students had aroused intense concern on the part of many Americans. The tennis agreement was one calculated to bring added prestige and money to the Vanderbilt tennis program. Vanderbilt worked out an intricate contract with the United States Tennis Association, one that promised considerable "profits" for Vanderbilt if the matches were well attended, possible losses otherwise. To protect Vanderbilt against any losses, the local NLT Corporation agreed to underwrite the event. By February the matches had already provoked the threat of massive protests, with most of the organizing led by the local NAACP and by some local churches. For students, now a bit nostalgic for the activist 1960s, here was a bona fide issue. Yet, campus opinion divided sharply, with everyone on both sides claiming to hate apartheid. The matches pushed Vanderbilt into the national limelight and led to policy statements by both Fields and Heard. Both appealed to the old policy of an open forum. The very nature of the opposition to the matches had turned them into a political issue, and thus Vanderbilt once again defended the principle of free expression. It promised to protect the rights of everyone on both sides of the argument, from protesters to those who wanted to attend the matches. The university endorsed neither side in the developing controversy and tried to do

701

everything possible to make it clear that it did not endorse apartheid in South Africa. Vanderbilt thus refused to cancel its contract and made ready to cope with protest and even possible violence.[13]

The Davis Cup matches considerably divided the campus. But, as during the student demonstrations of the 1960s, the administration never provided a very clear target. The majority of students, according to limited polls, endorsed the forum explanation and thus the holding of the matches. The consultative committee of the Faculty Senate voted to go ahead with the matches, while the senate itself passed a resolution condemning apartheid and expressing its regret that the Davis Cup competition obscured Vanderbilt's opposition to such a policy. Fourteen senators also signed a petition in opposition to the matches. The Divinity School and the university chaplain joined in opening Benton Chapel to opposition groups. Vanderbilt even subsidized a speak-out that allowed opponents a chance to address faculty and students. A faculty petition of 85 against the matches hardly balanced one of over 200 supporting the chancellor's and president's rationale for holding them. The division on campus meant that some faculty joined the protesting marchers during the games, or the first time in Vanderbilt history that professors had done so with impunity and no sense of administrative displeasure. Dean Sallie McFague (formerly TeSelle) of the Divinity School spoke out strongly against the matches and endorsed a strong opposition petition by her faculty. On the first day of the matches long but peaceful lines of marchers demonstrated before, but did not block entrance to, the gym. Smaller demonstrations followed until the matches ended. Smaller than normal crowds evaporated all hopes of great profits for Vanderbilt. Because of the controversy, NLT withdrew its sponsorship, but the United States Tennis Association relieved Vanderbilt of its $50,000 guarantee. Ironically, a reserve member of the South African team was a "coloured" Vanderbilt student from Cape Town, Peter Lamb, who defended holding the matches.

As a follow-up gesture, Fields addressed the Board of Trust on the much-agitated problem of investments by American companies in South Africa. Vanderbilt owned stock in approximately thirty-two companies with such investments. Fields opposed blanket devestment but suggested that the Vanderbilt proxy committee (a product of student activism back in 1971) selectively oppose any company policies that abetted apartheid in South Africa. The faculty-student-trustee committee, in a split vote just after the Davis Cup controversy, encouraged the board to cast votes against the management of two banks that loaned money to the South African government, or a rare example of moral concern affecting Vanderbilt's investment policies.[14]

The explosive Davis Cup controversy paralleled some climactic decisions about overall athletic policy. Enormous outside pressures, plus various allegations in the newspapers, led Chairman of the Board Fleming, Heard, and Fields all to issue public statements stressing that authority for athletic

Davis Cup protestors
(James Lawson, Jr., is speaking; Chaplain Beverly Asbury is to the left)

decisions lay within the university, and that Fields would assume administrative responsibility for any new policies adopted. Both a board committee and an administration-faculty committee completed studies by the spring of 1978. Thus, by the May board meeting Fields was ready to offer recommendations. He defended the athletic program as an inseparable part of the Vanderbilt tradition. He emphasized how much the teams strengthened the bond between Vanderbilt and its many constituencies, including the Nashville public. Although holding open a hope for a future Metro stadium, he announced the opening of planning for expansion of Vanderbilt's stadium to 45,000 or 50,000 seats. He stressed that Vanderbilt would try to attain excellence in everything it attempted, including athletics. He concluded with a careful but challengeable remark, that excellence in athletics need not compromise the central academic mission of Vanderbilt. Instead, pride in educational attainments could complement a proud athletic program if Vanderbilt continued to play by the rules and if its athletic program continued to live on its own income without diverting funds from academic departments.

He argued that this was possible, that Vanderbilt could win with scholar-athletes, and that it could win within the SEC. In these statements Fields appeased alumni and outside critics, chose the policy most acceptable to a majority of the board, but alarmed many faculty members by a stronger pro-athletic position than that taken by Branscomb or Heard. He also chose a policy that Heard could not fully endorse.[15]

Fields's first step in gaining athletic excellence was to announce the firing of Stapleton as athletic director. Technically, Stapleton resigned in June, 1978, but the coercion behind his resignation was documented by continued salary payments through his contract period of 1981 (paid, as were all higher administrative salaries, from a secret New York bank account controlled by the chairman and two vice-chairmen of the Board of Trust). Stapleton had become one of the devils in the piece, much hated by outside critics and purportedly sly and evasive. This handicap, and a tactless business manager, had offended many ticket purchasers. A committee very carefully screened new candidates for Stapleton's position before appointing Roy F. Kramer, a former Maryville College graduate and then football coach at Central Michigan University, for this most critical job, a job not only in recruiting coaches and athletes but in public relations. Kramer quickly solved many of the public relations problems and after the 1979 season fired the unpopular Pancoast and hired George MacIntyre as new football coach. MacIntyre slowly built a winning team by 1982, when Vanderbilt attended the Hall of Fame bowl. In 1980 Kramer replaced Wayne Dobbs as basketball coach with N. Richard Schmidt, even though in 1978–79 Dobbs's team had won eighteen games, and despite Dobbs's selection as SEC coach of the year. After Schmidt's teams suffered not only two losing seasons but morale problems, he was let go in 1981 in behalf of a talented, experienced C.M. Newton, a former Alabama coach who had moved to a position in the offices of the SEC. Newton, reasonably successful in his first two years, seemed to elicit the maximum performance from players of only average talent. Only major recruitment efforts could regain Vanderbilt's lost basketball status in the now very competitive SEC, an almost impossible assignment by 1983. In contrast to earlier years, basketball recruitment had become by 1984 a tougher problem than in football.

The stadium issue was even more sensitive than the choice of coaches. But it was critical to Fields's SEC commitment. His management task force completed a fifty-five-page stadium report in March, 1978. It covered seven different options, ranging from modest renovations to a new 45,000- to 50,000-seat stadium at a maximum cost of $14 million. With good luck, gate receipts could amortize all the options. The board committee chose a middle option—$7 million for extensive renovation, including a press box, and a new capacity of 45,000. In any case, the existing stadium needed extensive repairs, simply from the standpoint of engineering and safety. In November, 1979, the Executive Committee debated a formal motion to proceed with the stadium project. The strongest reservation was voiced by Chancellor Heard, who seemed finally to enjoy venting his doubts and frustrations over athletic policy, or what he called the "most intractable matter" of his seventeen years as chancellor. Thus his frustration closely matched that revealed in earlier comments by a retiring Kirkland and Branscomb.

Heard knew the board would accept the new stadium proposal. He thus felt free to speak his mind. The stadium project already threatened one of his principles—the financial independence of athletic programs. He believed the university would have to provide financing for the new stadium. Vanderbilt had already violated one of his hallowed principles—it had drawn students from outside existing academic programs (the Peabody agreement). All it had left was pride in adhering to the rules. But within the rules it seemed to be moving toward a position in which it would do anything possible to win. He pointed out, quite correctly, that Vanderbilt could not win in the SEC without special academic programs, such as those at Peabody, and special sources of funds, and thus not without compromising its stated academic goals and standards. He traced ten such added expedients or academic compromises adopted since 1962 and asked where it would all end. He reversed Fields's statement and said scholar-athletes could not win in the SEC. Gate receipts from academically respectable Vanderbilt teams could not build a new stadium. He thus supported views widely expressed in the Faculty Senate, predicted increasing faculty alienation from the athletic program, and asked for special commitments by the board to protect the financial resources of Vanderbilt's academic programs before it went ahead with the stadium. He predicted a series of new compromises, all necessary for victory, perhaps beginning with separate athletic dorms. On the vote to plan a $7 million addition, both Heard and Branscomb abstained and seven trustees including two of the women voted "no," or a comparatively rare dissent on an issue of this importance. To a certain extent the winning vote was a vote of confidence for Fields and his policies.[16]

The final stadium plans came to the Executive Committee of the board in March, 1980. Heard once again offered warnings. Professionalism was now a fact. Scandals were likely. Illegal gambling was extensive at Vanderbilt football games, even among the most fervent supporters of its athletic program. He had no evidence that winning teams had increased levels of giving. He even wistfully looked back and suggested that had he earlier stood firm against grants-in-aid to athletes he might have won the point. He was now prepared to move that Vanderbilt get out of the SEC and that it end all grants and any plans for a stadium. No one encouraged such a motion. Instead, the Executive Committee voted to enlarge the stadium to 41,000 by modernizing and enlarging the stands, all at a cost of approximately $11.6 million. Private patrons promised to market tax free bonds and, according to the plan, gifts plus gate receipts would retire them. In this sense Fields made good on the commitment not to divert funds from academic programs. Along with stadium renovation, the Executive Committee discussed what Heard saw as one of the inevitable next steps—special courses for athletes. Provost Holladay said he would bend on this issue only so far as special "gateway" or entry-level courses. Heard joined the other members of the committee in a unanimous vote on the funding details, and with this go-ahead the successful stadium renovation was completed by the fall season of 1981 (the long-range plans included completion of the open or northern end of the horseshoe, or an eventual capacity of 50,000). The new stadium lessened the pressures from other SEC teams, but in itself did not insure winning teams or Vanderbilt's ability, over time, to compete successfully in SEC football. By 1984 only one eventuality seemed all but certain—this most "intractable" problem will return to haunt future Vanderbilt chancellors.[17]

Fields's reassessment effort began in the fall of 1978 even as he struggled with athletic issues. A very capable reassessment panel set about evaluating administrative organization, support services, and academic programs, and worked throughout 1979. Its goal was a more rational allocation of resources. This meant a balance-sheet approach—saving through the elimination or curtailment of peripheral or unsuccessful academic and non-academic programs and the shifting of these savings to high-priority departments. By 1979 the sense of financial crisis had lessened, in part because of the early successes of the centennial campaign. Not austerity but a desire for rationality guided the delicate evaluations.

Fields, in the spirit of reassessment, helped consolidate the central administration in 1979 when Vice-President Purdy retired. Fields assumed personal responsibility for athletic matters, thus helping to eliminate one vice-president's position. Other tasks formerly assumed by Purdy went elsewhere. Jeff Carr, who had moved up from chief counsel to vice-president for governmental relations, now assumed overall responsibility for alumni affairs and publications and also took over some of the duties of the former secretary of the university (Robert McGaw also retired). The new provost, Wendell Holladay, assumed responsibility for student affairs. In addition to Carr and Holladay, the vice-president for medical affairs and the director of development also reported directly to Fields. But once again, as the reassessment panel prepared its final report, external events intruded, not only to force changes in the reassessment report but drastically to reduce its relative significance. George Peabody College for Teachers finally asked to merge with Vanderbilt.[18]

After so many aborted merger efforts in the past and particularly the last deeply frustrating effort of 1962, Peabody and Vanderbilt had backed away from merger talks and had instead sought closer cooperation in the 1960s and 1970s, cooperation exemplified by the common calendar agreement of 1963 and the athletic agreement of 1972. Peabody and Vanderbilt also continued as members of a Nashville University Center, that old dream of interuniversity cooperation that never quite died but never fulfilled many of the early, grandiose expectations. A small Ford Foundation grant in 1969 funded the University Center Council, made up of the chief officer and two delegates from the five cooperating institutions—Fisk, Meharry, Peabody, Scarritt, and Vanderbilt. The center developed its formal constitution in 1972 and hired an executive director. The council coordinated schedules, facilitated student registrations on neighboring campuses, coordinated programs and lectures, began some joint purchasing, supported library specialization, and arranged for a Metro bus to travel between Fisk and Vanderbilt. But by 1977 the center threatened to expire because of the end of foundation support. By then, four of the five schools were in trouble; only Vanderbilt was a strong, secure institution. Within the next five years Scarritt would practically go under, Fisk would face dire financial problems, and in 1981 Meharry briefly faced bankruptcy.

Peabody had greater strengths, but demographic trends proved devastating for colleges of education by the late 1970s. Declining enrollments left Peabody with unused facilities. Thus, Vanderbilt began leasing Confederate and East halls in 1978, or up to 200 dorm rooms. The problems at Peabody dated back to 1970 when austerity first became the rule. The college lost thirty faculty members in the next two years as it tried to reduce annual deficits. Inflation more than ate away meager salary increases, and several professors had to teach larger course loads. Some Ph.D. programs faced a loss of accreditation. In 1974 Peabody began sharply reducing its music program, moving toward a limited degree in music education. It also eliminated programs in business education, home economics, and modern languages, sold its demonstration school, cut courses in the arts and sciences, and began the elimination of all work in accounting. By 1978 the very survival of Peabody seemed to be at stake. Its undergraduate enrollment had dropped from 1,200 in 1972 to only 800, joined by a shrinking pool of approximately 1,200 graduate students.[19]

In this crisis Peabody president John Dunworth decided that neither Peabody nor any college of education could now survive without university affiliation. No such specialized college could continue to pay for a large campus, for all educational services, and for the academic courses needed for specialized degrees in education. Stringent measures had balanced Peabody's budget and saved its plant and endowment. The future threatened to erode these assets and to so weaken Peabody that it would have nothing to offer in merger talks. It seemed now or never. Short of a merger, Dunworth preferred liquidation to slow stagnation and decline. Of course, Dunworth first considered a merger with Vanderbilt. He persuaded his board to approve beginning negotiations with Vanderbilt by August of 1978, negotiations that he planned to carry out in complete secrecy. He originally met with Heard and then with Fields. He believed a merger, if at all possible, had to be effected quickly, before disappointed or threatened Peabody faculty, students, and alumni could organize resistance. Dunworth knew that he could not save the job of professors outside the area of education and human development. Unlike in the past, Peabody no longer bargained with Vanderbilt as an equal but as something close to a supplicant. Dunworth therefore sought one goal—a merger agreement that would guarantee an indefinite survival of a strong college of education. Without this guarantee he was unwilling to consider a merger with Vanderbilt or with any other university.

The first, confidential merger talks continued in September and October, 1978, while Heard was abroad. They climaxed in November and early December after his return. Because of the importance of the issue, both Heard and Fields took part in the discussions, although in the early stage Fields took the lead in evaluating options. His views also most shaped early discussions with Dunworth and with two Peabody deans. In these talks Dunworth was the eager suitor, Fields the shy and very reluctant partner. Fields drafted several testing papers, each of which, in rather heavy managerial jargon, explored the benefits and hazards of the merger from Vanderbilt's perspective. He found precious few benefits. The whole purpose of his reassessment was the curtailing of peripheral programs, the narrowing of focus. In the past a Peabody merger had made good sense; Vanderbilt had needed its resources in 1915, perhaps even as late as the 1950s. A merger made least sense in 1978.[20]

Vanderbilt did have a major stake in Peabody's survival. The more Vanderbilt officials thought about it the more important some of the interchanges seemed. Peabody provided a range of needed courses for Vanderbilt students, not only in education but physical education, accounting, music education, and some areas of psychology. Its faculty cooperated in VIPPS and in Medical Center research. Cooperative programs already encompassed student counseling, student health, the band, a choir, and—above all—joint athletic teams. Most important, Peabody shared an equity in the JUL and now provided indispensable dorm space for Vanderbilt students.

Despite such good reasons to consider a merger, Fields believed that it should not be considered on Peabody's terms. He wanted to acquire Peabody's assets but not at the price of guaranteeing the indefinite continuation of a full-fledged college of education. Instead, he talked of a research orientation, of graduate programs in human learning and teaching, or something close to a program in educational policy studies. At most, he wanted to guarantee continuation of the existing College of Education for only eight years, with Vanderbilt free at the end of that period to convert Peabody assets to whatever purposes it deemed desirable. For this meager commitment he wanted any merger agreement to insure that all merger costs would come from the Peabody endowment and that a future Peabody would continue to live on its own resources. He believed Vanderbilt should merge only if such would improve existing Vanderbilt academic programs, and only if the Peabody board would fully and completely surrender all its assets. In addition to these tough terms, Fields and Heard both made clear to Dunworth that a merger had to involve further time and study, not only by joint committees from the two boards but by faculty groups. This meant the courtship had to become public well before any formal engagement, let alone a legal marriage. Heard and Fields correctly anticipated intense faculty anxiety and concern at Vanderbilt, although nothing as compared to that at Peabody. Also, the constitution of the Faculty Senate required senate consultations before the addition of any new school or college.[21]

Given the terms offered by Fields, Dunworth dropped Peabody's courtship with Vanderbilt in December, 1978, seemingly to seek out other prospective partners. Whether he did this seriously or as a flirtatious ploy to pique Vanderbilt's interest remains a debated issue. Later, when the issue became public, he always claimed that the original Vanderbilt courtship failed because of differences over future Peabody priorities and missions. In December, Dunworth began talks with other universities outside Nashville, leaving Vanderbilt officials waiting and wondering if the final opportunity for a merger had already passed. Fields thought not. He believed that Vanderbilt should play a coy game, that a more compliant Peabody would soon renew its courtship.

Heard canceled a trip to the NCAA meeting in January just in case the merger talks resumed. But Fields remained cautious. On the basis of his Albany experience, he knew the dangers of a university's trying to do everything. The late 1970s was the worst possible time for university expansion. Vanderbilt should acquire a college of education only if it served a vital social need in the area, one that could not be met by other institutions, and only then if Vanderbilt could insure that it would be a college of the highest quality. Fields felt that Vanderbilt could gain many of these goals by a new plan of cooperation, something short of merger but which entailed Vanderbilt's providing, through contract, all the needed peripheral courses for Peabody. He simply did not believe that the Peabody board would formally consider any merger outside of Nashville. He believed Peabody would sooner or later join Vanderbilt on Fields's terms, as a small, graduate institution of education with an elite faculty and a limited number of Ph.D. candidates. To clinch his own assessment, Fields telephoned university administrators all over the country. The response was remarkably uniform—education colleges were weakest of all, caused more problems for chancellors and presidents than any other, and contributed least of all to university prestige. Incidentally, one pessimistic response came from his friend and vice-president for administration at Harvard, one Joe B. Wyatt. As a follow-up of these inquiries, Fields prepared a series of questions on the impact of merger, or of having to do without Peabody, and sent these questionnaires to deans and other administrative officers in February, 1979. He also had other members of his staff investigate the demand for secondary and elementary teachers and the prospects for educational colleges over the next decade. He began to receive responses in March. But before the inquiry ended, the

Vanderbilt board had approved a merger proposal, one that the Peabody board subsequently accepted. The campus inquiry thus contributed not so much to the decision to merge but to the details of a subsequent merger document.

The new Tennessee State University (TSU) proved to be the catalyst of merger. In 1977, under court orders, TSU (the former Tennessee A&I University) merged with the Nashville campus of the University of Tennessee, a downtown campus that catered largely to night school and commuting students. The new TSU had, without success, tried to work out a doctoral program in education with both Memphis State and Peabody. In January, 1979, some of its officials, joined by representatives of the State Board of Regents (the governing board of all the former state colleges), initiated confidential talks with Peabody officials. Too many people were now involved for the negotiations to remain secret. Nashville newspapers broke the story on February 13, and from then on every development and numerous rumors kept the public informed or misinformed about a major academic courtship of monumental importance for the city. Few Nashvillians had ever thought about a TSU-Peabody merger. Most had assumed that, somehow, as if by manifest destiny, Vanderbilt and Peabody would finally get together. Racial issues informed the speculation. TSU still had the image of a largely black school with low academic standards, characteristics that certainly influenced the outcries from Peabody faculty and students. Peabody's talks with distant universities, particularly Duke and George Washington, had raised serious alarm about the loss of a major campus and employer for the city. The TSU possibility raised high hopes among local citizens who had long sought a major public university for Nashville, among those who had supported an integrated TSU, and even among numerous Vanderbilt haters in the Nashville area.[22]

The early TSU-Peabody discussions seemed quite serious. Both sides talked as if merger were a certainty. By plan, the two boards (the Board of Regents and the Peabody board) were to take formal action in early March. In its March 10 meeting the State Board of Regents voted 11–1 in favor of a rather detailed merger proposal, although one that left ambiguous the rights of severed faculty members at Peabody. The state board asked for a full transfer of all Peabody resources, that Peabody become a college in TSU, and that Peabody retain programs in education, library science, and psychology. Continuing Peabody students would have been able to receive TSU degrees and, in return, enjoy much reduced tuition. If they wished, they could have received Peabody degrees by paying existing Peabody tuition. Perhaps most crucial, the merger required approval by the Tennessee legislature; time was short for such approval during the 1979 session. Thus, even as the *Tennessean* made the merger seem a near fait accompli, it really faced numerous and perhaps insurmountable hazards, among them a possible "no" vote by the Peabody board. Fields recognized all of this and once again urged caution.

710

His was the voice of one crying in the wilderness, for within a week Vanderbilt became the willing suitor. A marriage was more quickly consummated than anyone had ever dreamed possible.[23]

The TSU plan placed Vanderbilt in a ticklish position. If it tried to break the merger it risked charges of not only being a poor loser but of opposing the best interests of the majority of Nashville students, who could not afford Vanderbilt tuition, or even of being racist by blocking the one best chance for a successful experiment in integration. After the issue went public on February 13 and before the formal offer by the State Board of Regents, Heard publicly asked to resume negotiations, since he could now consult with the faculty and other Vanderbilt groups. Dunworth kept up the TSU talks. On March 6 Heard met with Wayne Brown, executive director of the Tennessee Higher Education Commission, to make clear that if given the opportunity to resume merger talks, Vanderbilt would seek ways either of achieving closer cooperation or a friendly merger. Fields sent copies of his inquiry questions to Dunworth, certifying the seriousness of Vanderbilt's continued interest. All along, Heard and key local board members had been much more receptive to merger than had Fields. The TSU scheme removed all of their lingering doubts.[24]

The TSU offer led to a flurry of activity by Heard and board members, particularly those in the Nashville area. Whether Dunworth bluffed or not, local board members were horrified at the prospect of Peabody's becoming a branch of TSU. This does not mean that they were concerned about blacks on a nearby campus, but that a state-owned Peabody would have had to give up many of its cooperative programs with Vanderbilt. TSU officials made clear that Peabody students could not continue to play on Vanderbilt's teams, and that Peabody might no longer be able to continue as a partner in JUL. Vanderbilt, even without a legal marriage, had lived with Peabody on such intimate terms as now to face many of the wrenching problems of a divorce, one that might get ugly and even involve extended litigation. Almost desperately, board chairman Sam Fleming asked what Vanderbilt could do, what initiatives it dare take. Heard confessed perplexity, except to make clear to Peabody that Vanderbilt was now ready to talk. At a crucial conference at Fleming's Gulf Stream, Florida, home, the Heard's and Fleming discussed options and decided to press ahead for a merger. Fleming opened informal discussions with several Peabody trustees but carefully avoided any moves to undermine the continuing discussions with TSU. More important by far, he drew upon the earlier studies, and Heard's assistance, to draft a formal Vanderbilt offer, one he presented to the Executive Committee of the Board on March 17. On the day before, Heard and Fields had checked this draft out with university vice-presidents, deans, the reassessment panel, the consultative committee of the Senate, and leaders of six student organizations. The Executive Committee endorsed Fleming's proposal, one that closely followed the terms of the TSU offer of a week earlier.[25]

711

Fleming cast his momentous March 17 offer in the form of a letter to Robert E. Gable, chairman of the Peabody board. Fleming reviewed the existing areas of cooperation and the recent history of merger talks. Vanderbilt was now fully willing to absorb Peabody's assets, to add four members of the existing Peabody board to the Vanderbilt Board of Trust, to provide for a continued evaluation of Peabody programs by a fifteen-member committee of visitors (eventually increased to twenty-two and made up of former Peabody board members), and to use all the existing Peabody endowment, after deducting merger costs, for the continued support of the college. It agreed to maintain the college as a professional school of education and human development but obligated Peabody, before the legal transfer took place, to cut all programs and faculty that duplicated those at Vanderbilt. Note that this was a letter of intent, setting forth guidelines for a future legal document that had to be approved by both boards of trustees. But, in general language it finally promised what Dunworth had bargained for—an open-ended, good-faith commitment by Vanderbilt to preserve the existing educational programs of Peabody, and thus to preserve the traditional identity of the college. Heard carried the letter to Peabody and on March 19 a very persuasive Fleming presented the proposal to the Peabody board. Its members debated for six hours before approving the terms of the letter by a vote of 32–0. Now the joint committees could begin drafting a more detailed merger document. This hasty marriage meant great gloom on the TSU campus. Vanderbilt later helped appease TSU by agreeing to a joint TSU-Peabody doctoral program in education.[26]

On April 27, 1979, both the Vanderbilt and Peabody boards agreed to a merger document—a Memorandum of Understanding. An immense amount of staff work went into this. Fields and Heard joined local trustees Fleming, Wilson, and Allen M. Steele on the merger committee. On the other side, Peabody members fought for the best possible terms in a period of sadness on the Peabody campus. The memorandum accepted on April 27 conformed to the general terms of Fleming's April letter, with one exception. The Vanderbilt board now agreed to absorb not only four members of the regular Peabody board as promised in February, but two additional board members beyond retirement age. These became life members of the Vanderbilt board, a generous concession by Vanderbilt except that it further increased the unmanageable size of the Vanderbilt board, which now had forty-two regular members plus up to twenty life members.

The memorandum provided for a final merger effective July 1, 1979. At this time Peabody was to become legally George Peabody College for Teachers of Vanderbilt University, a professional school of education and human development fully equal to all other Vanderbilt colleges and schools. Peabody resigned from JUL, thus conveying all assets to Vanderbilt and allowing Vanderbilt to revoke the trust indenture with continued protection of the rights of Scarritt. Vanderbilt absorbed approximately $11 million of

Peabody endowment; after merger expenses it retained over $9 million, and of this added $8.5 million to its pooled fund for the continued support of Peabody. Subject to a final review panel, Vanderbilt assigned to Peabody all responsibility in teacher training and certification, accepted existing undergraduate degree programs in elementary education, early childhood education, special education, and health and physical education (it soon transferred to Peabody responsibility for secondary education), but terminated all other undergraduate degree programs in the physical sciences, social sciences, and humanities, except in those psychological fields related to education and human development. Peabody retained all its master's degree programs in educational fields except for art and music education, and also its master's program in library science. It continued to award an Ed.D., but all Ph.D. work now came under the control of the Vanderbilt University Graduate School. Peabody retained its prestigious John F. Kennedy Center and several small research programs in education. Currently enrolled Peabody students continued as before, took required liberal arts courses in the College of Arts and Science, and received Peabody degrees upon graduation. Special provisions allowed lower tuition rates for continuing Peabody students, but new registrants came under the much higher Vanderbilt tuition rate (similar to Arts and Science). Special provisions permitted music and art students to complete work at other universities. Peabody alumni were to retain a degree of autonomy, with separate publications, but at the same time gained equal status in the Vanderbilt Alumni Association.[27]

All these agreements worked out better than anyone expected. Peabody slowly merged into Vanderbilt with almost no confusion or friction. The troublesome issue involved the loss of employment by Peabody personnel, both staff and faculty. The merger of supporting services left about forty wage employees out of work. Each of these received a parting bonus of 5 percent of annual wages for each year of service, or up to 75 percent of their annual pay. Laid-off workers could, of course, apply for any Vanderbilt vacancies and if successful retain seniority and benefits. Many found jobs at Vanderbilt. Dismissed faculty members faced the greatest problems in finding work, and these problems worried Vanderbilt administrators for the next several years. About the only consolation for Peabody faculty members was their preference for Vanderbilt over TSU; otherwise, they saw the merger as a sell-out of their interests. An indefinite number now faced extended unemployment in the worst possible job market. The faculty had vigorously protested merger and condemned Dunworth for his secret plotting without any faculty involvement. The Peabody faculty organized, issued strong statements, begged for independent studies before any faculty cuts, voted "no confidence" in Dunworth, and even staged one symbolic march on the Peabody administration building.

By the time of the April memorandum, Peabody had plans to terminate thirty-eight (later thirty-nine) faculty members (ninety-two remained). Of those dismissed, twenty-three had tenure. The severed faculty received termination notices on May 7 but with some powerful financial inducements for those willing to sign waivers against any future damage claims. Nontenured faculty received pay for one year plus $2,000 for relocation. Tenured faculty could either remain on duty for a final year or receive severance pay of one year's salary. In either case, they collected an additional bonus of 2 percent for each year of service and 1 percent for each remaining year until retirement age. For a few, who approached retirement age, this amounted to a paid leave plus a sizeable bonus. In addition, the new Vanderbilt University bent over backward to find new jobs or temporary employment for those with no work.

The threat of extensive faculty legal action, or AAUP investigations, slowly lessened. On an appeal from Peabody faculty members, the national AAUP sent letters to Heard and Dunworth stressing the rights of affected faculty members. It seemed unclear whether the merger procedures and the termination agreements violated AAUP tenure guidelines. The national AAUP never investigated Vanderbilt. The state branch of the AAUP condemned the dismissals in a resolution but took no further action. Larry S. Crist, a French professor, led a small minority of Vanderbilt professors who pledged solidarity with their Peabody colleagues and who urged the university to retain all tenured Peabody professors, if necessary by adding them to existing Arts and Science departments. By August 24, 1979, all Peabody tenured faculty had signed waivers, although several remained bitter and unemployed. In 1980 five still had failed to find jobs. Two nontenured faculty filed grievances; one hired an attorney and initiated legal action, but this was settled out of court.[28]

Such a sanguine description of the merger conceals numerous hurts and bruises. It took time and effort for many alumni on both sides to swallow the fait accompli. Vanderbilt students had long taken a snobbish view of Peabody, sneering at its purportedly lower academic standing and at crip courses in education. Peabody students had pride in their college and many felt deceived by its "capitulation" to a neighbor and rival. Even existing Peabody students faced a 10 percent annual increase in tuition, higher student activity fees, and the loss of valued programs in music and the arts. Of all the terminations, that of the music program probably left more intense regrets, along with a stranded music library. The most bitter student comments concerned identity issues, the loss of a distinct outlook, of a tolerant, equalitarian campus. One bitter Peabody graduate student expressed this view: "When I present my credentials a few years from now, I'd just as soon that no one know I technically graduated from the 'Harvard of the South'—where black students are mistaken for janitors, and frat boys who rate the bodies of passing women with large cardboard signs are considered cute and frisky rather than disturbed."[29]

For Vanderbilt, the merger suddenly expanded its campus by fifty-eight acres and solved many of its dorm and space problems. It pulled its enrollment above 9,000, its annual number of graduates to approximately 1,800. It

714

thus pushed Vanderbilt over the critical threshold from an unusually small graduate university to a mid-sized one. Vanderbilt gained about sixteen major buildings plus several small ones, sought-after apartment houses for married students, and even a president's home. It was able to sell some outlying lots and houses. In return for this and for the new space acquired and used by other parts of the university, and as a gesture of goodwill, Vanderbilt committed $700,000 a year for ten years to Peabody's operating budget.

In the euphoria of a smooth merger everyone forgot Fields's demurrals back in the fall of 1978. Perhaps Vanderbilt had acquired a sinking ship. The first four years after merger could prove very little, but Peabody clearly seemed a college with problems. As expected with the higher tuition, undergraduate enrollment at Peabody continued to drop (to only 336 in the fall of 1982), despite a few students who used Peabody as a back-door route into the more restrictive College of Arts and Science. Dunworth submitted his resignation, one of the necessary costs of merger. He had lost all credibility with his faculty. Hardy C. Wilcoxon, a Peabody psychology professor, agreed to serve as acting dean and helped smooth the transition. In October, 1980, a search committee recommended Willis D. Hawley as Peabody's new dean. He had come to Vanderbilt from Duke only in the preceding summer as professor of political science and director of the Center for Education and Human Development in VIPPS. His research on school desegregation gave him national recognition. But whether he could revive Peabody in the late 1980s remained problematic.

It may be impossible for a high-tuition college of education to compete for students in the South, given the number of public educational colleges. But a few omens favor Peabody, including enrollment increases in the fall of 1983 and a great sense of optimism in the faculty. A new, moderate demographic bulge is just entering the lower grades. A decade-long lack of demand for elementary and secondary teachers has sharply curtailed the number and the quality of education graduates, leading to early scarcities and what should be a rapid increase in demand, particularly for very able graduates. Suddenly, educational improvement has become a high national priority. Peabody will never try to compete with public universities in the massive training and certifying of teachers but will try to emphasize the quality training of master teachers, of educational administrators, and of college-level scholars. Vanderbilt's overall reputation should aid it in this mission. The demand for such elite educational leaders is sure to rise in the next decade, a demand that may lead to a minor boom among better colleges of education. If this should occur, then it is conceivable that Peabody will not shrink away but even thrive. The odds against such success remain very high.

While playing the merger game, Vanderbilt absorbed yet another school in 1981. But adoption of the Blair School of Music posed few of the risks and few of the challenges of Peabody. The story goes back to 1973 when Blair Academy faculty members approached Vanderbilt about some form of affiliation. The consultative committee of the Senate considered their inquiry and noted that any formal affiliation would have to go through normal channels in the College. In 1974 the faculty council of the College discussed Vanderbilt's music program and its possible relationship with Blair Academy. At that time Blair offered instruction largely to precollege youngsters. As of 1977, it ended its affiliation with Peabody and was on its own. In a report to a national accreditation panel in 1977, the Blair faculty announced its intention to remain an independent school of music but noted it would now seek a closer affiliation with Vanderbilt, by which it meant some relationship short of merger. In fact, it was already negotiating a lease of Vanderbilt land on Blakemore for its new home. Vanderbilt administrators viewed with apprehension the rapid curtailment of music programs at Peabody and thus welcomed a form of cooperation with Blair that would allow College undergraduates to take instrumental instruction. These efforts led to Blair's liberal lease, for forty-nine years at one dollar a year, of Vanderbilt land, on the condition that Vanderbilt approve its building plans and that the Blair staff accept Vanderbilt students for instruction (for a fee).[30]

The Peabody merger paralleled the planning of the new Blair building funded by $2.4 million from the Potter Foundation. When Vanderbilt approved the building plans, it had two major concerns, both of which suggested very close ties to Blair. It wanted plans consistent with a future rehearsal hall, one large enough for the Vanderbilt band, and it wanted library shelf space large enough to absorb the music library from Peabody. Concerns over the library space continued for months. Because of some problems of siting shelves, the space seemed barely adequate should the library ever move. Early in 1980 Vanderbilt also accepted an offer from Blair to maintain and safeguard pianos and other musical instruments moved over from Peabody. In June, 1979, Fields lunched with Justin Wilson, grandson of Justin Potter, son of board member David K. Wilson, and the key spokesman of the Blair Board. At that point, Wilson wanted Blair to remain independent, but for it to cooperate more closely with Vanderbilt.

In the fall of 1979, when Blair moved into its new building, the exact nature of its affiliation with Vanderbilt had to be further clarified. The Blair faculty wanted to teach music courses for credit and already looked ahead to some type of joint degree program. Perhaps more important, both the faculty and the Blair board had concluded that full university status would benefit Blair in its fund-raising efforts and aid its faculty in securing research grants. Merger would also clarify several technical problems about allocating costs for a building that from the beginning served joint purposes. For these reasons, the original request for merger came from Blair. Heard, who favored the merger, left the timing of such an offer up to David K. and Justin Wilson. Unlike the Peabody invitation, the Blair offer was very tentative and not at all urgent. Blair was solvent and successful and could go on indefinitely with a loose affiliation with Vanderbilt. It simply presented Vanderbilt with a fascinating opportunity.[31]

Once again Fields had to plot a merger strategy, right in the middle of the final reassessment process. He outlined his thinking to Heard on April 30 and then met on May 2, 1980, with what he called his management group (Fields, Holladay, McDowell, and Carr). He was once again challenged to fit another major expansion into reassessment and could do so only if Blair was a "new start" critical to Vanderbilt's mission. Blair's precollegiate program obviously was peripheral to Vanderbilt's goals and purposes. The justification had to be on two grounds—that Blair provide critical support for the music program of the College, and that it develop into a degree-granting school or conservatory. Within a month the management-level discussions had settled all doubts. Vanderbilt could not afford to pass up the opportunity. Thus, the administrative problem was strategic—how to make another merger palatable to a suspicious faculty. Fields planned a carefully orchestrated series of steps, beginning with legal merger and little more, later moving to the problems of expansion, of degrees, and even of conservatory status. A minimalist approach promised to disarm faculty fears and accomplish a quiet and harmonious merger. Thus, the final plan—to get Blair to make a formal offer, announce its generous terms to the campus in the fall of 1980, to downplay the importance of the merger, and to emphasize the small cost to Vanderbilt. After consultations on campus and in the Faculty Senate, the deal should go to the board by the end of the year. Once it had Blair, then Vanderbilt could carry out the extended studies needed to justify degree programs. Although the timing and scope of such expansion remained open, it is clear that the central administration and key board members had assumed such as all but inevitable from 1979 on. Merger was thereby only an opening gambit.[32]

Only one issue muddied the carefully orchestrated path to merger—the status of the Blair faculty. The terms of the offer to Blair seemed generous toward both sides. As in the case of Peabody, all Blair's assets came to Vanderbilt. This included not only a new building but income from almost $4 million in endowment plus an enviable reputation in Nashville. Fields thus endorsed merger as not only a boon to Vanderbilt but critical to the advancement of music in the Nashville community. Unlike Peabody, Blair seemed fully able to pay its own way, at least in its existing pre-college program, and had as secure a financial base as any school or college in the university. The old Blair board simply became a new advisory committee. But from consultations with the Vanderbilt faculty and discussions in the Faculty Senate, it became clear that the Vanderbilt faculty would not award faculty status even to the fourteen full-time instructors at Blair let alone to its twenty-three part-time teachers. Technically, the *Faculty Manual* limited the title and prerogatives of "faculty member" to degree-granting schools. This decision created great apprehension at Blair. In the merger document Blair instructors were designated artist-teachers, or something just below professors, and thus gained no representation on the Faculty Senate. But they could assume that this was a short-lived handicap, one to be corrected as soon as Blair began a degree program.

The Vanderbilt Board of Trust, in a special meeting, unanimously approved the merger agreement on December 22, 1980. Some members stressed that merger was pointless unless it involved a commitment to a future degree program. Thus, at the same time as the vote, the board approved the establishment of an ad hoc commission on the future of music at Vanderbilt, chaired by professor Ingram Bloch and made up of administrators, faculty, Blair teachers, and students. The merger was painless. Within a month Blair director John F. Sawyer began plans for a Vanderbilt orchestra, an innovation enthusiastically endorsed by the new commission and funded by the administration. In 1982, after extensive study and reports from two outside consultants, the commission recommended, as soon as feasible, that the College of Arts and Science establish a baccalaureate degree in music but with all music instruction, including academic as well as performance courses, located at Blair, a position opposed by some in the College of Arts and Science. It also recommended that Blair, when it had the requisite strength and funding, become a full school and offer a professional Bachelor of Music degree. On the matter of faculty status, it deemed it appropriate to consider awarding such status to some Blair teachers even before implementing either degree program. In fact, it would be difficult to recruit the five or six needed academic faculty members at Blair without awarding them such status. In 1983 the board approved in principle a professional degree program, authorized a search for a dean (Sawyer, as expected, gained this position), and approved preliminary plans for expanding the Blair building to absorb the Peabody music library. Possibly as early as 1985–86, Blair will become Vanderbilt's tenth degree-granting school.[33]

Just as Fields wrote his first extended report on the Blair merger in April, 1980, his reassessment panel, chaired by law professor Harold G. Maier, finally rendered its anxiously awaited report. It followed detailed studies on every program at Vanderbilt and even some extended surveys of student opinion. In most respects the report was anticlimactic. The panel found a dozen or so programs to cut or curtail in behalf of savings. Most controversial were proposals to close the moribund university press and to end all administrative costs for the Afro-American studies program. Less significant savings included the closing down of an old computer, eliminating a small graduate recruitment effort, closing a few lower administrative offices, curtailing publication budgets, cutting some staff in the Medical Center and in development, maintaining closer control over runaway computer use, increasing centralizing purchasing, and even a shifting of new women's athletic scholarships on to the self-supporting athletic department budget. These, plus savings in administration, funded over $1 million for high-priority goals, led by library improvements, improved faculty salaries, and additional support for faculty research. The panel identified several areas of possible future savings and at least targeted a few academic programs for early liquidation—engineering management, clinical education in the Law School, and the teacher training program still maintained in the College. It recommended a consolidation of fragmented area studies and of certain language offerings. Many of the recommendations simply confirmed, or justified, existing priorities or changes already under way.[34]

One final problem plagued Fields's five years as president—the status of women and minorities at Vanderbilt. These issues came to a head in 1981 in a controversy over the failure of Elizabeth Langland to gain tenure in the College of Arts and Science. The intensity of that controversy grew out of pent-up frustrations that had accumulated over the preceding decade. In the immediate aftermath of the Civil Rights Act of 1964 and of the first federal efforts to gain compliance with its antidiscrimination programs, almost all the focus at Vanderbilt had remained on blacks. As noted earlier, this issue joined with student activities on campus, and at least led to major efforts to recruit both black faculty and students. The first federal compliance report on Vanderbilt's affirmative action goals in 1968 noted numerous small problems, but again almost all these related to blacks. So did the focus of Vanderbilt's first affirmative action plan in 1969. Almost totally ignored in these years were numerous forms of discrimination against women, an old Vanderbilt tradition. But by 1970 women's issues began to come to the fore. Within two years women held center stage.

Nationally, the winds of change were readily felt by 1970. It was clear that Vanderbilt would have to change several policies relative to women. For example, the Board still retained its rigid quota on women in the College (one-third of the enrollment). And as late as 1969 the deans had voted to toughen nepotism rules for the faculty—ordinarily no more than one member of a family could serve in a department and if, for the good of the university, two held jobs, only one was eligible for tenure. In April, 1970, Heard warned the board that court decisions had already made illegal admission quotas for women in public colleges. Then in 1971 a visiting HEW team praised Vanderbilt for meeting targets on blacks but noted that its existing affirmative action plan was no longer adequate for it did not include mandated commitments on the hiring and promotion of females.

In 1971 various departments began seeking out women candidates. In 1970 the board had voted to waive the one-third rule for transfer students and, finally, in 1972 voted to phase out the quota over four years, ending up with a roughly equal number of men and women in the College. Nine die-hard trustees, mostly older men, voted against this break from a hallowed tradition. At almost the same time, a new organization—Professional Women at Vanderbilt—asked Heard to appoint a commission to study women's status at Vanderbilt and to develop a new plan for affirmative

719

action. Heard gladly appointed the commission in 1972. The early commission submitted an interim report in 1973, but changes in personnel and changes in the political climate helped delay a final report until 1976. While the commission investigated, women faculty and students organized, developed a sense of shared adversity, and began as militant an advocacy in behalf of women's rights as Vanderbilt had ever known.

Women students were as active as faculty members. An emerging self-consciousness on the part of women students went back for decades at Vanderbilt but became particularly noticeable about 1967. These early protests intertwined with student power issues, as in women students' struggle, eventually successful, to end all double standards in dorm rules. In fighting this battle they organized, protested, and began more aggressive efforts to gain power in student government. The next issue they engaged was greater equality in sports. Early in 1972 a female law student led an aggressive campaign by women to gain equal access to the indoor track and other facilities in the new McGugin Center. The athletic department controlled McGugin and claimed the authority to exclude all other students from facilities built for team athletes, but it had shared the facilities during certain hours with men students. The athletic department insisted that it had no separate facilities for women and thus turned down their early requests. The women presented their case both to the student affairs committee and the Faculty Senate, to the considerable embarrassment of the athletic department. Meanwhile, when women began using the track as freely as men no one tried to stop them.

Only one forbidden sanctuary remained, the sauna. Two young women decided to integrate it also in April of 1972. They purportedly called McGugin to find out if any rules prevented their use of the facility. No one had thought to formulate such a rule. They then simply went over to McGugin, stripped, and entered the sauna; no one apparently noticed except one startled male then using it. About five other males came in while they were there but no lines formed to see the show. This titillating escapade, of course, made the national news and led the athletic department to establish separate hours for women in the sauna. Women students were also successful in other areas. Since Memorial Gym was open to all men students, women won equal access and separate facilities in it. In 1972, in response to their entreaties and faculty support, the College opened the first course in women's studies, an experimental course that attracted about thirty-eight students. By 1982 a small women's studies program had grown to three or four courses each semester. In 1976 Vanderbilt women gained access to campus ROTC units.[35]

In 1972 Congress approved new amendments to its civil rights legislation. Title VII of the Civil Rights Act of 1964 already provided protections for faculty members and staff employees on such issues as employee procedures and salary and fringe benefits. The most comprehensive rules affecting women students were in Title IX of the Education Amendments of 1972,

720

although other titles further increased the now massive legal requirements that applied to all colleges accepting federal grants. Effective in 1974 and 1975, Title IX protected women students from discrimination relating to counseling, rules, marital or parental status, financial assistance, and athletics. The athletic provisions seemed most revolutionary and sent shock waves through campuses all over the country. In 1974 Vanderbilt began preparation for adherence while administrators prayed every night that Vanderbilt women would not want to form competitive teams. Of course, given the opportunity, they did want just this and now could demand completely equal treatment with men. By 1977 Vanderbilt had moved the director of women's physical education, Emily Harsh, up to assistant athletic director and had hired a women's basketball coach. In 1977 the university added $25,000 to existing funds for women athletes, employed a swimming coach, and began plans for grants-in-aid, which it first awarded in 1977–78 for basketball. The concessions followed determined actions by women students. In 1977 they threatened legal action under Title IX and even formed an activist group called Title IX in Tennessee, or TNT. By 1982, Vanderbilt's women's teams did about as well as men's in basketball, swimming, track, and tennis, but so far even basketball has suffered from very low attendance. In 1984 a talented women's basketball team won the National Invitational Tournament, the first national tournament ever won by a Vanderbilt basketball team.[36]

For faculty and staff women, all earlier efforts to gain attention and equal rights climaxed in the work of the Commission on the Status of Women. Its 1973 interim report barely suggested what was to come in 1976. In 1973 the critical issues seemed to be the small number of women at Vanderbilt, too few in fact to provide a data base to document discrimination. Consequently, the early commission tried to find out the number of women faculty members and to assess their status in rank and salary. The College had only 15 females to 263 males, no female chairpersons, only 2 full professors, and only 4 associate professors. Large departments such as English and history employed no women at all even though, nationally, approximately 25 percent of English Ph.D.s and about 12 percent in history went to women. The commission documented rules against part-time employment, or those nepotism rules that most handicapped wives. But it acknowledged recent efforts by the university to employ women and thus in a sense stated what had until recently been obvious at Vanderbilt—a bias in many key departments against appointing women professors. Because Vanderbilt entered the market for women at a very late date, its few women professors clustered in the lower ranks. Women had to be recruited increasingly from a very scarce supply, since affirmative action guidelines led colleges everywhere to seek out women.[37]

In 1975 the commission essentially began over again under the leadership of Jan Belcher (staff) and Antonina Gove (faculty). It submitted its draft

721

report to the administration and to deans in September, 1976. It resembled no earlier committee report at Vanderbilt; it shocked many administrators. In brief, the women revealed their bitterness and anger and thus submitted a tough, at points almost polemical, indictment of Vanderbilt. Because of ambiguities and some purported misquotations, the commission rewrote part of twenty pages before making public its book-length report, *Women at Vanderbilt*. It raked the university over the coals on a number of issues—failure to provide complete or adequate data, failure to conform to the recent requirements of Title IX, and above all for the fact that "women on this campus seldom receive equal treatment with men." Many of the detailed complaints involved staff. Here, women made up a majority of employees yet held a minority of administrative or leadership positions. Black women predominated in the lowest and most menial tasks. The commission found undergraduate women largely unaware of their newly won rights, the percentage of women in the Graduate School declining, and few women students ever able to take a course from a female because the university had so few women professors.

The sharpest criticisms involved the alleged plight of female faculty members—so few as to be almost invisible, isolated, subject to ridicule, underpaid, and unappreciated. Outside Nursing, women made up only 5.5 percent of the full-status faculty, and out of the confusion of statistics the commission doubted that the percentage of women had grown much between 1972 and 1975, despite a much higher rate of hiring. In only one College department did women make up as large a percentage as the number of accessible Ph.D.s in that field. Women still clustered in lower ranks. Outside the Medical School the university had only eleven tenured women, four of whom were in Nursing. Only three of these were full professors. On average, women in each rank received a lower salary than men, but the commission did not have the data needed to clarify the causes of this differential. In order to rectify what it saw as existing inequities, the commission submitted a series of recommendations: a university-funded office for women, child-care facilities, seminars by outside professionals to help eliminate sexist attitudes among administrators, new effort to collect data, a special office to help assure equal employment opportunities, more professional security forces and an escort service for women, better athletic facilities for women, more detailed affirmative action guidelines for staff employees, additional women's studies courses, expanded athletic programs for women, extra recruitment efforts on behalf of women graduate students, better gynecological services and counseling at the Student Health Center, various departmental strategies to increase women faculty, and even an effort to rid all official publications of sexist language or titles.[38]

The commission report appeared the fall before President Fields arrived at Vanderbilt. Over the next two years the central administration prepared responses to each commission recommendation, implementing some and justifying the rejection of others. Politically, the women placed greatest symbolic significance on their first recommendation—for what they would soon call a Women's Center. In 1977 the board approved the center, balancing this against its refusal to fund any child-care facilities (even these opened in 1983). In 1977 the board also edited the sexism from its bylaws, except for the title of chairman, and established a women's concerns committee. In 1978 Nancy Ransom was hired as director of the Women's Center, funded at $20,000 a year and located in one of the old Westside Row buildings. In the same year women organized the first of a continuing series of women's weeks. Administrative decisions and federal laws slowly nullified all earlier nepotism rules. The university also removed penalties for part-time appointees and in 1980 hired its first shared appointee, a husband-wife team that filled a single vacancy in geology.[39]

With increased federal pressures joining those of campus women, the university seemed to take strenuous measures to locate, evaluate, and hire women candidates for all vacancies. In 1982 the university had only one female academic dean (Nursing) but a steadily increasing percentage of females as associate and assistant deans. It then had only 9 female full professors compared with 214 male, but 34 associate professors to 138, and 62 assistant professors to 82, or sharp gains in the lower ranks, but numbers still distorted by the large staff in Nursing. Such gains did not always meet the demands of women, but in most cases they met or exceeded agreed-upon affirmative action guidelines. Meeting these guidelines required an enormous amount of staff effort, many new reports, and a continuous stream of complaints, investigations, or legal battles, with most involving staff rather than faculty. In the mid-1970s Vanderbilt seemed unable to keep up with all the legislation and thus seemed always to be behind in filing its affirmative action plan, which made up three volumes by 1977. As late as 1980 it had to sign a conciliation agreement with the U.S. Department of Labor because of its noncompliance with federal guidelines and its failure, among other things, to file a current affirmative action plan. Other universities had similar problems; in many cases the Vanderbilt violations were petty. And the rules kept expanding. For example, by 1980 Vanderbilt had to make expensive building modifications to meet new guidelines for disabled veterans and for handicapped people.[40]

In some ways Vanderbilt responded more effectively to women's demands than to blacks'. The women made most of the noise by the late 1970s. But at least the supply of women faculty candidates continued to climb, whereas the supply of black Ph.D.s stabilized and then declined. As a result, recruitment of blacks, particularly for a university like Vanderbilt, often proved almost impossible. Vanderbilt still suffered some disabilities because of its location. As late as 1972 two new black professors faced serious housing discrimination—a rented house that burned to the ground just before a black occupied it, threatening letters and a canceled contract on a purchased house for a second black. By the mid-1970s black enrollment also began to slip, from 130 undergraduates in 1976 to 117 in 1977 to only 105 in 1978. Major recruitment efforts, particularly in Engineering, raised the total number of blacks to 350 in 1980–81, a record number. The now less aggressive Afro-American Association condemned the virtual discontinuation of an Afro-American studies program in 1981 and was unable to do much to stimulate the development of black-oriented courses in academic departments. In 1982 the most explosive racial issue, one widely discussed and publicized, was triggered by student charges of racial discrimination in sororities and fraternities, not a new problem but one not agitated for almost a decade. The reports led to a plethora of pious pronouncements and soothing promises, to strong statements from student affairs officials, and even to a Faculty Senate resolution. Black students and faculty still felt isolated at Vanderbilt. Following the lead of students, black professors and administrators organized, but even in their combined strength remained an embarrassingly small group of twenty-seven by 1982. Of nineteen faculty members, several remained on part-time appointments. The Medical School, with six black faculty members, led all the other schools. In 1981 another small group formed as the Organization of Black Graduate and Professional Students. By then, the constant demand of the organized black faculty was more energetic recruitment, more blacks in higher administrative posts, and a black assistant provost or director of minority affairs.[41]

The Langland affair brought to the surface an immense fund of built-up resentment and frustration. No one, not even women or blacks, had quite realized the depth of alienation building on the campus. One reason for the breadth and depth of concern was that now, in one person, the plight of women and of alienated campus minorities seemed to join with the ever tense and threatening issue of tenure. For two decades students had protested the denial of tenure to beloved professors. Since almost anyone denied tenure has a loyal even if a small student following, most denials led to some hard feelings and, if publicized at all, to student charges that the university did not value good teaching. Thus, even if Elizabeth Langland had not been a woman, an adverse tenure decision for a popular young professor might have provoked some student petitions.

From the commission report of 1976 on, general but nonspecific charges of sexual bias or of extra handicaps for women had created the general impression that bias was normal at Vanderbilt. In 1980 the English department had voted against tenure for a young woman on the basis of her insufficient scholarly attainments. Because of earlier and apparently open discrimination against women in that department, and since no woman had yet gained tenure in English (Dean Stapleton had been a full professor back in the years before Vanderbilt had any tenure regulations), students proved receptive to her claims of discrimination. This case also helped establish a widespread assumption—should any woman ever be recommended for tenure in English, she obviously had full or even excessive credentials. Finally, Langland was part of the sisterhood, a small, increasingly cohesive, somewhat beleaguered group of women professors and committed feminists. Their emotional ties were deep, formed in an atmosphere of alienation and deep suspicions about the male establishment, and cultivated in a series of women's struggles on campus. Langland had chaired the committee on women's studies and had oriented much of her literary scholarship toward feminist issues. Her loss of tenure thus easily came to symbolize all the problems of women at Vanderbilt.

Only the sequence of events is clear. By university and College rules, Langland had to secure a favorable decision on her promotion to associate professor, and thus to a tenure position, by the end of the sixth year at Vanderbilt or by the spring of 1981. By the quite general criteria listed in the *Faculty Manual,* she would gain tenure only if her work had been at least competent in each of three overlapping areas—teaching, scholarship, and service to the University. The *Manual* emphasized that excellent work was desirable in each of these areas, and the College guidelines noted that tenure required distinction in either teaching or scholarship. Of course these qualitative criteria were far from precise and were fleshed out in a College-level statement on tenure. Their meaning also tends to vary through time. Effectively, people get tenure at Vanderbilt or at any other major university only if they are perceived to be as able and promising as other available candidates for the same position. When available candidates are scarce, effective tenure standards go down, as they did nationally in the 1960s. When the supply of scholars is high in a given field, then tenure requirements become more rigorous, for only by so raising these can a university maximize the relative strength of its faculty.

Faculty recruitment compares very closely to that of a professional baseball team. Every team is out to get the best possible players. A few internal factors may help qualify the competition in universities, factors such as "tenure density" (the percentage of faculty members in higher ranks), enrollment projections, and even on rare occasions humane considerations. And whatever the rules suggest, no contemporary university of Vanderbilt's quality will tenure professors unless they have a competitive record (call it excellent or distinctive) as productive scholars or scientists. Put in another way, scholarship is the equivalent of a baseball player's batting average, teaching comparable to that of fielding skills. One simply cannot make it in the majors without a competitive batting average. One has to be able to field also but, given a high batting average, a player can usually find a position on a team, such as a designated hitter (the equivalent of a research professor). This is the reality of the tenure game. No fuzzy language or a ton of encomiums about great teaching can change the facts.

Whether the system is fair or not, whether it conforms to sound educational policy, is another question. Much more than suggested by the baseball analogy, teaching and scholarship are interactive. Scholarship is a necessary preparation for teaching at a university level; graduate-level teaching often departs immediately from one's inquiry. A university pays its scholar-teachers to do two jobs simultaneously, and over the years about one-half of a professor's time should go into research or into appropriate creative work (music composition, painting, even set designs for someone in theater). If it does not, then professors should draw only half pay or teach more courses than they presently do. These priorities are subject to innumerable abuses, abuses that are endemic to academic life. Too often, scholarship translates into pedantic or routine inquiry, into a stream of unimaginative or jargon-infected publications, all of which contribute to an inane evaluative system based on the number or at times almost the weight of articles or books. Even when so vulgarized, the system still makes completed inquiry and usually some form of publication the sine qua non of tenure. And it is good to remember that tenure has both a socially redeeming purpose—to protect academic freedom, the right of unrestricted inquiry or teaching—and a professionally self-serving role—job security for professors.

On March 12, 1981, the tenured professors in the English department voted on Langland's promotion and tenure. In a divided vote (not unusual) fifteen approved and five opposed. Two English professors wrote supporting letters for Langland's file, but even they noted some deficiencies in her scholarship. Two professors who opposed her tenure wrote letters protesting her lack of scholarly attainments sufficient for the grant of tenure. In his advisory opinion, Dean Ernest Q. Campbell of the Graduate School also recommended against tenure. So much opposition branded this as a "very doubtful" case, one that a dean has to evaluate very carefully. In fact, on major campuses the likelihood of a dean's approval in the face of such a divided departmental vote would be well below 50 percent. Dean Jacque Voegeli faced a very tough decision strictly on the merits of the case and totally apart from its explosive political potential. Voegeli was aware of the political repercussions, kept the provost, president, and chancellor informed of his thinking, and submitted Langland's dossier to each of his superiors (only Heard favored tenure, but he would leave the decision up to Voegeli). Voegeli addressed detailed inquiries about her deficiencies in scholarship to the English department on May 19. In response to this inquiry, eight of sixteen contacted English professors wrote letters in support of Langland, although they placed greater emphasis upon her future promise than on past scholarly achievements. Finally, on June 12, or almost two weeks beyond the usual time of notification, Voegeli decided against tenure, a decision the dean of the College makes unilaterally. Legally, his decision is reversible only by an extraordinary act of the chancellor, but such a reversal would undermine the integrity of the tenure process and would amount to a vote of no confidence in a dean.

Voegeli questioned Langland's scholarship, not her teaching or university

726

contributions. At the time of his tenure decision she had only two published articles, one in a scholarly or refereed journal. In addition, she had another article accepted for publication, was coeditor of a yet unpublished but committed book-length volume in *Soundings* (a Vanderbilt publication) on the impact of women's studies, was coeditor of and contributor to another unpublished and unplaced volume on feminist issues relating to the novel, and author of an unpublished, revised dissertation that she had tried, heretofore unsuccessfully, to place with two university presses. By the usual standards applied in such cases, her published work was well below tenure standards, but an evaluation of scholarship was not so simple as that. The department and the dean had to evaluate all her completed scholarship, published or unpublished, and to assess the evaluation of six outside reviewers or referees. Of these six referees, three recommended tenure; two opposed it. One believed Langland deserved tenure if her subsequent book matched the quality of her essays. All but one referee, who was uniformly positive, mixed praise with criticism. (Note that brilliant, clearly publishable, but as yet unpublished work often suffices for favorable tenure decisions.)

By a traditional rule of the College, Voegeli sent his rejection notice only to the English department. The chairman then read it to Langland; she gained a copy only by request of her lawyers. The denial left Langland only one recourse within the university—an appeal to the Faculty Senate committee on professional ethics and academic freedom. She chose to by-pass this procedure and instead engaged lawyers to represent her in a contemplated complaint to the EEOC. Her counsel sought the needed documents from the university but, before filing the complaint, asked for a reassessment of her case by the university. This began a tortuous legal process that continued until at least 1984.[42]

Langland claimed discrimination against her on the basis of sex. In part she rested her claim on tenure patterns in the College. She claimed that the College did not hire and then tenure a single woman from 1971 to 1982 (true, but a bit misleading, as Voegeli had approved tenure for one woman during this period). In the same period it had employed eighteen women, all of whom eventually left Vanderbilt for a variety of reasons (only three failed to get tenure). The College had only two female full professors and only seven tenured women, 1.6 percent of its total. The procedural basis of her case rested upon her claim that the dean had misapplied the tenure criteria of the College, and that he had demanded a higher level of achievement from her than from male candidates. The charge focused on language in Voegeli's letter. She claimed that he had faulted her for insufficient evidence of "national stature" in her field, or a wording that was part of the stated standards for promotion to full professor, not to associate, in the College guidelines. But this overlooked the fact that the language he used was in the *Faculty Manual*, which takes precedence over the supplemental rules of individual colleges or schools.[43]

Dean Voegeli's decision was announced only in late spring. But even then a pro-Langland movement began to organize on campus. In October it incorporated as Women's Equity at Vanderbilt (WEAV), an organization committed to long-term goals but initially formed primarily to get a reversal of the Langland decision. It gained broad support among female, and some male, students, held fund-raising events, and began a defense fund for Langland. As late as 1982 a few graduating seniors withheld gifts to Vanderbilt to protest the Langland decision. Ironically, Heard, Fields, and Carr contributed to WEAV and endorsed its goals but stipulated that their gifts not be used to pay for legal processes against Vanderbilt. Students signed several petitions in behalf of Langland. Among students and among many lay supporters of Langland outside the university, her charge of sexual discrimination became gospel, so much a working assumption that no one seemed to question it. Apparently the statistical patterns in the College, the failure of so many women to remain at Vanderbilt or to gain tenure, governed this understanding of the Langland case. Also, the widely published views of Langland herself, her impressive list of services to Vanderbilt, and even her lengthy list of scholarly involvements seemed to clinch her claim.[44]

Few female faculty members at Vanderbilt, few Langland supporters who understood the tenure process, endorsed such a simple theory of overt bias. They knew that Dean Voegeli did not intentionally veto tenure for Langland because she was a woman. They knew that he was not a fool, that he harbored no self-conscious animus against women. In fact, given the political context and the demands of public relations, given Vanderbilt's anxiety to overcome past claims of racial or sexual bias, then all the pressures on Voegeli clearly mandated tenure for Langland. In this light, his decision was courageous, a political risk, one that might jeopardize his deanship. Many at Vanderbilt knew this. A majority of faculty members in the College supported high tenure standards, and thus the basis of the Langland decision (almost no one had access to the data needed to judge the scholarly issues). But a majority of women faculty members, including some of the most able professors at Vanderbilt, still felt that Voegeli made the wrong decision and that the interest of the university, including that of its students, required a reversal. Consequently, they begged for a new review, sought some mode of undoing what they perceived as a grievous mistake or an injustice. Two different and equally subtle perspectives undergirded such passionately held beliefs.

The first perspective directly concerns Langland's scholarship. By Vanderbilt's rules she deserved tenure if her scholarship met the nebulous criterion of being "competent." Translated into the realities of the process, she deserved tenure if her scholarly work was comparable to that of other assistant professors who had gained tenure in very recent years. This ultimately came down to qualitative, not quantitative, judgments, given the fact that Langland did have several unpublished articles and, most crucial in her field, a book-length manuscript available for the evaluation of experts in her field. Publication can be a diverting issue. Gaining publication for an article or a book helps a literary critic such as Langland because it confirms the merit of the work, as experts are involved in the acceptance process. Also, given contemporary publication standards, most able scholarship does eventually get published and so becomes more easily available to other scholars. But publication is not determinant in the tenure process; the quality of completed scholarship is. Thus, most critical for Langland were judgments about her scholarship, judgments made not primarily by Dean Voegeli but by the six experts in her own field, three selected by Langland, three selected by her colleagues in the English department.

Here is where the suspicions of other women scholars, even some who had not read her work, came to rest. They came to believe that Langland suffered from the subject matter of at least part of her work at Vanderbilt, a charge rejected by both the department and the dean. Langland's friends argued that, since she bid for tenure in English, only her publications in literary criticism had counted. Her edited volume on women's studies was thus irrelevant to the English department. Her other co-edited but unpublished manuscript, with its overt feminist perspective, also weighed very little in the evaluation. They knew that the key to promotion in departments such as English and history is writing not journal articles or assembling edited works but writing significant, original books. Such criteria all but excluded a share of Langland's unpublished writings. She had also solicited and accepted an appointment, by Voegeli, as chair of the women's studies committee, a post she held for three years. But this, they believed, won her no credits at all in her home department, not even for teaching. The problem, as campus women perceived it, was that neither outside referees nor departmental colleagues had credited her for a body of work that made a vital contribution to students and to the new field of women's studies. Beyond this, Langland and some supporters argued that she suffered from a type of institutional sexism, from a failure of male referees, or even of a discipline whose standards derived from male perspectives, to give value to feminist scholarship. From these perspectives, Langland could have suffered from a subtle form of discrimination that never took the form of overt bias.

The second perspective is quite different and finesses many of the subtle conflicts over scholarly credentials. Pervasive among women at Vanderbilt was a sense of isolation, and thus an almost universal cry—recruit and retain more women for the faculty. This feeling helps explain the wrenching sense of loss after the Langland announcement, a loss that led to tearful meetings of women faculty and even to one intense, highly emotional meeting with women members of the Board of Trust. From this perspective Langland had become essential to their cause—to recruit more women, to gain campus visibility and recognition, to create a critical mass of feminist scholarship, to add courses in women's studies, and to provide more role models for women students. Langland's loss of tenure symbolized their failure, seemed an eloquent witness to a lack of concern for these goals on the part of administrators (wrongly, perhaps, but one can see why they felt that way). Thus, their desolation, their sense of defeat, their ill-repressed anger or bitterness, responses that seemed disproportionate to one tenure decision. They believed that, for various educational reasons and as testimony to a concern for greater equity in the larger society, Vanderbilt badly needed more women on its faculties, and particularly in such traditionally underrepresented departments as English. Thus, quite literally, they saw sex as a legitimate criterion in appointment and in promotion, for at Vanderbilt sex had become, or should have become, at least a small component in the job description for new faculty positions.

The breadth and seriousness of the administrative response to the Langland case further elevated its significance. The case also brought to the surface all the ambiguities and unresolved equity problems connected with affirmative action. By talking almost immediately to lawyers and by announcing her early intent to file a complaint with EEOC, Langland created the primary context for further negotiation—a series of essentially legal confrontations between counsel for both sides, or what by 1983 amounted to perhaps the most difficult case ever handled by Jeff Carr and his associates in the university's legal office. Langland's no-compromise demand, channeled through her attorney, was for a reversal of the decision and thus the awarding of tenure, a request virtually impossible to satisfy even though the chancellor has a legal right to overturn Voegeli's decision. Had he done so, Voegeli would have had to resign, and with basic procedures so undermined by this precedent, it is difficult to envision anyone's taking his job. In other words, the university would have conceded a lack of integrity in the College tenure process if it had unilaterally reversed Voegeli's decision, however politically inviting such a reversal was by the early fall of 1981.

By August of 1981, Fields had tentatively adopted a mediating position—to allow Langland an extra year in the tenure track. The university would conduct a new tenure review in 1981–82 and, if she failed to get tenure this time, allow her the normal year of grace, meaning she could remain at Vanderbilt until the summer of 1983. Pursuant to this, the Executive Committee met in a special session on August 31, 1981, to consider the Langland problem. Heard expressed his perplexity on how to proceed. Then he asked the trustees for authority to depart from the procedures of the *Faculty Manual*, with three options as possibilities—to extend a year, to let the present decision stand, or to reverse it and award tenure by fiat of the chancellor. The discussions made clear that extension was the only likely option and so the committee granted the chancellor the authority to extend Langland's appointment for no more than two years.[45]

An extension created several hazards back on campus. No procedure seemed safe. One concern was how to square the decision with Voegeli. Throughout the discussions in Kirkland Hall, Provost Holladay kept bringing up a critical issue—support for a beleaguered dean who he firmly believed had rendered a conscientious decision. An extension, as Langland and her attorneys made clear repeatedly, fell far short of her demand for a reversal, so far short that she never fully accepted it as an alternative. She did not want a demeaning second chance, any special favors; she wanted a reversal of an earlier decision. Finally, an extension would violate tenure rules, invite future appeals for exceptions by everyone denied tenure, and would seem blatantly unfair to men of possibly comparable qualifications who had also failed to win tenure bids.

Fields tried to chart a safe path through these hazards. He began on August 26 by requiring Holladay to conduct a review of all thirty-nine earlier tenure decisions made by Voegeli to determine if he had always followed the criteria of the *Faculty Manual*, if he had done so in the Langland case, and if his decision in the Langland case was consistent with the other thirty-nine. A conscientious Holladay did the hard work. He found no inconsistency and no violation, a strong vote of confidence in Voegeli. To make it more emphatic, and as a means of presenting a public defense by the university, both Holladay and Fields presented their report to the assembled College faculty. This statement of the administration's view of the issue angered some Langland supporters and was resented by some of the faculty, as it preceded and therefore to some extent affected a planned discussion of tenure procedures. Even the subsequently polarized College debates and a narrow 1983 defeat of proposals to create a tenure review committee for the College related directly to the Langland case. But such a concerted and well-publicized vindication of Voegeli was only a preface to compromise. Fields concluded that despite a fair and consistent application of the rules and a justified judgment against Langland, he would still recommend that she be given an added year and another review. He justified such an exceptional procedure on two bases: the unusually large proportion of as yet unpublished work in Langland's file and the university's special commitment to attracting and promoting more women.[46]

Ultimately compromise failed, to the despair of many conciliatory groups on campus. Langland received the final offer of a second review on September 1. Her deadline for filing a formal complaint with EEOC was December 7, six months after the alleged injustice. The university refused to conduct a second review if such legal procedures were under way but gave every possible assurance that if, at any subsequent time, Langland wanted to make an EEOC complaint the university would not use the missed deadline as a defense. This seemed to mean that Langland could consider the offer of review on its own merit, but neither she nor her lawyers ever felt secure on this point. But they did engage in endless haggling about details, climaxing in a November 3 meeting between the two counsels plus Heard, Fields, and Holladay. Langland sensed the hazards of a second review and again resented any implications of a special second chance. She might lose on the second

731

review, since the same dean seemed likely to make the decision. She worried over a second departmental review (not needed, said the university) and over details about outside reviewers. As the December 7 filing date approached, the university gave up on any solution. Langland thus filed her EEOC complaint. But she was still tantalized by the chance of a further review, and on December 15 asked for the review to go on as earlier contemplated. At this point the university held to its earlier position—it could not undertake a review while a legal complaint pended.

This seemed to end all the negotiations. But several people on campus tried to get both sides to yield. Thus, in what amounted to a final negotiation effort, Langland in February, 1982, agreed to hold her EEOC complaint in abeyance pending the outcome of a review. But she and her attorney demanded far more concessions on the details of the review than Vanderbilt felt it could promise. Soon both sides claimed bad faith, or a frequent shift in position. Thus, Langland broke off the negotiations and deferred once again to the EEOC. In March, 1982, Langland accepted a new position at Converse College. A year later she filed a suit in the federal courts consistent with permission granted by the EEOC, and before it reached a final decision on her complaint. She again charged sex discrimination as part of a pattern at Vanderbilt and asked for restitution of her position, for tenure, and for compensation for all losses.[47]

After one postponement, the Langland case finally came to trial in October, 1983, before the U.S. District Court in Nashville. Judge C. Clure Morton presided. Because of an intervening illness, he was unable to render his decision until April 27, 1984. In her charges against Vanderbilt, Langland claimed a violation of contract under Tennessee law, a failure of Vanderbilt to live up to affirmative action guidelines agreed to in a conciliation agreement with EEOC, and a violation of Title VII of the Civil Rights Act of 1964—a more stringent application of tenure standards to her, a woman, than to male candidates. Only the last charge became a significant issue in the trial. Judge Morton believed that Voegeli had followed the wording of the *Faculty Manual*, which takes precedence over College rules, in justifying his denial of tenure, and that he had therefore violated no employment contract. He also believed that Voegeli had acted consistent with the EEOC guidelines when he delegated to departmental chairs Vanderbilt's accepted obligation to provide extra counsel to minority and women faculty, and that the chair of the English department had fulfilled this obligation to Langland.[48]

The judge's decisions left Langland's one substantial claim—that Voegeli discriminated in applying tenure standards. On this issue, Langland offered evidence that gained the serious consideration of Judge Morton, and which required a detailed response from Vanderbilt, particularly from Dean Voegeli. In fact, the trial was distinguished by the exceptional preparation and ability of the two major protagonists—Langland and Voegeli. Langland accepted a very difficult task—to prove that sexual discrimination lay behind her failure to gain tenure. Since she was unable to introduce overt evidence of such discrimination, she had to rely on circumstantial arguments. Implicit in her case was her contention that she deserved tenure according to Vanderbilt standards. Thus, her qualifications, particularly in scholarship, became a central issue in the trial. Langland used two tactics to make her case. The first involved statistical evidence which, she argued, established that a pattern of discrimination against women prevailed at Vanderbilt. The university admitted that the underrepresentation of women on its faculty did reflect pre-1964 discrimination but denied any such since then, and particularly in the College under the deanship of Voegeli. Based on Vanderbilt's efforts to hire women, and on the number recently recruited in the College, Morton denied any overall pattern of bias in employment. As for Voegeli's decisions on individual tenure cases (his rejection of three of four women candidates), Morton believed the small sample made suspect any statistical analysis.

Langland was therefore left with only one option—to try to document discrimination by a detailed comparison of nine tenure decisions made by Voegeli. Her testimony on this issue seemed persuasive, at least before the university's response, and it even elicited some much-publicized compliments from Morton, creating an early and mistaken belief that Langland was winning her case. This part of the trial also had one unfortunate result—it made public confidential and embarrassing evaluations of past tenure candidates at Vanderbilt. Langland tried to prove that two female candidates who failed to get tenure had qualifications equal to two paired males who did. In addition, she argued that her qualifications matched or exceeded that of five males who gained tenure. In one much-publicized case, and possibly her strongest, she also claimed that, for one black professor, Voegeli had relaxed his normal standards and awarded tenure, at least in part, because of race. On these issues, Voegeli's testimony, and the exact content of the files, proved conclusive. Morton found no evidence of any double standard, even in the case of the one black candidate, and found in each case details that distinguished the qualifications of admittedly borderline male candidates from those of Langland. In Morton's estimation, Voegeli had reason to deny tenure to Langland on the basis of her unacceptable achievement in scholarship. The circumstantial evidence failed to prove any sexual discrimination. Thus, he ruled for Vanderbilt and against Langland and assessed all costs to Langland. She plans an appeal.[49]

In a broader response to the issues raised by Langland, in the fall of 1981 President Fields appointed an ad hoc committee on the status of women and minorities at Vanderbilt. This committee, chaired by Peter J. Paris of the Divinity School, quickly bogged down in all the semantic, legal, and moral ambiguities of affirmative action. Rather consistently, a majority of the Vanderbilt faculty had expressed approval for extra recruitment efforts needed to identify female or black candidates but had opposed any favoritism for such candidates. In a very limited way, the Paris committee challenged this prevailing position. It stressed the need for more women and minorities on the Vanderbilt faculty, not only because of a need for cultural diversity or role models for black or women students, but in some cases because they could bring new sexually or racially related perspectives to traditional academic subjects. The committee recognized a present market reality—academic women and blacks are in scarce supply in the higher ranks, and thus command higher salaries than white males at a comparable level of experience and achievement. The committee made all the expected recommendations—for new and more imaginative recruitment tactics, for more administrative positions for women and blacks, for more blacks on the Board of Trust, and for more courses in black and women's studies.

It did more. It asked for a fund in excess of $100,000 to help deans and department chairs lure additional blacks and women to the Vanderbilt faculty. The fund, as subsequently established in the office of the provost, was to cover market-dictated additions to salaries or fringe benefits, or added recruitment costs, needed to hire women and blacks with academic qualifications equal to those of white, male competitors. Without such inducements, the committee believed Vanderbilt would be doomed, in the near future, to hiring only white males, particularly at the higher ranks. The fund meant that departments could still make offers only to the best qualified candidates, but with an understanding that the provost would add extra funds if such candidates happened to be female or black. By this limited financial incentive, Vanderbilt now made sex and race important job qualifications. The committee believed racial and sexual diversity were worth the extra cost. To get the diversity, Vanderbilt had to pay the going cost, as much so as when it seeks a winning football coach.[50]

Vanderbilt's two leaders—Heard and Fields—were unable to guide the final litigations of the Langland case. They both left office as of July 1, 1982, a year earlier than anyone had expected, since Heard had planned to retire at the end of twenty years as chancellor. A new opportunity hastened his decision. Officials of the Alfred P. Sloan Foundation approached him about a major three-year study of the presidential election process in America, a subject that related closely to Heard's earlier research as a political scientist. He began preliminary work on the project in 1981–82, drawing one-tenth of his salary from the foundation. On retirement, he retained his professorship in political science but established his project in the former president's home at Peabody and worked as a part of vipps. The board not only honored him by all the formalities but gave him special loan benefits to help him buy a new home. In late 1983 it voted to name the Vanderbilt University Library for Jean and Alexander Heard. Heard's retirement, by all administrative logic, required the resignation of President Fields. If Fields stayed on as an experienced president, a new chancellor would have found enormous difficulty in establishing his or her authority. In fact, the office of president no longer made any sense, for it fit the special circumstances of the 1970s. Thus in April,

1981, the Executive Committee of the Board voted to discontinue the office, and did so without consulting Fields. The elimination of his office clarified some ambiguities in Fields's position. It made him a clear candidate for chancellor, a post he very much wanted to fill and, after five years of crisis and of very demanding work, a post he thought he deserved.

He did not get it. Instead, he retained only his position as a tenured professor in the history department. As conscientious men and women who fail to get tenure will testify, universities rarely give any more than token awards for conscientious service. The future always places the greatest claim. Those who hire and fire have to choose on behalf of the ongoing welfare of the university, on behalf of future students and the larger society. Thus, over and over again the Board of Trust has sought new blood for chancellor. The one exception, the one possible parallel to Fields, was Oliver C. Carmichael, the one clear apprentice chancellor in Vanderbilt's history. And he was at the university almost too long, became responsible for too many difficult decisions, to inherit his kingdom. Fields did not have united faculty support. With it, he might have gained the chancellorship, despite the doubts or opposition of Heard. But the hectic years of his presidency had kept him too vulnerable on too many issues, had created too many enemies for him to have such support. The final enemies came out of the Langland case; strong supporters of blacks and women at Vanderbilt generally opposed Fields. Faculty judgments on his ability, on his leadership capability, varied immensely. Given this lack of consensus on the faculty, support that is almost impossible to gain by anyone as centrally involved in policy decisions as Fields, faculty members usually choose to gamble, to look ahead to a new leader. It is easy to invest one's hopes and dreams in some imagined chancellor. Frustrated constituencies always hope for a new start, for new priorities, and thus for fulfillment of their special goals.

Board members also have a stake in new leadership. The selection of a chancellor provides them their only critical leverage over the basic academic policies of the university. This suggests an outside search and the nomination of a new chancellor, clearly chosen by them, and one for a brief time necessarily subservient to their wishes. Local community input might have tipped the balance toward Fields. In the last two elections local boosters kept alive the candidacy of Sarratt and Purdy. Fields did not have such intense local support, had never played the alumni game, had not effectively cultivated local support. His position did not allow this luxury. His personality precluded it. He was neither a charmer nor a politician.

The board made a daring choice—Joe B. Wyatt, vice-president for administration at Harvard. For the first time in Vanderbilt's history it did not choose a scholar, instead selecting a man with limited academic experience and not widely known in academic circles. It also for the first time chose a candidate who was not nominated or supported by a faculty screening committee. Clearly, more than in the past, dominant members of the board wanted to set new directions for Vanderbilt. They made the most radical choice so far in Vanderbilt's history, a choice for discontinuity over continuity. Wyatt, a Texan, had made his early career in the business world and had specialized in the relatively new field of computer science. It is much too early to gauge the direction of his leadership at Vanderbilt, but his early speeches suggest his desire to improve the quality of the Vanderbilt faculty, and to realign Vanderbilt toward a greater partnership with large corporate enterprise, toward a greater emphasis upon technical fields, and toward a greater involvement in larger community concerns. In his early speeches he has expressed his sense of the magnitude of recent technological change, the enormous problems and possibilities this change offers to universities, and his desire that Vanderbilt lead American universities in adapting to a new era, to what he often calls the information revolution. But these priorities involve the next chapter of Vanderbilt's history, or finally one subject that is not fated to be part of this long history.

Postscript

ANY INSTITUTIONAL HISTORY has its pitfalls and limits. It cannot capture and express the unique experiences of those who make up a university community. In the perspective of its various citizens, there is not one Vanderbilt but hundreds. The images vary immensely. The points of convergence—campus, buildings, administrators, key faculty members—may be only a minute aspect of the Vanderbilt that some people know and either love or hate. In this history I have presented the university known by administrators, faculty, and students, and not the one known by parents of students, by such consumers of its services as hospital patients, by campus neighbors, or even by its many staff employees.

Throughout this history I have tried to give priority to what I consider the most vital constituency in any university—undergraduate students. They have a special status, one that comes closest to expressing the role of colleges and universities in American society. College, for most undergraduates, marks the leaving of the nest, the first escape from home and family, the first entry into a new and very different environment. The hazards rival the opportunities. The experience is not always exhilarating. But it is always memorable. Perhaps not more so than other nest-leaving experiences—a tour in the military, a new and distant job, extended foreign travel. But it is at least comparable to those in the intensity of the experience. Most people retain more detailed memories of their undergraduate years than any prior or subsequent four years of their lives. And for the same reasons, these are years of rapid personal maturation. These are not only memorable but very formative years, much more so for undergraduates than for graduate or professional students. Even early in Vanderbilt's history, when most professional students had no prior college experience, their more narrowly specialized training and their exemption from many of the frivolities as well as the varied intellectual challenges of the College helped insure a less challenging and liberating education.

I use the word "liberate" quite deliberately. Leaving the nest is, in part, to break free. But free for what? A college proffers numerous options, not only in intellectual pursuits but in social relationships. The presence of such options alone gives content to the new freedom. The discipline of college communal life sets necessary limits. For most students, college is their Brook

Farm, their brief and only experiment with an often troubling Utopia. Four years may be quite enough, even too much. The college interlude usually facilitates growth but in a sense it also prolongs a type of dependency.

A college is, at best, a highly subsidized commune. Students at Vanderbilt, at any excellent university, never pay the full cost of their education and few at Vanderbilt have to earn their own tuition. They are privileged, still enjoying enormous subsidies from parents and society, still preparing for a self-sufficient life, for their own special vocation. This gives them a last interval of freedom from certain cares of adult life but cannot but support a galling sense of prolonged dependency. But, at its best, college provides the rare interlude when one is liberated from the intellectual constraints of parents and the local community, even as one is free of the coming constraints imposed by a job and a demanding career. In this brief interlude between the parochialism of family, clan, or sect and the even more limiting parochialism of a firm or a specialized profession, a young adult can investigate and experiment with an array of new beliefs and new modes of behavior. Perhaps above all, he or she can enjoy more than ever before, and in all likelihood ever again, an environment that allows a large degree of personal exploration and personal honesty. At its best a college invites honesty—that is, it encourages students to report on the exact quality of their experience, to express their most unconventional beliefs. If the emperor is naked, they are the ones to shout forth the alarming news. The normal fears of exposure and censure, the wide array of constraints—to please, to adjust, to gain status, to win promotion—abate just a bit, even on occasion in classrooms, more often in dormitories or in various student interest groups. The same freedom from conventional constraints help open up an array of human contacts, invite new and deeper friendships, or another luxury of a special communal life.

The undergraduate schools of Vanderbilt have offered largely southern students such a brief flirtation with Utopia. In the classroom, in their social life, they have confronted new and in some cases very threatening or very challenging options. Not as many, not as threatening, as they would have confronted in large, more heterogeneous northern universities. Not the same options as at southern public universities or small liberal arts colleges. To dare even these comparative judgments is to ask the question that is critical to any university history, and a question I most frequently confront whenever one learns that I am involved with the history of Vanderbilt. What is unique about Vanderbilt? What, if anything, distinguishes it from other universities, particularly such southern and Methodist-derived cousins as Emory and Trinity-Duke? What is the special character of Vanderbilt, these qualities that make it so special to students and alumni? Some phrase the question in elusive terms. They talk about the "spirit" or "essence" of Vanderbilt as if such were apparent to any who knew it well, or to those who love it enough to engage and probe its deepest identity. I fear that, behind the competent assertions of such a special identity, lie images as diverse in nuances as are the people who try, so futilely, to express them in appropriate language. When pushed to the level of fine distinctions, no two people intend exactly the same image when they talk about Vanderbilt. But I suspect there are a few points of convergence in these necessarily individual and thus unique perspectives. I want to suggest a few of these.

Geography remains critical. Vanderbilt is in an increasingly prosperous and culturally elusive South. This is an inescapable fact. Whether this should have, whether administrators or faculty want it to have, major significance or not it still lurks as a vital aspect of Vanderbilt's identity. It is not just early Vanderbilt traditions, the self-conscious affirmations of the Agrarians, or the lingering perceptions of most outside observers that make Vanderbilt not only in, but so much of, the South, but also the continuing and vital self-awareness of most people at Vanderbilt, whatever their origin. In this sense no one can long escape Vanderbilt's southernness. Why this sectional identity remains so focal involves not so much the distinctive history of Vanderbilt as that of the Confederate South. The burdens of being a part of the South—exceptional poverty, racial subjection, educational backwardness, an inescapable sense of moral and cultural and intellectual inferiority—supports a regional self-consciousness that is still much more intense than that in New England or the Midwest. Thus, geography and an historic culture remain a more important distinguishing mark of Vanderbilt, as of a Duke or Emory or Tulane, than a Harvard or a Northwestern. Mixed in with this regional self-consciousness is a deep-rooted sense of inferiority, an acute consciousness of rank or status and thus a certain defensiveness, a craving for acceptance or certification. To cite such self-consciousness is not to argue that everyone means the same thing by Vanderbilt's southern identity, or even that most people give any very precise cultural content to the label "southern." When one tries to talk clearly about regional character, one usually flounders in all the ambiguities or perplexities that haunt attempts to capture national character.

Fortunately, some widespread images of the South reduce to measurable facts. Although linguists can distinguish several versions of southern speech, no one can miss the southern accents that so distinguish, and adorn, campus speech. Vanderbilt also has a reputation for friendliness and civility, for a more leisurely pace of life. It is hard to pin this one down, particularly since most American universities make the same claim. But these images may have a basis in not always flattering facts—in foreclosed southern economic opportunities that discouraged highly competitive habits, in a provincialism that abetted clan loyalties, in a loneliness that gave a special value to fellowship, in religious styles that supported warmth and generosity, even in work habits appropriate to a debilitatingly hot climate. At times the slow pace at Vanderbilt simply documents an unusual degree of incompetence or inefficiency in the staff. The civility may rest, at least in part, on cultural traditions in well-established families, on the sense of security fostered by affluence, by still intact family structures, and by the class and religious homogeneity of Vanderbilt students. Vanderbilt retains the character of a relatively small and intimate campus; the civility and warmth rivals that of a neighborhood or a club.

One cannot escape religion. Vanderbilt's Methodist origin still shapes it, much more than anyone might suspect by present appearances. Methodism, in the South, set the standard for a type of evangelical Christianity—doctrinely loose, emotionally warm, morally rigorous, and intellectually soft. At Vanderbilt's beginnings, Methodism retained a sectarian fervor and literalism. Not for long. Even as doctrinal distinctions lessened, Methodists became part of a generalized and respectable southern Protestant establishment, one that includes a large share of Baptists, Presbyterians, Disciples, and Episcopalians. Unlike in the North, it includes few Lutherans or Congregationalists. Because of the social and economic prominence of Vanderbilt students, few of them represent smaller evangelical sects, the Churches of Christ, or more orthodox or conservative wings of traditional denominations. In spite of a leavening body of Jewish and Roman Catholic students at Vanderbilt, the mainline Protestant profile is probably more deeply entrenched than at any other graduate-level university in the country. This adds to the class and economic homogeneity of the student body. It also reinforces very traditional, middle-class values—high career expectations, strong attachments to the conventional family, and at least loosely orthodox or conventional beliefs not only about the gods but about most political and social issues.

In religion, as in most other areas, most contemporary Vanderbilt undergraduates are in the respectable mainstream, relatively secure in their sense of identity. They reflect the mentality of the arrived, the established, the successful. This does not mean they are smug, although a few are. Many know guilt, have a deep concern for social problems. But it is the concern of those who are distanced from economic hardship and poverty, from status anxieties, from the frustrations of failure. In religion they are, to use William James's phrase, largely among the once-born, those who have not suffered the terrible self-doubts, the overwhelming sense of guilt or worthlessness and the overwhelming anxiety of the twice-born, of those who know or experience traumatic or liberating religious experiences, who become fervent believers or sectarian activists or fundamentalist crusaders. Neither have many of them suffered or enjoyed the intellectual perplexities that lead so many young adults to reject all the old gods, to move beyond theism or beyond any organized religion. Unlike on many northern campuses, where the majority of students may be atheists or agnostics, a clear majority of Vanderbilt students retain not only theist beliefs but are even relatively orthodox Christians or Jews, and a majority have direct ties to organized churches or synagogues.

Of course, such a religious profile is more typical than distinctive among more elite southern universities. The distinctive role of religion at Vanderbilt is more subtle. The early Methodist imprint, and the continued and vital role of a Divinity School, has helped make religion an important academic concern at Vanderbilt. Although Vanderbilt's intellectual contribution, at the national level, has been primarily literary, it is notable how much religious themes have been a part of that literary tradition. But is is equally notable that Vanderbilt has never, since the age of McTyeire and Garland, stood for any one doctrinal stance. Perhaps Kirkland set the pattern of a broadly tolerant, even at times almost vaporously ecumenical religious atmosphere. One affect of this has been a notable lack of insistent, rigorous intellectuality. One only has to compare Vanderbilt with any good Jesuit school, to those in the Puritan and Presbyterian tradition, or to the New York colleges dominated by Jewish intellectuals to appreciate this characteristic.

Vanderbilt students, by and large, have eschewed the sectarian dogmatism, the carefully cultivated and intensely argued convictions on philosophical or theological or political issues, that leads to ideological conflict and to the most sustained and rigorous intellectual engagement. Even at their best, Vanderbilt students, often supported by their faculty, have valued an apt metaphor more than a tight syllogism, civility and kindness more than dialectical skill, sound scholarship and high academic standards more than originality or sheer brilliance. This is not just my perception but that of almost a century of student critics. Over and over again, student journalists have pleaded for more serious intellectual engagement on the part of professors and students, often without realizing what this might mean. One cannot have it both ways. Civility and broad tolerance and even conventional scholarly standards are simply inimical to rigorous intellectual engagement, which requires a degree of conflict, of sectarian factionalism, of intense involvement, and a sharp and even aggressive intellectual style, and thus produces all manner of insecurities and anxieties.

Such norm-setting traits in undergraduates have complemented some related traits of Vanderbilt administrators and faculties. Vanderbilt has never stood for major educational or intellectual innovations. The one possible exception might be what is called the New Criticism, which grew in part out of the work of the Fugitives. But the Fugitives, least of all, spoke for the Vanderbilt administration, and they consistently reflected the beliefs of no more than a tiny minority of students or faculty. Generally, Vanderbilt has tenaciously clung to older pedagogic and academic traditions, resisted rapid changes, and thereby avoided most fads and fashions. The most apt, and perhaps most frequent, terms describing Vanderbilt have been the pair "integrity" and "high standards." On these rest the considerable respect that it has always enjoyed in the larger academic community. I do not mean by this that Vanderbilt has conformed to the highly intellectualized, even brilliant cultural reaction voiced by certain of the Agrarians. In their prophetic hands, reaction became a very un-Vanderbilt-like form of radicalism. Rather, Van-

741

derbilt administrators have generally resisted the trends of the times and only gradually adapted to the new, whether in curriculum, pedagogy, grading standards, rules for student conduct, or in broader social policy.

In one sense of the loaded and almost useless term, Vanderbilt has been a deeply "conservative" institution. Perhaps an even better label would be "preservative." Restraint, caution, and political prudence have characterized Vanderbilt's remarkably few chancellors, with Heard possibly the one exception. Its faculty has been unusually stable. More than in most institutions, save possibly the U.S. Senate, old men have generally held the preponderence of power, in part because so few key personnel ever leave Vanderbilt short of retirement. Thus, the profile of age and maturity, possibly of wisdom, best fits not only the Board of Trust but the administration and even the faculty. The dramatic exceptions only prove the rule. By exceptions I refer to dozens of young professors or administrators who have, with great frustration and ultimate futility, tried to institute idealistic or radical changes at Vanderbilt. The innovators, from a Joseph K. Hart to the curriculum reformers of the mid-1930s to a Howard Hartman have all had a tough time at Vanderbilt, for better or for worse.

A cautious resistance to rapid change does not mean that Vanderbilt has remained static. It does mean that, at Vanderbilt, adaptive change has lagged behind not only that of a few avowedly progressive or experimental colleges, but behind almost all American universities. From this restraint Vanderbilt has often clearly benefited, as in the 1930s when it finally reaped the returns of an almost unbelievable prudence in investment policies, or in the late 1970s when it did not have to struggle so very much to regain high grading standards or a demanding curriculum. At other times it has suffered, as in the early 1980s when, in the most difficult of times, it tried to undo earlier forms of racial and sexual exclusiveness. Often, by waiting longer to inaugurate new programs, as in business education or even in the fine arts, it has been able to profit from the trials and tribulations of more daring institutions. In this, as so many areas, it has minimized risk, a policy only in part tied to tight budgets. Its private status, of course, has insulated Vanderbilt from many of the political pressures that plague public institutions, at least until the last decade. This is why affirmative action programs and other outside mandates, each loaded down with its share of ambiguities, has created so many anxieties at Vanderbilt. Even the older sense of integrity, of Vanderbilt's adhering to certain standards or principles whatever the pressures, now seems a bit outdated or at least a political liability.

I doubt any early shifts in these Vanderbilt traditions, despite recent hints of radical new departures. When the Board of Trust met in 1982 to elect Chancellor Wyatt, a unanimous choice of its search committee, some of the language seemed strangely familiar. The chair of the search committee, William Vaughn, suggested that Vanderbilt had tried to find a chancellor like Heard, but "one with a vision, appropriate to this day and age." This sense of a new age, of a future dramatically different than the past, echoed some of Wyatt's own beliefs. But Vaughn went on to express the board's hopes at this time of a new beginning—that Wyatt could help raise Vanderbilt from the "upper rung of the second tier of private U.S. universities to the entering level of the top tier." In different words, this is the exact sentiment expressed at both the election of Branscomb and Heard. I do not think that Vaughn meant this remark as a confession of past failures. If he did he was unfair, for I am convinced that Vanderbilt navigated through the perilous 1960s and 1970s as successfully as any university in America. But in it also lurked the ever present frustration so evident at Vanderbilt. It seemed so often to move so close to an academic promised land but never quite get there.

Nothing is more hazardous than predictions about the future. Our lives are ever haunted by irony. So few of our expectations are ever realized, at least in the way we expected. What seems so obviously portended by Vanderbilt's present course may seem absurd or foolish five years from now. But, despite these hazards, I share a few anticipations. An era of growth and expansion is over, at least for the next decade. The enrollment pressures of the 1960s, the added schools of the 1970s, have given way to stable enrollments and limited pressures for new buildings or new schools. Thus, the immediate problems at Vanderbilt all involve upgrading academic standards and maintaining the needed financial support for such goals. Unlike any decade of the last ten, not a single college or school seems in such peril as to risk closure, although Nursing and possibly Peabody face intimidating challenges.

Academic improvements do not come easily or quickly. In the years after 1945, Vanderbilt, in many respects, enjoyed a near boom, an almost revolutionary improvement in faculty, in facilities, in enrollment, in the quality of its students, and in the number of schools and colleges. But even so, it has not moved much higher in the ranks of graduate-level universities. One has to run so hard to keep up with the pack. Holding one's present position is not easy. Comparative rankings are suspect, but in Vaughn's terms I do not expect Vanderbilt in the next twenty years to move into the "entering level of the top tier" of private universities, if that means the top ten. Such, if it occurred, would be an almost unprecedented achievement for any university. In other words, Vanderbilt will not soon be able to match a Harvard or a Yale, a Brown or a Stanford in overall resources, unless one of these suffers from abysmal leadership or a financial disaster. As in so many areas of American life, the largest and strongest institutions are always better able to take advantage of opportunities. If anything, the gap of quality widens rather than narrows. This is most true for universities, where tradition and funded assets (such as libraries) and reputation, all so slowly gained, are so determinant. Even the gradual shift of wealth and population toward the South, which in so many areas (increased gifts, a growing pool of applicants) has aided Vanderbilt, still has a more limited impact on higher education than on other institutions, again because of the uniquely conservative nature of universities.

The South, by its poverty, its racial exclusiveness, and its cultural backwardness, long insured Vanderbilt's lowly rank in any national perspective. That it is so much less a handicap today, although still a handicap, is Vanderbilt's single most promising augury for the near future.

I do not want to end with what might seem to some a near lament. I do not interpret these realistic assessments as even mildly pessimistic. For Vanderbilt, I suspect the "upper rung of the second tier" amounts to a notable achievement. It is a compliment to the struggle, the effort, of so many people who have given so much of their talent, affection, and money to Vanderbilt. It also documents some of Vanderbilt's strengths. For example, I doubt that students, anywhere in America, get a significantly better education than do present undergraduates in the College or professional students in Medicine and Divinity. The second-tier image, since it is predicated on a national perspective, strikes me as both more accurate and more challenging than the older, smug "Harvard of the South," an image that prevailed when the qualifying "South" excused so very much. The stated goal of moving up to the top tier may be an energizing one. It may help stimulate the needed efforts to strengthen some very weak graduate programs, to renew the Nursing School, to help the College of Arts and Science regain its earlier preeminence in the total university. But, unfortunately, Vanderbilt's status anxieties, its desire to gain a national reputation, may be stultifying, in the sense that it leads to imitation, to perennial efforts to catch up with a Harvard or a Yale. Instead, I believe Vanderbilt needs to nourish, to bring to a level of self-consciousness, its own distinctive traditions, its own special achievements and instructive failures, and to build on those. This requires self-understanding. The preface to such a search for identity, which also turns out to be the means for an endless creation of a new identity, is historical self-consciousness. To such a goal I dedicate this history.

Abbreviations

BOT   Vanderbilt University. "Minutes of the Board of Trust." Special Collections, Jean and Alexander Heard Library, Vanderbilt University.

Bull.   *Bulletin of Vanderbilt University* [title and department vary]. See also *Register.*

CHP   Centennial History Project [subjects and dates vary]. Special Collections, Jean and Alexander Heard Library, Vanderbilt University.

Chanc. Off.   Office of the Chancellor Records. Special Collections, Jean and Alexander Heard Library, Vanderbilt University.

Chr. Adv.   *Christian Advocate* [city varies].

coll.   collection

corr.   correspondence

ff   file folder

FM   Vanderbilt University. "Faculty Minutes." Special Collections, Jean and Alexander Heard Library, Vanderbilt University.

Fin. State-ments   Vanderbilt University, *Financial Statements of Vanderbilt University for Year Ending* . . . . [date varies]. Special Collections, Jean and Alexander Heard Library, Vanderbilt University.

HL   Jean and Alexander Heard Library, Vanderbilt University.

Meritt Coll.   Centennial History Project. "Admin. —Chanc. Kirkland-Meritt Material," [dates vary]. Special Collections, Jean and Alexander Heard Library, Vanderbilt University.

MS, MSS   manuscript, manuscripts

Quarterly   *Vanderbilt University Quarterly*

RG   record group

Reg.   *Register of Vanderbilt University* . . . [dates vary], *Announcement,* . . . [dates vary]. Nashville: n.p., [dates vary]. See also *Bulletin.*

SC   Special Collections, Jean and Alexander Heard Library, Vanderbilt University.

Notes

1. Birth Pains

1. *Journal of the General Conference of the Methodist Episcopal Church, South, May, 1854* (n.p.: n.p. [1854]), 304–305; *Chr. Adv.* (Nashville), May 1, 1856.

2. *Chr. Adv.* (Nashville), Apr. 16, 30, 1857; Clarence Moore Dannelly, "The Development of Collegiate Education in the Methodist Episcopal Church, South, 1846–1902" (Ph.D. diss., Yale Univ., 1933), 114–15.

3. T.O. Summers, ed., *Life and Papers of A.L.P. Green* (Nashville: Southern Methodist Publishing House, 1877), 241–42, 259–60, 262–64.

4. *Private Acts of the State of Tennessee, Passed at the First Session of the Thirty-Second General Assembly, for the Years 1857-8* (Nashville: n.p., 1858), 241; Dannelly, "Development of Collegiate Education," 117–18.

5. *Chr. Adv.* (Nashville), May 27; Nov. 11, 1858; June 17, 1859; *Daily Chr. Adv.*, May 12, 31; June 2, 1858.

6. *Chr. Adv.* (Nashville), Aug. 11, 1859; Dannelly, "Development of Collegiate Education," 116–17.

7. *Journal of the General Conference . . . April, 1866*, 133–34, 136, 239; Hunter Dickinson Farish, *The Circuit Rider Dismounts: A Social History of Southern Methodism, 1865–1900* (Richmond, Va.: Dietz Press, 1938), 87, 258–60, 262–63.

8. John J. Tigert, IV, *Bishop Holland Nimmons McTyeire, Ecclesiastical and Educational Architect* (Nashville: Vanderbilt Univ. Press, 1955), 124–26, 133–44, 154–57.

9. *Chr. Adv.* (Nashville), Apr. 4, 25; May 23; June 27, 1867.

10. Louise Dowlen, "Landon Cabell Garland: The Prince of Southern Educators, A Sketch," *Bull.* 38 (Jan. 15, 1938): 11; *Chr. Adv.* (Nashville), Oct. 9, 16, 23, 30; Nov. 6, 13, 1869; Apr. 16, 23, 30, 1870.

11. *Journal of the General Conference . . . May 1870*, 237, 240–43; *Round Table* (Nashville), June 14, 1890, J. T. McGill Coll., box 11, ff 177, SC.

12. McTyeire to Amelia McTyeire, Sept. 7, 1870–Nov. 4, 1871, McTyeire Corr., film 793, HL; William C. Johnson to Landon C. Garland in *Chr. Adv.* (Nashville), Oct. 18, 1890.

13. *Round Table* (Nashville), Apr. 26, July 5, 1890.

14. *Round Table* (Nashville), Apr. 26, 1890.

15. Ibid.

16. *Chr. Adv.* (Nashville), Feb. 3, 10, 1872; Summers, *A.L.P. Green*, 258–60; BOT, Jan. 26, 1872.

17. BOT, Jan. 26, 1872.

18. BOT, Jan. 27, 1872; *Central University Charter, Proceedings of the Board of Trust, and Address of the Board* (Nashville: Southern Methodist Publishing House, 1873), 8–13.

19. *Chr. Adv.* (Nashville), May 18, 1872; BOT, May 8, 9, 1872; *Central University Charter*, 3–7.

20. *Chr. Adv.* (Nashville), Mar. 2, 9, 23; Apr. 6, 27; May 4, 18, 1872; BOT, May 10, 1872.

21. BOT, Jan. 16, 17, 1873.

22. McTyeire to Amelia McTyeire, Mar. 12, 1873, McTyeire Corr.

23. Tigert, *McTyeire*, 30, 45–63, 67–71, 90, 93, 100–105, 109–15.

24. Ibid., 65–66.
25. McTyeire Sermons, McTyeire-Baskervill Papers, files 1–163, SC.
26. Tigert, *McTyeire,* 149–50, 154, 163–72.
27. See McTyeire to Amelia McTyeire, passim, McTyeire Corr.; Tigert, *McTyeire,* 49–50, 166, 229–30.
28. McTyeire to Amelia McTyeire, Mar. 12, 1873, McTyeire Corr.; Jane McTyeire Baskervill, MS memorandum on "Mrs. Frank A. Vanderbilt" in McTyeire-Baskervill Papers.
29. Tigert, *McTyeire,* 83–87, 190–91.
30. Baskervill, MS memorandum on "Mrs. Frank A. Vanderbilt."
31. Ibid.
32. Tigert, *McTyeire,* 187–200; Baskervill, MS memorandum on "Mrs. Frank A. Vanderbilt."
33. McTyeire to Amelia McTyeire, Mar. 12, 17, 1873, McTyeire Corr.
34. Ibid.; Tigert, *McTyeire,* 194–95.
35. McTyeire Corr.; *Charter and Amended Charter of Vanderbilt University* ([Nashville]: n.p., n.d.), 7–8; BOT, Mar. 26, 1873.
36. Vanderbilt to McTyeire in BOT, Mar. 26, 1873.
37. BOT, May 9, 1873; McTyeire to Vanderbilt, May 21, 1873; reply, May 26, 1873, McTyeire-Baskervill Papers; W.G.E. Cunnyngham to Garland, May 25, 1873; McTyeire to Garland, May 28, 1873, Landon Cabell Garland Papers, SC; *Union and American* (Nashville), May 4, 5, 1873; *Republican Banner* (Nashville), May 5, 8, 17, 1873; Tigert, *McTyeire,* 183–84.
38. McTyeire to Garland, May 28; Aug. 25; Sept. 13, 1873, Garland Papers; McTyeire to Vanderbilt, July 31, 1873, McTyeire-Baskervill Papers; Synopsis of Plans and Specifications for the University, approved Aug. 25, 1873, John J. Tigert Coll., SC; *Republican Banner* (Nashville) Apr. 29, 1874.
39. BOT, Apr. 29, 1874; June 18, 19, 1876; Vanderbilt to McTyeire, Dec. 2, 1875, Tigert Coll.
40. BOT, May 24, 1880.
41. BOT, Jan. 15, 1874.
42. "Report of the Committee on Education at the General Conference of 1878," in *Chr. Adv.* (Nashville), June 15, 1878.

2. Sect and Section

1. Daniel Coit Gilman, *The Launching of a University and Other Papers: A Sheaf of Remembrances* (New York: Dodd, Mead, 1906), 7–10, 27–30.
2. McTyeire to Amelia McTyeire, Mar. 17, 1874, McTyeire Corr., film 793, HL.
3. John J. Tigert, IV, *Bishop Holland Nimmons McTyeire: Ecclesiastical and Educational Architect* (Nashville: Vanderbilt Univ. Press, 1955), 213.
4. Emory Stevens Bucke, ed., *The History of American Methodism,* 3 vols. (New York: Abingdon Press, 1964), I:11–12, 14–29; Holland N. McTyeire, *A History of Methodism* (Nashville: Publishing House of The Methodist Episcopal Church, South, 1910), 14, 108–17.
5. Bucke, *American Methodism,* I:74–80, 95–96, 152–54, 185–89, 197–206, 213–16, 231–32; McTyeire, *Methodism,* 279–84, 314–19, 343–44, 391–92; Nathan Bangs, *A History of the Methodist Episcopal Church,* 4 vols. (New York: Phillips and Hunt, 1880), I:46–48, 151–67.
6. Bucke, *American Methodism,* I:29–40; McTyeire, *Methodism,* 52–53.
7. Bucke, *American Methodism,* I:32–33, 246; McTyeire, *Methodism,* 192–99.
8. Bucke, *American Methodism,* I:258–61, 301–303, 323–27; McTyeire, *Methodism,* 327.
9. McTyeire, *Methodism,* 59, 375–89; Bucke, *American Methodism.* I:188–89, 251–58; Hunter Dickinson Farish, *The Circuit Rider Dismounts: A Social History of Southern Methodism, 1865–1900* (Richmond, Va.: Dietz Press, 1938), 4–6.
10. Bucke, *American Methodism,* I:365–68, 428–33, 453–73.
11. Bucke, *American Methodism* II:322–26, 417–19, 642–44; Farish, *Circuit Rider Dismounts,* 65, 87–89.

12. Gilman, *Launching of a University*, 8, 41–43, 48–49; Francesco Cordasco, *Daniel Coit Gilman and the Protean Ph.D.: The Shaping of American Graduate Education* (Leiden: E.J. Brill, 1960), 54–92.

13. Richard A. Easterlin, "Regional Income Trends, 1840–1950," in Seymour E. Harris, ed., *American Economic History* (New York: McGraw-Hill, 1961), 525–47.

14. W.W.[oodford] Clayton, *History of Davidson County, Tennessee with Illustrations and Biographical Sketches of Its Prominent Men and Pioneers* (Philadelphia: J.W. Lewis, 1880), 133–40, 211–12, 292–98, 328–40; George H. Rogers, comp., *The Nashville and Edgefield Directory* (Nashville: Marshall & Bruce, 1878); J. Woolridge, ed., *History of Nashville, Tenn.* (Nashville: Publishing House of the Methodist Episcopal Church, South, 1890), 193–202, 330–40; Hollis Phillip Bacon III, "The Historical Geography of Ante-Bellum Nashville" (Ph.D. diss., George Peabody College for Teachers, 1955), 138, 140, 191–92, 200.

15. Don Harrison Doyle, "Urbanization and Southern Culture: Economic Elites in Four New South Cities (Atlanta, Nashville, Charleston, Mobile), c. 1865–1910," in Orville Vernon Burton and Robert C. McMath, Jr., eds., *Toward a New South? Studies in Post Civil War Southern Communities* (Westport, Conn.: Greenwood Press, 1982), 11–36; Woolridge, *History of Nashville*, 377–97, 432–36, 442–52; Lucius Salisbury Merriam, *Higher Education in Tennessee* (Washington, D.C.: Government Printing Office, 1893), 31, 41, 48–50, 261–73, 278–80, 282–85; Alfred Leland Crabb, *Nashville: Personality of a City* (Indianapolis: Bobbs-Merrill, 1960), 192–93, 200–202.

16. *Union and American* (Nashville), Apr. 29, 1874; *Republican Banner* (Nashville), Apr. 28, 29, 1874.

3. ACADEMIC FOUNDATIONS

1. Robert K. Hargrove, "Memorial Address—The Founders and Organizers of Vanderbilt University," *Vanderbilt Quarterly* 1 (May, 1901): 113–15; Louise Dowlen, "Landon Cabell Garland: The Prince of Southern Educators, A Sketch," *Bull. 38* (Jan. 15, 1938): 4, 31–33.

2. Garland to McTyeire, Feb. 16, 1874, John J. Tigert IV Coll., SC; to T.O. Summers, July 14, 1874; to William W. Folwell, July 22, 1874, both in Landon C. Garland Letterbooks, SC.

3. Dowlen, "Garland," 4–5, 8–16, 18–19, 23; Hargrove, "Memorial Address," 113–15; Charles Forster Smith, *Reminiscences and Sketches* (Nashville: Publishing House of the Methodist Episcopal Church, South, 1908), 4–8; Rebecca Agnew Holt and May Lightfoot Garland, "Landon Cabell Garland's Letter Book While President of the Northeast & Southwest Alabama Railroad Company, 1854–1855," *Alabama Historical Quarterly* 34 (Spring, 1972): 37–94.

4. Dowlen, "Garland," 10, 14, 20–30; Hargrove, "Memorial Address," 113–14; *Announcement, Vanderbilt University, First Session, 1875–6* (Nashville: n.p. 1875); quotation p. 14 in *Reg.*, 1875–81; Garland to McTyeire, Apr. 2, 1873, McTyeire Corr., film 793, HL; McTyeire to Garland, Apr. 7, 1873, Garland Papers, SC; letter from Judge H.W. Foote in *Chr. Adv.* (Nashville), Dec. 14, 1893.

5. McTyeire to Garland, Mar. 17, Apr. 7, May 28, 1873; A.L.P. Green to Garland, Apr. 22, 1873, Garland Papers; BOT, May 9, 1873; Garland to McTyeire, July 16, 1874, Garland Letterbooks; *Chr. Adv.* (Nashville), May 10, 1873; Garland to McTyeire, June 16, 1873, McTyeire Corr.; Garland to McTyeire, April 22, 1875, Tigert Coll.

6. BOT, Jan. 14, 16; Apr. 29, 1874; McTyeire to Garland, Jan. 17, 1874, Garland Papers; Garland to McTyeire, Feb. 26, 1874, Tigert Coll.

7. *Reg.*, 1875–76, pp. 9–12, 21–31.

8. Ibid., 11–13; 1876–77, pp. 23–27; Garland to McTyeire, Feb. 16, 1874, Tigert Coll.; McTyeire to Garland, Apr. 15, 1874, Garland Papers.

9. *Reg.*, 1875–76, pp. 13, 21–31; Landon C. Garland's Founders' Day Address in ibid., 1876–77, pp. 62–69; McTyeire to Garland, Apr. 15, 1874; Garland to Rev. William L. Plummer, Nov. 25, 1875, Garland Letterbooks; Garland to McTyeire, Apr. 6, 8, May 15, 1874, Garland Papers; BOT, Apr. 29, 1874; June 19, 1876.

10. BOT, May 9, 1873; Apr. 29, Sept. 30, 1874; May 3, 1875; Garland to Rudolph Koenig,

Paris, July 13, 1874; to Monsieur Salferr [?], Paris, July 14, 1874; to John Browning, London, July 16, 1874, Garland Letterbooks; Garland to McTyeire, June 20, [1874/75], Tigert Coll.; McTyeire to Garland, June 17, 1874, Garland Papers.

11. *Reg.,* 1875–76, p. 9; 1876–77, p. 17; Wilbur Fisk Tillett ff, reminiscences of "Chancellor Garland," Divinity School Archives, box 10, SC.

12. For McTyeire-Garland correspondence, see: McTyeire Corr., Apr. 2, 1873–July 11, 1874; Garland Letterbooks, July 11, 1874–Sept. 11, 1874; Garland Papers, Mar. 17, 1873–Sept. 3, 1874; Tigert Coll., Apr. 2, 1873–Apr. 19, 1874.

13. Charles Harold Poole, "Thomas O. Summers: A Biographical Study" (M.A. thesis, Vanderbilt Univ., 1957), 10–11, 43–44, 60–66, 90–95; Allen Johnson and Dumas Malone, eds., *Dictionary of American Biography,* 21 vols., 4 supp. (New York: Scribner's, 1928–74), 18: 207–8; A.L.P. Green to Garland, Dec. 20, 27, 1873, Garland Papers; BOT, May 27, 1878; June 14, 1886.

14. Johnson, *Dictionary,* 18: 113–14; *Reg.,* 1875–76, pp. 32–34; Garland to McTyeire, Sept. 24, 1873, McTyeire Corr.; Garland to J.C. Granbery, Aug. 30, 1874, Garland Letterbooks; Garland to McTyeire, Apr. 22, 1875, Tigert Coll.; *Chr. Adv.* (Nashville), Sept. 2, 1876; BOT, June 18, 1877.

15. BOT, Jan. 15, Sept. 30, 1874; McTyeire to Garland, Jan. 17, 1874, Garland Papers; Garland to McTyeire, Apr. 22, 1875, Tigert Coll.; Garland to McTyeire, Jan. 21, 1874, McTyeire Corr.

16. BOT, May 4, 1875; June 22, 1876; Johnson, *Dictionary,* 10:290; *Reg.,* 1875–76, pp. 25–26; 1876–77, pp. 31–32.

17. Johnson, *Dictionary,* 16:287.

18. Ibid., 20:373–74; Lawrence N. Powell, *New Masters: Northern Planters During the Civil War and Reconstruction* (New Haven: Yale Univ. Press, 1980), 16, 20–21, 33, 46.

19. Garland to McTyeire, Dec. 23, 1873, McTyeire Corr.; Eugene A. Smith to Garland, Oct. 27, Dec. 9, 1873; N.T. Lupton to McTyeire, Jan. 6, 1874; Smith to McTyeire, Jan. 11, 1874; Jos. A. Taylor to Garland, Mar. 17, 26, 1874, McTyeire Corr., film 792; *The National Cyclopedia of American Biography* (New York: James T. White, 1904), 294–95; BOT, Jan. 16, 1874; McTyeire to Garland, Jan. 17, 1874, Garland Papers.

20. BOT, Sept. 11, 1875; June 22, 1876; Garland to McTyeire, Sept. 2, 1875, Tigert Coll.; *Who Was Who in America,* vol. 1, *1897–1942* (Chicago: A.N. Marquis, 1943), 145.

21. BOT, Oct. 1, 1874; Garland to Milton D. Humphreys, Aug. 1874, Garland Letterbooks; Edwin Mims, *History of Vanderbilt University* (Nashville: Vanderbilt Univ. Press, 1946), 58; Johnson, *Dictionary,* 9:226–27, 377–78.

22. *Reg.,* 1875–76, passim.

23. See McTyeire-Garland Corr.: Garland Letterbooks, July 11, 1874–Sept. 11, 1874; McTyeire Corr., Apr. 2, 1873–July 11, 1874; Garland Papers, Mar. 17, 1873–June 24, 1875.

24. BOT, Jan. 16, Apr. 29, 1874; Timothy C. Jacobson, "Medical Center: A History of Science in Medicine" (unpublished MS in SC, [1982]), 45–52; *Reg.,* 1876–77, pp. 40–45; 1875–76, pp. 40–45; 1876–77, pp. 54–58; *Nashville Journal of Medicine and Surgery* 19 (1877): 100.

25. BOT, Jan. 14, 15, Apr. 29, 1874; May 3, 6, 7, 11, 25, 1875; June 18, 1876; July 7, 1887; J.H. Kirkland, "Twenty-Five Years of University Work," *Vanderbilt University Quarterly* 1 (1901): 88; *Chr. Adv.* (Nashville), July 18, 1874; *Daily American* (Nashville), June 21, 1876; "Records and Facts of Univ. History," McGill Coll., box 6, ff 99–100, SC.

26. "Records and Facts of Univ. History," McGill Coll., box 6, ff 99–100.

27. McGill Coll., box 7, ff 110–11.

28. *Reg.,* 1875–76, pp. 14–16, 18–19; BOT, June 18, 1877; for an example of an early Vanderbilt student's social life see George S. Clifford's Diary, Aug. 31, 1877–Nov. 12, 1877, SC.

29. FM, Sept. 23, 27; Oct. 8, 9; Nov. 23, 1875; Apr. 18, 1876; Oct. 23, 1877; BOT, June 18, 1877.

4. The Reign of King McTyeire

1. BOT, June 16, 1876.

2. BOT, June 20, 1877; May 28, 30, 31, 1878; Edward Joynes to Alexander Winchell, July 16, 1878, Winchell Letters, film 547, Alexander Winchell Papers, HL; Joynes to McTyeire, June 1, 3, 1878; McTyeire to Joynes, June 3, 1878, McTyeire Corr., film 792, HL; *Vanderbilt Austral*, Mar. 1879, pp. 6–7; Apr. 1879, p. 5.

3. BOT, May 29, 30, 1878; Special Staff of Writers, *History of Virginia*, 6 vols. (Chicago: American Historical Society), 4:154–55; *Vanderbilt Austral*, Apr. 1879, p. 5; for origin of Bachelor of Ugliness, see *Observer* 8 (June, 1886).

4. BOT, May 28, 1878; Garland to McTyeire, Apr. 19, 1875, John J. Tigert, IV Coll. SC; McTyeire to Garland, June 16, 1875, McTyeire/Garland Corr. SC; F. Garvin Davenport, "Scientific Interests in Kentucky and Tennessee, 1870–1890," *Journal of Southern History* 14 (Nov., 1948): 515–16.

5. Davenport, "Scientific Interests," 515–16; *Chr. Adv.* (St. Louis), May 22, 1878; *Chr. Adv.* (Nashville), June 1, 1878.

6. BOT, May 28, 1878; Thomas J. Dodd's "Vanderbiltiana," Thomas J. Dodd Papers, box 3, ff 14, SC; *Round Table* (Nashville), Apr. 26, 1890.

7. *Chr. Adv.* (Nashville), June 1, 1878; McTyeire to Alexander Winchell, June 5, 1878; Andrew D. White to Winchell, July 13, 15, 1878, Winchell Letters; Nashville *American*, June 16, July 19, 1878; *Round Table* (Nashville), Apr. 26, 1890; Alexander Winchell Diary, June 7, 28, 1878, film 505, HL; clipping from *Memphis Appeal*, June 23, 1878, in McTyeire Corr., film 792.

8. N.T. Lupton to Alexander Winchell, June 6, 1878, Winchell Letters; BOT, May 28, 1879; *Vanderbilt Austral*, Mar., 1879, p. 3; Apr. 1879, p. 3; May, 1879, pp. 3–4, 6–7.

9. BOT, Apr. 16, May 24, 28, 1879; McTyeire to Olin H. Landreth, May 15, 31, 1879, copies in SC; "Records and Facts of Univ. History," McGill Coll. box 6, ff 99–100, SC.

10. BOT, May 29, 1879; FM, May 21, 1880.

11. FM, May 29, 1879; May 21, 1880.

12. BOT, July 22, 1879; May 24, 26, 27, 1880; Dodd, "Vanderbiltiana."

13. BOT, May 29, 1881; May 31, 1882; McGill Coll., box 11, ff 170, 181; Charles Forster Smith, *Reminiscences and Sketches* (Nashville: Publishing House of the Methodist Episcopal Church, South, 1908), 44–45.

14. Dodd, "Vanderbiltiana"; H.H. White, "Vignettes of Vanderbilt: Sketches of University Personalities and Scenes," *Vanderbilt Alumnus* 29 (June, 1944): 8–9.

15. For strong friendships and correspondence between James H. Kirkland, William M. Baskervill, and Charles Forster Smith, see Charles Forster Smith Letters to James H. Kirkland, Feb. 15, 1880–Mar. 6, 1881, James H. Kirkland Papers, box 7, ff 128, SC; Smith to Kirkland, June 17, 1886; to President Battle, Apr. 19, 1886; Kirkland to his mother, Sept. 9, 1883; letter fragment, Smith to [Kirkland], [1884], Meritt Coll., Edwin Mims, *Chancellor Kirkland of Vanderbilt* (Nashville: Vanderbilt Univ. Press, 1940), 43–68.

16. BOT, May 25, 1881; May 28, 1883; July 14, 1886; *Reg.* 1880–81, p. 77; FM, May 3, 1881; Dodd, "Vanderbiltiana"; McGill Coll., box 11, ff 182.

17. BOT, May 25, 1880; May 29, July 11, 18, Sept. 1, 1882; May 28, 1883; Dodd, "Vanderbiltiana"; FM, May 29, 1883; Holland N. McTyeire will dated Jan. 18, 1887, copy in McTyeire-Baskervill Papers, box 2, ff 7, SC.

18. *Reg.*, 1884–85, p. 19; BOT, May 25, 1885.

19. BOT, May 25, 26, 1885; Mar. 2, June 14, 1886; Dodd, "Vanderbiltiana"; Nashville *American*, June 15, 17, 1885.

20. *Reg.*, 1885–86, pp. 4, 7; O.E. Brown, "Appreciation of Dr. Tillett's Life and Thought," pp.7–8, in Wilbur Fisk Tillett Coll., Divinity Archives, box 10, SC; *Chr. Adv.* (Nashville), May 8, 1886; BOT, June 14, 1886.

21. BOT, May 25, 27, Sept. 4, 1885; J.T. McGill to N.T. Lupton, Mar. 9, 1893, McGill Coll., box 1, ff 1.

22. BOT, Sept. 2, 4, June 18, Oct. 5, 20, 1885; Chas. F. Smith, "Professor Casimir Zdano-wicz," in McGill Coll., box 11, ff 186.

23. Dodd, "Vanderbiltiana"; BOT, June 16, 1886; June 13, 1887; Smith to Kirkland, June 17, 1886, Meritt Coll.

24. *Reg.,* 1881–82, p. 24–27; BOT, May 30, 1882; May 26, 1884; Jan. 16, 1886.

25. Robert A. McGaw, *The Vanderbilt Campus: A Pictorial History* (Nashville: Vanderbilt Univ. Press, 1978), 14; Smith, *Reminiscences,* 27, 33; *Alumnus* 11 (Jan., 1926): 61; *Reg.,* 1878–79, pp. 78–84; for an example of students' comments see *Observer* 3 (May, 1883): 11.

26. *Reg.,* 1880–81, p. 81; BOT, May 28, 1879; May 29, 1882; FM, Jan. 29, 1884.

27. *Reg.,* 1876–77, p. 28; 1877–78, pp. 28–31; FM, Apr. 17, 1877; BOT, May 28, 1883; for student's view of course work see George Clifford's Diary, esp. citations Sept. 13–15, 28, 1877; *Alumnus* 42 (Autumn, 1971): 10–11, 45; *Observer* 8 (Apr., 1886): 1–4.

28. BOT, Aug. 29, 1879; May 26, 1884; Jan. 1, June 14, Aug. 21, 1886; McGill Coll., box 6, ff 99; *Vanderbilt Austral,* Mar., 1879, pp. 3–4; *Observer* 6 (May 28, 1885): 24.

29. BOT, May 28, 1879; Jan. 18, May 28, 1883; *Reg.,* 1875–76, pp. 15–16; McGill Coll., box 6, ff 99; *Vanderbilt Austral,* May, 1879, pp. 3–4; Nashville *Banner,* Oct. 15, 1925.

30. BOT, May 28, 1883; Jan. 18, May 30, Oct. 23, 1883; June 15, 1886; *Observer* 4 (Dec., 1883): 3, 11–12.

31. FM, Sept. 2, Oct. 7, 1879; Oct. 18, 25, 1881; BOT, Aug. 29, Oct. 6, 1879; R.H. Crockett, *Observer* 14 (Apr. 1892): 319–22.

32. *Vanderbilt Austral,* May, 1879, p. 8; June, 1879, p. 9; BOT, June 16, 1886; see McGill Coll. for information on Vanderbilt alumni and the Alumni Association, esp. box 6, ff 110–112, box 7, ff 113–23; *Observer* 9 (June, 1887): 13.

33. *Vanderbilt Austral,* Apr., 1879, pp. 3–4; FM, Oct. 23, 1877; *Hustler,* Sept. 17, 1903; *Observer* 8 (Apr., 1886): 12; *Vanderbilt Comet* 2 (1887–88): BOT, June 15, 1886; *Constitution of the Tennessee Inter-Collegiate Baseball Association* (Nashville: Hasslock & Ambrose, Printers, 1887), 2–6, copy in William L. Dudley Papers, box 4, ff 64, SC.

34. *Vanderbilt Austral,* May, 1879, pp. 4–5; *Reg.,* 1875–76, pp. 14–15; 1879–80, p. 48; BOT, May 24, 1881; Sept. 1, 1882; May 28, 1883; May 26, 1884; *Observer* 7 (May, 1885): 18.

35. *Vanderbilt Austral,* Mar., 1879, pp. 6–7; Apr., 1879, pp. 5–6; *Observer* 6 (Oct., 1884): 17; see issues of *Observer,* 1882–87, for references to young women, especially under the "Locals" heading; *Observer* 3 (Mar., 1883): 28–29.

36. BOT, June 15, Sept. 27, 1881; Aug. 24, 1883; Tigert Coll., ff 3; *Vanderbilt Austral,* Apr., 1879, pp. 6–7.

37. BOT, May 29, 1879; *Vanderbilt Austral,* June, 1879, p. 9; *Reg.,* 1878–79, p. 88; Nashville *Daily American,* May 31, 1879; Kate Lupton, "Co-education at Vanderbilt University," *Observer* 10 (Mar., 1888): 46–49.

38. *Observer* 2 (Sept., 1882): 13; 2 (Jan., 1883): 77; 4 (Sept., 1883): 13; *Reg.,* 1882–83, p. 70; 1885–86, p. 74.

39. *Observer* 4 (May, 1883): 2–3; 4 (Jan. 1884): 9–13.

40. Ibid., 9 (June, 1887): 13–14.

41. Ibid., 3 (Mar., 1883): 23–24; 3 (Apr., 1883): 12; 5 (June, 1888): 9–14; 10 (Dec., 1887): 39.

42. Ibid., 3 (June, 1886): 7–9.

5. A Bid for Greatness

1. BOT, June 13, 15, 1887; N.C. Beasley, Q.M. Smith, and R.H. White, "Entrance and Graduation Requirements in College of Liberal Arts and Entrance Requirements to Professional Schools of Vanderbilt University, 1875–1927," Department of School Administration, George Peabody College for Teachers, Nashville, [1935] (typescript in SC), pp. 19–20, 28, 37.

2. BOT, Oct. 18, 1889; June 16, 1890.

3. BOT, June 15, Nov. 10, 1887; FM, May 31, Oct. 25, Nov. 22, 1887; Jan. 23, 1894.

4. BOT, June 15, 1887; June 18, 1894; FM, May 31, 1887.

5. Garland to McTyeire, July 7, 1887, in CHP.

6. BOT, June 13, 15, 1887; June 18, 1888; May 8, 1889; *Observer* 5 (Oct., 1887): 19–22; 10 (Nov., 1887): 10–16, 47–52; 10 (Dec., 1887): 15–20; 10 (Jan., 1888): 36–41; FM, June 21, 1888.

7. BOT, May 7, 1889; Feb. 15, 16, 1889; *Observer* 11 (Mar., 1889): 16, 43.

8. *Observer* 11 (Mar., 1889): 43–44.

9. BOT, May 7, 1889.

10. For information on Bishop Hargrove see unidentified newspaper clippings, McGill Coll., SC; Hargrove's presidential reports appear in BOT.

11. BOT, June 10, 1891; June 16, 1892.

12. Edwin Mims, *Chancellor Kirkland of Vanderbilt* (Nashville: Vanderbilt Univ. Press, 1940), 94–96; BOT, June 20, 21, 1893.

13. Mims, *Kirkland*, 3–4, 12–17, 21–42.

14. Ibid., 43–60; for information on Kirkland's years abroad see his letters to his mother, Meritt Coll.

15. Mims, *Kirkland*, 60–68; Kirkland to Mother, Nov. 4, 1883; Feb. 3, May 11, 27, June 11, Sept. 22, 1884; Apr. 5, May 24, July 25, Sept. 19, 1885; letter fragments [1885]; Apr. 19, 30, 1886; Kirkland to Wilbur, Apr. 1, 1886; Charles F. Smith to Kirkland, June 17, 1886; Mother to Kirkland, n.d., Meritt Coll.; BOT, June 16, 1886.

16. *Observer* 18, no. 1 [1894]: 1–13; 18 (Oct., 1895): 1–14; Mims, *Kirkland*, 118–19.

17. Mims, *Kirkland*, 74–79; *Observer* 16 (Oct., 1893): 33–34; *Hustler*, Apr. 28, 1898.

18. Kirkland to Mother, Sept. 9, 1885, Meritt Coll.

19. BOT, June 21, 1893; Mims, *Kirkland*, 89–90, 119–26; Kirkland to Mary Henderson, Apr. 1, July 5, Sept. 8, Oct. 8, 1895, Meritt Coll.; *Hustler*, Nov. 21, 1895.

20. See letters Kirkland to Mary Henderson Kirkland in Meritt Coll.; *Hustler*, Nov. 21, 1895.

21. BOT, June 13, 1887; *Reg.*, 1888–89, p. 138; 1889–90, p. 113.

22. BOT, Oct. 18, 1889; June 16, 1891; June 13, 14, 1892; FM, Apr. 9, 1889.

23. BOT, Nov. 10, 1887; FM, Apr. 9, 1889; *Observer* 13 (Jan., 1891): 43; 14 (Nov., 1891): 95–96; 16 (Jan., 1894): 179–83.

24. BOT, June 14, 15, 1892; June 17, 1901; FM, Mar. 7, 1895; *Observer* 14 (Apr., 1892): 303; 18, (Apr. 1896): 285; Richard Hofstadter and Walter P. Metzger, *The Development of Academic Freedom in the United States* (New York: Columbia Univ. Press, 1955), 427–28.

25. BOT, June 10, 12, 1891; Samuel Craig Cowart to Edith Denny White, Apr. 5, 1941, CHP, ff "Fac. Biog. Collins Denny (Vann Material)"; J.T. McGill Coll., box 11, ff 172, SC.

26. Lucius S. Merriam, *Higher Education in Tennessee*, Contributions to American Educational History 16 (Washington, D.C.: Government Printing Office, 1893), 148; BOT, June 14, 1892.

27. *Observer* 18 (Mar., 1896): 232; 18 (Apr., 1896), most of issue devoted to Garland; *Comet*, 1895, pp. 55–64; FM, Feb. 12, 1895.

28. BOT, June 18, 1894; *Hustler*, Apr. 19, 26, 1894; *Observer* 17 (Oct., 1894): 42–43.

29. FM, June 13, 1893; Sept. 7, 1899; BOT, June 19, 1893; *Observer* 23 (Oct., 1900): 37–38; Kirkland to Mary Henderson Kirkland, July 2, 5, Aug. 3, 1901, Meritt Coll.

30. BOT, June 18, 1900.

31. BOT, June 18, 1899; June 19, 1900.

32. FM, May 8, Sept. 18, 25, Oct. 9, 1900; *Comet*, 1900, pp. 31–32.

6. KIRKLAND'S APPRENTICESHIP

1. *Observer* 23 (Nov., 1900): 77–82; *Atlantic* 56 (Dec., 1885): 738–50.

2. *Observer* 10 (Dec., 1887): 50; FM, Mar. 26, Oct. 22, Nov. 12, 1895; Edwin Mims, *Chancellor Kirkland of Vanderbilt* (Nashville: Vanderbilt Univ. Press, 1940), 128–31; Alfred M. Meyer, "A History of the Southern Association of Colleges and Secondary Schools" (Ph.D. diss., George Peabody College of Teachers, 1933).

3. BOT, June 16, 17, 1890; June 10, 1891.

4. BOT, June 19, 1893.

5. BOT, June 10, 1890; June 13, 1898.

6. BOT, June 14, 1892; June 18, 1894.

7. BOT, June 18, 1894; Sept. 24, 1895; June 14, 1897; June 13, 1898; Mims, *Kirkland*, 107–13.

8. BOT, June 15, 1896; June 18, 1900; Mims, *Kirkland*, 113.

9. *Hustler*, Apr. 7, 1899; BOT, June 19, 1899; June 18, 1900.

10. BOT, June 18, 1900; June 19, 1905; June 15, 1908; *Hustler*, Apr., 1900.

11. BOT, June 18, 1899; June 18, 1900.

12. BOT, June 10, 1891; June 18, 1899; FM, May 8, 1900.

13. *Observer* 10 (Jan., 1888): 8–9; 23 (Nov., 1900): 101–102; BOT, June 19, 1893; *Hustler*, Mar. 22, 1894; Kirkland to Mary Henderson Kirkland, Oct. 29, [1901], Meritt Coll.

14. BOT, June 13, 1892; June 19, 1893; June 18, 1899.

15. Dillard Jacobs, *10^2 Years: A Story of the First Century of Vanderbilt University School of Engineering, 1875–1975* (Nashville: Vanderbilt Engineering Alumni Association, 1975), 12, 15–16, 21; BOT, June 19, 1893.

16. *Reg.*, 1894–95, p. 136; 1897–98, p. 140; 1898–99, p. 140; Jacobs, *10^2 Years*, 10, 19, 22, 27.

17. *Quarterly* 5 (Oct., 1905): 248–53; BOT, June 20, 1888; May 8, 1889; June 16, 1890; J.T. McGill Coll., ff 101, SC.

18. BOT, June 16, 1890; June 19, 1899; *Comet*, 1900, p. 22.

19. BOT, June 13, 1892; Observer 15 (Oct., 1892): 50; *Comet*, 1900, p. 21.

20. For enrollments and graduates of the Biblical Department see BOT and *Reg.*; Howard L. Boorman, ed., *Biographical Dictionary of Republican China* 2 (New York: Columbia Univ. Press, 1970): 137–42.

21. BOT, May 8, 1889; June 10, 1891; June 17, 1895; *Observer* 16 (Oct., 1893): 47.

22. BOT, June 17, 1889; June 17, 1890; June 11, 1891; June 14, 1897.

23. BOT, June 15, 16, 1882.

24. BOT, June 18, 19, 1900; *Observer* 23 (Nov., 1900): 64.

25. *Quarterly* 1 (May, 1901): 121–23; 1 (July, 1901): 194; *Observer* 23 (Nov., 1900): 66–67; BOT, Aug. 2, 1889.

26. *Quarterly* 1 (May, 1901): 120–23; BOT, June 15, 1897; June 13, 1898; June 18, 1899; FM, May 9, 1899.

27. Timothy C. Jacobson, "Medical Center: A History of Science in Medicine" (unpublished MS in SC, [1982]), 67, 70–72; BOT, June 18, 1894; June 17, 1895; Mims, *Kirkland*, 105–7; *Observer* 23 (Nov., 1900): 61–62.

28. BOT, June 17, 1895; Mar. 9, 1896; Jacobson, "Medical Center," 69, 72–76; *Observer* 23 (Nov., 1900): 61–62, 111.

29. Kirkland to Daniel Coit Gilman, Jan. 21, 1900, ff "Changing Status—Univ. Ctr.—Peabody Kirkland—Gilman letters 1897–1901," CHP.

30. Ibid.

31. Kirkland to Daniel Coit Gilman, Mar. 1, 1900; Jan. 15, 1901, [Gilman] to [Kirkland], Jan. 17, 1901, in ibid.

7. THE STUDENT PERSPECTIVE

1. *Observer* 15 (May, 1893): 396.

2. BOT, June 17, 1895; June 14, 1897; June 18, 1899.

3. *Observer* 12 (Mar., 1889): 1–2; see also issues of *Comet* in the 1890s for student attitudes.

4. *Hustler*, Sept. 19, 1895; Mar. 1, 1899; BOT, June 16, 1890; *Observer* 10 (June, 1888): 17; *Chr. Adv.* (Nashville), Oct. 22, 1887; FM, Oct. 24, 1893.

5. *Observer* 16 (Oct., 1893): 48–49; 17 (n.d. [1895]): 283; 22 (Nov., 1899): 69; FM, Apr. 24, 1889; Sept. 20, 1898.

6. *Alumnus* 49 (May–June, 1962): 29; *Comet*, 1894, pp. 36, 39.

7. *Reg.*, 1892–93, pp. 20, 106, 112; *Comet*, 1893, p. 42; *Observer* 12 (Jan., 1890): 18–20; 12 (Mar. 1891): 11–14; FM, Apr. 26, June 7, 11, 1892; *Alumnus* 49 (May–June, 1962): 29.

8. *Reg.*, 1894–95, p. 140; 1896–97, p. 138; 1899–1900, pp. 137–38; 1900–1901, p. 160; BOT, June 18, 1894, June 14, 1897; FM, June 16, 1894.

9. W.B. Nance, "Student Life at Vanderbilt," *Southern Magazine* 5 (Feb., 1895): 472, 474; *Observer* 12 (Oct. 1889): 6; 21 (Nov., 1898): 63; issues of *Comet* list the clubs and their members.

10. Nance, "Student Life," 472–73; *Observer* 11 (Oct., 1888): 14–15; FM, Oct. 14, 1890.

11. BOT, June 15, 1886; *Observer* 23 (Nov., 1900): 86–89; Nance, "Student Life," 474.

12. Nance, "Student Life," 474–75; Nashville *Banner*, Nov. 28, 1890; *Observer* 14 (Nov., 1891): 90, 96; 14 (Dec., 1891): 137–39.

13. Nance, "Student Life," 475–76; *Observer* 16 (Dec., 1893): 153–54; *Hustler*, Dec. 14, 1893; Nov. 23, Dec. 7, 16, 1897.

14. *Observer* 12 (Mar., 1889): 35; 16 (Nov., 1893): 88.

15. Ibid., 16 (Dec., 1893): 150; BOT, June 14, 1892; June 19, 1894; June 15, 1896; FM, May 23, 1893; *Commencement Courier*, June 13, 1896.

16. FM, Nov. 14, 16, 21, 25, Dec. 8, 1896; Nashville *American*, Nov. 15, 16, 18, 25, 26, 28, 1896; *Observer* (Nov., 1896): 81, 84–85.

17. BOT, June 14, 16, 1897; June 14, 1898.

18. *Comet*, 1887.

19. *Hustler*, Apr. 18, 1901.

20. *Observer* 22 (Mar., 1900): 215–16; *Hustler*, Mar. 23, 1900; May 18, 1900.

21. *Hustler*, Oct. 13, 1896; Apr. 22, Oct. 14, 1897; *Observer* 20 (Nov., 1896): 94–95; Robert A. McGaw, *The Vanderbilt Campus: A Pictorial History* (Nashville: Vanderbilt Univ. Press, 1978), 34–35.

22. Kirkland to Daniel Coit Gilman, Mar. 1, 1900, ff "Changing Status—Univ. Ctr.—Peabody Kirkland—Gilman letters 1897–1901," CHP, Frederick W. Moore, "The Twenty-Fifth Anniversary of the Opening of Vanderbilt University and the Presentation of Kissam Hall," *Quarterly* 1 (Mar., 1901): 6–16.

23. Moore, "Twenty-Fifth Anniversary," 11–36; Bishop R.K. Hargrove, "The Founders and Organizers of Vanderbilt University," *Quarterly* 1 (Mar., 1901): 99–115; *Hustler*, Oct. 18, 25, 1900.

24. *Hustler*, Oct. 25, 1900; J.H. Kirkland, "Twenty-Five Years of Vanderbilt University," *Quarterly* 1 (May, 1901): 86–98.

8. The Bishop's War

1. Nashville *Chr. Adv.*, Sept. 19, 1895; BOT, Sept. 24, 1895.

2. Kirkland to D.C. Gilman, Oct. 31, 1904, James H. Kirkland Papers, box 24, ff 2, SC.

3. BOT, June 13, 14, 23, 1904; Memorandum regarding the election of Dr. F.W. Moore as Dean of the Academic Department of Vanderbilt University in 1904, typed, copy in CHP, ff "Changing Status—M.E. Church, 1895–1904."

4. BOT, June 13, 14, 23, 1904.

5. BOT, June 23, 1904; *Quarterly* 4 (July, 1904): 213–14; newsclippings, n.d., Kirkland Papers, box "Newsclippings, I, 1887–1915," ff 5.

6. BOT, June 23, 1904.

7. Kirkland to D.C. Gilman, Oct. 31, 1904, Kirkland Papers, box 24, ff 2; J.H. Kirkland, "Recent History of Vanderbilt University," *Methodist Quarterly* 59 (Apr., 1910): 344–46, copy in Kirkland Papers, box 15, ff 14; newsclipping, n.d., in ibid., box "Newsclippings, I, 1886–1915," ff 6; *Quarterly* 5 (Oct., 1905): 262–65.

6. BOT, June 19, 20, 1905; Kirkland, "Recent History," 247–49; "Application for Amendment of Charter of Vanderbilt," June 14, 1892," copy in Chanc. Off. R.G. 3, box 13, ff "Vanderbilt Case"; Nashville *Banner*, Oct. 26, 1905; clippings from the Nashville *Banner*, Nashville *Tennessean and American*, Nashville *Chr. Adv.*, *Hustler*, and other newspapers and

church publications may be found in Kirkland Papers, box "Newsclippings, I, 1886–1915," and in Stella Vaughn Scrapbooks, SC.

9. E.E. Hoss to Kirkland, Sept. 13, 28, 1905, Kirkland Papers, box 26, ff 28; Kirkland to Hoss, Sept. 14, 29, 1905, in ibid., box 24, ff 3; Hoss to Charles B. Galloway, Sept. 19, 1905; Galloway to Hoss, Sept. 21, 1905, both quoted in "Deposition of E.R. Hendrix," *State, ex rel., A.W. Wilson et al. vs. Board of Trust of Vanderbilt University,* 3:575–77, SC; "Extract from Proceedings before the Vanderbilt University—College of Bishops Commission," Oct. 24–26, 1906, copy in CHP, ff "Changing Status—M.E. Church, 1905–1909."

10. *The Bristol Herald Courier,* n.d., and Collins Denny, "Board of Church Extension Report of the Committee on Memoirs. Bishop Elijah Embree Hoss," copies in CHP, ff "Admin.—Board of Trust—Trustee Hoss, E.E."; see also Hoss letters to Denny in Elizabeth Vann Papers, box 45, SC, for insights into Hoss's character.

11. E.E. Hoss to Charles B. Galloway, Jan. 18, 1905, cited in Ivan Lee Holt, *Eugene Russell Hendrix, Servant of the Kingdom* (Nashville: Parthenon Press, [1905]), 108.

12. *Quarterly* 5 (Oct., 1905): 262–66; "Assignment of Errors and Briefs on Behalf of Vanderbilt University and the Board of Trust," *State, ex rel., A.W. Wilson et al. vs. Board of Trust of Vanderbilt University,* 3:374–81; Nashville *American,* Dec. 3, 1909.

13. Nashville *Banner,* Oct. 26, 1905; "Assignment of Errors and Briefs", 385–89; Kirkland to Mary Kirkland, May 8, 12, 15, 1906, Meritt Coll.

14. Kirkland to Mary Kirkland, May 5, 8, 9, 11, 12, 15, 1906, Meritt Coll.; J.H. Kirkland (prepared by), "Statement for the Commission Appointed to Investigate Certain Questions Relating to the Charter and Status of Vanderbilt University," Aug. 15, 1906, *Argument before Vanderbilt Commission,* SC; Nashville *Tennessean,* May 28, 1906; Nashville *Banner,* May 12, 1906; BOT, June 18, 1906.

15. *Quarterly* 6 (July, 1906): 214–15; Nashville *Banner,* May 12, October 25, 1906; BOT, June 18, 29, 1906; June 17, 1907; Kirkland, "Statement for the Commission," and "Report of the Vanderbilt Commission" in *Argument before Vanderbilt Commission.*

16. "Report of the Vanderbilt Commission."

17. BOT, June 17, 18, 1907.

18. Newsclippings, n.d., Stella Vaughn Scrapbooks, ff 10; BOT, June 15, 1908.

19. *Peabody Fund Trustees, Proceedings,* 6 vols. (Cambridge [Mass.]: John Wilson and Son, 1916), 6: 93, 117, 134–37, 160, 213, 219–20, 300–303, 322–24; Charles E. Little, *George Peabody College for Teachers: Its Evolution and Present Status* (Nashville: George Peabody College for Teachers, 1912), 30–31.

20. Nashville *American,* Nov. 14, 1909.

21. William Lawrence, *Memoirs of a Happy Life* (Boston and New York: Houghton Mifflin, 1926), 267–76; Nashville *American,* Nov. 14, 1909; *Peabody Fund Trustees, Proceedings* 6 (Jan. 24, 1905), 259–60; Kirkland to D.C. Gilman, May 11, 22, Sept. 14, 1904, Kirkland Papers, box 24, ff 2; Gilman to Kirkland, Feb. 21, 1903, Dec. 17, 1904, ibid., box 26, ff 27; Kirkland to Mary Kirkland, Oct. 14, 26, 1904, Meritt Coll.

22. D.C. Gilman to Kirkland, Apr. 8, May 13, 1905, Kirkland Papers, box 26, ff 27; Kirkland to Gilman, May 16, 1905, ibid., box 24, ff 3; Kirkland to Mary Kirkland, Sept. 16, 1905, Oct. 1, 1906, Meritt Coll.

23. *Peabody Fund Trustees, Proceedings* 6 (Oct. 4, 1905), 285, 308; 6 (Jan. 31, 1910): 459; Nashville *American,* Nov. 14, 1909; Kirkland to Wallace Buttrick, Nov. 16, 1905, copy in CHP, ff "Changing Status—Univ. Ctr.—Peabody, 1904–1915."

24. *Peabody Fund Trustees, Proceedings,* 6 (Oct. 4, 1906): 308; 6 (Nov. 2, 1911): 528–41; Nashville *American,* Nov. 14, 1909.

25. Nashville *Banner,* Dec. 14, 1907, Dec. 28, 1909; Nashville *American,* Dec. 13, 1907; newsclippings, 1909, in Kirkland Papers, box "Newsclippings, I, 1886–1915," ff 17.

26. Nashville *Banner,* Aug. 9, Nov. 22, Dec. 28, 1909; Nashville *American,* Aug. 4, 8, 1909; newsclippings [1909], in Stella Vaughn Scrapbooks, ff 10, 11; newsclippings, n.d., Kirkland Papers, box "Newsclippings, I, 1886–1915," ff 13.

27. Newsclippings, [1909], Stella Vaughn Scrapbooks, ff 10; newsclippings [1909], Kirkland Papers, box "Newsclippings, I, 1886–1915," ff 14.

28. Nashville *American,* Sept. 12, 18, 20, 1909; House Bill No. 679, Senate Bill No. 512, *Senate Journal of the Fifty-Sixth General Assembly of the State of Tennessee.* . . , Jan. 4, 1909 (Nashville: McQuiddy Printing, 1909), 553, 795; copy of minutes of Jan. 1909 meeting of Biblical Department in St. Louis in CHP, ff "Changing Status, M.E. Church, 1905–1909"; Kirkland to W.K. Vanderbilt, Jan. 13, 1909; Vanderbilt to Kirkland, Jan. 13, 1909, copies in CHP, ff "Changing Status—M.E. Church, 1905–1909;" BOT, Oct. 25, 1910.

29. *Epworth Era,* Dec. 2, 16, 1909; Nashville *American,* Dec. 15, 16, 1909; Nashville *Banner,* Apr. 22, 1909; Nashville *Tennessean,* Apr. 23, 28, 1909; Kirkland to J.W. Moore, Dec. 16, 1909, Kirkland Papers, box 1, ff 73; *Wesleyan Chr. Adv.,* Dec. 10, 1909.

30. Kirkland to J.C. Bradford, Jan. 20, 1910, copy in CHP, ff "Changing Status—Univ. Ctr.—Peabody, 1904–1915"; BOT, July 8, 13, 1909; Feb. 28, Mar. 2, June 13, 1910; July 19, 1911; *Hustler,* Oct. 29, 1910.

31. Kirkland to Mary Kirkland, May 5, 6, 7, 9, 1910, Merritt Coll.; Nashville *American,* Nov. 16, 1909; *Nashville Chr. Adv.,* May 18, 1910; *Quarterly* 10 (Apr.–June, 1910), 64–65; newsclipping [1909], in Stella Vaughn Scrapbooks, ff 11; "A Memorial Concerning Vanderbilt University from the Alumni to the General Conference of the Methodist Episcopal Church, South, May 1910," in *Argument before Vanderbilt Commission.*

32. BOT, June 13, 14, 1911; Kirkland to J.W. Moore, Dec. 16, 1909, Kirkland Papers, box 1, ff 73; *Quarterly* 10 (Apr.–June, 1910): 64–65; *Hustler,* Oct. 29, 1910.

33. Kirkland to Mary Kirkland, May 13, 1910; Mary Kirkland to Kirkland, May 14, 1910, Meritt Coll.; *Nashville Chr. Adv.,* May 16, 1910.

34. BOT, June 13, 14, 1910; Nashville *Banner,* June 15, 1910; Nashville *American,* June 12, 15, 1910; newspaper clippings, 1910, in Stella Vaughn Scrapbooks, ff 13; *Nashville Chr. Adv.,* June 24, 1910.

35. Nashville *Tennessean,* June 23, 1910; clippings, 1910, Kirkland Papers, box "Newsclippings, I, 1886–1915," ff 21; BOT May 25, June 14, 1910.

36. BOT, June 14, Oct. 25, 1910; Nashville *American,* June 16, 1910; *Nashville Chr. Adv.,* July 15, 1910; *Hustler,* Oct. 29, 1910; see newsclippings in Kirkland Papers, box "Newsclippings, I, 1886–1915," ff 21; "Assignment of Errors and Brief on Behalf of Vanderbilt University and the Board of Trust," 344–46 in *Vanderbilt Law Suit, Supreme Court,* SC.

37. BOT, Oct. 25, 1910; Jan. 3, 1911; Nashville *Tennessean,* Dec. 23, 1910; Nashville *Banner,* Oct. 25, 26, 1910; newsclippings, n.d., Stella Vaughn Scrapbooks, ff 13, 14.

38. *Quarterly* 11 (Jan.–Mar. 1911): 22; 11 (Oct.–Dec. 1911): 254; 12 (Apr.–June, 1912): 86–88.

39. BOT, June 29, 1910; Bruce R. Payne to Edwin Mims, Dec. 31, 1910; Jan. 23, 1911; Feb. 24, 1912, Mims Corr., box 2, ff "Payne, Bruce R." nos. 1 and 2, SC; Kirkland to Mims, Jan. 22, 26, Apr. 10, 1911, Mims Corr., box 2, ff "Kirkland, J.H.," No. 1; newsclippings, n.d., Stella Vaughn Scrapbooks, ff 14.

40. BOT, Feb. 24, 1912; Kirkland to Edwin Mims, Jan. 7, 1911, Mims Corr., box 2, ff "Kirkland, J.H.," no. 1; Edward Neely Cullum, "George Peabody College for Teachers, 1914–1937" (Ph.D. diss., George Peabody College for Teachers, 1963), 185–89.

41. BOT, Apr. 6, Oct. 24, 1912; Wilbur F. Tillett, "Two Things I Did," undated memorandum, c. 1925, pp. 23–24, Divinity School Archives, RG 73, SC.

42. BOT, Feb. 24, Mar. 16, Apr. 13, June 15, 1914; June 9, 1915.

43. BOT, Feb. 22, 1913; Opinion of Chancellor John Allison in *Wilson vs. Board* in Appendix to Brief of Complaints in *Vanderbilt Law Suit, Supreme Court;* Nashville *Banner,* Mar. 21, 1914; *Hustler,* Feb. 21, 26, 1913; newsclippings, 1913, Stella Vaughn Scrapbooks, ff 20.

44. Nashville *Banner,* Mar. 21, 1914.

45. "Assignment of Errors and Brief on Behalf of Vanderbilt University and the Board of Trust" and "Statement of the Case, Brief and Argument on Behalf of the Realtors, College of Bishops of the Methodist Episcopal Church, South, et al.," both in *Vanderbilt Law Suit, Supreme Court.*

46. "Opinion of the Supreme Court of Tennessee in the Vanderbilt University Case," *Vanderbilt Law Suit, Supreme Court.*

47. Nashville *Banner,* Mar. 21, 1914; BOT, June 14, 1914.

48. BOT, June 14, 1914; *Quarterly* 14 (Jan.–Mar. 1914): 15–18; Nashville *Banner,* Mar. 23, 1914; Nashville *Tennessean,* Mar. 22, 1914; *Hustler,* Mar. 21, Apr. 11, 1914; E.E. Hoss to Collins Denny, Dec. 25, 1913, Elizabeth Vann Papers, box 45, ff 4; *Hustler* newsclippings, n.d., Stella Vaughn Scrapbooks, ff 14.

49. "The General Conference and the Vanderbilt Decision," Chanc. Off., RG 3, box 13, ff "Vanderbilt Case"; *Quarterly* 14 (Apr.–June, 1914): 83–89; 14 (July–Sept., 1914): 163–67; BOT, June 14, 1914.

50. BOT, June 14, 1914; newsclippings [1914], Stella Vaughn Scrapbooks, ff. 21.

9. THE HOME FRONT

1. Nashville *American,* Aug. 2, 1911; undated newsclippings and a letter from the committee of the Nashville Branch of the Alumni Association, Aug. 15, 1911, in Stella Vaughn Scrapbooks, ff 14, SC; newsclipping from the *Arkansas Democrat,* n.d., in James H. Kirkland Papers, box "Newsclippings, I, 1886–1915," ff 25, SC; *Hustler,* Apr. 30, May 17, 1913.

2. BOT, June 15, 1914.

3. *Hustler,* Feb. 19, 1913; *Reg.,* 1909–1910, pp. 9–10.

4. *Quarterly* 13 (Jan.–Mar., 1913): 34–38; 14 (Oct.–Dec., 1914): 259–89; BOT, June 14, 1915.

5. BOT, June 19, 1905.

6. *Quarterly* 1 (Oct., 1901): 296–97; 2 (July, 1902): 224; BOT, Feb. 20, 1903; June 15, 1908; June 14, 29, 1910; June 19, 1911; June 16, 1913; newsclippings, n.d., Stella Vaughn Scrapbooks, ff 15.

7. BOT, May 9, 1911; June 16, 1913; Apr. 12, June 14, 1915.

8. Newsclippings, n.d., Stella Vaughn Scrapbooks, ff 17; BOT, June 17, 1912.

9. Kirkland to Edwin Mims, May 12, [1906]; Dec. 31, 1910; Jan. 7, 1911, all in Mims Corr., box 2, ff "Kirkland, J.H.," SC; *Hustler,* Feb. 19, 1913; BOT, June 13, 1910, June 16, 1913; June 15–16, 1914.

10. *Reg.,* 1901–1902, pp. 142–45; 1914–1915, pp. 179–85; BOT, June 15, 1908; June 17, 1912.

11. FM, Sept. 18, 1906; Mar. 12, 1907; Dec. 10, 1912; Mar. 16, 1915; *Reg.,* 1914–1915, p. 56; *Quarterly* 10 (July–Sept. 1910): 172–73; *Observer* 29 (Mar., 1907): 337–42; 31 (Jan., 1909): 180–85.

12. FM, May 14, Sept. 17, 1907; *Quarterly* 7 (July, 1907): 177–79; 7 (Oct., 1907): 260–72; 7 (July, 1908): 202–204.

13. *Hustler,* Apr. 20, 1905; Elizabeth Denny Vann, "The Fire," typescript, CHP, ff "Vann Correspondence"; Nashville *American,* Apr. 21, 1905; Nashville *Banner,* Apr. 20, 1905; *Quarterly,* (Apr., 1905): 116–17; 6 (July, 1906): 189–90.

14. Vann, "The Fire"; *Quarterly* 5 (Apr., 1905): 116–17; 6 (July, 1906): 176–77; *Hustler,* Apr. 27, 1905; Nashville *Banner,* Apr. 25, 1905; BOT, June 7, 1907.

15. BOT, June 15, 1903; June 19, 1905; June 18, 1906; June 17, 1907; June 15, 1908; *Hustler,* May 4, 1905; Mar. 14, 1907; *Commencement Courier,* June 20, 1905.

16. *Hustler,* Sept. 28, 1905; Mar. 7, 1910; BOT, June 20, 1905; Nov. 14, 1907; June 15, 1908; June 14, 1909; *Quarterly* 5 (Oct., 1905): 272–80; Robert A. McGaw, *The Vanderbilt Campus: A Pictorial History* (Nashville: Vanderbilt Univ. Press, 1978), 54–61.

17. BOT, June 17, 1907; June 15, 1908; *Quarterly* 7 (July, 1907): 152, 160; McGaw, *Vanderbilt Campus,* 28–37.

18. *Quarterly* 6 (July, 1906): 189–91; 7 (July, 1907): 164–68; 8 (July, 1980): 183–85; 12 (July–Sept., 1912): 166–70; 13 (July–Sept., 1913): 200–201; BOT, June 17, 1912.

19. BOT, June 15, 1908; *Quarterly* 8 (July, 1908): 189–95; 9 (Jan., 1909): 3–9; McGaw, *Vanderbilt Campus,* 60–62.

20. BOT, June 19, 20, 1911; Apr. 6, June 20, 1912; June 15, 1914; June 14, 1915.

21. *Quarterly* 6 (July, 1906): 195–96; BOT, June 17, 1907; June 15, 1908; June 13, 1910; June 19, 1911; June 14, 1915.

22. Newsclippings, n.d., Stella Vaughn Scrapbooks, ff 9; *Quarterly* 12 (Apr.–June, 1912): 114–18; BOT, June 15–16, 1914; June 14, 1915.

23. *Quarterly* 8 (Jan., 1908): 34–38; 7 (July–Sept., 1912): 149–57; FM, Mar. 10, 1908.

24. *Alumnus* 5 (Feb., 1920): 115–18; BOT, June 14, 1915.

25. BOT, June 14, 1915; *Quarterly* 2 (Oct., 1902): 275; 3 (July, 1903): 184–87; 4 (July, 1904): 194–95; Nashville *Banner*, Oct. 4, 1902; *Reg.*, 1903–1904, p. 155; 1909–1910, p. 210; 1911–1912, p. 202; *Hustler*, Sept. 21, 1907.

26. BOT, June 15, 1908; June 13, 1910; June 15, 1915; *Quarterly* 15 (Oct.–Dec., 1915): 147–54.

27. *Quarterly* 7 (July, 1907): 153; 15 (Oct.–Dec., 1915): 255–58; BOT, June 15, 1903; June 13, 1904; June 14, 1909; June 15, 1914; *Hustler*, Oct. 11, 1906.

28. *Quarterly* 6 (July, 1906): 186; 13 (Apr., 1913): 124; BOT, June 17, 1907; June 19, 1911; McGaw, *Vanderbilt Campus*, 64.

29. Timothy C. Jacobson, "Medical Center: A History of Science in Medicine" (unpublished MS in SC [1982]), 1982), 73–79, 123–24; Nashville *American*, Aug. 5, 1909.

30. Jacobson, "Medical Center," 93–111, 117–20, 124–30, 132–34, 141–44; Abraham Flexner, *Medical Education in the United States and Canada: A Report to the Carnegie Foundation for the Advancement of Teaching*, Bulletin No. 4 (New York: [Carnegie Foundation for the Advancement of Teaching], c. 1910), 308; BOT, May 1, 30, June 16, 17, 1913.

31. Jacobson, "Medical Center," 144–48, 150–54; newsclippings, Stella Vaughn Scrapbooks, ff 14; BOT, May 1, 30, June 16, 17, 1913; Nashville *Banner*, May 31, 1913; McGaw, *Vanderbilt Campus*, 64–67.

32. Nashville *Banner*, May 31, June 19, July 15, 1913; newsclippings, Stella Vaughn Scrapbooks, ff 20, 26; Jacobson, "Medical Center," 154–60; Nashville *Tennessean and American*, June 19, 1913; *Quarterly* 13 (July–Sept., 1913): 209.

33. BOT, June 16, 1913; June 14, 1915.

34. BOT, June 20, 28, 1905; June 16, 1913; Elizabeth Vann, "Reminiscences," CHP, ff "Vann, Elizabeth."

35. *Hustler*, Dec. 8, 1904; Mar. 24, Dec. 17, 1910; Dec. 14, 1912; Feb. 19, 1913.

36. *Quarterly* 6 (Oct., 1906): 260; 9 (July, 1909): 148.

37. Ibid. 9 (July, 1909): 185; *Hustler*, May 21, 1908.

38. *Hustler*, Oct. 29, Nov. 19, 1908; Apr. 15, 1909; Apr. 1, 11, 1914.

39. *Reg.* 1911–12, p. 207; *Hustler*, Dec. 3, 1903; Sept. 22, 1904; Oct. 8, 1908; June 3, 1909; Dec. 3, 1910.

40. *Observer* 38 (Apr., 1915); *Hustler*, Mar. 17, Apr. 17, 1915; FM, May 11, 1915.

41. *Hustler*, Apr. 22, 1909; Feb. 27, 1913; Nov. 14, 1914; BOT, June 16, 1913; *Quarterly* 4 (Jan., 1904): 72; 11 (Oct.–Dec., 1911): 253.

42. Kirkland to Mary Kirkland, Sept. 18, 1902, Meritt Coll.; BOT, June 14, 1915; FM, Mar. 16, May 11, 1915.

43. BOT, June 13, 14, 1904; *Hustler*, Dec. 5, 1901; Dec. 11, 1902; Dec. 10, 1903.

44. *McGugin*, Alumni and Development Office Flyer, n.d.; *Hustler*, Oct. 6, Dec. 1, 1904; Sept. 28, Oct. 14, Dec. 7, 1905; Mar. 15, Nov. 8, 29, 1906; Dec. 19, 1907; Nashville *American*, Nov. 23, 1906; Nashville *Banner*, Nov. 23, 1906.

45. *McGugin*; *Hustler*, Apr. 25, Oct. 17, 24, Nov. 7, 1907; Oct. 1, Dec. 10, 1908; Stella Vaughn Scrapbooks, ff 9.

46. *Hustler*, Dec. 9, 1909; Oct. 19, 20, 26, Nov. 12, 30, 1910; Oct. 28, 1911; Dec. 11, 1912; *Commodore*, 1915, pp. 341–45.

47. Newsclippings, n.d., Stella Vaughn Scrapbooks, ff 14; *Hustler*, Oct. 5, 1905; Oct. 4, 11, 1906; Nov. 21, 28, Dec. 5, 1907; *Observer* 30 (Dec., 1907): 197–99.

48. *Hustler*, Sept. 17, 1902; Nov. 23, 1905; Nov. 8, 1908; Apr. 23, May 14, Oct. 15, 1908; Mar. 18, Sept. 30, 1909; Nov. 11, 1911; *Quarterly* 5 (July, 1905): 173; 6 (Oct., 1906): 314.

49. FM, Sept. 15, 1908; Oct. 3, 1910; Feb. 9, 16, 1915; *Hustler*, May 7, Oct. 15, 1908; Oct. 15, 1910.

50. *Hustler*, Nov. 9, 1910; Feb. 15, 25, Mar. 1, 1911; FM, Feb. 16, 1911.

51. *Observer* 34 (Dec., 1911): 82–85, 90–91; *Hustler*, May 6, 13, 1911; Oct. 16, 1912; Mar. 5, 1913; FM, Dec. 12, 1911.

52. FM, Dec. 12, 1911; Jan. 19, 1912; *Hustler*, Feb. 7, 1912.

53. *Hustler*, May 4, 1912; Feb. 15, 1913.

54. Ibid., Apr. 19, 23, 1913.

55. Ibid., Feb. 3, 6, 13, 17, 20, 1915.

10. NUTS AND BOLTS

1. BOT, Mar. 14, 1914; June 14, 1915; FM, Feb. 16, Mar. 16, Apr. 13, Sept. 27, 1915; "Suggestions Concerning Affiliation with George Peabody College" [May, 1914] (memorandum), History Department Archives, RG 62, box 1, ff 3, SC.

2. BOT, June 15, 1915; June 12, 1916; *Alumnus* 1 (Oct., 1915): 4; 2 (Jan., 1917): 67; 7 (Apr., 1922): 131.

3. BOT, June 14, 1915.

4. BOT, June 14, 1915; Feb. 3, Apr. 25, 1916; *Alumnus* 1 (Feb., 1916): 1, 3–7.

5. BOT, June 12, 1916; June 11, 1917; Jan. 9, 1918; *Alumnus* 1 (Mar., 1916): 5–6; 1 (May, 1916): 3–8; 2 (Oct., 1916): 8; 2 (Nov., 1916): 34; 2 (Jan., 1917): 61; 3 (Jan., 1918): 69–70; *Hustler*, Oct. 11, 14, 18, 21, 25, 28, Nov. 1, 1916.

6. *Alumnus* 2 (Mar., 1917): 115–18; 3 (Oct., 1917): 4; *Hustler* Jan. 13, 1917.

7. *Hustler*, Feb. 10, 28, Mar. 12, 1917; BOT, Apr. 19, 1917; FM, Apr. 10, 30, 1917; *Alumnus* 2 (Apr., 1917): 142–48.

8. *Hustler*, Feb. 14, 24, 28, Mar. 31, Apr. 18, 21, 25, 28, May 2, 5, 9, 1917; *Alumnus* 2 (Apr., 1917): 141; BOT, June 11, 1917.

9. *Alumnus* 3 (Oct., 1917); 3 (Nov., 1917): 37–38; 3 (Jan., 1918): 68; 3 (Mar., 1918): 136; *Hustler*, Apr. 4, May 12, 16, 1917; Mar. 9, Apr. 11, 1918; FM, June 9, 1917; BOT, June 10, 1918.

10. *Alumnus* 3 (Feb., 1918): 102–104; 3 (Mar., 1918): 140; 3 (Apr., 1918): 165–68; 4 (Feb., 1919): 76–77.

11. BOT, Sept. 25, Dec. 27, 1918; June 9, 1919; *Alumnus* 4 (Nov., 1918): 5–8, 27; FM, Sept. 28, 1918; *Hustler*, Nov. 11, 25, 1918.

12. *Hustler*, Jan. 6, 11, 25, 1919; *Commodore*, 1919; *Alumnus* 4 (Jan., 1919): 48; BOT, June 9, 1919; June 7, 1920.

13. BOT, Dec. 27, 1918; June 17, 1920; FM, Dec. 17, 1918; Mar. 11, 1919; *Hustler*, Feb. 8, Mar. 1, 29, 1919; Feb. 4, 1920; *Alumnus* 4 (Mar., 1919): 99–100; Nashville *Tennessean*, Mar. 4, 7, 1919; Committee Representing Student Body to Kirkland, n.d., Chanc. Off., RG 3, box 12, ff 7.

14. *Commodore*, 1920; BOT, June 7, 1920.

15. Nashville *Tennessean*, May 3, 4, 1919; Transcript of the Proceedings, Meeting Executive Committee of Board of Trust of Vanderbilt University, May 4, 1919, Minutes of Board of Trust Meetings, 1909–1920, RG 2, box 1, ff "Minutes 1919," SC (hereinafter cited as "Proceedings, May 4, 1919").

16. Nashville *Banner*, May 2, 3, 1919; Nashville *Tennessean*, May 2, 4, 21, 1919; *Hustler*, May 3, 1919; "Proceedings, May 4, 1919."

17. "Proceedings, May 4, 1919"; Nashville *Tennessean*, May 2, 1919; Nashville *Banner*, May 2, 1919.

18. "Proceedings, May 4, 1919"; BOT, May 4, 1919; Nashville *Tennessean*, May 2, 3, 4, 1919; Nashville *Banner*, May 2, 7, 10, 1919.

19. "Proceedings, May 4, 1919."

20. BOT, May 12, 21, 1919; FM, May 20, 21, 1919; Nashville *Tennessean*, May 21, 22, 1919; copy of report of Faculty Committee Investigating the Russell Scott Case, n.d., CHP, ff "Aca. Free.—Scott, Russell—1919."

21. *Alumnus* 4 (Feb., 1919): 69–71; 4 (Mar., 1919): 101; 4 (Apr., 1919): 133–35; 6 (Dec., 1920): 71–72; BOT, June 7, 1920.

22. *Bull.*, Feb., 1917, pp. 194–202, 214–15; Mar., 1920, p. 222; Feb., 1922, p. 224; Feb., 1924, pp. 228, 230–32; Feb., 1926, pp. 222–23; Feb., 1929, pp. 249–52; BOT, Sept. 27, Nov. 25, 1919; June 7, 1920.

23. *Alumnus* 5 (Jan., 1920): 68, 74–76; 9 (Nov., 1923): 39–40.

24. *Hustler*, Apr. 11, 1917; *Alumnus* 8 (Oct., 1922): 8; William C. Binkley, "The Contribution of Walter Lynwood Fleming to Southern Scholarship," *Journal of Southern History* 5 (1939): 143–54; undated newsclippings, Stella Vaughn Scrapbooks, ff 22, SC; BOT, June 6, 1926.

25. *Alumnus* 8 (Mar., 1923): 36.

26. BOT, June 11, 1928; *Bull.*, Feb., 1926, p. 13; *Hustler*, Jan. 12, 1922; Nov. 1, 1923; May 15, 1924; newsclippings [Aug., 1924], Stella Vaughn Scrapbooks, ff 17; Kirkland to Walter L. Randolph, Dec. 28, 1935; Guy L. Moser to Kirkland, Mar. 13, 1937; Kirkland to Gus Dyer, Mar. 16, 1937; Dyer to Kirkland, Mar. 17, 1937, all in Chanc. Off., RG 3, box 1, ff 54.

27. BOT, Oct. 5, 1928.

28. BOT, June 14, 1915; June 8, 1925.

29. BOT, June 12, 1916; June 9, 1919; June 12, 1922; *Bull.*, Feb., 1926, p. 12.

30. Kirkland to C.M. Sarratt, May 8, 1929, History Department Archives, RG 62, box 1, ff 6; Walter L. Fleming to Kirkland, May 22, 1928, ibid., ff 43; *Bull.*, Feb., 1930, pp. 13–17; BOT, Nov. 7, 1918.

31. Kirkland to Walter L. Fleming, Oct. 9, 1928, History Department Archives, RG 62, box 1, ff 16; Fleming to Kirkland, May 22, 1928, ibid., ff 43; circular sent to professors, Sept. 21, 1927, and Kirkland to Fleming, Apr. 1, 1927, ibid., box 2, ff 117; newsclipping [Mar. 21, 1927], Stella Vaughn Scrapbooks, ff 15.

32. Walter L. Fleming to Kirkland, May 22, 1928, History Department Archives, RG 62, box 1, ff 43.

33. BOT, June 10, 1918; Feb. 18, June 9, 1919; Walter L. Fleming to Kirkland, June 8, 1926, History Department Archives, RG 62, box 1, ff 16; *Alumnus* 3 (Jan., 1918): 71.

34. BOT, June 10, 1918; June 9, Sept. 27, 1919; June 7, 1920; June 11, 1923; June 7, 1926; Mar. 9, June 6, 1927; June 9, 1930; June 8, 1931; FM, June 11, 1924; Edwin Mims to Kirkland, Apr. 10, 1925, Chanc. Off., RG 3, box 2, ff "Edwin Mims."

35. BOT, June 13, 1922; June 7, 1926; June 11, 1928.

36. BOT, June 9, 1919; June 7, 1920; June 6, 1921.

37. *Alumnus* 3 (Mar., 1918): 131, 133–34; 8 (Oct., 1922): 8; 13 (Jan.–Feb., 1928): 93–94, 99, 104–105; BOT, June 9, 1924, June 8, 1925; Robert A. McGaw, *The Vanderbilt Campus: A Pictorial History* (Nashville: Vanderbilt Univ. Press, 1978), 70–75.

38. *Alumnus* 11 (Oct., 1925), entire issue devoted to the semicentennial.

39. Ibid., 11–19.

40. Ibid.

41. BOT, June 8, Oct. 26, 1925; *Alumnus* 11 (Oct., 1925): 5; 11 (Jan., 1926): 53; 11 (Feb., 1926): 87–94.

42. *Alumnus* 12 (Nov., 1926): 43, 45; 12 (Mar., 1927): 149; 14 (Nov.–Dec., 1928): 51; BOT, June 6, 1927; Nov. 27, 1928.

43. BOT, Feb. 2, June 8, 1931.

44. BOT, June 6, 1927; June 11, 1928; June 10, 1929; June 9, 1930; *Alumnus* 13 (Jan.–Feb., 1928): 93–94, 99.

45. BOT, June 11, 1923; June 9, 1924; June 6, 1927; June 11, 1928; June 10, 1929; June 6, 1930.

11. SCHOOLS LARGE AND SMALL

1. FM, Apr. 13, 1915; BOT, June 12, 1916; Dillard Jacobs, *10² Years: A Study of the First Century of Vanderbilt University School of Engineering, 1875–1975* (Nashville: Vanderbilt Engineering Alumni Association, 1975), 62–63; *Alumnus* 6 (Oct., 1920): 17–18.

2. Willis G. Waldo to Kirkland, July 14, 1928; Oct. 3, 24, 1930; Oct. 14, 1931, all in Chanc. Off., RG 3, box 4, ff "Waldo, W.G. (1927–40)"; BOT, Oct. 5, 1928; Jacobs, *10² Years,* 63; Bull., Feb., 1930, p. 272.

3. BOT, June 14, 1915; Feb. 16, June 7, 1920.

4. BOT, June 11, 1917; June 10, July 9, 1918; June 20, July 7, 1919; June 11, 1923; June 8, 1925; June 7, 1926; undated newsclipping, Stella Vaughn Scrapbooks, ff 19, SC.

5. BOT, Nov. 30, 1915; June 7, 1920; June 11, 1923; June 8, 1925; June 12, 1927; *Alumnus* 9 (May–June, 1924): 173.

6. BOT, June 12, 1922; June 8, 1925; June 6, 1927; June 10, 1929; Walter L. Fleming to Franklin Paschal, Nov. 8, 1927, History Department Archives, RG 62, box 2, ff 88, SC; *Alumnus* 12 (Jan., 1927): 83–84.

7. *Alumnus* 15 (Nov.–Dec., 1929): 27; BOT, June 7, 1926; June 10, 1929; Feb. 3, Mar. 28, 1930; *Hustler,* Oct. 11, 1929.

8. BOT, June 14, 1915; June 12, 1916; June 10, 1918.

9. *Bull.,* School of Religion, Apr., 1916, pp. 5–8, 11–12; BOT, June 12, 1916; June 10, 1918; June 9, 1919.

10. BOT, June 10, 1918; June 9, 1919; June 12, 1922; June 11, 1923; *Hustler,* Dec. 8, 1921.

11. BOT, June 8, 1925; June 6, 1927.

12. BOT, June 6, 1927; "The Vanderbilt University School of Religion," pamphlet in CHP, ff "Divinity School—Misc.—Documents"; *Bull.,* School of Religion, Aug. 1932, p. 32; newsclippings [Apr. 17, 1927], Stella Vaughn Scrapbooks, ff 19; *Alumnus* 14 (Jan., 1929): 91–92.

13. *Alumnus* 13 (Jan.–Feb., 1928): 93, 99; BOT, June 10, 1929; June 9, Oct. 16, 1930; Feb. 11, 1931.

14. BOT, June 11, 1917; Nov. 25, Dec. 31, 1919; *Alumnus* 5 (Jan., 1920): 69–72.

15. John Ettling, *The Germ of Laziness: Rockefeller Philanthropy and Public Health in the South* (Cambridge: Harvard Univ. Press, 1981), 49–57.

16. Ibid., 57–93.

17. Ibid., 97–121, 152–207.

18. Abraham Flexner, *Medical Education in the United States and Canada: A Report to the Carnegie Foundation for the Advancement of Teaching,* Bulletin No. 4 (New York: [Carnegie Foundation for the Advancement of Teaching], c. 1910); Timothy C. Jacobson, "Medical Center: A History of Science in Medicine" (unpublished MS in SC [1982]), 117–26, 150–56, 165–66, 171–74, copy in SC.

19. Jacobson, "Medical Center," 171–80; *Alumnus* 5 (Jan., 1920): 69–72; see Chanc. Off., RG 3, box 5, ff 31 for Kirkland/Abraham Flexner correspondence; confidential memorandum, Feb. 27, 1919, ibid.

20. BOT, Sept. 27, Nov. 25, Dec. 31, 1919.

21. G. Canby Robinson, *Adventures in Medical Education* (Cambridge: Harvard Univ. Press, 1957), 145–46; Robinson to Kirkland, Dec. 8, 31, 1919; Jan. 19, 26, 1920; Kirkland to Robinson, Jan. 28, 1920, all in Chanc. Off., RG 3, box 7, ff 51; Jacobson, "Medical Center," 168–70, 195–201; BOT, Feb. 16, 1920.

22. Robinson, *Adventures,* 146; Robinson to Kirkland, May 11, 1920, Chanc. Off., RG 3, box 7, ff 51; Robinson to Kirkland, ibid., ff 52; BOT, Dec. 31, 1919; Jacobson, "Medical Center," 208–10.

23. Jacobson, "Medical Center," 195–201, 209–10, 215–20; G. Canby Robinson, "The Relation of Medical Education to the Medical Plant," *Journal of the American Medical Association* 81 (July 28, 1923): 321–23; Robinson, *Adventures,* 158–59; Robinson to Wallace Buttrick, Sept. 3, 1920; to Abraham Flexner, Sept. 23, 1920; to Kirkland, Sept. 24, 1920, all in Chanc. Off., RG 3, box 7, ff 52.

24. Kirkland to G. Canby Robinson, May 27, 1921, Chanc. Off., RG 3, box 7, ff 51; Kirkland to Robinson, Oct. 7, 1920; Jan. 29, Feb. 9, 1921, ibid., ff 52; Charles Cason to Abraham Flexner, n.d. [1921], ibid., box 1, ff 33; Wallace Buttrick to Kirkland, Dec. 24, 1920, ibid., box 5, ff 21; Jacobson, "Medical Center," 222–28.

25. Edwin Mims, *History of Vanderbilt University* (Nashville: Vanderbilt Univ. Press, 1946), 358–61; Robinson's role is documented in the Robinson/Kirkland correspondence, Chanc. Off., RG 3, box 7, ff 52.

26. BOT, Nov. 25, 1919, June 6, 1921; June 9, 1924; June 25, 1925.

27. *Alumnus* 9 (Oct., 1923): 7; BOT, Sept. 14, 1923; Kirkland to G. Canby Robinson, Mar. 12, 1926, Chanc. Off., RG 3, box 7, ff 56.

28. For extensive correspondence between Robinson and Kirkland concerning the selection of medical school professors see Chanc. Off., RG 3, box 7, ff 54–56; BOT, June 9, 1924; Jan. 20, June 8, 1925; June 7, 1926.

29. Jacobson, "Medical Center," 269–72; *Bull.*, Feb., 1926, pp. 142–43; BOT, Mar. 30, June 8, 1925; newsclipping, n.d., Stella Vaughn Scrapbooks, ff 15.

30. *Bull.*, Feb., 1925, pp. 155–57; *Bull.*, School of Medicine, 1929–30, pp. 63, 73–74; *Bull.*, Feb., 1930, pp. 173–79; BOT, June 7, 1926; June 6, 1927; Jacobson, "Medical Center," 253–54; newsclipping, June 7, 1927; newsclipping, n.d., both in Stella Vaughn Scrapbooks, ff 15.

31. Jacobson, "Medical Center," 252–56; BOT, Dec. 22, 1925; June 7, Dec. 21, 1926; June 6, 1927.

32. BOT, June 7, 1926; June 6, 1927; June 11, 1928; June 9, 1930.

33. BOT, June 7, 1926; for extensive correspondence between Kirkland and the GEB see Chanc. Off., RG 3, box 5.

34. BOT, June 6, 1927; June 11, 1928; June 10, 1929; Kirkland to Trevor Arnett, Oct. 26, 1928, Chanc. Off., RG 3, box 5, ff 13; Kirkland to G. Canby Robinson, June 13, 1928; Robinson to Kirkland, Jan. 14, Apr. 27, 1928, all in Chanc. Off., RG 3, box 7, ff 56.

35. BOT, June 10, 1929; June 9, 1930.

36. *Commodore*, 1918, p. 122; 1924, p. 63.

37. G. Canby Robinson to Edwin R. Embree, May 3, Dec. 8, 1924, G. Canby Robinson MSS, Medical School Library, Vanderbilt University.

38. Edwin R. Embree to G. Canby Robinson, June 13, 1925; Robinson to Embree, May 19, 1925; Robinson to Abbie Roberts, Dec. 21, 1916; see extensive correspondence between Robinson, Bruce R. Payne, and the GEB, all in Robinson MSS; Robinson to Payne, Dec. 6, 1926; to Kirkland, Jan. 13, 1927, both in Chanc. Off., RG 3, box 7, ff 56; BOT, Mar. 17, 1925, *Alumnus* 40 (Apr., 1925): 135.

39. G. Canby Robinson to Edwin R. Embree, Dec. 9, 1925, Robinson MSS; to Kirkland, Nov. 4, 23, 1925, Chanc. Off., RG 3, box 7, ff 56; *Alumnus* 12 (Feb., 1927): 118; BOT, June 6, 1927; *Bull.*, School of Nursing, Aug., 1926; Walter Fleming to Kirkland, Apr. 5, 1926; to Edith Brodie, Apr. 22, 1926; "Recommendations by the Faculty of the College of Arts and Science Relating to a Combined Course in Nursing and Academic Work," May 11, 1926, all in History Department Archives, RG 62, box 3, ff 143.

40. Walter Fleming to Kirkland, May 25, 1928, History Department Archives, RG 62, box 3, ff 143.

41. BOT, Feb. 3, 1930; *Alumnus* 16 (Oct., 1939): 7.

12. College Life in the 1920s

1. FM, Apr. 9, 1918.

2. FM, May 13, 1919; Feb. 8, 1921; Apr. 11, 1922; *Hustler*, Jan. 10, 1924; *Alumnus* 7 (Oct., 1921): 3–4; 9 (Jan., 1924): 72.

3. FM, Feb. 8, 1921; BOT, June 12, 1922; *Bull.*, Feb., 1926, p. 225; *Alumnus* 13 (Jan.–Feb., 1928): 101.

4. *Bull.*, Feb., 1923, p. 106; BOT, June 8, 1925; June 6, 1927.

5. BOT, June 7, 1920; June 6, 1927; June 8, 1931; FM, Sept. 18, 1926; *Alumnus* 13 (May–June, 1928): 169; *Bull.*, Feb., 1930, p. 273.

6. Memorandum, "Suggestions Concerning Affiliation with the George Peabody College [May 1914]," History Department Archives, RG 62, box 1, ff 3, SC; Leonidas C. Glenn to Kirkland, Mar. 5, 1920, in John Dale Russell, "Staff Study No. 3, Historical Analyses of Cooperation Between George Peabody College for Teachers and Vanderbilt University," 1962, pp. 36–37, copy in CHP; BOT, June 11, 1928.

7. For statements by Payne belittling liberal arts programs see undated newsclippings, History Department Archives, RG 62, box 1, ff 3; Walter Fleming to Kirkland, Jan. 7, 1925; to W.D. Weatherford, June 5, 1925; to Bruce R. Payne, Jan. 24, 1925; undated memorandum, "Affiliations with Other Institutions"; Fleming to Kirkland, July 2, 1927, all in ibid., ff 4; to Kirkland, May 22, 1928, ibid., ff 43.

8. Walter Fleming to Kirkland, July 2, 1927, ibid., ff 4; to Kirkland, June 24, 1927, ibid., ff 16.

9. Walter Fleming to Kirkland, Feb. 19, 1926; July 2, 1927; Kirkland to Fleming, Feb. 25, 1926, Chanc. Off., RG 3, box 6, ff 2; Fleming to Kirkland, Feb. 18, 1929, History Department Archives, RG 62, box 1, ff 16; BOT, June 10, 1929; June 9, 1930.

10. BOT, June 9, 1919; *Alumnus* 4 (May, 1919): 171; for W.D. Weatherford/Kirkland correspondence see Chanc. Off., RG 3, box 6, ff 4; George Peter Antone, "Willis Duke Weatherford: An Interpretation of His Work in Race Relations, 1906–1946" (Ph.D. diss., Vanderbilt Univ., 1969), 125–45.

11. Jesse L. Cuninggim, "How the Doors Were Opened, or Problems Faced and Solutions Found in the Development of a College," c. 1947, typescript, Jesse L. Cuninggim Papers, Scarritt College Library; Jesse L. Cuninggim, "History of Scarritt College," c. 1943, unfinished MS, in ibid.; Mary Anna Howard, "A Decade in the History of Scarritt College for Christian Workers" (M.A. thesis, Scarritt College, 1937).

12. BOT, June 9, 1919; *Hustler*, Dec. 8, 1921; *Alumnus* 9 (Oct., 1923): 13.

13. BOT, June 9, 1919; June 7, 1920; *Alumnus* 1 (Nov., 1915): 7.

14. *Hustler*, Feb. 9, 1922; BOT, June 8, 1925.

15. *Hustler*, Oct. 1, 1921; BOT, June 12, 1922; June 8, 1925; FM, June 10, 1925.

16. *Hustler*, May 27, 1916; FM, June 10, 1916; *Vampire*, n.d. [May 13, 1916], Chanc. Off., RG 3, box 4, ff "*The Vampire*, 1916–1917."

17. *Jade*, Nov. 27, 1919, copy in CHP, ff "Students—Activities—Publication—*The Jade*"; *Alumnus* 5 (Nov., 1919): 51; H.C. Tolman, "Action of the Committee on Student Life and Interests in regard to the June Edition of *The Jade*," n.d.; L.B. Smelser to the Committee on Student Life and Interests, June 8, 1923, both in Chanc. Off., RG 3, box 6, ff 1; FM, Oct. 9, 1923; *Hustler*, Apr. 13, 1922; Oct. 25, Dec. 13, 1923.

18. *Hustler*, Jan. 24, Feb. 21, 1917; FM, Feb. 20, 1917; *Alumnus* 5 (Apr., 1920): 176–77.

19. BOT, June 7, 1920; *Hustler*, Nov. 25, 1918; May 20, 1920; *Alumnus* 2 (Oct., 1916): 3; 6 (May–June, 1921): 203; *Commodore*, 1918.

20. *Alumnus* 8 (Mar., 1923): 133; *Hustler*, Oct. 9, 1920; BOT, June 6, 1927; June 10, 1929; FM, Nov. 8, 1927.

21. *Alumnus* 5 (Apr., 1920): 176–77; 8 (Jan., 1923): 83; BOT, June 7, 1920.

22. BOT, June 19, 1899; June 14, 1915; June 7, 1920; Jan. 19, June 6, 1921; FM, Feb. 8, 1921.

23. BOT, June 11, 1923; June 11, July 1, 1925; *Alumnus* 8 (Mar., 1923): 133; 8 (Apr., May, June, 1923): 163, 166–67.

24. BOT, June 11, 1925; June 7, 1926; *Alumnus* 12 (Mar., 1927): 151.

25. *Hustler*, Feb. 27, 1918; *Alumnus* 5 (Apr., 1920): 178–80.

26. Nashville *Tennessean*, Mar. 30, 1927; Walter Fleming to Kirkland, Mar. 31, 1927, Kirkland Papers, box 4, ff 50, SC.

27. *Alumnus* 1 (Mar., 1915): 9; 2 (Jan., 1917): 70; 7 (Jan., 1922): 74; see clippings in Stella Vaughn Scrapbooks, ff 18, SC.

28. BOT, June 12, 1922; June 6, 1927; *Alumnus* 13 (Nov.–Dec., 1927): 47.

29. Regarding Glee Club see newsclippings in Kirkland Papers, box "Newsclippings, 1919–1950," ff 23.

30. *Alumnus* 1 (Nov., 1915): 4–5; 1 (Jan., 1916): 5–6; 2 (Jan., 1917): 65, 68; Edwin Mims, *History of Vanderbilt University* (Nashville: Vanderbilt Univ. Press, 1940), 286–87.

31. *Alumnus* 6 (Nov., 1920): 36; 6 (Dec., 1920): 85; 7 (Nov., 1921): 47–54; 8 (Nov., 1922): 35, 37–40; *Hustler,* Oct. 20, Dec. 8, 1921; Mar. 9, 1922; for information on Vanderbilt football also see Fred Russell and Maxwell E. Benson, eds., *Fifty Years of Vanderbilt Football* (Nashville: F. Russell and M.E. Benson, 1938), 32–48.

32. BOT, June 12, 1922; June 11, 1923; June 10, 1929; *Hustler,* Nov. 10, 1921; Jan. 19, 1922; *Alumnus* 7 (Nov., 1921): 37–38; 8 (Oct., 1922): 3–7, 9–13; 8 (Nov., 1922): 35, 37–40; 8 (Jan., 1923): 82; 9 (Nov., 1923): 49–53; *Commodore,* 1925, pp. 112–16.

33. *Alumnus* 11 (Jan., 1926): 67; 12 (Nov., 1926): 47–50; 14 (Nov.–Dec., 1928): 47–49, 53–54; 15 (Nov.–Dec., 1929): 29–30.

34. BOT, May 11, June 11, 1923; *Hustler,* Nov. 8, Dec. 6, 1924; Dan McGugin to Committee on Revision of By-Laws of Athletic Association, 1929, Alec Brock Stevenson Papers, Athletics, SC; *Alumnus* 5 (Mar., 1920): 150; 12 (Feb., 1927): 132–33.

35. *Alumnus* 8 (Apr., May, June, 1923): 186; 9 (Feb., 1924): 106; 14 (Nov.–Dec., 1928): 52.

13. FUGITIVES AND AGRARIANS

1. Louise Cowan, *The Fugitive Group: A Literary History* (Baton Rouge, La.: Louisiana State Univ. Press, 1959), 3–42; Louis D. Rubin, Jr., *The Wary Fugitives: Four Poets and the South* (Baton Rouge, La.: Louisiana State Univ. Press, 1978), 2–15; Thomas Daniel Young, *Gentleman in a Dustcoat: A Biography of John Crowe Ransom* (Baton Rouge, La.: Louisiana State Univ. Press, 1976), 37–40, 80–84, 90–93.

2. Rubin, *Wary Fugitives,* 13–14; Cowan, *Fugitive Group,* 5, 17–20; Rob Roy Purdy, ed., *Fugitives' Reunion: Conversations at Vanderbilt,* May 3–5, 1956 (Nashville: Vanderbilt Univ. Press, 1959), 32, 90–91, 123–28.

3. Young, *Gentleman,* 90–93.

4. Cowan, *Fugitive Group,* 20–22, 26–28; Rubin, *Wary Fugitives,* 15–21; John Crowe Ransom, *Poems About God* (New York: H. Holt, 1919).

5. Cowan, *Fugitive Group,* 24–26, 28–30; Rubin, *Wary Fugitives,* 15, 21; Michael O'Brien, *The Idea of the American South, 1920–1941* (Baltimore: Johns Hopkins Univ. Press, 1979), 119–20, 185.

6. Cowan, *Fugitive Group,* 30–35.

7. Ibid., 35–40; Daniel Joseph Singal, *The War Within: From Victorian to Modernist Thought in the South, 1919–1945* (Chapel Hill: Univ. of North Carolina Press, 1982), 232–34; O'Brien, *American South,* 136–39; Rubin, *Wary Fugitives,* 22–24, 64–67.

8. Cowan, *Fugitive Group,* 43–48; Rubin, *Wary Fugitives,* 2–3; *Fugitive* 1 (Apr., 1922): 1; (Oct., 1922): 66; (Dec., 1922): 98–100.

9. Cowan, *Fugitive Group,* 55–59, 77–79.

10. Rubin, *Wary Fugitives,* 23–29; *Fugitive* 1 (Apr., 1922): passim; *Jade,* 3 (Apr. 13, 1922); *Hustler,* Apr. 20, 1922; Cowan, *Fugitive Group,* 53–55.

11. Cowan, *Fugitive Group,* 105–106; *Fugitive* 2 (Apr.–May, 1923): 34.

12. Cowan, *Fugitive Group,* 106–108; Singal, *War Within,* 340–42; O'Brien, *American South,* 185–87; Young, *Gentleman,* 126–27.

13. Cowan, *Fugitive Group,* 118–27, 149; Rubin, *Wary Fugitives,* 47, 82–85, 147–48; Young, *Gentleman,* 137–45, 150–57, 164.

14. Cowan, *Fugitive Group,* 117–22, 139–40, 155–57, 190, 216–21.

15. Rubin, *Wary Fugitives,* 194–96; Cowan, *Fugitive Group,* 206–208; F. Garvin Davenport, Jr., *The Myth of Southern History: Historical Consciousness in Twentieth Century Southern Literature* (Nashville: Vanderbilt Univ. Press, 1967), 50–53; Donald Davidson, "The Vanderbilt Literary Tradition," *Alumnus* 41 (May–June, 1956): 7–8.

16. Rubin, *Wary Fugitives*, 154–55; O'Brien, *American South*, 137–38, 187–88; Edwin Mims, *The Advancing South: Stories of Progress and Reaction* (New York: Doubleday, Page, 1926), passim, but see esp. vii–xiv, 257–311.

17. Young, *Gentleman*, 6–8, 15, 60–61, 66.

18. Ibid., 151, 188–91, 311.

19. John Crowe Ransom, *God Without Thunder: An Unorthodox Defense of Orthodoxy* (New York: Harcourt, Brace, 1930), passim.

20. Singal, *War Within*, 232–33, 238–50; O'Brien, *American South*, 139–46.

21. O'Brien, *American South*, 185–87; Rubin, *Wary Fugitives*, 140–41, 158–60; Cowan, *Fugitive Group*, 149–50.

22. O'Brien, *American South*, 187–91.

23. Rubin, *Wary Fugitives*, 161–66; 168–72, 181–84, 252; O'Brien, *American South*, 193–95.

24. Twelve Southerners, *I'll Take My Stand: The South and the Agrarian Tradition* (New York: Harper, 1930; repr. New York: Harper Torch Books, 1962), ix–xxiv.

25. Ibid., xxiv–xxviii.

26. Ibid., xxviii–xxx.

27. Ibid., passim.

28. Ibid., 3–27.

29. Ibid., 94–96, 110–11, 114–21.

30. Ibid., 28–60.

31. Ibid., x, 249–64; Rubin, *Wary Fugitives*, 335–36.

32. Singal, *War Within*, 348–49.

33. O'Brien, *American South*, 163–68; Twelve Southerners, *Stand*, 61–91; Purdy, *Fugitives' Reunion*, 203–205.

34. O'Brien, *American South*, 146–49; Twelve Southerners, *Stand*, 155–66.

35. Twelve Southerners, *Stand*, 166–75.

36. Ibid., 122–54.

37. Ibid., 201–45.

38. Ibid., 176–200.

39. Ibid.

40. Jess Gilbert and Steve Brown, "Alternative Land Reform Proposals in the 1930s: The Nashville Agrarians and the Southern Tenant Farmers' Union," *Agricultural History* 55 (Oct., 1981): 352–53, 355–58.

41. Singal, *War Within*, 217–18, 250–52; O'Brien, *American South*, 176–78.

42. Young, *Gentleman*, 251–52, 257–59; see *American Review* 4 (1934–35) for articles by Davidson, Lytle, Ransom, Herbert Agar, Owsley, Fletcher, and others.

43. O'Brien, *American South*, 156–57; Herbert Agar and Allen Tate, *Who Owns America? A New Declaration of Independence* (Boston: Houghton Mifflin, 1936); see early issues of *Free America*.

44. Gilbert, "Alternative Land Reform Proposals," 352–53, 355–56; Agar and Tate, *Who Owns America?*, 80–93.

45. Paul K. Conkin, *Tomorrow a New World: The New Deal Community Program* (Ithaca, N.Y.: Cornell Univ. Press, 1959), 93–130, 182–84; Gilbert, "Alternative Land Reform Proposals," 360–63.

46. Frank L. Owsley, "The Pillars of Agrarianism," *American Review* 4 (Mar., 1935): 531–38.

47. Ibid., 538–47.

48. A Symposium, "The Agrarians Today," *Shenandoah* 3 (Spring, 1952): 14–33; Purdy, *Fugitives' Reunion*, 181–83; Donald Davidson, *Southern Writers in the Modern World* (Athens: Univ. of Georgia Press, 1958): 35–51; O'Brien, *American South*, 178–80, 206–209.

49. William C. Havard and Walter Sullivan, eds., *A Band of Prophets: The Vanderbilt Agrarians After Fifty Years* (Baton Rouge: Louisiana State Univ. Press, 1982), 8–9, 15–16.

14. HARD TIMES

1. BOT, June 8, 9, 1931; Feb. 1, June 6, 1932; Feb. 6, 1933; June 10, 1935; Feb. 3, 1936.

2. BOT, June 10, 1935; Feb. 3, 1936; *Fin. Statements, May 1, 1928*, pp. 6–11; April 30, 1930, pp. 12–24.

3. *Fin. Statements*, May 1, 1933, pp. 6–21; BOT, Feb. 6, 1933; Feb. 5, 1934; Feb. 4, June 10, 1935; Feb. 3, 1936.

4. BOT, June 6, 1932; Feb. 3, 1936.

5. *Bull., Reports of Chancellor and Other Administrative Officers*, 1933–1934, p. 17; BOT, Feb. 1, Apr. 11, June 6, July 7, 1932; *Alumnus* 17 (Feb., 1932): 101–103; *Hustler*, Apr. 8, 1932.

6. BOT, June 8, 1931; June 6, 1932; Feb. 6, 1933; Feb. 5, 1934; June 4, 1936; June 7, 1937; Feb. 1, 1940; see *Fin. Statements*, 1933–37, for university budgets and annual surpluses.

7. *Bull.*, Reports of Chancellor, 1938–1939, p. 112; "Faculty Committee's Requirements for Extra-Mural Projects with FREA [*sic*] Students," Oct. 10, 1934, and "National Youth Administration, Student Aid Program, 1937–38," Chanc. Off., RG 3, box 2, ff Henry G. Hart; BOT, Nov. 9, 1934; FM, Feb. 14, Nov. 14, 1933; Dec. 11, 1934; *Bull.: Register*, 1932–33, pp. 44–47, *Hustler*, Mar. 2, 1934.

8. *Hustler*, Oct. 21, 1932.

9. *Alumnus* 18 (Oct., 1932): 5, 15; *Bull.*, 1931–32, pp. 13, 15, 16, 18.

10. BOT, Nov. 20, 1934; Feb. 4, 1935; *Alumnus* 20 (Dec., 1934): 1, 3, 32; 20 (Jan./Feb., 1935): 7–8; 20 (Mar., 1935): 1, 3.

11. BOT, June 10, 1929; Feb. 1, 1932; Apr. 16, 1935.

12. FM, Mar. 11, 1930; Feb. 10, June 10, Dec. 8, 1931; Apr. 11, 1933; BOT, Apr. 11, 1933; Feb. 5, 1934.

13. BOT, Apr. 16, 1935; Oliver Cromwell Carmichael, "Adventures in Education" (typescript, undated, in SC), 137–39.

14. *Who's Who in American Education*, 12th ed., 19 vols. (Nashville: Who's Who in American Education, Inc., c. 1946), 12:212; Carmichael, "Adventures," 20, 24, 33–35, 42, 45–48, 68–69, 77, 79–80, 82–83, 88–89, 92–93, 98, 108–09, 117, 127–37.

15. Letters and Memorandums, F.C. Paschal to Kirkland, Apr. 1, 1935; C.M. Sarratt to Kirkland, Apr. 1, 1935; Edwin Mims to Kirkland, Apr. 1, 1935; W.C. Binkley to Kirkland, Mar. 30, 1935; F.J. Lewis to Kirkland, Mar. 30, 1935; all in Chanc. Off., RG 3, box 6, ff 5; BOT, Apr. 16, June 10, 1935; June 8, 1936.

16. *Bull.*, Reports of Chancellors, 1934–35, p. 25; 1938–39, pp. 112–13; BOT, Oct. 11, 1932; Feb. 6, June 12, 13, 1933; July 9, 1936; Feb. 1, 1937.

17. BOT, June 6, 1932; Oct. 18, 1933; Jan. 18, Mar. 7, 1934; Louis D. Rubin, Jr., *The Wary Fugitives: Four Poets and the South* (Baton Rouge: Louisiana State Univ., 1978), 252–53, 342.

18. *Alumnus* 17 (Mar., 1932): 138–39; 18 (Apr., 1933): 169–70; BOT, June 10, 1935.

19. Walter L. Fleming to Kirkland, May 12, 1924, History Department Records RG 62; box 1, ff 3, SC; *Typographical Bulletin* (Nashville), Dec. 16, 1921, copy enclosed with letter Whitefoord Cole to Kirkland, Dec. 17, 1921; Kirkland to Cole, Dec. 19, 1921; Cole to Kirkland, Dec. 20, 1921, all in Chanc. Off., RG 3, box 14, ff "Whitefoord R. Cole, 1921–1924;" Kirkland to Walter L. Randolph, Dec. 28, 1935; Guy L. Moser to Kirkland, Mar. 13, 1937; unsigned copy from Member of Congress to G.W. Dyer, Mar. 13, 1937; Kirkland to Dyer, Mar. 16, 1937, all in ibid., box 1, ff 54; W.E. Norvell, Jr., to Cole, Apr. 21, 1934; Cole to Norvell, Apr. 23, 1934; Kirkland to Cole, May 4, 1934, all in ibid., box 14, ff "Whitefoord Cole, 1929–1938;" *Hustler*, Apr. 13, 20, 1934.

20. BOT, June 10, 1929; Feb. 3, 1930; *Who Was Who in America* 2 (Chicago: A.N. Marquis, 1950): 238; Hart to Professor Walker, Nov. 26, 1929; Joseph K. Hart to Kirkland, Jan. 1, 1930; Kirkland to Hart, Jan. 7, 1930; Hart to Kirkland, Jan. 9, 11, 30, 1930, all in Chanc. Off., RG 3, box 2, ff "Joseph K. Hart, 1929–1934."

21. Joseph Kinmont Hart, *A Social Interpretation of Education* (New York: Henry Holt, 1929), passim, but see esp. xi–xx, 425–32.

22. D.C. Cabeen to Kirkland, June 5, 1934, and Joseph K. Hart to Kirkland, Apr. 11, 1933, in Chanc. Off., RG 3, box 2, ff "Joseph K. Hart, 1929–1934; *Hustler*, Mar. 24, Apr. 14, 1933.

23. Joseph K. Hart to Kirkland, May 25, 1932, Jan. 24, 1933, June 4, 1934; undated memorandum of student grades in Hart's classes, all in ff "Joseph K. Hart, 1929–1934."

24. Joseph K. Hart to Kirkland, June 4, 1934, in ibid.; *Hustler*, Mar. 30, 1934.

25. *Hustler*, Apr. 6, 1934; FM, Apr. 9, 1934.

26. *Hustler*, Apr. 13, 1934.

27. Joseph K. Hart to Kirkland, June 4, 1934; Minutes of Committee on Educational Policies Meeting, Apr. 5, 1934, in Chanc. Off., RG 3, box 2, ff "Joseph K. Hart, 1929–1934."

28. BOT, May 31, 1934; Curtis H. Walker to Kirkland, June 4, 1934; D.C. Cabeen to Kirkland, June 5, 1934; student petitions to Kirkland, June 5, 1934, all in Chanc. Off., RG 3, box 2, ff "Joseph K. Hart, 1929–1934."

29. BOT, June 12, 1934; Joseph K. Hart to Kirkland, June 9, July 22, 1934; Kirkland to Hart, July 2, 1934; W.W. Cook to Kirkland, Sept. 19, 1934, all in Chanc. Off., RG 3, box 2, ff "Joseph K. Hart, 1929–1934."

30. Kirkland to W.W. Cook, Sept. 21, 28, Oct. 4, Nov. 9, 1934; Cook to Kirkland, Sept. 26, Oct. 15, Nov. 8, 1934; Joseph K. Hart to Kirkland, Dec. 3, 1934, all in Chanc. Off., RG 3, box 2, ff "Joseph K. Hart, 1929–1934"; Joseph K. Hart, *Education for an Age of Power: The TVA Poses a Problem* (New York: Harper, 1935).

31. For evidence of faculty concern over issues raised by the Hart case see Herbert C. Sanborn to W.T. Hale, Jr., June 9, 1934, Chanc. Off., RG 3, box 2, ff "Joseph K. Hart, 1929–1934"; FM, June 9, Dec. 11, 1934; Jan. 8, 1935.

32. BOT, Feb. 1, 1932.

33. *Alumnus* 17 (Feb., 1932), 161; 17 (Mar., 1932): 141; 17 (Apr., 1932): 165.

34. BOT, Feb. 6, 1933; Feb. 5, June 12, 1934; Feb. 4, 1935.

35. BOT, June 10, 1935; Feb. 3, Apr. 29, May 26, June 8, 9, 1936; *Bull.*, Register, 1935–36, p. 242.

36. Stanley Lincoln Harbison, "The Social Gospel Career of Alva Wilmot Taylor" (Ph.D. diss., Vanderbilt Univ., 1975), 14; 30, 49–54, 61–64, 116–22, 128–29, 131–32, 143–57, 169–72, 178, 188–91, 193–98, 208–11.

37. Ibid., 213–17, 255–60, 270–71.

38. Ibid., 233–38, 245–49, 252–54, 274–82, 286–89, 370, 372, 380, 384–89.

39. Ibid., 258–67, 271–72, 326–27; Frank D. Alexander to Kirkland, June 6, 1936; Frank D. Alexander, June 25, 1936; Kirkland to Vernon Tupper, Sept. 17, 1936; mimeographed petitions signed by Taylor's former students, all in Chanc. Off., RG 3, box 4, ff "Alva W. Taylor, 1931–38."

40. Harbison, "Social Gospel Career," 325, 329–43, 349, 363–67, 370–95, 400–403.

41. Ibid., 269, 271–72.

42. *Bull.*, Register, 1930–1931, p. 299; 1934–35, p. 235; *Bull.*, School of Law 1934–1935, pp. 7, 15; BOT, June 13, 1933; June 17, 1934; June 10, 1935; *Hustler*, Sept. 28, 1934.

43. BOT, June 6, 1932; June 10, 1935; June 7–8, 1937.

44. BOT, Feb. 4, 1934; Apr. 16, May 22, June 10, 1935; June 8–9, 1936; Feb. 1, 1937; *Alumnus* 22 (Mar., 1937): 4.

45. BOT, June 9, 1930; June 12, 1932; Feb. 5, 1934; *Bull.*, School of Nursing, 1936–37, p. 27.

46. BOT, Feb. 5, 1934; Mar. 29, June 10, 1935; June 8–9, 1936.

47. *Almnus* 18 (Apr., 1933): 1, 172; *Bull.*, Register, 1932–33, p. 240; 1934–35, p. 234; 1933–34, p. 230; *Bull.*, Reports of Chancellor, 1930–1931, pp. 50–51; *Hustler*, Sept. 28, 1934.

48. *Bull.*, Reports of Chancellor, 1931–32, pp. 59, 63; *Hustler*, Dec. 2, 1932.

49. *Alumnus* 18 (Dec., 1932): 71, 78; 18 (Jan.–Feb., 1933): 199, 202; 20 (Mar., 1935): 4; 21 (Dec., 1935): 3; *Hustler* Jan. 24, 1930, Oct. 28, 1932; Alec B. Stevensen Papers, ff 34 "Football Schedules . . . 1932–1939," SC; BOT, Feb. 6, 1933.

50. BOT, Jan. 9, Feb. 4, 1935; Feb. 3, 1936; *Alumnus* 20 (Jan.–Feb., 1935): 4, 6; 21 (Jan.–Feb., 1936): 1, 3–4.

51. FM, Nov. 13, 1934; *Hustler*, Oct. 28, 1932; Nov. 16, Dec. 14, 1934; Feb. 8, Nov. 1, 1935; Feb. 21, Apr. 3, 10, 1936; *Vanderbilt Rustler*, n.d.

52. *Alumnus* 20 (March, 1935): 8; *Hustler*, Nov. 8, 1935; Mar. 27, 1936.

53. *Vanderbilt Patriot*, Apr. 29, 1936.

15. BETTER TIMES

1. BOT, June 12, 1934; June 10, 1940; Feb. 2, July 31, 1942; FM, June 8, 1935; Faculty Music Committee, "A Recommendation submitted by the Music Committee to the Faculty of Arts and Science of Vanderbilt University for Preliminary Action," in FM, June 8, 1935; *Bull.*, Register, 1942–1943, p. 48.

2. BOT, Feb. 7, 1938; June 10, 1940.

3. BOT, June 12, 1939; June 10, Dec. 23, 1940; Feb. 3, 1941; June 5–6, 1942; *Alumnus* 26 (Nov., 1940): 3–4.

4. BOT, July 9, Aug. 18, 1937; June 6–7, 1938; Feb. 1, 1943; *Alumnus* 23 (Oct., 1937): 12–13; 24 (Oct., 1938): 6.

5. BOT, June 6–7, 1938; June 12, 1939; June 10, 1940; June 10, 1941.

6. BOT, June 12, 1939; June 10, 1940.

7. BOT, June 10, 1940; Feb. 3, 1941.

8. BOT, Feb. 3, 1936.

9. *Bull.*, Reports of the Chancellor and Other Administrative Officers, 1940–1941, p. 34; *Bull.*, School of Engineering, Jan. 15, 1941, pp. 8, 30–32, 54; BOT, June 12, 1939; Feb. 3, 1941.

10. BOT, Feb. 3, 1936; Feb. 1, June 7, 1937; June 10, 1941, Feb. 7, 1944; *Bull.*, School of Law, 1939–40, p. 14; *Bull.*, School of Law, 1942–43, p. 35.

11. BOT, June 8, 1936; Feb. 1, June 7–8, 1937; Feb. 7, 1938; Jan. 26, 1939.

12. BOT, Oct. 4, 1935; June 25, 1936; Feb. 1, 1937; *Alumnus* 20 (Mar., 1937): 5.

13. BOT, Apr. 10, 1939; *Alumnus* 20 (May, 1939): 12; *Bull.*, School of Religion, Mar. 15, 1941, pp. 9, 29, 39–49; *Bull.*, Reports of the Chancellor and Other Administrative Officers, 1940–1941, p. 100.

14. *Bull.*, School of Medicine, 1937–1938, p. 10; BOT, June 7–8, 1937; June 10, 1940; Feb. 3, 1941; Timothy C. Jacobson, "Medical Center: A History of Science in Medicine" (unpublished MS in SC [1982]), 349–57; *Fin. Statements*, May 1, 1937, p. 66.

15. BOT, June 6–7, 1938; June 12, 1939; Feb. 3, 1941; *Bull.*, School of Nursing, 1939–40, pp. 8–9; "The Endowment of the Vanderbilt University School of Nursing," School of Nursing Archives, box 11, ff 18, SC.

16. *Alumnus* 24 (Jan.–Feb., 1939): 11; 24 (Apr., 1939):7.

17. BOT, Apr. 16, 1935; FM, Oct. 14, 1935.

18. FM, Dec. 9, 1935; Dec. 8, 1936; "Minutes of the Senior College Committee" (Nov. 15, 1935; Feb. 14, 1936), W.B. Jewell Papers, box 8, ff 8–19, SC.

19. "Minutes of the Senior College Committee" (Nov. 15, 1935; Feb. 14, 1936; Apr. 21, 1936; Oct. 27, 1936), Jewell Papers, box 8, ff 8–19; "Report of the Committee on the Senior College," in FM, Dec. 8, 1936.

20. FM, Dec. 8, 15, 1936.

21. "Minutes of the Senior College Committee" (Nov. 11, 16, 18, 1936), Jewell Papers, box 8, ff 8–19; Kirkland to F.C. Rand, Feb. 10, 1937, Chanc. Off., RG 3, box 4 (BOT), ff "Rand, F.C."

22. O.C. Carmichael, "Adventures in Education" (typescript, copy in SC), 142–43.

23. FM, Feb. 9, 1937; Kirkland to F.C. Rand, Feb. 10, 1937, Chanc. Off., RG 3, box 4 (BOT), ff "Rand, F.C."

24. FM, Apr. 6, 13, 1937, including "Preliminary Statement of Board of Review" and the "Report of the Board of Review."

25. Kirkland to F.C. Rand, Feb. 10, 18, Apr. 14, May 6, 1937, Chanc. Off., RG 3, box 4 (BOT), ff "Rand, F.C."; J. Chappell to F.L. Owsley, June 4, 1936, F.L. Owsley Papers, ff 1–17, SC; BOT, June 8, 1937.

26. BOT, May 3, 1937; F.C. Rand to Kirkland, Apr. 16, 1937; Kirkland to Rand, Apr. 14, 23, 1937, Chanc. Off., RG 3, box 4 (BOT), ff "Rand, F.C."

27. Kirkland to F.C. Rand, Apr. 19, 23, May 13, 1937; Rand to Kirkland, Apr. 22, 16, 1937, Chanc. Off., RG 3, box 4 (BOT), ff "Rand, F.C."; FM, May 4, 1937; *Bull.*, College of Arts and Science, 1937–38, p. 59; BOT, June 6–7, 1938; *Alumnus* 23 (Mar., 1938): 5.

28. Thomas Daniel Young, *Gentleman in a Dustcoat: A Biography of John Crowe Ransom* (Baton Rouge: Louisiana State Univ. Press, 1976), 272–75; Nashville *Tennessean*, May 26, 1937; BOT, June 7, 1937; Andrew Lytle to Frank Rand, June 1, 1937, Chanc. Off., RG 3, box 3, ff "John Crowe Ransom."

29. Young, *Gentleman*, 275, 278–85; for letters and telegrams protesting Ransom's proposed departure from Vanderbilt see Chanc. Off., RG 3, box 3, ff "John Crowe Ransom."

30. Young, *Gentleman*, 286–90; BOT, June 25, 1937.

31. Young, *Gentleman*, 151, 293–94, 356–58, 474; A Symposium, "The Agrarians Today," *Shenandoah* 3 (Spring, 1952): 14–16.

32. Young, *Gentleman*, 325–26, 341–42, 349–52.

33 Ibid., 321; Robert Penn Warren and Cleanth Brooks, Jr., *Understanding Poetry: An Anthology for College Students* (New York: H. Holt, 1938).

34. BOT, June 7, 25, 1937.

35. Carmichael, "Adventures," 143; BOT, Feb. 1, June 7–8, 1937; June 6–7, 1938; *Alumnus* 22 (June, 1937): 1–5.

36. BOT, June 8, 1937; Feb. 6, 1939; *Alumnus* 23 (Jan.–Feb., 1938): 3–9, 12–14.

37. *Alumnus* 23 (Jan.–Feb., 1938): 13; Carmichael, "Adventures," 144–45.

38. *Fin. Statements, April 30, 1938*, 30–33; BOT, Feb. 3, 1936; June 7, 1937; Feb. 7, 1938; Feb. 6, June 12, 1939.

39. BOT, June 12, 1939; June 2, 1944; June 8, 1945.

40. BOT, Feb. 6, 1939; Feb. 3, June 10, 1941; *Fin. Statements*, June 30, 1946, p. 48.

41. Kirkland to Trevor Arnett, Oct. 15, 1929, Chanc. Off., RG 3, box 5, ff 13; *Bull.*, Register, 1930–1931, pp. 30–31; BOT, June 9, 1930.

42. Kirkland to Trevor Arnett, Oct. 15, 1929; D.H. Stevens to Kirkland, Feb. 3, 1931; Trevor Arnett to Kirkland, Jan. 19, 1935, all in Chanc. Off., RG 3, box 5, ff 11–13; BOT, Feb. 1, 1932; June 13, 1933; A. Frederick Kuhlman, "Joint University Libraries, Nashville, Tennessee," in Allen Kent et al., eds., *Encyclopedia of Library and Information Science* 23 (New York: Marcel Dekker, 1975): 292–94.

43. Kuhlman, "Joint University Libraries," 292–94; Edwin Mims to David H. Stevens, Mar. 16, 1934; Kirkland to Trevor Arnett, Apr. 9, 1934; Stevens to Kirkland, Apr. 13, 1934; W.W. Brierley to Kirkland, Mar. 23, Apr. 5, 1935, all in Chanc. Off., RG 3, box 5, ff 11; BOT, Feb. 3, 1936.

44. Kuhlman, "Joint University Libraries," 292–94; unsigned letter from Chancellor of Vanderbilt University and President of Peabody College to Raymond D. Fosdick, [1936], Chanc. Off., RG 3, box 5, ff 9; BOT, Feb. 3, June 8–9, 1936; Feb. 7, 1938; W.W. Brierley to O.C. Carmichael, Dec. 8, 1937, Chanc. Off., RG 3, box 5, ff 8; *Alumnus* 23 (Jan.–Feb., 1938): 10.

45. BOT, Feb. 7, Dec. 5, 1938; Oct. 11, 1939; *Alumnus* 27 (Dec., 1941): 1–2; O.C. Carmichael to James G. Stahlman, Feb. 19, 1938, copy in CHP; promotional literature of Stahlman for library fund drive, J.L. Cuninggin Papers, Correspondence Regarding the Joint University Libraries, Scarritt Archives, Scarritt College, Nashville.

46. BOT, Aug. 18, 1937; June 12, 1939; Kirkland to Ben [Meritt], June 27, 1939; Spencer Jarnagin McCallie to Mrs. Kirkland, Aug. 17, 1939, Meritt Coll.; *Alumnus* 25 (Oct., 1939): 3–5.

47. BOT, Aug. 16, 1939; Feb. 2, 1942; *Alumnus* 27 (Dec., 1941): 1–7; "Program, Dedication Exercises, Joint University Library, Nashville, Tennessee," SC; *Peabody Reflector* 15 (Jan., 1942).

16. WAR TIMES

1. *Hustler,* Feb. 1, Nov. 15, 1935; Apr. 10, May 1, 1936; "The Stand for Revision of the Neutrality Law by Religious and Lay Leaders of America," Chanc. Off., RG 3, ff "Neutrality Legislation (1939)."

2. *Alumnus* 21 (May, 1936): 14; *Hustler,* Oct. 20, 1933; Oct. 27, Nov. 3, 10, 1939; Feb. 7, May 17, Dec. 13, 1940; May 9, 14, 23, Dec. 12, 1941; Oct. 16, 1942; BOT, July 12, 1940.

3. BOT, Feb. 1, 1937; Feb. 3, 1941; Feb. 2, 1942; James E. Stahlman to O.C. Carmichael, Mar. 13, 1941, Chanc. Off., RG 3, box 2, ff "Naval ROTC (1941)"; *Alumnus* 30 (Apr.–May, 1945): 4.

4. BOT, June 10, 1941; Feb. 2, June 5, 1942; June 4, 1943; June 5, 1945; *Alumnus* 27 (June, 1942): 13; FM, March 10, 1942; *Hustler,* Nov. 13, 1942; Apr. 6, 1944.

5. BOT, Feb. 7, 1944.

6. BOT, Feb. 5, July 12, 1940; Feb. 3, 1941; June 5, 1942; Feb. 1, 1943; Feb. 7, 1944; *Hustler,* Jan. 9, 1942; Oct. 21, 1943; H.H. Arnold to O.C. Carmichael, Apr. 9, 1942, Graduate School Files, RG 86, box 10, ff "Army Reserve Correspondence, April–August, 1942," SC; "Curriculum 'C' Pre-Meteorology Program," ibid., ff "Committee—University Pre-Meteorological Committee"; ibid., box 11, ff "Army."

7. BOT, June 9, 1941; Feb. 1, 1943; Albert L. Perkins to O.C. Carmichael, May 13, 1943, Graduate School Files, RG 86, box 10, ff "Detachment Commander"; H.L. Swint to Madison Sarratt, Apr. 13, 1943, ibid., ff "Course V—History, English, and Oral Communication"; *Hustler,* May 21, 1943.

8. *Alumnus* 30 (Dec., 1944): 3–4; (July–Aug., 1945): 4; BOT, June 9, 1941; Feb. 2, 1942; *Hustler,* Oct. 21, 1943; FM, Apr. 8, 1941.

9. BOT, Feb. 2, June 5–6, 1942; Feb. 1, June 4, 1943; Oct. 19, 1944; *Alumnus* 27 (Oct., 1942): 5; 30 (Oct.–Nov., 1944): 11; 30 (Jan–Feb., 1945): 4; 21 (Oct.–Nov., 1945): 5; *Hustler,* Nov. 20, 1942.

10. *Alumnus* 28 (June, 1943): 8; 30 (June, 1945): 3–4; BOT, Feb. 1, July 23, 1943.

11. BOT, May 29, 1942; Feb. 1, June 4, 1943; June 8, 1945; Alumnus 19 (June, 1934): 3; Vanderbilt University, *Reports of the Chancellor and Other Administrative Officers, Bulletin* 42 (1942): 15–16; Education Committee, Second Southern Rural Life Conference, *The School and Rural Community Living in the South* (Nashville: Southern Rural Life Council, George Peabody College for Teachers, [1947]).

12. FM, May 9, 1944; *Hustler,* Mar. 6, Apr. 10, 24, Oct. 16, 23, 1942; Dec. 3, 1945; BOT, Feb. 2, June 5–6, 1942; *Alumnus* 30 (Jan.–Feb., 1945): 5.

13. *Alumnus* 19 (Dec., 1933): 4; Henry G. Hart to Kirkland, Apr. 30, 1934, Chanc. Off., RG 3, box 2, ff "Henry G. Hart (1932–44)"; Hart to O.C. Carmichael, Dec. 22, 1941, with attached sheets, Chanc. Off., RG 3, box 2, ff "Henry G. Hart (1932–44)"; BOT, Feb. 2, 1942; Mar. 17, 1943.

14. Thomas A. Krueger, *And Promises to Keep: The Southern Conference for Human Welfare, 1938–1948* (Nashville: Vanderbilt Univ. Press 1967): 3–4, 16–24, 26, 84–92.

15. Ibid., 96–102; *Hustler,* Apr. 10, 24, May 1, 1942; Jan. 22, 1943; *Alumnus* 27 (May, 1942): 16.

16. *Hustler,* Nov. 13, 1942.

17. BOT, Mar. 17, 1943; Charlie [Charles Moss] to Jimmy [James G. Stahlman], Jan. 22, 1943, copy in CHP, ff "Student Activities—Miscellaneous, SCA and Religious Emphasis Week, 1943"; for student reactions see letters Ann Geddes Stahlman to Daddy [Stahlman], Jan. 25, 1943, and Mildred Thornton Stahlman to Daddy [Stahlman], Jan. 24, 1943, copies in "Student Activities—Miscellaneous, SCA and Religious Emphasis Week, 1943"; *Hustler,* Jan. 29, 1943.

18. Ann Geddes Stahlman to Daddy [James G. Stahlman], Jan. 25, 1943, copy in CHP, "Student Activities—Miscellaneous, SCA and Religious Emphasis Week, 1943"; Nashville *Banner,* n.d. [1943], clipping in ibid.; *Hustler,* Jan. 22, 29, Feb. 5, 1943.

19. Ann Geddes Stahlman to Daddy [James G. Stahlman], Jan. 25, 1943; Mildred Thornton Stahlman to Daddy [Stahlman], Jan. 24, 1943; Stahlman to R.C. Patterson, Apr. 19, 1945;

Charlie [Charles Moss] to Jimmy [Stahlman], Jan. 22, 1943; Stahlman to Frank C. Rand, Jan. 28, 1943; Stahlman to O.C. Carmichael, Jan. 28, 1943; Fitz Hall to Stahlman, Jan. 30, 1943, all are copies in CHP, ff "Student Activities—Miscellaneous, SCA and Religious Emphasis Week, 1943"; BOT, Feb. 1, 1943; *Hustler,* Feb. 5, 1943.

20. BOT, Mar. 17, 1943; *Hustler,* Jan. 22, 1943.

21. BOT, June 4, 1943; Charles E. Crouch and H.C. Nixon to O.C. Carmichael, May 31, 1944; Carmichael to Henry G. Hart, June 15, 1944; Helene B. Hart to Carmichael, Aug. 31, 1944, in Chanc. Off., RG 3, box 2, ff "Henry G. Hart (1932–44)."

22. *Alumnus* 20 (Mar., 1935), 4; 22 (Dec. 1936): 1–3; 23 (Dec., 1937): 6–7; 25 (Apr., 1940): 8; 27 (Dec., 1941): 8–9; 28 (Nov., 1942): 7–8; BOT, Jan. 9, Feb. 4, 1935; June 4, 1943.

23. BOT, Feb. 3, 1936; Feb. 5, June 10, Sept. 10, 1940; Feb. 3, Oct. 24, 1941.

24. O.C. Carmichael, "Adventures in Education" (typescript, copy in SC), 151; *Alumnus* 27 (May, 1943): 3; 29 (Apr.–May, 1944): 8; FM, Jan. 11, 1944.

25. BOT, Feb. 7, 1944; FM, Feb. 29, 1944.

26. FM, Oct. 10, 26, Nov. 6, Dec. 12, 1944; O.C. Carmichael to Frank C. Rand, Oct. 31, 1944, Chanc. Off., RG 3, box 4 (BOT) ff "Rand, F.C."

27. F.C. Rand to Edwin Mims, Oct. 27, 1944, Chanc. Off., ff "Rand, F.C."; BOT, Dec. 11, 1944; Feb. 5, 1945; FM, Dec. 12, 1944; *Alumnus* 31 (Dec., 1945): 5.

28. BOT, Feb. 8, 1946; Fitzgerald Hall to Chancellor Carmichael, Feb. 6, 1945; Alex Guerry to Hall, Mar. 12, 1945; Hall to Guerry, Mar. 14, 1945; Hall to the President of the Board of Trust, the Chancellor, and the Members of the Board of Trust of Vanderbilt University, Mar. 24, 1945, all in Chanc. Off., RG 3, box 2 (BOT), ff "Fitzgerald Hall."

29. Fitzgerald Hall to the President of the Board of Trust, the Chancellor, and the Members of the Board of Trust of Vanderbilt University, Mar. 24, 1945; A.B. Benedict to Hall, Mar. 25, 1945; J.E. Chappell to O.C. Carmichael, Mar. 26, 1945; F.C. Rand to Carmichael, Mar. 30, 1945; Hall to A.B. Benedict, Apr. 14, 1945; Hall to Carmichael, May 21, 1945, in Chanc. Off., RG 3, box 2 (BOT), ff "Fitzgerald Hall."

30. *Alumnus* 30 (Sept., 1945): 1; BOT, Feb. 4, 1946.

31. *Alumnus* 30 (Dec. 1944): 3–4; 30 (Apr.–May, 1945): 4; 31 (June, 1946): 1–2, 8; BOT, Feb. 4, Apr. 23, 1946.

32. *Alumnus* 31 (June, 1946): 9; BOT, June 2, 1944; June 7, 1946.

33. BOT, Feb. 4, June 7, 1946; Feb. 3, 1947.

34. BOT, Feb. 4, June 7, 1946; Feb. 3, June 6, 1947; *Alumnus* 31 (Jan.–Feb., 1946): 12–13.

35. *Alumnus* 31 (Mar., 1946): 1–6; 31 (Sept., 1946): 9–12; BOT, Feb. 7, 1944; Feb. 4, June 7, 1946; Feb. 3, 1947.

36. BOT, Feb. 4, June 7, 1946; Feb. 3, May 6, June 6, 1947.

37. O.C. Carmichael, "Adventures," 156–58; Carmichael to Frank C. Rand, Aug. 4, 11, 1945, Chanc. Off., RG 3, box 4 (BOT), ff "Rand, F.C."; BOT, Oct. 19, 1945.

38. BOT, Oct. 19, 1945; James G. Stahlman to George A. Sloan, May 31, 1946, copy in CHP, ff "Admin.—Chanc. Branscomb—(Selection of)"; Robert L. Garner, *This Is The Way It Was with Robert L. Garner* (Chevy Chase, Md.: n.p., Dec., 1972), 178.

39. James G. Stahlman to Robert L. Garner, Dec. 19, 1945; Stahlman to George A. Sloan, May 31, 1946, copies in CHP, ff "Admin.—Chanc. Branscomb—(Selection of)"; BOT, Dec. 28, 1945.

40. *Alumnus* 31 (Oct.–Nov., 1945): 1–2; C. Madison Sarratt to O.C. Carmichael, Apr. 5, 1946, Chanc. Off., box 6, ff 5.

41. James G. Stahlman to Robert L. Garner, Dec. 19, 1945, copy in CHP, "Admin.—Chanc. Branscomb—(Selection of)"; Harvie Branscomb to O.C. Carmichael, Sept. 1, 1942, Chanc. Off., RG 3, box 22, ff "Harvie Branscomb"; Harvie Branscomb, *Purely Academic: An Autobiography* (Nashville: limited ed. printed by Vanderbilt Univ., 1978), 106–107.

42. Branscomb, *Purely Academic,* 107; George A. Sloan to Jimmy [James G. Stahlman], Apr. 2, 1946, May 24, 1946; Stahlman to Sloan, May 31, 1946; memo of telephone conversation with Sloan, at Greenwich, Conn., Friday, May 31, 1946, beginning around noon, by Stahlman; V.J. Alexander to Stahlman, July 18, 1946, all copies in CHP, ff "Admin.—Chanc. Branscomb—

(Selection of)"; telegram, Harvie Branscomb to F.C. Rand, Apr. 12, 1946; Rand to C.M. Sarratt, Apr. 12, 1946, all in Chanc. Off., RG 3, box 4 (BOT), ff "Rand, F.C.''; C.M. Sarratt to O.C. Carmichael, July 9, 1946, Chanc. Off., RG 3, box 1, ff "Carnegie Foundation (1942–48)."

43. Frank C. Rand to Dean Branscomb, July 28, 1946, Chanc. Off., RG 3, box 22, ff "Harvie Branscomb"; Branscomb, *Purely Academic,* 108–109.

44. BOT, Feb. 4, 1946.

45. Branscomb, *Purely Academic,* 111–14.

17. AT THE TOP

1. Harvie Branscomb, *Purely Academic: An Autobiography* (Nashville: limited ed. printed by Vanderbilt Univ., 1978), 13, 15, 35–37, 41–46, 49, 51, 57–64, 68–75, 84–85, 87, 92–101, 103–105.

2. Ibid., 64, 86–87; Bennett Harvie Branscomb, *Jesus and the Law of Moses* (New York: Richard R. Smith, 1930); B. Harvie Branscomb, *The Gospel of Mark* (New York: Harper, n.d.).

3. BOT, Apr. 25, Dec. 30, 1952; May 1, 1953; *Major Benefactors of Vanderbilt University: A preliminary printing containing a representative selection from a more complete book now being compiled* (Nashville: Vanderbilt Univ., 1961), 34–36.

4. *Alumnus* 32 (Jan.–Feb., 1947): 5–7; BOT, Feb. 6, 1950.

5. Harvie Branscomb, "Strengthening and Enervating the Board of Trust" (n.d.), 1–2, in CHP, "Admin.—Chanc. Branscomb and the Board of Trust"; BOT, Dec. 5, 1949; Feb. 6, June 2, 1950; Branscomb, *Purely Academic,* 183–85.

6. Branscomb, "The Board of Trust," 8.

7. BOT, June 2, 1950; Branscomb, *Purely Academic,* 185–89, 196; Robert L. Garner, *This is the Way it Was with Robert L. Garner* (Chevy Chase, Md.: n.p., Dec., 1972), 182.

8. BOT, June 4, 1948; June 6, 1953; Jan. 11, 1956; May 9, 1958.

9. BOT, Apr. 13, 1948; June 8, July 17, 1951; May 6, 1955; May 4, June 13, 1956; June 17, 1959.

10. "Report of the Treasurer," *Fin. Statements* (June 30, 1946), 48; BOT, Oct. 10, 1952; May 4–5, 1962; *Alumnus* 47 (July–Aug., 1962): 5.

11. *Alumnus* 39 (Jan.–Feb., 1954): 9–11; *Hustler,* Jan. 8, 1954; *Bull.,* College of Arts and Science, 1946–48, p. 53; *Bull.,* Medicine, 1945–46, p. 41; BOT, Apr. 25, 1952.

12. Branscomb, *Purely Academic,* 199–200; BOT, Apr. 13, June 4, 1948; Dec. 15, 1949; Feb. 6, 1950; Dec. 19, 1951; Apr. 25, 1952; May 15–16, Sept. 15, 1959.

13. *Alumnus* 41 (Jan.–Feb., 1956): 2–3; 47 (July–Aug., 1962): 15; BOT, Apr. 10, 1957; Oct. 16, 1959; Oct. 7, 1960.

14. BOT, Oct. 7, 1960; Branscomb, "The Board of Trust," 15.

15. *Bull.,* College of Arts and Science, 1947–1948, p. 50; 1955–56, p. 34; 1958–59, p. 15; 1960–61, p. 15; 1962–63, p. 16; 1964–65, p. 17; BOT, June 3, 1949.

16. *Alumnus* 36 (Mar., 1951): 5; 37 (Oct.–Nov., 1951): 7; 43 (Mar.–Apr., 1958): 10; BOT, June 5, 1951; May 1, 1953.

17. Branscomb, *Purely Academic,* 193–94; BOT, May 4–5, 1962.

18. Robert A. McGaw, *The Vanderbilt Campus: A Pictorial History* (Nashville: Vanderbilt Univ. Press 1978), 82–83; BOT, June 6, Dec. 16, 1947; Nov. 4–5, 1955; Jan. 11, 1956.

19. McGaw, *Vanderbilt Campus,* 86–87, 91; *Alumnus* 39 (Mar.–Apr., 1954): 4–5; 47 (July–Aug., 1961): 4, 17; 48 (Sept.–Oct., 1962): 5; 49 (May–June, 1963): 28–29; BOT, June 25, 1952; Nov. 12, 1954; Apr. 13, 1960; May 4, 1963; *Bull.,* 1963–64, p. 476; *Vanderbilt Today* 1 (June, 1961): 3; *Hustler,* Dec. 14, 1962.

20. McGaw, *Vanderbilt Campus,* 86.

21. BOT, July 24, Oct. 10, 1952; Apr. 20, 1955; May 9, Oct. 1, 1958; Branscomb, *Purely Academic,* 123–24.

22. *Alumnus* 50 (May–June, 1965): 17–23; BOT, June 22, 1961; May 4–5, 1962.

23. Branscomb, *Purely Academic,* 111–12; BOT, June 4, 1948; May 6, Nov. 12, 1954.

24. BOT, May 4–5, Oct. 19–20, 1956; Nov. 1–2, 1957; Branscomb, *Purely Academic,* 117–18.

25. BOT, May 4–5, 1962.

26. BOT, May 4–5, 1956; May 20–21, 1960; May 5, 1961.

27. John Dale Russell, "Report of the Study of Closer Cooperation Between George Peabody College for Teachers and Vanderbilt University" (Nashville: n.p., May, 1962), 62–63, 69, 71; BOT, Apr. 25, Oct. 11, 1952; May 9, 1958.

28. Russell, "Closer Cooperation," ii, 69; Walter Stokes, Jr., to Sam M. Fleming, Feb. 10, 1961, copy in CHP, ff "Changing Status—Univ. Ctr.—Peabody, 1915–73"; Nashville *Tennessean,* May 12, 1961; Nashville *Banner,* May 11, 12, 1961.

29. Russell, "Closer Cooperation," 2–5, 12, 14–17.

30. "Comments Concerning Cooperation Vanderbilt University and George Peabody College for Teachers" [Apr. 9, 1962], Chanc. Off., RG 93, ff "Peabody—Vanderbilt Relations."

31. BOT, Feb. 2, 1948; June 3, 1949; Mar. 8, Apr. 17, 1950.

32. BOT, Feb. 2, 1948.

33. "Arts and Science Faculty Minutes, February 11, 1947," p. 1, in W.B. Jewell Papers, box 7, ff 7–2, SC; BOT, Feb. 2, Mar. 9, 1948; Jan. 19, 1949; Oct. 10, 1952; Feb. 10, 1953.

34. Chanc. Off., RG 3, box 3, ff "Salaries"; BOT, July 20, 1955; May 4, 1956; May 9, 1958; May 4–5, 1962.

35. BOT, Apr. 13, 1948; June 8, 1951.

18. In the Middle

1. *Bull.,* College of Arts and Science, Sept., 1963; *Bull.,* Graduate School, Oct., 1963.

2. BOT, Sept. 11, 1951; May 20–21, 1960; *Bull.,* College of Arts and Science, 1950–51, p. 9; 1952–53, p. 9; 1953–54, p. 15; 1955–56, p. 13.

3. A&S Dean, Annual Report, 1955–56, p. 2, submitted by E.P. Shahan, Apr. 10, 1956, RG 48, box 14, SC; FM, Feb. 1, 1952; Jan. 11, 1955, with attached sheets, Feb. 8, 1955, with attached sheets.

4. FM, Oct. 14, 1952; Jan. 13, 1953; Jan. 17, 1956, with attached "Recommendations of the Committee on the Course of Study"; Mar. 13, 1956; BOT, May 1, 1953; *Bull.,* College of Arts and Science, 1952–53, p. 66; A&S Dean, Annual Report, 1951–52, pp. 10–11, RG 48, box 2, SC; A&S Dean, Annual Report, 1952–53, p. 4, RG 48, box 14, SC; *Alumnus* 45 (Nov.–Dec., 1960): 13; *Hustler,* Sept. 18, 1959.

5. FM, Jan. 17, 1956, with attached "Recommendations of the Committee on the Course of Study"; Feb. 4, 18, 24, Mar. 4, with "A Proposal from the Educational Policy Committee for a Coordinated Program in Liberal Studies as Revised by the Faculty Council"; Apr. 8, 15, 29, May 6, 20, 1958; BOT, May 3, 1957.

6. A&S Dean, Annual Report, 1956–57, pp. 2–3, submitted by E.P. Shahan, Apr. 1957, RG 48; BOT, May 1, 1953; June 9, 1954; May 4, 1956; Harvie Branscomb, *Purely Academic: An Autobiography* (Nashville: limited ed. printed by Vanderbilt Univ., 1978), 138–39.

7. Branscomb, *Purely Academic,* 135–37; BOT, June 6, July 29, 1947; June 3, 1949.

8. Branscomb, *Purely Academic,* 118–19, 133–35.

9. For Graduate School enrollments and satistics on Ph.D.s and M.A.s awarded see Chancellor's Reports in BOT, May 1, 1953; May 20–21, 1960.

10. "University Press, Vanderbilt Planning Study, 1963–64," Chanc. Off.; BOT, May 6, 1955; May 15–16, Oct. 16–17, 1959.

11. For faculty publications see Chancellor's Reports in BOT, and books advertised and reviewed in the *Alumnus.*

12. BOT, May 28, June 4, 1948; June 20, 1949; May 9, 1958.

13. BOT, June 3, 1949; June 5, 1951; Apr. 25, 1952; May 6, 1954; July 6, 1962; *Bull.* College of Arts and Science, 1954–55, pp. 17–18; 1962, p. 123.

14. BOT, Apr. 25, 1952; June 22, 1961; Apr. 10, May 4–5, 1962; *Alumnus* 45 (May–June, 1960): 11; *Bull.*, College of Arts and Science, 1962, p. 111.

15. *Alumnus* 42 (Jan.–Feb., 1957): 5; *Bull.*, College of Arts and Science, 1956–57, pp. 19–20.

16. BOT, Apr. 25, 1952; May 6, 1955; May 9, 1958; *Bull.*, College of Arts and Science, 1956–57, p. 20; *Alumnus* 45 (Nov.–Dec., 1959): 6; Don D. Moore, "Walter Clyde Curry's Last Lecture," CHP, ff "Happy History—Personal Reminiscences."

17. *Bull.*, College of Arts and Science, 1956–57, pp. 118–20; BOT, Feb. 6, 1950; Branscomb, *Purely Academic,* 137.

18. BOT, June 3, 1949; Apr. 25, 1952; May 3, 1957; May 15–16, 1959; *Bull.*, School of Engineering, 1955–56, pp. 49–53; 1958, p. 37.

19. BOT, Jan. 9, May 20–21, 1960; May 5, 1961; May 4–5, 1962; May 3–4, 1963; *Bull.*, School of Engineering, 1961–62, pp. 10–11; *Alumnus* 45–46 (Nov.–Dec., 1960): 13.

20. BOT, June 6, 1947; June 3, 1949; June 2, 1950; Apr. 25, 1952; May 3, 1957; *Alumnus* 41 (Jan.–Feb., 1956): 3; *Bull.*, School of Law, 1960–61, pp. 10–12; Branscomb, *Purely Academic,* 173–75.

21. BOT, June 3, 1949; May 6, 1954; Apr. 10, 1957; May 9, 1958; May 15–16, 1959; May 20–21, 1960; *Alumnus* 47 (May–June, 1962): 6; Branscomb, *Purely Academic,* 173–76.

22. Branscomb, *Purely Academic,* 177.

23. Ibid.; BOT, June 6, 1947; Feb. 7, 1949; May 6, 1954.

24. BOT, Feb. 7, June 3, 1949; Timothy C. Jacobson, "Medical Center: A History of Science in Medicine" (unpublished MS in SC [1982]), 412–20; Branscomb, *Purely Academic,* 177–78.

25. Jacobson, "Medical Center," 421; BOT, Feb. 3, 1947; Feb. 2, June 4, 1948; Feb. 7, June 3, 1949; Branscomb, *Purely Academic,* 178–80.

26. *Alumnus* 34 (Sept., 1949): 10–11, 17; BOT, June 4, 1949; June 3, 1949; Jan. 30, Oct. 10, 1952; May 1, Oct. 23, 1953; Nov. 12, 1954; Jacobson, "Medical Center," 429–30; Branscomb, *Purely Academic,* 177–79.

27. BOT, Nov. 4, 1955; Mar. 20, May 3, 1957; Nov. 24, 1959; *Alumnus* 43 (July–Aug., 1958): 4.

28. BOT, June 4, 1948; Feb. 6, 1950; Feb. 5, June 8, Oct. 9, 27, 1951; Apr. 25, 1952.

29. *Alumnus* 43 (July–Aug., 1958): 41; BOT, Oct. 16–17, 1959; Oct. 7, 1960; May 5, 1961.

30. BOT, May 15–16, 1959; Mar. 24, 1961; July 6, 1962; William J. Darby to John B. Youmans, June 27, 1957, Chanc. Off., RG 3, box 86, ff "John W. Patterson, Dean School of Medicine, 1958–61 (Faculty and Staff Material)"; Darby to Patterson, Jan. 9, 1961, Chanc. Off., box 86, ff "John W. Patterson—Executive Faculty Agenda, Minutes, etc., 1961–62."

31. "Confidential Memorandum with Reference to the Current Difficulties in the School of Medicine," Office of the Chancellor to John W. Patterson, Mar. 5, 1962, Chanc. Off., RG 3, box 86, ff "John W. Patterson, Dean School of Medicine, 1962–"; Patterson to Harvie Branscomb, Feb. 17, 1962; Patterson to Amos Christie, Feb. 14, 1962, all in Chanc. Off., RG 3, box 86, ff "John W. Patterson, Dean School of Medicine, 1961–"; "Suggested Rules of Procedure for the School of Medicine, Vanderbilt University"; ballots in regard to the "Suggested Rules of Procedure"; Patterson to Branscomb, Feb. 2, 1962; and Patterson-Noyes correspondence, all in Chanc. Off., RG 3, ff "John W. Patterson—Executive Faculty Agenda, Minutes, etc., 1961–62"; BOT, Mar. 15, Apr. 10, May 4–5, 1962; Feb. 8–9, 1963.

32. BOT, June 6, 1947; June 3, 1949; June 2, 1950; May 6, 1954; July 6, 1962.

33. BOT, Nov. 5, 1954.

34. BOT, Sept. 13, 1954; May 5, 1961; Feb. 8–9, 1963.

35. *Bull.*, School of Religion, Feb. 15, 1948, p. 5; BOT, Apr. 25, 1952; Nov. 4, 1955; May 3, 1957; Jan. 11, 1958.

36. Branscomb, *Purely Academic,* 170–73; BOT, Oct. 19–20, 1956; May 20–21, 1960; *Alumnus* 42 (Sept.–Oct., 1956): 6.

37. BOT, Jan. 18, 1957; Oct. 1, 1958; June 17, 1959; *Alumnus* 42 (Jan.–Feb., 1957): 5.

38. BOT, Nov. 24, 1959; *Bull.*, Divinity School, 1961–62, p. 39.

39. BOT, Feb. 6, 1950.

40. BOT, June 8, 1951; *Alumnus* 36 (Mar., 1951): 2–4; Five faculty members to Branscomb, Mar. 7, 1951 [cover letter dated Mar. 15, 1951], Chanc. Off., RG 3, box 42, ff "College A&S Faculty, Donald Davidson"; Nashville *Tennessean*, Feb. 18, 1951.

41. BOT, June 8, 1951; Nashville *Tennessean*, Feb. 19, 1951; copies of New York *Times* and Nashville *Banner* editorials in Chanc. Off., box 118, ff "Subversive Control Bill, J. Frank Taylor, 1951–52."

42. BOT, May 1, 1953.

43. John Keith Benton to Harvie Branscomb, June 15, 1949; Benton to Nels F.S. Ferre, Dec. 9, 1949, Chanc. Off. box 55, ff "Nels Ferre—Controversy, 1949–56"; BOT, June 20, 1949.

44. Nels Frederick Solomon Ferre, *The Christian Understanding of God* (New York: Harper, 1951); *The Sun and the Umbrella* (New York: Harper and Row, 1953).

45. *Christian Century*, Aug. 24, 1955, and *Michigan Chr. Adv.*, Sept. 1, 1955, copies in Chanc. Off., RG 3, box 55, ff "Nels Ferre—Controversy, 1949–56"; for hostile letters and pamphlets regarding Ferre see Chanc. Off., RG 3, box 55, ff "Ferre Controversy, 1953–56."

46. Harvie Branscomb to J.C. Roberts, Feb. 24, 1954; Branscomb to Vance Alexander, Sept. 12, 1955; M.G. Lowman to Branscomb, June 27, 1956; Daniel M. Lyons to Branscomb, Mar. 18, 1954; copies of letters to Alexander, all in Chanc. Off., RG 3, box 55, ff "Nels Ferre—Controversy, 1949–56"; see also letters Alexander to Branscomb, RG 3, box 55, ff "Ferre Controversy, 1953–56."

47. Harvie Branscomb to F.W. Foote, Dec. 22, 1955; Branscomb to Vance Alexander, Sept. 12, 1955; letters from Branscomb to Ferre's critics, all in Chanc. Off., RG 3, box 55, ff "Nels Ferre Controversy 1949–56"; Branscomb to Horace H. Hull, Mar. 6, 1954, RG 3, box 55, ff "Ferre Controversy, 1953–56."

48. Harvie Branscomb to Nels Ferre, May 22, Oct. 10, 27, 1956; Toru Yamazuki to Ferre, n.d. [1956]; Ferre to Dean Benton, May 19, 1956; Ferre to Branscomb, Aug. 15, Oct. 13, Dec. 7, 1956; J.K. Benton Memorandum, May 16, 1956; Memorandum on conference between the Chancellor, Dean Benton, and Professor Ferre, May 16, 1956, all in Chanc. Off. RG 3, box 55, ff "Nels Ferre, 1955–56"; Branscomb to V.J. Alexander, Oct. 8, 1956, Chanc. Off., RG 3, box 101, ff "Race Relations (2), Non-Admission of Negroes to Law School, Fall 1956."

49. Harvie Branscomb to Vance J. Alexander, Dec. 23, 1953, Chanc. Off., RG 3, box 55, ff "Ferre Controversy, 1953–56"; John K. Maddin to Branscomb Feb. 3, 1953; Norman L. Parks to Branscomb, June 28, Aug. 6, 1951; Branscomb to Parks, July 9, 1951; Branscomb to E.B. Norton, May 13, 1952, all in Chanc. Off., RG 3, box 96, ff "Norman L. Parks, 1951–52."

50. William C. O'Brien to Harvie Branscomb, May 18, 1955; Branscomb to O'Brien, June 2, 1955; D.F. Fleming to Branscomb, Mar. 20, 1954, May 27, 1955; Vanderbilt University Inter-Office Correspondence, July 9, 1957, Chanc. Off., RG 3, box 56, ff "D.F. Fleming, 1957–62."

51. Ewing P. Shahan to Harvie Branscomb, Oct. 23, 1957; Branscomb to D.F. Fleming, Nov. 12, 1957; articles by Fulton J. Lewis; Fleming to Branscomb, July 7, 1959, Sept. 30, Dec. 7, 1960; R.R. Purdy to Fleming, Jan. 6, 1961, in Chanc. Off., RG 3, box 56, ff "D.F. Fleming, 1957–62."

52. L. Roy North to Harvie Branscomb, Mar. 30, 1962; Branscomb to L. Roy North, Apr. 5, 1962; to Crawford Wheeler, Mar. 30, 1962 with attached note from Wheeler and reviews of Fleming's book; to Herbert Sanborn, Feb. 21, 1962; to Mrs. Mary Low Weaver, June 11, 1962; reprint copy of "Academic Freedom and Tenure: The University of South Florida," from *AAUP Bulletin*, Spring, 1964, pp. 47–48; copy *News and Views*, May, 1962, all in Chanc. Off., RG 3, box 56, ff "D.F. Fleming, 1957–62."

53. Copy of *Bulletin: The Florida Coalition of Patriotic Societies*, July 2, 1962; Sam B. Smith to Harvie Branscomb, Aug. 6, 1962; reprint copy of "Academic Freedom and Tenure," all in Chanc. Off., RG 3, box 56, "D.F. Fleming, 1957–62."

54. D.F. Fleming to Alexander Heard, Dec. 13, 1963; to Harvie Branscomb, Dec. 10, 1963, Chanc. Off., RG 3, box 56, ff "Fleming, D.F., 1963–69."

55. Rob Roy Purdy to Harvie Branscomb, Aug. 17, 1961, Chanc. Off., RG 3, box 99, ff "Purdy, Rob Roy, Vice-Chancellor."

56. BOT, May 15–16, 1959.

19. ON THE BOTTOM

1. Harvie Branscomb, *Purely Academic: An Autobiography* (Nashville: limited ed. printed by Vanderbilt Univ., 1978), 127–28; BOT, June 8, 1958; May 5, 1961; *Bull.*, College of Arts and Science, 1955–1956, p. 277; *Bull.*, Graduate School, 1955–1956, pp. 32–34.

2. FM, Mar 2, 1955, appended report by Dean of Women, "Vanderbilt University Women's Scholarship Averages, 1953–1954"; *Bull.*, For Vanderbilt Coeds, 1946–1947; *Hustler*, Sept. 26, Oct. 3, 1958; Feb. 17, 1961; Mar. 8, 1963.

3. BOT, Oct. 27, 1951.

4. *Hustler*, Jan. 8, 1954.

5. *Hustler*, Jan. 6, 13, 1961.

6. Ibid., Mar. 30, Apr. 13, 1951; *Alumnus* 36 (Apr.–May, 1951): 2–3.

7. *Hustler*, Oct. 9, 16, 23, 30, 1959; Oct. 28, Nov. 4, 1960; Oct. 13, 1961.

8. Ibid., Apr. 8, Nov. 4, 1960; Sept. 16, 1961; Nov. 2, 1962.

9. Ibid., Dec. 1, 1950; Jan. 28, 1955; Jan. 12, Mar. 3, 1961; Deposition of Robert A. McGaw, Nov. 7, 1955, in the Circuit Court of Davidson County, Tenn., Robert L. Langford, Plaintiff vs. The Vanderbilt University, et al., Defendants, pp. 69–79, Chanc. Off., RG 3, box 132, ff "Complaint—Langford et al. 1956."

10. Plaintiff's Bill of Exceptions, in the Circuit Court of Davidson County, Tenn., Robert L. Langford, Plaintiff vs. The Vanderbilt University, et al., Defendants," pp. 4–5, 20–22, 28–29, Chanc. Off., RG 3, box 132, ff "Complaint—Langford et al. 1956"; *Hustler*, Sept. 24, Dec. 3, 1954.

11. *Hustler*, Jan. 28, Feb. 4, May 6, 1955; Plaintiff's Bill of Exceptions, p. 26.

12. See depositions of Dr. Harvie Branscomb and Robert A. McGaw in Chanc. Off., RG 3, box 132, ff "Complaint—Langford et al. 1956"; *Hustler*, Feb. 10, 1956; Sept. 19, 1958; *Alumnus* 42 (Sept.–Oct., 1956): 6–7.

13. *Alumnus* 34 (Oct.–Nov., 1948): 10–11, 14; 37 (Mar., 1952): 10–11.

14. Ibid. 35 (Mar., 1950): 6–8; *Hustler*, Apr. 11, 12, 1958.

15. *Hustler*, May 2, Oct. 3, 1958.

16. *Alumnus* 35 (Mar., 1950): 8–9.

17. Ibid., 34 (Dec., 1948): 7; *Hustler*, Oct. 23, 29, 1948; Oct. 3, 1952; Oct. 28, 1960; May 17, 1963.

18. *Alumnus* 35 (Jan.–Feb., 1950): 11–12; 35 (Mar., 1951): 6–7; 38 (Jan.–Feb., 1953): 5–6; 42 (Nov.–Dec., 1956): 5;42 (Jan.–Feb., 1957): 5; 45–46 (May–June, 1961): 6–7; 47 (July–Aug., 1961): 5; *Commodore* n.v. (1948): 178; n.v. (1949): 223–24; 65 (1950): 224–27; *Vanderbilt Commodores*, 1974–75, pp. 58, 68–69, 80–86, and *Vanderbilt Basketball Guide*, 1969–70, p. 15, in RG 25, SC.

19. *Hustler*, Oct. 10, 1947; Oct. 8, Dec. 3, 10, 1948; Dec. 1, 1961; *Alumnus* 37 (Dec., 1951): 7, 10–11; 38 (Jan.–Feb., 1953): 12; 38 (Mar.–Apr., 1953): 4–5; 41 (Jan.–Feb., 1956): 6; 47 (Mar.–Apr., 1962): 6–7.

20. Clarence P. Houston to Harvie Branscomb, Oct. 14, 1949; to Fred Lewis, Mar. 9, 1950; Lewis to Clarence P. Houston, Mar. 16, 1950, all in Chanc. Off., RG 3, box 18, ff "NCAA, 1945–1957"; Branscomb to Blake Van Leer, Mar. 10, 1951, Chanc. Off., RG 3, box 18, ff "Southeastern Conference 1941–59"; BOT, Oct. 27, 1951.

21. BOT, Feb. 5, Oct. 27, 1951.

22. Harvie Branscomb to Fred T. Mitchell, Oct. 10, 1951; to Rufus Harris, Nov. 20, 1951; Mitchell to Branscomb, Oct. 8, 1951; "Vanderbilt University proposes the following changes in the By-Laws of the Southeastern Conference" (n.d.); "Proposed Amendments to Southeastern Conference By-Laws," Nov. 21, 1951; "Meeting of Institutions of the Southeastern Confer-

ence" (n.d.); "Report of Committee on Limitation of Scholarships in Southeastern Conference" (n.d.), all in Chanc. Off., RG 3, box 18, ff "Southeastern Conference, 1941–1959"; *Alumnus* 37 (Oct.–Nov., 1951): 6; 37 (Dec., 1951): 6; Branscomb, *Purely Academic*, 150–51; reprint of Branscomb's "Intercollegiate Athletics in the Southern Association," *The Southern Association of Colleges and Secondary Schools*, Dec. 1952, in Chanc. Off., RG 3, box 18.

23. BOT, Apr. 25, 1952.

24. BOT, May 3, 1957, May 4, 19, 1962; FM, Apr. 30, 1957; Branscomb, *Purely Academic*, 151.

25. Branscomb, *Purely Academic*, 144–45.

26. BOT, Oct. 27, 1951; Apr. 25, 1952; May 6, 1958; Branscomb, *Purely Academic*, 145; *Hustler*, Nov. 14, 1952; *Alumnus* 37 (Apr.–May, 1952): 16–17.

27. *Alumnus* 40 (Mar.–Apr., 1955): 3–5; *Hustler*, Feb. 25, Mar. 4, Apr. 29, 1955; FM, Feb. 17, with appended "Report from the Faculty Committee Reviewing the Vanderbilt Fraternity System"; Mar. 2, with appended "Panhellenic Council and Interfraternity Report as Requested by Chancellor Branscomb" and "Report of Alumni Fraternity Counselling Committee," Mar. 9, 1955.

28. *Hustler*, Oct. 4, 11, 1957; BOT, May 3, 1957; Oct. 24–25, 1958; Mar. 10, May 15–16, 1959.

29. BOT, Mar. 10, Apr. 10, May 15–16, 1959; "Vanderbilt University Report and Recommendations on Fraternity-Sorority Policy," Apr., 1959, Chanc. Off., RG 3, box 61, ff "Fraternity Housing—Spring of 1959 (Important Documents)"; Supplement to *Alumnus*, May–June, 1959, Chanc. Off., RG 3, box 61, ff "Fraternities—Spring of 1959 (newspaper)"; *Hustler*, Apr. 17, 24, May 1, 8, 1959.

30. *Hustler*, Apr. 17, 24, May 1, 8, 15, Oct. 23, 1959; BOT, May 15–16, Oct. 16–17, 1959; for hostile alumni letters see Chanc. Off., RG 3, box 61, ff "Fraternities 1959 (Letters favoring present fraternity plan)"; *Alumnus* 47 (Nov.–Dec., 1961): 5; Branscomb, *Purely Academic*, 146–47.

31. *Hustler*, Mar. 6, 1959; J.G. Baker version of the Kirkland Tower Ghost, 1960, and Samuel F. Babbitt to Horace Kemp, May 25, 1959, CHP, ff "Happy History—J.G. Baker Tape and Documents—The Ghost of Kirkland Hall."

32. *Alumnus* 37 (June, 1952): 7–8; clippings from the Nashville *Banner*, May 19, 1952, and Nashville *Tennessean*, n.d. Dean for Student Life, RG 20, box 14, ff "Student Disturbances 1957–64," SC; Report from Miss Jameson (by telephone) concerning disturbances in Women's Dormitories Sunday night, May 18, dated May 18, 1952, CHP, ff "Student Disorders."

33. *Hustler*, Jan. 8, 21, 1954.

34. Ibid., Dec. 6, 13, 1957; Jan. 10, 17, 1958; Frederick B. Rentschler to Henry Lee Swint, Aug. 30, 1972, CHP, ff "Happy History, 1950–1969"; Madison Sarratt to Harold Bold, Dec. 23, 1957, Chanc. Off., RG 3, box 14, ff "Student Act.—Disorders"; Memorandum, Nora C. Chaffin to Harvie Branscomb, Nov. 29, 1957; Felix C. Robb to Samuel Babbitt, Dec. 2, 1952; Branscomb to Babbitt, Dec. 17, 1957; Chaffin to Babbitt, Feb. 17, 1958, Chanc. Off., RG 20, box 14, ff "Student Disturbances, 1957–64"; Nashville *Tennessean*, Nov. 27, 1957; Nashville *Banner*, Nov. 27, 1957; BOT Jan. 11, 1958.

35. *Hustler*, Jan. 21, 1954; Nov. 6, 1959; Mar. 1, 1963; Memorandum, Walter Parry to Sydney F. Boutell, Apr. 9, 1963, Chanc. Off., RG 20, box 14, ff "Student Disturbances, 1957–64".

36. *Hustler*, Oct. 21, 1960; Feb. 16, 1962; *Alumnus* 45-46 (Nov.–Dec., 1961): 12–13.

37. *Hustler*, Feb. 8, 1957; Apr. 21, May 12, 1961.

20. The Unwanted

1. Harvard Sitkoff, *The Struggle for Black Equality, 1954–1980* (New York: Hill and Wang, 1981), 19–20.

2. Harvie Branscomb, *Purely Academic: An Autobiography* (Nashville: limited ed. printed by Vanderbilt Univ., 1978), 153; Harvie Branscomb to Jonathan Daniels, Sept. 3, 1948, Chanc. Off., RG 3, box 101, ff "Race Relations, 1948–1955."

3. S.M. McMurray to Harvie Branscomb, Nov. 15, 1948; Branscomb to McMurray, Nov. 20, 1948, Chanc. Off., RG 3, box 101, ff "Race Relations, 1948–1955."

4. BOT, Feb. 2, 1948; Feb. 6, 1950; Branscomb, *Purely Academic,* 154.

5. BOT, June 20, 1949; Harvie Branscomb to C.A. Craig, Oct. 17, 1949; Robert E. Williams, Jr., to [Vanderbilt University], May 25, 1949; Cecil Sims to Branscomb, June 15, 1949, all in Chanc. Off., RG 3, box 101, ff "Race Relations, 1949–1955."

6. Branscomb, *Purely Academic,* 154–55; BOT, Oct. 10, 1952.

7. Nashville *Tennessean,* Feb. 13, 1953; Harvie Branscomb to Silliman Evans, Feb. 14, 16, 1953; Branscomb, "Statement released for publication to the Nashville *Banner* on February 13, 1953"; Nelson Fuson to Branscomb, Mar. 6, 1953, all in Chanc. Off., RG 3, box 101, ff "Race Issue—Tennessee newsstories, 1953–54"; Donald Davidson to Branscomb, May 3, 1953, Chanc. Off., RG 3, box 101, ff "Race Relations, 1949–1955."

8. BOT, May 1, 1953; Branscomb, *Purely Academic,* 153–56; Harvie Branscomb to James Pike, Mar. 16, 1953, Chanc. Off., RG 3, box 101, ff "Race Issue—Tennessee newsstories, 1953–54."

9. Sitkoff, *Black Equality,* 21–32; telegram, Frank G. Clement to Harvie Branscomb, Jan. 23, 1956; Branscomb to Clement, Jan. 26, 1956, Chanc. Off., RG 3, box 101, ff "Race Relations Issue (3)—General—1948–1957."

10. Harvie Branscomb to James A. Simpson, Sept. 17, 1954, Chanc. Off., RG 3, box 101, ff "Race Relations, 1948–1955"; newspaper clippings, n.d.; Branscomb to John T. Mendes, Mar. 12, 1956, both in Chanc. Off., RG 3, box 101, ff "Race Relations Issue (3)—General—1948–1957."

11. Branscomb, *Purely Academic,* 158; BOT, May 6, 1955; Sept. 28, 1956; letters, Branscomb to his critics, Chanc. Off., RG 3, box 101, ff "Race Relations Issue (2), Con—Admission of Negroes to Law School, Fall of 1956"; letters in support to Branscomb, Chanc. Off., RG 3, box 101, ff "Race Relations Issue (1), Pro—Admission of Negroes to Law School, Fall of 1956–1957."

12. V.J. Alexander to Harvie Branscomb, Sept. 28, 1956; "Independent Association of Alumni and Friends," Oct. 7, 1956, Chanc. Off., RG 3, box 101, ff "Race Relations Issue (2), Con—Admission of Negroes to Law School, Fall of 1956"; Vernon Sharp to Judge William H. Swiggart, Oct. 16, 1956, Chanc. Off., RG 3, box 101, ff "Race Relations Issue (3)—General—1948–1957"; *Alumnus* 42 (Nov.–Dec., 1956): 12–15; Branscomb, *Purely Academic,* 115–59.

13. For Branscomb's replies to letters concerning the Law School see esp. Branscomb to Dr. Mayhew W. Dodson, Oct. 29, 1956, Chanc. Off., RG 3, box 101, ff "Race Relations Issue (1), Pro—Admission of Negroes to Law School, Fall of 1956–1957"; to V.J. Alexander, Oct. 3, 8, 1956; to R.C. Crumbaugh, Oct. 17, 1956, Chanc. Off., RG 3, box 101, "Race Relations Issue (2), Con—Admission of Negroes to Law School, Fall of 1956."

14. Harvie Branscomb to C.C. Bankston, Jr., Jan. 30, 1957, Chanc. Off., RG 3, box 101, ff "Race Relations Issue (2), Con—Admission of Negroes to Law School, Fall of 1956"; William H. Nicholls to James Maina, Nov. 12, 1959; Branscomb to S. Walter Martin, Mar. 10, 1961, Chanc. Off., RG 3, box 101, ff "Race Relations, 1955–1963"; "Suggested Statement of Purposes," Mar., 1956; Hugh J. Morgan to Branscomb, Mar. 12, 1956; [Branscomb] to Morgan, Mar. 15, 1956, Chanc. Off., RG 3, box 101, ff "Race Relations Issue (3)—General—1948–1957."

15. See letters to Branscomb in Chanc. Off., RG 3, box 101, ff "Race Relations Issue (2), Con—Admission of Negroes to Law School, Fall of 1956."

16. James M. Lawson, Jr., application to Divinity School, May 19, 1958, and James M. Lawson, Jr., to Director of Admissions, Vanderbilt University, May 22, 1958, in Chanc. Off., box 76, ff "Lawson Case—Miscellaneous (Part II), Chancellor's Statements."

17. Ibid.; Court Records—Statement of Lawson conviction for violation of selective service

act; Frank Loveland, U.S. Dept. of Justice, to Harvie Branscomb, May 15, 1960, all in Chanc. Off., RG 3, box 101, ff "Lawson Case—Miscellaneous (Part II), Chancellor's Statements."

18. Arthur L. Foster's chronology of the Lawson Case, Dean of Divinity School, RG 73, box 12, ff "Lawson Case: Foster Document," pp. 1–2, hereinafter cited as "Foster Document."

19. Newsclipping from Nashville *Banner,* Mar. 1, 1960, Secretary of the University, RG 5, box 24, ff 7, "Lawson Case—Newspaper Clippings," SC; *Wesley Notes,* Mar. 7, 1960, Chanc. Off., RG 3, box 76, ff "Lawson Case—Miscellaneous (Part I) (Resolutions, etc.)."

20. Newsclippings from the Nashville *Banner,* Mar. 1, 2, 1960; Nashville *Tennessean,* Mar. 1, 1960, Chanc. Off., RG 3, box 76, ff "Lawson Case—Miscellaneous (Part III), Newspaper Clippings, etc."; Nashville *Banner,* Mar. 3, 1960, Secretary of the University, RG 5, box 24, ff 7, "Lawson Case—Newspaper Clippings."

21. "Foster Document," 3–5; newsclipping Nashville *Banner,* Mar. 1, 1960, Secretary of the University, RG 5, box 24, ff "Lawson Case—Newspaper Clippings."

22. J.M. Lawson, Jr., "Personal Statement, May 26, 1960," copy in CHP, ff "Divinity School—Students—Lawson Important Papers—Chanc.'s Files—Kirkland Hall."

23. Branscomb, *Purely Academic,* 161; Harvie Branscomb, "The Lawson Episode—Twenty Years Later," Nov. 15, 1980, Branscomb Papers, box 4, ff 34, "Branscomb-Vanderbilt University Lawson Affair," SC.

24. Branscomb, "The Lawson Episode—Twenty Years Later"; copy of letter, Harvie Branscomb to James W. Armsey, June 20, 1960, CHP, ff "Divinity School—Students—Lawson Important Papers—Chanc.'s Files."

25. Branscomb, "The Lawson Episode—Twenty Years Later"; "Foster Document," 5; BOT, Mar. 2, 1960; copy of memorandum, Robert McGaw to Branscomb, Aug. 26, 1960, CHP, ff "Divinity School—Students—Lawson Important Papers—Chanc.'s Files"; *Hustler,* Mar. 4, 1960.

26. Branscomb, *Purely Academic,* 161; Branscomb, "The Lawson Episode—Twenty Years Later"; Lawson, "Personal Statement, May 26, 1960," CHP, ff "Divinity School—Students—Lawson Important Papers—Chanc.'s Files—Kirkland Hall."

27. "Foster Document," 5, 7, 31–34; James E. Sellers to Mr. Frey, Feb. 16,1961, Dean of Divinity School, RG 73, box 12, ff "Lawson Case: Defense Fund," SC.

28. Branscomb, *Purely Academic,* 161–62; "Foster Document," 7–8; BOT, Mar. 2, 1960; *Hustler,* Mar. 4, 1960.

29. "Foster Document," 5, 8–9; Members of Divinity School to Bob [Robert Nelson], Mar. 2, 1960, Dean of Divinity School, RG 73, box 12, ff "Lawson Case: Documents Issued by Faculty, etc."; mimeograph of "The University's first public announcement," Mar. 3, 1960, Secretary of the University, RG 5, box 24, ff "Lawson Case—Statement of Vanderbilt University to American Association of Theological Schools," SC; Office of the Chancellor to Messrs. Purdy, Stambaugh, and McGaw, Sept. 6, 1960, Branscomb Papers, box 4, ff 34, "Branscomb—Vanderbilt University, Lawson Affair."

30. *Wesley Notes,* Mar. 7, 1960, Chanc. Off., RG 3, box 76, ff "Lawson Case—Miscellaneous (Part I) (Resolutions, etc.)"; see newsclippings, Chanc. Off., RG 3, box 76, ff "Lawson Case—Miscellaneous (Part III) Newspaper Clippings, etc."; see Dean of Divinity School, RG 73, box 12, ff "Lawson Case: Defense Fund"; "Foster Document," 14, 16, 27.

31. *Hustler,* Mar. 11, 1960; *Wesley Notes,* Mar. 7, 1960, Chanc. Off., RG 3, box 76, ff "Lawson Case—Miscellaneous (Part I) (Resolutions, etc.)"; "Foster Document," 15, 17; "This statement was made by Chancellor Harvie Branscomb of Vanderbilt University at the Arts and Science Faculty meeting on Tuesday, March 8, 1960," Chanc. Off., ff "Lawson Case—Miscellaneous (Part II)."

32. *Hustler,* Mar. 11, 1960; Leonard Beach, et al., "Recommendation of the Beach Committee," June 1, 1960, Branscomb Papers, box 4, ff 34 "Branscomb—Vanderbilt University, Lawson Affair."

33. *Hustler,* Mar. 25, 1960.

34. The Faculty of the Divinity School to the Vanderbilt Senate, Mar. 11, 1960, Dean of Divinity School, RG 73, box 12, ff "Lawson Case: Documents Issued by Faculty, etc.," SC; copy

of letter Harold S. Vanderbilt to Robert Nelson, Mar. 17, 1960, Secretary of the University, RG 5, box 24, ff "Lawson Case—Statement of Vanderbilt University to American Association of Theological Schools"; "Foster Document," 20–22; Nashville *Tennessean,* Mar. 23, 1960, Chanc. Off., RG 3, box 76, ff "Lawson Case—Miscellaneous (Part III) Newspaper clippings, etc."

35. "Foster Document," 24–27, 34–35.

36. Ibid., pp. 28–31, 33; copy of letter J. Robert Nelson to Harvie Branscomb, Mar. 23, 1960, CHP, ff "Divinity School—Students—Lawson Info. from Chanc.'s Files, I-44, Kirkland Hall."

37. BOT, May 20–21, 1960; J. Robert Nelson to Harvie Branscomb, May 18, 1960, Chanc. Off., RG 3, box 76, ff "Lawson Case—Miscellaneous (Part I) (Resolutions, etc.)"; "Foster Document," 34–37; copy of letter, Nelson to Branscomb, May 26, 1960; copy of "A Statement to the Admissions Committee of the Divinity School in Reply to the Recommendation for the Readmission of Mr. James Morris Lawson, Jr.," May 30, 1960; J.M. Lawson, Jr., "Personal Statement," May 26, 1960, all in CHP, ff "Divinity School—Students—Lawson Important Papers—Chanc.'s Files"; James M. Lawson, Jr., excerpts from prison diary, May 26, 1960; Branscomb to James Bennett, Director Federal Bureau of Prisons, May 3, 1960; Frank Loveland, Acting Director, U.S. Dept. of Justice to Branscomb, May 15, 1960, all in Chanc. Off., RG 3, box 76, ff "Lawson Case—Miscellaneous (Part III), Chancellor's Statements"; Branscomb to Board of Trust, May 30, 1960, Secretary of the University, RG 5, box 24, ff "Lawson Case—Statement of Vanderbilt University to American Association of Theological Schools."

38. "Foster Document," 28–29, 38, 41–42; J. Robert Nelson to Harvie Branscomb, May 30, 1960; Nine Members of Divinity School to Branscomb, May 30, 1960, both in Dean of Divinity School, RG 73, box 12, ff "Lawson Case: Documents Issued by Faculty, etc."

39. "Foster Document," 40–41; Everett Tilson to Editor of *British Weekly,* Feb. 7, 1961, in papers of the Vanderbilt Chapter of AAUP, RG 133 (one box only), ff "1960–61, AAUP," SC.

40. J. Robert Nelson to Faculty, June 1, 1960, Dean of Divinity School, RG 73, box 12, ff "Lawson Case: Documents Issued by Faculty, etc."; "Foster Document," 41–42; see Dean of Divinity School, RG 73, box 12, ff "Lawson Case: Applications for Faculty Positions in Wake of Resignations."

41. Nashville *Banner,* May 31, 1960.

42. See newspaper and magazine clippings in Secretary of the University, RG 5, box 24, ff "Lawson Case—Statement of Vanderbilt University to American Association of Theological Schools"; Secretary of the University, RG 5, box 24, ff "Lawson Case—*Christian Century* clippings"; ibid., ff 8, "Lawson Case—Newspaper and Magazine Clippings"; Chanc. Off., RG 3, box 78, ff "Lawson Case—Miscellaneous (Part III) Newspaper clippings, etc"; "Foster Document," 45–46.

43. "Foster Document," 46–60; BOT, June 3, 7, 1960; Walter Harrelson to Harvie Branscomb, June 4, 1960, CHP, ff "Divinity School—Students—Lawson Important Papers—Chanc.'s Files"; Statement by Chancellor Harvie Branscomb, June 7, 1960, Walter Harrelson to Chancellor Branscomb, June 7, 1960, both in Secretary of the University, RG 5, box 24, ff "Lawson Case—Statement of Vanderbilt Univeristy to American Association of Theological Schools."

44. John C. Wahlke to Louis Joughlin, June 17, 1960, ff "1960–61 AAUP"; "Minutes of the Special Meeting of the Vanderbilt Chapter AAUP, June 8, 1960"; "Resolution Unanimously Adopted by Vanderbilt Chapter of AAUP, Wednesday, June 8, 1960." Papers of the Vanderbilt Chapter of AAUP, RG 133, ff "Some 1960–61 Notes AAUP," SC; "Foster Document," 65–67.

45. "Foster Document," 58–59; Rob Roy Purdy to Harvie Branscomb, Aug. 17, 1961, Chanc. Off., RG 3, box 99, ff "Purdy, Rob Roy, Vice-Chancellor"; copy of Telegram, Medical School Professors to Harold Vanderbilt, June 12, 1960, CHP, ff "Divinity School—Students—Lawson Info. from Stahlman Papers"; telegram, Amos Christie to Harold S. Vanderbilt, June 10, 1960, CHP, ff "Divinity School—Students—Lawson Telegram, Drs. Christie & Scott to H.S. Vanderbilt, 10 June 1960; Reply, 12 June 1960."

46. John C. Wahlke to Louis Joughlin, June 17, 1960, Papers of the Vanderbilt Chapter of

AAUP, RG 133, "1960–61 AAUP"; "Foster Document," 69–72; J. Robert Nelson to Harvie Branscomb, June 9, 1960, CHP, ff "Divinity School—Students—Lawson Important Papers—Chanc.'s Files."

47. BOT, June 9, 1960; "Foster Document," 60–61, 71–73; [Harvie Branscomb], "The Lawson Episode: The Role of Dean Robert Nelson," Branscomb Papers, box 4, ff "Branscomb—Vanderbilt University, Lawson Affair."

48. Copy of letter, James G. Stahlman to Harvie Branscomb, June 17, 1960, CHP, ff "Divinity School—Students—Lawson Info. from Stahlman Papers"; "Foster Document," 72–73.

49. "Foster Document," 73–75; copy of letter, James G. Stahlman to Harvie Branscomb, June 17, 1960, CHP, ff "Divinity School—Students—Lawson Info. from Stahlman Papers."

50. "Foster Document," 73–75; copy of letter, James G. Stahlman to Harvie Branscomb, June 17, 1960, CHP, ff "Divinity School—Students—Lawson Info. from Stahlman Papers."

51. John C. Wahlke to Louis Joughlin, June 17, 1960, Papers of the Vanderbilt Chapter of AAUP, RG 133, ff. "1960–61, AAUP"; "Foster Document," 76–78.

52. Copy of Letter, James G. Stahlman to Harold S. Vanderbilt, June 11, 1960; copy of Proposals by O.H. Ingram and Stahlman, June 13, 1960, CHP, ff "Divinity School—Students—Lawson Info. from Stahlman Papers."

53. Copy of Proposals by Ingram and Stahlman, ibid.; Branscomb, *Purely Academic*, 162–63.

54. "Foster Document," 79–81; Harvie Branscomb, "A Statement to the Faculty of Vanderbilt University," June 13, 1960, Papers of the Vanderbilt Chapter of AAUP, RG 133, ff "1960–61, AAUP."

55. Nashville *Banner*, June 14, 1960; J. Robert Nelson, "Vanderbilt's Time of Testing," *Christian Century*, Aug. 10, 1960, in Secretary of the University, RGS, Box 24, ff "Lawson Case—*Christian Century* clippings"; Office of the Chancellor to Messrs. Purdy, Stambaugh and McGaw, Sept. 6, 1960, Branscomb Papers, Box 4, ff "Branscomb—Vanderbilt University, Lawson Affair."

56. "Foster Document," 81–85, 88–89; Rob Roy Purdy to Harvie Branscomb, Aug. 17, 1961, Chanc. Off., RG 3, Box 99, ff "Purdy, Rob Roy, Vice-Chancellor."

57. "Foster Document," 81–85, 88–91; James G. Sellers to Harold E. Fey, Feb. 6, 16, 1961, Dean of Divinity School, RG 73, Box 12, ff "Lawson Case: Defense Fund."

58. "Foster Document," 89–93.

59. Rob Roy Purdy to Harvie Branscomb, Aug. 22, 1960; Albert E. Barnett to Harvie Branscomb, July 6, 1960, Chanc. Off., RG 3, box 47, ff "Divinity School—Selection of new dean, June 1960–61."

60. "The Purpose of the Divinity School" [Oct. 31, 1960], Chanc. Off., RG 3, box 46, ff "Divinity School, 1957–1962;" BOT, Jan. 31, 1961; Harvie Branscomb to Earl Moreland, Nov. 30, 1960; to Ernest Colwell, Feb. 9, 1961, Chanc. Off., RG 3, Box 47, ff "Divinity School—Selection of new dean, June 1960–61."

61. Jas. A. Jones to Harvie Branscomb, Dec. 2, 1960; William L. Finch to Branscomb, Sept. 5, 1961, with attached report, Dean of Divinity School, RG 73, box 12, ff "Lawson Case: AATS Investigation."

62. Copy of Letter, Harvie Branscomb to James W. Armsey, June 20, 1960, CHP, ff "Divinity School—Students—Lawson Important Papers—Chanc.'s Files-Kirkland Hall."

63. John H. Stambaugh to Harvie Branscomb, Mar. 30, 1961, Chanc. Off., RG 3, box 101, ff "Race Relations 1955–1963"; Branscomb to Donald Davidson, Oct. 17, 1960, Chanc. Off., RG 3, box 42, ff "Donald Davidson, 1956–62."

64. Newsclippings, Harvie Branscomb to Paul D. Boone, Jan. 15, 1963, Chanc. Off., RG 3, box 101, ff "Race Relations, 1955–1963"; *Hustler*, Dec. 14, 1962.

65. *Hustler*, Jan. 4, 1963; Branscomb to W.M. Caskey, Jan. 17, 1963; to Jack Kershaw, Dec. 19, 1962; Robert A. McGaw, Press Release, Dec. 20, 1962, Chanc. Off., RG 3, box 101, ff "Race Relations, 1955–1963"; Wesley C. George, *The Biology of the Race Problem* (New York: Distribution by the National Putnam Letters Committee, 1962).

66. BOT, May 5, 1961; Mar. 15, May 4–5, 1962; *Hustler*, Feb. 9, 16, Apr. 20, 1962; John W. Wade to Harold S. Vanderbilt, Apr. 4, 1962; Leonard B. Beach to Harvie Branscomb, Mar. 13, 1962, Chanc. Off., RG 3, box 101, "Race Relations, 1955–1963"; Branscomb, *Purely Academic*, 165; College of Arts and Science, "Faculty Minutes," Apr. 17, 1962, SC; "A Communication from the University Senate to the Board of Trust adopted April 26, 1962, by unanimous vote of those members present and voting," CHP, ff "Race—Bd. of Tr. Mtg. (called 6/9/62)."

67. "A Communication from the University Senate to the Board of Trust adopted April 26, 1962 by unanimous vote of those members present and voting," CHP, ff "Race—Bd. of Tr. Mtg. (called 6/9/62)."

68. Branscomb, *Purely Academic*, 165; Harold S. Vanderbilt to Harvie Branscomb, Mar. 19, 28, Apr. 2, 29, 1962, Harold S. Vanderbilt Papers, box 3, ff 5, "Vanderbilt, H.S. Outgoing Correspondence—Integration at Vanderbilt," SC; BOT, May 4–5, 1962.

69. BOT, May 4–5, 1962; Harold S. Vanderbilt to Alec B. Stevenson, May 23, 1962, Vanderbilt Papers, ff 5, "Vanderbilt, H.S. Outgoing Correspondence—Integration at Vanderbilt."

70. Harold S. Vanderbilt to Harvie Branscomb, Apr. 24, 1962, Vanderbilt Papers, ff 5, "Vanderbilt, H.S. Outgoing Correspondence—Integration at Vanderbilt"; *Hustler*, May 11, 1962.

71. Sitkoff, *Black Equality*, 97–166, 197.

21. Leadership and Stewardship

1. Harold S. Vanderbilt to Dr. Amos Christie, Prof. J. Philip Hyatt, Prof. Willard B. Jewell, Prof. George W. Stucking, Dean John W. Wade, July 21, 1961; to Harvie Branscomb, June 12, 1962, both in Harold S. Vanderbilt Papers, box 3, ff 9, SC.

2. Officers of the Alumni Association to Harold S. Vanderbilt, May 10, 1962; Charles S. Trabue, Jr., to Vanderbilt, June 22, 1962, both in Vanderbilt Papers, box 3, ff 10; for examples of recommendations received by the board, see ibid., ff 11; R.R. Purdy to Chancellor Branscomb, Apr. 6, 1962, Chanc. Off., RG 3, box 105, ff "Salaries 1957–1966."

3. Willard B. Jewell to Henry C. Alexander, Oct. 14, 1961, with attached "Report of the Faculty Committee," Vanderbilt Papers, box 3, ff 11.

4. Don [Price] to [Henry] Alexander, Feb. 4, 17, 1962, Harvie Branscomb Papers, box 4, ff 32, SC.

5. Harold S. Vanderbilt to Prof. Jewell, Dec. 20, 1961; to Henry C. Alexander, Jan. 9, 1962; to the Officers of the Alumni Association, June 18, 19, 1962, Vanderbilt Papers, box 3, ff 9; Leonard Beach to Harold K. [*sic*] Vanderbilt, Feb. 28, 1962; W.B. Jewell to Vanderbilt, Jan. 5, 1962, May 20, 1962; John H. Stambaugh to Vanderbilt, May 30, 1962, all in ibid., ff 10.

6. Harold S. Vanderbilt to Henry C. Alexander, O.H. Ingram, and Eldon Stevenson, Jr., Mar. 30, 1962; to Alexander, Apr. 6, 14, 1962; to Alexander Heard, May 7, 1962, Vanderbilt Papers, box 3, ff 9; "Memorandum of Telephone Conversations between H.S. Vanderbilt and Two of the Nine Members of the President's Commission on Campaign Costs of which Dr. Heard was Chairman," May 16, 1962, ibid., ff 11.

7. Harold S. Vanderbilt to Alexander Heard, May 10, 25, 1962; to Eldon Stevenson, May 25, June 22, 1962; to Vanderbilt University Alumni and Alumni Association Officers, June 18, 19, 1962, Vanderbilt Papers, box 3, ff 9; Stevenson to John Sloan, May 28, 1962; telegram Harvie [Branscomb] to Vanderbilt, June 7, 1962, ibid., ff 10; Branscomb to Henry Alexander, Dec. 20, 1961; Heard to Stevenson, June 4, 1962, both in ibid., ff 11.

8. Interview in the *Hustler*, May 6, 1978; *Alumnus* 58 (Spring, 1973): 13-16.

9. *Southern Politics in State and Nation* (New York: Alfred A. Knopf, 1949); Alexander Heard, *A Two Party South* (Chapel Hill: Univ. of North Carolina Press, 1952).

10. *The Costs of Democracy* (Chapel Hill: Univ. of North Carolina Press, 1960).

11. Vanderbilt *Gazette*, Feb. 8, Oct. 9, 1963; May 1, 1964.

12. Mary Jane Werthan, "What's a Woman Trustee to Do?" *Alumnus* 55 (Jan.–Feb., 1970): 16–19.

13. BOT, Oct. 8, Nov. 1–2, 1968; Alexander Heard, "Recent Graduates to be Added to Board of Trust," *Alumnus* 54 (Nov.–Dec., 1968): 3.

14. "Young Trustees," *Alumnus* 58 (Spring, 1973): 23–25, 47.

15. "The Constitution of the Faculty Assembly and the University Senate," Apr., 1967. This and later, amended versions available from the secretary of the Faculty Senate.

16. Ibid.

17. The detailed reports of the Planning Study are in Chanc. Off., RG 3, boxes 79 and 80.

18. *Vanderbilt Planning Study Abstracts* (Nashville, 1964), 21–36; "The Vanderbilt Planning Study," *Alumnus* 50 (July–Aug., 1964): 25–27; "First Fruits of the Planning Study," ibid., (Sept.–Oct., 1964): 18–19; also see ibid. 51 (Nov.–Dec., 1965): 2–3; ibid. (Jan.–Feb., 1966): 2–3; ibid. (Mar.–Apr., 1966): 23.

19. *Planning Study Abstracts*, 198–211.

20. Ibid., 192–97, 219–21.

21. Ibid., 109–19.

22. Ibid., 26.

23. Ibid., 13–17; *Vanderbilt University Financial Report*, June 30, 1982.

24. "Campaign for Vanderbilt," *Alumnus* 52 (Sept.–Oct., 1966): 5–9; BOT, July 19–21, 1965.

25. "Benefactions of the Vanderbilt Family," *Vanderbilt University Financial Report*, June 30, 1981, p. 3; "Vanderbilt, Harold S., Estate of, 1973–74" in Board of Trust Records, RG 2, box 6, SC.

26. BOT, Aug. 1–3, 1974; for details of Sea Island Conference, see a series of folders in Board of Trust—Executive Committee, RG 2, box 7, SC.

27. BOT, Sept. 9, 1981.

28. See either BOT minutes or annual *Bulletins* for tuition information.

29. *AAUP Bulletin*, June, 1973, p. 240; Sept., 1978, p. 246; also see tables and statistics in *Academe*, July–Aug., 1982.

30. BOT, Nov. 5–6, 1965; Feb. 2, 1968.

31. *Hustler*, Dec. 1, 1967; *Newsweek*, Oct. 11, 1971; dozens of issues of the *Hustler* give an ongoing account of the controversy.

32. The new map and plan is in the *Hustler*, Mar. 16, 1973; also see ibid., Dec. 9, 1975; Apr. 25, 1978; Mar. 25, 1980.

33. The Clarke and Rapuano map is in the CHP. files.

34. The Dober report, *Context and Action*, is in the CHP files; *Hustler*, Apr. 7, 1970, contains a summary of the Dober report and maps.

35. The BOT minutes document the plans and costs of each of these new buildings. Specific citations seem superfluous.

36. BOT, Dec. 3, 1968; *Hustler*, Dec. 17, 1968; Jan. 7, Feb. 7, May 16, 1969.

37. See Board of Trust—Executive Committee, RG 2, box 7, SC, for the plans matured at Sea Island; BOT, Aug. 1–3, 1974.

38. BOT, Feb. 1, Mar. 8, Oct. 4, 1977.

22. THE CHANCELLOR, THE KIDS, AND SOME OLD MEN

1. BOT, May 14–15, 1965.

2. Ibid.

3. BOT, May 15–16, 1964; *Hustler*, Feb. 8, 22, Apr. 10, Nov. 8, 1963; Oct. 2, 23, 1964.

4. See Chanc. Off., RG 3, box 14, ff "Horton Early—Carl Braden Material."

5. *Hustler*, Apr. 23, May 7, Dec. 3, 10, 1965; Feb. 18, 1966.

6. For the records of annual Impact programs, see Chanc. Off., RG 3, box 68, numerous ff.

7. Ibid.; *Impact Magazine*, Apr. 4, 1967.

8. Nashville *Banner*, Mar. 23, 24, 25, 1967.

9. BOT, Apr. 4, May 5–6, 1967; Harold S. Vanderbilt telegram in Chanc. Off., RG 3, box 113, ff "Board of Trust, re: Carmichael, Stokely."

10. BOT, Apr. 4, 1967.

11. Senate Res. 2051, The American Legion Resolution of 5 April 1967, and a statement by Beverly Asbury, all in files of Impact, CHP; the correspondence is largely in ff marked "Controversial Speakers, 1967," Chanc. Off., RG 3, box 113; *Hustler,* Apr. 7, 1967.

12. Nashville *Banner,* Apr. 8, 10, 11, 12, 1967; Nashville *Tennessean,* Apr. 9, 10, 11, 1967; *Hustler,* Apr. 14, 1967.

13. Nashville *Banner,* April 10, 1967; Nashville *Tennessean,* April 11, 1967; *Time,* April 21, 28, 1967.

14. The correspondence of Stahlman and his full statement to the board are in the files on Impact, CHP; BOT, May 5, 6, 1967.

15. Stahlman correspondence in CHP; Nashville *Banner,* June 9, 1967.

16. Extensive files on Heard's offer from Columbia University are in boxes 25–26, Heard Personal Files, SC.

17. *Hustler,* May 5, 19, 1967.

18. See Chanc. Off., RG 3, box 68, ff "Heard: Quings."

19. *Hustler,* Nov. 14, 17, 1967; Feb. 6, 16, 23, 1968.

20. *Hustler,* Apr. 5, 12, 26, May 3, 1968.

21. Nashville *Banner,* Nov. 15, Dec. 1, 1968.

22. "A Demonstration," *Alumnus* 56 (May–June, 1969): 25.

23. *Versus,* May 8, 1970; *Hustler,* May 5, 8, 1970.

24. Alexander Heard, "Report on the Washington Assignment," *Alumnus* 56 (Sept.–Oct., 1970): 5–6.

25. *Versus,* Dec. 4, 1970; *Hustler,* Oct. 19, 1971; Vanderbilt *Gazette,* May 4, 1976.

26. Mary Brabston, "Memoirs of an Ex-Radical," *Alumnus* 63 (Winter, 1978): 7–10; *Hustler,* Sept. 15, 1970; Oct. 21, 28, 1972.

27. *Hustler,* Dec. 9, 1972; Oct. 12, 26, 1973; Chanc. Off., box 35, ff "Complaints—Gay Rights Association."

28. Heard to Charles W. Emerson, Jr., Dec. 21, 1972, Chanc. Off., RG 3, box 36, ff "Complaints—YSA/Gay Lib. Homosexual." Also in this folder are the several early drafts of this form letter.

29. Heard memorandum to Board of Trust, Apr. 26, 1974, in ibid.

30. See various issues of *Versus* in 1968 and 1969.

31. *Hustler,* Mar. 15, 1972; *Versus,* Sept. 17, 27, 1971.

32. BOT, Nov. 5, 1971.

33. *Versux [Versus],* Jan., 1979.

34. *Hustler,* May 6, 1969.

35. "V.U. Gets a Chaplain," *Alumnus* 52 (Sept.–Oct., 1966): 3; *Versus,* Apr. 30, 1971, and several subsequent numbers.

36. "A Study of the Chaplaincy at Vanderbilt," June, 1970, a report of the Chaplain's Advisory Committee, in files of the Academic Program Committee, BOT, Records of the Board of Trust, RG 2, SC.

37. *Hustler,* Dec. 1, 1967; Feb. 28, Sept. 23, 1969.

38. Ibid., Nov. 7, 1969; Oct. 9, 1970; Feb. 15, Oct. 8, 1971.

39. BOT, Feb. 8, 1967; see "Policies and Regulations for Undergraduate Students in Non-Curricular Matters, 1972–73," pp. 17–18.

40. BOT, Mar. 4, 1969; *Hustler,* Nov. 2, 1979.

41. BOT, June 30, 1964; *Hustler,* Dec. 3, 1965; Oct. 13, 1967; and numerous others.

42. *Hustler,* Nov. 1, 1963; May 1, 1964; Sept. 27, 1968; Sept. 25, 1970; and numerous others.

43. Ibid., Nov. 12, 1968; HEW report in BOT, Mar. 4, 1969.

44. *Hustler,* Feb. 25, 1969; "Director Named for Black Studies," *Alumnus* 56 (Jan.–Feb., 1971): 6.

45. James Stahlman to Dr. D.W. Stubblefield, June 2, 1967, CHP; also see other letters by Stahlman, CHP.

46. BOT, Dec. 3, 1968.

47. Ibid., Jan. 7, 1969; Heard to Branscomb, Jan. 8, 1969; and Branscomb to Heard, Jan. 10, 1969, CHP.

48. BOT, Jan. 7, 1969.

49. Hobbs letter in Chanc. Off., RG 2, box 75, ff "Lawson, James, Jr. (1968–69)."

50. BOT, Jan. 12, 1969.

23. ACADEMIC UPDATE

1. *Hustler,* Apr. 1, 1977.

2. Jacque Voegeli to Wendell Holladay, Apr. 9, 1979, in Chancellor's Files, Active Records, Kirkland Hall, ff "College of A&S."

3. John Donaldson, "The Undergraduate, A Campus Self-Study," *Alumnus* 55 (Jan.–Feb., 1970): 26–27; "Students to Aid in Public Policy," ibid. (Mar.–Apr., 1970): 7; *Bull.,* 1971.

4. For the final plan, see the *Bull.,* 1982–83.

5. *Chronicle of Higher Education,* Jan. 12, 1983.

6. "The Graduate School," *Alumnus* 54 (Mar.–Apr., 1969): 27; *Chronicle of Higher Education,* Sept. 29, 1982.

7. *Chronicle of Higher Education,* Jan. 19, 1983.

8. Ibid., Nov. 10, 1982.

9. Ibid.

10. Ibid.

11. *Vanderbilt Planning Study Abstracts* (Nashville, 1964), 227–34.

12. "A University Approach to Urban Problems," *Alumnus* 53 (May–June, 1968): 19–21.

13. Vanderbilt *Gazzete,* Dec. 18, 1974.

14. Erwin C. Hargrove, "Past, Present, and Future of the Institute," a memo to the chancellor, 1983, CHP.

15. *Planning Study Abstracts,* 261–63; *Hustler,* Apr. 28, 1972; Oct. 28, 1975; Sept. 10, 1979.

16. The Oberlin merger plan is in BOT, Dec. 17, 1965; also see Chanc. Off., RG 3, box 46, ff "Divinity School Merger with Oberlin."

17. Supplement to *Vanderbilt Financial Report,* June 30, 1981.

18. *Hustler,* Feb. 12, Nov. 9, 1971; Feb. 15, 18, 1972; Nov. 30, 1973; Mar. 16, 1976; Mar. 11, 1977; Jan. 12, 1979.

19. See Chanc. Off. RG 3, box 51, ff "Engineering School (Howard Hartman, Dean, 1974)."

20. *Hustler,* Sept. 1, 1972; Sept. 18, 1979; Oct. 31, 1980; BOT, Feb. 6, 1973.

21. *Hustler,* Jan. 25, 1980; BOT, Mar. 6, Nov. 9–10, 1973.

22. *Planning Study Abstracts,* 155–60; Emmett Fields, "From the President," *Alumnus* 165 (Winter, 1979): 3.

23. *Hustler,* Feb. 20, 1972; Aug. 25, 1979.

24. *Planning Study Abstracts,* 183–91; BOT, May 3–4, 1963.

25. *Hustler,* Nov. 16, 1971; Jan. 25, Sept. 6, 1972; BOT, Feb. 2, June 6, 1972.

26. *Hustler,* Sept. 6, 1972; Mar. 22, Dec. 2, 1977; Jan. 17, 1978; National League of Nursing to Emmett Fields, Dec. 7, 1979, Chancellor's Files, Active, Kirkland Hall, ff "Nursing School."

27. *Task Force Report,* 1981, Chancellor's Files, Active, Kirkland Hall, ff "Nursing School."

28. *Hustler,* Sept. 30, 1980.

29. *Vanderbilt University Financial Report,* June 30, 1982.

30. This too brief survey of Medical School history rests upon Board of Trust records, several articles in the *Alumnus* and *Hustler,* and at points upon Timothy C. Jacobson's "Medical Center: A History of Science in Medicine" (unpublished MS in SC [1982]). Adequate citations would number in the hundreds.

31. See Chanc. Off., RG 3, box 86, ff "Professional Services Plan for Clinic Faculty."

32. Ibid.

33. BOT, Apr. 8, 1969; Apr. 4, 1972; supplement to *Financial Report,* June 30, 1981.

34. Nashville *Tennessean,* Mar. 26, 1983.

35. Chancellor's files, Active, Kirkland Hall, ff "Medical School."

36. BOT, July 19–21, 1965; the committee report is in Chanc. Off., RG 3, box 96, ff "Management, Graduate School of, through 1966."

37. BOT, Apr. 4, May 5–6, 1967.

38. Igor Ansoff, "Management," *Alumnus* 55 (Nov.–Dec., 1969): 14–18; Jean Crawford, "The Graduate School of Management: An Experiment in Channeling Change," ibid., 19–24.

39. Igor Ansoff, "A Strategic Plan for the Graduate School of Management," Sept., 1968, CHP.

40. Ibid.

41. Most of the detailed information about the school is in a series of folders in Chanc. Off., RG 3, box 95.

42. Ibid.

43. BOT, Jan. 7, Feb. 4, May 2–3, 1975.

44. The task force report is in BOT, July 9, 1975; *Hustler,* Aug. 5, 1975; also see files in Chanc. Off., RG 3, box 95.

45. For the full, and rather complex, court ruling see Chanc. Off., RG 3, files, box 35, ff "Complaints: Lowenthal Suits."

46. BOT, Sept. 11, 1979; June 15, 1982; *Hustler,* Sept. 3, 1976.

47. BOT, June 31, 1980; July 28, 1981.

24. Presidential Politics

1. BOT, Apr. 27, 1976.

2. BOT, July 13, Oct. 21–23, 1976; also see over a cubic foot of planning records on executive reorganization in box 7, Board of Trust–Executive Committee, RG 2, SC.

3. BOT, Oct. 21–23, 1976; Vanderbilt *Gazette,* Jan. 12, 1977.

4. The preceding judgments rest on some still active records in Kirkland Hall, but even more on impressions gained from personal experience and several interviews.

5. Vanderbilt *Gazette,* Oct. 1, 1977; Jan. 16, 1978.

6. BOT, Nov. 10–11, 1967; May 4–5, 1973.

7. For the Quarterback Club speech see Chancellor's Files, Active, Kirkland Hall, ff "Athletics."

8. The atheltic record is abundantly documented in the *Hustler,* and *Alumnus.*

9. Alexander Heard, "A Report on Recommendations for the Vanderbilt Athletic Program," *Alumnus* 53 (Sept.–Oct., 1967): 9–11; "Jess Neely," ibid., 12–13.

10. BOT, Nov. 10–11, 1967; Nov. 7–8, 1969; Chancellor's Files, Active, Kirkland Hall, ff "Athletics."

11. BOT, May 5–6, 1972; Nov. 12, 1976.

12. BOT, Nov. 4–5, 1977.

13. See the ff "Davis Cup," in President's Files, Active, Kirkland Hall; Vanderbilt *Gazette,* Feb. 9, Mar. 3, May 16, 1978.

14. Ibid.; see also newspaper coverage in the *Hustler.*

15. Vanderbilt *Gazette,* May 16, 1978.

16. BOT, Mar. 7, 1978; Nov. 2, 1979.

17. BOT, Mar. 4, 1980.

18. Vanderbilt *Gazette,* Sept. 25, 1978.

19. Ibid., Nov. 1, 1975; *Hustler,* Mar. 3, 1972; Dec. 10, 1974; Nov. 12, 1976.

20. See President's Files, Active, Kirkland Hall, ff "Peabody—Merger Documents."

21. Ibid.

22. Ibid.

23. Ibid.; *Hustler,* Feb. 16, 27, Mar. 12, 1979.

24. President's Files, Active, Kirkland Hall, "Peabody Merger Documents."

25. Ibid.

26. Fleming to Gable, Mar. 17, 1979, ibid.; *Hustler,* Mar. 20, 1979.

27. Vanderbilt *Gazette,* May 16, 1979.

28. BOT, Mar. 17, Apr. 25, 1979; *Hustler,* Mar. 30, Apr. 20, Aug. 25, Oct. 16, 1979.

29. *Hustler,* Sept. 25, 1979.

30. See Chancellor's Files, Active, Kirkland Hall, on "Blair Academy."

31. Ibid.

32. Ibid.

33. Ibid.; BOT, Dec. 22, 1980; *Register,* Apr. 23, 1982.

34. The reassessment documents are in the President's Files, Active, Kirkland Hall; also see Vanderbilt *Gazette,* Oct. 26, 1979.

35. *Hustler,* Feb. 8, Apr. 18, 1972.

36. Dozens of issues of the *Hustler* document this story.

37. See Chanc. Off., RG 3, box 131, ff "Commission on the Status of Women."

38. *Women at Vanderbilt,* Report of the Chancellor's Commission on the Status of Women, 1972–1976 (1976).

39. Vanderbilt *Gazette,* July 31, 1977.

40. "Vanderbilt University Affirmative Action Plan, 1982," vols. I and II.

41. Chancellor's Files, Active, Kirkland Hall, ff "Integration" and "Association of Black Faculty and Black Administrators."

42. This account draws on the active files on the Langland Case in the Chancellor's Office, Kirkland Hall, and also from a detailed but unpublished "Summary and Analysis of the Langland Tenure Case" by Larry Diamond, June 10, 1982.

43. Ibid.

44. Chancellor's Files, Active, Kirkland Hall, "Langland Case."

45. Ibid.; BOT, Aug. 31, 1981.

46. *Register,* Dec. 18, 1981.

47. Chancellor's Files, Active, Kirkland Hall, "Langland Case"; and Diamond "Summary and Analysis."

48. *Elizabeth Langland v. Vanderbilt University, et al.,* U.S. District Court for the Middle District of Tennessee, Nashville Division, Apr. 27, 1984, No. 3-83-0115.

49. Ibid.

50. *Register,* Mar. 5, 1982.

Index

Fleming, Sam *(cont.)*
688, 702–703, 711, 712
Fleming, Walter L., 241–42, 244, 247, 248,
249, 250, 287, 292, 293–94, 304
Fletcher, John Gould, 321, 333–34, 339,
340
Fletcher, Joseph, 425–26
Flexner, Abraham, 204–205, 208, 230–31,
243, 267, 270, 271, 272, 273, 279, 281,
307, 675, 676
Flexner, Bernard, 307
Flexner, Simon, 269, 272
Florence Normal School, 357
Florida, University of, 697
Florida Coalition of Patriotic Societies, 512
Flowers, H. Fort, 657
fluid research fund, 382
Fogg, Francis B., 120
football at Vanderbilt: origins, 104, 135,
137–39; debate over, 139–40; beginning
of McGugin era, 214–17; in the twenties,
307–309, 311; in the depression, 378;
during World War II, 430–31; in the
fifties, 524, 525–26; recent trends, 597,
698, 700, 704; incidental references, 145,
234, 429
Foote, Mary Ella Calhoun, 251
Force, William F., 595
Ford, Ford Madox, 400
Ford Foundation, 459, 460, 470, 482, 483,
490, 492, 495, 496, 542, 574, 584, 597,
598–99, 658, 681, 688, 707
Fordham, Jefferson B., 439
Forrester, William Ray, 491
Forstman, H. Jackson, 660, 661
Fosdick, Harry S., 306–307
Foster, Arthur, 560
Frank, James, 318
Frank, John, 416
Frankfurter, Felix, 435
Fraser, Russell, 655
fraternities at Vanderbilt: legal recognition,
76–78, 80; in the nineties, 119, 134,
141; strains in a new century, 218–19,
296–97; in the depression, 377–78;
post-World War II growth, 516–18;
reform under Branscomb, 529–32; recent
history, 636, 642, 724; incidental
references, 37, 58, 209, 295, 422, 447,
478, 515
Free America, 342
Free University of Nashville, 638–39
Freeland, William, 426
Freeman, Ella, 90
French Department, 239, 484, 488, 654
Friends of the Library, 657
Frierson, William, 318
Frost, Robert, 317
Frye, William W., 421, 496
Fugitive, The, 299, 319–23, 329

Fugitives, The, 223, 230, 312, 313, 314–23,
344, 345, 346, 654, 741
Fulton, John E. ("Uncle Remis"), 305–306,
368
Fund for the Republic, 492
fund raising, 90, 113–14, 145–46, 193–94,
199–200, 231–32, 255–58, 259–60,
264, 266, 405–406, 411, 458, 460–61,
599–600, 600–601
Fundamentalist Church League of America,
512
Furman, Mary, 114, 193–94
Furman Hall, 128, 144, 194, 195, 196–97,
198, 243, 257, 260, 358, 609
Furman University, 697
Future War Vets, 380

Gable, Robert E., 712
Gage, George N., 392
Gaines, Francis P., 440, 442
Gaines Case of 1938, 539
Galloway, Charles B., 143, 154, 156, 157,
159, 175
Galloway Memorial Fund, 267
Galloway Memorial Hospital, 206, 267, 272,
273, 274
Gardner, Edwin S., 454
Garis, Roy, 245, 359
Garland, Landon C.: defense of theological
education, 7; role in founding Vanderbilt
University, 7–12; planning the campus,
19–20; early life, 39–41; as architect of
Vanderbilt's first academic program,
39–44; love of scientific machines,
44–45; role in selecting Vanderbilt's first
faculty, 46–53; emphasis on Christian
character, 46; establishment of Law and
Medical Departments, 54–55;
relationship to students, 75–82;
leadership in academic reform, 88–92;
role in restructuring university
government, 92–94; faculty recruitment
in the nineties, 103–105; death,
105–106; incidental references, 23, 25,
31, 35, 37, 56, 57, 65, 67, 68, 70, 71,
73, 74, 84, 87, 107, 116, 123, 130, 134,
139, 144, 180, 193, 243, 246, 600, 692,
741
Garland Hall, 257, 464, 609
Garner, Robert, 298, 621
Garrey, Walter A., 277–78, 421
Garrison, S.C., 413
Gates, Frederick T., 268, 269, 270
Gator Bowl (1955), 525
Gault, Alma E., 667
Gaventa, John, 629, 639, 642–43
Gay Rights Association, 633
Gelders, Joseph, 424
General Biology, Department of, 651–52
General Education Board (GEB), 151, 166,